Encyclopedia of the
ANCIENT GREEK WORLD

REVISED EDITION

David Sacks
Editorial Consultant Oswyn Murray

Revised by Lisa R. Brody

☑®
Facts On File, Inc.

Encyclopedia of the Ancient Greek World, Revised Edition

Facts On File, Inc.
132 West 31st Street
New York NY 10001

Library of Congress Cataloging-in-Publication Data
Sacks, David.
Encyclopedia of the ancient Greek world / David Sacks; editorial consultant,
Oswyn Murray; revised edition by Lisa R. Brody.—Rev. ed.
p. cm.
Revision of: 1st ed. New York: Facts On File, c1995.
Includes bibliographical references and index.
ISBN 0-8160-5722-2
1. Greece—Civilization—To 146 B.C.—Dictionaries. I. Murray, Oswyn.
II. Brody, Lisa R. III. Title.
DF16.S23 2005
938'.003—dc22   2004056429

Facts On File books are available at special discounts when purchased in bulk
quantities for businesses, associations, institutions, or sales promotions. Please call
our Special Sales Department in New York at (212) 967-8800 or (800) 322-8755.

You can find Facts On File on the World Wide Web at http://www.factsonfile.com

Produced by Schlager Group Inc.
Text design by Joan M. Toro
Cover design by Cathy Rincon
Illustrations by Margaret Bunson
Maps by Jeremy Eagle

Printed in the United States of America

VB Hermitage 10 9 8 7 6 5 4 3 2 1

This book is printed on acid-free paper.

For Rebecca and Katie Sacks.
—David Sacks

For Julia and Connor. Sas agapo.
—Lisa R. Brody

CONTENTS

LIST OF ILLUSTRATIONS AND MAPS

Greece and Neighboring Regions

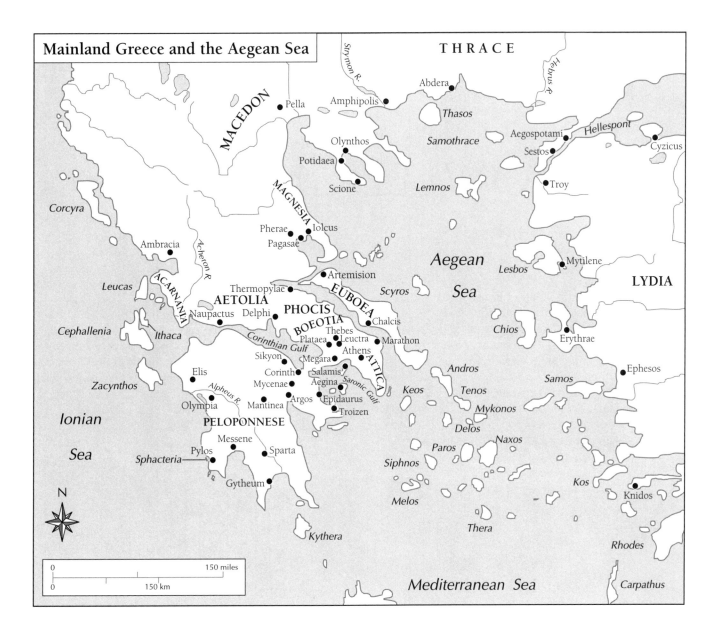

Mainland Greece and the Aegean Sea

THRACE

MACEDON

Strymon R.

Hebrus R.

Pella

Amphipolis

Abdera

Thasos

Samothrace

Aegospotami

Hellespont

Olynthos

Sestos

Cyzicus

Potidaea

Lemnos

Troy

Scione

MAGNESIA

Corcyra

Acheron R.

Ambracia

Pherae

Iolcus

Aegean

Sea

Lesbos

Mytilene

Pagasae

LYDIA

Leucas

ACARNANIA

Artemision

Scyros

Cephallenia

Ithaca

Thermopylae

EUBOEA

Chios

AETOLIA

PHOCIS

Erythrae

Naupactus

Delphi

BOEOTIA

Chalcis

Corinthian Gulf

Thebes

Marathon

Ephesos

Zacynthos

Sikyon

Plataea

Leuctra

Samos

Elis

Megara

Athens

ATTICA

Andros

Corinth

Salamis

Keos

Tenos

Alpheus R.

Mycenae

Aegina

Saronic Gulf

Mykonos

Olympia

Mantinea

Argos

Epidaurus

Troizen

Delos

Naxos

Ionian

PELOPONNESE

Paros

Sea

Messene

Siphnos

Sphacteria

Pylos

Sparta

Kos

Gytheum

Knidos

Melos

Thera

Rhodes

Kythera

Carpathus

Mediterranean Sea

N

0   150 miles

0   150 km

ix

ACKNOWLEDGMENTS

I am most grateful to several people for help. My former teacher Oswyn Murray, fellow of Balliol College and lecturer in ancient history at Oxford University, vetted the manuscript with the same patience and receptiveness that distinguished his tutorial sessions. I owe him a great deal, not only for the book's preparation, but also for my wider fascination with the ancient world. Two other scholars kindly donated their time to read sections and make comments: Gilbert Rose, professor of classics at Swarthmore College, and Christopher Simon, currently a visiting assistant professor of classics at the University of California, Berkeley. (Any factual errors here remain my own, however.)

I wish to thank my parents, Louis and Emmy Lou Sacks, for their unstinting encouragement. Ditto my good friend Jeffrey Scheuer. My thanks to Facts On File editor Gary Krebs, who kept the door open while the manuscript came together. Especially I must thank my wife, Joan Monahan, who brought home the family's bacon, day after day, during the four years consumed by this project.

—David Sacks

INTRODUCTION TO THE REVISED EDITION

The gleaming marble of the Parthenon in Athens. The poignant handclasp of a married couple on a tombstone in the Kerameikos. The perfect acoustics of the theater at Epidaurus. The vibrant characters of Homer and Euripides. The rhythmic decoration of a Geometric vase painting. The driving ambition of Alexander the Great. The mysterious oracle of Apollo at Delphi. The thrilling competition of the athletic festival at Olympia.

The ancient Greek world began to emerge in the eastern Mediterranean during the third millennium B.C.E. and continued until Rome conquered the region in the first century B.C.E. Many elements of modern Western civilization—including art, architecture, literature, philosophy, science, and medicine—rely on the cultural achievements of the ancient Greeks. Today a wide range of interdisciplinary scholars study the ancient Greek civilization; the goal of this revised encyclopedia is to present these scholars' new discoveries and reinterpretations in a concise and readable format that will appeal to a broad audience.

Greece is a peninsula in southeast Europe that projects into the Mediterranean, flanked by the Aegean Sea to the east and the Ionian Sea to the west. Its long coastline has numerous natural harbors and inlets for sea travel and maritime commerce that became essential to Greek civilization from its inception. Mainland Greece is also a mountainous country, with a landscape well suited to grazing sheep and goats, growing grape vines and olive trees, and building naturally defended citadels and cities.

The first truly Greek civilization was that of the Mycenaeans, around 1600–1200 B.C.E., modeled after the earlier, non-Greek Minoan civilization on the island of Crete. The centuries following the collapse of the Mycenaean civilization are variously called the Sub-Mycenaean period, the Greek Dark Ages, the Protogeo-

metric period, or the early Iron Age. During this time (ca. 1100–900 B.C.E.), the population of Greece decreased and was redistributed into isolated communities, literacy disappeared, and works of art and architecture became all but nonexistent.

The period from about 900 to 700 B.C.E., the Geometric era, was a time of renewal and growth for Greece. Communication and trade routes were renewed, literacy reemerged with a new written language adopted from the Phoenicians, and artistic creativity began to be expressed again. The Geometric Greeks also built sacred cult areas with altars and temples where they worshiped their gods with animal sacrifices and other offerings. The Greeks' prosperity continued into the early Archaic period (ca. 700–600 B.C.E.), which saw the rise of the political unit known as the *polis* (city-state). Coinage was invented, and monumental stone sculpture and architecture began to be created, probably due to influences from neighboring peoples such as the Egyptians.

In the 500s B.C.E., many of the new Greek city-states came to be ruled by tyrants, several of whom were strong patrons of the arts. The communities continued to flourish and trade increased. In Athens, the tyranny of the Peisistratid family was ended in 510 B.C.E., and after this a democratic government began to evolve. Around the same time, the massive Persian Empire began its attempts to conquer the Greeks. Despite being generally outnumbered, the Greeks (under the leadership of the Athenians) defeated the Persians; the victory was celebrated in public artworks by scenes of mythological battles where civilized forces triumph over barbaric ones (Gods vs. Giants, Greeks vs. Centaurs, Greeks vs. Amazons, and Greeks vs. Trojans).

The end of the Persian Wars in 479 B.C.E. marks the end of the Archaic period and the start of the classical period. The fifth century B.C.E. is viewed as a "golden age," especially in Athens under the leadership of the statesman Perikles. A monumental building program was undertaken on the Athenian Acropolis, including the temple of Athena, known as the Parthenon. By the late 400s B.C.E., tension had arisen between imperialist Athens and other Greek city-states, particularly Sparta and others in the Peloponnese. The resulting civil war, the Peloponnesian Wars, disrupted the entire Greek world and ended the domination of the Athenians.

In the mid-400s B.C.E., a new power began to appear in Greece: Macedon, under the rule of King Philip and his son, Alexander the Great. The Macedonian conquests, extending as far east as India, spread Hellenic culture throughout the ancient world and introduced a new, international era, known as the Hellenistic period. Cosmopolitan centers such as Alexandria, Athens, and Pergamon attracted large numbers of artists, philosophers, and scientists. Cults of foreign divinities such as Isis and Mithras became increasingly popular, alongside those of the traditional Olympian gods. By the 200s B.C.E., another new power appeared in the Mediterranean: Rome. In 146 B.C.E., Greece was made a Roman province, and the defeat of Cleopatra and Mark Antony at the Battle of Actium in 31 B.C.E. signaled the end of the Hellenistic period and the start of the Roman Imperial era.

Travel to Greece, motivated by interest in its ancient culture, began almost immediately, in the early Roman period. In the second century C.E., a traveler named Pausanias toured the mainland and wrote one of the world's earliest and most detailed guidebooks. His systematic accounts of ancient sites and sanctuaries, though sometimes flawed and often based on hearsay instead of observation, provide a fascinating source of information for modern scholars, to be used in conjunction with archaeological evidence.

In the medieval era, travelers to Greece were mainly pilgrims, passing through the country on their way to Jerusalem. They were less interested in contemplating the ancient Greek world than in reaching their ultimate destination as quickly as possible. In the early 15th century, however, an Italian named Cyriac of Ancona journeyed to Greece with antiquarian purposes in mind. His descriptions of ancient sites and drawings of visible ruins (particularly inscriptions) are another valuable source for today's Classical scholars.

After Cyriac, interest in ancient Greece waned for a while. Those Europeans of the 16th and 17th centuries who were curious about the ancient world tended to concentrate on Rome instead, though there were a few exceptions. One of these exceptions involved a group of scholars and artists led by the French marquis de Nointel in 1673–1674. One of these artists was Jacques Carrey, whose invaluable drawings of the Parthenon sculptures

help modern scholars reconstruct many pieces that were subsequently destroyed.

The real age of travel to Greece began in the 18th century, at a time when the "Grand Tour" came into fashion for large numbers of rich, educated Europeans. One group, the Society of Dilettanti, sponsored a number of significant expeditions to Greece and published several illustrated travel accounts. In 1748, they hired two architects, James Stuart and Nicholas Revett, to visit Athens and to draw as many ancient monuments as possible. Their meticulous work, published in four volumes between 1762 and 1816 as *The Antiquities of Athens,* is invaluable for information about many Athenian antiquities that were better preserved in the 18th century than they are today.

Other Europeans during the 18th and 19th centuries continued to visit Greece and to record the places and things of interest that they experienced. Some of the more significant travelers to the Greek world during this time include William Hamilton (1764), Richard Chandler (1764–1766), J. B. S. Morritt (1794–1796), Sir William Gell (1801–1834), Edward Dodwell (1801–1806), Colonel William Martin Leake (1802–1815), George Lord Byron (1809–1811, 1823–1824), Edward Lear (1848–1864), and Richard Farrer (1880–1882).

Today scholarship of the ancient Greek world is called classical studies, and the archaeology of ancient Greece is called classical archaeology. These fields developed gradually but constantly from the period of the early travelers to modern times. One early scholar whose work is sometimes said to mark the beginning of classical archaeology is the German Johann Joachim Winckelmann (1717–1768); his impressive *History of Art in Antiquity* sparked intense interest in the ancient Greece world during the Romantic era.

The earliest expeditions to Greece were really more about collecting than archaeology. In 1801, the British ambassador to Turkey, Lord Elgin, received a permit from the Turks to "excavate and remove" antiquities from the Athenian Acropolis. The sculptures that he took from the ruins of the Parthenon are now in the British Museum in London and are the object of heated controversy; the Greeks consider the "Elgin marbles" to be stolen cultural property and are anxious to have them returned. Elgin's undertaking was soon imitated; the Germans removed sculptures from the Temple of Aphaia at Aegina and the Temple of Apollo Epikourios at Bassae, and the French claimed Greek statues such as the Nike of Samothrace and the Venus de Milo.

In the mid- and late 19th century, the Greek government allowed the establishment of several foreign archaeological schools in Athens, such as the American School of classical studies. From this time on, foreign scholars wanting to excavate Greek sites or study Greek antiquities have been required to obtain permits and to be closely regulated; no more Greek artifacts would leave the country. classical archaeology gradually was transformed from a hobby of acquisition to a scientific pursuit, due in large part to the work of German scholars in the late 19th and early 20th centuries. Systematic excavations were begun at Olympia by the Germans (1875–1881), at Delphi by the French (1892–1903), and at Corinth by the Americans (1896 to the present).

Classical archaeology today is a highly specialized field, and excavations require the cooperation of experts from a variety of subspecialties. Despite the long history of travel to Greece and study of ancient Greek artifacts, new discoveries are being made all the time. Because of this, new publications in classical studies appear constantly, even about such well-studied subjects as the Parthenon frieze. New revisions of older publications, such as this *Encyclopedia of the Ancient Greek World,* are necessary and valuable for the same reason.

The original format of David Sacks's *Encyclopedia of the Ancient Greek World* has not been altered in this revised edition, but many of the entries have been edited and rewritten, and several new entries have been added. Most of the changes were specified by Sacks, but occasionally I found myself able to add further information due to my own experience and fields of expertise. I have also made a few stylistic modifications and a few format changes according to the publisher's guidelines. Overall, I have tried to do as little rewriting as possible, so that the original author's "voice" still predominates.

I also adjusted the spelling of several headword entries. Although Sacks used Latinized and Anglicized spellings in many instances, I have used modern transliterations of the ancient Greek as much as possible, retaining the Latinized ones only in cases where it would be far more familiar to the general reader: "Perikles" instead of "Pericles" and "Hephaistos" instead of "Hephaestus," for example, but "Corinth" instead of "Korinth" and "Aeschylus" instead of "Aischylos."

The change that I hope will provide the greatest benefit to the reader is the addition of specialized bibliographies ("Further reading") after each entry, supplementing the updated, general bibliography at the end of the book. In compiling these bibliographies, I have tried to include the most recent and scholarly sources on each topic, though this was limited to a degree by the necessity of citing only English-language works.

If this encyclopedia had been published when I myself was an undergraduate and graduate student in classical studies, I would have found it extremely beneficial. I have enjoyed preparing the revised edition and hope that my modifications have made the publication even more valuable. My hope is that current students, as well as other interested general readers, will read it and make reference to it, and that it will enrich their knowledge and appreciation of the ancient Greek world.

—Lisa R. Brody

INTRODUCTION TO THE ORIGINAL EDITION

About 2100 B.C.E. a migrant, cattle-herding, pony-riding people made their way into the Mediterranean landmass that today is called Greece. They entered overland from the north, probably the Danube basin, but their origins may have been farther northeast, for they spoke a language of the Indo-European linguistic family. Modern philologists believe that the ancestral Indo-European language—whose modern descendants include English, German, Gaelic, French, Farsi, Hindi, and modern Greek—evolved in the fourth millennium B.C.E. on the plains of southern Russia. This mother tongue then branched into different forms, carried in all directions by nomadic tribes. The group that reached Greece ca. 2100 B.C.E. brought with it an early form of the Greek language. These people can be called the first Greeks.

The land that they invaded was held by farmers who had probably immigrated centuries earlier from Asia Minor, a place with which they perhaps remained linked via an eastward trade network that included the Aegean island of Crete. They apparently knew seafaring and stone masonry—two skills that the nomadic Greeks did not yet have.

But the Greeks were the stronger warriors. They took over the country, probably by violence in the most desirable locales, but elsewhere perhaps by intermarriage (as may be reflected in the many Greek myths in which the hero marries the foreign princess). One apparent sign of conquest is the wrecked remnant of a pre-Greek palace that modern archaeologists call the House of the Tiles, at Lerna on the plain of Argos. Destroyed by fire ca. 2100 B.C.E., this may have been the home of a native ruler who led an unsuccessful defense of the fertile heartland of southern Greece. Yet at certain other sites, archaeologists have found no clear signs of violence—only continued habitation and the abrupt emergence of a new style of pottery, betokening the Greeks' arrival.

The region that the Greeks now took over—and that would henceforth be their homeland—is a huge, jagged, southward-pointing peninsula, with a coastline stretching nearly 2,000 miles. Beyond its shores, particularly to the southeast, are islands that beckon to sea travelers and traders. Through the peninsula's center, from north to south, runs an irregular line of mountain ranges, whose slopes in ancient times held forests of oak, beech, and fir—timber for generations of house builders and shipwrights. In a later era, the limestone formations in these mountains would yield marble for sculptors and architects. But the mountains also occupied most of the mainland's total area, leaving only 20 percent as arable land.

Aside from scattered pockets, the farmland lay mainly in three regions: the plains of Argos, Boeotia, and Thessaly, in southern, central, and northern Greece, respectively. These territories were destined to become early Greek centers of power, especially the region of Argos, with its capital at Mycenae.

The soil of much of Greece is red or orange from clay deposits, which served centuries of potters and sculptors. In ancient times the farmed plains and foothills produced wheat, barley, olives, grapes, figs, and pomegranates—crops that could survive the ferociously hot, dry Greek summer. Summer, not winter, is the barren season in Greece, as in other parts of the Mediterranean. Winters are relatively mild—cool and rainy, but far rainier on the mainland's western side. The eastern regions, although traditionally densely populated, are blocked by the central mountains from receiving the westerly rainy weather. Athens gets only about 15 inches of rainfall a year; Corfu, on the west coast, has three times that much.

In such a country, where farmland and water supplies were precious, the Greek invaders of ca. 2100 B.C.E. found most of the best locales already settled. The Greeks took over such settlements but kept their pre-Greek names. For that reason, the names of most ancient Greek cities do not come from the Greek language. Names such as *Athens*, *Corinth*, and *Mycenae* are not etymologically Greek; their original meanings are lost in prehistory. Relatively few ancient mainland sites have recognizably Greek names, among them Pylos ("the gate"), Megara ("the great hall"), Chalcis ("bronze city"), and Marathon ("fennel").

Eventually the Greeks acquired the civilizing arts of the people they had conquered. The Greeks learned shipbuilding, seamanship, and stoneworking—skills at which they excelled. More significantly, they borrowed from the non-Greeks' agrarian religion, which perhaps involved the worship of a mother goddess and a family of fertility deities. Non-Greek goddesses and beliefs, imported into Greek religion, complemented and refined the warrior Greeks' Indo-European–type worship of a sky father and male gods. A new spirituality was born.

Thus in the centuries after 2100 B.C.E. came the creative fusion of two cultures—one primitive Greek, one non-Greek. To these two elements was added a third: the example and influence of the dynamic, non-Greek, Minoan civilization of Crete. By 1600 B.C.E. such factors had produced the first blossoming of the Greeks, in the Bronze Age urban society called the Mycenaean civilization.

For reasons never adequately explained, the Greeks of the next 15 centuries showed a spiritual and intellectual genius that expressed itself in religious awe, storytelling, poetry, sports, the material arts, trade, scientific studies, military organization, and in the governments of their self-contained city-states, particularly Athens. Their legacy to modern global society is immense. The Greeks invented democracy, narrative history writing, stage tragedy and comedy, philosophy, biological study, and political theory. They introduced the alphabet to European languages. They developed monumental styles of architecture that in the United States are used for museums, courthouses, and other public buildings. They created a system of sports competitions and a cult of physical fitness, both of which we have inherited. In sculpture, they perfected the representation of the human body. In geometry, they developed theorems and terminology still taught in schools. They created the idea of a national literature, with its recognized great writers and the libraries to preserve their work. And (perhaps what most people would think of first) the Greeks bequeathed to us their treasure trove of myths, including a hero who remains a favorite today—Herakles, or Hercules.

The early Greeks learned much about art and technology from Near Eastern peoples such as the Egyptians and Phoenicians. But more usually the Greeks became the teachers of others. They were an enterprising, often friendly people, and—as sea traders, colonists, mercenary soldiers, or conquerors—they traveled the world from southern Spain to Pakistan. Everywhere they went, they cast a spell through the magnetic appeal of their culture and style of life.

Their most fateful protégés were the Romans, a non-Greek people of Italy. Influenced by imported Greek goods and ideas from the 700s or 600s B.C.E. onward, the Romans modeled their religion largely on the Greeks', using Greek deities to shape their native Roman gods. This early stage was followed by a more elaborate copying—of Greek coinage, architecture, and other arts—starting in the 300s B.C.E. When the Romans sought to create their own national literature, they naturally turned to Greek models in epic and lyric poetry, history writing, rhetoric, tragedy, and comedy. They also became important patrons of Greek artists and craftsmen.

But meanwhile Roman armies were capturing Greek cities and kingdoms—first in Italy and Sicily (300s–200s B.C.E.), then in mainland Greece, Macedon, and Asia Minor (100s B.C.E.), and finally in Syria and Egypt (first century B.C.E.). Roman generals and governors plundered centuries' worth of Greek sculptures and other art treasures, removing them from temples and public squares and shipping them to Rome. In most locales, the inhabitants became taxpaying subjects of the Roman empire. The Romans more or less put an end to the Greek achievement, even as they inherited it. The Roman poet Horace found a more hopeful phrasing for this when he wrote, about 19 B.C.E., "Captive Greece took mighty Rome captive, forcing culture onto rustic folk."

The Romans went on to conquer a domain that, at its greatest extent, stretched from Scotland to Mesopotamia. Their borrowed Greek culture became part of the permanent legacy of Europe and the eastern Mediterranean. Today we speak automatically of our "Greco-Roman" heritage. But there was no necessary reason for the Romans to imitate the Greeks (the two did not even speak the same language), except that the ambitious Romans saw these people as superior to them in the civilizing arts.

The Romans were by no means the only ones to fall under the Greek spell. Another such people were the Celts. Extant Celtic pottery and metalwork clearly show that the "La Tène" culture, emerging ca. 500 B.C.E. in Gaul (modern France, Switzerland, and Belgium), was inspired by Greek goods and influences, undoubtedly introduced up the Rhone River by Greek traders from Massalia (modern Marseilles, founded by Greeks ca. 600 B.C.E.). By the first century B.C.E. the Celts of Gaul were writing in the Greek alphabet and had learned from the Greeks how to grow olive trees and grape vines (the latter mainly for winemaking). The creation of the French wine industry is a legacy of the ancient Greeks.

Similarly, from the 200s B.C.E. onward, the powerful African nation of Nubia, in what is now northern Sudan, traded with Greek merchants from Ptolemaic Egypt. In time the Nubian upper class adopted certain Greek styles of life: for instance, queens of Nubia were using the Greek name Candace down to the 300s C.E.

Nor were the Jews immune to Greek influence, especially after the conquests of Alexander the Great (334–323 B.C.E.) created a Greco-Macedonian ruling class in the Near

East. In religion, Jewish monotheism was not much affected by Greek paganism. But in society and business, many Jews of Near Eastern cities adapted enthusiastically to the Greek world. They attended Greek theater, exercised publicly in Greek gymnasiums, and used the Greek language for commerce and public life. In Egyptian Alexandria (although not everywhere else), Greek-speaking Jews forgot their traditional languages of Hebrew and Aramaic. For the benefit of such people, a Greek translation of the Hebrew Bible began being produced in Alexandria during the 200s B.C.E. Thus, for many assimilated Jews of this era, Judaism was preserved in Greek form. Today a Jewish house of worship is known by a Greek word—synagogue (from *sunagogē*, "gathering place")—which is but one reminder of the Jews' fascination with the Greeks.

This encyclopedia attempts to give all the essential information about the ancient Greek world. Aimed at high-school and college students and general readers, the book tries to convey the achievements of the Greek world, while also showing its warts. (And warts there were, including slavery, the subordination of women, brutal imperialism, and the insanely debilitating wars of Greek against Greek.)

The encyclopedia's entries, from "Abdera" to "Zeus," range in length from about 100 to 3,000 words. The entries embrace political history, social conditions, warfare, religion, mythology, literature, art, philosophy, science, and daily life. Short biographies are given for important leaders, thinkers, and artists. Particular care is taken, by way of several entries, to explain the emergence and the workings of Athenian democracy.

The book's headwords include the names of real-life people (for example, Socrates), mythical figures (Helen of Troy), cities (Sparta), regions (Asia Minor), and institutions (Olympic Games), as well as many English-language common nouns (archaeology, cavalry, epic poetry, marriage, wine). Supplementing the text are more than 70 ink drawings, based mainly on photographs of extant Greek sculpture, vase paintings, architecture, and metalwork.

My research has involved English-language scholarly books and articles, ancient Greek works in translation, and many of the ancient Greek texts themselves. (I have used my own translations for quotations from Greek authors.) In writing this encyclopedia, I have tried to be aware of recent archaeological finds and other scholarly developments. My manuscript has been vetted by an eminent scholar. However, I have chosen and shaped the material for the general reader, not the scholarly one.

I have assumed that the reader knows nothing about the ancient Greeks and that he or she wants only the "best" information—that is, for any given topic, only the main points, including an explanation of why the topic might be considered important in the first place. I have tried to keep my language simple but lively and to organize each entry into a brisk train of thought. Although facts and dates abound in this book, I hope they only clarify the bigger picture, not obscure it.

In choosing the entries, I have had to abbreviate or omit much. Names or topics that might have made perfectly good short entries—Antaeus, grain supply, or Smyrna—have been reduced to mere cross-references in the text or to listings in the index. The reader is therefore urged to consult the index for any subject not found as an entry.

In time frame, the encyclopedia covers more than 2,000 years, opening in the third millennium B.C.E. with the beginnings of Minoan civilization and ending with the Roman annexation of mainland Greece in 146 B.C.E. Occasionally an entry will trace an ongoing tradition, such as astronomy, beyond the cutoff date. And short entries are given for a few Roman-era Greek authors, such as Plutarch (ca. 100 C.E.) and the travel writer Pausanias (ca. 150 C.E.), because their work sheds important light on earlier centuries. But most Greek personages and events of the Roman Empire, including the spread of Christianity, are omitted here as being more relevant to the Roman story than the Greek.

Within its 2,000-year span, the encyclopedia gives most attention to the classical era—that is, roughly the 400s and 300s B.C.E., which produced the Greeks' greatest intellectual and artistic achievements and most dramatic military conflicts. The 400s B.C.E. saw the Greeks' triumphant defense of their homeland in the Persian Wars, followed by Athens's rise as an imperial power. This was the wealthy, democratic Athens of the great names—the statesman Pericles, the tragedians Aeschylus, Sophocles, and Euripides, the historian Thucydides, the sculptor Phidias, and the philosopher Socrates. In these years the Pathenon arose and the fateful Peloponnesian War was fought, ending in Athens's defeat. The 300s B.C.E. brought the rise of Macedon and the conquest of the Persian Empire by the Macedonian king Alexander the Great. This was the time of the philosophers Plato and Aristotle, the historian Xenophon, the orator Demosthenes, and the swashbuckling Macedonian prince Demetrius Poliorcetes. Many of the topics that will bring readers to a book about ancient Greece fall within these two centuries.

In a book of this scope written by one person, certain preferences are bound to sneak in. I have tried always to be thorough and concise. But I have allowed slightly more space to a few aspects that I consider more likely than others to satisfy the general reader's curiosity. When I studied Greek and Latin at graduate school, my happiest hours were spent reading Herodotus. He was an Ionian Greek who, in the mid-400s B.C.E., became the world's first historian, writing a long prose work of incomparable richness about the conflict between the Greeks and Persians. And I find, with all humility, that I have favored the same aspects that Herodotus tends to favor in his treatment—namely, politics, personalities, legends, geography, sex, and war.

—David Sacks

CHRONOLOGY OF THE ANCIENT GREEK WORLD

Historical Events	Cultural Events

The Aegean Bronze Age

2200 B.C.E.	Minoan civilization begins in Crete	
2000 B.C.E.	First Greek speakers arrive in Greece	
1750 B.C.E.	Peak of Minoan civilization in Crete	
1700 B.C.E.	Palace at Knossos destroyed by earthquake or war and subsequently rebuilt	
1600 B.C.E.	Mycenaean civilization begins in Greece	
1628 B.C.E.	Eruption of volcano on the island of Thera	
1250 B.C.E.		Construction of the Lion Gate at Mycenae
1200 B.C.E.	Decline of Mycenaean civilization	
1185 B.C.E.	Traditional date of the Trojan War	

The Greek "Dark Age"

1100 B.C.E.	Greek colonies established in Ionia (Asia Minor)	

The Archaic Period

790 B.C.E.	Greek trading post established at Al Mina (Syria)	
776 B.C.E.		First Olympic Games
775 B.C.E.	Greek colony of Pithecusae founded in Italy	The Greeks adopt the alphabet from the Phoenicians
750 B.C.E.		Homer's *Iliad* and *Odyssey* written down
734 B.C.E.	Greek colony of Corcyra (modern Corfu) established	
733 B.C.E.	Greek colony of Syracuse established in Sicily	
730 B.C.E.	Greek colonies established in South Italy and Sicily	
720 B.C.E.	Beginning of the Lelantine War between Chalcis and Eretria	
700 B.C.E.	Greek colonies established around the Black Sea (Asia Minor)	Hesiod's *Works and Days* and *Theogony*
680 B.C.E.	End of the Lelantine War	

(continues)

	Historical Events	Cultural Events
650 B.C.E.	"Lykourgan" reforms instituted at Sparta Kypselos establishes tyranny at Corinth	
621 B.C.E.	Draco issues law code with capital punishments in Athens	
620 B.C.E.		Poetry of Alcman
595 B.C.E.	First Greek coins are minted by the state of Aegina	
594 B.C.E.	Solon becomes archon at Athens	
590 B.C.E.		Temple of Artemis at Corcyra built entirely in stone Poetry of Sappho
585 B.C.E.		Thales predicts solar eclipse
583 B.C.E.	Tyranny at Corinth is overthrown	
582 B.C.E.		First Pythian Games
581 B.C.E.		First Isthmian Games
573 B.C.E.		First Nemean Games
566 B.C.E.	First Panathenaic Festival in Athens	
560–527 B.C.E.	Tyranny of Peisistratus and his sons in Athens	
530 B.C.E.	Pythagoras establishes a school at Croton, in south Italy	
520 B.C.E.		Red-figure pottery style begins to replace black-figure style in Athens
510 B.C.E.	Expulsion of the tyrant Hippias from Athens	
508 B.C.E.	Kleisthenes introduces democratic reforms in Athens	
499 B.C.E.	The Ionian cities revolt against the Persian Empire	
498 B.C.E.	Hippocrates becomes tyrant at Gela	
495 B.C.E.	The Persians capture Miletus in Ionia	
490 B.C.E.	The Greeks defeat the Persians at the Battle of Marathon Gelon becomes tyrant at Gela	Pindar's *Pythian 6*
486 B.C.E.		Pindar's *Pythian 7*
485 B.C.E.	Gelon becomes tyrant at Syracuse	
483 B.C.E.	Themistokles persuades Athenians to create large naval fleet	

The Classical Period

	Historical Events	Cultural Events
480 B.C.E.	The Persians defeat the Greeks at the Battles of Thermopylae and Artemision The Persians occupy Attica and sack the Acropolis in Athens The Greeks defeat the Persians at the Battle of Salamis	
479 B.C.E.	The Greeks defeat the Persians at the Battles of Plataea and Mycale	
478 B.C.E.	Formation of the Delian League Hieron succeeds Gelon as tyrant at Syracuse	
476 B.C.E.		Pindar's *Olympian 1*
472 B.C.E.		Aeschylus's *The Persians*
470 B.C.E.		Pindar's *Pythian 1* and *Isthmian 2*
467 B.C.E.		Aeschylus's *Seven Against Thebes*
464 B.C.E.	The Messenians revolt from Spartan control	
463 B.C.E.		Aeschylus's *The Suppliants*
461 B.C.E.	Long Walls are begun connecting Athens and Piraeus	
458 B.C.E.		Aeschylus's *Oresteia* (*Agamemnon*, *Libation Bearers*, *Eumenides*)
454 B.C.E.	Treasury of Delian League moved from Delos to Athens	
451 B.C.E.	Perikles passes citizenship law in Athens	

(continues)

Historical Events	Cultural Events
450 B.C.E.	City plan is designed for Piraeus by Hippodamus
	Polykleitos's *Doryphoros* (*Spear Bearer*)
	Sophokles' *Ajax*
449 B.C.E. Peace of Kallias	
447 B.C.E.	The Parthenon in Athens is begun
446 B.C.E. Boeotia and Megara revolt from Athenian control	Pindar's *Pythian 8*
The Spartans invade Attica	
Thirty Years' Peace causes temporary end to hostility between Athens and Sparta	
442 B.C.E.	Sophokles' *Antigone*
440 B.C.E. Revolt of Samos	
438 B.C.E.	Pheidias's *Athena Parthenos* is dedicated on the Acropolis in Athens
431 B.C.E. Beginning of the Peloponnesian War	Euripides' *Medea*
Battle of Potidaea	Thucydides begins his *History of the Peloponnesian War*
	Empedokles forms his theory of four humors of the body
429 B.C.E. Perikles dies in the plague at Athens	Sophokles' *Oedipus the King*
428 B.C.E.	Euripides' *Hippolytus*
425 B.C.E. The Athenians defeat the Spartans at the Battle of Sphacteria (Pylos)	Aristophanes' *Acharnians*
	Herodotus's *History of Greece*
424 B.C.E.	Aristophanes' *Knights*
423 B.C.E.	Aristophanes' *Clouds*
421 B.C.E. Peace of Nikias begins, causing a temporary end to the Peloponnesian War	Aristophanes' *Peace*
420 B.C.E.	Sophokles' *Electra*
418 B.C.E. The Spartans defeat the Athenians and Argives at the first Battle of Mantineia	
415 B.C.E. Peace of Nikias ends	Euripides' *Trojan Women*
The Athenians send an expedition against Syracuse (Sicily)	
414 B.C.E.	Aristophanes' *Birds*
413 B.C.E. Nikias and the Athenians surrender in Sicily	
411 B.C.E.	Aristophanes' *Lysistrata*
409 B.C.E.	Sophokles' *Philoctetes*
405 B.C.E. The Spartans defeat the Athenians at the Battle of Aegospotami	Aristophanes' *Frogs*
Dionysius I becomes tyrant at Syracuse	Euripides' *Bacchae* and *Iphigeneia* (presented posthumously)
404 B.C.E. Athens surrenders to Sparta to end the Peloponnesian War	
Rule of Thirty Tyrants is established in Athens	
403 B.C.E. Democracy is restored in Athens	
401 B.C.E.	Sophokles' *Oedipus at Colonus*

The Late Classical Period

399 B.C.E. Trial and death of Socrates in Athens	
394 B.C.E. Beginning of Corinthian War	
388 B.C.E.	Aristophanes' *Wealth*
387 B.C.E.	Plato establishes the Academy in Athens
386 B.C.E. King's Peace treaty signed between the Spartans and the Persians	

(continues)

Historical Events	Cultural Events
382 B.C.E. Sparta seizes citadel of Thebes	
379 B.C.E. The Spartans are expelled from Thebes	
378 B.C.E. Spartan-Theban alliance	
375 B.C.E.	Xenophon's *Anabasis*
371 B.C.E. The Thebans defeat the Spartans at the Battle of Leuctra	
362 B.C.E. The Mantineians defeat the Spartans at the second Battle of Mantineia	
Dionysius II succeeds Dionysius I as tyrant of Syracuse	
360 B.C.E.	Xenophon's *Hellenica*
354 B.C.E.	Demosthenes' first public speech
350 B.C.E.	Praxiteles' *Aphrodite of Knidos*
	King Mausolus's tomb is constructed at Halicarnassus
343 B.C.E.	Aristotle becomes the tutor of Alexander the Great
338 B.C.E. The Macedonians defeat the Greeks at the Battle of Chaironeia	
336 B.C.E. Alexander the Great succeeds his father, Philip II, as king of Macedon	
335 B.C.E.	Aristotle establishes the Lyceum in Athens
334 B.C.E. Alexander invades Asia Minor	
333 B.C.E. Alexander defeats King Darius at the Battle of Issus and conquers Persia	
332 B.C.E. Alexander conquers Egypt	
327 B.C.E. Alexander conquers southern India	

The Hellenistic Age

Historical Events	Cultural Events
323 B.C.E. Death of Alexander the Great	
316 B.C.E.	Menander's *Misanthrope*
301 B.C.E. Alexander's successors fight at the Battle of Ipsus	
300 B.C.E. King Seleucus establishes his capital, Antioch, on the Orontes in Syria	
290 B.C.E.	Construction of the Colossus (statue of Helios) at Rhodes
280 B.C.E.	Construction of the lighthouse at Alexandria
197 B.C.E. The Romans defeat the Macedonians	
146 B.C.E. The Romans sack Corinth	
133 B.C.E. Pergamon comes under Roman control	
64 B.C.E. Syria comes under Roman control	
31 B.C.E. Octavian defeats Mark Antony and Cleopatra at the Battle of Actium	
30 B.C.E. Egypt comes under Roman control	

Abdera This important Greek city is situated on the north Aegean coast in the non-Greek region known as THRACE. Located on a coastal plain near the mouth of the river Nestos, Abdera was a depot for TRADE with local Thracian tribesmen and an anchorage on the shipping route between mainland Greece and the HELLESPONT. Traditionally said to have been founded by Herakles in honor of the hero Abderos, the city was actually first settled around 650 B.C.E. by colonists from the city of Clazomenae. Soon afterward it was destroyed by the Thracians and was reestablished by Greek colonists around 545 B.C.E. These settlers came from Teos—a city in the Greek region of western ASIA MINOR called IONIA—which they had abandoned to the conquering Persians under King CYRUS (1). Among the Tean settlers was a young man, ANACREON, destined to become the most famous lyric poet of his day.

Like other Greek colonies of the northern Aegean, Abdera prospered from Thracian trade, which brought GOLD and SILVER ore, TIMBER, and SLAVES (available as war captives taken in Thracian tribal wars). These goods in turn become valuable Abderan exports to mainland Greece and other markets. Local wheatfields and fishing contributed to the city's prosperity. The disadvantages were periodic Thracian hostility and the northern climate (cold and wet by Greek standards).

Lying directly in the path of the Persian invasion of the spring of 480 B.C.E., Abdera submitted to the Persian king XERXES and hosted him at legendary expense. After the Persian defeat (479 B.C.E.), Abdera became an important member of the Athenian-controlled DELIAN LEAGUE (478 or 477 B.C.E.). In 457 B.C.E. wealthy Abdera was paying an annual Delian tribute of 15 TALENTS (as much

as BYZANTIUM and more than any other state except AEGINA).

Although other Greeks considered the Abderans to be stupid, the city produced at least two important thinkers of the middle and late 400s B.C.E. the sophist PROTAGORAS and the atomist philosopher DEMOKRITUS. In these years Abdera, like other cities of the silver-mining north Aegean, was famous for the beauty of its COINAGE. The city's symbol on coins was an ear of wheat.

Abdera passed briefly to Spartan influence after Athens's defeat in the PELOPONNESIAN WAR (404 B.C.E.), but by about 377 B.C.E., it had become a member of the SECOND ATHENIAN LEAGUE. Seized by the Macedonian king PHILIP II around 354 B.C.E., Abdera remained within the Macedonian kingdom over the next 180 years. During the fourth century B.C.E., the city expanded to the south on an urban grid plan design. This part of Abdera included a strong fortification wall, an acropolis, and two busy harbors. Sacked by Roman troops in 170 B.C.E. during the Third Macedonian War, Abdera recovered to become a privileged subject city in the Roman Empire.

Excavations on the site from 1950 to 1966 uncovered the outline of the city wall (with a circuit of about 3.4 miles) and the precise grid pattern of the late Classical expansion. The older part of Abdera and its cemetery have been the subject of excavations since 1981.

See also COLONIZATION; PERSIAN WARS; ROME.

Further reading: J. M. F. May, *The Coinage of Abdera* (London: Royal Numismatic Society, 1966); Dorothy and Nicholas E. Leekley, *Archaeological Excavations in Central and Northern Greece* (Park Ridge, N.J.: Noyes Press, 1980); A. J. Graham, "Abdera and Teos," *Journal of Hellenistic Studies* 112 (1992): 44–73.

Abydos   *See* SESTOS.

Academy   The Akademeia was a GYMNASIUM and park about a mile outside ATHENS, sacred to the local hero Akademos. During the sixth century B.C.E., one of Athens's three gymnasiums was founded here. In around 387 B.C.E., PLATO bought land and buildings in this suburb and set up a school of PHILOSOPHY there, which can be counted as the Western world's first university.

Plato's aim was to train the future leaders of Athens and other Greek states. Students at the early Academy did not pay fees, and lessons probably took place in seminars similar to the disputations portrayed in Plato's written *Dialogues.* Teachings emphasized MATHEMATICS and the Platonic reasoning method known as dialectic. In its breadth of inquiry, the Academy of 386 B.C.E. was distinct from all prior Greek schools of advanced study, which taught only RHETORIC, poetry, or the argumentative techniques of the SOPHISTS.

Two great students of the early Academy were the mathematician-astronomer Eudoxus of KNIDOS and the philosopher ARISTOTLE. Aristotle was considered Plato's possible successor as president, but after the master's death Academy members voted Plato's nephew Speusippus as head (347 B.C.E.). Aristotle eventually set up an Athenian philosophical school of his own, called the LYCEUM.

Under Speusippus and his successors, the Academy's curriculum became more mathematical and abstract, until Arcesilaus of Pitane (president ca. 265–242 B.C.E.) redirected it toward philosophical SKEPTICISM. Arcesilaus and his distant successor Karneades (ca. 160–129 B.C.E.) both were known for their criticisms of the rival school of STOICISM.

After the Romans annexed Greece (146 B.C.E.), the Academy attracted students from all over the Roman—and later the Byzantine—Empire. The Academy survived more than 900 years from its founding, until the Christian Byzantine emperor Justinian closed it and the other pagan philosophical schools in 529 C.E.

The school's name has produced the English common noun *academy,* meaning a place of rigorous advanced study. The site of the Academy has been investigated by Greek archaeologists since 1920.

See also EDUCATION.

Further reading: P. A. Brunt, "Plato's Academy and Politics" in *Studies in Greek History and Thought* (Oxford: Clarendon Press, 1993), 282–342; David Fowler, *The Mathematics of Plato's Academy,* 2d ed. (Oxford: Clarendon Press, 1999).

Acarnania   This region of northwest Greece lies between the Gulf of Patras (to the south) and the Gulf of AMBRACIA (to the north). It was named for Acarnan, son of ALCMAEON (1) and grandson of AMPHIRAEUS, who was said to have first settled the area. Although largely mountainous, Acarnania contains a fertile alluvial plain along the lower Acheloös River. Acarnania was inhabited by rough Greek "highlanders" who in the 400s B.C.E. were still known for carrying weapons in public. Their main town was named Stratos, and their political structure was a loosely-knit union of rural cantons (later, of towns). Acarnania was bordered on the west and east by hostile neighbors—the Corinthian colonies of the seaboard and the inland people of AETOLIA. Because of these threats, the Acarnanians sought alliances with several great states of the Greek world.

As allies of ATHENS in the PELOPONNESIAN WAR, Acarnanian troops under the Athenian general DEMOSTHENES (2) wiped out most of the army of the Corinthian colony of Ambracia in three days (426 B.C.E.). In 338 B.C.E. Acarnania (with the rest of Greece) passed to the control of the Macedonian king PHILIP II. The Acarnanians were staunch allies of King PHILIP V in his wars against Aetolia and shared his defeat in the disastrous Second Macedonian War against ROME (200–196 B.C.E.). Thereafter, Acarnania passed into Roman hands.

See also ALCMAEON (1).

Further reading: Stewart I. Oost, *Roman Policy in Epirus and Acarnania in the Age of the Roman Conquest of Greece* (Dallas: Southern Methodist University Press, 1954).

Achaea   For most of ancient Greek history, the place-name Achaea was applied to two different regions of Greece: (1) the hilly northwest corner of the PELOPONNESE and (2) a small area in THESSALY. The Peloponnesian Achaea (the more important of the two) was twice organized into a 12-town Achaean League, with shared government and citizenship. The First Achaean League was established at some date before the fifth century B.C.E. and lasted through the fourth century. This confederation was dissolved soon after it joined in the wars against Philip II of MACEDON in 338 B.C.E. A Second Achaean League was founded in 280 B.C.E.

Achaea was important in the Greek colonization of the western Mediterranean. In the late 700s B.C.E., colonists from Achaean cities founded or cofounded important Greek settlements in southern ITALY, including CROTON and SYBARIS. These cities were part of the area that became known as MAGNA GRAECA, due to the large number of settlements established there by colonists from Greece.

One of the most important cities in Achaea was SICYON, on the Gulf of Corinth. Prior to 251 B.C.E., Sicyon had been ruled by a tyrant. When the tyranny was overthrown, the commander Aratus came to power (active 251–213 B.C.E.) Sicyon joined the Achaean League and became one of its leading members, so that the league soon emerged as the strongest power of mainland

Greece. By tapping the Greeks' hatred of Macedonian overlordship, Aratus united the northern Peloponnese against Macedon. The Achaean League and its allies forced the Macedonians to retreat from CORINTH in 247 B.C.E., and for a few years the democratic league was the last hope for that unfulfilled dream of Greek history: the creation of an independent, federal state of Greece.

In 227 B.C.E., the Achaean League became threatened by its rival Peloponnesian state, SPARTA, and it requested aid from its previous enemy, Macedon. This resulted in a tremendous reduction in power and prestige for the league. By the time that fighting erupted between Macedon and ROME, it became clear that the Achaean League could no longer survive alone. As a Roman ally (198 B.C.E. and after), the Achaean League encompassed most of the Peloponnese, including the important cities of Corinth, Sparta, and Messene. However, resistance to Roman interference led to the disastrous Achaean War of 146 B.C.E., in which the Romans sacked Corinth, dissolved the league, and made Achaea part of a Roman province.

See also ACHAEANS.

Further reading: E. S. Gruen, "Aratus and the Achaean Alliance with Macedon," *Historia* 21 (1972): 609–625; ———, "The Origins of the Achaean War," *Journal of Hellenic Studies* 96 (1976): 46–49.

Achaeans   The word *Achaioi* (Achaeans) is one of the terms used by the poet HOMER (ca. 750 B.C.E.) as a general name for the Greeks. In this, Homer probably preserves a usage of the Mycenaean Age (ca. 1600–1200 B.C.E.), when Achaioi would have been the Greeks' name for themselves. As a result, modern scholars sometimes use the name *Achaeans* to mean either the Mycenaeans or their ancestors, the first invading Greek tribesmen of about 2100 B.C.E.

Intriguingly, a place-name pronounced *Ahhiyawa* has been deciphered in the cuneiform annals of the Hittite people of ASIA MINOR (1300s–1200 B.C.E.). In the documents, the name indicates a strong foreign nation, a sea power, with which the Hittite kings were on polite terms. Possibly this foreign nation was the mainland Greek kingdom ruled from the city of MYCENAE. The Hittite rendering *Ahhiyawa* may reflect a Greek place-name, Achaiwia or "Achaea," meaning the kingdom of Mycenae.

In later centuries, the Greek place-name ACHAEA came to denote a region of the northwestern PELOPONNESE, far from Mycenae. Probably that name arose because surviving Mycenaeans took refuge there after their kingdom's downfall.

See also MYCENAEAN CIVILIZATION.

Achilles (Greek: Achilleus, perhaps meaning "grief") This preeminent Greek hero in the legend of the TROJAN WAR was the son of the hero PELEUS and the sea goddess Thetis. He figured in many tales but received his everlasting portrait as the protagonist of HOMER's epic poem the *Iliad* (written down around 750 B.C.E.). At the story's climax, Achilles slays the Trojan champion HECTOR in single combat, fully aware that his own preordained death will follow soon.

To the Greek mind, Achilles embodied the old-time heroic code, having specifically chosen a brief and glorious life over one that would be safe and obscure. Achilles recounts the terms of this choice in a well-known passage in the *Iliad*:

> My goddess mother says that two possible destinies bear me toward the end of life. If I remain to fight at Troy I lose my homecoming, but my fame will be eternal. Or if I return to my dear home, I lose that glorious fame, but a long life awaits me [book 9, lines 410–416].

The *Iliad*'s announced theme is "the anger of Achilles" (book 1, lines 1–2). Opening in the war's 10th year, the poem portrays Achilles as a glorious individualist, noble and aloof to the point of excessive pride. Still a young man, he has come to the siege of TROY from his native THESSALY at the head of a contingent of troops, his Myrmidons ("ants"). After quarreling justifiably with the commander in chief, King AGAMEMNON, over possession of a captive woman named Briseis, Achilles withholds himself and his men from the battlefield (book 1). Consequently, the Greeks suffer a series of bloody reversals (books 8–15). Achilles rebuffs Agamemnon's offered reconciliation (book 9) but relents somewhat and allows his friend PATROKLUS to lead the Myrmidons to battle (book 16). Wearing Achilles' armor, Patroklus is killed by Hector, who strips the corpse.

Mad with grief, Achilles rushes to battle the next day wearing wondrous new armor, forged for him by the smith god HEPHAISTOS at Thetis's request (books 18–20). After slaying Hector, he hitches the Trojan's corpse to his chariot and drags it in the dust to the Greek camp (book 22).

His anger thus assuaged, Achilles shows his more gracious nature in allowing Hector's father, the Trojan king PRIAM, to ransom the body back (book 24). At the *Iliad*'s end Achilles is still alive, but his death has been foretold (for example, in book 19, lines 408–417). He will be killed by the combined effort of the Trojan prince PARIS and the god APOLLO, patron of the Trojans.

Greek writers later than Homer provide details of Achilles' life before and after the *Iliad*'s events. At Achilles' birth his mother tried to make him immortal by dipping him into the river Styx (or into fire or boiling water, in other versions). But she was interrupted or otherwise forgot to immerse the baby's right heel, and this later proved to be the hero's vulnerable "Achilles' heel."

Knowing at the Trojan War's outset that her son would never return if he departed, Thetis arranged with Lykromedes, king of the island of Skyros, to hide Achilles, disguised as a girl, in the WOMEN's quarters of the king's palace. There Achilles fathered a son with Lykomedes' daughter Deidameia; the boy was named NEOPTOLEMUS. The Greeks, having heard a prophecy that they could never take Troy without Achilles' help, sent ODYSSEUS and other commanders to find Achilles, which they did.

At Troy, Achilles showed himself the greatest of warriors, Greek or Trojan. Among the enemy champions he slew were, in sequence: Cycnus, TROILUS, Hector, Queen Penthesilea of the AMAZONS, and the Ethiopian king MEMNON. At last Achilles himself died, after his vulnerable heel was hit by an arrow shot by Paris and guided by Apollo. (Various myths say that either the arrow was poisoned or the wound turned septic.) In Homer's *Odyssey* (book 11), Odysseus meets Achilles among the unhappy ghosts in the Underworld. But later writers assigned to Achilles a more blissful AFTERLIFE, in the Elysian Fields.

See also FATE; PROPHECY AND DIVINATION.

Further reading: P. R. Hardee, "Imago Mundi. Cosmological and Ideological Aspects of the Shield of Achilles," *Journal of Hellenistic Studies* 105 (1985): 11–31; K. C. King, *Achilles: Paradigms of the War Hero from Homer to the Middle Ages* (Berkeley: University of California Press, 1987); J. T. Hooker, "The Cults of Achilles," *Rheinisches Museum für Philologie* 131 (1988): 1–7; J. Burgess, "Achilles' Heel. The Death of Achilles in Ancient Myth," *Classical Antiquity* 14 (1995): 217–243.

acropolis (akropolis)   The word *acropolis* comes from the Greek "*akro*" ("high") and "*polis*" ("city"). It generally refers to a hilltop citadel and was a vital feature of most ancient Greek cities, providing both a refuge from attack and an elevated area of religious sanctity. The best-known acropolis is at ATHENS, where a magnificent collection of temples and monuments, built in the second half of the fifth century B.C.E., remains partially standing today. The most famous of these buildings is the PARTHENON, the temple of ATHENA Parthenos (the maiden). In terms of natural setting, the highest and most dramatic Greek acropolis was on the 1,800-foot mountain overlooking ancient CORINTH.

Most early societies naturally concentrated their settlements on raised areas, less vulnerable to attack than low-lying sites. In ancient Greece the royal palaces of the MYCENAEAN CIVILIZATION arose on the choicest of these hills (1600–1200 B.C.E.). The Mycenaean Greeks favored hilltops close to agricultural plains and not too near the sea, for fear of pirate raids. Typical Mycenaean sites include MYCENAE, TIRYNS, Athens, and Colophon (meaning "hilltop"), a Greek city in ASIA MINOR. Of the great classical Greek cities, only SPARTA—a post-Mycenaean settlement—had a puny, unfortified acropolis. Rather than depend on a defensive citadel, Sparta relied on its invincible army and on the mountain ranges enclosing the region.

The Athenian acropolis is a limestone-and-schist formation that rises about 300 feet above the lower town. There is evidence of occupation on the hill as early as the Neolithic period (ca. 6500–4500 B.C.E.), but its association with the goddess Athena probably dates from the Bronze Age (ca. 1200 B.C.E.), when a Mycenaean palace stood there. ARCHAEOLOGY reveals that the acropolis's upper sides were first enclosed in a man-made wall around this time; a later wall from ancient times still encloses the upper rock face today.

Numerous dedications have been found on the Athenian acropolis from the sixth century B.C.E., including a series of numerous "korai," statues of youthful women, terra-cotta statuettes, bronze vessels, and pottery.

Like other Greek citadels, the Athenian acropolis played a role in its city's turbulent politics. Kylon (ca. 620 B.C.E.) and PEISISTRATUS (ca. 560 B.C.E.) each began an attempted coup by seizing the acropolis. Later, as dictator (546–527 B.C.E.), Peisistratus beautified the site with new marble temples to the gods. The temple to Athena was still unfinished when the Persians sacked Athens in 480 B.C.E. and destroyed all the monuments on the acropolis. The city of Athens and its allies vowed in the Oath of Plataea not to rebuild the temples but to leave them in their ravaged state as a memorial to the barbaric sacrilege of the Persians.

Several years after the Persians had been defeated, around 450 B.C.E., the Athenian statesman PERIKLES reversed the Oath of Plataea and initiated a building program that resulted in the remarkable monuments now standing on the Athenian acropolis—a focus of international tourism in the ancient world, as today. Financing for Perikles' acropolis building program came from tribute paid by Athens's allies in the DELIAN LEAGUE. The fact that other Greek states paid for Athens's beautification caused angry debate at that time, both among the allies and within Athens itself.

The Athenian acropolis building program was supervised by the sculptor PHEIDIAS. In addition, several architects were involved, as well as hundreds of other artisans and laborers. In part because of this ambitious project, the mid-fifth century B.C.E. is considered the "golden age" of Classical Greece. Already in the early Roman period, Periklean Athens was held up as an ideal of culture and beauty. In addition to the Parthenon, the acropolis building program included the small, Ionic temple of Athena Nike (Athena of Victory), the unusual erechtheion (which housed the cults of Athena, POSEIDON, and the legendary king Erechtheus), and the monumental Propylaea (gateway).

In the Hellenistic and Roman periods, very little construction took place on the Athenian acropolis. In subsequent later periods, several of the buildings on the site were converted into Christian churches, Frankish houses, and Turkish houses and other buildings.

The Athenian acropolis, built ca. 400 B.C.E. The gateway was in the west, front center. The small temple of Athena Nike is on the right. *(Alison Frantz Photographic Collection, American School of Classical Studies at Athens)*

Several important monuments and sanctuaries from antiquity can also be found on the slopes of the acropolis, including the Theater of DIONYSUS, the Sanctuary of ASKLEPIOS, the Odeion of Herodes Atticus, the Shrine of the Nymphs, the shrine of Aphrodite and Eros, and the Odeion of Perikles.

See also ARCHITECTURE; KALLIAS; PERSIAN WARS; THUCYDIDES (2).

Further reading: Robin Rhodes, *Architecture and Meaning on the Athenian Acropolis* (Cambridge: Cambridge University Press, 1995); Harrison Eiteljorg, *The Entrance to the Athenian Acropolis before Mnesicles* (Dubuque, Iowa: Kendall/Hunt, 1995); Diane Harris, *The Treasures of the Parthenon and Erechtheion* (New York: Oxford University Press, 1995); Jeffrey Hurwit, *The Athenian Acropolis: History, Mythology, and Archaeology from the Neolithic into the Present* (Cambridge: Cambridge University Press, 1999).

Adonis A beautiful mortal youth, Adonis was a lover of the goddess APHRODITE. According to the usual version of the MYTH, he was the son of a Cypriot or Syrian princess who had fallen in love with her own father and became impregnated by him. Growing up, Adonis was loved by both PERSEPHONE and Aphrodite. When the two rival goddesses appealed to ZEUS, he decreed that Adonis should spend part of the year with each. (This myth resembles the similar tale of DEMETER and Persephone.)

Out hunting one day in the mountains of what is now Lebanon, Adonis was gored to death by a wild boar—the disguised form of the jealous god ARES, Aphrodite's occasional lover. Roses or anemones sprang from the dying youth's blood; these scarlet flowers recall Adonis's beauty and mortality.

At ATHENS and other cities of classical Greece, the death of Adonis was commemorated each summer in a WOMEN's festival lasting about eight days. At the culmination, women of all social classes would stream out of the city in a mourning procession, wailing for the slain Adonis and carrying effigies of him to be thrown into the sea. For this occasion, women would cultivate "gardens of Adonis"—shallow baskets of earth in which seeds of wheat, fennel, and flowers were planted, to sprout quickly and then die and be thrown into the sea. While probably symbolizing the scorched bleakness of the eastern Mediterranean summer, this strange rite also invites a psychological interpretation—as a socially permitted emotional release for Greek women, amid their repressed and cloistered lives.

The worship of Adonis is a prime example of Greek cultural borrowing from non-Greek peoples of the Near East. According to modern scholars, the Greek cult of

A pair of small personal altars showing the death of Adonis in the arms of Aphrodite. They were probably used to hold sacrificial burnt offerings during the women's festival. *(The J. Paul Getty Museum)*

Adonis derived from a Phoenician festival of the mother goddess Astarte and her dying-and-reborn lover Baalat or Tammuz. The center of this worship was the Phoenician city of BYBLOS. Around the 700s B.C.E., Greek or Phoenician merchants brought this worship from Byblos to Greece perhaps by way of the Greco-Phoenician island of CYPRUS. In the Greek version of the myth, the sex-and-fertility goddess Astarte becomes the love goddess Aphrodite.

The name Adonis is not Greek but rather reflects the Phoenician worshippers' ritual cry of *Adon*, meaning "lord." (Compare Hebrew *Adonai*, "the Lord.")

Further reading: J. G. Frazer, *Adonis, Attis, Osiris: Studies in the History of Oriental Religion*. 3d ed. (New Hyde Park, N.Y.: University Books, 1962); R. A. Segal, "Adonis: A Greek Eternal Child," in *Myth and the Polis*, edited by Dora Pozzi and John Wickersham (Ithaca: Cornell University Press, 1991), 64–84; J. D. Reed, "The Sexuality of Adonis," *Classical Antiquity* 14 (1995): 317–347.

Adrastus *See* SEVEN AGAINST THEBES.

adultery *See* MARRIAGE.

Aegean Sea The approximately 80,000-square-mile section of the eastern Mediterranean stretching between Greece and ASIA MINOR, the Aegean is bounded on the north by the coast of ancient THRACE and on the south by the island of CRETE. This body of water contained or bordered upon most of the important ancient Greek states. The sea was supposedly named for the mythical King Aegeus, father of the Athenian hero THESEUS; Aegeus was said to have drowned himself in this sea. In fact, its name may come from the Greek word *aigis*, "storm."

See also CHIOS; CYCLADES; GREECE, GEOGRAPHY OF; LESBOS; RHODES; SAMOS.

Further reading: H. M. Denham, *The Aegean: A Seaguide to Its Coasts and Islands* (London: Murray, 1963).

Aegina This small island state is situated in the Saronic Gulf, in southeast-central Greece. Only 33 miles square, the triangular island lies 12 miles southwest of the Athenian coast and five miles northeast of the nearest point on the Argolid. Aegina's capital city, also called Aegina, stood in the northwest part of the island, facing the Argolid and Isthmus.

In prehistoric times, Aegina was inhabited by pre-Greek peoples and then by Mycenaean Greeks. In the

Iron Age, the unfertile island gave rise to merchant seamen who claimed descent from the mythical hero Aeacus (son of ZEUS and the river nymph Aegina). In the late 600s and the 500s B.C.E., Aegina was a foremost Greek sea power, with a Mediterranean TRADE network rivaling that of CORINTH. In the 400s B.C.E., however, the island became a bitter enemy of nearby ATHENS. The Athenian statesman PERIKLES (mid-400s B.C.E.) called Aegina "the eyesore of Piraeus"—a hostile presence on the sea horizon, as viewed from Athens's main harbor.

The Aeginetans's trade routes have been difficult to trace, because they were simply the middlemen in the selling of most ware. Specifically, they manufactured no POTTERY of their own for modern archaeologists to find in far-off locales. But we know that Aeginetan trade reached EGYPT and other non-Greek Near Eastern empires. Around 595 B.C.E. Aegina became the first Greek state to mint coins—an invention probably learned from the kingdom of LYDIA, in ASIA MINOR. Made of SILVER and stamped with the image of a sea turtle, Aegina's COINAGE inspired other Greek states to start minting.

The 500s B.C.E. were Aegina's heyday. Relations with Athens had not yet soured. Aeginetan shippers brought Athenian black- and red-figure pottery to the ETRUSCANS of western ITALY; they probably also brought WINE, metalwork, and textiles. In exchange, the Etruscans gave raw metals such as silver and tin.

Aegina's prosperity is reflected in the grand temple of the goddess Aphaia (a local equivalent of ATHENA or ARTEMIS), built of local limestone soon after 500 B.C.E. Located near the island's northeast coast and still partly standing today, this Doric-style structure is the best-preserved early temple in mainland Greece. The building's pediments contained marble figures of mythical Greek heroes fighting at TROY; these important Archaic SCULPTURES were taken away by German archaeologists in 1811 C.E. and now are housed in the Antikensammlungen und Glyptotek in Munich.

Hostility with Athens flared in the late 500s B.C.E. The two states had become trade rivals, and Athens feared Aegina's navy, the largest in Greece at that time (about 70 ships). Hatred worsened when Aegina submitted to envoys of the Persian king DARIUS (1), the enemy of Athens (491 B.C.E.).

By about 488 B.C.E., Aegina and Athens were at war. The Athenians, urged by their statesman THEMISTOKLES, built 100 new warships, doubling their navy's size. But this Athenian navy fought alongside the Aeginetans in defending Greece against the invasion of the Persian king XERXES (480 B.C.E.).

After the Persians' retreat, Aegina joined SPARTA's alliance for protection against Athens. Nevertheless, in 459 B.C.E. the Athenians defeated an Aeginetan fleet, landed on the island, and besieged the capital. Defeated, Aegina was brought into the Athenian-controlled DELIAN LEAGUE and made to pay the highest tribute of any member, 30 TALENTS. Probably at this time Athens settled a garrison colony on the island. Aegina's anger and defiance in these years are suggested in certain verses by the Theban poet PINDAR, who had friends there.

According to the Thirty Years' Peace, agreed to by Athens and Sparta in 446 B.C.E., the Athenians were supposed to grant Aegina a degree of self-determination (*autonomia*). This promise was never kept. The resentful Aeginetans continually urged the Spartans against Athens until, at the outbreak of the PELOPONNESIAN WAR (431 B.C.E.), Athens evicted the Aeginetans and repopulated the whole island with Athenian colonists. The Aeginetans, resettled by Sparta, eventually were reinstalled on Aegina by the triumphant Spartan general LYSANDER (405 B.C.E.).

After some renewed hostility toward Athens in the CORINTHIAN WAR (395–386 B.C.E.), Aegina fades from history. Aegina is reached most easily today by a short ferry ride from the port of PIRAEUS. It is a quiet island and attracts tourists mostly for its beaches and for the lovely ruins of the Temple of Aphaia. Aegina is also known for its pistachios, said to be the best in Greece.

See also NAUCRATIS; PERSIAN WARS; WARFARE, NAVAL.

Further reading: Sonia de Neuhoff, *Aegina* (Milan: Apollo Editions, 1978); T. J. Figueira. *Aegina: Society and Politics.* 3d ed. (New York: Arno Press, 1998); K. Pilafidis-Williams, *The Sanctuary of Aphaia on Aegina in the Bronze Age* (Munich: Hirmer, 1998).

Aegospotami   Aigospotamoi, "goat's rivers," was a shoreline on the European side of the HELLESPONT, opposite the city of Lampsacus, where the strait is about two miles wide. There in September 405 B.C.E., the final battle of the PELOPONNESIAN WAR was fought. At one swoop, the Spartan commander LYSANDER eliminated the Athenian fleet and left the city of ATHENS open to blockade and siege. Within eight months of the battle, Athens had surrendered.

The battle was waged over possession of the Hellespont. In the summer of 405 B.C.E., Lysander slipped into the Hellespont with a fleet of about 150 warships. There he captured the Athenian ally city Lampsacus and occupied its fortified harbor. In pursuit came 180 Athenian warships—almost the entire Athenian navy—led by six generals drawn from a depleted Athenian high command.

The Athenians encamped opposite Lampsacus, on the open shore of Aegospotami. The next morning they rowed out toward Lampsacus to offer battle. But Lysander kept his fleet inside the harbor's defenses, which the Athenians were unwilling to attack. Returning late in the day to Aegospotami, the Athenians beached their ships and went ashore for firewood and food. Lysander sent out a few fast ships to spy on them.

This procedure continued for several days. The Athenian generals did not withdraw to the nearby port city of SESTOS, where a fortified harbor could offer defense; apparently they thought a withdrawal would allow Lysander to escape.

On the fifth evening the Athenian crews beached their ships as usual at Aegospotami and went ashore. This time the Spartan scout ships signaled back to Lysander's fleet—which immediately rowed out from Lampsacus and attacked. The Athenians were completely unprepared: many of their ships still lay empty as the Spartans reached them. Only one Athenian leader, KONON, got his squadron away; the other 170 or so Athenian ships were captured, with most of their crewmen. The Spartans collected their prisoners—perhaps 5,000 Athenians and allies—and put to death the 3,000 or so Athenians among them.

See also WARFARE, NAVAL.

Further reading: B. S. Strauss, "Aegospotamoi reexamined," *American Journal of Philology* 104 (1983): 24–35; G. Wylie, "What Really Happened at Aegospotamoi?" *L'Antiquité classique* 55 (1986): 125–141.

Aeneas (Greek: Aineias)   In Greek MYTH, Aeneas was a Trojan hero of royal blood, the son of the goddess APHRODITE and the mortal man Anchises. Aeneas's earliest appearance is as a minor character in HOMER's epic poem the *Iliad* (written down ca. 750 B.C.E.). He is shown as a respected figure, pious to the gods (who protect him in his overambitious combats with the Greek champions DIOMEDES and ACHILLES) The god POSEIDON prophesies that Aeneas will escape Troy's doom and that his descendants will rule future generations of Trojans (book 20).

Over later centuries, partly in response to Greek exploration and COLONIZATION in the western Mediterranean, there arose various non-Homeric legends describing how, after the fall of Troy, Aeneas voyaged westward, establishing cities in SICILY, ITALY, and elsewhere. In the first century B.C.E. the Roman poet Vergil amalgamated these tales in his patriotic Latin epic poem, the *Aeneid*. Vergil's Aeneas endures hardships and war in order to found the city of Lavinium and initiate a blood line that will eventually build the city of ROME. The Julio-Claudian emperors, including Julius Caesar and Augustus, claimed direct descent from Aeneas through his son, Ascanius (Iulus). Since Aeneas was the son of Aphrodite, this gave the Imperial family the right to assert that they were also related to the goddess (whom they called Venus). Aeneas was thus one of the very few Greek mythological figures who was more important in the Roman world than in the Greek.

See also TROJAN WAR.

Further reading: K. Galinsky, *Aeneas, Sicily, and Rome* (Princeton, N.J.: Princeton University Press, 1969); David West, trans. *The Aeneid,* 2d ed. (London: Penguin Books, 2003).

Aenus (Greek: Ainos)   This rich and important Greek trading city is situated on the northeastern Aegean coast, in the principally non-Greek region known as THRACE. Aenus was founded around 600–575 B.C.E. by colonists from CYME and other AEOLIAN GREEK cities of ASIA MINOR. The city lay advantageously at the mouth of the Hebrus River, in the territory of the powerful Odrysian Thracians. Like its distant Greek neighbor ABDERA, Aenus prospered from TRADE with the Thracians, who brought TIMBER, SLAVES, SILVER ore, and other precious resources for overseas export to the major markets of Greece.

Around 477 B.C.E. Aenus became an important member of the Athenian-controlled DELIAN LEAGUE. Around this time Aenus was minting one of the most admired silver coinages in the Greek world; the Aenian coins showed the head of HERMES, god of commerce. The city remained an Athenian ally during the PELOPONNESIAN WAR (431–404 B.C.E.); and it came under Spartan rule after Athens' defeat. Later Aenus passed to the region's dominant powers: MACEDON, PERGAMON, and, in the 100s B.C.E., ROME. A late tradition connected the founding of Aenus with the mythical Trojan-Roman hero AENEAS.

See also AEOLIS; COINAGE.

Further reading: J. M. F. May, *Ainos: Its History and Coinage 474–341 B.C.* (London: Oxford University Press, 1950).

Aeolian Greeks   This ethnic branch of the ancient Greeks was distinct from the two other main groups, the IONIAN GREEKS and DORIAN GREEKS. The Aeolians spoke a dialect called Aeolic and claimed a mythical ancestor, Aeolus (not the ruler of the winds in the *Odyssey,* but another Aeolus, son of the first Greek man, HELLEN).

During the epoch of MYCENAEAN CIVILIZATION (ca. 1600–1200 B.C.E.), the Aeolians seem to have been centered in central and northeastern Greece. But amid the Mycenaeans' violent end (ca. 1100–1000 B.C.E.), displaced Aeolians migrated eastward across the AEGEAN SEA. First occupying the large eastern island of LESBOS, these people eventually spread along the northwest coast of ASIA MINOR, in the region that came to be called AEOLIS.

By the 600s B.C.E. Aeolian Greeks inhabited Lesbos and Aeolis (in the eastern Aegean) and BOEOTIA and THESSALY (in mainland Greece). The strong poetic traditions of Aeolian culture reached their peak in the poetry of SAPPHO and ALCAEUS, written at Lesbos in the early 500s B.C.E.

See also GREEK LANGUAGE; LYRIC POETRY.

Further reading: S. Bommeljé, "Aeolis in Aetolia: Thuc. 3, 102, 5 and the origins of the Aetolian ethnos," *Historia* 37 (1988): 297–316.

Aeolic dialect   *See* GREEK LANGUAGE.

Aeolis   This region on the northwest coast of ASIA MINOR, was inhabited by AEOLIAN GREEKS. Extending from the Hermus River northward to the HELLESPONT, Aeolis was colonized by Aeolians in eastward migrations between about 1000 and 600 B.C.E.; the nearby island of

LESBOS apparently served as an operational base for these invasions. The major city of Aeolis was KYMĒ.

Aeolis prospered from east-west TRADE. However, the loose confederation of Aeolis' cities never achieved international power in the Greek world, and Aeolis was dwarfed in importance by its southern Greek neighbor, the region called IONIA.

Further reading: British Museum, Department of Coins and Medals, *Catalogue of the Greek Coins of Troas, Aeolis, and Lesbos,* edited by Warwick Wroth (Bologna: A. Forni, 1982).

Aeolus   *See* ODYSSEUS.

Aeschines   (ca. 400–320 B.C.E.) *Athenian orator*
Aeschines is remembered mainly as a political enemy of the famous orator DEMOSTHENES (1). In 346 B.C.E., when the Macedonian king PHILIP II was extending his power by war and intimidation throughout Greece, Aeschines and his mentor, Eubulus, belonged to an Athenian party that sought a negotiated peace with Philip; Aeschines served on two Athenian embassies to Philip that year. Aeschines' conciliatory speeches in the Athenian ASSEMBLY brought him into conflict with Demosthenes, who staunchly advocated war.

Soon Philip's flagrant expansionism had borne out Demosthenes' warnings, and Demosthenes brought Aeschines to court twice (346 and 343 B.C.E.) on charges that he had advised the Athenians irresponsibly, acting as Philip's paid agent. Although the bribery charge was probably false, Demosthenes' second prosecution nearly succeeded, with Aeschines winning the jury's acquittal by merely one vote.

Thirteen years later Aeschines struck back with a charge against an associate of Demosthenes named Ktesiphon, who had earlier persuaded the Athenians to present Demosthenes with a golden crown, in gratitude for his statesmanship. By a procedure known as *graphē paranomon*, Aeschines accused Ktesiphon of having attempted to propose illegal legislation in the assembly. Demosthenes spoke in Ktesiphon's defense; his speech, *On the Crown,* survives today and is considered to be Demosthenes' masterpiece of courtroom oratory. Defeated and humiliated, Aeschines retired to the island of RHODES.

Three of Aeschines' speeches are extant, each relating to one of his three court cases against Demosthenes. In the speech *Against Timarchus* (346 B.C.E.), Aeschines successfully defended himself by attacking Demosthenes' associate Timarchus, who was coprosecuting. Invoking an Athenian law that forbade anyone of bad moral character from addressing the court, Aeschines argued persuasively that Timarchus had at one time been a male prostitute. The speech is a valuable source of information for us regarding the classical Greeks' complex attitudes toward male HOMOSEXUALITY. Aeschines' speech *Against*

Ktesiphon (330 B.C.E.) also is interesting, for it gives a negative assessment of Demosthenes' career.

See also LAWS AND LAWCOURTS; RHETORIC.

Further reading: E. M. Harris, *Aeschines and Athenian Politics* (New York: Oxford University Press, 1995); R. L. Fox, "Aeschines and Athenian Democracy," in *Ritual, Finance, Politics. Athenian Democratic Accounts Presented to David Lewis* (Oxford: Clarendon Press, 1994), 135–155.

Aeschylus   (525–456 B.C.E.) *Famous playwright of fifth-century-B.C.E. Athens*
Aeschylus was one of the three most famous tragedians in Classical Athens; the other two were SOPHOKLES and EURIPIDES. He wrote 90 plays, of which only seven survive under his name; and of these, *Prometheus Bound* may not really have been written by him. Like other Athenian tragedians, Aeschylus wrote mainly for competition at the annual Athenian drama festival known as the City Dionysia, where three playwrights would each present three tragedies and a satyr play. Among Aeschylus's extant plays is the only complete Greek tragic trilogy to come down to us, the *Oresteia,* or *Oresteian Trilogy*—one of the greatest works of Greek literature.

Aeschylus's place in Western culture is due to his solemn vision of divine justice, which orders events on earth. He drew largely on MYTHS for his stories, and described his plays as morsels from the banquet of HOMER. He was also a pioneer of stage technique at a time when Greek drama was still crude, and he was a spokesman for the big, patriotic emotions that had been aroused by Athens's victory in the PERSIAN WARS (490–479 B.C.E.). Aeschylus won first prize at the Dionysian competition 13 times; after his death, his plays came to be seen as old-fashioned in theme and language.

Aeschylus was born into an aristocratic family of Eleusis, a city in Athenian territory. His father's name was Euphorion. Little is known of Aeschylus's life, but as a teenager he would have witnessed two great public events: the expulsion of the dictator HIPPIAS (1) (510 B.C.E.) and the institution of Athenian DEMOCRACY as fashioned by the reformer KLEISTHENES (1) (508 B.C.E.). In 490 B.C.E. Aeschylus took part in the single most important moment in Athenian history, fighting as a soldier in the Battle of MARATHON, which repulsed a Persian invasion (and in which his brother Cynegeirus was killed). Aeschylus also may have fought 10 years later at the sea battle of SALAMIS (1), where a much larger Persian invasion was defeated. His participation in these great events shaped his patriotism and his faith in an ordering divinity—themes that echo throughout his plays. These were beliefs shared by his audiences in the 480s–460s B.C.E.

One anecdote from Aeschylus's early years mentions a competition ca. 489 B.C.E. to choose the official epitaph for the Athenian dead at Marathon. Aeschylus's submitted poem was not selected, although he was an Athenian who had fought at the battle; the judges, finding that his poem lacked sympathy of expression, preferred the poem submitted by the poet SIMONIDES of Keos. A modern scholarly reconstruction of the two poems has shown that Simonides' poem characterized the dead men as saviors of Greece, but Aeschylus's as saviors of Athens. The episode is significant in showing Aeschylus's pro-Athenian outlook and his inclination toward the grand vision rather than the human details. Both of these traits tend to contrast Aeschylus with the younger tragedian Euripides, and it is no coincidence that the comic playwright ARISTOPHANES fictionally showed Aeschylus and Euripides competing in his comedy *Frogs* (405 B.C.E.).

Aeschylus presented his first tragedies in around 499 B.C.E. and won his first festival victory in 484 B.C.E., with a trilogy whose name we do not know. His tragedy *The Persians* was presented in 472 B.C.E. as part of a trilogy that won first prize, and its *chorēgos* (paying sponsor) was the rising young politician PERIKLES. *The Persians* apparently is modeled somewhat on *The Phoenician Women*, by the tragedian PHRYNICHUS. It is unusual in that its subject matter is drawn not from myths but rather from a recent event—namely, the Persian disaster at Salamis, as seen from the Persian viewpoint. The play's title describes the chorus (a group of Persian councillors), and the protagonist is Atossa, mother of the Persian king XERXES. In the simple plot, arrival of news of the calamity is followed by an invocation of the ghost of the great Persian king DARIUS (1), Xerxes' father. The Persians are presented theatrically, but with pathos and dignity, as victims of Xerxes' insane HUBRIS.

Shortly afterward, Aeschylus traveled to SICILY, to the wealthy court of the Syracusan tyrant HIERON (1) (patron also of such poets as Simonides and PINDAR). It was probably at this time that Aeschylus wrote a new play, *Women of Aetna* (now lost), to commemorate Hieron's founding of a city of that name, near Mt. Etna. Aeschylus returned to Athens to compete at the City Dionysia of 468 B.C.E., but he lost first place to a 28-year-old contestant named Sophokles.

Of Aeschylus's other extant work, the *Seven Against Thebes*—a pageant centering on the Theban king Eteocles' decision to meet his brother, Polynices, in combat to defend his city—was presented in 467 B.C.E. Another play, *The Suppliants*—about the Danaid maidens' flight from their suitors, the sons of Aegyptus—dates from around 463 B.C.E. The three plays of the *Oresteia*—*Agamemnon*, the *Libation Bearers*, and the *Eumenides*—were performed in 458 B.C.E.

Perhaps alarmed by growing class tensions at Athens, Aeschylus traveled again to Sicily, where he died at the age of 69; *Prometheus Bound*, if it is in fact by Aeschylus, may have been presented in Sicily in his final years. He was buried at GELA. Aeschylus's brief verse epitaph, which he supposedly prepared himself, ignored his many

literary honors and mentioned only that he had fought at Marathon.

The Oresteian trilogy, Aeschylus's greatest work, describes the triumph of divine justice working through a series of horrific events on earth. In the first play, *Agamemnon*, the vainglorious Agamemnon, fresh from his victory in the TROJAN WAR, is so misled by pride that he cannot see that his wife, the adulterous CLYTAEMNESTRA, plans to murder him. After the killing, their son, ORESTES, must avenge his father by slaying his mother in the trilogy's second play, the *Libation Bearers* (*Chōephoroi*). But this act in turn incites the wrath of supernatural fiends, the FURIES (Erinues), whose divine function is to avenge a parent's blood. In the third play, the *Eumenides*, Orestes is pursued by the chorus of Furies to Athens, where he is cleansed of his curse with the help of ATHENA and APOLLO. Tried for his murder before the Athenian law court of the AREOPAGOS, Orestes is acquitted, and his persecutors are invited to stay on at Athens as protective spirits—the "Kindly Ones" of the play's title. The *Eumenides* is simultaneously a bit of Athenian nationalism and a profound vision of civilized society as a place where the old, violent code of blood vengeance has been replaced by law.

Aeschylus was responsible for many innovations that soon became standard on the Athenian stage. He developed the use of lavish costumes and introduced a second speaking actor, thereby greatly increasing the number of possible speaking roles (since each actor could "double" or "triple" on roles). Aeschylus had a fondness for visual effects and wild, demonstrative choral parts, which his successors found crude. Yet in places his language has a spellbinding solemnity, and in the scenes leading up to the murders in the *Agamemnon* and *Libation Bearers*, he is a master of suspense.

His later life saw a period of serious political strife at Athens, between radical democrats and more right-wing elements. The brilliant left-wing statesman THEMISTOKLES was ostracized (ca. 471 B.C.E.) and forced to flee to PERSIA to avoid an Athenian death sentence, but his policies eventually were taken up by the young Perikles and his comrades. It is evident that Aeschylus was a member of this democratic party, not only from his 472 B.C.E. association with Perikles, but also from the plays he wrote. The Athenian navy is indirectly glorified in *The Persians*; there are muted, approving references to Themistokles in *The Persians* and *The Suppliants*; and a major aim in the *Eumenides* (458 B.C.E.) is to dignify the Areopagos, which in real life had recently been stripped of certain powers by left-wing legislation.

But Aeschylus's work was never partisan in a petty way: plays such as *The Suppliants* and the *Eumenides* end with hopeful reconciliation between opposing forces, and in this we can see the lofty, generous spirit of an artist who sought out the divine purpose in human affairs.

See also DIONYSUS; ELECTRA; EPHIALTES; PROMETHEUS; SEVEN AGAINST THEBES; THEATER.

Further reading: S. Goldhill, *Language, Sexuality, Narrative: The Oresteia* (Princeton, N.J.: Princeton University Press, 1984); Philip Vellacott, *The Logic of Tragedy: Morals and Integrity in Aeschylus' Oresteia* (Durham, N.C.: Duke University Press, 1984); C. J. Herington, *Aeschylus* (New Haven, Conn.: Yale University Press, 1986); Alan H. Sommerstein, *Aeschylean Tragedy* (Bari: Levante, 1996); Anthony J. Podlecki, *The Political Background of Aeschylean Tragedy,* 2d ed. (London: Bristol Classical Press, 1999); Harold Bloom, ed., *Aeschylus: Comprehensive Research and Study Guide* (Broomall, Pa.: Chelsea House, 2002).

Aesop (ca. 620–560 B.C.E.) *Supposed author of a number of moralizing fables, many involving animals as characters*
According to Greek legend, Aesop was a Phrygian slave on the island of SAMOS in the 500s B.C.E. He was said to have earned his freedom through his cleverness and lived afterward at the court of King Croesus of Sardis. On a visit to the oracle of APOLLO at DELPHI, Aesop openly criticized the priests there, who murdered him in their anger. Another version says that Aesop had been sent to Delphi by Croesus with gold as a gift to the citizens, but when he refused to distribute the money after seeing their greed, he instead sent it back to the king. The incensed Delphians then executed Aesop as a public criminal. A statue of Aesop was erected in Athens, carved by the famous Greek sculptor LYSIPPUS.

In fact, it is not certain whether Aesop existed as a real person. Aesop may just be a name around which certain ancient folktales gravitated, as with Homer and the epic poems attributed to him.

One of the best known of Aesop's fables tells of the race between the tortoise and the hare. The overconfident hare, stopping to nap in the middle of the race, loses to his slower but steadier opponent.

Animal parables also occur in extant verses by ARCHILOCHOS (ca. 650 B.C.E.), whose writings may have inspired some of the tales that we known as Aesop's.

Further reading: Anton Wiechers, *Aesop in Delphi* (Meisenheim, Germany: Hain, 1961); Ben E. Perry, *Studies in the Text History of the Life and Fables of Aesop* (Chico, Calif.: Scholars Press, 1981); J.-Th. A. Papademetriou, *Aesop as an Archetypal Hero* (Athens: Hellenic Society for Humanistic Studies, 1997); C. A. Zafiropoulos, *Ethics in Aesop's Fables. The Augustana Collection* (Leiden, Netherlands: E. J. Brill, 2001).

Aetolia Mountainous region of central Greece, north of the Corinthian Gulf, bordered on the west by ACARNANIA and on the east by the Mt. Parnassus massif. Interior Aetolia contained good farmland, but the southern mountains blocked Aetolia from the gulf and from outside influences. Through the 400s B.C.E. the Aetolians remained rugged Greek "highlanders," divided by tribal feuds and known for carrying weapons in public for self-defense.

During the PELOPONNESIAN WAR, Aetolia was invaded by the Athenian general DEMOSTHENES (2), who hoped to seize the eastward mountain route into enemy BOEOTIA. But the Aetolians, arrayed as javelin-throwing light infantry, defeated the cumbersome Athenian HOPLITES in the hills (426 B.C.E.).

In the late 300s B.C.E. Aetolia emerged as a force in the Greek resistance to the overlordship of MACEDON. By now the Aetolians had united into a single federal state— the Aetolian League. Aetolian towns shared a common citizenship, representative ASSEMBLY, and a war captain, elected annually; the capital city was Thermon. By the late 200s B.C.E. the aggressive league dominated most of central Greece, with alliances extending to the PELOPONNESE. Aetolia fell into conflict with its southern rival, the Achaean League, as well as with Macedon. In 218 B.C.E. the dynamic Macedonian king PHILIP V invaded Aetolia and sacked Thermon.

Aetolia was a natural ally for Philip's enemy, the imperialistic Italian city of ROME. Allied to Rome in the Second Macedonian War, the Aetolians helped defeat Philip at the Battle of Cynoscephalae (197 B.C.E.). However, disappointed by the mild Roman peace with Macedon, the Aetolians allied with the Seleucid king ANTIOCHUS (2) III against Rome (192 B.C.E.). After the Romans had defeated Antiochus, they broke the Aetolian League's power and made it a Roman subject ally (189 B.C.E.).

See also ACHAEA; WARFARE, LAND.

Further reading: W. J. Woodhouse, *Aetolia: Its Geography, Topography, and Antiquities* (New York: Arno Press, 1973); S. Bommeljé, et al., *Aetolia and the Aetolians: Towards the Interdisciplinary Study of a Greek Region* (Utrecht, Netherlands: Parnassus Press, 1987).

afterlife Throughout ancient Greek history, nearly all Greeks believed in some form of life after death. Only the philosophy called EPICUREANISM (after 300 B.C.E.) maintained unequivocally that the human soul died with the body. Because Greek RELIGION had no specific doctrine on the subject, beliefs in the afterlife varied greatly, from crude superstition to the philosopher PLATO's lofty vision (ca. 370 B.C.E.) of an immortal soul freed of its imperfect flesh and at one with absolute reality in another world.

The primitive concept that the dead somehow live on in their tombs never disappeared from Greek religion. The shaft graves at MYCENAE—datable to 1600–1550 B.C.E., at the dawn of MYCENAEAN CIVILIZATION—were filled with armor, utensils, and even pets and SLAVES killed in sacrifice, to comfort the deceased in the afterlife. This practice may have been inspired by the burial rites of Egyptian pharaohs, but the general idea seems to have survived in Greece for over 1,000 years. Greeks of the 400s and 300s B.C.E. were still offering food and drink at the graveside, as nourishment for the dead.

Another belief was that the souls of the dead traveled to an Underworld, the realm of the god HADES and his wife, PERSEPHONE. Unlike the modern concept of Hell, this "House of Hades" (as the Greeks called it) was not primarily a place of punishment. It was, however, a cold and gloomy setting, where the souls—after being led from the living world by the messenger god HERMES—endured a bleak eternity.

The earliest extant description of Hades' kingdom comes in book 11 of HOMER's epic poem the *Odyssey* (written down around 750 B.C.E.), when the living hero ODYSSEUS journeys there by ship to seek prophecy. The site is vaguely described as a grim shoreline of OCEANUS, at the edge of the living world. (Later writers tended to situate it underground.) There Odysseus recognizes the ghosts of some of his family and former comrades. He

A pottery statuette of a woman mourning the soul of a loved one carried to the Underworld; a tomb decoration *(Alison Frantz Photographic Collection, American School of Classical Studies at Athens)*

also sees the torments of three sinners—Tityus, TANTALUS, and SISYPHUS—who had betrayed the friendship of the gods. The only people to be excused from Hades' realm were those who had been granted divinity and who now resided with the other gods on Mt. OLYMPUS. These lucky few included HERAKLES and the twins CASTOR AND POLYDEUCES.

Gradually, concepts of reward and punishment were enlarged. Poets wrote of a place called Elysium (*Elusion*) where certain souls, chosen by the gods, enjoyed a happy afterlife. Also known as the Islands of the Blessed, this locale is described by the Theban poet PINDAR (476 B.C.E.) in terms of shady parklands and athletic and musical pastimes—in other words, the ideal life of the living Greek aristocrat. Post-Homeric sources placed ACHILLES there with other heroes, including the Athenian tyrannicides of 510 B.C.E. HARMODIUS AND ARISTOGEITON.

Similarly, legend began to specify a lowermost abyss in Hades' realm, a place called Tartarus. This was the scene of punishment for the evil TITANS and for the worst human sinners. (Post-Homeric sources add the DANAIDS and IXION to the group.) Typical punishments require the prisoner to endure eternal frustration of effort (Sisyphus, the Danaids) or desire (Tantalus).

Greek writers such as Plato began to describe the mythical judges who assigned each soul to Elysium, Tartarus, or the netherworld. These judges were MINOS and Rhadamanthys (who were brothers) and Aeacus, all of whom had once been mortal men. The concept of eternal judgment contains an obvious ethical message—a warning to act justly in this life—that resembles the later Christian view.

The well-known rivers of the Underworld are best described in Vergil's Latin epic poem, the *Aeneid* (ca. 20 B.C.E.). But the idea of rivers or lakes in Hades' kingdom goes back at least to the Greek poet HESIOD's *Theogony* (ca. 700 B.C.E.). The Greeks associated these Underworld waters with actual rivers of mainland Greece, apparently believing that the waters continued their course underground. The Styx ("hated") was an actual river in ARCADIA. The Acheron ("woeful") flowed in EPIRUS, near an oracle of the Dead. The Underworld's other rivers were Lethe ("forgetting"), Cocytus ("wailing"), and Pyriphlegethon or Phlegethon ("burning"). These dire names probably referred to Greek FUNERAL CUSTOMS rather than to any punishment for the souls.

Legend usually described the Styx as the Underworld's boundary. New arrivals were brought across by the old ferryman Charon, and Greek burial sites often included placing a coin in the corpse's mouth, to pay for this final passage. The monstrous many-headed dog KERBEROS stood watch on the Styx's inner bank, preventing the souls from leaving.

This grim Greek picture of the common man's afterlife eventually inspired a reaction: A number of fringe religious movements arose, assuring their followers of a happy afterlife. These were called mystery cults or mysteries (*mustēria,* from *mustēs,* "an initiate"). While centering on a traditional deity such as DIONYSUS, DEMETER, or Persephone, the mysteries claimed to offer the correct beliefs and procedures for admittance into Elysium. In Greek tombs of southern ITALY from about 400 B.C.E., archaeologists have discovered golden tablets inscribed with precise directions for the soul entering the Underworld: The soul is warned not to drink from the attractive spring of forgetfulness—"seen on the right, where the white cypress grows"—but from the lake of remembrance, beyond.

One mystery faith, ORPHISM, emphasized reincarnation (also known as transmigration). According to this belief, each person's soul passed, at death, into a newborn body, whether human or not. The new assignment was based on the person's conduct and belief in the prior life; bad souls descended through criminals, slaves, and animals, but a right-living soul ascended to kings and heroes, eventually gaining admittance to Elysium. This concept was adapted by the philosophers PYTHAGORAS (ca. 530 B.C.E.) and EMPEDOKLES (ca. 450 B.C.E.), who influenced Plato.

In the Hellenistic and Roman periods, other mystery religions from the eastern Mediterranean became extremely popular, including those of Osiris and Mithras. These cults welcomed worshippers of all ages, genders, and social status, and their teachings of a blissful afterlife were enhanced by their rituals of rebirth and reincarnation. At the same time, Judaism and Christianity developed from relatively minor local cults into the major religious institutions that they are today, eventually replacing the polytheistic belief systems of the ancient Greeks.

See also ELEUSINIAN MYSTERIES; HELLENISTIC AGE; PROPHECY AND DIVINATION.

Further reading: Jan M. Bremmer, *The Early Greek Concept of the Soul* (Princeton, N.J.: Princeton University Press, 1983); Robert Garland, *The Greek Way of Death* (Ithaca, N.Y.: Cornell University Press, 1984); Jan N. Bremmer, "The Soul, Death, and the Afterlife in Early and Classical Greece," in *Hidden Future. Death and Immortality in Ancient Egypt, Anatolia, the Classical, Biblical, and Arabic-Islamic World,* edited by Jan N. Bremmer, Th. P. J. van den Hout, and R. Peters (Amsterdam: Amsterdam University Press, 1994), 91–106; C. Penglase, "Some Concepts of Afterlife in Mesopotamia and Greece," in *The Archaeology of Death in the Ancient Near East,* edited by Stuart Campbell and Anthony Green (Oxford: Oxbow Books, 1995), 192–195; B. C. Dietrich, "Death and Afterlife in Minoan Religion," *Kernos* 10 (1997): 19–38.

Agamemnon   In MYTH, Agamemnon was the king of MYCENAE and ARGOS, son of ATREUS, the husband of

A gold mask portrait thought to be of Agamemnon, king of Mycenae, who led the expedition against Troy to recover Helen *(Alison Frantz Photographic Collection, American School of Classical Studies at Athens)*

KLYTEMNESTRA, and the commander of the allied Greek army in the TROJAN WAR. Agamemnon's earliest appearance in literature is in HOMER's epic poem the *Iliad* (written down around 750 B.C.E.), where he is portrayed negatively. Contrary to his name, which means "very steadfast," Agamemnon is shown to be an irresolute, arrogant, and divisive leader. His quarrel with the Greek champion ACHILLES over possession of a female war captive provokes Achilles to withdraw from the fighting and sets in motion the *Iliad's* tragic plot.

The events leading up to Agamemnon's command are told by Homer and later writers. The Greek-Trojan conflict began when Helen, wife of MENELAUS (Agamemnon's brother) was seduced by the Trojan prince PARIS and eloped with him. Agamemnon organized an expedition against TROY to recover Helen, but incurred Klytemnestra's hatred by sacrificing their daughter IPHIGENIA as a blood offering to the hostile goddess ARTEMIS, who was sending contrary winds to prevent the Greek ships' departure.

After the Greeks sacked Troy, Agamemnon sailed for home with his war booty, which included the captured Trojan princess CASSANDRA. But on the very day that they stepped ashore, Agamemnon and Cassandra were murdered by henchmen of Agamemnon's treacherous cousin Aegisthus, Klytemnestra's illicit lover. (This is Homer's version in the *Odyssey;* in later tales the king dies while emerging from his bath, stabbed by Aegisthus or axed by Klytemnestra.) It was left to Agamemnon's son ORESTES and daughter ELECTRA to avenge his murder.

Agamemnon's downfall is the subject of Athenian playwright AESCHYLUS's tragedy *Agamemnon* (458 B.C.E.), the first play in the Oresteian Trilogy.

See also HELEN OF TROY.

Further reading: Christopher Logue, *The Husbands: An Account of Books 3 and 4 of Homer's Iliad* (London: Faber, 1994); Donna F. Wilson, *Ransom, Revenge, and Heroic Identity in the Iliad* (New York: Cambridge University Press, 2002); Aeschylus, *Oresteia*, translated by Alan Shapiro and Peter Burian (New York: Oxford University Press, 2003).

Agathokles (361–289 B.C.E.) *Ruthless and flamboyant ruler of the Sicilian Greek city of SYRACUSE from 316 to 289 B.C.E.*

Agathokles was the last of the grandiose Syracusan TYRANTS. He challenged the mighty African-Phoenician city of CARTHAGE and captured most of SICILY from Carthaginians and fellow Greeks. His imperial reign in the Greek West was inspired partly by the example of ALEXANDER THE GREAT's successors in the East.

Agathokles did not come from the ruling class. Born in Thermae, in the Carthaginian-controlled western half of Sicily, he was the son of a Greek manufacturer of POT-TERY; enemies later derided Agathokles as a mere potter. Emigrating to Syracuse, he came to prominence as an officer in the Syracusan army. In 316 B.C.E. he overthrew the ruling Syracusan OLIGARCHY and installed himself as *turannos,* or dictator, with the common people's support.

Many adventures followed. Suffering a major defeat in battle against the Carthaginians, Agathokles was besieged by land and sea inside Syracuse (summer 311 B.C.E.). But he solved this predicament with an amazingly bold action: In August 310 B.C.E., when the Carthaginians briefly relaxed their naval blockade, Agathokles sailed from Syracuse harbor with 60 ships and a mercenary army of about 13,000 to invade Carthage itself.

His was the first European army to land in Carthaginian North Africa. But despite his victories over Carthaginian armies in the field, Agathokles failed to capture the city. Meanwhile, in Sicily, Syracuse held out against the Carthaginians; but a Sicilian-Greek revolt against Agathokles induced the tyrant to abandon his African army under his son Archagatus and return to Sicily. Eventually Archagatus and his brother were murdered by the army, which evacuated North Africa.

Agathokles made peace with the Carthaginians, giving up territories in west Sicily (306 B.C.E.). But he soon became the sole ruler of Greek-held eastern Sicily. In 304 B.C.E., patterning himself on Alexander the Great's heirs who were reigning as supreme monarchs in the East, Agathokles adopted the absolute title of king (*basileus*).

He then extended his power to Greek south ITALY and western mainland Greece. In about 300 B.C.E. he drove off the Macedonian king KASSANDER, who was besieging CORCYRA. Agathokles took over Corcyra and gave it, twice, as a dowry for his daughter Lanassa's two influential MARRIAGES, first to the Epirote king PYRRHUS (295 B.C.E.) and then to the new Macedonian king, DEMETRIUS POLIORKETES (ca. 291 B.C.E.). The aging Agathokles himself married a third wife, a daughter of the Greek Egyptian king PTOLEMY (1). But his hope of founding a grand dynasty faded when his son Agathokles was murdered by a jealous relative.

The elder Agathokles died at age 72, probably from jaw cancer. Although he had thwarted the Carthaginian menace, he left no legacy of good government for Sicily. However, his military exploits were influential in demonstrating that mighty Carthage was susceptible to invasion. The Romans would invade Carthage more effectively during their Second Punic War (202 B.C.E.).

Further reading: R. R. Holloway, "The Bronze Coinage of Agathocles," in *Greek Numismatics and Archaeology. Essays in Honor of Margaret Thompson,* edited by Otto Morkholm and Nancy Waggoner (Wetteren, Belgium: Editions NR, 1979), 87–95; M. B. Borba Florenzano, "Political Propaganda in Agathocles' coins," in *Actes du XIᵉ Congrès international de numismatique, Bruxelles 8–13 septembre 1991* (Louvain-la-Neuve, 1993), 71–77; M. Ierardi, "The Tetradrachms of Agathocles of Syracuse. A Preliminary Study," *American Journal of Numismatics* 7–8 (1995–1996): 1–73.

Agathon (ca. 450–401 B.C.E.) *Athenian tragic playwright of the late 400s B.C.E.*

Agathon was considered by the Athenians to be their fourth greatest tragedian after AESCHYLUS, SOPHOKLES, and EURIPIDES. Less than 40 lines of his work survive; these show a clever, polished style, influenced by the contemporary rhetorician GORGIAS and by the SOPHISTS. Agathon won his first drama competition at the annual festival known as the City Dionysia, in 416 B.C.E., with a tragic trilogy whose titles have not survived.

We know little of Agathon's life. But we do know that in 407 B.C.E. he left Athens—as Euripides had done—for the court of the Macedonian king Archelaus, and there (like Euripides), Agathon died.

From references in ARISTOTLE's *Poetics* we know that Agathon was an innovator. He often removed the chorus from the story's action, reducing the choral odes to mere interludes. In his day he was noteworthy for his tragedy *Antheus,* of which he invented the entire plot himself, rather than drawing on MYTH or history. His plots were overinvolved; Aristotle once criticized him for having crammed the entire tale of the TROJAN WAR into one play.

Agathon had personal beauty and apparently an effete manner. He appears as a fictionalized character in ARISTOPHANES' comedy *Thesmophoriazusae* (411 B.C.E.) and is burlesqued for his effeminacy—but not for his writing, which Aristophanes calls "good" (*agathos*). Agathon also appears as a character in the philosopher PLATO's dialogue the *Symposium* (ca. 370 B.C.E.), which is set at a drinking party at Agathon's house to celebrate his 416 B.C. competition victory.

See also THEATER.

Further reading: Pierre Leveque, *Agathon* (Paris: Societé d'édition Les Belles Lettres, 1955).

Agesilaos (444–360 B.C.E.) *Spartan king who reigned 399–360 B.C.E.*
Agesilaos led SPARTA during the city's brief phase of supremacy after the PELOPONNESIAN WAR. Although a capable battlefield commander, he steered Sparta into a shortsighted policy of military domination in Greece that eventually provoked the rise of a challenger state, THEBES.

The Athenian historian XENOPHON was a friend of Agesilaos and wrote an admiring biography of him, as well as including his exploits in the general history titled *Hellenica*. These two extant writings provide much of our information about Agesilaos.

A son of King ARCHIDAMUS of Sparta's Eurypontid royal house, Agesilaos was dynamic, pious, and lame in one leg. He became king after the death of his half brother, King Agis II. In 396 B.C.E. he took 8,000 troops to ASIA MINOR to protect the Spartan-allied Greek cities there from Persian attack. Marching inland through Persian-held west-central Asia Minor, Agesilaos defeated the Persians in battle before being recalled to Sparta (394 B.C.E.). His raid probably helped inspire the future conquests of ALEXANDER THE GREAT.

Agesilaos had been summoned home to help his beleaguered city in the CORINTHIAN WAR. Bringing his army overland through THRACE and THESSALY, he descended southward into hostile BOEOTIA, where he narrowly defeated a coalition army of Thebans, Argives, Athenians, and Corinthians at the Battle of Coronea (394 B.C.E.). Wounded, and with his army now too weak to occupy Boeotia, Agesilaos withdrew to Sparta. He commanded subsequent Spartan actions against ARGOS (391 B.C.E.), CORINTH (390 B.C.E.), ACARNANIA (389 B.C.E.), and defiant Thebes (378–377 B.C.E.).

His hostility toward the Theban leader EPAMINONDAS at a peace conference resulted in renewed war and a disastrous Spartan defeat at the Battle of LEUKTRA (371 B.C.E.). In the disarray that followed, Agesilaos helped lead the defense of the Spartan homeland, culminating in the stalemate Battle of MANTINEIA (362 B.C.E.).

After peace was made, the 82-year-old king sailed to EGYPT with 1,000 Spartan mercenary troops to assist an Egyptian prince's revolt against the Persians. (The expedition's purpose was to replenish Sparta's depleted revenues.) The revolt went awry, and Agesilaos died on the voyage home.

See also EURYPONTID CLAN.

Further reading: Paul Cartledge, *Agesilaos and the Crisis of Sparta* (Baltimore: Johns Hopkins University Press, 1987); M. A. Flower, "Agesilaus of Sparta and the Origins of the Ruler Cult," *Classical Quarterly* 38 (1988): 123–134; Charles D. Hamilton, *Agesilaus and the Failure of Spartan Hegemony* (Ithaca, N.Y.: Cornell University Press, 1991); D. R. Shipley, *A Commentary on Plutarch's Life of Agesilaos: Response to Sources in the Presentation of Character* (Oxford: Clarendon Press, 1997).

Agiad clan The Agiads (Agiadai) were the senior royal family at SPARTA, which had an unusual government in that it was ruled simultaneously by two kings. The Agiads, "descendants of Agis," traced their ancestry back to a legendary figure who was one of the sons of HERAKLES. As the senior house, the Agiads enjoyed certain ceremonial privileges over their partners, the EURYPONTID CLAN. Notable Agiad kings include the brilliant KLEOMENES (1) and Leonidas, the commander at the Battle of THERMOPYLAE.

Further reading: R. Martínez-Lacy, "The Application of the Concept of Revolution to the Reforms of Agis, Cleomenes, and Nabis at Sparta," *Quaderni di Storia* 46 (1997): 95–105; S. Hodkinson, "The Development of Spartan Society and Institutions in the Archaic Period," in *The Development of the Polis in Ancient Greece,* edited by Lynette Mitchell and P. J. Rhodes (London: Routledge, 1997), 83–102; A. Powell, *Athens and Sparta: Constructing Greek Political and Social History from 478 B.C.* (New York: Routledge, 2001).

agora The open "place of assembly" in an ancient Greek city-state. Early in Greek history (900s–700s B.C.E.), free-born males would gather in the agora for military duty or to hear proclamations of the ruling king or COUNCIL. In the more settled centuries that followed, the agora served as a marketplace where merchants kept open-air stalls or shops under colonnades.

Classical ATHENS boasted a grand agora—the civic heart of the city that dominated Greece. This area had been used as a cemetery as early as the third millennium B.C.E. Under the Athenian dictators PEISISTRATUS and HIPPIAS (1) (second half of the 500s B.C.E.), the agora was cleared to a rectangular open area of about 600 by 750 yards, bordered with grand public buildings. Devastated by the occupying Persians in 480–479 B.C.E., the agora was rebuilt in the later 400s to include temples, government buildings, and several colonnades, of which the best known was the Stoa Poikilē (painted colonnade). The agora continued to be the center of Athenian commercial and political life throughout antiquity. One of the most prominent buildings added to the space in the Roman period was the Odeion of Agrippa, built in 15 B.C.E.

The ancient Athenian agora has been excavated by the American School of Classical Studies since 1931. In the 1950s, the Hellenistic Stoa of Attalos was reconstructed on the east side of the agora, and today it serves as the site museum and as storage and office space for the excavation team. Another building that has been rebuilt, using a large amount of its original material, is the Doric temple on a hill overlooking the west side of the agora, the so-called Hephaisteion (previously misidentified as a temple of THESEUS and now generally identified as a temple of HEPHAISTOS), built around 449 B.C.E.

See also ARCHITECTURE; ASSEMBLY; DEMOCRACY; OSTRACISM; PAINTING; STOICISM.

Further reading: John McK. Camp, *The Athenian Agora: Excavations in the Heart of Classical Athens* (London: Thames and Hudson, 1986); American School of Classical Studies at Athens, *The Athenian Agora: A Guide to the Excavation and Museum,* 4th ed. (Athens, ASCSA, 1990).

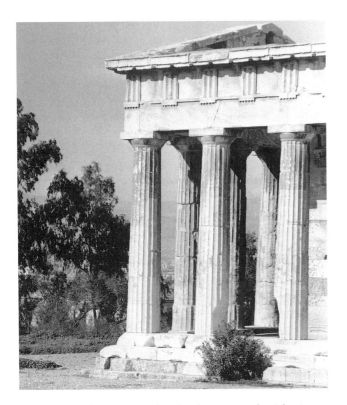

An example of the Doric order of architecture at the Athenian agora. There were eight columns front and back and 17 along both sides. A triangular gable or pediment in the roof front and back usually contained sculptures. *(Alison Frantz Photographic Collection, American School of Classical Studies at Athens)*

agriculture *See* FARMING.

Ajax (1) In the legend of the TROJAN WAR, Ajax (Greek Aias) was king of SALAMIS (1) and son of Telamon. After ACHILLES, he was the bravest Greek warrior at Troy. In HOMER's epic poem the *Iliad,* Ajax engages in many combats—for example, dueling the Trojan hero HECTOR to a standoff (book 7) and leading the Greeks in defense of their beached ships (book 13). Giant in size, stolid, and slow-spoken, Ajax embodies the virtue of steadfastness. He carries a huge oxhide shield and is often called by the poetic epithet "bulwark of the Achaeans." Homer implicitly contrasts him with his chief rival among the Greeks, the wily ODYSSEUS. Although the stronger of the two, Ajax loses a WRESTLING match to Odysseus's skill (*Iliad* book 23).

As described by Homer in the *Odyssey* (book 11), Ajax's death came from his broken pride over this rivalry. After Achilles was killed, Ajax and Odysseus both claimed the honor of acquiring his wondrous armor. The dispute was arbitrated by Trojan prisoners of war, who agreed that Odysseus had done more to harm the Trojan cause. Maddened with shame, Ajax eventually killed himself with his own sword. This tale is the subject of the extant tragedy *Ajax,* written around 450–445 B.C.E. by the Athenian playwright SOPHOKLES. Sophokles' Ajax is brought down by his flaws of anger and pride—and by a deep nobility that prevents him from accepting a world of intrigue and compromise personified by Odysseus.

See also ACHAEANS; HUBRIS.

Further reading: Joe P. Goe, *Genre and Meaning in Sophokles' Ajax* (Frankfurt: Athenaeum, 1987); Sophokles, *Ajax,* translated by Shomit Dutta (New York: Cambridge University Press, 2001).

Ajax (2) Often known as the lesser Ajax, this warrior was the son of Oileus and leader of troops from LOCRIS. In the legend of the TROJAN WAR, he was brave, swift-footed, arrogant, and violent. His savage behavior at the sack of TROY, unmentioned by the poet HOMER, is described by later writers. Finding the Trojan princess CASSANDRA in sanctuary at the goddess ATHENA's altar, Ajax pulled her away and raped her. He was hated by Athena, but his death, as described in Homer's *Odyssey* (book 4), occurred at POSEIDON's hands. On the homeward voyage from Troy, Ajax's ship was wrecked; he reached shore safely but sat atop a cliff declaring hubristically that he had beaten the gods. Poseidon, enraged, blasted him back into the sea.

See also HUBRIS.

Further reading: R. Rubenstein, "Ajax and Cassandra: An Antique Cameo and a Drawing by Raphael," *Journal of the Warburg and Courtauld Institutes* 50 (1987): 204–205; Joan B. Connelly, "Narrative and Image in Attic Vase Painting. Ajax and Kassandra at the Trojan Palla-

In the tragic play by Sophokles, Tekmessa covers Ajax's body after his suicide. The Brygos painter of this cup shows the sword entering through the back rather than through the stomach, a unique way to "fall on one's sword." *(The J. Paul Getty Museum)*

dion," in *Narrative and Event in Ancient Art,* edited by Peter J. Holliday (New York: Cambridge University Press, 1993), 88–129.

Akragas (**Acragas, modern Agrigento**) In antiquity, Akragas was the second-most-important Greek city of SICILY, after SYRACUSE. Today the site contains some of the best-preserved examples of Doric-style monumental Greek ARCHITECTURE.

Located inland, midway along the island's southern coast, Akragas is enclosed defensively by a three-sided, right-angled mountain ridge. The city was founded in about 580 B.C.E. by Dorian-Greek colonists from the nearby city of GELA and the distant island of RHODES. Akragas lay close to the west Sicilian territory of the hostile Carthaginians, and the city soon fell under the sway of a Greek military tyrant, Phalaris, who enlarged the city's domain at the expense of the neighboring native Sicans around 570–550 B.C.E. (Notoriously cruel, Phalaris supposedly roasted his enemies alive inside a hollow, metal bull set over a fire.)

Akragas thrived as an export center for grain to the hungry cities of mainland Greece. Local WINE, olives, and livestock added to the city's prosperity. Under the tyrant Theron (reigned 488–472 B.C.E.), Akragas became the capital of a west Sicilian empire. Theron helped defeat the Carthaginians at the Battle of HIMERA (480 B.C.E.) and

used Carthaginian war captives as labor for a grand construction program at Akragas. Among Theron's works was a temple of ZEUS, never finished but intended to be the largest building in the Greek world.

After ousting Theron's son and successor, Thrasydaeus, the Akragantines set up a limited DEMOCRACY (ca. 472 B.C.E.). Associated with this government was Akragas's most illustrious citizen—the statesman, philosopher, and physician EMPEDOKLES (ca. 450 B.C.E.). In Empedokles' time, Akragas underwent a second building program, whose remnants include the temples that stand today along the city's perimeter ridge as if guarding the site. The most admired of these is the beautifully preserved Temple of Concord (so-called today, perhaps really a temple of CASTOR AND POLYDEUCES).

Captured and depopulated by the Carthaginians in 406 B.C.E., Akragas was resettled by the Corinthian commander TIMOLEON (ca. 338 B.C.E.) but never recovered its former greatness. By about 270 B.C.E. the city was again a Carthaginian possession. As a strategic site in the First Punic War between CARTHAGE and ROME (264–241 B.C.E.), Akragas was twice besieged and captured by Roman troops. In 210 B.C.E. it was again captured by the Romans and soon thereafter repopulated with Roman colonists.

See also DORIAN GREEKS; ORPHISM; TYRANTS.

Further reading: A. Bruno, "Ancient Greek Water Supply and City Planning. A Study of Syracuse and Acragas," in *Technology and Culture* (1974): 389–412; M. Bell, "Stylobate and Roof in the Olympeion at Akragas," *American Journal of Archaeology* 84 (1980): 359–372.

Alcaeus (ca. 620–580 B.C.E.) *Lyric poet of the city of Mytilene on the island of Lesbos*
Born into an aristocratic family, Alcaeus was a contemporary and fellow islander of the poet SAPPHO. Like her he wrote love poems, but unlike her, he also wrote of his involvement in great events, such as the civil strife between Mytilene's traditional ARISTOCRACY and ascendant TYRANTS. Better as a poet than as a political analyst, Alcaeus was a spokesman for the old-fashioned aristocratic supremacy, which in his day was being dismantled throughout the Greek world.

Although no one complete poem by him has come down to us, the surviving fragments show his talent and give a dramatic biographical sketch. When Alcaeus was a boy in around 610 B.C.E., his elder brothers and another noble, PITTACUS, expelled the local tyrant. Soon Alcaeus was fighting under Pittacus's command in Mytilene's war against Athenian settlers in northwest ASIA MINOR. Alcaeus threw away his shield while retreating and (like ARCHILOCHOS, an earlier Greek poet) wrote verses about it.

When another tyrant arose in Mytilene, Alcaeus went into exile until the tyrant died. Alcaeus may have gone home—but only for a brief time—because soon his former comrade Pittacus was ruling singly in Mytilene, and Alcaeus and many other nobles were expelled. In his poetry Alcaeus raved against Pittacus as a "low-born" traitor and expressed despair at being excluded from the political life that was his birthright.

Apparently Alcaeus went to EGYPT, perhaps as a mercenary soldier. (Meanwhile, his brother joined the army of the Babylonian king Nebuchadnezzer and took part in the campaign that captured Jerusalem in 597 B.C.E.) At some point Alcaeus and his friends planned to attack Mytilene and depose Pittacus, but the common people stood by their ruler. Supposedly Pittacus at last allowed Alcaeus to come home.

Like Sappho, Alcaeus wrote in his native Aeolic dialect and used a variety of meters. A number of his extant fragments are drinking songs, written for solo presentation at a SYMPOSIUM. Even by ancient Greek standards, Alcaeus seems to have been particularly fond of WINE. He wrote hymns to the gods, including one to APOLLO that was much admired in the ancient world. In accordance with the upper-class sexual tastes of his day, he also wrote love poems to young men.

More than 550 years after Alcaeus's death, his poetry served as a model for the work of the Roman poet Horace.

See also GREEK LANGUAGE; HOMOSEXUALITY; HOPLITE.

Further reading: Anne P. Burnett, *Three Archaic Poets: Archilochus, Alcaeus, Sappho* (Cambridge, Mass.: Harvard University Press, 1983).

Alcestis   In MYTH, Alcestis was the wife of King Admetus of Pherae in THESSALY. She became Admetus's wife after he was able, with the god APOLLO's help, to fulfill her father Pelias's onerous precondition of yoking a lion and wild boar to a chariot and driving it around a racecourse.

Alcestis is best known for the story of how she voluntarily died in her husband's place. Apollo, discovering from the Fates that his mortal friend Admetus had only one day to live, arranged that Admetus's life be spared if a willing substitute could be found; the only one to consent was Alcestis. In EURIPIDES' tragedy *Alcestis* (438 B.C.E.), this old tale of wifely duty is recast as a disturbing account of female courage and male equivocation.

See also FATE.

Further reading: Euripides, *Alcestis,* translated by William Arrowsmith (New York: Oxford University Press, 1989); Charles Segal, *Euripides and the Poetics of Sorrow: Art, Gender, and Commemoration in Alcestis, Hippolytus, and Hecuba* (Durham, N.C.: Duke University Press 1993); Sarah W. Goodwin and Elisabeth Bronfen, eds., *Death and Representation* (Baltimore: Johns Hopkins University Press, 1993); Kiki Gounaridou, *Euripides and Alcestis: Speculation, Simulation, and Stories of Love in the Athenian Culture* (Lanham, Md.: University Press of America, 1998).

Alcibiades   (ca. 450–404 B.C.E.)   *Athenian general, politician, and social figure*
Alcibiades strongly influenced the last 15 years of the PELOPONNESIAN WAR between ATHENS and SPARTA. The mercurial Alcibiades embodied the confident Athenian spirit of the day. Although brilliant as a leader in battle, he was prone to dangerously grandiose schemes in war strategy and politics. His fellow citizens repeatedly voted him into high command, yet they mistrusted him for his private debaucheries and for his ambition, which seemed aimed at seizing absolute power of Athens. After his political enemies organized the people against him (415 B.C.E.), Alcibiades spent three years as a refugee turncoat, working for the Spartans (414–412 B.C.E.). Pardoned by Athens in its hour of need, he led the Athenians through a string of victories on land and sea (411–407 B.C.E.) that could have saved the city from defeat. But the Athenians turned against him once more, and he died in exile, murdered at Spartan request, soon after Athens surrendered.

As a flawed genius of tragic dimensions, Alcibiades is vividly portrayed in extant Greek literature. His Athenian contemporaries, the historians THUCYDIDES (1) and XENOPHON, describe him in their accounts of the Peloponnesian War. A biography of Alcibiades comprises one of PLUTARCH's *Parallel Lives,* written around 100–110 C.E. A fictionalized Alcibiades appears in dialogues written by the philosopher PLATO in around 380 B.C.E.

Alcibiades was born into a rich and powerful Athenian family during the Athenian heyday. His mother, Deinomache, belonged to the aristocratic Alcmaeonid clan. After his father, Kleinias, was killed in battle against the Boeotians (447 B.C.E.), Alcibiades was raised as a ward of Deinomache's kinsman PERIKLES, the preeminent Athenian statesman. Breeding and privilege produced a youth who was confident, handsome, and spoiled, and he became a rowdy and glamorous figure in the homosexual milieu of upper-class Athens; Plutarch's account is full of gossip about men's infatuated pursuit of the teenage Alcibiades. Later he also showed a taste for WOMEN, especially for elegant courtesans. He married an Athenian noblewoman, Hipparete, and they had two children, but Alcibiades' conduct remained notoriously licentious. We are told that he commissioned a golden shield, emblazoned with a figure of the love god EROS armed with a thunderbolt.

In his teens Alcibiades became a follower of the Athenian philosopher SOCRATES, who habitually tried to prompt innovative thought in young men bound for public life. This is the background for the scene in Plato's *Symposium* where a drunken Alcibiades praises Socrates to the assembled thinkers: According to Plato's version, the middle-age Socrates was in love with Alcibiades but never flattered the younger man or had sexual relations with him, despite Alcibiades' seductive advances.

Alcibiades reached manhood at the start of the Peloponnesian War. At about age 18 he was wounded in the

Battle of POTIDAEA (432 B.C.E.) while serving as a HOPLITE alongside Socrates. (Supposedly Socrates then stood guard over him during the combat.) Alcibiades repaid the favor years later at the Battle of Delion (424 B.C.E.). On horseback, he found the foot soldier Socrates amid the Athenian retreat and rode beside him to guard against the pursuing enemy.

Although an aristocrat, Alcibiades rose in politics as leader of the radical democrats, as his kinsman Perikles had done. He was only about 30 years old when he was first elected as one of Athens's 10 generals. Meanwhile, he pursued fame with scandalous extravagance, sponsoring no fewer than seven CHARIOTS at the OLYMPIC GAMES of 416 B.C.E.—the most ever entered by an individual in an Olympic contest. His chariots took first, second, and fourth places, and inspired a short poem by EURIPIDES. Many right-wing Athenians were alarmed by this flamboyance, so reminiscent of the grandiose TYRANTS of a prior epoch.

Alcibiades' political leadership was similarly reckless. In 420 B.C.E. he helped to sabotage the recent Peace of NIKIAS (which had been meant to end Spartan-Athenian hostilities), by convincing the Athenians to ally themselves with Sparta's enemy, the city of ARGOS. The outcome was a Spartan field victory over an army of Argives, Athenians, and others at the Battle of MANTINEIA (418 B.C.E.).

In 415 B.C.E. Alcibiades led the Athenian ASSEMBLY into voting for the most fateful undertaking of Athenian history—the expedition against the Greek city of SYRACUSE. (This huge invasion—by which Alcibiades hoped eventually to conquer SICILY and CARTHAGE—would later end in catastrophe.) Not trusting Alcibiades as sole commander, the Athenians voted to split the expedition's leadership between him and two other generals, including the cautious Nicias. But the force, with 134 warships, had barely reached Sicily when Athenian envoys arrived, summoning Alcibiades home to face criminal charges of impiety.

One accusation (possibly true) claimed that on a prior occasion Alcibiades and his friends had performed a drunken parody of the holy ELEUSINIAN MYSTERIES. A second accusation concerned a strange incident that had occurred just before the Sicilian expedition's departure: An unknown group had gone around overnight smashing the herms (HERMAI, marble figures of the god HERMES that stood outside houses throughout Athens), perhaps to create a bad omen against the invasion. Alcibiades was charged with this mutilation—although this charge was certainly false.

Knowing that these accusations had been orchestrated by his enemies to destroy him, Alcibiades accompanied the Athenian envoys by ship from Sicily but escaped at a landfall in southern ITALY. Crossing on a merchant ship to the PELOPONNESE, he sought refuge at Sparta, where his family had ancestral ties. The Athenians condemned him to death in absentia and confiscated his property.

In Alcibiades the Spartans found a most helpful traitor. At his urging, they sent one of their generals to Syracuse to organize that city's defense; within two years the Athenian invasion force was totally destroyed. Also on Alcibiades' advice, the Spartans occupied Dekeleia, a site about 13 miles north of Athens, to serve as their permanent base in enemy territory (413 B.C.E.). By now Athens had begun to lose the war.

In 412 B.C.E. Alcibiades went on a Spartan mission to the eastern Aegean to foment revolt among Athens's DELIAN LEAGUE allies and to help bring PERSIA into the war on Sparta's side. Yet the Spartans soon condemned Alcibiades to death—they mistrusted him, partly because he was known to have seduced the wife of the Spartan king Agis. With Sparta and Athens both against him, Alcibiades fled to the Persian governor of western ASIA MINOR. From there he began complex intrigues with commanders at the Athenian naval base on the nearby island of SAMOS in hopes of getting himself recalled to Athenian service.

His chance came in June 411 B.C.E., after the government at Athens fell to the oligarchic coup of the FOUR HUNDRED, and the Athenian sailors and soldiers at Samos defiantly proclaimed themselves to be the democratic government-in-exile. Alcibiades was invited to Samos and elected general. After the Four Hundred's downfall (September 411 B.C.E.), he was officially reinstated by the restored DEMOCRACY at Athens, although he stayed on active duty around Samos.

Then about 40 years old, Alcibiades began a more admirable phase of his life. The theater of war shifted to Asia Minor's west coast and to the HELLESPONT seaway, where Spartan fleets, financed by Persia, sought to destroy Athens's critical supply line of imported grain. Alcibiades managed to keep the sea-lanes open. His former ambition and recklessness now shone through as bold strategy and magnetic leadership. (For example, he once told the crews of his undersupplied ships that they would have to win every battle, otherwise there would be no money to pay them.) His best victory came in 410 B.C.E. at Cyzicus, where he surprised a Spartan fleet of 60 ships, destroying or capturing every one. In 408 B.C.E. he recaptured the strategic but rebellious ally city of BYZANTIUM. In 407 B.C.E., at the height of his popularity, he returned ceremoniously to Athens to receive special powers of command. Then he sailed back to war, destined never to see home again.

In 406 B.C.E. a subordinate of Alcibiades was defeated in a sea battle off Notion, near EPHESOS, on Asia Minor's west coast. The fickle Athenian populace blamed Alcibiades and voted him out of office. Alarmed, he fled from his fellow citizens a second time—only now he could not go to Sparta. He eventually settled in a private fortress on the European shore of the Hellespont. But, with Athens's surrender to Sparta in 404 B.C.E., Alcibiades had to flee from the vengeful Spartans, who now controlled all of Greece.

He took refuge with Pharnabazus, the Persian governor of central Asia Minor. But too many people desired Alcibiades' death. The Spartan general LYSANDER and the Athenian quisling KRITIAS feared that Alcibiades would lead the defeated Athenians to new resistance. At Spartan request, Pharnabazus sent men to kill him. Legend says that Alcibiades was abed with a courtesan when he awoke to find the house on fire. Wrapping a cloak around his left arm as a shield, he dashed out naked, sword in hand, but fell to arrows and javelins. The woman escaped and later had him buried.

So died the foremost Athenian soldier of his day. The historian Thucydides sums up the dual tragedy of Athens and Alcibiades: "He had a quality beyond the normal, which frightened people. . . . As a result his fellow citizens entrusted their great affairs to men of lesser ability, and so brought the city down." The Athenians' puzzlement over him is suggested in ARISTOPHANES' comedy *Frogs,* staged in 405 B.C.E., the year before Alcibiades' death. The play involves a poetry contest in the Underworld; the final question to the contestants is: "What do you think of Alcibiades?"

See also ALCMAEONIDS; HOMOSEXUALITY; PROSTITUTES.

Further reading: Walter M. Ellis, *Alcibiades* (New York: Routledge, 1989); Steven Forde, *The Ambition to Rule: Alcibiades and the Politics of Imperialism in Thucydides* (Ithaca, N.Y.: Cornell University Press, 1989); W. M. Ellis, *Alcibiades* (London: Routledge, 1989); E. F. Bloedow, "'Not the Son of Achilles, but Achilles himself': Alcibiades' Entry on the Political Stage at Athens." *Historia* 39 (1990): 1–19; ———, "On 'nurturing lions in the state': Alcibiades' Entry on the Political Stage at Athens," *Klio* 73 (1991): 49–65; ———, "Alcibiades: Brilliant or Intelligent?" *Historia* 91 (1992): 139–157; Plato, *Alcibiades,* edited by Nicholas Denyer (New York: Cambridge University Press, 2001).

Alcmaeon (1) In MYTH, Alcmaeon was a hero of the city of ARGOS. After his father, Amphiaraus, was killed in the exploit of the SEVEN AGAINST THEBES, Alcmaeon led the expedition of the Epigoni (Descendants) and captured THEBES. Then, in accordance with a prior vow to Amphiaraus, Alcmaeon murdered his own mother, Eriphyle, for her treacherous role in convincing Amphiaraus to join the doomed expedition. The dying Eriphyle cursed her son, wishing that no land on earth might welcome him.

Tormented by the FURIES for his crime, Alcmaeon fled from home. On advice he journeyed to ACARNANIA, where a recent strip of alluvial shore from the River Acheloos supplied a "new" land, unaffected by Eriphyle's curse. There Alcmaeon received absolution.

The story is similar to the myth of ORESTES, who was also compelled by duty to kill his mother. The horror and legalistic dilemma of this situation appealed to the classi-

cal Greek mind. Alcmaeon was the subject of at least two tragedies by the Athenian playwright EURIPIDES (late 400s B.C.E.).

Further reading: J. P. Small, "The Matricide of Alcmaeon," *Mitteilungen des Deutschen Archäologischen Instituts. Römische Abteilung* 83 (1976): 113–144.

Alcmaeon (2) *See* CROTON.

Alcmaeonids The Alkmaionidai (descendants of Alcmaeon) were a noble Athenian clan, active in politics in the 600s–400s B.C.E. The family claimed descent from a certain Alcmaeon (not the same as the Argive hero ALCMAEON or the physician Alcmaeon of CROTON). Although the Alcmaeonids were aristocrats, a few of them played major roles in the Athenian DEMOCRACY of the late 500s–mid-400s B.C.E. These included KLEISTHENES (1) and (by maternal blood) PERIKLES and ALCIBIADES.

As a group, the Alcmaeonids were not greatly trusted by other Athenians. They were suspected of plotting to seize supreme power, and they were considered to be living under a hereditary curse from the days when an Alcmaeonid commander had impiously slaughtered the conspirators of KYLON (632 B.C.E.).

The Alcmaeonids were thought to be responsible for the treasonous heliographic signal—the showing of the shield—that accompanied the Battle of MARATHON (490 B.C.E.). In the rash of OSTRACISMS of the 480s B.C.E.—aimed against suspected friends of the fallen tyrant HIPPIAS—two Alcmaeonid figures were expelled: Kleisthenes' nephew Megakles and XANTHIPPUS, who had married into the clan and was Perikles' father.

Perikles gained the people's trust by disassociating himself from the family; he avoided Alcmaeonid company and aristocratic gatherings in general. In 431 B.C.E., on the eve of the PELOPONNESIAN WAR, the hostile Spartans demanded that the Athenian people "drive out the curse," that is, by expelling Perikles. But the demand was ignored.

See also ARISTOCRACY; HARMODIUS AND ARISTOGEITON; TYRANTS.

Further reading: D. Gillis, "Marathon and the Alcmaeonids," *Greek, Roman, and Byzantine Studies* 10 (1968): 133–145; T. E. Surikov, "Perikles and the Alcmaeonidae," *Vestnik drevnej istorii* (1997): 14–35.

Alcman (654–611 B.C.E.) *Famous poet of* SPARTA
A plausible later tradition says Alcman was an Ionian Greek who had immigrated from ASIA MINOR; he was notorious for his supposed gluttony. Only a few fragments of his work have come down to us, but they include the earliest surviving example of a choral ode—a type of poem sung by a chorus of girls or men, to musical accompaniment, at a religious festival or other event. Choral poetry was in those years a distinctly Spartan art

form, and the Doric Greek dialect of Sparta was the language of the genre.

Alcman's 101-line fragment presents the final two thirds of a *partheneion*, a "maiden song." The fragment begins by recounting one of the adventures of the hero HERAKLES, then abruptly switches topic and starts praising by name the individual teenage girls who are singing the words. Certain passages seem intended for delivery by half choruses in playful rivalry. The poem obviously was composed for a specific occasion, perhaps a rite of female adolescence connected with the Spartan goddess ARTEMIS Orthia. Alcman's technique of layering mythology and personal references seems to anticipate the work of the greatest Greek choral poet, PINDAR (born 508 B.C.E.).

Intriguing for a modern reader are the emotionally charged statements that Alcman wrote for public recitation by these aristocratic girls. ("It is Hagesichora who torments me," the chorus says, referring to the beauty of a girl who may have been the chorus leader.) The nuances are sexual, and presumably the verses commemorate genuine emotions within this exclusive girls' group. In the surviving fragments of another *partheneion*, Alcman seems to be addressing the same topic. The situation resembles the female-homosexual style of life later described by the poet SAPPHO (ca. 600 B.C.E.).

In other extant verse, Alcman celebrates simple aspects of the natural world: birds, flowers, food. His buoyant, sophisticated poetry reflect a golden phase of Spartan history—the period of the city's triumph in the hard-fought Second Messenian War, before Sparta had completely become a militaristic society.

See also GREEK LANGUAGE; HOMOSEXUALITY; IONIAN GREEKS; LYRIC POETRY; MESSENIA.

Further reading: M. L. West, "Alcman and the Spartan Royalty," *Zeitschrift für Papyrologie und Epigraphik* 91 (1992): 1–15; Charles Segal, *Aglaia: The Poetry of Alcman, Sappho, Pindar, Bacchylides, and Corinna* (Lanham, Md.: Rowman & Littlefield, 1998); Claude Calame, *The Poetics of Eros in Ancient Greece* (Princeton, N.J.: Princeton University Press, 1999); G. O. Hutchinson, *Greek Lyric Poetry: A Commentary on Selected Larger Pieces* (New York: Oxford University Press, 2001).

Alexander the Great (356–323 B.C.E.) *Macedonian king and conqueror*

Alexander was the finest battlefield commander of the ancient world, and when he died of fever just before his 33rd birthday he had carved out the largest empire the world had ever seen, stretching 3,000 miles from the Adriatic Sea to the Indus River.

His principal achievement was the conquest of the empire of PERSIA, an event that remade the map of the ancient world. For 200 years previously, the Persian kingdom had been a menacing behemoth on the Greeks' eastern frontier. With Alexander's conquests, Persia ceased to exist as a sovereign power. The Persians' former territory—including their subjugated regions such as EGYPT and Mesopotamia—became Alexander's domain, garrisoned by Macedonian and Greek troops.

Alexander's sprawling realm quickly fell apart after his death, and there arose instead several Greco-Macedonian kingdoms of the East, including Ptolemaic Egypt, the SELEUCID EMPIRE, and Greek BACTRIA. These rich and powerful kingdoms carried Greek culture halfway across Asia and overshadowed old mainland Greece, with its patchwork of relatively humble city-states. Historians refer to this enlarged Greek society as the Hellenistic world.

At the start of his reign, the 20-year-old Alexander was the crowned king only of MACEDON—a crude Greek nation northeast of mainland Greece—and some of the credit for his triumphs must go to his father, King PHILIP II. When the tough, hard-drinking Philip fell to an assassin's knife in 336 B.C.E., he himself was preparing to invade Persian territory. Philip had devoted his reign to building a new Macedonian army, invincible in its CAVALRY and its heavy-infantry formation known as the PHALANX. He bequeathed to Alexander troops, home-base organization, and propaganda program needed for the Persian campaign.

Alexander conquered to rule, not to plunder. Whereas most Greeks despised non-Greeks as barbarians

Alexander the god. A generation after his death, Alexander is shown with the ram's horns of the Greek-Egyptian deity Zeus-Ammon on this silver four-drachma coin, minted around 285 B.C.E. in the north Aegean region of Thrace. *(The J. Paul Getty Museum, Gift of Lily Tomlin)*

(*barbaroi,* meaning "those who speak gibberish"), Alexander planned to introduce the Persian ruling classes into his army and government. This plan is sometimes referred to as Alexander's fusion policy.

Still, the man had serious flaws. He neglected his kingdom's future by exhausting himself in warfare while he delayed in fathering a royal successor. He was capable of dire cruelty when opposed. His heavy drinking led to disastrous incidents and hastened his death. His lack of long-range planning is shown by his conquest of the far-off Indus valley (327–325 B.C.E.)—how could he have hoped to manage such an immense domain? It has been said that Alexander died just in time, before he could see his empire collapse.

Knowledge of Alexander comes mainly from the surviving works of four ancient authors who lived centuries after him: Arrian, PLUTARCH, DIODORUS SICULUS, and the first-century C.E. Roman writer Curtius Rufus. Arrian, the most reliable of the four, was an ethnic Greek Roman citizen who served in the Roman government in the 120s–130s and devoted his retirement to writing. His thorough account of Alexander's campaigns, written in Greek, is believed to derive from the now-vanished campaign memoirs of Alexander's friend and general PTOLEMY (1). Plutarch's biography of Alexander, written around 110 C.E. is one of his *Parallel Lives* (short biographies comparing noble Greeks with noble Romans); here, Alexander's life story is paired with that of Julius Caesar.

Alexander (Alexandros, "defender") was King Philip's eldest legitimate child. His mother, Olympias, came from the ruling clan of the northwestern Greek region called EPIRUS. The tempestuous Olympias remained for 20 years the foremost of the polygamous Philip's wives. But the royal MARRIAGE was unhappy, and mother and son sided together against Philip.

As a mystical follower of the god DIONYSUS, Olympias was said to sleep with a giant snake in her bed as a pet and spiritual familiar. Apparently she convinced the young Alexander that in conceiving him she had been impregnated not by Philip but by ZEUS, king of the gods. This divine parentage would have put Alexander on a par with the noblest heroes of MYTH.

Such childhood influences gave Alexander a belief in his preordained greatness, a need to surpass his father and all other men, and an imperviousness to danger, pain, and fatigue. Ancient writers describe Alexander's yearning for adventure and exploration. He modeled his behavior on two legendary heroes—the world-civilizing HERAKLES and the great soldier ACHILLES.

Alexander was fair-skinned, fair-haired, and not tall. Although a dedicated soldier, he disliked all SPORT except hunting. He was sexually abstemious, once remarking that sleep and sexual intercourse both made him sad since they reminded him that he was mortal. When he did pursue love, he tended in his youth to prefer males. His lifelong intimate friend was Hephaistion, a Macedo-

nian noble. Later in life, Alexander had sexual relations with WOMEN; when he died he left behind two wives, one of whom was pregnant with his son. Alexander's bisexual development was in keeping with Greek upper-class custom.

Legend claims that at about age nine Alexander tamed the stallion Bucephalus (*Boukephalus,* "ox head"), after its trainer failed to do so. Bucephalus became Alexander's war-horse, carrying him into each of his major battles over the next 20 years.

To tutor the teenage Alexander, King Philip brought the Greek philosopher ARISTOTLE to Macedon. From about 343 to 340 B.C.E. Aristotle taught Alexander political science and literature, among other subjects. For the rest of his life, Alexander is said to have kept with him Aristotle's edited version of HOMER's *Iliad.* Also, in future years King Alexander supposedly sent specimens of unfamiliar plants and animals from Asia to his old tutor, to assist Aristotle's biological studies at the LYCEUM.

At age 16 Alexander held his first battlefield command, defeating a Thracian tribe on Macedon's northern frontier. Two years later, in 338 B.C.E., he commanded the Macedonian cavalry at the Battle of CHAERONEA, in which King Philip won control over all of Greece. (In all his battles, even as king, Alexander remained a cavalry commander, personally leading the charge of his 2,000 elite mounted assault troops known as the Companions.)

With Greece subjugated, King Philip next planned to "liberate" the Persian-ruled Greek cities of ASIA MINOR—and to seize the fabled wealth of Persian treasuries. For propaganda purposes, Philip arranged the creation of a federation called the Corinthian League, representing all the major mainland Greek states, except resistant SPARTA. League delegates dutifully elected Philip as war leader. But before Philip could invade Persian territory, he was assassinated in Macedon (summer 336 B.C.E.).

The killer, an aggrieved Macedonian nobleman, was slain as he tried to escape. The official verdict claimed that he had been bribed by the Persian king, Darius III. Yet suspicion also lights on Alexander and his mother, who had both recently fallen from royal favor. After Philip's death, Alexander was immediately saluted as the new Macedonian king.

The invasion was delayed for two more years. First Alexander was elected as the Corinthian League's new war captain, empowered to raise troops from mainland Greece and to make war against Persia, in revenge for the Persian king XERXES' invasion of Greece over 140 years before. But despite this pretence of alliance, the Greek city of THEBES revolted (335 B.C.E.). Alexander—who feared a Greek rebellion as the worst threat to his plans—angrily captured the city and destroyed it. Six thousand Thebans were killed; 30,000, mostly women and children, were sold as SLAVES.

Leaving behind a regent, ANTIPATER, to guard Greece and Macedon and organize reinforcements, Alexander invaded Persian territory in the spring of 334 B.C.E. He sailed across the HELLESPONT to northwestern Asia Minor with a small Macedonian-Greek force—about 32,000 infantry, 5,100 cavalry, and a siege train. His second-in-command was the 60-year-old Parmenion, who had been Philip's favorite general.

The events of the next 11 years, culminating in Alexander's conquest of Persia and the Indus Valley, can only be summarized here. Alexander's first battle victory came within a few days, at the River Granicus, where he defeated a smaller Persian army commanded by local Persian governors. The central action was a cavalry battle on the riverbank, after Alexander had led a charge across the river.

The Granicus victory opened Asia Minor to Alexander. There he spent the next year and a half, moving methodically south and east. Local Persian troops fell back to a few strongholds. The fortress of Sardis surrendered without a fight. The Persian garrisons at MILETUS and HALICARNASSUS resisted but succumbed to siege.

As local Greek cities opened their gates to Alexander, he set up democratic governments and abolished Persian taxes. But in Asia Minor's non-Greek territories, he merely replaced Persian overlordship with a similar system of obligation toward himself. Most non-Greek cities continued to pay tribute, now to Alexander. His governors were chosen either from his staff or from cooperative local gentry.

By the spring of 333 B.C.E. he had reached the province of Phrygia, in central Asia Minor. At the Phrygian capital of Gordion stood an ancient wagon supposedly driven by the mythical king MIDAS. The wagon's yoke carried a thong tied in an intricate knot, and legend claimed that whoever could untie the Gordian Knot was destined to rule Asia. According to the most familiar version, Alexander sliced the knot apart with his sword.

In November 333 B.C.E. Alexander defeated a second Persian army, this one commanded by King Darius himself. The battle took place in a seaside valley on the Gulf of Issus—the geographic "corner" where Asia Minor joins the Levantine coast—about 15 miles north of the modern Turkish seaport of Iskenderun. The mountainous terrain presents a string of narrow passes; it was a natural place for the Persians to try to bottle up Alexander.

At the Battle of Issus, Alexander had about 40,000 troops; Darius had about 70,000. Although half of Darius's army was inferior light infantry, they could have won the battle had not Darius fled in his chariot when Alexander and his Companion Cavalry charged into the Persian left wing. Darius's retreat caused most of his army to follow.

Darius had lost more than a battle. The captured Persian camp at Issus contained the king's wife (who was also his sister) and other family, who now became Alexander's hostages. Ancient writers emphasize that Alexander not only refrained from raping Darius's beauti-

ful wife, as was his due, but he also became friends with Darius's captive mother!

Oddly, rather than pursue the beaten Darius, Alexander chose to let him go. (Upon reaching Mesopotamia, Darius began raising another army.) Alexander turned south to the Levant, to capture the Persians' remaining Mediterranean seaboard. Most of PHOENICIA submitted. But the defiant island city of Tyre provoked an immense siege, which lasted eight months (332 B.C.E.). The siege's turning point came when the Greeks of CYPRUS rebelled from Persian rule and declared for Alexander, sending him 120 badly needed warships. Lashing these ships into pairs as needed, Alexander equipped some with catapults and others with siege ladders. When the ships' catapults had battered down a section of Tyre's wall, he led his shipborne troops inside. With exemplary cruelty, Alexander sold most of the 30,000 inhabitants into slavery.

Envoys from Darius offered peace: Darius would give his daughter in marriage to Alexander and cede all territory west of the Euphrates River. When the Macedonian general Parmenion commented that he would accept such terms if he were Alexander, the young king replied, "So would I, too, if I were Parmenion." Alexander dismissed the envoys.

In Egypt in the fall of 332 B.C.E., he received the Persian governor's surrender and was enthroned by the Egyptians as their new pharaoh (as Persian kings had customarily been). In the spring of 331 B.C.E. west of the Nile's mouth, he founded a city destined to be one of the greatest of the ancient world, ALEXANDRIA (1).

The final campaign against Darius came in the fall of 331 B.C.E. Alexander marched northeast from Egypt. King Darius, with a huge army levied from all remaining parts of the empire, awaited him east of the northern Tigris, near Gaugamela village, not far from the city of Arbela (modern Erbil, in Iraq).

The Battle of Gaugamela, also called the Battle of Arbela, was a huge, clumsy affair that has defied modern analysis. Alexander was greatly outnumbered. Against his 7,000 cavalry and 40,000 foot, the Persians had perhaps 33,000 cavalry and 90,000 foot. The Persians remained weak in the quality of their infantry, most of whom were Asiatic light-armed troops. But Darius intended a cavalry battle.

Darius launched a massive cavalry attack against both wings of Alexander's army. Somehow the cavalry's departure left Darius's own center-front infantry open to attack; Alexander led his Companion Cavalry charging across the open ground between the two armies' center fronts and struck the Persian infantry there. The melee brought the Macedonians close to Darius—who turned and fled in his chariot, just as at Issus. Soon all Persian troops were in retreat, despite having inflicted heavy losses on Alexander's men.

With his kinsman Bessus, Darius fled into the mountains toward Ecbatana (modern Hamadan, in Iran). For the second time, Alexander turned away from a defeated Darius and marched south, into Mesopotamia.

Alexander now declared himself king of Asia. At Babylon he received the submission of the Persian governor and appointed him as *his* governor there. This move is the first sign of Alexander's fusion policy. Soon he would reappoint other such governors and organize well-born Persian boys into units of cadets, to train for a Macedonian-Greek-Persian army.

From Babylon, Alexander headed southeast, overcoming some fierce resistance, into the Persian heartland. The royal cities of Susa and Persepolis surrendered, opening to him the fantastic wealth of the Persian kings. In April 330 B.C.E. at Persepolis, Alexander burned down the palace complex designed by King Xerxes. (Its impressive ruins are visible today.) According to one story, Alexander—usually so respectful of Persian royalty—set the fire during a drunken revel.

Alexander's claim to the Persian throne was confirmed by Darius's death (July 330 B.C.E.). Stabbed by Bessus's men in the countryside near what is now Tehran, Darius died just as Alexander's pursuing cavalry arrived. Alexander is said to have wrapped his cloak around the corpse. Bessus fled farther east and declared himself king, but Alexander had him hunted down and executed.

Still Alexander did not rest. The years 330–327 B.C.E. saw him campaigning in Bactria (northern Afghanistan) and Sogdiana (Uzbekistan and Tajikistan), where rugged mountain dwellers and horsemen had lived semi-independent of any Persian king. Subduing these people, Alexander took one of them as his bride—Roxane, the beautiful daughter of a Sogdian baron. No doubt the marriage helped to pacify the defiant region. But it is puzzling that the 29-year-old conqueror did not choose a marriage of wider political advantage.

By then he had won the entire domain over which his adversary Darius had ruled. Alexander's northeast frontier became dotted with garrison towns named ALEXANDRIA (2). But these years brought worsening relations between Alexander and certain Macedonian nobles who resented his solicitude toward the defeated Persians and his adoption of Persian customs. Between 330 and 327 B.C.E. several of Alexander's associates were executed for suspected treason. These included the 70-year-old Parmenion and the army's official historian, Kallisthenes, who was Aristotle's nephew. History does not record Aristotle's reaction.

In the summer of 327 B.C.E., Alexander led his army across the Hindu Kush Mountains and down into the plain of the Indus River (called India by the Greeks but today contained inside Pakistan). This region had at one time been part of the Persian Empire. Alexander's conquest required three arduous years, during which he encountered a fearsome new war machine—the Indian elephant, employed as "tank corps" by local rulers.

A battle fought in monsoon rains at the River Hydaspes (an Indus tributary, now called the Jhelum) was Alexander's military masterpiece. There he defeated his most capable adversary, the local king Porus. The captured Porus was confirmed as Alexander's governor of the region (May 326 B.C.E.).

In the fall of 326 B.C.E., at the Beas River, Alexander's men mutinied, refusing to continue east to the Ganges River. Angrily and reluctantly, Alexander turned west and south. The army had reached its easternmost point and was now on a roundabout route home.

At the resistant fortress of the Malloi (perhaps modern Multan, in Pakistan), Alexander's siege ladder collapsed behind him as he went over the enemy wall. Trapped inside, he was hit in the lung by an arrow. Although rescued, he nearly died. The damaged lung surely hastened his death, now less than two years away.

After a disastrous march west through the southern Iranian desert (325 B.C.E.), Alexander returned to the Persian royal cities. At Susa in 324 B.C.E. he held his famous marriage of East and West. Although he already had a wife, he now also married Darius' daughter Barsine, and 90 other Macedonian and Greek officers married high-born Persian women.

That year Alexander sent messages to the mainland Greeks requesting that they honor him as a living god. This request was granted but was met with derision at ATHENS and elsewhere—the Greeks of that era did not generally deify living people. If Alexander had a political purpose in this, it failed. By now he may have been losing his grip on reality.

At Ecbatana in the late summer of 324 B.C.E., Alexander's close friend Hephaistion died from fever and drinking. Alexander, frantic with grief, ordered a stupendously extravagant monument and funeral. He himself was drinking heavily. Reportedly, in these last days, the brooding Alexander would go to dinner dressed in the costumes of certain gods, such as HERMES or ARTEMIS.

Planning a naval expedition to Arabia, Alexander traveled in the spring of 323 B.C.E. to Babylon (which is humid and unhealthy in the warmer months). After several nights of drinking, he fell ill. He died 10 days later, on June 10, 323 B.C.E., in the palace of Nebuchadnezzar. The story that he was poisoned by Antipater's sons KASSANDER and Iolas—to preserve their father's power—is probably false. Legend claims that the dying Alexander, when asked to name his successor, replied, "The strongest."

Of his two widowed wives, Barsine was murdered by order of the pregnant Roxane, who gave birth to Alexander's only legitimate son, also named Alexander. Kassander, as ruler of Macedon, later murdered Roxane, her son, and Olympias. The empire broke into warring contingents under Alexander's various officers, known as the DIADOCHI, or Successors.

See also ANTIGONUS (1); HELLENISTIC AGE; HOMOSEXUALITY; RELIGION; WARFARE, LAND; WARFARE, NAVAL; WARFARE, SIEGE.

Further reading: Peter Green, *Alexander of Macedon 356–323 B.C.: A Historical Biography* (Berkeley: University of California Press, 1992); A. B. Bosworth, *Conquest and Empire: The Reign of Alexander the Great* (New York: Cambridge University Press, 1993); Robin Lane Fox, *Alexander the Great* (New York: Penguin Books, 1994).

Alexandria (1) This city in EGYPT was a major Mediterranean port both in ancient times and still today. Alexandria was founded in 331 B.C.E. by ALEXANDER THE GREAT, who established many Eastern cities. Located 20 miles west of the Nile's westernmost mouth, Alexandria was immune to the silt deposits that persistently choked harbors along the river. Alexandria became the capital of the hellenized Egypt of King PTOLEMY (1) I (reigned 323–283 B.C.E.). Under the wealthy Ptolemy dynasty, the city soon surpassed ATHENS as the cultural center of the Greek world.

Laid out on a grid pattern, Alexandria occupied a stretch of land between the sea to the north and Lake Mareotis to the south; a man-made causeway, over three-quarters of a mile long, extended north to the sheltering island of Pharos, thus forming a double harbor, east and west. On the east was the main harbor, called the Great Harbor; it faced the city's chief buildings, including the royal palace and the famous Library and Museum. At the Great Harbor's mouth, on an outcropping of Pharos, stood the lighthouse, built ca. 280 B.C.E. Destroyed in an earthquake in the early 1300s C.E., the lighthouse was reckoned as one of the SEVEN WONDERS OF THE WORLD for its unsurpassed height (perhaps 460 feet); it was a square, fenestrated tower, topped with a metal fire basket and a statue of ZEUS the Savior.

The library, at that time the largest in the world, contained several hundred thousand volumes and housed and employed scholars and poets. A similar scholarly complex was the Museum (Mouseion, "hall of the MUSES"). During Alexandria's brief literary golden period, around 280–240 B.C.E., the library subsidized three poets—KALLIMACHUS, APOLLONIUS, and THEOKRITUS—whose work now represents the best of Hellenistic literature. Among other thinkers associated with the library or other Alexandrian patronage were the mathematician Euclid (ca. 300 B.C.E.), the inventor Ktesibius (ca. 270 B.C.E.), and the polymath Eratosthenes (ca. 225 B.C.E.).

Cosmopolitan and flourishing, Alexandria possessed a varied population of Greeks and Orientals, including a sizable minority of JEWS, who had their own city quarter. Periodic conflicts occurred between Jews and ethnic Greeks.

The city enjoyed a calm political history under the Ptolemies. It passed, with the rest of Egypt, into Roman hands in 30 B.C.E., and became the second city of the Roman Empire.

Recently, archaeologists have been conducting underwater excavations in the harbor of Alexandria, discovering a rich array of monuments and artifacts from the Greek and Roman history of the city. These include the remains of over a dozen ships, dated from the fourth century B.C.E. to the seventh-century C.E., which are providing invaluable information about the trade networks between Alexandria and the rest of the ancient Mediterranean. Numerous fragments of buildings and statues have also been discovered, including several colossal blocks that appear to come from the Pharos lighthouse.

See also ASTRONOMY; HELLENISTIC AGE; MATHEMATICS; SCIENCE.

Further reading: William La Riche, *Alexandria: The Sunken City* (London: Weidenfeld & Nicolson, 1996); *Alexandria and Alexandrianism: Papers Delivered at a Symposium Organized by the J. Paul Getty Museum and the Getty Center for the History of Art and the Humanities and Held at the Museum, April 22–25, 1993* (Malibu, Calif.: J. Paul Getty Museum, 1996); Jean-Yves Empereur, *Alexandria Rediscovered* (New York: George Braziller, 1998); Theodore Vrettos, *Alexandria: City of the Western Mind* (New York: Free Press, 2001); M. S. Venit, *The Monumental Tombs of Ancient Alexandria: The Theater of the Dead* (New York: Cambridge University Press, 2002).

Alexandria (2) Several cities founded by ALEXANDER THE GREAT on his conquests eastward (334–323 B.C.E.) were named Alexandria. Among these were:

1. Modern-day Iskenderun (previously known as Alexandretta), in southeastern Turkey. Founded after Alexander's nearby victory at Issus (333 B.C.E.), the city guarded the mountain passes linking ASIA MINOR with the Levantine coast.
2. Modern-day Herat, in northwest Afghanistan.
3. A city at or near modern-day Kandahar, in southeast Afghanistan.

The grandiose Greek city recently excavated at the site called Aï Khanoum, in northern Afghanistan, may have been the Alexandria-in-Sogdiana mentioned by ancient writers.

See also COLONIZATION.

Al Mina This modern name refers to an ancient seaport at the mouth of the Orontes River, on the Levantine coast in what is now southern Turkey. In around 800 B.C.E. the town was settled as an overseas Greek trading depot—the earliest such post-Mycenaean venture that we know of—and it seems to have been the major site for Greek TRADE with the East for several centuries. Al Mina was surely the main source for Eastern goods that reached Greece and the islands during the "Orientalizing" period, roughly

750–625 B.C.E. This seaport was discovered purely by ARCHAEOLOGY in 1936 C.E. Some scholars believe that it may be the ancient site of Poseideion.

There is evidence of Bronze Age occupation in the area, but the main period of activity at Al Mina begins in the ninth century B.C.E., when the first Greeks must have arrived with permission of the Armenian-based kingdom of Urartu, which then controlled the region. The trading post was run by Greeks, Cypriots, and local Phoenicians, as shown by the types of pottery found at the site. Being a place where East and West mingled, Al Mina is the most probable site for the transmission of the Phoenician ALPHABET to the Greeks (ca. 775 B.C.E.).

Greek occupation of Al Mina continued until the fourth century B.C.E. (with a brief recession under Babylonian supremacy in the sixth century). Around 300 B.C.E., the site was displaced by nearby ANTIOCH and its seaport, Seleuceia.

See also CHALCIS; ERETRIA; PHOENICIA.

Further reading: A. Graham, "The Historical Interpretation of Al Mina," *Dialogues d'Histoire Ancienne* 12 (1986): 51–65; John Boardman, "Al Mina and History," *Oxford Journal of Archaeology* 9 (1990): 169–190; Joanna Luke, *Ports of Trade, Al Mina, and Geometric Greek Pottery in the Levant* (Oxford: Archaeopress, 2003).

alphabet The Greek alphabet, containing 24 to 26 letters (depending on locale and era), was adapted from the 22-letter alphabet of the ancient Phoenicians, sometime between 800 and 750 B.C.E. Prior to this time, Greek societies had used syllabic, pictographic scripts, where one character corresponded to a single syllable: e.g., in modern English, one symbol for "pen," two for "pencil." (Although simple in concept, a syllabic system requires several dozens or even hundreds of symbols to accommodate the various sounds in a language.) Once the alphabet came into use, the number of symbols was reduced because each symbol was assigned a precise sound, not an entire syllable. These alphabetic symbols (letters) can be used flexibly in innumerable combinations to fit different spoken languages.

It appears that the Greeks first encountered the alphabet through their commerce and trade activities, probably observing the record keeping of the Phoenician merchants. One place where such exchanges may have occurred was the north Levantine harbor of AL MINA, where Greeks and Phoenicians interacted from about 800 B.C.E. on. Other trading centers on CYPRUS, CRETE, or mainland Greece could also have supplied points of contact. One of the earliest forms of the Greek alphabet was written by the Greeks of CHALCIS (who were also prominent at Al Mina); by 700 B.C.E., many regional versions of the Greek alphabet had emerged. The Ionic version, as later adopted and modified at ATHENS, is the ancient form most familiar today.

The Greeks imitated the general shapes, names, and sequence of the Phoenician letters. Phoenician ⴲ (*aleph,* "an ox") became Greek Λ and was renamed *alpha.* Phoenician ⴴ (*bayt,* "a house") became Greek *beta,* β, and so on. All the Phoenician letters represented consonantal sounds, and most of these were retained by the Greeks—Greek β imitates the "b" sound of Phoenician ⴴ, for instance. Since the Phoenician alphabet did not include any vowels, the Greeks changed the meaning of seven of the letters in order to supply them. Thus Greek Λ represented the vowel sound "a," replacing the *aleph*'s glottal stop.

The Phoenician alphabet is loosely preserved in the modern Arabic and Hebrew alphabets. The ancient Greek letters live on in modern Greek, although several of them have acquired new pronunciations. The Greek alphabet was also adapted by the ETRUSCANS and the Romans to produce a Roman alphabet (ca. 600 B.C.E.) that is the direct ancestor of our modern Roman alphabet, among others.

See also PHOENICIA; ROME; WRITING.

Further reading: L. H. Jeffery, *The Local Scripts of Archaic Greece: A Study of the Origin of the Greek Alphabet and Its Development from the Eighth to the Fifth Centuries B.C.,* 2d ed. (New York: Oxford University Press, 1961); John Healey, *The Early Alphabet* (Berkeley: University of California Press, 1990); Henry R. Immerwahr, *Attic Script: A Survey* (New York: Oxford University Press, 1990); Martin Bernal, *Cadmean Letters: The Transmission of the Alphabet to the Aegean and Further West before 1400 B.C.* (Winona Lake, Ind.: Eisenbrauns, 1990); Roger Woodard, *Greek Writing from Knossos to Homer: A Linguistic Interpretation of the Origin of the Greek Alphabet and the Continuity of Ancient Greek Literacy* (New York: Oxford University Press, 1997); Marc-Alain Ouaknin, *The Mysteries of the Alphabet,* translated by Josephine Bacon (New York: Abbeville Press, 1999); Andrew Robinson, *The Story of Writing* (New York: Thames and Hudson, 1999); John Man, *Alpha Beta: How 26 Letters Shaped the Western World* (New York: Wiley, 2000).

Amazons In Greek MYTH, a tribe of female, horse-riding warriors was imagined as dwelling in northeast ASIA MINOR, or along the east coast of the BLACK SEA, or at other locales on the northeast fringe of the known world. Beneath layers of poetic elaboration, the Amazon myth may recall Hittite armed priestesses in Asia Minor in the second millennium B.C.E. An alternative source for the legends has been suggested by recent archaeological finds on the Ukrainian steppes, where 21 Scythian burial mounds have been excavated. In five of these tombs were found the bodies of young women buried along with their weapons: usually a quiver, bow, arrows, and two throwing spears.

Whatever its origin, the Amazon story exerted a strong influence on the Greek imagination. Amazon society was thought of as savage and exclusively female. To breed, the Amazons periodically mated with foreign males, and they discarded or crippled any resulting male babies. The Amazons wore clothes of animal skin and hunted with bow and arrow; to facilitate use of the bow, they would sear off their young girls' right breasts—hence their name, "breastless" (Greek: *amazoi*).

Appropriately, the Amazons worshipped ARTEMIS, virgin goddess of the hunt, and ARES, the war god. In Greek art, Amazons usually are shown wearing Scythian-style trousers, with tunics that reveal one breast; they are armed with bow, sword, or ax and carry distinctive crescent-shaped shields.

In HOMER's epic poem the *Iliad* (written down around 750 B.C.E.) the Amazons are mentioned as a distant people, previously warred upon by the Trojan king PRIAM and the Greek hero BELLEROPHON.

Later writers give the Amazons a role in the TROJAN WAR. The beautiful Amazon queen Penthesilea led a contingent of her tribeswomen to Troy to aid the beleaguered city after HECTOR's death; she was slain by the Greek champion ACHILLES, who then grieved over her death. Other tales develop the sexual overtones; for his ninth Labor, HERAKLES journeyed to the Amazons' land and fought them to acquire the belt (often called the "girdle") of their queen, Hippolyta. Similarly, the Athenian hero THESEUS abducted the Amazon queen Antiope; when her outraged subjects pursued them back to Athens and besieged the city, Theseus defeated them and (Antiope having been killed) married their leader. This Amazon bride, also named Hippolyta, bore Theseus's son, HIPPOLYTUS.

Certain tales associated the Amazons with the founding of EPHESOS and other Greek cities of Asia Minor. A later legend claimed that an Amazon queen met the real-life Macedonian king ALEXANDER THE GREAT on his Eastern campaign and dallied with him, hoping to conceive his child (ca. 330 B.C.E.).

The Amazons were in part a reverse projection of the housebound lives of actual Greek WOMEN, most of whom were excluded from the men's world, bereft of both political power and sexual freedom. Imaginary "male women" apparently were both fascinating and frightening to Greek men. On the one hand, the Greeks found tall, athletic women generally attractive, and the legend of hard-riding, overtly sexual Amazons seems designed in part to provide an enjoyable male fantasy.

On the other hand, the Amazons represented the kind of foreign, irrational power that was felt to threaten life in the ordered Greek city-state. A favorite subject in Greek art was the Amazonomachy, the battle between Greeks and Amazons; by the mid-400s B.C.E. the Amazonomachy had come to symbolize the Greeks' defeat of Eastern invaders in the PERSIAN WARS. An Amazonomachy is portrayed among the architectural marble carvings of the Athenian PARTHENON and on the shield of ATHENA PARTHENOS.

Further reading: W. B. Tyrrell, *Amazons, A Study in Athenian Mythmaking* (Baltimore: Johns Hopkins University Press, 1984); J. Blok, *The Early Amazons: Modern and Ancient Perspectives on a Persistent Myth* (New York: E. J. Brill, 1994); Lyn Webster Wilde, *On the Trail of the Women Warriors: The Amazons in Myth and History* (New York: St. Martin's Press, 2000).

Ambracia   This Corinthian colony of northwestern Greece is located north of the modern Gulf of Ambracia. The city was founded in around 625 B.C.E. as part of a string of northwestern colonies along CORINTH's trade route to ITALY.

Ambracia soon came into conflict with its non-Corinthian Greek neighbors in ACARNANIA and Amphilochia. In the PELOPONNESIAN WAR (431–404 B.C.E.), Ambracia fought as a Corinthian ally against ATHENS but was effectively neutralized in 426 B.C.E., when most of its army was wiped out by the brilliant Athenian general DEMOSTHENES (2).

In 338 B.C.E. Ambracia was occupied by troops of the Macedonian king PHILIP II. In 294 B.C.E. the city passed into the hands of King PYRRHUS of EPIRUS, who made it his capital. As a member of the Aetolian League, Ambracia was besieged and captured by the Romans in 189 B.C.E. It later became a free city of the Roman empire.

See also AETOLIA; PERIANDER.

Further reading: C. M. Kraay, "The Earliest Issue of Ambracia," *Numismatica e antichità classiche* 6 (1977): 35–52; ———, "The Coinage of Ambracia and the Preliminaries of the Peloponnesian War," *Numismatica e antichità classiche* 8 (1979): 37–59; V. Karatzeni, "Ambracia during the Roman Era," in *L'Illyrie méridionale et l'Epire dans l'antiquité, 3. Actes du IIIe Colloque international de Chantilly, 16–19 octobre 1996*, edited by Pierre Cabanes (Paris: De Boccard, 1999), 241–247.

Amphiaraus   *See* SEVEN AGAINST THEBES.

Amphictyonic League   This confederation of different peoples in central Greece was organized originally around the temple of DEMETER at Anthela (near THERMOPYLAE) and later around the important sanctuary of APOLLO at DELPHI. The league's name derives from the Greek *amphictiones,* "dwellers around." The 12 member states included THESSALY, BOEOTIA, LOCRIS, and PHOCIS. The league maintained its two sanctuaries, holding regular meetings of members' delegates and raising and administering funds. It was the league, for instance, that managed Delphi's PYTHIAN GAMES.

Further reading: Anthony Yannacakis, *Amphictyony, Forerunner of the United Nations* (Athens, 1947).

Amphipolis This Athenian colony is located near the north Aegean coast of the non-Greek region known as THRACE. Located about three miles inland, Amphipolis ("surrounded city") stood on a peninsula jutting into the Strymon River. Originally a Thracian town had occupied the site. The Athenian colony was established in 437 B.C.E., after a failed attempt in 462 B.C.E., when native Thracians massacred the settlers.

Amphipolis controlled the local bridge across the Strymon and hence the east-west route along the Thracian coast, as well as the north-south riverine route to the interior. As a local TRADE depot, Amphipolis was an important source of certain raw materials exported to ATHENS. Among these were GOLD and SILVER ore (mined from Thrace's Mt. Pangaeus district) and probably SLAVES, purchased as war prisoners from the feuding Thracian tribes. Shipbuilding TIMBER was another valuable local product, and it seems that Athenian warships were constructed right at Amphipolis.

In 424 B.C.E., during the PELOPONNESIAN WAR, the city was captured without a fight by the brilliant Spartan commander BRASIDAS. In 422 B.C.E., at the Battle of Amphipolis, Brasidas and the Athenian leader CLEON were both killed as the Athenians tried unsuccessfully to retake the city. Thereafter Amphipolis remained beyond Athenian control. Captured by King PHILIP II of MACEDON in 357 B.C.E., it became a Macedonian city and coin-minting center. After ROME's final defeat of Macedon in the Third Macedonian War (167 B.C.E.), Amphipolis passed into Roman hands.

A major archaeological monument near the site is the colossal Lion of Amphipolis, a grave marker erected in the 300s B.C.E.

See also THUCYDIDES (1).

Further reading: Oscar Broneer, *The Lion Monument at Amphipolis* (Cambridge, Mass.: Harvard University Press, 1941).

amphora *See* POTTERY.

Anacreon (ca. 575–485 B.C.E.) *Celebrated Greek lyric poet of the late 500s B.C.E.*

Anacreon was active at SAMOS and ATHENS but born at Teos, a Greek city of western ASIA MINOR. Witty, decadent, and evidently bisexual, Anacreon was the poet of pleasure. His sophisticated verses celebrate WINE, WOMEN, boys, and song—the vital ingredients at the SYMPOSIUM, or upper-class drinking party. Anacreon exemplified the wealth and sophistication of his native region of IONIA, which during the poet's own lifetime fell disastrously to Persian invasion.

Anacreon was in his teens or 20s when he joined the evacuation of Teos to escape the attacking Persians, ca. 545 B.C.E. Sailing north to the coast of THRACE, these refugees founded the city of ABDERA; one poem by Anacreon, presumably from this period, is an epitaph for an Abderan soldier slain in local fighting.

Before long, however, Anacreon had emerged at one of the most magnificent settings in the Greek world—the court of the tyrant POLYCRATES of Samos. There (where another great poet, IBYCUS, was installed) Anacreon won fame and fortune and became a favorite of the tyrant. In keeping with upper-class taste (and with Polycrates' own preference), Anacreon wrote many poems on homosexual themes, celebrating the charms of boys or young men.

In around 522 B.C.E., when the Persians killed Polycrates and captured Samos, Anacreon went to Athens. According to one tale, he escaped the Persian onslaught aboard a warship sent expressly by Hipparchus, the brother and cultural minister of the Athenian tyrant HIPPIAS (1). Anacreon thrived at Hippias's court (where the poet SIMONIDES was another guest). By the time of Hippias's downfall (510 B.C.E.), Anacreon had found new patrons among the aristocrats of THESSALY. Soon, however, he was back in Athens, where he seems to have been welcome despite his prior association with the tyrant.

His Athenian friends of these years include XANTHIPPUS (later the father of PERIKLES) and a young man named Kritias (the future grandfather of the oligarch KRITIAS and an ancestor of PLATO), to whom Anacreon wrote love poems. Anacreon seems to have created a cultural sensation at Athens; a red-figure vase made in about 500 B.C.E. shows a symposium scene with a figure labeled "Anacreon" wearing an Asian-style turban and playing an Ionian-style lyre. Surely Anacreon's long stay in Athens helped to introduce Ionian literary tastes, thus contributing to the city's grand cultural achievements in the following decades. He probably died at Athens, perhaps in around 490 B.C.E.; legend assigns to him an appropriate death, from choking on a grape seed. In later years the Athenians set up a statue of him on the ACROPOLIS.

Most of Anacreon's surviving poems are short solo pieces for lyre accompaniment, written to be sung at a symposium. In simple meters and simple Ionic language, these verses combine yearning with merriment. Whereas a poet like SAPPHO (ca. 600 B.C.E.) might earnestly describe love as a fire under the skin, Anacreon writes of love as a game of dice or a boxing match. "Boy with the virginal face," he writes, "I pursue you but you heed me not. You do not know you are the charioteer of my heart."

One poem (later imitated by the Roman poet Horace) compares a young woman to a frisky colt who needs the right fellow to mount her gently and break her in.

Another poem clearly presents the poet's sophisticated world: "Now golden-haired Love hits me again with a purple ball and tells me to play with the girl in colored sandals. But she comes from Lesbos, a cosmopolitan place, and finds fault with my gray hair. And she gapes at someone else—another girl!"

Among his other surviving work are hymns to ARTEMIS, EROS, and DIONYSUS. The corpus also includes 60 anonymous poems, not written by Anacreon but penned centuries after his death, in imitation of his style. These verses, called Anacreonta, had great literary influence in the Roman era.

See also GREEK LANGUAGE; HOMOSEXUALITY; LYRIC POETRY; MUSIC.

Further reading: Anacreon, *Anakreon: The Extant Fragments*, translated by Guy Davenport (Tuscaloosa: University of Alabama, Parallel Editions, 1991); Patricia Rosenmeyer, *The Poetics of Imitation: Anacreon and the Anacreontic Tradition* (New York: Cambridge University Press, 1992).

Anaxagoras (ca. 500–428 B.C.E.) *Greek philosopher, born in Clazomenae but active in Athens*
Coming from the intellectually advanced region called IONIA, in Greek ASIA MINOR, Anaxagoras played a vital role in introducing the study of PHILOSOPHY at Athens. As such, he was an important forerunner of the philosopher SOCRATES.

A teacher and friend of the Athenian statesman PERIKLES, Anaxagoras is said to have lived at Athens for 30 years, probably ca. 480–450 B.C.E. Supposedly he taught philosophy to the tragic playwright EURIPIDES. Eventually, however, Anaxagoras was charged with the criminal offense of impiety (*asebeia*, the same charge that would destroy Socrates 50 years later). The supposed offense was Anaxagoras's theory that the Sun is really a huge, red-hot stone—an idea that would logically deny the existence of the sun god, HELIOS—but probably the accusation was meant to harm Perikles. Anaxagoras fled Athens, apparently before the case went to trial, and was condemned to death in absentia. He settled at Lampsacus, in Asia Minor, near the HELLESPONT, where he founded a philosophical school and lived as an honored citizen.

Anaxagoras carried forth the Ionian tradition of natural philosophy—that is, of theorizing about the natural world. He is said to have written only one book (now lost). Our knowledge of his work comes mainly from sometimes contradictory references by later writers. He seems to have accepted PARMENIDES' doctrine that reality is unchanging and eternal, but he also was influenced by the atomist theories of DEMOCRITUS and LEUCIPPUS to the extent that he pictured a system of various "seeds" that bunch together in different combinations to constitute different material. Behind the movements of these seeds is "Mind" (*nous*), the universe's animating force, which is

infinite and aloof, but which is somehow reflected in human intelligence and other phenomena. These concepts help to explain Anaxagoras' best-remembered (although enigmatic) statement: "In everything there is a portion of everything except Mind. And there are some things in which there is Mind also."

An important figure in early Greek ASTRONOMY, Anaxagoras followed ANAXIMENES' theory that the Earth is flat and suspended in air, with the heavenly bodies rotating around it. Anaxagoras guessed that the Moon is closer to us and smaller than the Sun, and that its light is reflected from the Sun. His belief that the Sun, Moon, and stars are really huge stones was probably influenced by the fall of a large meteorite in the Hellespont district in 467 B.C.E.

See also ANAXIMANDER; PERSIAN WARS; THALES; THUCYDIDES (2).

Further reading: Daniel E. Gershenson, *Anaxagoras and the Birth of Physics* (New York: Blaisdell, 1964); Anaxagoras, *The Fragments of Anaxagoras*, edited with an introduction and commentary by David Sider (Meisenheim am Glan, Germany: Hain, 1981); Sven-Tage Teodorsson, *Anaxagoras' Theory of Matter* (Göteborg, Sweden: Acta Universitatis Gothoburgensis, 1982).

Anaximander (ca. 610–545 B.C.E.) *Early brilliant scientist and philosopher*
A pupil of THALES, Anaximander lived in MILETUS, in the flourishing Greek region called IONIA, in western ASIA MINOR. In modern opinion, Anaximander is the most distinguished of the three thinkers who comprised the Milesian School of natural philosophers. (The third is ANAXIMENES.) Anaximander also can be called the West's first astronomer and geographer.

Anaximander wrote the earliest known Greek prose work, a theoretical description and history of the natural world. This treatise has not survived, but a number of later ancient writers refer to it. It contained the first Greek map of the heaven and the Earth, and described the movements of the constellations. It was probably the first written attempt in the West to substitute SCIENCE for MYTH in explaining the universe.

Anaximander pictured the Earth as a cylinder suspended upright, with the flat ends at top and bottom; humans live on the top surface, surrounded by the heavens. While Thales had theorized that the Earth floats on water. Anaximander believed that the Earth is suspended in air, equidistant from all other heavenly bodies. This idea looks remarkably like a guess at the celestial law of gravity.

According to Anaximander, the primal element in the universe is not water, as Thales believed, but a more mysterious substance that Anaximander refers to as the *apeiron*, the "boundless" or "indefinite." He apparently imagined this *apeiron* as partaking of characteristics more usually ascribed to the gods. The *apeiron* is immortal, indestructible, the source of creation for the heavens and the Earth, and also the receptacle that receives and recirculates destroyed matter. Although abstruse, Anaximander's theory seems to point toward a pantheistic or monotheistic notion of a life force animating the universe; it also anticipates modern chemistry's discovery that basic matter is never really destroyed but only undergoes change.

Anaximander seems to have guessed at the biological process of evolution. He is recorded as having believed that humankind originally emerged from fishes to step forth onto land. He is also credited with constructing the first sundial in the Greek world, probably based on Babylonian examples.

Anaximander is said to have died around 545 B.C.E., the same year in which the proud, accomplished Ionian Greek cities were conquered by the Persian armies of King CYRUS (1).

See also ASTRONOMY; PHILOSOPHY.

Further reading: Robert Hahn, *Anaximander and the Architects: The Contributions of Egyptian and Greek Architectural Technologies to the Origins of Greek Philosophy* (Albany: State University of New York Press, 2001); Dirk Couprie et al., *Anaximander in Context: New Studies in the Origins of Greek Philosophy* (Albany: State University of New York Press, 2003).

Anaximenes (ca. 585–525 B.C.E.) *Early Greek philosopher and scientist*

Anaximenes lived at MILETUS, a prosperous Greek city in the region called IONIA, in western ASIA MINOR. Following his two greater predecessors, THALES and ANAXIMANDER, Anaximenes was the last important member of what is called the Milesian School of natural philosophers. Nothing is known of his life except that he wrote a book in "simple and unpretentious Ionic language," as one later writer described it. Although the book is lost to us, enough of it is paraphrased by other authors to give an idea of its message.

Like Thales and Anaximander, Anaximenes sought to identify a single, primal substance that is the basic element in the universe. Thales had said that this primal substance is water. Anaximenes, apparently observing that water is itself part of a larger process of condensation and evaporation, identified the universal element as *aër*—"air" or "mist."

The air, he said, is infinite and eternally moving. As it moves, it can condense into different forms: into wind, which produces cloud, which creates rain, which can freeze into ice. Contrarily, air can rarify itself to form fire. Cold is a result of condensation; heat, or rarefaction. This is why a person puffs through compressed lips to cool down hot food, but puffs through open lips to heat cold hands.

Anaximenes believed that the Earth was flat and floated on air in the cosmos. He considered air to be the divine, ordering force in the universe; it is said that he did not deny the existence of the gods, but claimed that the gods arose from air. Although much of Anaximenes' theory seems to derive from his two forerunners, his commonsensical attempt to explain material change was to have great influence on later philosophers, particularly on the atomist DEMOCRITUS.

See also PHILOSOPHY; SCIENCE.

Further reading: Jonathan Barnes, *Early Greek Philosophy* (New York: Penguin Books, 1987); Robin Waterfield, ed. *The First Philosophers: The Presocratics and Sophists* (New York: Oxford University Press, 2000).

Andokides (ca. 440–390 B.C.E.) *Athenian political figure and businessman*

The adventures of Andokides were associated with the downfall of his city in the PELOPONNESIAN WAR (431–404 B.C.E.). Four speeches are preserved under his name, although one of these "Against Alcibiades," is considered a later forgery.

Andokides was born into a prominent aristocratic family at ATHENS. As a member of a right-wing club, he was named as one of the conspirators in the Mutilation of the Herms in 415 B.C.E. To gain immunity from prosecution, Andokides confessed and named his co-conspirators—whether truthfully or not is unclear. Departing from Athens, he prospered elsewhere as a merchant, supplying needed oars at cost to the Athenian fleet at SAMOS.

Unluckily, Andokides' return to Athens in 411 B.C.E. coincided with the oligarchic coup of the FOUR HUNDRED, which brought to power men from the right-wing circles that had been harmed by his confession of four years before. He was then thrown into prison. Released, he left Athens again and resumed his trading. Eventually he was reinstated at Athens, after defending himself against certain charges in his speech "On the Mysteries" (ca. 400 B.C.E.).

As an Athenian ambassador to SPARTA in 392 B.C.E. during the CORINTHIAN WAR, Andokides helped negotiate a proposed Athenian-Spartan peace treaty, the terms of which are preserved in his speech "On the Peace."

Unfortunately, the Athenians rejected the terms and prosecuted the ambassadors, whereupon Andokides left Athens yet again. He died soon after.

See also OLIGARCHY; RHETORIC.

Further reading: Anna Missiou, *The Subversive Oratory of Andokides: Politics, Ideology, and Decision-making in Democratic Athens* (New York: Cambridge University Press, 1992); William D. Furley, *Andokides and the Herms: A Study of Crisis in Fifth-century Athenian Religion* (London: Institute of Classical Studies, 1996); Michael Gagarin and Douglas M. MacDowell, trans., *Antiphon and Andocides* (Austin: University of Texas Press, 1998).

Andromache In Greek MYTH, Andromache was a princess from southeastern ASIA MINOR who became the wife of the Trojan prince HECTOR. During the 10-year TROJAN WAR, her father, brothers, and husband were slain by the Greek hero ACHILLES. Her son, Astyanax, was executed by the Greeks after their capture of TROY, and Andromache became the slave of Achilles' son, NEOPTOLEMUS. She accompanied him home to EPIRUS and bore him a son, Molossus, ancestor of the royal Molossian tribe. She ended her days in Epirus, as wife of the refugee Trojan prince Helenus.

In HOMER's epic poem the *Iliad,* she appears as a gracious and stalwart lady whose future misery is clearly foreshadowed. As an embodiment of female suffering at the hands of conquerors, Andromache was a natural subject for the intellectual Greek playwright EURIPIDES; his tragedy *Andromache* (presented in about 426 B.C.E.) survives today, and Andromache also is prominent among the characters in his *Trojan Women* (415 B.C.E.).

Further reading: Grace-Starry West, "Andromache and Dido," *American Journal of Philology* 104 (1983): 257–267; Euripides, *Andromache,* translated by Susan Stewart and Wesley D. Smith (New York: Oxford University Press, 2001).

Andromeda *See* PERSEUS (1).

Antaeus *See* HERAKLES.

Antalcidas *See* KING'S PEACE, THE.

Antigone A mythical princess of the central Greek city of THEBES, Antigone was the daughter of the incestuous union of OEDIPUS and Jocasta. She is the heroine of an extant tragedy by the Athenian playwright SOPHOKLES. His *Antigone* (performed in about 442 B.C.E.) examines the conflict between law and moral obligation. Although Sophokles was drawing on an existing MYTH, most of the information available to us about Antigone comes from his play.

Antigone had two brothers, Eteokles and Polynices. In the disastrous expedition of the SEVEN AGAINST THEBES, Polynices led a foreign army to Thebes in an attempt to depose Eteokles, who, contrary to prior agreement, was monopolizing the kingship. The two brothers killed each other in single combat. The new Theban ruler, Kreon, decreed that the invader Polynices's corpse go unburied, thereby—according to Greek belief—denying Polynices's ghost a resting place in the Underworld. But Antigone chose her obligations of KINSHIP and RELIGION over her obligations as a citizen, and she covered the body with dust and did honors at the graveside. As punishment, Kreon sentenced her to be sealed alive in a vault. After being warned prophetically that he was offending the gods, Kreon relented: too late, for Antigone had killed herself. This brought calamity to Kreon's house, in the suicides of Kreon's son Haemon (who had been betrothed to Antigone) and of his wife, Eurydice.

Antigone was the subject of a lost play by EURIPIDES that seems to have followed a familiar folktale pattern. In this version, the condemned Antigone is handed over to Haemon for execution; instead he hides her in the countryside, and they have a son. Unaware of his royal lineage, the boy eventually makes his way to Thebes, where adventures and recognition follow.

See also AFTERLIFE; FUNERAL CUSTOMS.

Further reading: George Steiner, *Antigones* (New Haven, Conn.: Yale University Press, 1996); Nicholas Rudall, trans., *Antigone/Sophokles* (Chicago: Ivan R. Dee, 1998); Judith P. Butler, *Antigone's Claim: Kinship between Life and Death* (New York: Columbia University Press, 2000).

Antigonus (1) (ca. 382–301 B.C.E.) *Macedonian general and dynast*
Antigonus ruled ASIA MINOR and other parts of the Greek world in the tumultuous years after the death of ALEXANDER THE GREAT (323 B.C.E.). He is counted as one of the DIADOCHI, who carved up—and fought over—Alexander's vast domain. Antigonus and his son, the dynamic soldier DEMETRIUS POLIORKETES, came close to reconquering and reknitting Alexander's fragmenting empire. But Antigonus died in battle at the hands of a coalition of his enemies (301 B.C.E.). Much of our information about him comes from the later writer PLUTARCH's short biography of Demetrius.

Antigonus was nicknamed One-eyed (Monophthalmos), possibly from a war injury. Serving as one of Alexander's generals in the East, Antigonus was appointed governor of Phyrgia (central Asia Minor), around 333 B.C.E. His ascent truly began in 321 B.C.E. when the Macedonian regent ANTIPATER appointed him chief commander in Asia. In the next two decades, Antigonus's ambition of reuniting the empire brought him and his son into wars on land and sea against the four secessionist Diadochi—PTOLEMY (1) (who claimed EGYPT as his domain); KASSANDER (who claimed MACEDON and Greece); LYSIMACHUS (who claimed THRACE); and SELEUCUS (1) (who, having deserted from Antigonus's command, claimed vast tracts in Mesopotamia and the Iranian plateau).

Based at Celaenae, in southern Phrygia, Antigonus and Demetrius fought against the allied Diadochi over two periods, 315–312 B.C.E. and 307–301 B.C.E., in Syria, Asia Minor, Greece, and the Mediterranean. After Demetrius's spectacular naval victory over Ptolemy near Cyprian Salamis (306 B.C.E.), Antigonus adopted the title king (*basileus*)—that is, king of Alexander's empire. Soon after, each of the other Diadochi took the title king as well.

The downfall of Antigonus, aged about 80, came from a concerted campaign against him. With Ptolemy and Cassander helping elsewhere, Seleucus marched an army west out of Asia and joined Lysimachus in northern Phrygia. The Battle of the Kings was fought at Ipsus, in central Phrygia, in 301 B.C.E. Antigonus and Demetrius, with an army allegedly of 70,000 infantry, 10,000 cavalry, and 75 elephants, opposed Seleucus and Lysimachus's force of 64,000 foot, 10,500 horse, and 480 elephants. Demetrius, leading his cavalry, was drawn too far forward in the field and was cut off by the enemy's elephants. Antigonus was surrounded and killed; his last recorded words were: "Demetrius will come and save me." Demetrius survived the battle and fled to EPHESOS, to fight another day. Antigonus's kingdom was divided between Seleucus and Lysimachus.

Further reading: Richard Billows, *Antigonus the One-eyed and the Creation of the Hellenistic State* (Berkeley: University of California Press, 1990).

Antigonus (2) *See* MACEDON.

Antioch This rich and important Greek city on the northern Levantine coast is situated beside the Orontes River, about 15 miles inland from the Mediterranean Sea. King SELEUCUS Nikator, (1) creator of the SELEUCID EMPIRE, founded Antioch in 300 B.C.E. to be his Syrian provincial capital. He named it for his son, Prince Antiochos. The city thrived, eventually replacing Seleuceia-on-the-Tigris as the capital of the Seleucid Empire which reached from Macedonia to the borders of India. Antioch's port was another city named Seleuceia, at the mouth of the Orontes.

Antioch profited from its fertile plain and especially from its position on the age-old TRADE route between Mesopotamia and the Mediterranean. Militarily, it gave access north to ASIA MINOR, west to the Mediterranean, and east to the Asian continent. Antioch was the second city of the eastern Mediterranean, after Egyptian ALEXANDRIA (1); like Alexandria, it had an international population, including a large minority of JEWS.

Along with the remaining Seleucid domain, Antioch became a Roman possession in 63 B.C.E. In later times, Antioch became an important center in the spread of Christianity, as well as in the spread of heretical movements. The city continued to prosper through the Byzantine era until it was damaged by an earthquake and sacked by the Persians in the sixth century C.E. It was rebuilt by the emperor Justinian but was later taken again by the Persians, and then by the Arabs. Antioch was captured and recaptured several times in the following centuries, by the Byzantines, the Selçuks, the Crusaders, the Ottomans, the Egyptians, the French, and finally became part of Turkey in 1939.

In the HELLENISTIC AGE, a Greek sculptor named Eutychides of SIKYON, a pupil of LYSIPPOS, created for Antioch a BRONZE statue of Tyche that became extremely admired and famous. Tyche was the goddess of Fortune and the protector of cities; in the Hellenistic period almost every city began to worship its own unique Tyche, often modeled on the Tyche of Antioch. Eutychides represented her in a complex, twisted pose, seated on a rock, with her foot resting on the back of a youth swimming in front of her, a personification of the Orontes River. She wears a mural crown, in the form of a city fortification wall. The original statue does not survive, but it is reflected in numerous copies from the later Hellenistic and Roman periods.

See also SCULPTURE.

Further reading: Fatih Cimok, *Antioch on the Orontes.* 2d ed. (Istanbul: A Turizm Yayinlari, 1994).

Antiochos (1) *See* ANTIOCH; SELEUCID EMPIRE.

Antiochos (2) III (ca. 241–187 B.C.E.) *Capable and ambitious king of the Seleucid Empire (reigned 223–187 B.C.E.)*
Surnamed "the Great," Antiochos reconquered prior Seleucid holdings in the Iranian plateau and eastward, but came to grief on his western frontier against the expansionism of ROME. The Romans were alarmed by Antiochos's conquests in the Levant at the expense of

A portrait of King Antiochos I of the Seleucid dynasty, founded by one of Alexander's generals, Seleucus I. The depiction intentionally mimics those of Alexander the Great, with tangled hair and expressive eyes. *(The J. Paul Getty Museum, Gift of Chester B. Frantz)*

Ptolemaic EGYPT (202–198 B.C.E.), by his invasion of THRACE (196 B.C.E.), and finally by his invasion of Greece at the invitation of the Aetolian League (192 B.C.E.). In the Romans' Syrian War (192–188 B.C.E.), Antiochos was defeated in Greece and western ASIA MINOR and at sea. His peace treaty with Rome prohibited any further Seleucid military activity on the Mediterranean seaboard. This Treaty of Apamaea (188 B.C.E.) was a major step toward Rome's absorption of the Greek East. Antiochos died the following year.

See also AETOLIA.

Further reading: C. A. Kincaid, *Successors of Alexander the Great* (Chicago: Argonaut, 1969); John Ma, *Antiochus III and the Cities of Western Asia Minor* (New York: Oxford University Press, 1999); John D. Grainger, *The Roman War of Antiochus the Great* (Leiden, Netherlands: E. J. Brill, 2002).

Antipater (397–319 B.C.E.) *Macedonian general*
During King ALEXANDER THE GREAT's eastern campaigns (334–323 B.C.E.), Antipater served as Alexander's regent over MACEDON and the conquered land of Greece. He destroyed two Greek rebel uprisings: one in 331 B.C.E., led by the Spartan king Agis III, and the second in 323–322 B.C.E., when ATHENS and other states arose at news of Alexander's death.

With the Macedonian royal house in disarray, Antipater became nominal regent of Alexander's whole empire in 321 B.C.E. In his last years' struggle to keep the vast domain together, Antipater was aided by his friend ANTIGONUS (1), whom he made chief commander in Asia. But on Antipater's death, his own son KASSANDER seized Macedon and Greece, in defiance of Antigonus.

See also DIADOCHI.

Further reading: Christopher W. Blackwell, *In the Absence of Alexander: Harpalus and the Failure of Macedonian Authority* (New York: Peter Lang, 1999).

Antiphon (ca. 480–411 B.C.E.) *Athenian orator*
Antiphon was the mastermind behind the abortive right-wing coup of the FOUR HUNDRED in 411 B.C.E. at ATHENS. After the coup's failure, Antiphon chose to remain behind when most of his co-conspirators fled. Arrested, he was condemned for treason and executed. The historian THUCYDIDES (1) knew Antiphon and describes him as one of the most capable Athenians of the day. Antiphon rarely spoke in public before the ASSEMBLY or law courts, preferring instead to advise or to compose speeches for clients. His speech in his own defense at his treason trial was, according to Thucydides, probably the best courtroom speech ever made.

Antiphon's work survives in three rhetorical exercises for courtroom-speaking practice, plus two or three speeches written for actual court cases. The exercises are known as tetralogies, from their four-part structure—two speeches each by both prosecution and defense. The best known of the tetralogies concerns an imagined criminal case, apparently popular among contemporary thinkers, in which a boy at the GYMNASIUM has been killed accidentally by a thrown javelin. Who is guilty, the speech inquires: the one who hurled the weapon, or the weapon itself?

See also OLIGARCHY; PROTAGORAS; RHETORIC.

Further reading: R. C. Jebb, ed., *Selections from the Attic Orators: Being a Companion Volume to the Attic Orators from Antiphon to Isaeus* (New Rochelle, N.Y.: Caratzas Bros., 1983); Michael Nill, *Morality and Self-interest in Protagoras, Antiphon, and Democritus* (Leiden, Netherlands: E. J. Brill, 1985); Antiphon, *Orationes et Fragmenta*, translated by Michael Gagarin (New York: Cambridge University Press, 1997); Michael Gagarin and Douglas M. MacDowell, trans., *Antiphon and Andocides* (Austin: University of Texas Press, 1998); A. Tullin, "Slave Witnesses in Antiphon 5, 48," *Scripta Classica Israelica* 18 (1999): 21–24; Michael Gagarin, *Antiphon the Athenian: Oratory, Law, and Justice in the Age of the Sophists* (Austin: University of Texas Press, 2002).

Aphrodite Aphrodite was the ancient Greek goddess of love, sex, fertility, rebirth, and physical beauty. She was also closely associated with the sea. She is one of several deities (along with ZEUS, ATHENA, and APOLLO) whose earthly influence is most celebrated in Greek art and poetry.

Aphrodite's cult arrived in mainland Greece sometime between about 1200 and 900 B.C.E., probably imported from the island of CYPRUS, which had attracted Greeks in the COPPER TRADE. In MYTH, Cyprus was said to be the birthplace of Aphrodite, and in historical times the Cyprian city of Paphos had an important temple dedicated to the goddess.

The early Aphrodite of Cyprus was probably originally a fertility goddess similar to the Near Eastern goddess Ishtar-Astarte. Among the Greeks she came to personify sexuality and was devoutly worshipped as a universal force. Many local sanctuaries dedicated to Aphrodite arose throughout mainland Greece, and her cults often varied widely from place to place. In some areas, Aphrodite was considered a war goddess, which may have been the stimulus for her mythical association with ARES, the god of war.

Not surprisingly, Aphrodite was also considered to be the patron deity of PROSTITUTES. Her temple at CORINTH was famous in Roman times for its sacred prostitutes, whose fees went to the sacred treasury. This feature seems to have been unique in a Greek cult, and it probably developed in the prosperous harbor city of Corinth because of the Syrian-Phoenician influence that arose in the 700s B.C.E. through trade and commerce. Another important cult center for Aphrodite was Cythera, off the southern Peloponnesian coast.

In myth, Aphrodite's husband was the lame and deformed blacksmith god, Hephaistos. This attests the Greek sense of humor that sometimes pervaded their conceptions of the gods—the loveliest goddess being married to the ugliest of the gods. Dissatisfied, Aphrodite had several affairs with the handsome Ares. The goddess also took numerous mortal men as lovers, including the Trojan shepherd Anchises (their union produced the hero AENEAS) and the Cypriot youth ADONIS, whom jealous Ares eventually killed.

The origin of the name Aphrodite is unknown; the Greeks explained it as meaning "foam-born." A passage in HESIOD's epic poem the *Theogony* (ca. 700 B.C.E.) tells the best-known version of her birth. The primeval god CRONUS severed the genitals of his father, Uranos, and threw them into the sea. There, they generated a white foam (Greek: *aphros*). The goddess arose from this foam, fully formed, and stepped ashore at Cyprus. There is also another version of her birth, told in HOMER's epic *Iliad* and *Odyssey*, written down perhaps 50 years before Hesiod's time. There, Aphrodite is said to be the daughter of Zeus and the ocean nymph Dione.

Homer's Aphrodite is an oddly undignified character. In the *Iliad,* she tries to protect the Trojans and her Trojan son, Aeneas, but she ignominiously flees the battlefield after being wounded by the Greek hero DIOMEDES. Zeus then reminds the goddess that her province is love, not war (book 5). An episode in the *Odyssey's* book 8 tells how Aphrodite's cuckolded husband, Hephaistos, used a chain-link net to trap her and Ares together in bed, then dragged the ensnared pair before the assembled gods on MT. OLYMPUS.

Later legends made Aphrodite the mother (by Ares) of the boy-god EROS and also the mother (by the god HERMES) of Hermaphroditus, a creature with the sex organs of both genders.

Aphrodite's attributes included the dove, the myrtle leaf, and the woman's hand mirror; in later centuries these traits, like the rest of Aphrodite's worship, were borrowed by the Romans for their goddess Venus. Aphrodite's cult titles included Pandemos (of the whole people), Ourania (celestial), Pelageia (of the sea), and Philommeides (laughter-loving or genital-loving).

Aphrodite was one of the most popular subjects in ancient Greek art, inspiring numerous sculptors and painters. The first monumental statue to show a female nude was the statue of Aphrodite carved by PRAXITELES for KNIDOS around 340 B.C.E. Shown preparing for her bath, this representation was considered so scandalous that its original commissioner, Kos, rejected it in favor of a clothed image. The Knidian Aphrodite subsequently became one of the most famous statues in ancient Greece, and it inspired numerous nude and seminude representations of the goddess. One of these is the famous Venus de Milo, displayed in the Louvre in Paris. This second-century B.C.E. statue was found on the Greek island of MELOS and is apparently a copy of a lost original from the 300s B.C.E.

See also OCEANUS.

Further reading: Geoffrey Grigson, *The Goddess of Love: The Birth, Triumph, Death, and Return of Aphrodite* (New York: Stein and Day, 1977); Paul Friedrich, *The Meaning of Aphrodite* (Chicago: University of Chicago Press, 1978); Charlotte R. Long, *The Twelve Gods of Greece and Rome* (Leiden, Netherlands: E. J. Brill, 1987); Arianna S. Huffington, *The Gods of Greece* (New York: Atlantic Monthly Press, 1993); Giulia Sissa, *The Daily Life of the Greek Gods,* translated by Janet Lloyd (Stanford, Calif.: Stanford University Press, 2000); Stephanie Budin, *The Origin of Aphrodite* (Bethesda, Md.: CDL Press, 2003).

The goddess of love undressing for her bath. This Roman statuette copies a famous statue carved by Praxiteles around 350 B.C.E. and the first full-scale female nude in Greek art. *(The J. Paul Getty Museum)*

Apollo (Greek: Apollon) This important Greek god embodied certain high ideals of ancient Greek society. Apollo's association with human intellect, musical harmony, religious purity, and male beauty have led him to be called (in one modern scholar's phrase) "the most Greek of the gods."

According to MYTH, Apollo and his twin sister, the goddess ARTEMIS, were children of the demigoddess Leto and the great god ZEUS. The Greeks imagined Apollo as partaking of his father's wisdom and authority, but in a young form. Greek SCULPTURE and PAINTING portrayed him as muscular, handsome, and (often) in his late teens—at manhood's threshold but still wearing his hair long in a boy's fashion.

Apollo personified Greek male citizen youth. His name may mean "god of the assembly," and it seems to have been connected with the annual Greek festival of the Apelleia, at which 17-year-old males were initiated into the community.

The god was believed to oversee several facets of civilized life. As patron of MEDICINE and physicians, he could cure human illness or, contrarily, bring it on. As lord of MUSIC, poetry, and the MUSES, he inspired human poets and was often shown in art holding the bard's stringed instrument, the lyre. He was associated with Greek mathematical discoveries and philosophical thought. He was a patron of shepherds and archers. Along with the lyre, Apollo's most usual attribute was the archer's bow; the arrows with which he killed his enemies might be either solid or intangible and "gentle," bringing disease.

Apollo oversaw human religious purification and atonement. One myth, most famously retold in AESCHYLUS's tragedy *Eumenides* (458 B.C.E.), described how the god personally exonerated the hero ORESTES of blood guilt. In real life, certain priests of Apollo could provide rituals or advice intended to cleanse a person or place of religious pollution.

This giving of advice was related to Apollo's most famous aspect, the giving of prophecies. Through various oracles—that is, priests or priestesses who supposedly spoke for the god—Apollo might reveal the future and the will of his father, Zeus. Apollo was not the only Greek god of prophecy, but it was one of his oracular shrines that became the Greek world's most influential religious center—DELPHI, in central Greece.

Oracles of Apollo existed at other Greek locales as well, including CUMAE in western ITALY, Didyma and Claros on the western coast of ASIA MINOR, and sites along Asia Minor's southern coast. Delphi's preeminence was due to its role as religious adviser to the great colonizing expeditions that sailed from Greece in the 700s through 500s B.C.E. The god of Delphi was the protector of colonists; one of Apollo's many cult titles was Archegetis, "leader of expeditions."

The lord of harmony was linked with human restraint and moderation. Apolline ideals were expressed

Apollo, the god of youth, music, and prophecy, shown as a young man, would probably have been holding a bow and arrows, now missing. The statue is Roman (100s C.E.) in the style of the Greeks (400s B.C.E.). *(The J. Paul Getty Museum)*

in two famous proverbs carved on the Delphi temple wall: "Nothing in excess" and "Know thyself" (meaning "Know your human limitations").

Not every sanctuary of Apollo featured an oracle. After Delphi, Apollo's next most important sanctuary was on the tiny Aegean island of DELOS, his mythical birthplace.

Although adorned with architectural splendors, Delos had no oracle in historical times. Two other prominent, non-oracular shrines of Apollo were at Amyclae (near SPARTA) and at THEBES.

Modern scholars believe that Apollo's cult, like that of APHRODITE, entered Greek RELIGION relatively late—in the centuries after the collapse of the MYCENAEAN CIVILIZATION around 1200 B.C.E. Apollo may have emerged from the fusion of two older deities: a god of shepherds, brought southward by the DORIAN GREEKS in about 1100–1000 B.C.E., and a non-Greek, Semitic god of plague, imported from PHOENICIA around 1000–800 B.C.E. via the island of CYPRUS, where Greeks and Phoenicians mingled. If the primitive Dorian god was associated with tribal animal totems, this could help explain Apollo's many sacred animals, including the wolf, stag, swan, and dolphin. Apollo's familiar title Phoebus, often translated as "shining," more probably meant "fox god."

Similarly, Apollo's Near Eastern ancestry may be reflected in his Asia Minor cults and his mythical association with the non-Greek city of TROY, in Asia Minor. According to Greek legend, Apollo helped to found that city and in the TROJAN WAR he fought on the side of the Trojans, shooting arrows of plague into the Greek camp (*Iliad*, book 1) and later guiding the Trojan arrow that killed the Greek champion, ACHILLES.

Contrary to some modern belief, Apollo was not a sun god. Although a Greek philosophical theory of the 400s B.C.E. associated him with the Sun, this never became a sincere religious concept. Instead, the Sun had its own mythical personification, named HELIOS.

See also APOLLONIA; ASKLEPIOS; BASSAE; BOXING; CASSANDRA; COLONIZATION; CYRENE (1); CYRENE (2); EPIC POETRY; HERAKLITUS; HOMER; HOMOSEXUALITY; HYACINTHUS; ION (1); LYCEUM; LYRIC POETRY; NIOBE; PROPHECY AND DIVINATION; PYTHAGORAS; PYTHIAN GAMES.

Further reading: H. W. Parke, *The Oracles of Apollo in Asia Minor* (London: Croom Helm, 1985); Mary Barnard, *The Myth of Apollo and Daphne from Ovid to Quevedo: Love, Agon, and the Grotesque* (Durham, N.C.: Duke University Press, 1987); Jon Solomon, ed. *Apollo: Origins and Influences* (Tucson: University of Arizona Press, 1994); Leda Krontira, *Getting to Know Apollo's Delphi* (Athens: Ekdotike Athenon, 1996).

Apollodorus of Athens (Apollodoros) (ca. 180–120 B.C.E.) *Author of books on grammar, mythology, geography, and history; said to have written the* Bibliotheca *[Library]*
Apollodorus was born in Athens but spent much of his adult life studying and writing in the cultural center of Alexandria, where he was a pupil of the philologist Aristarchus. He left Alexandria around 146 B.C.E., perhaps for Pergamon, and eventually returned to his home city of Athens. Since Byzantine times Apollodorus has been said to have been the author of a famous mythological work called the *Bibliotheca* [Library], but this text as we have it today is actually a much later compilation, written in the first or second century C.E.

Apollodorus is known to have written several works that today survive only in tantalizing fragments. The *Chronica*, in four books, was a historical account of Greece from 1184 B.C.E. (said to be the fall of TROY) to 144/3 B.C.E. A later supplement continued the history down to at least 120/19 B.C.E. Apollodorus's work was based on the writings of his third-century B.C.E. predecessor, Eratosthenes, one of the first to try to establish a systematic chronology for events in Greek history. The surviving fragments of the *Chronica* are composed in iambic trimeter verse and show an eloquent writing style.

Another work by Apollodorus, mostly lost, was *On the Gods*. This 24-book mythological treatise was filled with attempts to explain the Greek gods in terms of rational principles. Apollodorus had studied STOICISM in Athens, and this work seems to have been greatly influenced by the teachings of that philosophical school. The surviving fragments of *On the Gods* are very different, in this respect, from the *Bibliotheca*, providing another reason to suspect that Apollodorus had nothing to do with the composition of the latter. The *Bibliotheca* is a traditional, conservative retelling of numerous Greek myths, closely based on the works of SOPHOKLES, EURIPIDES, HOMER, and APOLLONIOS.

Apollonia Several Greek cities bore this name, in honor of APOLLO, god of colonists. The most important Apollonia was located inland of the eastern Adriatic coast, in a non-Greek territory that is now Albania. The city was founded in about 600 B.C.E. by colonists from CORINTH and perhaps also from CORCYRA, as part of a Corinthian TRADE network extending westward to ITALY.

Other Greek cities named Apollonia included one on the Aegean island of Naxos, one on the western BLACK SEA coast, and one that was the port city of CYRENE (1).

See also COLONIZATION; EPIDAMNUS; ILLYRIS.

Further reading: H. Ceka, *Apollonia* (Tiranë, Albania: N. Sh. botimeve "Naim Frashëri," 1958); R. G. Goodchild, J. G. Pedley, and D. White, *Apollonia, the Port of Cyrene: Excavations by the University of Michigan 1965–1967* (Tripoli, Libya: Department of Antiquities, 1976).

Apollonius (ca. 295–230 B.C.E.) *Greek poet and scholar of Alexandria (1), in Egypt*
Apollonius's surviving epic poem, the *Argonautica*, presents the legend of JASON (1) and the Argonauts in their quest for the Golden Fleece. Impressive in its verbal beauty and presentation of character, the *Argonautica* is the only Greek epic to be preserved from the HELLENISTIC AGE (300–150 B.C.E.). The poem's scholarly subject matter, its often playful tone, and its concern with male and female sexual feel-

ings all reveal the values of the Alexandrian literary movement. Apollonius—along with his rival, KALLIMACHUS—epitomizes this sophisticated movement.

Although probably born in Alexandria, Apollonius is often known by the surname Rhodius (of RHODES), referring to the Greek island city where he spent the last part of his life. According to various sources, he began as the pupil of the established poet Kallimachus, but the two men became antagonists in a famous literary feud. This bitter quarrel—which the poets also pursued in their verses—was perhaps based partly on literary tastes. (The experimental Kallimachus objected to the writing of Homeric-style EPIC POETRY, with its familiar subject matter and long plot.) Another cause of enmity may have been King PTOLEMY (2) II's appointment of Apollonius as director of the great Library of Alexandria (ca. 265 B.C.E.). This prestigious job made Apollonius the most influential person in the Greek literary world and incidentally placed him in authority over Kallimachus, who also was employed at the Library (and who may have been passed over for the directorship).

Whether the disruptive feud played a part or not, Apollonius resigned from the Library post and withdrew to Rhodes, in order to write, or rewrite, his *Argonautica*. This relatively short epic—5,834 dactylic hexameter lines, in four books—skillfully combines traditional MYTH, scholarly erudition, and romance. The first two books describe the outward voyage from THESSALY to Colchis, at the eastern shore of the BLACK SEA, the admirable third book describes the Colchian princess MEDEA's self-destructive love for the hero Jason and the exploits relating to the fleece's capture; the last book recounts the Argonauts' escape homeward by way of a fantastical route that calls forth much geographical lore from the poet. The poem's flaw is a lack of cohesion in theme and tone, but it is noteworthy for being the first Greek epic to include psychological descriptions of a woman in love (possibly inspired from the stage tragedies of EURIPIDES). In this and other aspects, the *Argonautica* had a great affect on subsequent poetry, particularly on the Roman poet Vergil's epic work, the *Aeneid* (ca. 20 B.C.E.).

Apollonius also wrote prose treatises, epigrams, and scholarly poems on the foundations of certain cities, according to the literary taste of the day. Other than one extant epigram attacking Kallimachus, these writings survive only in fragments.

See also LYRIC POETRY; WOMEN.

Further reading: Charles Rowan Beye, *Ancient Epic Poetry: Homer, Apollonius, Virgil* (Ithaca, N.Y.: Cornell University Press, 1993); Mary Margolies DeForest, *Apollonius' Argonautica: A Callimachean Epic* (Leiden, Netherlands: E. J. Brill, 1994); V. H. Knight, *The Renewal of Epic: Responses to Homer in the Argonautica of Apollonius* (Leiden, Netherlands: E. J. Brill, 1995); Robert V. Albis, *Poet and Audience in the Argonautica of Apollonius* (Lanham, Md.: Rowman & Littlefield, 1996); Theodore Papanghelis

and Antononios Rengakos, eds., *A Companion to Apollonius Rhodius* (Leiden, Netherlands: E. J. Brill, 2001); R. J. Clare, *The Path of the Argo: Language, Imagery, and Narrative in the Argonautica of Apollonius Rhodius* (New York: Cambridge University Press, 2002).

Aratus (1)   *See* ACHAEA.

Aratus (2)   (ca. 315–240 B.C.E.) *Greek poet and philosopher*
Born in the city of Soli in southeastern ASIA MINOR, Aratus studied at ATHENS under the Stoic founder Zeno. There he met the future Macedonian king Antigonus II (reigned ca. 276–239 B.C.E.). Aratus became a court poet and physician to Antigonus, and it was at the king's request that he composed the long poem about ASTRONOMY, for which he is best known: the *Phainomena* (aspects of the sky). He also composed a second poem, *Prognostica* (signs of weather).

The *Phainomena* survives today. It is a didactic treatise that combines religious and philosophical lore with the astronomical theories of Eudoxus of KNIDOS (active ca. 350 B.C.E.) in explaining the movements of the heavenly bodies. The poem was immensely popular in the ancient world; it was admired and translated into Latin by Cicero. Later generations regarded Aratus as one of the four great Hellenistic poets, along with KALLIMACHUS, APOLLONIUS, and THEOKRITUS, but the relatively abstruse subject matter of his work leaves it virtually unread today.

See also HELLENISTIC AGE; STOICISM.

Further reading: Malcolm Campbell, ed., *Index Verborum in Arati Phaenomena = A Word-index to Aratus' Phaenomena* (New York: G. Olms, 1988); Emma Gee, *Ovid, Aratus, and Augustus: Astronomy in Ovid's Fasti* (New York: Cambridge University Press, 2000); D. Mark Possanza, *Translating the Heavens: Aratus, Germanicus, and the Poetics of Latin Translation* (New York: Peter Lang, 2004).

Arcadia   This mountainous, landlocked, central portion of the PELOPONNESE is bordered on the south by the territory of SPARTA and on the northeast by that of ARGOS. Arcadia was inhabited by a rugged breed of highlanders who claimed to have inhabited their mountain glens since before the Moon was born. The poverty and hardiness of the Arcadians is shown in their ancient reputation for eating acorns. Serving as HOPLITES, they were formidable warriors, and by the 400s B.C.E. they were producing mercenary soldiers for wars abroad.

Arcadia had few cities aside from the important group of TEGEA, MANTINEIA, and Orchomenus in the eastern plains, and (later) Megalopolis in the west. The area's history in the 500s–300s B.C.E. mostly involves feuding between Tegea and Mantinea and periodic resistance to Spartan domination. The Theban statesman EPAMINONDAS liberated Arcadia from Sparta at the battle of LEUCTRA (371 B.C.E.) and founded a new city, MEGALOPOLIS, in about 365 B.C.E. Megalopolis was a strategically located settlement formed by the amalgamation of numerous Arcadian villages, and it became the center of a new political/religious federation.

In the Hellenistic period, Arcadia was divided in its response to Macedonian domination, with Megalopolis supporting the northern power and the rest of the cities rebelling against them. From about 250 B.C.E., the Arcadians were members of the Achaean League. After being defeated by the Romans, Arcadia (like the rest of Greece) became part of the Roman province of Macedonia in 146 B.C.E. In the Roman period, the territory of Arcadia declined sharply in importance and population.

The Arcadians' dialect bore resemblance to that of the distant island of CYPRUS; scholars believe that this shared, unique dialect goes back to the language of the MYCENAEAN CIVILIZATION (ca. 1600–1200 B.C.E.). Both Arcadia and Cyprus seem to have been points of refuge for the Mycenaeans, whose civilization was destroyed by internal wars and by the invading DORIAN GREEKS of 1100–1000 B.C.E. Corroboratively, archaeological evidence reveals little settlement in Arcadia before about 1000 B.C.E.

In the cosmopolitan circles of the Hellenistic and Roman worlds (and later, in the European Renaissance), Arcadia was romanticized as the home of rustic virtues amid a mythical Golden Age. The Sicilian-Greek poet THEOKRITUS (ca. 265 B.C.E.) imagined Arcadia as an idyllic haunt of lovelorn shepherds and shepherdesses.

See also HELLENISTIC AGE.

Further reading: W. E. Thompson, "Arcadian Factionalism in the 360s," *Historia* 32 (1983): 149–160; M. E. Voyatzis, *The Early Sanctuary of Athena, Alea and other Archaic Sanctuaries in Arcadia* (Göteborg, Sweden: P. Astroms forlog, 1990); O. Palagia and W. Coulson, eds. *Sculpture from Arcadia and Laconia. Proceedings of an International Conference Held at the American School of Classical Studies at Athens, April 10–14, 1992* (Oxford: Oxbow Books, 1993).

archaeology   The science of archaeology involves the systematic study of past cultures through the recovery and analysis of material remains, including building debris, sculpture in stone, wood, metal, or clay, metal weapons and utensils, clay utensils, objects of wood or basketry, coins, jewelry, human and animal skeletons, plant remains, and written inscriptions. In most instances these objects are preserved by being buried protectively underground or by lying undisturbed for centuries on the sea floor.

POTTERY was ubiquitous in ancient households and provides by far the single most common source of archaeological data. Although clay vessels often break into numerous small fragments, those fragments are virtually indestructible and can be preserved in the ground for up to 10,000 years. Stone, in building and in SCULPTURE, also survives well, but many ancient structures have partially or completely disappeared because they were quarried for materials in later antiquity or the Middle Ages. Metal objects, particularly bronzes, were frequently melted down in later periods for reuse as sculpture, tools, or coins. Organic materials such as wood, textiles, and papyrus generally are not preserved, since they tend to disintegrate due to moisture and other conditions of the air and soil. Only in the arid atmosphere of Egypt and some other southern and eastern Mediterranean sites, or occasionally under water, have a few such materials been preserved from ancient Greek times.

The subfield of archaeology that studies Greek and Roman antiquities is traditionally called classical archaeology. It had its origins in art collecting, going back at least to the London-based Society of Dilettanti (founded 1733 C.E.), which financed a series of expeditions to Italy to produce sketches and written descriptions of visible remains, and to purchase numerous antiquities. The practice of excavation had begun by 1738, when Queen Maria of Naples sponsored the dig that discovered the ancient Roman city of Herculaneum. The finds there and at Pompeii sparked a tremendous interest in classical antiquity throughout western Europe. French, British, and German enthusiasts eagerly purchased excavation rights at sites in the eastern Mediterranean, often subsequently confiscating their discoveries. As a result, numerous Greek and Turkish national treasures were stored and displayed in western European countries. The most famous such case is the group of PARTHENON sculptures known as the Elgin Marbles, which is currently in the British Museum and is the subject of many heated debates as Greece tries to lobby for its return to Athens. Today, foreign archaeologists may receive permits to excavate in the Mediterranean countries, but all artifacts remain government property.

The most spectacular archaeological discoveries regarding the ancient Greek world took place in the later 19th century. Using intuition and reliance on descriptions in HOMER's *Iliad*, the wealthy German businessman and amateur archaeologist Heinrich Schliemann discovered and excavated the site of ancient TROY (1871–73). Schliemann next turned his attention to the mainland Greek city of MYCENAE (whose location was already known). Digging just inside the famous Lion's Gate in the summer of 1876, Schliemann discovered the group of treasure-filled, second-millennium tombs now known as Grave Circle A. Schliemann also excavated at Boeotian ORCHOMENUS and at TIRYNS. His work proved the historical basis of the Homeric poems and established the existence of a previously unsuspected Greek prehistory, dated around 1600–1200 B.C.E.—the MYCENAEAN CIVILIZATION. Similarly, starting in 1900 C.E. excavations by the British scholar Sir Arthur Evans at KNOSSOS and other sites in

CRETE brought to light the earliest great Aegean culture, the MINOAN CIVILIZATION.

In the century since Evans, archaeology has benefited from advanced technology, including aerial photography and electromagnetic search. Aerial viewing of terrain from aircraft at several thousand feet can reveal variations in the color of topsoil or of ripening crops that indicate the presence of buildings underneath. Electromagnetic search—typically conducted on foot, with hand-held equipment—can reveal the presence of buried material by indicating an obstruction to the soil's natural conductivity of electrical flow. Similarly, buried items of IRON or burned clay create a perceptible distortion in the area's natural magnetic field.

Modern underwater equipment such as submersible vessels, scuba gear, and the vacuum cleaner-like suction dredger have opened the sea floor to archaeology since the mid-20th century. Several dramatic Aegean finds have been made in recent years, including the sunken ancient trading ship lying off the island of Dokos, near the Argolid, in southern Greece. Possibly a remnant of the pre-Hellenic inhabitants of Greece, 2200 B.C.E., this very early discovery testifies to those people's shipbuilding skill and overseas TRADE routes—assets later taken over by the conquering Greeks.

Another valuable new technological advance in archaeological research is DNA analysis. Better retrieval processes on excavations recover increasing quantities of plant remains and bones (both human and animal), which can be subjected to genetic testing for identification of species, gender, population group, and disease.

Despite modern equipment, archaeology still relies much on "low-tech" tools as the trowel, brush, sieve, and icepick-like piolet. After removing an area's topsoil and sifting it for displaced remains, the archaeological team might divide the site into numbered quadrants, indicated by a gridwork of strings held aloft on poles. As digging proceeds with trowel, piolet, and brush, the team keeps meticulous records regarding the depth at which each discovered item was found. With some variation, earlier items tend to be located deeper underground, later items nearer the surface.

One of the greatest modern advances has been scholars' ability to assign a time frame to recovered items. Until recently, dates were assigned largely on the basis of associated information, such as excavation level, or how the item's shape compared with similar ones of known date. But recent technology allows for dating on the basis of some items' molecular structure. For example, carbon-14 dating measures the radioactive type of carbon that occurs in all living matter. Thermoluminescence reveals the number of loose electrons in certain material. Both methods can give approximate dates to some archaeological remains.

The most fruitful archaeological sites are ones that are no longer inhabited. For instance, much of our infor-mation about housing and town planning in the 300s B.C.E. comes from OLYNTHOS, a north Aegean Greek city abruptly destroyed by war in 357 B.C.E. and never reoccupied. Conversely, archaeology at ATHENS has been greatly restricted by the problem of how to requisition excavation sites in the middle of the modern Greek capital city. THEBES and PIRAEUS are two examples of modern Greek cities sitting atop ancient layers that remain largely untouched and inaccessible.

Among the more successful classical archaeological projects of recent years has been the excavation of the original city of Smyrna, near the modern Turkish seaport of Izmir. The site—containing remnants of houses, a temple of the goddess ATHENA, and an encircling wall—provides the best surviving example of a Greek city-state of the early 500s B.C.E.

See also DELOS; DELPHI; EPHESOS; EPIDAURUS; LEFKANDI; LINEAR B.

Further reading: K. Schuchardt, *Schliemann's Excavations: An Archaeological and Historical Study,* translated by Eugenie Sellers (New York: B. Blom, 1971); Dorothy Leakley, *Archaeological Excavations in Central and Northern Greece* (Park Ridge, N.J.: Noyes Press, 1980); Michael Grant, *The Visible Past: Greek and Roman History from Archaeology 1960–1990* (New York: Scribner, 1990); A. E. Raubitschek, *The School of Hellas: Essays on Greek History, Archaeology, and Literature* (New York: Oxford University Press, 1991); Ian Morris, ed., *Classical Greece: Ancient Histories and Modern Archaeologies* (New York: Cambridge University Press, 1994); Kenneth Sheedy, ed., *Archaeology in the Peloponnese: New Excavations and Research* (Oxford: Oxbow Books, 1994); W. Biers, *The Archaeology of Greece: An Introduction,* 2d ed. (Ithaca, N.Y.: Cornell University Press, 1996); Michael Shanks, *Classical Archaeology of Greece: Experiences of the Discipline* (New York: Routledge, 1996); James Delgado, ed., *Encyclopedia of Underwater and Maritime Archaeology* (New Haven, Conn.: Yale University Press, 1998); James Whitley, *The Archaeology of Ancient Greece* (New York: Cambridge University Press, 2001); Christopher Mee, *Greece: An Oxford Archaeological Guide* (Oxford: Oxford University Press, 2001).

Archidamus Dynastic name among the Eurypontid kings of SPARTA. The best known was King Archidamus II, who reigned from about 469 to 427 B.C.E. His reign was clouded by Spartan-Athenian hostility, culminating in the PELOPONNESIAN WAR. Impressed by Athenian sea power and wealth, Archidamus unsuccessfully urged his fellow Spartans to vote against war in 431 B.C.E. He predicted (correctly) that they would be bequeathing the war to their children.

After hostilities began, the aged Archidamus led the Spartan invasion of Athenian territory in 431, 430, and 428 B.C.E. and the attack on PLATAEA in 429 B.C.E. The war's first decade, from 431 to the Peace of NIKIAS in 421 B.C.E., is often known as the Archidamian War.

See also EURYPONTID CLAN.

Further reading: C. D. Hamilton, "Philip II and Archidamus," in *Philip II, Alexander the Great, and the Macedonian Heritage* (Washington, D.C.: University Press of America, 1982): 61–83; C. D. Hamilton, "The Early Career of Archidamus," *Echos du monde classique* 1 (1982): 5–20; E. F. Bloedow, "Archidamus, the 'Intelligent' Spartan," *Klio* 65 (1983): 27–49.

Archilochos (ca. 680–640 B.C.E.) *One of the earliest and greatest Greek lyric poets*
Archilochos was the bastard son of Telesikles, an aristocrat of the island of Paros, and a slave woman. Archilochos emigrated with a colonizing expedition that his father led to the northern Aegean island of THASOS (in a GOLD- and SILVER-mining region). There Archilochos served as a soldier, defending the colony against native Thracians. At some point he may have taken work as a mercenary to fight elsewhere. He is said to have died in battle.

As a poet, Archilochos was an innovative genius, the first person in Western culture to write movingly about his own experiences and emotions. There had been lyric poets before him, but he gave to his verses the kind of strong personal content that is considered to be the identifying feature of more modern poetry. Later generations of Greeks revered him as an artist of the caliber of HOMER, PINDAR, and SOPHOKLES.

Archilochos's work survives in some 100 fragments quoted by later writers. His favorite verse forms are iambic meters (which he pioneered as a form for satire) and the elegy (generally composed to be sung or recited to flute accompaniment). The personality that emerges in these verses is cynical, angry, proud, and vigorously heterosexual. Archilochos's illegitimate birth and adverse life seem to have given him an outsider's sardonic view of the world, yet he could also feel intense passions.

Archilochos writes of his love for and anger with the woman Neoboule and of his tender seduction of her younger sister. Other subjects include shipwreck, war, WINE, and the male organ. One famous fragment describes with jovial regret how he had to abandon his (expensive but heavy) shield in order to run away from the Thracians: "Let the shield go," the fragment ends, "I'll get another just as good." The antiheroic tone sounds almost modern and sets Archilochos apart from other voices of his age. Greek society frowned on a soldier's retreat and loss of shield, but that did not stop Archilochos from writing about it. Among later Greeks he had a reputation for being abusive in verse. According to legend, when Neoboule's father, Lycambes, reneged on his promise to give her in MARRIAGE to Archilochos, the infuriated poet circulated such withering satirical verses that

Lycambes, Neoboule, and the rest of the family hanged themselves out of shame.

See also AESOP; COLONIZATION; HOPLITE; LYRIC POETRY.

Further reading: Anne P. Burnett, *Three Archaic Poets: Archilochus, Alcaeus, Sappho* (Cambridge, Mass.: Harvard University Press, 1983); Carlos Miralles, *Archilochus and the Iambic Poetry* (Rome: Edizioni dell'Ateneo, 1983).

Archimedes (287–211 B.C.E.) *Inventor and mathematician from the Sicilian Greek city of Syracuse*
Archimedes' discoveries in geometry and hydrostatics (the study of the properties of standing water) were monumental, and represent a high point of Greek achievement.

A friend and adviser of King Hieron II, Archimedes was famous for his inventions, which included the Archimedes screw, still used today for drawing a continuous flow of water upward. Yet he dismissed engineering feats as pandering to a vulgar public and was prouder of his work in geometry, particularly his discovery that a sphere contained inside a cylinder will always have an area two-thirds that of the cylinder.

Regarding the weight-displacing abilities of the lever, Archimedes made the famous statement, "Give me a place to stand and I will move the world." But his best-remembered utterance concerns his discovery of the principle of specific gravity, after he was asked by King Hieron to determine whether a golden crown had been adulterated by baser metal. Pondering the problem in his bath at the GYMNASIUM (the story goes), Archimedes suddenly realized that he could compare the amount of water displaced by the crown with that displaced by an equal weight of pure GOLD. Delighted with his discovery, he ran naked through the street shouting "I have found it!— *heurēka!*" (or, as we render it today, "eureka").

During the Roman siege of Syracuse (213–211 B.C.E.), he constructed elaborate devices of defense, including a giant glass lens that focused sunlight on Roman warships in the harbor and set them afire. When the Romans captured the city, Archimedes was killed, supposedly because he enraged a Roman soldier by commanding "Don't disturb my circles" as the man found him pondering diagrams in the sand.

Of his written work, nine treatises survive in Greek and two others in later Arabic translation. Most of these deal with geometrical inquiries, particularly regarding circles, spheres, and spirals.

See also MATHEMATICS; SCIENCE.

Further reading: A. Wegener Sleeswyk, "Archimedes' Odometer and Waterclock," in *Ancient Technology. Symposium Athens. 30.3–4.4.1987* (Helsinki: 1990); 23–37; Sherman K. Stein, *Archimedes: What Did He Do Besides Cry Eureka?* (Washington, D.C.: Mathematical Association of America, 1999); G. M. Phillips, *Two Millennia of Mathematics: From Archimedes to Gauss* (New York: Springer, 2000).

architecture The ancient Greeks bequeathed a tremendous legacy to subsequent centuries of Western civilization in their architecture. The three "orders" that developed between the 600s and 300s B.C.E. remain central to architectural design even today and can be seen on the exteriors of such modern neoclassical public buildings as banks, museums, libraries, and city halls. These orders were known as Doric, Ionic, and Corinthian, and all describe variations on buildings where a solid upper structure (entablature) is supported by vertical columns.

Certain architectural elements are common to all three of the ancient Greek orders. The columns stand on a foundation course known as the *stylobate,* which is sometimes itself supported by two or three more courses. The columns have an upper part, the capital, which is the easiest means of distinguishing the three orders. Doric column capitals are relatively plain, with a rounded *echinus* sitting on a square *abacus.* Ionic capitals have spiral volutes at each corner, and Corinthian ones are derived from a floral design, representing baskets of acanthus leaves. Above the columns, the entablature includes a frieze, which on a Doric building consists of alternating elements called *triglyphs* and *metopes.* The blank metopes could be filled with painted images or carved reliefs. Ionic and Corinthian friezes were continuous, uninterrupted spans that were frequently filled with relief SCULPTURES. In every order, the temple's sloped roof had a triangular gable, or *pediment,* at the front and back. These pediments were often adorned with sculptures fastened to the wall behind. The figures often showed a scene from MYTH, and Greek sculptors used great ingenuity in devising arrangements that would accommodate the pediment's narrowing height at the outer edges. The sculptures were painted, to project the flesh, hair, clothing, and weaponry, and the pediment's background was also painted, usually a solid blue or red. In addition, the column capitals and the architectural moldings adorning other elements of the building would have been brightly painted in blue, red, and yellow.

The Doric and Ionic orders (both older than the Corinthian order) emerged in the 600s B.C.E. specifically for the construction of temples of the gods, which now began to be built of stone. Previously, cult buildings had generally been constructed of less permanent materials such as wood, thatch, and mud-brick. As cut stone (either limestone or marble) became the predominant building material, Greek architects began developing canonical systems of proportion and design for their work. Scholars believe that the Doric and Ionic orders are, to some extent, translations into stone of the wooden structures that came before. For example, certain purely ornamental details of the Doric style are best understood as preserving (in stone) the shapes of wooden beams and pegs that had been necessary structural elements of earlier, wooden temples. Also, the vertical fluting of Doric and Ionic columns may echo the grooving done by adze in the tree-trunk pillars of earlier temples. Since wood is rarely preserved in the archaeological record, however, no wooden structures survive from ancient Greece to compare with their stone successors.

The Doric order emerged in mainland Greece. The name (*Dorike arche* in Greek) refers to the style having originated at such prosperous Dorian-Greek cities as CORINTH and the Corinthian colony of CORCYRA. The earliest known all-stone building is the Temple of Artemis at Corcyra (modern Corfu), completed around 590 B.C.E. This temple was built of limestone—cheaper, more readily available, and easier to carve than marble—which later became the preferred material for Greek architects. Although only the building's foundations and parts of its western pediment survive today, modern scholars can reconstruct its probable appearance. Like all Greek temples, the heart of the cult building was a walled, rectangular, roofed structure (the *naos,* or cella) that housed the cult statue of the deity. The cella's single doorway was typically in the east, perhaps with two

The Ionic order was used specifically in the construction of temples of the gods. The top or capital of each column was decorated with this scroll-like pattern. (*Alison Frantz Photographic Collection, American School of Classical Studies at Athens*)

The Temple of Apollo at Corinth shows the fluted columns topped by rounded capitals of the Doric order in closer detail. *(Alison Frantz Photographic Collection, American School of Classical Studies at Athens)*

columns in the entranceway. The roof extended on all four sides around the cella and was supported on each side by at least one row of columns. At Corcyra—as at one of the most famous Greek temples, the Athenian PARTHENON (completed by 438 B.C.E.)—there are eight columns across the front and back, with 17 along each side (counting the corner columns twice). This eventually became the canonical proportion for a Greek temple, with "x" columns across the front and back and "2x + 1" along the sides.

Also in the 600s B.C.E., the Ionic order emerged at such wealthy Ionian-Greek cities as EPHESOS and MILETUS, on the west coast of ASIA MINOR. Ionic buildings were taller and lighter than Doric ones, and they were also far more ornate. Of the distinctive details in the Ionic order, the most obvious are the scroll-like volutes at the four corners of the column capital. A forerunner of the Ionic capital is the vegetal Aeolic capital, which survives in a carved stone form of the 600s B.C.E. from the Greek island of LESBOS (near the coast of Asia Minor).

Ionic columns are more slender than their Doric counterparts. Other distinctive Ionic features include the use of a decorative column base and a continuous frieze replacing the Doric-style metopes and triglyphs beneath the roof and pediments. This difference allowed the Ionic entablature to show continuous carvings around the entire building in the frieze. The most glorious building in the Ionic order was the huge temple of Artemis at Ephesos, constructed around 550–450 B.C.E. and considered to be one of the SEVEN WONDERS OF THE WORLD. Unfortunately, it and most other Ionic temples have disappeared over the centuries. Among the few Ionic structures standing today are the Erechtheion and the Temple of Athena Nike, both on the Athenian ACROPOLIS.

The Corinthian order arose in the 400s B.C.E. as an ornate variant on the Ionic form, using a design of stylized acanthus leaves for its column capital. Its early use was more decorative than structural and seems to have been confined to the interiors of certain structures in southern Greece. One of the first known Corinthian columns appears inside the Doric Temple of APOLLO at BASSAE (ca. 400–390 B.C.E.). The Corinthian order first appears on the exterior of a building (but still as an ornamental element) on the Monument of Lysikrates in Athens (334 B.C.E.). It is employed in the 300s B.C.E. at the rotunda of ASKLEPIOS's temple at EPIDAURUS and at the Temple of ATHENA at TEGEA. Later the design was thought to communicate imperial splendor and became a favorite of the Romans; a great example of a Corinthian temple in Greece is the Temple of Olympian Zeus in Athens, mostly built in the second century C.E. under the emperor Hadrian.

Greek architects were extremely talented and sophisticated, and in the Classical period they began incorporating certain refinements into their buildings to create a more "perfect" effect. One of the best-known examples of a building with such architectural refinements is the Athenian Parthenon. The horizontal courses of this structure (such as the stylobate and the entablature) curve upward in the center to counteract the natural optical illusion that a horizontal line, seen from a distance, appears to sag downward. In addition, the columns are carefully carved so that they are not perfectly straight but slightly cigar-shaped; this refinement is called *entasis.*

See also DORIAN GREEKS; IONIAN GREEKS; RELIGION.

Further reading: J. J. Coulton, *Ancient Greek Architects at Work: Problems of Structure and Design* (Ithaca, N.Y.: Cornell University Press, 1977); A. W. Lawrence, *Greek Architecture,* 5th ed. (New Haven, Conn.: Yale University Press, 1996).

archon Meaning "leader" or "ruler," the archon was a political executive in numerous ancient Greek states. Prior to the seventh century B.C.E., archons ruled for 10-year terms; before that they had been chosen to serve for life. In the democratic ATHENS of the mid-400s B.C.E. and later, the archonship was a prestigious but relatively narrow job, with executive and courtroom duties. Nine archons were selected annually by lot, from the Athenian upper and middle classes.

The three senior Athenian archons were the archon *basileus* (or king), the *polemarchos* (war leader), and the archon *eponumos* (eponymous). The *basileus* oversaw state religious functions and any related lawsuits. Religious and judicial duties also were assigned to the *polemarchos* (whose role as a military commander was discontinued soon after 490 B.C.E.). The *eponumos* had jurisdiction over cases of inheritance and other property rights. The man who served as archon *eponumos* also gave his name to the calendar year—that is, the year was henceforth known as that in which so-and-so had been archon.

A man (WOMEN were ineligible) might be an archon only once at Athens. After the end of his office, barring any disqualifying offense, he was enrolled for life in the judiciary council known as the AREOPAGOS.

See also DEMOCRACY; LAWS AND LAW COURTS.

Further reading: William B. Dinsmoor, *The Archons of Athens in the Hellenistic Age* (Amsterdam: A. M. Hakkert, 1966).

Areopagos In the democratic ATHENS of the mid-400s B.C.E. and later, the Areopagos was a special law court of 200–300 members, comprised of former ARCHONS. With regard to its origin, the Areopagos (the word in Greek means "hill of ARES," indicating the site where the court's building stood) was a remnant of Athens's old-time aristocratic government.

In the days of aristocratic rule, around 900–600 B.C.E., the Areopagos probably ran the city, acting as a legislative body and high court. As Athens developed in stages toward DEMOCRACY, however, the Areopagos gradually was shorn of power. Under SOLON (ca. 594 B.C.E.), a new COUNCIL preempted the Areopagos's legislative-executive duties, and a newly created court of appeals made the Areopagos's legal decisions no longer final.

As the job of Athenian archon became less exclusive and demanding (500s–400s B.C.E.), so did the Areopagos cease to function as a right-wing bastion. In 462 B.C.E. the radical reforms of EPHIALTES deprived the Areopagos of most of its important legal jurisdictions and distributed these among the citizens' ASSEMBLY, the council, and the other law courts. The Areopagos henceforth heard only cases of deliberate homicide, wounding, and arson.

In its capacity as a homicide court, the new, diminished Areopagos is celebrated in AESCHYLUS's tragedy the *Eumenides* (458 B.C.E.). In the second half of this play, actors portray the ancient Areopagos sitting in judgment over the mythical hero ORESTES for the murder of his mother. Aeschylus wrote the *Eumenides* during the period of civil turmoil following Ephialtes' reforms, and one of his intentions was to soothe the class strife of his fellow citizens.

See also ARISTOCRACY; LAWS AND LAW COURTS.

Further reading: Robert W. Wallace, *The Areopagos Council, to 307 B.C.* (Baltimore: Johns Hopkins University Press, 1989).

Ares The Greek god of warfare, Ares was one of the 12 principal gods, the son of ZEUS and HERA. Unlike his Roman counterpart, Mars, Ares was never considered by the Greeks to be a benevolent guardian figure. He was primarily a personification of battle, with little moral aspect. He was physically attractive—thus his amorous pairing with the beautiful APHRODITE—but cruel, arrogant, and bloodthirsty; he was disliked by most of the other Olympians.

There were relatively few major sanctuaries in Greece dedicated specifically to Ares' worship; only in THEBES was his cult important. He was also particularly associated with the land of THRACE and may have been Thracian in origin, although his name seems to be Greek. His sacred animals were the vulture and the dog.

In his epic poem the *Odyssey* (book 8), HOMER describes how the clever smith god HEPHAISTOS captured Ares making love with Hephaistos's wife, Aphrodite, by trapping them in an unbreakable chain-link net. The lovers were then dragged in front of all the gods; this irreverent tone is typical of much of Ares' treatment in myth and poetry; one passage in the *Iliad* (book 5) mentions that Ares was subdued by the demigods Otus and Ephialtes, imprisoned in a metal casket.

Fierce and impetuous, Ares had unhappy associations. Disguised as a wild boar, he jealously killed Aphrodite's mortal lover, the beautiful youth ADONIS. Ares' children by various mortal women included such violent characters as the Thracian Diomedes and the outlaw Cycnus, both slain by HERAKLES. He was also the father of the personifications Deimos (Fear) and Phobos (Terror). Ares and Aphrodite were the parents of EROS and of Harmonia, who became CADMUS's wife.

See also ATHENA.

Further reading: Charlotte R. Long, *The Twelve Gods of Greece and Rome* (Leiden, Netherlands: E. J. Brill, 1987); Arianna S. Huffington, *The Gods of Greece* (New York: Atlantic Monthly Press, 1993); Giulia Sissa, *The Daily Life of the Greek Gods*, translated by Janet Lloyd (Stanford, Calif.: Stanford University Press, 2000).

Argonauts *See* JASON (1).

Argos Major city of the eastern PELOPONNESE, located three miles inland, on the western rim of the Argive plain, at the neck of the large peninsula known as the Argolid. The city's patron deity was the goddess HERA, whose Argive cult was very ancient, going back to the pre-Greek mother goddess worshipped there. In its early days, Argos was one of the foremost cities of Greece. But after about 600 B.C.E. SPARTA displaced Argos in the control of the Peloponnese, and thereafter Argos's story was one of decline and subordination, despite flashes of ambition.

With its farmland and twin citadels, Argos was a fortress and cult center by the early Bronze Age (ca. 2100 B.C.E.). The Greeks' conquest of the region may perhaps be shown by local ARCHAEOLOGY in the burned remnants of the House of the Tiles at Lerna, near Argos. During the Greek MYCENAEAN CIVILIZATION (ca. 1600–1200 B.C.E.), Argos shared preeminence with the overlord city of MYCENAE, just across the plain, and with nearby TIRYNS.

Argos's importance in this era is suggested by the city's prominent role in Greek MYTH, as the home of PERSEUS (1), of ATREUS and his royal family, and of many other heroes. In general, Argos seems to have supplanted Mycenae in later folk memory (or perhaps Mycenae was once called Argos). In the epic poems of HOMER, the term *Argive*—along with *Achaean* and *Danaan*—simply means "Greek."

During the Dorian-Greek invasion of about 1100–1000 B.C.E., Argos became a Dorian city and the Dorians' base for their conquest of southern Greece. Thereafter Argos remained supreme in the Peloponnese for over 400 years until the rise of Sparta, farther south. In the mid-600s B.C.E. Argos enjoyed a brief peak of power under its dynamic King PHEIDON, who defeated the Spartans at the Battle of Hysiae (669 B.C.E.) and extended his rule across the Peloponnese. Pheidon may also have been the first to introduce coinage into mainland Greece, as well as a new system of weights and measures. But soon Sparta and CORINTH had become the great southern Greek powers, while Argos withdrew into isolation, occasionally emerging to fight (and lose to) Sparta. Argos's worst defeat came at the Battle of Sepeia (494 B.C.E.), at the hands of the Spartan king KLEOMENES (1). This disaster brought the Spartans right up to the walls of Argos (where, according to legend, the Argive poet Telesilla rallied her fellow citizens and led a counterattack of armed Argive WOMEN).

During the Persian king XERXES' invasion of Greece (480–79 B.C.E.), Argos alone of the Peloponnesian states remained neutral, in effect siding with the Persians. Internal strife, possibly caused by the trauma of Sepeia, now resulted in the OLIGARCHY's overthrow and the rise of a DEMOCRACY on the Athenian model. Argos allied itself to ATHENS in 461, 420, and 395 B.C.E., but did so without realizing its potential as a rival to Sparta. In 226 B.C.E., Argos joined the Achaean League and came under Roman control in 146 B.C.E.

Argos was famous for its Classical school of SCULPTURE. Its best-known member was the sculptor POLYKLEITOS, who worked in the mid-400s B.C.E. and was particularly renowned for his statues of men. He wrote a treatise on the perfect proportions of the human figure and illustrated it with a BRONZE statue of a warrior called the Spear-bearer (Greek: Doryphoros). His original work does not survive but is preserved in numerous copies from the Roman period.

See also ACHAEA; DORIAN GREEKS; PELOPONNESIAN WAR; THEMISTOKLES.

Further reading: R. A. Tomlinson, *Argos and the Argolid: From the End of the Bronze Age to the Roman Occupation* (London: Routledge and Kegan Paul, 1972); Thomas Kelly, *A History of Argos to 500 B.C.* (Minneapolis: University of Minnesota Press, 1976); Christopher Pfaff, *The Architecture of the Classical Temple of Hera* (Princeton, N.J.: American School of Classical Studies, 2003).

Arion (600s B.C.E.) *Greek lyric poet*
Arion was active at the wealthy court of the tyrant PERIANDER in CORINTH, around 620 B.C.E. He was born on the Aegean island of LESBOS—where strong artistic traditions produced other poets of this era, including SAPPHO, ALCAEUS, and TERPANDER—and he became famous as a performer who sang his own verses, as well as other poets', while accompanying himself on the kithara (a type of lyre). The Greek historian HERODOTUS described Arion as "the best singer in the world."

Arion is credited with imposing artistic order on the dithyramb, a song sung by a chorus in honor of the god DIONYSUS. Apparently he systematized the performance so that the singers stood stationary, grouped in a circle; he may have assigned a specific subject to each song. These developments would later contribute to the emergence of Greek stage tragedy. None of Arion's compositions survives today.

But Arion is best remembered for the charming legend that he rode on a dolphin's back through the sea. According to the tale told by Herodotus, Arion—returning from a lucrative performance tour of the Greek cities of SICILY and ITALY—took passage on a ship from Italy to Corinth. But he was forced to jump overboard when the crew decided to steal his money. As the ship sailed on, Arion was picked up at sea by a dolphin—an animal sacred to the god APOLLO, who was also the patron of poets. Carried to Cape Taenarum, on the southern coast of the PELOPONNESE, Arion made his way back to Corinth, arriving ahead of the ship. When the ship's crew reached Corinth, they were confronted by Arion and the ruler, Periander.

The legend may have a kernel of truth. According to modern scientific studies, the sea mammals known as dolphins and porpoises are the only wild animals to be attracted to humans. It is not unusual for dolphins to flock around a human swimmer at sea.

See also MUSIC; LYRIC POETRY; THEATER.

Further reading: A. W. Picard-Cambridge, *Dithyramb, Tragedy, and Comedy,* 2d ed. (Oxford: Clarendon Press, 1962); Lonzo, Anderson, *Arion and the Dolphins: Based on an Ancient Greek Legend* (New York: Scribner, 1978).

Aristides (Aristeides) (ca. 530–465 B.C.E.) *Athenian soldier and statesman who was one of the founders of the Athenian empire*
Aristides was instrumental in creating the Athenian-controlled alliance of Greek states known as the DELIAN LEAGUE. He was surnamed "the Just" for his reputedly fair dealings in politics and in diplomacy with other Greek states.

According to the later Greek writer PLUTARCH, Aristides was one of the Athenian generals at the Battle of MARATHON (490 B.C.E.). Yet in 482 B.C.E. the Athenians voted to ostracize him—amid a rash of OSTRACISMS in the 480s B.C.E. This might have been an outcome of Aristides' political conflict with THEMISTOKLES.

As required by the ostracism law, Aristides withdrew from ATHENS, expecting to be in exile for 10 years. However, two years later he was recalled to help against the Persian king XERXES' invasion of Greece. Elected as a general by the Athenians, he served alongside his former enemy Themistokles. Aristides fought at the Battle of SALAMIS (1) (480 B.C.E.) and, reelected as general for the following year, commanded the Athenian contingent at the land BATTLE OF PLATAEA (479 B.C.E.).

As a general again in 478 B.C.E., Aristides led the Athenian squadron in the allied Greek naval liberation of BYZANTIUM and much of CYPRUS. When the arrogance of the Spartan commander Pausanias alienated the other Greeks, Aristides began his diplomatic efforts to secure a mutual-defense alliance between Athens and the eastern Greek states. When the resulting Delian League was formed, in the summer of 478 or 477 B.C.E., Aristides won admiration for his fair assessment of the annual contribution due from each member state.

Aristides seems to have been widely contrasted with the wiliness and rapacity of Themistokles. At the performance of AESCHYLUS's tragedy *SEVEN AGAINST THEBES* in Athens in 467 B.C.E., when certain lines were spoken concerning the hero Amphiaraus's wisdom and righteousness, the entire audience turned to look at Aristides in his seat.

Aristides is said to have died poor, having refused to enrich himself dishonestly through office.

Further reading: Plutarch, *The Lives of the Noble Grecians and Romans,* translated by John Dryden (New York: Modern Library, 1979); Barbara Scardigli, ed., *Essays on Plutarch's Lives* (Oxford: Clarendon Press, 1994).

aristocracy   The word comes from the Greek *aristokratia* and means "rule by the best." It refers to an early form of government in some Greek city-states whereby power was shared by a small circle whose membership was defined by privilege of noble birth. This ruling circle—often confined to one clan—tended to monopolize wealth, land, and military and religious office as well as government. The typical instrument of aristocratic rule was the COUNCIL (*boulē*), a kind of omnipotent senate that decided laws and state policies.

Aristocracies arose to supplant the rule of kings, after the fall of MYCENAEAN CIVILIZATION around 1200–1100 B.C.E. (Some Greek states, such as ARGOS and SPARTA, seem to have retained kings who were merely the first among aristocratic equals.) By the 600s B.C.E., however, growth in TRADE and revolutionary developments in warfare had resulted in the breakup of the old aristocratic monopoly, as a new class of citizen—the middle class—acquired wealth and military importance. In some cities, such as CORINTH, conflict between aristocrats and commoners produced revolutions that placed popular TYRANTS in power; elsewhere, the new middle class gradually was granted political power. In these cases, the aristocracy became an OLIGARCHY (rule by the few—the mass of poorer citizens still were excluded from power). Although oligarchies resembled aristocracies in certain ways, such as the council, they notably lacked the old requirement of the noble blood.

See also HOPLITE; POLIS.

Further reading: Paul L. MacKendrick, *The Athenian Aristocracy, 399 to 31 B.C.* (Cambridge, Mass.: Harvard

University Press, 1969); Oswyn Murray, *Early Greece,* 2d ed. (Cambridge, Mass.: Harvard University Press, 1993); Martin Ostwald, *Oligarchia: The Development of a Constitutional Form in Ancient Greece* (Stuttgart: F. Steiner, 2000).

Aristogeiton   *See* HARMODIUS AND ARISTOGEITON.

Aristophanes   (ca. 450–385 B.C.E.)   *Athenian comic playwright*

In antiquity, Aristophanes was recognized as the greatest classical Athenian writer of comedy. Eleven of his 30 or so plays have survived in their entirety. These 11 plays supply our only complete examples of fifth-century-B.C.E. Athenian "Old Comedy" and show the highly political nature of that art, with plots and jokes devoted to current events. Aristophanes' work provides valuable information about Athenian public opinion during the PELOPON-NESIAN WAR (431–404 B.C.E.).

As suggested by his name (meaning "noblest showing"), Aristophanes probably came from an aristocratic family. On the basis of a reference in Aristophanes' play *Acharnians,* some scholars believe that the playwright owned land on the Athenian-occupied island of AEGINA. The satirical spirit of his comedies provides no clear proof of Aristophanes' own political beliefs, but he probably identified with the intellectual, anti-left-wing, and basically antiwar Athenian noble class (the class that provided the military's CAVALRY and that is sympathetically portrayed in Aristophanes' play *Knights*). Without being fully antidemocratic, Aristophanes' comedies mock the excesses of Athenian DEMOCRACY: namely, the people's fickle abuse of power and the political pandering and vulgarity of the demagogues.

But any aspect of Athenian life was fair game for Aristophanes, whose weapons were parody, burlesque, and comic exaggeration. Against members of his own leisured class, he derides the dishonest quibbling of the SOPHISTS, and the abstruse brainwork of the philosopher SOCRATES and the tragedian EURIPIDES. These men and many of his other targets were Aristophanes' contemporaries, who might be found in the audience at a play's performance.

Athenian comedy was performed at two state-sponsored festivals: the Lenaea, in midwinter, and the grander holiday called the City Dionysia, in early spring. Each play was part of a three-way competition.

By a convention of the era, most of Aristophanes' plays are titled according to the group character of the onstage chorus. His earliest play, *Banqueters* (427 B.C.E.), was presented when he was probably in his early 20s. Neither that work nor his comedy of the next year, *Babylonians,* has survived, but we know that *Babylonians* daringly portrayed the Greek subject allies of the Athenian empire as SLAVES, grinding at the mill. Coming at a moment when ATHENS was relying heavily on allied loy-

alty against the Spartan enemy in the Peloponnesian War, the play provoked the powerful left-wing politician KLEON to prosecute Aristophanes. (We do not know the exact charge.) The prosecution failed, and Aristophanes' mocking pen was eventually turned against Kleon.

Acharnians, performed at the Lenaea of 425 B.C.E., is Aristophanes' earliest surviving work. The plot involves an Athenian farmer who makes a private peace with the Spartans while the Athenian military fights on. The play's pro-peace message foreshadows the more urgent antiwar themes of Aristophanes' *Peace* (421 B.C.E.) and *Lysistrata* (411 B.C.E.). Without being defeatist, *Acharnians* spoke to a city disillusioned in its hopes of an early victory, and the play received first prize.

Knights, performed at the 424 B.C.E. Lenaea, is Aristophanes' most political play: It amounts to a vicious attack on the politician Kleon, who at that time was standing for election to Athens's board of generals. In *Knights,* Kleon clearly appears in the character of a flattering, scheming slave named Philodemos ("lover of the people"). Philodemos's foolish and elderly master is Demos ("the people"), and the plot involves Philodemos's vulgar competition with a sausage vendor for Demos's affection. The Athenians approved of Aristophanes' mockery of Kleon, and *Knights* received first prize. However, the real-life Kleon still won the election.

Clouds ridicules the real-life Socrates as a crackpot scientist and corrupt teacher of sophistry and RHETORIC. The play won only third prize at the 423 B.C.E. City Dionysia, being defeated by KRATINUS's masterpiece, *The Bottle.* The next year saw the *Wasps,* which parodies Athenian litigiousness and the elderly Athenians' enthusiasm for jury duty. Like *Knights,* this play contains liberal mockery of Kleon (who had sponsored a law increasing jury pay). Kleon's death in battle in 422 B.C.E. deprived Aristophanes of his favorite comic butt.

Peace was presented at the City Dionysia of 421 B.C.E., just a few days before or after the Peace of NIKIAS was concluded, which supposedly ended the Peloponnesian War. This plot involves the rescue of the goddess Peace from her prison pit. Despite its topical subject, *Peace* received only second prize.

Aristophanes' comedies of the years 420–415 B.C.E. have not come down to us. By the time of his next extant work, *Birds* (414 B.C.E.), the playwright had begun to move away from political topics in favor of themes more generally social. In *Birds,* two Athenians, in despair over the city's litigiousness, fly off and create a bird city in the sky, Cloud-cuckoo-land (Nephelokokkugia). *Birds* contains some of Aristophanes' finest theatrical effects, particularly in its onstage chorus of birds. The play won second prize at the City Dionysia.

The year 411 B.C.E. brought two comedies about WOMEN's issues. *Thesmophoriazusae* (women celebrating the Thesmophoria festival) amounts to a satire on the tragedies of Euripides; the story involves a scheme by the

Athenian women to destroy Euripides on account of his plays' revealing portrayal of women. *Lysistrata* imagines the Athenian women organizing a sex strike to compel the men to make peace in the Peloponnesian War (which by now was turning disastrously against Athens). The comedy combines bawdiness with a sincere, conciliatory, antiwar message.

Frogs, which won first prize at the Lenaea in 405 B.C.E., is considered Aristophanes' masterpiece. The comic protagonist is the god DIONYSUS, who journeys to the Underworld to fetch back the tragedian Euripides (who in fact had died the previous year). But once in the Underworld, Dionysus is compelled to judge a contest between Euripides and AESCHYLUS (died 456 B.C.E.), as to who was the greater tragedian. Deciding in favor of Aeschylus, the god brings *him* back, instead, to save Athens. Part of *Frogs'* appeal is its pathos: Performed barely a year before Athens' final defeat in the war, the play conveys a giddy sense of desperation.

Aristophanes' career continued after the war's end for perhaps 20 years, but we have only two plays from this final period. *Ecclesiazusae* (women in the assembly) was presented in 392 or 391 B.C.E. In this play, the Athenian women, tired of the men's mismanagement, take over the government and proclaim a communist state.

Wealth (388 B.C.E.) is Aristophanes' latest surviving comedy. Plutus, the god of wealth, is blind, which explains why riches are inappropriately distributed in the world. But when Wealth regains his sight in the story, attempts at redistribution create social chaos. *Wealth* clearly belongs to the less political, more cosmopolitan "comedy of manners" of the 300s B.C.E.

See also ASSEMBLY; EUPOLIS; MENANDER; THEATER.

Further reading: Kenneth J. Dover, *Aristophanic Comedy* (Berkeley: University of California Press, 1972); E. David, *Aristophanes and Athenian Society of the Early Fourth Century B.C.* (Leiden, Netherlands: E. J. Brill, 1984); Lauren Taaffe, *Aristophanes and Women* (New York: Routledge, 1993); Douglas MacDowell, *Aristophanes and Athens: An Introduction to the Plays* (New York: Oxford University Press, 1995); G. Van Steen, *Venom in Verse: Aristophanes in Modern Greece* (Princeton, N.J.: Princeton University Press, 2000).

Aristotle (384–322 B.C.E.) *Greek philosopher and scientist*
A man of immense learning and curiosity, Aristotle (Aristoteles) can be seen as the most influential Western thinker prior to the 19th century C.E. Aristotle spent 20 years as the student of the great Athenian philosopher PLATO, but he eventually rejected his teacher's otherworldly doctrines to concentrate on better understanding the material world around him. Aristotle was as much interested in defining problems as in finding answers, and he created categories of systematic research that are still used today, including "logic," "biology," and "physics."

His writings established a scholarly tradition of study that formed a foundation for all subsequent scientists and philosophers. He also founded a new scholarly community in Athens, the LYCEUM, which became one of the greatest centers for advanced study in the ancient world.

His chief accomplishment in PHILOSOPHY was in devising the first system of logic—the system now known as Aristotelian syllogistic, which provided a cornerstone of logic studies for centuries. In SCIENCE his work was epochmaking. He pioneered the studies of biology and zoology (among others), and he divorced science from philosophy, setting scientific method on its future course of empirical observation.

Of his many writings, less than one-fifth have survived—about 30 treatises. Yet these few works came to dominate European higher learning during the Middle Ages and Renaissance. Among his other accomplishments, Aristotle was one of the first political scientists, cataloguing and analyzing the various forms of government in the Greek world and beyond. His extant treatise *Politics* is now probably his most widely read work, having become a virtual textbook for college political science courses.

Although he spent more than half his adult life in ATHENS, Aristotle was never an Athenian citizen. He was born in a minor town named Stagirus (later Stagira), in the Greek colonial region called CHALCIDICĒ, on the northwest Aegean coast near the Greek kingdom of MACEDON. Aristotle's father, Nicomachus, was the court physician to the Macedonian king Amyntas III. Aristotle's career was destined to be shaped by both the Macedonian connection and by the medical tradition's emphasis on observation and diagnosis. The family was probably rich; hence Aristotle's ability to travel and to devote himself to study.

After Nicomachus' death, 17-year-old Aristotle was sent to Athens to join Plato's philosophical school, the ACADEMY (367 B.C.E.). Eventually recognized as Plato's foremost pupil and possible successor at the Academy, Aristotle remained there for 20 years until Plato's death (347 B.C.E.). In the election of the Academy's new president, Aristotle was passed over—which may be why he then left Athens with a number of friends and followers. They traveled to northwest ASIA MINOR, where they set up a school at the town of Assos at the invitation of Hermias, a local Greek ruler who was a Persian vassal. Evidently Aristotle became a close friend of Hermias, for he married Hermias's adopted daughter, Pythias. But when Hermias was arrested and executed for some unknown reason by the Persians, Aristotle and his followers sailed to the nearby Greek island of LESBOS, and stayed in the city of MYTILENE. By then Aristotle's group included a well-born man of Lesbos named Theophrastus, who became his protégé and later his successor as head of his philosophical school.

At the landlocked lagoon of Pyrrha, in central Lesbos, Aristotle conducted many of the observations of marine animals recorded in his zoological writings. His method of field observation and documentation—an innovation in his own day—was destined to set the pattern for all future biological study.

In around 343 B.C.E. the 41-year-old Aristotle accepted an invitation from King Philip, by then the most powerful man in the Greek world, to go to Macedon to tutor Philip's 13-year-old son, Alexander (who was destined to conquer the Persian Empire and be known to history as ALEXANDER THE GREAT). Aristotle spent about three years providing a higher education for the prince and some of his retinue. The curriculum probably included political science—Aristotle wrote two (lost) treatises for Alexander, *On Kingship* and *On Colonists*—as well as studies in literature and biology. Aristotle gave Alexander an edited version of HOMER's *Iliad* that the young warrior supposedly carried with him for the rest of his life. According to legend, King Alexander would later send Aristotle specimens of unfamiliar Eastern plants and animals to study. Beyond this, however, Aristotle's influence on Alexander was not profound, and the teacher probably went home to Stagirus after Alexander began serving as regent for his father, in 340 B.C.E.

In 335 B.C.E., after Alexander had inherited the throne, Aristotle returned to Athens to establish his own philosophical school there. He opened the school in rented buildings outside the city, on the grounds of a GYMNASIUM known as the Lyceum ([Lukeion], named for its grove sacred to the god APOLLO in his cult title Lukeios). Aristotle's Lyceum period (335–323 B.C.E.) is the third and most important phase of his life.

The Lyceum enjoyed special resources and status—Alexander supposedly donated the immense sum of 800 TALENTS—and was protected by the local Macedonian authorities. Without doubt, the Lyceum provided Aristotle with the means to engage in the encyclopedic array of inquiries for which he is remembered. The school resembled a modern university in some ways, with general courses alongside "graduate" research projects under the master's guidance. Among such delegated projects was a description of the individual governments (or "constitutions") of the 158 most important Greek cities; of these 158 analyses, only one survives today—the *Constitution of Athens* (*Athenaion Politeia*), our major source of information for the workings of the Athenian DEMOCRACY.

Supposedly, Aristotle would lecture to general audiences in the morning and to the advanced scholarly circle in the afternoon. It is said that he had a habit of walking around (*peripatein*) while lecturing and that his listeners walked with him—which gave to the community its title of the Peripatetic School. (However, the name may come from the roofed courtyard, *peripatos,* that was a physical feature at the Lyceum or at a later site.) In personal demeanor, Aristotle is said to have dressed elegantly or even foppishly and to have spoken with an upper-class lisp.

During these years at Athens, Aristotle's wife, Pythias, died, and he lived with a common-law wife, Herpylla. Aristotle had two children: a daughter named Pythias, after her mother, and a son, Nicomachus, by Herpylla. Nicomachus is remembered in the title of Aristotle's *Nicomachean Ethics,* so called because the son supposedly edited the work after his father's death.

With Alexander's sudden death in the East (323 B.C.E.), anti-Macedonian feeling erupted at Athens, and a criminal charge of impiety was lodged against Aristotle. The 61-year-old scholar fled, supposedly remarking that he was saving the Athenians from committing a second sin against philosophy (a reference to their execution of SOCRATES for impiety in 399 B.C.E.). Aristotle took refuge at the nearby city of CHALCIS, where his mother had been born and where a Macedonian garrison was in control, and there he died in the following year (322 B.C.E.).

As previously mentioned, less than one-fifth of Aristotle's writings are represented in the 30 works that have come down to us. The vanished work—bits of which survive as quotations cited by later ancient authors—included poems, letters, essays, and Platonic-style dialogues. Many of these were polished literary pieces, intended for a general readership: In a later century, the Roman thinker Cicero described Aristotle's writing style as "a river of gold." This praise would not be appropriate for the 30 surviving items, which often make for difficult reading.

Ironically, most of these extant writings probably were never meant for publication. Many seem to be Aristotle's lecture notes for his more advanced courses of study. These "treatises" or "esoteric writings," as they are sometimes called, contain passages that are notoriously difficult—either overly condensed or repetitive—with apparent cross-references to works now lost. The titles and sequence of these preserved treatises are not Aristotle's choice, but rather are the work of ancient editors after Aristotle. However, the 30 treatises do provide a good sampling of Aristotle's mature thought, covering logic, metaphysics, ethics, scientific inquiries, literary criticism, and political science.

Aristotle's six treatises on logic (*logikē*, meaning "the art of reasoning") are sometimes mentioned under the collective title Organon, or "tool"—that is, of thought. Of these works, the best known is the one titled *Prior Analytics,* which contains Aristotle's system of syllogistic. (A syllogism is a form of reasoning consisting of two premises and a conclusion. The classic form of syllogism is: [1] Socrates is a man. [2] All men are mortal. Therefore, [3] Socrates is mortal.) The *Prior Analytics* examines the various forms of syllogistic thought.

Other extant treatises include studies of the natural world: *Physics, On the Heavens, Meteorology, Generation of Animals,* and the admired *History of Animals* (so called traditionally, although *Zoological Researches* would better translate the Greek title), which presents many careful descriptions of different species. The very notions of genus and species—general type, specific type—are among the categories devised by Aristotle.

Aristotle's theory of reality is found in his *Metaphysics,* or "Beyond Physics" (a title created by an ancient editor, originally signifying only that the book followed the *Physics* in sequence). Here—in a criticism and radical adaptation of Plato's theory of Forms—Aristotle explains how universal qualities are rooted in particulars. For example, a specific dog partakes of universal "dogness" along with all other canines, yet this dogness has no existence apart from the world's flesh-and-blood dogs. Book 12 of the *Metaphysics* presents Aristotle's well-known picture of God as the unmoved mover—pure intelligence, uninvolved in the world's day-to-day occurrences.

In book 1 of the *Nicomachean Ethics,* Aristotle identifies the attainment of happiness as the highest good, and he defines happiness as an activity of the soul in conformity with virtue (*aretē*). Book 2 is famous for defining virtue as the mean (*mesotēs*) between two extremes of behavior: Courage, for example, falls between cowardice and recklessness; generosity falls between stinginess and extravagance.

In the *Rhetoric,* Aristotle examines the art of public speaking in terms of its desired goal, persuasion. The *Poetics* analyzes the nature of literature and offers the famous Aristotelian observation that stage tragedy provides a cleansing (*katharsis*) of the audience's emotions of pity and fear.

See also ASTRONOMY; EDUCATION; MEDICINE.

Further reading: G. E. R. Lloyd, *Aristotelian Explorations* (New York: Cambridge University Press, 1996); Jonathan Barnes, *Aristotle: A Very Short Introduction,* 2d ed. (Oxford: Oxford University Press, 2000); Adrian Oldfield, *Ordered Cities, Ordered Souls: An Introduction to Greek Political Thought* (London: Routledge, 2003).

Aristoxenus   *See* MUSIC.

armies   *See* ALEXANDER THE GREAT; CAVALRY; HOPLITE; PELOPONNESIAN WAR; PERSIAN WARS; PHALANX; WARFARE, LAND.

arms and armor   *See* CAVALRY; HOPLITE; WARFARE, LAND.

art   *See* ARCHITECTURE; PAINTING; POTTERY; SCULPTURE.

Artemis   Greek goddess of wilderness, wild animals, and the hunt, also associated with childbirth and the Moon. Although her worship was of secondary rank in most cities of mainland Greece, she was a principal deity for many Greeks of ASIA MINOR. At EPHESOS, for example, she was the primary city deity and was honored with a huge temple, begun in the mid-500s B.C.E. and counted as one of the SEVEN WONDERS OF THE WORLD.

In MYTH, Artemis was the twin sister of the god APOLLO; their parents were the great god ZEUS and the demigoddess Leto. Impregnated by Zeus, Leto fled from Zeus's jealous wife, HERA, and found refuge on the island of DELOS, in the AEGEAN SEA. There she gave birth to the divine twins. Artemis was born first and, while only a few minutes old, helped her mother give birth to Apollo. For this reason, the Greeks considered her to be a goddess of childbirth, even though she is a virgin with no children of her own. She is also the guardian of young girls, before they become women.

Artemis and Apollo grew to be skilled archers. With their arrows, they slew a number of Leto's enemies, including the 14 children of the arrogant NIOBĒ. Niobē had boasted that she was superior to the goddess because she had borne seven sons and seven daughters, while Leto had only one of each. Artemis also shot the enormous hunter ORION, who had tried to rape her; his body now hangs as a constellation in the sky.

Statuette of Artemis, goddess of wilderness, wild animals, and the hunt, shown with her bow and holding a fawn *(Alison Frantz Photographic Collection, American School of Classical Studies at Athens)*

Like ATHENA and HESTIA, Artemis was a virgin goddess. Imagined as a lithe young woman, she was said to roam mountain forests and uncultivated lands, hunting the beasts and, contrarily, overseeing their safety and reproduction. Her most famous title, mentioned by the poet HOMER (ca. 750 B.C.E.), was Potnia Theron, "mistress of wild animals." In art she often was shown accompanied by deer, bears, or similar beasts, and myths told of her retinue of NYMPHS—female creatures embodying the spirit of wilderness places. Among her human devotees described in myth were the Athenian prince HIPPOLYTUS and the female warriors known as AMAZONS. Two regions dear to Artemis were the mountains of CRETE and ARCADIA.

In the classical Greek mind, Artemis's virginity probably suggested the sanctity of wilderness places. A legend tells how the Theban prince Actaeon, while out hunting with his hounds, accidentally found Artemis bathing naked in a stream. Enraged to have her modesty compromised, the goddess changed Actaeon into a stag, whereupon his own hounds mauled him to death.

Although she had no children of her own, Artemis was concerned with birth and offspring among both animals and humans. One of her titles was Kourotrophos ("nurse of youths"). Like the goddess HERA, Artemis watched over WOMEN in labor. They would call on her in their distress, remembering the birthing pains of Leto. Women who died in childbirth, or who died suddenly from other natural causes, were said to have been killed by Artemis's arrows.

The puzzle of why the Greeks would have a virgin fertility goddess can perhaps be explained. Artemis may combine two different heritages, of which the fertility concept is the older. The name Artemis seems not to come from the Greek language, and scholars believe that this goddess—like Athena and Hera—was not originally Greek. Rather, Artemis represents a religious survival from the non-Greek peoples who inhabited the Aegean region before the first Greek invaders arrived in about 2100 B.C.E. A goddess of mountains and beasts is portrayed on surviving gemstones and other artwork of the second millennium B.C.E. from Minoan Crete. This unnamed goddess, or series of goddesses, is shown walking with a lion and standing between rampant lions. She appears to be a deity of wilderness abundance. Presumably the conquering Greeks appropriated this regal Lady of Animals into their own RELIGION, during the second millennium B.C.E., changing her into Zeus's daughter. This origin would explain the Greek Artemis's ties to Crete. Artemis's virginity could have been an aspect created by the Greeks, perhaps because the original fertility-Artemis had no husband in the mythology.

Even in historical times, certain cults of Artemis emphasized fertility over virginity. The Artemis worshipped at Ephesus was a mother figure, influenced by the contemporary cult of the goddess Cybele, from the Phrygian territory in interior Asia Minor. The Ephesian Artemis's cult image, of which numerous copies survive today, depicted a crowned goddess with numerous objects attached to her breast (thought today to represent bulls' testicles and to symbolize fertility). Artemis in Asia Minor thus appears to have been very unlike the virgin huntress of mainland Greek religion.

In Greece, one of the main cult sites for Artemis was at Brauron, where a festival (the Brauronia) was held every four years. Another peculiar cult existed at SPARTA. At the annual festival of Artemis Orthia (the surname's meaning is lost to us), Spartan boys endured a public ordeal of whipping as they tried to steal cheeses from the goddess's altar. This brutal rite, dating at least from the 400s B.C.E., had deteriorated into a tourist attraction by the days of the Roman Empire.

See also MINOAN CIVILIZATION.

Further reading: Charlotte R. Long, *The Twelve Gods of Greece and Rome* (Leiden, Netherlands: E. J. Brill, 1987); C. Sourvinou-Inwood, *Studies in Girls' Transitions: Aspects of the Arkteia and Age Representation in Attic Iconography* (Athens: Kardamitsa, 1988); Arianna S. Huffington, *The Gods of Greece* (New York: Atlantic Monthly Press, 1993); Giulia Sissa, *The Daily Life of the Greek Gods,* translated by Janet Lloyd (Stanford, Calif.: Stanford University Press, 2000).

Artemisia   *See* HALICARNASSUS.

Artemision   This harbor and ship-beaching site on the north shore of EUBOEA, off the eastern coast of Greece, was named for a local temple of the goddess ARTEMIS. The site overlooks a six-mile-wide channel whose opposite shore lies along the Magnesian peninsula of THESSALY. In this channel, during the PERSIAN WARS, the allied Greek navy first opposed the invading navy of King XERXES (summer of 480 B.C.E.). The Battle of Artemision was fought nearly simultaneously with the land battle of THERMOPYLAE, 40 miles away, and was part of a Greek strategy to block the Persian southward advance at two neighboring bottlenecks, on land and sea, north of central Greece. Like Thermophylae, Artemision was a marginal Persian victory that nevertheless helped to boost Greek morale.

The allied Greek fleet had about 380 warships, with the largest contingent supplied by ATHENS (180 ships). The Persian ships—which in fact were manned by subject peoples, such as Phoenicians, Egyptians, and IONIAN GREEKS—may have numbered 450 or more. This fleet recently had been reduced, from perhaps 600 ships, by storms off Thessaly.

The battle began when the Persian fleet left its base on the channel's Thessalian shore and rowed out in an enveloping crescent formation against the Greeks. In its Phoenician contingent, the Persian side had the better sailors and faster vessels, but these advantages were reduced in the chaotic press of battle.

The fight was something of an infantry battle on the water. The Persians preferred boarding tactics to ramming: They fought by bringing their ships alongside the Greeks' and sending over the thirty Persian foot soldiers who rode aboard each ship. The Greeks fought back with their own ships' soldiers, about 40 per vessel. After substantial mutual damage, the two fleets returned to their harbors. But upon receiving news of the Greek defeat at Thermophylae, the Greeks withdrew southward.

Artemision contributed to the strategic Greek naval victory at SALAMIS (1), about three weeks later. The Artemision losses weakened the Persian fleet and narrowed Xerxes' options for using it; he decided against sending a squadron to raid Spartan territory (which might have been successful in breaking up the Greek alliance). For the Greeks, Artemision supplied a lesson. It probably helped convince the Greek commanders that, to offset the enemy fleet's better maneuverability, they would have to offer battle in a narrower channel than the one at Artemision—a channel such as the one at Salamis.

In modern times, the Artemision waters have yielded up one of the finest artworks of the ancient world: an over-life-sized BRONZE statue of the god ZEUS, from about 455 B.C.E. Lost with an ancient shipwreck and recovered by underwater ARCHAEOLOGY in the 1920s, the statue now stands in the National Museum in Athens, along with another bronze sculpture from the same shipwreck, a Hellenistic horse and jockey.

See also SCULPTURE; WARFARE, NAVAL.

Further reading: Carol Mattusch, *Classical Bronzes: The Art and Craft of Greek and Roman Statuary* (Ithaca, N.Y.: Cornell University Press, 1996); Sean Hemingway, *The Horse and Jockey from Artemision: A Bronze Equestrian Monument of the Hellenistic Period* (Berkeley: University of California Press, 2004).

Asklepios This mythical Greek physician-hero was eventually worshiped as a god of MEDICINE. The cult of Asklepios blossomed in the 300s B.C.E., partly in response to a new spirit of individualism, which sought a more personal RELIGION. Asklepios's cult was centered on his sanctuary at EPIDAURUS, in the northeastern PELOPONNESE. Sick people flocked there to acquire, for a fee, cures supposedly provided by the god.

The myth of Asklepios is told in a choral ode by the poet PINDAR, performed in about 470 B.C.E. At this time Asklepios was still regarded as a mortal hero who had lived and died long before. He was the son of APOLLO and the Thessalian woman Koronis, but was brought up by the centaur Chiron after Apollo destroyed Koronis for her infidelity. Medicine was one of Apollo's arts, and his son, taught by Chiron, came to excel as a physician. Unfortunately, Asklepios overstepped the boundary of human knowledge when, at the plea of the goddess ARTEMIS, he resurrected a previously dead man (HIPPOLYTUS, a favorite

of Artemis). The high god ZEUS, recognizing Asklepios's skill as a threat to natural order, immediately killed both men with a thunderbolt.

In the latter 400s B.C.E., Asklepios became associated with divine healing. It is unclear why he should have grown to rival his mythical father, Apollo, as patron of physicians, but in any case Asklepios began to be worshipped as a god. His cult center at Epidaurus became a shrine for invalid pilgrims, comparable to that of Lourdes, in France. Its growth and popularity at this particular time were likely due in part to the plague that devastated Athens in 430 B.C.E.

The Epidaurus cult was based on a process known as incubation, whereby a worshipper who sought a cure would spend a night in a dormitory associated with the temple, and be visited by the god in a dream. The next morning, perhaps, the god's priests would interpret the dream and dispense specific medical advice. Many existing inscriptions attest to this procedure's success, whether the explanation lies in the worshippers' autosuggestion or in pious fraud on the part of priests who might impersonate the nocturnal god. But Epidaurus and other Asklepian shrines contained genuine health-promoting facilities, such as baths and GYMNASIUMS. Major Asklepian sanctuaries, established through the Epidaurus priesthood, arose at ATHENS (420 B.C.E.); PERGAMON (300s B.C.E.); and the Italian, non-Greek city of ROME (291 B.C.E.). At Rome, the god's name was latinized to Aesculapius.

Asklepios's totem was a sacred snake; a snake normally lived at each of his shrines. Greek art often protrayed the Asklepian snake as wrapped around another of the god's emblems, the physician's staff. Asklepios's snake and staff survive today as the symbol of the modern medical profession.

See also CENTAURS; HIPPOCRATES.

Further reading: Nikolaos Faraklas, *Epidaurus: The Sanctuary of Asclepios* 2d ed. (Athens: Lycabettus Press, 1972); Mabel Lang, *Cure and Cult in Ancient Corinth: A Guide to the Asklepeion* (Princeton, N.J.: American School of Classical Studies, 1977); R. A. Tomlinson, *Epidauros* (Austin: University of Texas Press, 1983); Emma J. Edelstein, *Asclepius: A Collection and Interpretation of the Testimonies* (Salem, N.H.: Ayer, 1988); Sara Aleshire, *Asklepios at Athens: Epigraphic and Prosopographic Essays on the Athenian Healing Cults* (Amsterdam: J. C. Gieben, 1991).

Asia See EUROPE AND ASIA.

Asia Minor This peninsular landmass, 292,260 miles square, forms a western subcontinent of Asia. Also known as Anatolia, this territory comprises much of modern Turkey. In Greek and Roman times, Asia Minor contained important Greek cities, particularly in the central west coast region called IONIA.

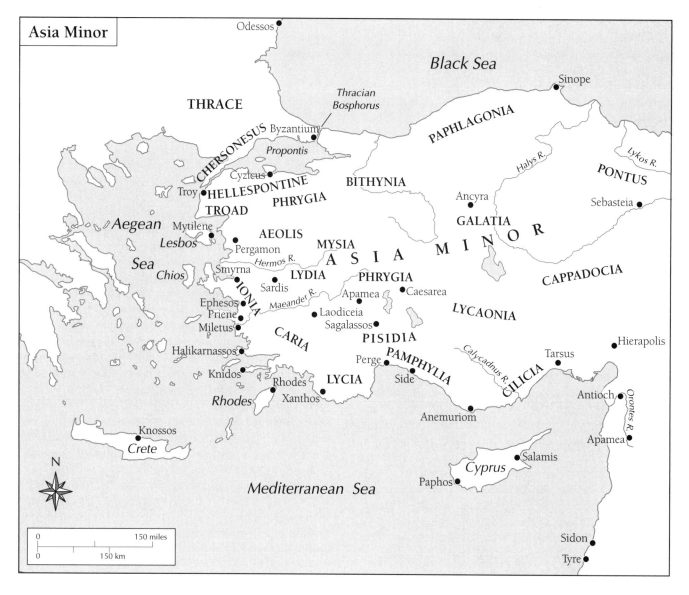

Asia Minor

The name Asia Minor (lesser Asia) came into use among the Romans not long before the birth of Jesus; for the Greeks of prior centuries, the region was simply called Asia. At its northwest corner, Asia Minor is separated from the European continent by the narrow BOSPORUS and HELLESPONT waterways and the SEA OF MARMARA. The hospitable west coast—fertile, temperate, with fine harbors—opens onto the AEGEAN SEA; large inshore islands include (from north to south) LESBOS, CHIOS, SAMOS, and RHODES. Asia Minor's southern coast faces the greater Mediterranean; its north coast faces the BLACK SEA. North and south coasts give rise to steep mountains. The Pontic Range, alongside the north coast, offered TIMBER and raw metals in ancient times. The Taurus Range, in the south, intrudes on the shoreline and limits the number of harbors and habitable sites. Stretching eastward, the long Taurus chain also restricts land

travel between southeast Asia Minor and northern Syria, narrowing the route to a series of mountain passes, such as the Cilician Gates, north of Tarsus. Inland of the mountains, Asia Minor is an often-arid plateau.

By the early second millennium B.C.E., before the first Greeks arrived, Asia Minor was controlled by the Hittites, who ruled out of the north-central interior. Probably with the Hittites' permission, Mycenaean Greeks set up trading posts along the west coast in around 1300 B.C.E. (as suggested by the troves of Mycenaean POTTERY found at MILETUS and other sites). The Greeks were looking for raw metals—copper, tin, GOLD, and SILVER, all mined in the Asia Minor interior—and for luxury goods, such as carved ivory, available through TRADE routes from Syria and Mesopotamia. The legend of the TROJAN WAR surely reflects (distortedly) the Mycenaean Greeks' destruction of an actual, non-Greek fortress town in northwest Asia Minor, a town we call TROY, which evidently was interfering with inbound Greek shipping in the Hellespont (ca. 1200 B.C.E.).

After the Hittite Empire collapsed (ca. 1200 B.C.E.), central Asia Minor came under control of an Asian people called the Phrygians. Their name survived in the central region, known as Phrygia. In these years the new technology of IRON-working, previously monopolized by the Hittites, spread from Asia Minor to mainland Greece (before 1050 B.C.E.). Greek legend claimed that the world's first ironworkers were the Chalybes, a mountain people of northeastern Asia Minor.

Asia Minor's west coast then came under steady Greek invasion, amid the migrations accompanying the downfall of Mycenaean society in mainland Greece. By 1000 B.C.E. Greeks of the Ionian ethnic group had settled in the region thereafter called Ionia; the foremost states here were Miletus, Samos, Chios, and EPHESOS. Greeks of the Aeolian type, using Lesbos as their base, colonized Asia Minor's northern west coast, thereafter called AEOLIS (ca. 1000–600 B.C.E.). Greeks of Dorian ethnicity occupied sites around the southern west coast (ca. 900 B.C.E.), including HALICARNASSUS, KNIDOS, and the islands of Cos and Rhodes. Seizing the best harbors and farmlands, the arriving Greeks ejected the non-Greek peoples. One such people were the Carians, who survived in the southwestern region called Caria.

Greek settlement spread to Asia Minor's northern and southern coasts during the great age of COLONIZATION (ca. 750–550 B.C.E.). In the north, CYZICUS, on the Sea of Marmara, and SINOPE, midway along the Black Sea coast, were among the colonies founded by Miletus in an attempt to control the Black Sea trade route. On the south coast, the principal Greek cities were (from west to east) Phaselis, Perge, Aspendus, and Side.

The Greek settlements prospered along their sea routes and caravan routes. The cities of Ionia produced the poet HOMER (ca. 750 B.C.E.) and the earliest Greek achievements in SCIENCE, PHILOSOPHY, and monumental ARCHITECTURE (600s–500s B.C.E.). But there were also non-Greek nations of the interior to contend with. The marauding Kimmerians overran Phrygia and besieged Ephesos (ca. 600 B.C.E.). The kingdom of LYDIA dominated the west coast (by 550 B.C.E.) and then fell to the Persian king CYRUS (1) (546 B.C.E.).

By the late 500s B.C.E. all of Asia Minor was under the jurisdiction of the Persian king, who ruled and collected tribute through governors called satraps. The two chief satraps of western Asia Minor were based at the former Lydian capital of Sardis and at Dascylion, on the Sea of Marmara. At the end of the PERSIAN WARS, the Greek naval counteroffensive liberated most of Asia Minor's western Greek cities (479–477 B.C.E.). Persian puppet governments were expelled in favor of Athenian-style DEMOCRACY, and the Greek cities became tribute-paying members of the Athenian-dominated DELIAN LEAGUE.

Passing to Spartan control by the end of the PELOPONNESIAN WAR (404 B.C.E.), these cities were ignominiously handed back to PERSIA by the terms of the KING'S PEACE (386 B.C.E.).

ALEXANDER THE GREAT's invasion of Asia Minor (334 B.C.E.) reliberated the Greek cities and brought them into a suddenly enlarged Greek world. Alexander restored local democracies and abolished tribute. After his death (323 B.C.E.), Asia Minor became a battleground for his warring successors. ANTIGONUS (1) ruled from his Phrygian citadel of Celanae, but upon his death at the Battle of Ipsus (in Phrygia, in 301 B.C.E.), Asia Minor was parceled out between LYSIMACHUS and SELEUCUS (1). Seleucus destroyed Lysimachus at the Battle of Corupedium (in Lydia, in 281 B.C.E.) and brought Asia Minor into the sprawling SELEUCID EMPIRE. But the emergence of the city of PERGAMON, inland on the middle west coast, created a local rival for power (mid-200s B.C.E.). By the early 100s B.C.E., Pergamon was one of the most beautiful and prosperous Greek cities.

The Pergamene kings cooperated with the encroaching nation of ROME, and—after helping a Roman army defeat the Seleucids at the Battle of Magnesia (189 B.C.E.)—Pergamon obtained control of most of Asia Minor. The entire region passed into Roman hands with the death of the last Pergamene king (133 B.C.E.). Later the non-Greek kingdom of Pontus arose against Roman authority.

See also AEOLIAN GREEKS; BRONZE; DIADOCHI; DORIAN GREEKS; HELLENISTIC AGE; IONIAN GREEKS; MYCENAEAN CIVILIZATION.

Further reading: George M. A. Hanfmann, *From Croesus to Constantine: The Cities of Western Asia Minor and Their Arts in Greek and Roman Times* (Ann Arbor: University of Michigan Press, 1975); James Mellaart, *The Archaeology of Ancient Turkey* (Totowa, N.J.: Rowman and Littlefield, 1978); Seton Lloyd, *Ancient Turkey: A Traveller's History of Anatolia* (Berkeley: University of California Press, 1989); Ekrem Akurgal, *Ancient Civilizations and Ruins of Turkey: from Prehistoric Times until the End of the Roman Empire*, translated by John Whybrow and Mollie Emre, 8th ed. (Istanbul: NET Turistik Yayinlar, 1993); David Parrish, ed., *Urbanism in Western Asia Minor: New Studies on Aphrodisias, Ephesos, Hierapolis, Pergamon, Perge, and Xanthos* (Portsmouth, R.I.: Journal of Roman Archaeology, 2001).

Aspasia (ca. 470–410 B.C.E.) *Common-law wife of the Athenian statesman Perikles*
After divorcing his legal wife, Perikles lived with Aspasia from about 450 B.C.E. until his death in 429 B.C.E.

Aspasia was an immigrant from MILETUS and thus was a resident alien at ATHENS. Perikles, being an Athenian citizen, was prohibited from marrying her (according to a law of 451 B.C.E., which he himself had sponsored).

Historians traditionally have theorized that Aspasia was either herself a prostitute (*hetaira*) or that she at least managed a "house" of *hetairai,* but some modern scholars dismiss this information as being a daring joke of Athenian stage comedy. Contemporary comic playwrights such as KRATINUS, EUPOLIS, and ARISTOPHANES made vicious public fun of Perikles' liaison with Aspasia.

Witty and well educated, Aspasia seems to have had a captivating personality. She is said to have given lessons in RHETORIC, and the Athenian philosopher SOCRATES supposedly enjoyed conversing with her.

The 430s B.C.E. at Athens saw a rash of politically motivated prosecutions indirectly aimed at Perikles; the immediate targets included Aspasia and Perikles' friends PHEIDIAS and ANAXAGORAS. Aspasia was accused of impiety (*asebeia*)—a common charge against intellectuals—and she also may have been accused of procuring freeborn Athenian ladies for Perikles' pleasure. At trial she was acquitted after Perikles made a personal appeal to the jurors, during which he uncharacteristically burst into tears.

She and Perikles had a son, also named Perikles. Although ineligible for Athenian citizenship because his mother was alien, the younger Perikles was enrolled as a citizen at his dying father's request, in about 429 B.C.E. In 406 B.C.E. the younger Perikles was one of six Athenian generals executed by public order for failing to rescue Athenian survivors after the sea battle of Arginusae, during the PELOPONNESIAN WAR.

Aspasia provides an example of the kind of success that an ambitious woman might find in a society that generally excluded WOMEN from power and wealth. Although further disadvantaged by being alien, she achieved a degree of influence and security by attaching herself to a powerful man.

See also EDUCATION; MARRIAGE; METICS; PROSTITUTES.

Further reading: Madeleine M. Henry, *Prisoner of History: Aspasia of Miletus and Her Biographical Tradition* (Oxford: Oxford University Press, 1995); S. Blundell, *Women in Classical Athens* (London: Bristol Classical Press, 1998).

assembly The word used to translate the Greek word *ekklēsia*—the official gathering of citizens in a Greek DEMOCRACY for the purpose of public debate and vote. At democratic ATHENS in the 400s and 300s B.C.E., the assembly was the sovereign body of government.

Admission to the Athenian assembly was open to all male citizens over age 18 (in theory about 30,000–40,000 men; in practice about 5,000). Under the radical democracy there were no property requirements for admission, and the 300s B.C.E. saw the introduction of a small payment for attendance, comparable to our modern jury pay.

The Athenian assembly met at least 40 times per year, with extra meetings as called for by the COUNCIL or by the board of generals. In the 400s B.C.E. the usual place of meeting was the Pnyx ("Packing Place"), a smoothened hillside west of the ACROPOLIS. There the people might vote on issues by show of hands; if written balloting was required—such as in an OSTRACISM vote—then the AGORA would be used. In debate, any Athenian had the right to address the assembly; a chairman of the day presided; and rules of order were maintained. Foreign ambassadors and other noncitizens might be allowed to address the assembly on issues of state.

Usually the assembly could debate and vote only on those topics placed on the agenda by the council; however, the assembly could (by vote) require the council to list a certain topic for the next meeting. Like other instruments of Athenian government, the assembly enjoyed courtroom powers. For example, it had the final verdict in certain serious criminal cases. By its vote the assembly passed laws, declared war, made peace, inflicted individual sentences of death or exile, and elected the army's generals and other important executives. The power of the assembly during Athens' imperial heyday can be seen in the Mytilenean Debate—described in THUCYDIDES' (1) history of the PELOPONNESIAN WAR (book 3)—where the fate of every man, woman, and child of the rebellious city of MYTILENE was decided in public debate at Athens in 427 B.C.E.

Further reading: M. H. Hansen, *The Athenian Ecclesia: A Collection of Articles, 1976–1983* (Copenhagen: Museum Tusculanum Press, 1983); ———, *The Athenian Assembly in the Age of Demosthenes* (New York: B. Blackwell, 1987); ———, *The Athenian Ecclesia II: A Collection of Articles, 1983–1989* (Copenhagen: Museum Tusculanum Press, 1989); Chester G. Starr, *The Birth of Athenian Democracy: The Assembly in the Fifth Century B.C.* (New York: Oxford University Press, 1990); James L. O'Neil, *The Origins and Development of Ancient Greek Democracy* (Lanham, Md.: Rowman & Littlefield, 1995); John Thorley, *Athenian Democracy* (New York: Routledge, 1996); M. H. Hansen, *The Athenian Democracy in the Age of Demosthenes: Structure, Principles, and Ideology,* translated by J. A. Crook (Norman: University of Oklahoma Press, 1999).

astronomy The ancient Greeks pioneered the study of astronomy in the Western world, cataloguing the stars and identifying five of the planets (besides the Earth). Most important, they developed several geometric models that tried to explain the movements of the heavenly bodies in terms of concentric spheres and other orbital paths. Unfortunately, the Greeks incorrectly placed Earth at the center of the universe. This geocentric theory was brought to a false perfection by Ptolemy of ALEXANDRIA (1), around 135 C.E. With Ptolemy's revisions, the geocentric model seemed to account for all heavenly motion observable to the unaided eye. (The Greeks possessed no telescopic lenses, only crude sighting devices.)

Ptolemy's system was so persuasive that it remained canonical in late antiquity and the Middle Ages, before it was finally ousted in 1543 C.E. by Copernicus' heliocentric model, which correctly placed the Sun at the center of the solar system. Ironically, the ancient Greek astronomer Aristarchus of SAMOS (ca. 275 B.C.E.) had produced a simple heliocentral model, but this had been bypassed in favor of the more apparently promising geocentric one.

Like other ancient peoples lacking precise calendars, the earliest Greeks relied on the rising and setting of the constellations in order to gauge the FARMING year. The poet HESIOD's versified farming almanac, *Works and Days* (ca. 700 B.C.E.) mentions certain duties as signaled by the stars—for instance, grapes are to be picked when the constellation ORION has risen to a position overhead, in early autumn.

In the verses of HOMER (ca. 750 B.C.E.) and other early poets, the Earth is imagined as a disk surrounded by the stream of Ocean (*Okeanos*). The early philosopher-scientist THALES of MILETUS (ca. 585 B.C.E.) elaborated on this concept, picturing a world that floats like a log on a cosmic lake of water. Thales' successor ANAXIMANDER (ca. 560 B.C.E.) devised the first, crude astronomical theory; he saw the world as a cylinder or disk suspended in space, with the cylinder's flat top constituting the inhabited world and the visible sky comprised of a series of fitted rings forming a hemisphere. The Sun, Moon, and stars are holes in these rings, through which we glimpse a distant celestial fire.

An obvious weakness of Anaximander's theory was its inability to explain the puzzling movements of the planets. The five planets known to the Greeks were Mercury, Venus, Mars, Jupiter, and Saturn (to use modern names). To the naked eye they look like bright stars, but their individual, looping progress through the night skies earned them the Greek name *planētai,* or "wanderers."

The planets' movements were first plausibly explained by the brilliant mathematician Eudoxus of KNIDOS, who was a student of PLATO at the ACADEMY at ATHENS (ca. 350 B.C.E.). Eudoxus held that all heavenly movements are caused by the circular rotations of 27 concentric spheres, with the Earth at their center. All of the proper stars exist on the single, outermost sphere (according to Eudoxus), but each planet employs no fewer than four concentric spheres, which spin along different axes to produce the planet's irregular course. Similarly, Sun and Moon are governed by three spheres each. Greater precision seemed to be achieved when more spheres were added by Eudoxus' younger contemporary Callipus of CYZICUS and by the great ARISTOTLE (both ca. 330 B.C.E.).

Another astronomer of this Athenian intellectual heyday was Heraclides Ponticus (like Eudoxus, a younger associate of Plato at the Academy). Using the geocentric model, Heraclides suggested that the Earth itself rotates on its axis. All of these thinkers approached astronomy as a challenge in geometry, not physics; there seem to have been no theories regarding what mechanical forces would cause the spheres to move. Understandably, the Greeks had no knowledge of astrophysics; topics such as gravity or the chemical compositions of stars were largely unexplored.

Aristarchus of Samous was a follower of Aristotelian Peripatetic School at Athens, around 275 B.C.E. Rejecting the Eudoxan model, Aristarchus invented the heliocentric theory, which correctly posited that the Earth and planets revolve around the Sun and that the Earth spins on an axis. Like prior astronomers, Aristarchus imagined the stars as spread along a vast outer sphere—but thought that this sphere was stationary. He also correctly believed that the stars' apparent movement is an illusion created by the Earth's orbit. Few of Aristarchus's writings survive, and we know of his theory mainly from later authors.

This heliocentric theory was not accepted in antiquity for two reasons. First, it ran counter to prevailing religious-philosophical beliefs by removing humankind from the center of creation. Second, it failed to account satisfactorily for the absence of stellar parallax—in other words, if the Earth moves through space, then the stars should be seen to slide sideways in their progress overhead, which they do not seem to do. (In fact, the stars do shift their angles minutely as the Earth orbits past, but their immense distance from the Earth makes this variation invisible to the naked eye.)

The next great name in Greek astronomy is Apollonius of Pergē (a Greek town in southwestern ASIA MINOR), who was active at Alexandria around 200 B.C.E. A mathematical genius, Apollonius revolutionized the geocentric theory by abandoning Eudoxus's cumbersome spheres in favor of two different models explaining celestial movement in terms of irregular orbits called eccentrics and epicycles. For example, the epicyclical theory imagined a planet shooting around in a small circle while at the same time orbiting in a much larger circle around the Earth.

One of antiquity's few practical astronomers was Hipparchus of Nicaea (a Greek city in western Asia Minor). Active at RHODES around 135 B.C.E. Hipparchus invented or improved the sighting device known as the dioptra, and was the first to map and catalogue approximately 850 stars.

The work of Apollonius and Hipparchus laid the groundwork for the greatest astronomer of the ancient world, Claudius Ptolemaeus, usually known as Ptolemy (but not a member of the Macedonian-Egyptian royal dynasty that used that name). A Greek-blooded Roman citizen of Alexandria, Ptolemy was active around 127–140 C.E., under the Roman Empire. His written masterpiece was the *Almagest,* which has survived in medieval Arabic translation. (That title is the Arabic form for the unofficial Greek title *Megistē,* "the greatest," i.e.

textbook.) In 13 books, the *Almagest* presented the sum total of astronomical knowledge of the day, as enlarged by Ptolemy's own work on the geocentric model. Aided by his pioneering use of the sighting device known as the armillary astrolabe (the forerunner of the medieval astrolabe), Ptolemy also enlarged Hipparchus' star map, among his many other achievements.

See also ARATUS (2); MATHEMATICS; OCEANUS; PYTHAGORAS.

Further reading: Theodor S. Jacobsen, *Planetary Systems from the Ancient Greeks to Kepler* (Seattle: University of Washington Press, 1999); Jean Claude Pecker, *Understanding the Heavens: Thirty Centuries of Astronomical Ideas from Ancient Thinking to Modern Cosmology,* edited by Susan Kaufman (New York: Springer, 2001); Ronald Brashear, *Star Struck: One Thousand Years of the Art and Science of Astronomy* (Seattle: University of Washington Press, 2001).

Astyanax   *See* ANDROMACHE; HECTOR.

Atalanta   In MYTH, Atalanta was an Arcadian or Boeotian heroine of the athletic, forest-ranging, virginal type (in the pattern of the goddess ARTEMIS and of the AMAZONS). Beloved by the hero Meleager, Atalanta joined him in the CALYDONIAN BOAR HUNT. But the best-known legend about Atalanta concerns her MARRIAGE. Unwilling to be wed, she declared that she would submit only to the man who could beat her in a footrace. According to one version, she would follow the racing suitor with a spear and stab him as she overtook him. She was finally won by a suitor named Melanion (or Hippomenes) who, with the goddess APHRODITE's help, had acquired three golden apples. During the race he dropped these treasures one by one in Atalanta's way; pausing to acquire them, she lost the contest. Their son was named Parthenopaeus ("born of the virgin").

Further reading: J. Barringer, "Atalanta as Model: The Hunter and the Hunted," *Classical Antiquity* 15:1 (1996): 44–76; Thomas Scanlon, *Eros and Greek Athletics* (Oxford: Oxford University Press, 2002).

Athena (often Athene)   This important Greek goddess was the guardian of the city of ATHENS—whose name she shared—and the patron of wisdom, handicraft, and the disciplined aspect of war. Athena was worshiped on the ACROPOLIS of several Greek cities, including ARGOS and SPARTA. But her most significant shrine was on the Athenian acropolis, where a succession of temples culminated, in 438 B.C.E., in the building that is the gem of ancient ARCHITECTURE: the PARTHENON, or Temple of Athena the Virgin.

The name Athena, like the name Athens, is not actually Greek; the ending *-na* belongs to the language of the non-Greek people who preceded the Greeks as the inhab-itants of mainland Greece. In her pre-Greek form, Athena was probably a patron deity of kings, whose hilltop palaces she guarded as an idol shown clad in armor; in her ultimate origins she may be related to armed goddesses of the ancient Near East, such as the Mesopotamian Ishtar. After about 2100 B.C.E., when ethnic Greek invaders began taking over the land of Greece, Athena became incorporated into the developing Greek RELIGION (as did other pre-Greek goddesses, including HERA and ARTEMIS). Keeping her armor and her association with the hilltop, Athena entered Greek MYTH as the daughter of the great god ZEUS. This transition was under way by the Mycenaean era (1600–1200 B.C.E.), as is suggested by the mention of a "Lady of Atana" on a surviving Mycenaean clay tablet, inscribed in LINEAR B script and dated by archaeologists to 1400 B.C.E.

The charming myth of Athena's birth from the head of Zeus is told by the poets HESIOD (ca. 700 B.C.E.) and PINDAR (467 B.C.E.). It seems that Zeus swallowed his first wife, Metis, when she was pregnant. He did this because a prophecy had warned him that Metis would otherwise bear a son destined to depose his father. But Zeus soon felt a terrible headache. And when the smith god HEPHAISTOS helpfully split open Zeus' skull, the goddess Athena sprang out—adult, in full armor, giving a war shout. This tale surely contains a primitive religious-political motive: namely, it shows absolutely that the goddess is Zeus's daughter and hence subordinate to him. The story also symbolizes how Zeus and Athena both partake of cleverness (Greek: *mētis*). The birth scene is a favorite subject on surviving Greek vase paintings from the 600s B.C.E. onward.

As goddess of organizational wisdom, Athena was thought to guide the typical Greek city-state (not only Athens). Her cult titles included Boulaia, "goddess of the COUNCIL," and Polias, "goddess of the city." In these functions she resembled Zeus, who was god of cosmic order and whose titles included Poleios, "lord of the city." In later centuries she naturally became associated with the academic wisdom of PHILOSOPHY.

As a protector of civilized Greek life, Athena was prominent in myths of order versus chaos. She was imagined as fighting gallantly in the gods' primeval war against the rebellious GIANTS. A famous section of the Great Altar of PERGAMON, sculpted around 180 B.C.E. and now in Berlin, shows Athena hauling the subdued Giant leader, Alcyoneus, by his hair. In other myths she repeatedly appears as a counselor to heroes struggling against monsters and villains. She helps HERAKLES with his Twelve Labors, ODYSSEUS with his homecoming, and PERSEUS (1) with the killing of MEDUSA.

As a war goddess, Athena overlapped with the war god ARES. But where the brutal Ares embodied war's madness and waste, Athena tended to represent the more glorious aspects—strategy, discipline, national defense. She was said to have introduced such military inventions as the ship, the horse bridle, and the war chariot. In HOMER's epic poem the *Iliad* (written down around 750 B.C.E.), she is the Greeks' staunch ally against the Trojans, accompanying her chosen warriors into battle. She intervenes to aid her favorite, DIOMEDES, and, in the poem's climactic section, helps ACHILLES to slay the Trojan HECTOR. Early in the poem, however, she restrains Achilles from an act of violence against the Greek commander, AGAMEMNON, for she is also a deity of reason and control.

In poetry and art, Athena's war gear includes a breastplate, helmet, spear, and shield of some sort. Sometimes her shield is the supernatural aegis (*aigis*), associated also with Zeus. Homer describes the aegis as a fearsome storm cloud, but by the mid-600s B.C.E. vase painters were picturing it as a goatskin mantle on Athena's left arm or covering her breast, tassled with live snakes and showing the vanquished Medusa's face. Later the aegis became styled as a round metal shield, embossed with Medusa's image.

Statue of Athena, goddess of wisdom and protector of the city of Athens, shown leaning on her shield *(Alison Frantz Photographic Collection, American School of Classical Studies at Athens)*

Among peaceful duties, Athena was said to have invented weaving, spinning, and other domestic crafts performed by WOMEN in the ancient Greek world. She was also the patron of carpenters, potters, and (like the god Hephaistos) of metalworkers. Her relevant title was Erganē, "worker woman."

The Athenians credited her with introducing the cultivation of the olive, a staple of the ancient Greek diet and economy. Legend said that Athena and the god POSEIDON had competed publicly over who would become the Athenians' patron deity. Poseidon stabbed his trident into the acropolis summit, bringing forth a saltwater well; but alongside it Athena planted the first olive tree, and she was judged the winner by the people. The saltwater well and sacred olive tree were features of the Athenian acropolis in historical times.

Athena was pictured as stately and beautiful, although stern. In Homer's verses, Zeus calls her by the fond nickname *glaukopis*, "gray eyes" or "bright eyes." Her virginity—a trait she had in common with the goddesses Artemis and HESTIA—may perhaps harken back to her primeval form as a defender of the citadel: She is inviolate, like the fortress that she oversees. Her famous Athenian cult title was Parthenos, "the virgin," and her very old title Pallas was likewise understood as meaning "virgin." In myth, the Palladion was an image of Athena, sent down from heaven and worshipped by the Trojans.

By the late 400s B.C.E. Athena had two sanctuaries on the Athenian acropolis. One was the Parthenon, housing a 35-foot-tall, GOLD-and-ivory statue of Athena Parthenos; the other was the Erectheion, housing a smaller, immemorably old, olivewood statue of Athena Polias. This simple wooden idol was revered at the midsummer festival of the Panathenaia ("all Athens")—considered to be Athena's birthday—when the people ceremoniously brought a new woolen gown (*peplos*) up to the goddess. An especially large celebration, held every fourth year, was called the Great Panathenaia. At another festival, in early summer, the Polias statue was carried down to the sea to be washed.

The Greeks identified their gods with certain animals; Athena was associated with snakes and, particularly, owls. Folklore claimed that owls were wise, like their goddess. Modern scholars believe that Athena's links with the owl, snake, and olive tree were all survivals of her primitive, pre-Greek cult, dating back to the third millennium B.C.E.

See also FARMING; MINOAN CIVILIZATION; PARIS; PHEIDIAS.

Further reading: C. J. Herrington, *Athena Parthenos and Athenia Polias: A Study in the Religion of Periclean Athens* (Manchester, U.K.: Manchester University Press, 1955); Jenifer Neils, *Goddess and Polis: The Panathenaic Festival in Ancient Athens* (Princeton, N.J.: Princeton University Press, 1992); ———, ed., *Worshipping Athena* (Madison: University of Wisconsin Press, 1996);

Susan Deacy and Alexandra Villing, *Athena in the Classical World* (Leiden, Netherlands: E. J. Brill, 2001).

Athenian democracy   *See* DEMOCRACY.

Athens   This is the foremost city of ancient Greece and one of the three most important ancient cities that shaped Western civilization, along with ROME and Jerusalem. The culture produced by the rich and confident Athens of the mid-400s B.C.E.—in THEATER, ARCHITECTURE, SCULPTURE, and PHILOSOPHY—provides a cornerstone of our modern society. Most important, Athens was the birthplace of DEMOCRACY (*dēmokratia,* "power by the people").

The physical city, beautified by the wealth of empire, was a marvel to the ancient world—as it is today for the tourists and scholars who visit Athens (now the modern Greek capital). With some justification the Athenian statesman PERIKLES described his city as "the greatest name in history . . . a power to be remembered forever." Defeat in the PELOPONNESIAN WAR (431–404 B.C.E.) broke Athens's imperial might, but the city remained politically important for the next century and culturally influential for the rest of antiquity.

An advantageous site helped make the city great. Located in southeast-central Greece, in the peninsular landmass called ATTICA, Athens lies amid the region's largest plain, where grain and olives were grown in historical times. The plain is surrounded by mountains and has three major rivers running through and near the city: the Eridanos, the Ilissos, and the Kephissos. Athens lies approximately four miles from the shore of the Saronic Gulf, and its primary geographical feature is the 300-foot-tall, rock-formed hill later known as the ACROPOLIS. This defensible position dominated the plain and, being four miles inland of the Saronic Gulf, gave access to the sea without inviting naval attack.

The locale was inhabited long before the first Greek-speaking tribesmen arrived around 2000 B.C.E. Archaeological excavations on the Acropolis have found evidence of occupation as far back as the Neolithic period. The name Athens (Athenai) is pre-Greek and is associated with the city's patron goddess, ATHENA, who is likewise pre-Greek. Evidently the early Greek invaders appropriated these two related names (whose original meanings are lost to us). During the flourishing Greek MYCENAEAN CIVILIZATION (1600–1200 B.C.E.), Athens was a second-rank power—overshadowed by MYCENAE, THEBES, and other centers.

Greek MYTH claims that the unification of Attica under Athenian control was brought about by the Athenian king THESEUS. This legend probably recalls a real-life event of the late Mycenaean era. In later centuries this unification (*sunoikismos,* "synoecism") was celebrated at an annual Athenian festival called the Sinoikia. Among the resources of the Attic countryside that then passed to Athenian control were the fertile plain of Eleusis, the marble of Mt. Pentelicus, and, most important, the raw SILVER of Mt. Laurion. In a later era, Laurion silver would provide the Athenian COINAGE and help finance the social and military programs of the democracy.

A united Attica was able to resist the invading DORIAN GREEKS who swept southward through Greece after the collapse of Mycenaean society (around 1100 B.C.E.). Legend tells how the last Athenian king, Kodrus, sacrificed his life to save Athens from Dorian capture. Other legends describe Athens as a rallying point for Greek refugees whose homes in the PELOPONNESE had been overrun by the Dorians. These refugees, of the Ionian ethnic group, migrated eastward to establish cities on the ASIA MINOR coast that in later centuries retained cultural and political ties to Athens.

Following the depressed years of the DARK AGE (1100–900 B.C.E.), Athens emerged as a mainland commercial power, alongside CORINTH, CHALCIS, and a few other cities. In the 800s–700s B.C.E., Athenian workshops produced a widely admired Geometric-style POTTERY eventually imitated throughout Greece. At Athens, as at other prosperous Greek cities, there arose a monied middle class—mainly manufacturers and farmers—who resented being excluded from political power.

Like other Greek states, Athens at this time was governed as an ARISTOCRACY. A small circle of noble families monopolized the government and judiciary and owned most of the land. The general population was unrepresented, its political function being mainly to pay taxes, serve under arms, and obey the leaders' decrees. The emergence of democracy involved a drastic revamping of Athens' government in the 500s and 400s B.C.E., to the point where the citizens' ASSEMBLY comprised the sovereign, decision-making body.

This process required improvization, compromise, and bloodshed. In about 632 B.C.E. an adventuring nobleman named KYLON tried to exploit middle-class unrest to make himself tyrant of Athens, but the coup failed. Popular demand for a permanent, written law code was left unsatisfied by the aristocratically biased legislation of DRACO (ca. 624 B.C.E.), but SOLON's radical reforms (ca. 594 B.C.E.) averted revolution and laid the foundations for Athenian democracy. In foreign affairs, Athens defeated its nearby rival MEGARA (1) for control of the island of SALAMIS (1). Athenian COLONIZATION in the HELLESPONT district—at Sigeum and the CHERSONESE—foreshadowed Athens's imperial control of that region in future years.

Despite Solon's legislation, class tensions remained keen enough for PEISISTRATUS to seize power as tyrant (mid-500s B.C.E.). Under his enlightened rule, Athens advanced commercially and artistically. Supplanting Corinth as the foremost mainland mercantile power, Athens monopolized the pottery market, exporting Athenian black-figure ware throughout the Mediterranean.

Athens and Its Monuments

to Academy

to Eleosis

Panathenaic Way

Kerameikos

Athens

Dipylon Gate

Eridanus R.

Sacred Gate

to Marathon

to Salamis

Hephaisteion —

Stoa of Attalus

to Piraeus

Tholos —

South Stoa —

Erechtheion

Northern Long Wall

Parthenon

City Wall

Lyceum

Areopagus

Hill of the Nymphs

Pnyx

Ilissus R.

Odeion of Pericles

to Lyceum

Stoa of Eumenes

Theater of Dionysus

Hill of the Muses

Temple of Olympian Zeus

Stadium

to Pireus

to Cape Sunion

Middle Long Wall

Southern Long Wall —

to Phaleron

N

/// \\\   Elevation

═══   Roads

0   500 yards

0   500 m

Athens became a cultural center, as Peisistratus and his son and successor, HIPPIAS (1), attracted poets, sculptors, and other craftsmen from throughout the Greek world.

The expulsion of Hippias in 510 B.C.E. brought on the birth of democracy. The reforms of KLEISTHENES (1) (508 B.C.E.) broke the aristocracy's residual influence by means of administrative changes based on the redivision of the population into 10 new tribes. A citizens' COUNCIL of 500 became the guide and executive for the popular assembly, which in practice numbered about 5,000 men. The assembly held regular meetings in the Pnyx ("packing place"), a hollowed-out hillside about 500 yards west of the acropolis. In around 507 B.C.E. the Athenians repulsed an attack by the Spartan king KLEOMENES (1) that was aimed at dismantling the fledgling democracy. The optimism of the following years helped the Athenians to repel a Persian invasion force at the Battle of MARATHON, outside Athens (490 B.C.E.).

By 500 B.C.E., the physical city had begun to take on its classical layout. Probably by then a surrounding wall had been built (although only later walls have survived in

remnants). Atop the acropolis, which was sacred to Athena and other gods, old temples of wood or limestone were being replaced by marble structures. At the acropolis's southeast base stood an open-air THEATER dedicated to the god DIONYSUS, where performances of the newborn Athenian art-forms of tragedy and comedy were held. Northwest of the acropolis lay the AGORA—the city's commercial center. Some distance northwest of the agora, beyond the Dipylon Gate, stood an industrial suburb, the Kerameikos ("potters' quarter"), at the outer edge of which lay the aristocratic families' elaborate graveyards, still visible today.

Under leadership of the left-wing statesman THEMISTOKLES, the Athenians developed PIRAEUS as a seaport and amassed the biggest navy in Greece, 200 warships. This navy played a paramount role in defending Greece against the invasion of the Persian king XERXES (480 B.C.E.). Athens was evacuated before the advancing Persians—who burned and sacked the empty city twice, in 480 and 479 B.C.E.—but the Athenians fought on in their warships and helped destroy the Persian navy at the sea battle of Salamis.

The defeat of Xerxes' invasion created an outpouring of confidence—and an influx of money—that made Athens into the cultural capital of the Greek world. First the city wall, torn down by the Persians, was rebuilt and enlarged, despite Spartan objections (479 B.C.E.); remnants of this four-mile-long "Themistoklean Wall" survive today. In the Greek naval counteroffensive against Persian territories, Athens now took the lead, organizing the Greek city-states of the AEGEAN SEA and the Asia Minor coast into an Athenian-controlled coalition, the DELIAN LEAGUE (478 or 477 B.C.E.). The league's most prominent officer was the conservative Athenian statesman KIMON. Delian member states paid dues—in the form of silver or military service—which in time came to be used strictly for Athens's advantage.

Athenian aggressions in mainland Greece—against AEGINA, BOEOTIA, PHOCIS, and CORINTH—brought Athens into intermittent conflict with those states' powerful ally, Sparta (459–446 B.C.E.). Meanwhile the left-wing statesman Perikles became heir to Themistokles' policies of sea empire and resistance to Sparta. Perikles tightened Athens's control over the Delian allies, and he built the LONG WALLS, connecting Athens to its naval base at Piraeus in a continuous fortification (461–456 B.C.E.). After arranging peace with PERSIA, he initiated a building program (448 B.C.E.) to replace the temples destroyed in 480–479 B.C.E. This program, supervised by the sculptor PHEIDIAS, turned Athens into the grandest city of the Greek world. Among the famous constructions still standing today are the PARTHENON, Propylaia, Erechtheion, and Temple of Athena Nikē (all on the acropolis), and the admirably preserved temple of the god HEPHAISTOS in the agora.

The middle and late 400s B.C.E. saw the Athenian high noon. The tragic playwrights AESCHYLUS, SOPHOKLES, and EURIPIDES, the painter Polygnotus, the intellectual movement of the SOPHISTS, the comic playwright ARISTOPHANES, the historian THUCYDIDES (1), and the West's first great ethical philosopher, SOCRATES, all lived in Athens during these years. From other Greek cities craftsmen, poets, and businessmen flocked to Athens, swelling Attica's population to over 200,000 (including SLAVES) and making the city fully dependent on imports of Ukrainian grain, supplied by Perikles' far-reaching naval program.

Fear of Athenian expansionism led Sparta, Corinth, and Boeotia to start the Peloponnesian War (as we call it), in 431 B.C.E. Despite the outbreak of plague (430 B.C.E. and later), the Athenian navy and maritime network could have brought the city safely through the conflict, had the citizens not wasted lives and resources in a vainglorious attempt to conquer SYRACUSE, in Greek SICILY (415–413 B.C.E.). This calamitous defeat threw Athens on the defensive, while the Spartans, with the help of Persian money, were able to develop a navy, subvert Athens's Delian allies, and attack the Athenian lifeline in the Hellespont. With

their fleet destroyed (405 B.C.E.), the Athenians surrendered after an eight-month siege (404 B.C.E.). The victorious Spartans pulled down the Long Walls. Despite urgings from the Thebans and Corinthians to destroy Athens, the Spartans spared the city, installing the short-lived dictatorship of the THIRTY TYRANTS.

Athens quickly recovered, joining another war against Sparta (395–387 B.C.E.) and organizing another maritime coalition, the SECOND ATHENIAN LEAGUE (377 B.C.E.). In spite of the eloquent harangues of the statesman DEMOSTHENES (1), the Athenians proved ineffectual against the military-diplomatic campaigns of King PHILIP II of MACEDON. After sharing in the defeat of CHAIRONEIA (338 B.C.E.), Athens received lenient treatment as Philip's subject city; the league, however, was disbanded. Athens revolted against Macedonian rule after the death of ALEXANDER THE GREAT (323 B.C.E.), but defeat brought an end to Athens's foreign policy ambitions, and a Macedonian garrison was then installed at Piraeus (322 B.C.E.). Under the Macedonian king KASSANDER, Athens was governed by the enlightened Demetrius of Phaleron (317–307 B.C.E.). Liberated by the warrior prince DEMETRIUS POLIORKETES, Athens reverted periodically to Macedonian control, until the coming of ROME broke Macedon's power (167 B.C.E.).

The 300s B.C.E. marked the greatest days of Athenian philosophy, starting with the establishment of PLATO's school of higher learning, the ACADEMY (ca. 385 B.C.E.). In 335 B.C.E., Plato's former pupil ARISTOTLE opened a rival school, the LYCEUM. Among other influential philosophical movements to emerge at that time at Athens were EPICUREANISM (ca. 307 B.C.E.) and STOICISM (ca. 300 B.C.E.). Athens still retained a foremost position in the arts, producing, among other talents, the sculptor PRAXITELES (ca. 350 B.C.E.) and the playwright MENANDER (ca. 300 B.C.E.).

The HELLENISTIC AGE saw Athens's creative output begin to diminish as new centers of wealth and patronage arose, including ALEXANDRIA (1) and PERGAMON.

In 86 B.C.E., Athens revolted in an attempt to free itself from Roman rule, but the general Sulla sacked the city and demolished the fortification walls that had been build under Themistokles four centuries earlier. In the Imperial period, Athens regained some of its former glory, being appreciated by the Romans for its rich cultural history and becoming a prestigious center of EDUCATION. The philosophical schools continued to be active until 529 C.E., when they were closed by the emperor Justinian. Athens remained an important city in the Byzantine Empire until 1204. It was subsequently occupied by the Franks until 1456 and then by the Turks until 1821. At this time, the Greeks finally obtained their freedom, and in 1833 the city of Athens was proclaimed the new nation's capital.

See also CORINTHIAN WAR; PAINTING; PERSIAN WARS; POLIS; TRADE; TYRANTS.

Further reading: John Travlos, *Pictorial Dictionary of Ancient Athens* (New York: Hacker, 1980); John McK. Camp, *The Archaeology of Athens* (New Haven, Conn.: Yale University Press, 2001); Mark Munn, *The School of History: Athens in the Age of Socrates* (Berkeley: University of California Press, 2003).

Atlantis The legend of Atlantis ("island in the Atlantic") first appears in two dialogues, the *Timaeus* and the *Critias*, written in about 355 B.C.E. by the Athenian philosopher PLATO. Plato describes Atlantis as a vast, wealthy island or continent that had existed 9,000 years before in the Atlantic Ocean. This domain was an ideal society, inhabited by an advanced and virtuous people who conquered eastward to Europe and Africa. But their greed for power grew, until the angry gods sent a deluge to submerge the island.

Despite our modern-day fascination with this legend, it seems clear that Atlantis never existed as described. Plato probably made up the tale as a parable of self-destructive pride. Some modern scholars believe that Plato's story may record some 1,100-year-old folktale telling of the decline of MINOAN CIVILIZATION in the Aegean region. ARCHAEOLOGY has yielded information about the volcanic island of Thera (modern Santorini), which was under the influence and/or control of the Minoans and was destroyed by a massive eruption of its volcano in the 1600s B.C.E. This eruption caused most of the island to become submerged, and it created tidal waves and clouds of ash throughout the eastern Mediterranean, including on the island of CRETE. Plato's Atlantis may be a distorted memory of the destruction of Thera or the downfall of Minoan Crete, projected beyond the Mediterranean world.

See also HUBRIS; THERA.

Further reading: Lewis Spence, *The History of Atlantis* (New York: Gramercy Books, 1996); Rodney Castleden, *Atlantis Destroyed* (New York: Routledge, 1998); Richard Ellis, *Imagining Atlantis* (New York: Alfred A. Knopf, 1998).

Atlas In MYTH, Atlas was one of the TITANS (the race of demigods that ruled the universe before the emergence of the Olympian gods). After the Titans' overthrow by the gods, Atlas was condemned by ZEUS to hold up the sky on his shoulders for eternity. The Greeks associated Atlas with the far West. By the mid-400s B.C.E. he was identified with the Atlas mountain range in North Africa, and his name had been given to the Atlantic Ocean (Greek *Atlantikos*, "of Atlas").

Atlas was said to be the father of the HESPERIDES (daughters of Evening), who tended the fabled garden in the West where golden apples grew. When the hero HERAKLES arrived to fetch a few such apples for his twelfth Labor, Atlas offered to get them for him if he would kindly support the sky in the meantime. Returning with three golden apples, Atlas intended to leave Herakles holding up the celestial canopy, but Herakles was able to trick Atlas into resuming his assigned burden. The incident is portrayed on a famous marble relief carving from the Temple of Zeus at OLYMPIA.

See also OLYMPUS, MT.

Atreus This mythical king of MYCENAE was the father of the heroes AGAMEMNON and MENELAUS, who in poetry are often referred to as the Atreidai (the sons of Atreus).

Atreus and his brother Thyestes labored under a hereditary curse received by their father, PELOPS. The events of their own lives perpetuated this curse. Thyestes offended Atreus by seducing his wife and stealing a golden ram, a token of the kingship. Atreus banished his brother, but then, pretending to be reconciled, invited him to a banquet. At the feast, Atreus treacherously served the cooked flesh of Thyestes' own children, which the unwitting guest ate. Upon realizing the horror, Thyestes invoked a curse on his brother and departed. This curse was fulfilled when Thyestes' surviving son Aegisthus helped murder Agamemnon after the latter's return from the TROJAN WAR. The banquet of Atreus and Thyestes was a favorite reference in later Greek and Roman poetry. The Roman statesman-philosopher Seneca (ca. 60 C.E.) wrote a tragedy *Thyestes*, presenting the monstrous events onstage.

See also CLYTAEMNESTRA; ORESTES.

Further reading: Maria H. Lübeck, *Iphigeneia, Agamemnon's Daughter: A Study of Ancient Conceptions in Greek Myth and Literature Associated with the Atrides* (Stockholm: Almqvist & Wiksell International, 1993).

Attalus *See* PERGAMON.

Attica Attica refers to the territory of ATHENS. Named perhaps from the Greek word *aktē*, "promontory," it is a triangular peninsula in southeast-central Greece, extending southward into the AEGEAN SEA. The peninsula's neck is bordered by BOEOTIA (to the north and northwest) and by the territory of MEGARA (1) (to the northwest). Attica's western sea is the Saronic Gulf, containing the islands SALAMIS (1) and AEGINA, among others.

With 1,000 square miles, Attica is about half the size of Massachusetts. The mountainous terrain reaches four separate peaks: Mt. Hymettus in the southwest (near Athens); Mt. Pentelicus halfway up the east coast; Mt. Parnes in the north-central area; and Mt. Laurion at the southern tip.

Attica's natural resources played vital roles in making Athens a major commercial power, starting in the 500s B.C.E., particularly significant was the SILVER mined at Laurion. An admired marble was quarried at Pentelicus and Hymettus, and the superior clay in the Attic soil was important for Athens' domination of the Greek POTTERY market in the 800s–700s and 500s–400s B.C.E.

The mountains and hills of Attica enclose four discrete farming plains, which from prehistoric times determined the groupings of settlement. There is (1) the large plain of Athens, (2) the southern plain of the Mesogeia ("midland"), (3) the small northeastern flatlands of MARATHON and Aphidna, and (4) the one truly fertile plain, at Eleusis in the west. The prominence of Eleusis as a food source is reflected in the ancient, state-run ELEUSINIAN MYSTERIES, which celebrated the goddess DEMETER's gift of grain to humankind. Other crops grown in the rather thin Attic soil included vines, figs, and olives.

Among other important locales was Sounion, at Attica's southern tip, where a famous temple of Poseidon was built in the 440s B.C.E.

See also ATHENA; KLEISTHENES (1); DEME; DEMOCRACY; PELOPONNESIAN WAR; PERSIAN WARS; PIRAEUS; THESEUS.

Further reading: *Studies in Attic Epigraphy, History, and Topography: Presented to Eugene Vanderpool* (Princeton, N.J.: American School of Classical Studies, 1982); Erika Simon, *Festivals of Attica: An Archaeological Commentary* (Madison: University of Wisconsin Press, 1983); Mark Munn, *The Defense of Attica: The Dema Wall and the Boiotian War of 378–375 B.C.* (Berkeley: University of California Press, 1993).

B

Bacchae *See* EURIPIDES; MAENADS.

Bacchus *See* DIONYSUS.

Bacchylides (ca. 515–450 B.C.E.) *Greek lyric poet from the island of Keos*

Bacchylides' work survives mainly in the form of 20 choral poems—14 victory odes and six dithyrambs—discovered in an Egyptian papyrus in 1896 C.E. He is known to have written many other verses for choruses, including hymns that survive in a few fragments. Despite his lack of genius, Bacchylides showed genuine artistic virtues, including clarity of expression and a talent for narrative.

Bacchylides seems to have been born sometime between 515 and 506 B.C.E. He was the nephew (sister's son) and protégé of the famous poet SIMONIDES, and it was to Simonides' sponsorship that Bacchylides owed much of his worldly success. He seems to have followed his uncle's footsteps from early on and to have been employed by some of the same patrons. Like Simonides, Bacchylides wrote dithyrambs for poetry competitions at ATHENS. (The dithyramb, a precursor of Athenian stage tragedy, was a narrative poem on a mythological subject; it was sung in public performance by a chorus, one of whose members would take on a solo role in character.) Two of Bacchylides' extant dithyrambs present imaginative episodes from the life of the Athenian hero THESEUS. In around 476 B.C.E., Bacchylides accompanied the 80-year-old Simonides to the court of HIERON (1), ruler of the Sicilian-Greek city of SYRACUSE. There Bacchylides and Simonides are said to have been engaged in an unfriendly rivalry with the Theban poet PINDAR, who was visiting Sicily in those years and was probably close to Bacchylides' age.

Bacchylides was greatly admired in antiquity for his elegant and polished writing style. In the Hellenistic period, he was considered by the scholars of Alexandria to be one of the nine canonical Greek lyric poets. He was a brilliant storyteller, and his poems were often focused on moments of intense emotion or suspenseful action. He seems to have been influenced by contemporary Greek tragedy, for he incorporates genres such as the dramatic dialogue into his poems. Modern knowledge of Bacchylides' work was greatly increased by a papyrus discovery in 1896, which expanded the surviving corpus of his poetry from approximately 100 fragments to over 1,000 lines of verse.

Bacchylides and Pindar both composed victory odes for Hieron. Hieron's victory in the horserace at the OLYMPIC GAMES (476 B.C.E.) is commemorated in Bacchylides' Ode 5 as well as in Pindar's Olympian Ode 1; similarly, Hieron's victory in the chariot race at the PYTHIAN GAMES (470 B.C.E.) produced Bacchylides' Ode 4 and Pindar's Pythian 1. But when Hieron won his coveted Olympic chariot victory in 468 B.C.E., it was Bacchylides, not Pindar, who was assigned to write the celebratory ode.

This poem, Ode 3, is Bacchylides' most successful work. It addresses a rich dictator who, although at his peak of prestige, was in failing health, with only a year to live. The poem is full of sad reminders of human transience, couched in terms that are lovely despite being wholly conventional: *Life is short and troubled,* the poet says, in essence, *and hope is treacherous. Be ready for death tomorrow or 50 years hence. The best a mortal man can do is worship the gods and live a good life.* The poem is spun around the central legend of the Lydian king CROESUS, who fell from wealth and power to defeat, before being saved by the god APOLLO. The ode's consolation in the face of death and its muted warning against the sin of pride may have proved poignant to Hieron. In closing, the poet refers to himself as the "the nightingale of Keos"—a charmingly modest and apt self-description.

See also HUBRIS; LYRIC POETRY; THEATER.

Further reading: A. P. Burnett, *The Art of Bacchylides* (Cambridge, Mass.: Harvard University Press, 1985); David Campbell, ed., *Greek Lyric: Bacchylides, Corinna, and Others.* Loeb Classical Library, no. 461 (Cambridge, Mass.: Harvard University Press, 1992); Charles Segal, *Aglaia: The Poetry of Alcman, Sappho, Pindar, Bacchylides, and Corinna* (Lanham, Md.: Rowman and Littlefield, 1998); Ilja Leonard Pfeijffer and Simon Slings, eds., *One Hundred Years of Bacchylides: Proceedings of a Colloquium Held at the Vrije Universiteit Amsterdam* (Amsterdam: VU University Press, 1999); G. O. Hutchinson, *Greek Lyric Poetry: A Commentary on Selected Larger Pieces* (New York: Oxford University Press, 2001).

Bactria   Corresponding roughly to what is now northern Afghanistan, Bactria was an important province of the Persian Empire in the mid-500s to mid-300s B.C.E. In 330 B.C.E. the region was captured by the Macedonian king ALEXANDER THE GREAT, during his conquest of the Persian domain. Bactria's significance for Greek history is that, after being assigned heavy settlements of Alexander's veteran soldiers, the region developed into a far-eastern enclave of Greek culture.

Following Alexander's death (323 B.C.E.), Bactria passed into the east Greek SELEUCID EMPIRE, but by 255 B.C.E. it had revolted under a leader named Diodotus, who became its first king. Prospering from its central Asian TRADE routes, this Greek kingdom lasted for over a century and enveloped what is now southern Afghanistan, western Pakistan, southern Uzbekistan, and southeastern Turkmenistan. The Bactrian kings—of which there seem eventually to have been two rival dynasties, reigning out of different capitals—minted a superb COINAGE, stamped with royal portraits. Today surviving Bactrian coins provide some of the most realistic portraiture from the ancient Greek world.

Among the principal Bactrian cities were two named ALEXANDRIA (2)—modern Kandahr and Herat, in Afghanistan. The remarkable remnants of a Greek-style GYMNASIUM and temple discovered at Aï Khanoun, in northern Afghanistan, mark the site of another city—probably also named Alexandria—that thrived under Bactrian kings. But by 100 B.C.E. Bactria had fallen, overrun by Asian nomads.

See also HELLENISTIC AGE.

Further reading: Paul Bernard, *Ai Khanum on the Oxus: A Hellenistic City in Central Asia* (London: Oxford University Press, 1967); W. W. Tarn, *The Greeks in Bactria and India* (Chicago: Ares Publishers, 1985); Frank Lee Holt, *Alexander the Great and Bactria: The Formation of a Greek Frontier in Central Asia* (Leiden, Netherlands: E. J. Brill, 1988); C. C. Lamberg-Karlovsky, *Bactria: An Ancient Oasis Civilization from the Sands of Afghanistan* (Venice: Erizzo, 1988); Frank Lee Holt, *Thundering Zeus: The Making of Hellenistic Bactria* (Berkeley: University of California Press, 1999); H. Sidky, *The Greek Kingdom of Bactria: From Alexander to Eucratides the Great* (Lanham, Md.: University Press of America, 2000).

Bassae (Bassai)   This site in southwest ARCADIA, contains a remarkable temple to APOLLO EPIKOURIOS, now reconstructed. Bassae (meaning "ravines") is located on the remote slopes of Mt. Cotilion. The austere Doric-style temple was begun in about 450 B.C.E. and completed perhaps 30 years later. It was designed by Iktinus, the architect of the Athenian PARTHENON and almost certainly predates the Parthenon (begun in 447 B.C.E.).

Built atop a narrow mountain ridge, the temple necessarily has a north-south orientation (as opposed to the

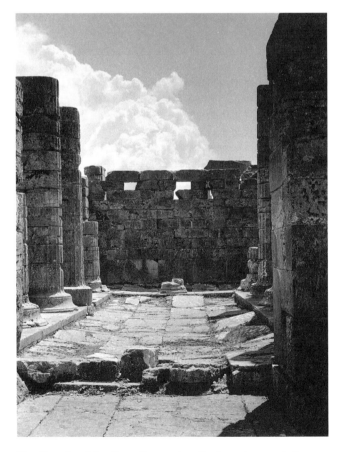

The Temple of Apollo at Bassae is a Doric-style temple begun in 450 B.C.E. A single Corinthian column once stood in this interior. *(Alison Frantz Photographic Collection, American School of Classical Studies at Athens)*

typical east-west). Instead of using marble that would have had to be transported to the remote site, the temple is built of gray local limestone. Its most famous feature is the single Corinthian-style column that stands in the back of the interior. The column's original capital disappeared in the 19th century C.E. but was previously noted and sketched as having acanthus-leaf decorations on four sides. This makes it the earliest known example of a Corinthian column.

The temple is adorned by SCULPTURES, figures carved in relief on a continuous frieze that ran around the interior of the cella. This frieze, stripped off and carted away in the 19th century, now stands in the British Museum in London. The style of the frieze suggests that it may have been carved some years after the temple itself was complete, perhaps in the early fourth century B.C.E. The subject of the Bassae frieze depicts scenes of battle between Greeks and AMAZONS and between Lapiths and CENTAURS. These two favorite subjects of Greek temple carving convey the theme of (Greek) order versus (barbarian) chaos and are thus appropriate to a Greek god of culture such as Apollo. Similar images existed also among the sculptures of the Parthenon.

The interesting combination of orders on the Temple of Apollo at Bassae—Doric columns and proportions, Ionic-style continuous frieze, and Corinthian interior column—shows a sense of experimentation and innovation on the part of the architect, Iktinos. Similar features are also present in the Parthenon, which is also a mostly Doric building with an Ionic-style sculpture frieze.

See also ARCHITECTURE.

Further reading: Fred Cooper, "The Temple of Apollo at Bassai. Observations on Its Plan and Orientation," *AJA* 72 (1968): 103–111; Fred Cooper, *The Temple of Apollo Bassitas* (Princeton, N.J.: American School of Classical Studies, 1992); I. Jenkins and D. Williams, "The Arrangement of the Sculptured Frieze from the Temple of Apollo Epikourios at Bassai," in *Sculpture from Arcadia and Laconia. Proceedings of an International Conference Held at the American School of Classical Studies at Athens, April 10–14, 1992,* edited by O. Palagia and W. Coulson (Oxford: Oxbow Books, 1993), 57–77; N. Kelly, "The Archaic Temple of Apollo at Bassai. Correspondences to the Classical Temple," *Hesperia* 64 (1995): 228–277.

Bellerophon This mythical hero came to be associated with a flying horse named Pegasus, who was created when PERSEUS cut off the head of the Gorgon MEDUSA. The goddess ATHENA helped Bellerophon capture and tame Pegasus by giving him a golden bridle; the three figures are frequently shown together in Greek art. Pegasus is not mentioned, however, in the earliest surviving references to Bellerophon, found in Homer's *Iliad* (written down around 750 B.C.E.). Another myth about the hero says that he tried to ascend Mt. Olympus on his winged

On the inside of this Spartan *kylix,* or cup, the hero Bellerophon battles the Chimera, a fire-breathing monster. Bellerophon holds the reins of his horse, Pegasus, while Pegasus strikes at the Chimera with his hooves and Bellerophon uses his spear. *(The J. Paul Getty Museum)*

steed but was struck down by ZEUS, angered at the mortal's HUBRIS.

Like HERAKLES and other Greek heroes, Bellerophon was assigned a series of impossible-seeming tasks, which he accomplished. His adventures began when he resisted the advances of Anteia (or Stheneboea), the wife of King Proteus of ARGOS (or TIRYNS). Humiliated, she claimed he had tried to seduce her, and so Proteus sent him away with an encoded letter for the king of Lycia, in ASIA MINOR. The letter requested that the king kill the bearer. Obligingly, the king sent Bellerophon to fight the Chimera and the AMAZONS, among other hazards. But the hero triumphed and eventually married the king's daughter, Philonoë.

Later versions of the MYTH—such as in the poet PINDAR's 13th Olympian ode (466 B.C.E.)—had Bellerophon assisted by the winged Pegasus. Bellerophon was honored as a hero in the city of Corinth, and Pegasus appeared as a symbol of the city on Corinthian COINAGE.

Further reading: M. Low Schmitt, "Bellerophon and the Chimaera in Archaic Greek Art," *American Journal of Archaeology* 70 (1966): 341–347; K. Schefold, *Gods and Heroes in Late Archaic Greek Art,* translated by Alan Griffiths (New York: Cambridge University Press, 1992); H. Hoffman, "Bellerophon and the Chimaira in Malibu. A Greek Myth and an Archaeological Context," in *Studia Varia from the J. Paul Getty Museum* (Malibu, Calif.: J. Paul Getty Museum, 1993), 63–70.

Bion *See* CYNICS.

birth control   Women in ancient Greece generally married at a young age, and their primary functions in society were to maintain the household and to bear children. At the same time, parents preferred to produce small numbers of their children because they would need to provide dowries for each daughter and to divide their estates equally among all their sons. The high infant mortality rate, however, as well as the chances that a grown child would die in childbirth or in battle, led parents to conceive extra children to safeguard the future of the family estate. In the 400s B.C.E., the Athenian statesman Perikles recognized that the increasing population was a problem for the maintenance of personal estates, and he enacted a citizenship law intended to stem the growth of the population.

In the medical treatise *Nature of Women* by the Greek physician HIPPOCRATES (ca. 460–390 B.C.E.), there is only a brief discussion of contraception. It advises that a woman should drink a thick mixture of beans and water, which will prevent her from getting pregnant for a year. Other ancient medical writers such as Dioskorides and Soranos provide evidence for herbal oral contraceptives, most of which have been tested in modern times and seem to be truly effective.

In addition to actual contraceptives, the ancient Greeks utilized several other means of population control, including homosexuality, anal intercourse, and extramarital sex with prostitutes or slaves. Although Hippocrates was philosophically against the idea of intentional abortion, it was certainly practiced, as was exposure of unwanted infants (or an infant of an unwanted gender).

See also MARRIAGE; MEDICINE; PROSTITUTES.

Further reading: Agnus McLaren, *A History of Contraception from Antiquity to the Present Day* (Oxford: Basil Blackwell Press, 1990); J. M. Riddle, *Contraception and Abortion from the Ancient World to the Renaissance* (Cambridge, Mass.: Harvard University Press, 1992); J. M. Riddle, *Eve's Herbs: A History of Contraception and Abortion in the West* (Cambridge, Mass.: Harvard University Press, 1997).

black peoples   The ancient Greeks were acquainted with people of the Negroid race. During the second and first millennia B.C.E. the Greeks had periodic contact with EGYPT, culminating in ALEXANDER THE GREAT's conquest of the land in 322 B.C.E. Although most Egyptians were of Semitic blood, some were of Negroid blood, with also an intermingling of the two races. As is the case in Egypt today, many inhabitants may have had dark skin, with Semitic or Negroid physical features in varying degrees. People of black African descent played important roles as soldiers, administrators, priests, and sometimes pharaohs.

Moreover, the Greeks knew about Egypt's southern neighbor—the powerful nation called Nubia or Kush (also spelled Cush). Located along the Nile in what is now northern Sudan, Nubia was inhabited by black Africans, with possibly an admixture of Semitic blood. Nubia was a trading partner and periodic enemy of the pharaohs' Egypt; during the third to first millennia B.C.E. the two nations warred intermittently over a shared, shifting frontier that lay south of the first Nile cataract (modern-day Aswan). Nubia was an important supplier of GOLD ore to Egypt, and Nubian troops often served as mercenaries in Egyptian service.

By the mid 700s B.C.E. the Nubians had reorganized themselves and had begun a large-scale invasion of Egypt, the conquest of which was completed in around 715 B.C.E. by the Nubian ruler Shabako (or Shabaka). The period from about 730 to 656 B.C.E., when Nubian pharaohs ruled part or all of Egypt, is called by modern historians the 25th Dynasty of Egypt. But Assyrian invaders toppled the dynasty, and Egypt passed to other hands.

In the early 500s B.C.E. Nubia came under military pressure from a resurgent Egypt. The Nubians removed their capital southward to Meroë, situated between the fifth and sixth Nile cataracts (about 120 miles north of modern-day Khartoum). This "Meroitic" Nubian kingdom flourished for 900 years as an African society independent of Egypt and of Egypt's successive conquerors—the Persians, the Greco-Macedonian Ptolemies, and the Romans.

Among the Greeks, such facts became the stuff of legend. HOMER's epic poems, the *Iliad* and *Odyssey*, written down around 750 B.C.E., make reference to a people known as *Aithiopes* (Greek: "burnt-face ones"). Beloved of the gods, they dwelt far to the south, in the land called *Aithiopia.* It was the force of the southern sun, the early Greeks believed, that crisped these people's faces. Greek MYTH told of an Aithiopian king, MEMNON, who led an army northward to help defend TROY during the TROJAN WAR but was killed in single combat with the Greek hero ACHILLES. This episode (not described by Homer) was recounted in a now-vanished Greek epic poem usually called the *Aethiopis.* It is not known whether this legend contains any kernel of historical truth.

Homer and other early writers give no clear location for Aithiopia. But by the early 400s B.C.E. the Greeks had come to equate it specifically with the nation of Nubia, south of Egypt. The Greek historian HERODOTUS, visiting Egypt circa 450 B.C.E., heard tales about Aithiopia-Nubia. According to Herodotus, the Aithiopians were said to be "the tallest and most attractive people in the world" (book 3). Herodotus also mentions that Aithiopian troops, armed with spear and bow, served in the Persian king XERXES' invasion of Greece in 480 B.C.E. (Although not part of the Persian Empire, Nubia seems to have been enrolled as a diplomatic friend of PERSIA.)

In modern times, the place-name Aithiopia (latinized to Ethiopia) has been applied to an African nation located far southeast of ancient Nubia. Confusingly, however, modern historians of the ancient world sometimes use the terms Ethiopia and Ethiopian in the old, Greek sense, to denote ancient Nubia. Egypt's 25th Dynasty is often referred to as the Ethiopian Dynasty.

As a result of contact with black people of Egypt and Nubia, ancient Greek artists began portraying blacks in statuary, metalwork, vase paintings, and the like; the earliest surviving examples date from the 500s B.C.E. One of the finest pieces is an Athenian clay drinking cup, realistically shaped and painted to represent the head of a black youth (ca. 525 B.C.E.). The hero Memnon appears on several extant vase paintings; usually he is shown with distinctly Negro facial features.

Another black man in Greek art was the evil Busiris. According to Greek legend, Busiris was an Egyptian king, a son of the god POSEIDON; capturing any foreigners who entered Egypt, he would sacrifice them on the altar of the god ZEUS. But at last the Greek hero HERAKLES arrived and—in a scene popular in vase paintings—killed Busiris and his followers. This odd tale may distortedly recall Greek relations with Egypt amid the downfall of the 25th (Nubian) Dynasty in the mid 600s B.C.E.

Alexander the Great's conquest of the Persian Empire brought Egypt into the Greek world, thus opening Nubia and other parts of West Africa to Greek exploration and TRADE. Around 280–260 B.C.E. Egypt's king PTOLEMY (2) II sent explorers and merchants sailing along the Red Sea coast as far as modern-day Somalia, and up the Nile to Nubian Meroë and beyond. Ptolemy's goal was the acquisition of gold and other goods, particularly live African elephants for military use. Subsequent Ptolemies maintained these African trading and diplomatic ties, which incidently brought Greek influences to the ruling class in Nubia. We know, for example, that the Greek name Candace was used by Nubian queens from this era until the 300s C.E.

See also NAUCRATIS; POTTERY; XENOPHANES.

Further reading: Joyce L. Haynes, *Nubia: Ancient Kingdoms of Africa* (Boston: Museum of Fine Arts, 1992); Stanley Burstein, ed., *Ancient African Civilizations: Kush and Axum* (Princeton, N.J.: M. Wiener, 1998).

Black Sea This modern name refers to the 168,500-square-mile oblong sea bordering ASIA MINOR on the south and Ukraine and southwestern Russia on the north. Attractive for its access to Asia Minor's metal TRADE and Ukraine's vast wheatfields, the Black Sea became ringed by Greek colonies, from around 700 B.C.E. onward. The Greeks called it Pontos Euxeinos, "the hospitable sea." But this name was intentionally euphemistic, insofar as fierce native inhabitants and a cold and stormy climate might make the region distinctly inhospitable.

The Black, or Euxine, Sea was opened up by explorers from the Greek city of MILETUS, on the west coast of Asia Minor. The Milesians' first goal was to acquire copper, tin, GOLD, and other raw metals of interior Asia Minor, and one of their early colonies was SINOPE, located

halfway along the southern Black Sea coast. In the next 100 years, colonies from Miletus (and a few other east Greek cities) arose around the entire Black Sea.

Along the northern coastlines, the principal Greek cities were Olbia (meaning "prosperous"), at the mouth of the River Bug, and PANTICAPAEUM, on the east coast of the Crimean peninsula. These sites offered the very valuable resource of grain, grown as surplus by farmers in the interior and purchased by the Greeks for export to the hungry cities of mainland Greece. By 500 B.C.E. the north Black Sea coast was a major grain supplier, especially for ATHENS. This shipping route placed strategic importance on two narrow waterways—the BOSPORUS and the HELLESPONT—that help connect the Black Sea to the AEGEAN SEA.

See also AMAZONS; COLONIZATION; HECATAEUS; HERODOTUS; JASON (1); SHIPS AND SEAFARING.

Further reading: Marianna Koromila, *The Greeks in the Black Sea: From the Bronze Age to the Early Twentieth Century* (Athens: Panorama, 1991); Neal Ascherson, *Black Sea* (New York: Hill and Wang, 1995); Gocha R. Tsetkhladze, ed., *The Greek Colonisation of the Black Sea Area: Historical Interpretation of Archaeology* (Stuttgart: Franz Steiner, 1998).

Boeotia This northwest-southeast-elongated region of central Greece is bordered by PHOCIS to the northwest, by the Straits of EUBOEA to the northeast, and by the Corinthian Gulf to the southwest. Central Boeotia consists of a mountain-girt plain that provided rich FARMING and the raising of horses. In the plain's southeast corner lay the major Boeotian city, THEBES. The second city was

Boeotian artwork circa late 700s B.C.E. used decorative repeated patterns. The painted swastikas represent the good magic of rotating wheels or drills for making fire. *(Alison Frantz Photographic Collection, American School of Classical Studies at Athens)*

ORCHOMENOS, in the plain's northwest corner, opposite Thebes.

South of Thebes, Boeotia shared an ill-defined border with the Athenian territory, along the east-west line of Mt. Parnes and Mt. Kithairon. The historically important Boeotian town of PLATAEA lay just north of Kithairon. Farther northwest stood Boeotia's tallest mountain, Helicon (about 5,800 feet).

The Boeotian heartland comprised one of the centers of MYCENAEAN CIVILIZATION (around 1600–1200 B.C.E.)—as suggested by Thebes's prominent place in Greek MYTH. The name Boeotia refers to the raising of cattle (*boes*) and specifically commemorates the Boiotoi, a Greek people who invaded the region, migrating south from THESSALY circa 1100 B.C.E. The Boeotians of historical times spoke a form of the Aeolic dialect, related to the dialect of Thessaly and that of the east Aegean island of LESBOS. Boeotians were reputed to be boorish and ignorant, although prosperous. "Boeotian pig" was a Greek epithet. But Boeotia's literary tradition produced the poets HESIOD, PINDAR, and CORINNA.

With the exception of Plataea, the Boeotian towns followed Thebes as enemies of ATHENS, starting in the late 500s B.C.E. Boeotia was a target of Athenian expansionism, and the Athenians actually occupied Boeotia for a decade, 457–447 B.C.E. Soon thereafter the towns formed a Boeotian League, under Theban dominance, for mutual defense and a jointly decided foreign policy. The Boeotian army then emerged as one of the best in Greece, distinguished by a large CAVALRY force in addition to strong infantry. At the Battle of Delium in 424 B.C.E., during the PELOPONNESIAN WAR, the Boeotians defeated the invading Athenians and ended their hope of reconquering the region. Later, under the Theban commander EPAMINONDAS, the Boeotian League broke the might of SPARTA (371 B.C.E.) and became the foremost power in Greece, before falling to Macedonian conquest (338 B.C.E.).

Boeotia's central location and flat interior often made it a battleground—"the dancing floor of War," Epaminondas called it. Famous Boeotian battlefields included Plataea (479 B.C.E.), LEUCTRA (371 B.C.E.), and CHAIRONEIA (338 B.C.E.).

See also GREECE, GEOGRAPHY OF; GREEK LANGUAGE; MUSES; PERSIAN WARS; PLATAEA, BATTLE OF; WARFARE, LAND.

Further reading: Albert Schachter, *Cults of Boiotia* (London: University of London, Institute of Classical Studies, 1981); John M. Fossey, *Topography and Population of Ancient Boiotia* (Chicago: Ares Publishers, 1988).

Bosporus (Bosphorus) This narrow, zigzagging, 18-mile-long channel flows southwestward from the BLACK SEA to the SEA OF MARMARA. Beyond the Marmara, the current continues south and west through the HELLESPONT channel to the AEGEAN SEA. Like the Hellespont, the Bosporus borders part of northwestern ASIA MINOR; it was considered to be a dividing line between EUROPE AND ASIA.

Shorter and generally narrower and swifter-flowing than the Hellespont, the Bosporus ranges in width from 2.5 miles to 400 yards. Its name, "cow ford" or "ox ford," was in ancient times said to refer to the mythical wanderings of IO, a woman loved by the god ZEUS and transformed into cow by Zeus's jealous wife, HERA. But the name may refer to a more mundane cattle crossing.

Around 513 B.C.E., the Persians under King DARIUS (1)—preparing to cross from Asia to Europe for their invasion of Scythia—spanned the Bosporus with a pontoon bridge consisting of about 200 ships anchored in a row. This was a remarkable engineering feat in the ancient world, although not as amazing as the Persians' bridging of the Hellespont, a wider channel, 30 years later. In modern times the Bosporus, now a part of Turkey, was not bridged until 1973.

The Bosporus and Hellespont were the two bottlenecks along the shipping route between the Black Sea and the Aegean. This route had become crucial by about 500 B.C.E. when ATHENS and other cities of mainland Greece were becoming dependent on grain imported from the northern Black Sea coast. As a natural site where shipping could be raided or tolled, the Bosporus, like the Hellespont, offered wealth and power to any state that could control it. This, combined with the excellent commercial fishing in the strait and its value as a ferry point, helps to explain the prosperity of the Bosporus's most famous city, BYZANTIUM, located at the southern mouth. Athens controlled the Bosporus in the 400s B.C.E. by holding Byzantium as a subject ally.

See also THRACE.

Further reading: John Freely, *The Bosphorus* (Istanbul: Redhouse Press, 1993); Yusuf Mardin, *Bosphorus Through the Ages* (Ankara: T. C. Kültür Bakanligi, 1995); Rhonda Vander Sluis, *From the Bosphorus: A Self-guided Tour* (Istanbul: Çitlembik, 2000).

boulē *See* COUNCIL.

boxing An important SPORT among the ancient Greeks, boxing was however less popular than the two other combat sports, WRESTLING and PANKRATION.

Our knowledge of Greek boxing comes mainly from extant literature, artwork, and inscriptions (on tombs and religious offerings). Because HOMER's epic poem the *Iliad* describes a boxing match in book 23, we know that the Greeks were practicing boxing by at least the mid-700s B.C.E., when the Homeric poems were written down. Possibly the early Greeks learned the sport from MINOAN CIVILIZATION of the ancient Aegean region (2200–1400 B.C.E.). A surviving fresco from Minoan THERA, painted around 1550 B.C.E., shows two boys engaging in what appears to be a stylized form of boxing.

The sport's patron god was APOLLO, a deity of the civilizing arts. During historical times boxing was the sort of discipline that a wealthy young man in a Greek city-state might practice at a local GYMNASIUM. Like other Greek sports of the pre-Roman era, boxing was purely an amateur pastime. The best boxers could hope to compete in the men's or boys' category at the OLYMPIC GAMES or at one of the other great sports festivals.

The Greeks had no boxing rings; official contests might take place on an unfenced sand floor in an outdoor stadium, where the referee would keep the two opponents in a fighting proximity. More brutal than today's sport, Greek boxing did not recognize different weight classes; the advantage tended to go to the heavier man. The match had no rounds, but continued until one man either lost consciousness or held up a finger, signaling defeat. Boxers were allowed to gouge with the thumb but were forbidden to clinch or grab. Certain vase paintings show a referee using his long stick to beat a clinching boxer.

Down through the 400s B.C.E. boxers often wore protective rawhide thongs wrapped around their hands. During the 300s B.C.E. the thongs developed into a heavier, more damaging form, with a hard leather knuckle pad. For practice only, boxers might use soft gloves similar to our modern boxing gloves. Boxers tended to attack the face—ancient artwork and inscriptions commemorate broken noses and damaged eyeballs. It was not unusual for a boxer to die from injuries. A wonderful artistic representation of a Greek boxer is a bronze statue from the Hellenistic period, now in the Terme Museum in Rome. Here, the athlete is seated on a rock after his event, bruised and bloodied, still wearing the leather strips wrapped around his knuckles, his ears and nose swollen from having received many blows in his career.

Although champions came from all over the Greek world, boxing was particularly associated with the grim discipline of SPARTA. The Athenian philosopher PLATO's dialogue *Gorgias* (ca. 386 B.C.E.) mentions "the boys with the cauliflower ears," referring to the antidemocratic, upper-class Athenian youth who practiced boxing in imitation of Spartan training.

See also EDUCATION; OLIGARCHY.

Further reading: Nancy B. Reed, *More Than Just a Game: The Military Nature of Greek Athletic Contests* (Chicago: Ares, 1998); William Blake Tyrell. *The Smell of Sweat: Greek Athletics, Olympics, and Culture* (Wauconda, Ill.: Bolchazy-Carducci Publishers, 2004); Stephen G. Miller, *Ancient Greek Athletics* (New Haven, Conn.: Yale University Press, 2004).

Brasidas (d. 422 B.C.E.) *Dynamic Spartan general of the* PELOPONNESIAN WAR
His successes against Athenian holdings on the north Aegean coast in 424–422 B.C.E. helped to offset Athenian victories elsewhere and bring about a mood of stalemate, resulting in the Peace of NIKIAS. Brasidas's great triumph was his capture of the vital Athenian colony of AMPHIPOLIS (early 423 B.C.E.). He died at the Battle of Amphipolis, successfully defending the city from an Athenian army under KLEON.

Brasidas saw that the way to attack an impregnable ATHENS was to destroy its northeastern supply lines. His northern campaign was an early, crude, land-bound version of the strategy that would later win the war for SPARTA, in the naval campaigns of 413–404 B.C.E.

See also THUCYDIDES (1).

Further reading: G. Wylie, "Brasidas. Great Commander or Whiz-kid?" *Quaderni urbinati di cultura classica* 41 (1992): 75–95; Donald Kagen, *The Peloponnesian War* (New York: Viking, 2003).

bronze An alloy of copper and tin, usually in a nine-to-one ratio, bronze supplied the most useful metal known during the third and second millennia B.C.E. It replaced prior uses of copper in weaponry, tools, and artwork throughout the Near East and Mediterranean.

Fortified by its measure of tin, bronze is harder than copper, but it melts at the same relatively low temperature—2,000 degrees Fahrenheit. Molten bronze can be intricately shaped by casting—that is, by being poured into a mold. Once cooled, the bronze item can be sharpened or shaped further.

This technology was invented in the Near East before 3000 B.C.E. and had spread to Minoan CRETE by around 2500 B.C.E. Whether the first arriving Greek tribesmen of about 2100 B.C.E. already had their own bronze weapons is unknown, but in the centuries after they occupied mainland Greece they steadily increased their bronze-working skill, especially for warfare. As shown by ARCHAEOLOGY, bronze was providing the Greek MYCENAEAN CIVILIZATION with swords and spear-points before 1500 B.C.E., and by 1400 B.C.E. Mycenaean metalsmiths had mastered the technique of casting bronze plates, then hammering them out to make helmets and body armor. The Mycenaeans used bronze plowshares, sickles, ornaments, and vessels for drinking and cooking.

The potential disadvantage of bronze was that one of its two component metals, tin, could be difficult for the Greeks to acquire. Whereas the Greeks mined copper on the islands of EUBOEA and CYPRUS, tin had to be purchased through expensive, long-range TRADE with ASIA MINOR and western Europe. Tin was mined intensively by native peoples in what is now Cornwall, in southwest England; it then traveled overland—brought by non-Greek middlemen—to trade outlets on the Mediterranean.

The collapse of Mycenaean society and the invasion of mainland Greece by the DORIAN GREEKS (around 1100–1000 B.C.E.) temporarily destroyed in the tin routes. Compelled to find a replacement for bronze, the

A bronze statue of a youth, formed by casting the molten bronze in a mold, early 400s B.C.E. *(Alison Frantz Photographic Collection, American School of Classical Studies at Athens)*

Greeks began mining and working IRON. Just as bronze had supplanted copper, so iron now replaced bronze in many objects, such as plowshares and sword blades. But bronze working returned, alongside ironworking, once the tin supplies were renewed. In ancient technology, bronze was far more malleable than iron, and bronze remained essential wherever shaping or thinness was required.

During the great trading expansion of the 800s–500s B.C.E., the mainland Greeks imported and copied the artful bronzework of cauldrons, hand mirrors, and other artifacts from the Near East. Bronze helmets, breastplates, and shield facings were standard equipment for Greek HOPLITE armies (around 700–300 B.C.E.). The foremost Greek city of about 700 B.C.E. was CHALCIS, whose name probably refers to bronze (Greek: *chalkos*). Now and later, bronze provided a favorite material for SCULPTURE; one technique was to pour the molten metal into a wax mold that had a clay or plaster core, to produce a hollow statue.

Tin supplies were always a concern. The lure of tin brought Greek traders into the western Mediterranean by 600 B.C.E., when the Greek colony of MASSALIA was founded. A major tin supplier was the Celtic kingdom of Tartessus, in southern Spain. (Perhaps none of this tin was mined locally; it may all have come from Cornwall.) Competition over metal supplies brought the western Greeks into conflict with similarly aggressive traders—the Carthaginians. Around 500 B.C.E. the Carthaginians probably destroyed Tartessus, but by then the Greeks had found new tin suppliers, in ITALY and what is now France.

Bronze objects generally do not survive as well in the archaeological record as artifacts made of stone, terracotta, or glass. This is due in part to corrosion of the metal and in part because many bronze objects were melted down in later periods for reuse. A large percentage of surviving bronzes come from ancient shipwrecks such as the one discovered near Cape Artemision, which yielded numerous significant bronze artifacts, including the famous over-life-size statue of ZEUS now in the National Museum in Athens.

See also BRONZE AGE; CARTHAGE SCULPTURE; SINOPE; WARFARE, LAND.

Further reading: Caroline Houser, *Greek Monumental Bronze Sculpture* (London: Thames and Hudson, 1983); Carol Mattusch, *Classical Bronzes* (Ithaca: Cornell University Press, 1996); Veronica McGeehan Liritzis, *The Role and Development of Metallurgy in the Late Neolithic and Early Bronze Age of Greece* (Jonsered, Sweden: Paul Astroms Förlag, 1996); Conrad M. Stibbe, *The Sons of Hephaistos: Aspects of the Archaic Greek Bronze Industry* (Rome: L'Erma di Bretschneider, 2000).

Bronze Age   This term used by modern archaeologists and historians describes the phase of Asian and European human prehistory that falls roughly between 3500 and 1000 B.C.E. Coming after the Neolithic or New Stone Age, the Bronze Age is considered to have spread from Near East to various other regions over several centuries. The era was marked by improved metallurgy that produced the alloy BRONZE as the prime substance for tools of war, agriculture, and industry. For the kings and lords who could produce or buy it, bronze replaced copper, obsidian, and flint. IRON—destined to replace bronze for many uses—was not yet in use.

The Bronze Age saw the birth of the earliest great civilizations of the Near East and the eastern Mediterranean. These include the Sumerian kingdom in Mesopotamia (which arose around 2800 B.C.E.), the Egyptian Old Kingdom (ca. 2660 B.C.E.), the MINOAN CIVILIZATION in CRETE (ca. 2000 B.C.E.), the Hittite kingdom in ASIA MINOR (ca. 1650 B.C.E.), and the MYCENAEAN CIVILIZATION of mainland Greece (ca. 1600 B.C.E.).

By scholarly convention, the Bronze Age in mainland Greece is divided into three phases, called Early Helladic (ca. 2900–1950 B.C.E.), Middle Helladic (ca. 1950–1550 B.C.E.), and Late Helladic (ca. 1550–1100 B.C.E.), with each phase subdivided into stages I, II, and III. Much of

Early Helladic covers an epoch prior to the Greeks' appearance on the scene, when mainland Greece was still inhabited by a non-Greek people (who used bronze, although not extensively). The violent arrival of the first primitive Greeks is usually placed between Early Helladic II and III, around 2100 B.C.E. The flowering of Greek Mycenaean culture corresponds to the Late Helladic era. The Mycenaeans' downfall marks the end of the Bronze Age and the advent of the DARK AGE in Greece.

Further reading: J. Lesley Fitton, *The Discovery of the Greek Bronze Age* (Cambridge, Mass.: Harvard University Press, 1996); Donald Preziosi and Louise Hitchcock, *Aegean Art and Architecture* (Oxford: Oxford University Press, 1999); Curtis N. Runnels and Priscilla Murray, *Greece Before History: An Archaeological Companion and Guide* (Stanford, Calif.: Stanford University Press, 2001); Keith Branigan, ed., *Urbanism in the Aegean Bronze Age* (London: Sheffield Academic Press, 2001); Tracey Cullen, ed., *Aegean Prehistory: A Review* (Boston: Archaeological Institute of America, 2001).

Bucephalus   *See* ALEXANDER THE GREAT.

building   *See* ARCHITECTURE.

burial   *See* FUNERAL CUSTOMS.

Byblos   This city was the northernmost of ancient PHOENICIA's three major seaports, together with Sidon and Tyre. Today the site of Byblos is about 26 miles north of Beirut, in Lebanon.

Called Gebal ("citadel") by the Phoenicians, Byblos was one of the earliest cities of the Near East probably occupied by around 5000 B.C.E. In the Phoenician heyday of the 900s–700s B.C.E., Byblos was the nation's capital, with a powerful navy and TRADE routes extending to Greece and EGYPT.

Contact between Greek and Bybline traders, at such ports as AL MINA, in Syria, and Citium, in CYPRUS, was a crucial factor in transmitting certain Near Eastern advantages to the emerging Greek culture, including the ALPHABET (around 775 B.C.E.). Byblos at this time was the major export center for papyrus (primitive "paper" made from the pith of Egyptian water plants and used as a cheap substitute for animal skins in receiving WRITING). Byblos's monopoly in this trade is commemorated in the early Greek word for papyrus, *biblos*. That word, in turn, yielded Greek *biblion*, "book," and *bibliotheka*, "library," which survive in such familiar words as Bible, bibliophile, and French *bibliothèque* ("library").

Byblos's political fortunes in the era 700–300 B.C.E. followed those of greater Phoenicia, and the city quickly faded in importance after the founding of the nearby Seleucid-Greek city of ANTIOCH (300 B.C.E.).

A French archaeologist, Ernest Renan, did some investigating of Byblos in 1860, but systematic excavation did not begin until the 1920s. The ruins visible today represent a long series of successive cultures present at the site: Phoenician, Egyptian, Assyrian, Persian, Roman, Arab, Crusader, and Ottoman. There is abundant evidence of trade from all periods; Byblos appears always to have been a major commercial center and an important link between the Near East and the Mediterranean.

See also ADONIS.

Further reading: Maurice Denand, *Byblos: Its History, Ruins, and Legends,* translated by H. Tabet (Beirut: Catholic Press, 1964); Nina Jidejian, *Byblos through the Ages,* 2d ed. (Beirut: Dar el-Machreq, 1971); Alessandra Nibbi, *Ancient Byblos Reconsidered* (Oxford: D. E. Publications, 1985).

Byzantium   A celebrated Greek city on the European side of the southern mouth of the BOSPORUS channel, Byzantium is now the Turkish metropolis of Istanbul.

Founded in the mid-600s B.C.E. by Greeks from MEGARA (1), the city was called Buzantion in Greek. Supposedly it took its name from the colonists' leader, Buzas; more probably, it was the name of a preexisting settlement of native Thracians. The Greek city thrived amid Thracian tribes hungry for Greek goods.

Byzantium enjoyed a superb location on a peninsula jutting between the Bosporus mouth and the Sea of MARMARA. Alongside the peninsula's landward base lay the mouth of the Golden Horn River, providing rich fishing and access to the interior. More important, Byzantium controlled the Bosporus. Greek merchant ships—full of precious grain from the BLACK SEA coast, bound for cities of mainland Greece—would sail south through the channel. Byzantium's navy was able to impose tolls on this passing traffic.

Byzantium was held as a strategic point by successive imperial powers: PERSIA (ca. 513–478 B.C.E.), ATHENS (478–404 B.C.E.), and ROME (mid-100s B.C.E. onward). As a member of the Athenian-dominated DELIAN LEAGUE in the 400s B.C.E., Byzantium played a vital role in Athens's control of the Black Sea grain route. We know that in 457 B.C.E. wealthy Byzantium was paying a relatively high yearly Delian tribute—15 TALENTS. The city revolted unsuccessfully against Athens twice (440 and 411 B.C.E.).

Passing to Spartan influence at the end of the PELOPONNESIAN WAR (404 B.C.E.), the Byzantines soon became disenchanted with their new masters. By about 377 B.C.E. they were again Athenian allies. The Macedonian king PHILIP II unsuccessfully besieged Byzantium in the winter of 340–339 B.C.E.

Amid the wars of the DIADOCHI in the late 300s B.C.E., Byzantium was able to keep its independence. The city suffered attacks from the CELTS, who invaded much of the Greek world in the early 200s B.C.E., and

C

Cadmus (Greek: **Kadmos**) In Greek MYTH, Cadmus was a prince of the Phoenician city of Tyre and founder of the Greek city of THEBES. Young Cadmus's sister at Tyre was EUROPA, whom the god ZEUS abducted in the shape of a bull. Cadmus was assigned by his father, King Agenor, to find the vanished Europa. Leading a band of men to central Greece, he consulted the god APOLLO through the oracle at DELPHI. Apollo advised Cadmus to abandon the search and instead follow a cow that he would find outside the temple; he should establish a city wherever the cow lay down to rest. Accordingly, the cow led Cadmus to the future site of Thebes, about 50 miles away. There Cadmus built the Cadmea, which became the citadel of the later city.

Several adventures accompanied this foundation. To gain access to the local water supply, Cadmus had to slay a ferocious serpent, the offspring of the war god ARES. When Cadmus consecrated the dead monster to the goddess ATHENA, she appeared and told him to sow the serpent's teeth in the soil. Immediately there sprang up a harvest of armed men to oppose him, but Cadmus cleverly threw a stone into their midst, thereby setting them to fight one another. The surviving five of these warriors joined Cadmus's service and became the ancestors of the Theban nobility, known as the Sown Men.

After enduring eight years' servitude to Ares in expiation for having killed his serpent son, Cadmus was allowed to marry Harmonia, daughter of Ares and APHRODITE. As a wedding gift, Harmonia received a wondrous necklace that bestowed irresistible attraction on its wearer; this necklace would play a role in the next generations' misfortunes, in the adventure of the SEVEN AGAINST THEBES.

Reigning as king of Thebes, Cadmus civilized the crude local Greeks by teaching them how to write. He and Harmonia had four daughters, all of whom suffered unhappy fates: Semele (later the mother of the god DIONYSUS); Ino (who was driven mad by the goddess HERA); Agave (whose son PENTHEUS would be destroyed by Dionysus); and Autonoe (whose son Akteon would be destroyed by the goddess ARTEMIS). In old age, Cadmus and Harmonia emigrated to the northwest, where they ruled over the Illyrians and eventually were changed into serpents.

The Cadmus legend—a Phoenician prince civilizing and ruling part of Greece—presents an odd combination. Although the Greeks had extensive contact with the Phoenicians in the 900s–700s B.C.E., this myth seems to commemorate an earlier period of Greek contact with the Near East, possibly during the Mycenaean era (around 1200 B.C.E.).

See also ALPHABET; ILLYRIS; MYCENAEAN CIVILIZATION; PHOENICIA.

Further reading: Ruth Edwards, *Kadmos the Phoenician: A study in Greek Legends and the Mycenaean Age* (Amsterdam: Adolf M. Hakkert, 1979).

calendars Each city-state in the ancient Greek world had its own calendar, generally based on the cycles of the Moon and closely connected to the various religious festivals that took place in each city-state throughout the year. Best known today is the Athenian calendar, reconstructed from evidence provided by ancient Greek inscriptions and literary references.

The Athenian calendar year consisted of 12 months, each containing either 29 or 30 days, depending on the timing of the new moon. These months had the following names: Hekatombaion, Metageitnion, Boedromion, Pyanepsion, Maimakterion, Posideon, Gamelion, Anthesterion, Elaphebolion, Mounichion, Thargelion, and Skirophorion. The Greeks considered certain days each month to be sacred to various divinities; for example, the seventh day of each month was sacred to Apollo. Other major festivals took place annually; the primary celebration dedicated to Athena, the PANATHENAIA, occurred on the 28th day of Hekatombaion, though the festival probably lasted for three or four days.

Since having 12 months of 29 or 30 days resulted in 354-day-long years, the Athenians would occasionally have an "intercalary year" of 13 months, to keep the festivals aligned with the course of the seasons. Sometimes they would even insert extra days into their regular months, so that the festivals would remain in accord with the lunar cycles.

The Athenians also had another, civil calendar that coexisted with the festival calendar. It was based on prytanies: periods of time in which each of the Athenian tribes served as prytanies, or committees, of the COUNCIL. The prytany calendar consisted of 366 days, divided into six prytanies that were 37 days in length and four that were 36 days.

Another useful chronological tool for classical Athens is the so-called ARCHON list. In the Classical period, the city was ruled by an archon, elected annually, whose name would be used to designate the year of his office. Ancient authors including Diodorus of Siculus compiled lists of the Attic archons for chronological purposes, and modern scholars have utilized them as an important source for reconstructing the ancient Athenian calendar.

Hellenistic and Roman authors also used another way of reckoning time in ancient Greece: the Olympiad. This term referred to the four-year span including the year in which the OLYMPIC GAMES were held, plus the three following years until the next Games.

Further reading: W. Kendrick Pritchett and O. Neugebauer, *The Calendars of Athens* (Cambridge, Mass.: Harvard University Press, 1947); Benjamin Meritt, *The Athenian Year* (Berkeley: University of California Press, 1961); Alan Samuel, *Greek and Roman Chronology: Calendars and Years in Classical Antiquity* (Munich: C. H. Beck, 1972); Jon Mikalson, *The Sacred and Civil Calendar of the Athenian Year* (Princeton, N.J.: Princeton University Press, 1975).

Callias See KALLIAS.

Callimachus (Greek: Kallimachos) (ca. 310–240 B.C.E.)
The most admired lyric poet of the HELLENISTIC AGE
Born in the Greek city of CYRENE (1) in North Africa, Callimachus lived and wrote at Egyptian ALEXANDRIA (1)

during the brief literary golden age under King Ptolemy II (reigned 285–274 B.C.E.). Of Callimachus's voluminous output—a reported 800 scrolls' worth—only six hymns and some 60 epigrams survive whole. Several dozen fragments of other poems exist, and more of his verses are being discovered in the sands of Egypt. (One sizable fragment was published from papyrus in 1977.) Callimachus's best-known work, now lost, was the *Aetia* (Origins), a collection of narrative elegies in four books totaling about 7,000 lines; this erudite and digressive poem presented MYTHS and descriptions explaining the origins of places, rites, and names throughout the Greek world.

Callimachus was the Alexandrian poet par excellence: witty, scholarly, and favoring brief forms and cerebral topics. He was an "in" poet, composing for an "in" group of sophisticated readers or, more accurately, *listeners,* to whom he would read aloud. Among his pupils were APOLLONIUS of Rhodes, Eratosthenes, and Aristophanes of BYZANTIUM. A bitter rivalry existed between Callimachus and Apollonius; their dispute, based partly on differing poetic tastes, was the most famous literary quarrel of the ancient world. Callimachus's work remained immensely popular in later literary circles; 200 years after his death, his style and values were influencing such Roman poets as Catullus, Propertius, and Ovid.

Emigrating from Cyrene to EGYPT, the young Callimachus began his career as a schoolteacher in a suburb of Alexandria. Eventually attracting royal patronage, he was installed at Alexandria's famous Library, with the huge job of cataloguing the several hundred thousand books there. His resultant catalogue, called the *Pinakes,* or Tablets, supposedly ran to 120 volumes and must have taken 10 years; it would have included lists of titles, biographical sketches of authors, and literary criticism. Apparently it was an admirable piece of scholarship, and it testifies to the scholarly, cataloguing urge that also infused his poetry.

Callimachus never reattained the prestigious post of director of the Library, but rather was passed over in favor of Apollonius after the retirement of the director Zenodotus. This development sparked or fueled the two men's quarrel. The enmity was part of a larger literary dispute between the writers of lengthy, narrative EPIC POETRY, based on HOMER's *Iliad* and *Odyssey,* and poets such as Callimachus, who considered epic irrelevant to modern society. "A big book is a big evil," Callimachus wrote. Although he did compose certain lengthy poems toward the end of his life, he seems to have objected specifically to the continuous plot and familiar subject matter of the Homeric-style epic; rather, Callimachus's longer poems were innovative and episodic.

Callimachus's epigrams have been praised for their sincere emotion and their charming word use; they include epitaphs and expressions of sexual desire. The most admired epigram poignantly describes the writer's feelings on learning of the death of his fellow poet Heraclitus. One of Callimachus's surviving hymns, known today as Hymn 1, describes the mythical birth and rearing of the god ZEUS. Famous in antiquity, this Hymn to Zeus set a standard of court poetry by drawing subtle parallels between the king of the gods and King Ptolemy II.

No information exists regarding a wife or children for Callimachus. He seems to have been one of those strictly homosexual Greek men who shunned MARRIAGE. Of his surviving epigrams, every one of the erotic poems celebrates the charms of boys. He lived to about age 70, highly esteemed and enjoying the patronage of Ptolemies; certain of his verses, such as his poem on Queen Arsinoë's death (270 B.C.E.), sound like the public presentations of a court poet laureate.

See also HOMOSEXUALITY; LYRIC POETRY.

Further reading: Peter Bing, *The Well-Read Muse: Present and Past in Callimachus and the Hellenistic Poets* (Göttingen, Germany: Vandenhoeck and Ruprecht, 1988); Stanley Lombardo and Diane Rayor, trans., *Callimachus: Hymns, Epigrams, Select Fragments* (Baltimore: Johns Hopkins University Press, 1988); G. O. Hitchinson, *Hellenistic Poetry* (New York: Clarendon Press, 1990); M. A. Harder, R. F. Regtuit, and G. C. Wakker, eds., *Callimachus* (Groningen, Netherlands: Egbert Forster, 1993).

Callinus (Greek: Kallinos) (mid-600s B.C.E.) *One of the earliest Greek lyric poets whose work (in part) has come down to us*

Callinus was a native of the Greek city of EPHESOS in ASIA MINOR and wrote patriotic verses encouraging his countrymen in their defense against the Kimmerians, a nomadic people from southwestern Russia who were ravaging Asia Minor in those years. In the single substantial fragment by him that survives, Callinus reminds his audience how honorable it is to fight for city and family and how death finds everyone eventually.

Callinus is the first known writer of the verse form known as the elegy, which was intended for recital to flute accompaniment.

See also LYRIC POETRY; MUSIC.

Further reading: Douglas E. Gerber, ed., *A Companion to the Greek Lyric Poets* (Leiden, Netherlands: E. J. Brill, 1997); ———, ed. and trans., *Greek Elegiac Poetry: From the Seventh to the Fifth Centuries B.C.* (Cambridge, Mass.: Harvard University Press, 1999).

Calydonian Boar Hunt One of many Greek MYTHS recounting the destruction of a local monster. King Oeneus of Calydon (a region in AETOLIA) offended the goddess ARTEMIS by forgetting to sacrifice to her. In retaliation, she sent a monstrous boar to ravage the countryside. To hunt the beast, Oeneus's son Meleager collected a band of heroes, including the virgin huntress ATALANTA, with whom Meleager was in love. After much effort, the heroes succeeded in killing the creature, the honor of the first spear thrust going to Atalanta. At Meleager's insistence, she then received the edible portions of the boar. But this insulted Meleager's maternal uncles, who were also part of the hunt, and in the ensuing fight, Meleager slew them.

Upon hearing the news, Meleager's mother, Althaea, took vengeance on her son. She had in her possession a half-burned log, with the following significance: years before, just after Meleager's birth, Althaea had been visited by the three goddesses of FATE, the Moirai, who informed her that her baby son would live only until the log then on the fire should be burned away. Subverting the prophecy, Althaea had quenched the fire and preserved the half-burned log in a chest. Now, in anger at her brothers' murder, she threw the log on the fire, and Meleager died.

The boar hunt was a favorite subject in vase painting and other artwork. Among surviving representations is a panel on the Athenian black-figure François vase (ca. 570 B.C.E.).

See also POTTERY.

Further reading: Daniel Butterly, *The Reckless Heart: Meleager and Atalanta* (Oak Park, Ill.: Bolchazy-Carducci, 1986); Judith Barringer, "Atalanta as Model: The Hunter and the Hunted," *Classical Antiquity* 15.1 (1996): 44–76.

Calypso This beautiful nymph played a role in the MYTH of ODYSSEUS, as told in HOMER's epic poem the *Odyssey* (book 5). The name Kalupso means "concealer." A daughter of ATLAS and the sea goddess Thetis, she lived alone on a remote island, where she received the shipwrecked Odysseus. As Odysseus's lover, she detained him for seven years, promising to make him immortal if he stayed; but he insisted on returning to his wife and kingdom. At ZEUS's command, Calypso helped him build a boat on which to put to sea.

In the structure of the *Odyssey*, Calypso supplies a benevolent doublet to the sinister CIRCE (who also detains Odysseus seductively, for one year). Odysseus's seven years with Calypso can be interpreted as representing the distractions of pleasure versus the duties of leadership.

See also NYMPHS; WOMEN.

Further reading: Thomas Gelzer, *How to express emotions of the soul and operations of the mind in a language that has no words for them as exemplified by Odysseus and Calypso (Odyssey V, 1–281)* (Berkeley: Center for Hermeneutical Studies in Hellenistic and Modern Culture, 1988); Gregory Crane, *Calypso: Backgrounds and Conventions of the Odyssey* (Frankfurt am Main, Germany: Athenaeum, 1988).

Cappadocia *See* ASIA MINOR.

Caria *See* ASIA MINOR.

Carthage This major non-Greek city of North Africa is located about 10 miles from the modern city of Tunis. Carthage was founded by Phoenician settlers from Tyre around 800 B.C.E. to be an anchorage and trading post for Phoenician merchant ships in the western Mediterranean. The Phoenician name Kart Hadasht means "New City"; the Greeks called it Karchedon and the Romans, Carthago.

Governed as an OLIGARCHY under two presiding officials called shophets, Carthage thrived by commerce. It became a foremost power of the ancient world, with a feared navy to protect its trading monopolies in the western Mediterranean. The Carthaginians maintained trading bases such as Gades and Malaca (modern Cadiz and Malaga, both in southern Spain), from which they acquired valuable raw metals. The Carthaginians traded with the Greeks, as indicated by the troves of Corinthian POTTERY discovered at Carthage by modern archaeologists. But Carthage is important in Greek history mainly as an enemy and occasional overlord of the Greek cities in Magna Graecia.

Greeks and Carthaginians had first come into conflict when the Greeks intruded into Carthaginian trading waters in the western Mediterranean. Around 600 B.C.E. a Carthaginian fleet was defeated by Phocaean Greeks in the vicinity of MASSALIA (modern-day Marseille, in southern France). About 60 years later a joint fleet of Carthaginians and ETRUSCANS successfully drove the Greeks away from Corsica.

The Greeks and the Carthaginians fought intensely for almost 300 years over the territory of Sicily, whose coast lies about 130 miles from Carthage. This conflict eventually ended in favor of the Carthaginians, who also dominated the island of Sardinia. Carthage's greed for Sicily, however, eventually brought on conflict with the rising Italian city of ROME. The resulting three Punic Wars (264–241 B.C.E., 218–201 B.C.E., and 149–146 B.C.E.) ended in the complete destruction of Carthage by the Romans.

Prosperous Carthage won the admiration of the philosopher ARISTOTLE (mid-300s B.C.E.), whose treatise *Politics* contains a remarkable section that favorably compares the Carthaginian government with that of certain Greek cities. But another Greek writer describes—and ARCHAEOLOGY confirms—the gruesome Carthaginian custom of sacrificing upper-class children in time of public crisis, to ensure the god Baal-Ammon's care of the city.

Carthage's ancient monuments are poorly preserved today because the city's ruins were pillaged by many different groups as sources of marble; the Cathedral of Pisa is one of many later structures said to be built largely out of Carthaginian spoils. In modern times, further destruction to the remains of Greek and Roman Carthage has been done by the construction of the Tunisian railroad system. The most impressive of the surviving monuments from that era is the aqueduct, over 50 miles long.

See also AGATHOCLES; BRONZE; DIONYSIUS (1); GELON; HIMERA; PHOCAEA; PHOENICIA; SILVER; TRADE.

Further reading: David Soren, Aicha Ben Abed Ben Khader, and Hedi Slim, *Carthage: Uncovering the Mysteries and Splendors of Ancient Tunisia* (New York: Simon and Schuster, 1990); Serge Lancel, *Carthage* (Paris: Fayard, 1992); Henry R. Hurst, *The Sanctuary of Tanit at Carthage in the Roman Period: A Reinterpretation. Journal of Roman Archaeology Supplement no. 30* (Portsmouth, R.I.: Journal of Roman Archaeology, 1999); Dexter Hoyos, *Hannibal's Dynasty: Power and Politics in the Western Mediterranean, 247–183 B.C.* (London: Routledge, 2003).

caryatid The Greeks used this name for their type of decorative pillar represented as a clothed woman, holding up a ceiling structure with her head. The most famous caryatids are the six in marble from the south porch of the Athenian Erechtheion (built in 421–406 B.C.E.); the best preserved one of these is now in the British Museum in London. The Greeks also made hand mirrors that

Marble caryatids holding up the south porch of the Athenian Erechtheion, built 421–406 B.C.E. *(Alison Frantz Photographic Collection, American School of Classical Studies at Athens)*

scholars call "caryatid mirrors," because the handle is in the form of a woman, with the reflective disk of the mirror above her head.

Supposedly the name caryatid referred to the region of Caryae in LACONIA, where WOMEN traditionally danced with baskets on their heads. In any case, the sight of women carrying water pitchers or laundry baskets in this way was a familiar one in the ancient Greek world and certainly contributed to the design. The male equivalents of caryatids were called Atlantes, from the mythological figure ATLAS, who held up the heavens with his head.

See also ARCHITECTURE.

Further reading: Lamia Doumato, *The Erechtheum* (Monticello, Ill.: Vance Bibliographies, 1980); Lenore O. Keene Congdon, *Caryatid Mirrors of Ancient Greece: Technical, Stylistic, and Historical Considerations of an Archaic and Early Classical Bronze Series* (Mainz am Rhein, Germany: Philip von Zabern, 1981).

Cassander   *See* KASSANDER.

Cassandra (Greek: Kassandra, Alexandra)   In MYTH, Cassandra was a daughter of King PRIAM of TROY. She is mentioned in HOMER's *Iliad* simply as the loveliest of Priam's daughters, but later writers—particularly the Athenian playwright AESCHYLUS, in his *Agamemnon* (458 B.C.E.)—present her as a tragic heroine. Cassandra was beloved by the god APOLLO, who wooed her by offering her the power of prophecy. She accepted the gift but still refused his advances. Apollo could not revoke his gift, but he decreed vindictively that no one would ever believe her predictions.

In the TROJAN WAR, the Trojans ignored Cassandra's frantic plea not to take the Greeks' giant wooden horse into the city. When the Greeks emerged from the horse to sack Troy, Cassandra was dragged away from the altar of the goddess ATHENA and raped by AJAX (2) the Locrian. Afterward, Cassandra was allotted as concubine to the Greek grand marshal, King AGAMEMNON. On her arrival with Agamemnon at his kingdom of MYCENAE, Cassandra and Agamemnon were murdered by Agamemnon's wife, KLYTEMNESTRA. Naturally, Cassandra foresaw her own and Agamemnon's death but was unable to prevent them.

Cassandra is a frequent figure in Greek art, especially in Athenian vase paintings. The scene most commonly depicted shows the young princess kneeling and holding on to the statue of Athena, as Ajax drags her away. She is usually shown nude in these scenes—even in periods when Greek artists almost always depicted women fully clothed—in order to convey that Ajax is about to rape her. Cassandra also appears often in Greek and Roman literature; in addition to Aeschylus's drama, her tragic story is also told by APOLLODORUS, Vergil, and Pausanias.

Our modern expression "to be a Cassandra" or "to play Cassandra" is applied to someone who habitually predicts that bad things will happen.

See also PROPHECY AND DIVINATION.

Further reading: J. B. Connelly, "Narrative and Image in Attic Vase Painting. Ajax and Kassandra at the Trojan Palladion," in *Narrative and Event in Ancient Art*, edited by Peter J. Holliday (New York: Cambridge University Press, 1993), 88–129; H. Jackson, "A Black-Figure Neck-Amphora in Melbourne. The Nudity of Kassandra," *Mediterranean Archaeology* 9–10 (1996–1997): 53–75; M. Maaskant-Kleibrink, "Bearers of Idols. Iphigeneia, Kassandra, and Aeneas," in *La Glyptique des mondes classiques. Mélanges en homage á Marie-Louise Vollenweider*, edited by Mathilde Avisseau Broustet (Paris: Bibliothéque nationale de France, 1997), 23–34.

Castor and Polydeuces   These mythical twin heroes were worshipped as gods, especially at SPARTA and other Dorian-Greek cities. The cult of Castor and Polydeuces was an early cultural export to the Romans, who latinized the youths' names to Castor and Pollux.

The distinction between mortal hero and immortal god played a central role in the MYTH. According to the story, the Spartan king Tyndareus had a wife, LEDA, whom the god ZEUS raped or seduced. Leda bore two pairs of twins: the girls KLYTEMNESTRA and Helen (later known as HELEN OF TROY) and the boys Castor and Polydeuces. One version says that both boys were the immortal sons of Zeus—hence they were called the Dioskouroi, "the youths of Zeus." But a different tradition says that only Polydeuces was Zeus's child and thus immortal, while Castor, fathered by Tyndareus, was doomed to die like other humans.

The boys grew up inseparable and devoted to each other. Polydeuces became a champion boxer, Castor a famous horseman. They had three major adventures: they raided Athenian territory to rescue their sister Helen after she was kidnapped by the Athenian king THESEUS; sailed with the Argonauts under the Thessalian hero JASON (1) to capture the Golden Fleece; and abducted the two daughters of the Messenian nobleman Leucippus, who sent in pursuit his nephews Idas and Lynceus (to whom the young women had been betrothed). In the ensuing fight, Idas, Lynceus, and Castor were all killed. But Polydeuces prayed to his father, Zeus, who resurrected Castor on the condition that the twins thereafter divide their lot, living together one day among the gods and the next day in the Underworld. HOMER's epic poem the *Odyssey* mentions that "the grain-giving earth holds them, yet they live . . . One day they are alive, one day dead" (book 11).

Like HERAKLES (another hero turned god), the Dioskouroi were thought to be sympathetic to human needs and were worshipped widely by the common people. As patron gods of seafarers, they averted shipwreck, and their benevolent presence supposedly was indicated by the electrical phenomenon that we call St. Elmo's fire (whereby the mast and rigging of a sailing ship would seem to sparkle during a thunderstorm). They also were identified with the constellation known as the Twins (Gemini).

Often pictured as riding on white horses, the Dioskouroi embodied the spirit of military youth. At the Battle of the Sagras River (late 500s B.C.E.), the divine twins were believed to have appeared in person to aid the army of LOCRI (a Dorian-Greek city in south ITALY) against the army of CROTON (a nearby Achaean-Greek city). This miracle was copied by the Romans, who claimed that the Dioskouroi helped them to win the Battle of Lake Regillus against the Latins in about 496 B.C.E.

See also AFTERLIFE; BOXING; DORIAN GREEKS; ROME; SHIPS AND SEAFARING.

Further reading: E. A. Mackay, "The Return of the Dioskouri. A Reinterpretation of the Scene on the Reverse of the Vatican Amphora of Exekias," *American Journal of Archaeology* 83 (1979): 474–476; P. J. Connor, "Twin Riders. Dioskouri?" *Archäologischer Anzeiger* (1988): 27–39; H. A. Shapiro, "Cult Warfare. The Dioskouri between Sparta and Athens," in *Ancient Greek Hero Cult. Proceedings of the Fifth International Seminar on Ancient Greek Cult, Göteborg, 21–23 April 1995,* edited by Robin Hägg (Stockholm: Svenska Institutet I Athen, 1999), 99–107.

Catana (Greek: **Katane**) This Greek city on the east coast of SICILY is situated at the foot of volcanic Mt. Etna. Set at the northeastern rim of a large and fertile plain, this site is now the Sicilian city of Catania. The locale was seized in about 729 B.C.E. by Greek colonists from the nearby city of NAXOS (2), who drove away the region's native Sicels. This attack was part of the Greeks' two-pronged capture of the plain; the other captured site was Leontini.

Catana possessed one of the Greek world's first law codes, drawn up by a certain Charondas, probably in the early 500s B.C.E. As an Ionian-Greek city, Catana took part in ethnic feuding between Ionians and DORIAN GREEKS in Sicily. By 490 B.C.E. the city had fallen under the sway of its powerful Dorian neighbor to the south, SYRACUSE. In 476 B.C.E Syracusan tyrant HIERON (1) emptied Catana, exiling its inhabitants to Leontini, and repopulated the site with his Greek mercenary troops. The "new" city, renamed Aetna, was celebrated by the visiting Athenian playwright AESCHYLUS in a play (now lost), titled *Women of Aetna.* But after Hieron's death, the former Catanans recovered their city by force and gained independence (461 B.C.E.).

Catana provided the Athenians with a base against Syracuse in 415 B.C.E., during the PELOPONNESIAN WAR. In 403 B.C.E. Catana was recaptured by the Syracusans under their tyrant DIONYSIUS (1). For the next 150 years,

despite moments of independence provided by such saviors as the Corinthian commander TIMOLEON (339 B.C.E.) and the Epirote king PYRRHUS (278 B.C.E.), Catana remained a Syracusan possession. Seized by the Romans in 263 B.C.E., during the First Punic War, Catana become an important city of the Roman Empire.

See also COLONIZATION; IONIAN GREEKS; LAWS AND LAW COURTS; ROME.

Further reading: Tobias Fischer-Hansen, ed., *Ancient Sicily* (Copenhagen: Museum Tusculanum Press, 1995); Giovanni Pugliese Carratelli, ed., *The Greek World: Art and Civilization in Magna Graecia and Sicily* (New York: Rizzoli, 1996).

cavalry Although citizens wealthy enough to own horses were socially important in ancient Greek cities such as Athens (called *hippeis,* "knights"), ancient Greek warfare generally emphasized the foot soldier over the horse soldier. It took the tactical genius of the Macedonian kings PHILIP II and his son ALEXANDER THE GREAT (mid-300s B.C.E.) to raise cavalry to even a prominent secondary position. One reason for cavalry's inferior status lay in the mountainous terrain of mainland Greece, which was resistant to the strategic movement of horsemen and to horse-breeding itself; in most regions, only the very rich could afford to raise horses.

During the 700s to 300s B.C.E., when Greek citizen-soldiers supplied their own equipment, a city's cavalry typically consisted of rich men and their sons. Cavalry contingents were therefore small in most Greek armies. Only on the horse-breeding plains of THESSALY, BOEOTIA, and Greek SICILY did large cavalry corps develop.

In those days, cavalry was not so effective a "shock" troop as it would become in later centuries. The Greeks knew nothing of the stirrup—a vital military invention that enables a rider to "stand up" in the saddle and lean forward strenuously without falling off. (The stirrup probably came out of Siberia around 550 C.E.) Nor had the horseshoe or the jointed bit yet been invented. The Greeks knew only small breeds of horses prior to the late 300s B.C.E. (when Alexander's conquests introduced larger breeds from the Iranian plateau). Therefore, in battle, cavalry was not usually strong enough to ride directly against formations of infantry. The juggernaut charges of medieval Europe's armored knights were still 1,500 years in the future.

Ancient Greek artwork and certain writings—such as the historian XENOPHON's treatise *On Horsemanship* (ca. 380 B.C.E.)—suggest what a horse soldier looked like. He might wear a corset of linen or leather, with a BRONZE helmet (open-faced, to leave his vision clear). He probably carried no shield, or at most a small wooden targe attached to his left forearm. The Greek cavalry weapon was a spear for jabbing (not usually for throwing); unlike the long lance of a medieval knight, this spear was only

This marble carving from the Parthenon frieze, circa 432 B.C.E., shows Athenian cavalry cadets. These wealthy young men supplied their own horses and drilled at local riding tracks and in countryside maneuvers. *(Alison Frantz Photographic Collection, American School of Classical Studies at Athens)*

about six feet long. We know from battle scenes in Greek art that the horseman used his spear for a downward thrust, often overhand from the shoulder: the spear was not couched in the armpit for the charge, since the impact probably would have knocked the stirrupless rider off his horse. If the spear was lost, the horseman would rely on the IRON sword tied into a scabbard at his waist. As in other eras of military history, the preferred cavalry sword was a saber—that is, it had a curved cutting edge, designed to slash downward rather than to stab.

Horsemen of the 500s and 400s B.C.E. were needed for scouting and supply escort, and in combat they had the job of guarding the vulnerable infantry flanks. When one side's infantry formation began to dissolve into retreat, the cavalry of both sides might have crucial roles to play, either in running down the fleeing enemy, or (on the other side) in protecting the foot soldiers' retreat. Descriptions of ancient battles make clear that a disorderly retreat could become a catastrophe once the withdrawing infantry was overtaken by enemy horsemen. Among such examples is the plight of Athenian HOPLITES pursued by Boeotian cavalry after the Battle of Delium (424 B.C.E.), during the PELOPONNESIAN WAR.

The kingdom of MACEDON had a strong cavalry in its horse-breeding barons, whom King Alexander I (ca. 480 B.C.E.) organized into a prestigious corps of King's Companions. Whereas cavalry had previously formed only a small part of the Greek military, it made up nearly one-sixth of Alexander's forces on his Asiatic expeditions. The Macedonian army included an equal number of heavy and light cavalry; the light were armed with a special lance (the *sarissa*), while the heavy-armed riders were accompanied by a mounted servant and probably another freight-bearing horse. The subsequent innovations of Philip and Alexander brought cavalry into the heart of battle. Cavalry became the offensive arm, to complement the more defensive role of the heavy-infantry PHALANX. The Macedonian phalanx would stop the enemy infantry attack and rip gaps in its battle order, and the cavalry would then attack these vulnerable gaps before the enemy could reorganize. In this case cavalry could charge against massed infantry, since the charge was directed not against the enemy's waiting spear-points but against open ground. Into such a gap Alexander led the Macedonian cavalry at the battles of CHAIRONEIA (338 B.C.E.) and Gaugamela (331 B.C.E.). Prior to Alexander's conquests, the Persians possessed the most numerous and formidable cavalry known to the Greeks. All noble-born Persian boys were taught to ride and shoot with the bow.

During the HELLENISTIC AGE (300–150 B.C.E.), the importance of cavalry generally declined in favor of heavy-armed infantry forces. Alexander's successors in the eastern Mediterranean did experiment with such Persian-influenced cavalry as mounted archers and javelin men. They also developed horse and rider teams protected by chain-mail armor and known as *kataphraktai,* "enclosed ones." These cataphracts pointed the way toward the Parthian heavy cavalry of the Roman era and the armored knights of the Middle Ages.

See also PERSIA; WARFARE, LAND.

Further reading: I. G. Spence, *The Cavalry of Classical Greece: A Social and Military History with Particular Reference to Athens* (New York: Oxford University Press, 1993); Leslie J. Worley, *Hippeis: The Cavalry of Ancient Greece* (Boulder, Colo.: Westview Press, 1994); John McK. Camp II, *Horses and Horsemanship in the Athenian Agora* (Athens: American School of Classical Studies at Athens, 1998); Robert E. Gaebel, *Cavalry Operations in the Ancient Greek World* (Norman: University of Oklahoma Press, 2002).

Celts (Greek: Keltoi)   This race of people speaking an Indo-European language emerged from central Europe in a series of invasions after about 750 B.C.E. Among the places they occupied were France, Spain, and Britain. Today Celtic languages and culture still exist in Ireland, Scotland, Wales, and Britanny (in France), and the Celts are commemorated in place-names such as Galicia (in modern Spain) and Gaul (Gallia, the Roman name for ancient France). The Celts were known for their physical size and beauty, their natural spirituality, and their undisciplined fierceness in battle. The distinctive Celtic armament was the long, oblong shield.

Celtic society was tribal and agricultural, with walled towns for commerce and defense, but few cities. Although not a literary people (at that time), they developed an admirable material culture, especially in metallurgy. Early Celtic culture reached maturity around 400–100 B.C.E., in the La Tène style of art and metal design (named for an archaeological site in Switzerland).

By 600 B.C.E. Greek merchants in the western Mediterranean were dealing with Celtic peoples in Spain and France in order to acquire metals such as tin and SILVER. The Spanish Celtic kingdom of Tartessus had friendly dealing with Greek merchants from PHOCAEA. From the Phocaean colony at MASSALIA (modern Marseille), Greek goods and culture slowly spread inland among the Celts of Gaul, prompting the subsequent emergence of the La Tène civilization.

But the Greeks and Celts collided in the 200s B.C.E., when Celtic tribes descended the Danube, invaded mainland Greece from the north, and overran the sanctuary at DELPHI (279 B.C.E.). Another column of invaders crossed the HELLESPONT to attack ASIA MINOR, where they were contained after being defeated in battle by the Seleucid king Antiochus I (ca. 273 B.C.E.). The Greeks admired the valor of the Celts even while they considered them to be brutish barbarians, memorializing them in Hellenistic Greek statues like the *Dying Gaul,* erected in the city of PERGAMON and known today from later Roman copies.

Settling in north-central Asia Minor, immigrant Celts formed the kingdom of Galatia. Amid the neighboring Greeks and Phrygians, the Galatians maintained Celtic customs and language for centuries. In the first century C.E. Galatia contained an early Christian community, and these Galatians are commemorated in the New Testament, as recipients of a letter from St. Paul.

See also BRONZE; CARTHAGE; TRADE; WINE.

Further reading: David Rankin, *Celts and the Classical World* (London: Routledge, 1996); Peter Berresford Ellis, *Celt and Greek: Celts in the Hellenic World* (London: Constable, 1997); John Collis, *The Celts: Origins and Reinventions* (Stroud, U.K.: Tempus, 2003); Barry W. Cunliffe, *The Celts* (Oxford: Oxford University Press, 2003); Peter Berresford Ellis, *The Celts: A History* (New York: Carroll and Graf, 2004).

centaurs (Greek: kentauros)   These legendary creatures were part human, part horse; usually imagined as having a male horse's body with a male human torso and head emerging above the horse's chest. This shape is portrayed on the earliest surviving likeness of a centaur—a baked-clay figurine from the 900s B.C.E., decorated in Geometric style, discovered at LEFKANDI, in central Greece. However, certain other early images in art show human forelegs, with a horse's body and rear legs. The original meaning of the Greek word is not clear to us.

In Greek MYTH, centaurs had occupied the wild regions of THESSALY and ARCADIA in the old days; they represented the uncivilized life, before the general establishment of Greek laws and city-states. Although capable of wisdom and nobility, they were fierce, oversexed, and prone to drunkenness. The best-known myth about the centaurs, mentioned in HOMER's *Iliad* and *Odyssey,* is their battle with the Lapiths, a human tribe of Thessaly. The gathering began as a friendly banquet to celebrate the wedding of the Lapith king Perithoos, but the centaurs got drunk on WINE and tried to rape the Lapith women. In the ensuing brawl, the centaurs were defeated. As a symbol of savagery versus civilization, this battle was a favorite subject of Classical Greek art. It appeared, for instance, in the architectural SCULPTURES on the Athenian PARTHENON and on the Temple of ZEUS at OLYMPIA (mid-400s B.C.E.).

Another myth tells how a centaur named Nessos offered to carry HERAKLES' second wife, Deianeira, across a river but then tried to rape her. Herakles shot the creature with poisoned arrows, but before Nessos died he gave to Deianeira the poisoned blood-soaked garment that would later cause Herakles' death. A more benevolent centaur was Chiron, or Cheiron, the wise mountain-dweller who served as tutor to heroes, including JASON, ASKLEPIOS, and ACHILLES.

See also AMAZONS; GIANTS.

Further reading: P. B. C. Baur, *Centaurs in Ancient Art, the Archaic Period* (Berlin: K. Curtius, 1912); A. Lebessi, "The Relations of Crete and Euboea in the Tenth and Ninth Centuries B.C. The Lefkandi Centaur and his Predecessors," in *Minotaur and Centaur. Studies in the Archaeology of Crete and Euboea Presented to Mervyn Popham*, edited by Doniert Evely, Irene Lemos, and Elizabeth S. Sherratt (Oxford: Tempus Reparatum, 1996), 146–154; J. Michael Padgett et al., *The Centaur's Smile: The Human Animal in Early Greek Art* (New Haven, Conn.: Yale University Press, 2003).

Chaironeia (Chaeronea) The northernmost town of BOEOTIA, Chaironeia is located in the Kephissos River valley, on the main route between central and northern Greece. There in the summer of 338 B.C.E. the Macedonian king PHILIP II defeated an allied Greek army, to make Greece a subject state of MACEDON.

The decisive Battle of Chaironeia was one of the most consequential fights of ancient history—not only for politics, but for the development of battlefield tactics. The Greek army, comprised mainly of contingents from Boeotia and ATHENS, had a slight advantage in numbers: 35,000 HOPLITES (heavily armed infantry) against Philip's 30,000, with about 2,000 CAVALRY on each side. The allied Greeks comfortably guarded the route southward—their battle line filled the valley side to side, from the town's citadel on their left, to the river on their right. The Athenian hoplites, 10,000 strong, occupied the army's left wing; in the center were various levies and a company of 5,000 mercenaries; and on the right wing were 12,000 Boeotians, including the men of THEBES, the best soldiers in Greece. The position of honor, on the extreme right wing, was given to the Theban Sacred Band, an elite battalion of 300, consisting entirely of paired male lovers.

Philip, on horseback behind his army's right wing, brought his men southward through the valley in an unusual, slantwise formation, which was destined to become a model Macedonian tactic. The Macedonian PHALANX was angled so that the right wing advanced ahead of the center and the center ahead of the left wing. Holding back on the Macedonian left wing was the cavalry, commanded by Philip's 18-year-son, Prince Alexander (later known to history as ALEXANDER THE GREAT).

Philip's battlefield plan was a refinement of tactics used by the Thebans themselves at LEUKTRA more than 30 years before. Like the Thebans at Leuktra, Philip planned to hit his enemies at their strongest point: their right wing. But Philip's inspired innovation was to precede this blow with a disruptive feint against the enemy's left wing in the hope of creating a gap along the long line of massed Greek soldiery.

According to a statement by a later ancient writer, it is possible that Philip staged a retreat of his right wing during the battle. Presumably the Macedonians withdrew by stepping backward in good order, with their 13-foot-long pikes still facing forward. The disorganized Athenians followed, in deluded triumph. But in fact, the overexcited Athenians were drawing their army's left wing forward, with the Greek troops in the center following suit. Eventually gaps appeared in the Greek battle line, as various contingents lost contact with one another. On the Greek far right, the Theban Sacred Band stood isolated from the rest of the army. It was then that Prince Alexander led his cavalry charging down the valley, followed by the reserve Macedonian infantry.

The Sacred Band was surrounded and overrun by Alexander's cavalry. Meanwhile Philip, off on the Macedonian right, ordered an end to his false retreat. His men pressed forward against the Athenians, who scattered and fled. The Macedonians pursued, killing 1,000 Athenians

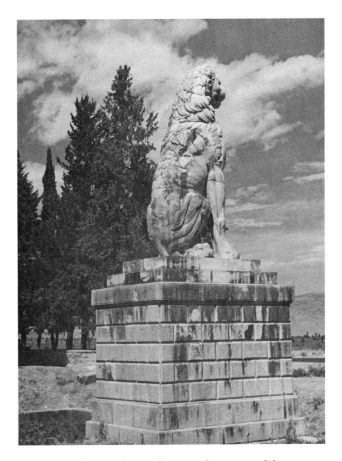

The Lion of Chaironeia watches over the graves of the Sacred Band and the burial mound of the Macedonian dead. *(Alison Frantz Photographic Collection, American School of Classical Studies at Athens)*

and taking 2,000 prisoners. Among the fugitives was DEMOSTHENES (1), the great Athenian orator and enemy of Philip's.

After the battle, the corpses of the Sacred Band lay in the serried ranks of their disciplined formation. Of their 300 men, only 46 had survived. The rest were buried on the battlefield, where their 254 skeletons were discovered by archaeologists in the 19th century. The Battle of Chaironeia marks an important point in Greek military history, since it demonstrated the vast superiority of organized forces such as the Macedonian phalanx over traditional Greek hoplite warfare. This victory also established Macedonia as the supreme power in Greece. The defeated Athenians, treated relatively leniently by their conquerors, dissolved their naval confederacy and joined Philip's new Hellenic League. The Macedonians next marched into the Peloponnese and easily established control there before moving forward with Philip and Alexander's ultimate plan of invading Persia.

Today the site of Chaironeia is marked by an 18-foot-tall marble lion, sculpted in ancient times, overlooking the Sacred Band's graves and the burial mound of the Macedonian dead. The lion was discovered in pieces in 1818 and restored on a 10-foot-tall plinth. In addition to the graves of the Thebans, excavated in 1879 by George Soteriadis, archaeological investigations at Chaironeia have revealed the ancient theater and the acropolis with its Hellenistic fortification walls, as well as occupation remains from the prehistoric period.

See also HOMOSEXUALITY; WARFARE, LAND.

Further reading: Hugo Montgomery, *The Way to Chaeronea: Foreign Policy, Decision-making, and Political Influence in Demosthenes' Speeches* (Irvington-on-Hudson, N.Y.: Columbia University Press, 1983).

Chalcedon   *See* BYZANTIUM.

Chalcidicē   The northwestern coast of the AEGEAN SEA, Chalcidicē is located in what eventually became Macedonian territory, north of Greece proper. It is distinguished by three peninsulas, each about 30 miles long, jutting into the Aegean and providing harbors and natural defenses. These three, west to east, were called Pallene, Sithonia, and Acte (meaning "promontory" in Greek).

Originally inhabited by Thracians, the region was colonized in the latter 700s B.C.E. by Greeks from the city of CHALCIS; they established about 30 settlements and gave the region its Greek name, "Chalcidian land." Among later Greek arrivals were Corinthians who, around 600 B.C.E., founded the important city of POTIDAEA on the narrow neck of the Acte peninsula. Another prominent city was OLYNTHOS, founded in the 400s B.C.E., north of Potidaea.

Chalcidicē offered precious TIMBER, SILVER ore, and SLAVES, and controlled the coastal shipping route to the HELLESPONT. The prosperous Chalcidic towns had become tribute-paying members of the Athenian-dominated DELIAN LEAGUE by the mid-400s B.C.E., but in the spring of 432 B.C.E. Potidaea revolted unsuccessfully against the Athenians. More revolts followed the arrival of the Spartan general BRASIDAS in 432 B.C.E., during the PELOPONNESIAN WAR. The town of Scione, recaptured by the Athenians in 421 B.C.E., was treated with exemplary cruelty: All men of military age were killed and the WOMEN and children were sold as slaves.

Chalcidicē endured a generation of Spartan rule after SPARTA's victory in the Peloponnesian War (404 B.C.E.), yet meanwhile the Chalcidic towns organized themselves into a federation, with a shared citizenship and government and with Potidaea as the capital (ca. 400 B.C.E.). In the 370s B.C.E. this Chalcidic League joined the SECOND ATHENIAN LEAGUE. But renewed Athenian interference with Potidaea drove the Chalcidic Greeks to make an alliance with the ambitious Macedonian king PHILIP II (356 B.C.E.). Resistance to Philip led to war, in which Philip captured and destroyed Olynthus and Potidaea (348 B.C.E.). Henceforth the region was ruled by MACEDON.

Chalcidicē revived under the Macedonian king Kassander (reigned 316–298 B.C.E.). He built a grand new city, Kassandreia, on the site of the ruined Potidaea.

See also ARISTOTLE.

Further reading: J. A. Alexander, "Cassandreia during the Macedonian Period: An Epigraphical Commentary," in *Archaia Macedonia*, edited by V. Laourdas and C. Makaronas (Thessaloniki, 1970).

Chalcis   This important city is situated midway along the west coast of the large inshore island called EUBOEA, in east-central Greece. Chalcis was strategically located on the narrow Euripus channel, so it was able to control all shipping through the Euboean Straits. Inland and southward, the city enjoyed the fertile plain of Lelanton.

Inhabited by Greeks of the Ionian ethnic group, Chalcis and its neighbor ERETRIA had emerged by about 850 B.C.E. as the most powerful cities of early Greece. Chalcis—its name refers to local copper deposits or to worked BRONZE (both: *chalkos*)—thrived as a manufacturing center, and its drive for raw metals and other goods placed it at the forefront of Greek overseas TRADE and COLONIZATION ca. 800–650 B.C.E. Seafarers from Chalcis and Eretria established the first Greek trading depot that we know of, at AL MINA on the north Levantine coast (ca. 800 B.C.E.). A generation later, in western ITALY, they founded the early Greek colonies PITHECUSAE and CUMAE.

Around 735 B.C.E. the partnership of Chalcis and Eretria ended in conflict over possession of the Lelantine plain. Chalcis apparently won this LELANTINE WAR (by 680 B.C.E.), and the city and its new ally CORINTH then dominated all Greek westward colonization. Among the

This helmet, with its elaborate decoration, was probably ceremonial not battle armor. It is a light Chalcidian helmet, with hinged cheekpieces. The griffin on top and the wings over the ears are usually associated with gods and heroes. *(The J. Paul Getty Museum)*

westward colonies founded by Chalcis in this era were RHEGIUM, in southern Italy, and NAXOS (2) and ZANCLĒ, in SICILY. In the late 700s B.C.E., Chalcis also sent colonists to the north Aegean region eventually known as CHALCIDICĒ (Chalcidian land). BUT BY THE MID-600s B.C.E. Chalcis was being eclipsed in commerce by Corinth.

According to tradition, Chalcis's last king was killed in the Lelantine War, after which the city was governed as an ARISTOCRACY led by the *hippobotai* (horse-owners), Chalcidian nobles. In 506 B.C.E. these aristocrats, with help from nearby BOEOTIA, made war on ATHENS and its newly democratic government. Chalcis was completely defeated, and a portion of the *hippobotai's* land was confiscated for an Athenian garrison colony.

Chalcis contributed 20 warships to the defense of Greece in the PERSIAN WARS (480–479 B.C.E.). Soon after, Chalcis and all the other Euboean cities were compelled to join the Athenian-led DELIAN LEAGUE. In 446 B.C.E., Chalcis led a Euboean revolt from the league, but Athens crushed this harshly, exiling the *hippobotai*. A successful

revolt followed later, amid the Delian uprisings of the later PELOPONNESIAN WAR (411 B.C.E.). However, after a bitter taste of Spartan overlordship, Chalcis joined the SECOND ATHENIAN LEAGUE (378 B.C.E.).

The Macedonian king PHILIP II conquered the Greeks in 338 B.C.E. and placed a garrison in Chalcis. For the next 140 years or more, Chalcis served as a Macedonian stronghold—one of the Macedonians' four "fetters" of Greece.

In 194 B.C.E. the Romans ejected the Macedonian garrison; however, as a member of the anti-Roman Achaean League, Chalcis was besieged and captured by the Romans in 146 B.C.E. The city recovered, to play a role in the empire of ROME.

See also ACHAEA; ALPHABET; GREECE, GEOGRAPHY OF; IONIAN GREEKS; MACEDON.

Further reading: S. C. Bakhuizen, *Studies in the Topography of Chalcis on Euboea: A Discussion of the Sources* (Leiden, Netherlands: E. J. Brill, 1985); E. Sapouna-Sakellaraki, *Chalkis: History, Topography, and Museum,* translated by W. Phelps (Athens: Ministry of Culture, Archaeological Receipts Fund, 1995).

chariots The chariot—an axled, two-wheeled vehicle typically pulled by horses—played a small but picturesque role in Greek history. Around 1600–1200 B.C.E., the kings of the MYCENAEAN CIVILIZATION kept fleets of war chariots, as indicated by archaeological evidence (including Mycenaean grave stones and wall paintings and texts of LINEAR B tablets listing inventories of chariots and chariot parts). The Mycenaean chariot was probably made of wood plated with BRONZE, with upright sides and front. It was drawn by two horses and carried two soldiers—the driver and a passenger armed with spears or arrows.

Although the chariot would have served well for display and for sportsmanlike Mycenaean battles on the plains of ARGOS, BOEOTIA, and THESSALY, it must have had very limited use elsewhere, in the hilly Greek terrain. Modern scholars believe the Mycenaean copied the chariot's use from Near Eastern armies—either from the Hittites of ASIA MINOR or the New Kingdom Egyptians—without themselves having a clear tactical need for such a vehicle. Evidently the Mycenaeans were attracted to the machine's pure glamour.

Mycenaean chariots are commemorated in HOMER's *Iliad* (written down around 750 B.C.E. but purporting to describe events of around 1200 B.C.E.). Homer describes chariots as two-horse, two-man vehicles that bring aristocratic heroes such as ACHILLES and HECTOR to and from the battle. For actual fighting, the warrior leaps to the ground while the driver whisks the chariot to the sidelines. Modern scholars doubt that this poetic picture is accurate. Homer, presumably without realizing his mistake, has represented Mycenaean chariots as being used exactly as horses were used in his own day—to carry noble champions to battle. In fact (says the modern theory), like their Hittite and Egyptian counterparts, Mycenaean chariots seem to have taken part directly in combat—in charges, sweeps, and similar tactics—with an archer or spearman stationed inside each vehicle.

After the destruction of Mycenaean society and the ensuing DARK AGE (ca. 1100–900 B.C.E.), the Greek chariot became used purely for SPORT, in races held at the great religious-athletic festivals. Because of this new function, the chariot evolved a new design. They were usually one-man vehicles drawn by four horses or, sometimes, by four mules. During the 700s–100s B.C.E., the most prestigious competition in the entire Greek world was the race of horse chariots at the OLYMPIC GAMES. Coming last in the sequence of Olympic events, this race involved dozens of chariots in 12 laps around the stadium's elongated track, for a total distance of almost nine miles. Like the later chariot races of imperial ROME, the Greek sport offered considerable danger of collisions and other mishaps. For instance, at the PYTHIAN GAMES of 482 B.C.E., the winning chariot finished alone in a starting field of 41 vehicles.

The official competitors in a chariot race were not usually the drivers (who were professionals), but the people sponsoring the individual chariots. It was a sport for the rich, requiring large-scale breeding and training of horses. For Greek aristocrats and rulers, an Olympic chariot victory was the crowning achievement of public life. To help celebrate such a triumph, a winner might commission a lyric poet such as PINDAR (ca. 476 B.C.E.) to write a victory song.

Among the more famous chariot owners was the flamboyant Athenian politician ALCIBIADES. For the Olympic Games of 416 B.C.E., he sponsored no less than seven chariots, which finished first, second, and fourth.

See also ARISTOCRACY; PELOPS; WARFARE, LAND.

Further reading: P. A. L. Greenhalgh, *Early Greek Warfare: Horsemen and Chariots in the Homeric and Archaic Ages* (Cambridge: Cambridge University Press, 1973); J. H. Crouwel, *Chariots and Other Means of Land Transport in Bronze Age Greece* (Amsterdam: Allard Pierson Museum, 1981); J. H. Crouwel, *Chariots and Other Wheeled Vehicles in Iron Age Greece* (Amsterdam: Allard Pierson Museum, 1992); Robert E. Gaebel, *Cavalry Operations in the Ancient Greek World* (Norman: University Of Oklahoma Press, 2002).

Charon *See* AFTERLIFE; FUNERAL CUSTOMS.

Charybdis *See* SCYLLA.

Chersonese The Chersonēsos ("peninsula") was a 50-mile-long arm of the northeastern Aegean coast, alongside northwestern ASIA MINOR. The peninsula's eastern shore forms the western side of the HELLESPONT—the 33-mile-long strait that was a crucial part of the ancient TRADE route to the BLACK SEA. To control the Hellespont, great powers such as ATHENS and MACEDON sought to hold the Chersonese. In modern times this region is known as Gallipoli, the scene of bloody fighting in World War I.

Although part of the non-Greek land of THRACE, the Chersonese began receiving Greek colonists from LESBOS and MILETUS by the 600s B.C.E. Athenian settlers arrived in the early 500s B.C.E. The elder Miltiades, an Athenian, ruled most of the Chersonese as his private fief (mid-500s B.C.E.). His nephew and successor, the famous MILTIADES, abandoned the area to Persian invasion.

After the PERSIAN WARS, the Chersonese settlements were dominated by Athens through the DELIAN LEAGUE. In 338 B.C.E. the region passed to the Macedonian king PHILIP II. Thereafter it was held by various Hellenistic kingdoms, until the Romans conquered Greece and Macedon in the mid-100s B.C.E.

The Chersonese had two chief cities, both Greek: SESTOS, which was the commanding fortress of the Hellespont; and Cardia, on the peninsula's western side.

Further reading: A. J. Graham, "A Dedication from the Chersonese at Olympia," in *Nomodeiktes. Greek Studies in Honor of Martin Ostwald,* edited by Ralph M. Rosen and Joseph Farrell (Ann Arbor: University of Michigan Press, 1993), 331–338; G. Greatrex, "Procopius and Agathias on the Defenses of the Thracian Chersonese," in *Constantinople and Its Hinterland. Papers from the Twenty-seventh Spring Symposium of Byzantine Studies, Oxford, April 1993,* edited by Cyril Mango and Gilbert Dagron (Brookfield, Vt.: Variorum, 1995), 125–129.

Chilon (500s B.C.E.) *Spartan EPHOR who is credited with certain developments in SPARTA's government and foreign policy*
Apparently, Chilon increased the ephors' power to counterbalance the two Spartan kings, and he probably launched Sparta's policy of hostility to TYRANTS throughout Greece. He also organized Sparta's individual alliances with other states—including CORINTH and SIKYON—into a permanent network of mutual defense, which modern scholars call the Peloponnesian League.

Revered at Sparta after his death, Chilon was counted as one of the SEVEN SAGES of Greece. His political heir was the Spartan king KLEOMENES (1), who reigned ca. 520–489 B.C.E.

Further reading: Constantine Cavarnos, *The Seven Sages of Ancient Greece: The Lives and Teachings of the Earliest Greek Philosophers, Thales, Pittacos, Bias, Solon, Cleobulos, Myson, Chilon* (Belmont, Mass.: Institute for Byzantine and Modern Greek Studies, 1996).

Chios This large Aegean island, 30 miles long and 8–15 miles wide, lies close to the coast of ASIA MINOR. The main city, also named Chios, was situated on the island's east coast (five miles across from the Asian mainland) and was one of the foremost Greek city-states. The island, known for its scenic beauty, is extremely mountainous; its highest peak is Mt. Elias, with an elevation of 4,160 feet. Agricultural products from Chios are similar to those in mainland Greece, including olives, figs, grapes (for making wine), and mastic. Herds of sheep and goats graze everywhere. The island also has some good marble quarries and other geological natural resources.

Occupied around 1000 B.C.E. by IONIAN GREEKS from mainland Greece, Chios thrived as a maritime power whose exports included a renowned WINE as well as textiles, grain, figs, and mastic (a tree resin used for varnish). Chios figured prominently in the cultural achievements of the east Greek region known as IONIA. The island is said to have been the birthplace of the poet HOMER (born probably around 800 B.C.E.); in later centuries a guild of bards, the Homeridae, or sons of Homer, were active there. Chios was also known as an international slave emporium, supplying the markets of Asia Minor and itself employing many SLAVES for FARMING and manufacturing.

During the Greek wars of the 700s–600s B.C.E., Chios tended to ally itself with MILETUS, against such nearby rivals as Erythrae and SAMOS. In government, the emergence of certain democratic forms at Chios is shown in an inscription (ca. 560 B.C.E.) that mentions a "People's Council"—possibly a democratically elected COUNCIL and court of appeals. This democratic apparatus may have been modeled on the recent reforms of SOLON at ATHENS.

Like the rest of Ionia and Asia Minor, Chios fell to the conquering Persian king CYRUS (1) in around 545 B.C.E. In the ill-fated IONIAN REVOLT against Persian rule, Chios contributed 100 warships, which fought gallantly at the disastrous Battle of Lade (494 B.C.E.). Later the avenging Persians devastated Chios.

Following the liberation of Ionia during the PERSIAN WARS (479 B.C.E.), Chios became a prominent member of the Athenian-dominated DELIAN LEAGUE. Chios chose to make its Delian annual contributions in warships rather than in SILVER—one of the few league members to do so. For 65 years Chios proved the most steadfast of any Athenian ally. The Athenians paid Chios the compliment of coupling its name with that of Athens itself in public prayer at each Athenian ASSEMBLY. But in 412 B.C.E., with Athens's power dissolving during the PELOPONNESIAN WAR, Chios initiated the revolt of the Delian subject cities. Chios staved off the vengeful Athenians, and by 411 B.C.E. the island was firmly controlled by Athens' enemy, SPARTA.

After 30 years of Spartan domination, the Chians joined the SECOND ATHENIAN LEAGUE, but in 354 B.C.E. revolted from Athens again. During the 200s B.C.E., in resistance to the SELEUCID EMPIRE's designs, Chios joined the Aetolian League. The island passed to Roman control in the next century.

The archaeological remains of ancient Chios are sparse and poorly preserved, primarily because its major city is located beneath the island's modern capital. Some rescue excavations hare have revealed bits and pieces from antiquity, and sporadic archaeological investigations have also been carried out in other parts of the island.

See also AETOLIA; DEMOCRACY.

Further reading: John Boardman, *Excavations in Chios, 1952–1955: Greek Emporio* (London: Thames and Hudson, 1967); Charalampos Bouras, *Chios,* translated by David Hardy (Athens: National Bank of Greece, 1974); Sinclair Hood, *Excavations in Chios, 1938–1955: Prehistoric Emporio and Ayio Gala* (London: Thames and Hudson, 1981); Michael Balance, *Excavations in Chios, 1952–1955: Byzantine Emporio* (London: Thames and Hudson, 1989); Anna Lemos, *Archaic Pottery of Chios: The Decorated Styles* (Oxford: Oxford University Committee for Archaeology, 1991).

choral poetry *See* LYRIC POETRY.

chorus *See* LYRIC POETRY; THEATER.

Cilicia *See* ASIA MINOR.

Cimon *See* KIMON.

Circe (Greek: Kirke) In MYTH, a beautiful goddess and witch, was the daughter of the sun god HELIOS and his wife, Perse. Circe dwelt on a magical island in the West, in a stone house with enchanted wolves and lions. Her name seems derived from *kirkos,* "hawk."

Circe plays a sinister but exciting role in Homer's epic poem the *Odyssey* (book 10). When the homeward-bound Greek hero ODYSSEUS brings his ship to her island and sends half his crew ashore to scout, she welcomes them with a magic drink that turns them into pigs. Odysseus goes to their rescue, armed with a magical herb called moly (*molu*)—the gift of the god HERMES—that makes him immune to Circe's spells. Odysseus forces her to restore his men's human shapes. Then, at her invitation, he lives with her for a year as her lover, but finally demands that she give him directions for his continued voyage home. Circe's advice (book 12) enables Odysseus to resist the deadly SIRENS and avoid other dangers. Circe is one of two supernatural women who became Odysseus's lovers during his wondrous voyage; the other is CALYPSO.

Generations of Greeks after Homer elaborated Circe's story. Her home was sometimes identified with Monte Circeo, a promontory midway along the west coast of ITALY. According to one story, she bore Odysseus's son

Telegonus, who later unwittingly killed his father. In APOLLONIUS's epic poem, the *Argonautica*, Circe welcomes JASON (1) and MEDEA after their escape from the kingdom of Colchis.

Further reading: Gregory Crane, *Calypso: Backgrounds and Conventions of the Odyssey* (Frankfurt am Main, Germany: Athenaeum, 1988); Judith Yarnall, *Transformations of Circe: The History of an Enchantress* (Urbana: University of Illinois Press, 1994).

city-state   *See* POLIS.

Cleisthenes (1)   *See* KLEISTHENES (1).

Cleisthenes (2)   *See* KLEISTHENES (2).

Cleomenes (1)   *See* KLEOMENES (1).

Cleon   *See* KLEON.

Cleopatra (Kleopatra)   *Dynastic female name of the Macedonian royal family in the 300s* B.C.E., *later used by the Macedonian-descended Ptolemies of* EGYPT.
The name means "glory of her father" in Greek. The famous Cleopatra—Cleopatra VII, daughter of Ptolemy XII—was the last Ptolemaic ruler of Egypt and also the last Hellenistic ruler outside Roman control. Upon her death in 30 B.C.E., Egypt was annexed by ROME.
See also HELLENISTIC AGE; PTOLEMY (1).

Further reading: S. B. Pomeroy, *Women in Hellenistic Egypt: From Alexander to Cleopatra* (New York: Schocken Books, 1984); Lucy Hughes-Hallett, *Cleopatra: Histories, Dreams, and Distortions* (New York: Harper and Row, 1990); Michael Grant, *Cleopatra* (London: Phoenix Press, 2000); Susan Walker and Peter Higgs, eds., *Cleopatra of Egypt: From History to Myth* (London: British Museum, 2001); Michel Chauveau, *Cleopatra: Beyond the Myth*, translated by David Lorton (Ithaca: Cornell University Press, 2002).

clothing   The ancient Greeks did not have a commercial fashion industry; most clothing, typically made of linen, cotton, or wool, was woven in the home. Wives and their female servants often spent much of their day indoors, spinning yarn and weaving cloth on a loom. Greek women were very skilled in the arts of weaving and embroidery, and garments often included elaborate border designs. Clothing was simple and loose-fitting, with only a few basic forms and much similarity between outfits worn by men and women.

Scholars today have several sources for obtaining information about ancient Greek clothing, including written documents and images in Greek SCULPTURE and vase painting. Both men and women wore a tunic, generally sleeveless, which was called a *chiton*. This garment was created from a rectangular piece of cloth (usually linen or cotton) that was folded in a certain way around the body and pinned on one shoulder. The woman's tunic generally reached to the floor and would frequently be worn under a mantle or cloak (known as a *himation*), which was also created from a rectangle of woven cloth, usually wool. The man's tunic could either fall to the feet (in Ionian fashion) or merely to the knees or above (in the Dorian fashion). The shorter tunic was often worn by workmen, farmers, and soldiers, who wore it underneath their body armor. Like women, men might also wear a *himation*. For horseback riding, younger men often wore a distinctive wide cloak known as a *chlamys*.

For women, the *chiton* and *himation* combination was an Ionian style that became popular in mainland Greece in the early fifth century B.C.E., after the Persian invasion. Earlier, women generally wore a simple woolen garment called a *peplos*. This dress was also created from a large rectangle of cloth, and it was usually fastened at the shoulders and belted at the waist.

This maiden is called the Peplos Kore because she wears the long flowing woman's tunic called a peplos. Notice her long plaited hair, fashionable for both men and women. *(Alison Frantz Photographic Collection, American School of Classical Studies at Athens)*

From the Parthenon frieze, a rider wearing a petasos, the low, broad-rimmed hat worn by travelers, hunters, and others to keep off the hot Greek sun *(Alison Frantz Photographic Collection, American School of Classical Studies at Athens)*

Greek men, who spent much of their day outdoors in the hot Mediterranean sun, often wore various types of hats. Travelers, workmen, and sailors might wear a conical cap known as a *pilos;* ODYSSEUS is frequently shown wearing one of these. Travelers, hunters, and others sometimes wore a low, broad-rimmed hat called a *petasos;* one is often seen on the head of the messenger god HERMES. The footwear of choice for heavy walking was either sandals or leather boots; otherwise, clogs or slippers were worn.

See also POTTERY.

Further reading: David Symons, *Costume of Ancient Greece* (New York: Chelsea House Publishers, 1988); Ioanna Papantoniou, *Greek Dress: From Ancient Times to the Early 20th Century,* translated by David A. Hardy (Athens: Commercial Bank of Greece, 2000); Lloyd Llewellyn-Jones, ed., *Women's Dress in the Ancient Greek World* (London: David Brown Book Co., 2002).

Clytaemnestra *See* KLYTEMNESTRA.

Cnidus *See* KNIDOS.

coinage The first coins came into use in the 600s B.C.E. But long before then the ancient Greeks traded (by barter) and understood the concepts of value and profit. Among the Greeks, the forerunners of the coin were certain implements used for representing high value. One such was the bar of SILVER, usually called an ingot. Several ingots might comprise the monetary unit known as the TALENT (Greek *talanton,* "weight"), equivalent to just under 58 pounds of silver. Another precious metal of those days was IRON. The Greeks developed a high-level currency based on the iron rods (*oboloi*), traded by the handful (*drachmē*). These rods remained in circulation down through the 500s B.C.E. and even later in the reclusive city of SPARTA.

The invention of coins—easily stored, transported, and counted—marked an improvement over ingots or rods. The first nation on Earth to mint coins was most likely the kingdom of LYDIA in ASIA MINOR, around 635 B.C.E. The Lydians were not Greek, but the Greeks seem to have imported and studied this new Lydian invention. Modern archaeologists have uncovered Lydian coins composed of electrum (an alloy of silver and GOLD) at the ancient Greek city of EPHESOS, in Asia Minor. Stamped with a lion figure "seal of approval" as a royal guarantee of weight and purity, these Lydian coins may have been given to pay large groups of artisans or mercenary soldiers, who surely included Greeks. Before long, Greeks were minting their own coins, copied from the Lydian ones.

According to ancient writers, the first Greek minting state was AEGINA (probably around 595 B.C.E.). The Aeginetan coins were silver, in three sizes that cleverly employed the denominations already existing for iron rods. The smallest coin was called the obol, the next the drachm, and the largest the didrachm (two drachmas), or statēr. The Aeginetan statēr showed a sea turtle, the city symbol. The other two early Greek coining states were ATHENS (ca. 575 B.C.E.) and CORINTH (ca. 570 B.C.E.)—both, like Aegina, trading and maritime powers.

By the 400s B.C.E., every important Greek state was minting its own coins, as a sign of independence and an aid to TRADE. There was not yet a uniform system of denominations; rather, each city tended to follow one of two available systems. Silver remained the prime coining metal (gold being a scarce resource for the Greeks). But coinages of BRONZE, to cover lower denominations, began in the mid-400s B.C.E. By the mid-300s B.C.E., gold coins were being minted by certain states such as MACEDON, which had local supplies of gold ore.

Unlike some modern currency, a Greek coin was intended to contain an unadulterated amount of precious metal equal to the face value: The stamp on the coin was meant to guarantee this. The earliest Greek coins were stamped on only one side. To prepare such a coin, the smith would place a blank, heated disk of metal on an anvil atop a shallow die bearing the engraved shape of the intended imprint. The disk was then punched into the die by a rod (Greek: *charaktēr*), hammered at one end. The resulting coin would bear a relief created by the die on one side (the "obverse") and a mere indentation on the other (the "reverse"). By about 530 B.C.E. the Greeks had learned to make two-sided coins by using a rod whose lower end also bore an engraved die.

To judge from the hundreds of specimens surviving today, Greek coins were intended as objects of beauty and as means of civic propaganda. Extant coins bear such charming or stirring emblems as the Athenian owl, the Corinthian winged horse Pegasus, and the man-faced, bull-bodied river god of GELA. In the Hellenistic period, coins also became a medium for accurate profile portraiture; it is from coins that we know what certain ancient personages looked like. In the late 300s B.C.E., for instance, the successors of ALEXANDER THE GREAT paid homage to his memory—and laid claim to his empire—by issuing coins showing his portrait and, later, their own. This was a dramatic change from earlier Greek numismatic convention, which was generally to depict deities, heroes, or their attributes, never portraits of real people. The Hellenistic coin portraits also served as objects of political propaganda, since Alexander and the DIADOCHOI were shown wearing divine attributes, such as HERAKLES' lion skin, DIONYSUS's leopard skin, and ZEUS Ammon's bull's horns.

Greek coinage changed at this time, in the aftermath of Alexander's conquest of the Persian Empire. Under Hellenistic kings ruling vast territories in an enlarged Greek world, there arose uniform coinages used over large areas and not necessarily differing from city to city. Of the older Greek states, only Athens and Rhodes continued minting. Important coining states of the 200s and 100s B.C.E. included Macedon, the SELEUCID EMPIRE, Hellenistic EGYPT, PERGAMON, and the Greek leagues of ACHAEA and AETOLIA. Also, the Greco-Macedonian kings of BACTRIA commemorated themselves in a series of remarkably vivid personal portraits on coins. The naturalism in these representations had a significant influence on the super-realistic portraiture of Republican Rome that would develop in the 100s B.C.E.

Most Greek coinage ceased during the Roman conquests in the two centuries before Jesus. Henceforth the Greeks relied mainly on coins minted by the imperial city of ROME.

See also ATHENA; BELLEROPHON; HELLENISTIC AGE; HIMERA.

Further reading: Gilbert K. Jenkins, *Ancient Greek Coins,* 2d ed. (London: Seaby, 1990); Otto Mørkholm, *Early Hellenistic Coinage: From the Accession of Alexander to the Peace of Apamea (336–188 B.C.)* (New York: Cambridge University Press, 1991); John Melville-Jones, *Testimonia numaria: Greek and Latin Texts Concerning Ancient Greek Coinage* (London: Spink, 1993); Ian Carradice, *Greek Coins* (Austin: University of Texas Press, 1995); Glyn Davies, *A History of Money: From Ancient Times to the Present Day* (Cardiff: University of Wales Press, 2002).

colonization Even prior to the conquests of ALEXANDER THE GREAT (ca. 334–323 B.C.E.), the ancient Greek world stretched from Libya and southern France to CYPRUS, ASIA MINOR, and the Crimean peninsula. This Greek proliferation around the Mediterranean and BLACK SEA took place during the great colonizing era of the 700s through the 500s B.C.E., when Greek cities extended their TRADE routes (and alleviated domestic food shortages and other population problems) by sending out shipborne expeditions of young male colonists. Sailing along sea routes already scouted by Greek traders, these colonists might travel considerable distances to descend on a land typically occupied by a vulnerable, non-Greek people (such as in eastern SICILY). But coasts defended by powerful kingdoms such as EGYPT or Assyria were never colonized by early Greeks.

The colonists' new city would retain the laws, traditions, and religious cults of the mother city, or *mētropolis*. Metropolis and colony would typically enjoy cordial relations and trade agreements; for example, SYRACUSE, in Sicily, was surely bound to export surplus grain to its hungry mother city, CORINTH.

The earliest Greek colonizing took place during the MYCENAEAN CIVILIZATION around 1600–1200 B.C.E. The Mycenaean Greeks founded settlements on Cyprus and on the west coast of Asia Minor. But the great age of colonization began in the mid-700s B.C.E., after trade and improved seamanship had begun the expansion of the Greek world. Parts of HOMER's epic poem the *Odyssey* (written down circa 750 B.C.E.) seem colored by a contemporary interest in trade and exploration around Sicily and the Adriatic Sea. Most modern knowledge of this period comes from archaeological evidence—building sites, POTTERY types, occasional inscriptions—and from literary sources such as the fifth-century-B.C.E. historians HERODOTUS and THUCYDIDES (1) and the Roman geographer Strabo.

The earliest datable colony was established circa 775 B.C.E. by Greeks from the commercial cities of CHALCIS and ERETRIA, in central Greece. It was a trading station on the island of PITHECUSAE, six miles off the Bay of Naples, on the central west coast of ITALY. The location reveals a purely mercantile motive; the settlement was intended as a safe haven for trade with the ETRUSCANS of mainland Italy. Later the Pithecusans crossed to the mainland, to found CUMAE.

In the 730s B.C.E. expeditions from mainland Greece ventured to the fertile east coast of Sicily; NAXOS (2) and ZANCLĒ were founded by Chalcis, and Syracuse by Corinth. By then the colonists were setting sail primarily for farmland. The later 700s B.C.E. saw colonies planted in southern coastal Italy: RHEGIUM (from Chalcis), TARAS (from SPARTA), and SYBARIS and CROTON (from ACHAEA). The colonists' hunger for Italian grainfields is symbolized in the ear-of-wheat emblem on coins minted by the Achaean colony of Metapontum, on the Italian "instep." In time, the entire southern Italian coastline, from "heel" to "toe," became dotted with Greek cities.

The north Aegean coast of THRACE received colonists by the late 700s B.C.E. Ousting the native Thracians, Greeks mainly from Chalcis occupied the region subsequently called the Chalcidian land—CHALCIDICĒ. Not far away, the island of THASOS was occupied by Greeks from the island of Paros. Later colonies on the Thracian coast included ABDERA, AENUS, and AMPHIPOLIS. The region offered farmland and valuable resources for export: grain, TIMBER, SLAVES, SILVER, and GOLD.

Farther east, the Black Sea and its approaches were colonized almost single-handedly by MILETUS. Of perhaps two dozen Milesian colonies here, the most important included SINOPE (founded circa 700 B.C.E.), CYZICUS (circa 675 B.C.E.), and PANTICAPAEUM (late 600s B.C.E.). But the city with the grandest destiny was BYZANTIUM, founded circa 667 B.C.E. by colonists from MEGARA (1). Among the assets of the Black Sea region were the boundless wheatfields of the Ukraine and the metals trade of Asia Minor.

Circa 730 B.C.E. the Corinthians established CORCYRA (modern Corfu) on the northwestern coast of GREECE, 80 miles across the Adriatic from the "heel" of Italy. Later the Corinthians compensated for a Corcyrean rebellion by creating new northwestern colonies, including AMBRACIA, APOLLONIA, and Leucas (630–600 B.C.E.).

The North African Greek city of CYRENE (1), destined for commercial greatness, was founded by colonists from the humble island of THERA, circa 630 B.C.E. To the northwest, Greeks from PHOCAEA endured Carthaginian hostility in order to establish MASSALIA (modern Marseille, in southern France) and other far-western Greek colonies, circa 600 B.C.E.

Like other great endeavors in the ancient world, colonization was a mixture of the utilitarian and the religious. The mother city would appoint an expedition leader, or "oikist" (oikistēs), who would organize the departure, lead the conquest of new land, and rule the new city as king or governor. Before departure, the oikist would seek approval for the project from the god APOLLO's oracle at DELPHI. Apollo was the patron of colonists—one of his titles was Archagetēs, "leader of expeditions"—and several colonies were named for him, including Apollonia on the Adriatic and Apollonia on the Black Sea. He was the only god who could sanction a colonizing expedition, and it was probably by careful politicking that the priesthood at Delphi was able to make its oracle of Apollo more important than any other. In the late 500s B.C.E. a Spartan prince Dorieus set out to found a colony without gaining Delphi's approval; eventually he and his followers were massacred by non-Greeks in western Sicily.

By the 500s B.C.E. colonizing had become regulated as a tool of imperialism, with great powers planting garrison colonies in militarily desirable areas. Athenian designs on the HELLESPONT in the late 500s B.C.E. brought Athenian colonists to Sigeum, in northwest Asia Minor,

and to the Thracian CHERSONESE. The imperial ATHENS of the 400s B.C.E. punished its rebellious subject allies by establishing cleruchies (klērouchiai), which were land-grabbing Athenian colonies that acted as garrisons. Among the states to receive these onerous colonies were Chalcis, AEGINA, and LESBOS.

The use of military colonies was developed in the 330s–320s B.C.E. by Alexander the Great. He established over 70 new cities in the wake of his conquests, including several named ALEXANDRIA (1 and 2). These foundations were intended to settle veterans while also guarding lines of supply. The far-flung Greco-Macedonian settlements—such as the ancient city represented by Greek-style ruins at Aï Kanoun, in northern Afghanistan—played a crucial role in hellenizing the East during the HELLENISTIC AGE (300–150 B.C.E.).

Alexander's successors in EGYPT and the SELEUCID EMPIRE continued his practice of founding garrison settlements, either within the kingdom or along a frontier. The most successful of such foundations was the Seleucid city of ANTIOCH (330 B.C.E.). In many instances, they renamed and gave generous benefactions to existing cities rather than founding entirely new settlements. A major purpose of Hellenistic rulers' colonization was to allow the valuable Greco-Macedonian soldier class to breed and create a new generation to become heavy infantry.

See also BOSPORUS; BRONZE; ILLYRIS; MARMARA, SEA OF; SHIPS AND SEAFARING.

Further reading: Irad Malkin, *Religion and Colonization in Ancient Greece* (Leiden, Netherlands: E. J. Brill, 1987); Carol Dougherty, *The Poetics of Colonization: From City to Text in Archaic Greece* (New York: Oxford University Press, 1993); Jack Cargill, *Athenian Settlements of the Fourth Century B.C.* (Leiden, Netherlands: E. J. Brill, 1995); A. J. Graham, *Collected Papers on Greek Colonization* (Leiden, Netherlands: E. J. Brill, 2001).

comedy *See* THEATER.

commerce *See* TRADE.

Conon *See* KONON.

Corcyra (Greek: Kerkyra) This major Greek city of the Adriatic coast is located on the lush and attractive inshore island now known as Corfu. The city was situated on a peninsula on the island's east coast, opposite the Greek mainland region called EPIRUS. Corcyra was one of the earliest Greek colonies, founded around 734 B.C.E. by settlers from CORINTH.

Located only 80 miles across the Adriatic from the Italian "heel," Corcyra provided a vital anchorage on the coastal TRADE route from Greece to ITALY and SICILY. Corcyra also enjoyed local trade with the Illyrians, a non-Greek people who supplied SILVER ore, TIMBER, SLAVES, tin (for BRONZE making), and wildflowers (for perfume-making). Agriculturally, the island was (and is) known for dense growths of olive trees.

Unlike most Greek colonies, Corcyra rebelled violently against its mother city. In 664 B.C.E., as mentioned by the Athenian historian THUCYDIDES (1), Corcyra and Corinth fought the first sea battle on record; Thucydides neglects to state who won. Around 610 B.C.E., the Corinthian tyrant PERIANDER brought Corcyra temporarily to heel. At some point the two cities cooperated in founding the Adriatic colony of EPIDAMNOS, but Corinth continued to establish its own colonies in the area, partly to guard against Corcyrean hostility.

It was at prosperous Corcyra around 580 B.C.E. that the first large, all-stone Greek building was erected—a temple of ARTEMIS, designed in the newly emerging Doric style. This building has been called the Gorgon temple, on account of its pedimental sculptures showing the Gorgon MEDUSA flanked by beasts. Today the temple survives only in its west pediment, preserved in the Corfu Museum.

Despite having one of the most powerful navies in Greece, Corcyra remained neutral in the PERSIAN WARS. Later its bitter relations with Corinth played a role in igniting the PELOPONNESIAN WAR (431–404 B.C.E.). These events began in 435 B.C.E., when Corcyra was drawn into conflict with Corinth over relations with Epidamnus. A Corcyrean fleet of 80 ships defeated 75 invading Corinthian ships at the Battle of Leukimme, off Corcyra's southeast coast. To defend against retaliation, the Corcyreans allied with the powerful city of ATHENS. The next episode saw 10 Athenian warships ranged alongside 110 Corcyrean ships against a Corinthian fleet of 150. This was the important Battle of Sybota (433 B.C.E.), fought off the mainland near Corcyra and ending in a Corinthian victory. As a consequence of this battle, Corinth urged SPARTA to declare war against Athens.

Corcyra fought in the Peloponnesian War and suffered greatly. The city was being governed as a pro-Athenian DEMOCRACY when a group of Corcyrean right-wingers launched a coup, hoping to swing Corcyra over to the Peloponnesian side. The coup failed, bringing on a gruesome civil war (427–425 B.C.E.). Thucydides' sympathetic but objective description of the Corcyrean *stasis* (civil strife) is one of the great set pieces in his history of the Peloponnesian War (book 3).

Later in the war, Corcyra was a staging base for Athens's disastrous invasion of SYRACUSE (415 B.C.E.). In 410 B.C.E. Corcyra ended its alliance with Athens. But in 375 B.C.E. Corcyra joined the SECOND ATHENIAN LEAGUE as protection against Spartan domination.

With its wealth and strategic position, Corcyra became a bone of contention among the rival dynasts after the death of the Macedonian king ALEXANDER THE GREAT (323 B.C.E.). The city was occupied variously by Macedonians, Syracusans, Epirotes, and Illyrians, before passing to the empire of ROME (229 B.C.E.). It served for many years as a Roman naval base.

See also AGATHOKLES; ARCHITECTURE; COLONIZATION; ILLYRIS; WARFARE, NAVAL.

Further reading: J. B. Wilson, *Athens and Corcyra: Strategy and Tactics in the Peloponnesian War* (Bristol, U.K.: Bristol Classical Press, 1987); Alkestis Spetsieri-Choremi, *Ancient Kerkyra* (Athens: Archaeological Receipts Fund, 1991); Athena Dountsi, *Corfu Island of Colours, Island of Light* (Smyrni, Greece: Topio Publications, 1996); John Melville-Jones, ed., *Studies in the Architecture of Dalmatia and Corfu* (Venice: Filippi, 2001).

Corinna (Korinna) (sixth-fifth centuries B.C.E.?) *Female lyric poet from Tanagra in Boeotia*
Corinna is one of the few female authors known from ancient Greece. Hellenistic and Roman authors believed her to have been a contemporary and rival of the Theban poet PINDAR (ca. 518–438 B.C.E.). Some modern literary scholars, however, date her work as late as the second century B.C.E., since the earliest sources that mention her come from the first century B.C.E.

The Roman traveler Pausanias says that Corinna won a poetry competition against Pindar, and a monument was subsequently erected in her honor. Aelian says that she actually defeated Pindar five times, and that he bitterly called her a sow.

Fragments of Corinna's poetry are preserved on papyrus texts from the Roman era, and these show that she generally wrote on mythological subjects, often focusing on local Boeotian legends. One of her poems, for instance, tells of a singing contest between the personifications of two Boeotian mountains. Her writing, as it is preserved for us, uses a Boeotian dialect and seems to have been elegant but simple and direct in style.

A marble statuette now in the Musée Vivenel at Compiègne, France, is inscribed with the name "Korinna" and depicts a youthful woman holding a scroll. It appears to be a Roman period copy of an original statue from around 320 B.C.E., which would suggest that Corinna could not have lived as late as some scholars believe.

Further reading: Archibald Allen and Jiri Frel, "A Date for Corinna," *Classical Journal* 68 (1972): 26–30; J. M. Snyder, *The Woman and the Lyre. Women Writers in Classical Greece and Rome* (Carbondale: Southern Illinois University Press, 1989); D. Clayman, "Corinna and Pindar," in *Nomodeiktes: Greek Studies in Honor of Martin Oswald,* ed. R. M. Rosen and J. Farrell (Ann Arbor: University of Michigan Press, 1993); W. S. Henderson, "Corinna of Tanagra on Poetry," *Archaeologica Classica* 38 (1995): 29–42; J. Balmer, *Classical Women Poets* (Newcastle-upon-Tyne, U.K.: Bloodaxe Books, 1996); C. Segal, *Aglaia: The Poetry of Alcman, Sappho, Pindar, Baccylides,* *and Corinna* (Lanham, Md.: Rowman, 1998); A. Stewart, "Nuggets: Mining the Texts Again," *American Journal of Archaeology* 102 (1998): 271–282.

Corinth (Greek: Korinthos)

This major city of the northeastern PELOPONNESE was known in antiquity for its manufacturing and seaborne TRADE. Located on the narrow isthmus that connects southern and central Greece, Corinth prospered in large part because of its geography. It guarded the land route along the isthmus, and it controlled harbors on both shores: eastward on the Saronic Gulf and westward on the aptly named Corinthian Gulf. In addition, the city's lofty ACROPOLIS—the "Acrocorinth," a limestone mountain standing just outside the lower town—gave Corinth a nearly impregnable citadel. It was also on top of this peak that the sanctuary to the city's patron goddess, APHRODITE, was located.

The area of ancient Corinth was occupied continuously from the Late Neolithic period through the Bronze and Iron Ages, but no architectural remains from those periods have been discovered. The city's peak of prosperity came in the 600s and early 500s B.C.E., when its international shipping network came to dwarf those of other mainland Greek cities. Although it lost this preeminence to ATHENS in the fifth century B.C.E., Corinth remained a center for commerce and luxury throughout ancient history. Among its most lucrative tourist attractions were the sacred PROSTITUTES that belonged to the Temple of Aphrodite.

The name Korinthos is not originally Greek, containing as it does the *nth* sound that identifies certain words that survive from the language of the pre-Greek inhabitants of Greece. The invading Greek-speaking tribesmen around 2100 B.C.E. took over an existing, pre-Greek settlement and retained the non-Greek name. After the fall of the MYCENAEAN CIVILIZATION, around 1100–1000 B.C.E., the region was inhabited by the DORIAN GREEKS. Later MYTHS connect the Dorian conquest of Corinth with that of ARGOS, farther south.

By the 700s B.C.E., the Dorian city eventually became governed as an ARISTOCRACY, dominated by an endogamous clan called the Bacchiads. It was these rulers, around 700 B.C.E., who commissioned the first Temple of APOLLO at Corinth, one of the earliest Greek buildings to be roofed with terra-cotta tiles. This temple was destroyed around 580 B.C.E. and replaced a generation later with a larger building, seven columns of which remain standing today on the so-called Temple Hill. Because of these important temples, many scholars today consider Corinth to be the birthplace of the monumental ARCHITECTURE that we know as the Doric order; the more elaborate Corinthian order would emerge much later.

Under the Bacchiads, Corinth was the foremost Greek port and manufacturing center, known to HOMER and other poets by the epithet *aphneios,* "wealthy."

Corinthian shipbuilding was renowned. Imports included textiles, worked metal, and carved ivory from the non-Greek kingdoms of western Asia. Exports included POTTERY in the beautiful painted styles now known as Protocorinthian and Corinthian. This pottery dominated all markets from about 700 to 550 B.C.E., when it gradually became superseded by Athenian black-figure ware.

Corinth's exports traveled beyond the Greek world. One avid market was the powerful non-Greek people called the ETRUSCANS, in northern and central ITALY. Excavations at Etruscan sites have revealed immense troves of Corinthian pottery; such remains surely indicate the presence of other export goods that have not survived in the archaeological record, such as perfumes, textiles, and metalwork.

To provide anchorages and local depots along the western trade route, Corinth founded two colonies around 734 B.C.E., both destined to become great cities in their own right: SYRACUSE, on the southeast coast of SICILY, and CORCYRA, on an Adriatic island off the west coast of Greece. Corcyra, however, rebelled against its mother city, and Corinthian-Corcyran hostilities would later be an important cause of the PELOPONNESIAN WAR (431–404 B.C.E.).

Meanwhile, prosperity brought violent political change to Corinth in the seventh century B.C.E., as the middle class chafed under the Bacchiads' monopoly of power. In about 657 B.C.E, a revolution toppled the aristocrats and installed a popular leader, KYPSELOS, as dictator (*tyrannos*). Kypselos usually is considered to be the earliest of the Greek TYRANTS; soon this pattern of revolution swept the other major cities of Greece as well.

Under Kypselos and his son PERIANDER (reigned ca. 625–585 B.C.E.), Corinth prospered and reached new commercial heights. New northwestern colonies—AMBRACIA, APOLLONIA, and others—were founded to develop further the western trade route and guard the approaches to the Corinthian Gulf. With Periander's paving of a five-mile-long dragway across the isthmus's narrowest section, merchant ships could be trundled on trolleys between the eastern and western seas, thus eliminating the long voyage around the Peloponnese and bringing to Corinth a rich revenue in tolls from non-Corinthian shipping. The influential ISTHMIAN GAMES were also instituted around this time.

After Periander's death, his successor was quickly deposed in favor of a constitutional OLIGARCHY that remained Corinth's typical form of government down to Roman times. During the late 500s B.C.E., Athens arose as Corinth's commercial rival. The two cities remained friendly, however, and 40 Corinthian warships fought alongside the Athenian fleet against the invasion of the Persian king XERXES in 480 B.C.E.

By the mid-400s B.C.E., however, Corinth (along with its ally SPARTA) was feeling the threat of an expansionist, democratic Athens. Alarmed by an Athenian alliance with Corcyra (433 B.C.E.), Corinth urged Sparta and the other Peloponnesian states to declare war on Athens. The resulting Peloponnesian War enveloped the Greek world for nearly 30 years and saw Corinthian naval and land troops in many battles. The fighting ended in defeat for Athens and exhaustion of Corinth.

Rebelling from the onerous rule then imposed by Sparta, Corinth fought against its former ally (and alongside Athens, Argos, and other states) in the CORINTHIAN WAR of 395–386 B.C.E. In these troubled years the city also underwent a brief democratic coup. In 338 B.C.E., Corinth shared in the failed defense of Greece against King PHILIP II of MACEDON. Corinth was occupied by a Macedonian garrison and remained a Macedonian holding until 243 B.C.E., when it was liberated by the statesman Aratus for the Achaean League. But in 222 B.C.E., Corinth returned again to Macedonian control.

When the Romans took Greece from the Macedonians in 196 B.C.E., Corinth again became the foremost city of the Achaean League. Greek resistance to Roman interference, however, led to the disastrous Achaean War of 146 B.C.E., in which Corinth was captured and sacked by Roman troops led by consul Lucius Mummius. The Roman senate decreed that the city should be burned down and its art treasures be either sold or carried off to Rome. This pillaged art is said to have increased the Greek influence on the emerging Roman imperial culture. The city experienced a period of depopulation and depression until 44 B.C.E., when it was refounded as a Roman colony under the direction of Julius Caesar.

Historians usually consider the destruction of Corinth in 146 B.C.E.—and the associated annexing of ACHAEA as part of a Roman province—as the end of the ancient Greek world. Although other Greek cities thrived under Roman rule and Corinth itself eventually revived, mainland Greece as a political entity had ceased to exist. Greece had become part of ROME.

Travelers and archaeologists became interested in the site of ancient Corinth at an early date, since the ruins of the Temple of Apollo have remained visible since antiquity. The area surrounding the temple has been extensively excavated under the auspices of the American School of Classical Studies at Athens ever since 1896. Artifacts from the site are kept in the Corinth Museum, and results from the excavations have been published in the ongoing Corinth series and in the scholarly journals *Hesperia* and the *American Journal of Archaeology*.

See also BELLEROPHON; COINAGE; COLONIZATION; GREECE, GEOGRAPHY OF; HOPLITE; LELANTINE WAR.

Further reading: Mario A. Del Chiaro, ed., *Corinthiaca: Studies in Honor of Darrell A. Amyx* (Columbia: University of Missouri Press, 1986); Elizabeth Langridge-Noti, *A Corinthian Scrapbook: One Hundred Years of American Excavations in Ancient Corinth* (Athens: Lycabettus Press, 1996); Richard Rothaus, *Corinth, the First City of Greece:*

An Urban History of Late Antique Cult and Religion (Leiden, Netherlands: E. J. Brill, 2000); Charles K. Williams II and Nancy Bookidis, eds., *Corinth, the Centenary, 1896–1996* (Princeton, N.J.: American School of Classical Studies at Athens, 2003).

Corinthian order   *See* ARCHITECTURE.

Corinthian War   This name is given by modern historians to the conflict of 395–386 B.C.E., fought between SPARTA (with its allies) and an alliance of CORINTH, ATHENS, BOEOTIA, ARGOS, EUBOEA, and the kingdom of PERSIA. The grand alliance was remarkable for combining traditional enemies in a united campaign against Spartan supremacy. This anti-Spartan axis introduces the politics of the next generation, when the Boeotian city of THEBES would emerge to challenge and finally defeat Sparta (371 B.C.E.).

The background of the Corinthian War is Sparta's victory over Athens in the huge PELOPONNESIAN WAR (404 B.C.E.), which marked the beginning of Sparta's oppressive rule over all the Greek states, former friend and foe alike. Claiming also to protect and rule the Greek cities of ASIA MINOR, Sparta came into conflict with the Persian king Artaxerxes II (399–395 B.C.E.). As a result, Persian funds became available for the anti-Spartan alliance in Greece.

The course of the war is described in the account titled *Hellenica*, by the Athenian historian XENOPHON (who was present at some of the events). The Spartan general LYSANDER invaded Boeotia at the head of a Spartan-allied army, but was defeated and killed by the Thebans at the Battle of Haliartus (395 B.C.E.). The next summer the Spartans defeated an allied army in battle outside Corinth, but this was counterbalanced when a Spartan fleet was destroyed by the Athenian admiral KONON, leading a Persian-Athenian fleet at the Battle of KNIDOS, off the coast of Asia Minor (394 B.C.E.).

Meanwhile, the Spartan king AGESILAOS, summoned home from campaigning against Persian land forces in Asia Minor, led his army along the north Aegean coastline into northeastern Greece. Descending southward, he invaded Boeotia. At the desperate Battle of Coronea (394 B.C.E.), Agesilaus narrowly defeated an allied army but then withdrew southward toward Sparta without attacking any Boeotian cities.

Thereafter the war became bogged down with maneuverings around Corinth and Argos. In around 392 B.C.E. Corinth, traditionally an OLIGARCHY, underwent a short-lived democratic coup. But the most important event of the war was its ending: The fighting stopped in 386 B.C.E., when Persia withdrew its support after King Artaxerxes II had negotiated a separate peace with Sparta. According to this treaty, known as the KING'S PEACE, Sparta ceded the Greek cities of Asia Minor and CYPRUS back to Persian control. This notorious treaty unmasked Sparta once and for all as an oppressive power, bent on dominating mainland Greece even at the cost of selling out the eastern Greek cities. The rise of Thebes in the following years was buoyed partly by widespread anger at this treaty.

See also EPAMINONDAS; IONIA.

Further reading: Charles D. Hamilton, *Sparta's Bitter Victories: Politics and Diplomacy in the Corinthian War* (Ithaca, N.Y.: Cornell University Press, 1979); John Buckler, *Aegean Greece in the Fourth Century* B.C.E. (Leiden, Netherlands: E. J. Brill, 2003).

council   Evidence in HOMER's epic poems and in the LINEAR B tablets indicates that a council (*boulē*) of king's advisers was an important facet of government in primitive Greek societies (around 1600–1000 B.C.E.). As the age of kings gave way to the age of ARISTOCRACY (around 1000–600 B.C.E.), a Greek city-state's council more or less became the government, combining legislative, executive, and judiciary powers. In this era ATHENS was governed by an aristocratic council called the AREOPAGOS, whose several hundred members, probably serving for life, were drawn exclusively from the city's narrow circle of noble families.

The democratic reforms of KLEISTHENES (1) (ca. 508 B.C.E.) removed the Areopagos from the heart of government in Athens and created instead a council of 500 members selected annually from upper- and middle-income citizens. (By the late 400s B.C.E., lower-income citizens apparently were admitted.) Under the Athenian DEMOCRACY of the 400s and 300s B.C.E., the council had important legislative and executive duties but was always subordinate to the sovereign ASSEMBLY of citizens.

The most important job of the Athenian council was to prepare the agenda for the 40 assembly meetings each year. Specifically, the council drafted the proposals to be debated at the next assembly—apparently the assembly could vote only on proposals prepared beforehand by the council. Council meetings might include debate and voting, the hearing of citizens' petitions, the summoning of witnesses, and other information-gathering, for which the council had high authority. Like the assembly, the council had judicial duties. The councillors could act as judge and jury in trying cases of certain state offenses, such as misconduct by officials.

The council also served as an executive body, responsible for the enactment and enforcement of the assembly's decisions and for much of the day-to-day running of the state. The council received foreign ambassadors, had responsibility for the care of public buildings, and oversaw the construction of new warships and the maintenance of the fleets and dockyards for Athens's all-important navy. The council seems to have been especially important in administering finances: Among other duties, it audited the books of all outgoing officials who had handled public funds.

The citizens who served on the council were not career politicians or public servants, but rather were amateurs fulfilling a public duty not so different from our modern jury duty. The 500 council members for the year were selected by lot, in procedures at the 139 local city wards, or DEMES (*dēmoi*). Only male citizens over the age of 30 were eligible—there, as everywhere else in the Athenian government, WOMEN were excluded. By the late 400s B.C.E., councillors were receiving state pay for their service. (This important provision, enabling less-wealthy citizens to serve, probably began in around 457 B.C.E. amid the left-wing reforms of EPHIALTES and PERIKLES.)

Each new council began its term in midsummer, at the start of the Athenian year. Aside from festivals and days of ill omen, the members met daily, usually in the council chamber in the AGORA. By nature of its selection, the council always consisted of 10 50-man contingents from the 10 Athenian tribes. Each of these 50-man groups took one turn, through the year, as the council's presiding official, or *prytaneis*.

Although Athens is the place for which we have the most information about the workings of the government and the council, almost every ancient Greek city-state had a council, with similar responsibilities and powers. At Sparta, for instance, the government was nominally a joint monarchy. There was also a council that consisted of the two kings plus 28 aristocrats, all of whom were retired from military service (thus over 60 years old). Sparta also had an assembly that consisted of all the Spartan males; this group selected the members of the council and approved or vetoed council motions. Above all in terms of power, however, was a small group of five men, known as the ephorate, which ultimately had supreme control over all the other governmental branches. Councils probably played similar roles in other nondemocracies, maintaining a secondary importance to the omnipotent tyrant, dictator, or monarch.

See also LAW AND LAW COURTS; POLIS.

Further reading: John Thorley, *Athenian Democracy* (London: Routledge, 1996).

cremation   *See* FUNERAL CUSTOMS.

Crete   The largest and southernmost island of the AEGEAN SEA, Crete is long and thin in shape—about 160 miles long and 30–40 miles wide—and on a map it extends horizontally east-west. The island's western shore lies only about 65 miles southeast of the mainland Greek PELOPONNESE and about 200 miles northeast of the Libyan coast. Crete's eastern shore is 130 miles from the coast of ASIA MINOR. Due partly to this dominant position on the sea routes linking the Aegean with the Egyptian and Near Eastern worlds, Crete in the late third millennium B.C.E. gave birth to a brilliant BRONZE AGE culture, the MINOAN CIVILIZATION. The Minoans were not Greeks, but they are considered as marking the start of Greek prehistory, since they deeply influenced the emerging Greek MYCENAEAN CIVILIZATION of the mainland.

The traditional Greek name Krētē is not a genuine Greek word and may reflect the vanished language of the Minoans. Crete's terrain rises in mountainous humps, peaking at 8,000 feet mid-island at Mt. Ida and in the west at the White Mountains. Limestone formations include caves, some of which housed important religious cults in antiquity. Arable land is found in small lowland pockets, where olives, grapes, and grain were farmed, and the many upland plateaus offered grazing for livestock. Mountain TIMBER provided shipbuilding material and a prized export.

Ancient populations tended to favor the warmer and drier eastern half of the island, especially the flatter north coast. ARCHAEOLOGY reveals that the humans first came to Crete in the Neolithic era, around 5000 B.C.E. These seaborne pioneers, coming perhaps from the Levant, brought the island's first pigs, sheep, and cattle. Newcomers arrived around 2900 B.C.E., possibly from Asia Minor, bringing BRONZE weapons to Crete and intermarrying with the existing people. From this fusion there arose, around 2200 B.C.E., the Minoan civilization, the earliest great nation on European soil. The seafaring Minoans traded with EGYPT and the Levant, and dominated the Aegean.

The Minoan kings' capital was the north-central city of KNOSSOS, inland of the modern seaport of Irakleion. At Knossos in 1900 C.E. the British archaeologist Sir Arthur Evans discovered the remnants of an elaborate palace complex, begun in around 1950 B.C.E. and reaching its existing form in around 1700 B.C.E. Other surviving Minoan monuments on Crete include the palace at Phaistos (mid south coast, across the island from Knossos), the villas at Hagia Triada (Phaistos, harbor town), the palace at Mallia (eastern north coast), and the remnants of a Minoan town at Gournia (eastern north coast). Current knowledge of the Minoans comes largely from the archaeology of these sites. Minoan artworks found in excavation are collected in the Irakleion archaeological museum.

The Minoan sites on Crete tell a tale of vigorous construction after 1950 B.C.E. and of fiery ruin in around 1400 B.C.E. or soon after. The cause of this simultaneous destruction was probably an invasion of Crete by Mycenaean Greeks from the mainland. Oddly, the Mycenaeans seem to have abandoned Crete after the palaces' destruction.

In around 1000 B.C.E. a new people occupied the island. These were the DORIAN GREEKS, who had previously invaded southward through mainland Greece, overrunning the Peloponnese and continuing their conquests by sea. For the rest of antiquity, Crete remained a Dorian-Greek island, with governmental and social institutions that resembled those at SPARTA.

Dorian Crete was divided into city-states governed as military aristocracies. The chief of these were Knossos, CORTYN (in the south-central island), and, later, Kydonia (modern Khania, on the western north coast). As was the case at Sparta, Dorian-Greek nobles ruled over a population of rural serfs—probably the descendants of the subjugated non-Dorians.

The island was active in the seaborne expansion of the Greek world in the later 700s and 600s B.C.E. Cretan colonists helped to found the city of GELA, in southeastern SICILY, and Cretan workshops exported an admired

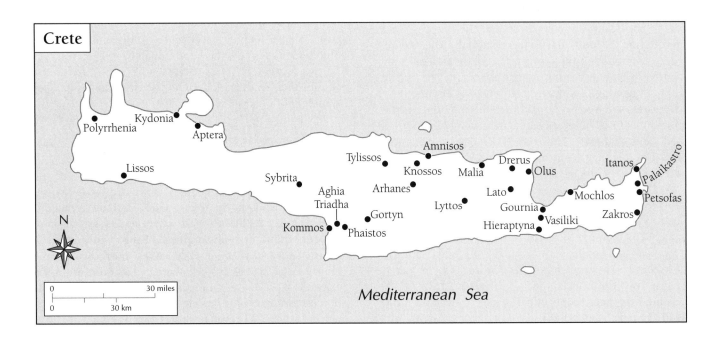

Geometric-style POTTERY and contributed to the style of statuary now known as Daedalic. But gradually the Cretan cities withdrew into isolation, and Crete declined amid internal conflicts, mainly between Knossos and Gortyn. By the late 200s B.C.E. the island had become notorious as a haunt of pirates. Order was restored by the Romans, who annexed Crete in 67 B.C.E. and made it part of a Roman province.

The Cretans were the best archers in the Greek world (where archery was generally not practiced), and many Greek armies from the 400s B.C.E. onward employed Cretan bowmen as mercenaries. Cretans also had the reputation of being liars.

The RELIGION of Dorian Crete was distinguished by certain cults and beliefs that probably contained pre-Greek, Minoan elements. It was said that the great god ZEUS, as a baby, had been hidden in a cave on Crete's Mt. Dicte to save him from his malevolent father, CRONUS. More amazing to classical Greeks was the Cretans' claim that the immortal Zeus was born and died annually on Crete and that his tomb could be seen at Knossos. This "Zeus" may have been the surviving form of a mythical son or consort of the prehistoric Minoan mother goddess.

See also ARISTOCRACY; ARTEMIS; ATLANTIS; COLONIZATION; GREEK LANGUAGE; HELOTS; ROME; SCULPTURE; SHIPS AND SEAFARING.

Further reading: Adam Hopkins, *Crete: Its Past, Present, and People* (London: Faber, 1977); Manolis Andronikos, *Herakleion Museum and Archaeological Sites of Crete* (Athens: Ekdotike Athenon, 1985); J. Wilson Myers, Eleanor Emlen Myers, and Gerald Cadogan, *The Aerial Atlas of Ancient Crete* (Berkeley: University of California Press, 1992); Jan Driessen and Colin F. Macdonald, *The Troubled Island: Minoan Crete Before and After the Santorini Eruption* (Austin: University of Texas at Austin, Program in Aegean Scripts and Prehistory, 1997); Yannis Hamilakis, *Labyrinth Revisited: Rethinking 'Minoan' Archaeology* (Oxford: Oxbow Books, 2002).

Croesus (Greek: Kroisos) (ca. 595–520 B.C.E.) *Last king of* LYDIA, *a powerful non-Greek nation of west-central* ASIA MINOR

Croesus inherited the throne at age 35 from his father, Alyattes, and reigned ca. 560–546 B.C.E., until his country was conquered by the Persian king CYRUS (1).

Croesus' wealth was proverbial. Friendly toward the Greek world, he was a patron of the god APOLLO's shrine at DELPHI and was the first foreign ruler to form an alliance with a mainland Greek state, SPARTA. Closer to home, he subdued the Greek cities of western Asia Minor, but dealt benevolently with them as subjects.

On his eastern frontier he met disaster. Seeking to conquer east-central Asia Minor from the Persians, Croesus led an army across the River Halys, the border between Lydia and the Persian domain. After an inconse-

Head and shoulders of the Anavyssos Croesus. Croesus reigned around 560–546 B.C.E. over the kingdom of Lydia. *(Alison Frantz Photographic Collection, American School of Classical Studies at Athens)*

quential battle against King Cyrus, Croesus returned to Lydia, where Cyrus, following quickly, defeated and captured him. Croesus's subsequent fate is unknown. One legend says he was carried off by his divine protector Apollo to safety in the magical land of the Hyperboreans.

Like other Eastern despots, Croesus inspired the Greek imagination. The tales told about him by the historian HERODOTUS (ca. 435 B.C.E.) are a fascinating mix of fact and storytelling. With his grand style and sudden fall, Croesus represented for the Greeks a real-life example of HUBRIS—excessive pride that leads to a divinely prompted blunder in judgment, which leads to disaster.

One legend claims that, at the height of Croesus's reign, he was visited by the Athenian sage SOLON. Croesus asked Solon to name the happiest man he had ever seen, expecting to hear himself named, but Solon explained to Croesus that no man may be called "happy" until he is dead; before then, he is merely lucky. This Greek proverb later reappears at the end of SOPHOKLES' tragedy *Oedipus the King*.

The best-known story tells how, before his campaign against PERSIA, Croesus consulted the Delphic Oracle. He was advised that if he crossed the Halys River he would destroy a mighty empire. Heartened by this prophecy, he decided to march. Unfortunately, the mighty empire destroyed turned out to be his own.

See also MIDAS; PROPHECY AND DIVINATION.

Further reading: G. M. A. Hanfmann, "On the Palace of Croesus," in *Festschrift für Frank Brommer,* edited by Ursula Höckmann and Antje Krug (Mainz am Rhein, Germany: Philip von Zabern, 1977), 145–154; H. W. Park, "Croesus and Delphi," *Greek, Roman, and Byzantine Studies* 25 (1984): 208–232; H. I. Flower, "Herodotus and Delphic Traditions about Croesus," in *Georgica: Greek Studies in Honor of George Cawkwell,* edited by Michael A. Flower and Mark Toher (London: University of London, Institute of Classical Studies, 1991), 57–77; Andrew Ramage and Paul Craddock, *King Croesus' Gold: Excavations at Sardis and the History of Gold Refining* (Cambridge, Mass.: Harvard University Press for the Archaeological Exploration of Sardis, 2000); F. Hartog, "Myth into Logos. The case of Croesus, or the Historian at Work," in *From Myth to Reason? Studies in the Development of Greek Thought,* edited by Richard Buxton, 2d ed. (New York: Oxford University Press, 2001), 183–195.

Cronus (Greek: Kronos) In MYTH, the primeval king of the TITANS and father of ZEUS and other gods. According to HESIOD's epic poem the *Theogony,* Cronus was born to GAEA (Mother Earth) and Uranus (Ouranos, "Sky"). On his mother's advice, Cronus castrated his father with a sickle and ruled in his place.

Cronus married his own sister, Rhea, who bore him the gods HESTIA, DEMETER, HERA, HADES, POSEIDON, and, last, Zeus. But Cronus had been warned that his offspring would subdue him, and so he swallowed each newborn child. Finally, at Zeus's birth, Rhea tricked her husband—presenting him with a stone wrapped in swaddling clothes—and spirited the infant off to CRETE. Eventually Cronus was made to vomit up all his swallowed children, who (still alive) followed Zeus in revolt against their father. A different vein of legend, at odds with this grim picture, described Cronus as supervising a time of innocence and blessing—if not in heaven, at least on earth. Cronus's reign was said to have marked the Golden Age of human history, when people lived without greed, violence, toil, or need for laws.

The name seems to have no meaning in the Greek language. Like other elements of the Greek Creation myths, the Cronus story may have derived from non-Greek, Near Eastern sources. Specifically, it resembles the tale of the Mesopotamian god Kumarbi, which was current in the second millennium B.C.E. Modern scholars believe that the Cronus myth may have come to Greece via the Phoenicians, with whom the Greeks had extensive trading contacts in 900–700 B.C.E.

At classical ATHENS there was a feast of Cronus, the Kronia, celebrated in midsummer, just after the Greek New Year. The Kronia was probably a harvest festival, and Cronus was often portrayed in art as carrying a sickle, the harvester's tool. (The sickle also was the weapon he used to castrate his father.)

The primitive figure of Cronus was the object of attempted rationalization during the Athenian Enlightenment of the 400s–300s B.C.E. A theory claimed that his name was not really Kronos but rather Chronos, "time," and that his myth of impious violence to father and children was simply an allegory for the ravages of time. This confused interpretation created an image that, surviving 2,500 years, can be seen every New Year's—old Father Time, holding his emblematic sickle.

See also PHOENICIA; RELIGION.

Further reading: M. van der Valk, "On the God Cronus," *Greek, Roman, and Byzantine Studies* 26 (1985): 5–11; Samuel L. Macey, *Patriarchs of Time: Dualism in Saturn-Cronus, Father Time, the Watchmaker God, and Father Christmas* (Athens: University of Georgia Press, 1987).

Croton (Greek: Kroton; modern Crotone) This important Greek city is situated on the southern rim of the Gulf of Taranto, on the "sole" of south ITALY. Located high above a small double harbor, near fertile farmland, Croton was founded by colonists from ACHAEA, probably around 710 B.C.E. The city carved out a sizable domain at the expense of the local Italian inhabitants, the Brutii.

Around 530 B.C.E., the Samian-born philosopher PYTHAGORAS founded his mystical school of study at Croton and apparently helped to run the city government, as an OLIGARCHY. By the late 500s B.C.E., prosperous Croton had a famous school of MEDICINE, producing, among others, the philosopher-physician Alcmaeon. Another distinguished citizen of the day was Milon the Strongman, a champion in WRESTLING at the OLYMPIC and PYTHIAN GAMES. Several other athletes from Croton also achieved great success in these Panhellenic festivals from 588 B.C.E. onward.

The city's zenith came in 510 B.C.E., when it destroyed its archrival, the Italian Greek city SYBARIS. But Croton soon was weakened by conflicts with two other Italian Greek cities, RHEGION and LOCRI, and with the Brutii. Croton was captured and plundered in 379 B.C.E. by the Syracusan ruler DIONYSIUS (1). Exhausted by the wars that accompanied ROME's expansion through Italy in the 300s and 200s B.C.E., Croton eventually became a Roman subject state.

Just outside the city, on the coast, is located the important Sanctuary to Hera Lacinia, one column of which remains standing today. This Doric temple reached its height in the fifth century B.C.E.; later it was sacked by the Syracusan tyrant Dionysus and, afterward, by the Romans. Much of the structure was reused as building material by inhabitants from the Roman era and later. No other remains from the Greek period at Croton are visible, but a few buildings from the Roman period have been located in the Hera sanctuary. Many artifacts were excavated there and are now on display in the Crotone National Archaeology Museum.

Further reading: W. L. Gale, *The Sacred Tripod: Kroton and Its Coins* (Mosman, N.S.W.: Ocean Spray Pty., 1995); Roberto Spadea, *The Treasures of Hera: Magna Grecian Antiquities from Southern Italy* (Milan: Edizioni ET, 1998).

Cumae (Greek: Kume) This ancient Greek city of Campania, on the west coast of ITALY, is located just north of the Bay of Naples, 10 miles west of modern-day Naples.

Cumae was one of the earliest datable Greek colonies, established by Euboean Greeks who moved ashore from their nearby island holding of PITHECUSAE around 750 B.C.E. One story claims that the new city included eastern Greek settlers who named it for their native CYMĒ, in ASIA MINOR.

The founding of Italian Cumae marks an early milestone in Greek COLONIZATION, namely the decision by a band of Greeks to make a first landing on the Italian coast. Possibly they went ashore at the invitation of the ETRUSCANS, a powerful Italian people who were avid consumers of Greek goods and who had a stronghold at nearby Capua.

Cumae thrived, supplying the Etruscans with Corinthian painted POTTERY, Euboean worked BRONZE, and other wares. It sent out colonists of its own, founding ZANCLĒ (modern Messina, in SICILY, around 725 B.C.E.) and Neapolis ("new city," modern Naples, around 600 B.C.E.), among other settlements. As a northern outpost of Greek culture in Italy, Cumae played a crucial role in the hellenization of the Etruscans.

But Cumae's relations with the Etruscans eventually worsened, and in the late 500s B.C.E. the Cumaean leader Aristodemus twice defeated Etruscan armies (and then made himself tyrant of the city). In 474 B.C.E. in alliance with the Syracusan tyrant HIERON (1), Cumae won a great sea battle against the Etruscans and crushed their power. But in 421 B.C.E. the city fell to another Italian people, the Samnites, and later passed to the Romans. Throughout antiquity Cumae was known for its oracle, told by a priestess called the Sibyl.

The Sibyl of Cumae was a beautiful mortal woman who obtained her oracular powers after the god APOLLO became attracted to her and offered to grant any wish if she would spend a night with him. She asked that she might live for as many years as grains of sand she could squeeze into her hand. Apollo agreed, but Sibyl reneged and rejected his advances. She was therefore cursed with the literal fulfillment of her wish—eternal life but not eternal youth. She got older and older, eventually shriveling into a tiny, frail body that was confined in a jar or a cage. She did not need to eat or to drink, since she could not die of hunger or of thirst. She hung from the branch of a tree at the mouth of a cave and stayed there, uttering occasional oracles to those who approached. The Romans kept a sacred collection of her prophecies in their primary temple, the Capitolium.

European travelers and archaeologists began to explore Cumae in the middle of the nineteenth century C.E., hoping to discover the actual site of the Cumaean oracle, which had been described in sources from the fourth century C.E. It was thought several times to have been found until finally, in 1932, the Italian archaeologist Amadeo Maiuri discovered a long, trapezoidal-shaped tunnel that seems to correspond to the late antique description of the Sibyl's grotto. The identification of this tunnel remains controversial, however, and some archaeologists believe instead that it served a military function.

See also PROPHECY AND DIVINATION; ROME; TYRANTS.

Further reading: Raymond Schoder, *Ancient Cumae* (New York: Scientific American, 1963); A. G. MacKay, *Ancient Campania* (Hamilton, Ont.: Vergilian Society, 1972); H. W. Parke, *Sibyls and Sibylline Prophecy in Classical Antiquity,* edited by B. C. McGing (London: Routledge, 1988).

Cyclades This group of islands in the AEGEAN SEA roughly forms a circle, *kuklos,* around the holy isle of DELOS. Aside from Delos, the major Cyclades were Naxos (1), Paros, Andros, Keos, THERA, and MELOS. All the islands are mountainous and arid, with little good agricultural land. Only Naxos and Melos have enough pasture area to produce and export sheep and goat milk cheeses. Some of the Cyclades (Santorini, Melos) are volcanic in origin. Most of them had an economy based on seafaring and trade. They provided convenient ports of call for ships en route from Greece to Asia Minor, and major trading harbors emerged at islands such as Delos and Syros.

Naxos, the largest and most fertile of the Cyclades, was known in antiquity for its WINE and its associated worship of the god DIONYSUS. It also was home to an important school of SCULPTURE from the Archaic period onward. In its marble quarries, archaeologists have found several colossal male statues (kouroi), unfinished and abandoned. Paros was even more famous for its high-quality marble, prized in the 500s and 400s B.C.E. as a material for sculpture due to its fine grain. Melos is perhaps best known today as the spot where the Louvre Museum's statue of APHRODITE (the Venus de Milo) was found. In antiquity, this volcanic island was an important source of obsidian, desired for making blades and other cutting tools as early as 2000 B.C.E.

The Cyclades enjoyed a flourishing civilization in the third and second millennia B.C.E., well before the Greeks arrived. Archaeological evidence such as surviving POTTERY gives a picture of two-way TRADE with Minoan CRETE. By 1600 B.C.E. these pre-Greek Cyclades had come under direct control of Crete. After 1400 B.C.E. the Cyclades seem to have been ruled by Mycenaean Greeks from the mainland. Before 1000 B.C.E. most of the Cyclades were occupied by migrating IONIAN GREEKS. For the main centuries of Greek history, the Cyclades were inhabited by ethnic Ionian Greeks; of the principal islands, only Melos and Thera were settled by DORIAN GREEKS.

The Cyclades fell to the invading Persians in 490 B.C.E., Naxos, resisting, was ravaged. At the end of the PERSIAN WARS, most of the islands joined the DELIAN LEAGUE, headquartered at Delos but led by ATHENS (478 B.C.E.). The league died with Athens' defeat in the PELOPONNESIAN WAR (404 B.C.E.), but by 377 B.C.E. most of the islands had joined the SECOND ATHENIAN LEAGUE. With the rest of Greece, they passed into the hands of the Macedonian king PHILIP II in 338 B.C.E. During the HELLENISTIC AGE (300–150 B.C.E.), the Cyclades were a bone of contention mainly between the Greek dynasties of MACEDON and EGYPT. In the mid-100s B.C.E. they passed to the domain of ROME.

Further reading: R. L. N. Barber, *The Cyclades in the Bronze Age* (Iowa City: University of Iowa Press, 1987); Ann-Louise Schallin, *Islands Under Influence: The Cyclades in the Late Bronze Age and the Nature of Mycenaean Presence* (Göteborg, Sweden: Paul Aströms Förlag, 1993); Pat Getz-Gentle, *Stone Vessels of the Cyclades in the Early Bronze Age* (University Park, Pa.: Pennsylvania State University Press, 1996); Martin van Schaik, *The Marble Harp Players from the Cyclades* (Utrecht: Dutch Study Group on Music Archaeology, 1998); Cyprian Broodbank, *An Island Archaeology of the Early Cyclades* (New York: Cambridge University Press, 2000).

Cyclops (plural: Cyclopes)   A type of mythical, gigantic, semihuman monster, first described in HOMER's epic poem the *Odyssey* (written down around 750 B.C.E.). The name Kuklops, "round eye," refers to the one large eye that such creatures had in midforehead. Descended from the earth goddess GAEA and her husband, Uranus (Ouranos, "Sky"), the Cyclopes dwelt in a distant land (sometimes identified as eastern SICILY), with no cities or laws. The *Odyssey* (book 9) describes the hero ODYSSEUS's violent encounter with the Cyclops POLYPHEMOS.

A slightly different tradition, presented in HESIOD's epic poem the *Theogony* (ca. 700 B.C.E.), made the Cyclopes a guild of supernatural, one-eyed blacksmiths, who forged thunderbolts for the great god ZEUS. These Cyclopes were associated with the smith god, HEPHAISTOS. The classical Greeks ascribed to the Cyclopes the building of certain ancient walls made of huge blocks without mortar, such as the walls at TIRYNS. In reality, these had been built by Mycenaean Greeks around 1300 B.C.E., but to later generations they looked like the work of giants. The term cyclopean was used to describe such masonry.

See also MYCENAEAN CIVILIZATION.

Further reading: Bernard Evslin, *The Cyclopes* (New York: Chelsea House, 1987); Warcwick Hutton, *Odysseus and the Cyclops* (New York: M. K. McElderry Books, 1995); Anne F. Rockwell, *The One-Eyed Giant and Other Monsters from the Greek Myths* (New York: Greenwillow Books, 1996); Judith Kazantzis, trans., *In Cyclops' Cave: The Odyssey Book IV Lines 105–566/Homer* (Warwick, U.K.: Greville, 2002).

Cylon   *See* KYLON.

Cyme   *See* KYME.

Cynics   The English words *cynic* and *cynicism* describe an informal, embittered frame of mind. But the original Cynics comprised a major Greek philosophical movement, which arose in the early 300s B.C.E. The name Kunikoi, "doglike," derived from one of the movement's pioneers, DIOGENES of SINOPE (400–325 B.C.E.), whose austere and immodest way of life won him the nickname the Dog (Kuon). Unlike other philosophies, Cynicism was never organized around a formal place of study. Although overshadowed in the 200s B.C.E. by two new and partly derivative schools of thought, STOICISM and EPICUREANISM, Cynicism nevertheless continued to attract a following in response to the spiritual crisis in the HELLENISTIC AGE (300–150 B.C.E.). In the first century C.E. the cities of the Roman Empire teemed with traveling Cynic beggars.

The Cynics taught a radical doctrine of moral self-sufficiency. They renounced wealth and social convention, preferring to go homeless, do no work, wear simple clothes or rags, and avoid such niceties as finding privacy before relieving themselves. They sought knowledge and harmony through a liberation from materialism. But, far from withdrawing to live as hermits, they chose to dwell in cities and (often) to travel from city to city, preaching. They would sermonize and hold philosophical discussions on streetcorners and were notorious for their outspokenness. Their lampoons against vice and pride were often directed personally against passersby.

The movement's roots lay with the Athenian philosopher SOCRATES (469–399 B.C.E.). Although not himself a Cynic, Socrates was known for his austerity and his habit of questioning people on the street. After Socrates' death, one of his followers, Antisthenes, an Athenian, lived in exaggerated imitation of Socrates' plain living. In a modified Socratic belief, Antisthenes taught that happiness comes from personal virtue (*aretē*), not from pleasure, and that the best virtue comes from triumph over hardship.

Antisthenes was the first Cynic, but the movement's most famous master was Diogenes, who began as Antisthenes' pupil. Other important Cynics included Bion of Borysthenes and Menippus of Gadara (early 200s B.C.E.); Menippus adapted the Cynics' haranguing speaking style to a written form that was a precursor of the literary satire later produced by the Romans.

With their doctrine of self-improvement through painful effort, the Cynics revered the mythical hero HERAKLES, whose twelve Labors were seen as an ideal example of moral victory and self-liberation.

See also PHILOSOPHY; POLIS.

Further reading: Donald R. Dudley, *A History of Cynicism from Diogenes to the 6th Century A.D.*, reprint (Chicago: Ares, 1980, 1937); Luis Navia, *The Philosophy of Cynicism: An Annotated Bibliography* (Westport, Conn.: Greenwood Press, 1995); Luis Navia, *Classical Cynicism: A Critical Study* (Westport, Conn.: Greenwood Press, 1996); R. Bracht-Branham and Marie-Odile Goulet-Caze, eds., *The Cynics: The Cynic Movement in Antiquity and its Legacy* (Berkeley: University of California Press, 1996); Luis Navia, *Diogenes of Sinope: The Man in the Tub* (Westport, Conn.: Greenwood Press, 1998).

Cyprus This large eastern Mediterranean island, 140 miles long, was an eastern frontier of the Greek world. Located 60 miles off the coast of northern Syria and 50 miles south of ASIA MINOR's southern coast, Cyprus played a vital role in TRADE warfare between East and West. The island's Oriental contacts and remoteness from mainland Greece gave rise to a distinctive, sometimes peculiar, Greek culture.

As shown by ARCHAEOLOGY, the island was host to a flourishing non-Greek civilization, derived from Asia Minor, during the first half of the second millennium B.C.E. After about 1400 B.C.E. Cyprus was intensively colonized by Mycenaean Greeks from mainland Greece. What lured them to Cyprus was copper—the major component of the alloy BRONZE, upon the Mycenaeans depended for war and FARMING. Cyprus had the richest copper deposits in the eastern Mediterranean; the English word *copper* comes from the Latin term *Cyprium aes,* "the Cypriot metal." A copper ingot eventually became the island's emblem on COINAGE.

Greek Cyprus was largely undisturbed by the collapse of MYCENAEAN CIVILIZATION in mainland Greece (around 1200–1000 B.C.E.). The island's spoken Greek dialect, unaffected by any change or immigration, retained certain characteristics of old Mycenaean Greek. Other Mycenaean survivals included the Cypriot Syllabary (as it is now called), a primitive form of writing using pictograms, employed on Cyprus around 700–200 B.C.E.

In the 800s B.C.E. the seafaring Phoenicians, seeking copper and shipping stations, established a stronghold in southeast Cyprus: Kart Hadasht, "new city," called Kition by the Greeks and Kittim in the Bible. The Phoenicians, in steady conflict with the Greeks, remained a powerful presence and later served as puppets of the Persian overlords. Meanwhile Cyprus became a place where Greeks

could observe and imitate Phoenician shipbuilding, trade techniques, and religious beliefs. The Phoenician cult of ADONIS may have reached Greece by way of Cyprus, as probably did a more important religious borrowing from the Near East—the cult of the goddess APHRODITE.

The Cypriot Greeks became expert seafarers. By 700 B.C.E. their population was centered in eight cities, roughly ringing the island's east-south-west perimeter. Each city had its own king; foremost of these Greek cities was Salamis (often called Cypriot Salamis, to distinguish it from the island near ATHENS). Located on a hospitable bay on Cyprus's east coast, site of modern Famagusta, Salamis commanded the shipping run to north Syria. The ninth city of Cyprus was Phoenician Citium; in later centuries it became partially Greek.

In 525 B.C.E. Cyprus submitted to the conquering Persians. As Persian subjects, the Cypriots—both Greeks and Phoenicians—supplied warships and crews for their overlords' campaigns. The Cypriot Greeks joined the IONIAN REVOLT against Persian rule but were defeated (ca. 497 B.C.E.). Modern archaeology at the southwest city of Paphos has uncovered the lower levels of an ancient Persian siege mound, littered with hundreds of bronze arrowheads—the remnants of Greek defensive arrow volleys from the city's walls.

In the mid-400s B.C.E. Cyprus was a bone of contention between the Persians and imperial Athens. The Athenian commander KIMON had begun a large-scale attempt to liberate Cyprus when he died there (450 B.C.E.), and the island relapsed into Persian-Phoenician control, despite the hellenic cultural program of the dynamic king Evagoras of Salamis (ca. 411 B.C.E.). By the terms of the KING'S PEACE (386 B.C.E.), the mainland Greeks recognized Persian mastery of Cyprus.

In 332 B.C.E., after the Macedonian king ALEXANDER THE GREAT had invaded the Persian Empire, Greek Cyprus dramatically joined his side and contributed 120 warships for the conqueror's massive siege of Tyre. After Alexander's death, PTOLEMY (1), the Macedonian-born ruler of EGYPT, captured Cyprus despite suffering a naval defeat by his enemy DEMETRIUS POLIORCETES off Salamis (306 B.C.E.). Ptolemy suppressed Cyprus' traditional nine kingships, replaced them with democratic forms, and established an Egyptian overlordship that lasted until 58 B.C.E., when the island was taken over by the Romans.

See also GREEK LANGUAGE; PHOENICIA; SHIPS AND SEAFARING; WARFARE, NAVAL.

Further reading: Vassos Karageorghis, *The A. G. Levantis Foundation and the Cultural Heritage of Cyprus* (Athens: The Foundation, 1990); ———, *Cyprus Museum and Archaeological Sites of Cyprus,* translated by Kay Cicellis, 2d ed. (Athens: Ekdotike Athenon, 1991); A. T. Reyes, *Archaic Cyprus: A Study of the Textual and Archaeological Evidence* (New York: Oxford University Press, 1994); Veronica Tatton-Brown, *Ancient Cyprus,* 2d ed.

(London: British Museum Press, 1997); Vassos Karageorghis, *Cypriote Archaeology Today: Achievements and Perspectives* (Glasgow: University of Glasgow, Glasgow Archaeological Society, 1998); Paul Aström, *A Century of International Cyprological Research* (Nicosia: Bank of Cyprus Foundation, 2000); Vassos Karageorghis, *Early Cyprus: Crossroads of the Mediterranean* (Los Angeles: J. Paul Getty Museum, 2002).

Cypselus *See* KYPSELOS.

Cyrene (1) (Greek: **Kyrene**) This major Greek city of North Africa, near modern-day Benghazi in eastern Libya, was founded by DORIAN GREEKS from the island of THERA around 630 B.C.E. Located inland, on a hill surrounded by fertile plains, Cyrene thrived in TRADE with mainland Greece, which lay 300 miles due north across the Mediterranean. (CRETE was 200 miles northeast.) Through its harbor town of Apollonia, Cyrene exported grain, woolens, oxhides, and silphium—a local plant, prized as a laxative and digestive. Far surpassing Thera in wealth and power, Cyrene established local colonies of its own and was an important early outpost of the Greek world.

The circumstances of Cyrene's foundation are well known, thanks to an account by the historian HERODOTUS (ca. 435 B.C.E.) and a surviving inscription, dating from the 300s B.C.E., claiming to record the Therans' decision to send out ships of colonists 300 years earlier. The expedition was organized to relieve overpopulation and water shortage on Thera. Although volunteers were welcome, one son from each family was required to join, the penalty for default being death. The sea route to the intended landfall had already been explored by Greek traders from Crete. The Theran colonists, landing on the then-fertile Libyan coast, were at first welcomed by the native Libyans.

Cyrene's foundation offers one of the clearest examples of the role played by APOLLO, patron god of colonists, and by Apollo's oracle at DELPHI, in central Greece. The Theran expedition and its leader were approved beforehand by Delphic Apollo, and the new city was named for the god. (The name Kyrēnē is related to Kouros, "young man," a cult title of Apollo.)

Early Cyrene was governed by kings of a family named the Battiads, or "sons of Battus." (Battos, "stammerer," was supposedly the name of the original expedition's leader.) The dynasty customarily used the royal names Battus and Arcesilaus (meaning "leader of the people"). A prominent king was Battus II, surnamed the Lucky, under whom the city attracted a new influx of Greek settlers and fought off a Libyan-Egyptian attack in about 570 B.C.E. In this era Cyrene founded its own nearby colonies: Barca and Euhesperides (modern Benghazi). The territory of these Greek cities, in the "hump" of eastern Libya, was named Cyrenaica, as it is still called today.

Cyrene submitted to the Persians in around 525 B.C.E., but the Battiads remained in power, amid some dynastic violence, until about 440 B.C.E., when Arcesilaus IV was deposed in favor of an Athenian-style DEMOCRACY. Remote from the political centers of the Greek world, Cyrene was unaffected by the PELOPONNESIAN WAR (431–404 B.C.E.) but was absorbed into the domain of ALEXANDER THE GREAT after he reached EGYPT in his invasion of the Persian empire (332 B.C.E.). On Alexander's death in 323 B.C.E. the city passed to PTOLEMY (1), the Macedonian-born ruler of Egypt. Ptolemy removed the city's democracy and installed a liberal OLIGARCHY, which he could better control.

Under lenient Egyptian rule, the city reached a peak of prosperity in the late 300s and 200s B.C.E., with a public building program and such cultural ornaments as a native school of PHILOSOPHY—the Cyrenaics, founded by Aristipus, a follower of SOCRATES. In the mid-200s B.C.E. the Cyrenaic cities banded into a federation, which remained part of Egypt until the 100s B.C.E., when the Romans began to interfere in Egyptian administration. In 74 B.C.E., Cyrenaica became a province of the Roman domain.

See also COLONIZATION; CYRENE (2); ROME.

Further reading: Charles Hyslop, *Cyrene and Ancient Cyrenaica, a Guidebook* (Tripoli: Government Press, 1945?); Shimon Applebaum, *Jews and Greeks in Ancient Cyrene* (Leiden, Netherlands: E. J. Brill, 1979); Graeme Barkes, John Lloyd, and Joyce Reynolds, eds., *Cyrenaica in Antiquity* (Oxford: B. A. R., 1985); S. E. Kane, "Sculpture from Cyrene in Its Mediterranean Context," in *Ancient Marble Quarrying and Trade. Papers from a colloquium held at the annual meeting of the Archaeological Institute of America, San Antonio, Texas, December 1986,* edited by J. Clayton Fant (Oxford: B. A. R., 1988), 127–138.

Cyrene (2) (Greek: **Kyrene**) In MYTH, this nymph was beloved by the god APOLLO. Cyrene lived in THESSALY, where she delighted in the woodlands and in hunting wild beasts.

Apollo spied Cyrene one day as she wrestled with a lion on Mt. Pelion. He immediately fell in love with her for her beauty and "manly" strength. The god carried her off in his golden chariot to Libya in North Africa. There, on a hill surrounded by fertile plains, Apollo founded the Greek city that he named CYRENE (1), for her to rule. She bore him a hero son, Aristaeus, who introduced to humankind such civilizing arts as beekeeping and cheese making.

The legend of Cyrene reveals at least two layers. The earlier layer—describing Apollo and the nymph in Thessaly—appears in a fragment by the epic poet HESIOD, who wrote in about 700 B.C.E. (before the Greeks founded the city of Cyrene, in about 630 B.C.E.). In the original version, Apollo probably did not carry his beloved off to North Africa—a detail not needed for the story. But at some point, perhaps around 600 B.C.E., the older tale was developed into a political "foundation myth," explaining the origin of the city of Cyrene. This later legend is told in the poet PINDAR's ninth Pythian ode, written in abound 474 B.C.E. for an athlete of Cyrene.

See also NYMPHS.

Further reading: Jennifer Larson, *Greek Nymphs: Myth, Cult, Lore* (New York: Oxford University Press, 2001).

Cyrus (1) (Greek: Kyros) (ca. 580–529 B.C.E.)
This Persian king and conqueror ruled from 559–529 B.C.E. and built PERSIA into a vast empire. Cyrus also brought Persia to its first, hostile contact with the Greek world. Despite this, Cyrus was viewed by later Greek thinkers as a model of the wise and righteous ruler; the historians HERODOTUS (ca. 435 B.C.E.) and XENOPHON (ca. 380 B.C.E.) both wrote about his life in legendary terms.

Cyrus—sometimes called Cyrus the Great or Cyrus II—was the grandson of a prior King Cyrus and son of King Cambyses. He ruled after the death of his father. The Persians at that time were a simple, seminomadic people of the southwestern Iranian plateau; they and their king were subordinate to a kindred people, the Medes. Cyrus revolted against the Medes, captured their capital city of Ecbatana, and made himself supreme king. Henceforth the Persians were the dominant people. The Medes became their inferiors, and there arose a new imperial dynasty—Cyrus's family, called the Achaemenids (descendants of Achaemenes).

The domain that Cyrus had seized was one of the three great powers of western Asia; the others were the kingdoms of LYDIA and Babylonia. Over his 20-year reign, Cyrus eliminated these two rival kingdoms and carved out an empire stretching from the AEGEAN SEA to Afghanistan.

First, provoked by the (undoubtedly welcome) aggression of the Lydian king CROESUS, Cyrus marched to ASIA MINOR in 546 B.C.E. and conquered Lydia. It was then that he encountered the Greek cities of IONIA, in western Asia Minor, which had been privileged subject states under Croesus. After some resistance, the Greeks of Asia Minor submitted to the Persians (around 545 B.C.E.). These events could be described as the starting point of the PERSIAN WARS.

Later Cyrus seized the city of Babylon and its empire—in effect avenging the Babylonian subjugation of the JEWS—a triumph for which he is praised in the Old Testament book of Isaiah. He seems to have governed benevolently, allowing nations to keep their laws and religious customs once they had offered submission. He died in battle on his northeastern frontier (perhaps modern-

day Uzbekistan) and was succeeded by his son Cambyses (530 B.C.E.).

Further reading: A. Cizek, "From the Historical Truth to the Literary Conventions. The Life of Cyrus the Great Viewed by Herodotus, Ctesias, and Xenophon," *L'Antiquité classique* (1975): 531–552; H. A. Storck, "The Lydian Campaign of Cyrus the Great in Classical and Cuneiform Sources," *Ancient World* 19 (1989): 69–76; H. G. Dakyns, trans., *The Education of Cyprus/Xenophon* (Rutland, Vt.: C. E. Tuttle, 1992); Christopher Nadon, *Xenophon's Prince: Republic and Empire in the 'Cyropaedia'* (Berkeley: University of California Press, 2001).

Cyrus (2) *See* XENOPHON.

Cyzicus (Greek: Kyzikos) This Greek seaport of northwestern ASIA MINOR is situated on the south coast of the SEA OF MARMARA, about 60 miles east of the HELLESPONT. Lying in the territory of the non-Greek Mysians, Cyzicus was founded by Greeks from MILETUS, around 675 B.C.E. According to legend, the city was named for an ancient native King Cyzicus, who had been killed in a mishap involving the Greek hero JASON (1) and his Argonauts.

Cyzicus was located on the southern tip of an inshore island called Arctonnessus ("bear island," now a peninsula of the Turkish mainland). The site commanded a double harbor, formed by the narrow channel between island and shore; this superior anchorage became an important station along the Greek shipping route to the BLACK SEA. Cyzicus thrived from TRADE by sea and by the land routes from interior Asia Minor; it also enjoyed rich local fisheries.

From the late 500s until the late 300s B.C.E., Cyzicus minted coins of electrum (an alloy of GOLD and SILVER) in the high denomination known as the statēr. Stamped with the city's emblem, a tuna, Cyzicene statērs were renowned for their beauty and reliable measure.

By about 493 B.C.E. the city had submitted to the conquering Persian king DARIUS (1). Liberated by the Greek counteroffensive after 479 B.C.E., Cyzicus joined the Athenian-led DELIAN LEAGUE and (a sign of its prosperity) contributed a sizable annual tribute of nine silver TALENTS.

Revolting from Athenian rule in the Delian uprising of 411 B.C.E., during the PELOPONNESIAN WAR, Cyzicus welcomed a Spartan-Peloponnesian fleet under the Spartan commander Mindarus. The following spring, 410 B.C.E., saw one of the war's great sea battles, off Cyzicus. The Athenian commander ALCIBIADES, arriving with 86 warships, surprised the 60 Spartan ships at their naval exercises and cut them off from Cyzicus harbor. The Spartans fled in-shore and moored. When Alcibiades brought some of his ships ashore, the Spartan commander, Mindarus, also led some of his men ashore, but was killed in the fighting. The Athenians captured the entire enemy fleet with the exception of one squadron, set afire by its fleeing crew. The victorious Alcibiades extorted large sums of money from Cyzicus to pay his crews, but sailed off without doing other damage to the recaptured rebel city.

After passing into the empire of ALEXANDER THE GREAT (334 B.C.E.), Cyzicus was absorbed into the east Greek SELEUCID EMPIRE around 300 B.C.E. The city continued to prosper, enjoying good trade relations with the Seleucids' rivals, the kings of nearby PERGAMON. Like other portions of western Seleucid territory, Cyzicus came under Roman control around 188 B.C.E.

See also COINAGE.

Further reading: Alfred R. Bellinger, *Greek Coins from the Yale Numismatic Collection. III, A Hoard of Bronze Coins of Cyzicus* (New Haven, Conn.: Yale University Press, 1952); D. M. Bailey, "A Grave Group from Cyzicus," *Journal of Glass Studies* 34 (1992): 27–34.

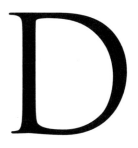

Daedalus (Greek: **Daidalos**) This mythical Athenian inventor was regarded as a patron hero of craftsmen. According to legend, Daedalus invented carpentry and woodworking, among other skills. But he fled from ATHENS after murdering his nephew-apprentice, who showed signs of surpassing him in talent. Traveling to CRETE, Daedalus constructed a number of fabulous works, including the mechanical cow in which Queen Pasiphaë was able to quench her unnatural lust for a bull. Imprisoned by the enraged king MINOS on account of the Pasiphaë episode, Daedalus and his son, Ikaros, escaped by flying away on mechanical wings attached to their arms. But Ikaros, despite his father's warning, soared too close to the Sun, which melted the adhesive wax on his wings, and plummeted to his death in the AEGEAN SEA. Ikaros' fatal flight has often been interpreted as a metaphor for HUBRIS and overreaching ambition.

Landing in SICILY, Daedalus was protected by the native king Cocalus. The mighty Minos, arriving in pursuit, was murdered at Cocalus's order. Daedalus stayed in Sicily and built a number of works.

In real life, the classical Greeks—especially the Sicilian Greeks—ascribed to Daedalus many existing ancient monuments whose origin they could not otherwise explain. Supposedly he was the first sculptor to free the statue's arms from its sides and show the eyes open.

The Athenians commemorated Daedalus in a DEME (city ward) named Daidalidai, "the descendants of Daedalus." The Athenian philosopher SOCRATES (469–399 B.C.E.), a sculptor or stonecutter by profession, claimed personal descent from Daedalus—perhaps jokingly or symbolically.

See also LABYRINTH; SCULPTURE.

Further reading: John Boardman, "Daedalus and Monumental Sculpture," *Panepistemion Kretes. Pepragmena tou D' Diethnous Kretologikou Synedriou (Irakleion 29 August–3 September 1976)* (Athens): 43–47; Sarah P. Morris, *Daidalos and the Origins of Greek Art* (Princeton, N.J.: Princeton University Press, 1995).

Damokles (300s B.C.E.) *Syracusan courtier during the reign of the tyrant DIONYSIUS (1).*
Damokles praised the luxury and power of a ruler's life, until one day Dionysius ordered Damokles to be feasted at a banquet, underneath a downward-pointing sword, suspended by a single hair. Various Roman authors, including Horace and Persius, tell this story; the object lesson was that a ruler's life, for all its splendors, is fraught with worry and fear.

Further reading: L. J. Sanders, *Dionysius I of Syracuse and Greek Tyranny* (London: Croom Helm, 1987); Brian Caven, *Dionysius I: War-lord of Sicily* (New Haven, Conn.: Yale University Press, 1990).

Danaids *See* DANAUS.

Danaus In Greek MYTH, Danaus and Aegyptus were brothers who lived in EGYPT and had 50 children each; Aegyptus had all boys, Danaus, all girls (the Danaidai, "daughters of Danaus.") When the children reached maturity, Aegyptus insisted that his sons marry their cousins, the Danaids. Danaus refused and fled with his daughters to the Greek city of ARGOS, where they were received as suppliants. When the sons of Aegyptus arrived in pursuit, Danaus—to spare the Argives harm—consented to the 50-

fold marriage. But he secretly instructed his daughters to murder their husbands on their wedding night. All obeyed except for Hypermnestra (whose name is translatable as "excessive wooing" or "special intent"); she spared her husband, Lynceus, and helped him to escape.

Danaus was enraged to learn of Hypermnestra's disobedience, but she was acquitted by an Argive law court following a plea by the love goddess APHRODITE. Lynceus later returned, killed Danaus, ruled Argos with Hypermnestra, and founded a dynasty of Argive kings. The other Danaids remarried among the Argives; their descendants were known as the Danaans (Danai), a name that in the epic poems of HOMER simply means "Greeks." The tale of the Danaids was the subject of a trilogy by the Athenian tragedian AESCHYLUS; one play from this trilogy survives, the *Suppliant Maidens* (463 B.C.E.).

According to one story, the 49 guilty Danaids were punished after death for their outrage to the MARRIAGE bed. In the Underworld, they are forced forever to fetch water in leaky jars or sieves.

The odd myth of Danaus possibly presents a distorted reflection of some contact between Egypt and the Mycenaean Greeks, around 1600–1200 B.C.E.

See also AFTERLIFE; MYCENAEAN CIVILIZATION.

Further reading: David Grene and Richmond Lattimore, eds., *Aeschylus II: The Suppliant Maidens; The Persians; Seven Against Thebes; Prometheus Bound*, 2d ed. (Chicago: University of Chicago Press, 1991).

Dardanelles   *See* HELLESPONT.

Darius (1) I (ca. 550–486 B.C.E.) *King of* PERSIA *from 522 to 486* B.C.E.

Darius was known for his soldiering and administrative abilities. His reign saw hostilities intensify between the Persian Empire and its relatively weak western neighbors, the Greeks.

Although not the son of a king, Darius was of Persian royal blood. Coming to the throne at around age 30, following the death of the childless king Cambyses, Darius soon advanced the empire's boundaries. On the northwestern frontier, he subdued several eastern Greek states, including SAMOS, CHIOS, LESBOS, and BYZANTIUM. He was the first Persian king to cross into Europe, bridging the BOSPORUS and the Danube and leading an expedition against the nomads of western Scythia (ca. 512 B.C.E.). This expedition failed, but Darius did gain the submission of THRACE and MACEDON, which brought his domain right up to the northeastern border of mainland Greece. The Persian Empire had reached its greatest extent, stretching (in modern terms) from Pakistan to Bulgaria and southern EGYPT. It was the largest empire the world had yet seen.

Darius ruled strictly but wisely. He was the first Persian ruler to mint coins, and he reorganized the empire

into 20 provinces, or "satrapies," each governed by a satrap, answerable to the king. (In a future century, this apparatus would be taken over en bloc by the Macedonian conqueror ALEXANDER THE GREAT.) Darius built a road system with relay stations for mounted messengers; this Persian "pony express" became a marvel of the ancient world. He aggrandized the city of Susa as his capital and began work on a summer capital at Persepolis. Darius practiced the Zoroastrian faith, but he enforced Persian tolerance toward the religions of subject peoples, such as JEWS and Greeks. One ancient Greek inscription records Darius's show of respect for the god APOLLO.

Darius employed Greek subjects as soldiers and craftsmen; his personal physician was a Greek, Democedes of CROTON. But in 499 B.C.E. the empire's Greek cities erupted in rebellion. This IONIAN REVOLT was finally crushed by Darius (in 493 B.C.E.), but meanwhile it had drawn in two free cities of mainland Greece to fight against Persia: ATHENS and ERETRIA. Angry at these two cities, Darius sent a seaborne expedition to capture them. At the ensuing Battle of MARATHON (summer of 490 B.C.E.), the Persians were unexpectedly defeated by the Athenians.

This distant defeat must have mattered little to the mighty Darius. When he died, it was his son and successor, XERXES, who mobilized the full strength of Persia against mainland Greece.

See also PERSIAN WARS.

Further reading: Jack Martin Balcer, *The Persian Conquest of the Greeks, 545–450 B.C.E.* (Konstanz: Universitätsverlag Konstanz, 1995); Philip De Souza, *The Greek and Persian Wars, 499–386 B.C.* (New York: Routledge, 2003).

Darius (2) III   *See* ALEXANDER THE GREAT.

Dark Age   This term is sometimes used by modern historians to describe the time period from approximately 1100 to 800 B.C.E. on mainland Greece, after the fall of the MYCENAEAN CIVILIZATION. The era is called "dark" because of its grimness—archaeological evidence creates a picture of widespread destruction, depopulation, and impoverishment. The literate and artistic culture of the Mycenaeans seems to have disappeared, and the population shifted from cosmopolitan palace sites into small, isolated villages. Trade with other civilizations of the Mediterranean ceased. This period was named in imitation of the Dark Ages of medieval Europe (around 476–1000 C.E.), which similarly saw chaos after the fall of a dominant civilization, the Roman Empire.

The Greek "Dark Age" also makes reference to modern ignorance of the events of these years, since the amount of material culture that survives from this period is very slight. This fact, however, is gradually starting to change as archaeologists are beginning to learn more about the era, and many scholars now prefer to use the term "Iron Age" to describe this period in Greek history.

See also DORIAN GREEKS; IRON; GREEK LANGUAGE; LEFKANDI.

Further reading: Vincent Robin d'Arba Desborough, *The Greek Dark Ages* (London: Benn, 1972).

death *See* AFTERLIFE; FUNERAL CUSTOMS; HADES; PHILOSOPHY; RELIGION.

Delian League This is the modern name for the Athenian-controlled alliance of Greek states, mostly in and around the AEGEAN SEA, that arose at the end of the PERSIAN WARS (ca. 478 B.C.E.) and lasted, with much erosion, until ATHENS's defeat in the PELOPONNESIAN WAR (404 B.C.E.). The league—based for its first 25 years at the sacred island of DELOS—was formed as a mutual-defense pact against PERSIA, but eventually became the basis for an Athenian naval empire in the Aegean. The number of league member states swelled to about 200 by the mid-400s B.C.E. In exchange for Athenian protection, these member states paid an annual tribute (although a few powerful allies, such as SAMOS, CHIOS, and LESBOS, chose to supply warships instead). The allies' tribute, paid in TALENTS of SILVER, was originally used to finance league naval operations, but later came to be used by the Athenians to aggrandize and fortify their own city. By the start of the Peloponnesian War (431 B.C.E.), the Delian League had become an Athenian weapon against not Persia but SPARTA.

The history of the league is one of Athens's increasing arrogance and authoritarianism toward its subject allies. The milestones in this process are (1) the removal of the league treasury from Delos to Athens (454 B.C.E.); (2) the Peace of KALLIAS, which formally ended hostilities with Persia but also ended the league's logical reason for existence (449 B.C.E.); (3) the revolt of Samos, which, although not the first rebellion within the league, came close to succeeding (440 B.C.E.); and (4) the reassessment of 425 B.C.E., by which league members had their annual dues doubled or trebled, as Athens strove to raise funds for the Peloponnesian War. After the Athenian disaster at SYRACUSE (413 B.C.E.), many league members revolted and went over to the Spartan side in the war; among these rebellious states were Chios, MILETUS, BYZANTIUM, MYTILENE, EPHESOS, THASOS, and the cities of EUBOEA. But after the war, Spartan domination proved so loathsome that many former allies returned to Athens to form a SECOND ATHENIAN LEAGUE.

Partial lists exist of the Delian League members and their annual tributes for certain years of the mid-400s B.C.E. These lists were preserved as inscriptions cut into marble and set up on the Athenian ACROPOLIS. The state that paid by far the most tribute was Athens's old enemy AEGINA—a crushing 30 talents a year. For other states, the tribute may have been demanding but not punitive:

ABDERA and Byzantium paid 15 talents each in 457 B.C.E. (more later, after the reassessment); Paros was paying 16 talents by the mid-400s; AENUS, CYMĒ, and Lampsacus each paid 12 talents; Miletus and Perinthus, 10. League membership offered many attractions—and not just access to the cultural glories of Athens. The league was based partly on the notion that Athenian-style DEMOCRACY was available to the member states, and lower- and middle-class citizens usually supported league membership. (Sparta, on the other hand, always appealed to the upper class; "liberation" by Sparta meant local rule by an OLIGARCHY.)

See also ARISTIDES; EGYPT; KIMON; KLEON; THUCYDIDES [2].

Further reading: Russell Meiggs, *The Athenian Empire,* 2d ed. (Oxford: Clarendon Press, 1979); P. J. Rhodes, *The Athenian Empire* (Oxford: Clarendon Press, 1985); Robin Osborne, ed. *The Athenian Empire,* 4th ed. (London: London Association of Classical Teachers, 2000).

Delium *See* PELOPONNESIAN WAR; WARFARE, LAND.

Delos This island in the AEGEAN SEA is situated in the center of the CYCLADES group. Inhabited by pre-Greek peoples in the third millennium B.C.E., Delos was occupied around 1050 B.C.E. by IONIAN GREEKS from the mainland. As the mythical birthplace of the divine APOLLO and ARTEMIS, Delos eventually became the second-greatest sanctuary of Apollo, after DELPHI. By the 700s B.C.E., Delos was the scene of a yearly Aegean festival in the god's honor.

The island's scant two-square-mile area contained temples and monuments, including a famous artificial lake with swans and geese sacred to Apollo. Much of ancient Delos can be seen today, thanks to more than a century of French ARCHAEOLOGY on the site. One of its most impressive surviving monuments is the famous Lion Terrace, with its five surviving marble lions from the 600s B.C.E. Other important ruins on the site include the Temples of Apollo and Artemis, a theater, Sanctuaries of the Foreign Gods (including cults of Egyptian and Syrian divinities), workshops, warehouses, and several residential buildings from the Hellenistic and Roman periods.

Delos's sanctity made it politically attractive to various Greek rulers. Both the Athenian tyrant PEISISTRATUS (ca. 543 B.C.E.) and the Samian tyrant POLYCRATES (ca. 525 B.C.E.) held public ceremonies there. In 478 or 477 B.C.E., Delos became the headquarters and treasury of the DELIAN LEAGUE, the Aegean-Greek alliance organized by ATHENS against PERSIA. But in 454 B.C.E., amid increased authoritarianism, the Athenians removed the league treasury from Delos to Athens.

However, Athenian stewardship of Delos continued. In 426 B.C.E., during the PELOPONNESIAN WAR, the Athenian general NIKIAS conducted ceremonies to resanctify the island in gratitude for Apollo's ending of the plague at Athens. The Athenians built a new temple to the god and inaugurated a new festival, called the Delia, to be celebrated every four years.

After Athens's defeat in the war (404 B.C.E.) and a generation of hated Spartan rule, Delos in 387 B.C.E. became the capital of a new Athenian-led alliance, the so-called SECOND ATHENIAN LEAGUE. In the late 300s B.C.E. Delos became the center of another Aegean alliance, the League of Islanders, most likely established by the Macedonian commander ANTIGONUS (1). In the 200s B.C.E. Macedonian kings were patrons of the island; one of their gifts was the Stoa of PHILIP V, a colonnade that still is partly standing today. This friendship with MACEDON brought Delos into hostility with ROME. After their victory in the Third Macedonian War (167 B.C.E.), the Romans handed over Delos to their allies the Athenians, who colonized the island.

Under Roman-Athenian control, Delos became a thriving free port. In the 100s B.C.E. it was the notorious center of the Greek slave trade. Later it dwindled in importance and was abandoned. Today, the island of Delos can be reached only by caique (a small boat) from the island of Mykonos. The passage is often rough, and in certain weather conditions it will not be made.

See also SLAVES.

Further reading: Petros Themelis, *Mykonos—Delos: Archaeological Guide* (Athens: Apollo Editions, 1971); Nicholas Rauh, *The Sacred Bonds of Commerce: Religion, Economy, and Trade Society at Hellenistic Roman Delos, 166–87 B.C.* (Amsterdam: J. C. Gieben, 1993).

Delphi   A sanctuary of the god APOLLO in central Greece, Delphi was the most influential of all ancient Greek shrines and contained the most famous of the Greek world's oracles, or priestly soothsayers. The Delphic oracle was a priestess, the Pythia, who would go into a trance or seizure to speak Apollo's answers to suppliants' questions. During Delphi's busy heyday, in the 500s B.C.E., as many as three Pythias held the office at once.

Located about 2,000 feet above sea level, Delphi sits on a southern spur of Mt. Parnassus, north of the central Corinthian Gulf, in the region once known as PHOCIS. The name Delphi may commemorate Apollo's cult title *Delphinios* (meaning dolphin or porpoise). The site, terraced into the mountainside, was thought to be the center of the world, and one of Delphi's relics was a carved "navel stone" (*omphalos*) symbolizing this geographic position. Delphi served as a meeting place for the AMPHICTYONIC LEAGUE, a powerful coalition of central Greek states. Because of its oracle and its sports competition held every four years, the PYTHIAN GAMES, Delphi attracted religious pilgrims and other visitors from all over the Greek world.

Delphi's buildings were ruined by an earthquake and scavengers in late antiquity but have been excavated and partly reconstructed by French archaeologists since the end of the 19th century C.E. They now comprise the single most spectacular collection of surviving Greek monuments.

Long before the first Greek invaders arrived around 2100 B.C.E., Delphi was a holy place of the pre-Greek inhabitants. Modern ARCHAEOLOGY at Delphi has uncovered traces of these people's religious sacrifices but do not reveal what kind of deity was worshipped. Perhaps in those early days Delphi was the seat of a non-Greek oracular priestess. According to Greek tradition, the shrine's original name was Pytho. Greek MYTH tells how the young Apollo took over Pytho after slaying its protector, the serpent Python. In the Greek historical era (700s B.C.E.), a sacred serpent was part of Apollo's cult there. Also, a second god, DIONYSUS, was said to inhabit Delphi during the winter months, when Apollo was absent.

It is not known when the earliest temple to Apollo was built at Delphi but it is known that the building was replaced twice during historical times. A stone temple, dating from the 600s B.C.E., burned down in 548 B.C.E. and was replaced by an elaborate Doric-style building, completed in about 510 B.C.E. with the help of the powerful Alcmaeonid clan of ATHENS. That structure collapsed in an earthquake in 373 B.C.E. and was replaced by the Doric-style, limestone temple that partly survives today.

Amid a clutter of smaller buildings, the grand temple stood atop its terraced platform in the center of a walled, rectangular, hillside enclosure. The site's secondary structures eventually included colonnades, meeting halls, a theater where the Pythian Games' musical and dramatic contests were held, and a dozen or so "treasuries" (small, elegant stone buildings erected by various Greek states to hold statuary, relics, and other precious offerings to the god).

Today the Doric-style Treasury of the Athenians is the only treasury standing, reconstructed by modern archaeologists to look as it did in 490 B.C.E., when the Athenians built it to commemorate their victory over the Persians at MARATHON. Another important treasury was built in about 525 B.C.E. by the island of Siphnos; financed by the island's GOLD mines, this treasury was meant to surpass all others in size and beauty. The Delphi Museum now holds part of the Siphnian treasury's frieze; its marble carvings, showing the mythical combat between gods and GIANTS, supply one of the best surviving examples of early Greek architectural SCULPTURE.

Within the temple was the holy sanctum where the Pythia gave Apollo's prophecies. After a ritual purification, a suppliant (males only) could enter the Pythia's presence and hand over his written question for the god. Some suppliants might seek guidance on personal matters—MARRIAGE, business, and the like—while others would be representing city governments on questions of public importance. The Pythia would go into a trance or fit (it is possible that she inhaled some sort of narcotic vapor) and would then deliver the god's answer in sometimes unintelligible exclamations, which an attending priest would render into hexameter verse.

The facts behind this soothsaying cannot be fully explained. Clearly some pious fraud was involved. Like the medieval Vatican, Delphi was a rich, opportunistic organization, with widespread eyes and ears. The suppliants tended to be wealthy men, whose dealings and affiliations might be well known. The priesthood could learn about upcoming questions while individual suppliants or their messengers made the long and public pilgrimage to Delphi. Nor were the god's answers often clear; of the 75 Delphic responses that are reliably recorded by ancient historians or inscriptions, most are either vague, commonsensical, or nonsensical.

The most notorious answers, as reported by the historian HERODOTUS, were gloriously ambiguous. When the Lydian king CROESUS inquired in about 546 B.C.E. if he should invade Persian territory, the oracle replied that if he did so a mighty empire would be destroyed. So Croesus invaded—but the empire that fell was his own.

Delphi reached its peak of power early in Greek history. The shrine became important amid the great movement of overseas Greek COLONIZATION, beginning in the mid-700s B.C.E. Apollo was the god of colonists, and by skillful politicking, the priests at Delphi were able to position "their" Apollo as the official sanction for all Greek colonizing expeditions. Delphi's prestige was further enhanced around 582 B.C.E., when a reorganization of the Pythian Games made them into a major event of the Greek world.

By endorsing TYRANTS such as the Corinthian KYPSELOS (mid-600s B.C.E.), the Delphic oracle attracted gifts and support from this new class of Greek rulers. Delphi also won the patronage of non-Greek kings in ASIA MINOR—including Croesus and the Phrygian MIDAS—who sought to establish contacts and allies in mainland Greece.

But Delphi's eastern contacts brought about its undoing, for when the Persians prepared to invade Greece shortly before 480 B.C.E. the Delphic oracle advised the Greeks to surrender. The Delphi priesthood may have hoped to see their shrine become the capital of Greece under Persian occupation. Several major Delphic prophecies in these years warned (with only slight equivocation) that Greek resistance would be futile. But in fact the Greeks triumphed over the invaders in the PERSIAN WARS of 490–479 B.C.E. The Delphic priesthood was henceforth stigmatized for its defeatism as well as for its reputed susceptibility to bribery.

Nevertheless, Delphi remained politically influential through the 300s B.C.E. and remained a central religious shrine for more than 600 years after that, down to the late Roman Empire. The oracle was shut down around 390 C.E. by order of the Christian Roman emperor Theodosius, in his campaign to eliminate pagan rites throughout his domain.

The site of Delphi began to be investigated by French travelers, architects, and archaeologists in the 19th century C.E. Intensive excavations began in 1892, revealing and restoring its spectacular ruins and publishing numerous excavation reports and guidebooks. Today, Delphi is one of the most popular tourist destinations in Greece (as it was in antiquity), and most of the finds from the site are displayed in the local museum.

See also ALCMAEONIDS; CELTS; PHILIP II; PROPHECY AND DIVINATION; RELIGION.

Further reading: T. Dempsey, *The Delphic Oracle: Its Early History, Influence, and Fall* (New York: B. Blom, 1972); Petros Themelis, *Delphi: The Archaeological Site and the Museum* (Athens, Ekdotike Athenon, 1983); Catherine Morgan, *Athens and Oracles: The Transformation of Olympia and Delphi in the Eighth Century B.C.* (New York: Cambridge University Press, 1990); Elena Partida, *The Treasuries at Delphi: An Architectural Study* (Göteborg, Sweden: Paul Aströms Förlag, 2000); Manoles Andronikos, *Delphi*, translated by Brian de Jongh, 2d ed. (Athens: Ekdotike Athenon, 1993).

deme (*dēmos*) This term refers to a village or city ward constituting part of a larger territory. It usually is used to describe the political wards of ATTICA (the 1,000-square-mile territory of ATHENS), as organized by the democratic reformer KLEISTHENES (1) in 508 B.C.E. The Attic demes numbered 139 and ranged in type from city neighborhoods to townships to patches of rural area.

The demes were the foundation blocks of the Athenian DEMOCRACY: for example, the 500-man Athenian COUNCIL drew its members from each deme, in proportion to population. The demes' headquarters maintained local census figures, with each male citizen formally enrolling on his 19th birthday. There were kept deeds of property and other legal documents and there "town meetings" were held.

Further reading: C. William Eliot, *Coastal Demes of Attika: A Study of the Policy of Kleisthenes* (Toronto: University of Toronto Press, 1962); John Traill, *The Political Organization of Attica: A Study of the Demes, Trittyes, and Phylai, and Their Representation in the Athenian Council* (Princeton, N.J.: American School of Classical Studies at Athens, 1975); Robin Barrow, *Athenian Democracy*, rev. ed. (London: Bristol Classical Press, 1999).

Demeter One of the 12 Olympian gods, Demeter was worshipped as the goddess of grain, agriculture, and fertility. For an agrarian society like ancient Greece, this divinity was clearly of the utmost importance in daily life and religion. Unlike many other major Greek goddesses, Demeter seems to have been purely Greek in origin. Her name is Greek: "de-meter" probably means "spelt mother" (spelt is a type of grain). In MYTH, Demeter bore a daughter to ZEUS, called Kore ("maiden"). At an early date, however, Kore seems to have been assimilated into a more complex, pre-Greek deity called Persephone, who was the queen of the dead.

Demeter's primary sanctuary was at the town of Eleusis, located 15 miles northwest of ATHENS in the fertile Thriasian plain. There, the prestigious and stately ELEUSINIAN MYSTERIES were held in honor of Demeter and her daughter. This cult, celebrating the goddess's gift of grain to mortals, surely arose from Eleusis's importance as a center of production for barley and wheat.

The most famous myth about Demeter and Kore-Persephone tells how the young maiden was abducted by HADES, the Greek god of death and king of the Underworld. She was gathering flowers in a meadow when the earth opened and Hades emerged in his fiery chariot and carried her below. Frantically seeking her missing daughter, Demeter neglected her duties and let the earth go barren and the grain wither. Her search eventually brought her to Eleusis, where, disguised as an old woman, she

Demeter, goddess of grain and fertility, with her daughter Persephone or Kore *(Alison Frantz Photographic Collection, American School of Classical Studies at Athens)*

was hospitably received at the home of the local king. In an attempt to restore fertility to the earth, Zeus decreed that Kore should return to the upper world. Unfortunately, she had eaten several pomegranate seeds while in Hades' realm, so she was partly obligated to remain in the Underworld. Zeus decided that Kore would henceforth spend four months of every year below ground as Hades' wife and the other eight months on earth with her mother. The myth offers an explanation or allegory for the unproductivity of the soil during the harsh winter months, when Demeter mourns her child, as well as the renewal of the land in the spring, when Kore is restored to her. At the same time, it "explains" why Eleusis is Demeter's cult center.

In some versions of the myth, Demeter's search is localized in SICILY—for instance, to light her way by night she lights two torches at volcanic Mt. Etna. Such details evidently emerged from the important cult of Persephone observed by the Sicilian Greeks.

See also FARMING; ORPHISM.

Further reading: Kevin Clinton, *Myth and Cult: The Iconography of the Eleusinian Mysteries* (Stockholm: Svenska Institutet i Athen, 1992); Kevin Clinton, "The Sanctuary of Demeter and Kore at Eleusis," in *Greek Sanctuaries: New Approaches,* edited by Nanno Marinatos and Robin Hägg (London: Routledge, 1993); Helene Foley, ed., *The Homeric Hymn to Demeter: Translation, Commentary, and Interpretive Essays* (Princeton, N.J.: Princeton University Press, 1994); L. Nixon, "The Cults of Demeter and Kore," in *Women in Antiquity: New Assessments,* edited by R. Hawley and B. Levick (London: Routledge, 1995); Tamara Agha-Jaffar, *Demeter and Persephone: Lessons from a Myth* (Jefferson, N.C.: McFarland, 2002).

Demetrius Poliorkētēs (337–283 B.C.E.) *Macedonian-born soldier and ruler*
Brilliant but unstable, Demetrius received the surname Poliorkētēs (the besieger) on account of his spectacular yet unsuccessful siege of the city of RHODES in 305 B.C.E.

Demetrius's father, ANTIGONUS (1), served as a general under the Macedonian king ALEXANDER THE GREAT and was his governor in ASIA MINOR. After Alexander's death (323 B.C.E.), Antigonus sought to maintain Alexander's empire against the secessionist claims of the other DIADOCHI (the successors to Alexander), including KASSANDER, PTOLEMY (1), LYSIMACHUS, and SELEUCUS (1). Demetrius was positioned for power at age 15, when he married Phila, the daughter of the Macedonian regent ANTIPATER. By age 25, Demetrius had become his father's field commander and admiral, in this doomed cause of reuniting the empire.

From Antigonus's base in central Asia Minor, Demetrius led his fleets to and fro across the eastern Mediterranean. In 307 B.C.E. he captured ATHENS, ejected

Kassander's governor, and proclaimed that Athens was free. After nearly 17 years of Cassander's overlordship, the Athenians welcomed the conquering Demetrius with adulation.

Demetrius's most famous victory came the following spring, 306 B.C.E., in the sea battle off the Cyprian city of Salamis. With 108 warships, he totally defeated Ptolemy's fleet of 140 (albeit smaller) warships. Ptolemy lost 120 ships and thousands of shipboard mercenaries; he also lost CYPRUS and command of the sea for the next 20 years. On the basis of this victory, Antigonus proclaimed himself and Demetrius to be joint kings of Alexander's empire. However, in the following year (spring of 304–spring 303 B.C.E.) Demetrius failed in his efforts to capture Rhodes. Rhodes was an important trading city and potential naval base for Ptolemy, but Demetrius's willful decision to waste a year on the siege when he had already captured the more important island of CYPRUS demonstrates his flaws as commander.

Meanwhile Demetrius's enemy Kassander had recaptured central Greece and was besieging Athens. With a fleet of 330 warships and transports, Demetrius sailed from Rhodes and rescued Athens a second time, then defeated Kassander's army at THERMOPYLAE (304 B.C.E.). Demetrius spent that winter at Athens, carousing with his courtesans, whom he installed in the PARTHENON. The following year he liberated central and southern Greece from Kassander's troops. Although he still had Phila as his wife, he also married Deidameia, sister of the Epirote king PYRRHUS. These years mark Demetrius and his father's peak of power.

Soon, however, their enemies had allied against them. At the huge Battle of Ipsus, in central Asia Minor (301 B.C.E.), Antigonus and Demetrius were defeated by the combined forces of Seleucus and Lysimachus. Demetrius, leading 10,000 CAVALRY, pressed his attacks too far forward and was cut off by the enemy's elephant brigade, containing 480 beasts. Meanwhile Antigonus was surrounded and killed. Surviving, Demetrius fled to EPHESOS and rallied a fleet, but the disastrous defeat had left him a mere pirate, without a kingdom.

Kassander's death (297 B.C.E.) and the subsequent turmoil in MACEDON provided an opportunity to acquire that country's throne (to which Demetrius had a claim through his marriage with Phila). By 294 B.C.E. he was king of Macedon and by 289 had reestablished his old control over Greece. Yet the following year he lost this kingdom also, when his foolhardy scheme to attack Seleucus in Asia Minor resulted in his army's desertion. In 285 B.C.E., the 51-year-old Demetrius was captured in Asia Minor by Seleucus. Comfortably imprisoned, Demetrius idly drank himself to death with WINE. Antigonus II, who was Demetrius's son by Phila, eventually left a stable dynasty on the Macedonian throne.

See also WARFARE, NAVAL; WARFARE, SIEGE.

Further reading: Christos Patsavos, *The Unification of the Greeks under Macedonian Hegemony* (Athens: C. Cacoulides, 1965); Edward Newell, *The Coinages of Demetrius Poliorcetes* (Chicago: Obol International, 1978).

democracy The form of government that we call democracy (Greek: *dēmokratia*, "power by the people") was invented at ATHENS in the late 500s and early 400s B.C.E. "It is called a democracy because it is directed, not by a privileged few, but by the populace," explained the Athenian statesman PERIKLES in his Funeral Oration of 431 B.C.E. (as recounted by the historian THUCYDIDES (1)). The Athenian democracy was a marvel and inspiration to the Greek world, as it remains today; one reason for Athens's successful imperialism in the 400s B.C.E. was the city's appeal to the underprivileged classes in Greek cities governed as old-fashioned oligarchies. It was not the Athenian army and navy that SPARTA feared so much as the menace of Athenian-sponsored democracies taking over the rest of Greece.

Current knowledge of the Athenian democracy comes partly from literary sources, such as the political speeches of DEMOSTHENES (1) (mid-300s B.C.E.) and other orators and the comedies of ARISTOPHANES (late 400s B.C.E.). The most important extant literary source is a treatise preserved among the works of ARISTOTLE (mid-300s B.C.E.) titled the *Constitution of Athens* (*Athēnaion Politeia*), which briefly describes the different branches of Athenian government. Filling out this meager picture is the archaeological evidence, such as several dozen surviving decrees of the Athenians of this era, preserved as inscriptions in stone.

Democracy at Athens was forged by the political reforms of SOLON (ca. 594 B.C.E.) and KLEISTHENES (1) (508 B.C.E.). The immediate purpose was to assuage the Athenian middle class, who supplied the backbone of the HOPLITE army and whose discontent was creating the threat of civil war and of usurpation by TYRANTS. Similarly, lower-class Athenians benefited politically when Athens's need to maintain a large navy made the urban poor important as naval oarsmen (400s B.C.E.). The losers in these reforms were members of the traditional Athenian ARISTOCRACY, who had previously monopolized political office and decision making. Yet by the early 400s B.C.E. individual aristocrats such as THEMISTOKLES and Perikles had adapted to the new reality and were holding power as left-wing champions of the common people.

The sovereign governing body of the Athenian democracy was the citizens' ASSEMBLY (*ekklēsia*). This was open to all 30,000 to 40,000 adult male Athenian citizens but was usually attended by only about 5,000. (Although individual WOMEN were classed as citizens or noncitizens, they had no political voice either way.) The assembly convened 40 times a year, normally in a natural hillside auditorium called the Pnyx. There, by public debate and vote, the people directed foreign policy, revised the laws, approved or condemned the conduct of public officials, and made many other state decisions. The assembly's agenda was prepared by the 500-member COUNCIL (*boulē*), which also had important executive duties in enacting the assembly's decrees. Councillors were ordinary Athenian citizens of the upper or middle classes, chosen by lot to serve for one year.

It was essential to the Athenian democracy that its public officials not have much individual power. There was no such office as president of Athens. Perikles enjoyed 20 years of nearly unrivaled influence because he was the leader of a political party (the left wing) and because he was able to win the people's trust. But, in terms of elected office, Perikles was always just a *stratēgos*—a military general, one of 10 such elected annually at Athens. Having endured the tyrannies of PEISISTRATUS and HIPPIAS (1) (late 500s B.C.E.), the Athenians feared that other politicians might try to take over the government, and the odd procedure known as OSTRACISM existed as a safeguard against anyone even suspected of thirsting for supreme power.

Aside from the generalships, Athenian state offices tended to be narrowly defined. The top civilian jobs were the nine archonships, which by the mid-400s B.C.E. were filled by lot, annually, from candidates among the upper and middle classes. An ARCHON might supervise various judicial or religious procedures; the most prestigious post was the *archon eponymos*, where the officeholder's personal name was used to identify the calendar year. Beneath the archonships were the 400-odd lesser executive jobs for the day-to-day running of the Athenian state, such as the commissioners of weights and measures and the commissioners of highway repair. These posts were filled by Athenian citizens, normally chosen by lot to serve for one year with pay. The prominent use of lottery was part of a radical-democratic theory of government which held that an honest lottery is more democratic than an election, because lotteries cannot be unduly influenced by a candidate's wealth or personality. However, elections were used to award certain posts, such as naval architects, army officers, and liturgists.

A liturgy (*leitourgia*, "public duty") was a prestigious service that a rich Athenian might undertake at his own expense. The most prominent liturgy was the *triērarchia*, whereby a citizen would finance, out of pocket, the maintenance of a naval warship for a year. In the mid-300s B.C.E. 1,200 citizens were recognized as rich enough to be nominated as trierarchs.

Jury duty was a vital aspect of the democracy. Athenian jury panels had considerable courtroom authority and discretion (more akin to modern judges than modern juries), and jurymen were paid reasonably well (although less than an able-bodied man could earn in a day). Consequently, jury duty was known as a resort of old men wishing to pass the time profitably. This social pattern is mocked by Aristophanes in his comedy *Wasps* (422 B.C.E.). Juries were filled by volunteers—male citizens over age 30—who were enrolled at the start of the Athenian year.

Jury pay, like the salaries for other government jobs, presented an important political card for Athenian statesmen in the 400s and 300s B.C.E. By increasing such payments, left-wing politicians could please the crowd and genuinely broaden the democracy's base by making such jobs more accessible to lower-income citizens. Perikles introduced jury pay (in about 457 B.C.E.) and his imitator KLEON increased it (in about 423 B.C.E.).

Democracy at Athens was an expensive proposition. Classical Athens was an imperial power, enjoying monetary tribute from its DELIAN LEAGUE subject cities as well as a publicly owned SILVER mine. Such revenues financed the democracy's programs and helped prevent power from being monopolized by the wealthiest citizens.

See also DEME; LAWS AND LAW COURTS; OLIGARCHY; POLIS.

Further reading: Cynthia Farrar, *The Origins of Democratic Thinking: The Invention of Politics in Classical Athens* (New York: Cambridge University Press, 1987); D. L. Stockton, *The Classical Athenian Democracy* (New York: Oxford University Press, 1990); Donald Kagen, *Pericles of Athens and the Birth of Democracy* (New York: Maxwell Macmillan International, 1991); M. H. Hansen, *The Athenian Democracy in the Age of Demosthenes: Structure, Principles, and Ideology* (Cambridge, Mass.: B. Blackwell, 1991): Edward Harris, *Aeschines and Athenian Politics* (New York: Oxford University Press, 1995); Deborah Boedeker and Kurt A. Raaflaub, eds., *Democracy, Empire, and the Arts in Fifth-Century Athens* (Cambridge, Mass.: Harvard University Press, 1998); Nicholas F. Jones, *The Associations of Classical Athens: The Response to Democracy* (New York: Oxford University Press, 1999); Jon Hesk, *Deception and Democracy in Classical Athens* (New York: Cambridge University Press, 2000).

Demokritos (Democritus) (ca. 460–390 B.C.E.) *Philosopher of the Greek city of* ABDERA
Demokritos was born to a noble, wealthy family, and his education included instruction in astronomy and theology by several Chaldaean scholars who were sent to Abdera by the Persian king XERXES. When grown, he traveled around the ancient world (including EGYPT, Ethiopia, PERSIA, and India), searching for wisdom. He was particularly interested in Pythagorean teachings, and he studied under the philosopher LEUCIPPUS.

Demokritos and Leucippus together share the credit for having developed the concept of material PHILOSOPHY that is now called the atomic theory. In a remarkable anticipation of 20th-century physics, the atomists decided that the basic components of matter are tiny particles, which they called *atomoi,* "indivisible." These indivisible particles, infinite in shape and number, move in the void and combine variously; their movements and changes produce the compounds of the visible world.

Modern scholars are unsure how to apportion credit for the atomic theory between Leucippus and Demokritos. It was probably the master's original idea, expanded and blended into a theory of ethics by Demokritos. He believed, for example, that moderation and knowledge can produce happiness because they protect the soul's atoms from turmoil. He argued also that nature, space, and motion were all infinite and eternal. He discussed laws of movement caused by impact, distinguishing between primary and secondary motion, action and reaction.

Demokritos was a prolific author, said to have written 70 treatises on subjects such as MATHEMATICS and MUSIC, as well as physics and ethics. His atomist theory was published in a book called the *Little World-system,* probably written to complement Leucippus's *Big World-system.* (Alternatively, both works may have been written by Demokritos.) None of Demokritos's works survives. Although many fragments are quoted by later authors, these come mostly from the ethical works, not from the atomist writings.

Within a century of Demokritos's death, his ideas greatly influenced the philosopher Epicurus (ca. 300 B.C.E.), the founder of EPICUREANISM. In later centuries, Demokritos was sometimes remembered as the "laughing philosopher," possibly because of his ethical emphasis on happiness or cheerfulness (*euthymie*). The Roman author Seneca says that Demokritos was constantly laughing to mock the foolishness of humanity.

See also PYTHAGORAS; SCIENCE.

Further reading: Paul Cartledge, *Democritus* (New York: Routledge, 1999); C. C. W. Taylor, trans., *The Atomists, Leucippus and Democritus: Fragments* (Toronto: University of Toronto Press, 1999).

Demosthenes (1) (384–322 B.C.E.) *Greatest of the Athenian orators*

Demosthenes is best known for opposing the Macedonian king PHILIP II's ambitions in Greece in 351–338 B.C.E. Although his rallying of his countrymen against Philip brought defeat for ATHENS and could not save Greece from subjugation, it also produced the finest surviving political speeches of the ancient Greek world. Demosthenes was not a great statesman; his defiance of Philip led him to urge foolhardy extremes, and he was badly distracted by Athenian political infighting. But he was a true patriot, for which, under Macedonian rule, he eventually paid with his life.

Demosthenes was born into the well-off middle class—his name means "strength of the people"—but his father, who owned an arms-manufacturing business, died when Demosthenes was seven, and the boy's brothers dissipated the estate. The young Demosthenes' first public speech was directed against his brother Aphobus and an associate, in a lawsuit over Demosthenes' withheld inheritance. Although skinny, awkward, and dour, Demosthenes soon gained prominence as a paid attorney in private cases, and then began serving as an assistant prosecutor in public trials. He also began speaking in the Athenian political ASSEMBLY on questions of public importance.

Alarmed by Philip's aggressions in the northeast, Demosthenes in 351 B.C.E. delivered his *First Philippic,* urging the Athenians to recapture their old colony of AMPHIPOLIS from the Macedonians. Demosthenes' military advice was not heeded. When Philip besieged the Greek city of OLYNTHOS, in the CHALCIDICE region (349 B.C.E.), Demosthenes, in his three speeches called the *Olynthiacs,* again urged an Athenian military expedition to save the town; again the Athenians voted down such an action.

Meanwhile, Demosthenes was embroiled in partisan conflicts with his Athenian enemies, notably Eubulus and the orator AESCHINES. Demosthenes and Aeschines had been amicable partners on an embassy to MACEDON to make peace with Philip in 346 B.C.E. But after Philip made a mockery of the peace by immediately marching into central Greece, occupying THERMOPLYLAE and taking control of DELPHI, Demosthenes began his long and bitter feud with Aeschines, denouncing him as Philip's paid lackey.

In 340 B.C.E. Demosthenes engineered an Athenian alliance with the vital northeastern city of BYZANTIUM; this spurred Philip to declare war on Athens and besiege Byzantium (unsuccessfully). As Philip led his army south into Greece in 338 B.C.E. Demosthenes proposed and established an alliance with THEBES, resulting in an Athenian-Theban army that confronted the Macedonian advance at CHAIRONEIA, in northern BOEOTIA. The Battle of Chaironeia, fought in the summer of 338 B.C.E., was a disastrous Greek defeat. Demosthenes fought on the field as an Athenian HOPLITE and joined the Athenian retreat; according to one story, when the fleeing Demosthenes' cloak got tangled in a bush, he shouted, "Don't kill me! I'm Demosthenes!"

After the battle, however, he became the leader of the moment, organizing Athens's defense and arranging for grain imports. Demosthenes was not persecuted by the Macedonians when they came to terms with Athens, and he was chosen by the city to deliver the funeral oration for the Athenians slain at Chaironeia. The Athenians later awarded him an honorific crown or garland for his state services, and when Aeschines accused him of improper conduct in this (330 B.C.E.), Demosthenes won such a resounding acquittal with his extant defense speech *On the Crown* that Aeschines emigrated from Athens in humiliation. Later, however, Demosthenes was condemned for embezzlement and was exiled from the city.

Meanwhile, Philip's son and successor ALEXANDER THE GREAT had died at Babylon after conquering the Persian

Empire (323 B.C.E.), and the time looked ripe for a Greek rebellion against Macedonian rule. Recalled to Athens, Demosthenes helped organize this revolt, which was crushed by the Macedonian governor ANTIPATER. Demosthenes fled from Athens and committed suicide as Antipater's men were closing in. He is said to have died by drinking the poison that he always carried in a pen.

See also FUNERAL CUSTOMS; LAWS AND LAW COURTS; RHETORIC.

Further reading: Arthur Wallace Picard-Cambridge, *Demosthenes and the Last Days of Greek Freedom, 384–322 B.C.* (New York: AMS Press, 1978); Ian Worthington, ed., *Demosthenes: Statesman and Orator* (New York: Routledge, 2000); Harvey Yunis, ed., *On the Crown/Demosthenes* (New York: Cambridge University Press, 2001).

Demosthenes (2) (d. 413 B.C.E.) *Accomplished Athenian general of the Peloponnesian War*
By developing the use of light-armed javelin men in hilly terrain, Demosthenes made a lasting contribution not only to the Athenian war effort but to the progress of Greek military science. He was the first commander to compensate for the limited mobility of the heavy-infantry HOPLITE.

Defeated by light-armed skirmishers in the hills of AETOLIA (426 B.C.E.), Demosthenes took the lesson to heart in his next campaign that same season, against the northwestern Greek city of AMBRACIA. With a force of Athenian hoplites and light-armed local allies, Demosthenes destroyed nearly the entire Ambracian army.

In 425 B.C.E. came his greatest triumph: the Battle of PYLOS and the capture of nearly 200 Spartan hoplites on the inshore island of Sphacteria. Archers and javelin men played a crucial role in the final assault. The operation was commanded by the Athenian politician KLEON who undoutedly used Demosthenes' troops and battle plan. By then Demosthenes was acting as Kleon's unofficial military adviser; after Kleon's death (422 B.C.E.), Demosthenes seems to have fallen into disfavor. He was not elected to another generalship until 413 B.C.E., when he was sent to reinforce the Athenian general NIKIAS at the disastrously stalled Athenian siege of SYRACUSE.

There Demosthenes commanded the rear guard in the calamitous Athenian retreat. Surrounded, he eventually surrendered, and was later put to death by the Syracusans.

See also WARFARE, LAND.

Further reading: Joseph Roisman, *The General Demosthenes and His Use of Military Surprise* (Stuttgart, Germany: F. Steiner, 1993); Donald Kagen, *The Peloponnesian War* (New York: Viking 2003); J. F. Lazenby, *The Peloponnesian War: A Military Study* (London: Routledge, 2004).

Diadochoi   This term, meaning "successors," refers to the generals of the Macedonian king ALEXANDER THE GREAT. After Alexander's death in 323 B.C.E., they

emerged to lay claim to—and fight over—parts of his vast empire, which stretched from Greece to the Indus River.

The chaotic campaigns and maneuverings of the Diadochoi lasted for over 25 years and divided Alexander's empire permanently into smaller Hellenistic kingdoms whose boundaries were more or less settled by about 280 B.C.E.

ANTIGONUS (1) and his son DEMETRIUS POLIORKETES were based in ASIA MINOR and sought to preserve and rule the entire empire as it had been under Alexander. They failed in this attempt, but retained power in Asia Minor and founded the Antigonid Dynasty. PTOLEMY (1) seized EGYPT and founded his dynasty there. SELEUCUS (1) took control of areas in the Near East and parts of the old Persian Empire, establishing the powerful Seleucid Dynasty. KASSANDER claimed MACEDON and Greece, and LYSIMACHUS took THRACE. The Macedonian regent ANTIPATER was active in the early years after Alexander's death, as the overlord to Antigonus. In addition, an able commander named Eumenes posed an early threat but was driven eastward out of Asia Minor by Antigonus, then was killed.

See also HELLENISTIC AGE.

Further reading: R. M. Errington, "Diodorus Siculus and the Chronology of the Early Diadochoi, 320–311 B.C.," *Hermes* 105 (1977): 478–504; Richard Billows, *Antigonos the One-Eyed and the Creation of the Hellenistic State* (Berkeley: University of California Press, 1990); Helen Lund, *Lysimachus: A Study in Early Hellenistic Kingship* (New York: Routledge, 1992).

dialects   *See* GREEK LANGUAGE.

Diodorus Siculus (first century B.C.E.) *Greek historian born at Agyrium, in central SICILY*
Diodorus the Sicilian (as his surname means) lived in the first century B.C.E. and wrote a world history, from earliest times to the end of Julius Caesar's Gallic Wars (54 B.C.E.). Much of the work is lost, but books 11–20 survive fully and provide much information (and some misinformation) about events in Greek history of the 400s and 300s B.C.E. While Diodorus sometimes relies on inferior source material, he provides the best available account for many events of the 300s, such as the wars of the DIADOCHI.

Further reading: R. M. Errington, "Diodorus Siculus and the Chronology of the Early Diadochoi, 320–311 B.C." *Hermes* 105 (1977): 478–504; Kenneth Sacks, *Diodorus Siculus and the First Century* (Princeton, N.J.: Princeton University Press, 1990); P. McKechnie, "Diodorus Siculus and Hephaestion's Pyre," *Classical Quarterly* 45 (1995): 418–432; P. J. Stylianou, *A Historical Commentary on Diodorus Siculus, Book 15* (New York: Oxford University Press, 1998); C. Rubincam, "Did Diodorus Siculus Take Over Cross-references from His Sources?" *American Journal of Philology* 119 (1998): 67–87.

Diogenes (ca. 400–325 B.C.E.) *Best known of the Cynic philosophers*
As an extreme devotee of Cynic simplicity and rejection of social convention, Diogenes voluntarily lived in a brutish and immodest manner that supposedly won him the nickname "the Dog" (Kuon). From this, his followers became known as Kunikoi, or CYNICS. Diogenes did not, however, start the Cynic movement; it had been founded by an Athenian, Antisthenes.

Diogenes was born in the Greek city of SINOPE, on the southern coast of the BLACK SEA. He learned the Cynic's creed upon moving to ATHENS in middle age. According to one story, he was taught by Antisthenes himself, after pursuing him relentlessly for instruction.

Living homeless and impoverished, sleeping in public colonnades or in an overturned clay storage jar (not exactly the "bathtub" of legend), Diogenes traveled to CORINTH and probably to other cities, preaching the Cynic doctrine of spiritual self-sufficiency. Despite his avowed apathy to social matters, he seems to have been a skilled exhibitionist, attracting the attention of passersby while preaching his sermons. He is said to have walked the streets with a lit lamp in daylight, remarking that he was searching for an honest man. Another story claims that he threw away his only possession, a cup, after watching a boy scoop up cistern water with his hands. Supposedly Diogenes also had the scandalous habit of masturbating in the public places where he lived—a practice he defended by saying he wished he could satisfy hunger as easily, by just rubbing his stomach.

According to legend, when the young Macedonian king ALEXANDER THE GREAT visited Corinth in 335 B.C.E. he found Diogenes at some public haunt and asked if he could do anything for Diogenes. "Yes," replied the sage. "Move a little, out of my sunlight." Later the king declared, "If I were not Alexander, I would be Diogenes." (That is, If I did not have my conquests to pursue, I would emulate Diogenes' asceticism.)

Further reading: Luis Navia, *Classical Cynicism: A Critical Study* (Westport, Conn.: Greenwood Press, 1996); Luis Navia, *Diogenes of Sinope: The Man in the Tub* (Westport, Conn.: Greenwood Press, 1998).

Diomedes This mythical Greek hero of ARGOS played a significant role in the TROJAN WAR. He was the son of the Calydonian hero Tydeus and the Argive princess Deipyle, and later became the king of AETOLIA. As a young man, Diomedes avenged his father's death at THEBES by helping to capture the city in the expedition of the Epigoni (Descendants).

In HOMER's epic poem the *Iliad,* Diomedes is represented as one of the bravest of the Greeks, on a par with AJAX (1) and ACHILLES. He was a favorite of ATHENA, and he was said to be not only a superb fighter but also a good councillor. He engaged in single combat with HECTOR and AENEAS, and he wounded the goddess APHRODITE and the war god ARES himself, in two separate battles (book 5). Along with ODYSSEUS, Diomedes made a night raid on the Trojan allies' camp and killed the Thracian champion Rhesus (book 10). These two soldiers also joined together in carrying off the Trojan statue of Athena known as Palladion, one of the fated preconditions for the city's capture. In tales told by later writers, Diomedes and Odysseus were sometimes said to have brought the wounded hero PHILOKTETES from the island of Lemnos.

Diomedes survived the war and returned home to Argos. According to one version, he found when he arrived that the goddess Aphrodite had caused his wife, Aegiale, to be unfaithful. Distressed, he departed Greece again and sailed to Magna Graecia in ITALY, where he founded a new city called Argyripa and remarried.

See also SEVEN AGAINST THEBES.

Further reading: D. C. Kurtz, "The Man-Eating Horses of Diomedes in Poetry and Painting," *Journal of Hellenic Studies* 95 (1975): 171–172; B. Kirigin, "Archaeological Evidence for the Cult of Diomedes in the Adriatic," in *Studi sulla Grecità di Occidente* (Rome: L'Erma di Bretschneider, 1998), 63–110.

Dionysius (1) (ca. 430–367 B.C.E.) *Ruthless and dynamic dictator of the Sicilian Greek city of Syracuse*
Dionysius reigned from 405 to 367 B.C.E. Like other Sicilian TYRANTS, he was able to seize supreme power largely due to the external threat of Carthaginian domination. A brilliant battlefield commander—he introduced the first Greek use of siege artillery, in the form of arrow-shooting giant crossbows—Dionysius confined the expansionist Carthaginians to the western third of SICILY. Ruling also over Greek southern ITALY, he was, for a time, master of the Greek West. He is best remembered for briefly hosting the Athenian philosopher PLATO at his court (387 B.C.E.).

Dionysius became a promising young soldier-politician in the democratic Syracuse of the late 400s, and he married the daughter of the statesman Hermocrates. Amid renewed Carthaginian attacks on the Sicilian Greeks, Dionysius was elected to the Syracusan board of generals (406 B.C.E.). Supplanting his colleagues, he easily convinced the Syracusan people to vote him supreme powers, for they were seeking a military savior.

Over the next 15 years Dionysius stymied the Carthaginian advance in Sicily, while quelling uprisings at home and subduing many Sicilian Greeks and native Sicels. He destroyed the Sicilian Greek city of NAXOS (2) and captured and sacked the Carthaginian stronghold of Moyta, at Sicily's western tip, after a famous siege (398 B.C.E.). Twice he beat back the Carthaginians from the walls of Syracuse. By 390 B.C.E., peace had been made with the island's two domains—Carthaginian (west) and Syracusan (east)—now officially recognized.

Dionysius next sought conquest over southern Italy. Allied with the Italian-Greek city of LOCRIS and the native Lucanii, he destroyed the Italian-Greek city of RHEGIUM (in about 387 B.C.E.). But a renewed Carthaginian war in Sicily brought battlefield defeat and loss of territory.

Dionysius's cruelty and greed were notorious: He constantly needed money to finance his campaigns. Yet he was also a cultured man who wrote tragedies and owned relics (including a desk and writing tablets) that had belonged to the great Athenian playwrights AESCHYLUS and EURIPIDES. Dionysius's death at about age 64, supposedly came from the effects of his carousing after receiving the news that his play *Hector's Ransom* had won first prize at an Athenian tragedy competition.

He was succeeded by his son Dionysius II, a far less capable leader.

See also CARTHAGE; THEATER; WARFARE, SIEGE.

Further reading: L. J. Sanders, *Dionysius I of Syracuse and Greek Tyranny* (New York: Methuen, 1987); Brian Caven, *Dionysius I: War-Lord of Sicily* (New Haven, Conn.: Yale University Press, 1990).

Dionysius (2) II   *See* SYRACUSE.

Dionysus   This Greek god was associated with several different spheres of power. On one hand, he was the god of wine, agriculture, and earthly fertility. He was also the patron god of theater. Furthermore, he was a god of mystery cults and religious possession. Like the goddess DEMETER, the cult of Dionysus was more popular among the Greek common people than among the aristocrats.

The distinguishing feature of Dionysus was that he inspired humans to escape from daily life through either physical intoxication or spiritual frenzy. Worshippers achieved a divinely motivated ecstasy (*ekstasis,* "standing outside oneself"), in which the human personality briefly vanished, supposedly replaced by the identity of the god himself.

In MYTH, Dionysus was the son of ZEUS and the Theban princess Semele (a daughter of CADMUS). Semele was pregnant with Zeus's child when Zeus's jealous wife, HERA, approached her in disguise and convinced her to ask Zeus this favor: that he should visit her in his true shape. When Semele made this request, Zeus reluctantly appeared to her as a thunderbolt, which killed Semele but made her unborn child immortal. Zeus incubated the fetus in his thigh until it was ready to be born. Hera persecuted the child by sending monsters, but the young Dionysus evaded or survived their torments and was at last welcomed by the other deities as the 12th god on Mt. OLYMPUS.

In some form, Dionysus probably existed in Greek RELIGION by about 1200 B.C.E., since his name seems to appear on LINEAR B tablets from Mycenaean-era PYLOS. Many modern scholars, however, think that Dionysus

This kantharos, a cup with two high handles, has a mask of Dionysus, the god of wine, on one side. Such an elaborate cup with molded masks may have been intended for dedication to the gods in a temple or a tomb rather than for actual use. *(The J. Paul Getty Museum)*

evolved from the fusion of a local Greek nature divinity with a more complex god imported from ASIA MINOR or THRACE. Some ancient Greeks also believed that Dionysus came from one of these non-Greek, uncivilized lands. The god's name may mean "son of Zeus," or alternatively it may mean "god of Nysa" (referring to Mt. Nysa in Phrygia).

The Greeks sometimes called him Bacchos (the name later adopted as Bacchus when the Romans borrowed the god for their religion). Greek myth included many stories of Dionysus's human female followers called Bacchae or MAENADS. These women would leave their homes and roam the mountains in frenzied bands, dancing and singing in the god's honor. EURIPIDES' tragedy *The Bacchae* (405 B.C.E.) recounts how Dionysus returned to his mother's city of THEBES to claim divine worship and discovered that his uncle, the Theban king Pentheus ("lamenting"), had prohibited the god's worship and persecuted his followers. Incensed, Dionysus retaliated by inspiring the Theban women to wander the countryside as Maenads, including Pentheus's own mother, Agave. Then, in human disguise, the god convinced the young king to follow them. The women spied Pentheus in a tree and, in their intoxicated state thought that he was a wild animal, so they hunted him down and tore him limb from limb.

In actual Greek ritual, Dionysian worship and possession was not quite as grotesque. No doubt his followers got agreeably drunk at festivals honoring Dionysus, as people in more recent centuries have done at country fairs and on St. Patrick's Day. There was also symbolic possession in the wearing of masks. Dionysus had several annual festivals at ATHENS, the most important one being the City Dionysia or Greater Dionysia, held in early spring. At this festival in early times, masked worshippers would impersonate the god, speaking words in his character. By the late 500s B.C.E., these rites had developed into the beginnings of Athenian stage comedy.

The main sites of Dionysus's worship in Greece were Athens, BOEOTIA, and the Aegean island of Naxos; all were important vine-growing regions. As a vegetation god, Dionysus was associated with all fruit-bearing trees and with the pine and plane trees. His fertility aspect was suggested in the unquenchable lust of his attendant creatures, the SATYRS and *Silenoi*. Sexual relations did not play a major role in his myths (that was the province of the goddess APHRODITE), but Dionysus did have one well-known lover, the Cretan princess Ariadne, whom he carried off from Naxos after she had been abandoned there by the Athenian hero THESEUS.

Dionysus was a popular subject in Attic vase painting. At first, in the 500s and 400s B.C.E., he was always portrayed as a bearded man. Later representations tended to show him as a beardless youth or child. He is generally represented wearing a wreath of grape leaves and, like the Maenads, he carries a special staff with vines wrapped around one end, called a *thyrsos*. He also frequently carries a drinking cup and sometimes rides regally on a leopard.

For the classical Greeks, Dionysus represented the irrational aspect of the human soul. The frenzies wrought by Dionysus were the natural complement to the virtues of reason and restraint embodied in the god APOLLO. Symbolically, Dionysus was said to inhabit Apollo's sanctuary at DELPHI during the latter's annual winter absence. During the HELLENISTIC AGE (300–150 B.C.E.), amid the growing hunger for personal religion, Dionysus was one of the few Greek deities whose worship produced a mystery cult, offering the hope of a happy AFTERLIFE to its initiates.

See also LYRIC POETRY; MUSIC; NYMPHS; ORPHISM; THEATER; PRAXITELES.

Further reading: Walter F. Otto, *Dionysus: Myth and Cult*, reprint, translated by Robert B. Palmer (Dallas, Tex.: Spring Publications, 1981, 1986); Alain Daniélou, *Gods of Love and Ecstasy: The Traditions of Shiva and Dionysus* (Rochester, Vt.: Inner Traditions, 1992); Andrew Dalby, *Bacchus: A Biography* (London: British Museum, 2003).

Dioskouroi   *See* CASTOR AND POLYDEUCES.

dithyramb   *See* LYRIC POETRY; THEATER.

divination   *See* PROPHECY AND DIVINATION.

divorce   *See* MARRIAGE.

Dodona   This famous sanctuary and oracle of the god ZEUS is located in a region of northwest Greece called EPIRUS. Although purely Greek in origin, the sanctuary was very ancient, and it retained primitive aspects in historical times. It lay mainly out in the open, and its central feature was an ancient oak tree, sacred to Zeus. In response to an applicant's questions, the god spoke in the oak leaves' rustlings, which were then interpreted by the priests; a sacred dove may also have been part of the cult. HOMER's epic poem *The Iliad* (written down around 750 B.C.E.) describes Zeus's priests at Dodona "sleeping on the ground, with unwashed feet." By the time of the historian HERODOTUS (ca. 435 B.C.E.), three priestesses had somehow replaced the male priests. These priestesses called themselves "doves" (*peleiades*).

Although never as influential as the oracle of the god APOLLO at DELPHI, Dodona was the religious-political center of northwest Greece. There is evidence of cult activity at Dodona as early as the eighth century B.C.E., but building activity did not begin on the site until the 300s. The cult reached its peak of popularity in the 200s B.C.E., and the Epirote king PYRRHUS made it the religious capital of his domain. It was destroyed by the Aetolians in 219 B.C.E. but rebuilt almost immediately by the Macedonian king PHILIP V. Activity continued then until the Romans destroyed the site again (167 B.C.E.).

The first archaeological investigation of Dodona took place by N. Karapanos in 1873–1875, confirming the location of the sanctuary and uncovering numerous artifacts. From 1913 to 1932, some additional excavation was done by the Greek Archaeological Society. Systematic excavation began in the 1950s under D. Evangelides and S. Dakaris, and since 1981 the work has continued under the auspices of the Archaeological Society, funded by the University of Ioannina. Conservation and restoration completed since 1961 have focused particularly on the beautiful theater and stadium. Other monuments whose remains are visible at Dodona include the Temple of Zeus, the council house, and the ACROPOLIS.

See also AETOLIA; PROPHECY AND DIVINATION.

Further reading: H. W. Parke, *The Oracles of Zeus: Dodona, Olympia, Ammon* (Oxford: Blackwell, 1967); Sotirios Dakaris, *Archaeological Guide to Dodona*, translated by Elli Kirk-Defterou (Ioannina, Greece: Cultural Society, 1971); Sotirios Dakaris, *Dodona* (Congleton, U.K.: Old Vicarage, 1994).

Dorian Greeks   This term refers to one of the three main ethnic branches of the ancient Greek people; the other two were the IONIAN and AEOLIAN GREEKS. Archaeological evidence, combined with a cautious reading of Greek MYTH, indicates that Dorian invaders overran mainland GREECE around 1100–1000 B.C.E., in the last wave of violent, prehistoric Greek immigration. Emerging (probably) from the northwestern Greek region called EPIRUS, the Dorians descended southward, battling their fellow Greeks for possession of desired sites. They bypassed central Greece but occupied much of the PELOPONNESE and the isthmus and Megarid. Taking to ships, the Dorians then conquered eastward across the southern AEGEAN SEA and won a small area of southwestern ASIA MINOR. The Dorian invasion obviously was associated with the collapse of MYCENAEAN CIVILIZATION, but recent scholarship considers the invasion to be an effect, rather than a cause, of the Mycenaeans' downfall. Similarly, some historians have believed that the Dorians' success was due to their possession of IRON weapons—superior to the defenders' BRONZE—but it seems equally likely that all Greeks acquired iron-forging only after the Dorian conquest.

The word Dorian (Greek: *Dorieus*) may be related to the Greek word *doru,* "spear." Ancient legend also connected the name of the hero Dorus, son of HELLĒN. A small Dorian region called Doris, in the mountains of central Greece, was erroneously thought to be the people's original homeland.

By the classical era (400s B.C.E.), the important Dorian states included the Peloponnesian cities of CORINTH and ARGOS, the Aegean islands of CRETE and RHODES, and the Asian Greek cities of HALICARNASSUS and KNIDOS. Farther afield, prosperous Dorian colonies existed in SICILY (particularly SYRACUSE), in southern ITALY, and in Libya, at CYRENE (1). But the most important Dorian site, and the one that other Dorians looked to as their protector, was the militaristic city of SPARTA, in the southeastern Peloponnese.

Dorian states were distinguished by their dialect (called Doric) and by their peculiar social institutions, including a tripartite tribal division and the brutal practice—at Sparta, Crete, Syracuse and elsewhere—of maintaining an underclass of serfs, or HELOTS. Due largely to the superior armies of Sparta, the Dorians were considered the best soldiers in Greece, until the 300s B.C.E. saw the emergence of non-Dorian BOEOTIA.

Although Dorian cities such as Corinth were at the forefront of Greek TRADE and culture in the 700s and 600s B.C.E. by the following centuries the Dorians had acquired the reputation for being crude and violent (at least in the eyes of the Athenians and other Ionian Greeks). Ethnic tensions between Dorians and Ionians in mainland Greece and Sicily reached a bloody crisis in the

PELOPONNESIAN WAR (431–404 B.C.E.). During the HELLENISTIC AGE (300–150 B.C.E.), Syracuse, Rhodes, and Halicarnassus were among the Dorian states important in commerce and art.

See also ACRAGAS; AEGINA; CORCYRA; DARK AGE; GELA; GREEK LANGUAGE; LOCRI; MEGARA (1); MELOS; MESSENIA; SICYON; TARAS.

Further reading: Elizabeth M. Craik, *The Dorian Aegean* (London: Routledge and Kegan Paul, 1980); Kazimierz Lewartowski, *The Decline of the Mycenaean Civilization: An Archaeological Study of Events in the Greek Mainland* (Wrocław, Poland: Wydawnictwo Polskiej Akademii Nauk, 1989); Jonathan M. Hall, *Ethnic Identity in Greek Antiquity* (New York: Cambridge University Press, 1997); Irene S. Lemos, *The Protogeometric Aegean: The Archaeology of the Late Eleventh and Tenth Centuries B.C.* (New York: Oxford University Press, 2002).

Doric dialect   *See* GREEK LANGUAGE.

Doric order   *See* ARCHITECTURE.

Doris   *See* DORIAN GREEKS.

Draco (600s B.C.E.) *Athenian statesman who supposedly gave the city its first written code of law, circa 621 B.C.E.*
Draco's laws were aristocratically biased and egregiously harsh, involving wide use of the death penalty. One later thinker remarked that the laws had been written in blood, not ink. Draco's severity is commemorated in the English word "Draconian," used to describe excessively harsh law or administration. Within 30 years, Draco's code was replaced by that of the great lawgiver SOLON (ca. 594 B.C.E.)

See also ARISTOCRACY; LAWS AND LAW COURTS.

Further reading: Ronald S. Stroud, *Drakon's Law on Homicide* (Berkeley: University of California Press, 1968); Michael Gagarin, *Drakon and Early Athenian Homicide Law* (New Haven, Conn.: Yale University Press, 1981); Alexander Tulin, *Dike Phonou: The Right of Prosecution and Attic Homicide Procedure* (Stuttgart, Germany: B. G. Teubner, 1996); Edwin Carawan, *Rhetoric and the Law of Draco* (New York: Oxford University Press, 1998).

drama   *See* THEATER.

E

education Literacy became widespread at a surprisingly early date in the ancient Greek world. Surviving public inscriptions and historical anecdotes suggest that, in the more advanced Greek states, a majority of at least the male citizens could read and write by around 600 B.C.E.—barely 175 years after the Greeks had first adapted the Phoenician ALPHABET. The impetus for this learning was probably not love of literature but the necessity of TRADE—a need that included the middle and lower-middle classes.

As today, literacy and numeracy were taught to boys at school. The earliest surviving reference to a school in the Western world occurs in the history of HERODOTUS (ca. 435 B.C.E.), in reference to the year 494 B.C.E. on the Greek island of CHIOS. Similarly, school scenes first appear on Athenian vase paintings soon after 500 B.C.E. Schools were private, fee-paid institutions. There were no state-funded schools at this time and no laws requiring children to receive education. There were separate schools for girls (coeducation did not exist), but girls' schooling was generally not as widespread or thorough as boys'.

In classical ATHENS (400s–300s B.C.E.), a boy's schooling usually began at age seven, and many of the lower-income students probably left after the three or four years needed to learn the basic skills. For the rest, there might be as much as 10 years' elementary school, under three types of teachers. The *grammatistēs* gave lessons in reading, WRITING, arithmetic, and literature. Literary studies emphasized the rote memorization of passages from revered poets, particularly HOMER and (in later centuries) the Athenian tragic playwrights of the 400s B.C.E., SPORT comprised the second branch of Greek education, under a coach (*paidotribēs*). WRESTLING and

gymnastics were among the preferred disciplines. Militaristic states such as SPARTA greatly emphasized sports as a preparation for soldiering; the rugged art of BOXING was considered a typically Spartan boy's sport. Sparta was unusual in encouraging gymnastics training for girls.

The third teacher, the *kitharistēs,* gave instruction in MUSIC—specifically, in singing and playing the lyre for the recitation of LYRIC POETRY. This branch of Athenian-style education may have been less esteemed outside of Athens. Supposedly, the Macedonian king PHILIP II once rebuked his young son Alexander after the boy's musical performance at a banquet. "Are you not ashamed, my son, to play the lyre so well?" Philip asked the future king ALEXANDER THE GREAT (340s B.C.E.).

At age 18 an Athenian male became known as an *ephebos* (youth) and began two years of military training; similar programs existed at other Greek states. That a rich young man might then resume his studies was a practice that evolved at Athens in the mid- and late 400s B.C.E. The pioneers in this practice were the SOPHISTS and teachers of RHETORIC who came flocking to Athens. Charging high fees, tutors such as PROTAGORAS of ABDERA and GORGIAS of Leontini gave lessons in disputation and public speaking to young men planning to enter public life. The Athenian philosopher SOCRATES (469–399 B.C.E.), while not himself a sophist, occupies an important place in this evolution, as does the Athenian orator ISOKRATES (436–338 B.C.E.). Such tutors answered a growing need at Athens for higher education.

Socrates and the sophists paved the way for the Western world's first university—the ACADEMY, established by the Athenian philosopher PLATO in an area just outside the city wall, in around 385 B.C.E. The Academy was known as a school of PHILOSOPHY, but offered lectures and advanced study in many areas that might not be associated with philosophy, such as MATHEMATICS. An even broader range of study was offered at the LYCEUM, founded at Athens by ARISTOTLE (ca. 335 B.C.E.). Two other major philosophical schools, of EPICUREANISM and STOICISM, were established at Athens by about 300 B.C.E. During the HELLENISTIC AGE (300–150 B.C.E.), education became even more widespread, leading to great advances in philosophy, mathematics, medicine, and science. New centers of higher learning arose around the Mediterranean, at cities such as ALEXANDRIA (1) and PERGAMON, both of which maintained tremendous libraries.

See also ASTRONOMY; HOMOSEXUALITY; SCIENCE; WOMEN.

Further reading: M. L. Clarke, *Higher Education in the Ancient World* (London: Routledge and Kegan Paul, 1971); Robin Barrow, *Greek and Roman Education* (Basingstoke, U.K.: Macmillan, 1976); Nigel M. Kennell, *The Gymnasium of Virtue: Education and Culture in Ancient Sparta* (Chapel Hill: University of North Carolina Press, 1995); Martin D. Carcieri, *Democracy and Education in Classical Athens and the American Founding* (New York: P. Lang, 2002).

Egypt Located in northeast Africa, Egypt was (and is) a non-Greek land situated approximately 600 miles southeast of mainland Greece. Its territory includes about 700 miles of land along the lower Nile River, with coastlines along the Mediterranean Sea and the Red Sea. At the beginning of the Greek era, in the second millennium B.C.E., Egypt was already a magnificent kingdom that was far more culturally advanced than Greece. When the MYCENAEAN CIVILIZATION of mainland Greece began to emerge around 1600 B.C.E., it was probably strongly influenced by the Egyptian Middle and New Kingdoms. The royal tombs at MYCENAE, for instance, may have been inspired by the pyramids and graves of the Egyptian pharaohs. The Greek MYTH of DANAUS and Aegyptus—among other tales—seems to commemorate some early Greek-Egyptian contact. The Mycenaeans would have visited Egypt for TRADE purposes, for service as hired mercenaries, and/or for pirate raids. It is very probable that the "Sea Peoples" who ravaged Egypt's Mediterranean coast around 1100 B.C.E. included groups of displaced Mycenaeans fleeing from social collapse in Greece.

For several centuries in the first millennium B.C.E., Greek merchants were banned by the Egyptian pharaohs. As a result, Egypt never influenced the ripening Archaic Greek culture of the 700s B.C.E. as strongly as did another Near Eastern civilization, PHOENICIA. Around 650 B.C.E., however, the termination of this policy allowed Greek traders to set up an emporium in the Nile delta. At this site, called NAUKRATIS, the Greeks offered SILVER ORE and SLAVES in exchange for Egyptian grain and luxury goods

such as carved ivory. The Greek poet BACCHYLIDES (ca. 470 B.C.E.) mentions grain ships bringing a fat profit home from Egypt. The Naukratis trade brought Egyptian artwork in quantity to Greece, to be imitated by Greek artists. Egyptian statuary, for example, was extremely influential for the stylistic development of the famous Greek *kouroi* statues in the early and mid-500s B.C.E.

Greek soldiers were always more welcome in Egypt than merchants, and by 600 B.C.E., pharaohs were hiring Greek HOPLITE mercenaries to fight in their wars. One piece of evidence for this phenomenon is a graffito scratched onto a colossal statue at Abu Simbel, 700 miles up the Nile, by a Greek soldier in about 591 B.C.E.

Egypt was conquered by the Persian king Cambyses in 525 B.C.E. As a Persian subject state, Egypt contributed warships and crews in the PERSIAN WARS against Greece. In 460 B.C.E., a Greek invasion force—120 ships of the Athenian-led DELIAN LEAGUE—sailed into the Nile to attack the city of Memphis, held by a Persian garrison. The invasion was destroyed by the Persians in 455 B.C.E., and Egypt remained securely under Persian control for another 120 years.

In 332 B.C.E., the Macedonian king ALEXANDER THE GREAT captured Egypt as part of his conquest of the Persian Empire. On Egypt's Mediterranean coast, Alexander founded a city destined to be one of the greatest of the ancient world, ALEXANDRIA (1).

When Alexander died, one of his successors, a Macedonian general named PTOLEMY (1), took control of Egypt and founded a dynasty there. With its brilliant capital at Alexandria, Ptolemaic Egypt became the wealthiest and most important kingdom in the HELLENISTIC AGE (300–150 B.C.E.). Culture thrived, attracting philosophers and poets from all over the Mediterranean. The Ptolemies adopted the apparatus of the pharaohs and modernized it, creating an immense, efficient civil service for drawing taxes from the Egyptian peasantry who worked the fertile Nile valley.

In foreign affairs, another of the Hellenistic kingdoms soon emerged as the enemy of Ptolemaic Egypt: the Syrian-based SELEUCID EMPIRE. Between 274 and 168 B.C.E., these two kingdoms fought the six Syrian Wars, disputing their common boundary in the Levant. The Ptolemies continued to rule Egypt until the Roman conquest of 30 B.C.E. The last Ptolemaic ruler was the famous Cleopatra VII.

See also BLACK PEOPLES; DIADOCHOI; GOLD; HERODOTUS; PTOLEMY (2) II; SCULPTURE; WARFARE, LAND; WARFARE, NAVAL.

Further reading: Shelley Wachsmann, *Aegeans in the Theban Tombs* (Leuven: Peeters, 1987); Jaromir Málek, *Egyptian Art* (London: Phaidon, 1999); Sally-Ann Ashton, *Ptolemaic Royal Sculpture from Egypt: The Interaction between Greek and Egyptian Traditions* (Oxford: Archaeopress, 2001).

ekklesia   *See* ASSEMBLY.

Elea   *See* PARMENIDES.

Electra (Elektra)   In MYTH, Electra was a daughter of King AGAMEMNON of MYCENAE and his queen, KLYTEMNESTRA. Not mentioned by HOMER, her first known literary appearance comes in STESICHORUS's poem, *The Oresteia* (ca. 590 B.C.E.). In Classical Athenian tragedy, she appears as a main character in the story—retold by each of the three great tragedians—of how her brother ORESTES avenged Agamemnon's murder by slaying Klytemnestra and her lover, Aegisthus.

In AESCHYLUS's play *The Libation Bearers* (458 B.C.E.), Electra welcomes Orestes and supports his scheme to kill their hated mother and Aegisthus. In SOPHOKLES' *Electra* (ca. 418–410 B.C.E.), she acts similarly and is the primary focus of the play. In EURIPIDES' *Electra* (ca. 417 B.C.E.), however, she appears obsessively hateful and jealous of her mother, who has denied Electra the chance to marry, thereby punning on her name: *alektron* ("without marriage"). In this version, Electra wields an ax and actually helps Orestes to kill Klytemnestra (offstage), then goes wild with guilt. Euripides' treatment of Electra's character provides one of the best extant examples of that playwright's innovative interest in psychology and the plight of WOMEN in Greek society.

Further reading: Friedrich Solmsen, *Electra and Orestes: Three Recognitions in Greek Tragedy* (Amsterdam: Noord-Hollandsche U.M., 1967); Leona MacLeod, *Dolos and Dike in Sophokles' Elektra* (Leiden, Netherlands: E. J. Brill, 2001).

elegy   *See* LYRIC POETRY.

elephants   Although elephants were not native to Greece, elephant ivory was used for carving as early as the late Bronze Age (ca. 1400 B.C.E.). The raw material was imported from Syria, Egypt, and/or North Africa. The animal itself is first mentioned in Greek sources by Herodotus, writing in the fifth century B.C.E., although the historian does not appear to have ever seen one himself. Slightly later, in the late fifth and early fourth centuries B.C.E., Ctesias wrote extensively about the elephants he saw in Persia and India while he was court physician for the Persian king Artaxerxes II. The fourth century B.C.E. scholar Aristotle was also familiar with elephants and describes them in several passages.

Hannibal of Carthage is famous for having used elephants successfully in battle against the Romans during the Punic Wars. In fact, there were precedents for Hannibal's actions in the military tactics of ancient Greece. Alexander the Great encountered elephants in battle several times. The first instance occurred in 331, when he fought the Persian king Darius at Gaugamela, although the animals do not appear to have taken part in the fighting at this battle, and Alexander does not seem to have been fazed by them. He encountered them several more times during his subsequent conquest of India and needed to devise new strategies for these encounters, since his horses would not willingly face the Indian elephants. During the Indian conquest, Alexander received numerous elephants as tribute for his victories and began to use them for hauling heavy equipment and possibly even in the front lines of subsequent battles. Coins minted under Alexander frequently feature elephants, and some show the conqueror wearing an elephant-skin helmet instead of his customary Herakles-like lion's skin. After Alexander's death, his successors fought fiercely over his territory, and historians tell us that elephants were featured in several of these battles. At the Battle of Ipsus (301 B.C.E.), for example, the 480 elephants of King SELEUCUS (1) helped to destroy his enemy, ANTIGONUS (1).

The Greeks acquired their elephants from India as well as from Africa. Typically ridden by a handler and an archer or javelin man, the war elephant provided a kind of live "tank." Deployed usually to screen the PHALANX and charge ahead, elephants were effective mainly as weapons of terror, to scare horses and soldiers not accustomed to them.

In 280 B.C.E., King Pyrrhus of Epirus used 20 elephants in his war against the Romans. At first, this strategy was successful because few Italians had seen the huge animals before, and they tended to panic at the sight. The elephants could be used to frighten the horses of the Roman cavalry and send them into a stampede. By 275 B.C.E., the Roman warriors had learned that they could defeat Pyrrhus and his troops by wounding the elephants with their spears, causing them to run around in pain and to trample their own men. The use of these unmaneuverable beasts diminished by the mid-200s B.C.E. By that time many commanders had learned to deflect their charges with arrow or javelin volleys or to let them pass harmlessly through by having the troops open corridors in their path.

Further reading: H. H. Scullard, *The Elephant in the Greek and Roman World* (London: Thames and Hudson, 1974).

Eleusinian Mysteries   This important Athenian religious cult in honor of the grain goddess DEMETER was observed at the town of Eleusis (which lies 15 miles northwest of ATHENS, in the region's main wheat- and barley-growing plain). The cult was given the title "Mysteries" (*mustēriai*, from *mustēs*, "an initiate") because of its secretive nature. Only those who had been formally initiated could participate, and details of the rites (which seem to have been harmless enough) were forbidden to be revealed publicly. The Eleusinian Mysteries were a rare form of worship in classical Greece (mid-400s B.C.E.), where city-states emphasized public cults; later, however, in the HELLENISTIC AGE (300–150 B.C.E.), mystery religions began to proliferate.

The cult was run by the Athenian state and was officiated by two noble families of Eleusis: the Eumolpidae and the Kerykes. Despite the emphasis on secrecy, the requirements for initiation were lenient: Anyone of Greek speech and without blood guilt was eligible to join. This inclusion of SLAVES and WOMEN is remarkable. The initiate's oath of secrecy was taken seriously; no knowledgeable ancient writer has left us a description of the rites, and in the 400s B.C.E. such prominent men as the playwright AESCHYLUS and the politician ALCIBIADES were investigated or prosecuted for supposedly revealing the mysteries. Clearly the initiates' conduct was thought to affect the goddess Demeter's goodwill and the all-important fertility of the grainfields.

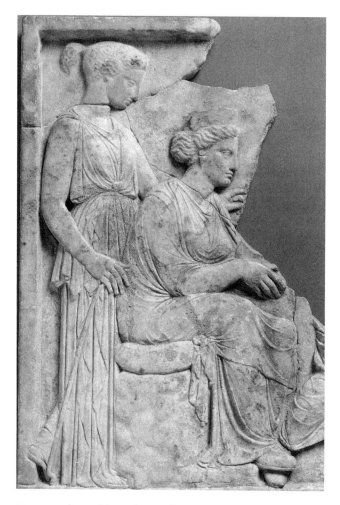

Demeter, the goddess of agriculture, sits on a rock; her daughter Kore stands behind her holding the key to the temple. These deities were worshipped by the cult Eleusinian Mysteries in hopes of a better afterlife. *(The J. Paul Getty Museum)*

The "bible" of the mysteries was the central myth of Demeter. According to legend, the death god HADES stole away Demeter's daughter Korē (also called PERSEPHONE). Demeter searched the world for her, letting the fields go barren in her grief; and the god ZEUS restored order by allowing Korē-Persephone to remain with her mother for eight months out of every year.

The mysteries probably reenacted this story every spring, as a kind of pageant, with dance and incantation. At the climactic, secret, nocturnal ceremony in Demeter's temple, the priest would hold up an ear of grain amid reverent silence. The "doctrine" of the mysteries was probably very simple: thanksgiving for Demeter's gift to the living and the hope that she and her daughter Persephone would take further care of the initiates' souls in the Underworld. This hope of a happy AFTERLIFE became a cornerstone of later mystery cults.

See also DEMETER; ORPHISM.

Further reading: Robert F. Healey, *Eleusinian Sacrifices in the Athenian Law Code* (New York: Garland, 1990); Kevin Clinton, *Myth and Cult: The Iconography of the Eleusinian Mysteries: The Martin P. Nilsson Lectures on Greek Religion, Delivered 19–21 November 1990 at the Swedish Institute at Athens* (Stockholm: Svenska Institutet i Athen, 1992); Maureen B. Cavanaugh, *Eleusis and Athens: Documents in Finance, Religion, and Politics in the Fifth Century B.C.* (Atlanta, Ga.: Scholars Press, 1996); Margaret M. Miles, *The City Eleusinion* (Princeton, N.J.: American School of Classical Studies, 1998).

Eleusis　*See* ATTICA; ELEUSINIAN MYSTERIES.

Elis　In about 471 B.C.E., the inhabitants of this plain in the western PELOPONNESE established a city, also called Elis, as their political center. The Eleans had charge of the highly important OLYMPIC GAMES, the sports-and-religious festival held every four years in honor of the god ZEUS. The actual site of the games was the sanctuary and sports complex known as OLYMPIA. Since Olympia lay closer to the city of Pisa than to the city of Elis, there was intermittent strife between Elis and Pisa for control.

Formidable soldiers, the Eleans remained staunch allies of SPARTA until 420 B.C.E., when events led them to make alliances with Sparta's enemies ATHENS and ARGOS, in the PELOPONNESIAN WAR. Later, still an enemy of Sparta, Elis made an alliance with ARCADIA (369 B.C.E.). In the 200s B.C.E. it was an enemy of Arcadia and a member of the Aetolian League.

See also AETOLIA; PHEIDON.

Further reading: N. B. Crowther, "Elis and the Games," *L'Antiquité classique* 57 (1988): 301–310; J. Roy, "The Perioikoi of Elis," in *The Polis as an Urban Centre and as a Political Community, Symposium August 29–31, 1996,* edited by Mogens Herman Hansen (Copenhagen: Munksgaard, 1997), 282–320; Nicholas F. Yalouris,

Ancient Elis: Cradle of the Olympic Games (Athens: Adam Editions, 1996); J. Roy, "Thucydides 5, 49, 1–50, 4. The Quarrel Between Elis and Sparta in 420 B.C. and Elis' Exploitation of Olympia," *Klio* 80 (1998): 360–368; N. Yalouris, "The Cultural and Intellectual Dimension of Ancient Elis and Olympia," in *Homère chez Calvin*, edited by Pierre Lipschutz (Geneva: Droz, 2000), 435–443.

Empedokles (ca. 495–430 B.C.E.) *Influential early philosopher*
Empedokles was born to an aristocratic family of the Sicilian Greek city of ACRAGAS. As a thinker, poet, statesman, and physician he became a semilegendary figure among his contemporaries. He is plausibly said to have helped establish DEMOCRACY at Acragas after the expulsion of the reigning tyrant, in about 472 B.C.E., and he supposedly declined a public offer of kingship. He is said to have later been exiled from Acragas. He was an admired orator, who reportedly tutored the greatest Greek orator of the next generation, GORGIAS of Leontini.

His philosophy, partly inspired by the Italian-based Greek philosophical schools of PARMENIDES and PYTHAGORAS, was presented in two epic poems in hexameter verse, *On Nature* and *Purifications;* he is said to have recited the latter at the OLYMPIC GAMES. About 450 verses of these poems (approximately one-tenth of their combined total) survive today as quotations in works by later writers. The poems' ideas had a profound effect on subsequent thinkers, including ARISTOTLE.

On Nature introduced the concept, later fundamental to Aristotle's physics, that all matter derives from four elements: air, water, fire, and earth. These elements are eternal and unchanging; apparent creation and destruction in the world merely indicates the ceaseless reorganizations of these four elements into new ratios. Love (Philia) and Strife (Neikos) are cosmic forces seeking to unify and divide, respectively. Empedokles' theory of elements has been interpreted as a correction of Parmenides' belief that ultimate reality is unified and immobile. Here Empedokles probably helped inspire the elemental theories of the early "atomists," DEMOCRITUS and LEUCIPPUS.

The *Purifications* was concerned with humankind's Original Sin and restoration—ideas that had already been developed in the mystic ORPHISM of Acragantine aristocratic circles. Empedokles apparently identified the primal sin as the first shedding of blood and eating of meat. Tainted by this ancestral pollution, the individual human soul must be purified through a series of incarnations, bringing the soul through the round of elements to a renewed state of bliss. In the *Purifications'* most famous verse, Empedokles declares, "Already I have been a boy and a girl, a bush and a bird, and speechless fish in the sea." The Orphic-derived notion of the soul's transmigration was also a feature of Pythagorean belief, taught at certain Greek cities of nearby southern ITALY. While not a Pythagorean himself, Empedokles was clearly influenced by such teachings.

See also AFTERLIFE; MEDICINE; SCIENCE.

Further reading: Raymond A. Prier, *Archaic Logic: Symbol and Structure in Heraclitus, Parmenides, and Empedocles* (The Hague: Mouton, 1976); Peter Kingsley, *Ancient Philosophy, Mystery, and Magic: Empedocles and Pythagorean Tradition* (New York: Oxford University Press, 1995).

Epaminondas (Greek: Epameinondas) (ca. 410–362 B.C.E.) *Brilliant Theban statesman and general*
Epaminondas engineered the rise of THEBES as the foremost Greek city, in defiance of SPARTA. He destroyed the legend of Spartan military invincibility and ended Sparta's domination of Greece that had lasted for 35 years since Sparta's victory in the PELOPONNESIAN WAR.

Epaminondas became involved in Thebes's public affairs in 379 B.C.E., from which time onward he became the city's primary statesman. His main interest was in having Thebes control the other cities of BOEOTIA, and he did this by engaging in war with the seemingly omnipotent Spartans. As an elected commander in 371 B.C.E., Epaminondas quarreled with the Spartan king AGESILAOS at a peace conference. The resulting Spartan invasion of Theban territory, however, ended in an unexpected Theban triumph, due to Epaminondas's brilliant strategy at the Battle of LEUKTRA.

After this victory, the Thebans began to assert themselves further against powerful Spartan dominance of mainland Greece. Marching into the PELOPONNESE in the winter of 370–369 B.C.E., Epaminondas liberated ARCADIA from Spartan overlordship and (then or later) established his "big city," Megalopolis, to be the center of an Arcadian league.

Soon afterward, Epaminondas entered the Spartan-ruled region of MESSENIA, where he founded another city, Messene, to be a political center against Sparta. The Theban liberation of Messenia had a devastating effect on Sparta, which had traditionally relied for subsistence on Messenian grain, grown by the Messenian serfs known as HELOTS.

Epaminondas's later exploits included further invasions of the Peloponnese and a naval expedition against the Athenians. In 362 B.C.E. he again led an army into the Peloponnese, to oppose a Spartan threat against Arcadia. Although the Battle of MANTINEIA was another Theban victory, Epaminondas died there from wounds. He was the greatest leader to emerge in the tumultuous half century between the end of the Peloponnesian War (404 B.C.E.) and the rise of MACEDON (350s B.C.E.).

See also WARFARE, LAND.

Further reading: Victor Davis Hanson, *The Soul of Battle: From Ancient Times to the Present Day, How Three Great Liberators Vanquished Tyranny* (New York: Anchor Books, 2001).

Ephesos   This Greek city of IONIA, on the central west coast of ASIA MINOR, was known for its TRADE and its elaborate cult of the goddess ARTEMIS. Founded around 1050 B.C.E. by IONIAN GREEKS from mainland Greece, Ephesos lay at the mouth of the Cayster River, at a site that commanded the coastal farming plain, the riverine route inland, and the sea passage to the nearby Greek island of SAMOS.

Ephesos was one of the Greek world's foremost cities during the Ionian heyday of the 600s and 500s B.C.E. Although never a great seagoing power like its neighbor and trade rival MILETUS, Ephesos thrived as a terminus for caravans from the Asian interior and as an artisan center; its ivory carving was famous. In the mid-600s B.C.E. Ephesos withstood attack by a nomadic people, the Kimmerians, who had swept westward through Asia Minor. Patriotic resistance was urged in verses by the Ephesian poet CALLINUS (whose surviving fragments are among the earliest extant Greek LYRIC POETRY). But Ephesos's most famous resident was the early Greek philosopher HERAKLEITOS (ca. 500 B.C.E.).

Around 600 B.C.E. the city's oligarchic government gave way to a line of TYRANTS. This regime, however, was relatively short-lived and ended in the mid-500s B.C.E. when, along with the rest of Ionia, Ephesos fell to the Lydian king CROESUS. Soon thereafter, the city was again conquered by an outside force, this time the Persian king CYRUS (1).

The city fared better than other Ionian cities under the Persians. Although it joined in the ill-fated IONIAN REVOLT of 499 B.C.E., it apparently made a timely surrender and avoided the worst retaliations, while the Persians' sack of Miletus in 494 B.C.E. removed Ephesos's main rival. In 479 B.C.E. Ephesos was liberated, along with the rest of Ionia, by the mainland Greeks.

Ephesos then became part of the Athenian-controlled DELIAN LEAGUE (478 B.C.E.), but joined the general Delian revolt against ATHENS toward the end of the PELOPONNESIAN WAR (in 411 B.C.E.). As an important Spartan naval base, Ephesos served the commander LYSANDER in his defeat of an Athenian fleet at the nearby Battle of Notion (406 B.C.E.), and after the war Ephesos continued as a Spartan base for sea operations against PERSIA. But with the KING'S PEACE of 386 B.C.E., Ephesos and all other Asian Greek cities passed back to Persian rule, until they were again liberated in 334 B.C.E., by ALEXANDER THE GREAT.

The city then embarked on its second era of greatness. Rebuilt at a new site by the Macedonian dynast LYSIMACHUS around 294 B.C.E., Ephesos became an emporium of the HELLENISTIC AGE, rivaled only by ALEXANDRIA (1) and ANTIOCH. Ephesos passed into the influence of the Seleucid kings in the mid-200s B.C.E., then to the kingdom of PERGAMON and, finally, in 133 B.C.E., to ROME. In Roman times it continued to be a great city of the East. One of the most important features of Ephesos was its cult of Artemis, which had originated in the 700s B.C.E. and lasted through the Roman period. The image of the goddess known from dozens of Roman-era copies is very different from typical Greek representations of Artemis as the virgin huntress. The Artemis of Ephesos stands very rigidly upright and her dress is covered with many round objects, often described as female breasts but more recently thought to be bulls' testicles (in any event, symbols of fertility).

The earliest cult structure at Ephesos consisted of a marble platform and altar, constructed in the early sixth century B.C.E. In about 560 B.C.E., under one of the tyrants, a magnificent new temple was begun, later considered one of the SEVEN WONDERS OF THE WORLD. This temple, known as the Artemision, was the largest Greek building of its day, measuring 358 feet in length and 171 feet in width. It was designed by two prominent Cretan architects, Chersiphron and Metagenes. Apparently not completed until about 430 B.C.E., it was burned down in 356 B.C.E. by an arsonist who wanted his deed to be remembered forever.

The Ephesians soon rebuilt the Artemision, involving several of the best Greek sculptors of the day in its design and decoration. This second temple was burnt by the Goths in 263 C.E. and later completely destroyed by the Christians.

Archaeological research at Ephesos was begun in 1863 by an English architect, John Turtle Wood, who was looking for the site of the famous Artemision. He discovered its marble platform finally in 1869. Investigations by the Austrians began in 1895 and have continued to the present day, only interrupted by the two world wars. Today, excavation is combined with programs of conservation and restoration to further enrich visitors' understanding of the site; approximately 2 million tourists walk among the ruins each year.

Further reading: Recep Meriç, *Ephesus: Archaeological Guide* (Izmir, Turkey: Ticaret Matbaacilik, 1971); S. Erdemgil, et al., *The Terrace Houses in Ephesus* (Istanbul: Hitit Color, 1987); *Ephesus Museum Catalogue* (Istanbul: Hitit Color, 1989); Sabahattin Türkoglu, *The Story of Ephesus,* translated by Bahar Atlamaz (Istanbul: Arkeoloji ve Sanat Yayinlari, 1995); Peter Scherrer, ed., *Ephesus: The New Guide* (Istanbul: Ege Yayinlari, 2000).

Ephialtes (b. ca. 500 B.C.E.) *Left-wing Athenian statesman and mentor of PERIKLES*
Born into a humble family, Ephialtes arose in the 460s B.C.E. as the democratic leader against the conservative party of KIMON; in this, he was the political heir of THEMISTOKLES.

In 462 B.C.E., taking advantage of Kimon's recent disgrace, Ephialtes and Perikles proposed stripping the powers and jurisdictions from the conservative law court known as the AREOPAGOS. The proposals were passed, but within a year Ephialtes was dead—probably murdered by political reactionaries. The mantle of leadership of the left wing passed to Perikles.

See also DEMOCRACY.

Further reading: D. W. Roller, "Who Murdered Ephialtes?" *Historia* 38 (1989): 257–266; L. A. Jones, "The Role of Ephialtes in the Rise of Athenian Democracy," *Classical Antiquity* 6 (1987): 53–76; L. G. Hall, "Ephialtes, the Areopagos, and the Thirty," *Classical Quarterly* 40 (1990): 319–328; E. G. Bloedow, "Pericles and Ephialtes in the Reforms of 462 B.C.," *Scholia* 1 (1992): 85–101; J. L. Marr, "Ephialtes the Moderate?" *Greece and Rome* 40 (1993): 11–19; James L. O'Neil, *The Origins and Development of Ancient Greek Democracy* (Lanham, Md.: Rowman & Littlefield, 1995); T. E. Rihill, "Democracy Denied. Why Ephialtes Attacked the Areiopagus," *Journal of Hellenic Studies* 115 (1995): 87–98; Anthony J. Podlecki, *Perikles and His Circle* (London: Routledge, 1998); H. F. Mueller, "Ephialtes Accusator. A Case Study in Anecdotal History and Ideology," *Athenaeum* 87 (1999): 425–445.

ephor The title of an annually elected chief official at SPARTA and other Dorian Greek states. This term suggests "one who watches over." The Spartan ephors, who numbered five by the 400s B.C.E., served as an important counterweight to the two Spartan kings. The ephors oversaw the kings' administration and personal conduct; they could summon the kings to their presence or prosecute them. Two ephors always accompanied a king on campaign (a sign of the Spartan fear of the corrupting outside world). Every month ephors and kings exchanged oaths to observe each other's authority.

See also CHILON; LYKOURGOS (1).

Further reading: P. A. Rohe, "The Selection of Ephors at Sparta," *Historia* 29 (1980): 385–401; P. J. Rhodes, "The Selection of Ephors at Sparta," *Historia* 30 (1981): 498–502; Michael Whitby, *Sparta* (Edinburgh: Edinburgh University Press, 2002).

epic poetry The earliest and greatest works of extant Greek literature are the two long narrative poems titled the *Iliad* and *Odyssey*, ascribed to the poet HOMER. Employing dactylic hexameter verse and a distinctive, elevated vocabulary, the *Iliad* and *Odyssey* typify the Greek literary genre called *epikē* (from *epos*, "word").

Today most scholars recognize that the *Iliad* and *Odyssey*—written down around 750 B.C.E., soon after the invention of the Greek ALPHABET—represent the final stage in a prior tradition of unwritten verse composition, stretching back some 500 years to the second millennium B.C.E. This unwritten poetry-making is today known as oral composition. The foremost geographic region for this poetic tradition was the eastern Greek area called IONIA.

In preliterate cultures, poetry serves a mnemonic purpose: The rhyme and rhythm of a poem or song make the words easier to remember. Many preliterate societies have used poetry (in unwritten forms) for the memorization and recital of legends and folktales. In the early Greek world, oral poetry typically recounted tales from Greek MYTH—tales of olden-day heroes and their interactions with the gods.

These stories were preserved and retold by a professional class of bards or minstrels known as *aoidoi* or *rhapsoidoi* (rhapsodes, "song-stitchers"). The skill of these bards lay in their knowledge of the vast mythological material and in their ability to select and shape episodes for public recitation. This oral poetry was sung or recited in the flowing rhythm of dactylic hexameter. (Greek poetry did not employ rhyme; the GREEK LANGUAGE had too many natural rhymes for this to be considered beautiful.) An idea of the bard's function is communicated in book 8 of the *Odyssey*, where the blind minstrel Demodocus recites to his own accompaniment on the lyre at a royal feast. The technique by which a bard might draw on familiar subject matter while composing individual lines spontaneously from a mental trove of formulaic expressions has been illuminated in modern times by Milman Parry's studies of oral composition in Serbia and Croatia in the 1930s C.E.

The second well-known Greek epic poet is HESIOD (ca. 700 B.C.E.). The rural, middle-class Hesiod was an individualist in the art: In his *Works and Days* he fitted the epic verse form to a most unusual content, a moralizing farming calendar.

But the main epic tradition is exemplified by Homer's poems of aristocratic war and voyaging. We know that, by about 550 B.C.E., there existed about 10 other epic poems—written down after the *Iliad* and *Odyssey*, shorter than they, and probably inspired by them. Known collectively as the epic cycle (*epikos kuklos*), these poems taken together recounted a loose mythical world history from the Creation to the aftermath of the TROJAN WAR. Among the non-Homeric epics were the *Oedipodia*, the *Thebaïd*, and the *Epigoni*, recounting the tragic history of the ruling house of the city of THEBES (including the tales of OEDIPUS and of the SEVEN AGAINST THEBES). But most of the epic cycle described episodes of the Trojan War not recounted in Homer; these poems included the *Cypria*, *Little Iliad*, *Destruction of Troy*, and *Homecomings*.

Today the non-Homeric epics exist only in fragments quoted by later writers. But many of the legends that they described have been preserved for us—in Athenian stage tragedy (400s B.C.E.), in the prose works of ancient scholars, and in such later epics as the Roman Ovid's *Metamorphoses*.

By the mid-500s B.C.E., epic composition had died out in favor of newer forms, such as LYRIC POETRY and then THEATER. Epic was revived in a more self-conscious, literary form in the mid-200s B.C.E. by the Alexandrian poet APOLLONIUS. The Alexandrian epic tradition strongly affected Roman literature, culminating in the Roman poet Vergil's patriotic masterpiece, the *Aeneid* (ca. 20 B.C.E.).

See also ACHILLES; JASON (1); MUSIC; ODYSSEUS.

Further reading: G. B. Nussbaum, *Homer's Metre: A Practical Guide for Reading Greek Hexameter Poetry* (Bristol, U.K.: Bristol Classical Press, 1986); Chet A. Van Duzer, *Duality and Structure in the Iliad and the Odyssey* (New York: P. Lang, 1996); Barbara Graziosi, *Inventing Homer: The Early Reception of Epic* (New York: Cambridge University Press, 2002).

Epicureanism This influential Greek philosophical school of the HELLENISTIC AGE (300–150 B.C.E.) and after was founded by Epicurus. Born at SAMOS to an Athenian father in about 341 B.C.E., Epicurus (Greek: Epikouros) resided at ATHENS from the late 300s B.C.E. until his death in 270 B.C.E. There he and his followers lived in privacy and simplicity on his property (a house and garden), where he taught pupils. The fact that these pupils included SLAVES and WOMEN is a sign of Epicurus's innovative and liberal outlook, by ancient Greek standards.

His doctrine of Epicureanism was a daring intellectual breakthrough. For the Epicureans, the purpose of life was pleasure (*hēdonē*), as derived from a simple, even ascetic, mode of existence. Pursuits that brought pain, ill health, frustration, anxiety, or unending desire were not considered appropriate pleasures. Since the chief cause of pain is unsatisfied desire, Epicureans were taught to limit their desires rather than seeking to satisfy each one. The ideal state of the soul is freedom from agitation (*ataraxia*); this can be achieved through temperance and study. Teaching his followers to renounce political ambition, with its cares and corruptions, Epicurus went boldly against the traditional grain of the Greek city-state and anticipated the more personal, individualistic values of Hellenistic society.

On the metaphysical side, Epicureanism relied on the atomist theory of DEMOKRITOS and LEUCIPPUS. Epicurus concluded that, because the human soul is composed of atoms like the body, these atoms must disperse at the person's death. In other words, the soul dies with the body. And thus there is no such thing as an AFTERLIFE. It was this revolutionary idea that led to much criticism of Epicureanism by religious circles in the ancient world.

Also offensive to religious thinkers was the Epicurean idea that the gods, although they exist, are completely detached from human events. Like good Epicureans themselves, the gods live in contentment and self-restraint. Humans should revere them, but not hope for favors or fear their anger.

Although it remained overshadowed by the rival school of STOICISM, Epicureanism did influence later thinkers, such as the Roman poets Lucretius and Horace

(who lived more than 200 years after Epicurus). Ironically, because Epicurus's own voluminous writings have been lost to us, scholars have relied largely on Lucretius's philosophical epic poem *De Rerum Natura* (*On the Nature of Things*) in order to reconstruct the tenets of Epicureanism.

Epicureanism suffered from "bad press" through the centuries, insofar as its beliefs flatly contradicted both ARISTOTLE and Christianity. The Epicurean doctrine of pleasure has been misunderstood as vulgar hedonism, and this is reflected in our modern English word *epicure*, meaning someone with well developed tastes in food, wine, and the like.

Further reading: Elizabeth Asmis, *Epicurus' Scientific Method* (Ithaca, N.Y.: Cornell University Press, 1984); Richard Hibler, *Happiness Through Tranquility: The School of Epicurus* (Lanham, Md.: University Press of America, 1984); Robert Strozier, *Epicurus and Hellenistic Philosophy* (Lanham, Md.: University Press of America, 1985); R. W. Sharples, *Stoics, Epicureans, and Sceptics: An Introduction to Hellenistic Philosophy* (London: Routledge, 1996); Diskin Clay, *Paradosis and Survival: Three Chapters in the History of Epicurean Philosophy* (Ann Arbor: University of Michigan Press, 1998); Dane R. Gordon and David B. Suits, eds., *Epicurus: His Continuing Influence and Contemporary Relevance* (Rochester, N.Y.: RIT Cary Graphic Arts Press, 2003); Norman Lillegard, *On Epicurus* (Belmont, Calif.: Wadsworth/Thompson Learning, 2003).

Epicurus *See* EPICUREANISM.

Epidamnos This Greek city is located on the eastern Adriatic shore, at the site of modern-day Durazzo in Albania. Founded in the late 600s B.C.E. by colonists from CORCYRA and CORINTH, Epidamnos occupied an isthmus beside a harbor in the non-Greek region known as ILLYRIS. The city was ideally located as an anchorage on the coastal route to ITALY and as a depot for TRADE with the Illyrians. Prosperity eventually brought class warfare, however, as Epidamnus's middle class rose up against their aristocratic rulers.

By 435 B.C.E. the citizens had established a DEMOCRACY and expelled the aristocrats, who in turn besieged the city. The democrats appealed to Corinth for help. But nearby Corcyra sent out its powerful navy, which captured Epidamnos for the aristocrats and also defeated the Corinthian fleet at the sea battle of Leukimme (435 B.C.E.), fought off of Corcyra island. This conflict between Corinth and Corcyra was an important cause in igniting the PELOPONNESIAN WAR (431–404 B.C.E.).

Epidamnos itself remained remote from the great events of the 400s and 300s B.C.E. Eventually known by a new name, Dyrrhachium, the city passed to King PYRRHUS of EPIRUS (ca. 280 B.C.E.) and thereafter into the expanding empire of ROME.

See also ARISTOCRACY.

Further reading: S. C. Bakhuizen, "Between Illyrians and Greeks. The Cities of Epidamnus and Apollonia," *Iliria* 16, no. 1, (1986): 165–177.

Epidaurus This city in the northeastern Peloponnese, facing the Saronic Gulf, was famous in antiquity for its sanctuary of the physician hero-god ASKLEPIOS. The cult was established as early as the sixth century B.C.E., but its peak popularity was reached in the fourth and third centuries B.C.E. A great temple of Asklepios was built in the 300s B.C.E. as the center of a large complex devoted to healing and worship. Inside the temple was a huge GOLD-and-ivory statue of the god, shown seated with two of his emblems: a staff in one hand and a serpent under the other. The site also included a GYMNASIUM, baths, hostels, lesser shrines, and a magnificent THEATER for dramatic presentations.

As the focus of pilgrimages by invalids seeking cures from the hero-god, Epidaurus combined aspects of a modern spa with those of medieval healing shrines. Suppliants would spend the night in a dormitory associated with the temple, and there (supposedly) they would be visited by the god in a dream. This process, known as incubation, is attested in many surviving inscriptions of the ancient Greek world. The next morning, the priests of Asklepios would give the worshipper specific medical advice, including regimens to be followed in the nearby facilities.

In modern times, large numbers of tourists constantly visit Epidaurus to view the ruins of the sanctuary, particularly, the magnificent and well-preserved theater. Built in two stages, during the late 300s B.C.E. and the mid-100s B.C.E., this building was already praised in the second century C.E. by the Roman traveler Pausanias. Today, the theater is the venue for a festival of modern theatrical performances every summer.

Systematic archaeological excavation of Epidaurus was begun in 1879 by the Greek Archaeological Society, under the direction of P. Kavvadias. Work on the sanctuary took place in several phases: 1879–1926, 1942–1943, 1948–1951, and 1974–present. Since 1985, significant conservation and restoration efforts have been undertaken.

See also MEDICINE; PELOPONNESIAN WAR.

Further reading: Alison Burford, *The Greek Temple Builders at Epidauros; A Social and Economic Study of Building in the Asklepian Sanctuary, during the Fourth and Early Third Centuries B.C.* (Toronto: University of Toronto Press, 1969); Theodore Papadakis, *Epidauros: The Sanctuary of Asclepios,* 5th ed. (Munich: Verlas Schnell & Steiner, 1976): R. A. Tomlinson, *Epidauros* (Austin: University of Texas Press, 1983); S. E. Iakovidis, *Mycenae-Epidaurus, Argos-Tiryns-Nauplion: A Complete Guide to the Museums and Archaeological Sites of the Argolid,* translated by Kay Cicellis (Athens: Ekdotike Athenon, 1990); Lynn

LiDonnici, *The Epidaurian Miracle Inscriptions: Text, Translation, and Commentary* (Atlanta, Ga.: Scholars Press, 1995).

Epirus (Greek: *epeîros,* "the mainland") This northwest region of mainland Greece is bordered on the west by the Adriatic Sea and on the east by the Pindus mountain range. Epirus was a humid and forested region, inhabited by 14 tribes or clans, some of Dorian-Greek descent and others of non-Greek, Illyrian blood. The ruling clan, the Molossians, claimed to be descended from the hero NEOPTOLEMOS.

Epirus contained two primitive but important religious sanctuaries: the ancient oracle of ZEUS at DODONA; and an oracle of the dead, situated along the River Acheron, where an entrance to the Underworld was believed to be.

A political backwater for most of Greek history, Epirus came into prominence briefly under its dynamic Molossian king PYRRHUS (319–272 B.C.E.), who made AMBRACIA his capital. Later Epirus sided with MACEDON against the encroaching Romans. After the Roman victory in the Third Macedonian War (167 B.C.E.), Epirus passed to Roman rule.

See also AFTERLIFE; DORIAN GREEKS; ROME.

Further reading: N. G. L. Hammond, *Epirus: The Geography, the Ancient Remains, the History and Topography of Epirus and Adjacent Areas* (Oxford: Clarendon Press, 1967); Arthur Foss, *Epirus* (London: Faber, 1978); T. J. Papadopoulos, "Tombs and Burial Customs in Late Bronze Age Epirus," *Aegeum* 1 (1987): 137–142; M. B. Sakellariou, ed., *Epirus 4000 Years of Greek History and Civilization* (Athens: Ekdotike Athenon, 1997); N. G. L. Hammond, "The Ethne in Epirus and Upper Macedonia," *Annual of the British School of Athens* 95 (2000): 345–352; James Wiseman and Konstantinos Zachos, eds., *Landscape Archaeology in Southern Epirus, Greece I* (Princeton, N.J.: American School of Classical Studies at Athens, 2003).

Erechtheion *See* ACROPOLIS; ARCHITECTURE; ATHENA.

Eretria This city is located on the large island of EUBOEA, in east-central Greece. Located midway along the island's west coast, Eretria was established around 800 B.C.E., apparently by Ionian-Greek refugees from the nearby site now called LEFKANDI. Eretria allied itself with its important neighbor, CHALCIS, and together these cities were among the most prominent in the Greek world during the early era of TRADE and COLONIZATION (ca. mid-800s to mid-600s B.C.E.). The Eretrians and Chalcidians set up trading depots on the coasts of Syria and ITALY, and founded the first Greek colonies in Italy and SICILY. Later these two cities warred over the fertile Lelantine plain, which lay between them; Eretria seems to have fared somewhat the worse in this LELANTINE WAR (around

720–680 B.C.E.), and soon both Euboean cities had been surpassed by CORINTH and ATHENS.

In 499 B.C.E. the Eretrians sent five warships to aid the Greek IONIAN REVOLT against Persian rule in ASIA MINOR. This tiny expedition bore disastrous fruit in 490 B.C.E., when a Persian seaborne army captured the city and burned it in retaliation. After the PERSIAN WARS (490–479 B.C.E.), Eretria was forced to join the Athenian-run DELIAN LEAGUE. With the rest of Euboea, Eretria revolted from Athens unsuccessfully in 446 B.C.E. and successfully in 411 B.C.E. Chafing under Spartan domination, Eretria joined the SECOND ATHENIAN LEAGUE (377 B.C.E.) but again revolted (349 B.C.E.). Along with the rest of Euboea, Eretria came under control of the Macedonian king PHILIP II in 338 B.C.E. With the rest of Greece, Eretria passed to Roman control in the mid-100s B.C.E.

See also AL MINA; CATANA; CHALCIDICE; CUMAE; IONIAN GREEKS; MARATHON; NAXOS (2); PITHECUSAE; ZANCLE.

Further reading: Efi Sapouna Sakellaraki, *Eretria: Site and Museum,* translated by David Hardy (Athens: Ministry of Culture, Archaeological Receipts Fund, 1995); N. Toogood, "Athens Aids Eretria: A State's Jurisdiction over Its Citizens' Actions," *Classical Quarterly* 47 (1997): 295–297; N. G. L. Hammond, "Eretria's Colonies in the Area of the Thermaic Gulf," *Annual of the British School at Athens* 93 (1998): 383–399; Keith Walker, *Archaic Eretria: A Political and Social History from the Earliest Times to 490 B.C.* (London: Routledge, 2004).

Erinna (ca. 600 B.C.E.) *Female poet who probably lived on the Greek island of Telos, near the coast of southwestern* ASIA MINOR

Erinna was a friend of SAPPHO and was best known for her 300-line poem called *The Distaff,* which was composed in memory of a young woman or girl who had died unmarried. Only four lines survive, written in Erinna's native Doric dialect; these fragments present a touching picture of the dead girl's sweet personality and unfulfilled life. Like her character, Erinna later died unmarried, at the young age of 19. Our knowledge of her life comes from a passage by Eustathius, who is unsure whether the poet came from Telos, Teos, LESBOS, or RHODES. He also says that the ancient Greeks "thought her verses rivaled those of Homer." Since so little is known of Erinna's life, its details remain unclear and controversial; some modern scholars believe that she was not Sappho's contemporary but that she lived in the 300s B.C.E. instead.

Further reading: Diane J. Rayor, *Sappho's Lyre: Archaic Lyric and Women Poets of Ancient Greece* (Berkeley: University of California Press, 1991).

Erinyes *See* FURIES.

Eros *Greek god of love*
Eros is often described as the son of the love goddess APHRODITE. While Aphrodite personified a universal sexual principle, Eros represented more the romantic feelings that one has for a specific person.

Eros arrived relatively late in Greek religion; he does not appear in the epic poems of HOMER (written down around 750 B.C.E.). There, the word *eros* is simply a common noun denoting sexual desire. The god first appears in literature in HESIOD's epic poem, *The Theogony* (ca. 700 B.C.E.), where he is described as the most beautiful of the gods. He is said to have been born from Chaos, along with the goddess Earth, and is an attendant of Aphrodite.

Later versions of Greek MYTH make Eros the son of Aphrodite by either ARES or HERMES, and he is conceived of as a thoughtless, mischievous child with golden wings. He appears as such, for example, in the lyric poems of ANACREON (ca. 520 B.C.E.). His attributes, the bow and piercing arrows, were first mentioned, as far as we know, by the Athenian playwright EURIPIDES (ca. 430 B.C.E.). Eros's frequent companions included Anteros (god of mutual love), Pothos (longing), Himeros (desire), Peitho (persuasion), the MUSES, and the Graces.

As a god of male beauty or of fertility, Eros had cults in BOEOTIA and at ATHENS; his most important site of worship was at Thespiae in Boeotia. His cult image there was an ancient, unworked stone, and every fifth year the Boeotians held a festival, the Erotia, in his honor. The love story of Eros and Psyche (soul) was a philosophical allegory that arose in the 300s B.C.E.

Borrowed by the Romans, Eros became the Roman god Cupid (Latin *cupido,* meaning "desire").

Further reading: James Gollnick, *Love and the Soul: Psychological Interpretations of the Eros and Psyche Myth* (Waterloo, Ontario: Wilfrid Laurier University Press, 1992); Anne Carson, *Eros the Bittersweet* (Normal, Ill.: Dalkey Archive Press, 1998); Paul Ludwig, *Eros and Polis: Desire and Community in Greek Political Theory* (New York: Cambridge University Press, 2002); Sonia Cavicchioli, *The Tale of Cupid and Psyche: An Illustrated History* (New York: George Braziller, 2002).

Eteocles *See* SEVEN AGAINST THEBES.

Ethiopia *See* BLACK PEOPLES.

Etruscans This powerful non-Greek people occupied the region of northwest ITALY now known as Tuscany. By the 700s B.C.E. they controlled a domain extending south to Campania, on the Bay of Naples. When the first Greek traders began arriving at the Campanian coast after 775 B.C.E., it was probably the Etruscans, as overlords of the region, who invited the newcomers to make a permanent colony at CUMAE.

The Etruscans' significance for Greek history is twofold: (1) as avid consumers of Greek goods, they provided an important overseas market for the Greeks in the 700s–500s B.C.E.; and (2) having imbibed Greek material culture and RELIGION, they then transmitted aspects of this to their non-Etruscans subject cities, including the Latin town of ROME. The Etruscans were a crucial early link between the Greek and Roman worlds.

The Greeks called the Etruscans Tursenoi and believed, perhaps rightly, that they had emigrated from ASIA MINOR. The Etruscans were able seafarers, with a reputation for piracy. Their craving for Greek goods has been proven by ARCHAEOLOGY. Excavations in Tuscany since the early 1800s C.E. have unearthed vast troves of Corinthian POTTERY. This surviving pottery is a clear sign of a much-larger TRADE in goods that have not survived, such as textiles, metalwork, and WINE. The importance of this foreign market for CORINTH can be seen in the systematic founding of Corinthian western colonies—CORCYRA, AMBRACIA, and others (mid-700s to 600 B.C.E.)—to serve as anchorages on the coastal route to Italy. Later (500s B.C.E.) the Athenians dominated this market—as evidenced from archaeological finds of Athenian black- and red-figure pottery in Italy. What the Etruscans may have supplied in exchange was raw metal: tin (for BRONZE-making), lead, and SILVER.

The Etruscan culture was extremely rich and is becoming increasingly illuminated by modern scholars as new research is done into this fascinating civilization. Most of our knowledge about Etruscan religious beliefs comes from excavation of their elaborate tombs, created (like the Egyptian pyramids) to serve as homes for the soul in the AFTERLIFE. They had an extensive pantheon, and many of their deities eventually became associated with similar Greek gods and goddesses. The Etruscans believed strongly in predestination and divine will; special priests were trained as Augurs to interpret signs and omens for the general public.

The alphabet is another aspect of the Etruscan civilization that was strongly influenced by the Greeks. Through interactions with the Greek colonists at Cumae and at PITHECUSAE in the early and mid-700s B.C.E., the Etruscans adopted and adapted Greek letters to create their own writing system. The earliest complete Etruscan inscription appears on a proto-Corinthian vase found at Tarquinia, dated to about 700 B.C.E. Earlier than this, however, are some spindle whorls that have been discovered, marked with the single letter *alpha,* which date to about 720–710 B.C.E. It appears, therefore, that the transmission of the alphabet from the Greek colonists to the Etruscan educated classes probably occurred around 725 B.C.E., and the new style of communication spread rapidly around Italy. Most Etruscan inscriptions are written from right to left, and there is little or no punctuation. Writing seems to have been used primarily for dedications, proprietary inscriptions, economic transac-

tions, and funerary epitaphs; there may also have been extensive Etruscan literature, but none has survived.

Eventually the Etruscans came into conflict with their proliferating Greek guests. In alliance with the Carthaginians, the Etruscans defeated the Phocaean Greeks in a naval campaign near Corsica (around 545 B.C.E.). Soon, however, they suffered defeats on land from the Greek leader Aristodemus of Cumae (524–505 B.C.E.). In 474 B.C.E. the Etruscans lost their claim to Campania forever, when they were defeated in a sea battle off Cumae, at the hands of the Syracusan tyrant HIERON (1). The Etruscans continued as a power in their northern home region for another 200 years but were finally absorbed by their former subjects, the Romans.

See also CARTHAGE.

Further reading: Mario Torelli, *Etruria,* 2d ed. (Rome: Laterza, 1982); Larissa Bonfante, ed., *Etruscan Life and Afterlife: A Handbook of Etruscan Studies* (Detroit: Wayne State University Press, 1986): Anette Rathje, *The Etruscans: 700 Years of History and Culture,* translated by Judith Green (Rome: Edizioni daga, 1989); Paula Kay Lazrus, *Discovering the Etruscans* (Rome: L'Erma di Bretschneider, 1990); Nigel Spivey and Simon Stoddart, *Etruscan Italy* (London: Batsford, 1990); Ellen Macnamara, *The Etruscans* (London: British Museum Publications, 1990; Gösta Säflund, *Etruscan Imagery: Symbol and Meaning,* translated by Peter Fraser (Göteborg, Sweden: P. Astroms Forlag, 1993); Sybille Haynes, *Etruscan Civilization: A Cultural History* (Los Angeles: J. Paul Getty Museum, 2000).

Euboea   This large inshore Greek island, nearly 100 miles long, runs parallel to the east coast of central Greece, alongside the regions of LOCRIS, BOEOTIA, and ATTICA. Euboea lies closest to the mainland at a narrow channel called the Euripus. There lay the most important Euboean city, CHALCIS. Close to Chalcis in locale and importance was ERETRIA; the other significant town was Karystos, on the island's southern coast.

The island's name means something like "rich in cattle." It emerged from the DARK AGE around 900 B.C.E. as an Ionian-Greek region. Chalcis and Eretria soon became the two foremost cities of early Greece, both in TRADE and in COLONIZATION. Eventually, however, the two cities fought for possession of the fertile Lelantine plain, which stretched between them; this LELANTINE WAR (ca. 720–680 B.C.E.) was remembered as the first major conflict in Greek history. Later the island was a target of Athenian expansionism, as ATHENS and Chalcis became enemies. The Athenians defeated the Chalcidians and seized part of the Lelantine plain for Athenian colonists (506 B.C.E.).

During the PERSIAN WARS, the Persians landed an expedition on Euboea and destroyed Eretria (490 B.C.E.); in 480 B.C.E. the Euboeans supplied crews and warships against the invaders, and the major sea battle of ARTEMISION was fought off the northwestern tip of Euboea. After the war the Euboean cities were coerced into joining the Athenian-controlled DELIAN LEAGUE, from which the whole island unsuccessfully revolted in 446 B.C.E. The Athenian reconquest of Euboea was personally led by PERIKLES, who installed Athenian garrison colonies. However, a successful revolt followed amid Athens's decline during the PELOPONNESIAN WAR (411 B.C.E.).

In about 377 B.C.E., after chafing under Spartan domination, the Euboean cities joined the SECOND ATHENIAN LEAGUE, but revolted again, in 349 B.C.E. After 338 B.C.E. the island was under control of the Macedonian king PHILIP II, who garrisoned Chalcis as one of his strategic holds on the Greek mainland. Thereafter Euboea remained in Macedonian hands until 196 B.C.E. Eventually it became part of the Roman province of Macedonia (146 B.C.E.).

See also GREECE, GEOGRAPHY OF.

Further reading: Rosalinde Kearsley, *The Pendent Semi-circle Skyphos: A Study of Its Development and Chronology and an Examination of It as Evidence for Euboean Activity at Al Mina* (London: University of London, Institute of Classical Studies, 1989); Sara Wheeler, *An Island Apart: Travels in Evia* (London: Abacus, 1993); Doniert Evely, Irene S. Lemos, and Elizabeth Susan Sherratt, *Minotaur and Centaur: Studies in the Archaeology of Crete and Euboea Presented to Mervyn Popham* (Oxford: Tempus Reparatum, 1996); D. Vanhove, *Roman Marble Quarries in Southern Euboea and the Associated Road Systems* (Leiden, Netherlands: E. J. Brill, 1996).

Eubulus *See* AESCHINES.

Euclid (Eukleides) *See* MATHEMATICS.

Eumenes (1) *See* DIADOCHOI.

Eumenes (2) *See* PERGAMON.

Eumenides *See* EURIPIDES; FURIES.

Euphorion (b. 276 B.C.E.) *Poet and scholar of the HELLENISTIC AGE*
Born at CHALCIS, in EUBOEA, Euphorion wrote epic poems and epigrams, typically short pieces on mythological subjects. Although little of his work survives today, it was influential and admired in the Graeco-Roman world, and it inspired Roman poets such as Catullus and his circle (ca. 60 B.C.E.) and Vergil (ca. 30 B.C.E.). He was also one of the favorite authors of the Roman emperor Tiberius in the first century C.E.

Some of Euphorion's compositions included *Hesiod, Alexander, Apollodorus,* and *Arius.* His most ambitious work was entitled *Mopsopia* ("Miscellanies") and consisted of five books; it was a collection of Attic fables and histories. Although Euphorion was not born wealthy, he married a rich widow; this enabled him to continue to pursue his creative endeavors without concern for his financial state. Upon meeting the Seleucid king Antiochos II (223–187 B.C.E.), he was appointed the head of the library at ANTIOCH.

Further reading: M. Dickie, "Poets as Initiates in the Mysteries. Euphorion, Philicus, and Posidippus," *Antique und Abendland* 44 (1998): 49–77.

Eupolis (ca. 446–411 B.C.E.) *One of the three masters of classical Athenian comedy, along with ARISTOPHANES and KRATINUS*
Titles of 19 plays by Eupolis are known. None of these has survived complete, but many fragments of his work exist, quoted by later writers. In his relatively short career (429–411 B.C.E.), Eupolis won first prize in annual Athenian drama-competitions at least four times—three times at the midwinter festival known as the Lenaea and once at the City Dionysia, a grand event held in early spring. Eupolis died in the HELLESPONT region, on duty in one of the Athenian naval campaigns of the later PELOPONNESIAN WAR.

In the tradition of comedy under the Athenian DEMOCRACY, Eupolis's plays seem to have been political, obscene, and insulting to various public figures. *The Golden Age* (424 B.C.E.) ridiculed the powerful left-wing politician KLEON. *The Demes* (412 B.C.E.) showed great Athenians of bygone years arising from the dead to counsel a city in turmoil.

See also THEATER.

Further reading: Gregory W. Dobrov, *The City as Comedy: Society and Representation in Athenian Drama* (Chapel Hill: University of North Carolina Press, 1997); David Harvey and John Wilkins, *The Rivals of Aristophanes: Studies in Athenian Old Comedy* (London: Duckworth and the Classical Press of Wales, 2000).

Euripides (ca. 485–406 B.C.E.) *Youngest and most controversial of the three great Athenian tragedians of the 400s B.C.E.*
Euripides' place in literature alongside AESCHYLUS and SOPHOKLES is due to his insight into human psychology (especially abnormal psychology, such as madness or obsessive love), his frequent and sympathetic use of female characters (unusual for a classical Greek male), and his bold questioning of the traditional religious ideas in the Greek MYTHS. His best-known plays include *Medea* (431 B.C.E.), *Hippolytus* (428 B.C.E.), *The Trojan Women* (415 B.C.E.), and *The Bacchae* and *Iphigenia in Aulis* (both presented posthumously, perhaps in 405 B.C.E.). These and other works show protagonists (often female) caught in the grip of obsession or disaster, in tales that combine suspense and human detail with brooding questions about the nature of the universe and of the supposed gods.

Criticism of Euripides, both ancient and modern, often focuses on the playwright's tendency to distort certain myths to such an extent that it approaches caricature, with gods sometimes portrayed as repulsive personalities (e.g., HERA in *Herakles Insane* and APOLLO in *Ion*). Euripides' contemporaries clearly found his religious irreverence to be disturbing; although he competed 22 times at Athenian festival drama competitions, he was awarded first place only five times (as compared with Aeschylus's 13 and Sophokles' 24 in their lifetimes). Still, he was always considered thought-provoking enough to be allowed a hearing. The Athenian officials never rejected his application to compete. The ambivalent Athenian attitude toward Euripides is shown in ARISTOPHANES' comedy *The Frogs* (405 B.C.E.), presented soon after Euripides' death. In this play, Euripides and Aeschylus hold a contest in the Underworld for the privilege of returning to ATHENS, and Euripides loses.

Euripides was said to have written 120 plays, of which 80 titles are known. More of his works are preserved today than of any other Athenian playwright: 18 tragedies and one satyr play by Euripides have survived complete, as opposed to only six or seven by Aeschylus and seven by Sophokles. This generous legacy has perhaps hurt Euripides' reputation among modern thinkers, since, unlike the other two tragedians, his surviving plays include work that is not his best.

Little is known about Euripides' life. He came from a family of Phyle outside Athens that might have been wealthy. Tradition holds (probably falsely) that he was born on the same day as the Greek naval victory over the Persians at SALAMIS (1) (480 B.C.E.). His first play was entered in the dramatic competition at Athens when he was 25 years of age; this drama (*The Pleiades*), was awarded third place.

Unlike Sophokles, Euripides was not politically active, but he did compose a funerary hymn for NIKIAS, DEMOSTHENES, and the other Athenians slain in the disastrous expedition to SYRACUSE during the PELOPONNESIAN WAR (415–413 B.C.E.). He was very interested in philosophy and was associated with the intellectual movement of the SOPHISTS, who often presented disturbing ideas to their contemporaries. It was supposedly at Euripides' home that the sophist PROTAGORAS recited a treatise that cast doubt on the existence of the gods. He was also said to be friends with the philosophers ANAXAGORAS and SOCRATES, as well as with the politician and general ALCIBIADES. Like many intellectuals, he was thought to be hostile to the radical Athenian DEMOCRACY.

These political and philosophical leanings made Euripides an object of enmity in Athens, and in 408 B.C.E. he left the city on a self-imposed exile, eventually settling in Macedonia at the invitation of the Macedonian king Archelaus, an enthusiastic literary patron. Euripides' unhappy personal life may have also led him to leave Athens; twice married, he was supposedly surly and reclusive. He died and was buried at Pella in 406 B.C.E., and a cenotaph was also erected in his honor at Athens. It is said that Sophokles, at the next Dionysia, dressed his chorus in mourning for his deceased rival.

Euripides' surviving plays show a range of subject matter and philosophical treatment. His object, more often than not, is emotion. The chorus is used somewhat differently in his plays than in many of his contemporaries' works; it is generally a nonessential element rather than a major part of the dramatic action.

Medea, a play about the mythical queen who eventually kills her children out of obsessive hatred for her husband, is now considered one of the greatest Greek tragedies. Interestingly enough, however, the Athenian judges at the City Dionysia drama competition in 431 B.C.E. awarded *Medea*'s three-play group only third prize. Euripides did win first prize at the competition in 428 B.C.E., however, with his *Hippolytus*, an insightful play that features a psychological portrait of the mythical queen Phaedra and her hopeless love for her stepson, HIPPOLYTUS.

The Trojan Women—one of a trilogy of plays about the TROJAN WAR—was performed in 415 B.C.E., at the height of the Peloponnesian War. Opening after TROY's capture by the Greeks, the play catalogues the woes that befall the royal Trojan female captives (HECUBA, ANDROMACHE, and CASSANDRA) at the hands of the bullying conquerors—who are themselves unknowingly doomed to meet disaster on their voyage home. The play is a clear protest against Athenian imperialism, including the Athenians' contemporary expedition against Syracuse and their destruction of the resistant, helpless Aegean island of MELOS. The Athenians voted the trilogy second prize.

The Bacchae, produced after Euripides' death, presents the story of the god DIONYSUS's destruction of his kinsman, the Theban king Pentheus. The play is admired as a study of human delusion and a disturbing inquiry into the cruelty of the gods.

See also IPHIGENIA; MAENADS; MEDEA.

Further reading: Christopher Collard, *Euripides* (Oxford: Clarendon Press, 1981); Shirley A. Barlow, *The Imagery of Euripides: A Study in the Dramatic Use of Pictorial Language* (Bristol, U.K.: Bristol Classical Press, 1986); Marc Huys, *The Tale of the Hero Who Was Exposed at Birth in Euripidean Tragedy: A Study of Motifs* (Leuven, Belgium: Leuven University Press, 1995); Daniel A. Mendelsohn, *Gender and the City in Euripides' Political Plays* (New York: Oxford University Press, 2002); Philip Freund, *The Birth of Theatre* (London: Peter Owen, 2003).

Europa (Greek Europē, "wide eyes") In Greek MYTH, Europa was a Phoenician princess of the city of Tyre. Seeing her by the Mediterranean shore, the great god ZEUS became inflamed with desire. He changed himself into a handsome bull and enticed her to climb atop his back, then swam quickly out to sea to the island of CRETE. There Europa bore the god two sons, the Cretan princes MINOS and Rhadamanthys. (Some versions add the hero Sarpedon.) Meanwhile, Europa's brother KADMOS began a futile search for her, during which he crossed to Greece and eventually founded the city of THEBES.

The myth may reflect in some dark way Mycenaean-Greek relations with the Near East and Crete ca. 1400–1200 B.C.E. The modern English word *Europe,* meaning the continent, seems to derive from this mythical character's name.

See also EUROPE and ASIA; MYCENAEAN CIVILIZATION; PHOENICIA.

Further reading: P. B. S. Andrews, "The Myth of Europa and Minos," *Greece and Rome* 16 (1969): 60–66; Judith M. Barringer, "Europa and the Nereids. Wedding or Funeral?" *American Journal of Archaeology* 95 (1991): 657–667; Martin Robertson, "Europa and Others. Nostalgia in Late Fifth Century Athenian Vase-painting," in *Kotinos. Festschrift für Erika Simon,* edited by Heide Froning, Tonio Hölscher, and Harald Mielsch (Mainz, Germany: Philip von Zabern, 1992), 237–240; R. S. P. Beekes, "Where Europa Bathed," *Mnemosyne* 48 (1995): 579–581.

Europe and Asia The English words *Europe* and *Asia* both come from the ancient Greeks. By the 700s B.C.E. the Greeks had developed the notion that these were two different continents, separated by the AEGEAN SEA. The Greek word Europē seems to have been derived from the name of the mythical princess EUROPA. As used as a place-name, the word originally referred to central Greece. *Asia* originally denoted interior ASIA MINOR, east of the Greek-settled region called IONIA.

As Greek TRADE and COLONIZATION opened up the Mediterranean and other waterways (800–500 B.C.E.); the name *Europe* was applied to the coastlines of SICILY, ITALY, France, Spain, and the western and northern BLACK SEA. Similarly, the region indicated by the name *Asia* grew with time. After the Eastern conquests of ALEXANDER THE GREAT (334–323 B.C.E.), Asia came to include the Near East, PERSIA, and other lands, east to the Indus and Ganges River valleys. But EGYPT was usually considered to be outside both Asia and Europe.

In Greek MYTH, a character named Asia is a nymph, sometimes described as the wife of PROMETHEUS. In fact, the Greeks may have taken that name around 1200 B.C.E. from the Hittites, whose word *Assuiuva* denoted western Asia Minor.

See also HECATEAUS; HERODOTUS; NYMPHS.

Eurydice *See* ORPHEUS.

Eurypontid clan The Eurypontids (eurupontidai) were the junior royal family at SPARTA, a city that had an unusual government insofar as it was ruled simultaneously by two kings. The Eurypontids traced their ancestry back to a legendary King Eurypontis, one of the sons of HERAKLES.

Eurypontid kings took second place in protocol to their partners, the Agiad kings, but they tended to share power equally. Among the best-known Eurypontids was the King ARCHIDAMUS who reigned ca. 469–426 B.C.E.

See also AGIAD CLAN; DORIAN GREEKS.

Further reading: E. I. McQueen, "The Eurypontid House in Hellenistic Sparta," *Historia* 39 (1990): 163–181.

Euxine *See* BLACK SEA.

F

family *See* KINSHIP.

farming Mainland Greece is a mountainous country, and ancient Greek society was shaped by the scarcity of farmland. Individuals owning land in the plains tended to be much richer and more elevated socially than those who farmed the foothills. Hilly terrain dictated cultivation of olive trees, grape vines, and other fruit-bearing plants that thrive on rough ground.

MYCENAEAN CIVILIZATION (1600–1200 B.C.E.) was a feudal society based on sheep- and cattle-ranching, which involved baronial estates worked by serfs. Cattle rustling and meat feasts are two favorite activities of the aristocrats in HOMER's *Illiad* and *Odyssey* (written around 750 B.C.E. but reflecting the Mycenaean world of some 500 years prior). The classical Greek religious custom of sacrificing cattle and sheep to the gods is clearly a Mycenaean vestige. Preoccupation with grazing is reflected in such regional names as EUBOEA and BOEOTIA, containing the Greek root *boes,* "cattle."

The social upheavals of the DARK AGE and years following (around 1100–700 B.C.E.) saw the emergence of smaller holdings, owned by nobles, yeomen, or poor subsistence farmers. Developments in metallurgy brought an improved plowshare, tipped with IRON rather than BRONZE (ca. 1050 B.C.E.). By the start of the historical era (750 B.C.E.), Mycenaean-style ranches survived mainly on the plains of THESSALY; elsewhere, a more efficient use of the land arose in the raising of crops.

Information on Greek farming in this epoch comes from the Boeotian poet HESIOD's verse calendar *Works and Days* (ca. 700 B.C.E.) and from agricultural writers of later years. Details are added by archaeological evidence, ranging from farming scenes on vase paintings to recovered ancient pollen spores. The primary Greek farm crops were grain, olives, grapes (mainly for winemaking); other fruits such as apples, pears, figs, and pomegranates; and beans and other greens. Barley was the most common grain grown in mainland Greece, but by the 400s B.C.E. imports of Ukrainian and Sicilian wheat were displacing barley on the market at many cities. Millet was grown for fodder. Flax was grown for weaving into linen. The ancient Greeks knew about cotton, which was cultivated in EGYPT but could not be grown easily on Greek terrain. However, North American–type corn (maize) was unknown to the Greeks, as were tomatoes and potatoes.

Crucial to the ancient Greek economy was olive cultivation, which in the Aegean dates back at least to the Minoan era (ca. 2000 B.C.E.). Eventually the Greeks had more than 25 varieties of olive; they used olive oil for cooking, washing, lamp fuel, religious devotions, and as a treatment for athletes. Olive oil was a principal export of the city of ATHENS, where the olive tree was honored in MYTH as the goddess ATHENA's gift to the city.

Early Greek farmers had to let a field lie fallow every other year (or sometimes two years for each one cultivated), so the soil could replenish its nutrients. But by around 400 B.C.E. the Greeks had discovered the much more productive method of raising different crops in annual rotation on the same land. The Greeks did their plowing and grain-sowing in October, at the start of the rainy season. In order to plow a field, a farmer would guide a wooden rig behind a pair of yoked oxen. (Ancient Greek horse breeds were too small for draft, aside from pulling CHARIOTS.) Plowing was hard work. Unlike the much-improved plowshare of medieval northern Europe, the ancient Greek tool did not turn the soil but only scratched the surface, and the plowman had to keep pushing the blade into the earth as he proceeded.

Grain grew through the relatively mild Greek winter and was harvested in May. During the parching Greek summer the crop was winnowed and stored. September brought a second harvest—of grapes, olives, and other fruit.

In the HELLENISTIC AGE, the small farms that had existed in earlier Greek history began to be replaced by large agricultural estates (which would eventually influence the development of elaborate villas in the Roman era). These estates, worked in many instances by slaves or serfs, helped generate an agricultural surplus. They generally clustered around newly developed towns and small cities, whose merchants facilitated the trade of the farmed goods. This commercial element of Hellenistic farming went along with the increased internationalism of the society and the constant trade and communication that took place among the Mediterranean civilizations.

See also ASTRONOMY; ELEUSINIAN MYSTERIES; GREECE, GEOGRAPHY OF; MINOAN CIVILIZATION; SPORT.

Further reading: Victor Davis Hanson, *Warfare and Agriculture in Classical Greece* (Pisa, Italy: Giardini, 1983); Signe Isager and Jens Erik Skydsgaard, *Ancient Greek Agriculture: An Introduction* (London: Routledge, 1992); B. Wells, ed., *Agriculture in Ancient Greece: Proceedings of the Seventh International Symposium at the Swedish Institute at Athens, 16–17 May, 1990* (Stockholm: Svenska Institutet i Athen, 1992); Alison Burford, *Land and Labor in the Greek World* (Baltimore: Johns Hopkins University Press, 1993); Maria S. Marsilio, *Farming and Poetry in Hesiod's Works and Days* (Lanham, Md.: University Press of America, 2000).

fate This supernatural power is imagined as preordaining certain on all human events. In Greek MYTH and RELIGION, a belief in fate paradoxically existed alongside the belief in the divine guidance and decision making of ZEUS and his subordinate gods.

The main words for fate were *moira* and *aisa*, also translatable as "lot" or "share"—a person's fate is what has been apportioned to him or her. Obviously the final and most dramatic item of human fate is death. Greek notions of fate are best understood as elaborating on the simple knowledge that every person will die and that the gods are unwilling or unable to prevent this.

The god Zeus was imagined as working in harmony with fate or somehow causing fate. One of his titles was Moiragetēs, "leader of fate." HOMER's epic poem the *Iliad* (written down around 750 B.C.E.) repeatedly shows Zeus holding a pair of golden scales and weighing the respective dooms (*kēres*) of two human antagonists on the battlefield; the warrior indicated by the heavier pan is doomed. Zeus will not avert a doomed warrior's fate—even his beloved human son Sarpedon is fated to die, slain by the Greek warrior PATROKLOS (book 16). Con-

versely, the angry god POSEIDON in the *Odyssey* cannot completely destroy the hero ODYSSEUS, because Odysseus is fated to survive his voyage and return home (book 5). But the hero ACHILLES in the *Iliad* is aware of a choice in his fate: He can either stay and die gloriously, fighting at TROY, or can return home and live to a safe, undistinguished old age (book 9).

The personification of fate as three goddesses, the Moirai, is first clearly described in HESIOD's epic poem the *Theogony* (ca. 700 B.C.E.). Hesiod presents the Moirai as the daughters of Zeus and the goddess Themis. They are imagined as working at the womanly task of spinning—drawing out a thread of yarn that determines or represents each person's life. Into the thread may be woven sorrow, wealth, travel, and the like. Hesiod names the three fates Clotho (spinner), Lachesis (disposer of lots), and Atropos (unavoidable). Later writers distinguished the goddesses' duties, with Clotho spinning the thread, Lachesis measuring it out, and Atropos snipping it. Either the cutting produced the person's death or, in another version, the thread was entirely spun out and cut at the baby's birth, to contain the person's future.

The pretty conceit of divine spinners was probably more important to poets than to the Greek religious public. But the Moirai were widely worshipped as goddesses of childbirth and as promoters of good harvest. Athenian brides, for instance, brought cuttings of their hair as offerings to the fates.

See also PROPHECY AND DIVINATION.

Further reading: M. E. Reesor, "Fate and Possibility in Early Stoic Philosophy," *Phoenix* 19 (1965): 285–297; B. C. Dietrich, *Death, Fate, and the Gods. The Development of a Religious Idea in Greek Popular Belief and in Homer,* 2d ed. (London: Athlone Press, 1967); G. Giannakis, "The 'Fate-as-Spinner' Motif. A Study on the Poetic and Metaphorical Language of Ancient Greek and Indo-European, 1," *Indogermanische Forschungen* 103 (1998): 1–27.

food and meals The people of ancient Greece enjoyed a flavorsome and extremely varied diet. All around the hilly countryside, olives, grapes, and figs were harvested, and in some of the more fertile plains, grains such as wheat, barley, and millet were grown as well. The olives were manufactured into olive oil and the grapes into wine. Herds of goats ranged everywhere and provided milk and cheese. People also raised chickens and ate eggs frequently. Fish and other kinds of seafood (squid, octopus, shrimp, and the like) were an extremely important part of the Greek diet. Other types of meat were sometimes available in the markets of the larger city-states; only the flesh of animals that had been hunted in the wild was eaten—never domesticated animals. In general, meat was eaten rarely and was primarily reserved for religious sacrifices.

The importance of the olive and olive oil in the ancient Greek diet and economy is illustrated by a MYTH about the goddess ATHENA. She and POSEIDON were arguing over which deity would be the patron of the city of ATHENS. ZEUS decreed that the winner would be the one who gave the more valuable gift to the city. Poseidon struck the ground with his trident, and a salt-water spring erupted out of the earth. Then Athena produced the olive tree. Her gift was immediately judged to be the better one, and Athens was hers. To this day, olive oil remains one of Greece's most important agricultural products and exports.

In HOMER's epics, the Greeks ate their meals while sitting, but by the Classical period diners regularly reclined on couches called *klinai*. When WOMEN were allowed to be present for meals (only in the home, with the family), they sat upright while the men reclined. Women depicted in Greek art as reclining at a meal are meant to be PROSTITUTES ("hetairai").

The ancient Greeks did not use knives or forks, eating primarily with their fingers. They did occasionally use a spoon or a piece of hollowed-out bread for eating soups and other liquids. They also used pieces of bread to wipe their hands after eating (the bread was then given to dogs); not until the Roman era were napkins used.

See also FARMING.

Further reading: William J. Slater, ed., *Dining in a Classical Context* (Ann Arbor: University of Michigan Press, 1991); John Wilkins, David Harvey, and Mike Dobson, eds., *Food in Antiquity* (Exeter, U.K.: University of Exeter Press, 1995); Andrew Dalby, *Siren Feasts: A History of Food and Gastronomy in Greece* (London: Routledge, 1996); Peter Garnsey, *Food and Society in Classical Antiquity* (New York: Cambridge University Press, 1999).

Four Hundred, The   This Oligarchic committee briefly seized power at ATHENS in 411 B.C.E., during the PELOPONNESIAN WAR. The Four Hundred were led by the politician Pisander and by the orator ANTIPHON. Taking advantage of the absence from Athens of large numbers of working-class, pro-democratic citizens (who were manning the large fleet in operation at SAMOS), the conspirators began intimidating the populace in the spring of 411 B.C.E. with a series of political murders and demonstrations. The coup d'état was performed in June in the Athenian ASSEMBLY. Led by Pisander, the plotters pushed through a number of revolutionary decrees, amounting to a dismantling of the DEMOCRACY; all existing executive posts were abolished and a new COUNCIL, of 400 men (replacing the democratic council of 500), was appointed.

The conspirators ruled Athens for the duration of the summer. But the Athenian troops on distant Samos remained staunchly pro-democratic, perpetuating the Athenian democracy by holding their own assemblies and elections. After a home-defense war fleet dispatched by the Four Hundred was defeated by the Spartans in the Straits of EUBOEA, the oligarchs were discredited and overthrown (in September of 411 B.C.E.). Pisander fled to SPARTA; Antiphon, disdaining to flee, was tried and executed under the restored democracy.

See also OLIGARCHY.

Further reading: H. C. Avery, "Critias and the Four Hundred," *Classical Philology* 58 (1963): 165–167; G. Adeleye, "Theramenes and the Overthrow of the 'Four Hundred,'" *Museum Africum* 2 (1973): 77–81; G. Adeleye, "Critias, Member of the Four Hundred?" *Transactions of the American Philological Association* 104 (1974): 1–9; G. Pesely, "Andron and the Four Hundred," *Illinois Classical Studies* 20 (1995): 66–76; Donald Kagen, *The Peloponnesian War* (New York: Viking, 2003).

funeral customs   Despite the cremation of slain heroes described in HOMER's epic poems, the Greeks outside of the DARK AGE (around 1100–900 B.C.E.) generally buried their dead. The elaborate tombs of Mycenaen kings have

This marble gravestone from about 510 B.C.E. shows a life-size man named Aristion in soldier's armor. He may have died in battle; his name means "one of the noblest." *(Alison Frantz Photographic Collection, American School of Classical Studies at Athens)*

Athenian gravestone, circa 535 B.C.E., standing nearly 14 feet tall. The monument shows a carved likeness of the dead person topped with a guardian sphinx. *(Alison Frantz Photographic Collection, American School of Classical Studies at Athens)*

supplied archaeologists with most of their information about Greek prehistory for the era 1600–1200 B.C.E. The Greeks of historical times, after about 750 B.C.E., had their own burial customs. Their need to cover a corpse with earth was not simply a matter of hygiene or decorum; it was believed that the sight of a dead body would offend the Olympian gods, and that the dead person's ghost could not enter the Underworld until the body had been covered. This helps explain the insistence of SOPHOKLES' tragic heroine ANTIGONE on sprinkling dirt over her slain brother's corpse, although forbidden by a ruler's decree from doing so. As Antigone's action suggests, such a "burial" could be merely ceremonial, performed with a few handfuls of dirt.

For a regular funeral (Greek: *taphē*), the body was bathed and clothed. At the home, it was laid out and mourned over by relatives and household (Greek: *prothesis*). In the Classical period, excessive lamentation actually was forbidden by law at ATHENS; there seems to have been a deep-seated fear that WOMEN's lamenting might bring the dead back to life. The body would then be carried on a stretcher to the place of burial (Greek: *ekphora*), where it would be placed in a coffin or—for the rich of a certain era—a stone sarcophagus ("flesh-eater"). Certain marble sarcophagi, carved with beautiful reliefs showing scenes of hunting and war, are among the finest Greek SCULPTURE of the late 300s–200s B.C.E. At the graveside, offerings of food and drink might be left—to "refresh" the dead in the grave or for the journey to the Underworld.

After the burial, the grave would receive some kind of marker. Again, for the wealthy, there was marble—specifically, the type of monument known as a *stēlē*, with an idealized portrait of the dead. At Athens, the Kerameikos district, just outside the northwest city wall, contained monumental graveyards owned by aristocratic families, many marked by elaborate stelai. These gravestones provide important archaeological evidence about Athenian family groups and religious customs and beliefs, as well as artistic styles and development. Sculptured grave stelai in Athens date from the Archaic and Classical periods; in the 300s B.C.E. such ostentatious commemorations were outlawed in favor of small, undecorated columnar markers.

For public funerals, such as the mass observances by which the classical Athenians honored their war dead, a prominent citizen might be chosen to deliver a speech (or, alternatively, compose a poem) honoring the departed. This kind of funerary speech was known by the adjective *epitaphios*, from which comes our word "epitaph." The most famous funeral oration of the ancient world was delivered by the Athenian statesman PERIKLES in the first year of the PELOPONNESIAN WAR (431 B.C.E.). As recounted by the historian THUCYDIDES (1), Perikles speech presents a glorification of the Athenian DEMOCRACY, for which the men had died.

See also AFTERLIFE; MYCENAEAN CIVILIZATION.

Further reading: Donna Kurtz and John Boardman, *Greek Burial Customs* (London: Thames and Hudson, 1971); Ian Morris, *Burial and Ancient Society: The Rise of the Greek City-State* (New York: Cambridge University Press, 1987); William G. Cavanagh and Christopher Mee, *A Private Place: Death in Prehistoric Greece* (Jonsered, Sweden: P. Aströms förlag, 1998); G. J. Oliver, ed., *The Epigraphy of Death: Studies in the History and Society of Greece and Society of Greece and Rome* (Liverpool, U.K.: Liverpool University Press, 2000); Janet Burnett Grossman, *Greek Funerary Sculpture: Catalogue of the Collections at the Getty Villa* (Los Angeles: J. Paul Getty Museum, 2001).

Furies (Greek: Erinues) In Greek RELIGION and MYTH, the Furies were horrible female spirits of divine retribution. Tormenting their victims by nonphysical means—inciting fear and madness—they especially punished the crime of murdering a family member. But they might pursue oath-breakers or anyone else who had broken a bond of society. Their best-known appearance in literature is in AESCHYLUS's tragedy *Eumenides* (458 B.C.E.), where they constitute the play's 12-member chorus. In the story, they torment the hero ORESTES, who has slain his mother.

In HESIOD's Creation poem, the *Theogony* (ca. 700 B.C.E.), they are described as being the daughters of GAEA (Mother Earth), born from the spattered blood of the castration wound that CRONUS inflicted on his father, Uranus (Ouranos, "Sky").

The Furies were usually worshipped under some euphemistic name; Aeschylus's title *Eumenides* means "kindly ones." An altar to them as the Dreaded Goddesses, at the foot of the Athenian ACROPOLIS, became associated with the curse of the Alcmaeoid family.

See also ALCMAEON (1); ALCMAEONIDS; KYLON; ELECTRA.

Further reading: A. L. Brown, "Eumenides in Greek Tragedy," *Classical Quarterly* 34 (1984): 260–281; H. Lloyd-Jones, "Erinyes, Semnai Theai, Eumenides," in *Owls to Athens. Essays on Classical Subjects Presented to Sir Kenneth Dover* (New York: Oxford University Press, 1990), 203–211; S. B. Matheson, "Hounded by Furies," *Yale University Bulletin* (1997–1998): 18–29.

G

Gaea (Gaia, Ge) This goddess was the Greek personification of the earth (as opposed to the elements of sea sky), but unlike the grain goddess DEMETER, Gaea was not a central deity of Greek RELIGION. Her name reflects the Greek common noun for "land," *ge* or *ga*. Gaea had several significant cult sites, particularly at the Greek colonies in SICILY. She was worshipped for her fertility as *kourotrophos*, "bearer of children," and also as a goddess of mortality. The corresponding goddess in Roman mythology was called Tellus.

According to the creation myth in HESIOD's epic poem *The Theogony* (ca. 700 B.C.E.), Gaea emerged from primeval Chaos, then gave birth to Pontos ("Sea") and Uranus (*Ouranos*, "Sky"), whom she married. Their monstrous children included the TITANS, the Cyclopes, and the "Hundred-handed Ones" (Hekatoncheires). When their son CRONUS castrated his father, fertile Gaea was impregnated by the spattered blood and gave birth to the FURIES and the GIANTS. She also bore several children to Pontos, including Nereus, Thaumas, Phorcys, Ceto, and Eurybia. Later she also produced other offspring, including the giants TYPHON (who had a hundred heads), Antaeus, and Tityus, and the legendary kings of Athens Erechtheus and Kekrops.

In Greek MYTH, the Giants and Typhon impiously attacked the immortal gods atop Mt. OLYMPUS. The subsequent battle between the gods and the Giants (the *gigantomachy*) was a frequent subject in Classical art, particularly in ATHENS, as a symbol of civilization vs. barbarianism.

See also CYCLOPS; ZEUS.

Further reading: Evelyn B. Harrison, "Alkamenes' Sculptures for the Hephaisteion, 1. The Cult Statues," *American Journal of Archaeology* 81 (1977): 265–287; Th. Hadzisteliou-Price, *Kourtrophos: Cults and Representations of the Greek Nursing Deities* (Leiden, Netherlands: E. J. Brill, 1978); Mary B. Moore, "Ge," *Lexicon Iconographicum Mythologiae Classicae IV, 1* (Zurich: Artemis Verlag, 1988), 171–177.

Galatea *See* POLYPHEMUS; PYGMALION.

Galatia *See* ASIA MINOR; CELTS.

Games *See* ISTHMIAN GAMES; NEMEAN GAMES; OLYMPIC GAMES; PANATHENAIA; PYTHIAN GAMES; SPORT.

Ganymede In Greek MYTH, Ganymede was a handsome Trojan prince, son of King Tros. The earliest surviving mention of him, in HOMER's epic the *Iliad* (written down around 750 B.C.E.) says that Ganymede was abducted by the gods to be cupbearer for the great god ZEUS on Mt. OLYMPUS; in exchange, Ganymede's father received a herd of wondrous horses.

Later versions add that the boy was stolen by Zeus himself in the shape of an eagle, or that the eagle was sent by Zeus. Unlike Homer, poets such as THEOGNIS (ca. 542 B.C.E.) portrayed the abduction as a rape, assuming that Zeus desired Ganymede sexually. Modern scholars believe that this sexual nuance is not intended in the original tale told by Homer; the added homosexual coloration would seem to reflect new upper-class values that arose after Homer's time, perhaps in the late 600s B.C.E. The version adopted by the ETRUSCANS of ITALY included the sexual aspect. The Etruscan rendition of the boy's name was Catamitus, a word that eventually went into Latin and subsequently into our own language as the pejorative noun *catamite,* meaning "a male who receives sexual penetration."

In Greek vase painting of the 500s and 400s B.C.E., Ganymede is portrayed as an idealized youth or boy with long hair. Sometimes he holds a playing hoop (suggesting boyhood) and a rooster (Zeus's courting gift).

See also HOMOSEXUALITY.

Further reading: E. K. Gazda, "Ganymede and the Eagle. A Marble Group from Carthage," *Archaeology* 34 (1981): 56–60.

Gaugmela, battle of   *See* ALEXANDER THE GREAT.

Gela   This Greek city is situated on the southeastern coast of SICILY, near the mouth of the river Gelas. Founded in about 688 B.C.E. by DORIAN GREEKS from CRETE and RHODES, Gela was a small city on a fertile plain that enjoyed prosperity. In around 580 B.C.E. it established its important daughter city, ACRAGAS, farther west on the south coast. Gela was ruled by a horsebreeding ARISTOCRACY until the late 500s B.C.E., when (like other cities of the Greek world) it passed into the hands of TYRANTS.

Gela became the most powerful Sicilian city around 490 B.C.E., after the Geloan tyrant Hippocrates conquered much of eastern Sicily. But Gela's preeminence ended when Hippocrates' successor, GELON, captured the great city of SYRACUSE in 485 B.C.E. and made it his capital, going so far as to transplant the richer half of Gela's population to Syracuse.

By the mid-400s B.C.E. the tyrants had fallen from power, but Dorian Gela remained an ally of Dorian Syracuse against the region's Ionian-Greek cities. Gela assisted Syracuse's triumphant defense against the Athenian invasion of 415–413 B.C.E. In the 300s B.C.E., with Sicily a battleground between the Greeks and the Carthaginians, Gela suffered from the exploits of Greek tyrants such as AGATHOKLES, who executed 4,000 Geloans for suspected treason. In 311 B.C.E. Gela's population was entirely transplanted to a new city by the tyrant Phintias of Acragas.

Further reading: Pietro Griffo, *Gela: A Sicilian Town Founded by the Greeks* (Genoa, Italy: Stringa, 1963); Pietro Griffo and Leonard von Matt, *Gela: The Ancient Greeks in Sicily* (Greenwich, Conn.: New York Graphic Society, 1968); G. Kenneth Jenkins, *The Coinage of Gela* (Berlin: De Gruyter, 1970); Jaimee Pugliese Uhlenbrock, *The Terracotta Protomai from Gela: A Discussion of Local Style in Archaic Sicily* (Rome: L'Erma di Bretschneider, 1988).

Gelon   (ca. 540–478 B.C.E.)   *Dictator or tyrant (turannos) of the Greek cities GELA and SYRACUSE, in Sicily*
An able military commander, Gelon is remembered for his defeat of the Carthaginians at the Battle of HIMERA (480 B.C.E.)—an event that made him the most powerful individual in the Greek world.

As his name suggests, Gelon was descended from the first Greek colonists of Gela. He was an aristocrat, and before seizing power he served as a leader of CAVALRY for the Geloan tyrant Hippocrates (who carved out a small empire in eastern Sicily). After Hippocrates' death, Gelon dispossessed the tyrant's sons and assumed full power, at about age 50.

In 485 B.C.E., Gelon captured Syracuse, the foremost city of Sicily. Making Syracuse his new capital, Gelon grandiosely transferred the richer half of Gela's population there, as well as the richer citizens of other captured Greek towns. (Other Sicilian tyrants soon copied this ruthless new practice of transplantation.) Gelon installed his brother HIERON (1) as tyrant of Gela and allied himself with Theron, tyrant of ACRAGAS, taking Theron's daughter Demareta as one of his wives.

Meanwhile, the Greek world was being threatened by two foreign empires, the Persians in the East and the Carthaginians in the West. Around 481 B.C.E. a delegation of mainland Greeks went to Syracuse to appeal for Gelon's aid against the coming invasion of Greece by the Persian king XERXES. Gelon offered to contribute a large force on the condition that he himself receive chief command of either the Greek army or navy. When these two options were rejected, Gelon sent the ambassadors away, remarking that they seemed better equipped with generals than with troops.

In 480 B.C.E.—coinciding with the Persian invasion of Greece—the Carthaginian leader Hamilcar sailed from North Africa with an army and landed on Sicily's north coast. But a Greek army under Gelon destroyed Hamilcar and his force at the Battle of Himera.

After making peace with CARTHAGE and imposing on them a huge indemnity of 1,000 TALENTS, Gelon began a program of propagandistic cultural display. He dedicated lavish offerings at the sanctuaries of DELPHI and OLYMPIA, in Greece; he enlarged and adorned Syracuse with public building; and he minted a celebrated victory-issue coin, called the Demareteion (after his wife). When Gelon died, he was succeeded by his brother Hieron, who proved to be a less popular ruler.

See also COINAGE; PERSIAN WARS; TYRANTS.

Further reading: A. G. Woodhead, *Greeks in the West* (London: Thames and Hudson, 1962); T. J. Dunbabin, *Western Greeks: The History of Sicily and South Italy from the Foundation of the Greek Colonies to 480 B.C.* (Oxford: Clarendon Press, 1968); A. M. McCann, "The Riace Bronzes. Gelon and Hieron I of Syracuse?" in *From the Parts to the Whole. Acta of the 13th International Bronze Congress. Cambridge, Massachusetts, May 28–June 1, 1996,* edited by Carol Mattusch, Amy Brauer, and Sandra E. Knudsen (Portsmouth, R.I.: Journal of Roman Archaeology, 2000), 97–105.

Geometric pottery   *See* POTTERY.

This golden hairnet was made to be worn over a bun at the back of the head (ca. 100 B.C.E.). The woman depicted in the center may be the Ptolemaic queen Arsinoe III. Gold jewelry was reserved for nobles because of its rarity. *(The J. Paul Getty Museum)*

geometry   *See* MATHEMATICS.

Geryon   *See* HERAKLES.

Giants   In MYTH, the Gigantes were a primeval race of monsters who unsuccessfully rebelled against ZEUS and the other gods, piling Mt. Ossa atop Mt. Pelion in order to assault Mt. OLYMPUS. In the Creation myth in HESIOD's epic poem *Theogony* (ca. 700 B.C.E.), the Giants are described as children of Mother Earth, GAEA (her name is reflected in theirs). She gave birth to them after being impregnated by the blood of the god Uranus (Ouranos, "Sky"), which fell to earth when Uranus was castrated by his son CRONUS. The Giants were sometimes portrayed in art as large, snake-legged humanoids.

The Gigantomachy (battle with the giants) was one of the most popular mythological subjects in Greek art and poetry, symbolizing the victory of civilization over savagery. On grand artistic vistas, such as the architectural sculptures of the PARTHENON, the battle might be shown in conjunction with the fight between CENTAURS and Lapiths or the battle between Greeks and AMAZONS. The Gigantomachy was also the primary subject of the wonderful high-relief frieze on the Great Altar of ZEUS at PERGAMON, one of the major sculptural monuments of the HELLENISTIC AGE. Later writers embellished the tale, adding that the gods enlisted the hero HERAKLES after being warned that they must include a mortal in order to win.

See also ATHENA; THESSALY; ZEUS.

Further reading: Max Kunze, *The Pergamon Altar: Its Rediscovery, History, and Reconstruction* (Berlin: Staatliche Museem zu Berlin, Antikensammlung, 1991); N. T. de Grummond, "Gauls and Giants, Skylla and the Palladion. Some Responses," in *From Pergamon to Sperlonga. Sculpture and Context* (Berkeley: University of California Press, 2000), 255–277.

gold   Ancient Greeks prized gold for the casting of precious SCULPTURE and other artifacts. However, gold as a mineral deposit was scarce in the Aegean region. The source for the gold used for the royal tomb offerings at MYCENAE around 1550 B.C.E. is unknown. The ore may have come from EGYPT or ASIA MINOR, traveling by way of TRADE or plunder of war.

By the 600s B.C.E. Greek pioneers were prospecting for gold at Mt. Pangaeus, on the Aegean coast of THRACE. Despite the hostility of the native Thracians, the Greeks, based in the nearby island of THASOS, panned the streams of Pangaeus and perhaps dug mines; SILVER seems to have been more abundant there than gold. Eventually Pangaeus was seized by imperial ATHENS (mid-400s B.C.E.) and then by the Macedonian king PHILIP II (mid-300s B.C.E.). The nearby Athenian colony at AMPHIPOLIS was strategic to these interests. Another Aegean gold source, closer to mainland Greece, was the Greek island of Siphnos, in the western CYCLADES. The Siphnian mines financed the construction of an elegant treasury building at DELPHI, ca. 525 B.C.E. before the mines were ruined by natural flooding.

Most gold probably reached early Greece through trade with non-Greek nations beyond the Aegean basin. Trading partners in the 600s and 500s B.C.E. included the Asia Minor kingdoms of Phrygia and LYDIA, where gold could be panned from certain rivers, and where such kings as MIDAS and CROESUS, fabled for their wealth, ruled. In Lydia, a gold-silver alloy called electrum—panned from the rivers where it formed naturally—supplied the metal for the world's first coins, around 635 B.C.E. The Greeks, however, rarely used gold for their COINAGE; since gold was so difficult for them to acquire, they minted with silver and, eventually, with BRONZE.

In the mid-500s B.C.E. the gold fields of Asia Minor and Mesopotamia passed into the hands of the conquering Persians, who continued the gold trade. Like other precious goods, gold became more plentiful for the Greeks of the HELLENISTIC AGE (around 300–150 B.C.E.), after the conquests of the Macedonian king ALEXANDER THE GREAT had opened up the mines and treasure troves of the Persian empire.

See also PHEIDIAS.

Further reading: Dyfri Williams and Jack Ogden, *Greek Gold: Jewellery of the Classical World* (London: British Museum Press, 1994); Aikaterini Despini, *Ancient Gold Jewellery,* translated by Alexandra Doumas (Athens: Ekdotike Athenon, 1996); Andrew Ramage and Paul Craddock, *King Croesus' Gold: Excavations at Sardis and the History of Gold Refining* (Cambridge, Mass.: Harvard University Press for the Archaeological Exploration of Sardis, 2000).

Gordian Knot   *See* ALEXANDER THE GREAT.

Gorgias (ca. 483–376 B.C.E.) *Greek orator of the east-coast Sicilian Greek city of Leontini*
Visiting ATHENS on a political embassy in 427 B.C.E., Gorgias created a cultural sensation with his highly wrought style of public speaking. His display pieces, using rhyme, alliteration, and rhythmical parallel clauses, were soon widely imitated at Athens; his visit marked a revolution in ancient Greek RHETORIC. Gorgias periodically returned to Athens to teach; his greatest pupil was the Athenian orator ISOKRATES. Gorgias's influence has been noted in the works of the historian THUCYDIDES (1) and the playwright AGATHON.

Because of his love of the ingenious and shameless argument, Gorgias was associated with the intellectual movement of the SOPHISTS. One of his surviving speeches, the *Encomium of Helen,* is a defense of the mythical HELEN OF TROY and her adulterous, disastrous elopement with the Trojan prince PARIS. The speech shows Gorgias's soothing, jingling style, which apparently seeks to charm the listener by incantation.

A dignified, amiable Gorgias appears as a character in PLATO's fictional dialogue *Gorgias* (written around 380 B.C.E.).

Further reading: George Kimball Plochmann and Franklin E. Robinson, *A Friendly Companion to Plato's Gorgias* (Carbondale: Southern Illinois University Press, 1988); Robert Wardy, *The Birth of Rhetoric: Gorgias, Plato, and Their Successors* (London: Routledge, 1998); Scott Consigny, *Gorgias, Sophist and Artist* (Columbia: University of South Carolina Press, 2001); Bruce McComiskey, *Gorgias and the New Sophistic Rhetoric* (Carbondale: Southern Illinois University Press, 2002).

Gorgons   *See* MEDUSA.

Gortyn   This city of central CRETE was settled by the DORIAN GREEKS after about 1000 B.C.E. By 500 B.C.E. it was a flourishing city, the largest on the island. In the first century B.C.E. Gortyn became the capital of the Roman province of Crete and Cyrenaica.

Archaeological excavations of the ancient town in the 1880s uncovered the now-famous marble inscription called the Law Code of Gortyn, carved in about 500 B.C.E. The code, written in the Doric dialect, addresses such civil-law issues as land tenure, mortgages, and the status of SLAVES. Although the surviving inscription contains no sections on criminal law, the Gortyn code remains the most important, single, extant source for Greek law prior to 300 B.C.E.

See also GREEK LANGUAGE; LAWS AND LAW COURTS; WRITINGS.

Further reading: A. E. Jackson, "The Bronze Coinage of Gortyn," *Numismatic Chronicle* 11 (1971): 37–51; M. Gagarin, "The Organization of the Gortyn Law Code," *Greek, Roman, and Byzantine Studies* 23 (1982): 129–146; S. V. Spyridakis, "Notes on the Jews of Gortyna and Crete," *Zeitschrift für Papyrologie und Epigraphik* 73 (1988): 171–175; I. Morris, "The Gortyn Code and Greek Kinship," *Greek, Roman, and Byzantine Studies* 31 (1990): 233–254; M. Gagarin, "The Economic Status of Women in the Gortyn Code. Retroactivity and Change," in *Symposium 1993. Vorträge zur griechischen und hellenistischen Rechtsgeschichte. Graz-Andritz, 12–16 September 1993* (Cologne: Böhlau, 1994), 61–71; M. Gagarin, "The First Law of the Gortyn Code Revisited," *Greek, Roman, and Byzantine Studies* 36 (1995): 7–15; P. Perlman, "Gortyn. The First Seven Hundred Years, 1," in *Polis and Politics. Studies in Ancient Greek History. Presented to Mogens Herman Hansen on His Sixtieth Birthday, August 20, 2000,* edited by P. Flensted-Jensen, T. H. Nielsen, and L. Rubenstein (Copenhagen: Museum Tusculanum Press, University of Copenhagen, 2000), 59–89.

grain supply   *See* BLACK SEA; EGYPT; FARMING; HELLESPONT; SICILY; THRACE.

Greece, climate and landscape of

Greece is a peninsula in the Mediterranean Sea, flanked to the east by the Aegean Sea and to the west by the Adriatic. It has an area of approximately 82,000 square miles and an extremely variable landscape. Within its boundaries are high mountain ranges such as the Pindus, long valleys, rough hills, flat plains, and networks of small rivers. The long, meandering coastline is one of the Greek landscape's most distinctive features and has always caused its inhabitants to foster a close relationship with the sea and its bounty.

The Aegean islands are also part of Greece, including the CYCLADES, the Sporades, and the Dodecanese. The largest of these islands is CRETE, to the south of mainland Greece—not far from the coast of EGYPT in North Africa. There are also many smaller islands, some of which are virtually uninhabited.

In antiquity, as in modern times, Greece enjoyed a generally mild climate, with intermittent rain during the winter and dry heat during the summer. The blazing sun of the summer months is tempered somewhat by seasonal winds known as the Meltemia. Some of the highest mountains receive snow, but the rest of the country rarely sees temperatures drop much below freezing. The unpredictable amount of rainfall that Greece receives makes its agriculture-based economy somewhat precarious, and various systems of irrigation and crop rotation were therefore developed and refined at a very early date.

The vegetation in Greece is quite extensive and varied, with more than 6,000 indigenous species of plants having been identified thus far.

Further reading: Oliver Rackham and Jennifer Moody, *The Making of the Cretan Landscape* (New York: Manchester University Press, 1996); John Victor Luce, *Celebrating Homer's Landscapes: Troy and Ithaca Revisited* (New Haven, Conn.: Yale University Press, 1998); Paul Halstead and Charles Frederick, *Landscape and Land Use in Postglacial Greece* (Sheffield, U.K.: Sheffield Academic Press, 2000); Guy Hedreen, *Capturing Troy: The Narrative Functions of Landscape in Archaic and Early Classical Greek Art* (Ann Arbor: University of Michigan Press, 2001); Jamie Morton, *The Role of the Physical Environment in Ancient Greek Seafaring* (Leiden, Netherlands: E. J. Brill, 2001).

Greece, geography of

The key to Greece's history lies in its geography. The mountainous terrain compartmentalized the country into separate population centers, with distinctive dialects, cultures, and politics. This is the background of the Greek "city-state," or POLIS. The rough terrain also placed great economic importance on the few rich FARMING plains. The earliest Greek culture, the MYCENAEAN CIVILIZATION (ca. 1600–1200 B.C.E.) was centered mainly on the two major farmlands of southern and central Greece: the Argive plain, containing the cities of MYCENAE, ARGOS, and TIRYNS; and the twin Boeotian plains, containing THEBES and ORCHOMENOS.

Threatened by famine, Greek cities fought desperate wars over farmland. The first fully remembered conflict in Greek history was the LELANTINE WAR, fought for control of the plain lying between the central Greek cities of CHALCIS and ERETRIA (ca. 720–680 B.C.E.). In the south, the rising state of SPARTA waged a series of wars to annex the plain of MESSENIA (mid-700s–600 B.C.E.).

Cities unable to retain or capture farmland might take to shipping—for Greece comprises a large, ragged peninsula that juts into the northeastern Mediterranean, and many Greek cities lie near the sea. After acquiring seafaring skills from the prehellenic inhabitants of the land (second millennium B.C.E.), and after copying the technologies and trade routes of the brilliant Phoenicians (around 900–800 B.C.E.), the Greeks emerged as a great seagoing people. The vast enlargement of the Greek world through overseas TRADE and COLONIZATION (around 800–500 B.C.E.) was in part due to individual states using seafaring to solve their problems of lack of food supply and employment. The tiny Greek state of AEGINA, perched on a rocky island, became rich as a middleman in overseas trade (500s–early 400s B.C.E.). The city of ATHENS became a superpower through its strong navy (400s–300s B.C.E.).

Cities could prosper by controlling critical points on a trade route—a sea channel, an anchorage, or a mountain road. The best example is CORINTH, superbly located on the narrow isthmus stretching northeastward from the PELOPONNESE. By land, Corinth commanded the route north to central Greece. By sea, Corinth possessed two harbors, facing east and west across the midpoint of Greece, which enabled the city to develop trade routes in both directions, to the Near East and to ITALY and SICILY.

Of strategic importance were the mountains of north-central Greece. Any invading army marching southward from the northeast was forced to face a defensible bottleneck at the mountain pass of THERMOPYLAE, in southern THESSALY. Themopylae played a repeated role in Greek military history, most famously as the site of a failed Greek defense in the PERSIAN WARS (480 B.C.E.), but also in the machinations of the Macedonian king PHILIP II (in 346–338 B.C.E.).

The Macedonian kings who kept Greece subjugated in the 200s B.C.E. recognized four "fetters" or "keys" of Greece—four critical geographic points, possession of which were vital for control. The fetters were Corinth, Chalcis (guarding the narrows of the Euboean Straits), the Athenian port city of PIRAEUS, and the coastal stronghold of Demetrias, beside Thessaly's Gulf of Pagasae (near modern Volos).

See also ACARNANIA; AEGEAN SEA; AETOLIA; ATTICA; BOEOTIA; CHALCIDICE; EPIRUS; EUROPE AND ASIA; EUBOEA;

IONIAN SEA; LOCRIS; MACEDON; PHOCIS; SHIPS AND SEAFAR-
ING; THRACE.

Further reading: E. H. Warmington, *Greek Geography* (New York: AMS Press, 1973); Patricia Jeskins, *The Environment and the Classical World* (London: Bristol Classical Press, 1998).

Greece, history of *See* ALEXANDER THE GREAT; ATHENS; COLONIZATION; CORINTH; DARK AGE; DIADOCHOI, HELLENISTIC AGE; MACEDON; MINOAN CIVILIZATION; MYCENAEAN CIVILIZATION; PELOPONNESIAN WAR; PERSIAN WARS; ROME; SPARTA; THEBES; TRADE; TYRANTS.

Greek language The ancient Greek language was one of the Indo-European family of languages that now includes English, German, Russian, Persian, and such Latin-derived romance languages as French, Italian, and Spanish. These tongues show certain resemblances in grammar and vocabulary (e.g., English "father," ancient Greek *patr,* ancient Latin *pater*). According to modern linguistic theory, the prototype of all these languages was spoken by a group of people living in the Caucasus region (now in southern Russia) in the third millennium B.C.E. At some later date, this people—or, at least, their language—begun to spread outward, presumably by migration and conquest.

In 1952 C.E., British architect Michael Ventris deciphered the LINEAR B language of the MYCENAEAN CIVILIZATION and confirmed that the Mycenaeans of 1400–1200 B.C.E. spoke an early form of Greek. It seems that probably in about 2100 B.C.E., people coming into Greece from the Danube basin brought the developing Greek language with them; these people can be called the first Greeks. In later centuries, the Greek language continued to contain many words of non-Greek etymology, presumably derived from the pre-Greek inhabitants' language. Often distinguished by the endings *-nthos, -sos,* or *-ene,* these words include names of local plants, certain gods' names, and many place-names in mainland Greece. Examples include CORINTH (Korinthos), HYAKINTHOS, acanthus (akanthos), NARCISSUS (Narkissos), and ATHENA (Athene), as well as words like *thalassa,* "sea," and *nesos,* "island."

The final stage of development for the ancient Greek language came with the end of the Mycenaean civilization, soon after 1200 B.C.E. As this society fell, Greece became subject to a new immigration of Greeks—the DORIAN GREEKS, speaking their own dialect of the language. The story of what happened in the following centuries has been pieced together by ARCHAEOLOGY, philology, MYTH, and a few precious references by later Greek authors.

Entering central Greece from the northwest around 1100 B.C.E., the Dorians failed to capture the territory of ATHENS. Farther south, however, they overran almost all of the PELOPONNESE (although mountainous ARCADIA

held out), and they continued conquering by sea across a band of the southern AEGEAN SEA, to CRETE and southwestern ASIA MINOR. In historical times, this swath of territory was distinctive for the Dorian culture and Doric dialect shared by its various inhabitants. The best-known Dorian city was SPARTA. Modern linguists tend to group the Doric dialect into a larger category known as West Greek, which includes the language of the ancient Greeks around the western Corinthian Gulf.

Meanwhile, around 1000 B.C.E., other migrations from mainland Greece were taking place. The AEOLIAN GREEKS of BOEOTIA and THESSALY, buffeted by the invading Dorians, sent refugees fleeing eastward across the Aegean to the island of LESBOS and beyond, to northwestern Asia Minor. These disparate areas became known by their shared Aeolic dialect.

The most fateful migration, however, was of those Ionian-ethnic Greeks whom the Dorians had chased from the Peloponnese. These Ionians emigrated across the Aegean to the central west coast of Asia Minor, where they eventually flourished as the rich and advanced society of IONIA. Athens and the CYCLADES islands remained Ionian territory, all distinguished by their Ionic dialect. The Athenian language developed as a subcategory of Ionic, called Attic (after the Athenian home territory of ATTICA).

Such were the three main divisions of Greek language and culture, although other regional categories existed as well. The highlanders of Arcadia spoke a very old form of Greek that retained aspects of ancient Mycenaean speech and that resembled the speech of another, but very distant, Greek enclave on the island of CYPRUS. Modern scholars call this shared dialect Arcado-Cyprian.

See also ALPHABET; EPIC POETRY; IONIAN GREEKS; LABYRINTH; LYRIC POETRY; MYCENAE; RELIGION; SHIPS AND SEAFARING; TIRYNS; WRITING.

Further reading: P. S. Costas, *An Outline of the History of the Greek Language with Particular Emphasis on the Koine and Subsequent Periods* (Chicago: Ares, 1979); Leonard R. Palmer, *The Greek Language,* 2d ed. (Norman: University of Oklahoma Press, 1996); G. Horrocks, *Greek: A History of the Language and Its Speakers* (London: Longman, 1997).

gymnasium Referring to a sports complex, the Greek word *gumnasion* comes from the verb *gumnazo,* "exercise" (from the adjective *gumnos,* "naked" or "loinclothed," which was how Greek athletes usually trained and competed). Typically located outside a city's walls, the gymnasium featured a running track, a WRESTLING court, and fields for throwing the javelin and discus; also, rooms for changing, oiling down, and so on. A more elaborate type might also include parklands, colonnaded walks, and a horse-riding track.

Gymnasiums first appeared in the 500s B.C.E. They were usually state-run institutions open to men and boys

Depiction of youths in a gymnasium. Greek athletes usually trained and competed naked or loinclothed, as shown here. *(Alison Frantz Photographic Collection, American School of Classical Studies at Athens)*

of the citizen classes. Within this group, the majority of regular customers would be aristocrats and other leisured rich, who did not need to work for a living. The gymnasium played a central role in the Greek city-state, fostering male competition and camaraderie. Schoolboys would receive training in SPORT, and men would pass their time in exercise and conversation. The gymnasium was also central to the male-homosexual climate of the 500s–300s B.C.E., the place where men could observe, and try to meet, boys and youths.

With its gathering of educated people, the gymnasium was a natural scene for philosophical discussion—at least in ATHENS during its age of intellect (400s and 300s B.C.E.). The Athenian philosopher SOCRATES often could be found in one or another of the city's gymnasiums, conversing with his following of aristocratic men. Two Athenian gymnasiums, the ACADEMY and the LYCEUM, gave their names to nearby philosophical schools, set up by PLATO and ARISTOTLE, respectively (300s B.C.E.). The intellectual and social-sexual energy of the Athenian gymnasium is conveyed in certain of Plato's fictional dialogues, such as the *Charmides*.

See also ARISTOCRACY; EDUCATION; HOMOSEXUALITY; POLIS.

Further reading: Fikret K. Yegül, *The Bath-Gymnasium Complex at Sardis* (Cambridge, Mass.: Harvard University Press, 1986); S. L. Glass, "The Greek Gymnasium. Some Problems," in *The Archaeology of the Olympics. The Olympics and Other Festivals in Antiquity. Papers of an international symposium, Los Angeles, April 5–6, 1984* (Madison: University of Wisconsin Press, 1988), 155–173; N. B. Crowther, "Euexia, Eutaxia, Philoponia. Three Contests of the Greek Gymnasium," *Zeitschrift für Papyrologie und Epigraphik* 85 (1991): 301–304; Nigel M. Kennel, *The Gymnasium of Virtue. Education and Culture in Ancient Sparta* (Chapel Hill: University of North Carolina Press, 1995).

H

Hades In MYTH, this was the god of the Underworld and the brother of ZEUS and POSEIDON. The name Hades ("the unseen") properly refers to the god and not his kingdom. Unlike the Judeo-Christian Satan, Hades is not evil; as king of the dead, he rules a domain in nature that complements the happier realm of his brother Zeus. Hades is, however, rather colorless. He has no MYTH, except for his abduction of PERSEPHONE. By Zeus's decree, she lives with Hades as his queen for four months of every year.

Hades does not appear as frequently in Greek art as some of the other divinities. When he is represented, he is generally shown as an older, bearded god (like his brothers, Zeus and Poseidon), with gloomy features. He is sometimes shown standing with the three-headed dog Kerberos or holding a pickax and cornucopia. Most often, however, Hades appears in Greek art as the abductor of Persephone. One of the most spectacular examples of this scene is the wall painting on one of the tombs at Vergina, dated around 350 B.C.E.

Like other gods of death or ill omen, Hades often was worshipped under euphemistic titles. One of the most common of these was Pluton, "the Rich One," probably referring to the rich metal ore in the ground. The early Romans, in adapting Greek RELIGION to their own use, adapted this title as the name for their god of the dead, Pluto.

See also AFTERLIFE.

Further reading: T. A. S. Tinkoff-Utechin, "Ancient Painting from South Russia. The Rape of Persephone at Kerch," *Bulletin of the Institute of Classical Studies, University of London* 26 (1979): 13–26; B. Lincoln, "The Rape of

Persephone. A Greek Scenario of Women's Initiation," *Harvard Theological Review* 72 (1979): 223–235; A. D. Trendall, "A Campanian Lekanis in Lugano with the Rape of Persephone," *Numismatica e antichità classiche* 10 (1981): 165–195; L. Albinus, *The House of Hades. Studies in Ancient Greek Eschatology* (Aarhus, Denmark: Aarhus University Press, 2000).

Halicarnassus This Greek seaport of southwestern ASIA MINOR is situated in the non-Greek territory known as Caria. Founded around 900 B.C.E. by DORIAN GREEKS from Troezen (in the eastern PELOPONNESE), Halicarnassus lay at the northern shore of what is now called the Bay of Gökova, in Turkey. As a gateway to and from the southeastern AEGEAN SEA, the city had a lively commercial culture, combining Carian and Dorian-Greek elements. Halicarnassus was part of the local Dorian federation, centered at nearby KNIDOS.

Like other east Greek cities, Halicarnassus flourished in the 600s and 500s B.C.E., was captured by the Persians in about 545 B.C.E., and endured a series of Persian-run Greek TYRANTS. Remarkably, one such tyrant was a woman, named Artemisia, who accompanied the Persian king XERXES on his invasion of Greece and led a naval squadron against the mainland Greeks at the Battle of SALAMIS (1) (480 B.C.E.).

Halicarnassus's most famous native—the first known writer of history, HERODOTUS—fled the city in about 460 B.C.E. after taking part in a failed coup against another tyrant, Lygdamis. By 450 B.C.E., however, Halicarnassus was a DEMOCRACY and a member of the Athenian-led DELIAN LEAGUE. In 412 B.C.E., during the PELOPONNESIAN

WAR, the city became a major Athenian naval base, after other sites had been lost to widespread revolt by the Delian allies. Later Halicarnassus reverted to Persian control, by the terms of the KING'S PEACE (386 B.C.E.).

Under Persian rule, Halicarnassus became one of the most beautiful and dynamic cities of the Greek world. The ruler Mausolus—Carian by birth but reigning under Persian suzerainty—glorified the city as his capital, building a circuit wall, public monuments, dockyards, and a citadel (ca. 370 B.C.E.). The crown of the building program was his own monumental tomb, the famous Mausoleum, planned and begun by Mausolus himself and continued after his death by his adoring widow, Artemisia (who was also his sister). It is unclear whether the monument was ever completely finished.

Now vanished, but described in detail by ancient authors, the Mausoleum was a colossal structure that towered over the city of Halicarnassus and its busy harbor. It measured 120×100 feet at its base and stood 140 feet tall. Because of its tremendous size and splendor, the Mausoleum was considered one of the SEVEN WONDERS OF THE WORLD. It was a squared, pyramidal structure of white marble with a colonnade at its base, ascending in layers to a sculpted chariot group at the top, probably representing the sun god, HELIOS. Mausolus commissioned four of the greatest Greek sculptors of his time to work on his tomb: Skopas, Timotheos, Leochares, and Bryaxis, as well as a famous Greek architect, Pytheos. The building was adorned with numerous freestanding and relief sculptures (some now displayed in the British Museum), including a battle between Greeks and AMAZONS, a battle between Lapiths and CENTAURS, a hunting scene, and over-life-sized of Mausolus's family and ancestors.

The Mausoleum was destroyed by an earthquake in the 14th century C.E., and many of its stones were taken by the Knights of Rhodes as building material for the castle they erected in the harbor of Halicarnassus in 1415–1437. In 1856, Charles Thomas Newton began exploring the site of the Mausoleum; he found several sculptures and took them back to England. Systematic excavation of the site was later undertaken by Danish archaeologists in 1966 and has continued to the present day.

Defended by a Persian garrison, Halicarnassus was besieged and captured by the Macedonian king ALEXANDER THE GREAT in 334 B.C.E., and passed into his empire. His successors warred over it, with the Ptolemies of EGYPT eventually winning possession (200s B.C.E.). The city came under Roman rule in the 100s B.C.E.

Further reading: G. B. Waywell, "The Mausoleum of Halicarnassus," in *The Seven Wonders of the Ancient World,* edited by Peter A. Clayton and Martin J. Price (London: Routledge, 1988), 100–123; P. Pedersen, "Town-planning in Halicarnassus and Rhodes," in *Archaeology in the Dodecanese [Symposium, Copenhagen, April 7th to 9th 1986],* edited by Søren Dietz and Ioannis Papachristodoulou (Copenhagen: National Museum of Denmark, 1988),

93–103; Tullia Linders and Pontus Hellström, eds., *Architecture and Society in Hecatomnid Caria: Proceedings of the Uppsala Symposium 1987* (Uppsala, Sweden: Almquist and Wiksell International, 1989); Christ Scarre, ed., *The Seventy Wonders of the Ancient World: The Great Monuments and How They Were Built* (London: Thames and Hudson, 1999); Diana Bentley, *The Seven Wonders of the Ancient World* (New York: Oxford University Press, 2001).

Harmodius and Aristogeiton Known as the tyrannicides (tyrant slayers), these two young male Athenian aristocrats became semilegendary figures after they died while assassinating Hipparchus, younger brother of the Athenian dictator HIPPIAS (1), in 514 B.C.E. Far from ending Hippias's reign at ATHENS, the assassination brought on repression from the ruler; but Harmodius and Aristogeiton's bravery and sacrifice—and the fact that the two men were linked by romantic love—struck a sentimental chord in their fellow Athenians.

Harmodius and Aristogeiton were kinsmen in an ancient noble clan. In accordance with the usual pattern of upper-class Greek homosexual pairings, Aristogeiton was the protective older lover, perhaps in his late 20s; Harmodius was probably in his late teens. When Harmodius ignored the unwelcome advances of Hipparchus, the thwarted Hipparchus insulted Harmodius's sister in public.

In revenge, Aristogeiton plotted with Harmodius and a few sympathizers to murder the dictator Hippias and overthrow the regime. But the plot went awry. At the summer festival of the PANATHENAIA, Harmodius and Aristogeiton, attacking with daggers, had the chance to kill only Hipparchus. The young Harmodius was slain by bodyguards. Aristogeiton, escaping into the crowd, was later captured and tortured to death.

After Hippias was expelled from Athens by other forces in 510 B.C.E., the dead tyrannicides came to be seen as forerunners of the newly installed DEMOCRACY and were commemorated with yearly religious sacrifices and a famous public statue. At the same time, they were viewed by the upper class as models of aristocratic conduct. One symposiastic song praised them in mythical terms, including the stanza "Dearest Harmodius, they say surely you are not dead but live forever in the Islands of the Blessed, with swift-footed Achilles and Diomedes."

The Athenian historian THUCYDIDES (1), in his history of the PELOPONNESIAN WAR, devotes an unusual digression to the subject of the tyrannicides, trying to correct the exaggerated, unhistorical stories about them.

See also ACHILLES; AFTERLIFE; ARISTOCRACY; DIOMEDES; HOMOSEXUALITY; SYMPOSIUM; TYRANTS.

Further reading: C. W. Fornara, "The Cult of Harmodius and Aristogeiton," *Philologus* 114 (1970): 155–180; Sture Brunnsåker, *The Tyrant-Slayers of Kritios and Nesiotes: A Critical Study of the Sources and Restorations,* 2d ed. (Stockholm: Svenska Institutet i Athen,

1971); Michael W. Taylor, *The Tyrant Slayers: The Heroic Image in Fifth Century B.C. Athenian Art and Politics,* 2d ed. (Salem, N.H.: Ayer, 1991); Aileen Ajootian, "A Day at the Races. The Tyrannicides in the Fifth-century Agora," in *Stephanos. Studies in Honor of Brunilde Sismondo Ridgway,* edited by Kim Hartswick and Mary Sturgeon (Philadelphia: University Museum, University of Pennsylvania, 1998), 1–13; K. A. Raaflaub, "Zeus Eleutherios, Dionysus the Liberator, and the Athenian Tyrannicides. Anachronistic Uses of Fifth-century Political Concepts," in *Polis and Politics. Studies in Ancient Greek History. Presented to Mogens Herman Hansen on his Sixtieth Birthday, August 20, 2000,* edited by P. Flensted-Jensen, T. H. Nielsen, and L. Rubenstein (Copenhagen: Museum Tusculanum Press, University of Copenhagen, 2000), 249–275.

harpies (Greek: harpuiai) In MYTH, the harpies were winged female demons who would fly down to steal food, people, and so on; their name means "snatchers-away." They are mentioned in HOMER's epic poem the *Odyssey* (written down around 750 B.C.E.) as carrying off the daughters of the hero Pandareus. HESIOD's *Theogony* (ca. 700 B.C.E.) describes them as three in number, named Celaeno ("dark"), Ocypete ("swift-wing"), and Aello ("storm"). The harpies are most familiar from APOLLONIUS's epic poem, the *Argonautica* (ca. 245 B.C.E.). There they are said to torment the Thracian king Phineus on a regular basis by flying down, snatching away his food, and departing, leaving their feces on everything.

Possibly the harpies originated as spirits or personifications of the wind. In their general role as winged, malevolent females, they resemble the FURIES and the SIRENS.

Further reading: J. Lerner, "A Note on Sassanian Harpies," *Iran* 13 (1975): 166–171; R. J. Rabel, "The Harpies in the Eneid," *Classical Journal* 80 (1984–1985): 317–325; Ann E. Farkas, Prudence Harper, and Evelyn B. Harrison, eds., *Monsters and Demons in the Ancient and Medieval Worlds. Papers Presented in Honor of Edith Porada* (Mainz am Rhein, Germany: Philip von Zabern, 1987).

Hecataeus (ca. 550–490 B.C.E.) *Early geographer and "logographer" (travel writer)*
Hecataeus lived in the Greek city of MILETUS, in ASIA MINOR. On the basis of travels in EGYPT, Scythia, the Persian interior, and elsewhere, he wrote a prose treatise called the *Periodos Gēs,* or "Trip Around the World" (which today survives only in fragments quoted by later writers). The book accompanied a map Hecataeus had made—perhaps painted onto textile or incised on a copper plate—showing the world as he had encountered it; although this was not the world's first map, the map

and book together were revolutionary for Greek learning. We know that the book gave accounts of local histories, customs, and so on. There were two volumes: *Europe* and *Asia.* Hecataeus is an important forerunner of the world's first historian, HERODOTUS (born ca. 485 B.C.E.).

We know almost nothing about Hecataeus's life. His father was said to have been a landowner at Miletus, and Hecataeus must have been wealthy to undertake his travels. He surely had contacts among Miletus's merchant community, for his journeys included sites along the Milesian shipping route northeastward to the BLACK SEA. Herodotus mentions Hecataeus amid events of the IONIAN REVOLT against Persian rule (499–493 B.C.E.). He saw that Hecataeus was present at the first Milesian war council and advised against the revolt. Herodotus tells us no more about Hecataeus; perhaps he was killed in the Persian capture of Miletus in 493 B.C.E.

In addition to his travel book, Hecataeus wrote a treatise called *Geneologies,* about the legendary pedigrees of noble Greek families and mythical heroes. The few surviving fragments of this work suggest a strong rationalizing purpose: For example, DANAUS could not have had 50 daughters as the MYTH claims, but perhaps 20. The book's opening words announce the writer's logical approach: "I write what I believe to be the truth. For the stories of the Greeks are many and laughable."

See also EUROPE AND ASIA; IONIA.

Further reading: William A. Heidel, *Hecataeus and the Egyptian Priests in Herodotus, Book II* (New York: Garland, 1987); S. West, "Herodotus' Portrait of Hecataeus," *Journal of Hellenic Studies* 111 (1991): 144–160.

Hecatē This mysterious and sinister goddess was associated with night, witchcraft, ghosts, the Moon, and the supernatural danger of the crossroads. Hecatē was very much a chthonian deity, whom the Greeks attempted to propitiate by leaving out monthly "Hecatē's suppers." She had shrines at crossroads, apparently intended to keep her away. To our knowledge, she had no MYTH.

Her name means "One Hundred" in Greek and may have originated as a euphemism for some unspoken name. Hecatē was probably a survival of a pre-Greek goddess of black magic.

See also RELIGION.

Further reading: Charles M. Edwards, "The Running Maiden from Eleusis and the Early Classical Image of Hekate," *American Journal of Archaeology* 90 (1986): 307–318; Bernard Evslin, *Hekate* (New York: Chelsea House, 1988); S. I. Johnston, *Hekate Soteira. A Study of Hekate's Roles in the Chaldean Oracles and Related Literature* (Atlanta: Scholar's Press, 1990); Stephen Ronan, *The Goddess Hekate* (Hastings, U.K.: Chthonios, 1992); Robert Von Rudloff, *Hekate in Ancient Greek Religion* (Victoria, B.C.: Horned Owl Publishers, 1999).

Hector In MYTH, this Trojan prince was the eldest son of King PRIAM and Queen HECUBA, and the commander of TROY's forces in the TROJAN WAR. His lasting portrait occurs in HOMER's epic poem the *Iliad,* which reaches its climax in Hector's death at the hands of the Greek hero ACHILLES.

Although Achilles is the *Iliad's* protagonist, Hector is by far the poem's most sympathetic character—brave, generous, a devoted husband, father, and son. His poetic epithets include *hippodamos,* "tamer of horses." He is a civilized figure, remarkably unselfish as compared with his Greek counterparts. Also unlike them, he is shown as having a domestic role. One of the most poignant scenes in the *Iliad* occurs in book 6, when Hector visits his wife, ANDROMACHE, and their child, Astyanax, for what will be the last time. He bids them farewell, revealing his certainty that doom will overtake him, his family, and the city of Troy. He tells Andromache how he would much prefer to die in battle than live to see her captured by the Greeks: "May I lie dead, and may the heaped-up earth cover me, before I hear your cries as they drag you into captivity" (lines 463–464).

Hector's deeds in the story include his single combat with the Greek hero AJAX (1) (who gets somewhat the upper hand before it ends in a draw) and his attack with his men against the Greeks' camp and the beached Greek ships (which he almost succeeds in burning up). In the course of this action, Hector slays the Greek warrior PATROCLUS, who has entered the fray dressed in the armor of his friend Achilles. This fateful act sets the scene for Hector's single combat with the enraged Achilles the next day.

In the *Iliad's* climactic scene (book 22), Hector waits for Achilles on the plain in front of Troy, despite the appeals of his parents from the city walls. But he turns and flees as Achilles approaches. After a long chase on foot, the heroes duel. Achilles kills Hector, ties the corpse to his chariot, and drags it back to camp. Later relenting, he allows Priam to ransom the body, and the *Iliad* ends with Hector's funeral.

Unlike many of Homer's Trojans, Hector has a Greek name ("warder-off"). We know that this name was used by at least one Greek prince in ASIA MINOR in the 700s B.C.E.; Hector's name and portrayal might possibly be based on some Greek leader living in the era when the *Iliad* was written down (around 750 B.C.E.).

Further reading: James Redfield, *Nature and Culture in the Iliad: The Tragedy of Hector* (Durham, N.C.: Duke University Press, 1994); A. T. Murray, trans., *Homer, Iliad. Loeb Classical Library,* revised by William F. Wyatt (Cambridge, Mass.: Harvard University Press, 1999).

Hecuba (Greek: Hekabē) In MYTH, Hecuba was the wife and queen of the Trojan king PRIAM. She was the mother of the princes HECTOR and PARIS and 18 of Priam's other sons. Later writers also assign to her a daughter, Polyxena.

In HOMER's epic poem the *Iliad* (written down around 750 B.C.E.), Hecuba is a secondary character, regal and gracious. Later writers, describing her relentless sorrows and decline after TROY's fall, treat her as a symbol of ruined happiness. She is portrayed as a Greek captive in two of EURIPIDES' surviving tragedies, *Trojan Women* (415 B.C.E.) and *Hecuba* (424 B.C.E.). Hecuba presents her vengeance on the Greek champion Polymnestor, who had killed Polyxena as a sacrifice to ACHILLES' ghost. Lured into Hecuba's tent, Polymnestor is blinded, and his two young sons murdered, by her waiting women. Later authors, such as the Roman Ovid, describe Hecuba's death; forgiven for her violence against Polymnestor, she was handed over as a prize to ODYSSEUS. But her hatred of him was such that she was supernaturally transformed into a snarling, barking dog. In this shape, she leapt into the sea. Her grave became a landmark, Cynos Sema (dog's tomb), along the HELLESPONT.

Further reading: Judith Mossman, *Wild Justice: A Study of Euripides' Hecuba* (Oxford: Clarendon Press, 1995); Timberlake Wertenbaker, trans., *Hecuba by Euripides* (Woodstock, Ill.: Dramatic Publishing, 1996); Nicholas Rudall, trans., *The Trojan Women/Euripides* (Chicago: Ivan R. Dee, 1999).

Helen of Troy In MYTH, this Spartan princess of great physical beauty was the daughter of the god ZEUS and the Spartan queen LEDA.

Helen was married to the Spartan king MENELAUS. But at the prompting of the love-goddess APHRODITE, Helen eloped with the handsome Trojan prince PARIS. This infatuation was the cause of the disastrous TROJAN WAR, which was to end, after a 10-year siege, in Troy's destruction and the death of Paris and many others, Trojan and Greek. HOMER's epic poem the *Iliad* shows Helen installed at Troy, protected and admired by the people to whom she has brought so much trouble. She is portrayed as a glamorous and gracious lady, well aware of her reprehensible position. In one famous scene (book 5), the Trojan elders, admiring her beauty, agree once again that she is worth fighting for. In Homer's *Odyssey,* Helen is shown living contentedly again with Menelaus back in Sparta, after the war.

Later writers elaborated on Helen's story. In one version, Menelaus intends to kill her after the Greeks take Troy, but, on seeing her, forgives her. The most famous reworking of Helen's story was the *Palinodia* of the Sicilian Greek poet STESICHORUS (ca. 590 B.C.E.), which claimed that Helen had never left Sparta at all; rather, the gods had sent a phantom-Helen with Paris to Troy, so that Troy's doom might be fulfilled.

At SPARTA Helen was worshipped as a goddess associated with TREES and nature. This divine Helen was probably a survival of a pre-Greek goddess—one of many who infiltrated Greek RELIGION in various guises.

See also EURIPIDES; GORGIAS.

Further reading: Jack Lindsay, *Helen of Troy: Woman and Goddess* (London: Constable, 1974); George A. Kennedy, *The Story of Helen: Myth and Rhetoric* (St. Louis, Mo.: Washington University Press, 1987); Robert Meagher, *Helen: Myth, Legend, and the Culture of Misogyny* (New York: Continuum Publishing Co., 1995); Robert Meagher, *The Meaning of Helen: In Search of an Ancient Icon* (Wauconda, Ill.: Bolchazy-Carducci, 2002).

Helios In MYTH, the god Helios was the personification of the Sun. Helios was not important in Greek RELIGION, except for his nationalistic cult on the island of RHODES. Elsewhere he was more of a poetic fancy—a charioteer who drives his horses across the sky each day and returns by night, sailing in a giant cup around the stream of ocean, to start again next morning. His best-known myth told how he had a human son, Phaëthon, who won his father's permission to drive the solar chariot in Helios's place for one day. But Phaëthon, unable to control the reins, careened too close to the Earth, until the god ZEUS was forced to kill him with a thunderbolt, to save the world from fire.

As the god who sees everything from above, Helios was sometimes invoked as the guarantor of oaths. Some myths give him the minor function of bringing news to the gods of certain events that he has witnessed.

In the philosophical climate of the 400s B.C.E., there arose a theory identifying Helios with the major god APOLLO. Later writers of the ancient world sometimes referred to Apollo as a sun god, and this idea persists in popular belief today; but in Greek myth the Sun generally had its own god.

As the patron deity of Rhodes, Helios was honored with a grand annual festival. This cult was clearly shaped by non-Greek, Oriental beliefs. The famous Colossus of Rhodes, built in about 275 B.C.E. outside the harbor of Rhodes city, was a giant statue of the sun god. It was considered to be one of the SEVEN WONDERS OF THE WORLD.

See also OCEANUS.

Hellas *See* HELLĒN.

Hellēn In MYTH, this figure was the father of the Greek people. Hellēn—who should not be confused with the princess HELEN OF TROY—had three sons: Dorus, Aeolus, and Xuthus. From these came the main ancient Greek ethnic branches—the DORIAN GREEKS, the AEOLIAN GREEKS, the IONIAN GREEKS, and the Greeks of ACHAEA (the latter two categories are named for Xuthus's sons, Ion and Achaeus). According to the myth, this is why the Greek people are known collectively as the Hellēnes, "the sons of Hellēn."

The art on this lekythos, a container used for precious perfumed oils, depicts the moment when Paris, the Trojan prince, meets Helen, the wife of Spartan king Menelaus. The goddess of love blesses their meeting as she flies over them in a chariot. *(The J. Paul Getty Museum)*

Hellenistic World, ca. 240 B.C.E.

The legend's purpose was simply to explain the origins of these various ethnic groups. In true fact the name *Hellēnes* seems to be derived from the word *Hellas*, which was the Greeks' name for mainland Greece.

Hellenistic Age This term is used by scholars to describe the era of the enlarged, cosmopolitan Greek world of approximately 300–150 B.C.E. Unlike the word *Hellenic,* which refers straightforwardly to the Greeks, the word *Hellenistic* comes from a verb *Hellazein,* "to speak Greek or identify with the Greeks," and refers to the Greek-influenced societies that arose in the wake of ALEXANDER THE GREAT's conquests (334–323 B.C.E.). This Hellenistic world extended from southern France to northern Afghanistan. Its characteristic nature was a mingling of Greek and Eastern cultures, particularly in the Near East and in ASIA MINOR. The political units of the Hellenistic world were the rich and large kingdoms of Alexander's successors—MACEDON, Ptolemaic EGYPT, the SELEUCID EMPIRE, and, eventually, PERGAMON—and

the Syracusan monarchy. Gone was the society built around the traditional Greek POLIS, or city-state, where citizens debated public policy in political assemblies and served as soldiers in time of war. In the Hellenistic world, kings did the governing, war was the business of professionals, and citizens turned to more individualistic pursuits, such as mystery religions and new, more personal philosophies.

Mainland Greece lay under Macedonian rule for much of the Hellenistic era. ATHENS, still a revered "university town," was no longer the cultural center of the Greek world. That honor had passed to Egyptian ALEXANDRIA (1) and secondarily to ANTIOCH, Pergamon, and SYRACUSE. At these places, rich kings sponsored courts full of scientists and poets.

The Hellenistic world was absorbed by ROME in several stages. Syracuse fell to Roman siege in 211 B.C.E. The Romans dismantled the Macedonian kingdom in 167 B.C.E., after the Third Macedonian War. Mainland Greece was occupied by the Romans in 146 B.C.E., after the

Achaean War. In 133 B.C.E. the Greek cities of Asia Minor were bequeathed to the Romans by the last king of Pergamon (effective 129 B.C.E.), and the remnants of the Seleucid kingdom and Ptolemaic Egypt were annexed by Rome in the first century B.C.E.

See also AFTERLIFE; APOLLONIUS; ARCHIMEDES; ASTRONOMY; BACTRIA; DIADOCHOI; DIONYSUS; EPICURE-ANISM; KALLIMACHUS; MATHEMATICS; MEDICINE; PHALANX; RELIGION; RHODES; SCIENCE; SCULPTURE; SKEPTICISM; STO-ICISM; THEOCRITUS; WARFARE, LAND; WARFARE, NAVAL; WARFARE, SIEGE.

Further reading: John Onians, *Art and Thought in the Hellenistic Age: The Greek World View, 350–50 B.C.* (London: Thames and Hudson, 1979); Stanley M. Burstein, ed., *The Hellenistic Age from the Battle of Ipsos to the Death of Kleopatra VII* (New York: Cambridge University Press, 1985); J. J. Pollitt, *Art in the Hellenistic Age* (New York: Cambridge University Press, 1986); Peter Green, *Alexander to Actium: The Historical Evolution of the Hellenistic Age,* 2d ed. (Berkeley: University of California Press, 1993); Helmut Koester, *History, Culture, and Religion of the Hellenistic Age,* 2d ed. (New York: W. de Gruyter, 1995).

Corinthian-style columns and other Greek architectural remnants at Palmyra, in the Syrian desert. Palmyra, an oasis town on the caravan route between Damascus and Mesopotamia, flourished in the Hellenistic world that arose in the wake of Alexander's conquests. From ca. 300 B.C.E. to 64 B.C.E. Palmyra owed allegiance to the Seleucid kings; thereafter, it was a half-Greek, half-Syrian frontier city of the Roman Empire. These columns were part of a grandiose sanctuary of the local god Bel, built in C.E. 32. *(Margaret Bunson)*

Hellespont This thirty-three-mile-long sea strait separates the Gallipoli peninsula from the northwestern coast of ASIA MINOR. Through this channel, which ranges between one and five miles wide, a strong current flows southwestward from the Sea of MARMARA to the AEGEAN SEA. Also known as the Dardanelles, the Hellespont is the more western of two bottlenecks—the other being the BOSPORUS—along the shipping route to the BLACK SEA. Like the Bosporus, the Hellespont traditionally has been considered a boundary between the continents of EUROPE AND ASIA.

The ancient Greek name Hellēspontos, "Hellē's Sea," was said to commemorate the young daughter of Athamas, a mythical king of EUBOEA. According to legend, Hellē fell to her death in the strait when she slipped off the back of the flying ram that was carrying her and her brother to safety from their stepmother. (This was the first episode in the story of JASON (1) and the Golden Fleece.)

As a bottleneck where shipping could be attacked or tolled systematically, the Hellespont was a critical link in the eastern TRADE route. The opportunities of this locale, combined with the channel's excellent commercial fishing, raised several local cities to wealth and prominence. The earliest and most important of these was TROY, situated on the Asian side, just outside the strait's western mouth. Archaeological evidence suggests that a wealthy Troy, inhabited by non-Greeks, was destroyed abruptly around 1220 B.C.E.—probably by Mycenaean Greeks driven to remove Troy's disruption of metal imports to Greece.

As the Black Sea region began supplying grain for the cities of mainland Greece, control of the Hellespont became crucial to the ambitious, food-importing city of ATHENS. By 600 B.C.E. Athenian colonists were warring with settlers from LESBOS over possession of Sigeum, near the old site of Troy. By the mid-400s B.C.E. Athens had a naval base at the Hellespontine fortress of SESTOS, on the European shore. There all westbound, non-Athenian, merchant grain ships were subject to a 10 percent tax, which would be reimbursed if the ship brought its cargo to Athens's port.

During the later PELOPONNESIAN WAR, Athenian and Spartan navies fought no fewer than three battles in the Hellespont (411 and 405 B.C.E.), as the Spartans sought to destroy Athens's lifeline of imported grain. The third such battle, the Spartan victory at AEGOSPOTAMI, won the war for SPARTA.

Besides Sestos, prominent Greek cities of the Hellespont included Abydos and Lampsacus, both on the Asian shore. The fact that Abydos faced Sestos across the channel's narrowest part (one mile wide) helped to inspire the charming legend of Hero and Leander. This tale described how a man of Abydos (Leander) swam the Hellespont every night to visit his mistress in Sestos.

See also ALCAEUS; CHERSONESE; PERSIAN WARS.

Further reading: W. L. Adams, "Cassander and the Crossing of the Hellespont, Diodorus 17, 17, 4," *Ancient World* 2 (1979): 111–115; N. G. L. Hammond and L. J. Roseman, "The Construction of Xerxes' Bridge over the Hellespont," *Journal of Hellenic Studies* 116 (1996): 88–107.

helots   These publicly owned serfs, or noncitizens, farmed the land in virtual captivity, providing food for the citizen population of a given state. Unlike SLAVES, these serfs kept their own language, customs, and communities on the land (which of course they did not own). They were typically the descendants of a once-free people, either Greek or non-Greek, who had been conquered in a prior era.

The public use of serfs may have been a tradition specifically of the DORIAN GREEKS, because most of the attested locales were Dorian (including CRETE and SYRACUSE). The serfs were known by various names; at ARGOS, for instance, they were called *gumnētes*, or "naked ones." But the most notorious use of such people was at SPARTA, where they were called *helotai*, or helots. This name supposedly came from the town of Helos ("marsh"), annexed and subjugated by Sparta in the late 700s B.C.E. By 600 B.C.E. further Spartan conquests had created helots in two large geographic areas: LACONIA (the territory around Sparta) and MESSENIA (the large plain west of Laconia's mountains). These people were Dorian Greeks, just like their conquerors, the Spartans.

Although helot farm labor freed Sparta's citizens to concentrate on war, this subjugated population had a warping affect on the Spartan mentality. Between Messenia and Laconia, the helots outnumbered their Spartan masters, and the fear of a helot revolt—such as that of 464 B.C.E.—kept the Spartan army close to home and drove Sparta to repressive measures. The Krypteia ("secret society") was an official Spartan group dedicated to eliminating subversive helots.

Helots might accompany Spartan armies to war, serving as soldiers' servants or as skirmishers. But such loyalty did not win Spartan trust. In 424 B.C.E., during the PELOPONNESIAN WAR, the Spartans decreed that they would honor those helots who claimed to have done the best battlefield service for Sparta. Two thousand helots came forward in the belief that they would be made Spartan citizens. But the treacherous Spartans, having thus identified the most spirited of the helots, eventually murdered them.

See also PYLOS.

Further reading: I. M. Diakonoff, "Slaves, Helots, and Serfs in Early Antiquity," *Acta Antiqua Academiae Scientiarum Hungaricae* 22 (1974): 45–78; L. J. Piper, "Spartan Helots in the Hellenistic Age," *Ancient Society* 15–17 (1984–1986): 75–88; R. J. A. Talbert, "The Role of the Helots in the Class Struggle at Sparta," *Historia* 38 (1989): 22–40; B. Jordan, "The Ceremony of the Helots in Thucydides, IV, 80," *L'Antiquité classique* 59 (1990): 37–69; J. A. Dearman, "Nabis of Sparta and the Helots," *Palestine Exploration Quarterly* 122 (1990): 41–46; M. Whitby, "Two Shadows. Images of Spartans and Helots," in *The Shadow of Sparta* [Colloquium Cardiff 1991], edited by Anton Powell and Stephen Hodkinson (New York: Routledge for the Classical Press of Wales, 1994), 87–126; P. Hunt, "Helots at the Battle of Plataea," *Historia* 46 (1997): 129–144; N. Luraghi and Susan E. Alcock, eds., *Helots and Their Masters in Laconia and Messenia: Histories, Ideologies, Structures* (Washington, D.C.: Center for Hellenic Studies, Trustees for Harvard University, 2003).

Hephaistos (Hephaestus)   The lame smith god, patron of craftsmen, was worshipped mainly at ATHENS and other manufacturing centers. Hephaistos was also the god of fire and volcanoes, and this more primitive aspect was probably his original identity. He had an important cult on the volcanic Greek island of Lemnos, and he was also associated with volcanic Mt. Etna in SICILY. To the imaginative Greeks, these volcanoes must have suggested a blacksmith's furnace.

According to HOMER, Hephaistos was the son of ZEUS and HERA, though HESIOD calls him only the son of Hera. He was born ugly and lame, which horrified and embarrassed his mother, since the gods were generally beautiful and perfect. In her shame, Hera threw her son down from Mt. OLYMPUS into the ocean, where he was rescued and raised by ocean nymphs. In some versions of the MYTH, the god was only born ugly (not physically deformed), and it was the fall from Olympus that lamed him.

While being raised by the nymphs, Hephaistos began to create many wonderful works of art and craft, including a beautiful golden throne with invisible chains that would entrap the sitter. He sent it to Hera, who sat down and was immediately imprisoned. The gods then summoned Hephaistos back to Olympus; he did not want to return, but eventually DIONYSUS got him drunk and managed to bring him back. The return of Hephaistos to Olympus was a favorite subject in Greek art. Once back among the gods, Hephaistos took his mother's side in a quarrel between her and Zeus, and this time Zeus threw him down from the mountain. He fell for nine days and nights and finally landed on the island of Lemnos, which became a favorite place of his. Some versions of Greek myth actually attribute Hephaistos's lameness to this fall instead of the first one.

As the craftsman god, Hephaistos was often closely linked with ATHENA, and they stood together in the Hephaisteion in the Athenian AGORA. In the *Odyssey,* he was married to APHRODITE; the Greeks found it amusing to think of the ugliest god wed to the most beautiful goddess. The love-goddess had many extramarital affairs, not least of which an ongoing relationship with the god of war, ARES. Tired of her adulteries, Hephaistos fashioned a marvelous chain-link net, with which he captured his wife and Ares together in bed. Then he hauled them, netted, before the assembled gods. Hephaistos also played a minor role in many other Greek myths, providing such marvelous handiwork as the invincible armor of ACHILLES. The Romans adopted Hephaistos's myth and cult, attaching these to their fire god, Vulcan (*Volcanus*).

See also SEVEN AGAINST THEBES.

Further reading: Evelyn B. Harrison, "Alkamenes' Sculptures for the Hephaisteion, 1. The Cult Statues," *American Journal of Archaeology* 81 (1977): 265–287; H. A. Shapiro, *Art and Cult under the Tyrants in Athens. Supplement* (Mainz am Rhein, Germany: Philip von Zabern, 1995).

Hera One of the most important Greek deities, Hera was the eldest daughter of CRONUS and Rhea, and she later married her own brother, ZEUS. She was worshipped by the Greeks as the patron of WOMEN and MARRIAGE. She had major cult centers at the city of ARGOS (a very ancient cult) and on the island of SAMOS, but she was worshipped throughout the Greek world, particularly in the PELOPONNESE. Her name means "lady" in Greek. Her powers in nature complement those of Zeus. She controls storm clouds and lightning, and her attendants are the Seasons and Iris, goddess of the rainbow.

In MYTH, Hera cuts a strong figure—an independent wife, but jealous of Zeus's many extramarital amours. In one famous scene in HOMER's epic poem the *Iliad,* she seduces her husband as part of a scheme to distract him from observing the TROJAN WAR and aiding the Trojans (book 14). Other stories represent her as oppressively cruel toward her rivals—that is, toward the female humans and demigods who involuntarily attracted Zeus's lust. Among such persecuted rivals were Leto (who gave birth to Zeus's children APOLLO and ARTEMIS) and Io. But the most important example is Hera's enmity toward the hero HERAKLES, son of Zeus and the mortal woman Alkmene. Hera is Herakles' constant antagonist and is reconciled with him only at the end of his labors, at Zeus's command.

Hera's children by Zeus are ARES, HEPHAISTOS, Eileithyia (goddess of childbirth), and Hebe (goddess of youth). In art, she appears as a mature, physically attractive woman. She is usually represented seated on a throne, wearing a diadem and a veil. The cow and the cuckoo are often associated with her. The Romans identified Hera with their goddess Juno.

Despite her Greek name and her place in Greek RELIGION, Hera was probably not Greek in origin. It has been plausibly suggested that she is a vestige of the mother goddess who was the primary deity of the non-Greek occupants of Greece before the first Greeks arrived around 2100 B.C.E. The immigrating Greeks conquered the land and assimilated this goddess's cult into their own religion, to a position subordinate to the Greek father god, Zeus. This goddess's original name is not known, nor is it certain whether this assimilation took place because it was politically expedient or because it was religiously attractive to the early Greeks.

Further reading: Karl Kerényi, *Zeus and Hera: Archetypal Image of Father, Husband, and Wife,* translated by Christopher Holme (London: Routledge & Kegan Paul, 1976); Joan O'Brien, *The Transformation of Hera: A Study of Ritual, Hero, and the Goddess in the Iliad* (Lanham, Md.: Rowman & Littlefield, 1993); Isabelle Clark, "The Gamos of Hera: Myth and Ritual," in *The Sacred and the Feminine in Ancient Greece,* edited by Sue Blundell and Margaret Williamson (London: Routledge, 1998), 13–26; Christopher Pfaff, *The Architecture of the Classical Temple of Hera* (Princeton, N.J.: American School of Classical Studies at Athens, 2003).

Heraclitus (Greek: Herakleitos) (ca. 500s B.C.E.) *Early philosopher, of the Greek city of EPHESOS, in western ASIA MINOR*

Almost nothing is known of his life. He is said to have been of high aristocratic lineage and of an arrogant and reclusive nature. Some of the writings ascribed to him are derisive of the democratic politics at Ephesos.

Heraclitus was the last of the great Ionian thinkers who, in the 500s B.C.E., pioneered the study that we call PHILOSOPHY. His writings consisted of a collection of prose proverbs, fashioned in an oracular style. A number of individual proverbs have come down to us in quotations by later writers. Although often obscure in wording, these aphorisms seem to show remarkable originality in their search for universal order amid worldly flux.

Where his Ionian predecessors—THALES, ANAXIMANDER, and ANAXIMENES—had looked for cosmic unity in some elemental substance such as water or mist, Heraclitus sought it in the universe's defining arrangement (Greek: *logos*). He saw everything in the world as part of single, continuous process of change—"All things flow" and "You cannot step into the same river twice" are two of his more famous sayings. This change, he said, is regulated by a balance or measure typically involving the conflict of opposing forces. Heraclitus found deep significance in the opposing tensions employed in the stringing of the musician's lyre and the archer's bow (both of which were inventions associated with the god APOLLO, lord of harmony and order). Heraclitus evidently saw the lyre and bow's "backward-stretched unity" (Greek: *palintonos harmoniē*) as a key to understanding the cosmos.

Similarly, many of Heraclitus's proverbs seek to show that opposites such as hot and cold are actually related or connected. "The road up and the road down are one and the same," he wrote, apparently referring to a footpath that leads both ways (so to speak), up and down a mountain. Other surviving proverbs suggest an innovative belief in one God, reflecting this notion of cosmic unity—for example, "The god is day, night, winter, summer, war, peace, satiety, hunger."

The cosmic order was somehow maintained by fire, according to Heraclitus. He believed that a person's soul was a kind of fire, which could be harmfully "dampened" by bad behavior such as sexual excess or drunkenness. Spiritually healthy souls remained dry; after death they would be able to reach higher places in the heavens.

A brilliant but eccentric thinker, Heraclitus did not inspire an immediate following. However, in the 200s B.C.E. the philosophical movement called STOICISM honored his memory and adapted some of his ideas.

See also IONIA.

Further reading: Joel Wilcox, *The Origins of Epistemology in Early Greek Thought: A Study of Psyche and Logos in Heraclitus* (Lewiston, N.Y.: E. Mellen Press, 1994); Dennis Sweet, *Heraclitus: Translation and Analysis* (Lanham, Md.: University Press of America, 1995); Richard Geldard, *Remembering Heraclitus* (Hudson, N.Y.: Lindisfarne Books, 2000).

Herakles (Hercules)   The most popular of all Greek mythical heroes, Herakles was famous for his strength, courage, and generosity of spirit. By virtue of his 12 Labors performed for the good of humankind, Herakles was worshipped as both god and man throughout antiquity. Philosophical schools such as STOICISM saw him as an ideal of human fortitude. The early Christians called him a forerunner of Christ. Better known today by his Roman name, Hercules, the hero continues to have a life of his own in such pop culture media as comic books, films, and advertising. Herakles is one of our single most vital legacies from ancient Greece.

His name means "glory of HERA." In the legends that have come down to us, the goddess Hera is his implacable enemy. But given the hero's name, it seems plausible that at some early stage of Greek mythology (ca. 1200 B.C.E.), Hera was his divine patron and he her servant, performing his helpful labors at her command. Possibly the Greek Herakles derived from a pre-Greek god or hero—a servant or consort of the mother goddess who was worshipped on the Argive plain long before the first Greeks arrived, around 2100 B.C.E.

In MYTH, Herakles was associated with both of the two centers of Mycenaean Greece—the Argive plain and

the Theban plain. Born at THEBES, he was the son of Alkmēnē, a princess of MYCENAE or TIRYNS. Alkmēnē was married to Amphitryon, but Herakles' true father was the great god ZEUS, who had visited Alkmēnē disguised as her husband. (Herakles had a mortal twin brother, Iphikles, begotten by Amphitryon.)

The goddess Hera, chronically jealous of her husband's infidelities, was Herakles' enemy from the first. She sent two snakes to kill the twins in their cradle, but the baby Herakles strangled them. Hera continued to plague him throughout his life and was reconciled with him only after his death and transformation into a god.

As a child at Thebes, Herakles showed strength but wildness. When his MUSIC teacher tried to beat him for misbehavior, Herakles brained the man with a lyre. Later his weapons were the club and the archer's bow. He defended Thebes from an attack from the city of ORCHOMENUS and married the Theban princess Megara. But when Hera blighted him with a fit of madness, he killed Megara and their children. (This episode is described in EURIPIDES' surviving tragedy *Herakles*, ca. 417 B.C.E.) Seeking expiation at the god APOLLO's shrine at DELPHI, Herakles was instructed by the priestess to return to his parents' home region in the PELOPONNESE and place himself in servitude for 12 years to his kinsman Eurystheus, king of Tiryns.

The tasks set by Eurystheus comprise the famous 12 Labors (*athloi* or *ponoi*), which are the heart of the Herakles myth. In each case, Herakles had either to destroy a noxious monster or to retrieve a prize. The Labors' objectives begin with the elimination of certain local monsters in the Peloponnese, but gradually the goals become more distant and fabular until, by the last two Labors—capturing the monstrous dog KERBEROS from the Underworld and fetching apples from the supernatural sisters called the Hesperides—Herakles was symbolically conquering death.

The 12 Labors were (1) kill the lion of Nemea, (2) kill the hydra (water snake) of Lerna, (3) capture alive the boar of Erymanthus, (4) capture the hind (female deer) of Keryneia, (5) destroy the birds of Stymphalia, (6) cleanse the stables of King Augeas of ELIS, (7) capture the bull of CRETE, (8) capture the horses of the Thracian king Diomedes, (9) fetch the belt ("girdle") of the queen of the AMAZONS, (10) steal the cattle of the monster Geryon, in the far West, (11) fetch Kerberos from the realm of HADES, and (12) bring back some of the golden apples from the Hesperides' garden, in the far West. The hero accomplished these tasks, albeit with the goddess ATHENA's occasional help, and so he won purification for his crime.

Besides the Labors, Herakles had many mythical exploits, in part because so many Greek cities wanted to claim an association with him. In a dispute with the Delphic oracle, he tried to steal Apollo's holy tripod from the sanctuary. He sailed with the Thessalian hero JASON (1) in the quest for the Golden Fleece. He vanquished the wrestler Antaeus, a Giant who was son of POSEIDON. And, after a quarrel with the Trojan king Laomedon, Herakles raised an army and captured TROY, in the generation before the TROJAN WAR.

When Nessos the centaur tried to rape Herakles' second wife, Deianeira, the hero killed him with arrows dipped in venom of the Lernean hydra. But the dying centaur gave Deianeira his bloody shirt, convincing her that it could be used as a love charm on Herakles, if needed. Later, seeking to retain the love of her unfaithful husband, Deianeira laid the shirt on his shoulders. Herakles died in rage and excruciating pain from the venom-soaked blood (as described in SOPHOKLES' tragedy *The Women of Trachis*, ca. 429–420 B.C.E.). But on the funeral pyre Herakles' mortal part was burned away, and he ascended as a god to Mt. OLYMPUS. There he was welcomed by his divine father, reconciled with Hera, and married to Zeus and Hera's daughter, the goddess Hebe.

In art, Herakles usually appears as a strong, bearded man wearing the skin of the Nemean Lion, which he slew in his first labor; he also holds a club. He often has the physiognomy of a boxer, with a broken nose and swollen, "cauliflower" ears. His 12 labors were extremely popular subjects for Greek artists, especially vase painters. They are also depicted on a series of architectural reliefs adorning the Temple of Zeus at OLYMPIA.

In a politically angled legend, the DORIAN GREEKS claimed descent from Herakles. Supposedly the Heraklidae (the "sons of Herakles"), reclaiming their lost birthright, had led the Dorians in their invasion of central and southern Greece, around 1100–1000 B.C.E.

See also AFTERLIFE; AGIAD CLAN; CENTAURS; CYNICS; EURYPONTID CLAN; GIANTS.

Further reading: Birgitta Bergquist, *Herakles on Thasos: The Archaeological, Literary, and Epigraphic Evidence for His Sanctuary, Status, and Cult Reconsidered,* English text revised by Neil Tomkinson (Uppsala, Sweden: Almquist & Wiksell, 1973); Gudrun Ahlberg-Cornell, *Herakles and the Sea-monster in Attic Black-figure Vase-painting* (Stockholm: Svenska Institutet i Athen, 1984); Frank Brommer, *Herakles: The Twelve Labors of the Hero in Ancient Art and Literature,* translated by Shirley J. Schwarz (New Rochelle, N.Y.: A. D. Caratzas, 1986); Rainer Vollkommer, *Herakles in the Art of Classical Greece* (Oxford: Oxford University Committee for Archaeology, 1988); Kathryn Lasky, *Hercules: The Man, The Myth, the Hero* (New York: Hyperion Books for Children, 1997); Mark W. Padilla, *The Myths of Herakles in Ancient Greece: Survey and Profile* (Lanham, Md.: University Press of America, 1998).

Hercules *See* HERAKLES.

Hermes In MYTH, Hermes was the son of the great god ZEUS and the demigoddess Maia (daughter of ATLAS); he was also the messenger of the gods. In human society, he was the patron of land travel, heralds, commerce, weights and measures, RHETORIC, guile, thieves, WRESTLING, and other SPORT. Hermes was an attractive and picturesque deity, somewhat resembling his half brother, the god APOLLO. As the mythical inventor of the lyre, Hermes was a minor patron of poetry, which was normally Apollo's province.

In origin, Hermes may have been a protector of wayfarers, commemorated by roadside stone piles or carved images. His name most probably comes from the Greek word *herma* (plural: *hermai*), meaning "pile of marker stones." In an era when travel was uncomfortable and dangerous, Hermes safeguarded travelers and was worshipped at crossroads in particular.

In art, Hermes is portrayed as a beautiful youth, often in traveler's or herald's garb. He frequently wears a broad-brimmed, flat hat known as a *petasos*, and his swiftness is represented by the wings on his golden sandals. His primary attribute is a staff known as a *caduceus*; it is composed of three pieces, one forming the handle and the other two entwined in a knot at one end. These latter two were later replaced by serpents. The caduceus was a herald's staff, an emblem of peace and neutrality.

The legend of Hermes' birth is told in the charming *Homeric Hymn to Hermes,* composed around 675 B.C.E. The god was born at dawn on Mt. Cyllene in ARCADIA. By noon he was playing music on the lyre, which he had invented, using a tortoise shell as a sounding board. That same evening, he ventured out and stole a herd of 50 cattle belonging to Apollo. The story shows the mixture of creativity and dishonesty that characterized the mythical Hermes. He was also believed to guide the souls of the dead to the Underworld. Other legends name him as a lover of APHRODITE, who bore him a child, an androgynous creature named Hermaphroditus (from which we get the modern English word "hermaphrodite").

By the 400s B.C.E., Greek cities such as ATHENS contained stylized *hermai,* erected at streetcorners and in the AGORA. These were bronze or marble pillars sacred to the god, with only the face and genitals sculpted. Shortly before the Athenian sea expedition against SYRACUSE during the PELOPONNESIAN WAR (415 B.C.E.), the hermai throughout the city were mutilated overnight—probably by gangs of defeatist right-wingers, seeking to cast bad omens over the expedition by doing outrage to the god of travel.

See also AFTERLIFE; ALCIBIADES; ANDOKIDES; MUSIC.

Further reading: Antoine Faivre, *The Eternal Hermes: From Greek God to Alchemical Magus,* translated by Joscelyn Godwin (Grand Rapids, Mich.: Phanes Press, 1995).

Herodas (Herondas) (200s B.C.E.) *Writer of "mimes"* (*Greek:* mimiamboi, *"satirical sketches"*)

Little is known about the life of Herodas, but it is thought that he lived on the island of Cos. An ancient papyrus discovered in the collection of the British Museum in the 1800s C.E. has provided us with seven of his detailed urban scenes in verse. They range in length from 85 to 129 lines each, and their titles include "The Matchmaker," "The Pimp," "The Schoolmaster," "The Cobbler," "The Jealous Woman," "The Confidantes," and "A Visit to Asklepios." The best of the poems give delightful portraits of these interesting and amusing characters.

Further reading: Giuseppe Mastromarco, *The Public of Herondas* (Amsterdam: J. C. Gieben, 1984).

Herodotus (ca. 484–420 B.C.E.) *Greek historian from HALICARNASSUS in southwest ASIA MINOR*
Herodotus is known for his detailed, surviving account of the PERSIAN WARS, which had culminated when he was a child. This lengthy history describes how the Persian expansion westward after the mid-500s B.C.E. was eventually defeated by the Greeks' defense of their homeland in 480–479 B.C.E. Herodotus is considered the world's first historian, the first writer ever to make systematic factual inquiries into the past. He has been called the father of history.

Prior to him, there had been only "logographers"—writers of travelogue, recounting local sights and local histories. Although Herodotus himself traveled widely to acquire local lore, his major accomplishment was that he arranged his voluminous material around a central theme and that he was the first to try to explain historical cause and effect. This approach is summed up in his opening words: "Here is the account of the inquiry (Greek: *historiē*) of Herodotus of Halicarnassus, in order that the deeds of men not be erased by time, and that the great and miraculous works—both of the Greeks and the barbarians—not go unrecorded, and, not least, in order to show what caused them to fight one another."

Herodotus was inspired by a predecessor. Forty or 50 years before his time a Milesian Greek logographer named HECATAEUS had written a travel account of EGYPT, Scythia, and other locales. Herodotus mentions Hecataeus's work with disdain but apparently borrows from it liberally. Herodotus began by imitating Hecataeus, visiting Egypt and the Scythian BLACK SEA coast early on. He probably intended to write a Hecataean-style travelogue. But at some point Herodotus warmed to a second inspiration—the mythical TROJAN WAR, as described in HOMER's *Iliad* and other Greek EPIC POETRY. If the Trojan War was seen as the original clash between East and West, then the Persian Wars could be explained in the same light, as part of an ongoing, destructive pattern.

Another idea of Herodotus's, that pride goeth before a fall, was perhaps borrowed from contemporary Athenian stage tragedy. In Herodotus, the grandeur of monarchs often leads to foolhardy decisions resulting in disaster. This is conveyed clearly in his literary portrait of the Persian king XERXES, whose vanity and arrogance resulted in the Persians' failed invasion of Greece and the deaths of so many good men on both sides. Herodotus himself never observed Xerxes, and his treatment of the king probably owes much to literary imagination. Herodotus's lecherous, violent, cowardly but aesthetic-minded and occasionally gracious Xerxes is one of the most enjoyable villains in Western literature.

We know little of Herodotus's life. He was born in Halicarnassus, a Greek city of international commerce that at the time was still ruled by Persian overlords and included a second non-Greek people, called Carians. Herodotus's father had a Carian name, Lyxes; the family was probably an affluent merchant clan of Greek-Carian blood.

Perhaps around age 25, Herodotus fled into exile after his involvement in a failed coup against the city's reigning tyrant. By 454 B.C.E. the tyrant had fallen and Halicarnassus was part of the Athenian-controlled DELIAN LEAGUE. Despite this, Herodotus never returned home, but rather spent the next decade traveling and writing. Beside Egypt and Scythia, he evidently journeyed throughout mainland Greece, Asia Minor, and the Levantine seaboard. His travels were probably helped by a Persian-Greek peace treaty that ended hostilities at that time (in about 449 B.C.E.).

Sometime in the 440s–420s B.C.E. Herodotus became known in the Greek world for giving paid readings aloud of his work-in-progress. He is said to have sought quick notoriety by reading at OLYMPIA during the Games. The Athenians supposedly voted to pay him the astounding sum of 10 TALENTS out of gratitude for his favorable portrayal of their city. He certainly had ties to ATHENS (which by then had become the cultural center of Greece). Supposedly, the Athenian playwright SOPHOKLES wrote verses to Herodotus, and the noble Athenian clan of the ALCMAEONIDS seems to have been a major source of information for him. Although Herodotus's history is generally respectful of Athens's rival, SPARTA, he does in one passage credit Athenian naval resistance as the single factor that saved Greece in the Persian Wars (book 7).

In 443 B.C.E., Herodotus joined an Athenian-sponsored project to colonize a city, Thurii, in southern ITALY. He died there in around 420 B.C.E. These last 20 years probably saw him traveling, giving readings, and revising his work. His history was being published in (or near) its present form by 425 B.C.E., when the Athenian comic playwright ARISTOPHANES parodied its opening passages in his play *Acharnians*.

Herodotus's native tongue was probably the Doric Greek dialect of Halicarnassus, but he wrote his history in Ionic—the dialect generally used for prose explication—and used a clear, pleasant, storytelling style. On its completion, this history was the longest Greek prose work ever written. Later editors divided it into nine "books." Not only is it far and away our major written source for the Persian Wars and prior events in Greece and PERSIA in the 700s–500s B.C.E., but it also makes for delightful reading. In telling his story, Herodotus shows himself interested in war, politics, and the gods, also in personality, gossip, and sex. Unusual for a classical Greek writer, Herodotus is fascinated by WOMEN and their influence in a man's world both East and West.

Remarkably, a large part of his story is told from the Persian viewpoint. In this Herodotus was imitating such Athenian stage tragedy as AESCHYLUS's play *The Persians,* which describes the Battle of SALAMIS (1) from the Persian side. Some of Herodotus's Persian scenes were surely fabricated by the author, but it is equally clear that he conducted original research, interviewing individual Persians as well as Greeks. Despite the fact that Persia was the Greeks' enemy, Herodotus portrays many Persians as brave and noble and shows a deep respect for their culture. The later Greek writer PLUTARCH accused Herodotus of being *philobarbaros,* "overfond of foreigners."

Literary pioneer though he was, Herodotus shows certain endearing flaws. He often strays from his main narrative with digressions. Although dedicated to finding out historical causes, he sometimes fastens on trivial or fairytale causes. For example, he claims (in book 3) that the attack of the great Persian king DARIUS (1) on Greece was prompted by the bedroom persuasion of his wife. Further, Herodotus is not above telling the occasional tall tale—claiming, for instance, that he visited Babylon, even though his work lacks any description of that majestic Mesopotamian city. Besides being called the father of history, Herodotus has also been called the father of lies.

Nevertheless, his history was a monumental achievement: the first rational inquiry into the past. In this, he paved the way for his successor, the Athenian historian THUCYDIDES (1).

See also EUROPE AND ASIA; GREEK LANGUAGE; HUBRIS; KALLIAS.

Further reading: John Hart, *Herodotus and Greek History* (New York: St. Martin's Press, 1982); Kenneth H. Waters, *Herodotos, the Historian: His Problems, Methods, and Originality* (Norman: University of Oklahoma Press, 1985); John Gould, *Herodotus* (London: Weidenfeld and Nicolson, 1989); J. A. S. Evans, *Herodotus, Explorer of the Past: Three Essays* (Princeton, N.J.: Princeton University Press, 1991); James S. Romm, *Herodotus* (New Haven, Conn.: Yale University Press, 1998); John L. Myres, *Herodotus, Father of History* (Oxford: Clarendon Press, 1999).

heroes *See* MYTH.

Herondas *See* HERODAS.

Hesiod (ca. 700 B.C.E.) *Greek epic poet, one of the earliest whose verses have survived*

Together with HOMER, who lived perhaps 50 years earlier, Hesiod is often considered a pioneer of early Greek litera-

ture. Two major works by him are extant. One is his *Theogony,* or *Birth of the Gods,* which describes the world's creation and the origins of the Olympian gods and lesser deities. The other is called *Works and Days,* a kind of farmer's almanac laced with practical advice on how to live a good life through honest work. For modern readers, *Theogony* is a treasury of information for Greek MYTH, while *Works and Days* provides a unique picture of early Greek rural society, as well as evidence for Greek astronomy and timekeeping. In addition to these two works, we also have preserved the first few lines of a third poem, *The Shield of* HERAKLES.

Hesiod's two surviving poems give some autobiographical details. He lived in the central Greek region of BOEOTIA, in a town called Ascra ("bad in winter, worse in summer, not good anytime," as he describes it in *Works and Days*). His father had abandoned a seafaring life and moved there from CYME, in ASIA MINOR. In *Theogony,* Hesiod says that he received the gift of song from the MUSES when he was tending sheep on Mt. Helicon as a boy. Later he won a prize in a poetry contest during funeral games at nearby CHALCIS. Hesiod quarreled with his brother Perses, who had apparently stolen part of Hesiod's inheritance, and *Works and Days* was written partly as an instructional rebuke to Perses. The poet's personality, as conveyed in the poems, is surly, practical, and conservative—an old-fashioned Greek yeoman farmer who happens to have a poetic gift.

Hesiod's *Theogony* is a major source for ancient Greek beliefs about the creation of the world and the origins of the Greek pantheon. It tells how only Chaos and Earth existed in the beginning, and how all the gods are descended from them. Hesiod divides time into five major epochs: the Golden Age (under CRONUS), the Silver Age (under ZEUS), the Bronze Age (a period of upheaval and war), the Heroic Age (the time of the Trojan War), and the Iron Age (his own time, the imperfect present). In addition to providing facts and genealogies about the gods, *Theogony* also supplies evidence of Near Eastern influence on the formative Greek culture of the 700s and 600s B.C.E., for a number of Hesiod's myths closely resemble certain older legends from Mesopotamia. This influence occurred from Greek TRADE with the Near East via Phoenician middlemen.

See also CRONUS; EPIC POETRY; PHOENICIA.

Further reading: Robert Lamberton, *Hesiod* (New Haven, Conn.: Yale University Press, 1988); Friedrich Solmsen, *Hesiod and Aeschylus* (Ithaca, N.Y.: Cornell University Press, 1995); Carlo Odo Pavese and Paolo Venti, *A Complete Formular Analysis of the Hesiodic Poems: Introduction and Formular Edition* (Amsterdam: A. M. Hakkert, 2000); Richard Gotshalk, *Homer and Hesiod: Myth and Philosophy* (Lanham, Md.: University Press of America, 2000); Jenny Strauss Clay, *Hesiod's Cosmos* (New York: Cambridge University Press, 2003).

Hesperides *See* HERAKLES.

Hestia Goddess of the hearth and of domestic fire, Hestia ("hearth") was the least important of the 12 Olympian deities. She was the sister of ZEUS, and little MYTH was attached to her name. Having refused to marry, Hestia remained a virgin and lived as a kind of respected spinster aunt on Mt. OLYMPUS.

Her cult, however, was important. In an era before manufactured matches, the hearth was the crucial place where cooking fire was maintained perpetually, winter and summer. The hearth helped to preserve order and civilization, and many governmental buildings had public hearths that symbolized the public good. Accordingly, Hestia was the patron goddess of town halls and similar; one of her epithets was *boulaia*, "she of the council house."

See also COUNCIL.

Further reading: O. Hansen, "Hestia Boulaia at Erythrai," *L'Antiquité classique* 54 (1985): 274–276; Helen North, "Hestia and Vesta: Non-identical Twins," in *New Light from Ancient Cosa: Classical Mediterranean Studies in Honor of Cleo Rickman Fitch,* edited by Norma Wynick Goldman (New York: P. Lang, 2001), 179–188; Jean-Pierre Vernant, "Hestia-Hermes: The Religious Expression of Space and Movement in Ancient Greece," in *Antiquities,* edited by Nicole Loraux, Gregory Nagy, and Laura Slatkin (New York: New Press, 2001), 112–133.

hetairai *See* PROSTITUTES.

heterosexuality In ancient Greece, the distinction between HOMOSEXUALITY and heterosexuality was far less pronounced than it is in modern society. Most men (we know less about the sexual habits and inclinations of Greek WOMEN) were bisexual. It was of utmost importance in Greek culture for men and women to marry and produce children. This was the most essential sexual relationship, but not necessarily the most fulfilling one for all couples, especially since many marriages were arranged for political or financial reasons by the prospective husband and the bride's parents. Wives were often much younger and less experienced than their husbands, suggesting that men tended to look elsewhere for nonprocreative sexual satisfaction. These extramarital affairs could be heterosexual (usually involving SLAVES or PROSTITUTES) or homosexual (usually with younger men or boys).

Further reading: David Konstan and Martha Nussbaum, eds., *Sexuality in Greek and Roman Society* (Providence, R.I.: Brown University Press, 1990); Natalie Kampen, ed., *Sexuality in Ancient Art: the Near East, Egypt, Greece, and Italy* (New York: Cambridge University Press, 1996); Bruce Thornton, *Eros: The Myth of Ancient Greek Sexuality* (Boulder, Colo.: Westview Press, 1997); Ann Olga Koloski-Ostrow and Claire L. Lyons, eds., *Naked Truths: Women, Sexuality, and Gender in Classical Art and Archaeology* (London: Routledge, 1997); Eva Cantarella, *Bisexuality in the Ancient World,* 2d ed., translated by Cormac O. Cuilleanáin (New Haven, Conn.: Yale University Press, 2002); Martha Nussbaum and Juha Sihvola, eds., *The Sleep of Reason: Erotic Experience and Sexual Ethics in Ancient Greece and Rome* (Chicago: University of Chicago Press, 2002); Laura McClure, ed., *Sexuality and Gender in the Classical World: Readings and Sources* (Oxford: Blackwell, 2002).

Hieron (1) (d. 467 B.C.E.) *Dictator of the Greek cities* GELA *and* SYRACUSE *in* SICILY
Hieron ("holy one") became the most powerful individual in the Greek world around 470 B.C.E. He had come to power under his brother GELON, who ruled in Syracuse and appointed him as his governor in Gela. On Gelon's death, Hieron succeeded as lord (*turannos*, "tyrant") of Syracuse, the foremost city of the Greek West (478 B.C.E.). Although less popular than his brother, Hieron ruled in grand style. He formed an alliance with the other great Sicilian-Greek tyrant, Theron of ACRAGAS. When the Greeks of CUMAE, in western ITALY, appealed for help against the encroaching ETRUSCANS, Hieron achieved his greatest triumph—his sea victory at Cumae, in the Bay of Naples, which broke the Etruscans' sea power forever and removed them as a threat to the Italian Greeks (474 B.C.E.).

At home he consolidated his power through social engineering and cultural display. He continued the Sicilian rulers' ruthless practice of transplantation, removing 10,000 citizens of CATANA in order to reestablish the site as a new, Dorian-Greek city, Aetna. The "founding" of Aetna was commemorated in the tragedy *Women of Aetna* by the Athenian playwright AESCHYLUS, who visited Hieron's court at the ruler's invitation around 470 B.C.E.

Other luminaries of Hieron's court were the great Theban choral poet PINDAR and the poets SIMONIDES and BACCHYLIDES of Keos. Pindar and Bacchylides were commissioned to write poems celebrating Hieron's prestigious victories in horse- and chariot-racing at the OLYMPIC and PYTHIAN GAMES (476–468 B.C.E.). Hieron is the addressee of Pindar's famous First Olympian ode and First Pythian ode.

Hieron died, probably of cancer, and was succeeded by his son Deinomenes. By 466 B.C.E. however, Syracuse had overthrown the tyranny and installed a DEMOCRACY in its place.

See also CHARIOTS; TYRANTS.

Further reading Ralph E. Doty. trans., *Hieron: A New Translation/Xenophon* (Lewiston, N.Y.: Edwin Mellen Press, 2003).

Hieron (2) II *See* SYRACUSE.

Himera This Greek city, located midway along the northern coast of SICILY, was founded in about 649 B.C.E.

by colonists from ZANCLĒ in northeastern Sicily. Himera's most famous citizen was the poet STESICHORUS (ca, 590 B.C.E.). Himera was a Greek frontier town, close to the Carthaginian-controlled western part of Sicily. In the late summer of 480 B.C.E., the vicinity of Himera was the site of a great battle in which a Greek army totally defeated an invading force from CARTHAGE.

In the years prior to the battle, the town was ruled by a Greek tyrant, Terillus, who eventually was ejected by Theron, tyrant of ACRAGAS. Terillus appealed to his ally, the Carthaginian leader Hamilcar, and in 480 B.C.E. Hamilcar sailed from North Africa with a large army to reinstate Terillus and conquer Greek Sicily. Landing in Sicily, the Carthaginians marched on Himera, but outside the town Hamilcar and his army were destroyed by an allied Greek force under GELON, the tyrant of SYRACUSE. According to legend, the battle was fought on the very same day as another great victory of liberation, the sea battle of SALAMIS (1), against the invading Persians in mainland Greece.

To commemorate the victory at Himera, Gelon minted what is perhaps the most beautiful coin of the 400s B.C.E.—the SILVER Syracusan decadrachm known as the Demareteion.

The Carthaginians' defeat stymied their ambitions in Sicily for three generations. But in 409 B.C.E. they captured Himera and razed it in vengeance.

See also COINAGE; TYRANTS.

Further reading: Colin M. Kraay, *The Archaic Coinage of Himera* (Naples: Centro Internazionale di Studi Numismatici, 1983).

Hipparchus   *See* HIPPIAS (1).

Hippias (1)   (b. ca. 565 B.C.E.) *Athenian dictator who reigned 527–510 B.C.E.*

Hippias was the son and successor of PEISISTRATUS. Succeeding his father as ruler at about age 40, he aggrandized ATHENS with public works, ambitious diplomacy, and economic projects. Under him, the city continued its emergence as the future cultural capital of Greece. Hippias's younger brother Hipparchus brought to Athens two of the greatest poets of the era: ANACREON and SIMONIDES. But the days of Greek TYRANTS like Hippias were numbered by the late 500s B.C.E., and Hippias eventually was ousted by Athenian opposition and Spartan intervention.

In 510 B.C.E. the Spartan king KLEOMENES led an army to Athens, against Hippias. The Spartans had been urged to do so by the oracle at DELPHI, but Kleomenes himself surely wanted to stop Hippias's diplomatic overtures to the Persian king DARIUS (1). Kleomenes probably feared that Hippias was planning to submit to Darius in order to retain personal power.

Aided by Athenians who were hostile to the tyranny, the Spartans surrounded Hippias and his followers on the ACROPOLIS. Hippias abdicated in exchange for a safe-conduct out. His departure brought to an end more than 35 years of Peisistratid rule at Athens, setting the stage for the political reforms of KLEISTHENES (1) and the full-fledged Athenian DEMOCRACY.

Traveling eastward to PERSIA, Hippias became an adviser at Darius's court. In 490 B.C.E., when the Persians launched their seaborne expedition against Athens, Hippias (by now nearly 80) accompanied the Persian army. Apparently he was intended as the puppet ruler.

He guided the Persian fleet to the sheltered bay at MARATHON, about 26 miles from Athens. It was there, more than 50 years before, that Hippias had helped his father, Pisistratus, bring a different invading army ashore. But this time fortune favored the defenders, and the Persian force was totally defeated by the Athenians at the famous Battle of Marathon. Hippias withdrew with the Persian fleet and, according to one story, died on the return voyage.

See also ALCMAEONIDS; HARMODIUS AND ARISTOGEITON; PERSIAN WARS; POTTERY; THEATER.

Further reading R. T. Williams, "The Owls and Hippias," *Numismatic Chronicle* 6 (1966): 9–13; W. G. Forrest, "The Tradition of Hippias' Expulsion from Athens," *Greek, Roman, and Byzantine Studies* 10 (1969): 227–286; F. J. Frost, "Toward a History of Peisistratid Athens," in *The Craft of the Ancient Historian. Essays in Honor of Chester G. Starr,* edited by John Eadie and Josiah Ober (Lanham, Md.: University Press of America, 1985), 57–78; H. A. Shapiro, "Oracle Mongers in Peisistratid Athens," *Kernos* 3 (1990): 335–345; R. D. Griffiths, "Hippias' Missing Tooth (Hdt. 6, 107)." *Ancient History Bulletin* 8 (1994): 121–122; John McK. Camp, "Before Democracy. Alkmaionidai and Peisistratidai," in *The Archaeology of Athens and Attica under the Democracy. Proceedings of an international conference held at the American School of Classical Studies at Athens, December 4–6, 1992,* edited by W. D. E. Coulson (Oxford: Oxbow Books, 1994), 7–12.

Hippias (2)   *See* SOPHISTS.

Hippocrates (1)   (ca. 460–377 B.C.E.) *Greek physician and medical writer*

A native of the Dorian-Greek island of Kos, near southwestern ASIA MINOR, Hippocrates is usually considered to be the founder of scientific medical practice.

Hippocrates was born into an elite family of priests who had accumulated many traditions of healing and wellness. As he grew to adulthood, he traveled throughout Greece to practice healing and to study PHILOSOPHY. He returned to Kos and established a school of MEDICINE that became renowned in the ancient world. While not the first Greek doctor, Hippocrates was apparently the first to systematize the existing knowledge and procedures and to ground medical practice in solid observation rather than theory. The later writer Celsus (ca. 30 C.E.) remarked that Hippocrates separated medicine from PHILOSOPHY.

Of the 72 medical treatises that have survived from the Hippocratic school, it is uncertain whether any were written by Hippocrates himself. These writings do, however, convey the spirit of the school through certain shared traits, such as their emphasis on observation and diagnosis. The treatises include *Airs, Waters, and Places,* which describes the effects of different climates on health and psychology, and *The Sacred Disease,* a discussion of epilepsy (concluding that there is nothing sacred about it). Many later Greek physicians, including the famous Galen, wrote commentaries on the works of Hippocrates.

All new doctors coming out of the ancient Hippocratic school would take the Hippocratic Oath. In this vow, the speaker swore to honor the brotherhood of the school, never to treat a patient with any purpose other than healing, never to give poison or induce abortion, and never as a doctor to enter a house with any ulterior motive, such as seduction of SLAVES. A modified form of this oath is still administered to medical school graduates today, 2,400 years later.

Further reading: William A. Heidel, *Hippocratic Medicine* (New York: Arno Press, 1981); Owsei Temkin, *Hippocrates in a World of Pagans and Christians* (Baltimore: Johns Hopkins University Press, 1991); Jody Rubin Pinault, *Hippocratic Lives and Legends* (Leiden, Netherlands: E. J. Brill, 1992); Jacques Jouanna, *Hippocrates,* translated by M. B. DeBevoise (Baltimore: Johns Hopkins University Press, 1999); David Cantor, ed., *Reinventing Hippocrates* (Burlington, Vt.: Ashgate, 2002).

Hippocrates (2)   *See* GELA; GELON.

Hippodamus (mid-400 B.C.E.) *Town planner, born at MILETUS but active in the service of Periklean ATHENS*
Around 450 B.C.E., Hippodamus designed the grid pattern for the Athenian port city of PIRAEUS (his design is still in use there today), and he probably did likewise for the Athenian-sponsored colony of Thurii, in southern ITALY. Such urban grid street systems are often today called by the adjective "Hippodamian." Hippodamus was one of the colonists who emigrated to Thurii circa 443 B.C.E. ARISTOTLE's *Politics* (ca. 340 B.C.E.) mentions his affected physical appearance—long hair and adorned robes in the Ionian manner.

See also IONIAN GREEKS.

Further reading: Ferdinando Castagnoli, *Orthogonal Town Planning in Antiquity,* translated by Victor Caliandro (Cambridge, Mass.: MIT Press, 1971): H. R. McCredie, "Hippodamos of Miletos," in *Studies Presented to George M. A. Hanfmann,* edited by David Gordon Mitten, John Griffiths Pedley, and Jane Ayer Scott (Cambridge, Mass.: Fogg

Art Museum, 1971), 95–100; A. Burns, "Hippodamus and the Planned City," *Historia* 25 (1976): 414–428.

Hippolyta   *See* AMAZONS; HERAKLES; TESEUS.

Hippolytus   In MYTH, Hippolytus was the son of the Athenian king THESEUS and the Amazon queen Hippolyta. After his mother's death, he grew to manhood at ATHENS as a hunter and male virgin, devoted to the goddess ARTEMIS. The love goddess APHRODITE, irked by Hippolytus's celibacy, caused Theseus's young wife, the Cretan princess Phaedra, to fall in love with Hippolytus, her stepson. Rebuffed by him, she hanged herself but left behind a letter accusing him of rape. Theseus, not believing his son's declarations of innocence, banished him and then cursed him. The curse was effective (as being one of three wishes that Theseus had been granted by his guardian, the god POSEIDON), and a monstrous bull emerged from the sea while Hippolytus was driving his chariot on the road. Hippolytus's terrified horses threw him from the chariot, and so his death was fulfilled in the manner suggested by his name: "loosed horse," or stampede. Theseus learned the truth from Artemis after it was too late.

Our main source for the legend is the admirable, surviving tragedy *Hippolytus* (431 B.C.E.) by the Athenian playwright EURIPIDES. In the play, Hippolytus appears as priggish and lacking in compassion, while Phaedra is convincingly imagined as an unhappy woman in the unwelcome grip of an obsession.

A later legend claimed that Hippolytus was restored to life by the physician-hero ASKLEPIOS. But then the god ZEUS, fearing a disruption of natural order, killed both men with a thunderbolt.

See also AMAZONS.

Further reading: Hazel E. Barnes, *Hippolytus in Drama and Myth* (Lincoln: University of Nebraska Press, 1960); James L. Sanderson and Irwin Gopnik, eds., *Phaedra and Hippolytus; Myth and Dramatic Form* (Boston: Houghton Mifflin, 1966).

Hipponax (mid-500s B.C.E.) *Greek lyric poet of EPHESOS*
Banished by one of the city's Persian-controlled TYRANTS around 540 B.C.E., Hipponax supposedly lived as a beggar in nearby Clazomenae. His wrote satirical poems in various meters, with the flavor of the gutter. He was said to have been the inventor of parody; one of his surviving fragments is a mock-Homeric description of a glutton.

Hipponax is credited with inventing the *skazon,* or "lame" iambic meter—which, to the Greek ear, had a halting, comic affect, appropriate to satire.

See also IONIA; LYRIC POETRY.

Further reading Carlos Miralles and Jaume Pòrtulas, *The Poetry of Hipponax* (Rome: Edizioni dell'Ateneo, 1988).

Homer (Greek: Homeros) According to tradition, Homer was the earliest and greatest Greek poet. Two epic poems were attributed to him: the *Iliad* and the *Odyssey*, which present certain events of the mythical TROJAN WAR and its aftermath. These two works, totaling about 27,800 lines in dactylic hexameter verse, were fundamental references for MYTH in ancient Greece. Greeks of subsequent centuries looked to them for insight into the gods' nature, for answers to moral questions, and for inspiration for new literature. The Athenian playwright AESCHYLUS (ca. 460 B.C.E.) described his own tragedies as "crumbs from the banquet of Homer." It is token of the Greeks' reverence for the *Iliad* and the *Odyssey* that both these long poems survived antiquity. Each poem's division into 24 "books," still used in modern editions, was made long after Homer's time by editors at ALEXANDRIA (1) in the early 100s B.C.E.

Despite a few legends, nothing is known about the life of Homer, whose name in ancient Greek may mean "hostage." Although the Greeks definitely believed that Homer was a real person, this is less strongly accepted by modern scholars. It is not impossible, in fact that the *Iliad* and the *Odyssey* were each composed by a different person, since the two poems differ in tone and narrative style. The *Odyssey*, which relies far more than the *Iliad* on fable and folktale, may have been written much later than the *Iliad*. Furthermore, given the collaborative nature of preliterate Greek EPIC POETRY, either poem or both could have been created by a group of poets, rather than by a single author. Assuming that Homer did exist, it is not even known that "he" was a man, except that the ancient Greek world's social structure makes it likely.

If there was a historical figure named Homer, he may have lived sometime between 850 and 750 B.C.E. The *Iliad* and the *Odyssey* were probably first written down around 750 B.C.E., after the invention of the Greek ALPHABET, but evidently both poems were fully composed before that date. They were probably created by the oral techniques of preliterate Greek epic poetry—that is, by a centuries-old method of using memorized verses, stock phrases, and spontaneous elaboration, without WRITING. Assuming that Homer did exist, it is not known if he wrote the poems down (or dictated them to scribes) in the mid-700s B.C.E., or whether he was long dead when others wrote down his verses, preserved by oral retelling. He may have been a bard who performed at the court of some Greek noble or king—much like the character Demodocus in book 8 of the *Odyssey*, who earns his livelihood singing traditional tales to entertain upper-class men and women.

The *Iliad* and the *Odyssey* reveal no autobiographical information. A single supposed autobiographical item is found in the *Hymn to Delian Apollo*, one of 34 choral songs to the gods that the ancient Greeks ascribed to Homer. In the hymn, the unnamed poet describes himself with these words: "If anyone should ask you whose song is sweetest, say: 'Blind is the man, and he lives in rocky CHIOS.'" Many ancient Greeks believed this to be a true description of the mysterious Homer, although modern scholars are wary of accepting it. Several cities claimed to be Homer's birthplace, and later writers believed variously that he was from Chios, Smyrna, ATHENS, EGYPT, or ROME. That Homer lived in the Greek region called IONIA, on the west coast of ASIA MINOR is suggested by the mainly Ionic dialect of his poems and by the fact that Ionia was at that time the most culturally advanced part of the Greek world. In later centuries Chios was home to a guild of bards who called themselves the Homeridae (sons of Homer).

More important than the poet's identity are the values and traditions on which his poetry is based. Homer and other bards of his day sang about an idealized ancestral society that was 500 years in the past. Homer's audience imagined this bygone era as an Age of Heroes, when men of superior strength, courage, and wealth lived in communion with the gods. Homer's aristocratic protagonists—ACHILLES in the *Iliad* and ODYSSEUS in the *Odyssey*—live by a code of honor that shapes all their actions. For them, disgrace was the worst possible fate—far worse than death. If a man's honor was slighted, then the man was obliged to seek extreme or violent redress.

Although Homer's poems purport to depict the ancient Greek society that scholars now call the Bronze Age—the era of the MYCENAEAN CIVILIZATION, they are actually better illustrations of Homer's own time. The institutions of the Greek POLIS that appear in the epic poems, for example, are those that existed in the 700s B.C.E., not in the 1200s. On the other hand, the poet does demonstrate some knowledge of actual Bronze Age practices and artifacts; the boar's tusk helmet worn by the Greek warriors resembles actual helmets found in Mycenaean tombs depicted on Mycenaean wall paintings and POTTERY.

Greek MYTH contains hundreds of stories from the Age of Heroes. Homer's genius lay in selecting certain tales and imposing order on the material, to fashion (in each epic poem) a cohesive, suspenseful narrative, with vivid character portraits. Contrary to some popular belief, the *Iliad* does not describe the entire Trojan War and fall of TROY. It rather focuses on certain episodes involving the Greek champion Achilles during the tenth and final year of the siege; the action of the poem takes place over a period of only seven weeks. It tells of the "anger of Achilles"—that is, his quarrel with the Greek commander AGAMEMNON, after Agamemnon had needlessly slighted Achilles' honor. Achilles' withdrawal from the battlefield causes difficulty for the Greeks, culminating in the death of Achilles' friend PATROKLOS at the hands of the Trojan prince HECTOR. At the story's climax (book 22), Achilles slays Hector in single combat, even though he knows that this act is ordained by FATE to seal his own doom. The *Iliad* ends not with Achilles' death or Troy's fall—those events are still in the future—but with Hector's funeral, after Achilles finally allowed the Trojans to ransom back the corpse.

The *Odyssey*, although it stands on its own merits, provides a loose sequel to the *Iliad*. In this story, the war has finally ended, Troy having fallen to the Greeks. The wily and resourceful Greek hero Odysseus, king of ITHACA, is making his way home to his kingdom amid supernatural adventures, both violent and sexual. Like the *Iliad*, the *Odyssey* displays narrative skill in maintaining suspense. Daringly not introducing the protagonist until book 4, the poem opens with the scenes at the disrupted kingdom of Ithaca, where more than 100 arrogant suitors (assuming Odysseus to be dead) have taken over the palace and are individually wooing his intelligent and gracious wife, PENELOPE, while threatening his oldest son, TELEMACHOS. The reader or listener thus observes the consequences of Odysseus's absence and shares in his family's longing for his return. We then meet Odysseus, who is nearing the end of his journey. Aided by the goddess ATHENA, he returns to Ithaca in disguise (book 14) and scouts out the dangerous situation at the palace before revealing his identity, slaying the suitors, and reclaiming his wife and kingdom (book 22–23). The suspense that precedes this violent climax is remarkably modern in tone and explains why Homer's epics have remained so popular for so many centuries.

See also GREEK LANGUAGE; WARFARE, LAND.

Further reading: Roberto Salinas Price, *Atlas of Homeric Geography* (San Antonio, Tex.: Scylax Press, 1992); Albert B. Lord, Stephen Mitchell, and Gregory Nagy, eds., *The Singer of Tales*, 2d ed. (Cambridge, Mass.: Harvard University Press, 2000); Ione Mylonas Shear, *Tales of Heroes: The Origins of the Homeric Texts* (New York: A. D. Caratzas, 2000); Barbara Graziosi, *Inventing Homer: The Early Reception of Epic* (New York: Cambridge University Press, 2002); Martin L. West, ed. and trans., *Homeric Hymns, Homeric Apocrypha, Lives of Homer* (Cambridge, Mass.: Harvard University Press, 2003).

homosexuality   Ancient   Greek   literature   and   art clearly show that certain types of homosexual relationships were considered natural and even admirable in many Greek cities during the epoch between about 600 B.C.E. and the spread of Christianity. Especially, male homosexuality was encouraged in some (not all) forms. Love between males was seen as harmonious with other Greek social values, such as athletic skill, military courage, and the idealization of male youth and beauty (reflected also in surviving Greek SCULPTURE). Such relationships provided males with a romance not usually found in MARRIAGE, since Greek society generally viewed WOMEN as morally and intellectually inferior.

Female homosexuality was also an approved practice in some locales, at least in the 600s–500s B.C.E. Extant

The hero Achilles, at right, bandages a wound for his friend Patroclus, in a red-figure scene from an Athenian cup, ca. 500 B.C.E. The painting conveys Patroclus's distress and Achilles' sympathetic concentration; the sexuality of the two men is suggested by the gratuitous peek at Patroclus's genitals. Although the *Iliad* never portrays Achilles and Patroclus as lovers, the Greeks after Homer came to view the pair as models for aristocratic, military, male homosexuality. *(Margaret Bunson)*

verses by the poets SAPPHO and ALCMAN document sexual feelings and acts between aristocratic young women on the Aegean island of LESBOS and SPARTA, both around 600 B.C.E. Also, a single sentence in the work of the later writer PLUTARCH suggest that at Sparta it was usual for mature women to have affairs with unmarried girls. But little other information survives regarding love between women. The silence is due partly to scarcity of extant writings by Greek women and partly to the fact that female homosexuality was not encouraged as widely as its male counterpart. Relations between females may even have been forbidden in certain cities that had male-homosexual traditions, such as ATHENS in the 400s B.C.E.

The ancient literary sources for information on Greek homosexuality include LYRIC POETRY composed between about 600 and 100 B.C.E., Athenian stage comedy of the 400s B.C.E., the works of the philosopher PLATO and the historian XENOPHON (both of them Athenians writing in the early 300s B.C.E.), and Athenian courtroom speeches of the 300s B.C.E. The visual evidence consists mostly of vase paintings from the 500s and 400s B.C.E., some showing courtship or sex between males. As is usual for any aspect of ancient Greek society, much of the extant source material is from Athens. There is, however, an important series of graffiti inscriptions from the Aegean island of THERA that provide evidence for homosexual attractions and relations there. The graffiti are dated to around 600 B.C.E. and include verses praising certain boys for their beauty and their dancing ability. Two of the inscriptions, written by the same man, boast more explicitly about a sexual conquest of a younger boy. Other Greek states—including Sparta, ELIS, CHALCIS, and especially THEBES—also had important male-homosexual cultures, linked to the training and esprit of citizen armies.

The Thera graffiti supports the theory that homosexuality as a social norm arose in Greece in the late 600s B.C.E. Modern scholars have found no homosexual content in the poetry of HOMER (ca. 750 B.C.E.), HESIOD (ca. 700 B.C.E.), or ARCHILOCHOS (ca. 660 B.C.E.). Expressions of homosexual desire, however, do appear in the extant verses of Sappho (ca. 600 B.C.E.) and SOLON (ca. 590 B.C.E.).

This new social custom probably derived in part from the military reorganizations that swept Greek cities after the arrival of HOPLITE tactics in the 600s B.C.E. Other, related social changes at this time included the glorification of masculinity and (at Sparta) the elimination of family life by the mass military training of boys. The Greeks tended to associate homosexuality with manliness and soldiering. Significantly, the IONIAN GREEKS of ASIA MINOR were reputed to be the softest, the least military, and the least interested in homosexual pursuits, of all Greek peoples.

The ancient Greeks did not classify a person as strictly homosexual or heterosexual, as modern society tends to do. The Greeks assumed that an attractive, young individual of either gender could inspire sexual desire in either gender. Adult male citizens—the one class of people who had sexual freedom—often led private lives that were bisexual. (Yet not always; the Greeks did recognize that some men preferred one or the other gender exclusively.)

Male citizens were expected to marry female citizens and beget children, but evidently most men were not in love with their wives, as the society did not encourage this. Instead, a husband was legally and morally free to seek partners outside of marriage. (Wives enjoyed no such privilege.) Possible partners for a married or unmarried man included male or female PROSTITUTES and SLAVES, who were of the lower social ranks and who received payment or sustenance in exchange for giving sexual favors. However, if a male citizen wished for romance with someone who was his social equal—that is, if he wished to conduct courtship and seduction, with the possibility of mutual love and admiration—then his choices were limited. In most cities, the wives and daughters of citizens were often kept away from public places, and their chastity was protected by severe laws. There

was only one kind of publicly approved romance available for people of the citizen classes—namely, the romance that might arise between a mature man and younger male.

This pairing—older male citizen/younger male citizen—was the classic pattern of ancient Greek homosexual love, as idealized in legend and art. This was the love pursued especially by wealthier and aristocratic citizens. Perhaps the best-known couple in this tradition were the Athenian tyrannicides of 514 B.C.E. HARMODIUS AND ARISTOGEITON.

The younger male was typically a well-bred boy between about 12 and 20 years old—that is, between early puberty and full maturity. Youths around ages 16 and 17 were considered especially desirable as being in the prime of beauty. The young man or boy would be the passive partner, the recipient of the older man's courtship and gifts. The most handsome and accomplished youths became glamorous social figures, over whom men would conduct fierce rivalries. The teenage aristocrat ALCIBIADES was one such figure, and Plato's dialogue *Charmides* includes a vivid scene where the teenage Charmides enters a GYMNASIUM followed by a boisterous crowd of quarreling admirers. But only citizen males were allowed to woo such love objects; any male slave who pursued a citizen boy in this way was liable to dire punishment.

Among the qualities the classical Greeks admired in their boys were masculinity and bodily strength. Such attributes are clearly indicated in several hundred surviving Greek vase paintings showing images of boys or young men, often labeled with the inscribed word *kalos,* "beautiful." (These are the famous kalos vases, the homosexual "pin-ups" of ancient Greece.) Boys with more feminine bodies or mannerisms were apparently not much sought after in the 500s and 400s B.C.E., although they seem to have come into vogue by the late 300s.

Painted scenes of Greek homosexual couples nearly always show the older male as bearded, indicating adulthood. He might be in his 20s, 30s, or possibly 40s—anywhere from about five to 25 years older than his partner. The younger male always appears as beardless. Written evidence reveals that—in fifth-century B.C. Athens, but not always elsewhere—young men were considered no longer desirable once they began sprouting facial hair. Probably at around age 20 a young Athenian would feel social pressure to relinquish his junior sex role. He might maintain a close friendship with his former lover(s), but he would now be ready to take on the adult role, as the active pursuer of a younger male. This change by him was part of his larger transition to adulthood and to his full identity as a citizen.

Men could meet boys and youths at public places and upper-class venues such as gymnasiums, riding tracks, religious sacrifices and processions, and city streets where boys traveled to and from school. The sons of wealthy homes went out accompanied by a *paidagogos,* a slave whose duties included keeping would-be suitors away. Part of the pursuer's challenge might lie in intimidating or evading the paidagogos, in order to make the boy's acquaintance.

Once a suitor had won the approval of the boy's father, the courtship progressed through stages that included the suitor giving gifts; a typical gift often appearing on vase paintings is a live rooster. Together the two males would partake of upper-class recreations such as SPORT, hunting, and the drinking party known as the SYMPOSIUM, where politics or intellectual topics might be discussed.

In a society that did not foster close ties between father and son, the suitor served as a role model. He played a vital part in the boy's EDUCATION, helping to improve the boy's athletic skills, military aptitude, and general readiness for manhood. At Sparta, for example, legend claimed that after a boy once cried out in pain during a fistfight, the boy's lover was punished for failing to teach manliness.

Beyond mere instruction, a lover might provide a boy with financial help and career contacts that supplemented, perhaps vastly, what the boy's family could provide. At Thebes the lover customarily supplied the younger man's first suit of armor (no small expense). At Athens many a politician, lawyer, and poet seems to have gotten his career start as a handsome boy, meeting older men who would become his benefactors and allies.

The relationship between man and boy was thought to be mutually inspiring; the man strove to be admirable in his public conduct; the boy strove to be worthy of the man. In Elis and Thebes, where love relationships often continued after the younger male reached adulthood, it was customary to station lovers side-by-side in battle, on the theory that each would fight more fiercely if observed by his partner. At Thebes this theory led to the creation, in around 378 B.C.E., of an elite, 300-soldier unit called the Sacred Band, comprised entirely of paired lovers.

Exactly what sexual activity was involved in such relationships is not clear to modern scholars; sexual customs evidently varied from region to region. In general the Greeks valued sexual restraint, much as they valued the ability to endure hunger or fatigue. Apparently one school of thought believed that lovers should practice abstinence. Plato, in his dialogue *The Symposium,* glorifies male homosexual love as a search for beauty and truth, yet he argues that love in its most exalted form involves no sexual contact—the famous "Platonic love." Similarly Xenophon, while describing homosexual pairings at Sparta, makes the surprising statement that Spartan law severely punished any man who had sexual relations with a boy. On the other hand, extant vase paintings (mostly from Athens) show more than one form of general activity between males.

The question is: Was the younger male typically subjected to sexual penetration by the older? The answer seems to be that at Thebes and certain other Greek cities this was socially permitted, while at Athens and at many other cities it was officially discouraged but it sometimes occurred anyway. At Athens the "better sort" of older partner did not try to seduce his beloved, as revealed by an anecdote in Xenophon's memoirs where the Athenian philosopher SOCRATES rebukes the young man KRITIAS for his unseemly lust for the boy Euthydemus. Socrates says that Kritias wants "to rub himself against Eurthydemus the way itchy pigs want to rub against stones." For sexual outlet, Greek men had recourse to their wives, concubines, and male and female prostitutes and slaves. Citizen boys—at Athens and Sparta, at least—were supposed to be kept pure (although that rule might be disobeyed).

This complicated outlook was part of the Greeks' attitude toward sex in general. Sex was seen as a form of power: One partner was considered dominant and one subordinate in any relationship. Typically the dominant partner was the male whose penis entered a bodily orifice of the other person. The recipient's submission was proof of inferior status. Although there was an awareness that women could enjoy sex—as suggested in the legend of the seer TEIRESIAS—the Greeks were uncomfortable with the idea that any subordinate partner could feel pleasure. Sex was for the dominant person's benefit.

In all sexual relations, an adult male citizen was expected to dominate. Males who willingly received sexual penetration were supposed to be either slaves or prostitutes—noncitizens, unlucky in their servitude or poverty. Any male citizen who wanted to be penetrated sexually was considered bizarre and morally debased. A citizen who gave his body for money was deemed a prostitute and was liable to lose most of his citizenship rights. This was the background of the speech *Against Timarchus* (346 B.C.E.), in which the Athenian orator AESCHINES convinced an Athenian court that his enemy Timarchus had prostituted himself in his younger days.

The contradiction in Greek homosexual love was that it placed young male citizens in danger of being sexually subordinated and thus dishonored. Any boy might receive expensive gifts from an admirer; many a boy probably succumbed to a lover's seduction. What distinguished this behavior from a prostitute's? The answer lay partly in monogamy. A boy who gave sexual favors might avoid disrepute by not being promiscuous and by choosing a worthy, discreet lover. A second way to avoid dishonor may have been by limiting sexual contact to an activity known today as intercrural intercourse (shown on vase paintings). This involved the two males standing or lying face to face, with the older man moving his penis between the younger's clamped thighs. Because the younger male was not actually being penetrated, this submission was probably thought of as being less degrading.

Modern scholars believe that the homosexual themes in Greek MYTH all represent a relatively late layer, added after 600 B.C.E. In other words, legends about friendships between males had existed without homosexual nuance for centuries prior; these include the tales of GANYMEDE and the god ZEUS, of PELOPS and the god POSEIDON, and of the heroes ACHILLES and PATROKLOS. Eventually these myths received a sexual coloring, reflecting real-life social norms of the 500s B.C.E. and later. Legend claimed that Greek homosexual practices had been initiated by the Theban king Laius (father of OEDIPUS), when he carried off the boy Chrysippus.

Homosexuality continued to be practiced during the Roman era, often, but not exclusively, between masters and slaves. As Christianity grew in popularity and influence, however, it began to be far less tolerated and moved out of mainstream society. All major Christian writers of the 300s and 400s C.E. express an emphatically negative attitude toward homosexuality.

See also ANACREON; CHAIRONEIA; HYACINTHOS; IBYCUS; KALLIMACHUS; PINDAR; POTTERY; THEOGNIS.

Further reading: Kenneth J. Dover; *Greek Homosexuality* (New York: Vintage Books, 1980); Wayne R. Dynes and Stephen Donaldson, eds., *Homosexuality in the Ancient World* (New York: Garland, 1992); Thomas K. Hubbard, *Homosexuality in Greece and Rome: A Sourcebook of Basic Documents* (Berkeley: University of California Press, 2003).

hoplite This term refers to the heavy infantryman of the Greek world, from about 700–300 B.C.E. The famous land campaigns of the 400s B.C.E.—in the PERSIAN WARS and the PELOPONNESIAN WAR—were fought by hoplite armies. In the late 300s B.C.E., hoplite tactics were superseded by the tactics of the Macedonian PHALANX.

The early hoplite was named for his innovative shield, the *hoplon*, which was round, wide (three feet in diameter), heavy (about 16 pounds), and deeply concave on the inside; it was made of wood reinforced with BRONZE, often with a bronze facing. The soldier held the shield by passing his left forearm through a loop on the inside center and then gripping a handle at the far inside edge. This arrangement helped with the necessary task of keeping the shield rigidly away from the man's chest. The shield was notoriously difficult to hold up for a long period of time; a hoplite fleeing from battle always threw away his cumbersome shield, and even victorious soldiers could lose their shields in the melee. In militaristic societies such as SPARTA, keeping your shield meant keeping your honor, as indicated by the Spartan mother's proverbial command to her son: "Return with your shield or upon it."

The rest of the hoplite's armor, or panoply, included a helmet—typically beaten from a single sheet of bronze and topped with a crest of bronze or horsehair—and a bronze breastplate and greaves (metal shin guards); under the breastplate the man would wear a cloth tunic. The offensive weapons were a six- to eight-foot-long spear for thrusting (not throwing) and a sword of forged IRON, carried in a scabbard at the waist. By various modern estimates, the whole panoply weighed 50–70 pounds, and it seems that, on the march and up until the last moments before battle, much of a hoplite's equipment was carried for him by a servant or slave.

A hoplite did not normally fight alone; he was trained and equipped to stand, charge, and fight side by side with his comrades, in an orderly, multiranked formation. The hoplite relied foremost on his spear, thrusting

Hoplites prepared for battle, carrying the hoplon, or round, wide, heavy shield held by passing the left arm through a loop on the inside center. *(Alison Frantz Photographic Collection, American School of Classical Studies at Athens)*

overhand at the enemy while trying to shield himself from their spear-points. The sword was used if the spear was broken or lost.

The armor's weight, plus the need to keep in formation, meant that hoplites could not charge at full speed for any distance. Two hundred yards would seem to be the farthest that hoplites actually could run and still be in a condition to fight.

Yet this heavy armor did not make the hoplite invulnerable. It was not practical for armor to cover a man's neck, groin, or thighs, and these were left exposed. References in ancient poetry and art make it clear that deadly wounds to the neck and groin were common, as were fatal blows to the head (possibly received from an inward denting of the helmet). Sometimes the bronze breastplate could be pierced—as demonstrated by evidence that includes the recently recovered remains of a Spartan hoplite, buried at a battle-site with the fatal, iron spear-point lodged inside his chest.

Hoplites could fight effectively only on level ground; hilly terrain scattered their formation and left the individual soldiers open to attacks from lighter-armed skirmishers. Similarly, hoplites who broke ranks and became isolated—in retreat, for example—were easy prey for enemy CAVALRY.

On warships, hoplites served as "marines." There they were armed mainly with javelins (for throwing) and were employed in grapple-and-board tactics. Soldiers unlucky enough to fall overboard would be dragged to the bottom by their heavy armor.

Hoplite armies began their history as citizen armies. In most Greek cities, each man up through middle age who could afford the cost of a panoply was required to serve as a hoplite if his city went to war. (Alternatively, those rich enough to maintain horses might serve in the cavalry.) In states governed as oligarchies, a man had to be of hoplite status or better in order to be admitted as a citizen. What distinguished a DEMOCRACY such as ATHENS was that the Athenian citizenry included men whose income level was below the hoplite level.

There also existed professional hoplites, recruited for service in the pay of some other power, whether Greek or foreign. The best-known mercenary from Greek history is the Athenian XENOPHON who, with 10,000 Greek hoplites, marched deep into the Persian Empire in 401 B.C.E., in the service of a rebel Persian prince.

See also OLIGARCHY; PHEIDON; ARCHILOCHOS; WARFARE, LAND; WARFARE, NAVAL.

Further reading: Antonio Santosuosso, *Soldiers, Citizens, and the Symbols of War: From Classical Greece to Republican Rome, 500–167 B.C.* (Boulder, Colo.: Westview Press, 1997); Anthony M. Snodgrass, *Arms and Armor of the Greeks* (Baltimore: Johns Hopkins University Press, 1999); Hans van Wees, "The Development of the Hoplite Phalanx: Iconography and Reality in the Seventh Cen-

tury," in *War and Violence in Ancient Greece,* edited by Hans van Wees (London: Duckworth and the Classical Press of Wales, 2000), 125–166.

hubris (**sometimes written as** *hybris*)   This term refers to human arrogance or excessive pride, which usually leads to disaster. Implicit in much of Greek MYTH, the concept of hubris received its full expression in Greek tragedy. Typically, a tragic hero would undergo a series of emotional/psychological stages, including *koros* (excess, overindulgence), *hubris* (pride, arrogance), and *ate* (ruin, destruction). A prime example of hubris is AGAMEMNON's decision to tread on the purple tapestry in AESCHYLUS's tragedy *Agamemnon*—a wanton desecration of expensive finery that called down upon Agamemnon the wrath of the gods. Extreme examples of hubris include mythical villains such as IXION of SISYPHUS, who betrayed the friendship of the gods.

In Athenian legal parlance, hubris had a second meaning: assault against an Athenian citizen. The term was used in the sense of statutory rape or any kind of violence. As in the primary definition of hubris, the concept involved an unacceptable flouting of boundaries.

See also AJAX (2); TANTALUS; THEATER; XERXES.

Further reading: N. R. E. Fisher, "The Law of 'Hubris' in Athens," in *Nomos. Essays in Athenian Law, Politics, and Society,* edited by Paul Cartledge, Paul Millett, and Stephen Todd (New York: Cambridge University Press, 1990), 123–138; D. Cohen, "Sexuality, Violence, and the Athenian Law of 'Hubris'," *Greece and Rome* 38 (1991): 171–188; N. R. E. Fisher, *Hybris: A Study in the Values of Honour and Shame in Ancient Greece* (Warminster, U.K.: Aris and Philips, 1992); D. L. Cairns, "Hybris, Dishonour, and Thinking Big," *Journal of Hellenic Studies* 116 (1996): 1–32; J. M. J. Murphy, "'Hubris' and 'Superbia': Differing Greek and Roman Attitudes Concerning Arrogant Pride," *Ancient World* 28 (1997): 73–81.

Hyacinthos (**Greek: Huakinthos**)   In Greek MYTH, Hyacinthos was a handsome Spartan youth loved by the god APOLLO. While Apollo was teaching him how to throw the discus one day, the jealous West Wind god, Zephyros, sent the discus flying back into the young man's skull. Hyacinthos lay dying, and from his blood there sprang the type of scarlet flower that the Greeks called the hyacinth (perhaps our iris or anemone, but not what is called the hyacinth now).

Hyacinthos was honored in a three-day early-summer festival throughout the Spartan countryside. His tomb was displayed at Apollo's shrine at Amyclae, near SPARTA. One ancient writer noted that Hyacinthos's statue at Amyclae showed a bearded, mature man, not a youth.

The name Hyacinthos is pre-Greek in origin, as indicated by its distinctive *nth* sound. Modern scholars believe that Hyacinthos's cult dates back to pre-Greek times and that he was originally a local non-Greek god, associated with a local flower but not imagined as a young man and not yet associated with the Greek god Apollo. Sometime in the second millennium B.C.E., Hyacinthos was adapted to the RELIGION of the conquering Greeks and was made into a human follower of Apollo. The element of romantic love between them may have been added later, after 600 B.C.E.

See also GREEK LANGUAGE; HOMOSEXUALITY.

Further reading: Machteld Mellink, *Hyakinthos* (Utrecht: Kemink, 1943); B. C. Dietrich, "The Dorian Hyacinthia. A Survival from the Bronze Age," *Kadmos* 14 (1975): 133–142; L. Bruit, "The Meal at the Hyakinthia. Ritual Consumption and Offering," in *Sympotica. A Symposium on the Symposium, Oxford, 4–8 September 1984,* edited by Oswyn Murray (New York: Oxford University Press, 1990), 162–174.

I

Ibycus (mid-500s B.C.E.) *Lyric poet, known particularly for his love poetry*

Coming from the Greek city of RHEGIUM, located in the "toe" of ITALY, Ibycus supposedly refused an offered dictatorship and traveled instead to the east Greek island of SAMOS, where he flourished at the wealthy court of the tyrant POLYCRATES, around 535 B.C.E.

Only a few fragments of Ibycus's verses survive, either quoted by later ancient writers or discovered recently in ancient papyri from EGYPT. It is known that Ibycus's work featured two very different genres of Greek LYRIC POETRY: mythological storytelling, as developed previously by the poet STESICHORUS, another western Greek; and short, personal love poems.

The love-poem tradition comes from the eastern Greeks, a product of the sophisticated cities of IONIA and LESBOS. In keeping with the upper-class tastes of the time, the feeling expressed in these poems was homosexual. Such poems usually were written by a man of aristocratic blood to proclaim his infatuation for some teenager or young man of equal social status. Ibycus was considered one of the great poets of this genre, and his articulate poetry shows great passion and sensitivity. He has the personal reputation of being crazy for the love of boys.

Ibycus's verses included choral poetry—poems to be sung or chanted by choruses at religious festivals or other great occasions. Recently discovered fragments suggest that Ibycus pioneered the choral form known as the victory ode (*epinikion*), years in advance of the poets SIMONIDES and PINDAR.

Ibycus is perhaps best known for the dubious story of his death. He was supposedly attacked by robbers in a deserted place and died saying that his murder would be avenged by the cranes that were flying overhead. Later, in the city, one of the murderers, seeing some cranes, declared, "Look! The avengers of Ibycus." The statement drew an inquiring crowd, and the killers were apprehended. Appropriately, Ibycus's extant verses show a love of the natural world, especially of birdlife.

See also HOMOSEXUALITY.

Further reading: G. O. Hutchinson, *Greek Lyric Poetry: A Commentary on Selected Larger Pieces: Alcman, Stesichorus, Sappho, Alcaeus, Ibycus, Anacreon, Simonides, Bacchylides, Pindar, Sophokles, Euripides* (New York: Oxford University Press, 2001); Bonnie MacLachlan, "Personal Poetry," in *A Companion to the Greek Lyric Poets,* edited by Douglas E. Gerber (Leiden, Netherlands: E. J. Brill, 2001).

Icarus *See* DAEDALUS.

Iliad *See* ACHILLES; HOMER; TROJAN WAR.

Ilium *See* TROY.

Illyris This non-Greek territory of the Adriatic coast, northwest of Greece, corresponds roughly to modern Albania. Organized into warlike tribes that were hungry for Greek goods, the Illyrians played a role in the development of northern Greece. The Corinthian colonies EPIDAMNOS (founded around 625 B.C.E.) and APOLLONIA (founded around 600 B.C.E.) conducted TRADE with the Illyrians, acquiring TIMBER, SLAVES, raw metals, and wildflowers (for perfume-making).

In the 300s and early 200s B.C.E., the Illyrians were enemies of the kings of MACEDON and EPIRUS. The Illyrians raided these kingdoms and, in turn, suffered annexation of their own territories. By the late 200s B.C.E. the Illyrians were fighting against Roman armies, until both Illyris and Macedon were defeated and occupied by the Romans in the Third Macedonian War (171–167 B.C.E.). Illyrian territory supplied part of the Roman province of Illyricum.

See also PHILIP II; PYRRHUS; ROME.

Further reading: John J. Wilkes, *The Illyrians* (Cambridge, Mass.: B. Blackwell, 1992).

Io In MYTH, Io was a woman of the city of ARGOS. The great god ZEUS loved her, but to conceal her from his jealous wife, HERA, he changed Io into a young cow. After several misadventures she was restored by Zeus to human shape in EGYPT, and there bore him a son, whose descendants were the DANAIDS.

This odd myth might possibly reflect Mycenaean-Greek attempts to connect the Egyptian cow-goddess Hathor with the Argive worship of Hera in the shape of a cow.

See also DANAUS; MYCENAEAN CIVILIZATION; RELIGION.

Further reading: Robert Duff Murray, *The Motif of Io in Aeschylus' Suppliants* (Princeton, N.J.: Princeton University Press, 1958); A. M. Dale, "The Transformation of Io. Ox.Pap. 23, 2369," *Classical Review* 10 (1960): 194–195; B. Freyer-Schauenburg, "Io in Alexandria," *Mitteilungen des Deutschen Archäologischen Instituts. Römische Abteilung.* 90 (1983): 35–49; J. M. Davison, "Egyptian Influence on the Greek Legend of Io," in *The Archaeology, Geography, and History of the Egyptian Delta in Pharaonic Times. Proceedings of Colloquium, Oxford, 29–31 August 1988* (Oxford: Discussions in Egyptology, 1989), 61–74.

Ion (1) This mythical ancestor of the IONIAN GREEKS was the son of the god APOLLO. According to legend, Creusa, daughter of the Athenian king Erechtheus, was seduced by the god and bore Ion in secret. Apollo took Ion away. Later Ion discovered the secret of his birth and subsequently became king of ATHENS. The legend was the subject of an extant tragedy by EURIPIDES (ca. 410 B.C.E.).

See also HELLĒN.

Further reading: K. H. Lee, trans., *Ion/Euripides* (Warminster, U.K.: Aris & Phillips, 1997); Katarina Zacharia, *Converging Truths: Euripides' Ion and the Athenian Quest for Self-definition* (Leiden, Netherlands: E. J. Brill, 2003).

Ion (2) (ca. 490–421 B.C.E.) *Tragic playwright and social figure of the island of* CHIOS
A wealthy aristocrat, Ion wrote tragedies (all now lost) on mythological subjects for competition in the theater festivals at ATHENS. In 452 B.C.E., after winning first prize in two categories (tragedy and dithyramb) at the major annual festival known as the City Dionysia, he made a gift of Chian WINE to every Athenian citizen.

Ion was one of the more versatile writers in the Classical period. In addition to his dramatic plays, he also composed poetry, historical writings, and a set of lively memoirs, which survive as fragments quoted by later authors. Equally at home in Athens or Chios, he hobnobbed with some of the greatest Athenians of the mid-400s B.C.E., including the statesman KIMON (whose affability Ion contrasts with the coldness of PERIKLES) and the tragedian SOPHOKLES (whose charm and wit Ion conveys).

Ion embodied the spirit of the Athenian empire, which saw cultured and talented people flocking to Athens from all over the Greek world.

See also LYRIC POETRY; THEATER.

Further reading: D. Thomas Benediktson, *Literature and the Visual Arts in Ancient Greece and Rome* (Norman: University of Oklahoma Press, 2000).

Ionia This Greek-occupied central part of the west coast of ASIA MINOR was named for Greeks of the Ionian ethnic group who invaded around 1050–950 B.C.E., displacing prior, non-Greek inhabitants. In later centuries the Asian IONIAN GREEKS retained links with the most important Ionian-Greek city of old Greece, ATHENS.

By the 700s B.C.E. an Ionian League had been formed from 12 states of the Asia Minor coast. These were: the islands of CHIOS and SAMOS, and the mainland cities of PHOCAEA, Klazomenae, Erythrae, Teos, Kolophon, Lebedus, EPHESOS, Priēnē, Myus, and MILETUS. At least one other local city, Smyrna, could claim Ionian kinship but was not a league member. The league held meetings at the Panionium, a sanctuary of the god POSEIDON at Cape MYCALĒ. There were internal rivalries and even wars, especially between the two preeminent powers, Miletus and Samos.

In TRADE, naval power, and culture, Ionia was at the forefront of the early Greek world. The poet HOMER lived and composed in Ionia, possibly in Chios (ca. 750 B.C.E.). In the 600s and 500s B.C.E., Miletus and Phocaea planted colonies from the BLACK SEA to southern Spain, and traded with EGYPT and other non-Greek empires. The JEWS of the Levant knew Ionia as "Javan"—mentioned in the biblical book of Ezekiel (early 500s B.C.E.) for its exports of SLAVES and worked BRONZE. Woolen textiles were another prized Ionian export.

The term *Ionian Enlightenment* sometimes is used to describe the intellectual explosion that occurred, chiefly at Miletus, in the 500s B.C.E. There Western SCIENCE and PHILOSOPHY were born together, when THALES, ANAXIMANDER, and ANAXIMENES first tried to explain the world in rational, nonreligious terms. In Ionia there arose the grandest Greek temples of the 500s B.C.E., at Ephesos, Samos, and Didyma (near Miletus). The decorative schemes developed for such buildings are still employed today, in the Ionic order of ARCHITECTURE.

But this confident culture existed precariously alongside the restless Asiatic empires of the interior. The non-Greek kingdom of LYDIA warred constantly against the Ionians and finally conquered them under King CROESUS (mid-500s B.C.E.). Croesus dealt favorably with Ionia, but in 546 B.C.E. the Persian king CYRUS (1) rode out of the East to defeat Croesus and seize his kingdom.

Ionia, after brief resistance, became a tribute-paying part of the Persian Empire. Many Ionians left home; the populations of Phocaea and Teos sailed away en masse. Throughout the cities, the Persians installed unpopular Greek puppet rulers. After the doomed IONIAN REVOLT (499–493 B.C.E.), Persian rule was harshly reaffirmed.

In the Persian invasions of mainland Greece (490 and 480 B.C.E.), Ionian troops and ships' crews were made to fight as Persian levies against their fellow Greeks. In 479 B.C.E. a seaborne force of mainland Greeks landed in Ionia, beat a Persian army at the Battle of Mycale, and liberated Ionia.

The leadership of an exhausted Ionia now passed to Athens, which established the DELIAN LEAGUE as an Ionian kinship—based mutual alliance against PERSIA (478 B.C.E.). Eventually, however, the onus of tribute and the fading of the Persian threat served to disenchant the allies. Samos revolted spectacularly (but unsuccessfully) against Athens in 440 B.C.E., and once the tide had turned against Athens in the PELOPONNESIAN WAR (after 413 B.C.E.), Chios, Miletus, Ephesus, and other Ionian states went over to Athens's enemy, SPARTA.

After Athens's defeat by Sparta (404 B.C.E.), Ionian freedom was short-lived. Spartan overlordship was worse than Athenian, and in 386 B.C.E. Sparta cynically handed Ionia back to the Persians, by the terms of the KING'S PEACE. Ionia was liberated again in 334 B.C.E., by ALEXANDER THE GREAT's invasion of the Persian Empire. Under Alexander, the Ionian cities enjoyed DEMOCRACY and freedom from paying tribute.

Several Ionian cities, notably Ephesus and Smyrna, went on to thrive in the HELLENISTIC AGE (300–150 B.C.E.) and Roman eras. But Ionia as a distinctive culture was finished.

See also ANACREON; ANAXAGORAS; HECATAEUS; HERACLITUS; KALLIAS; PERSIAN WARS; PYTHAGORAS; XENOPHANES.

Further reading: H. M. Denham, *The Ionian Islands to the Anatolian Coast. A Sea-guide* (London: J. Murray, 1982); J. M. Balcer, "Fifth Century B.C. Ionia. A Frontier Redefined," *Revue des études anciennes* 87 (1985): 31–42; George Bean, *Aegean Turkey,* 2d ed. (London: Murray, 1989); K. Dimitrov, "The Greek Cities in Ionia, Karia, and the Western Black Sea Area during the Early Hellenistic Age," in *100 Jahre österreichische Forschungen in Ephesos. Akten des Symposions, Wien 1995,* edited by H. Friesinger

and F. Krinzinger (Vienna, 1999), 179–184; C. Souyoud-zoglou-Haywood, *The Ionian Islands in the Bronze Age and Early Iron Age, 3000–800 B.C.* (Liverpool, U.K.: Liverpool University Press, 1999).

Ionian Greeks This Greek cultural and linguistic group is distinct from other ethnic groups, such as the DORIAN GREEKS and AEOLIAN GREEKS. The adjective *Ionic* usually refers to dialect of the Ionians or to the distinctive architectural style—the Ionic order—that was developed in Ionia for monumental buildings of stone.

After the collapse of MYCENAEAN CIVILIZATION and the subsequent Greek migrations (around 1150–950 B.C.E.), the Ionians were left occupying various sites in and around the AEGEAN SEA—namely, ATHENS, EUBOEA, most of the CYCLADES islands, and IONIA (as it came to be called), on the west coast of ASIA MINOR. Starting in the mid-700s B.C.E., Ionian-Greek seafarers colonized parts of ITALY, SICILY, the BLACK SEA coasts, and the northwestern Aegean region known as CHALCIDICĒ, among other regions.

Claiming descent from a common ancestor, ION (1), the far-flung Ionian Greeks retained a sense of kinship. In Sicily and southern Italy, Ionian cities banded together for protection against hostile Dorian settlements. During the 400s B.C.E., imperial Athens made the propagandistic claim to be the protector of all the Ionian Greeks.

In contrast to the stolid Dorians, the Ionians had the reputation for being intellectual, artistic, unsoldierly, elaborate in dress, and luxury-loving. Intriguingly, Ionian societies—other than Athens—were thought to be the least conducive to HOMOSEXUALITY.

See also ARCHITECTURE; DELIAN LEAGUE; GREEK LANGUAGE.

Further reading: G. L. Huxley, *The Early Ionians* (New York: Humanities Press, 1966); H. D. Westlake, "Ionians in the Ionian War," *Classical Quarterly* 29 (1979): 9–44; C. J. Emlyn-Jones, *The Ionians and Hellenism: A Study of the Cultural Achievement of Early Greek Inhabitants of Asia Minor* (London: Routledge & Kegan Paul, 1980); J. H. M. Alty, "Dorians and Ionians," *Journal of Hellenistic Studies* 102 (1982): 1–14; Carl Roebuck, *Ionian Trade and Colonization* (Chicago: Ares, 1984).

Ionian Revolt This failed rebellion of the Greek cities of ASIA MINOR against the Persian king DARIUS (1) marks the beginning of the PERSIAN WARS. Emanating from the prosperous Greek region called IONIA, the revolt lasted more than five years (499–493 B.C.E.) and might have succeeded but for internal rifts and weak leadership. The war demonstrated to the Persians that, in order to secure their western frontier, they would have to invade and subjugate mainland Greece itself.

In the mid-500s B.C.E. the Greeks of Asia Minor and the eastern Aegean islands had been engulfed by the Persian Empire. Persian rule was moderate (in the absence of resistance), but the Greeks had to pay tribute and contribute ships, soldiers, and craftsmen to Persian wars and other projects. Seagoing states such as MILETUS, which had previously built up networks of TRADE, found commerce dampened by the Persians (who at this stage in their history were antimercantile). Greek discontent was rife—particularly against the Greek TYRANTS whom the Persians had set up as their puppet rulers in the cities.

Information about the revolt comes from the Greek historian HERODOTUS (ca. 435 B.C.E.). The rebellion began in an Ionian-Greek fleet that was returning home from naval duty for the Persians. The ships' crews and officers rose up and arrested those tyrants who were serving aboard as squadron commanders. The ringleader of this mutiny was Aristogoras of Miletus, himself one of the tyrants. Advised by his father-in-law, Histiaeus, Aristagoras became leader of the revolt.

The home cities followed. At SAMOS, CHIOS, LESBOS, and EPHESOS, tyrants were deposed in favor of DEMOCRACY. Two cities of mainland Greece, ATHENS and ERETRIA, sent warships as aid—an anti-Persian act that would later have dire consequences for both cities.

The Athenians and Eretrians sailed home again after an allied land raid against Sardis, the Persians' main base in Asia Minor (498 B.C.E.). Meanwhile the revolt spread to other Greek regions under Persian rule: BYZANTIUM, the HELLESPONT, and the Greek cities of CYPRUS.

The Persians subsequently launched a methodical counteroffensive. With a navy supplied by their subject state PHOENICIA, the Persians landed in Cyprus and besieged the rebel cities. As Persian armies campaigned through western Asia Minor, the erratic Aristagoras found himself unpopular with his fellow Greeks. He relinquished command and sailed to the north Aegean coast to prepare a refuge in case of defeat, but he was killed by native Thracians.

The climactic battle came in 494 B.C.E. Seeking to destroy the Persians at sea, the Greeks assembled a large fleet (353 warships) from the nine major states still combatant. But the Greek side was divided by jealousies and mistrust, while the Persians offered preferential treatment for quick surrender. When the Greek fleet rowed out to fight the Battle of Lade, off Samos, 49 Samian warships hoisted sail and fled. Most of the other Greek ships followed, leaving only the Chians and Milesians to fight and lose.

The Persians took fierce vengeance on the defeated Greeks. Samos was spared, but Miletus was besieged, sacked, and depopulated, its people transported to interior PERSIA or sold as SLAVES. Returning eventually to their more usual leniency, the Persians reduced the cities' tribute and replaced the old systems of tyrant puppets with democratic governments. But Ionia—the birthplace of Western SCIENCE and PHILOSOPHY—had ceased to exist as a culture or a mercantile power.

See also MARATHON; PHRYNICHUS; WARFARE, NAVAL.

Further reading: Daniel Gillis, *Collaboration with the Persians* (Wiesbaden, Germany: Steiner, 1979); P. B. Georges, "Persian Ionia under Darius: The Revolt Reconsidered," *Historia* 49 (2000): 1–39.

Ionian Sea This name, both modern and traditional, refers to the southward extension of the Adriatic Sea, which separates western Greece from southern ITALY and eastern SICILY. Principal islands in this sea are ITHACA and Corfu (ancient CORCYRA).

Confusingly, the Ionian Sea is nowhere near the ancient Greek territory of IONIA (located some 300 miles to the east, on the ASIA MINOR coast). Nor was the Ionian Sea region inhabited by Greeks of the Ionian ethnic group. The name probably derives from the Greek term *Ionian Gulf* (Ionios Kolpos), used by ancient writers to denote the Adriatic. That term possibly dates back to the 800s–700s B.C.E. when the Adriatic was being explored by Ionian-ethnic Greek seafarers from EUBOEA.

See also COLONIZATION; IONIAN GREEKS.

Further reading: George Gissing, *By the Ionian Sea* (London: Richards Press, 1963); John Keahey, *A Sweet and Glorious Land: Revisiting the Ionian Sea* (New York: Thomas Dunne Books, 2000).

Ionic dialect *See* GREEK LANGUAGE.

Ionic order *See* ARCHITECTURE.

Iphigeneia In MYTH, she was the daughter of KLYTEMNESTRA and AGAMEMNON, king of MYCENAE and grand marshal of the Greek army in the TROJAN WAR. At the war's outset the Greek fleet assembled at Aulis—a port in BOEOTIA, in the Euripus channel—but departure for TROY was perpetually delayed by contrary winds, sent by the hostile goddess ARTEMIS. Agamemnon, learning through a seer the divine cause of his troubles, agreed to sacrifice his daughter Iphigeneia to propitiate the goddess' anger. Iphigeneia was summoned to Aulis on the pretense that she was to marry the Greek champion ACHILLES; on arrival, she was either killed or (in some versions) carried away by the goddess Artemis to safety among the distant Tauroi, a tribe on the Crimean peninsula of the northern BLACK SEA. The Athenian playwright EURIPIDES follows the latter version in his tragedy *Iphigeneia at Tauris* (ca. 413 B.C.E.). In any case, this affair was the cause of Klytemnestra's hatred toward her husband, and she then schemed to murder him after his return from Troy.

Further reading: C. A. E. Luschnig, *Tragic Aporia: A Study of Euripides' Iphigenia at Aulis* (Berwick, Australia: Aureal, 1988); W. S. Merwin and George E. Dimock Jr., trans., *Iphigeneia in Aulis/Euripides* (New York: Oxford University Press, 1992); Richmond Lattimore, trans., *Iphigeneia in Tauris/Euripides* (New York: Oxford University Press, 1992); Maria Holmberg Lübeck, *Iphigeneia, Agamemnon's Daughter: A Study of Ancient Conceptions in Greek Myth and Literature Associated with the Atrides* (Stockholm: Almqvist & Wiksell, 1993).

iron   Cheaper and easier to acquire than BRONZE, iron began replacing bronze in mainland Greece around 1050 B.C.E. as the metal of choice for swords, spear-points, ax heads, hammerheads, and other cutting or striking tools.

As produced by ancient foundries, iron and bronze were about equal in their toughness; iron's advantage lay in the fact that it was far more plentiful than bronze, both for the Greeks and for other ancient peoples. Bronze, on the other hand, is an alloy of copper and tin, and tin is very scarce in the eastern Mediterranean. Ancient Greek bronze production depended on long-range routes of TRADE, to provide tin. But iron ore—which needs only refining, not mixing—could be found in parts of mainland Greece and ASIA MINOR, among other Mediterranean locales.

Ancient iron forging involved repeated heating and hammering of the metal in order to refine it, weld it into workable quantities, and finally shape it. This process—far different from the casting of molten bronze—apparently was invented around 1500 B.C.E. by non-Greek peoples in the region now known as Armenia. At first the technology was kept secret and monopolized by the Hittite overlords of Armenia and Asia Minor. But after the Hittite Empire's collapse around 1200 B.C.E., ironworking quickly spread through eastern Mediterranean regions, both Greek and non-Greek. This was the era of social upheaval and migration that historians refer to as the early Iron Age. One reason why iron-working spread amid violence was that iron democratized warfare: A warrior no longer needed to be rich, or a rich man's follower, in order to have a superior weapon.

The arrival of ironworking in Greece can be connected to the final disappearance of MYCENAEAN CIVILIZATION and the invasion of the DORIAN GREEKS around 1100–1000 B.C.E. Either the Dorians used iron weapons in conquering Greece or (more likely) they arrived with bronze weapons but, having destroyed the old Mycenaean trade routes, found themselves without bronze supplies and immediately embraced the new metal. The Dorians possibly learned iron forging via maritime contact with the eastern Mediterranean island of CYPRUS, which was a meeting place of East and West.

The foremost early Greek ironworking cities included ATHENS, CORINTH, CHALCIS, and ERETRIA. Iron's importance in this economy can be seen in the Greeks' use of iron rods as a primitive form of currency. Only gradually were these replaced by the use of coins, in the 500s B.C.E.

By the 600s B.C.E. the Greeks had developed seaborne trade routes to major iron sources outside of Greece, in the western Mediterranean. These locales included western ITALY (where the ETRUSCANS traded with iron ore mined on the island of Elba) and southern Spain.

Ancient foundries never developed the technique, mastered during the European Middle Ages, of casting iron—that is, of heating iron hot enough to pour into a mold. For this application, bronze remained the premier metal. Throughout antiquity, bronze continued to supply such items as military breastplates, helmets, decorative tripods, and SCULPTURE, where casting or intricate shaping was required.

See also COINAGE; HEPHAISTOS; PITHECUSAE; WARFARE, LAND.

Further reading: Michail Yu Treister, *The Role of Metals in Ancient Greek History* (Leiden, Netherlands: E. J. Brill, 1996).

Iron Age   *See* IRON.

Isaeus (ca. 420–350 B.C.E.)   *Greek orator, active at ATHENS*
Isaeus may have been a native Athenian. He is said to have been a pupil of the orator ISOKRATES and a teacher of the great DEMOSTHENES (1). Of Isaeus's speeches, 11 survive. They are all courtroom speeches, dealing with disputed inheritance and other civil matters. Isaeus provides us with much of our information about Athenian laws of inheritance in the 300s B.C.E.

See also LAWS AND LAW COURTS; RHETORIC.

Further reading: Richard F. Wevers, *Isaeus: Chronology, Prosopography, and Social History* (The Hague: Mouton, 1969); John Frederic Dobson, *The Greek Orators* (Chicago: Ares, 1974); Stephen Usher, *Greek Oratory: Tradition and Originality* (New York: Oxford University Press, 1999); Deborah Kamen, *Isaeus' Orations 2 and 6* (Bryn Mawr, Pa.: Thomas Library, Bryn Mawr College, 2000).

Ischia   *See* PITHECUSAE.

Isokrates (436–338 B.C.E.)   *Influential Athenian orator, educator, and pamphleteer*
Isokrates' importance for Greek history is in his attempts to make the Greeks unite in a military crusade against the Persian empire. His most significant written work was his *Philippus,* or *Address to Philip* (346 B.C.E.). This work,

which survives today, was an "open letter" addressed to King PHILIP II of MACEDON, calling on the king to lead such a campaign. The letter surely came as a propaganda blessing to the opportunistic Philip, who was preparing to subdue Greece. Perhaps it was Isokrates who first inspired Philip's further ambition to conquer PERSIA (an ambition eventually fulfilled by Philip's son ALEXANDER THE GREAT).

Born into a wealthy family, Isokrates studied RHETORIC under the famous GORGIAS. Like certain other Greek orators, Isokrates wrote speeches for his clients to deliver themselves. He rarely, if ever, argued in court or spoke in the Athenian political ASSEMBLY. But his indirect influence was great. His students of rhetoric included the future historian Androtion and the future orator ISAEUS. At some point Isokrates had a school on the island of CHIOS.

It was the news of the humiliating terms of the KING'S PEACE (386 B.C.E.) that fired Isokrates' vision of the Greeks uniting to liberate the Greek cities of ASIA MINOR. Isokrates' first published pamphlet on the subject was the *Panegyricus* (380 B.C.E.), an idealistic tract that pictured ATHENS and SPARTA leading the crusade. The *Panegyricus* strongly anticipates the letter to Philip, written 24 years later. In the intervening years Isokrates somewhat shamelessly addressed similar pleas to other rulers of the Greek world, including the Spartan king AGESILAUS and the Syracusan tyrant DIONYSIUS (1).

But Isokrates' idealism could not stem Philip's ambition of conquering Greece. After the failure of a final plea following the Battle of CHAERONEA (338 B.C.E.), the 98-year-old Isokrates starved himself to death.

Ancient writers knew of 60 works by Isokrates; we possess 21. Six of these are court speeches; the rest are political pamphlets. He wrote with an elegant, masterful style, including careful choice of words and expressions. The rhythm of his prose greatly influenced later writers, both Greek and Roman.

See also EDUCATION; LAWS AND LAW COURTS.

Further reading: Yun Lee Too, *The Rhetoric of Identity in Isocrates: Text, Power, Pedagogy* (New York: Cambridge University Press, 1995); Takis Poulakos, *Speaking for the Polis: Isocrates' Rhetorical Education* (Columbia: University of South Carolina Press, 1997).

Isthmian Games This was one of the four Greek-international sports-and-religious festivals; the other three were the OLYMPIC, PYTHIAN, and NEMEAN GAMES. The Isthmian Games, or Isthmia, took place every two years at CORINTH (located on the isthmus of central Greece). The festival honored the god POSEIDON, and the ritual prize for the victors was a garland of wild celery. The games were first organized during the early 500s B.C.E.

Further reading: Elizabeth Gebhard, "The Sanctuary of Poseidon on the Isthmus of Corinth and the Isthmian Games," in *Mind and Body: Athletic Contests in Ancient Greece,* edited by Olga Tzachou-Alexandri (Athens: Ministry of Culture, 1989).

isthmus *See* CORINTH; PELOPONNESE.

Italy Like SICILY, Italy contained a number of powerful Greek cities in ancient times. Two separate regions of the Italian peninsula saw intensive COLONIZATION by the land- and commerce-hungry Greeks, around 750–550 B.C.E. One region is now called Campania, on the Bay of Naples on the Italian west coast. There the Euboean settlement of CUMAE became the first Greek landfall in Italy and one of the very earliest Greek colonies anywhere (around 750 B.C.E.). The attraction was TRADE with the powerful ETRUSCANS.

The other major focus of COLONIZATION was in the south, along the south coast of the Italian "toe" and "instep." There the Spartan colony of TARAS (founded around 700 B.C.E.) occupied the best harbor in Italy, on what is now called the Gulf of Taranto. Other Greek cities of south Italy included SYBARIS, CROTON, RHEGIUM, LOCRI, Metapontum, and Siris. The main attraction at these sites was farmland, which the Greeks seized from the native Brutii and Lucanii.

The Greek name Italia—applying originally only to the south coast of the Italian "toe"—was probably a Greek rendering of a local Italian place-name: Vitelia, "calf land." The "heel" of Italy originally had a different Greek name, Iapygia. Later the name Italia, passing into the Latin language of the conquering Romans, came to be applied to the entire peninsula, north to the Alps.

To the Greeks of southern Italy, coming from mountainous and overpopulated Greece, the land of Italy seemed to extend forever. The Greeks gave the region a nickname—Great Greece, Megalē Hellas—or (as it has been more traditionally known, in its Latin name) Magna Graecia.

By the 400s B.C.E. the Italian Greeks were subject to influence and control by the successive rulers of the Sicilian-Greek city of SYRACUSE. In the 200s B.C.E., after centuries of war with each other and with their Italian neighbors, the Greek cities of Italy became absorbed by the expansionist power of ROME.

See also AGATHOKLES; DIONYSIUS (1); HIERON (1); PARMENIDES; PITHECUSAE; POSEIDONIA; PYTHAGORAS.

Further reading: Margaret Guido, *Southern Italy. An Archaeological Guide. The Main Prehistoric, Greek, and Roman Sites* (Park Ridge, N.J.: Noyes Press, 1983); S. C. Bakhuizen, "Italy and Sicily in the Perception of the Early Greeks," *Mededelingen van het Nederlands Instituut te Rome* 48 (1988): 9–25; S. L. Dyson, "Reconstructing the

Italy and Sicily

Landscape of Rural Italy," in *Earth Patterns. Essays on Landscape Archaeology* (Charlottesville: University Press of Virginia, 1990), 245–253.

Ithaca   This small (44 square miles) island of the northwest coast of Greece is located outside the Gulf of Patras. Beautiful but unfertile, its coastline fretted with inlets of sea, Ithaca was inhabited throughout ancient times yet played almost no role in Greek history. It is best remembered as the domain of the Greek king ODYSSEUS. Archaeological excavations have uncovered POTTERY and house foundations from the Mycenaean era, confirming the island's importance around 1200 B.C.E., when Odysseus would have lived.

See also IONIAN SEA; MYCENAEAN CIVILIZATION.

Further reading: John Victor Luce, *Celebrating Homer's Landscapes: Troy and Ithaca Revisited* (New Haven, Conn.: Yale University Press, 1998).

Ixion A villain of Greek MYTH, Ixion was a prince of the Lapith tribe of THESSALY who murdered his father-in-law so as to avoid paying the bride price for the MARRIAGE. Although pardoned by the great god ZEUS, Ixion next schemed to seduce Zeus's wife, the goddess HERA. But Zeus, aware of Ixion's plan, deceived Ixion with a facsimile of Hera, shaped from a cloud. (Supposedly Ixion's semen impregnated the cloud-Hera, which gave birth to the race of CENTAURS.)

At Zeus's order, Ixion was whipped until he repeated the words "Benefactors deserve honor." Then he was tied to a fiery wheel and sent spinning through the sky—or through the Underworld—for eternity. Ixion was one of several great sinners of Greek legend—others include SISYPHUS and TANTALUS—whose crime involved betraying the friendship of the gods.

See also AFTERLIFE; HUBRIS.

Further reading: D. R. Blickman, "The Myth of Ixion and Pollution for Homicide in Archaic Greece," *Classical Journal* 81 (1985–1986): 193–208.

Jason (1) (Greek: Iason, "healer") In MYTH, this Thessalian hero led the Argonauts (sailors of the ship *Argo*) to the distant land of Colchis, to acquire the fabulous Golden Fleece. The tale of the Argonauts is mentioned in HOMER's *Odyssey* (written down around 750 B.C.E.) and elaborated in PINDAR's fourth Pythian ode (462 B.C.E.), but the main source is APOLLONIUS's clever Alexandrian epic, the *Argonautica* (ca. 245 B.C.E.).

The Argonaut tale seems to combine two different layers: (1) a very ancient legend going back to Mycenaean times (second millennium B.C.E.), of significance for Mycenaean centers in THESSALY and BOEOTIA; and (2) later traders' tales of the Sea of MARMARA and the BLACK SEA, developed during the Greek exploration of that region in the 700s and 600s B.C.E. In the earlier version (now lost), the Argonauts may have sailed to a fabled land called Aea, somewhere at the edge of the world. But the surviving version has the Argonauts voyaging to Colchis, a real (although distant), non-Greek region on the eastern Black Sea. (Colchis was an emporium for caravans from north-central Asia, and by the 500s B.C.E. the Milesian Greeks had a TRADE depot there.)

In the myth, Jason was the son of Aeson and heir to the kingship of the Thessalian city of Iolcus (modern Volos, the region's only seaport). As a child, he was smuggled away by his mother after Aeson's stepbrother Pelias had seized the throne. Raised in the Thessalian wilds by the wise Cheiron—the centaur who regularly tutors mythical young heroes—Jason returned as a young man to Iolcus, to claim his birthright. He entered the city with one sandal missing, having lost it crossing a river. Pelias—knowing by that foretold sign to beware of this man—immediately persuaded the newcomer to go out in search of the Golden Fleece.

This fleece was the skin of winged, golden-fleeced ram, which in prior times the gods had supplied to carry the young Phrixus and Hellē (the children of the Boeotian hero Athamas) away from their evil stepmother. Carried eastward through the sky, Hellē had lost her grip and fallen off, drowning in the waterway thenceforth called the HELLESPONT (in her honor). Her brother had safely reached the far-off land of Colchis, where he sacrificed the ram to ZEUS the Savior.

Jason, aided by his divine patron, HERA, then assembled an expedition consisting of the noblest heroes in Greece. The roster varies, but the most familiar names include: the Calydonian hero MELEAGER; the female warrior ATALANTA; the brothers PELEUS (father of ACHILLES) and Telamon (father of AJAX [1]); the Thracian musician ORPHEUS; the Spartan twins CASTOR AND POLYDEUCES; the twins Calais and Zetes (sons of the North Wind); and the greatest of heroes, HERAKLES (who soon gets "written out" of the story, so as not to monopolize the adventures).

Their ship was the *Argo*, built by a shipwright named Argos, who went along on the expedition. The Argonauts were sometimes called by the name MINYANS (*Minuai*), which was also the name of the ruling family of the Boeotian city ORCHOMENOS. These Boeotian Minyans may have figured in the early (lost) version of the myth.

Sailing northeastward from Greece to the Black Sea, the heroes had several adventures. They dawdled for a year on the Aegean island of Lemnos, busily impregnating the man-hungry Lemnian WOMEN, who had all murdered their husbands out of resentment of the latter's Thracian slave girls. Finally continuing to the Sea of Marmara, the Argonauts were welcomed by the native king Cyzicus, but he was killed by them in a mishap. Soon

Herakles was separated from the expedition, having gone ashore to search for his page, Hylas.

Still in the Marmara, the Argonauts rescued the old, blind Thracian king Phineus who, for some offense, was living in eternal torment. The HARPIES, hideous winged female demons, would relentlessly fly down to snatch away his food and leave behind their feces. The Argonauts Calais and Zetes, who could fly, chased away the harpies forever. In gratitude, Phineus gave Jason advice on how to slip through the Symplegades, the Clashing Rocks (which are a mythical rendering of the narrow BOSPORUS channel, leading into the Black Sea).

At the eastward end of the Black Sea, the adventurers reached Colchis, where the evil king Aeëtes set his conditions for surrendering the fleece. One of the Argonauts must plow a field with a pair of fire-breathing BRONZE bulls and sow the magical dragon's teeth (remnants of the hero CADMUS's adventure at THEBES), which Aeëtes had in his possession. From the seeds, there would arise armed men, who must be conquered.

Aeëtes was sure that these conditions could never be met. But his sorceress daughter MEDEA, having fallen in love with Jason (at APHRODITE's hand, from Hera's bidding), provided the hero with a magic ointment to make him invulnerable for a day. Thus Jason was able to fulfill Aeëtes' terms. Then the Argonauts fled Colchis with the fleece and Medea (who had stolen the fleece for them after charming to sleep the dragon that guarded it).

Aeëtes led his ships in pursuit. But Medea, who had brought her young brother Apsyrtus aboard the *Argo*, now murdered the child and cut him up, throwing the body sections into the sea. Aeëtes and his followers halted, collecting the royal corpse for burial.

The Argonauts returned to Thessaly, either the way they had come or via a fantastical route up the Danube and into the Mediterranean. Apollonius's *Argonautica* ends with the return to Iolcus. Other writers describe how Jason and Medea took vengeance on Pelias by fatally tricking him into climbing into a cauldron of boiling water that was supposed to rejuvenate him.

Driven from Iolcus by Pelias's son, Jason and Medea hung up the Golden Fleece in the temple of Zeus at Orchomenos. They settled at CORINTH, where the final chapter of Jason's drama was played out, as described in EURIPIDES' tragedy *Medea* (431 B.C.E.). Jason divorced Medea, intending to marry Glauce, daughter of the Corinthian king Creon. Medea, insane with rage, avenged herself by killing Glauce, Creon, and her own two children by Jason. She then fled to ATHENS. Jason, meanwhile, had set up the *Argo* on land and dedicated it to the god POSEIDON. As he slept beneath the ship's stern one day, a section fell off and killed him.

See also CENTAURS; CYZICUS; EPIC POETRY; SHIPS AND SEAFARING.

Further reading: Tim Severin, *The Jason Voyage: The Quest for the Golden Fleece* (New York: Simon and Schus-

ter, 1985); G. J. Smith and A. J. Smith, "Jason's Golden Fleece," *Oxford Journal of Archaeology* 11 (1992): 119–120; R. L. Hunter, *The Argonautica of Apollonius: Literary Studies* (New York: Cambridge University Press, 1993); James J. Clauss, *The Best of the Argonauts: The Redefinition of the Epic Hero in Book 1 of Apollonius' Argonautica* (Berkeley: University of California Press, 1993); Peter Green, trans., *The Argonautika by Apollonios Rhodius* (Berkeley: University of California Press, 1997); Calvin S. Byre, *A Reading of Apollonius Rhodius' Argonautica: The Poetics of Uncertainty* (Lewiston, N.Y.: Edwin Mellen Press, 2002).

Jason (2) (d. 370 B.C.E.) *Tyrant of Pherae in* THESSALY, *reigning ca. 385–370 B.C.E.*
In a period of political turmoil throughout Greece, he united Thessaly under himself and tried to forge it into a major power. An ally of THEBES, he negotiated a treaty between Thebes and SPARTA after the Spartan defeat at LEUKTRA (371 B.C.E.) but was assassinated the following year. In history he stands as a precursor to the Macedonian king PHILIP II (reigned 359–336 B.C.E.), who may have modeled himself on Jason to some extent. In warfare, Jason developed the use of primitive siege artillery—a military science later taken up by Philip.

See also TYRANTS; WARFARE, SIEGE.

Further reading: A. G. Woodhead, "IG II² 43 and Jason of Pherae," *American Journal of Archaeology* 61 (1957): 367–373; J. Mandel, "Jason, the Tyrant of Pherae, Tagus of Thessaly, as Reflected in Ancient Sources and Modern Literature. The Image of the New Tyrant," *Rivista storica dell'antichità* 10 (1980): 47–77; F. W. Mitchel, "The Rasura of IG II² 43. Jason, the Pheraian Demos, and the Athenian League," *Ancient World* 9 (1984): 39–58.

Jews The Jews and the Greeks, despite their respective importance in ancient history, had little to do with each other prior to the 300s B.C.E. An independent Jewish kingdom, with its capital at Jerusalem, ceased to exist in 586 B.C.E, when the Babylonians captured Jerusalem and removed the population to Babylon. This Babylonian Exile ended in 539 B.C.E., when the Persian king CYRUS (1) conquered much of the Near East. A proponent of religious freedom, CYRUS permitted his new Jewish subjects to return to their homeland in the Levant, though not all did so.

It was now that the Jews came into contact with another subject-people of the Persians—Greeks from IONIA, in western ASIA MINOR. The biblical prophet Ezekiel (late 500s B.C.E.) wrote disdainfully of the profit-minded Greek traders of "Javan" (Ionia), trading in SLAVES and worked BRONZE. The Greek historian HERODOTUS (ca. 435 B.C.E.) knew of the Jews—he called them "Palestinian Syrians"—and listed them among the naval levies serving in the Persian king XERXES' invasion of Greece in 480 B.C.E.

The destruction of the Persian Empire by the Macedonian king ALEXANDER THE GREAT between 334 and 323 B.C.E. left Macedonian and Greek governors over the various Jewish pockets of the Near East. By about 300 B.C.E. Alexander's domain had fragmented into the large Greco-Macedonian kingdoms of the HELLENISTIC AGE. Ptolemaic EGYPT seized Jerusalem and the southern Levant, while the SELEUCID EMPIRE ruled Babylon and other Jewish-inhabited regions. Consequently Jewish immigrants flooded such newly founded Hellenistic cities as Egyptian ALEXANDRIA (1) and Seleucid ANTIOCH. Alexandria in particular developed an important Jewish minority that occasionally endured ethnic violence from the Greek population.

Jewish monotheism was not deeply affected by the polytheistic RELIGION of the Greeks. However, the glamorous Greek style of life attracted many of the wealthier Jews, creating an assimilated, pro-Greek class. This process occurred not only in the Hellenistic cities but also in Jerusalem itself (where at least one Greek-style GYMNASIUM and THEATER were each built in the 100s B.C.E.). Greek nomenclature infiltrated Judaism; the word *synagogue,* for example, is Greek ("assembly place"). Greek influence can be seen in several surviving customs in the ceremonial Jewish Passover meal. The ritual drinking of cups of WINE and the prayerbook references to dining in a reclining position, for example, are best understood as elements borrowed from the Greek drinking party known as the SYMPOSIUM.

With Greek the language of commerce, administration, and secular law in the Hellenistic kingdoms, the emigrant Jewish communities began to forget the Hebrew tongue. In Alexandria this process had taken hold by around 260 B.C.E., when certain books of the Jewish Bible began appearing in Greek translation. The complete Greek translation of the Jewish Bible—a work supposedly ordered by the Macedonian-Egyptian king PTOLEMY (2) II and conducted by 70 scholars—became known as the Septuagint (from the Latin *septuaginta,* "seventy"). In the Greco-Roman world of later centuries, the Septuagint contributed greatly to the survival of Judaism and the spread of Christianity.

In 198 B.C.E. the Seleucid king ANTIOCHUS (2) III conquered much of the Levant, including the Jewish heartland. There the next generation saw the best-known, tragic encounter between Jews and Greeks—the Maccabean Revolt of 167–164 B.C.E., which is commemorated in the Jewish festival of Hanukkah. The biblical First Book of Maccabees describes how certain rural Jews rebelled after the Seleucid king Antiochus IV tried to impose Greek religious customs and convert the temple at Jerusalem into a temple of the Greek god ZEUS. The spreading revolt was led by Judas Maccabee ("the hammer"), of the priestly Hasmonaean family. Judas defeated Seleucid armies in battle and recaptured the Jerusalem temple, but the rebellion decayed into a Jewish civil war of anti-Greek versus pro-Greek factions. Finally, in 142 B.C.E., the rebels ejected the Seleucid garrison from the citadel at Jerusalem. For the next 80 years the Jews of the Levant comprised a sovereign nation ruled by a Hasmonaean dynasty. But in 63 B.C.E. the country fell to the Roman legions of Pompey the Great.

The Romans established local governors to control their new province of Judea, and the Jews did not fare well under this management. The Romans desired conformity from the inhabitants of their empire, and many old Jewish customs suffered as a result. Like many other growing religious sects, including Christianity, Judaism seems to have been both fascinating and threatening to the Romans, and Jews were often persecuted for their beliefs and traditions.

Much of our knowledge about Judaism in the late first century B.C.E. and first century C.E. comes from a Greek writer named Philo, called Iudaeus, "the Jew." He visited Rome in 39 C.E. as an ambassador to the Emperor Caligula, representing the Jewish people and their anger over an imperial edict that they must erect statues of the emperor in their synagogues. A scholar and philosopher, Philo wrote several works in the style of Plato, mostly concerned with blending the tenets of Platonism and Judaism.

Further reading: M. Stern, *Greek and Latin Authors on Jews and Judaism. Edited with Introduction, Translations, and Commentary. 1. From Herodotus to Plutarch* (Jerusalem: Israel Academy of Sciences and Humanities, 1976); S. Applebaum, *Jews and Greeks in Ancient Cyrene* (Leiden, Netherlands: E. J. Brill, 1979); A. D. Momigliano, "Greek Culture and the Jews," in *The Legacy of Greece. A New Appraisal,* edited by M. I. Finley (New York: Oxford University Press, 1981), 325–346; C. Zuckerman, "Hellenistic Politeumata and the Jews. A Reconsideration," *Scripta Classica Israelica* 8–9 (1985–1988): 171–185; J. Reynolds and R. Tannenbaum, *Jews and God-fearers at Aphrodisias. Greek Inscriptions with Commentary* (Cambridge: Cambridge Philological Society, 1987); Elias J. Bickerman, *The Jews in the Greek Age* (Cambridge, Mass.: Harvard University Press, 1988); D. S. Barrett, "Ancient Hellenism and the Jews. A Study in Attitudes and Acculturation," in *Greek Colonists and Native Populations. Proceedings of the First Australian Congress of Classical Archaeology. Sydney, 9–14 July 1985* (New York: Oxford University Press, 1990), 543–550; D. R. Edwards, *Religion and Power. Pagans, Jews, and Christians in the Greek East* (New York: Oxford University Press, 1996); M. Williams, ed., *The Jews Among the Greeks and Romans. A Sourcebook* (Baltimore: Johns Hopkins University Press, 1998); M. Goodman, ed., *Jews in a Graeco-Roman World* (Oxford: Clarendon Press, 1998); H. G. Snyder, *Teachers and Texts in the Ancient World: Philosophers, Jews, and Christians* (London: Routledge, 2000).

Jocasta   See OEDIPUS.

Kallias (Callias) (400s B.C.E.) *Athenian nobleman and diplomat, active in the early and mid-fifth century B.C.E.*
Kallias's family was the richest in ATHENS, renting out slave labor to the state SILVER mine at Laurion. Despite his upper-class background, Kallias became a political follower of the radical democrat PERIKLES. During Perikles' preeminence, Kallias was the foremost diplomat for Athens.

Kallias made at least one embassy to King Artaxerxes I of PERSIA, in about 461 B.C.E. Most modern scholars accept the theory, previously disputed, that in about 449 B.C.E. Kallias negotiated an end to the Greek-Persian hostilities known as the PERSIAN WARS. Apparently the Peace of Kallias in part protected the Athenian-allied Greek cities of western ASIA MINOR, prohibiting the Persians from sailing or marching west past certain set boundaries. For their part, the Athenians may have agreed to dismantle the fortifications of the Asia Minor Greek cities.

See also DELIAN LEAGUE; IONIA; SLAVES.

Further reading: J. Walsh, "The Authenticity and the Dates of the Peace of Callias and the Congress Decrees," *Chiron* 11 (1981): 31–63; E. Badian, "The Peace of Callias," *Journal of Hellenic Studies* 107 (1987): 1–39; Lisa Kallet-Marx, "The Kallias Decree, Thucydides, and the Outbreak of the Peloponnesian War," *Classical Quarterly* 39 (1989): 94–113; A. B. Bosworth, "Plutarch, Callisthenes, and the Peace of Callias," *Journal of Hellenic Studies* 110 (1990): 1–13; R. A. Moysey, "Thucydides, Kimon, and the Peace of Kallias," *Ancient History Bulletin* 5 (1991): 30–35; L. J. Samons II, "Kimon, Kallias, and Peace with Persia," *Historia* 47 (1998): 129–140.

Kassander (Cassander) (Greek: Kassandros) (ca. 360–297 B.C.E.) *Macedonian general and ruler*

Kassander was one of the several DIADOCHI (Successors) who carved up the empire of ALEXANDER THE GREAT after the latter's death in 323 B.C.E. He was the son of the Macedonian general ANTIPATER, who served as regent in MACEDON during Alexander's eastward campaigns (334–323 B.C.E.). Kassander joined Alexander's army in Asia in 324 B.C.E. He and the king seem to have disliked each other bitterly, and Kassander is mentioned by ancient writers as a suspect in theories that Alexander died from poisoning. After Antipater's death (319 B.C.E.), Kassander seized control of Macedon and most of Greece. He executed Alexander's mother, Olympias, Alexander's widow, Roxane, and Alexander's young son, Alexander III.

In the following years Kassander joined the other secessionist Diadochi—SELEUCOS (1), PTOLEMY (1), and LYSIMACHUS—in resisting the efforts of ANTIGONUS (1) to reunite Alexander's empire. After Kassander died, his dynasty in Macedon lasted only a few years before falling to the descendants of Antigonus.

Further reading: Daniel Ogden, *Polygamy, Prostitutes, and Death: The Hellenistic Dynasties* (London: Duckworth with the Classical Press of Wales, 1999).

Kerberos (Cerberus) In MYTH, this monstrous dog guarded the inner bank of the river Styx, at the entrance to the Underworld. According to HESIOD's epic poem the *Theogony*, Kerberos had 50 heads. A later, more familiar version gave him three heads and outgrowths of snakes. Kerberos would fawn on the ghosts arriving at the infernal kingdom, but became vicious toward anyone who tried to leave.

Kerberos was the target of HERAKLES' eleventh Labor. The hero visited the Underworld and won permission from the god HADES to bring the dog temporarily to the upper world. Dragging Kerberos to the city of TIRYNS, Herakles mischievously frightened his taskmaster, King Eurystheus. This was a favorite scene in ancient Greek artwork. One famous Athenian black-figure vase (530s B.C.E.), now in the Louvre, shows the timid king hiding inside a storage jar as the hound of Hell is led in.

See also AFTERLIFE.

Further reading: Bernard Evslin, *Cerberus* (New York: Chelsea House, 1987).

Kimon (Cimon) (ca. 505–450 B.C.E.) *Athenian soldier and conservative statesman in the 460s B.C.E.*
Kimon briefly dominated Athenian politics but succumbed to the failure of his pro-Spartan policy. He was the political enemy of the radical democrats, and his decline after 462 B.C.E. marked the rise of the young left-wing politician PERIKLES. In foreign policy, Kimon was the last great Athenian enemy of PERSIA, and his death ushered in a Greek-Persian peace treaty that officially concluded the PERSIAN WARS.

Kimon was born into a rich and eminent family, the Philaïds. His father was the Athenian soldier MILTIADES; his mother, Hegesipyle, was daughter of a Thracian king. By the 470s B.C.E., Kimon was regularly being elected to the office of general. He assisted ARISTIDES in the organization of the DELIAN LEAGUE (ca. 478 B.C.E.), and from 476 to 462 B.C.E. he was the premier Athenian soldier, leading the league's expeditions against the Persians. He became known particularly as a sea commander.

Kimon's height of success came in 469 or 466 B.C.E. (the exact date is unknown) when, with 200 league warships, he totally destroyed a Persian fleet and army at the River Eurymedon, midway along the south coast of ASIA MINOR. In purely military terms, the Eurymedon was the greatest Greek victory over Persia prior to the campaigns of ALEXANDER THE GREAT (334–323 B.C.E.).

At home, this success established Kimon in Athenian politics. Gracious and well-connected (his first or second wife, Isodice, was of the powerful Alcmaeonid clan), Kimon now emerged as leader of the conservative opposition. He blocked left-wing reforms and advocated an old-fashioned policy of hostility toward Persia and friendship with SPARTA. He even gave one of his sons the striking name Lacedaemonius, "Spartan."

Kimon's downfall came after he persuaded the ASSEMBLY to send him with an Athenian infantry force to assist the Spartans against their rebellious subjects, the Messenians (462 B.C.E.). This expedition ended in fiasco; the Spartans—fighting a serf rebellion—apparently found the Athenian soldiers' pro-democratic sentiments alarming and sent the Athenians home. Humiliated, Kimon now saw his conservative party swept out of power by democratic reforms sponsored by EPHIALTES and Perikles. In the following year, 461 B.C.E., the angry Athenians voted to ostracize Kimon.

Although the OSTRACISM law allowed a victim to return home after 10 years, this event ended Kimon's power and policies. Soon Athens began a full-fledged war against Sparta and its allies (460 B.C.E.). In 457 B.C.E., when the Athenian army was about to battle the Spartans near Tanagra, in BOEOTIA, the exiled Kimon arrived, asking permission to fight alongside his countrymen. Permission was refused but, according to one story, he was specially recalled to Athens soon after.

Kimon died while leading Athenian troops against the Persians in CYPRUS. He was remembered for his nobility and bravery, but his policies were at odds with Athens's destiny as a radical democracy that would dominate the rest of Greece.

See also ALCMAEONIDS; KALLIAS; MESSENIA; WARFARE, NAVAL.

Further reading: Plutarch, *Life of Kimon,* translated by A. Blamire (London: Institute of Classical Studies, University of London, 1989); Johan Henrik Schreiner, *Hellanikos, Thukydides and the Era of Kimon* (Aarhus, Denmark: Aarhus University Press, 1997).

King's Peace This treaty between SPARTA and the Persian king Artaxerxes II, drawn up in 386 or 387 B.C.E., is sometimes known as the Peace of Antalcidas (from the name of a Spartan ambassador). The agreement ended recent Spartan-Persian hostilities in the CORINTHIAN WAR and severed PERSIA's alliance with Sparta's enemeis, ATHENS, CORINTH, BOEOTIA, and ARGOS. But the notorious aspect of the treaty was Sparta's renunciation of its former claim to protect the Greek cities of IONIA and of other parts of ASIA MINOR. The King's Peace ceded the Greek cities of Asia Minor and CYPRUS back to the Persian king, even though these cities had been liberated by the Greeks after the PERSIAN WARS.

For the Persians, the King's Peace marked a high point in their designs against Greece, a return to the western conquests of DARIUS (1) (around 500 B.C.E.). For the Greeks, the peace unmasked the "real" Sparta from its pretense of being a liberator. Amid the resulting anti-Spartan anger, Athens was able to attract allies for its new SECOND ATHENIAN LEAGUE (around 377 B.C.E.), and the city of THEBES began to emerge as a rival to Sparta. It was then (380 B.C.E.) that the Athenian orator ISOKRATES began to publish pamphlets urging the Greeks to unite and liberate Ionia by invading the Persian Empire—a plea that would later bear fruit in the conquests of the Macedonian king ALEXANDER THE GREAT (334–323 B.C.E.).

Further reading: R. Seager, "The King's Peace and the Balance of Power in Greece, 386–362 B.C." *Athenaeum* 52 (1974): 36–63; R. K. Sinclair, "The King's Peace and the Employment of Military and Naval Forces, 387–378," *Chiron* 8 (1978): 29–54; George L. Cawkwell, "The King's Peace," *Classical Quarterly* 31 (1981): 69–83; E. Badian, "The King's Peace," in *Georgica. Greek Studies* *in Honour of George Cawkwell,* edited by Mark Flowers and Mark Toher (London: University of London, Institute of Classical Studies, 1991), 25–48.

kinship   From earliest times, Greek society was organized along multiple levels of kinship. The largest and simplest divisions were the different Greek ethnic groups, chiefly the IONIAN, AEOLIAN, and DORIAN GREEKS. All Dorian and many Ionian settlements were originally subdivided into citizens' groupings called *phylai* (usually translated as "tribes"). Dorian cities such as SPARTA or SYRACUSE had three phylai. Ionian cities such as ATHENS or MILETUS might have had four or more. Undoubtedly the phylai predate the Greek cities and reflect the tribal organizations of a nomadic era in the BRONZE AGE.

Appropriate to this primitive origin, the phylai were religious-military societies with inherited membership, centered on aristocratic families. Phylai were themselves divided into groups called *phratriai* (brotherhoods), whose members were *phrateres* (brothers). This Greek word—connected in origin to other Indo-European words such as Latin *frater* and English *brother*—described men who were not literally brothers but who fought together in the retinue of aristocratic war leaders. In HOMER's epic poem the *Iliad* (written down around 750 B.C.E.), the Greek leader AGAMEMNON is advised to marshal the army into battalions consisting of men from the same tribe and phratry. Early Sparta (around 700 B.C.E.) had 27 phratries, probably nine from each tribe.

Like other aspects of Greek citizenship and military life, the phratry was mainly the province of adult, citizen males. During the era of Greek aristocratic rule (around 1000–600 B.C.E.), a man did not need to be of noble blood to belong to a phratry, but he did have to be associated with one of the aristocratic families—for example, as a spear-carrier in war. For the individual citizen, the phratry provided aristocratic patronage and an extended family, giving assurance of support in legal proceedings, blood feuds, and similar events.

At the head of each phratry was a *genos* or (plural) *genē*. The *genos* was an aristocratic clan—a group of kinsmen claiming a single noble ancestor through male descent. A *genos* typically had a name formed with a Greek suffix meaning "the sons of"—for example, the Athenian Alcmaeonidae (sons of the ancestor Alcmaeon) and the Corinthian Bacchiadae (sons of Bacchis). As a center of political power, religious authority, and military might, the *genos* dominated the (larger and less elite) phratry, but presumably a phratry might be headed by more than one *genos*. We know the names of about 60 Athenian *genē;* they were also called by the blanket term *Eupatridai,* "sons of noble fathers."

With the arising middle-class challenge to aristocratic rule in the 600s–400s B.C.E., the old-fashioned, aristocratic-based phyle and phratry in many Greek cities were completely reorganized by political decree. At Sparta this occurred probably under the reforms of LYKOURGOS (1), around 650 B.C.E. At Athens such revamping was at the heart of the democratic reforms of KLEISTHENES (1) (ca. 594 B.C.E.). Abolishing the four traditional Athenian phylae, Kleisthenes created 10 new phylae and reconstituted the phratries so as to include newly enfranchised, lower-income citizens.

In the democratic Athens of the 400s and 300s B.C.E., the phratry remained a vital social-political entity, connecting the individual citizen with the political life of the state. As a young child and again as a teenager, the young male citizen was presented by his father and near kinsmen to his *phrateres* at the altar of ZEUS Phratrios, the Zeus of the Phratry. The adolescent presentation—at which the youth dedicated his newly shorn childhood hair to the god—signified the young man's entrance into the community. Later in the man's life, his *phrateres* witnessed his betrothal ceremony and feasted at his MARRIAGE. Less elaborately, it was at the local phratry office that a female Athenian's name would be enrolled, thus assuring her of the rights (regarding marriage, public assistance, etc.) available to citizen WOMEN.

See also ARISTOCRACY; DEMOCRACY; POLIS.

Further reading: W. E. Thompson, "Attic Kinship Terminology," *Journal of Hellenic Studies* 91 (1971): 110–113; Robert J. Littman, "Kinship in Athens," *Ancient Society* 10 (1979): 5–31; S. C. Humphreys, "Kinship Patterns in the Athenian Courts," *Greek, Roman, and Byzantine Studies* 27 (1986): 57–91; Robert J. Littman, *Kinship and Politics in Athens, 600–400 B.C.* (New York: P. Lang, 1990); Ian Morris, "The Gortyn Code and Greek Kinship," *Greek, Roman, and Byzantine Studies* 31 (1990): 233–254; S. D. Lambert, *The Phratries of Attica* (Ann Arbor: University of Michigan Press, 1998); Christopher P. Jones, *Kinship Diplomacy in the Ancient World* (Cambridge, Mass.: Harvard University Press, 1999).

Kleisthenes   (1)   (Cleisthenes)   (ca.   560–500   B.C.E.)
Athenian statesman of the late 500s B.C.E.
Kleisthenes is usually considered to be the father of Athenian DEMOCRACY. He began his career as a privileged aristocrat in a political arena of TYRANTS and aristocrats; but, whether through pure ambition or genuine convictions, he used his influence to reorganize the government to enlarge the common people's rights.

Born into the noble Athenian clan of the ALCMAEONIDS, Kleisthenes was the son of the politician Megakles and of Agariste, daughter of the Sicyonian tyrant KLEISTHENES (2). The younger Kleisthenes served as ARCHON (525 B.C.E.) under the Athenian tyrant HIPPIAS (1), but was later banished with the rest of the Alcmaeonids, on Hippias's order.

After Hippias's ouster (510 B.C.E.), Kleisthenes returned to Athens and became leader of one of two rival political parties. When his opponent Isagoras was elected archon (508 B.C.E.), Kleisthenes struck back. According to the historian HERODOTUS, writing some 70 years later, Kleisthenes "took the common people (*dēmos*) into partnership." Kleisthenes proposed, in the Athenian ASSEMBLY, certain radical reforms to increase the common people's rights at the expense of the aristocrats. This program made Kleisthenes the most powerful individual at Athens, with all the common people behind him. His reforms continued a process begun by the lawmaker SOLON nearly 90 years prior and transformed Athens into a full democracy, the first in world history.

Kleisthenes' changes were extensive and complicated. The enabling first step was to improve the rights of the mass of poorer citizens (the laborers and peasants, called *thētes*). The thētes were disadvantaged by the traditional system of four Athenian tribes (*phulai* or phylai). These tribes, which supplied the basis for public life in the city, were traditionally dominated by aristocratic families. Kleisthenes overhauled the tribal system, replacing the four old phylai with 10 new ones. Each new tribe was designed to include a thorough mix of Athenians—farmers with city dwellers, aristocrats and their followers with middle-class people and *thētes*. The effect was to reduce greatly the influence of the nobles within each tribe.

To create his new, "mixed-up" tribes, Kleisthenes reorganized the political map of ATTICA, the 1,000-square-mile territory of Athens that included all Athenian citizens. It was now, if not earlier, that Attica became administratively divided into about 139 DEMES—*dēmoi*, "villages" or local wards. By means of Kleisthenes' complicated gerrymandering, each new tribe was made to consist of several demes (an average of about 14, but the actual numbers varied between six and 21). Typically these tribal-constituent demes were unconnected by geography, traditional allegiances, and the like. The new tribes thus were relatively free from aristocratic domination and from the localism and feuding associated with aristocratic domination. Across the map of Attica, the traditional pockets of local-family influence were, in effect, broken up.

With his 10 tribes as a basis, Kleisthenes democratized other aspects of the government. The people's COUNCIL was enlarged from 400 to 500 members, now consisting of 50 citizens from each tribe, chosen by lot from a pool of upper- and middle-class candidates. The Athenian citizens' assembly received new powers, such as the judicial right to try or review certain court cases. But these radical changes did not go unchallenged. Kleisthenes' rival Isagoras appealed to the Spartan king KLEOMENES (1), who marched on Athens with a small Spartan force. Kleisthenes and his followers fled (507 B.C.E.). But when Kleomenes attempted to replace the new democracy with an OLIGARCHY consisting of Isagoras and his followers, the Athenian populace rose in resistance. Kleomenes and his army were besieged atop the

Athenian ACROPOLIS, then were allowed to withdraw, taking Isagoras with them.

Kleisthenes returned to Athens, but soon his prominence was over. He may have involved himself in diplomatic overtures to the Persian king DARIUS (1), and if so he would have been disgraced in the ensuing anti-Persian sentiment. But when Kleisthenes died, he received a public tomb in the honorific Kerameikos cemetery, just outside Athens. His democratization of Athens would be taken further by the radical reforms of EPHIALTES and PERIKLES, in the mid-400s B.C.E.

See also KINSHIP; OSTRACISM.

Further reading: C. William J. Eliot, *Coastal Demes of Attika: A Study of the Policy of Kleisthenes* (Toronto: University of Toronto Press, 1962); Charles W. Fornara, *Athens from Cleisthenes to Pericles* (Berkeley: University of California Press, 1991); Christian Meier, *Athens: A Portrait of the City in its Golden Age,* translated by Robert Kimber and Rita Kimber (New York: Metropolitan Books, 1998); Sarah Pomeroy et al., *A Brief History of Ancient Greece: Politics, Society, and Culture* (New York: Oxford University Press, 2004).

Kleisthenes (2) (500s B.C.E.) *Tyrant of the Peloponnesian city of Sikyon and maternal grandfather of the Athenian statesman KLEISTHENES (1)*

Kleisthenes ruled Sikyon from about 600 to 570 B.C.E., when the city was one of the foremost commercial and military powers in Greece. He extended his influence to DELPHI by leading a coalition against PHOCIS in the First Sacred War (ca. 590 B.C.E.) and crowned his achievements with a chariot victory at the OLYMPIC GAMES (ca. 572 B.C.E.). His wealth and prestige are apparent in the historian HERODOTUS's tale of how Kleisthenes hosted his daughter Agariste's 13 suitors at his palace for a year, observing them in SPORT, discourse, and so on, and gauging their aristocratic qualifications for marrying his daughter. The suitors came from various parts of the Greek world, but Kleisthenes favored two Athenians: Megakles, son of Alcmaeon of the clan of the ALCMAEONIDS, and Hippocleides, son of Teisander of the Philaïd clan.

On the day appointed to announce his choice, Kleisthenes held a great feast, at which the suitors competed in two final contests, lyre-playing and public speaking. Hippokleides, who outshone the others, was the one whom Kleisthenes had by now secretly chosen. But as more WINE was drunk, Hippokleides requested a tune from the flute-player and boldly began to dance. Then he called for a table and danced atop it, while Kleisthenes watched with distaste. And when Hippokleides started doing handstands on the table, beating time with his legs in the air, Kleisthenes cried out, "O, son of Teisander, you have danced away your wedding!" To which the young man replied, "Hippokleides doesn't care" ("ou phrontis Hippokleidei").

The story became proverbial as an example of aristocratic detachment and *joie de vivre*. Agariste's hand in MARRIAGE went to Megacles, and their son was Kleisthenes, the Athenian statesman (born in about 560 B.C.E.).

See also MUSIC; TYRANTS.

Further reading: J. Boardman, "Herakles, Delphi, and Kleisthenes of Sikyon," *Revue archéologique* (1978): 227–234; P. J. Bicknell, "Herodotus 5.68 and the Racial Policy of Kleisthenes of Sikyon," *Greek, Roman, and Byzantine Studies* 23 (1982): 193–201; D. Ogden, "Cleisthenes of Sicyon," *Classical Quarterly* 43 (1993): 353–363; V. Parker, "Some Aspects of the Foreign and Domestic Policy of Cleisthenes of Sicyon," *Hermes* 122 (1994): 404–424.

Kleomenes (1) (Cleomenes) (d. 490 B.C.E.) *Dynamic and ambitious king of SPARTA*

Kleomenes reigned ca. 520–490 B.C.E. His efforts to expand Spartan power beyond the PELOPONNESE, along with his resistance to Persian encroachment, mark him as one of the dominant personalities of the late 500s B.C.E. Unfortunately, our major source for his reign, written by the historian HERODOTUS (ca. 435 B.C.E.), is tainted by Spartan official revisionism that tries to diminish Kleomenes' importance.

The son of King Anaxandridas of the Agiad royal house, Kleomenes was awarded the kingship in victorious rivalry against his half brother Doreius. Soon Kleomenes was taking aim against the Athenian dictator HIPPIAS (1). Kleomenes wanted to end Hippias's reign in order to bring ATHENS into the Spartan alliance. In addition, Hippias's diplomatic overtures to the Persian king DARIUS (1) had made Kleomenes fear that Hippias was maneuvering to assist a Persian invasion of mainland Greece. In 510 B.C.E. Kleomenes entered Athens with an army, ejected Hippias, and withdrew. But Kleomenes was mistaken in expecting that this would result in an Athenian OLIGARCHY friendly to Sparta. Instead, there occurred peaceful revolution, producing the Athenian DEMOCRACY (508 B.C.E.).

Kleomenes returned with an army in 508 or 507 B.C.E., intending to overthrow the new government. He captured the Athenian ACROPOLIS but found himself besieged there by the Athenian populace and withdrew under truce. His later attempt to organize a full Spartan-allied attack on Athens was blocked by the other Spartan king, Demaratus, and by Sparta's ally CORINTH (which at that time was still friendly with Athens).

Despite a request from the Greek city of MILETUS, Kleomenes wisely declined to send Spartan troops overseas to aid the IONIAN REVOLT against the Persians (499 B.C.E.). He had an enemy nearer home to attend to — Sparta's Peloponnesian rival, ARGOS. In 494 B.C.E., at the Battle of Sepeia, on the Argive plain, Kleomenes obliterated an Argive army and marched his Spartans to the walls of Argos. But the city withstood Kleomenes' siege, a

failure that later was to be used against him by his enemies at Sparta.

In around 491 B.C.E. Persian envoys went to Sparta asking for earth and water, the tokens of submission to PERSIA. Probably at Kleomenes' prompting, the Spartans threw the Persians down a well, telling them they would find plenty of earth and water there. But other states, notably AEGINA, did submit. When Demaratus blocked Kleomenes' desired retaliation against Aegina, Kleomenes decided to rid himself of this uncooperative partner. He persuaded Demaratus' kinsman Leotychides to claim the kingship on grounds that Demaratus has been an illegitimate child, and he bribed the oracle at DELPHI to support this claim. Demaratus was deposed and succeeded by Leotychides.

Around 490 B.C.E. Kleomenes was in THESSALY. According to Herodotus, the king was in hiding because his disgraceful intrigues against Demaratus had been exposed. However, it seems more likely that Kleomenes was still at the height of power and working to organize Greek resistance to Persia. He then visited ARCADIA, a Peloponnesian region traditionally under Spartan control. By then he may have been aiming at an ambitious goal— to resist the Persians by creating a unified Peloponnesian state, under his personal dictatorship. Possibly he even tried to gain support from the Spartan serfs known as HELOTS, promising them freedom in exchange.

After returning to Sparta, Kleomenes died violently. According to the official version, he took his life in a fit of insanity. But it looks as if he were assassinated by conservative Spartan elements. His successor was his half brother, Leonidas, who was fated to die at the Battle of THERMOPYLAE (480 B.C.E.), resisting the Persian invasion that Kleomenes had tried to prevent.

See also AGIAD CLAN; KLEISTHENES (1); PERSIAN WARS.

Further reading: Bernadotte Perrin, trans., *Plutarch's Lives* (Cambridge, Mass.: Harvard University Press, 1993); William G. G. Forrest, *A History of Sparta*, 2nd ed. (London: Bristol Classical Paperbacks, 1995); Robert Parker, *Cleomenes on the Acropolis: An Inaugural Lecture Delivered before the University of Oxford on 12 May 1997* (Oxford: Clarendon Press, 1998).

Kleomenes (2) *See* SPARTA.

Kleon (Cleon) (d. 422 B.C.E.) *Athenian demagogue (rabble-rouser) of the early PELOPONNESIAN WAR*

For seven years after the death of the statesman PERIKLES (429–422 B.C.E.), the left-wing Kleon was the foremost politician in ATHENS. Although not really a soldier, he was the one person at the time who—by his bold planning and determination—could have won the war for Athens. But when he was killed in battle, the Athenian war leadership passed temporarily to the cautious NIKIAS.

Most information about Kleon comes from the written work of his contemporary, the Athenian historian

THUCYDIDES (1). The normally objective Thucydides viewed Kleon with distaste and underestimated his importance. Similarly, Kleon was despised by the Athenian comic playwright ARISTOPHANES, who mocked him in the *Knights* (424 B.C.E.) and other comedies as a crowd-pleasing opportunist. Yet despite the disapproval of such intellectuals, Kleon probably was widely viewed as Perikles' legitimate successor. Although Kleon came to prominence by attacking the aging Perikles (431 B.C.E.), he also imitated Perikles in his obsessive loyalty to the Athenian common people (*dēmos*), who were his power base. That is why, in the *Knights*, Aristophanes uses the name Philodemos (lover of the people) for his character who is a caricature of Kleon.

The son of a rich tanner of hides, Kleon was an accomplished orator who could whip up public opinion in the Athenian ASSEMBLY; he is said to have introduced a more vulgar and demonstrative mode of public speaking. He reached his peak of power in 425 B.C.E., after Athens had gained the advantage in the fighting against the Spartans at PYLOS. Accusing the Athenian generals of incompetence, Kleon won command of the entire Pylos campaign by acclamation of the assembly. He journeyed to Pylos, where—helped by the Athenian general DEMOSTHENES (2)—he won a total victory over the supposedly invincible Spartans.

Then preeminent in Athenian politics, Kleon presumably is the one who prompted the notorious "Thoudippos Decree" (425 B.C.E.), which authorized a reassessment of the annual tribute to be paid to Athens by its DELIAN LEAGUE allies. The decree resulted in a doubling or tripling of the amounts due from individual allied states. Around the same time, Kleon sponsored a law increasingly jury pay, to the advantage of lower-income citizens.

Elected as a general for 422 B.C.E., he led an Athenian army to the north Aegean coast, to recapture the area from the Spartan commander BRASIDAS. But at the Battle of AMPHIPOLIS, Kleon was defeated and killed. Thucydides mentions that he was running away when an enemy skirmisher cut him down.

See also DEMOCRACY; LAWS AND LAW COURTS; MYTILENE.

Further reading: Lowell Edmunds, *Cleon, Knights, and Aristophanes' Politics* (Lanham, Md.: University Press of America, 1987); W. Robert Connor, *The New Politicians of Fifth-Century Athens* (Indianapolis: Hackett, 1992).

Klytemnestra (Clytaemnestra) In MYTH, Klytemnestra was the wife and murderer of King AGAMEMNON of MYCENAE and, according to different versions of the tale, her father was either the god ZEUS or Leda's husband, the Spartan king Tyndareus. Klytemnestra had the famous HELEN OF TROY for a twin sister and CASTOR AND POLYDEUCES for her brothers. Her name, Klutaimnēstra, probably means "famous wooing" or "famous intent."

As Agamemnon's wife, Klytemnestra bore a son, ORESTES, and two daughters, ELECTRA and IPHIGENIA. But she grew to hate her husband when he chose to sacrifice Iphigenia to appease the goddess ARTEMIS, who was sending contrary winds to block the Greeks' sailing fleet at the start of the TROJAN WAR. During Agamemnon's 10-year absence at TROY, Klytemnestra became the lover of Agamemnon's cousin Aegisthus, and the two plotted to kill the king on his return. In the act, they also killed the Trojan princess CASSANDRA, whom Agamemnon had brought home as his war prize.

Afterward, Klytemnestra and Aegisthus ruled as queen and king at Mycenae. They were eventually killed in vengeance by Orestes, with Electra assisting.

Klytemnestra's character shows a growth in strength and evil during the centuries of Greek literature. Where she is first mentioned in HOMER's epic poem the *Odyssey* (written down around 750 B.C.E.), she is overshadowed by the vigorous Aegisthus, who seduces her and plots the murder. But in AESCHYLUS's tragedy *Agamemnon* (performed in 458 B.C.E.), Klytemnestra is the proud and malevolent prime mover, and Aegisthus is just her effete, subordinate lover. In the play, she persuades the newly arrived Agamemnon to tread atop a priceless tapestry; he thereby unwittingly calls down heaven's anger on himself. Then she leads him to his bath, where she murders him and Cassandra.

Agamemnon is the first play of Aeschylus's Oresteian Trilogy. In the following play, the *Choēphoroi* (or *Libation Bearers*), Klytemnestra and Aegisthus are slain by Orestes. As she dies, she calls down the avenging EURIES upon her son. A hateful Klytemnestra is portrayed also in SOPHOKLES' tragedy *Electra* and EURIPIDES' tragedy *Electra* (both ca. 417 B.C.E.). In vase painting, Klytemnestra sometimes is shown as wielding a double ax against Agamemnon or Cassandra or (unsuccessfully) against Orestes.

See also HUBRIS; THEATER.

Further reading: Sally MacEwen, ed., *Views of Clytemnestra, Ancient and Modern* (Lewiston: Edwin Mellen Press, 1990); Francine Viret Bernal, "When Painters Execute a Murderess: The Representation of Clytemnestra on Attic Vases," in *Naked Truths: Women, Sexuality, and Gender in Classical Art and Archaeology,* edited by Ann Olga Koloski-Ostrow and Claire L. Lyons (London: Routledge, 1997); Kathleen Komar, *Reclaiming Klytemnestra: Revenge or Reconciliation* (Urbana: University of Illinois Press, 2003).

Knidos (Cnidus) This prosperous Greek city is situated on the southwestern coast of ASIA MINOR. Founded around 900 B.C.E. by DORIAN GREEKS from mainland Greece, Knidos and its neighbor HALICARNASSUS were the two important Dorian cities of Asia Minor, and were part of a larger eastern Mediterranean Dorian federation including the islands of KOS and RHODES.

Knidos stood on the side of a lofty promontory jutting into the sea, and it thrived as a seaport and maritime power. In search of raw metals such as tin, the Knidians founded trade depots on the Lipari Islands and elsewhere in the western Mediterranean. When the Persians attacked Asia Minor under King Cyrus (1) in 546 B.C.E., the Knidians tried to convert their city into an inshore island by digging a canal across the peninsula. Finding the work slow and injurious, they consulted the Oracle of Delphi and were told to abandon resistance and make submission.

After the liberation of Greek Asia Minor in 479 B.C.E., Knidos became a tribute-paying member of the Delian League, under Athenian domination. In 413 B.C.E., with Athens losing ground in the Peloponnesian War, Knidos joined the general Delian revolt and became a Spartan ally. In 394 B.C.E., during the Corinthian War, the Athenian admiral Konon destroyed a Spartan fleet in a battle off Knidos.

Returned to Persian overlordship by the terms of the King's Peace (386 B.C.E.), Knidos was reliberated in 334 B.C.E. by the Macedonian king Alexander the Great. In about 330 B.C.E. the city's public and commercial buildings were rebuilt near the tip of its peninsula to take advantage of the superior harbor there. By then the city had reached its height of prosperity, being renowned for its exported Wine and its school of Medicine. Knidos housed a statue that was considered to be the most beautiful in the world: the naked Aphrodite carved in marble by Praxiteles in the 360s B.C.E. According to one ancient writer, people would voyage to Knidos expressly to view this work.

During the Hellenistic Age, Knidos became subject to Ptolemaic Egypt (200s B.C.E.). By the later 100s B.C.E. the city was part of the empire of Rome.

See also Bronze; Persian Wars.

Further reading: Christine M. Havelock, *The Aphrodite of Knidos and Her Successors: A Historical of the Female Nude in Greek Art* (Ann Arbor: University of Michigan Press, 1995).

Knossos This was the chief city of the island of Crete for most of antiquity. Located in the north-central part of the island, about three miles inland, Knossos had a good harbor—the site of the modern seaport of Irakleion—and also guarded a major land route southward across the middle of Crete. Knossos was the capital city of the Minoan civilization, which thrived on Crete around 2200–1450 B.C.E. and controlled a naval empire in the Aegean Sea. Although the Minoans were not themselves Greek, they stand at the threshold of Greek history insofar as they deeply influenced the emerging Greek Mycenaean civilization (ca. 1600–1200 B.C.E.). The name Knossos is in origin a pre-Greek word, probably from the lost Minoan language.

Knossos today is one of the world's most important archaeological sites, containing remnants of the largest Minoan palace, the seat of the Minoan rulers. First erected in around 1950 B.C.E. and then rebuilt and enlarged after earthquakes in around 1700 and 1570 B.C.E., the palace was first revealed to modern eyes by the British archaeologist Sir Arthur Evans in 1900 C.E. The building and envisions, excavated almost continuously since then, have yielded such well-known Minoan artwork as the Bull's Head Rhyton and the Toreador Fresco, now in the Irakleion archaeological museum.

Built mainly of large blocks of Cretan limestone, the palace survives today mostly as a network of foundations and wall remnants covering five and a half acres. Around a central, square courtyard measuring 82 by 180 feet, the building contained pillared hallways, staircases, and hundreds of rooms and storage chambers in a mazelike configuration. There were two or even three upper floors, now partly reconstructed. Among the palace's splendors was running water, carried in clay pipes. The building's size and complexity—unequaled in 1700 B.C.E outside the urban centers of Egypt and Mesopotamia—probably inspired the later Greek legend of the Cretan Labyrinth.

Remarkably, the palace had no enclosing wall; the Minoans evidently trusted in their navy for defense. Nevertheless, the palace was completely destroyed by fire in around 1400 B.C.E. or soon after, and was never rebuilt. As shown by Archaeology, every other known Minoan site on Crete also was destroyed at this time. The cause for such widespread ruin may have been an invasion of Crete by warlike Mycenaeans from the Greek mainland. Intriguingly, it seems that the Knossos palace already had been occupied by certain Mycenaeans prior to its destruction. This conclusion is reached because the palace debris of this era has yielded up nearly 4,000 clay tablets, inscribed with inventory notes written in the Greek Linear B script, identical to the script later used at Mycenaean sites on the mainland. But whoever it was who destroyed the palace, evidently Knossos and all of Crete abandoned thereafter by Mycenaeans.

In around 1000 B.C.E., Crete was occupied by new conquerors—the Dorian Greeks, invading from the Peloponnese. Knossos, with its superior location, became Dorian Crete's foremost city-state. Like the other Cretan cities, it was governed as a military Aristocracy, with social and political institutions similar to those at Sparta. Dorian-ethnic nobles ruled over a rural population of non-Dorian serfs.

Knossos shared in Crete's general decline after the 600s B.C.E. By the late 200s B.C.E. it had fallen into a debilitating conflict with its Cretan rival city, Gortyn. When the Romans annexed Crete in 67 B.C.E., they chose Gortyn over Knossos as their provincial capital.

For the classical Greeks, Knossos kept its associations with a dimly remembered, fictionalized Minoan

The dolphin fresco in the queen's great hall or megaron in Knossos, capital city of the Minoan civilization. The site is now a modern seaport on Crete, which accounts for the marine life theme. *(Alison Frantz Photographic Collection, American School of Classical Studies at Athens)*

past. The myths of DAEDALUS, MINOS, and THESEUS describe Knossos as a city of grandeurs and horrors.

See also GREEK LANGUAGE; HELOTS.

Further reading: Anna Michailidou, *Knossos: A Complete Guide to the Palace of Minos,* translation by Alexandra Doumas and Timothy Cullen (Athens: Ekdotike Athenon, 1998); Susan Sherratt, *Arthur Evans, Knossos, and the Priest-king* (Oxford: Ashmolean Museum, 2000); J. A. MacGillivray, *Minotaur: Sir Arthur Evans and the Archaeology of the Minoan Myth* (London: Pimlico, 2001).

Konon (ca. 444–390 B.C.E.) *Athenian admiral active from 414–392 B.C.E.*
Born into a noble family at ATHENS, Konon commanded fleets in the final years of the PELOPONNESIAN WAR. At

the disastrous Athenian naval defeat at AEGOSPOTAMI (405 B.C.E.), Konon alone of all the commanders got his squadron safely away from the Spartan ambush.

In the CORINTHIAN WAR (395–386 B.C.E.) he was active in developing the navy of Athens's ally PERSIA. Leading an Athenian squadron fighting alongside the Persians, Konon destroyed a Spartan fleet at the Battle of KNIDOS (394 B.C.E.). With funds from the Persian king Artaxerxes II, Konon oversaw the rebuilding of Athens's LONG WALLS. But his dreams of re-creating the Athenian empire died when the Persians switched sides in the war (392 B.C.E.). Konon died soon thereafter.

Further reading: C. D. Hamilton, "On the Perils of Extraordinary Honors. The Cases of Lysander and Conon," *Ancient World* 2 (1979): 87–90; H. D. Westlake, "Conon and Rhodes. The Troubled Aftermath of Snyoecism," *Greek, Roman, and Byzantine Studies* 24 (1983): 333–344; B. S. Strauss, "Thrasybulus and Conon. A Rivalry in Athens in the 390s B.C.," *American Journal of Philology* 105 (1984): 37–48; D. A. March, "Konon and the Great King's Fleet, 396–394," *Historia* 46 (1997): 257–269.

Korē   *See* DEMETER; PERSEPHONE.

Kratinus (Cratinus) (ca. 520–422 B.C.E.) *One of the three great comic playwrights of classical Athens, alongside Aristophanes and Eupolis*
Kratinus was Aristophanes' older contemporary and rival, and greatly influenced him. Apparently Kratinus's relied even more on obscene farce and personal derision of public figures than those of Aristophanes.

Kratinus's comedies, of which 27 titles and some 460 fragments survive, were presented in the mid-400s down to 423 B.C.E. We know he won first prize nine time in competitions at the two major Athenian drama festivals, the City Dionysia (in early spring) and the Lenaea (in midwinter). His titles, often styled as plural nouns, include *The Thracian Women, The Soft Fellows, The Dionysuses,* and *The Odysseuses* (which apparently used the chorus as ODYSSEUS' crew and included a large model of his ship.)

No complete play by Kratinus survives, but there exists a synopsis of his *Dionysalexandros* ("Dionysus-Paris"), performed in about 430 B.C.E. There the god DIONYSUS substitutes for the Trojan prince PARIS in judging the famous beauty contest of the three goddesses. Deciding in Aphrodite's favor, the god acquires the beautiful HELEN OF TROY as his reward but is terrified by the approach of Paris himself; farcical action follows, including the start of the TROJAN WAR. The play—clearly a burlesque on the recent outbreak of the very real and serious PELOPONNESIAN WAR—contained much indirect ridicule of the Athenian statesman PERIKLES, who was cast as the meddling Dionysus, while his common-law wife, ASPASIA, doubtlessly received a few hits as Helen.

Kratinus's final success came in 423 B.C.E., with his comedy *The Bottle.* The year before Aristophanes' *Knights* had publicly mocked Kratinus as a drunken has-been; this year Kratinus responded with a comic self-portrait featuring: a character named Kratinus; his estranged wife, Komoidia (comedy); his sluttish girlfriend, Methē (drunkenness); and the tempting pretty-boy Oiniskos (little wine). The play contained the proverb that an artist who drinks only water can never create anything worthwhile. *The Bottle* won first place at the City Dionysia, well over Aristophanes' *Clouds,* which took third. Kratinus died shortly thereafter.

See also THEATER.

Further reading: David Harvey and John Wilkins, eds., *The Rivals of Aristophanes* (London: Duckworth and the Classical Press of Wales, 2000).

Kritias (Critias) (ca. 460–403 B.C.E.) *Athenian oligarch*
As leader of the THIRTY TYRANTS, who ruled ATHENS by terror in 404–403 B.C.E., Kritias was one of the true villains of Athenian history.

Born into an aristocratic clan, Kritias was pupil of certain SOPHISTS and of the philosopher SOCRATES. Kritias was an elder kinsman of the philosopher PLATO (specifically, cousin to Plato's mother) and was also the uncle and guardian of Plato's uncle Charmides. Both Kritias and Charmides appear as glamorous, youthful figures in several of Plato's (fictional) dialogues, written in the first quarter of the 300s B.C.E.

As a suspected enemy of the DEMOCRACY, Kritias was arrested but then released after the incident of the Mutilation of the Herms (415 B.C.E.), during the PELOPONNESIAN WAR. Later Kritias proposed to the Athenian ASSEMBLY the decree recalling the exiled Alcibiades (probably in 411 B.C.E.), but when the Athenians turned against Alcibiades again (406 B.C.E.), Kritias apparently suffered incidental blame and was banished. He went in exile to THESSALY.

Like other exiles, Kritias was recalled as part of the peace terms imposed on Athens by the victorious Spartans at the end of the Peloponnesian War, in 404 B.C.E. He was then elected to the dictatorial, pro-Spartan government commonly known as the Thirty Tyrants. The Athenian historian XENOPHON, who lived through these events, portrays Kritias as leader of the Thirty's extremist faction, against the more moderate THERAMENES. Kritias directed the Thirty's reign of terror, executing anyone who was likely to organize resistance or whose personal wealth was attractive. He eventually denounced his colleague Theramenes and had him executed. Kritias's crowning outrage was to arrange the mass execution of 300 men (probably the entire male citizen population) of the nearby town of Eleusis.

In early 403 B.C.E. the Thirty were toppled. Kritias was killed, with Charmides and others, in street-fighting at PIRAEUS. The hatred of Kritias's memory played a role in the prosecution of his former teacher Socrates under the restored democracy (399 B.C.E.).

A man of intelligence and talent, Kritias wrote LYRIC POETRY, tragedies, and prose. His prose style was admired, and one of his works, now lost, was titled "Conversations" (Homilia). It is possible that this was a model for Plato's literary dialogues. As a thinker, Plato seems to have inherited some of his uncle's authoritarian nature.

Further reading: R. G. Bury, trans., *Timaeus; Critias; Cleitophon; Menexenus; Epistles/Plato,* reprint (Cambridge, Mass.: Harvard University Press, 1999, 1929); Tomás Calvo and Luc Brisson, eds., *Interpreting the Timaeus-Critias: Proceedings of the IV Symposium Platonicum: selected papers* (Sankt Augustin: Academia Verlag, 1997).

Kylon (Cylon) (600s B.C.E.) *Athenian aristocrat*
Kylon attempted to seize supreme power at ATHENS, in about 632 B.C.E., at a time when the city was still governed

as an ARISTOCRACY. He and his followers captured the Athenian ACROPOLIS. But the common people did not rise in support, and government forces besieged the conspirators. Kylon escaped but his men were massacred, despite having claimed sanctuary at religious altars. This mishap was the origin of the "Alcmaeonid curse"—the taint of pollution considered to lie perpetually on the entire clan of the ALCMAEONIDS, because one of the clan, Megakles, had overseen the massacre.

See also FURIES; TYRANTS.

Further reading: D. Harris-Cline, "Archaic Athens and the Topography of the Kylon Affair," *Annual of the British School at Athens* 94 (1999): 309–320.

Kymē   Kymē was the southernmost and main city of AEOLIS, a Greek region on the northwestern coast of ASIA MINOR. Like other cities of Aeolis, it was settled in about 900 B.C.E. by AEOLIAN GREEKS who had migrated eastward, via LESBOS, from mainland Greece. As indicated by the name (meaning wave or sea), the city was a port, advantageously located alongside the mouth of the Hermus River (which allowed trading contact with interior Asia Minor).

Kymē's fortunes followed those of the Aeolis region. Captured by the Persians around 545 B.C.E., Kymē took part in the failed IONIAN REVOLT in 499–493 B.C.E. Liberated by the Greeks at the end of the PERSIAN WARS (479 B.C.E.), Kymē became part of the Athenian-controlled DELIAN LEAGUE. After ATHENS's defeat in the PELOPONNESIAN WAR (404 B.C.E.), Kymē reverted to Persian control by the terms of the KING'S PEACE (386 B.C.E.). By about 377 B.C.E., Kymē had joined the SECOND ATHENIAN LEAGUE. After ALEXANDER THE GREAT's death (323 B.C.E.), Kymē passed through the SELEUCID EMPIRE and the kingdom of PERGAMON, before becoming part of the Roman Empire in the 100s B.C.E.

Kymē's best-known citizen was the historian Ephoros (ca. 400–330 B.C.E.), who wrote a world history as well as a history of Kymē, neither of which has survived. An inferior scholar, Ephorus was notorious for including in his world history such comments as "In this year the citizens of Kymē were at peace."

See also CUMAE.

Further reading: Jan Bouzek, ed., *Kyme I: Anatolian Collection of Charles University* (Prague: Univerzita Karlova,

1974); Jan Bouzek, Philippos Kostomitsopoulos, and Iva Ondrejová, eds., *Kyme II: The Results of the Czechoslovak Expedition* (Prague: Univerzita Karlova, 1980).

Kypselos (Cypselus) (600s B.C.E.)   *Corinthian dictator*
Kypselos reigned ca. 657–625 B.C.E., after seizing the city from the oppressive, aristocratic Bacchiad clan. CORINTH was at that time the foremost commercial power in Greece, and Kypselos gained control by leading a revolution of the affluent middle class that had previously been denied political power. Kypselos reigned mildly and is said to have kept no bodyguard. But as usurper and dictator, he usually is counted as one of the first Greek TYRANTS, who began arising in the mid-600s B.C.E. to wrest power violently from the aristocratic ruling class throughout the Greek world.

According to a folktale recorded by the Greek historian HERODOTUS (ca. 435 B.C.E.), Kypselos was born to a Bacchiad mother and a non-Bacchiad father. Members of the Bacchiad clan, alerted by a prophecy that the baby was destined to destroy them, arrived to kill him. But Kypselos's mother hid him in a wooden chest (*kypselē*) and outwitted the assassins.

This concept of the blessed but hunted infant is a Near Eastern mythological theme that recurs in the stories of Moses, Sargon the Assyrian, CYRUS (1) the Persian, and Jesus. The Greeks—having learned this type of legend from the Phoenicians, around 900–700 B.C.E.—applied it to certain Greek mythical heroes, such as OEDIPUS. Herodotus's tale evidently derives from propaganda that Kypselos himself issued during his reign; a cedarwood chest, supposedly the one used to hide the infant Kypselos, was eventually kept on display in the Temple of HERA at OLYMPIA.

Kypselos and his son and successor, PERIANDER, increased Corinth's power through TRADE and manufacturing. Export markets were developed in Etruscan ITALY and other western locales, and Corinthian vase painting blossomed into the perfection of style that modern scholars call Early Corinthian.

See also ETRUSCANS; POTTERY; PROPHECY AND DIVINATION.

Further reading: A. Andrewes, *The Greek Tyrants* (London: Hutchinson, 1956); S. I. Oost, "Cypselus the Bacchiad," *Classical Philology* 67 (1972): 10–30.

L

Labyrinth In MYTH, the Labyrinth was the mazelike palace designed by the Athenian craftsman DAEDALUS at KNOSSOS, in CRETE, to house the monstrous Minotaur. The Athenian hero THESEUS, making his way through the Labyrinth's corridors with the help of the Cretan princess Ariadne, slew the Minotaur. The classical Greeks described any kind of architectural maze as a labyrinth (*laburinthos*)—much as we use the word today.

Like other myths, this one contains a kernel of fact: The name *Labyrinth* was probably applied to the Minoan palace at Cnossus, sometime in the second millennium B.C.E. *Laburinthos* was not originally a Greek word, as shown by its distinctive *nth* sound (which distinguishes such other pre-Greek names as CORINTH and HYACINTHOS). It was probably a Minoan word, meaning "house of the double ax"—the two-headed ax (*labrys*) being a Minoan royal symbol.

See also GREEK LANGUAGE; MINOAN CIVILIZATION; MINOS.

Further reading: W. H. Matthews, *Mazes and Labyrinths: Their History and Development* (New York: Dover, 1970); J. Kraft, "The Cretan Labyrinth and the Walls of Troy. An Analysis of Labyrinth Designs," *Opuscula Romana* 15 (1985): 79–86; Rodney Castleden, *The Knossos Labyrinth: A New View of the 'Palace of Minos' at Knossos* (London: Routledge, 1990); Penelope R. Doob, *The Idea of the Labyrinth from Classical Antiquity through the Middle Ages* (Ithaca, N.Y.: Cornell University Press, 1990); Hermann Kern, *Through the Labyrinth: Designs and Meanings over 5000 Years,* translated by Abigail Clay (New York: Prestel, 2000); Jeff Saward, *Labyrinths and Mazes: the Definitive Guide to Ancient and Modern Traditions* (Stroud, U.K.: Gaia, 2003).

Laconia This word refers to the local territory of SPARTA, in the southeastern PELOPONNESE and apparently was a shortened form of the region's alternate name, Lacedaemon.

Of the Peloponnese's three southern peninsulas, Laconia included the eastern (Cape Malea) and middle one (Cape Taenarum). The two capes and much of the interior consist of limestone mountains; two ranges—Mt. Parnon in the east and Mt. Taygetus in the west—run north to south. Between these mountain ranges lay the fertile Eurotas River valley, which widens southward to the Laconian Gulf. In the north, Laconia shared a mountainous (and often-disputed) border with ARCADIA and the territory of ARGOS. To the west, beyond the Taygetus range, lay the region of MESSENIA.

In the second millennium B.C.E., Laconia was the site of a thriving Mycenaean-Greek kingdom; the semimythical king MENELAUS would have ruled there. Overrun by DORIAN GREEKS circa 1100–1000 B.C.E., Laconia eventually produced a number of Dorian settlements, including Sparta, in the upper Eurotas valley. By about 700 B.C.E. Sparta had conquered the Eurotas down to the sea. The town of Gytheum, on the western Laconian Gulf, became Sparta's port. The Eurotas farmland became the home of the Spartan elite, the "true" Spartans (Spartiatai). Other parts of Laconia were inhabited by Spartan citizens of lesser social rank—the PERIOIKOI ("dwellers about"). Together these two groups comprised the Spartan free population, the Lacedaemonians (*Lakedaimonioi*).

The name *Laconia* has provided the modern English word *laconic,* referring originally to the Spartan brevity of speech.

See also HELOTS.

Further reading: Jan M. Sanders, ed., *Philolakon: Lakonian Studies in Honour of Hector Catling* (London: British School at Athens, 1992); W. G. Forrest, *A History of Sparta,* 2d ed. (London: Bristol Classical Paperbacks, 1995); William G. Cavanagh, *The Laconia Survey: Continuity and Change in a Greek Rural Landscape* (London: British School at Athens, 1996); William G. Cavanagh and Susan E. C. Walker, eds., *Sparta in Laconia: Proceedings of the 19th British Museum Classical Colloquium Held with the British School at Athens and King's and University Colleges, London 6–8 December 1995* (London: British School at Athens, 1998).

Lampsacus   *See* HELLESPONT.

Laocoön   A Trojan priest of APOLLO, in the MYTH of the TROJAN WAR, Laocoön was the brother of Anchises and uncle of the hero AENEAS. After the Greeks had apparently abandoned the siege of TROY, leaving behind the wooden Trojan Horse, Laocoön objected vehemently to the Trojans' plan to bring the horse within the city's walls. (In fact, the horse was full of Greek soldiers.) To stifle Laocoön's objections, and thus fulfill the ordained doom of Troy, the goddess ATHENA sent two huge serpents from the sea. These enwrapped Laocoön and his two small sons and crushed them to death.

Further reading: Margarete Bieber, *Laocoon: The Influence of the Group since Its Discovery,* 2d ed. (Detroit: Wayne State University Press, 1967); S. Howard, "Laocoon Rerestored," *American Journal of Archaeology* 93 (1989): 417–422; B. Fehr, "The Laocoon Group, or the Political Exploitation of a Sacrilege," in *Religion and Power in the Ancient Greek World. Proceedings of the Uppsala Symposium 1993,* edited by Pontus Hellström and Brita Alroth (Stockholm: Alqvist & Wiksell International, 1996), 189–204.

lapiths   *See* CENTAURS.

laws and law courts   By the 700s B.C.E.—and probably long before—Greek states had developed official and public procedures for administering justice. No information is available on laws or law courts during the Mycenaean era (around 1600–1200 B.C.E.), but HOMER's epic poem the *Iliad* (written down around 750 B.C.E.) mentions a public trial as one of the scenes embossed on the shield of ACHILLES (book 18). In the scene, elders seated in a city's AGORA arbitrate a dispute between two men over payment of blood money for a murder done by one of the two. A crowd stands around, and heralds call for order.

The judges at such court cases would have been the individuals who ran the city government—that is, the aristocratic COUNCIL or a committee thereof. The ancient Greeks never distinguished between the judiciary and the legislative or executive branches, as modern American society does; there was no class of professional judges. Rather, in early Greek history (around 900–500 B.C.E.), the judges might be the same men who decreed the laws, commanded the army, oversaw the state RELIGION, and owned most of the land. Such law courts obviously were biased in favor of aristocratic plaintiffs and defendants, and this unfairness contributed to the popular anger that produced the Greek TYRANTS (600s B.C.E.) and, later, the Athenian DEMOCRACY (500s B.C.E.).

Systems of law differed from one city-state to another. Before the invention of the Greek ALPHABET, the law would have been handed down by oral tradition, with officials and their underlings memorizing whole legal codes. But in the 600s B.C.E., with the spread of WRITING in the Greek world, laws came to be written down for permanence and easy reference. (By contrast, written law codes had existed in the Near East since at least 1800 B.C.E.)

The writing-down of Greek legal codes came in response to the tense political climate of the 600s B.C.E., as middle-class citizens demanded fair, permanent, and publicly accessible laws. Naturally this was also an occasion for legal reforms and revisions. The earliest written Greek law code was supposedly composed by a certain Zaleucus at LOCRI, in Greek southern ITALY, around 662 B.C.E. At ATHENS, new laws were drafted and written down under DRACO (ca. 625 B.C.E.) and SOLON (ca. 594 B.C.E.). Solon's laws, carved into wooden blocks, were displayed for centuries afterward in the Athenian agora. Today the law code of the city of GORTYN partly survives in a lengthy inscription, carved in stone in about 450 B.C.E.

Law codes covered civil cases such as disputes over inheritance and land boundaries, as well as criminal cases such as homicide and forgery. A comparison with American laws shows some surprising differences. For instance, in Athens in the 400s–300s B.C.E., raping a nonslave woman was merely a finable offense, but a man who seduced such a woman could be punished much more severely. (The legal theory here was that rape was a spontaneous crime while seduction was not only premeditated but corruptive to the woman's morals and to the Athenian household.) The most serious crime at Athens was homicide; conviction brought the death penalty for an intentional killing or exile for an unintentional one (aside from an excusable accident or self-defense). Penalties for other crimes included loss of citizenship or confiscation of property.

Most information on the day-to-day workings of Greek law courts comes from the democratic Athens of the 400s–300s B.C.E. Sources include inscriptions, courtroom speeches, and factual references in the writings of PLATO, ARISTOTLE, and other thinkers. Cases were heard by large groups of jurors, often numbering 501 but otherwise ranging between about 201 and 2,501. Odd numbers were employed to avoid a tie jury vote—unlike modern American juries, ancient Greek juries did not need to reach a unanimous verdict.

The jurors were ordinary Athenian citizens, chosen by lottery. But their responsibilities far surpassed those of modern American jurors. Although an Athenian courtroom had an officiating magistrate to maintain procedure, there was no learned judge to interpret the law, enforce the rules of evidence, or pass sentence. These decisions were made by the jury itself, on the basis of the speeches and examination of witnesses by prosecutor and defendant (or, in a civil case, by the two disputants).

Similarly, there was no state-employed district attorney, whose job was to prosecute in court. State prosecutions were usually brought by volunteers; any adult male citizen could do so. A private individual might decide to prosecute out of civic duty or for public attention toward a political career. In case of conviction, the prosecutor might be entitled to a portion of the defendant's paid fine or confiscated property. Frivolous prosecution was discouraged by a law requiring the prosecutor to pay a fine himself if his case won less than one-fifth of the jury vote. Nevertheless, the courts undoubtedly became the scene of personal and political vendettas, and it is no coincidence that the Athenians were known to be a litigious people.

See also Aeschines; Andokides; Antiphon; Areopagos; aristocracy; Aristophanes; Catana; Kleon; Demosthenes (1); homosexuality; Isaeus; Isokrates; Lykourgos (1); Lykourgos (2); Lysias; marriage; Perikles; Pittakos; prostitutes; Protagoras; rhetoric; slaves; Socrates; women; Zeus.

Further reading: N. Robertson, "The Laws of Athens, 410–399 B.C. The Evidence for Review and Publication," *Journal of Hellenic Studies* 110 (1990): 43–75; Robin Osborne, "Law and Laws. How Do We Join Up the Dots?" in *The Development of the Polis in Archaic Greece,* edited by Lynette Mitchell and P. J. Rhodes (London: Routledge, 1997), 74–82; J. Whitley, "Cretan Laws and Cretan Literacy," *American Journal of Archaeology* 101 (1997): 685–661; C. Carey, "The Shape of Athenian Laws," *Classical Quarterly* 48 (1998): 93–109.

Leda In myth, this beautiful woman was the wife of the Spartan king Tyndareus. The god Zeus became infatuated with her and raped her, approaching her in the shape of a swan. Leda bore two sets of twins, all of whom had important destinies: Helen of Troy and Klytemnestra, and Castor and Polydeuces. According to a familiar pattern of Greek storytelling, it was sometimes claimed that only one member of each pair of twins was Zeus's child, the other being Tyndareus's. Helen and Polydeuces were Zeus's children, and hence eligible for immortality. In some versions, the two pairs of twins were hatched from two giant bird eggs.

Further reading: M. Maaskunt-Kleibrink, "Leda on Ancient Gems," in *Classicism to Neo-Classicism. Essays*

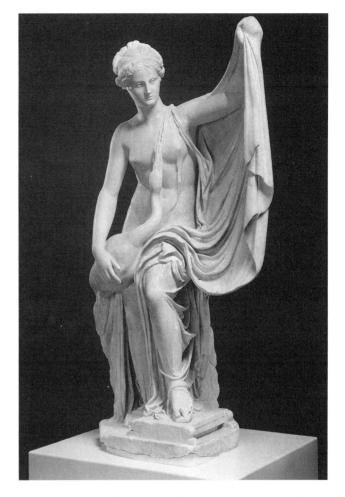

Zeus came to Leda in the form of a swan. Many statues show this popular myth. Here Leda pulls the swan into her lap and hides behind her cloak. *(The J. Paul Getty Museum, Gift of J. Paul Getty)*

Dedicated to Gertrud Seidman, edited by Martin Henig and Dimitris Plantzos (Oxford: Archaeopress, 1999), 19–27.

Lefkandi This modern village and archaeological site is situated on the Lelantine plain, on the west coast of the island of Euboea. In the 1960s C.E. British excavations there found traces of an ancient settlement whose earliest level predated the Greeks' arrival (around 2100 B.C.E.). As a Greek town, the site apparently prospered during the Mycenaean era and later, down to about 825 B.C.E., before being abandoned around 700 B.C.E.

Lefkandi has shed rare light on Greek life during the Dark Age (around 1100–900 B.C.E.). The pride of Lefkandi's archaeological yieldings is the so-called Hero's Tomb, excavated in the 1980s C.E. by the British School of Archaeology at Athens. This surprisingly rich grave of a warrior is located under the floor of a long and narrow, apsidal building dated to the first half of the 10th century

B.C.E. The warrior was cremated, and he was buried alongside a woman, who was inhumed. The burial also contained rich grave goods, including ornaments of GOLD imported from the East. An adjacent burial shaft with the skeletons of four horses further attests the wealth and social importance of the Lefkandi warrior. The tomb's evidence of affluence and TRADE has forced historians to revise their otherwise grim picture of Dark Age Greece.

Lefkandi's apparent abrupt decline after 825 B.C.E. seems related to the emergence of the nearby ancient city of ERETRIA. ARCHAEOLOGY suggests that Eretria arose abruptly, in prosperity, around 825 B.C.E., and modern historians have guessed that Lefkandi was the original city of the Eretrians. Lefkandi sits halfway along the Lelantine plain between Eretria (southeast) and CHALCIS (northwest). Probably under pressure from nearby Chalcis, Lefkandi was abandoned and a new settlement, Eretria, was founded farther away from Chalcis.

See also LELANTINE WAR.

Further reading: L. H. Sackett and M. R. Popham, "Lefkandi. A Euboean Town of the Bronze Age and the Early Iron Age (2100–700 B.C.)," *Archaeology* 25 (1972): 8–19; M. R. Popham, E. Touloupa, and L. H. Sackett, "The Hero of Lefkandi," *Antiquity* 56 (1982): 169–174; C. M. Antonaccio, "Lefkandi and Homer," in *Homer's World. Fiction, Tradition, Reality,* edited by Øivind Anderson and Matthew Dickie (Bergen, Norway: P. Aström, 1995), 5–27; J. A. K. E. de Waele, "The Layout of the Lefkandi Heroon," *Annual of the British School at Athens* 93 (1998): 379–384.

Lelantine War   The earliest Greek conflict for which any reliable historical record exists, this war was fought around 720–680 B.C.E. between the neighboring cities of CHALCIS and ERETRIA, on the west coast of the large island of EUBOEA, in central Greece. Chalcis and Eretria were the most powerful Greek cities of the day; they had previously cooperated in overseas TRADE and COLONIZATION ventures. But now they fought over possession of the fertile plain of Lelanton, which stretched between them.

According to the Athenian historian THUCYDIDES (1) (ca. 410 B.C.E.), the Lelantine War marked the first time that the Greek world divided itself into alliances on one side or the other. It seems to have been a primitive world war, in which the most powerful Greeks states squared off with each other according to traditional local enmities: MILETUS (Eretria's ally) versus its old rival and neighbor SAMOS (Chalcis's ally); CHIOS (Eretria's side) versus its mainland neighbor Erythrae (Chalcis's side); and SPARTA (Chalcis's) against its bitter enemy, the neighboring region of MESSENIA (Eretria's).

The fighting between Chalcis and Eretria on the Lelantine plain may have been an old-fashioned, gentlemen's affair. One later writer reports seeing an old inscription recording the belligerents' agreement not to use "long-distance missiles"—that is, arrows, javelins, and slingstones. Another inscription mentions CHARIOTS, a very old-fashioned military device. These battles were probably fought by dueling aristocrats rather than by the massed concentrations of HOPLITE citizen-soldiers who would come to define warfare in the mid-600s B.C.E.

The war ended around 680 B.C.E., apparently with Chalcis as the marginal winner. In any case, both cities soon were overtaken as commercial and military powers by Corinth, Sparta, and ATHENS. But the war's alliances had lasting effects. With the help of Corinth and Samos, Sparta later conquered Messenia. And seafaring Corinth, shut out of the BLACK SEA by its "Lelantine" enemy Miletus, instead enlarged its grain supplies and foreign markets in SICILY and ITALY.

See also WARFARE, LAND.

Further reading: Donald William Bradeen, *The Lelantine War and Pheidon of Argos* (Lancaster, Pa.: Transactions of the American Philological Association, 1947).

Leonidas   *See* THERMOPYLAE.

Leontini   *See* CATANA; SICILY.

lesbianism   *See* HOMOSEXUALITY; SAPPHO.

Lesbos   The largest island (630 square miles) of the eastern AEGEAN SEA, Lesbos is situated near the northwestern coast of ASIA MINOR. According to Greek MYTH, the island was named for the grandson of Aeolos, founder of the AEOLIAN GREEKS. The original inhabitants of Lesbos may have been descendants of the civilization of TROY. Pottery found through ARCHAEOLOGY there shows that occupation was continuous from at least the Late Neolithic period to the Geometric period.

In around the 900s B.C.E., Lesbos was conquered by the Aeolians, who had migrated east from the Greek mainland regions of THESSALY and BOEOTIA. In the following centuries, Lesbos was the departure point for further Aeolian expeditions that colonized the northwest Asia Minor coast. During the eighth century B.C.E., the foremost city of Lesbos, MYTILENE, controlled most of the cities across the water on the coast of Asia Minor, up to the HELLESPONT. By the 600s B.C.E., Lesbos had become the homeland of a thriving Aeolian culture.

The island prospered by seaborne TRADE, both with mainland Greece and with the eastern Mediterranean kingdoms of LYDIA and EGYPT. Lesbos's tradition of poetry making found its culmination in the verses of SAPPHO (ca. 600 B.C.E.). Lesbos's heyday also saw the political reforms of the Mytilenian statesman PITTACUS (ca. 600 B.C.E.) and the short-lived appearance of Aeolic-style temple architecture at Mytilene and Nape (early 500s B.C.E.). But the golden age had ended by the time the Persians captured the island in 527 B.C.E.

Under CYRUS (1), Lesbos was subject to the Persian Empire and joined the futile IONIAN REVOLT in 499 B.C.E. The island was finally set free from Persian domination in 479 B.C.E., after the battle at Mykale. Lesbos then became an ally of the Athenians, although most of the island revolted again in 428 B.C.E.; this rebellion was severely put down the following year. The Spartan general LYSANDER took command of Lesbos in 405 B.C.E., but it again reverted to Athenian control in 392 B.C.E. For the rest of the Greek era, the island constantly switched between being an independent state and being variously under Athenian, Spartan, Persian, and Macedonian control, finally coming under Roman domination in 88 B.C.E.

See also PERSIAN WARS.

Further reading: Joseph Braddock, *Sappho's Island: A Paean for Lesbos* (London: Constable, 1970); Raymond Kenneth Levang, *Studies in the History of Lesbos* (Minneapolis: Levang, 1972); Peter Green, *Lesbos and the Cities of Asia Minor* (Austin: University of Texas Press, 1984); Nigel Spencer, *A Gazetteer of Archaeological Sites in Lesbos* (Oxford: Tempus Reparatum, 1995); *Lesbos: From Sappho to Elytis* (Mytilene; Topio, 1995); Liza Evert (photographs), *Aeolian Lesbos* (Athens: Constellation Books, 1995).

Leto *See* APOLLO; ARTEMIS.

Leukippos (Leucippus) (ca. 480–420 B.C.E.) *Greek philosopher, credited with inventing the "atomic" theory of natural philosophy*
Probably a native of MILETUS, in ASIA MINOR, Leukippos believed that matter was composed of tiny particles, which he called *atomoi,* an adjective meaning "indivisible." According to him, all creation, destruction, and change are accomplished by the perpetual reorganization of these atoms into new combinations. The atomic theory forms the basis of much of modern physical science.

The basic facts of Leukippos's life and works are unknown. Leukippos was probably older than his pupil DEMOKRITOS, who was born in 460 B.C.E. Even Leukippos's birthplace is debated; some believe he was from Abdera or Elea, in Greek southern ITALY. He developed the atomic theory together with Demokritos, to some degree; it is not entirely possible to determine the individual views and contributions of these two philosophers. No written works survive under Leukippos's name, but two preserved treatises usually attributed Demokritos— *The Great World-system* and *On the Mind*—were probably written by his teacher. From the latter work is a quotation that seems to define Leukippos's basic philosophies: "Nothing happens in vain, but everything from reason and of necessity."

Further reading: Maurice Crosland, ed., *The Science of Matter: A Historical Survey* (Philadelphia: Gordon and Breach Science Publishers, 1992); Andrew Pyle, *Atomism*

and Its Critics: Problem Areas Associated with the Development of the Atomic Theory of Matter from Democritus to Newton (Bristol, U.K.: Thoemmes Press, 1995); C. C. W. Taylor, trans., *The Atomists, Leucippus and Democritus: Fragments: A Text and Translation with a Commentary* (Toronto: University of Toronto Press, 1999).

Leuktra (Leuctra) An ancient village in northern BOEOTIA, Leuktra was the site of one of the most eventful battles in Greek history. There, in the summer of 371 B.C.E., the legend of Spartan invincibility was destroyed when an army of Spartans and allies under King Kleombrotos met defeat by a force of Thebans and allies commanded by the Theban leader EPAMINONDAS. In the battle's aftermath, Epaminondas simply removed SPARTA as a first-class power, mainly by liberating the Spartan-ruled HELOTS of MESSENIA (362 B.C.E.). Sparta, previously master of Greece, never recovered its former power, and the mantle of Greek leadership passed (briefly) to THEBES.

The Battle of Leuktra is described in detail by XENOPHON in his *Hellenica* (ca. 360 B.C.E.). At the heart of the Theban victory was Epaminondas's decision to place the Theban Sacred Band on his battle lines' left wing, deepening it to 50 rows, against the Spartans' more usual 12-man depth. Epaminondas's intent was to destroy the Spartans along their strongest front—their right wing, where the elite "Spartiates" (the Spartan upper class) were arrayed and where the king commanded personally. Traditionally, Greek armies had won their battles on their right wings. The better troops customarily were stationed there, and, due to the battle rows' natural drift rightward, the advancing right wing tended to overlap (advantageously) the enemy left—for both armies. Victory, prior to Leuktra, lay in winning on the right while withstanding the enemy's advantage on its right; traditionally, the left wing performed more poorly. Epaminondas's tactic was to make his left wing the better-performing, by deepening it.

The success was devastating. The Spartan right was pushed back and crushed by the heavy Theban left, and the Spartan left wing scattered in retreat. Nearly 1,000 from the Spartan-led army were killed, including King Kleombrotos and 400 other Spartiates. The Theban side lost 47 men.

Epaminondas's innovation—striking at the enemy's strongest point—changed the nature of Greek warfare. Within a few decades, the technique had been elaborated by the Macedonian king PHILIP II.

See also CHAIRONEIA; WARFARE, LAND.

Further reading: E. David, "Revolutionary Agitation in Sparta after Leuctra," *Athenaeum* 58 (1980): 299–308; C. J. Tuplin, "The Leuctra Campaign. Some Outstanding Problems," *Klio* 69 (1987): 72–107; V. Hansen, "Epameinondas, the Battle of Leuktra (371 B.C.), and the Revolution in Greek Battle Tactics," *Classical Antiquity* 7

(1988): 190–207; J. DeVoto, "Pelopidas and Kleombrotos at Leuktra," *Ancient History Bulletin* 3 (1989): 115–117.

Linear B   This modern name refers to a pre-alphabetic form of WRITING used by the Mycenaean Greeks, around 1400–1200 B.C.E. This was a syllabary script; it basically employed about 90 symbols, each representing a vowel-consonant combination, with pictograms sometimes added to help identify certain words. Linear B was revealed to modern eyes in 1900 C.E. by archaeologist Sir Arthur Evans in his excavations at Mycenaean-era KNOSSOS, on the island of CRETE. The writing, incised into clay tablets, had been incidentally preserved when the tablets were fired during the violent burning of the palace, around 1400 B.C.E. Evans named the then-undeciphered script Linear B to distinguish it from an earlier, Minoan script found at Knossos, called Linear A.

Soon similar tablets were found at PYLOS, THEBES, and MYCENAE, at archaeological levels corresponding to about 1200 B.C.E. In each case the inscriptions had been preserved by unintended firing of the clay. To date, over 5,000 tablets have been discovered.

Linear B was finally deciphered in 1952 by British architect Michael Ventris. Ventris's breakthrough showed that the writing's language was an early form of Greek—that is, when the symbols are correctly sounded out, they yield words that are Greek. This discovery confirmed the assumption (not previously proven) that the Mycenaeans had spoken Greek. The deciphered tablets were revealed to be palace records—inventories, lists of employees and administrative notes—that have shed valuable light on the organization and material culture of late Mycenaean society.

Evidently the Mycenaeans acquired Linear B writing by adapting Minoan Crete's Linear A script to the Greek language. Linear A—which records a vanished, non-Greek language—remains largely undeciphered to this day.

See also ALPHABET; MINOAN CIVILIZATION; MYCENAEAN CIVILIZATION.

Further reading: D. Gary Miller, *Ancient Scripts and Phonological Knowledge* (Amsterdam: J. Benjamins, 1994); Leonard R. Palmer, *The Greek Language* (Norman: University of Oklahoma Press, 1996); Andrew Robinson, *The Man Who Deciphered Linear B: The Story of Michael Ventris* (New York: Thames and Hudson, 2002).

literacy   *See* WRITING.

literature   *See* EPIC POETRY; LYRIC POETRY; THEATER; WRITING.

Locri   A city on the east coast of the "toe" of ITALY, Locri was founded around 700 B.C.E. by Dorian-Greek colonists from LOCRIS, in central Greece. The city's official name was Lokroi Epizephurioi, "West Wind Locrians." After ejecting the native Sicels from the area, the Greek settlers established a well-run OLIGARCHY, called the Hundred Houses. Locri boasted the Greek world's earliest written law code, attributed to the statesman Zaleucus (ca. 622 B.C.E.).

A sprawling community defended by a wall more than four miles long, Locri feuded with neighboring Italian peoples and with CROTON and RHEGIUM, two nearby Greek cities inhabited by non-Dorians. In around 500 B.C.E. the Locrians—supposedly aided by the divine twins CASTOR AND POLYDEUCES—won a famous victory over the Crotonians at the Battle of the Sagras River.

Locri's allies included the powerful Dorian-Greek city of SYRACUSE, in eastern SICILY. In around 387 B.C.E. Locri helped the Syracusan tyrant DIONYSIUS (1) to destroy Rhegium. But Locri was later weakened by the wars that accompanied the expansion of ROME through the Italian peninsula, and the city surrendered to Hannibal of Carthage in 216 B.C.E., but was conquered by the Romans in 205 B.C.E. It gradually diminished in importance during the Roman era.

Archaeological ruins on the site of Locri include the city wall, built in the fourth or third century B.C.E., urban complexes of roads and houses, a theater, and a Doric temple, possibly dedicated to Olympian ZEUS. Also nearby is another, unidentified temple with a decorative SCULPTURE group on the roof consisting of a Nereid between the two DIOSKOUROI. In addition, a large cemetery has been excavated to the northeast of the city, including graves mostly of the 700s and 600s B.C.E., but some of later periods as well.

See also DORIAN GREEKS; LAWS AND LAW COURTS.

Further reading: A. De Franciscis, "Ancient Locri," *Archaeology* 11 (1958): 206–212; C. Sourvinou-Inwood, "The Boston Relief and the Religion of Locri Epizephyrii," *Journal of Hellenic Studies* 94 (1974): 126–137; E. Badian, "Athens, the Locrians, and Naupactus," *Classical Quarterly* 40 (1990): 364–369; Torben Melander, "The Import of Attic Pottery to Locri Epizephyrii. A Case of Reinterpretation," in *Pots for the Living, Pots for the Dead,* edited by Annette Rathje, Margatta Nielsen, and Bodil Bundgaard Rasmussen (Copenhagen: Museum Tusculanum Press, 2002), 59–82; James Redfield, *The Locrian Maidens: Love and Death in Greek Italy* (Princeton, N.J.: Princeton University Press, 2003).

Locris   This bipartite region in the mountains of central Greece is divided by the states of PHOCIS and Doris. West Locris—or Ozolian Locris, named for a local tribe—bordered the northern Corinthian Gulf from NAUPACTUS eastward to Crisa, the harbor of DELPHI. The heart of West Locris was the fertile coastal valley of Amphissa. East Locris—or Opuntian Locris, named for its center at Opus—lay along the Euboean Straits on the mainland's east coast, from THERMOPYLAE southward to a border with BOEOTIA.

East Locris, governed as a 1,000-man OLIGARCHY, was the more advanced of the two regions. It sent colonists to found LOCRI, in southern ITALY, around 700 B.C.E., and was minting coins in the 300s B.C.E. The Locrians were DORIAN GREEKS, but their dialect (called Northwest Greek by modern scholars) was one shared by many of the peoples dwelling around the western Corinthian Gulf.

See also GREEK LANGUAGE.

Further reading: John M. Fossey, *The Ancient Topography of Opountian Locris* (Amsterdam: Gieben, 1990).

Long Walls, the   These walls were built between 461 and 456 B.C.E. at the urging of the Athenian statesman PERIKLES, to connect ATHENS with its port city of PIRAEUS, four miles away. The completed Long Walls consisted of two parallel walls, about 200 yards apart. The result was to make Athens and Piraeus into a single, linked fortress, suppliable by sea and easily in contact with its navy. By building the Long Walls, Periklean Athens became the Greek naval power par excellence.

The Long Walls, however, affected civilian concerns in Athens as well. The city was henceforth connected with the "party of the Piraeus"—the pro-democratic, lower-income citizens who supplied the bulk of the navy's crews. These people began exercising more power in the Athenian ASSEMBLY, resulting in the left-leaning Periklean legislation of these years, such as the introduction of jury pay (457 B.C.E.). This political association was so odious to certain Athenian right-wingers that in 457 B.C.E. a band of Athenian extremists hatched a treasonous plot to deliver the Long Walls to the Spartans. The scheme was discovered and averted.

After the outbreak of the PELOPONNESIAN WAR (431 B.C.E.), the Long Walls permitted Perikles to employ his tortoiselike land strategy of abandoning the countryside to Spartan invasion and collecting the rural Athenian populace within the city's fortifications. The area between the Long Walls became crowded with refugees, resulting in the disastrous plague of 430–427 B.C.E.

After Athens's defeat in the war, the Long Walls were pulled down by Spartan order, to the MUSIC of flutes (404 B.C.E.). The Athenian leader KONON rebuilt the walls in 393 B.C.E., but after 322 B.C.E., under Macedonian overlordship, they gradually fell into disuse. Hardly any trace of them remains today.

See also DEMOCRACY; OLIGARCHY; WARFARE, NAVAL; WARFARE, SIEGE.

Further reading: David H. Conwell, "The Athenian Long Walls: Chronology, Topography, and Remains" (Ph.D. diss. University of Pennsylvania Press, 1992).

Lotus Eaters   *See* ODYSSEUS.

love   *See* APHRODITE; EROS; HOMOSEXUALITY; LYRIC POETRY; MARRIAGE.

Lyceum   This grove and GYMNASIUM outside ATHENS was sacred to the god APOLLO under his title *Lukeios*, "wolf god." The area, described by several ancient writers, was located to the east of the city wall and included several buildings: an exercise room, a dressing room, roads or running tracks, walkways, cult sanctuaries dedicated to Apollo, HERMES, and the MUSES, seating areas, and colonnaded stoas. It was at the Lukeion or Lyceum that ARISTOTLE opened his philosophical school, in 335 B.C.E. The Lyceum operated as a rival to the ACADEMY, which was the Athenian philosophical school founded by PLATO. Unlike the Academy, whose teachings were based on the study of MATHEMATICS, Aristotle's Lyceum focused on nature and the physical world.

In around 286 B.C.E., after the death of Aristotle's successor, THEOPHRASTUS, the Aristotelian school relocated to new buildings at Athens, donated by Theophrastus in his will. According to one version, the new site included a colonnaded walk (Greek: *peripatos*), which gave the institution its famous name, the Peripatetic School. Theophrastus's successor, Straton of Lampsacus, was the last great thinker to preside over the school (ca. 286–269 B.C.E.).

The Peripatetics suffered a decline in influence in the later 200s B.C.E. Whereas Aristotle and Theophrastus had overseen inquiries into every known branch of SCIENCE and PHILOSOPHY, later scholars focused mainly on literary criticism and biography writing; the movement acquired a reputation for pedantry. The decline may have resulted partly from the gradual disappearance of many of Aristotle's original writings, and when these were rediscovered and published in the first century B.C.E., the school did enjoy a partial revival. But by then the Peripatetics were being permanently overshadowed by other Greek philosophical movements, primarily STOICISM and EPICUREANISM, which were flourishing among the Romans. The word *lyceum* survives in the modern French word for school: "lycée."

Further reading: J. P. Lynch, *Aristotle's School. A Study of a Greek Educational Institution* (Berkeley: University of California Press, 1972).

Lycia   *See* ASIA MINOR.

Lydia   This wealthy and advanced non-Greek kingdom of western ASIA MINOR was centered at the city of Sardis, on the Hermus River. It bordered on the regions of Caria, to the south, and Phrygia, to the east. As a military and trading power—with riverborne GOLD and SILVER deposits, and access to eastern caravan routes—Lydia dominated Asia Minor in the 600s–500s B.C.E., before falling to the Persian conqueror CYRUS (1), in 546 B.C.E. Lydia's significance for Greek history lies in its relations, both hostile and friendly, with the Greeks of IONIA, on the coast of Asia Minor.

Lydia was the first non-Greek nation to take an active part in Greek affairs. King Gyges (ca. 670 B.C.E.) sent gifts to the god APOLLO'S shrine at DELPHI, in mainland Greece. King CROESUS, another patron of Delphi, also made a treaty of friendship with SPARTA (ca. 550 B.C.E.). Yet in that same era the Lydian kings repeatedly attacked the Ionian cities, particularly MILETUS, coveting them as outlets to the sea. Finally submitting to Croesus, these Greek cities became privileged subject states under Lydian rule.

Lydia was probably the first nation on earth to mint coins (ca. 635 B.C.E.). This invention was quickly copied by certain Greek cities.

Like certain other Asian peoples, the Lydians had a formidable CAVALRY; they also pioneered early techniques of siege warfare. But after Croesus succumbed to the Persian assault, Lydia became a western province of the Persian Empire.

Although not independent thereafter, Lydia retained a cultural identity. After the conquests and death of ALEXANDER THE GREAT (334–323 B.C.E.), Lydia became a province of the Hellenistic SELEUCID EMPIRE. In the 100s B.C.E. Lydia passed briefly into the kingdom of PERGAMON, before being absorbed into the empire of ROME. Several sites in Lydia have been investigated by archaeologists, but the most important of these is Sardis, which has been systematically excavated since 1958 by the Archaeological Exploration of Sardis, headquartered at Harvard University. The excavation team, consisting of American and Turkish scholars and students, continues to work there, uncovering and restoring monuments from the Lydian period, as well as from later eras.

See also COINAGE; PERSIA; WARFARE, SIEGE.

Further reading: E. N. Lane, "Two Notes on Lydian Topography," *Anatolian Studies* 25 (1975): 105–110; Andrew Ramage, *Lydian Houses and Architectural Terracottas* (Cambridge, Mass.: Harvard University Press, 1978); G. M. A. Hanfmann, "On Lydian Sardis," in *From Athens to Gordion. The Papers of a Memorial Symposium for Rodney S. Young Held at the University Museum the Third of May 1975*, edited by Keith DeVries (Philadelphia: University Museum, University of Pennsylvania, 1980), 99–107; C. H. Greenwalt Jr. and L. J. Majewski, "Lydian Textiles," in *From Athens to Gordion. The Papers of a Memorial Symposium for Rodney S. Young Held at the University Museum the Third of May 1975*, edited by Keith DeVries (Philadelphia: University Museum, University of Pennsylvania, 1980), 133–140; Nicholas Cahill, "Lydian Houses, Domestic Assemblages, and Household Size," in *Across the Anatolian Plateau: Readings in the Archaeology of Ancient Turkey*, edited by David C. Hopkins (Boston: American School of Oriental Research, 2002), 173–186.

Lykourgos (1) This semilegendary, early Spartan lawgiver was said to have founded the government and social organization of classical SPARTA. The Spartans revered the memory of Lykourgos, yet today little is known of his life or even when he lived.

By the most plausible modern theory, Lykourgos arose as a political savior in about 665 B.C.E., after Sparta had been disastrously defeated in a war with ARGOS. In the decades following this defeat, Sparta completely reorganized itself as a militaristic state, devoted to the HOPLITE style of warfare and governed as a moderate OLIGARCHY built around the hoplite class of citizens. The name given to this new form of government was *eunomia:* "good law" or "good discipline." It is reasonable to see this swift, comprehensive change as the work of individual political genius.

In later centuries the Spartans preserved the text of a brief "commandment" (*rhētra*), supposedly written by Lykourgos as the basis for his reforms.

Further reading: J. T. Hooker, "The Life and Times of Lykourgos the Lawgiver," *Klio* 70 (1988): 340–345; Richard J. A. Talbert, trans., *Plutarch on Sparta* (New York: Penguin Books, 1988).

Lykourgos (2) (ca. 390–324 B.C.E.) *Athenian orator and statesman of the mid-300s B.C.E.*
Known for his fierce public prosecutions of various enemies, Lykourgos was an able administrator, who received a special commission to oversee the city's finances. He was active in opposition to the Macedonian king PHILIP II, before Philip's conquest of Greece (338 B.C.E.). One speech by Lykourgos survives, *Against Leokrates* (331 B.C.E.).

See also LAWS AND LAW COURTS.

Further reading: David G. Romano, "The Panathenaic Stadium and Theater of Lykourgos. A Re-Examination of the Facilities on the Pnyx Hill," *American Journal of Archaeology* 89 (1985): 441–454.

lyric poetry Like Greek EPIC POETRY, lyric had its origins in MUSIC. *Lurika melē* (lyric verse) meant a solo song in which the singer accompanied him- or herself on the stringed instrument known as the lyre. These brief songs were distinct from epic verse, which told traditional tales of the deeds of heroes, using an on-flowing rhythm (the hexameter). Lyric used other meters, to convey more personal or immediate messages. Of the earliest lyric poets whose verses have survived, SAPPHO (ca. 600 B.C.E.) is the art's greatest practitioner.

Lyric poetry was developed by the AEOLIAN GREEKS and the DORIAN GREEKS. Aeolian-style lyric consisted of short rhythmical lines, accompanied by stringed instruments. They were personal songs, full of passionate emotions such as love and hatred, joy and sorrow. The Dorians developed a more complex genre of choral lyric, designed for performance in religious festivals. Their songs were therefore not as personal, since they were meant to be sung in public. They are accompanied by strings and flutes, and they had longer lines and a rhythm that was better suited for dancing. The Dorians also developed a greater variety of types of songs, enlarging the category of *lyric*.

One of these forms of song was the elegy, which had its own distinctive meter and was sung to the music of a flute (*elegos*); obviously, for this type of song, the singer used an accompanist. One natural setting for the elegy was the aristocratic drinking party known as the SYMPOSIUM, where female SLAVES would provide flute music as well as other pleasures. The Ephesan poet KALLINUS (ca. 640 B.C.E.) produced what are probably our earliest surviving elegiac verses, urging his countrymen to defend themselves against the marauding Kimmerians. The Spartan TYRTAEUS (ca. 630 B.C.E.) wrote elegies in a similar vein. The elegies of ARCHILOCHUS (ca. 640 B.C.E.) are more angry and personal, and those of ANACREON (ca. 520 B.C.E.) reflect a life that was fun-loving and decadent. One subcategory of elegy was the epigram, which was typically a brief poem, composed for inscription in stone; the epitaph, or gravestone inscription, was one type of epigram.

Another specialized lyric meter was the *iambos*, used by Archilochus, HIPPONAX (ca. 540 B.C.E.), and others for conveying satire and derision. Eventually iambic meter was adopted by Athenian playwrights as sounding natural for individual speaking parts in stage comedy and tragedy.

The term *lyric* also encompassed the category of choral poetry. These verses, in various meters, were written for public performance by a chorus—of men, boys, or girls—usually at a religious festival. Typically accompanied by lyre music, the chorus (usually 30 members) would dance and present interpretive movements.

The many categories of choral lyric include the *paian*, (religious hymn of praise), the maiden song (*parthenaion*), the dirge (*threnos*), and the victory ode (*epinikion*). The greatest Greek choral poet, PINDAR (ca. 470 B.C.E.), is best remembered for his victory odes, which celebrated various patrons' triumphs at such panhellenic festivals as the OLYMPIC GAMES. Another form of choral was the dithyramb, which was a song narrating a mythological story. At ATHENS, dithyrambs were performed at festivals of the god DIONYSUS and included the wearing of masks and the impersonation of characters in the story. By the mid-500s B.C.E., this practice had given birth to a crude form of stage tragedy.

See also ALCMAN; BACCHYLIDES; KALLIMACHUS; SIMONIDES; STESICHORUS; THEATER.

Further reading: Richard Lewis, *Muse of the Round Sky: Lyric Poetry of Ancient Greece* (New York: Simon and Schuster, 1969); Anthony Podlecki, *The Early Greek Poets and Their Times* (Vancouver: University of British Columbia Press, 1984); W. J. Henderson, "Criteria in the Ancient Greek Lyric Contests," *Mnemosyne* 42 (1989): 24–40; Paul Allen Miller, *Lyric Texts and Lyric Consciousness: The Birth of a Genre from Archaic Greece to Augustan Rome* (London: Routledge, 1994).

Lysander (ca. 445–395 B.C.E.) *Leading Spartan commander of the later* PELOPONNESIAN WAR *and aftermath*
First appointed as an admiral in 408 B.C.E., Lysander pursued a strategy to capture the HELLESPONT waterway from the Athenians, and it was in the Hellespont that he won the sea battle of AEGOSPOTAMI (405 B.C.E.), which virtually won the war for SPARTA. After besieging ATHENS, Lysander received the Athenian surrender, occupied the city, and installed the puppet government of the THIRTY TYRANTS (404 B.C.E.). Similarly, he set up oligarchic governments in former Athenian ally cities.

However, the Spartan king Pausanias reversed Lysander's policies, abandoning the Thirty and permitting the restoration of DEMOCRACY at Athens and elsewhere (403 B.C.E.). Lysander became shut out of power by Pausanias and his colleague AGESILAUS. As a field commander at the outbreak of the CORINTHIAN WAR (395 B.C.E.), Lysander invaded BOEOTIA but was killed in battle against the Thebans.

Further reading: C. D. Hamilton, "Lysander, Agesilaus, Spartan Imperialism, and the Greeks of Asia Minor," *Ancient World* 23 (1992): 35–50.

Lysias (ca. 459–380 B.C.E.) *Athenian orator*
Of Lysias's reportedly 200 speeches, 32 survive today. These provide an important source for our knowledge of the Athenian law courts.

Like other orators, Lysias wrote speeches for clients but did not personally plead in court. (He was forbidden to do so, since he was a resident alien, or metic.) His father, Kephalos, a Syracusan by birth, had a lucrative shield manufactory in PIRAEUS. (It is this Kephalos who, with Lysias's brother Polemarchus, is featured in the opening episode of PLATO's fictional dialogue *The Republic*.) Evidently the family knew SOCRATES and moved in intellectual circles.

Under the THIRTY TYRANTS (404 B.C.E.), Polemarchus was put to death and the family's wealth confiscated. Lysias escaped to MEGARA (1), returning under the restored DEMOCRACY of 403 B.C.E. His major speeches, such as his *Against Eratosthenes*—in which Lysias prosecuted a surviving member of the Thirty—were delivered in the period after this return.

See also LAWS AND LAW COURTS; METICS; RHETORIC.

Further reading: Christopher Carey, ed., *Trials from Classical Athens* (London: Routledge, 1997); Stephen Usher, *Greek Oratory: Tradition and Originality* (New York: Oxford University Press, 1999); Alan Boegehold, "At Home. Lysias 1, 23," in *Polis and Politics: Studies in Ancient Greek History*, edited by P. Flensted-Jensen, T. H. Nielsen, and L. Rubinstein (Copenhagen: Museum Tusculanum Press, 2000); S. C. Todd, trans., *Lysias* (Austin: University of Texas Press, 2000); A. Wolpert, "Lysias 1 and the Politics of the Oikos," *Classical Journal* 96 (2000–2001): 415–424.

Lysimachus (ca. 360–281 B.C.E.) *Macedonian general and one of the* DIADOCHOI *(successors) who carved up the empire of* ALEXANDER THE GREAT.

During Alexander's lifetime, Lysimachus was one of his close friends and bodyguards. After Alexander's conquest of the Persian Empire and his sudden death (323 B.C.E.), Lysimachus claimed a domain encompassing THRACE and northwest ASIA MINOR. He took the title of King of Thrace in 306 B.C.E. and built a royal capital, Lysimacheia, on the west coast of the CHERSONESE.

Lysimachus's primary enemy was ANTIGONUS (1), who sought to reconquer Alexander's entire empire from a base in Asia Minor. Lysimachus joined forces with SELEUCUS (1), and together they defeated Antigonus at the Battle of Ipsus in Asia Minor (301 B.C.E.), dividing his territory between themselves. In 287 B.C.E., Lysimachus and another ally, PYRRHUS, expelled Antigonus's son, DEMETRIUS POLIORKETES, from MACEDON and THESSALY. Pyrrhus took control of the lands at first, but the following year Lysimachus drove him out and established himself as the king of Macedon.

In 281 B.C.E., Lysimachus was defeated and killed by his former ally Seleucus at the Battle of Corupedium, in Asia Minor. Lysimachus's patchwork kingdom did not survive him, but instead was divided between the Seleucids and the Antigonids of Macedon.

Further reading: S. M. Burstein, "Lysimachus and the Cities. The Early Years," *Ancient World* 14 (1986): 19–24; Helen S. Lund, *Lysimachus: A Study in Early Hellenistic Kingship* (London: Routledge, 1992).

Lysippos   *See* SCULPTURE.

M

Macedon This outlying Greek kingdom north of THESSALY is situated inland from the Thermaic Gulf, on the northwest Aegean coast. In modern reference, the name *Macedon* usually refers to the political entity, as opposed to the general territory called Macedonia. Macedon's heartland was the wide Thermaic plain, west of the modern Greek city of Thessaloniki, where the rivers Haliacmon and Axius flowed close together to the sea. The widely separated upper valleys of these rivers supplied two more regions of political and economic importance. Elsewhere the country was mountainous and forested. Its name came from an ancient Greek word meaning highlanders.

Macedon was inhabited by various peoples of Dorian-Greek, Illyrian, and Thracian descent, who spoke a Greek dialect and worshipped Greek gods. Prior to the mid-400s B.C.E. Macedon was a mere backwater, beleaguered by hostile Illyrians to the west and Thracians to the east, and significant mainly as an exporter of TIMBER and SILVER to the main Greek world.

Unification and modernization came gradually, at the hands of kings of Dorian descent. Alexander I "the Philhellene" (reigned ca. 485–440 B.C.E.) began a hellenizing cultural program and minted Macedon's first coins, of native silver. The ruthless Archelaus I (413–399 B.C.E.) built forts and roads, improved military organization, chose PELLA as his capital city, and glorified his court by hosting the Athenian tragedians EURIPIDES and AGATHON (both of whom died in Macedon).

Macedon emerged as a major power in the next century. The brilliant Macedonian king PHILIP II (359–336 B.C.E.) created the best army in the Greek world and annexed territory in THRACE, ILLYRIS, and Greek CHAL-CIDICĒ, then subjugated Greece itself (338 B.C.E.). His son and successor, ALEXANDER THE GREAT (336–323 B.C.E.), conquered the Persian Empire and made Macedon, briefly, the largest kingdom on earth.

In the turmoil after Alexander's death, Macedon was seized by a series of rulers until the admirable king Antigonus II anchored a new, stable dynasty there (ca. 272 B.C.E.). This century saw Macedon as one of the three great Hellenistic powers, alongside Ptolemaic EGYPT and the SELEUCID EMPIRE. Macedonian kings controlled Greece, with garrisons at CORINTH, at the Athenian port of PIRAEUS, and elsewhere. In 222 B.C.E. the Macedonian king Antigonus III captured the once-indomitable city of SPARTA.

To counter Macedonian domination, there arose two new Greek federal states, the Achaean and Aetolian leagues (mid-200s B.C.E.). The Macedonian king PHILIP V (221–179 B.C.E.) punished the Aetolians but came to grief against a new European power—the Italian city of ROME. Philip's two wars against Roman-Aetolian armies in Greece—the First and Second Macedonian wars (214–205 and 200–197 B.C.E.)—ended with Macedon's defeat and the Roman liberation of Greece (196 B.C.E.).

Macedon's last king was Philip's son Perseus (179–167 B.C.E.). After defeating Perseus in the Third Macedonian War (171–167 B.C.E.), the Romans imprisoned him and dismantled his kingdom. In 146 B.C.E. the region was annexed as a Roman province, called Macedonia. A lot of current archaeological work is being done in the region of Macedon, particularly at sites like Pella, Dion, Edessa, and especially Vergina, where the royal Macedonian tombs have been discovered.

See also ACHAEA; AETOLIA; DORIAN GREEKS; HELLENISTIC AGE; KASSANDER; phalanx; PYRRHUS.

Further reading: N. G. L. Hammond, "The King and the Land in the Macedonian Kingdom," *Classical Quarterly* 38 (1988): 382–391; N. G. L. Hammond, *The Macedonian State: Origins, Institutions, and History* (New York: Oxford University Press, 1989); Peter Green, *Alexander of Macedon, 356–323 B.C.: A Historical Biography* (Berkeley: University of California Press, 1991); Eugene N. Borza, *In the Shadow of Olympus: The Emergence of Macedon,* 2d ed. (Princeton, N.J.: Princeton University Press, 1992); Alfred S. Bradford, ed., *Philip II of Macedon: A Life from the Ancient Sources* (Westport, Conn.: Praeger, 1992); N. G. L. Hammond, *Philip of Macedon* (London: Duckworth, 1994).

maenads (Greek: *mainadai,* "mad-women") In MYTH, the maenads were the frenzied female devotees of the god DIONYSUS. Usually imagined as Thracian WOMEN, the maenads symbolized the obliteration of personal identity and the liberation from conventional life that came with Dionysus's ecstatic worship. Clothed in fawn- or panther-skins, crowned with garlands of ivy, the maenads would

A satyr and maenad dance on this Greek-Etruscan antefix, 475 B.C.E. The maenad holds krotala, or castanets. An antefix was a decorated upright roof tile set along the edges of the roof of a building. *(The J. Paul Getty Museum)*

rove across mountains and woods, to worship the god with dancing and song. In their abandon, they would capture wild animals and tear them limb from limb, even eating the beasts' raw flesh. Also known as the Bacchae, the maenads were female counterparts of the male SATYRS, but, unlike the satyrs, they were never comical figures. The maenads' rites are unforgettably portrayed in the Athenian tragedian EURIPIDES' masterpiece, *The Bacchae* (405 B.C.E.).

Although certain women's religious groups of central Greece did practice a midwinter ritual of "mountain dancing" (Greek: *oreibasia*) in Dionysus's honor, the maenads as presented in art and literature were not real. Rather, they were mythical projections of the self-abandonment found in Dionysus' conventional cult. Perhaps the idea of the maenads originated in savage, real-life Dionysian festivals in the non-Greek land of THRACE.

Further reading: Renate Schlesier, "Mixtures of Masks: Maenads as Tragic Models," in *Masks of Dionysus,* edited by Thomas H. Carpenter and Christopher A. Faraone (Ithaca, N.Y.: Cornell University Press, 1993), 89–114; Guy Hedreen, "Silens, Nymphs, and Maenads," *Journal of Hellenic Studies* 114 (1994): 47–69; L. B. Joyce, "Maenads and Bacchantes. Images of Female Ecstasy" (Ph.D. diss., UCLA, 1997); Jenifer Neils, "Others Within the Other: An Intimate Look at Hetairai and Maenads," in *Not the Classical Ideal: Athens and the Construction of the Other in Greek Art,* edited by Beth Cohen (Leiden, Netherlands: E. J. Brill, 2000), 203–226; Ross Shepard Kraemer, *Women's Religions in the Greco-Roman World: A Sourcebook* (New York: Oxford University Press, 2004).

magic Magic and magicians were quite commonplace in ancient society, and the practice of magic was closely related to Greek religion and science. Spells, enchantments, and curses of various types have been found in inscriptions, and on stone and other materials. In MYTH, the most celebrated magicians were female: CIRCE in Homer's *Odyssey* and MEDEA in the story of JASON (1) and the Argonauts. The goddess Hekate is often associated with magical rites and herbs, and she is the divinity invoked by Medea in the play of that name by EURIPIDES (431 B.C.E.).

Probably the most common types of spells in the ancient world were love spells and curses. Love magic is mentioned in numerous literary sources from the time of Homer through the Roman era. In the *Iliad,* HERA uses APHRODITE's magic belt to seduce her straying husband, ZEUS. ARISTOTLE and other scientific writers provide information about the many plants, minerals, and animals believed to have magical and aphrodisiacal powers. In addition, many magical gemstones have survived that appear to be love amulets; they bear short Greek inscriptions and amorous scenes typically involving Aphrodite and EROS.

Curse tablets are another important source of information about ancient Greek magic. The most effective means of cursing an individual was thought to involve writing the name of the person along with magical formulas and/or symbols on a small strip of lead. The inscribed lead tablet was then buried in or near a tomb or thrown into a well, spring, or river. Sometimes the tablet was pierced with a nail, presumably to increase the potency of the curse.

Further reading: David Godwin, *Light in Extension: Greek Magic from Homer to Modern Times* (St. Paul, Minn.: Llewellyn, 1992); Hugh Parry, *Thelxis: Magic and Imagination in Greek Myth and Poetry* (Lanham, Md.: University Press of America, 1992); Hans Dieter Betz, *The Greek Magical Papyri in Translation, including the Demotic Spells*, 2d ed. (Chicago: University of Chicago Press, 1996); Christopher Faraone and Dirk Obkink, eds., *Magika Hiera: Ancient Greek Magic and Religion* (New York: Oxford University Press, 1997); Valerie Flint et al., *Witchcraft and Magic in Europe: Ancient Greece and Rome* (London: Athlone Press, 1999); Matthew Dickie, *Magic and Magicians in the Greco-Roman World* (London: Routledge, 2001); S. R. Asirvatham, C. O. Pache, and J. Watrous, eds., *Between Magic and Religion: Interdisciplinary Studies in Ancient Mediterranean Religion and Society* (Lanham, Md.: Rowman and Littlefield, 2001); Daniel Ogden, *Magic, Witchcraft, and Ghosts in the Greek and Roman Worlds: A Sourcebook* (New York: Oxford University Press, 2002).

Magna Graecia *See* ITALY.

Mantineia An important city of ARCADIA located in the central Arcadian plain, Mantineia emerged around 500 B.C.E. from an amalgamation of villages. The name *Mantineia*, suggesting holiness, may refer to a religious dedication at the city's founding. Mantineia was the implacable rival of its 10-mile-distant neighbor, TEGEA. The two cities fought over their boundary and the routing of the destructive water courses through the plain. Also, Mantineia tended to be the enemy of the mighty Spartans, who coveted Arcadia.

Mantineia became a moderate DEMOCRACY around 470 B.C.E.—probably due to Athenian involvement—and in 420 B.C.E., during the PELOPONNESIAN WAR, Mantineia joined an anti-Spartan alliance of ATHENS, ARGOS, and ELIS. This led to a Spartan invasion and a Mantineian defeat at the first Battle of Mantineia (418 B.C.E.). In 385 B.C.E. the Spartan king AGESILAUS captured the city and pulled down its walls; but after the Spartans' defeat at LEUKTRA (371 B.C.E.), the Mantineians built the majestic fortifications whose remnants still stand today. In 362 B.C.E. Mantineian troops fought on the Spartan side and shared in the Spartan defeat at the second Battle of Mantineia, where the Theban commander EPAMINONDAS was

killed in his hour of victory. This battle marked the final Theban invasion of the Peloponnese.

The city was captured and destroyed by the Macedonian king Antigonus III in 223 B.C.E., during his campaign that captured SPARTA. Mantineia was later reestablished under the name Antigoneia.

Mantineia began to be excavated in the early 20th century by the French Archaeological School at Athens. These investigations uncovered the ancient theater, the council house, and the AGORA. The Greek Archaeological Service undertook new excavations at the site in 1985–1995 and revealed the locations of several cult sanctuaries.

Further reading: S. Hodkinson and H. Hodkinson, "Mantineia and the Mantinike: Settlement and Society in a Greek Polis," *Annual of the British School at Athens* 76 (1981): 239–296.

Marathon This town in the Athenian territory of ATTICA is situated three miles from the sea and about 26 miles northeast of ATHENS, along a main road. The coastal plain at Marathon saw one of history's most famous battles, when an Athenian army defeated a seaborne invasion force sent by the Persian king DARIUS (1) (summer of 490 B.C.E.). The Persians, masters of western Asia, were thought to be invincible. The victory at Marathon saved Athens from subjugation and came to be viewed as a nearly mythical event—the gods were said to have smiled on the city and its fledgling DEMOCRACY. Among many later commemorations of the battle was a famous wall PAINTING in Athens's AGORA.

The name *Marathon* may have referred to wild fennel (Greek: *marathon*) in the area. More than 50 years before the battle, Marathon town played a role in the rise to power of the Athenian tyrant PEISISTRATUS. Like other towns of eastern Attica, Marathon held traditional allegiance to Peisistratus's family, and it was at Marathon's hospitable coast that Peisistratus landed an army by sea, to capture Athens (546 B.C.E.). His son HIPPIAS (1) rode with the army that day. Hippias later succeeded his father as tyrant of Athens, but was ousted in 510 B.C.E. Making his way to PERSIA, he became one of King Darius's advisers. Then, in 490 B.C.E., Hippias returned with a Persian invasion fleet, which he guided to the shore near Marathon.

Darius had sent the Persian force to punish two mainland Greek cities, ERETRIA and Athens, for their role in the recent IONIAN REVOLT against Persia. Hippias, then nearly 80 years old, was intended as the Persians' puppet ruler in Athens. Apparently he had been in secret contact with partisans inside Athens who had promised to hand the city over to the invaders.

The ancient Greek historian HERODOTUS, who is the main extant information source for the Marathon campaign, says that the Persian fleet numbered 600 ships. A more accurate figure may have been 200. The fleet carried a land army of perhaps 20,000: armored spearmen, archers, and the formidable Persian CAVALRY, well suited to fighting on the Marathon plain.

After destroying Eretria, the Persian troops disembarked at Marathon to attack Athens. Against them came marching a HOPLITE army of about 9,000 Athenians, plus perhaps 600 from Athens' faithful ally PLATAEA. The Spartans too had promised to send aid, but their troops were delayed at home by certain religious obligations—a typical case of excessive Spartan piety. By the time they arrived, the fight was over.

The opposing armies faced each other for several days, retiring to their respective camps at night. The Greeks, who had no horsemen or archers, were unwilling to attack: They were outnumbered, probably two to one, and they feared the Persian cavalry. The Greeks' advantage was their BRONZE armor (heavier and more extensive than the Persians') and their organized hoplite tactics; man for man, they were to prove the better foot soldiers.

The Athenian command, at this point in history, consisted of 10 generals overseen by a *polemarchos*, or "war leader." Five of the generals wanted to march back to defend the walls of Athens; but the other five led by the brilliant MILTIADES, convinced the polemarch, Kallimachus, to attack. Apparently the timing involved a chance to catch the Persians without their cavalry; the Persian horsemen may have been reembarking to sail elsewhere, when the Athenian army charged.

Advancing quickly across the mile that separated the armies, the Greeks crashed into the Persian infantry ranks and sent both wings fleeing. In the center, the Persian spearmen stood firm but were destroyed when the two Greek wings—Athenians on the right and Plataeans on the left—wheeled inward in an unusual pincer movement.

The retreating Persians were slaughtered as they ran for their ships waiting inshore. The Greeks pursued them into the sea, right up to the ships. There Kallimachus was killed. All but seven Persian ships got away, leaving behind 6,400 dead soldiers. The Athenians had lost 192. Later the Athenian and Plataean dead were buried on the battlefield, under a mound still visible today.

A runner was sent to Athens to report the victory. (Twenty-five centuries later this run would be commemorated in the marathon footrace, first organized for the 1900 C.E. 'Paris Olympics.) Meanwhile, on distant Mt. Pentelicus, behind the battlefield, a shield was seen flashing in the morning sun—probably a heliographic signal to the Persian fleet. Presumably Hippias's Athenian partisans were reporting themselves ready to launch their coup d'état. But no coup was ever attempted: The traitors were frightened off by news of the Athenian victory.

The Persian fleet sailed south and west around Cape Sunium, intending to land closer to Athens. But when they found the Athenian army waiting there, having marched from the battlefield, the Persians set sail for Asia. For the Persian command, the battle had demonstrated that future military action against mainland Greece would require a large army of occupation; 10 years later they would return with one.

The victory was a source of Greek religious awe. Legend claimed that the mythical Athenian hero THESEUS had been seen fighting alongside the Greeks and that an Athenian long-distance messenger had met the god PAN while running through the Arcadian wilds en route to SPARTA. For centuries afterward the battlefield was said to be haunted at night by the noise of combat.

Marathon inspired the confident outlook of a young generation of Athenians, who would defeat the Persians again (480–479 B.C.E.) and go on to forge an Athenian Empire. When the Athenian playwright AESCHYLUS died in 456 B.C.E., after a life full of honors, he recorded only one achievement in his epitaph: that he had fought at Marathon.

See also OSTRACISM; PERSIAN WARS.

Further reading: Konstantinos P. Kontorlis, *The Battle of Marathon: and The Recent Archaeological Discoveries Made There*, 2d ed. (Athens: K. Kontorlis, 1973); Alan Lloyd, *Marathon: The Story of Civilizations on Collision Course* (New York: New American Library, 1975); J. A. S. Evans, "Herodotus and the Battle of Marathon," *Historia* 42 (1993): 279–307; Basil Petrakos, *Marathon*, translated by Alexandra Doumas (Athens: Archaeological Society at Athens, 1996); N. A. Doenges, "The Campaign and Battle of Marathon," *Historia* 47 (1981): 1–17.

marble   *See* ARCHITECTURE; SCULPTURE.

Marmara, Sea of   This modern name refers to the roughly diamond-shape saltwater body, 140 miles long and 40 miles wide at most, that connects the BOSPORUS and HELLESPONT seaways, along the northwestern coast of ASIA MINOR. The Greeks called this sea the Propontis—the "foresea" (i.e., in front of the BLACK SEA). The Propontis supplied a link in the crucial Greek TRADE route that brought metals and grain westward from the Black Sea.

Although not originally part of the Greek world, the Propontis had begun attracting Greek COLONIZATION by the early 600 B.C.E. Greek exploration is reflected (distortedly) in certain episodes in the legend of JASON (1) and the Argonauts.

The major Greek cities on the shores of the Propontis were CYZICUS and BYZANTIUM. The sea's abundant fish runs were commemorated in Cyzicus's COINAGE, which used a tuna as the city's emblem.

Further reading: H. Buitenhuis, "Note on Archeozoological Research around the Sea of Marmara," *Anatolica* 20 (1994): 141–144.

marriage   The ancient Greeks were monogamous; only the Macedonian royal house and certain other marginal traditions allowed for multiple wives. Women married young; brides were frequently around 14 years of age. Grooms were generally chosen by a young girl's parents and tended to be as much as 20 years older than the bride. Marriages were frequently motivated by political and economic considerations.

Very little is known about actual marriage traditions in the BRONZE AGE or at the time of HOMER. The evidence of the Homeric epics shows that gifts were always exchanged between the groom and the bride's parents or guardians; these attested to the new alliance being forged between the two families. Homeric heroes sometimes obtained a wife by winning her in a competition or by abducting her in time of warfare. When Troy fell, the women of the city were taken by the Greeks as wives and concubines.

Most of our information about Greek marriage traditions comes from Athens in the 400s–300s B.C.E. There, marriage arrangements generally included a dowry paid to the groom by the family of the bride. The union was considered complete upon the groom's ritualized acceptance of the dowry or his promise to do so.

The Greek goddess of marriage was HERA, but the wedding ceremony did not involve any priests or priestesses. The ritual, for wealthier families, consisted of a wedding feast typically held at the house of the bride's father. Another important element of the ceremony was the bride's offering her childhood toys and clothing to the gods, symbolizing that she was undertaking the transition to adulthood and would no longer need these items. After the meal, the veiled bride left her father's home and accompanied her husband in a procession to his house— her new home. The revelers followed, and when the bride and groom entered the wedding chamber the well-wishers stood outside the closed door and sang the *epithalamion* (outside-the-bedroom song).

The primary purpose of marriage in ancient Greece was to produce children, and WOMEN were generally judged by their success or failure to do so. In the Athenian marriage ceremony, the bride's guardian would announce, "I give this woman for the begetting of legitimate offspring." The question of legitimacy was extremely important and had consequences for Athenian citizenship. The statesman PERIKLES sponsored a series of laws in 451 B.C.E. that decreed that an Athenian citizen could legally marry only another citizen, and citizenship for children was limited to the legal offspring of such marriages.

The exclusive emphasis on procreation rather than love, in a society that otherwise tended to devalue women, made most Greek marriages unromantic. It was considered entirely appropriate for husbands to find sexual adventure outside marriage—with SLAVES or PROSTITUTES, or in the homosexual pursuits of the GYMNASIUM and other male gathering places. The husband's businesslike view of marriage is conveyed in the words of a male Athenian courtroom speaker of the mid-300s B.C.E.:

"Prostitutes we have for our pleasure, concubines for our daily refreshment, but wives to give us legitimate children and be faithful guardians of our homes" (*Against Neaera,* 122; ascribed to DEMOSTHENES [1]).

In Athens, a husband's extramarital liaisons were not punishable as adultery unless they happened to involve another man's wife. Legally, adultery was defined as sex between a married woman and a man other than her husband—the offense was that it defied the husband's authority and created the possibility of illegitimate children. In cases of adultery, both the erring wife and her male lover could be severely punished. (Due to a lack of evidence, it is not known what the classical Athenians' attitude might have been toward wives taking female lovers, but it too was probably very disapproving. In any event, a wife's secluded, housebound life offered few chances to find lovers of any type.)

Greek divorce was simple. A husband could just dismiss his wife from the house, or a wife could decide to walk away. To petition for the return of her dowry, however, a woman had to present herself in a court of law, which was always biased in favor of her husband. For example, when Hipparette, the estranged wife of the Athenian statesman ALCIBIADES (ca. 420 B.C.E.), arrived at court for this purpose, Alcibiades appeared, lifted her up, and carried her home unchallenged.

See also ADONIS; ASPASIA; HETEROSEXUALITY; HOMOSEXUALITY; LAWS AND LAW COURTS.

Further reading: C. Zaccagnini, "On Late Bronze Age Marriage," in *Studi in onore di Edda Bresciani*, edited by S. F. Bondi (Pisa: Giardini, 1985), 593–605; P. Walcot, "Romantic Love and True Love. Greek Attitudes to Marriage," *Ancient Society* 18 (1987): 5–33; Aphrodite Avagianou, *Sacred Marriage in the Rituals of Greek Religion* (New York: P. Lang, 1991); C. B. Patterson, "Marriage and the Married Woman in Athenian Law," in *Women's History and Ancient History,* edited by Sarah B. Pomeroy (Chapel Hill: University of North Carolina Press, 1991), 48–72; John H. Oakley and Rebecca H. Sinos, *The Wedding in Ancient Athens* (Madison: University of Wisconsin Press, 1993); Cheryl Anne Cox, *Household Interests: Property, Marriage Strategies, and Family Dynamics in Ancient Athens* (Princeton, N.J.: Princeton University Press, 1998); V. Sabetai, "Marriage Boiotian Style," *Hesperia* 67 (1998): 323–334; Fiona Macdonald, *Women in Ancient Greece* (New York: Peter Bedrick Books, 1999).

Massalia This Greek seaport in southern France is located just east of the mouth of the Rhône River; in modern times it is the major French city of Marseille. Massalia was established in about 600 B.C.E. by long-range Greek seafarers from PHOCAEA, in ASIA MINOR; the founding was associated with a sea battle in which the Phocaeans defeated rival Carthaginians in the area.

The Ligurian tribes of the region apparently welcomed the Greeks. Massalia prospered through TRADE with the Ligurians as well as with the CELTS of interior Gaul and the Celtic kingdom of Tartessus in southern Spain. The Massaliote Greeks soon established their own Mediterranean colonies, including Nicaea (modern Nice) and Emporion (meaning "seaport"—modern Ampurias, in southern Spain). These contacts supplied the raw metals—SILVER, IRON, tin, and lead—that the Massaliotes craved for manufacturing or lucrative export to Greece. In exchange the Greeks offered luxury goods, such as worked BRONZE. Greek goods made their way into the continent: Modern ARCHAEOLOGY has discovered Greek bronzes of the 500s B.C.E. (cauldrons, a helmet, vasehandles) in southern Spain, southern France, and at a site 100 miles southeast of Paris.

Another important Greek export was WINE, the key that unlocked the wealth of native peoples. Like the French fur traders of the 1600s C.E. who took brandy into the Canadian wilderness to sell to Indians for pelts, so did the ancient Greeks take Greek wine into interior Gaul, introducing it among the Celtic tribes. A later Greek writer (ca. 20 B.C.E.) described how cheaply the Celts sold their SLAVES for wine, "trading a servant for a drink." In time, the peoples of southern France learned how to cultivate their own grapes. The creation of the French wine industry is not the least cultural legacy of the ancient Greeks.

This infusion of Greek influences up the Rhône in the 500s B.C.E played a vital role in shaping the Celtic "La Tène" culture that was to emerge in Gaul in the next century. From the Greeks, the Gauls learned improved methods of FARMING, fortification, and local administration. They copied the Greek ALPHABET, which Julius Caesar would find still in use throughout Gaul in 59 B.C.E. Aspects of the Gauls' religious beliefs may have been shaped by images of the Greek gods. One ancient writer observed that it seemed as if Gaul had become part of Greece.

Around 310–306 B.C.E. a Massaliote seafarer named Pytheas sailed through the Straits of Gibraltar and around the British Isles, perhaps reaching as far as Norway, in search of the sources of traded tin and other goods. Later ancient writers plausibly describe his exploration.

Massalia was known for the stability of its aristocratic government. Remote from the agitations of mainland Greece, the city thrived without social conflict, while keeping contact with the Greek homeland through such means as a Massaliote treasury house at DELPHI. For centuries, Massalia's only principal enemy was CARTHAGE, and Massalia finally allied itself with the Italian city of ROME against Carthage in the Second Punic War (218–201 B.C.E.). In 125 B.C.E. hostility from local tribes compelled Massalia to appeal to Rome, resulting in the Roman occupation of the region. The Romans called this territory "the province," Provincia—modern Provence.

Excavations began at Massalia after World War II, when the Greek theater was located. A sanctuary of the goddess Kybele and parts of the Roman harbor have also been investigated. Other remains discovered include houses from the Archaic through the Roman eras, a Hellenistic marble quarry, a cemetery, and some early Christian churches.

See also ARISTOCRACY; SHIPS AND SEAFARING.

Further reading: A. N. Oikonomides, "Greek Inscriptions from the Ancient City of Massalia," *Ancient World* 11 (1985): 53–60; B. B. Shefton, "Massalia and Colonization in the North-western Mediterranean," in *The Archaeology of Greek Colonisation. Essays Dedicated to Sir John Boardman*, edited by Gocha Tsetskhladze and Franco De Angelis (Oxford: Oxbow Books, 1994), 61–86; A. Trevor Hodge, *Ancient Greek France* (Philadelphia: University of Pennsylvania Press, 1999).

mathematics The study of mathematics represents the most permanent achievement of ancient Greek thought. Many aspects of modern mathematics, particularly the rules and nomenclature of geometry, derive from the Greeks.

The Greek term *mathematikē* simply means "learning." From the 500s B.C.E. the Greeks saw mathematics as an ideal study and exercise of pure intellect, relevant to PHILOSOPHY. The mystic philosopher PYTHAGORAS (ca. 530 B.C.E.) sought the secrets of the universe in numbers, while PLATO (427–347 B.C.E.) undoubtedly found inspiration for his theory of Forms in the analogy of perfect mathematical concepts. The Greeks were not the only ancient mathematicians—the Babylonians (especially) and Egyptians were also masters in the field—but the Greeks' abiding contribution was their practice of devising rigorous proofs for their theorems.

Like modern peoples, the Greeks counted by 10s, but their numerical symbols were awkward. (Arabic numerals had not been invented yet.) By the 400s B.C.E. Greek numbers were represented mainly by modified letters of the Greek ALPHABET in accumulative combinations. For example, 6,000 was written as ⌐ᴬX ; 6,852 was ⌐ᴬX⌐ᴴHHH⌐ᴬII . While arithmetic calculations could be difficult, plane and solid geometry came more naturally to the Greeks, partly from the age-old inspiration of FARMING patterns and boundary demarcation—the Greek word *geometria* means "land survey." The study of geometry was at the heart of early Greek ASTRONOMY, as brilliant mathematicians such as Eudoxus of KNIDOS (ca. 350 B.C.E.) and Apollonius of Pergē (ca. 200 B.C.E.) devised geometric models to explain the heavenly bodies' movements.

As for the accumulation of mathematical knowledge, a brief sketch must suffice here. By about 500 B.C.E. Pythagoras had discovered the geometric theorem that still bears his name, which states that the squared value of the hypotenuse of a right triangle is equal to the sums of the squares of the two adjacent sides. The very concept of square numbers was a Pythagorean discovery; the category was used for numbers that could be shown as dots forming a square, such as:

$$. \quad . \quad .$$
$$. \quad . \qquad . \quad . \quad .$$
$$. \quad . \ (4) \quad \text{or} \quad . \quad . \quad . \ (9)$$

These and other principles probably had been uncovered by the Babylonians centuries before, but the Greeks most likely made independent discoveries rather than somehow copying Babylonian technique.

Most likely, the earliest Greek mathematical textbook was the now-lost *Elements of Geometry* by Hippocrates of CHIOS, in about 430 B.C.E. (He is not be confused with his contemporary, the physician HIPPOCRATES (1) of Kos.) Mathematics were emphasized at Plato's Athenian school of higher learning, the ACADEMY (founded in about 385 B.C.E.). The most important mathematician of the day was Plato's pupil Eudoxus, who lived around 390–340 B.C.E. None of his writing survives, but he apparently developed the general laws of geometric proportion that now comprise Euclid's book 5. Eudoxus is probably the one who discovered that a cone will always cover one-third of the area covered by a cylinder with the same base and height.

By 300 B.C.E. the Greek-Egyptian city of ALEXANDRIA (1), with its royally endowed Library and Museum, had emerged as a new Greek center of learning. Among the city's mathematicians was Euclid (Eukleidēs), who wrote a textbook titled *Elements* (*Stoicheia*), which survives today. Divided into 13 "books," the *Elements* sets forth the total mathematical knowledge of the day. Euclid was not an original thinker, but he did provide a systematic statement of definitions and problems, featuring clear and methodical proofs. His terminology and methods became canonical, and not just for the ancient world. The *Elements'* first six books, on topics in plane geometry, were used in barely revised form as a textbook for European and North American schools up to the early 20th century.

The next century saw the acme of Greek mathematics in the work of two geniuses, ARCHIMEDES of SYRACUSE (ca. 287–212 B.C.E.) and Apollonius of Pergē (active ca. 200 B.C.E.). Although best remembered today as an inventor and physicist, Archimedes did groundbreaking mathematical work; his extant writings include part of *On the Sphere and the Cylinder, On Conoids and Spheroids,* and the *Sand Reckoner* (in which he invented a system for denoting very large numbers). Of all his life's achievements, he is said to have been most proud of a certain geometric proof, namely, that a cylinder circumscribing a sphere will always have an area in ratio 3-2 to the sphere.

Apollonius was born at a Greek city of southern ASIA MINOR and studied mathematics at Alexandria with the followers of Euclid. Later he sought the patronage of King Attalus I of PERGAMON. Apollonius' major treatise, *Conics,* has survived in most part and provides a milestone in post-Euclidean solid geometry. From Apollonius, for example,

come the modern names by which the three types of conic sections are known: ellipse, parabola, and hyperbola.

The most famous practical application of mathematics in the ancient world was that of Eratosthenes of CYRENE (1), who was head of the Alexandrian Library ca. 245–194 B.C.E. and who used simple geometric principles to calculate the Earth's polar circumference. Eratosthenes discovered that an upright stick would cast no shadow at noon on the summer solstice at Syene (modern Aswan, in southern EGYPT), while at the same moment a stick at Alexandria would cast a small shadow at a 7.2-degree angle. Believing Alexandria to be due north of Syene at a distance of 5,000 stades, Eratosthenes multiplied 5,000 by 50, in ratio to the calculation $50 \times 7.2 = 360$. To the resultant figure of 250,000 stades he added 2,000 more, to offset possible error. Assuming Eratosthenes' stade measure to equal 200 yards, then his figure for the Earth's north-south circumference equals about 28,636 miles; assuming a stade measure of 175 yards (as seems more likely, from the Alexandria-Syene figure), then Eratosthenes' figure equals about 25,057 miles. This is remarkably close to the modern measurement of 24,805 miles.

See also SCIENCE.

Further reading: G. E. R. Lloyd, "Science and Mathematics," in *The Legacy of Greece: A New Appraisal,* edited by M. I. Finley (New York: Oxford University Press, 1981), 256–300; Oswald A. W. Dilke, *Mathematics and Measurement* (London: British Museum Publications, 1987); D. J. O'Meara, *Pythagoras Revived. Mathematics and Philosophy in Late Antiquity* (New York: Oxford University Press, 1990); R. Netz, "Classical Mathematics in the Classical Mediterranean," *Mediterranean Historical Review* 12 (1997): 1–24.

Mausolus   *See* HALICARNASSUS.

Medea   In MYTH, the daughter of King Aeëtes of Colchis and the niece of the witch CIRCE. Medea herself was a sorceress; her name, Medeia, means "cunning." In the story of JASON (1) and the Argonauts, as told by the epic poet APOLLONIUS (ca. 245 B.C.E.), the young Medea fell in love with the handsome hero when he arrived at Colchis in search of the Golden Fleece. Against her father's interest, she helped Jason with magic ointments and instructions, and escaped with him and the fleece aboard the ship *Argo.*

Later, on arriving at the city of Ioclus, in THESSALY, Medea helped Jason avenge himself on his enemy; King Pelias. First, she boiled a cauldron of water and magic herbs for Jason's old father, Aeson. After submerging himself in the boiling water, Aeson emerged as a young man. Medea then suggested that Pelias's daughters do the same for him. But this time she supplied useless herbs, and when the king entered his daughters' bath he was boiled to death.

Ousted from Ioclus by Pelias's son, Jason and Medea settled at CORINTH, where they had a son and daughter.

What followed is the subject of Euripides' tragedy *Medea* (431 B.C.E.). Learning that Jason planned to desert her and marry Glauce—daughter of the Corinthian king—Medea went insane with anger. She sent Glauce a robe and tiara smeared in poison; this resulted in the death of both the bride and her father. Next, to avenge herself fully on Jason, Medea stabbed both of their young children to death, then flew off in a magic chariot, taking refuge with the Athenian king Aegeus (father of Theseus). Euripides' *Medea* provides an almost modern study of pathological jealousy and hatred, emanating from a woman wronged. The play is often considered to be almost feminist in its portrayal of the strong-willed, clever protagonist and her articulation of the injustices done to women in the ancient Greek world and other patriarchal societies (lines 215ff). She had betrayed her father and her country to be with Jason, and thereby made herself dependent on him. She fulfilled the primary purpose of a Greek wife in bearing him legitimate offspring. The tragic chorus is therefore sympathetic to her and her grievances. Her extreme reaction and her choice to slaughter her own children, however, is not only unfeminine, it is very un-Greek, and at this point she loses the support of the chorus, the playwright, and the audience.

Further reading: C. Sourvinou-Inwood, "Myths in Images. Theseus and Medea as a Case Study," in *Approaches to Greek Myth*, edited by Lowell Edmunds (Baltimore: Johns Hopkins University Press, 1990), 395–445; James Clauss and Sarah Iles Johnston, eds., *Medea: Essays on Medea in Myth, Literature, Philosophy, and Art* (Princeton, N.J.: Princeton University Press, 1997).

Medes *See* Persia.

medicine Modern knowledge of ancient Greek medicine comes largely from the surviving works of medical writers of antiquity, from references in the works of nonmedical writers, and from artwork depicting medical scenes. The greatest Greek medical writer was Galen of Pergamon, who lived in the 100s C.E. In the centuries before Galen, existing medical knowledge was organized and written down by Hippocrates (1) of Kos and his followers (late 400s B.C.E. and after) and by various physicians based at Alexandria (1).

To a surprising degree, the Greeks distinguished medicine from religion or superstition. Although Apollo, Asklepios, and other gods were believed to have healing powers—and although crude healing magic existed—such beliefs did not prevent the development of scientific methods. Since the Greeks lacked such modern marvels as antibiotics and anesthesia, surgery was a drastic and dangerous recourse. Ancient texts describe a number of surgical tools used by Greek physicians, and examples of them have been discovered in many archaeological excavations. These tools include scalpels, hooks (for lifting blood vessels or tissue and retracting the edges of a wound), forceps, bone drills, bone forceps, catheters, and vaginal speculums. One type of surgery that the Greeks performed was trepanning, a dangerous technique involving a hole being drilled into the skull to relieve pressure on the brain. This process is mentioned in writings of the 400s B.C.E., and a skeleton that survived such an operation was recently excavated on the island of Chios, dated to ca. 250 B.C.E. There was also no knowledge of microorganisms as the cause of disease. But a knowledge of dietetics, healing herbs, primitive orthopedics, and techniques of bandaging provided the beginnings of Greek medicine in the centuries prior to 400 B.C.E. Physicians employed numerous herbs in their treatments, many of which are still considered to be effective by alternative medicine practitioners today. An extensive treatise on herbal medicine was written by Aristotle's pupil Theophrastus in the 300s B.C.E.

There was no medical licensing in ancient Greece. Physicians were considered to be on par with skilled craftsmen such as poets or architects. The historian Herodotus mentions a famous Greek doctor, Democedes of Croton, who in the late 500s B.C.E. became the court physician to the tyrant Polycrates of Samos and then to the Persian king Darius (1). But it is Hippocrates (ca. 460–377 B.C.E.) who provides the first milestone.

On his native island of Kos, Hippocrates in about 430 B.C.E. established a school to create standards of medical and ethical procedure: The modern "Hippocratic Oath" is one legacy of this school. The Hippocratics emphasized careful observation and diagnosis. Among the writings known as the Hippocratic Collection (produced by Hippocrates' followers in the late 400s and early 300s B.C.E.), the two books entitled *Epidemics*—presenting 42 case histories of severely ill patients—are unequaled in clarity by any extant European medical writing prior to the 16th century C.E. Modern readers of the *Epidemics* are able to identify cases of diphtheria and typhoid fever from the symptoms described. It is a testament to the medical ignorance of the day, and to the honesty of the writer, that about 60 percent of the *Epidemics'* cases end with the patient's death.

Another Hippocratic writing is a treatise whose title is traditionally translated as *On the Nature of Man*. Written around 400 B.C.E., this work presents the famous (but incorrect) theory of the Four Humors, destined to dominate medical thought for the next 2,000 years. According to the theory, the human body consists of four elementary fluids—blood, phlegm (*pituita*), yellow bile (*cholē*), and black bile (*melancholia*)—whose correct proportion maintains health and whose imbalance causes illness. One crude procedure of the day was to apply heated metal cups to a patient's skin, in an attempt to draw off any excessive humors; gravestones and other surviving artwork sometimes show the physician with two metal cups, as a badge of profession. The practice of bleeding a patient, to purge "excessive" blood, was another misguided procedure inspired by the Four Humors belief.

The 300s B.C.E. saw a growing interest in anatomy, due partly to the biological studies of ARISTOTLE and his school, the LYCEUM. Anatomical knowledge was greatly advanced by two Alexandrian physicians of the middle and late 200s B.C.E.—Herophilus of Chalcedon and Eristratus of Keos, whose respective writings survive only in fragments but whose work is described by the Roman writer Celsus (first century C.E.). Working separately, Herophilus and Eristratus were among the first to perform dissection on the human body—and, according to rumor, they also practiced human vivisection in the name of medical knowledge, using condemned criminals handed over by royal permission. These doctors and their colleagues added greatly to the knowledge of human circulation and respiration, and several of the anatomical terms coined by them survive in use today.

In the Roman era, many of the herbs and tools used by Greek physicians continued to be utilized, but medicine generally became increasingly scientific and respected. With the establishment of a professional Roman army in 90 B.C.E., the need for practical medical treatments became greater. The emperor Augustus formed a professional military medical corps, with higher status and significant benefits. By the early first century C.E., a formal medical school had been established, including specialized training in fields such as internal medicine, urology, and ophthalmology.

See also SCIENCE.

Further reading: E. D. Phillips, *Aspects of Greek Medicine*, 2d ed. (Philadelphia: Charles Press, 1987); P. Potter, *Short Handbook of Hippocratic Medicine* (Quebec: Editions du Sphinx, 1988); J. Longrigg, *Greek Rational Medicine. Philosophy and Medicine from Alcmaeon to the Alexandrians* (London: Routledge, 1993); Darrel W. Amundsen, *Medicine, Society, and Faith in the Ancient and Medieval Worlds* (Baltimore: Johns Hopkins University Press, 1996); J. Longrigg, *Greek Medicine from the Heroic to the Hellenistic Age: A Sourcebook* (London: Duckworth, 1998).

Medusa   In MYTH, this winged female monster had hair of snakes and a face that caused any humans who looked at it to turn to stone. Medusa ("cunning") was mortal but had two immortal sisters, Sthenno ("strong") and Euryalē ("wide jumping"). Known collectively as the Gorgons ("grim ones"), they lived together in the far West. With the aid of the goddess ATHENA, the Greek hero PERSEUS severed Medusa's head and put it in a bag. The head—with its abiding ability to petrify an onlooker—aided Perseus in his subsequent adventures. The head was later given to Athena, who set it in the center of her cloak known as the aegis.

Clearly, in early Greek or pre-Greek RELIGION, Medusa and her sisters had an apotropaic function; that is, they were worshipped or represented as protective

The head of Medusa decorates the back of this bronze hand mirror. Medusa's gaze, with its ability to turn the observer to stone, was used in Greek art to ward off evil. Maybe the artist was also making a point about beauty and ugliness. *(The J. Paul Getty Museum)*

demons who could scare away evil from the community. The protective head of Medusa was said to be buried under the AGORA at Perseus's city, ARGOS. By the 600s B.C.E., Medusa (or an unspecified Gorgon) had became a favorite subject in PAINTING and SCULPTURE, particularly at CORINTH and at Corinthian colonies such as CORCYRA. Portrayed as a winged running demon grimacing at the viewer, the monster would be shown in vivid colors. Probably the best-known surviving example is the Gorgon pediment sculpture from the temple of ARTEMIS at Corcyra (ca. 600–580 B.C.E.).

Further reading: Stephen R. Wilk, *Medusa: Solving the Mystery of the Gorgon* (New York: Oxford University Press, 2000).

Megara (1)   This city of south-central Greece is located in the widening, northeastern isthmus region known as the Megarid. Lying in a fertile valley near the Saronic Gulf and the island of SALAMIS (1), Megara is surrounded on three sides by mountains, which separate the city from the regions of ATHENS (to the north east), CORINTH (to the southwest), and THEBES (to the north). In particular, the southwestern mountain range, the Geranea, formed a natural barrier between central Greece and the PELOPONNESE, and was of strategic importance in Greek history.

After a promising start, the city slipped into a largely unhappy pattern of resistance to its powerful neighbors. Megara was founded by DORIAN GREEKS who had invaded the Peloponnese (ca. 1100 B.C.E.). Unlike older Greek cities founded by pre-Greek inhabitants, Megara has a name that actually means something in Greek: "the great hall." In the age of TRADE and COLONIZATION (ca. 800–550 B.C.E.), Megara was a foremost power, exporting its prized woolens and establishing the colonies Megara Hyblaea, on the east coast of SICILY (ca. 750 B.C.E.), and Heraklea Pontika, on the south shore of the BLACK SEA (ca. 560 B.C.E.). In the LELANTINE WAR (ca. 720–680 B.C.E.), Megara sided with ERETRIA, the enemy of Megara's neighbor and rival, Corinth.

Like other commercial cities of this era, Megara came under the sway of TYRANTS. A certain Theagenes (ca. 630 B.C.E.) seized power after leading the common people in slaughtering the nobles' cattle. Theagenes was the father-in-law of the Athenian aristocrat KYLON and seems to have played a role in Kylon's failed coup at Athens (ca. 625 B.C.E.). Later the tyrant fell.

Engulfed by class war between nobles and commoners, the city declined, losing border land to Corinth and the coveted island of Salamis to Athens (mid-500s B.C.E.). The poems of the Megarian aristocrat THEOGNIS (ca. 540 B.C.E.) are filled with hatred toward the common people, signifying the discord that drained Megarian power in these years.

As part of the Spartan alliance, the Megarians fought on sea and land against the Persian king XERXES' invasion of Greece (480–79 B.C.E.). Later, after seeking help against Corinth in a border dispute, Megara allied itself with Athens (460 B.C.E.). The Athenians occupied the region and helped set up a DEMOCRACY at Megara. They also built "long walls," extending the mile's distance between Megara and its port of Nisaea, on the Saronic Gulf. The walls turned Megara and Nisaea into a linked fortress, suppliable directly by sea and impregnable by land.

Ironically, Megara's defenses came into use against Athens. In the 430s B.C.E. the Megarians withdrew from the Athenian alliance, encroached on Athenian territory, and murdered an Athenian herald. The Athenian statesman PERIKLES responded with the notorious Megarian Decree, which attempted to starve the Megarians into submission by placing embargoes on their food imports and their export trade. This hostile act alarmed the Spartans and other Greeks, and played a role in causing the PELOPONNESIAN WAR (431–404 B.C.E.).

As a Spartan ally near Athenian territory in the war, Megara was a constant target for the Athenians, who invaded the Megarid with a huge force in 431 B.C.E. and kept invading—without capturing the city—every year until 421 B.C.E. In 424 B.C.E. a faction within Megara attempted to betray the city to the Athenian general DEMOSTHENES (2); he seized Nisaea and the Long Walls, but Megara itself was saved by the Spartan general BRASIDAS.

A brief phase of prosperity came in the 300s B.C.E., when the city was host to a school of SCULPTURE and to the Megarian School of PHILOSOPHY (founded by Eukleides, a disciple of the Athenian SOCRATES). Thereafter, although still inhabited, Megara fades from history.

Further reading: Ronald Legon, *Megara: The Political History of a Greek City-state to 336 B.C.* (Ithaca, N.Y.: Cornell University Press, 1981); Hans R. Goette, *Athens, Attica, and the Megarid: An Archaeological Guide,* 2d ed. (London: Routledge, 2001).

Megara (2)   *See* HERAKLES.

Meleager   *See* CALYDONIAN BOAR HUNT.

Melian Dialogue   *See* MELOS; THUCYDIDES (1).

Melos   This small island of the western AEGEAN SEA is part of the island group known as the CYCLADES. ARCHAEOLOGY reveals that in the pre-Greek "Cycladic" culture of the third millennium B.C.E. Melos was the exclusive source of obsidian—a volcanic glass that when quarried and honed, supplied axblades, plowshares, and the like, in the days before general use of metals. By the 1600s B.C.E. Melos was an ally or subject of Minoan CRETE and by 1400 B.C.E. was part of the Aegean empire of the Mycenaean Greeks.

Around 1000 B.C.E. Melos was occupied by DORIAN GREEKS from LACONIA. With its capital city, also called Melos, in the north of the island, Melos existed as a Dorian state amid the predominantly Ionian-Greek Cyclades. By about 475 B.C.E. the Cyclades were the heart of the Athenian-dominated DELIAN LEAGUE, of which Melos was not a member.

Melos remained neutral at the outbreak of the PELOPONNESIAN WAR between ATHENS and SPARTA (431 B.C.E.). The Athenians attacked Melos in 426 B.C.E., and in 416 B.C.E. they again landed there, demanding that Melos join the Delian League. The Melians refused, preferring to look for help from their kinsmen the Spartans. This "Melian Dialogue" provides one of the set pieces of THUCYDIDES' (1) history of the Peloponnesian War (book 5). Although the dialogue often has been interpreted as an argument between Might and Right, it seems clear that Thucydides' heart is with the Athenians, who deliver their argument in terms of expedience and common sense. In any case, Melos city was besieged and captured by the Athenians, who enslaved and deported the islanders and planted an Athenian garrison colony there.

The celebrated statue called the Venus de Milo, now in the Louvre, is a marble APHRODITE discovered at Melos in 1820 C.E. ("Milo" being the Italian form of Melos.) Dated to the 100s B.C.E., it is probably a copy of a lost original of the 300s B.C.E.

See also BRONZE AGE; MINOAN CIVILIZATION; MYCENAEAN CIVILIZATION.

Further reading: Colin Renfrew and Malcolm Wagstaff, eds., *An Island Polity: The Archaeology of Exploitation in Melos* (New York: Cambridge University Press, 1982); Greg Curtis, *Disarmed: The Story of the Venus de Milo* (New York: Alfred A. Knopf, 2003).

Memnon   In Greek MYTH, Memnon was an Ethiopian king, son of the dawn goddess Eos and the mortal man Tithonus. Memnon, whose name means "resolute," led a contingent of his countrymen to TROY, to help defend the city against the Greeks in the TROJAN WAR. In battle Memnon slew NESTOR's son Antilochus, but was himself killed by the Greek champion, ACHILLES. The dawn goddess carried away her son's corpse, and the great god ZEUS revived him as an immortal in heaven. The story of Memnon was told in a now-lost epic poem, the *Aithiopis*.

Memnon was a favorite subject of Greek vase painting in the 500s and 400s B.C.E. Like other mythological figures from Ethiopia, he was sometimes shown with distinctly negroid facial features. During the HELLENISTIC AGE (300–150 B.C.E.), the Greeks in EGYPT associated Memnon with certain preexisting monuments of the ancient pharaohs, including the so-called Colossi of Memnon—two huge sandstone statues of Pharaoh Amenophis III, seen at Luxor today.

See also BLACK PEOPLES.

Further reading: W. D. E. Coulson and M. E. Clark, "Memnon and Sarpedon," *Museum Helveticum* 35 (1978): 65–73; D. V. Bothmer, "Euphronios and Memnon? Observations on a Red-Figured Fragment," *Metropolitan Museum Journal* 22 (1987): 5–11; R. D. Griffith, "The Origin of Memnon," *Classical Antiquity* 17 (1998): 212–234.

Menander (Greek: **Menandros**) (ca. 342–219 B.C.E.) *Athenian comic playwright*
Menander is the last great Athenian literary artist whose writings have survived from antiquity. He wrote over 100 plays, yet only one complete work exists today: *The Misanthrope* (Greek: *Duskolos*). Portions of other plays are known from quotations by later ancient authors and by modern archaeological discoveries of papyrus remnants in EGYPT, where Menander was apparently a favorite author of the Greco-Roman educated classes during the Roman Empire.

Little is known of his life. He grew up in an ATHENS that was well past its imperial prime and was dominated (like all of Greece) by the powerful kingdom of MACEDON. Menander apparently moved in the highest circles of Athenian society and politics. He studied under the Aristotelian philosopher THEOPHRASTUS and was a friend of Demetrius of Phalerum, an Athenian who served as governor for the Macedonian king KASSANDER. Demetrius's overthrow in 307 B.C.E. is said to have put Menander in temporary danger.

In 321 B.C.E., at about age 20, Menander won his first drama-victory, when his comedy *Anger* (not extant today) took first prize at an Athenian festival. His surviving masterpiece, *The Misanthrope,* won first prize in 316 B.C.E., at the midwinter festival called the Lenaea. Among his plays that survive in part today are *The Woman from Samos, The Hated Lover,* and *The Girl with the Short Haircut.*

Menander died after having won first prize eight times—a respectable but not dazzling record. However, his reputation grew soon after his death, and he came to be considered one of the classic Athenian authors. His plays served as models for the work of the Roman comic playwrights Plautus (ca. 200 B.C.E.) and Terence (ca. 150 B.C.E.)

For modern readers, *The Misanthrope* was discovered on an ancient papyrus only in 1958 C.E. (The French comic playwright Molière may have known the title but did not have the play as a model for his own *Misanthrope,* performed in 1666 C.E.) Set in the Athenian countryside, Menander's fanciful tale involves an old farmer, Knemon, who loathes humanity and lives, secluded, with his daughter. A rich young man, falling in love with the daughter, poses as a rustic laborer in order to win her hand in MARRIAGE. He succeeds after pulling Knemon out of a well where the old man has fallen.

Ancient and modern scholars have seen Menander's work as the high point of the "New Comedy" (ca. 321–264 B.C.E.), which marks the last phase of evolution for Athenian stage comedy. "Old Comedy," as developed by ARISTOPHANES and others in the 400s B.C.E., was the product of the powerful Athenian city-state; Menander and the New Comedy are products of the more cosmopolitan and uncertain HELLENISTIC AGE, where most citizens lived cut off from major political events. Whereas Old Comedy presented fantasy, political satire, and obscene farce, New Comedy offered realistic settings and domestic plots, often "boy meets girl." In keeping with other conventions of New Comedy, Menander's plays show a great reduction in the onstage role of the comic chorus, which is used only for song-and-dance interludes. Menander's witty comedies of manners are still highly relevant today and are well appreciated by modern audiences.

See THEATER.

Further reading: A. W. Gomme and F. H. Sandbach, *Menander, A Commentary* (New York: Oxford University Press, 1973); Dana F. Sutton, *Ancient Comedy: the War of the Generations* (New York: Maxwell Macmillan International, 1993); Netta Zagagi, *The Comedy of Menander: Convention, Variation, and Originality* (Bloomington: Indiana University Press, 1995); J. Michael Walton and Peter

D. Arnott, *Menander and the Making of Comedy* (Westport, Conn.: Greenwood Press, 1996); Susan Lape, *Reproducing Athens: Menander's Comedy, Democratic Culture, and the Hellenistic City* (Princeton, N.J.: Princeton University Press, 2004).

Menelaus   In MYTH, this king of Lacedaemon was the younger brother of King AGAMEMNON of MYCENAE. Menelaus was married to the Spartan princess Helen, later known as HELEN OF TROY. At the prompting of the love goddess APHRODITE, Helen abandoned Menelaus to elope with the Trojan prince PARIS. It was to punish this outrage that Agamemnon organized the Greek expedition against TROY, in the TROJAN WAR.

In the *Iliad* (book 3) Menelaus agrees to settle the entire war by single combat with Paris. Menelaus overwhelms his rival, but is deprived, by Aphrodite, of the chance to kill him. In the *Odyssey* Menelaus is shown briefly, back home with Helen and reconciled with her.

Further reading: Christopher Logue, *The Husbands: An Account of Books 3 and 4 of Homer's Iliad* (New York: Farrar, Straus and Giroux, 1995).

Messana   *See* ZANCLĒ.

Messenia   The southwest region of the PELOPONNESE, Messenia's eastern frontier is separated from the Spartan region of LACONIA by the lofty Mt. Taygetus range. On the west and south, Messenia is bounded by the sea, and in the north, it borders ELIS and ARCADIA. Largely mountainous, Messenia includes the westernmost of the Peloponnese's three southern peninsulas, Cape Akritas.

The heart of the region is the Messenian plain, one of the most fertile areas of mainland Greece; it opens southward around the river Pamisus to the Messenian Gulf. On the west coast, a second, narrower plain was home to a thriving kingdom in Mycenaean times, around 1400–1200 B.C.E. Later Greeks remembered this kingdom by the name PYLOS and associated it with the mythical king NESTOR. This domain vanished prior to or during the invasion of the DORIAN GREEKS, around 1100–1000 B.C.E., and consequently, Messenia became a Dorian region.

Messenia had a tragic history, being the most complete victim of Spartan domination. In the 700s B.C.E. the Spartans, crossing the Taygetus range, began their long campaign of conquest. The First and Second Messenian wars (ca. 730–710 B.C.E. and ca. 650–620 B.C.E.) were bitter conflicts; the Messenian leaders Aristodemus and Aristomenes were later remembered for their failed, heroic defense. By 620 B.C.E. the Messenian plain was in Spartan hands, and those Messenians who had not fled were virtually enslaved as Spartan-owned HELOTS.

Under the helot system, the Messenians were serfs, owned in common by the Spartan state. They were not deported to Sparta, but were left on the Messenian land (which they no longer owned), to farm it and produce food for their overlords. Half of all their produce went to Sparta.

The Messenians were allowed to maintain their local cults, customs, and family structures, but they were brutalized and terrorized. The Spartan poet TYRTAEUS writes of a Messenian's hopeless drudgery and his dutiful mourning when his Spartan master dies. Discipline was maintained by Spartan garrisons and by the Krypteia—the Spartan "secret society" whose job was to identify and do away with subversive helots. The Spartan's ferocity toward the Messenians—who were, after all, their fellow Dorian Greeks—comprised the single most warped aspect of the Spartan mentality.

The Third Messenian War was a rebellion sparked by news of a devastating earthquake at Sparta (464 B.C.E.). The revolt died with the surrender of the Messenian hilltop fortress of Ithomē ("the step"), in about 460 B.C.E. At least some of the Messenian defenders were permitted to depart under safe-conduct, and the Athenians later relocated them to NAUPACTUS, a city on the northwest shore of the Corinthian Gulf.

During the PELOPONNESIAN WAR (431–404 B.C.E.) Messenian helots served their Spartan masters loyally while, on the other side, refugee Messenians fought as valuable Athenian allies. After the Athenian victory at the site called Pylos, on Navarino Bay (425 B.C.E.), the Athenians built a fortified naval base there. But the hoped-for Messenian revolt against Sparta never materialized.

Messenia was finally liberated in 369 B.C.E. by the Theban statesman and general EPAMINONDAS, after his destruction of a Spartan army in 371 B.C.E. Under Epaminondas's guidance, the Messenians founded a city, Messene (modern Messini), to be the capital of the new, free territory. Messene and Messenia thrived for a century but suffered in the 200s and 100s B.C.E. from the intervention of MACEDON and the Achaean League, before passing into the hands of ROME after 146 B.C.E.

See also ACHAEA; DEMOSTHENES (2); ZANCLĒ.

Further reading: Nikos Kaltsas, *Ancient Messene* (Congleton, U.K.: Old Vicarage, 1994); Piotr Dyczek, *Pylos in the Bronze Age: Problems of Culture and Social Life in Messenia* (Warsaw: Wydawnictwa Uniwersytetu Warszawskiego, 1994); Petros G. Themelis, *Ancient Messene: Site and Monuments,* translated by A. Makres (Amaroussio, Greece: D & G Kalofolias, 1998); N. Luraghi and S. E. Alcock, eds., *Helots and Their Masters in Laconia and Messenia: Histories, Ideologies, Structures* (Washington, D.C.: Center for Hellenic Studies, Trustees for Harvard Universities, 2003).

meter   *See* EPIC POETRY; LYRIC POETRY.

metics   These resident aliens had legal status in Greek cities. A metic (Greek: *metoikos,* "dweller among") was usually a Greek who had immigrated to a Greek city other than his birthplace. Metics abounded in the wealthier and more populous Greek cities, but their existence is best attested at ATHENS.

The rules for acquiring metic status and the legal restrictions applying to metics somewhat resembled those surrounding resident aliens in the United States today. The applicant had to be sponsored by a citizen, had to register in an Athenian DEME (city ward), and had to pay a special annual tax. Metics owed the state certain public duties and military service, usually as crewmen in the Athenian navy. They could not set foot inside (much less vote at) the Athenian political ASSEMBLY, usually could not own land, and could not marry an Athenian citizen. In exchange, metics enjoyed the courts' protection, the right to engage in business, and a recognized position in the community. At Athens, much of the import-export and manufacturing was in the hands of metics, some of whom became very rich. One example is the Syracusan-born Kephalos, father of the orator LYSIAS. The most famous person who was a metic at Athens was ARISTOTLE.

See also POLIS.

Further reading: David Whitehead, *The Ideology of the Athenian Metic* (Cambridge: Cambridge Philological Society, 1977).

Midas The last king of the wealthy, non-Greek nation of Phrygia, in ASIA MINOR, Midas reigned through the late 700s B.C.E. He was said to be the first non-Greek to send gifts to the god APOLLO's shrine at DELPHI, that is, the first foreign ruler to open diplomatic relations with mainland Greece. He also was said to have married the daughter of the king of the east Greek city of CYMĒ, in Asia Minor. Midas died when his kingdom was overrun by the nomadic Kimmerians, in about 696 B.C.E.

On account of his fabulous wealth, Midas—like the later king CROESUS of LYDIA—became a figure in Greek legend. Best known is the tale of the Midas Touch. Offered any wish by the god DIONYSUS, Midas asked that whatever he touched might turn to GOLD. But, finding that this ruined the food that he touched, he prayed to lose the gift. In another version, it was his daughter whom he accidentally turned to gold.

Further reading: L. E. Roller, "Midas and the Gordian Knot," *Classical Antiquity* 3 (1985): 256–271; M. C. Miller, "Midas as the Great King in Attic Fifth-century Vase-painting," *Antike Kunst* 31 (1988): 79–89; A. J. N. W. Prag and D. Thimme, "Reconstructing King Midas. A First Report," *Anatolian Studies* 39 (1989): 159–165; O. W. Muscarella, "King Midas of Phyrgia and the Greeks," in *Anatolia and the Ancient Near East. Studies in Honour of Tahsin Özgüç,* edited by Kutlu Emre (Ankara, Turkey: Press of the Turkish Historical Foundation, 1989) 333–344; E. Simpson, "'Midas' Bed' and a Royal Phrygian Funeral," *Journal of Field Archaeology* 17 (1990): 69–87.

Miletus This Greek city, located on the central west coast of ASIA MINOR, was preeminent in TRADE, COLONIZATION, and cultural achievements in the 600s–500s B.C.E. Situated at the mouth of the river Maeander, Miletus enjoyed communication seaward and inland. The city, originally located on the coast, today lies approximately five miles from the sea. Archaeological evidence shows that this advantageous site was occupied in the second millennium B.C.E. first by Minoans, then by Mycenaean Greeks, and last by non-Greek Carians. Around 1000 B.C.E., IONIAN GREEKS arrived and founded the historical Miletus, which became the southernmost city of the Greek region known as IONIA.

The patron god of Miletus was APOLLO. In addition to the temple dedicated to him within the boundaries of the city itself, the Milesians also worshipped at the important local oracular cult located at Didyma, approximately 12 miles away.

The people of Miletus were expert seafarers and led the way in the expansion of the Greek world in the 600s B.C.E. They exported prized woolen textiles and metalwork, and they founded a remarkable string of colonies along the trade route to the BLACK SEA, as far as the distant Crimea.

By the late 600s B.C.E., Miletus was ruled by TYRANTS. In the mid-500s B.C.E., Miletus and the rest of Ionia were conquered by King CROESUS of LYDIA, only to be conquered shortly thereafter by the Persian king CYRUS (1). From about 546 to 499 B.C.E., Miletus enjoyed privileged status under the Persians, who maintained control through a series of Greek puppet rulers.

In the 500s B.C.E., the wealthy city witnessed the twin birth of PHILOSOPHY and SCIENCE, as the Milesian School of natural philosophers—THALES, ANAXIMANDER, and ANAXIMENES—took the first, revolutionary steps toward explaining the universe in nonreligious terms. Another innovative Milesian thinking of the day was the geographer HECATAEUS.

The city's heyday, however, was ending. After leading the doomed IONIAN REVOLT against Persian domination, Miletus was captured, sacked, and depopulated by the vengeful Persians (probably in 493 B.C.E.). The survivors were settled inside PERSIA. Miletus recovered, but slowly and not as a major power; EPHESOS soon surpassed it as the most important of the Ionian cities. After Ionia was liberated by the Greeks in 479 B.C.E., Miletus joined the Athenian-dominated DELIAN LEAGUE. Then governed as a DEMOCRACY, the city remained an Athenian ally for much of the PELOPONNESIAN WAR. In 412 B.C.E., however, Miletus revolted from Athens and became a naval base for the Spartan side. In 386 B.C.E., the Spartans returned Miletus and the rest of Ionia to Persian rule, according to the terms of the KING'S PEACE.

In 334 B.C.E., Ionia was again freed of Persian rule, this time by the Macedonian king ALEXANDER THE GREAT, who stormed Miletus to capture it from a Persian garrison.

In the HELLENISTIC AGE (ca. 300–150 B.C.E.), Miletus enjoyed self-rule, prosperity, and an admirable building program sponsored by such Hellenistic rulers as the Seleucids and the Attalids of PERGAMON. Unfortunately, the gradual silting up of the harbor brought economic decline.

Miletus was not highly regarded by the Romans, and it was eclipsed by its neighbors Ephesos and Smyrna, especially in the first century C.E. In the second century C.E., the city experienced a brief renaissance, as donors such as the empress Faustina sponsored major new building projects in the city center.

Excavations at Miletus were begun by German archaeologists in the late 19th century C.E. and have continued with few interruptions to the present. An archaeological museum at the site contains many of the artifacts discovered there.

See also CYZICUS; MINOAN CIVILIZATION; MYCENAEAN CIVILIZATION; PANTICAPAEUM; PHRYNICHUS; SINOPE.

Further reading: Krzystof Nawotka, *Boule and Demos in Miletus and Its Pontic Colonies from Classical Age until Third Century A.D.* (Wrocław, Poland, Poland: Wydawnicto, Zaklad Narodowy im. Ossolinskich, 1999).

Miltiades (ca. 550–489 B.C.E.) *Athenian general and politician*
Miltiades masterminded the Athenian victory over the invading Persians at the Battle of MARATHON (490 B.C.E.) and afterward enjoyed a brief preeminence at ATHENS before succumbing to political enemies. He was the first of a series of dynamic Athenian leaders in the 400s B.C.E.

Born into the rich and aristocratic Philaïd family, he began his career under the Athenian tyrant HIPPIAS (1). In around 522 B.C.E. Miltiades left Athens for the Thracian CHERSONESE—the 50-mile-long peninsula that forms the European side of the HELLESPONT—to rule the region, inherited from his maternal uncle, the elder Miltiades.

There the young Miltiades reigned as *tyrannos* (dictator) over native Thracians and Athenian colonists, but served as a vassal of the Persian king DARIUS (1). Miltiades married a Thracian king's daughter, who bore his son KIMON. Like other eastern Greek rulers, Miltiades took part in Darius's expedition across the Danube into Scythia (ca. 513 B.C.E.). However, after participating in the doomed IONIAN REVOLT against Darius, Miltiades fled back to Athens (493 B.C.E.).

Athens, by then a full-fledged DEMOCRACY, was entirely different from the place that Miltiades had left 30 years before. In the turbulent political climate, Miltiades had enemies who resented his prior dictatorship in the Chersonese and his association with Hippias. But before long Miltiades moved to the political fore, being elected as one of Athens' generals for the year 490 B.C.E.

That summer, when a seaborne Persian army landed at Marathon with the aim of capturing Athens, it was Miltiades who convinced the Athenian commander-in-chief to attack, rather than just defend the city walls. The Battle of Marathon—a complete victory by an outnumbered force over a supposedly invincible foe—was one of the crucial moments in Greek history. The unique battle plan, involving an enveloping tactic by the army's wings, probably came from Miltiades.

His glory lasted barely a year. Ambitious, he led a 70-ship Athenian fleet to seize Paros, a wealthy Greek island that had submitted to Darius. But the attack failed, and the 60-year-old Miltiades, with a badly injured knee, returned to face public anger at Athens. The left-wing leader XANTHIPPUS accused Miltiades of deceiving the Athenian people. The hero of Marathon was tried and convicted in the ASSEMBLY and fined a ruinous 50 TALENTS. Soon Miltiades died from his gangrenous injury, and the fine was paid by the young Kimon (himself destined to become the foremost Athenian soldier and statesman of his day).

Among the ancient artifacts now displayed at the OLYMPIA museum is a Greek HOPLITE helmet discovered by archaeologists in 1961 C.E. and inscribed with the words in Greek, "Miltiades dedicated this to Zeus." Presumably it is Miltiades' own helmet, worn at the Battle of Marathon and afterward given as an offering to the king of the gods and the lord of victory.

See also PERSIAN WARS; ZEUS.

Further reading: Debra Hamel, *Athenian Generals: Military Authority in the Classical Period* (Leiden, Netherlands: E. J. Brill, 1998).

Mimnermus (latter 600s B.C.E.) *Early Greek lyric poet of Colophon, in western ASIA MINOR*
Mimnermus's work survives only in fragments. He was a writer of the elegy—a form meant to be sung to flute accompaniment—and many of his verses were love poems addressed to a flute girl named Nanno. Mimnermus was a forerunner of the later love elegists of ALEXANDRIA (1) and imperial ROME. His best-known fragment deals with a topic destined to become a favorite of Greek and Latin poets: the transience of youth and the implacable approach of old age and death.

See also LYRIC POETRY.

Further reading: Archibald Allen, *The Fragments of Mimnermus: Text and Commentary* (Stuttgart, Germany: F. Steiner, 1993); S. R. Slings, *Symposium, Speech, and Ideology: Two Hermeneutical Issues in Early Greek Lyric, with Special Reference to Mimnermus* (Amsterdam: Koninklijke Nederlandse Akademie van Wetenscappen, 2000).

Minoan civilization Based on the Aegean island of ancient CRETE, this accomplished palatial society flourished from roughly 2200 to 1400 B.C.E. The name "Minoan civilization" refers to a mythological Cretan ruler, King MINOS, and was invented in 1900 C.E. by the British archaeologist Sir Arthur Evans. Evans was the first to discover the remains of this wealthy, sophisticated culture in his excavations at the site of KNOSSOS.

The Minoans were not Greeks, and their language, RELIGION, and social structures were not Greek. Most of what is known or can be guessed about the Minoans comes from modern ARCHAEOLOGY on Crete. (The little island of THERA also has yielded an important Minoan site.) Evidence suggests that the Minoans emerged from a fusion between existing Cretan inhabitants and invaders from ASIA MINOR during the era 2900–2200 B.C.E. These people became master seafarers and built a society inspired partly by contact with the Egyptian Old Kingdom (ca. 2650–2250 B.C.E.). By about 1900 B.C.E. the Minoans were acquiring an AEGEAN SEA empire and were constructing palaces on Crete—at KNOSSOS, Phaistos, Mallia, and Khania—that were bigger and more elaborate than any buildings outside the Near East. So confident were the Minoans in their naval power that they declined to encircle their palaces with defensive walls.

Wealth came from Cretan FARMING and fishing, from taxes paid by subject peoples in the CYCLADES and other Aegean locales, and from long-distance TRADE. Minoan objects discovered by archaeologists outside Crete indicate two-way commerce with EGYPT, Asia Minor, and the Levant as well as with western ITALY (a region that offered raw tin and copper, the components of BRONZE). But much Minoan trade, especially after 1600 B.C.E., was with the northwestern Aegean mainland now called Greece, where Greek-speaking tribes had been settling since about 2100 B.C.E.

The Minoans' importance for Greek history is that they supplied the model for the Greeks' MYCENAEAN CIVILIZATION, which arose on the mainland around 1600 B.C.E. The Mycenaean fortress palaces at MYCENAE, TIRYNS, and elsewhere were warlike imitations of Minoan palaces on Crete. Mycenaean skills in metalworking, POTTERY-making, and other handicrafts were improved by copying Cretan models. The Mycenaean form of WRITING—a syllabary script that modern scholars call LINEAR B, invented soon before 1400 B.C.E.—was copied from the Minoan system (a yet-undeciphered script called Linear A). Eventually the Mycenaeans were ready to challenge Minoan supremacy in the Aegean.

Daily scenes of the Minoans' life are preserved on some of their beautiful art objects, which include cut gems, worked GOLD, terra-cotta figurines, vase paintings, and frescoes. Sensuous and modern-seeming in design, Minoan pictorial art favors sea animals and other subjects from nature. Religious scenes often show a goddess (or priestess) with a subordinate male figure or with wild beasts, such as lions, in tame postures. Evidence of this kind leads many scholars to conclude that Minoan religion was centered on a mother goddess or a group of goddesses overseeing nature and bounty. Aspects of Minoan worship apparently infiltrated Greek religion in the cult of certain goddesses, such as ARTEMIS and HERA.

The Minoans ascribed religious or magical power to dancing and to the remarkable athletic performance now known as bull leaping. Minoan reverence for the bull is probably reflected in Greek MYTHS of later days, such as the interrelated tales of Minos and of THESEUS and the Minotaur, or the tale of HERAKLES and the Cretan bull.

Minoan high society probably revolved around a priest-king or priest-queen whose capital city was Knossos and whose royal emblem was the *labrys*, a double-headed ax. Scenes in art suggest a confident, vivacious life at court. Upper-class WOMEN—portrayed as wearing flounced skirts and open-breasted tunics—apparently played prominent roles in court life (as opposed to the secluded existence of women in Greece in later centuries).

The material level enjoyed by the Minoan ruling class was probably unsurpassed anywhere before the late 19th century C.E. The Knossos palace, reaching three stories in parts, boasted clay-piped plumbing and a clever system of air wells to bring light and ventilation to interior rooms. COINAGE had not yet been invented, but Minoan wealth was measured in luxury items and in farm surplus such as sheep, pigs, and olive oil (great quantities of which were stored at Knossos).

The Minoan golden age on Crete, around 1900–1450 B.C.E., was a time of peace but was troubled by natural disasters. Archaeology at Cnossus shows that the palace was destroyed twice by earthquake, in about 1730 and 1570 B.C.E. Around 1480 B.C.E. Cretan coastal regions suffered damage and depopulation, from some natural disaster.

The Knossos palace, on high ground, survived, but new archaeological signs of distress in the mid-1400s B.C.E. include proliferation of war equipment and the first appearance on Crete of the horse (presumably imported as a tool of war). Overseas, Minoan pottery from this time is absent from certain sites—a sign of disrupted trade routes. Presumably a foreign enemy or number of enemies, taking advantage of Cretan natural disaster, had begun to cut into the Minoan Empire. These enemies surely included groups of Mycenaean Greeks.

In about 1400 B.C.E. or soon after, all the Cretan palaces were destroyed by fire, presumably in war. The most obvious explanation for this simultaneous destruction is a Mycenaean invasion of Crete. Intriguingly, archaeological evidence suggests that, prior to this invasion, Mycenaean Greeks had already taken over the Knossos palace and that it was they who were destroyed in the palace's ruin. There may have been rival Mycenaean armies, battling each other for control of Crete.

Although the Mycenaean victors seem to have abandoned Crete soon after 1400 B.C.E., the Minoan culture was finished.

See also ATLANTIS; BRONZE AGE; DAEDALUS; LABYRINTH; SHIPS AND SEAFARING.

Further reading: Susan Sherratt, *Arthur Evans, Knossos, and the Priest-king* (Oxford: Ashmolean Museum, 2000).

Minos According to Greek MYTH, Minos was a Cretan king who ruled the AEGEAN SEA with fleets of warships in olden times. A son of the god ZEUS and the Phoenician princess EUROPA, Minos was born in CRETE with his two brothers, Rhadamanthys and Sarpedon. As a young man at the royal city of KNOSSOS, Minos married Pasiphaë, daughter of the sun god, HELIOS. During a dispute over who should become the next king of Crete, Minos prayed to the god POSEIDON to send a bull from the sea as a sign of divine favor. The bull emerged, thus assuring Minos of the kingship; but the pure-white animal was so beautiful that Minos neglected to sacrifice it to Poseidon, as he had promised to do.

In retaliation, the god inspired Pasiphaë with an unnatural lust for the animal, and she acquired—from the immigrant Athenian craftsman DAEDALUS—a wooden device that disguised her as a cow. In this costume she approached the bull and was mounted by it. She conceived its child, which proved to be a grotesque creature, half human, half bull—the Minotaur (Greek: Minotauros, "the bull of Minos").

To hide the Minotaur, Minos angrily ordered the meddling Daedalus to build the palace known as the LABYRINTH. Then Minos imprisoned Daedalus and his son, Icarus, inside a tower. But Daedalus escaped from Crete on mechanical wings. (Icarus fell to his death en route.)

By ship, Minos pursued Daedalus to SICILY, where he was treacherously murdered in his bath by King Cocalus's daughters, who did not want to relinquish the miraculous inventor Daedalus. Zeus then installed Minos as one of the judges of the dead in the Underworld.

The Minos legend probably represents the Greeks' distorted memory of the great days of Cretan wealth and naval power, around 1950–1450 B.C.E. For this reason, in 1900 C.E. the pioneering British archaeologist Sir Arthur Evans coined the adjective "Minoan" to describe that real-life civilization on Crete. The name Minos is not Greek in origin and may possibly have been a hereditary royal title of the Minoan rulers.

See also AFTERLIFE; MINOAN CIVILIZATION.

Further reading: P. B. S. Andrews, "The Myth of Europa and Minos," *Greece and Rome* 16 (1969): 60–66; Alexandre Farnoux, *Knossos. Searching for the Legendary Palace of King Minos,* translated by David J. Baker (New York: H. N. Abrams, 1996).

Minotaur *See* LABYRINTH; MINOS; THESEUS.

Minyans (Greek: Minuai) In MYTH, the Minyans were a powerful Greek clan that had controlled parts of BOEOTIA and THESSALY in the old days. This legend probably commemorates an actual northern Greek dynasty of the Mycenaean era, around 1200 B.C.E. Relatedly, in the Thessalian-based legend of JASON (1) and the Argonauts, the Argonauts traditionally are referred to as Minyans.

The modern term *Minyan Ware* was coined by archaeologist Heinrich Schliemann in 1880 C.E. to describe a kind of POTTERY he had discovered at the Boeotian city of ORCHOMENOS. The pottery, now dated to around 1900 B.C.E., usually is considered to have been made by early Greeks—that is, by early descendants of the Greek-speaking invaders who occupied mainland Greece after about 2100 B.C.E.

See also MYCENAEAN CIVILIZATION.

Further reading: F. J. Tritsch, "Minyans and Luvians," in *Acta of the 2nd International Colloquium on Aegean Prehistory. The First Arrival of Indo-European Elements in Greece. Athens, April 5–11, 1971,* edited by Elly Arditis (Athens: Ministry of Culture and Science, 1972), 43–45; J. H. Crouwel, "Pot-marks on Grey Minyan Ware," *Kadmos* 12 (1973): 101–108; J. B. Rutter, "Stone Vases and Minyan Ware. A Facet of Minoan Influence on Middle Helladic Laconia," *American Journal of Archaeology* 83 (1979): 464–469; J. B. Rutter, "Fine Gray-burnished Pottery of the Early Helladic III Period. The Ancestry of Gray Minyan," *Hesperia* 52 (1983): 327–355.

Mitylene *See* MYTILENE.

Muses These Greek goddesses oversaw poetry, MUSIC, dance, and the arts in general. The word *Muse* (Greek: Mousa) is related to *mousikē*, "music." In MYTH, they were the daughters of ZEUS and Mnemosyne—that is, the god of universal order and the goddess Memory—and this is surely a metaphor for the reliance on verse rhythm and the singer's memory in the traditional technique of oral composition, prior to the spread of literacy.

The Muses, together or individually, were imagined as inspiring human song and poetry. HOMER's *Odyssey* (written around 750 B.C.E.) opens with an appeal to an unspecified Muse to help the poet sing about his subject. In his epic poem *Theogony* (ca. 700 B.C.E.), HESIOD describes how the Muses approached him on Mt. Helicon, in BOEOTIA, and breathed the gift of song into him. Hesiod named nine goddesses, but it was only a later elaboration that assigned to each Muse a separate function. The nine were Kalliope, Klio, Euterpe, Terpsichore, Erato, Melpomene, Thalia, Polyhymnia, and Urania.

See also APOLLO; EPIC POETRY; WRITING.

Further reading: B. S. Ridgway, "Musings on the Muses," in *Beiträge zur Ikonographie und Hermeneutik. Festschrift für Nikolaus Himmelmann,* edited by Hans-Ulrich Cain, Hanns Gabelmann, Dieter Salzmann (Mainz am Rhein, Germany: Phillip von Zabern, 1989), 265–272; R. Cohon, "Hesiod and the Order and Naming of the Muses in Hellenistic Art," *Boreas* 14–15 (1991–1992): 67–83; Angeles Arrien, *The Nine Muses: A Mythological Path to Creativity* (New York: Tarcher/Putnam, 2000).

A depiction of three muses who together or individually were imagined to inspire human song and poetry. Note the musical instruments and parchment scroll. *(Alison Frantz Photographic Collection, American School of Classical Studies at Athens)*

music Greek music—*mousikē,* "the art of the MUSES"—was closely connected to dancing and to the recitation of Greek poetry. Greek poetic meter was a form of rhythm, and verses were sung or chanted to the accompaniment of various instruments. Ancient music is understood today primarily through descriptions in ancient literary sources; very few pieces of actual music are preserved. Musical rhythm generally consisted of a single melodic line; there was no complex harmony as in modern musical works.

The ancient Greeks considered the Homeric age to represent a musical "golden age." The primary instrument used to accompany the EPIC POETRY sung by bards (such as HOMER, if he did exist) was the *phorminx,* a type of stringed instrument played by plucking, also known as a lyre. The earliest known actual musician was the lyric poet TERPANDER of LESBOS, who lived in the 600s B.C.E.

In the age of LYRIC POETRY, new musical instruments became popular for accompanying the verses: the *kithara,* another type of lyre, and the *aulos,* a wind instrument

often described as a flute but really more like our clarinet or oboe. The lyre's sound was considered dignified and soothing, while flute music was more exciting. The lyre was associated with the god APOLLO, lord of order and harmony. The ennobling and civilizing power of music was emphasized in legends of the great lyre musicians, such as ORPHEUS, who could charm wild beasts with his song, or Amphion, whose music brought stones trooping of their own accord to build the perimeter wall of THEBES. By contrast, the aulos was associated with the riotous god DIONYSUS.

By the mid-600s B.C.E., the lyre had begun to be used to accompany more and more types of verse, including elegy (originally intended for flute music). Early surviving verses of elegy—such as those by the poets KALLINUS (mid-600s B.C.E.) and TYRTAEUS (ca. 630 B.C.E.)—convey military-patriotic themes intended to rouse and encourage an audience. Other forms of flute poetry included the dithyramb, which was a choral song sacred to Dionysus. Descended from the dithyramb (by the late 500s B.C.E.)

was the choral ode of Athenian stage tragedy, developed by PINDAR, also accompanied by flutes. In the 400s B.C.E., a new class of professional musicians arose, the best known of whom were Phrynis of MILETUS (ca. 450 B.C.E.), his pupil Timotheus of Miletus, and the Athenian playwright EURIPIDES. Ancient Greek music flourished through the Classical period and into the HELLENISTIC AGE, but dwindled as an art from under the Romans.

Musical instruments had important functions in many different aspects of ancient Greek life. Instruction in lyre playing formed an important part in the EDUCATION of upper- and middle-class boys at ATHENS. The flute, on the other hand, was generally considered an instrument of professional musicians, including SLAVES and PROSTITUTES. Flutes supplied lively dance music, as well as background music for SPORT competitions and for the drinking party known as the SYMPOSIUM. From the

A bigger, more elaborate form of lyre, called the kithara, was used for public performance. It was played with both hands, plucked with bare fingers, and strummed with an ivory plectrum. *(Alison Frantz Photographic Collection, American School of Classical Studies at Athens)*

mid-seventh century B.C.E. on, flute players always accompanied the Spartan army as it marched into battle, to keep the soldiers in step and to rouse their courage. Stately flute music was also used in the background at sacrifices and other religious ceremonies.

Greek MYTH ascribed the invention of the lyre to the god HERMES. In fact, the Greeks probably adopted the instrument in the second millennium B.C.E. from the Cretan MINOAN CIVILIZATION. The simplest form of the lyre had a sound box of tortoiseshell (or a wooden facsimile), with strings of animal gut stretched down from a crossbar between two extended horns. Most lyres had seven strings, though archaeological evidence suggests that some had as many as 12. Unlike the modern harp, the lyre had strings of a uniform length, but a skilled musician could vary the sound by stopping a string partway with the bare fingers of his left hand; sound was made by using an ivory plectrum in his right hand to pluck the strings.

The ancient flute could be made of wood, ivory, or bone, with a double reed in the mouthpiece. Representations of musicians in Greek art often show a player blowing a pair of flutes simultaneously, sometimes strapped around his or her head.

The question of Greek musical notation is obscure. Surviving artwork never shows musicians reading musical notes, but it is believed that some form of written musical notation did exist by the late 400s B.C.E.

A major advance in ancient musical theory was developed by the Greek philosopher PYTHAGORAS (ca. 530 B.C.E.), who sought in music the secrets of the universe. He developed ratios that explained the tones made by dividing a stretched string, making music a branch of MATHEMATICS as well as an art. PLATO (427–347 B.C.E.) also studied music reverently, believing that it represented a powerful force for either good or ill, with the ability to mold human character permanently.

The best-known musical theorist of ancient Greece was Aristoxenus (active ca. 330 B.C.E.), who was born at TARAS and studied under ARISTOTLE at the LYCEUM in Athens. Two of his works survive in part: *Principles and Elements of Harmonics* and *Elements of Rhythm.*

See also PYTHIAN GAMES.

Further reading: Solon Michaelides, *The Music of Ancient Greece: An Encyclopaedia* (London: Faber, 1978); Martin L. West, *Ancient Greek Music* (New York: Oxford University Press, 1994); Thomas Mathiesen, *Apollo's Lyre: Greek Music and Music Theory in Antiquity and the Middle Ages* (Lincoln: University of Nebraska Press, 1999); Egbert Pöhlmann and Martin L. West, eds., *Documents of Ancient Greek Music: The Extant Melodies and Fragments* (Oxford: Clarendon Press, 2001).

Mycalē This mountain peninsula on the central west coast of ASIA MINOR is situated opposite the island of

SAMOS, in the Greek-inhabited region known as IONIA. On Mycalē's north side was a sanctuary area called the Panionium, where delegates from the 12 Ionian cities met and where an annual Ionian festival was held. The site was sacred to POSEIDON.

In late summer of 479 B.C.E., at the end of the PERSIAN WARS, Cape Mycalē was the scene of a small but significant land battle, resulting in the liberation of Ionia after about 75 years of Persian domination. This battle supposedly occurred on the same day as the decisive Battle of PLATAEA, in mainland Greece.

At the Battle of Mycalē, a Greek force of about 4,400 HOPLITES landed from ships and destroyed a Persian army twice as large. More significantly, the Greeks then were able to burn the Persians' beached warships—numbering perhaps 100—which had comprised the last remnant of the Persian navy. (The rest had been destroyed at the Greek sea victory at SALAMIS the year before.) Without a navy, PERSIA became temporarily helpless to defend its other east Greek possessions, such as the HELLESPONT district or the island of CYPRUS, and these regions fell to the Greek counteroffensive in the following months.

The Greek commander in chief at Mycalē was the Spartan king Leotychides, at the head of a Spartan contingent. But—according to the version told by the historian HERODOTUS—the brunt of the fighting was borne by the Athenian contingent, under command of the soldier-politician XANTHIPPUS.

In the battle's aftermath, Xanthippus and other Athenian commanders enrolled the nearby Aegean island states in a common alliance against Persia. This union led quickly to the creation of the DELIAN LEAGUE, the power base for the Athenian Empire during the next 75 years.

Further reading: I. McDougall, "The Persian Ships at Mycale," in *Owls to Athens. Essays on Classical Subjects Presented to Sir Kenneth Dover,* edited by E. M. Craik (New York: Oxford University Press, 1990), 143–149.

Mycenae This Greek city in the northeast PELOPONNESE had great significance in early Greek history. Situated in the hills at the northeastern edge of the Argive plain, Mycenae was the capital of a rich and accomplished early Greek culture (around 1600–1200 B.C.E.). The name MYCENAEAN CIVILIZATION was coined by the pioneering German archaeologist Heinrich Schliemann on the basis of his excavations at Mycenae in the 19th century C.E. The ARCHAEOLOGY of the site has provided the single most important source of information about the Mycenaean Greeks, who left behind no written history.

The origins of the name "Mycenae" are mysterious and appear to predate the Greek occupation of the site, since the Greek name Mukēnai has no apparent meaning in the GREEK LANGUAGE. Some modern scholars believe that it comes from the word for indentation, referring to

This beaten-gold mask from Mycenaean times ca. 1550 B.C.E. was placed over the face of a male corpse. It is probably a portrait of the man made during his lifetime. *(Alison Frantz Photographic Collection, American School of Classical Studies at Athens)*

Mycenae's location in a recess of the Argive plain. Ancient authors such as PAUSANIAS (2) (ca. 150 C.E.) believed that the name came from the Greek word *mukēs,* "mushrooms." In other instances, it is said to refer to an eponymous heroine named Mycene, the daughter of the hero Inachus.

Mycenae was one of the first places occupied by the invading Greek tribesmen of about 2100 B.C.E., but it predates their arrival. Archaeology shows that the site—commanding the fertile plain to the south and the land route northward to the isthmus—was first inhabited around 3000 B.C.E. by Neolithic settlers. The Greek takeover of the region may be indicated in the destruction of a pre-Greek palace (often called the House of the Tiles) at Lerna, at the opposite edge of the Argive plain, around 2100 B.C.E. Greek presence is almost certainly indicated in changes in style of POTTERY found at Mycenae, datable to about 1900 B.C.E.

Greek Mycenae's preeminence by the midmillennium is clearly shown by the 31 lavish royal tombs now called Grave Circle A and Grave Circle B and dated to about 1550 B.C.E. and 1650 B.C.E., respectively. Circle A, located atop Mycenae's ACROPOLIS, was discovered by Schliemann; the tombs' treasure of GOLD and SILVER gave the first archaeological proof of the existence of an early-Greek high civilization.

Mycenae's heyday came in 1400–1200 B.C.E., when the huge limestone walls and hilltop citadel were built. In about 1260 B.C.E. the city received its most distinctive surviving feature: the Lion Gate, surmounted by rampant carved-limestone lions (now headless).

To this era belongs the supreme Mycenae later recalled in the MYTHS of the classical Greeks—the city "rich in gold" (as the poet HOMER called it), with a high king who was overlord of many lesser Greek rulers. The legendary AGAMEMNON, king of Mycenae, raises an army against TROY, by summoning his various vassal kings. This is probably an accurate reflection of Mycenae's feudal dominance in the Mycenaean age.

Archaeology also tells the tale of the city's decline in the 1200s B.C.E. A series of burnings culminated around 1200 B.C.E. in major destruction, which probably indicates internal strife or several defeats at the hands of other Mycenaean-Greek cities. There followed perhaps three generations of depopulation, culminating in Mycenae's final ruin, possibly at the hands of the invading DORIAN GREEKS (around 1120 B.C.E.).

Later Mycenae existed as a Dorian town whose inhabitants probably lived amid the ruins of vanished grandeur. Men of Mycenae fought as allies of SPARTA against the Persians at THERMOPYLAE (480 B.C.E.) and PLATAEA (479 B.C.E.). This Mycenae was destroyed by its powerful neighbor ARGOS around 468 B.C.E., but reemerged in the 200s B.C.E.

The ruins of Mycenae were first investigated by the British Lord Elgin in 1802, who concentrated on the monumental tomb outside the city, the so-called Treasury of ATREUS. The city itself was discovered and first excavated by Schliemann in 1874–1876. Greek archaeologists followed and carried out campaigns from 1876 to 1877 and 1884 to 1902. In the 20th century, the British School of Archaeology at Athens obtained rights to the site and excavated much of the area in 1920–1923, 1939, and 1950–1957. From the 1950s to the present, British and the Greek archaeologists have collaborated in excavating and restoring the Mycenaean remains, and a new museum is planned for the site.

See also ATREUS; TROJAN WAR.

Further reading: George Mylonas, *Mycenae, Rich in Gold* (Athens: Ekdotike Athenon, 1983); E. B. French, *Mycenae: Agamemnon's Capital. The Site and Its Setting* (Charleston, S.C.: Tempus, 2002).

Mycenaean civilization   This term is used by modern scholars to describe the earliest flowering of mainland Greek culture, around 1600–1200 B.C.E. The Mycenaeans were Greeks whose warlike society rose and fell long before the era of classical Greece. The classical Greeks of around 400 B.C.E. half remembered their Mycenaean forebears as a race of heroes, celebrated in MYTH and EPIC POETRY.

In world prehistory, the Mycenaeans comprised the last of several great civilizations to emerge in the eastern Mediterranean during the BRONZE AGE. The Mycenaeans' urban building, military organization, and TRADE seem to have been partly copied from a few preexisting, non-Greek, Bronze Age cultures—namely, the Middle and New Kingdoms of EGYPT, the Hittite kingdom of ASIA MINOR, and especially, the MINOAN CIVILIZATION of CRETE.

The adjective "Mycenaean" was coined in 1876 C.E. by the pioneering German archaeologist Heinrich Schliemann, on the basis of his spectacular discoveries at the site of MYCENAE, in the northeastern PELOPONNESE, in southern Greece. The Mycenaeans lived before the era of history-writing, and thus most details of their story—such as their rulers' names or the reasons why their entire society collapsed in fiery ruin around 1200 B.C.E.—remain unknown. Modern knowledge relies mostly on artifacts uncovered by ARCHAEOLOGY at a few sites, such as Mycenae, TIRYNS, and PYLOS (in the Peloponnese) and THEBES, ORCHOMENOS, and ATHENS (in central Greece). The artifacts include POTTERY, stone carvings, jewelry, and armor—most of it found in the tombs of rulers—as well as the remnants of Mycenaean stone palaces and defenses. Particularly, the sites of Mycenae and Tiryns still show huge fortifications built by Mycenaean inhabitants in the 1300s and 1200s B.C.E.

In addition, a few sites have yielded primitive Mycenaean written records, inscribed on clay tablets that seem to date from about 1400 B.C.E. or 1200 B.C.E., depending on the site. Written in a script that modern scholars call LINEAR B, the records have been deciphered mainly as lists of inventory—produce, livestock, military equipment—and accounts of goods-distribution, religious rites, and similar daily events. The tablets provide precious information on the social structure, economy, and RELIGION of the Mycenaeans, as well as on the early-stage GREEK LANGUAGE that they spoke.

Aside from archaeology, some insight into the Mycenaeans has been gained from a cautious reading of HOMER's epic poems, the *Iliad* and the *Odyssey*. Although written circa 750 B.C.E., more than 400 years after the Mycenaeans' disappearance, these poems derive from oral tradition that stretches back to the Mycenaeans. It is believed that the poems faithfully record certain aspects of Mycenaean upper-class life—such as the warrior code and the network of local kings—amid distortions and overlays.

The first Greek-speaking tribes arrived in mainland Greece around 2100 B.C.E., from the Danube region. But 500 years went by before the emergence of the culture that we call Mycenaean: The remarkable social and technological changes of these intervening centuries can only be guessed at. No doubt the Greeks were deeply influenced by the non-Greek people they had conquered, and from them the Greeks probably learned skills such as stone masonry, ship-building, navigation, the cultivation of the olive and certain other crops, and the worship of certain female deities (with associated, new spiritual concepts). Similarly, the Greeks were inspired by the palace society of Minoan Crete.

The Mycenaean era began around 1600 B.C.E., as archaeology reveals. Several sites in Greece came under control of powerful rulers who were buried in elaborate tombs, unlike the simple graves of prior centuries. And within a few generations the tomb designs altered again, suggesting further dynastic changes and evolving organization. The six treasure-filled tombs at Mycenae known as Grave Circle A—built in the era 1550–1500 B.C.E. and discovered intact by Schliemann—provide clear proof of the rulers' wealth and overseas contacts. For example, the tombs contain items of GOLD that were shaped by Greek smiths, but the raw metal probably came from Asia Minor or Egypt. The warlike nature of these leaders is suggested by the many weapons left as offerings in the tombs.

In Greece's terrain, where mountain ranges separate the flatlands, the Mycenaeans apparently emerged as four or so major kingdoms, each based at a large farming plain. Two of these domains were in the Peloponnese: the plain of ARGOS (with its capital at Mycenae) and the plain of MESSENIA (capital at Pylos). One was in central Greece: the plain of BOEOTIA (with the cities Thebes and Orchomenos vying for supremacy). And one was in the north, on the great plain of THESSALY (capital at Iolkos). Lesser kingdoms probably existed as well. But the greatest domain was Mycenae, as indicated by its signs of superior wealth and by the testimony of Greek myth. In Homer's *Iliad*, the Mycenaean king AGAMEMNON is the supreme commander, to whom all other kings, such as ODYSSEUS and NESTOR, owe obedience.

One event of the Mycenaean era that modern scholars are sure of is that by around 1450 B.C.E. Mycenaeans had taken over the Cretan palace at KNOSSOS—probably as the result of a Mycenaean naval invasion of Crete. Mysteriously, the Mycenaeans seem to have abandoned Crete soon thereafter, around 1400 B.C.E. But the years of occupation there taught Mycenaean rulers certain organizational skills—such as improved architectural techniques and the use of Cretan WRITING (adapted at this time, as the Linear B script)—that ushered in 200 years of the Mycenaean heyday in mainland Greece, around 1400–1200 B.C.E.

It was now that the Mycenaeans built their own palaces, adapted from the Minoan palaces on Crete. Mycenae and Tiryns were turned into elaborate, high-walled castles; other palaces, such as at Pylos, arose without huge defenses. The social and economic structure of these centers is partly revealed by the Linear B tablets. The palace was the seat of the king (*wanax* in Mycenaean Greek); beyond the capital city, a network of outlying villages paid taxes, obeyed the king's laws, and relied on him for defense against other rulers. That palace was also a center of industry, where metalworkers, weavers, perfumers, and many other crafts people turned out finished goods, to enrich the king or to be distributed by him. Raw materials came from local taxes (sheep's wool, for example) and from overseas trade.

A lion hunt inlaid on a Mycenaean dagger, deposited as an offering in a royal tomb ca. 1575 B.C.E. Two hunters carry distinctive hourglass-shaped oxhide shields. *(Alison Frantz Photographic Collection, American School of Classical Studies at Athens)*

The premier metal for war and industry was BRONZE (the use of IRON being introduced to the Greek world only later). The search for bronze's two components—copper and tin—led Mycenaean sea traders far and wide. Large remains of Mycenaean pottery in CYPRUS show that parts of that copper-rich island were colonized by Mycenaeans. On the western Asia Minor coast, the site of MILETUS probably became a Mycenaean trading colony, mainly for the acquisition of raw metals. Toward the other end of the Mediterranean, extant pottery suggests a Mycenaean presence in western ITALY, where tin could be found.

The Mycenaean rulers commanded armies of heavy infantry. The soldiers' standardized equipment, including bronze breastplates and helmets, is recorded on Linear B tablets. Various evidence paints a picture of Mycenaean kings or princes leading Viking-like raids overseas, of which the biggest were the (presumed) invasions of Crete and Cyprus. On certain Linear B tablets, SLAVES are mentioned by names that suggest they came from Asia Minor; probably they were captured in Mycenaean raids there. The Greek myth of JASON (1) and the Argonauts may distortedly commemorate such as overseas expedition. But the Mycenaean kingdoms fought also against each other: the legend of the SEVEN AGAINST THEBES seems clearly based on actual warfare between Mycenae and Thebes.

By about 1250 B.C.E. the Mycenaean world had come under pressure, due partly to upheavals in the Near East. The decline of the Hittite kingdom in Asia Minor probably brought a gradual closing of the Mycenaeans' eastern trade routes. Deprived of raw metals for industry and conquest, Mycenaean society began to whither. The Greek legend of the TROJAN WAR may recall the Mycenaeans' attempt to keep trade routes open by removing the interfering, non-Greek, Hellespontine city TROY, around 1220 B.C.E.

Finally, it seems, the Mycenaean kingdoms turned against each other and destroyed each other, in a desperate bid for survival. Archaeology clearly reveals the fiery ruin of Thebes, Mycenae, and other centers in the 50 years leading down to 1200 B.C.E. At Pylos, the final days are dramatically indicated in emergency troop movements and religious sacrifices recorded on Linear B tablets.

Modern historians used to believe that this wholesale destruction was the work of outsiders—specifically, DORIAN GREEKS invading from the northwest. But more recent scholarship concludes that the Dorian invasion, in about 1100 B.C.E., was merely opportunistic; the Mycenaeans had already exhausted themselves through internal war.

In the villages outside of the wrecked palaces, Mycenaean society survived on an impoverished scale during the 1100s B.C.E. Social change in these rural areas can be glimpsed in the development of a certain Greek word: The official title *quasireu,* which during the Mycenaean heyday had indicated a local sheriff (a relatively low posi-

tion), gradually changed to *basileus* and took on a new meaning, "king." These men became the new local rulers within the disintegrated Mycenaean kingdoms.

See also ACHAEA; ACHAEANS; ARCADIA; ATREUS; CHARIOTS; DARK AGE; FUNERAL CUSTOMS; PERSEUS (1); SHIPS AND SEAFARING; WARFARE, LAND.

Further reading: Konstantinos Kontorlis, *Mycenaean Civilization: Mycenae, Tiryns, Asine, Midea, Pylos,* 2d ed. (Athens: K. Kontorli, 1985); K. A. Wardle and Diana Wardle, *Cities of Legend: The Mycenaean World* (London: Bristol Classical Press, 1997); Michael L. Galaty and William A. Parkinson, eds., *Rethinking Mycenaean Palaces: New Interpretations of an Old Idea* (Los Angeles: University of California Press, 1999); Bryan Feuer, *Mycenaean Civilization: An Annotated Bibliography through 2002,* rev. ed. (Jefferson, N.C.: McFarland, 2004).

mystery cults *See* AFTERLIFE; DIONYSUS; ELEUSINIAN MYSTERIES; ORPHISM; SAMOTHRACE.

myth The Greek word *mythos* simply refers to any narrative, factual or not. In modern use, the term has come to mean a popular story elaborated over several generations. Myths are sometimes based on a kernel of historical fact and are often significant for understanding the mass mentality of an ancient people. Since they often involve gods or other supernatural beings, mythology is sometimes considered a facet of ancient religion, but Greek myths frequently address nonreligious topics as well.

The myths of ancient Greece, like those of other cultures, originated in a variety of ways and for a variety of purposes. Some have a moral, such as the need to be hospitable to strangers or the need for humility. Other myths are "etiological," attempting to explain local geographic features, religious rites, or other phenomena not fully understood by other means. Related to this type of story is the propagandistic "charter myth," which seeks to sanctify a local custom or social institution—examples include the myth connecting the DORIAN GREEKS with the prestigious sons of HERAKLES, or the myth claiming that the city of CYRENE (1) was founded by the god APOLLO for his mistress, named CYRENE (2). In addition, three major themes dominate the myths and legends from ancient Greece; the creation of the world, activities of the gods, and activities of heroes.

Many Greek myths appear to be based on distorted memories of the Aegean BRONZE AGE, including the MINOAN CIVILIZATION (ca. 2200–1400 B.C.E.) and the MYCENAEAN CIVILIZATION (ca. 1600–1200 B.C.E.). Later generations of Greeks regarded the Mycenaean age, in particular, as an Age of Heroes. Since the Minoans and Mycenaeans do not appear to have kept written histories, certain real-life events were commemorated by heroic songs handed down through the years and elaborated in a tradition of oral EPIC POETRY. There are many examples of such semihistorical myths, including THE-SEUS and the Minotaur, the SEVEN AGAINST THEBES, and the TROJAN WAR.

A remarkable number of Greek myths have survived antiquity. Their quantity and diversity are due in part to the fact that literacy took hold very quickly in Greek society after the invention of the Greek ALPHABET, probably occurring within the span of a single generation around 775–750 B.C.E. Many legends previously maintained by oral traditions were written down around that time. The earliest and most important of these writings are HOMER's *Iliad* and *Odyssey*. Many other ancient authors include mythological content in their works, such as the Boeotian epic poet HESIOD, the Theban choral poet PINDAR, the Athenian tragedians AESCHYLUS, SOPHOKLES, and EURIPIDES, the Alexandrian poets KALLI-MACHUS and APOLLONIUS, and the Roman poet Ovid. In the Christian era, myths survived as symbolic allegories, often being retold to conform to contemporary religious beliefs. From antiquity to the present, Greek mythology has had a constant and unmistakable influence on the development of the arts in Western civilization, including painting, sculpture, literature, and music.

See also CALYDONIAN BOAR HUNT; JASON (1); ODYSSEUS; OEDIPUS; ORESTES; PERSEUS; ZEUS.

Further reading: John Pinsent, *Greek Mythology* (New York: Harper & Row, 1983); Jan Bremmer, *Interpretation of Greek Mythology* (London: Routledge, 1988); Lowell Edmunds, ed., *Approaches to Greek Mythology* (Baltimore: Johns Hopkins University Press, 1990); Richard Stoneman, *Greek Mythology: An Encyclopedia of Myth and Legend* (Hammersmith, London: Aquarium Press, 1991); Fritz Graf, *Greek Mythology: An Introduction,* translated by Thomas Marier (Baltimore: Johns Hopkins University Press, 1993); Iain Thompson, *Ancient Greek Mythology* (Edison, N.J.: Chartwell Books, 1996).

Mytilene The principal city of the eastern Greek island of LESBOS, in ancient times and still today (under the name Mitilini). Located on the island's southeastern shore, 12 miles from the northern west coast of ASIA MINOR, Mytilene was a prosperous Greek seaport, connecting East and West.

Archaeological study of the ancient site has been hampered by the modern city, but we know that this advantageous locale was occupied before the arrival of the first Greeks. We also know that the name Mytilene—sometimes rendered as Mitylene—is not Greek, for the ending *-ene* is similar to the endings of other pre-Greek place-names. Mycenaean-Greek POTTERY from about 1200 B.C.E. has been discovered on Lesbos; very possibly the seafaring Mycenaeans captured Mytilene at this time. Later, around 1000 B.C.E., the city became a refuge for eastward-migrating AEOLIAN GREEKS. During 1000–900 B.C.E., Mytilene was an important departure point for

further Aeolian colonizing, along the northwest Asia Minor coast.

By 625 B.C.E. Mytilene was a leading city of the eastern Greek world. Lesbos's traditions of LYRIC POETRY reached their zenith with the Mytileneans SAPPHO (ca. 600 B.C.E.) and ALCAEUS (ca. 590 B.C.E.). In this era the city was governed as an ARISTOCRACY. The chief clan was the Penthilidae, who had the oppressive habit of arbitrarily beating people with clubs in the street. Class tensions were enflamed by an overseas military failure—Mytilene's loss of the Hellespontine colony of Sigeum to Athenian settlers (ca. 600 B.C.E.).

TYRANTS arose in Mytilene to lead the common people against the nobles. But civil war was averted by the statesman PITTACUS, who served as an elected 10-year dictator (ca. 590–580 B.C.E.) and was later enshrined as one of the SEVEN SAGES of Greece. The turmoil of this era is conveyed in the poems of Pittacus's enemy Alcaeus.

In about 522 B.C.E. Mytilene and the rest of the island fell to the advancing Persians under King DARIUS (1). The Mytileneans joined the doomed IONIAN REVOLT against Persian rule and distinguished themselves by their cowardice at the sea battle of Lade (494 B.C.E.). Liberated by the Greek counteroffensive at the end of the PERSIAN WARS (479 B.C.E.), Mytilene became a leading member of the Athenian-controlled DELIAN LEAGUE. For the next 50 years, Mytilene was one of the few league states to pay its annual obligation in the form of warships and crews rather than in SILVER.

During the PELOPONNESIAN WAR (431–404 B.C.E.), Mytilene twice revolted unsuccessfully against Athenian rule. The first revolt (428–427 B.C.E.) ended with Athenian troops occupying the island. Afterward, there occurred a famous debate in the ASSEMBLY at ATHENS, where a decision to destroy Mytilene and execute the adult male population was rescinded by a revote. This Mytilenean Debate forms a set piece in book 3 of the war history written by THUCYDIDES (1). After the second revolt was crushed (412 B.C.E.), the Mytileneans lost their fleet, their city walls, and much of their farmland to the vengeful Athenians. With the defeat of Athens in 404 B.C.E., a reduced Mytilene came under Spartan control.

After a generation of Spartan oppression, Mytilene joined the SECOND ATHENIAN LEAGUE, in about 377 B.C.E. In 333 B.C.E. the city fell briefly to the Persian navy but was liberated by the conquering Macedonian king ALEXANDER THE GREAT. After Alexander's death (323 B.C.E.), Mytilene and Lesbos passed to various Hellenistic rulers. Acquired by the kings of nearby PERGAMON in 188 B.C.E., Mytilene was part of the domain bequeathed to the Romans by the Pergamene king Attalus III in 133 B.C.E. The city soon became part of the Roman province of Asia.

See also GREEK LANGUAGE.

Further reading: P. Krentz, "Xenophon and Diodorus on the Battle at Mytilene, 406 B.C.," *Ancient History Bulletin* 2 (1988): 128–130; C. Williams and H. Williams,

"Excavations at Mytilene (Lesbos), 1987," *Echos du monde classique* 7 (1988): 135–149; ———, "Excavations at Mytilene (Lesbos), 1988," *Echos du monde classique* 8 (1989): 167–181; ———, "Excavations at Mytilene (Lesbos), 1989)," *Echos du monde classique* 9 (1990): 181–193; ———, "Excavations at Mytilene (Lesbos), 1990," *Echos du monde classique* 10 (1991): 175–191; H. J. Mason, "Mytilene and Methymna: Quarrels, Borders, and topography," *Echos du monde classique* 12 (1993): 225–250; C. Williams and H. Williams, "Excavations at Mytilene (Lesbos), 1994," *Echos du monde classique* 14 (1995): 95–100.

N

names Unlike modern Americans, ancient Greek males and females typically carried only one personal name—for example, Socrates. In formal address, a man or boy might be specified by a patronymic (his father's name): "Themistokles, son of Neokles." However, at some Greek cities, specifically ATHENS, the use of the patronymic was discouraged due to social-leveling legislation aimed at removing distinctions and stigmas of lineage. Hence "Themistokles of the DEME of Phrearrus" was the preferred form. The masculine or feminine ending of a name clearly distinguished the person's gender—Diotima and Elpinice are female; Perikles and Diodorus, male.

Greek names, like those in German and certain other Indo-European tongues, usually contained common words in compound form. The Greek female name Cleopatra means "glory of her father." One of the elements might typically be a deity's name, as in Herodotus, "given by HERA." Two male names popular after the 500s B.C.E. were Demetrius and Dionysius, which were adjectival forms of the names of well-loved agrarian gods, DEMETER and DIONYSUS.

Because the keeping of horses was a sign of wealth, many aristocratic names included the proud element *hippo*—: Philip (Philippos), "horse-lover," Hippocrates, "horse power," Xanthippe, "yellow horse." For some reason, an aristocratic boy usually was not named after his father, but often after a grandfather—for example, KLEIS-THENES (1) and (2), and THUCYDIDES (1) and (2). Collectively, members of a noble clan might be known by a family name—such as the ALCMAEONIDS (descendants of Alcmaeon).

Not only bluebloods had identifying names. Children of left-wing families might receive names with such polit-ically charged elements as Demo—("the people") or Iso—("equality")—for instance, Demosthenes, "the people's strength," or Isodice, "equal justice."

Acquired nicknames came into use, mainly for royalty, starting in the late 300s B.C.E. The Macedonian soldier-prince Demetrius was honored with the surname Poliorketēs, "the city-besieger"; his father, ANTIGONUS (1), was Monophthalmos, "the one-eyed." And the conquering Macedonian king Alexander was surnamed Megas "the Great."

See also ALEXANDER THE GREAT; DEMETRIUS POLIORCETES.

Further reading: M. Golden, "Names and Naming at Athens. Three Studies," *Echoes du monde classique* 5 (1986): 245–269; P. M. Fraser and E. Matthews, *A Lexicon of Greek Personal Names, 1. The Aegean Islands, Cyprus, Cyrenaica* (New York: Oxford University Press, 1987); E. Carney, "Eponymous Women. Royal Women and City Names," *Ancient History Bulletin* 2 (1988): 134–142; A. B. Tataki, *Ancient Beroea Prosopography and Society* (Athens: National Hellenic Research Foundation, 1988); C. Habicht, "Notes on Attic Prosopography. Coincidence in Father-Son Pairs of Names," *Hesperia* 59 (1990): 459–462; Carolyn Higbie, *Heroes' Names, Homeric Identities* (New York: Garland, 1995); M. J. Osborne, *The Foreign Residents of Athens: An Annex to the Lexicon of Greek Personal Names: Attica* (Leuven, Belgium: Peeters, 1996); Simon Hornblower and Elaine Matthews, eds., *Greek Personal Names: Their Value as Evidence* (New York: Oxford University Press, 2000).

Narcissus In MYTH, this handsome Boeotian youth, son of the river god Kephisus and the nymph Liriopē, fell in love with his own reflection in a pond. In one version, he pined away and died of hopeless longing, in another, he stabbed himself with a dagger in frustration. From his body or blood there arose the white flower that the ancient Greeks called the *narkissos* (possibly a type of iris or lily, but not the same as our modern narcissus flower). This tale has produced the English words *narcissism* and *narcissistic*.

Narcissus's connection with a local flower, along with the pre-Greek *issos* ending of his name, suggest that he was originally a god or demigod of the pre-Greek peoples, absorbed into Greek mythology during the second millennium B.C.E.

See also GREEK LANGUAGE; HYACINTHUS; NYMPHS; RELIGION.

Further reading: E. Pellizer, "Reflections, Echoes, and Amorous Reciprocity. On Reading the Narcissus Story," in *Interpretations of Greek Mythology,* edited by Jan Bremmer (London: Croom Helm, 1987), 107–120; M. Nelson, "Narcissus. Myth and Magic," *Classical Journal* 95 (1999–2000): 363–389.

Naukratis This ancient port city of EGYPT is situated about 50 miles inland, on the westernmost branch of the Nile River. In the later 600s B.C.E. the pharaohs assigned Naukratis as the one emporium for all Greek TRADE in Egypt. The city then became the site of Greek temples and offices where various Greek states were represented. As listed by the historian HERODOTUS, these states included the great seagoing powers of the day: AEGINA, SAMOS, CHIOS, MILETUS, PHOCAEA, MYTILENE, and RHODES. The name *Naukratis* seems to be Greek, meaning "ship power"—that is, shipping place.

Archaeological excavations at Naukratis, combined with written references, give some idea of the commerce between Greece and Egypt in the 600s–500s B.C.E. Much of this trade apparently consisted of Greek SILVER ore and SLAVES (both acquired in the northern Aegean) exchanged for Egyptian grain, which was shipped by Greek merchants at a large profit to the hungry cities of the Greek world. Egyptian luxury goods, such as carved ivory, were also exported.

Like other port cities throughout history, Naukratis offered its share of men's entertainment. Herodotus describes Naukratis as "a place for lovely courtesans" (*hetairai*). Certain verses by the Greek poet SAPPHO (ca. 600 B.C.E.) lament the predicament of Sappho's brother, ensnared at Naukratis by a fascinating *hetaira* on whom he has squandered his fortune.

Naukratis's fortunes declined after 525 B.C.E., when the Persian occupation of Egypt disrupted the Greek trade. After ALEXANDER THE GREAT's conquest of Egypt (332 B.C.E.), Naukratis was completely eclipsed by the founding of nearby ALEXANDRIA (1).

See also PROSTITUTES.

Further reading: M. S. Venit, *Greek Painted Pottery from Naukratis in Egyptian Museums* (Winona Lake, Ill.: Eisenbrauns, 1988); B. Muhs, "The Great Temenos of Naukratis," *Journal of the American Research Centers in Egypt* 31 (1994): 99–113; William Coulson, *Ancient Naukratis* (Oxford: Oxbow Books, 1996); H. Bowden, "The Greek Settlement and Sanctuaries at Naukratis. Herodotus and Archaeology," in *More Studies in the Ancient Greek Polis*, edited by Mogens Herman Hansen and Kurt Raaflaub (Stuttgart, Germany: Franz Steiner Verlag, 1996), 17–37; Albert Leonard Jr., *Ancient Naukratis: Excavations at a Greek Emporium in Egypt* (Atlanta: Scholars Press, 1998); Astrid Möller, *Naukratis: Trade in Archaic Greece* (New York: Oxford University Press, 2000); K. Smolárikova, "The Great Temenos at Naukratis Once Again," *Archív orientální* 68 (2000): 571–578.

Naupactos This seaport of West LOCRIS is situated at the mouth of the Corinthian Gulf. Naupactos' position controlling the gulf's narrow outlet made the town a natural naval base—its name in Greek means "shipbuilding." In the mid-400s B.C.E. Naupactos was captured by ATHENS and repopulated with fugitives from MESSENIA who had unsuccessfully revolted from Spartan rule (464–460 B.C.E.). During the PELOPONNESIAN WAR (431–404 B.C.E.), Naupactos was the main Athenian naval base in western Greece; it was off Naupactos that the Athenian admiral Phormion won his two brilliant sea victories over Peloponnesian fleets in 429 B.C.E.

After Athens's defeat in the war, Naupactos passed to the state of ACHAEA. In 338 B.C.E. the Macedonian king PHILIP II gave Naupactos to his ally, the state of AETOLIA. Naupactos had lost its importance by the 100s B.C.E., when the Aetolian League was defeated by ROME.

Further reading: E. Badien, "Athens, the Locrians, and Naupactus," *Classical Quarterly* 40 (1990): 364–369.

Nausicaa This princess of the virtuous Phaeacians is featured prominently in HOMER's *Odyssey.* In one of the poem's most charming episodes (book 6), she leads her waiting women to wash clothes at a stream and there encounters the shipwrecked hero ODYSSEUS. Approaching naked and shielded only by a leafy branch, Odysseus unintentionally scares away the servants, but not Nausicaa. Inspired by the goddess ATHENA, she supplies food and clothing to the hero, then shows him the way to her father's palace, where he is suitably received.

Further reading: F. Brommer, "Theseus and Nausicaa," *Journal of the Walters Art Gallery* 38 (1980): 364–369; J. Boardman, "No, No, Nausicaa," *Journal of the Walters Art Gallery* 39 (1981): 38.

navies *See* WARFARE, NAVAL.

navigation *See* SHIPS AND SEAFARING.

Naxos (1) *See* CYCLADES.

Naxos (2) The first Greek colony in SICILY, Naxos was also one of the earliest Greek colonies anywhere. Situated on a promontory on the island's east coast, at the foot of Mt. Etna, Naxos was a natural landfall for westbound ships rounding the "toe" of ITALY from the northeast. Naxos was founded in about 734 B.C.E. by Greeks from CHALCIS under a leader named Thucles. Supposedly, the expedition included Greeks from the Aegean island of Naxos, who gave the new city its name.

Naxos itself seems to have been intended only as a Greek foothold in Sicily: Six years after its founding, Thucles and his followers drove the native Sicels from the fertile plain of Catania and founded the cities of CATANA and Leontini. These cities and others, such as nearby SYRACUSE, soon exceeded Naxos in importance.

By the early 400s B.C.E. Naxos was ruled by Syracusan TYRANTS. As an Ionian-Greek city in a realm dominated by DORIAN GREEKS, Naxos became a target of ruthless social engineering when the Syracusan tyrant HIERON (1) depopulated it and moved the people to Leontini (476 B.C.E.).

Reconstituted, Naxos made an alliance with ATHENS against Syracuse in 415 B.C.E., during the PELOPONNESIAN WAR, and served as an Athenian base for the disastrous expedition against Syracuse. In 403 B.C.E. Naxos was captured and razed by the Syracusan tyrant DIONYSIUS (1).

See also COLONIZATION.

Further reading: Maria Costanza Lentini, ed., *The Two Naxos Cities: A Fine Link between the Aegean Sea and Sicily: 14–30 June 2001, University of Athens . . . 6–31 July 2001, Archaeological Museum of the Island of Naxos: exhibition of objects from the Museums of Sicilian and Cycladic Naxos: fruit of a collaboration between the Soprintendenza BB.CC.AA. di Messina and the University of Athens and the 21st Ephorate of the Cyclades* (Palermo, Italy: Regione Sicilia, Assessorato dei Beni Culturali e Ambientali e Pubblica Istruzione, 2001).

Nemean Games One of the four great sports-and-religious festivals of ancient Greece, the Nemean Games were celebrated along with the OLYMPIC, PYTHIAN, and ISTHMIAN GAMES. Sacred to the god ZEUS, this festival was held every other year at the valley and sanctuary called Nemea in the northeastern PELOPONNESE, in the region of ARGOS but close to the town of Cleonae. There, according to myth, the hero HERAKLES instituted the games after slaying the Nemean Lion—the first of his 12 Labors. In fact, the Nemean festival first became important in 573 B.C.E., when Argos took over its administration from Cleonae and enlarged it on the model of the Olympic Games. Around 415 B.C.E., the games were removed from Nemea to Argos, until they were returned to the sanctuary in the 330s B.C.E. At this time, there was a large

amount of building activity at Nemea, including the Temple of Zeus, the stadium, and a bath complex. The games were moved again to Argos (permanently, this time) in 271 B.C.E., although Aratos of SIKYON made an unsuccessful attempt to reinstate the games at Nemea in 235 B.C.E.

At the beginning of each competition, the participating athletes would gather and swear an oath to the god Zeus. The prize for victors was a garland of wild celery (as at the Isthmian Games).

The ruins of a Doric-style temple of Zeus, built around 340–320 B.C.E., have been excavated in Nemea. The temple was destroyed by earthquakes in late antiquity. Near the temple, archaeologists have discovered the remains of the ancient stadium, where the athletes competed in the Nemean Games. It was built around 330 B.C.E., perhaps on the site of some earlier structure. The stadium was in use until around 271 B.C.E., when the games ceased to be held at Nemea. During the Roman and Early Christian eras, the stadium was used for farming and herding animals.

Nemea was visited by European travelers in the 18th century C.E., but the first archaeological excavations took place in 1884, under the French School of Archaeology. An American team under the auspices of the University of Cincinnati and the American School of Classical Studies began work at Nemea in the 1920s and 1930s. A new expedition took place in the 1960s, under Charles K. Williams II, again sponsored by the American School of Classical Studies. From 1973 to the present, Nemea has been the subject of investigation by Stephen G. Miller, professor of classics at the University of California at Berkeley. Recent work at the site includes the construction of a new museum, the reconstruction of the temple of Zeus, and the revival of the Nemean Games as a modern annual athletic event.

Further reading: Stephen G. Miller, "Tunnel Vision. The Nemean Games," *Archaeology* 33 (1980): 54–56; Stephen G. Miller, "The Theorodokoi of the Nemean Games," *Hesperia* 57 (1988): 147–163; Paula Perlman, "The Calendrical Position of the Nemean Games," *Athenaeum* 67 (1989): 57–90; Olga Tzachou-Alexandri, ed., *Mind and Body: Athletic Contests in Ancient Greece* (Athens: Ministry of Culture, National Hellenic Committee I.C.O.M., 1989); Stephen G. Miller, *Nemea: A Guide to the Site and Museum* (Berkeley: University of California Press, 1990); Stephen G. Miller, "The Stadium at Nemea and the Nemean Games," in *Proceedings of an International Symposium on the Olympic Games, 5–9 September 1988,* edited by William Coulson and Helmut Kyrieleis (Athens: Deutsches Archaeologisches Institut Athen, 1992), 81–86; Darice E. Birge, *Excavations at Nemea* (Berkeley: University of California Press, 1992–2001).

Neoptolemos A Greek mythical hero of the island of Scyros, Neoptolemos was the son of the Thessalian hero

ACHILLES and the princess Deidameia. Neoptolemos ("new warrior") was begotten while Achilles was hiding among the WOMEN of Scyros in an attempt to avoid serving in the TROJAN WAR.

HOMER's epic poem the *Odyssey* mentions that Neoptolemos himself went to TROY after his father's death. He was summoned by the Greeks, who had learned in a prophecy that Neoptolemos's presence was a fated precondition of the city's fall. Although Neoptolemos would have been only about 10 years old at that time, this detail was overlooked in the legend, and he was said to have fought fiercely at Troy, winning the nickname Pyrrhus ("fiery" or "red").

Neoptolemos was one of the select Greek commandoes who hid inside the Trojan Horse. During the capture of the city, he slew the Trojan king PRIAM—despite the fact that Priam had taken sanctuary at the altar of the great god ZEUS. This brutal act brought the hatred of the Trojans' patron god APOLLO against Neoptolemos.

According to one version, Neoptolemos was killed after the war in a dispute at Apollo's shrine at DELPHI. Another version says he sailed to EPIRUS, in northwestern Greece, where he fathered the ruling clan, the Molossians. In historical times the Molossians used the hero's nickname, Pyrrhus, as a given name. The most famous such person was the Epirote king PYRRHUS (reigned 297–272 B.C.E.).

See also ANDROMACHE.

Further reading: E. Suárez de la Torre, "Neoptolemos at Delphi," *Kernos* 10 (1997): 153–176.

Nereids *See* NEREUS.

Nereus In MYTH, Nereus was a minor sea god, a kind of old man of the sea. He and his wife, Doris (the daughter of OCEANUS), had 50 daughters, known as the Nereids (Greek: Nereidai "daughters of Nereus"). These sea-dwelling young goddesses, often imagined as fish-tailed, have been favorite subjects of art and poetry since ancient times. The best known of the Nereids were Amphitritē, who married the Olympian sea god POSEIDON, and Thetis, who married the mortal PELEUS and gave birth to the hero ACHILLES.

The name Amphitritē is not Greek, and surely derives from the language of the prehistoric people who occupied the land of Greece before the first Greek-speaking tribes arrived, around 2100 B.C.E. The Nereids are probably survivals of the pre-Greek people's RELIGION.

See also ARTEMIS; NYMPHS.

Further reading: R. Glynn, "Herakles, Nereus, and Triton. A Study of Iconography in Sixth Century Athens," *American Journal of Archaeology* 85 (1981): 121–132.

Nestor In MYTH, Nestor was the king of PYLOS, in the southwestern PELOPONNESE, and the most elderly of the Greek commanders in the TROJAN WAR. Nestor—the son and successor of King Neleus—was probably imagined as being over the age of 50 when the war began and over the age of 60 at its conclusion. HOMER's *Iliad* and *Odyssey* give a charming portrait of an admirable but garrulous old man, often ineffectual in combat and councils of war. In both poems he delivers meandering but lively speeches recalling his youthful achievements.

The *Iliad* presents Nestor's fond relationship with his soldier-son Antilochus but omits the tale of Antilochus's death. We know from other ancient sources that Antilochus was killed while defending his father from the Ethiopian champion MEMNON. In the *Odyssey*, Nestor is shown safely back in Pylos, where he welcomes the prince TELEMACHOS in the latter's search for his father, ODYSSEUS.

Further reading: O. Murray, "Nestor's Cup and the Origins of the Greek Symposium," *Annali di archeologia e storia antica* 1 (1994): 47–54; Keith Dickson, *Nestor: Poetic Memory in Greek Epic* (New York: Garland, 1995).

Nikē The goddess of Victory, Nikē oversaw winning in war or SPORT. Like many other minor deities, Nikē was more a symbol than an important character in Greek MYTH. The name Nikē was sometimes reduced to an epithet of the goddess ATHENA—Athena Nikē, the patron of victory through strategy.

From the 500s B.C.E. onward, Nikē was picturesquely shown in art as having two feathery wings. She became a favorite subject after the Greek triumph in the PERSIAN WARS, and was often associated with the god ZEUS—most famously in the colossal statue of Zeus sculpted by PHEIDIAS for the temple at OLYMPIA. In this monument (completed in about 430 B.C.E., now lost, but represented on coins), Nikē appeared standing on the god's upturned palm.

The best-known surviving Nikē in art is the marble statue called the Winged Victory of Samothrace, sculpted around 190 B.C.E. and now in the Louvre. In the Greco-Roman world, Nikē often was shown on coins and medallions, sometimes elevated, garlanding a victorious general's head.

See also PARTHENON; SAMOTHRACE.

Further reading: B. S. Ridgway, "The Nike of Archermos and Her Attire," in *Chios. A Conference at the Homerion in Chios, 1984,* edited by J. Boardman and C. E. Vaphopoulou-Richardson (New York: Oxford University Press, 1986), 259–274; Ira S. Mark, *The Sanctuary of Athena Nike in Athens. Architectural Stages and Chronology. Hesperia Supplement 26* (Princeton, N.J.: American School of Classical Studies in Athens, 1993); M. H. Jamison, "The Ritual of the Athena Nike Parapet," in *Ritual, Finance, Politics. Athenian Democratic Accounts Presented to David Lewis,* edited by Robin Osborne and Simon Hornblower (New York: Oxford University Press, 1994), 307–324; Erika Simon, "An Interpretation of the Nike

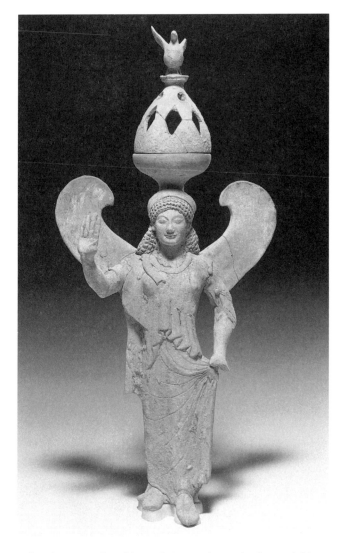

Nikē, the winged goddess of victory, forms the base of this incense burner, probably used to offer thanks. A bird sits atop the incense bowl. Nikē's pose and costume are identical with large-scale marble statues carved about 480 B.C.E. *(The J. Paul Getty Museum)*

Nikias ("victorious") was the son of Niceratus, of a distinguished Athenian family whose income came from the leasing of large numbers of SLAVES to work the Athenian SILVER mines at Laurion. Upon the death of PERIKLES (429 B.C.E.), the soldierly Nikias became the heir to Perikles' defensive strategy in the Peloponnesian War.

As a politician, Nikias headed the conservative peace party, composed of the upper class and the smallholding farmers. Nikias's opponent and personal enemy was the pro-war radical democrat KLEON. After Kleon's death, Nikias arranged the short-lived peace with SPARTA that bears his name—the Peace of Nikias (421 B.C.E.).

In 415 B.C.E. Nikias was appointed alongside the generals ALCIBIADES and Lamachus to command a 134-ship armada to besiege and capture Syracuse, in SICILY. Unfortunately, the 55-year-old Nikias disapproved of the ambitious venture and, after Alcibiades was recalled, Nikias proved to be a dangerously indecisive leader. The death of Lamachus, combined with Nikias's kidney ailment, contributed to the deteriorating situation, despite Nikias's field victory at the River Anapus (late 415 B.C.E.). By summer of 413 B.C.E. the Athenians—although reinforced by fresh troops—were surrounded by the enemy on land and sea, after Nikias had hesitated too long to abandon the siege and sail away. Leading a hopeless attempt to escape overland, Nikias was captured by the Syracusans amid the slaughter of his men at the River Assinarus. He was later executed by the Syracusans.

See also DELOS; DEMOSTHENES [2].

Further reading: R. Seager, "After the Peace of Nicias. Diplomacy and Policy 421–416 B.C.," *Classical Quarterly* 26 (1976): 249–269; Donald Kagan, *The Peace of Nicias and the Sicilian Expedition,* 2d ed. (Ithaca, N.Y.: Cornell University Press, 1991); J. C. Trevett, "Nikias and Syracuse," *Zeitschrift für Papyrologie und Epigraphik* 106 (1995): 246–248; J. E. Atkinson, "Nicias and the Fear of Failure Syndrome," *Ancient History Bulletin* 9 (1995): 55–63; Lisa Kallet, *Money and the Corrosion of Power in Thucydides: The Sicilian Expedition and Its Aftermath* (Berkeley: University of California Press, 2001).

Temple Parapet," in *The Interpretation of Architectural Sculpture in Greece and Rome,* edited by Diana Buitron-Oliver (Washington, D.C.: National Gallery of Art, 1997), 126–143; J. de Waele, "The Temples of Athena Nike on the Acropolis of Athens. Ancient Measurements and Design," *Pharos* 5 (1997): 27–48.

Nikias (ca. 470–413 B.C.E.) *Athenian general and politician of the PELOPONNESIAN WAR*

Rich and devoutly religious, Nikias served his city loyally. But his hesitancy and befuddlement in the Athenian campaign against SYRACUSE (415–413 B.C.E.) produced an epic disaster that destroyed an Athenian force of perhaps 50,000 men, including Nikias himself.

Niobē In MYTH, Niobē was the wife of the Theban hero Amphion. As the mother of six youths and six maidens, Niobē boasted arrogantly that she was superior to the demigoddess Leto, who had borne only two children—the deities APOLLO and ARTEMIS. Angered at this affront to their mother, Apollo and Artemis hunted down, with bow and arrow, all 12 of Niobē's children. Niobē wept ceaselessly until, on the 10th day of her lamenting, the god ZEUS turned her to stone. The stone was said to be located in ASIA MINOR, on the slopes of Mt. Sipylos, in Phrygia. It is described by the Roman traveler PAUSANIAS (2), as well as other ancient authors.

As a symbol of maternal grief, Niobē became a popular subject in ancient Greek literature and art. This tale is first told in HOMER's *Iliad,* as background to the grief of the parents of the slain Trojan hero HECTOR. Niobē was also featured in tragedies by AESCHYLUS and SOPHOKLES, and her transformation is one of the main stories in the Roman poet Ovid's *Metamorphoses.* Scenes of Niobē trying to shield her children from the arrows of Apollo and Artemis also appear on Greek vases. The most famous artistic representation of Niobē and her children was a marble SCULPTURE group taken from Greece to Rome in the early imperial era; it survives only in a Roman copy, and the original may have been by one of the famous Greek sculptors PRAXITELES or Skopas. As a symbol of maternal grief, Niobē became a popular subject in Greco-Roman art and poetry.

See also HUBRIS.

Further reading: R. M. Cook, *Niobe and Her Children* (Cambridge: Cambridge University Press, 1964); H. M. Fracchia, "The Mourning Niobe Motif on South Italian Art," *Echos du monde classique* 6 (1987): 199–205.

numbers   *See* MATHEMATICS.

nymphs   The nymphai were mythical female spirits of the wilderness, representing the beauty and fertility of nature. They were daughters of ZEUS or of other gods, but they themselves were not usually immortal. Rather, they were like leprechauns, living for centuries in the wild and avoiding contact with humans.

Usually imagined as young and amorous, nymphs were associated with the god DIONYSUS and his coterie of lusty male SATYRS. (This association is behind the pseudopsychiatric term *nymphomaniac,* meaning a woman with obsessive sexual desire.) Individual nymphs of MYTH include CALYPSO, lover of the hero ODYSSEUS, and CYRENE (2), lover of the god APOLLO. In the ancient GREEK LANGUAGE, *nymphē* could also mean a young marriageable woman.

Eventually these pretty wilderness creatures became the subject of poets' elaborations, especially in the Hellenistic and Roman eras, after 300 B.C.E. There we find specialized categories of nymphs, such as the Naiads (stream nymphs) and the Dryads or Hamadryads (tree nymphs).

Like the NEREIDS and other demigoddesses, the nymphs may date back to the RELIGION of the pre-Greek people who inhabited the land of Greece before 2100 B.C.E.

Further reading: Guy Hedreen, "Silens, Nymphs, and Maenads," *Journal of Hellenic Studies* 114 (1994): 47–69; Judith Barringer, *Divine Escorts: Nereids in Archaic and Classical Greek Art* (Ann Arbor: University of Michigan Press, 1995); Jennifer Larson, *Greek Nymphs: Myth, Cult, Lore* (New York: Oxford University Press, 2001).

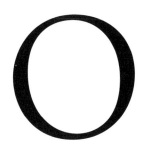

Oceanids *See* OCEANUS.

Oceanus In MYTH, Okeanos was a river that encircles the world and serves as the underground source for all earthly rivers. The poet HESIOD described the river god Oceanus as one of the primeval offspring of Ouranos ("Sky") and GAEA (Mother Earth). Oceanus and his wife, Tethys, produced the 3,000 Oceanids, the "daughters of Oceanus." These Oceanids were NYMPHS inhabiting bodies of water and other wilderness sites. In HOMER's *Iliad* and *Odyssey*, Oceanus was associated with the far West; there he flowed past shores inhabited by such fabulous creatures as MEDUSA, Geryon, and the Hesperides.

The notion of an encircling world stream is common to many mythologies. The Greeks may have borrowed it from the Near East, since the word Okeanos does not seem to be Greek. But the Greeks soon added their own layer, when their concept of *Okeanos* became colored by rumors of the Atlantic sea, lying west of the Mediterranean. The Greeks chose the word of Okeanos to identify the Atlantic, once they began to venture beyond the straits of Gibraltar in the wake of the pioneering Phoenicians (600s B.C.E.). The English word *ocean* of course derives from Okeanos.

See also ATLANTIS; ATLAS; HERAKLES; PHOENICIA.

Odysseus In MYTH, this wily king of ITHACA (a small island on the northwest coast of Greece) was a captain of the Greeks in the TROJAN WAR. Odysseus's 10-year-long journey home from TROY, and his strategy to rid his kingdom of troubles brewed by his absence, constitute the story of the 12,000-line epic poem the *Odyssey*. Written down around 750 B.C.E. and ascribed in ancient times to the poet HOMER, the *Odyssey*—with its associated poem, the *Iliad*—stands at the beginning of Western literature, as one of the greatest works of Western literature.

The name Odysseus means "angry." The Romans, in retelling the myth, latinized the name to Ulixes, from which we get the form Ulysses. In some versions, Ulysses or Odysseus was said to be secretly the son of the cunning hero SISYPHUS, begotten on Antikleia, wife of the Ithacan king Laertes. In any case, Odysseus was raised as Laertes' son and succeeded him as king after Laertes abdicated in old age. Soon, however, Odysseus was summoned, along with other Greek vassal kings, to bring troops and ships to the expedition against Troy organized by King AGAMEMNON of MYCENAE. Odysseus left behind a dedicated and highly intelligent wife, PENELOPE, and their infant son, TELEMACHOS. The Trojan War itself was to last for 10 years.

In the *Iliad,* which describes events of the war's 10th year, Odysseus appears as one of the foremost Greek commanders, valiant in combat and wise in counsel. He often is associated with the Greek hero DIOMEDES. Together they make a night raid against the Trojan allies (book 10) and later, amid fierce fighting, they stop a Greek retreat (book 11). Being the swiftest-running Greek aside from ACHILLES, Odysseus wins the footrace at the Funeral Games of PATROKLOS (book 23). He also wrestles the hero AJAX (1) to a draw, using skill to offset his opponent's greater strength. Later Greek writers, such as SOPHOKLES (400s B.C.E.), enlarged on the rivalry between these two heroes, contrasting the cleverness or deviousness of Odysseus with the simplicity or honesty of Ajax.

Odysseus's character was one of courage, wisdom, levelheadedness, and perseverance. He was an eloquent speaker and often served as ambassador or negotiator. His cleverness was sometimes sneaky and scheming, qualities that made him a successful spy as well. Although he is an accomplished soldier, he prefers to use persuasion rather than force. On his long voyage home to Ithaca from Troy, he resisted dozens of alluring temptations and remained steadfast in returning to his wife and family. Odysseus generally appears in Greek art as a bearded man, wearing the short, rounded cap of a sailor or traveler.

The chronological sequence of Odysseus's homeward progress—not presented in this simple order in the *Odyssey*—is as follows: Leaving the ruins of Troy, he and his 12 ships raid the coast of THRACE but are beaten off by the warlike Cicones (book 9). Thereafter the voyage enters the realm of fable and is no longer geographically recognizable. (However, certain of its supernatural landmarks seem to be associated with the shores of southern ITALY and eastern SICILY, which real-life Greek mariners were exploring in the 800s and 700s B.C.E.)

The voyagers' next landfall is among the friendly Lotus-eaters, who are perpetually narcotized by their magical *lotos*-fruit food. Fleeing from this seductive danger, the squadron puts ashore in the territory of the one-eyed monsters known as Cyclopes (book 9). Odysseus is captured by one of them, named POLYPHEMOS, but escapes after blinding the creature. Polyphemos prays to his father, the god POSEIDON, for revenge.

Next Odysseus and his ships reach the island of the hospitable wind king, Aeolis (book 10). Aeolis gives Odysseus a tied-up bag containing all the winds except the favorable one needed for Odysseus's voyage home. But out at sea, while Odysseus sleeps, his men greedily open the mysterious bag: The released winds blow the ships back to the isle of Aeolis, who refuses to help again. Later, Odysseus loses all ships and crews except his own to the cannabalistic Laestrygonians.

The hero's ship arrives at the island of the beautiful witch CIRCE (book 10). After saving his men from Circe's evil magic, Odysseus becomes her lover. She tells him that in order to reach home he must journey down to the Underworld and consult the ghost of the seer TEIRESIAS. In the Underworld (book 11) Odysseus observes the ghosts of several prominent people, including his own mother and such former comrades as Achilles and Ajax.

After lingering with Circe for a year, Odysseus reembarks, having received Circe's directions for reaching home. His ship bypasses the SIRENS, survives the channel of SCYLLA and the whirlpool Charybdis, and reaches the island where the cattle of the sun god, HELIOS, graze. There, despite his warnings, his men slaughter the cattle for food. Consequently, the ship is destroyed at sea by the thunderbolt of the great god ZEUS. Everyone aboard perishes except Odysseus, who drifts to the isle of the amorous CALYPSO (book 12).

Seven years later, at Zeus's command, Calypso allows Odysseus to depart in a boat of his own construction (book 5). But he is shipwrecked again, this time by Poseidon, in vengeance for Polyphemos's distress. With the help of the goddess ATHENA, Odysseus reaches the land of the virtuous Phaeacians and encounters the princess NAUSICAA, who directs him to the palace of her father, King Alcinous (book 6). There the hero, welcomed royally (books 7–8), tells the tale of his wanderings since Troy (books 9–12).

By then nearly 10 years have passed since Troy's destruction and Odysseus's departure for home and nearly 20 years have gone by since he first left Ithaca. Unknown to Odysseus, Ithaca has meanwhile fallen prey to more than 100 visiting lords and petty kings who crowd the palace, competing to marry the presumably widowed Penelope; she remains elusive, in the hope that Odysseus might yet return. The prince Telemachos, now a young man, has gone abroad in search of his father, hoping to free his home from the loathsome suitors.

The *Odyssey*'s entire second half (books 13–24) describes Odysseus's return to Ithaca, his espionage there in disguise as a beggar, and how—with the help of Athena, Telemachos, and two trusted retainers—he destroys the suitors, reclaims his wife and throne, and restores harmony to the island.

The story of Odysseus's death, not told in the *Odyssey,* was described in a later epic poem, now lost, called the *Telegonia.* Tiresias in the Underworld had predicted that Odysseus's death would come from the sea, but Odysseus reigned for many happy years on Ithaca. Meanwhile his three illegitimate sons by Circe grew to manhood. The youngest, Telegonus ("distant born"), set out to meet his father and somehow encountered Odysseus en route, not knowing who he was. A fight ensued, and Telegonus slew Odysseus. (This episode bears comparison with the similar tale of OEDIPUS.) The weapon that Telegonus used was a sharp fishbone, thereby fulfilling the terms of Tiresias's prophecy.

Odysseus is the best-known example of the "trickster" type of Greek mythical figure. Other tricksters from Greek myth include the god HERMES, the demigod PROMETHEUS, and Odysseus's putative father, Sisyphos.

See also AFTERLIFE; EPIC POETRY; PROPHECY AND DIVINATION.

Further reading: D. Williams, "Ajax, Odysseus, and the Arms of Achilles," *Antike Kunst* 23 (1980): 137–145; P. Walcot, "Odysseus and the Contest of the Bow. The Comparative Evidence," in *Studi Micenei ed Egeo-anatolici* 25 (Rome: Edizioni dell'Ateneo & Bizzari, 1984), 357–369; P. J. Connor, "The Cup and the Sword. Odysseus Intimidates Circe on a Column-krater in Sydney," *Archäologischer Anzeiger* (1988): 41–53; S. Symeónoglou, "The Wanderings of Odysseus," in *The Hellenic Diaspora from Antiquity to Modern Times, 1. From Antiquity to 1453. Proceedings of the First International*

Congress, Montreal, 17–22.IV.1988, edited by John Fossey (Amsterdam: J. C. Gieben, 1991), 37–43; T. J. McNiven, "Odysseus on the Niobid Krater," *Journal of Hellenic Studies* 109 (1989): 191–198; W. Donlan, "Political Reciprocity in Dark Age Greece. Odysseus and his Hetairoi," in *Reciprocity in Ancient Greece,* edited by C. Gill, N. Postlethwaite, and R. Seaford (New York: Oxford University Press, 1998), 51–71.

Odyssey *See* HOMER; ODYSSEUS.

Oedipus In MYTH, Oedipus was a Theban king who could not escape his FATE. He married a woman who, unbeknown to him, was his own mother, Jocasta (Iocastē). The story is mentioned in HOMER's *Odyssey,* but the classic telling of the Oedipus tale is the Athenian playwright SOPHOKLES' extant tragedy *Oedipus the King* (presented ca. 429–420 B.C.E.).

Oedipus was the son of Laius, king of THEBES, and Jocasta, his wife. Warned by prophecy that his son would kill him, Laius abandoned the infant on Mt. Kithaeron, after first running a spike through the baby's feet—from which the child later got his name, Oidipous, "swollen foot." As in all such folktales, the infant did not die but was rescued, in this case by a Corinthian shepherd, servant of the Corinthian king. This king and his wife, being childless, were happy to adopt the boy and pass him off as their own.

Nevertheless, the young Oedipus was taunted by others for being adopted, and eventually he went to DELPHI to ask the god APOLLO who his real parents might be. The oracle withheld this information but told Oedipus that he would kill his father and marry his mother. Disgusted, Oedipus decided never to return to CORINTH. Journeying by chance toward Thebes, he fell into a dispute at a crossroads with a stranger. Not knowing that this was Laius, his own father, Oedipus killed him. Then he reached Thebes, which was at that time being terrorized by a supernatural female monster, the Sphinx.

When the Sphinx encountered people, she would ask them a riddle, and eat them when they failed to guess the answer. The riddle asked: "What goes on four legs at morning, two at noon, and three at evening?" Oedipus deduced the correct answer: a human being. (The "legs" represent, respectively, the baby's hands and knees, the adult's upright legs, and the elderly person's legs and cane.) At this point the Sphinx either killed herself or was killed by Oedipus. Acclaimed by the Thebans, Oedipus now married the newly widowed queen, Jocasta, whom he did not know to be his mother. In most versions they had four children: the girls ANTIGONE and Ismenē and the boys Eteokles and Polynices. These children were also doomed to unhappy ends.

In Sophokles' play, these events are revealed through Oedipus's own careful investigations (prompted by a plague and famine in Thebes that can be resolved only by discovering the murderer of Laius). Jocasta hanged herself in grief, and Oedipus blinded himself and abdicated his throne, going into exile with Antigone. In Sophokles' play *Oedipus at Colonus* (performed 401 B.C.E.), the aged hero is shown as having wandered to Colonus, an outlying Athenian village (and Sophokles' own home). There Oedipus disappeared from earth, having been taken up by the gods.

The subject of Oedipus and the Sphinx was a popular one of vase painting in the 400s B.C.E.

See also PROPHECY AND DIVINATION; SEVEN AGAINST THEBES.

Further reading: Edmunds, Lowell, *Oedipus: The Ancient Legend and Its Later Analogues* (Baltimore: Johns Hopkins University Press, 1985); J. Bremmer, "Oedipus and the Greek Oedipus Complex," in *Interpretations of Greek Mythology,* edited by J. Bremmer (London: Croom Helm, 1987), 41–59.

oligarchy Meaning "government by the few" (*oligoi*), an oligarchy in ancient Greece referred to a city-state in which only a small minority of the citizens (usually the wealthiest) could be admitted to political power. The rest of the citizens had certain rights and protections, but they lacked any important say in the governing of the state.

ARISTOTLE and other ancient political thinkers discussed oligarchy and the distinctions between it and an ARISTOCRACY (where the government was controlled by a few chosen because of their familial lineage). In oligarchies, the exclusive ruling circle consisted of rich men, not only men of noble birth. Of course, there was some overlap between these two groups, and oligarchy usually represented a development from aristocracy, due to urbanization and commercialization in the 700s–400s B.C.E. The inroads made by wealth against privileges of birth are well documented in the indignant verses of aristocratic poets such as THEOGNIS (ca. 550 B.C.E.).

Oligarchy and DEMOCRACY were the two main opposing government forms of Classical Greece (400s–300s B.C.E.). The champion of oligarchies everywhere was SPARTA, and its enemy was ATHENS, the beacon of democracy (whose citizens, nevertheless, included an angry pro-oligarchic minority). The PELOPONNESIAN WAR (431–404 B.C.E.) was in part a conflict between these two forms of government. Sparta's ruling group was called the "council of elders" (*gerousia*), made up of the two kings plus 28 other wealthy men. Five annually elected officials called *ephors* also exercised considerable power, particularly concerning judgment and punishment.

Other prominent oligarchies of the 400s B.C.E. included CORINTH, THEBES, and LOCRI (in Greek ITALY).

See also HOPLITE; POLIS.

Further reading: J. M. Moore, trans., *Aristotle and Xenophon on Democracy and Oligarchy* (Los Angeles:

University of California Press, 1975); W. G. Forrest, "Democracy and Oligarchy in Sparta and Athens," *Echos du monde classique* 2 (1983): 285–296.

olives   *See* FARMING.

Olympia   Sanctuary and sports complex, sacred to the great god ZEUS, in the region known as ELIS, in the western PELOPONNESE. This was the site of the most important panhellenic festival of ancient Greece, the OLYMPIC GAMES. The name Olympia refers to Olympian Zeus—that is, Zeus, king of the gods on Mt. OLYMPUS. (However, Mt. Olympus itself stands in THESSALY, in northeastern Greece, hundreds of miles from Olympia.)

The elaborate complex, which has been partly restored by archaeologists since 1829, lay in a pleasant valley, near the confluence of the rivers Alphaeus and Kladeus. ARCHAEOLOGY has revealed traces of pre-Greek settlement and it may be that Olympia—like DELPHI and certain other Greek sanctuaries—was a holy place for the inhabitants of the land long before the first Greek invaders arrived circa 2100 B.C.E. The site was inhabited by Greeks of the Mycenaean era (around 1600–1200 B.C.E.), but Olympia truly emerged after 776 B.C.E., the traditional date for the first Olympic Games.

In its heyday, Olympia contained hostels, restaurants, a meeting hall, and many other amenities, but it was never a city in the political sense, for it had neither citizens nor a government. The heart of Olympia was the sacred precinct, or Altis—a walled enclosure whose name apparently comes from *alsos*, "grove." From early times the Altis contained a temple of the goddess HERA and a shrine to the hero PELOPS (mythical founder of the Games). In 457 B.C.E. the magnificent Doric-style temple of Zeus was completed inside the Altis. This building was wrecked by an earthquake at the end of antiquity, but the foundations and platform are visible today, as are the temple's huge, collapsed column drums (made of a limestone visibly comprised of fossilized shellfish). The temple's pedimental sculptures, partly preserved and now displayed in the Olympia Museum, showed two mythical scenes: the battle between Lapiths and CENTAURS at King Pirithoos's wedding, and the chariot race of Pelops and Oinomaus. The temple housed a colossal cult statue of Zeus, fashioned by the Athenian sculptor PHEIDIAS (ca. 430 B.C.E.) and reckoned as one of the SEVEN WONDERS OF THE WORLD for its size and solemn majesty.

The statue, about 40 feet high, showed the god seated, enthroned. One ancient viewer objected that Zeus's head was so close to the roofbeams that he could not have stood up without taking off the roof, but in the temple's darkened interior this disproportion was probably not obvious. The god's flesh was made of ivory; his cloak, sandals, and accoutrements were GOLD. A human-size figure of the goddess NIKĒ, in ivory and gold, stood atop his right-hand palm, and his left hand held a scepter of various precious metals, tipped with a golden eagle. His cloak was inlaid with images of animals and lilies, and on his head was a golden wreath of facsimile olive leaves.

This statue had the power to awe those who stood before it. The Roman orator Quintilian (ca. 70 C.E.) stated that it added something to human religion. The great work survived through the Roman era until the 400s C.E. when, having been removed to the eastern Roman capital at Constantinople, it was accidentally destroyed in a fire. Our scanty knowledge of the statue's appearance comes from its image on ancient Elean coins and its description by the travel writer PAUSANIAS (2) (ca. 150 C.E.).

Modern archaeological excavations at the site of Phidias's workshop at Olympia have uncovered traces of ivory and gold, and terra-cotta molds (apparently for the casting of Zeus's golden cloak). Also, rather spectacularly, a red-figure ceramic jug has been found, inscribed with Phidias's name—his "office coffee mug."

Other ancient splendors of Olympia included many statues of prior victors and a row of 12 treasury houses, built between about 600 and 480 B.C.E. by various rich states of the Greek world, to hold offerings to the god. Of these, the Treasury of the Sikyonians has been reconstructed by modern archaeologists. Along the valley were the structures for the sporting events: a huge GYMNASIUM; a hippodrome for horse and chariot races; and a stadium (now fully restored) for footraces, where 40,000 spectators could be seated on grass embankments that had no need of benches.

Olympia was first excavated by French archaeologists in 1829, and their finds began to be transported to the Louvre. The Greek government intervened and stopped the excavation. In about 1875, German archaeologists resumed investigation of the site, and work by the German Institute of Archaeology in Athens continues at Olympia to the present day.

See also ARCHITECTURE; MILTIADES; SCULPTURE.

Further reading: Theodora Karaghiorga, *Ancient Olympia* (Athens: Apollo Editions, 1971); Nikolaos Yalouris, *Olympia: Altis and Museum,* 2d ed., translated by Paul J. Dine (Athens: Art Editions Meletzis and Papadakis, 1973); G. Schneider, "Bronze Casting at Olympia in Classical Times," *Masca Journal* 6 (1898): 17–24; Manolis Andronikos, *Olympia,* 2d ed., translated by Brian de Jongh (Athens: Ekdotike Athenon, 1990); Catherine Morgan, *Athletes and Oracles: The Transformation of Olympia and Delphi in the Eighth Century B.C.* (New York: Cambridge University Press, 1990).

Olympic Games   These were the oldest and most important of the ancient Greek sports-and-religious festivals. Open to all male, free-born Greeks, the Olympic Games were held every four years in honor of the god

ZEUS, at OLYMPIA, in the western PELOPONNESE. Traditionally the games were said to have been established by the hero HERAKLES, or alternatively by the hero PELOPS, but in practical terms the Greeks recognized 776 B.C.E. as the inaugural date, the date at which a record of victors was first begun.

The games were administered by the people of ELIS (the general region of Olympia). However, after King PHEIDON of ARGOS marched his troops into Olympia and took over the games in (probably) 668 B.C.E., he handed Olympia over to be run by the people of the nearby town of Pisa. The Pisans held Olympia for about 90 years, until the Eleans, with Spartan support, won it back (in about 580 B.C.E.).

In the earliest years, the contests took place all on one day and consisted of only two events: WRESTLING and the footrace (one lap of the stadium). Later, perhaps after King Pheidon's intervention, the games were enlarged to include races for saddle horses and for horse- and mule-drawn CHARIOTS. By 471 B.C.E. the games spanned five days—involving competitions, religious sacrifices, and feasting—and included most of the famous sports events of classical Greece: BOXING; PANKRATION; the PENTATHLON; boys' categories in footrace, wrestling, and boxing; and, the final event of the sequence, the footrace for men in armor. A separate festival, in honor of the goddess HERA, was organized and run by WOMEN and included footraces and dances for girls in three age groups. For every contest, the prize for victory was nothing more than a garland of olive leaves.

The games were of immense political and social importance. To Olympia every four years crowded the most influential people (almost exclusively men) of the Greek world, as spectators and competitors. Statesmen such as the Syracusan tyrant HIERON (1) (ca. 468 B.C.E.) and the Athenian ALCIBIADES (ca. 416 B.C.E.) spent fortunes developing chariot teams to enroll at the games. Famous writers such as HERODOTUS and EMPEDOKLES gave readings at Olympia, probably at privately organized side events. Drinking parties of the rich and powerful took place. The spirit of the Olympic Games—religious fervor and aristocratic pride—can be found in the victory odes of the Theban poet PINDAR (ca. 470 B.C.E.).

The four-year cycle between Olympic festivals was known as an Olympiad and was used as a chronological device in the ancient world. For instance, "the 67th Olympiad" signified the period that we would call 512-508 B.C.E., which began 264 years (66 by 4 years) after the first Olympiad (776 B.C.E.). Sometimes the ancients remembered a specific year by noting that that was the year when so-and-so won the footrace at Olympia.

The most striking aspect of the games was the Olympic Truce, which was announced by heralds in all major cities of mainland Greece months before the start of each Olympic festival. Whatever wars might be in progress elsewhere, the region of Elis and the site of

Olympia were sacrosanct for the truce. During the PELOPONNESIAN WAR, for example, visitors from enemy cities coexisted peacefully at Olympia during the games. In 420 B.C.E. the Spartans, having attacked Elean territory after the truce was declared, were barred from competing that year. To enforce the ban, several thousand troops from Elis, ARGOS, and MANTINEIA (all enemies of Sparta) guarded Olympia during the competition. A more notorious truce-breaking occurred in 364 B.C.E., when the Pisans and Arcadians invaded Olympia and fought a battle against the Eleans that raged within the sanctuary itself.

The games remained prestigious—although less central—in the Roman era (after about 150 B.C.E.), and survived nearly to the end of antiquity. In 393 C.E. they were abolished by an edict of the Byzantine emperor Theodosius I that prohibited all pagan festivals.

The first modern Olympics were organized in Athens in 1896 by a Frenchman named Baron Pierre de Coubertin. Fourteen nations sent teams to participate, but the majority of the athletes were from Greece. The events included track and field events, fencing, weightlifting, rifle and pistol shooting, tennis, cycling, swimming, gymnastics, and wrestling. One race was added that was not part of the ancient festival: the 40-kilometer race that began at the site of MARATHON and finished in the Olympic Stadium. The marathon supposedly commemorates the run of a soldier named Pheidippides, said to have run to Athens with news of the Greeks' victory against the Persians at Marathon in 490 B.C.E.

See also SPORT.

A bronze jockey, ca. 668 B.C.E., minus his horse but still holding part of the reins. Races for saddle horses were a later addition to the Olympic Games. *(Alison Frantz Photographic Collection, American School of Classical Studies at Athens)*

Further reading: G. Nagy, "Pindar's Olympian 1 and the Aetiology of the Olympic Games," *Transactions of the American Philological Association* 116 (1986): 71–88; Richard Woff, *The Ancient Greek Olympics* (New York: Oxford University Press, 1999); Ulrich Sinn, *Olympia: Cult, Sport, and Ancient Festival,* translated by Thomas Thornton (Princeton, N.J.: M. Wiener, 2000); Terence Measham, Elisabeth Spathari, and Paul Donnelly, *1000 Years of the Olympic Games: Treasures of Ancient Greece. Exhibition* (Sydney: Powerhouse, 2000); Hugh M. Lee, *The Program and Schedule of the Ancient Olympic Games* (Hildesheim, Germany: Weidmann, 2001); W. Lindsay Adams and Larry R. Gerlach, *The Olympic Games: Ancient and Modern* (Boston: Pearson Custom Publishing, 2002); Judith Swaddling, *The Ancient Olympic Games* (London: British Museum, 2004); Stephen G. Miller, *Ancient Greek Athletics* (New Haven, Conn.: Yale University Press, 2004).

Olympias *See also* ALEXANDER THE GREAT.

Olympus, Mt. The tallest mountain in mainland Greece, Mt. Olympus was, in MYTH, the celestial home of ZEUS and most of the other important gods. The massif, whose height reaches 9,570 feet, rises in the region of THESSALY, in northeastern Greece.

The religious awe that Mt. Olympus inspired probably had to do with the mystery of its summit, often cloaked in stormclouds appropriate to the weather god Zeus. The massif also served as a barrier to any invasion force moving southward from MACEDON, and it may have represented an important milestone for the first immigrating Greeks of around 2100 B.C.E.

Throughout Greek literature, Mt. Olympus is identified as the royal court of Zeus—the "Olympian"—and of his foremost subordinate gods. These 12 Olympian gods, aside from Zeus, were: HERA, POSEIDON, APOLLO, ARTEMIS, ATHENA, APHRODITE, ARES, DEMETER, DIONYSUS, HERMES, and HESTIA. They comprised the important deities for most spheres of life, with the exception of the Underworld.

See also AFTERLIFE; HADES; RELIGION.

Further reading: Ilias Venezis, *Mount Olympos* (Athens, 1957).

Olynthos This major Greek city is situated in the northwestern Aegean region known as CHALCIDICĒ. Located on the coastal plain of the Chalcidic mainland, at the head the Gulf of Torone, Olynthos was originally a settlement of the non-Greek, native Bottiaeans. It was occupied by local Chalcidic Greeks after the non-Greek settlement was destroyed by the army of the Persian king XERXES, in 479 B.C.E.

With its southern neighbor POTIDAEA, Olynthos became one of the two premier cities of Chalcidice. After

Potidaea revolted from the Athenian-controlled DELIAN LEAGUE (432 B.C.E.), Olynthos served as a regional fortress against the retaliatory Athenian invasion. Soon thereafter, Olynthos became the capital of the newly formed local federation known as the Chalcidic League.

In 349 B.C.E. war broke out between the Chalcidic League and the aggressive Macedonian king PHILIP II. Philip besieged Olynthos. Despite the efforts at ATHENS of the statesman DEMOSTHENES (1) to organize military aid for Olynthos (in his three extant speeches called the *Olynthiacs*), Philip captured the city with the help of traitors within (348 B.C.E.). He razed Olynthos to the ground and sold the inhabitants as SLAVES. Reports of the pitiful condition of these captives provided Demosthenes with material for more of his speeches, the famous *Philippics*. Demosthenes' *Third Philippic* (341 B.C.E.) contains the comment that a visitor to the Olynthos site would never know that a city had stood there.

Olynthos was excavated by American archaeologists in 1928–1934 C.E. and published extensively in a 14-volume series, *Excavations at Olynthus,* by David M. Robinson. More recent work has been done at the site by Nicholas Cahill, who has created a database (available online at http://www.stoa.org/olynthus/) containing all the artifacts found in the houses during Robinson's excavations, room-by-room. The site, free from any later buildings, has provided one of the clearest pictures of the floor plans of ordinary ancient Greek houses. The city was laid out on a grid pattern, an admirable example of the Greek town planning that developed in the mid-400s B.C.E. Over a hundred houses are visible in plan, most dating from the late 400s and early 300s B.C.E.

See also ARCHAEOLOGY; HIPPODAMOS.

Further reading: Lisa C. Nevett, *House and Society in the Ancient Greek World* (New York: Cambridge University Press, 1999); Nicholas Cahill, *Household and City Organization at Olynthus* (New Haven, Conn.: Yale University Press, 2002).

orators *See* RHETORIC.

Orchomenos Three ancient Greek cities were known by this name, the most important being "Minyan" Orchomenos in BOEOTIA, in central Greece. The other two cities called Orchomenos were located in ARCADIA and THESSALY. The name seems to be Greek, meaning "place of the strong battle rank."

The site of Boeotian Orchomenos was first excavated by archaeologist Heinrich Schliemann in 1880 C.E. Buildings uncovered from the Mycenaean era (1600–1200 B.C.E.) include a palace and an elaborate tomb. Such remnants—along with certain hints in extant Greek myth—indicate that Orchomenos was one of the wealthiest Mycenaean-Greek cities, surpassing its neighbor and enemy, THEBES.

This Mycenaean Orchomenos was the seat of a rich and powerful clan named the MINYANS (Minuai), who may originally have come from the Thessalian Orchomenos. The Boeotian city thrived from its location—controlling the land route through central Greece—and from its fertile farmland, claimed by the engineered draining of nearby Lake Kopaïs.

But by the main centuries of ancient Greek history, Orchomenos had declined greatly, due to Thebes's dominance and the refilling of Lake Kopaïs. Orchomenos fought as a Theban ally against ATHENS in the PELOPONNESIAN WAR (431–404 B.C.E.) but sided with SPARTA against Thebes during the CORINTHIAN WAR (395–386 B.C.E.). After Thebes had replaced Sparta as the foremost Greek power (371 B.C.E.), revenge was swift. Orchomenos was destroyed by the Theban-led Boeotian League in 364 B.C.E. It was rebuilt, then again destroyed in 349 B.C.E.

See also ARCHAEOLOGY; MYCENAEAN CIVILIZATION; POTTERY.

Further reading: Penelope Mountjoy, *Orchomenos V: Mycenaean Pottery from Orchomenos, Eutresis, and Other Boeotian Sites* (Munich: Verlag der Bayerischen Akademie der Wissenschaften, 1983): F. E. Winter, "Arcadian Notes 1. Identification of the Agora Buildings at Orchomenos and Mantinea," *Echos du monde classique* 6 (1987): 235–246; F. E. Winter, "Arcadian Notes 2. The Walls of Mantinea, Orchomenos, and Kleitor," *Echos du monde classique* 8 (1989): 189–200; Katie Demakopoulou, ed., *Troy, Mycenae, Tiryns, Orchomenos: Heinrich Schliemann, the 100th Anniversary of his Death: Athens, National Archaeological Museum, 15th June–2nd September 1990, Berlin, Altes Museum, 4th October 1990–15th January 1991* (Athens: Ministry of Culture of Greece, 1990).

Orestes In MYTH, Orestes was the son of King AGAMEMNON and KLYTEMNESTRA, of the city of MYCENAE (alternatively, of the city of ARGOS). In the best-known version of the tale, told by the Athenian playwright AESCHYLUS in his Oresteian Trilogy (presented in 458 B.C.E.), Orestes murders his mother and her lover, Aegisthus, in vengeance for their murder of his father. But having broken the bonds of nature by committing matricide, Orestes is driven mad by the demonic FURIES, the agents of divine punishment. Orestes flees to DELPHI—and then, in Aeschylus's version, to ATHENS—and is eventually cleansed of his sin. The Greeks were intrigued by the horror and legalism of Orestes' dilemma—compelled by filial duty to avenge his father (even against his mother), but doomed to be punished for doing so. A similar myth developed around the Argive hero ALCMAEON (1).

The earliest surviving version of the story is a mention in HOMER's epic poem the *Odyssey* (written down around 750 B.C.E.). There Orestes has killed Aegisthus, who (in this version) is the principal culprit in Agamemnon's murder. It is not stated specifically whether Orestes also killed Klytemnestra, but it is implied. Homer says nothing of the Furies.

The Furies may have been introduced into the story by STESICHORUS (ca. 580 B.C.E.), the sophisticated Sicilian-Greek poet whose work had a strong influence on Aeschylus and other later writers. Stesichorus wrote a narrative poem called the *Oresteia*, which survives only in fragments. In this version the Furies pursued Orestes and APOLLO gave him a special bow, designed to ward them off.

The Orestes story also is told in surviving plays by SOPHOKLES and EURIPIDES. A side-by-side comparison of the three great Athenian tragedians' versions sheds light on their differing values and messages. Aeschylus is concerned (primarily) with settling Orestes' controversial position in the world order and (secondarily) with glorifying the playwright's beloved Athens. Orestes is introduced in the second play of Aeschylus's trilogy, the *Libation Bearers* (*Choëphoroi*), as having been ordered by Apollo to take vengeance on Klytemnestra and Aegisthus. Assisted by his friend Pylades and sister ELECTRA, Orestes can hardly bring himself to kill his mother but, having done so, he is immediately assailed by the Furies. The trilogy's third play, the *Eumenides* (kindly ones), features Orestes' legal acquittal at the hands of the Athenian homicide court, the AREOPAGOS, with the help of Apollo and ATHENA.

The version presented in Sophokles' *Electra* (ca. 418–410 B.C.E.) is closer to the simple Homeric story. Orestes shows only a little natural reluctance to do the deed, and afterward there are no Furies. Euripides in his *Orestes* (408 B.C.E.) and *Electra* (probably 417 B.C.E.) seeks to bring out the myth's most disturbing implications. His Orestes emerges, not as a heroic figure, but as an enthusiastic killer who has sexual feelings for his own sister. After the crime, the Furies (not shown onstage) are made to be simply phantoms of Orestes' troubled mind. In Euripides' *Iphigenia in Tauris* (ca. 413 B.C.E.), Orestes must expiate his guilt by journeying to the Crimean peninsula, at the edge of the known world.

Orestes' slaying of Aegisthus was a popular subject of vase painting and SCULPTURE in the 500s and 400s B.C.E. Ancient Greek artists also frequently depicted Orestes in the Sanctuary of Apollo at Delphi, where he sought sanctuary from the angry Furies. The location is represented either with the *omphalos* (the naval of the world) or the sacred Delphic tripod. Orestes himself is a handsome youth, often shown in heroic nudity wearing a *chlamys* (cloak) and holding a sword.

Further reading: William Whallon, *Problem and Spectacle: Studies in the Oresteia* (Heidelberg, Germany: Winter, 1980); D. J. Conacher, *Aeschylus' Oresteia: A Literary Commentary* (Toronto: University of Toronto Press, 1989); James Diggle, *The Textual Tradition of Euripides' Orestes* (New York: Oxford University Press, 1991); Ann Batchelder, *The Seal of Orestes: Self-reference and Authority* in *Sophokles' Electra* (Lanham, Md.: Rowman & Little-field, 1995); Deborah Boedeker, "Hero Cult and Politics in Herodotus: The Bones of Orestes," in *Cultural Poetics in Archaic Greece: Cult, Performance, Politics*, edited by Carol Dougherty and Leslie Kurke (New York: Oxford University Press, 1998), 164–177.

Orion In MYTH, this hunter of enormous size was particularly skilled with the bow and arrow. He is variously described as the son of the Earth goddess GAEA or as the son of the god POSEIDON and Euryalē the Gorgon. Orion was killed by the goddess ARTEMIS. His offense may have been his arrogant challenge of Artemis to a discus-throwing contest or his attempted rape of one of her attendants. Or his great hunting prowess may have proved to be an affront to the jealous goddess of the hunt. In any case, his huge corpse was set in the sky as the constellation Orion.

Further reading: Michael Speidel, *Mithras-Orion: Greek Hero and Roman Army God* (Leiden, Netherlands: E. J. Brill, 1980); Joseph Fontenrose, *Orion: The Myth of the Hunter and the Huntress* (Berkeley: University of California Press, 1981).

Orpheus In Greek MYTH, Orpheus was a Thracian lyre-player and singer of supernatural ability. Although THRACE was a savage, non-Greek land, Orpheus was a civilizing influence; his song could charm not only humans and beasts, but trees and stones as well. He served as one of the Argonauts who sailed with the Thessalian hero JASON (1) to win the Golden Fleece. But the best-known story about Orpheus tells how when his wife, Eurydicē, died from snakebite, he ventured down into the Underworld to seek the god HADES' permission to bring her up from the dead. Permission was granted, on condition that Orpheus not look back as Eurydicē followed, until they should reach the upper world. But as they approached the upper world Orpheus, not hearing her footsteps behind him, did look back, and with a cry Eurydicē disappeared forever.

Despondent, Orpheus neglected all other WOMEN, thereby infuriating the Thracian women—or, more specifically in some versions, those female followers of the god DIONYSUS known as MAENADS. These women tore Orpheus limb from limb in the course of a Dionysian frenzy and pitched his head into the Thracian River Hebrus. The head floated, singing, out to sea, to the Aegean island of LESBOS.

The background to these legends is uncertain. Orpheus may have been an actual poet and musician, perhaps of royal blood, in Thrace around 700 B.C.E. He was said to be the founder of the mystic religious cult known as ORPHISM, which arose in the Greek world in the 600s B.C.E. and revered certain religious poems supposedly written by him. He also was said to have introduced male HOMOSEXUALITY among the Thracians, in consequence of his later aversion to women. Alternatively, he was said to have lived celibate after Eurydicē's death.

For the classical Greeks, Orpheus symbolized the civilizing or soothing power of MUSIC. One well-known Athenian vase painting of around 500 B.C.E. shows him playing his lyre and singing to a group of charmed (but fierce-looking) Thracian warriors. The Athenian playwright AESCHYLUS wrote a tragic trilogy (now lost) about Orpheus.

See also LYRIC POETRY.

Further reading: D. A. Amyx, "The Orpheus Legend in Art," *Archaeological News* 5 (1976): 25–41; F. Graf, "Orpheus, a Poet among Men," in *Interpretations of Greek Mythology*, edited by J. Bremmer (London: Croom Helm, 1987), 80–106; Joan M. Erikson, *Legacies: Prometheus, Orpheus, Socrates* (New York: Norton, 1993); Ilona J. Jesnick, *The Image of Orpheus in Roman Mosaic: An Exploration of the Figure of Orpheus in Graeco-Roman Art and Culture with Special Reference to Its Expression in the Medium of Mosaic in Late Antiquity* (Oxford: Archaeopress, 1997).

Orphism This religious cult probably arose in the 600s B.C.E., with followers eventually at ATHENS and the Greek cities of SICILY and southern ITALY. Orphism's beliefs were set down in religious poems supposedly composed by the Thracian musician ORPHEUS. These poems, now lost, are known from mentions by later writers.

Orphism emphasized a belief in the transmigration of souls. This concept, later adapted by the Greek philosophers PYTHAGORAS (ca. 530 B.C.E.) and EMPEDOKLES (ca. 450 B.C.E.), claimed that a dead person's soul generally goes on to inhabit another life form, whether human, animal, or vegetable. Like the ELEUSINIAN MYSTERIES and other mystery cults, Orphism promised its followers a happy existence in the AFTERLIFE.

The Orphic MYTH centered on a holy infant named Zagreus, who was seen as an alter ego of the god DIONYSUS. In this peculiar tale, perhaps derived from Thracian legend, the great god ZEUS seduced or raped his own daughter, the goddess PERSEPHONE. She bore the baby Zagreus, whom Zeus intended to make supreme among the gods. However, the jealous TITANS, after luring the child to their midst, tore him limb from limb and ate him. Zeus angrily blasted the Titans with a thunderbolt, incinerating them. From their ashes emerged the first humans. Zagreus's living heart, saved from the butchery, was now swallowed by Zeus, who passed it on supernaturally in begetting his next divine son, Dionysus.

In Orphic belief, Zagreus's ghoulish murder was a kind of Original Sin, in which all humans shared. Consequently, atonement had to be made to Zagreus's bereaved mother, Persephone, who, as queen of the Underworld, judges people after death. Apparently Orphism viewed the cycle of transmigration as a kind of purgatory: Only by living successive lives (on earth and also in the Underworld) could a person's soul be cleansed of its Original

Sin. Reincarnation might mean reward or punishment, depending on Persephone's judgment of one's conduct in a prior life. The soul might descend to inhabit beasts or paupers, or ascend to statesmen and heroes. The Orphic devotee hoped eventually for release from this round of reincarnations. "I have escaped from the wheel of pain," one Orphic verse announces, referring to the achievement of bliss in the other world. The golden leaves discovered by archaeologists in Greek tombs of southern Italy from around 400 B.C.E., containing precise instructions for the soul's procedure on reaching the Underworld, are thought to be Orphic documents.

Related to this spiritual preparation, Orphism also involved strict behavioral taboos. Orphics were notorious for abstaining from hunting and meat-eating, and even from wearing wool. They also were known for sexual abstinence—or at least for discouraging heterosexual intercourse—in order to thwart pregnancy; pregnancy was lamentable because it imprisoned another soul in a human body. The Orphics said that the body (*soma*) was the tomb (*sēma*) of the soul. The higher life was the purified soul's existence in Persephone's realm.

Orphism's otherworldliness and contempt for bodily existence recommended it to the Athenian philosopher PLATO (ca. 370 B.C.E.). But its strict code of behavior struck many Greeks as crankish and kept Orphism on the mystic fringe.

Further reading: W. K. C. Guthrie, *Orpheus and Greek Religion: A Study of the Orphic Movement* (London: Methuen, 1952); M. Christopoulos, "The Spell of Orpheus. Orpheus and the Orphic Religion Movement," *Métis* 6 (1991): 205–222; Ralph Abraham, *Chaos, Gaia, Eros: A Chaos Pioneer Uncovers the Three Great Streams of History* (San Francisco: HarperSanFrancisco, 1994); Barry Sandywell, *The Beginnings of European Theorizing: Reflexivity in the Archaic Age* (London: Routledge, 1996).

ostracism   This political practice was unique to Athenian DEMOCRACY in the 400s B.C.E., whereby the people could vote to banish any citizen for 10 years. Created in reaction to the tyrannies of PEISISTRATUS and HIPPIAS (1), ostracism was intended for use against wealthy politicians who, while not guilty of wrongdoing, might still be suspected of hoping to seize supreme power.

Once a year, at an appointed time in winter, the citizens in ASSEMBLY voted on whether an ostracism should be held that spring—no candidates were named. If the majority voted yes, then the ostracism vote itself took place a few months later. There each citizen had the chance to write down the name of one person for exile. Because clay potsherds were the ancient world's equivalent of scrap paper, each voter used a sherd (Greek: *ostrakon*, plural: *ostraka*), on which to scratch the intended victim's name. The potsherds gave this unique practice its name, *ostrakismos*. The vote was secret, with

officials making sure no one handed in more than one ballot. If a quorum of 6,000 votes was reached, then the man with the most votes had to remove himself from the city within 10 days.

Ostracism in ancient Greece was not a criminal punishment. The ostracized individual was not considered a felon or a traitor; he retained his Athenian citizenship and property while absent and was allowed to return after a period of 10 years. During the state emergency of the PERSIAN WARS, two Athenians under ostracism, ARISTIDES and XANTHIPPUS, were allowed to return immediately (480 B.C.E.).

According to ARISTOTLE's treatise the *Constitution of Athens*, the ostracism law was created by the reformer KLEISTHENES (1) in about 508 B.C.E., soon after the expulsion of Hippias. Clearly, the law was aimed against Hippias's friends who might dream of reinstating a dictator. But what puzzles modern scholars is that the people did not vote their first ostracism until 487 B.C.E. (The victim was Hippias's kinsman Hipparchus.) This 20-year delay has led some historians to suggest that the ostracism law really was created soon after the Battle of MARATHON (490 B.C.E.), but was later falsely ascribed to Kleisthenes.

After Hipparchus, four more men were soon ostracized amid the political turmoil of the 480s B.C.E., and it is thought that about eight others fell victim during the rest of the 400s B.C.E. These included the left-wing statesman-soldier THEMISTOKLES (ca. 471 B.C.E.) and the conservative statesman-soldier KIMON (462 B.C.E.). This clearly shows that ostracism had quickly become a tool by which the two political parties could attack each other. Many other Athenians were named as ostracism candidates but did not receive majority votes—as indicated by the 64 names compiled from the several thousand *ostraka* discovered in modern archaeological excavations of the Athenaian AGORA and other sites.

The last successful ostracism was of the demogogue Hyperbolus (417 B.C.E.), after which the law fell out of use.

See also THUCYDIDES (2).

Further reading: Rudi Thomsen, *The Origin of Ostracism. A Synthesis* (Copenhagen: Gyldendal, 1972); A. E. Samuel, *Death and Taxes: Ostraka in the Royal Ontario Museum* (Toronto: A. M. Hakkert for the American Society of Papyrologists, 1971–1976); Kathleen McNamee, *Abbreviations in Greek Literary Papyri and Ostraca* (Chico, Calif.: Scholars Press, 1981); V. J. Rosirach, "Some Fifth and Fourth Century Views on the Purpose of Ostracism," *Tyche* 2 (1987): 161–170; J. L. Marr and N. Worswick, "The Institution of Ostracism at Athens," *Ostraka* 3 (1994): 285–290; D. C. Mirhady, "The Ritual Background to Athenian Ostracism," *Ancient History Bulletin* 11 (1997): 13–19; John F. Oates, *Checklist of Editions of Greek, Latin, Demotic, and Coptic Papyri, Ostraca, and Tablets* (Oakville, Conn.: American Society of Papyrologists, 2001).

P

paean *See* LYRIC POETRY.

Paestum *See* POSEIDONIA.

painting For the painting of scenes and portraits, the Greeks used various surface materials, including POTTERY, wooden panels, stone walls, leather, and textiles. Of these, only pottery has preserved Greek painting in any quantity, due to the ceramic's durability and the paint being baked into the clay during firing. Secondarily, there exist some examples of tomb paintings—from walls of graves or the insides of coffins—that were preserved underground. But most other Greek paintings have vanished over time, as their surfaces crumbled to dust.

The paintings on pottery can reveal only a certain amount about general Greek painting, because pottery was a miniaturist discipline, with colors limited to those that would survive firing. Modern scholars must therefore rely partly on indirect evidence, such as ancient writers' descriptions of specific paintings and techniques and certain surviving mosaics and wall paintings of the Roman era, believed to be copies of earlier Greek paintings.

Aegean painting traditions predate the Greeks. By the third millennium B.C.E. the Minoan peoples were making pigments by processing and grinding down various vegetation, and were painting lively murals at their palaces in CRETE. Among several existing examples is the famous Toreador Fresco (ca. 1500 B.C.E.). Minoan whorl designs, sea-life subjects, and human figures helped inspire Mycenaean-Greek paintings on walls and pottery, from the 1500s B.C.E. onward.

Examples of Greek painting in the centuries after the Mycenaeans' fall are represented now mainly by works on pottery: the whorls and other designs of the Protogeometric style (ca. 1050–900 B.C.E.), the stick-figure human and animal silhouettes of the Geometric style (ca. 900–700 B.C.E.), and the colors, detail, and primitive depth perception of the ripe Corinthian style (ca. 625–550 B.C.E.).

CORINTH was a center for painting in the 600s B.C.E., and one rare surviving example of nonvase painting of this era is a wooden plaque of ca. 500 B.C.E., found at a site near Corinth. The painting shows a sacrificial procession, in a style reminiscent of the Corinthian vase painting that had peaked a century before. With its vivid red, blue, and flesh tones, the work suggests the color range available to the ancient Greek painter—well beyond the restricted colors of the vase painter. The painting's background is white, which would remain the chosen background color for decades to come.

ATHENS arose to replace Corinth as the artistic center of Greece in the mid-500s B.C.E. By about 460 B.C.E. the splendors of the Athenian AGORA included a Painted Colonnade (Stoa Poikilē) where large wall paintings on mythological and patriotic subjects were displayed. This era produced the first Old Master of Greek painting—the artist Polygnotos, born at THASOS but active at Athens in the 470s–450s B.C.E. He is best remembered for two mythological wall paintings, neither of which survives: a scene of the fall of TROY, in the Painted Colonnade, and a scene of the Underworld, painted at the Meeting House at DELPHI. Polygnotos apparently used no foreshortening but did innovatively convey depth by showing his human figures standing at different levels—a device that subsequently appears in Athenian vase painting. He also pioneered the technique called encaustic, which used heated wax for applying colors. Micon of Athens is another painter remembered for public wall paintings in these years.

The use of perspective is said to have developed at Athens in the mid-400s B.C.E. partly through the production of painted backdrops for Athenian stage performances. The second half of the 400s B.C.E.—the Athenian cultural heyday—saw greater use of shading to indicate depth: The great name of the day was Apollodoros of Athens, surnamed *skiagraphos*, "shade painter." His younger contemporary and imitator Zeuxis—from Greek ITALY but active at Athens circa 430–400 B.C.E.—was known for his illusionary realism. Supposedly Zeuxis's outdoor paintings of grapes attracted hungry birds. Apollodoros, Zeuxis, and the painter-sculptor Parrhasius (active at Athens in these years) were all known for their mythological subjects. But scenes from everyday life—a woman spinning, young WOMEN playing at dice—are indicated by later Roman copies of lost originals.

With Athens's decline after the PELOPONNESIAN WAR (431–404 B.C.E.), the Peloponnesian city of SIKYON emerged briefly as a painting center. But it was the Macedonian king ALEXANDER THE GREAT (reigned 336–323 B.C.E.) who inspired a revival of Greek painting, at his wealthy court. The best-known surviving painting of this school comes from the Macedonian city of Aegai (modern Vergina, in northern Greece), from a wall of the royal tombs excavated in 1977 C.E. The scene shows HADES, the god of death, abducting the maiden goddess PERSEPHONE. Factual subjects are indicated by the admirable Roman mosaic from the "House of the Faun" at Pompeii (first century C.E.), showing the Persian king Darius III fleeing from Alexander at the Battle of the Issus; this is believed to be a copy of a Greek painting of the late 300s B.C.E., presumably commissioned by Alexander or one of his followers. The crowded battle scene shows intricate use of detail and foreshortening.

The HELLENISTIC AGE (300–150 B.C.E.) saw changes that anticipate the surviving examples of Roman painting (first centuries B.C.E. and C.E., mainly). These include development of landscape and other backgrounds to the extent of dwarfing the foreground figures and a new value placed on *trompe l'oeil* affects, such as mural-painted false windows or corridors, opening to realistic background scenes. Subjects became more whimsical while expert techniques were forgotten, and by about 50 C.E. the Roman writer Pliny the Elder could describe painting as a dying art.

See also ARCHITECTURE.

Further reading: V. J. Bruno, *Form and Color in Greek Painting* (London: Norton, 1977); Martin Robertson, *Greek Painting* (New York: Rizzoli, 1979); D. von Bothmer, *Greek Vase Painting*, 2d ed. (New York: Metropolitan Museum of Art, 1987); G. P. Schaus, "The Beginning of Greek Polychrome Painting," *Journal of Hellenic Studies* 108 (1988): 107–117; Stelios Lydakis, *Ancient Greek Painting and Its Echoes in Later Art* (Los Angeles: J. Paul Getty Museum, 2004).

Palladion   *See* ATHENA.

Pallas   *See* ATHENA.

Pan   This minor but picturesque Greek deity was the god of flocks, shepherds, and mountain pastures. His worship was centered in the rural area of ARCADIA, from which it spread eventually throughout Greece. Various myths describe Pan as the son of HERMES and a nymph, Dryops, or as the son of Hermes and PENELOPE. The *Homeric Hymn to Pan* says that his name comes from the Greek word for "all" and signifies that he delighted all the Olympian gods. He was, however, often associated with DIONYSUS and the NYMPHS.

Pan is represented in art as a small male figure with the horns, legs, hooves, and tail of a goat; he has a thick beard, a snub nose, and pointed ears. Famous images of Pan include the *Barberini Faun* at Munich, the *Dancing Faun* at Naples, and the Pan of PRAXITELES at Rome.

He loved music and dancing, and frequently appears playing a reed pipe or flute, which he was said to have invented; it is called a *syrinx* or, in colloquial English, a panpipe. Pan was said to have been particularly fond of the poet PINDAR and his LYRIC POETRY, and Pindar reciprocated by erecting a shrine to Pan in front of his house. At ATHENS, Pan had a sanctuary on the ACROPOLIS and annual festivities involving torch races. The Athenians adopted his worship after an incident associated with the Battle of MARATHON (490 B.C.E.), in which the god supposedly appeared to an Athenian dispatch runner in Arcadia.

Pan had a tendency to appear suddenly to passersby, and he was generally feared by travelers. As a result, any sudden fright without an obvious cause came to be attributed to Pan, leading to the English word "panic."

Further reading: P. J. Riis, "A Colossal Athenian Pan," *Acta Archaeologica* 45 (1974): 124–133; Dorothy Zayatz Baker, *Mythic Masks in Self-Reflexive Poetry: A Study of Pan and Orpheus* (Chapel Hill: University of North Carolina Press, 1986); Philippe Borgeaud, *The Cult of Pan in Ancient Greece,* translated by Kathleen Atlass and James Redfield (Chicago: University of Chicago Press, 1988); F. Bader, "Pan," *Revue de philology, de littérature, et d'histoire anciennes* 63 (1989): 7–46; Luba Freedman, *The Classical Pastoral in the Visual Arts* (New York: P. Lang, 1989); P. Flourentzos, "The Iconography of the God Pan in Cypriot Sculpture," *Report of the Department of Antiquities, Cyprus* (1989): 121–126; John Boardman, *The Great God Pan: The Survival of an Image* (New York: Thames and Hudson, 1998).

Panathenaia   This Athenian festival was celebrated annually in midsummer, and especially elaborately

Amphorae filled with oil pressed from olives from the sacred trees of Athena were given as prizes in the Panathenaic Games. One side of the amphora showed Athena and included the inscription "from the games at Athens"; the other side showed the event won. *(The J. Paul Getty Museum)*

be the birthday of the city's patron goddess, ATHENA, the festival included sacrifices, sports competitions, and a procession of citizens (illustrated on the famous PARTHENON frieze). At the fourth-yearly celebration— called the Great Panathenaia—the procession would carry a new *peplos,* or lady's gown, up to the Athenian ACROPOLIS. There the *peplos* would be presented to the ancient olivewood statue of Athena Polias ("of the city") that was housed, after about 410 B.C.E., in the Erechtheion.

Further reading: Jiri Frel, *Panathenaic Prize Amphoras* (Athens: Esperos, 1973); J. D. Mikalson, "Erechtheus and the Panathenaia," *American Journal of Philology* 97 (1976): 141–153; R. Develin, "From Panathenaia to Panathenaia," *Zeitschrift für Papyrologie und Epigraphik* 57 (1984): 133–138; Jenifer Neils, ed., *Goddess and Polis: The Panathenaic Festival in Ancient Athens* (Hanover, N.H.: Hood Museum of Art, Dartmouth College, 1992); Jenifer Neils, ed., *Worshipping Athena: Panathenaia and Parthenon* (Madison: University of Wisconsin Press, 1996); Gregory Nagy, *Plato's Rhapsody and Homer's Music: The Poetics of the Panathenaic Festival in Classical Athens* (Washington, D.C.: Center for Hellenic Studies, Trustees for Harvard University, 2002).

Pandora *See* PROMETHEUS.

pankration This one-on-one combative SPORT in antiquity combined BOXING and WRESTLING. The rules allowed for punching, kicking, strangleholds, and twisting of arms and fingers; only biting and gouging were forbidden. Opponents fought naked, sometimes with light boxing thongs to protect their hands. Victory occurred when a contestant either signaled surrender or was unable to continue. The bout was overseen by a referee, but pankration ("total strength" or "complete victory") was a brutal sport: Contestants sometimes died from injuries.

Pankration was an important event at the OLYMPIC GAMES and other major athletic festivals. Successful pankratiasts were celebrities throughout the Greek world. Ancient vase paintings and stone carvings show pankration scenes, and further details are given by ancient writers and athletes' tombstone inscriptions.

Pankration was a relative latecomer to Greek sport. It is not mentioned in HOMER's poems or in any writing before the 400s B.C.E.

Further reading: Michael Poliakoff, *Combat Sports in the Ancient World: Competition, Violence, and Culture* (New Haven, Conn.: Yale University Press, 1987); Olga Tzachou-Alexandri, ed., *Mind and Body: Athletic Contests in Ancient Greece* (Athens: Ministry of Culture, National Hellenic Committee I.C.O.M., 1989).

every fourth year. Although its roots were in prehistory, the Panathenaia ("all-Athens") was instituted by the Athenian tyrant PEISISTRATUS in the mid-500s B.C.E., to serve as a nationalist-religious holiday. Considered to

Panticapaeum (Pantikapaion, "ditch town") This important Greek colony on the northern BLACK SEA coast was founded around 625 B.C.E. by settlers from MILETUS. Panticapaeum guarded the Straits of Kerch in the eastern Crimean Peninsula, in what is now southern Ukraine. With access to the interior steppes along the river Don, the city thrived from the export of Ukrainian grain to the distant cities of the central Greek world. In the era around 438–404 B.C.E., under the powerful Thracian-Greek dynasty of the Spartocids, Panticapaeum became the premier supplier of grain to imperial ATHENS. Threatened in later centuries by local Scythian and Sarmatian peoples, Panticapaeum passed into the hands of King Mithridates VI of Pontus, who made it his capital (110 B.C.E.). After Mithridates' defeat by the Romans, the city came under control of ROME (63 B.C.E.).

Further reading: Gocha R. Tsetskhladze, ed., *The Greek Colonisation of the Black Sea Area: Historical Interpretation of Archaeology* (Stuttgart, Germany: F. Steiner, 1998); John Boardman, *The Greeks Overseas: Their Early Colonies and Trade,* 4th ed. (London: Thames and Hudson, 1999): N. Z. Kunina, "Decorated Glass Medallions from the Necropolis of Panticapaeum," in *Northern Pontic Antiquities in the State Hermitage Museum,* edited by J. Boardman, S. Solovyov, and G. R. Tsetskhladze (Leiden, Netherlands: E. J. Brill, 2001), 199–203; E. N. Khodza, "A Terracotta Bust from Panticapaeum," in *Northern Pontic Antiquities in the State Hermitage Museum,* edited by J. Boardman, S. Solovyov, and G. R. Tsetskhladze (Leiden, Netherlands: E. J. Brill, 2001), 205–229; Gocha R. Tsetskhladze and A. M. Snodgrass, *Greek Settlements in the Eastern Mediterranean and the Black Sea* (Oxford: Archaeopress, 2002); D. V. Grammenos and E. K. Petropoulos, eds., *Ancient Greek Colonies in the Black Sea* (Thessaloníki: Archaeological Institute of Northern Greece, 2003).

papyrus   *See* WRITING.

Paris   In MYTH, this handsome Trojan prince was the son of King PRIAM and Queen HECUBA. The name Paris (which has nothing to do with the capital city of France) means "wallet" in Greek. It may have been a nickname, since Paris had another name, Alexander (Greek: Alexandros, "defender").

With the help of the goddess APHRODITE, Paris seduced Helen, wife of King MENELAUS of Lacedaemon, and stole her away to TROY. This provoked the TROJAN WAR, in which the Greeks besieged Troy for 10 years to get Helen back. At the war's end, Paris was dead, Troy destroyed, and Helen was contentedly reunited with Menelaus.

In HOMER's *Iliad,* which presents events of the war's 10th year, Paris is portrayed as affable but irresponsible, in contrast to his elder brother, the champion HECTOR. In the *Iliad* (book 3) Paris challenges Menelaus to single combat but is nearly killed, and is saved only by Aphrodite's intervention. The goddess carries him back to his bedchamber within the walls of Troy and summons Helen to join him there.

The other tales of Paris's life were told in various post-Homeric works, including two epic poems now lost, the *Cypria* ("Tales of Cyprus") and *Little Iliad.* The narrative is as follows: Hecuba, while pregnant with Paris, dreamed that she gave birth to a flaming torch (a reference to the fated destruction of Troy). On the advice of soothsayers, the infant Paris was handed over to be killed, but—as in all similar Greek legends, such as that of OEDIPUS—the entrusted servant merely abandoned the baby in the wild. Rescued by shepherds, Paris grew to manhood and reclaimed his royal title after an incident of recognition at Troy.

The Judgment of Paris, the hero's most famous adventure, was recounted in the *Cypria* and was a favorite subject in Greek vase painting and other art from the 600s B.C.E. onward. After the goddess Eris ("strife") had set off a female rivalry in heaven (by offering a golden apple inscribed "For the fairest"), the goddesses HERA, ATHENA, and Aphrodite invited Paris to judge a beauty contest among them. They presented themselves naked to the young man. He chose the love goddess Aphrodite, whose bribe had been to promise him the world's most beautiful woman. Paris thus won Helen and the favor of Aphrodite. But henceforth he and all the Trojans suffered the hatred of Hera and Athena.

In the war's 10th year, sometime after the Greek champion ACHILLES had slain Hector, it was Paris, with the god APOLLO's help, who killed Achilles. Paris shot an arrow that struck Achilles in his only vulnerable spot, his right heel, and the wound proved fatal. Later Paris was slain by the Greek hero PHILOKTETES. Helen was briefly married to Paris's brother or half-brother Deiphobus, before rejoining with Menelaus after the war.

See also EPIC POETRY; HELEN OF TROY.

Further reading: P. Connor, "Erotes at Work. Paris and Helen on a Red-figured Hydria in Hildesheim (PM 1252)," *Mediterranean Archaeology* 2 (1989): 51–64.

Parmenides (ca. 515–440 B.C.E.) *The most important Greek philosopher before* SOCRATES
Parmenides was a native of the Greek city of Elea, in southwest ITALY. A member of a wealthy, influential family, he was said to have served Elea as a statesman and lawgiver. One of his teachers was supposedly the immigrant philosopher XENOPHANES. Parmenides was known for having lived an exemplary life, and later Greeks talked of an ideal "Parmenidean life." He founded a school of philosophy at Elea, known as the Eleatic School. He visited ATHENS at least once, when he was about 65 years old, and then became acquainted with

Socrates. This occasion is the setting for the Athenian philosopher PLATO's fictional dialogue *Parmenides*.

Parmenides' significance to PHILOSOPHY lies in his breakthrough theory that the material world as we observe it is not real. Prior to Parmenides, the foremost philosophers sought out essential reality by searching for the fundamental ingredient of the material world (hence the use of the name *material philosophers* to describe such thinkers). THALES (ca. 570 B.C.E.) decided that the basic element is water; ANAXIMENES (ca. 546 B.C.E.) called it *aer*, or mist. For Parmenides, however, the real world is not what we see and feel around us; he believed that it can be understood only by mental contemplation. Reality is an ideal world, a timeless unity, free of change, variation, generation, or destruction. Parmenides' notion of an ideal world, inherited in part from the Pythagoreans, would later contribute significantly to Plato's Theory of Forms (mid-300s B.C.E.).

Parmenides was best known for his didactic poem, *On Nature*, composed in hexameter verse and using the oracular language of religious revelation. The poem was divided into two parts, "The Way of Truth," and "The Way of Seeing." Of these, the former seems to have been the more important part, and fortunately about 150 lines of it survive today. "The Way of Truth" describes how an unnamed goddess instructs the poet that only the statement "It is"—or "It exists"—can be valid. Nothing, the goddess says, does not exist.

Further reading: Scott Austin, *Parmenides: Being, Bounds, and Logic* (New Haven, Conn.: Yale University Press, 1986); Karl R. Popper, *The World of Parmenides: Essays on the Presocratic Enlightenment* (London: Routledge, 1998); Victor Caston and Daniel W. Graham, eds., *Presocratic Philosophy: Essays in Honour of Alexander Mourelatos* (Aldershot, U.K.: Ashgate, 2002); Martin J. Henn, *Parmenides of Elea: A Verse Translation with Interpretive Essays and Commentary to the Text* (Westport, Conn.: Praeger, 2003).

Parnassus, Mt. *See* DELPHI.

Parthenon This temple is dedicated to the goddess ATHENA the Virgin (*Parthenos*), built atop the highest part of the Athenian ACROPOLIS in 447–432 B.C.E. Still partly standing today, the Parthenon is considered the most glorious building of the ancient world—the epitome of the Doric order of ARCHITECTURE and the embodiment of the classical Greek values of harmony and proportion. The Parthenon crowned a rich and powerful ATHENS that was the cultural capital of Greece. The temple was a focus of international tourism in ancient times, as it still is today; its survival for nearly 2,500 years is due to its superior design and workmanship. In fact, the Parthenon would be in far better shape today had it not been blown half apart in 1687 C.E. amid fighting between Turks and Vene-

tians, when a Venetian cannonball ignited a Turkish powder magazine inside the building.

The Parthenon was constructed in the statesman PERIKLES' building program, overseen by the sculptor PHEIDIAS and meant to celebrate the conclusion of hostilities with PERSIA. Designed by the architects Iktinus and Kallikrates, the temple was intended as the building program's masterpiece. The Parthenon stood close to the site of a prior temple of Athena, which had been burned down by the occupying Persians of 480 B.C.E.

Intriguingly, the Parthenon never housed the ancient, olivewood statue of Athena Polias (which was eventually placed in the nearby Erechtheion 1000). The Parthenon was devoted to a grander, more modern vision of goddess and city. The Parthenon's cult statue was a 35-foot-high, GOLD-and-ivory figure of Athena, sculpted by Phidias. Although this statue is lost, marble copies and descriptions by ancient writers give some idea of its appearance. The goddess wore a warrior's helmet, sleeveless robe, and biblike aegis. On the palm of her right hand stood a human-size statue of the goddess NIKĒ (Victory). Athena's left hand grasped the top rim of an upright shield, which stood grounded by her left leg; a giant snake coiled within the shield, and a long spear stood upright in the crook of her left arm. The flesh of Athena and Nikē was sculpted in ivory; the rest was gold.

The temple, measuring 228 feet by 101 feet at the top of its entrance stairs, is built almost entirely of marble quarried at Mt. Pentelicus, near Athens. It has 17 columns at each side and eight columns across the front and back, rather than the more usual six.

Like other elaborate ancient Greek temples, the Parthenon had its upper structures adorned by painted, marble SCULPTURE. There were carved figures at the two pediments (the triangular gables at front and back), at the metopes (plaques along the sides), and along the frieze (the continuous paneling that ran around the outside top of the inner block, or cella). The pedimental sculptures were carved entirely in the round. The east pediment showed the mythical birth of Athena from the head of ZEUS; the west showed the contest between Athena and POSEIDON for mastery of Athens.

The metopes' figures were carved nearly in the round. They showed various mythical combats, each symbolizing the triumph of civilization over barbarism or West over East—a victory that, to the classical Greek mind, had been actually reenacted in the recent PERSIAN WARS. The combats in sculpture were on the east, gods versus GIANTS; on the south, Lapiths versus CENTAURS; on the west, Greeks versus AMAZONS; and on the north, the TROJAN WAR.

The frieze carvings were in bas-relief. They were unique in Greek temple sculpture for showing not a mythical scene but a scene from real-life Athens—namely, the procession at the festival of the PANATHENAIA. This

The northwestern view of the Parthenon today. Many of the decaying sculptures of the upper structure were removed in 1800–1812 by the British ambassador to Greece, Thomas Bruce, Lord Elgin. The Elgin Marbles remain in London's British Museum. *(Alison Frantz Photographic Collection, American School of Classical Studies at Athens)*

daring glorification of contemporary Athens must have struck some ancient observers as crass or sacrilegious.

Through decay and vandalism over the centuries, many of the sculptures fell or were torn from their high places. In 1800–1812 C.E., the British ambassador to Greece—Thomas Bruce, Lord Elgin—bought and removed many of the sculptures; these "Elgin Marbles" are displayed in the British Museum. At the Parthenon today, modern casts of the Panathenaic frieze replace those carted off by Lord Elgin.

See also CAVALRY.

Further reading: Rhys Carpenter, *The Architects of the Parthenon* (Harmondsworth, U.K.: Penguin, 1970); Frank Brommer, *The Sculptures of the Parthenon: Metopes, Frieze, Pediments, Cult-statue,* translated by Mary Whittall (London: Thames and Hudson, 1979); John Boardman, *The Parthenon and Its Sculpture* (Austin: University of Texas Press, 1985); L. Kallet-Marx, "Did Tribute Fund the Parthenon?" *Classical Antiquity* 8 (1989): 252–266; D. Harris, *The Treasures of the Parthenon and Erechtheion* (Oxford: Clarendon Press, 1995); E. B. Harrison, "The Web of History. A Conservative Reading of the Parthenon Frieze," in *Worshipping Athena: Panathenaia and Parthenon,* edited by Jenifer Neils (Madison: University of Wisconsin Press, 1996): 198–214; J. J. Pollitt, "The Meaning of the Parthenon Frieze," in *The Interpretation of*

Architectural Sculpture in Greece and Rome, edited by Diana Buitron-Oliver (Washington, D.C.: National Gallery of Art, 1997), 50–65; Olga Palagia, *The Pediments of the Parthenon,* 2d ed. (Leiden, Netherlands: E. J. Brill, 1998); J. Boardman, "The Parthenon Frieze. A Closer Look," *Revue archéologique* (1999): 305–330; S. A. Pope, "Financing and Design. The Development of the Parthenon Program and the Parthenon Building Accounts," in *Miscellanea Mediterranea,* edited by R. Ross Holloway (Providence: Center for Old World Archaeology and Art, Brown University, 2000), 61–69; M. R. Lagerlöf, *The Sculptures of the Parthenon: Aesthetics and Interpretation* (New Haven, Conn.: Yale University Press, 2000); Manolis Korres, *Stones of the Parthenon* (Los Angeles: J. Paul Getty Museum, 2000); Jenifer Neils, *The Parthenon Frieze* (New York: Cambridge University Press, 2001); Mary Beard, *The Parthenon* (Cambridge, Mass.: Harvard University Press, 2003).

Patroklos   In HOMER's epic poem the *Iliad,* Patroklos is the close friend of the Greek hero ACHILLES in the TROJAN WAR. Patroklos is the older of the two. In the *Iliad* (book 22) he charges into battle wearing Achilles' armor (with Achilles' permission) to rally the retreating Greeks. Slain by the Trojan champion HECTOR, Patroklos is avenged ferociously by Achilles, who kills numerous

Trojans, including Hector. Book 23 describes Patroklos's funeral games.

The Greeks of the 500s B.C.E. and later, judging Patroklos and Achilles by the social standards of those days, assumed that the two men were sexual partners, in the familiar aristocratic pattern of an older man educating and protecting a younger. But the *Iliad* never states this to be, and modern scholars believe that such socially sanctioned male couplings were not part of the poet Homer's world (around 750 B.C.E.) nor part of the Mycenaean world (around 1200 B.C.E.) that inspired the *Iliad*. The modern consensus is that Homer imagined Patroklos strictly as Achilles' comrade and confidant.

See also HOMOSEXUALITY.

Further reading: Dale Sinos, *Achilles, Patroklos and the Meaning of Philos* (Innsbruck, Austria: Institut für Sprachwissenschaft der Universität Innsbruck, 1980); Steven Lowenstam, *The Death of Patroklos: A Study in Typology* (Königstein, Germany: Hain, 1981); A. Petropoulou, "The Interment of Patroklos (Iliad 23, 252–57)," *American Journal of Philology* 109 (1988): 482–495; David Konstan, *Friendship in the Classical World* (New York: Cambridge University Press, 1997).

Pausanias (1)   *See* PERSIAN WARS; PLATAEA, BATTLE OF.

Pausanias (2) (mid-100s C.E.) *Greek travel writer, said to have been a physician from* ASIA MINOR
Pausanias' surviving prose work, *A Description of Greece,* is a valuable source of information on the physical monuments and local histories of all the important mainland Greek cities and sanctuaries, including ATHENS, SPARTA, DELPHI, and OLYMPIA.

Further reading: W. H. S. Jones, trans., *Description of Greece/Pausanias* (Cambridge, Mass.: Harvard University Press, 1979); C. Habicht, "Pausanias and the Evidence of Inscriptions," *Classical Antiquity* 3 (1984): 40–56; H. Whittaker, "Pausanias and His Use of Inscriptions," *Symbolae Osloenses* 66 (1991): 171–186; K. W. Arafat, "Pausanias' Attitude to Antiquities," *Annual of the British School at Athens* 87 (1992): 387–409; J. Elsner, "From the Pyramids to Pausanias and Piglet," in *Art and Text in Ancient Greek Culture,* edited by Simon Goldhill and Robin Osborne (New York: Cambridge University Press, 1994), 224–254; L. Rubinstein, "Pausanias as a Source for the Classical Greek Polis," in *Studies in the Ancient Greek Polis,* edited by Mogen Herman Hansen and Kurt Raaflaub (Stuttgart, Germany: F. Steiner, 1995), 211–219; K. W. Arafat, *Pausanias' Greece: Ancient Artists and Roman Rulers* (New York: Cambridge University Press, 1996); Christian Habicht, *Pausanias' Guide to Ancient Greece* (Berkeley: University of California Press, 1998); Susan E. Alcock, John F. Cherry, and Jas Elsner, eds., *Pausanias: Travel and Memory in Roman Greece* (New York: Oxford University Press, 2001).

Pegasus   *See* BELLEROPHON.

Peleus   This mythical hero was the father of ACHILLES. Peleus's father was Aeacus, king of AEGINA and a son of the god ZEUS. As an adult, Peleus had various misadventures—including murdering his half brother and accidentally killing a man during the CALYDONIAN BOAR HUNT—before arriving in THESSALY. There he married the sea goddess Thetis, a daughter of NEREUS. The match was arranged by Zeus, who (knowing that Thetis's son was preordained to be greater than his father) was anxious that she marry a mortal, rather than a god. But in order to win the resentful Thetis's hand in MARRIAGE, Peleus had to defeat her in a WRESTLING bout, during which she took on various harmful shapes: fire, water, a lion, a serpent, and an ink-squirting cuttlefish.

Later, when Thetis abandoned him and the baby Achilles, Peleus took the boy to be raised by the centaur Chiron in the glens of Thessaly's Mt. Pelion. Eventually Peleus and Thetis were reconciled, and Peleus was made immortal in repayment for his hardships.

See also CENTAURS.

Further reading: E. G. Pemberton, "The Name Vase of the Peleus Painter," *Journal of the Walters Art Gallery* 36 (1977): 63–72; K. Danali-Giole, "Dionysus and Peleus. Problems of Interpretation in Athenian Black-Figured Vases," *Archaeognosia* 6 (1989–1990): 109–118.

Peirithoos   *See* CENTAURS; THESEUS.

Peisistratus (ca. 600–527 B.C.E.) *Dictator or tyrannos who ruled* ATHENS *from 546 to 527 B.C.E.*
Like other Greek TYRANTS of that era, Peisistratus seized supreme power in his city with the common people's support, at the expense of the aristocrats. His benevolent reign removed the nobles' grip on Athenian government and marked a step in the city's difficult progress from ARISTOCRACY to DEMOCRACY in the 500s B.C.E.

Peisistratus ("adviser of the army") was himself born into an Athenian aristocratic family. Before taking power, the dynamic and affable Peisistratus came to the political fore when he led an army against Athens's enemy, the city of MEGARA (1). He then set out to make himself dictator, by exploiting the volatile atmosphere of Athenian class tensions.

Despite the prior democratic reforms of the statesman SOLON (594 B.C.E.), Athenian politics and adjudication at this time were still dominated by the nobility. This dominance was resented by the middle class, which supplied the backbone of the army. When Peisistratus entered politics, the countryside held two opposing factions, divided along lines of region and class: the right-wing party of the plain, led by a certain Lykourgos; and the more democratic party of the coast, led by Megakles of the Alcmaeonid clan.

Peisistratus created a third, more left-wing party, by organizing a peasant following and styling himself as the champion of the common people. He then convinced the Athenian ASSEMBLY to vote him an escort of bodyguards. Legend claims that the aged Solon, who was Peisistratus's kinsman, warned the Athenians against the man's intentions, but Peisistratus, using his bodyguards, was able to seize the ACROPOLIS and become tyrant (in about 561 B.C.E.).

Soon pushed into exile by the combined effort of the two other factions, he was reinstated with the help of his former rival Megakles. But when this alliance broke down, Peisistratus fled once more (around 556 B.C.E.). In around 546 B.C.E. he was back, leading a Greek mercenary army hired with a fortune he had made in SILVER-mining ventures in THRACE. Sailing from ERETRIA, the invaders landed near the town of MARATHON, where Peisistratus's family had its regional following. There Peisistratus was joined by other Athenians who wanted an end to aristocratic strife. On the road to Athens, Peisistratus defeated a government army at the Battle of Pallene, and the city was his again.

Peisistratus ruled shrewdly and moderately for 19 more years. He took aristocratic hostages but indulged in no vendettas or confiscations. He maintained Solon's laws and certain trappings of democratic government (although he also made sure that his own supporters held the top posts). He taxed reasonably—his tax on farm revenue, for instance, was 5 percent—and in return, he provided lavish building programs and public relief.

Like other dictators, Peisistratus aimed to make his city great. He assured Athens of a food supply by developing military outposts along the HELLESPONT, at Sigeum and in the Thracian CHERSONESE. These guarded the shipping lane for precious grain from the BLACK SEA. He elaborated Athens' national festivals, such as the PANATHENAIA, and encouraged industry and commerce. Under him, Athenian black-figure POTTERY reached its artistic peak and dominated the Mediterranean market. In SCULPTURE, ARCHITECTURE, and primitive THEATER, Peisistratus's Athens moved toward its amazing achievements in the next century. He fostered an Athenian patriotic culture that was partly intended to compete with cities such as CORINTH and partly intended to erase the old, local, aristocratic factionalism at home. His reign brought Athens forward in its progress from being a second-tier power in the 600s B.C.E. to being the capital of the Greek world in the 400s B.C.E.

Peisistratus died peacefully and was succeeded by his eldest son, HIPPIAS (1), whose reign was more troubled.

See also ALCMAEONIDS.

Further reading: A. Podlecki, "Solon or Peisistratus? A Case of Mistaken Identity," *Ancient World* 16 (1987): 3–10; R. R. Holloway, "Peisistratus' House," *Numismatica e antichità classiche* 28 (1999): 83–96; Heleen Sancisi-Weerdenburg, ed., *Peisistratos and the Tyranny: A Reap-praisal of the Evidence* (Amsterdam: J. C. Gieben, 2000); Sarah Pomeroy, *A Brief History of Ancient Greece: Politics, Society, and Culture* (New York: Oxford University Press, 2004).

Pelias *See* JASON (1).

Pella The capital city of the kingdom of MACEDON, from about 410 B.C.E. until the Roman conquest of 167 B.C.E., Pella is located in the Thermaic coastal plain, about 25 miles northwest of the modern Greek seaport of Thessaloníki. The city was in existence by the mid-400s B.C.E. and was chosen by the Macedonian king Archelaus I as his capital. In this, Pella replaced the old royal capital at nearby Aegai (modern Vergina). Archelaus, who reigned 413–399 B.C.E., made Pella a showplace of Greek building and culture.

At Pella ruled such mighty Macedonian kings as PHILIP II, ALEXANDER THE GREAT, and PHILIP V, in the 300s and 200s B.C.E. But under Roman rule Pella was totally overshadowed by the development of Thessaloníki.

The first archaeological excavations took place at Pella between 1957 and 1964 C.E. These campaigns uncovered the remains of elaborate houses with beautiful mosaic floors (dated ca. 300 B.C.E.). The subjects of these floors include a Lion Hunt, a Stag Hunt, the Abduction of Helen, an Amazonomachy, and a scene of the god DIONYSUS riding on a leopard's back. Restoration work during these years included some of the walls and colonnade of the house with the Dionysus mosaic. In 1976, archaeologists returned to Pella, and these excavations continue today. Several additional buildings have been discovered, including the Macedonian palace, located on the northernmost hill of the city and covering an area of six hectares. The AGORA, in the center of the city, consists of a large open square surrounded by colonnades and commercial/administrative rooms. Other houses, sanctuaries, and cemeteries have also been excavated, and part of the house with the Abduction of Helen mosaic has been restored. Artifacts are exhibited in the archaeological museum at the site.

Further reading: Photios Petsas, *Pella: Alexander the Great's Capital* (Thessaloníki: Institute for Balkan Studies, 1978); Maria Siganidou and Maria Lilimpaki-Akamati, *Pella: Capital of Macedonians*, translated by David Hardy (Athens: Ministry of Culture, Archaeological Receipts Fund, 1996); Bonnie Kutbay, *Palaces and Large Residences of the Hellenistic Age* (Lewiston, N.Y.: Edwin Mellen Press, 1998); M. Lilimpaki-Akamati, "Recent Discoveries in Pella," in *Excavating Classical Culture: Recent Archaeological Discoveries in Greece,* edited by Maria Stamatopoulou and Marina Yeroulanou (Oxford: Beazley Archive and Archaeopress, 2002), 83–90.

Peloponnese (Peloponnēsos) ("Island of PELOPS") This wide, jagged, mountainous peninsula of southern

Greece measures 132 miles north to south and 134 east to west (maximum) and is connected with central Greece by the seven-mile-wide Isthmus of CORINTH. Other major sites in the Peloponnese include MYCENAE, SIKYON, EPIDAURUS, OLYMPIA, SPARTA, PYLOS, Messene, Mistra, and Stymphalos. In classical times the Peloponnese was the heartland of Dorian-Greek culture—the "other" Greece, in conflict with democratic, Ionian-Greek ATHENS.

Despite a coastline hundreds of miles long, the Peloponnese has few natural harbors; only Corinth and the Argos region became great from seaborne TRADE. Coastal geography includes four mountainous peninsulas jutting southward into the AEGEAN SEA; from west to east, these four capes were named Acritas, Taenarum, Malea, and (far to the northeast) Scyllaeum. Between these peninsulas, the sea forms three wide gulfs, whose shoreline typically features a fertile alluvial plain. Important events of Greek history centered on these three coastal flats named, from west to east, the plains of MESSENIA, LACONIA, and ARGOS.

It was on the plain of Argos that Greek civilization began, around 1600 B.C.E. There stood the chief group of Mycenaean-Greek cities: Mycenae, Argos, and TIRYNS. After the MYCENAEAN CIVILIZATION's downfall, the Peloponnese was largely overrun by DORIAN GREEKS, around 1100–1000 B.C.E. But one Mycenaean contingent fled inland to the mountains of the central Peloponnese, to reemerge in historical times as the hard-bitten "highlanders" of ARCADIA. Of the Dorian settlements, one in particular grew to power—Sparta ("the sown land"), located in interior Laconia. By 600 B.C.E. the Spartans had conquered Messenia as well as Laconia, thus controlling the entire southern Peloponnese.

Two other principal Peloponnesian regions were ELIS, in the west, and ACHAEA, in the northwest. The inhabitants of these two regions were not Dorians but had affinities in race and language with the Greeks of AETOLIA and other areas north of the Corinthian Gulf.

See also FARMING; GREECE, GEOGRAPHY OF; GREEK LANGUAGE.

Further reading: K. Adshead, *Politics of the Archaic Peloponnese. The Transition from Archaic to Classical Politics* (Aldershot, U.K.: Avebury, 1986); G. D. R. Sanders and I. K. Whitbread, "Central Places and Major Roads in the Peloponnese," *Annual of the British School at Athens* 85 (1990): 333–361; Kenneth A. Sheedy, ed., *Archaeology in the Peloponnese: New Excavations and Research* (Oxford: Oxbow Books, 1994); Peter Levi, *A Bottle in the Shade: A Journey in the Western Peloponnese* (London: Sinclair-Stevenson, 1996); W. Josing, *Greece: The Mainland—Peloponnese; An Up-to-date Travel Guide with 163 Color Photos and 23 Maps,* 2d ed. (Munich: Nelles, 2000); A. D. Rizakis and S. Zoumbaki, *Roman Peloponnese* (Paris: Diffusion de Boccard, 2001); Robin Hägg, ed., *Peloponnesian Sanctuaries and Cults: Proceedings of the Ninth International Symposium at the Swedish Institute at Athens, 11–13 June 1994* (Stockholm: Svenska Institutet i Athen, 2002).

Peloponnesian War This was the world war of ancient Greece, in which SPARTA and its allies defeated ATHENS and its allies after 27 years of intermittent fighting, 431–404 B.C.E. The defeat ended Athens's 75-year reign as the richest and most powerful Greek city and left Sparta in control of an exhausted Greece.

The Greeks called this conflict "the war between the Peloponnesians and the Athenians." One side consisted of Sparta and its core allies throughout the PELOPONNESE, grouped into a Spartan-led alliance known as the Peloponnesian League. The Athenian side included most of the islands and cities of the AEGEAN SEA and western ASIA MINOR—perhaps 200 states in all—organized into the Athenian-controlled DELIAN LEAGUE. Most of the Delian League states were peopled by IONIAN GREEKS, while the Spartan side consisted largely of DORIAN GREEKS. With some important exceptions, the war was fought along these ethnic lines, Ionians versus Dorians.

The fighting ranged across the Greek world, from eastern SICILY to BYZANTIUM, but the war often was mired in stalemate because Sparta remained invincible on land and Athens supreme at sea. Against the mainly defensive Athenian strategy, the cautious Spartans frequently proved ineffectual.

Low military technology contributed to the standoff. Greek armies of the 400s B.C.E. had not yet developed the tactics and machinery for storming fortified cities. Siege warfare was a slow and expensive game of encircling the enemy city and waiting for its defenders to succumb to starvation, fear, or betrayal. A fortified city suppliable by sea, such as Athens, was impossible to capture unless the besieger also could block the harbor.

Sparta finally gained the upper hand in the war after two critical changes occurred. First, the Athenian disaster at SYRACUSE (413 B.C.E.) inspired a widespread revolt of Athens's unhappy Delian League allies. Second, the non-Greek empire of PERSIA formed an alliance with Sparta (412 B.C.E.) and brought Persian funds to finance Spartan war fleets. Gradually Sparta was able to challenge Athenian naval supremacy, and the Spartan naval victory at AEGOSPOTAMI (405 B.C.E.) made Athens's surrender inevitable (404 B.C.E.). The victorious Spartans—over the objections of some of their allies—spared the defeated city from destruction.

Modern knowledge of the war comes partly from archaeological evidence (such as inscribed Athenian legislative decrees) but mostly from the works of ancient writers—principally the Athenian historian THUCYDIDES (1), who served briefly as a general in the war and produced a highly reliable history of it. Thucydides' account, unfinished, breaks off in describing the events of 411 B.C.E. The war's final years, 411–404 B.C.E., are recorded in the first part of the *Hellenica*, by the Athenian XENOPHON. Xenophon, like Thucydides, witnessed some of the events he describes. A third contemporary source was the Athenian comic playwright ARISTOPHANES, who addressed war politics in such plays as *Acharnians* (performed in 425 B.C.E.) and *Peace* (421 B.C.E.). Later sources include the biographer PLUTARCH (ca. 100 C.E.).

In one famous passage, Thucydides states that the ultimate cause of the war was Spartan fear of the growth of Athenian power. More than Athens's navy and army, however, Sparta feared Athens's magnetic cultural appeal and the appeal of Athenian DEMOCRACY. Thus, the Peloponnesian War was partly a conflict between two political ideologies—radical democracy, embodied by Athens and most of its allies, and the old-fashioned government of OLIGARCHY, championed by Sparta. Sparta's control of the Peloponnese depended on the oligarchic ruling class in the ally cities. The politically excluded underclass in

Greece during the Peloponnesian War

ILLYRIA

Epidamnos

MACEDON

EPIRUS

Corfu

THESSALY

BOEOTIA
Thebes
Leuctra
Athens
Corinth
Piraeus
PELOPONNESE
Elis
Argos
Olympia
Aegina
MESSENIA
Pylos
Sparta
Sphacteria
LACONIA
Kythera

THRACE

Amphipolis

Thasos

Olynthos

Lemnos

Aegospotami

Troy

Mytilene
Lesbos

Euboea

Chios

Melos

CYCLADES

Black Sea

Byzantium

PHRYGIA

PERSIAN EMPIRE

IONIA
Ephesos

Samos

Miletus

Knidos

Rhodes

Aegean Sea

CRETE

Mediterranean Sea

Athens and the states in the Delian Confederacy

Allies of Athens

Sparta and allied states

Neutral states

▲ Ally of Athens in Magna Graecia

0   100 miles
0   100 km

N

these cities posed a tremendous potential threat, liable to be exploited by the agents of democratic Athens.

Similarly, in almost every democratic city allied with Athens, a few rich right-wingers secretly wished for oligarchy. Athens itself contained such people; they seized power briefly in 411 B.C.E. The defections and attempted defections of cities on each side in the war came partly from this internal struggle between rich and poor, one side naturally pro-Spartan, the other naturally pro-Athenian. The most devastating civil strife occurred at the northwestern Greek city of CORCYRA, which at the war's start was an important Athenian ally but which then (427 B.C.E.) succumbed to riots between democrats and oligarchs.

An immediate cause of the Peloponnesian War was Athens's cavalier attitude toward the Thirty Years' Peace of 446 B.C.E., which had ended prior hostilities between Athens and Sparta. Although this religiously sanctioned treaty had guaranteed that Athens would not interfere with other mainland Greek cities, the treaty was flouted by the Athenian statesman PERIKLES, who apparently saw a future war as inevitable. The most provocative Athenian violations were domination of AEGINA and designs against MEGARA (1). The notorious Megarian Decree, passed at Athens in about 433 B.C.E., effectively prohibited the Megarians from conducting TRADE throughout the Athenian empire.

Next, Athens slipped into an undeclared war against CORINTH, an important Spartan ally. First, the Corinthian navy defeated a joint Corcyrean-Athenian fleet at Sybota, near Corcyra island (433 B.C.E.), then Corinthian and Athenian land troops fought outside POTIDAEA (432 B.C.E.). Incited by the Corinthians, the Peloponnesian League voted for war against Athens (432 B.C.E.). The Athenian ASSEMBLY, on Perikles' urging rejected Spartan ultimatums (fall and winter of 432–431 B.C.E.). Both sides prepared for war.

The Spartan bloc was joined by THEBES and other cities of BOEOTIA (a central Greek region northwest of Attica traditionally hostile to Athens). This caused the peninsular Athenian home region of ATTICA to face enemies along its entire land frontier.

Athens was ready, however, with its navy of 200 warships, its impregnable fortifications (including the LONG WALLS, linking the city to its harbor at PIRAEUS), and its huge financial reserve, supplied by the tribute-paying Delian League allies. Foremost among the Delian states were the eastern Aegean islands of LESBOS and CHIOS, which contributed warships and crews to Athens's navy. Outside of the league, Athens had several nontribute-paying allies, including Corcyra, the Boeotian city of PLATAEA (a traditional enemy of Thebes), and the northwestern regions of ACARNANIA and Amphilochia.

The Athenian war strategy was innovative and odd. Faced with a numerically superior enemy land army that boasted the best soldiers in Greece (the Spartans, The-

bans, Eleans, and Arcadians), Perikles planned to avoid land battles. Instead, Athens would rely on static defense by land and amphibious attacks by sea. If the Spartans attacked Athens, as expected, the Athenians would wait out the assault, relying on the city's fortifications and sea imports of food and supplies. Meanwhile, Athenian war fleets could sail from Piraeus even if a Spartan army was outside the walls. Carrying land troops aboard, Athenian fleets could attack enemy coastal sites. These attacks might be intended as either harassments or as wholesale attempts to capture enemy cities.

The drastic aspect of Perikles' strategy was that it would abandon the Athenian countryside to the Spartans. The Athenian rural population would be housed in camps within the Long Walls and the walls of the city and Piraeus—at least for the summer campaigns if not for the whole war. The farmers' livestock would be evacuated to the Athenian-controlled island of EUBOEA.

Perikles apparently believed that his one-sided strategy would not be needed for long. He seems to have expected that Sparta's allies would be demoralized and that the war would end in about three years. In fact, however, events were destined to take a far different turn.

The war's first military action was a failed Theban night attack against Plataea (spring of 431 B.C.E.). Then, in midsummer, the Spartan king ARCHIDAMUS led a Peloponnesian army of 24,000 HOPLITE infantry into Athenian territory. Events followed much as Pericles had forseen. Archidamus devastated crops and farm buildings in the evacuated countryside but was powerless against Athens's walls. After perhaps a month the Peloponnesians withdrew. This pattern of ineffectual Spartan invasion would recur in several following summers. The war's first 10 years (431–421 B.C.E.) are sometimes known as the Archidamian War, after the Spartan king who led these initial attacks.

After Archidamus had marched away that first year, Perikles himself led 13,000 hoplites and 100 warships against nearby Megara. But, like so many assaults against fortified cities in the Peloponnesian War, this one failed—as did Perikles' similar attack on EPIDAURUS the following year.

In the summer of 430 B.C.E., Athens suffered its first catastrophe of the war. When the Spartan army invaded for the second time, and the Athenian rural population again gathered within the walls, a deadly plague broke out at Athens (the disease's identity is unknown to us). The cramped, unsanitary conditions of the Athenian refugees provided a breeding ground for the contagion, which raged for the next year and a half and recurred briefly two years after that (427 B.C.E.). Eventually one-fourth of the population, perhaps 50,000 people, had died.

The plague removed Athens's initial advantage in the war, creating problems in manpower and leadership. Perikles himself died of the sickness in 429 B.C.E., at about age 65. Most significantly, the plague encouraged the Spartans by seeming to show the will of the gods.

In 429 B.C.E. the Spartans began besieging the defiant little city of Plataea. Two years later, the starving inhabitants surrendered (after half the garrison had escaped in a nighttime breakout through the Spartan siege lines). To please their Theban allies, the Spartans executed the male prisoners—200 Plataeans and 25 Athenians—and sold the WOMEN as SLAVES. Later, the empty town was leveled. Many Greeks felt that Plataea's destruction was an impious act, because during the PERSIAN WARS Plataea had been the site of a famous oath sworn by the Spartans and other Greeks, promising forever to honor the city.

The Athenians, now deprived of Perikles, sought more aggressively to drive Sparta's allies out of the war. Based at the West Locrian seaport of NAUPACTUS in northwestern Greece, the Athenian admiral Phormion won two spectacular naval victories against larger, Corinthian-led fleets (429 B.C.E.). In 426 B.C.E. the Athenian general DEMOSTHENES (2) brought an army of light-armed Acarnanians and Amphilochians to victory against their traditional enemy, the Corinthian colony of AMBRACIA. Demosthenes failed to capture Ambracia, but his experiences in the hilly, wooded terrain taught him the possible advantage of javelin men and slingers over heavier-armed hoplites. The subsequent Athenian development of light-armed projectile troops was one of the few tactical advances of the Peloponnesian War.

Meanwhile the important Delian League city of MYTILENE, capital of Lesbos, revolted against Athens (428 B.C.E.) but fell to a besieging Athenian force (427 B.C.E.). Back in Athens, the citizens' assembly debated how to punish the captured Mytileneans. Rescinding a vote led by the Athenian politician KLEON for massacre of the entire adult male population and enslavement of the women and children, the assembly voted a lesser penalty—execution of the 1,000 Mytileneans judged responsible for the rebellion. Certain speeches of this Mytilenean Debate provide a famous scene in Thucydides' history (book 3). Later, amid the war's increasing brutality, the Athenians would begin treating rebellion more cruelly.

Kleon, now emerging as Perikles' political heir, was a leader who could have won the war for Athens. Although not a military man by training, he embodied an aggressive, can-do spirit that was at odds with the Perikles-derived passivity of much of the Athenian officer class. In partnership with Demosthenes, Kleon would soon give Athens the upper hand in the war.

This critical campaign began when Demosthenes established an Athenian naval base at PYLOS, in the southwestern Peloponnese, only about 50 miles west of Sparta (425 B.C.E.). The ensuing fighting between Athenians and Spartans at Pylos, which took place in the city's harbor and on the nearby island of Sphacteria ("wasp place"), ended in an Athenian victory and was one of the most consequential events of the war. Kleon, who was present

at Pylos as an elected Athenian general, encouraged Demosthenes to attack the 420 elite Spartan soldiers trapped on Sphacteria, of whom 292 surrendered and survived.

Taken as prisoners to Athens, the 292 Spartans served as diplomatic pawns until 421 B.C.E., when they were returned home. That their government welcomed them back rather than punishing them for their surrender—as a prior generation of Spartan leaders might have done—is a sign of how valuable their bloodstock was thought to be, amid Sparta's long-term problem of falling birthrate.

Sparta then faced its low point in the war. Its supposedly invincible army had been humiliated, while the Athenian fort at Pylos became a rallying point for rebellious Messenians. At Athens, the Pylos victory made Kleon politically supreme, ushering in a period of Athenian military boldness in pursuit of total victory (425–421 B.C.E.). Spartan peace overtures were rebuffed. An imperialistic tone is evident in the surviving Athenian inscription called the Thoudippos Decree, which effectively doubled the tribute owed to Athens by its Delian League subject allies (autumn of 425 B.C.E.). But Kleon's aggressive policy brought some Athenian setbacks. Particularly, a foolhardy Athenian invasion of Boeotia was defeated at the land battle of Delium, fought near a temple of Delian Apollo alongside the Straits of Euboea (autumn of 424 B.C.E.).

More bad news followed for Athens. The brilliant Spartan general BRASIDAS, having marched a small Peloponnesian army to the north Aegean coast, convinced several Delian League subject towns to defect to the Spartan side. Then, in a night attack, he captured the strategic Athenian colony of AMPHIPOLIS (December of 424 B.C.E.). The city's loss caused an outrage at Athens; without possessing a single ship, Brasidas had dealt a blow to Athens' northeastern shipping route and had opened the threat of a wider north Aegean revolt. The Athenian general inside Amphipolis apparently had been killed or captured, while the other Athenian general in the vicinity had arrived with a naval squadron too late to save the city. This general was Thucydides, the same man whose written history of the war is our major source. Blamed by his countrymen for the loss, Thucydides was banished from Athens.

A new Spartan king, Pleistoanax, viewed these successes mainly as bargaining chips to end the war, but a year's truce for peace talks passed inconsequentially (spring 423—422 B.C.E.). In the north, meanwhile, Brasidas ignored the truce and continued to bring local towns into revolt against Athens.

Promising to recapture Amphipolis and eliminate Brasidas, Kleon sailed from Athens in the summer of 422 B.C.E. with 30 warships and a small army. But for all his pugnacity, Kleon was not an experienced tactician; while scouting the terrain around Amphipolis, he and his force were surprised by a sortie from the city, led by Brasidas. In the fight, the Athenians retreated with 600 dead, including Kleon—but Brasidas too had been killed. The

Battle of Amphipolis removed at once the two most war-like leaders of the day.

In March of 421 B.C.E., the two sides agreed to a peace that was intended to last 50 years. (In fact, it lasted barely three.) Modern scholars call this treaty the Peace of NIKIAS, named for the cautious soldier-politician who was then the leading Athenian. The peace's terms amounted to a triumph for Athens, which was left free to maintain its empire and to recapture rebellious subject cities. It was all that Perikles could have hoped for. The peace was followed quickly by an alliance between Athens and Sparta, designed to give them dual hegemony over the rest of Greece.

The losers in this process were the Spartan ally states, which had endured hardship only to see their interests ignored. Certain states then began looking for a new leader in the Peloponnese. This they found in the previously neutral, east Peloponnesian city of ARGOS.

By 420 B.C.E. an anti-Spartan axis had arisen, consisting of Argos, MANTINEA, ELIS, and—surprisingly—Athens, which flouted the Peace of Nikias. The driving force behind this Athenian policy was ALCIBIADES, a volatile, left-wing aristocrat, perhaps 30 years old, who had emerged as Nikias's political opponent. Alcibiades embodied the reckless mood of an Athenian citizenry that—far from being exhausted by 11 years of war—was overconfident from the advantageous peace.

Provoked by the four-city alliance, the Spartans marched. At the Battle of Mantinea, in the central Peloponnese, a Spartan-led army of 3,600 hoplites crushed a roughly equal force of Argive, Mantinean, Elean, and Athenian troops (418 B.C.E.). The alliance dissolved, bringing Elis and Mantinea back into the Spartan fold. Hostilities between Athens and Sparta did not recommence outright, but the angry Spartans awaited their chance.

In 416 B.C.E., the Athenians—tightening their control over their Aegean sea routes—landed a force on the Cycladic island of MELOS. The Melians were Dorian Greeks, descended from Spartan colonists. They had shown prior hostility to Athens and were now commanded to submit to Athenian rule, but Melian leaders refused the Athenian demands. Political-philosophical arguments purporting to be the positions of both sides are presented in the famous Melian Dialogue in Thucydides' history (book 5). Besieged, the Melians were starved into surrender. The Athenians killed all adult male prisoners and sold the women and children into slavery. The island was later repopulated with Athenian colonists.

The year 415 B.C.E. brought the most fateful event of the war—the Athenian expedition against the city of Syracuse, in southeastern Sicily. A wealthy, seafaring, Dorian-Greek democracy, Syracuse was an ally of Sparta and the enemy of the Ionian Greeks of Sicily and southern Italy.

At Alcibiades' urging, the Athenian assembly voted to send out a major force. The intended capture of Syracuse would give Athens control of the wheatfields that supplied grain to Corinth and other Spartan-allied cities. Although Alcibiades was the natural choice to lead the expedition, the Athenians mistrusted him because of his flamboyant and licentious private life. So they split the command among three generals—Alcibiades, Nikias (who had opposed the whole idea of the venture), and the able Lamachus.

Just before the departure, an act of religious terrorism occurred. Under cover of darkness, a group (probably pro-peace, right-wing conspirators) smashed the carved faces and genitals of the stone effigies of the god HERMES, called herms (hermai), that stood in front of houses throughout Athens. This sacrilegious event is known as the Mutilation of the Herms. Undoubtedly intended to create a bad omen against the expedition, the act succeeded well, because the Athenian people irrationally turned their suspicion on the commander Alcibiades.

The armada consisted of 134 warships, 130 supply ships, 5,100 hoplites, and 1,300 archers, javelin men, and slingers (mostly allies and mercenaries), plus about 20,000 crewmen. It sailed in late spring, but Alcibiades was soon summoned back to Athens to face impiety charges. He instead fled to Sparta, where he gave strategic advice against his fellow Athenians. Among other things, he advised that a Spartan officer be sent to Syracuse to organize the city's defense.

The Athenian attack on Syracuse stalled under the indecisive, ailing, 55-year-old Nikias, who took nearly a year to settle down to a siege (the spring of 414 B.C.E.). Outside the city wall, Athenian troops began constructing a siege wall to cut off the city's landward side; on the seaward side, Athenian naval patrols kept the Syracusan navy (about 80 warships) bottled inside the harbor. When Lamachus was killed in a skirmish at the siege works, Nikias took sole command. Meanwhile, the pessimistic Syracusans were urged to resistance by their statesman-general Hermocrates.

The tide turned when a Spartan general, Gylippos, led a small army of Peloponnesians and Sicilian Greeks into Syracuse on the landward side, around the incomplete Athenian siege wall. Gylippos blocked completion of the Athenians' wall and captured their naval base at the mouth of the bay known as the Greek Harbor. This loss forced the Athenians henceforth to beach their ships on an exposed shore at the head of the bay, where they could be bottled in by the Syracusan navy. As troops and supplies trickled into Syracuse by land and sea, the besiegers became the besieged.

In the spring of 413 B.C.E., in response to Nikias's appeal for help, a second Athenian armada sailed for Syracuse: 73 warships carrying 5,000 Athenian and allied hoplites and 3,000 light-armed troops. The force brought two generals, Eurymedon and (Athens's finest battlefield commander of the war) Demosthenes.

By then—with Nikias's warships having been defeated in a sea battle in the Great Harbor—the Athenian position at Syracuse was so vulnerable that the reinforcements were simply entering a death trap. Demosthenes and Eurymedon urged an evacuation by sea, but Nikias (still the senior general) hesitated, believing he could yet take the city. An unlucky eclipse of the moon (August 27, 413 B.C.E.) led the superstitious Nikias to delay further. Another sea battle in the Great Harbor brought a second Athenian defeat and the death of Eurymedon. When Nikias finally gave the order to evacuate by sea (September of 413 B.C.E.), the Syracusan navy blocked the Athenians from leaving the harbor mouth. Driven back to shore, the Athenians abandoned their dead and wounded and marched inland, hoping to escape to the neutral territory of the native Sicels. The bedraggled refugees numbered perhaps 40,000, largely crewmen from the ships.

"No prior Greek army had ever endured such a reversal. They had come to enslave others, but were now fleeing in fear of slavery themselves." So writes Thucydides, whose solemn account of the Athenians' final destruction (book 7) is the most moving section in his history. On the seventh day, the Athenian rear column, under Demosthenes, was surrounded and captured. The Athenian main column, under Nikias, was surrounded the next day in a riverbed and massacred with arrows and javelins. Of the approximately 7,000 captured, most died in captivity or were sold as slaves. Nikias and Demosthenes were captured and put to death.

It was the worst disaster in Athenian history: Losses included perhaps 50,000 men, 173 warships, and immense expense. Yet such were Athens's financial and spiritual resources that the city fought on for nearly another nine years (413–404 B.C.E.). In mainland Greece, the war had recommenced. In the spring of 413 B.C.E., the Spartans had invaded Athenian territory for the first time since 425 B.C.E. However, they did not withdraw entirely at the summer's end, but fortified the site called Decelea, about 13 miles north of Athens, to be a permanent base in Athenian territory.

Under personal command of the Spartan king Agis II, Decelea served Sparta much as Pylos had served Athens—as a front-line fort for raids and for rallying of the enemy's disaffected underclass. Thucydides says that 20,000 skilled Athenian slaves escaped to Decelea during the remaining war years.

The Spartan presence at Decelea threw Athens finally onto the defensive; overland communication outside the walls became a hardship. The Athenian CAVALRY was now obliged to make daily patrols against Spartan war parties in the Athenian countryside. Local resources, such as food and SILVER ore, became less available, and the Athenians grew increasingly reliant on purchased supplies imported by ship.

The Peloponnesian War's final nine years are sometimes known as the Ionian War, because the major campaigns shifted to the eastern Aegean and the shorelines of Asia Minor (particularly to the Greek region of west-

ern Asia Minor called IONIA). There lay the most important Athenian allies and the sea routes bringing resources westward to Athens; the most essential of these imports was grain, brought by merchant ships from the ports of the BLACK SEA. The vulnerable links in the sea route were the narrow waterways of the HELLESPONT and BOSPORUS, which Athenian forces controlled out of the naval base at SESTOS. It was against these regions that the Spartans directed their operations, aiming first to dislodge the unhappy and heavily taxed Athenian allies, and then to block Athens's supply route and bring the city to starvation.

Sparta's new role as a naval power was made possible because Athens had lost nearly three-fourths of its navy at Syracuse, and because Sparta now found a source of funds for its own shipbuilding and crews' wages, in an alliance with the Persian king Darius II (412 B.C.E.). In exchange, Darius received the right to reclaim the Greek cities of Asia Minor after the war.

The year after the Sicilian disaster saw the Greek world turn against Athens. Warships from the Peloponnese and Dorian Sicily began to invade the eastern Aegean. The Delian League unraveled amid revolts. The first rebel was Chios, with its considerable navy, followed by MILETUS, EPHESOS, PHOCAEA, CYMĒ, RHODES, Mytilene, and others. Of Athens's greatest east Aegean possessions, only the island state of SAMOS remained loyal. The Athenians responded with new war fleets, built with emergency funds. Samos became Athens's eastern naval base, as amphibious operations began against the rebels. Miletus and Dorian-Greek KNIDOS became Sparta's eastern naval bases.

By the winter of 412–411 B.C.E., the scene was set for Alcibiades' return. After earning the mistrust of his Spartan masters, Alcibiades had fled to Persian protection in western Asia Minor, and from there conducted secret intrigues with the Athenians at Samos to get himself recalled to Athens's service. His chance came when the oligarchic FOUR HUNDRED seized power at Athens, and the Athenian sailors and soldiers at Samos formed a democratic government-in-exile (June of 411 B.C.E.). Alcibiades was brought to Samos and elected as a general.

At Athens, the government of the Four Hundred, using untrained emergency crews, suffered a naval defeat against Peloponnesian ships in the Straits of Euboea (summer of 411 B.C.E.). With all of Euboea now in revolt against Athens, the disgraced Four Hundred soon fell from power.

The next four years marked the final Athenian high point of the war, under Alcibiades' leadership. The Spartans suffered a disastrous naval defeat at Alcibiades' hands at CYZICUS (410 B.C.E.) and soon offered peace on generous terms. The overconfident Athenians, however, rejected the offer as insufficient. In 408 B.C.E. Alcibiades captured the strategically vital, rebellious Delian city of Byzantium, and the next year he was recalled to Athens to receive extraordinary powers of command.

But when Alcibiades returned to the east Aegean in the autumn of 407 B.C.E., he faced a ruthless new opponent—the Spartan LYSANDER, commanding a fleet at Ephesos. After Lysander defeated a lieutenant of Alcibiades in a sea battle (spring of 406 B.C.E.), Alcibiades was blamed at Athens and was not reelected as general. Knowing that his life was in danger from his ungrateful fellow citizens, the greatest naval commander of the day retired to an estate beside the Hellespont.

Athens—foolishly trying to re-create its lost empire—was running out of resources. To man the newest fleet off the blocks, the Athenians resorted to enlisting slaves and resident aliens as oarsmen (a duty usually taken by lower-income Athenian citizens). In August of 406 B.C.E. these motley crewmen won the huge sea battle of Arginusae ("the white islands") off Mytilene. But the triumph was soured when the crews of the Athenian disabled vessels—about 5,000 men—perished in a storm immediately afterward. At Athens, hysteria reigned over the failure to rescue the crews; six of the responsible naval commanders, including Perikles' son, were executed. Worse, on the urging of the demagogue Kleophon, the assembly again rejected Spartan peace proposals.

Now a weak and inexperienced Athenian naval command led an irreplaceable force of about 200 ships. In the summer of 405 B.C.E., the wily Lysander sailed from Ephesus with 150 ships and slipped into the Hellespont, where he captured Lampsacus. When an 180-ship Athenian fleet arrived in pursuit, Lysander ambushed and destroyed it at the sea battle of Aegospotami ("the goat's rivers"). The Athenian navy had ceased to exist.

Spartan forces converged on the fortress of Athens, which endured six months of siege, without food imports. At last, the starving inhabitants voted to accept Sparta's terms—peace in exchange for the destruction of certain city fortifications, the surrender of overseas holdings and of most of the remaining warships, the recall of political exiles, and a military alliance with Sparta. The city capitulated in April of 404 B.C.E. Lysander's forces occupied Athens and Piraeus. The Long Walls were torn down to the MUSIC of flutes. It was the end of Athens as the dominant power in Greece.

See also CORINTHIAN WAR; EURIPIDES; KONON; SOCRATES; SOPHOKLES; THERAMENES; THIRTY TYRANTS, THE; WARFARE, LAND; WARFARE, NAVAL; WARFARE, SIEGE.

Further reading: John Wilson, *Athens and Corcyra: Strategy and Tactics in the Peloponnesian War* (Bristol, U.K.: Bristol Classical Press, 1987); Donald Kagen, *The Fall of the Athenian Empire* (Ithaca, N.Y.: Cornell University Press, 1987); I. G. Spence, "Perikles and the Defense of Attika During the Peloponnesian War," *Journal of Hellenic Studies* 110 (1990): 91–109; Barry S. Strauss, *Fathers and Sons in Athens: Ideology and Society in the Era of the Peloponnesian War* (Princeton, N.J.: Princeton University Press, 1993); Charles D. Hamilton and Peter Krentz, eds., *Polis and Polemos: Essays on Politics, War, and History in Ancient Greece, in Honor of Donald Kagen* (Claremont, Calif.: Regina Books, 1997); John F. Lazenby, *The Peloponnesian War: A Military Study* (London: Routledge, 2004).

Pelops   In Greek MYTH, Pelops was a prince of a non-Greek kingdom in ASIA MINOR—either LYDIA or Paphlagonia. His father was TANTALUS, who was a son of the god ZEUS and who offended the gods in an infamous episode. Pelops eventually emigrated to southern Greece, where he supposedly founded the OLYMPIC GAMES and fathered the line of kings at MYCENAE. He is commemorated in the name of the southern Greek peninsular region, the PELOPONNESE (Greek: Peloponnēsos, "island of Pelops"). The name Pelops (dark face) may refer to his Asian origin.

The best-known version of the Pelops story is told in the poet PINDAR's First Olympian ode, written in 476 B.C.E. As a youth in Asia Minor, Pelops became the favorite of POSEIDON (god of horses as well of the sea), who taught Pelops to be a great horseman and charioteer. Arriving in Greece, Pelops went to Pisa (the future site of OLYMPIA). There he asked for the hand in MARRIAGE of Hippodameia, the daughter of King Oinomaus.

Oinomaus secretly intended that his daughter never marry, either because he harbored an incestuous desire for her or because he knew a prophecy that his son-in-law would kill him. His terms of courtship were that anyone might carry Hippodameia off by chariot, but Oinomaus would follow and, upon overtaking, could spear the suitor. Twelve or 13 men had already died in this manner; their heads were nailed above the gates of Oinomaus's palace.

But Pelops cleverly bribed Oinomaus's groom, Myrtilus, to remove the linchpins from his master's chariot axle and replace them with wax. In the contest, Oinomaus's chariot collapsed and the evil king was dragged to death behind his horses. Pelops then married Hippodameia and became king of Pisa. Later he deceitfully killed Myrtilus, either to avoid acknowledging his help or to avoid sharing Hippodameia's favors with him, as promised. But the dying Myrtilus cursed Pelops and his family, and the curse proved effective. Pelops's son ATREUS and grandson AGAMEMNON ruled households riven by bloodshed.

The myth of Pelops and Oinomaus was in part etiological—that is, it explained the origin of a custom, namely the Olympic chariot race. In historical times Pelops was worshiped as a hero at Olympia, where his purported tomb was located. At Olympia's Temple of Zeus, the sculptures on the east pediment showed Pelops and Oinomaus preparing for the fateful chariot race, with Zeus standing between them and looking toward his grandson Pelops.

See also CHARIOTS.

Further reading: W. J. Slater, "Pelops at Olympia," *Greek, Roman, and Byzantine Studies* 30 (1989): 485–501; G. Howie, "Pindar's Account of Pelops' Contest with Oenomaus. With a Translation of Olympian 1," *Nikephoros* 4 (1991): 55–120; Helmut Kyrieleis, "Zeus and Pelops in the East Pediment of the Temple of Zeus at Olympia," in *The Interpretation of Architectural Sculpture in Greece and Rome,* edited by Diana Buitron-Oliver (Washington, D.C.: National Gallery of Art, 1997), 13–28.

Penelope   In MYTH, Penelope was the Spartan-born wife of the Ithacan king ODYSSEUS; their son was TELEMACHOS. She faithfully awaited her husband's return during his 20-year absence—10 years fighting the TROJAN WAR and another 10 years for his homeward voyage.

In HOMER's epic poem the *Odyssey,* Penelope appears as a gracious and clever lady. Since about the seventh year of Odysseus's disappearance during his voyage from TROY, she has been pressured to assume him dead and to marry one of the 108 suitors—local nobles and nearby kings—who have flocked to the palace at ITHACA. She puts them off by claiming she cannot remarry until she finishes weaving a shroud for Odysseus's elderly (but still living) father, Laertes. Every night she secretly unravels what she has woven that day, so that the work never progresses. At length the deceit is discovered, and she is compelled to make known the day on which she will choose a new husband. Finally she announces that she will marry whoever can bend and string Odysseus's mighty bow, then shoot an arrow through the empty sockets of 12 axheads sunk in a line. In fact, it is Odysseus himself who performs this feat, having returned to Ithaca disguised as a beggar. Then he slaughters the suitors and reclaims his throne (*Odyssey* books 21–22).

Afterward, Penelope and Odysseus lived happily for years. After his death—according to one post-Homeric version—Penelope married Telegonus, who was Odysseus's son by CIRCE.

Further reading: Marylin A. Katz, *Penelope's Renown: Meaning and Indeterminacy in the Odyssey* (Princeton, N.J.: Princeton University Press, 1991); Nancy Felson, *Regarding Penelope: From Character to Poetics* (Princeton, N.J.: Princeton University Press, 1994); D. Buitron-Oliver and B. Cohen, "Between Skylla and Penelope. Female Characters of the 'Odyssey' in Archaic and Classical Greek Art," in *The Distaff Side. Representing the Female in Homer's Odyssey,* edited by Beth Cohen (New York: Oxford University Press, 1995), 29–58; W. E. Helleman, "Penelope as Lady Philosophy," *Phoenix* 49 (1995): 283–302; Barbara Clayton, *A Penelopean Poetics: Reweaving the Feminine in Homer's Odyssey* (Lanham, Md.: Lexington Books, 2004).

pentathlon   The "fivefold contest," the pentathlon was one of the most prestigious events at such Greek athletic festivals as the OLYMPIC GAMES, beginning in 708 B.C.E. Originally, contestants competed in the footrace, the long jump, the discus throw, and the javelin throw. The two men scoring the highest in these events were then selected for the final contest, a WRESTLING match. The winner of this was declared to be the pentathlete. BOXING was added to the agenda in 688 B.C.E., and the PANKRATION was added in 648 B.C.E. The pentathlon continued to be called by that name, even though it came to include more than five events.

The modern pentathlon was invented by Baron Pierre de Coubertin, the founder of the modern Olympic Games. It first took place in 1912 C.E. at the Games in Stockholm, Sweden. The events chosen for the pentathlon were intended to appeal to the military and included equestrian show jumping, shooting, fencing, swimming, and cross-country running.

Further reading: S. G. Miller, "The Pentathlon for Boys at Nemea," *California Studies in Classical Antiquity* 8 (1975): 199–201; M. K. Langdon, "Scoring the Ancient Pentathlon. Final Solution?" *Zeitschrift für Papyrologie und Epigraphik* 78 (1989): 117–118; G. Waddell, "The Greek Pentathlon," in *Greek Vases in the J. Paul Getty Museum, 5* (Malibu, Calif.: J. Paul Getty Museum, 1991), 99–106; D. F. Jackson, "Philostratos and the Pentathlon," *Journal of Hellenic Studies* 111 (1991): 178–181; V. Matthews, "The Greek Pentathlon Again," *Zeitschrift für Papyrologie und Epigraphik* 100 (1994): 129–138; H. M. Lee, "Yet Another Scoring System for the Ancient Pentathlon," *Nikephoros* 8 (1995): 41–55.

Penthesilea   *See* AMAZONS.

Pentheus   *See* DIONYSUS.

Pergamon   One of the wealthiest and most important Greek cities of the later HELLENISTIC AGE (ca. 250–133 B.C.E.), Pergamon is located on the north-central west coast of ASIA MINOR, about 15 miles inland in the hills along the River Caïcus. The city thrived from local SILVER mines and exports of grain, textiles, and parchment (Greek: *pergamēnē*).

In the classical period, Pergamon was one of many Greek cities of the region called AEOLIS. Soon after 300 B.C.E. Pergamon became a subject city of the sprawling SELEUCID EMPIRE. By 262 B.C.E., however, the Pergamenes were led by Philetairos and his adopted son Eumenes and revolted from Seleucid rule. The royal dynasty of the Attalids—"the sons of Attalus" (Philetairos's father)—brought the city to its zenith. Pergamon dominated Asia Minor and became a center of Greek culture, with a royal library that was second in size only to the one at Egyptian ALEXANDRIA (1).

Eumenes' successor was King Attalus I (reigned 269–197 B.C.E.). He defeated the invading CELTS, resisted the ambitions of the Macedonian king PHILIP V, and wisely sided with the Romans against Philip in the Second Macedonian War (200–197 B.C.E.). Attalus's friendship with ROME helped assure Pergamon's survival amid Roman conquest of the eastern Mediterranean. When Attalus III died in 133 B.C.E., he bequeathed his kingdom to the Romans.

The grandeur of ancient Pergamon is suggested in the Great Altar of ZEUS, erected by King Eumenes II (reigned 197–159 B.C.E.) and now housed in the Pergamon Museum in Berlin. Carved with marble bas-reliefs showing the gods' mythical combat with the GIANTS, the altar is one of the most admired surviving Hellenistic artworks.

The site of Pergamon, terraced cleverly into high hills, was mostly excavated by German archaeologists in 1875–1886. Current work at the site primarily involves conserving and restoring the fantastic ruins for the many visitors. The city is one of the most dramatic ancient Greek sites in Turkey, with grand vistas from the ACROPOLIS and from the steep auditorium of the ancient THEATER.

See also WRITING.

Further reading: Esther V. Hansen, *The Attalids of Pergamon,* 2d ed. (Ithaca, N.Y.: Cornell University Press, 1971); Max Kunze, *The Pergamon Altar: Its Rediscover, History, and Reconstruction* (Berlin: Staatliche Museem zu Berlin, Antikensammlung, 1991); U. Westermark, "Bronze Coins of Pergamon," *Numismatica e antichità classiche* 20 (1991): 147–159; Ann Kuttner, "Republican Rome Looks at Pergamon," *Harvard Studies in Classical Antiquity* 97 (1995): 157–178; R. Dreyfus and E. Schraudolph, *Pergamon: The Telephos Frieze from the Great Altar* (San Francisco: Fine Arts Museums of San Francisco, 1996); N. T. de Grummond and B. S. Ridgway, eds., *From Pergamon to Sperlonga: Sculpture and Context* (Berkeley: University of California Press, 2000).

Periander (ca. 650–585 B.C.E.) *Dictator of* CORINTH *from about 625 to 585 B.C.E.*

The son and successor of KYPSELOS, Periander reigned energetically over a city that was the most prosperous in Greece. Combining total power with wise statesmanship, he was the most famous example of the breed of Greek rulers known as TYRANTS. Later generations counted him among the SEVEN SAGES of Greece.

Periander extended his power through the Greek world by war and diplomacy. He brought Corinth's rebellious colony CORCYRA to heel and captured the Peloponnesian city of EPIDAURUS. Looking to western ASIA MINOR, he forged ties with the Greek city of MILETUS and the non-Greek kingdom of LYDIA. Asked to arbitrate in a war between ATHENS and MYTILENE, he in effect judged in favor of Athens. This act inaugurated a period of Corinthian-Athenian friendship. (The two cities had a mutual trading rival, AEGINA.)

In TRADE, Periander brought Corinth to new heights. Responding to the great demand for Corinthian goods among the ETRUSCANS of western ITALY, Periander enlarged the westward shipping route, establishing Adriatic colonies such as APOLLONIA and EPIDAMNOS to serve as anchorages and local depots. In the distant northeastern region called CHALCIDICĒ, Periander founded the colony of POTIDAEA. Apparently he also pursued trade with EGYPT, as suggested by the Egyptian royal name Psammetichus that he gave to his son.

Exploiting Corinth's geography, Periander constructed a ships' dragway (Greek: *diolkos*) across the seven-mile-wide isthmus that separates the Saronic Gulf from the Corinthian Gulf. A stretch of this stone roadbed, with grooves for trolley wheels, remains visible today. The *diolkos* provided Greek merchant ships with an east-west overland shortcut across central Greece—and provided Corinth with revenue from tolls.

Periander's city was the cultural capital of mainland Greece. Poets such as the famous ARION came to Periander's court. The tyrant's public-building program stimulated the development of the form of monumental ARCHITECTURE known as the Doric order. In painted POTTERY, Corinthian artists achieved the style that we call Corinthian and that monopolized the Mediterranean market in that day.

Periander could be ruthless. He used surveillance and intimidation against Corinthians who might pose a threat to his power, and he executed the most important of them. After one of Periander's sons was killed in Corcyra (probably as governor), Periander took 300 boys from Corcyra's foremost families and shipped them as a gift to the Lydians, to be turned into eunuchs. (As it happened, they were rescued.) Periander's passions were uncontrolled: Gossip claimed that he murdered his beloved wife, Melissa, in an irrational rage of jealousy and then, in remorse, had sexual intercourse with her corpse.

Dying at an old age, Periander left his dynasty beleaguered. His son Psammetichus reigned for three years before being ousted in favor of a liberal OLIGARCHY.

See also COLONIZATION.

Further reading: J. P. Vernant, "From Oedipus to Periander: Lameness, Tyranny, Incest in Legend and History," in *Oxford Readings in Greek Religion,* edited by Richard Buxton (New York: Oxford University Press, 2000).

Perikles (ca. 495–429 B.C.E.) *Greatest Athenian statesman*

Despite his aristocratic blood, Perikles entered politics as a left-wing radical and by the mid-440s B.C.E. was preeminent in the government, steering ATHENS through its heyday of power and cultural achievement. More than any other individual, Perikles shaped classical Athens as a radical DEMOCRACY and naval power, as a center of learning, and as a city of architectural splendors, ascending to the PARTHENON. Perikles' ambitious vision created this Athens that (to use his own phrase) was an EDUCATION to the rest of Greece. As his influence increased, however, his political policies became increasingly imperialist, despite his left-wing roots. He ended his days in disfavor, after his belligerence toward other Greek states had provoked the PELOPONNESIAN WAR and his defensive military strategy had brought plague and demoralization to his city.

Perikles never held any such post as "president" of Athens, since no such job existed under the democracy. His highest title was *stratēgos,* "military general," a post to which the Athenians elected 10 different men annually. Unlike most other generals, however, Perikles was elected at least 20 times; we know that he served without interruption from 443 to 430 B.C.E.

Perikles' source of power was the *dēmos*—the common people, the mass of lower- and middle-income citizens. He was a politician they trusted to protect them against the rich and to guide the city. A rigorously intellectual man, Perikles was an accomplished orator, whose speeches in the public ASSEMBLY could sway his listeners to vote for his proposals.

Most of our knowledge of him comes from the Athenian historian THUCYDIDES (1), who wrote ca. 430–400 B.C.E., and from the biographer PLUTARCH, who wrote ca. 100 C.E. Thucydides is especially helpful because he knew Perikles personally and understood his politics. Some details are added by other writers and by inscriptions recording Periklean-inspired legislation.

Perikles' father was XANTHIPPUS, a distinguished Athenian soldier-politician. Perikles' mother was Agariste, a niece of the Athenian statesman KLEISTHENES (1) and a member of the noble clan of the ALCMAEONIDS. The family's wealth and influence no doubt helped Perikles enter politics, but he soon disassociated himself from the Alcmaeonids and from other right-wing connections.

At about age 23 he served as *chorēgos* (paying sponsor) for AESCHYLUS's stage drama *The Persians* (472 B.C.E.). Perikles' involvement in this politically charged play identifies him as a follower of the beleaguered left-wing Athenian statesman THEMISTOKLES. In the 480s B.C.E. Themistokles had pushed two interrelated programs—radical democracy and a buildup of the navy. The lower-income citizens who followed Themistokles were the same men who served as crews in the labor-intensive warships. Gradually Perikles emerged as Themistokles' political heir.

In 463 B.C.E., at about age 32, Perikles (unsuccessfully) prosecuted the conservative leader KIMON for bribery. The following year Perikles assisted the radical reformer EPHIALTES in proposing legislation that dismantled the power of the AREOPAGOS. Ephialtes' death and Kimon's OSTRACISM (both in 461 B.C.E.) left Perikles as

the foremost Athenian politician. His influence can be seen in the next decade, in Athens' left-leaning domestic policies and in its bellicose stance toward SPARTA and certain other Greek states, such as AEGINA.

In 461 B.C.E. Perikles urged the creation of the LONG WALLS, which were to stretch four miles from Athens down to its harbor at PIRAEUS. Completed in about 457 B.C.E., the walls turned Athens into an impregnable naval fortress. They also brought Piraeus's laborers and citizen-sailors more directly into Athenian politics.

Around 457 B.C.E. Perikles sponsored a bill creating jury pay. This important democratic measure effectively opened jury duty to lower-income citizens. It was probably also Perikles who, sometimes in the mid-400s B.C.E., instituted public assistance for the poorest citizens.

By 460 B.C.E. Athens had slipped into an undeclared war against Sparta and its allies. Repeatedly elected as general, Perikles led a seaborne raid against the enemy city of SIKYON (in about 454 B.C.E.) and led an Athenian fleet to the BLACK SEA to make alliance with Greek cities there that could supply precious grain to Athens (452 B.C.E.).

In about 449 B.C.E. Perikles convinced his fellow citizens to accept an offered peace with PERSIA, officially ending the PERSIAN WARS. To mark the event and to glorify the city, Perikles initiated a public building program, directed by the sculptor PHEIDIAS. This program—which created most of the famous buildings still standing today on the Athenian ACROPOLIS—amounted to a show of dominance over Athens's Greek ally states in the DELIAN LEAGUE. The league had been formed (around 478 B.C.E.) as a mutual-defense alliance against Persia, but now Perikles was demonstrating that, rather than reduce or forgive the allies' war dues on account of the new peace, Athens would continue collecting dues and would use them as it pleased.

Perikles' imperialism is also evident in the use of Athenian garrison colonies (known as cleruchies) to punish and guard resistant Delian League states. Among the Greek regions that received these hated, land-grabbing, Athenian settler communities were Aegina, EUBOEA, and the Cycladic island of Naxos.

As reported by Thucydides, Perikles' grim imperialism is summarized in a speech to the Athenian assembly in 430 B.C.E., after the outbreak of the Peloponnesian War. "It is no longer possible for you to give up your empire," Perikles told the people. "You hold the empire as a tyrant holds power: you may have been wrong to take it, but you cannot safely let it go." He went on in the speech to glorify Athens as "the greatest name in history . . . the greatest power that has ever yet arisen, a power to be remembered forever."

In 446 B.C.E. the Spartans invaded Athenian territory. Although Perikles was able to appease them with bribery and diplomatic concessions, the resulting Thirty Years' Peace was unpopular at Athens. Perikles was attacked by an Athenian right-winger named THUCYDIDES (2)—not the historian, but his maternal grandfather. By 443 B.C.E. Perikles and his followers had rallied, convincing the Athenian people to ostracize Thucydides.

Having become preeminent, Perikles became inaccessible. The biographer Plutarch records a change in Perikles' personality at this point; no longer the straightforward man of the people, Perikles adopted a formal style that Plutarch calls "aristocratic or even kingly." More than just indulging in arrogance, Perikles apparently was seeking to keep control of the people and to make himself impervious to bribery or undue influence. He became known for never accepting an invitation to dinner or to the drinking parties where rich men discussed politics. His cold, rational aloofness earned him the nickname "the Olympian" (as though he were a god of Mt. OLYMPUS).

His supremacy was severely tested by the revolt of the Delian League allies SAMOS and BYZANTIUM (440 B.C.E.). The defeat of Samos required a huge Athenian naval effort, and Perikles' generalship seems to have come in for some criticism on the Athenian comic stage. In 440 or 439 B.C.E. Perikles sponsored a law suspending the performance of all comedy for three years.

He endured an indirect political attack in around 438 B.C.E, when his friends Pheidias and ANAXAGORAS were charged with the crime of impiety. ASPASIA, Perikles' common-law wife, might have been a third defendant. Pheidias and Anaxagoras each departed from Athens at this time.

In the late 430s B.C.E., when hostilities with Sparta and CORINTH loomed, Perikles apparently saw war as inevitable, and refused to appease. It was undoubtedly he who advised the Athenians to make their fateful defense pact with CORCYRA (433 B.C.E.), which Corinth found so alarming, and he was likewise the author of the bellicose Megarian Decree (432 B.C.E.), directed against the nearby city of MEGARA.

When the Peloponnesian War broke out (431 B.C.E.), Perikles advised defense by land and offensive strikes by sea. With his faith in Athens's immense resources and fortifications, he convinced the rural citizens to evacuate their homes and contain themselves within the city walls, while the invading Spartans ravaged the countryside. This strategy backfired, however, when plague broke out among the Athenian refugees in their unsanitary encampments and swept the city (430 B.C.E.). At the same time, large Athenian expeditions failed to capture either Megara or (in a siege directed by Perikles himself) EPIDAURUS.

The angry Athenians voted to depose the 65-year-old Perikles from office and fine him a crushing 10 TALENTS. Relenting, they elected him as general for the following year. But in that year, 429 B.C.E., he died, probably of the plague.

Perikles had two sons by an Athenian wife, whom he divorced for Aspasia around 450 B.C.E. By a law of his own sponsoring, Perikles, being an Athenian citizen, could not legally marry Aspasia, who was an immigrant from MILETUS, but they lived together for 20 years until his death. Their son, named Perikles, was made an Athenian citizen by a special vote of the assembly, but he was one of the six Athenian generals executed by the people after the sea battle of Arginusae in 406 B.C.E.

See also FUNERAL CUSTOMS; KALLIAS; KLEON; KRATINUS; LAWS AND LAW COURTS; MARRIAGE; PROTAGORAS; RHETORIC; SOPHOKLES; THEATER; WARFARE, NAVAL; WOMEN.

Further reading: A. Andrews, "The Opposition to Perikles," *Journal of Hellenic Studies* 98 (1978): 1–16; Donald Kagen, *Pericles of Athens and the Birth of Democracy* (New York: Free Press, 1991); A. L. Boegehold, "Perikles' Citizenship Law of 451/0 B.C.," in *Athenian Identity and Civic Ideology,* edited by A. L. Boegehold and A. C. Scafuro (Baltimore: Johns Hopkins University Press, 1994), 57–66; Editors of Time-Life Books, *What Life Was Like at the Dawn of Democracy: Classical Athens 525–322 B.C.* (Alexandria, Va.: Time-Life Books, 1997); A. J. Podlecki, *Perikles and His Circle* (London: Routledge, 1998); B. S. Ridgway, "An Issue of Methodology. Anakreon, Perikles, Xanthippos," *American Journal of Archaeology* 102 (1998): 717–738.

perioikoi (perioeci) The Greek term *perioikoi* means dwellers around and describes certain second-class citizens in some Greek states. Perioikoi were typically freeborn and native; they had basic legal protections and obligations, such as military service, but were excluded by birth from taking part in government. By occupation, many were smallholding farmers.

This citizen class existed at ARGOS, CRETE, THESSALY, and elsewhere. But the perioikoi usually are spoken of in connection with SPARTA, where they were literally "dwellers around," inhabiting the foothills and secondary sites around the Eurotas River valley. The heart of this fertile plain was reserved for true Spartans—the Spartiatai. Together, Spartiates and perioeci constituted the united people known as Lakedaimonioi.

See also LACONIA; POLIS.

Further reading: A. Andrews, "Argive 'perioikoi,'" in *Owls to Athens. Essays on Classical Subjects Presented to Sir Kenneth Dover,* edited by E. M. Craik (New York: Oxford University Press, 1990), 171–178; J. Roy, "The Perioikoi of Elis," in *The Polis as an Urban Centre and as a Political Community. Symposium, August 29–31 1996,* edited by Mogens Herman Hansen (Copenhagen: Munksgaard, 1997), 282–320; N. M. Kennell, "From Perioikoi to Poleis. The Laconian Cities in the Late Hellenistic Period," in *Sparta. New Perspectives,* edited by S. Hodkinson and A. Powell (London: Duckworth, 1999), 189–210.

Peripatetic School *See* LYCEUM.

Persephone This Greek goddess was the queen of the Underworld and the wife of the god HADES. In MYTH, Persephone was identified with Kore, the daughter of the grain goddess, DEMETER. Modern writers, for the sake of thoroughness, sometimes refer to her as Kore-Persephone.

Persephone appears to have been the name of a pre-Greek, native goddess who was probably a judge and ruler among the spirits of the dead. When the Greeks first entered the Greek mainland around 2100 B.C.E., they amalgamated her into their own religion. Persephone, whose name is translatable as "destroyer" in Greek, was identified with the minor Greek goddess Kore ("maiden").

The Persephone, or Kore, of Greek myth was the daughter of Demeter and the great god ZEUS. Her most significant myth, first told by HESIOD (ca. 700 B.C.E.), tells how she was gathering flowers one day when her uncle, the god Hades, abducted her to become his queen in the Underworld. After searching frantically for her and causing the earth to become barren, the anxious Demeter appealed to Zeus. He ruled that Persephone should be returned to her mother on earth, but because she had eaten four seeds of a pomegranate while in the Underworld, she was required to spend four months of every year with her husband and eight months in the upper world. The Classical Greeks interpreted the goddess's double name as a sign of her dual nature: Kore the maiden on earth and the sterner Queen Persephone below. Neither Persephone nor Hades, however, was thought of as evil; death was seen as a natural part of the life-cycle.

By the 600s B.C.E., Persephone had also become part of the fringe cult called ORPHISM. This cult involved a complicated belief in reincarnation after death, believing that only by living successive lives (on earth as well as in the Underworld) could a person's soul achieve eternal bliss. Persephone, as the judge of the dead, directed each soul's sequence of transmigrations, according to how piously the person had lived each prior life.

Orphism became particularly popular among the Greeks of SICILY and southern ITALY. Consequently, Persephone became a major goddess of the Sicilian Greeks, and her myth became localized in Sicily. It was supposedly near the city of Henna (modern Enna) that Hades abducted Persephone, and supposedly volcanic Mt. Etna served as the hearth where Demeter lit two torches for searching by night. Such details obviously represent a later layer of the Persephone myth. The goddess was also adopted into the Roman pantheon, where she was called Proserpina.

In art, Persephone is frequently represented with a regal scepter and a small box. Other attributes include a torch or torches, a cornucopia, ears of corn, pomegranates, or a rooster (symbol of a new life as it signals a new day). Some of the most famous images of Persephone, including a fabulous 4th-century B.C.E. wall painting at the Macedonian site of Vergina, show her being carried away by Hades.

See also AFTERLIFE; ELEUSINIAN MYSTERIES.

Further reading: G. Kuntz, *Persephone: Three Essays on Religion and Thought in Magna Graecia* (Oxford: Clarendon Press, 1971); B. Lincoln, "The Rape of Persephone. A Greek Scenario of Women's Initiation," *Harvard Theological Review* 72 (1979): 223–235; N. Bookidis and R. Stroud, *Demeter and Persephone in Ancient Corinth* (Princeton, N.J.: American School of Classical Studies in Athens, 1987); Christine Downing, ed., *The Long Journey Home: Re-visioning the Myth of Demeter and Persephone for Our Time* (Boston: Shambhala, 1994); Ann Suter, *The Narcissus and the Pomegranate: An Archaeology of the Homeric Hymn to Demeter* (Ann Arbor: University of Michigan Press, 2002); Tamara Agha-Jaffar, *Demeter and Persephone: Lessons from a Myth* (Jefferson, N.C.: McFarland, 2002).

Perseus (1) In MYTH, Perseus was a hero of ARGOS and TIRYNS, and the slayer of the monster MEDUSA. The story of his birth is one of the most picturesque Greek legends. King Acrisius of Argos had a beautiful daughter, Danaë, but he was warned by a prophecy that he was destined to be killed by any son born to her. So he locked her in a tower or a bronze chamber in order to prevent anyone from approaching her. But the great god ZEUS came to her in the form of a shower of GOLD, and in due time she bore a son, whom she named Perseus (destroyer).

Acrisius, surprised to learn of these developments, put Danaë and Perseus to sea in a chest, which drifted south through the Aegean. Coming ashore at Seriphos, an island of the CYCLADES, mother and child were welcomed by the local king, Polydectes. There Perseus grew to manhood. Polydectes—intending to force Danaë to marry him, and wanting Perseus out of the way—sent the young man on a seemingly deadly mission: to go to the far West (or far South), find the three demon sisters known as the Gorgons, and bring back the head of the one called Medusa. The Gorgons were so hideous that merely looking at any one of them would cause a person to turn to stone. Undaunted, Perseus set off, with sword and shield.

On the advice of the goddess ATHENA, Perseus consulted the Graiai—three old sisters who had one eye and one tooth among them. Stealing their one eye until they would help him, Perseus received directions for finding the Gorgons' home. He also received from them a pair of winged flying shoes and a cap that would turn him invisible, as well as a pouch for carrying Medusa's severed head. Flying invisible to the land of the Gorgons, he sneaked up on Medusa with his face averted, guiding himself by watching her harmless reflection in his shield. Shearing off her head, he immediately hid it in his satchel, since even the head itself could turn people to stone. Perseus flew off, still invisible, evading Medusa's two sisters.

Perseus, wearing his cap of invisibility, cuts off the head of Medusa. *(Alison Frantz Photographic Collection, American School of Classical Studies at Athens)*

Soaring over the sea toward Seriphos, he then saved the Ethiopian princess Andromeda from a sea monster. (Andromeda's parents had planned to sacrifice her, to save their kingdom from the god POSEIDON's wrath.) Perseus killed the monster, married Andromeda, and resumed his journey by ship with her. At Seriphos, Perseus rescued his mother, using Medusa's head to turn Polydectes and his followers to stone. Then, leaving the island in the hands of Polydectes' righteous brother Dictys, Perseus returned with Andromeda to his native Argos.

The prophecy that Perseus would kill his grandfather Acrisius was fulfilled when the hero, throwing the discus in competition, inadvertently struck and killed Acrisius, who was sitting among the spectators. Leaving the throne of Argos to a kinsman, Perseus became the king of Tiryns and, according to one tradition, founded the nearby city of MYCENAE. One of his sons, Perses, supposedly became the father of the Asian people known as the Persians.

The Perseus tale may distortedly recall the political unification of the Argive plain in early Mycenaean times (ca. 1600 B.C.E.), as well as Mycenaean naval conquests in the Cyclades and beyond.

See also MYCENAEAN CIVILIZATION.

Further reading: E. Phinney Jr., "Perseus' Battle with the Gorgons," *Transactions of the American Philological Association* 102 (1971): 445–463; Jocelyn M. Woodward, *Perseus: A Study in Greek Art and Legend* (New York: AMS Press, 1976); J. H. Oakley, "Danae and Perseus on Seriphos," *American Journal of Archaeology* 86 (1982): 111–115; E. Pemberton, "A Late Corinthian Perseus from Ancient Corinth," *Hesperia* 52 (1983): 64–69; J. H. Oakley, "Perseus, the Graiai, and Aeschylus' 'Phorkides'," *American Journal of Archaeology* 92 (1988): 383–391.

Perseus (2) *See* MACEDON.

Persia The vast, rich, non-Greek kingdom of Persia played a crucial role in Greek history—largely as an antagonist, but also as an employer, overlord, or ally for many Greeks, especially those in ASIA MINOR. The Persian Empire reached its height around 500 B.C.E., at which time it stretched westward from the Indus Valley (modern Pakistan) to THRACE and MACEDON, on the northeastern border of Greece, with EGYPT also included. Encompassing about 1 million square miles, unified by a complex network of roads, and ruled by an absolute monarch, Persia was the greatest empire the world had ever seen.

The Persians originated as a nomadic, pastoral people in the western Iranian plateau. We know that by 850 B.C.E. they were calling themselves the Parsa and their territory (which shifted constantly) was known as Parsua. By the 600s B.C.E., the Persians had settled in the southwest Iranian plateau, bounded on the west by the Tigris River and on the south by the Persian Gulf; this region came to be their heartland. In these years, the Persians were subjects of the kindred Medes, another Iranian people. As vassals of the Medes, the Persian kings reigned out of their provincial capital at Susa, near the head of the Persian Gulf.

In 549 B.C.E., the Persian king CYRUS (1) led a revolt against the Median overlords. The Persians captured the Median capital and imposed a new dynasty—a Persian one. Henceforth the Persians were the ruling class; the Medes became their subordinates, although still partners in the empire.

Cyrus's conquest of western Asia Minor in 546 B.C.E. brought the Persians into contact with the Greeks in the cities of IONIA. The Persians made plans to conquer mainland Greece under King DARIUS (1) in the early fifth century B.C.E. but, amazingly, were defeated by the relatively puny Greek states. This conflict, known as the PERSIAN WARS, refers primarily to the invasions in 490 and 480–479 B.C.E.

The vast size of the Persian Empire eventually proved to be its undoing, as the delegation of power to local governors gradually weakened the king's central authority. When the Macedonian king ALEXANDER THE GREAT invaded the Persian Empire in 334 B.C.E. with a mere 37,000 soldiers, he encountered a disunified realm under a weak monarch, ripe for destruction. By the time of Alexander's death (323 B.C.E.), Persia was ruled as a Greek-Macedonian kingdom, eventually known as the SELEUCID EMPIRE. The Iranian cultures of the central plateau, however, continued to thrive and reclaimed power by the second century B.C.E.

See also AGESILAUS; CAVALRY; CYPRUS (1); DARIUS (1); DELIAN LEAGUE; HERODOTUS; KALLIAS; KING'S PEACE; XENOPHON.

Further reading: J. M. Cook, *The Persian Empire* (New York: Schocken Books, 1983); John Boardman, ed., *Persia, Greece, and the Western Mediterranean, c. 525 to 479 B.C.*, 2d ed. (New York: Cambridge University Press, 1988); John Sharwood Smith, *Greece and the Persians* (Bristol, U.K.: Bristol Classical Press, 1990); Jack M. Balcer, *A Prosopographical Study of the Ancient Persians Royal and Noble, c. 550–450 B.C.* (Lewiston, N.Y.: Edwin Mellen Press, 1993); Josef Wiesehöfer, *Ancient Persia: From 550 BC to 650 AD*, translated by Azizeh Azodi (London: I. B. Tauris, 1996); John Curtis, *Ancient Persia*, 2d ed. (London: British Museum Publications, 2000); Pierre Briant, *From Cyrus to Alexander: A History of the Persian Empire*, translated by Peter T. Daniels (Winona Lake, Ind.: Eisenbrauns, 2002).

Persian Wars   Although the Greeks and Persians were in intermittent conflict for over 200 years, the term *Persian Wars* refers mainly to the campaigns of 490 and 480–479 B.C.E., in which the Greeks successfully defended mainland Greece against two Persian invasions. These were the famous campaigns of MARATHON, THERMOPYLAE, and SALAMIS (1).

The Persian Wars were immensely important for Western civilization. The Greeks, a relatively small and disunified nation, unexpectedly defeated the greatest empire on earth. Afterward, this experience compelled the Greeks to identify themselves culturally. The world's first real historian, the Greek HERODOTUS, writing in the mid-400s B.C.E., chose the Persian Wars as his story to tell; it was the greatest understandable event in human memory, and it distinguished the Greek from the "barbarian." Similarly, the amazing Athenian cultural achievements of the 400s and 300s B.C.E.—in THEATER, PHILOSOPHY, SCULPTURE, ARCHITECTURE, and the development of DEMOCRACY—were products of a confidence or arrogance adopted because of the Persian Wars. Had the invading Persians won and had Greece become just another province of their empire, there would have been no brilliant Athenian century to serve as the foundation of modern culture.

The first stage of the conflict was the Persians' westward push into ASIA MINOR in the mid-500s B.C.E., when the Persian king CYRUS (1) conquered the east Greek region known as IONIA. Cyrus and his successors ruled moderately but demanded tribute, labor, and military service from their Greek subjects, governing them by means of Greek puppet rulers.

In 513 B.C.E. the Persian king DARIUS (1) led an army across the BOSPORUS and received the submission of THRACE and MACEDON. Southwest of Macedon, the land of Greece itself was still free, but for how long? It seemed obvious that the Persians would attack eventually, and equally obvious—to many—that Greece would fall. Certain Greeks began making friendly overtures to their expected overlords. A new verb appeared in the Greek language: Mēdizein, "to Medize," or to collaborate with the Medes (i.e., with the Persians). Among the most egregious Medizers were those local Greek despots known as TYRANTS (*tyrannoi*), who hoped to retain power and become the Persians' puppets after the conquest. Another Medizing force was the priesthood of the god APOLLO at DELPHI. The Persian kings had traditionally sent gifts to Delphi in order to develop contacts inside Greece; apparently the priesthood now decided that a Persian conquest would be to their god's advantage. During the Persian Wars, therefore, the Delphic oracle consistently gave advice that was defeatist in tone.

The IONIAN REVOLT of 499–493 B.C.E. saw the Greek cities of Asia Minor rise up, ill-fatedly, against their Persian masters. Before being crushed, the revolt attracted help from two cities of mainland Greece: ATHENS and ERETRIA. This intervention backfired, convincing the Persians to subdue Greece immediately. Soon Persian heralds appeared in the cities and islands of Greece, demanding the tokens of earth and water that were the formal symbols of submission to the Persian king. Many frightened Greek states obeyed, but the Athenians, in a violation of diplomatic sacrosanctity, threw the Persian envoys into the condemned criminals' pit. At SPARTA the envoys were thrown down a well, where (they were told) there was plenty of earth and water. Thus did the militaristic state of Sparta, with the best army in Greece, signal its intention to stand alongside Athens, against Persia.

Darius had at his court an Athenian adviser, HIPPIAS (1), the former tyrant of Athens who had been expelled in 510 B.C.E. Darius resolved to capture Athens and install the aged Hippias as his puppet. In the summer of 490 B.C.E. a Persian seaborne expedition crossed the AEGEAN SEA, landed at Eretria, destroyed that city, and sailed south to the coastal town of Marathon, about 26 miles from Athens. There a Persian army of perhaps 20,000 troops disembarked; with them was Hippias. But at the Battle of Marathon the attackers were totally defeated by 9,000 Athenians and a few hundred Plataeans, in a plan devised by the general MILTIADES.

After Darius's death, his son and successor, XERXES, decided to invade Greece in full force. He gathered a massive army, perhaps 300,000 land troops, including subject peoples as well as Persian regulars. His navy, numbering perhaps 600 warships, was drawn from seafaring provinces such as PHOENICIA, EGYPT, and Greek Ionia. Other preparations included spanning of the HELLESPONT with twin bridges of boats, a marvel of Persian engineering skill.

Preparations were under way on the Greek side as well. At Athens the brilliant statesman and general THEMISTOKLES convinced the democratic ASSEMBLY to vote to build 100 new trireme warships, thereby giving Athens about 180 ships in all—the biggest navy of any Greek city. Themistokles foresaw that the defense of Greece would depend on fighting at sea. The Persians' land army was too vast to destroy; but cripple their navy, and the army would founder—from lack of transport, supply, and communication. With a large fleet, Athens could be protected or, if need be, evacuated.

The uneasy alliance of Greek states, dominated by the land power Sparta, mapped out a grand strategy. The terrain and shoreline of Greece naturally compel a southward-moving invader through a series of bottlenecks on land and sea, and the Greek plan was basically to fight at certain defensible bottlenecks—a mountain pass, a sea channel—where the invader's advantage of superior numbers would be canceled. On land, the Greeks would avoid battle in the open plains, where the mighty Persian CAVALRY would rule. Similarly, for a sea fight, a narrow channel would tend to offset the superior seamanship of the Persians' elite contingent, the Phoenicians.

One advantage for the Greeks, of which they were not yet fully aware, was that their HOPLITE heavy infantryman was better than the Persian counterpart—not in courage, but in equipment and training. The hoplite wore a BRONZE breastplate and helmet, and carried a bronze-plated shield and a thrusting spear up to eight feet long; the Persian trooper wore less armor and carried a shorter spear and a shield made only of wickerwork. In the crush of battle, the hoplites usually could push through. But hoplites were not invincible, and the Persians had the greatest advantage in numbers.

Led by Xerxes, the Persians crossed the Hellespont and descended through Thrace and Macedon (spring of 480 B.C.E.). A Greek army marched to the mountain gorge of Tempe, in northern THESSALY, but then abandoned the site as being too far forward, in hostile territory. Thessaly submitted to the Persians, and the Greeks drew up a line of defense on Thessaly's southern frontier, at two interrelated sites: the mountain pass of Thermopylae and the six-mile-wide sea channel at ARTEMISION, on the northern shore of EUBOEA.

Simultaneous battles were fought on land and sea. The Battle of Thermopylae was a heroic Greek blunder; an army under the Spartan king Leonidas held the pass for three days but never received reinforcements, and was overrun. More creditable was the sea fight at Artemision, where about 370 Greek warships met an enemy fleet that had been badly reduced—perhaps to 450 ships, from 600—by recent storms. The battle was a marginal Persian

victory, but it showed the Greeks what they could do against the much-vaunted Phoenician crews, and it apparently encouraged the Greek admirals in their strategy of relying on narrow waterways to offset the enemy's advantages.

The defenders retreated south through central Greece. BOEOTIA submitted to the invaders and, like Thessaly, was forced to supply troops to fight against their fellow Greeks. In a dramatic decision, the Athenians voted to evacuate their city to the enemy: They would not stay and surrender. The noncombatants were transported to safe locales nearby, and the Athenian troops and warships remained on duty in the Greek forces. Athens was occupied and sacked by the Persians.

The summer was ending. Certain Greek commanders wanted to retreat farther south, to the naturally defensible Isthmus of CORINTH, but Themistokles and the Spartan commanding admiral, Eurybiades, pressed to offer battle at sea, in the one-mile-wide channel east of the island of Salamis, in the Saronic Gulf. There the Greek fleet stationed itself. Although Xerxes could have chosen to bypass, he overconfidently ordered his navy to attack the Greeks inside the channel, and the result was a complete Greek victory at the Battle of Salamis.

Suddenly the tables had turned. With his armada now in tatters, Xerxes was in danger of being trapped in Europe. Taking much of his army, he hurried back to the Hellespont before the Greek navy could arrive to sever the bridges there. Meanwhile, his able general Mardonius stayed in Greece with a force of perhaps 60,000.

Mardonius wintered in Thessaly and marched south again in the spring of 479 B.C.E.; his army was supplemented by collaborationist Greek troops from Thessaly and Boeotia. Athens, still evacuated, was reoccupied and burned. Mardonius reached the northeastern outskirts of MEGARA (1), the Persian high-water mark in Europe, but on news of an approaching Greek force he withdrew toward THEBES, the main Boeotian city, which was friendly to the Persians. The Greek army—nearly 39,000 Spartan, Peloponnesian, and Athenian hoplites, commanded by the Spartan general Pausanias—approached the town of PLATAEA in the late summer. Pausanias declined to attack, probably fearing what Mardonius's cavalry could do on the Boeotian plain. After almost two weeks of waiting—while both armies were plagued by a shortage of food and water—Mardonius launched a surprise attack. He was killed and his army destroyed at the Battle of Plataea.

Historians debate whether it was Salamis or Plataea that saved Greece from Persian conquest. Probably the Persians' invasion was doomed once they had lost most of their fleet at Salamis. Greece, a mountainous country, does not lend itself to being conquered by a strictly land-bound army. Had the Persians won at Plataea, they would probably have lost the war anyway. The Greeks would have retreated south to the isthmus, to beat them there.

That same year, 479 B.C.E., saw the Greek counteroffensive begin. Supposedly on the same day as the Battle of Plataea, an amphibious Greek force under the Spartan king Leotychides landed at Cape MYCALĒ in western Asia Minor; the Greeks beat a Persian army and burned the remaining Persian fleet. Ionia had been liberated; over 90 years would pass before the Persians could reclaim it. By winter an Athenian fleet under the general XANTHIPPUS had captured the Hellespont after destroying the Persian garrison at SESTOS. In 478 B.C.E. the Spartan Pausanias took BYZANTIUM and the Bosporus. There the Spartans dropped out of the counteroffensive, but the Athenians—calculatedly building an empire—carried on their liberation of the east Greeks in Asia Minor and CYPRUS.

Around 449 B.C.E., Persia negotiated a peace treaty with Athens, and hostilities ceased. But the Persian kings continued to scheme for the recovery of their lost territory of Ionia. As the patriotic Greek alliances of 480 B.C.E. dissolve into the PELOPONNESIAN WAR (431–404 B.C.E.) and CORINTHIAN WAR (395–386 B.C.E.), Persia eventually began to help Sparta in exchange for a free hand in Ionia. It took ALEXANDER THE GREAT, with his dismantling of the Persian Empire in 334–323 B.C.E., finally to make peace between Persia and the Greeks.

See also DELIAN LEAGUE; KALLIAS; KIMON; KING'S PEACE; WARFARE, LAND; WARFARE, NAVAL.

Further reading: Jack M. Balcer, "The Persian Wars against Greece. A Reassessment," *Historia* 38 (1989): 127–143; J. F. Lazenby, *The Defence of Greece, 490–479 B.C.* (Warminster, England: Aris & Phillips, 1993); Jack M. Balcer, *The Persian Conquest of the Greeks, 545–450 B.C.* (Konstanz, Germany: Universitätsverlag Konstanz, 1995); Philip de Souza, *The Greek and Persian Wars, 499–386 B.C.* (New York: Routledge, 2003).

Phaedra *See* HIPPOLYTUS; THESEUS.

Phaethon *See* HELIOS.

phalanx The noun *phalanx* refers to a battle formation of heavy infantry and is used by ancient Greek writers from HOMER (ca. 750 B.C.E.) onward. Modern scholars usually reserve the word to describe the distinctive battle order of the Macedonian and Hellenistic heavy infantry (mid-300s to mid-100s B.C.E.). These soldiers employed equipment and tactics invented by the Macedonian king PHILIP II (around 357 B.C.E.) and perfected by his son ALEXANDER THE GREAT. In several battles of the latter 300s B.C.E., the Macedonian phalanx proved itself superior to the classic HOPLITE armies of the Greek city-states.

Designed as an improvement on hoplite tactics, the Macedonian phalanx consisted of about 9,000 men arranged in orderly rows, one behind the other, up to 16 in number, with several hundred men in each row. Every man carried a 13- to 14-foot-long pike, called a *sarissa*.

When the first five rows presented their sarissas forward, a hedge of metal pike-points was formed, extending in serried rows to about 10 feet ahead. As the phalanx moved forward, these points pushed toward the enemy with great force. Behind the first five rows, the soldiers kept their sarissas upright, waiting to move forward as their comrades in front fell.

Because hoplites and other heavy infantrymen of the day were armed only with six- to eight-foot-long jabbing spears, the phalanx enjoyed an advantage in reach and in density of offered weapons; the enemy formation could present its spears only from a depth of two or three rows. Also, the rows of the phalanx tended not to crush together as tightly as did rows of hoplites or other troops, and this made combat somewhat less exhausting for men in the phalanx.

Because the sarissa needed to be held with two hands, the man's shield was strapped to his left forearm or shoulder, without engaging the hand. This shield was necessarily smaller than the kind carried by Greek hoplites. In general, Macedonian soldiers seem to have worn less armor than their hoplite counterparts, using leather or cloth for helmets and corsets, in place of BRONZE. While this allowed the phalanx men greater maneuverability and endurance (and less expense for equipment), it also left them vulnerable to archers and javelin men, who might easily stay out of reach. Another weaknesses of the phalanx (one shared by the hoplite formation) was its unshielded right flank and rear.

The proper use of the phalanx involved coordination with CAVALRY and light-armed infantry to guard the flanks and chase away enemy projectile troops. In combat, the phalanx's natural function was defensive—to hold the enemy's charge and damage his formation, while the cavalry looked for a weak point to attack.

The Hellenistic kingdoms of the 200s and 100s B.C.E. continued the legacy of Macedonian-style warfare, but the phalanx became enlarged to such unwieldy sizes as 20,000 men. The wars of ROME against MACEDON and the SELEUCID EMPIRE saw the phalanx beaten repeatedly—at Cynocephalae (197 B.C.E.), at Magnesia (186 B.C.E.), and at Pydna (167 B.C.E.)—by the newly developed Roman legions. The legions of the Roman army were successful against the Greek phalanx due to their increased flexibility and maneuverability. The Roman legion was divided into numerous subsections, each of which could operate independently if an opportunity arose to take advantage of a gap in the opposing phalanx. Also, in contrast to the phalanx which required all of its troops to engage together at the start of a battle, the Roman legion was composed of several battle lines that could act as reserves for the troops in front of them, if necessary. These adjustments in organization and strategy contributed to the immense success of the Roman military machine from the first century B.C.E. onward.

See also CHAIRONEIA; HELLENISTIC AGE; PHILIP V; WARFARE, LAND.

Further reading: Hans vans Wees, "The Homeric Way of War. The 'Iliad' and the Hoplite Phalanx, 1," *Greece and Rome* 41 (1994): 1–18; ———, "The Homeric Way of War. The 'Iliad' and the Hoplite Phalanx, 2," *Greece and Rome* 41 (1994): 131–155; Victor Davis Hanson, "From Phalanx to Legion 350–250 BC," in *The Cambridge Illustrated History of Warfare: The Triumph of the West,* edited by Geoffrey Parker (New York: Cambridge University Press, 1995), 32–49; Antonio Santosuosso, *Soldiers, Citizens, and the Symbols of War: From Classical Greece to Republican Rome, 500–167 B.C.* (Boulder, Colo.: Westview Press, 1997); R. H. Storch, "The Archaic Greek Phalanx, 750–650 B.C.," *Ancient History Bulletin* 12 (1998): 1–7; Hans van Wees, "The Development of the Hoplite Phalanx: Iconography and Reality in the Seventh Century," in *War and Violence in Ancient Greece,* edited by Hans van Wees (London: Duckworth and the Classical Press of Wales, 2000), 125–166.

Pheidias (ca. 490–425 B.C.E.) *Athenian sculptor*

Pheidias's masterpiece was the colossal GOLD-and-ivory cult statue of the god ZEUS, constructed around 430 B.C.E. for Zeus's temple at OLYMPIA and considered one of the SEVEN WONDERS OF THE WORLD for its size and solemn majesty. Today, however, Pheidias is best remembered for his work on the Athenian PARTHENON and for the prestige he achieved as an associate of the Athenian statesman PERIKLES.

Pheidias was the son of a man called Charmides (an Athenian aristocratic name that also crops up in the family of PLATO). The family was probably affluent enough that the young Pheidias was free to pursue his art. His genius encompassed not only SCULPTURE but also PAINTING, engraving, and metalworking.

One of Pheidias's early works (ca. 456 B.C.E.) was a 30-foot-high BRONZE statue of the armored Athena Promachos (the Defender), which stood among the outdoor statues on the Athenian ACROPOLIS. The gleam from the point of the goddess' upright spear was said to be visible to ships as far as 15 miles away. Another early work was Pheidias's bronze statue known as the Lemnian Athena, commissioned by inhabitants of the island of Lemnos (probably Athenian colonists were recent settlers there). This work's grace and dignity were much admired in ancient times.

In about 448 B.C.E., Pheidias was chosen as the artistic director of the public-building program organized by Perikles to commemorate the end of the PERSIAN WARS. It was in this job that Pheidias oversaw the building of the Parthenon and the execution of the temple's famous architectural sculptures. We do not know whether Pheidias himself carved any of these. But he did sculpt one central work, the 35-foot-high gold-and-ivory cult statue of the goddess ATHENA that stood inside the Parthenon.

The Parthenon statue was completed by about 438 B.C.E., but soon Pheidias had to pay for his success, as criminal charges were brought against him by politicians hoping to discredit his friend Perikles. Pheidias was accused of having stolen some of the gold entrusted to him for the statue's construction. This charge was disproved when the gold plates—which Pheidias had constructed as detachable—were taken off the statue and weighed.

A second accusation, of impiety was even more damaging. Pheidias had incurred this charge by supposedly including likenesses of himself and his patron Perikles amid the relief figures on the shield of Athena. There, in a battle scene of Greeks versus AMAZONS, Pheidias was said to have portrayed himself as a bald old man hurling a rock and Perikles as a warrior about to spear an Amazon.

Perhaps as a result of his legal troubles, Pheidias left Athens soon after the Parthenon Athena was in place. (A later legend, claiming that he died in an Athenian prison, is untrue.) Around this time he won the prestigious commission to sculpt his second giant gold-and-ivory statue, at Olympia. The Olympian cult statue of Zeus was arguably the most important religious statue of the Greek world.

Further reading: J. A. K. E. de Waele, "Wondering about a World Wonder. Phidias' Work in Olympia," *Kodaibunka* 46 (1994): 15–28; A. Corso, "Competition between Myron, Pheidias, and Polykleitos," *Numismatica e antichità classiche* 24 (1995): 173–188; Evelyn B. Harrison, "Pheidias," in *Personal Styles in Greek Sculpture,* edited by Olga Palagia and J. J. Pollitt (New York: Cambridge University Press, 1996), 16–65; Nigel Spivey, *Understanding Greek Sculpture: Ancient Meanings, Modern Readings* (New York: Thames and Hudson, 1997); B. Lundgreen, "A Methodological Enquiry. The Great Bronze Athena by Pheidias," *Journal of Hellenic Studies* 117 (1997): 190–197; Kenneth D. S. Lapatin, *Chryselephantine Statuary in the Ancient Mediterranean World* (New York: Oxford University Press, 2001).

Pheidon (600s B.C.E.) *Powerful king of ARGOS who probably reigned ca. 675–655 B.C.E.*

Pheidon brought his city to a brief preeminence at the expense of its perennial enemy, SPARTA. With his army, Pheidon seized the sacred site of OLYMPIA and personally took over management of the OLYMPIC GAMES—"the most arrogant thing ever done by a Greek," according to the ancient Greek historian HERODOTUS. Probably after this coup, Pheidon introduced a uniform system of weights and measures throughout the PELOPONNESE (a step meant to extend Argive control over TRADE).

The philosopher ARISTOTLE, in his treatise *Politics,* written around 340 B.C.E., states that Pheidon began as a king and ended as a tyrant (Greek: *tyrannos*). This means not that Pheidon's rule grew more harsh but that, after coming to the Argive throne by legal succession, he seized absolute power, probably at the expense of the city's aristocrats and with the support of the middle class. As such he anticipated the first wave of Greek TYRANTS, who began taking power violently at CORINTH, SIKYON, and other cities in the mid-600s B.C.E.

It was almost certainly under Pheidon that the Argives reorganized their army for HOPLITE tactics and became the best soldiers in Greece. In 669 B.C.E. an Argive army soundly defeated a Spartan army at the Battle of Hysiae, in the eastern Peloponnese. According to the most plausible modern explanation, this battle marked the triumph of Argive hoplites over an enemy still using the older, disorganized tactics. It may have been in the following year that Pheidon marched his army across the Peloponnese to Olympia.

See also WARFARE, LAND.

Further reading: Donald Kagen, "Pheidon's Aeginetan Coinage," *Transactions of the American Philological Association* 91 (1960): 121–136; Z. Rubinson, "Pheidon of Argos. Military Reformer or Capitalist?" *Rendiconti. Instituto Lombardo* 105 (1971: 636–642; Carol G. Thomas, "Pheidon (c. 600 B.C.), King of Argos," in *Great Leaders, Great Tyrants?: Contemporary Views of World Rulers Who Made History,* edited by Arnold Blumberg (Westport, Conn.: Greenwood Press, 1995), 242–247.

Philemon   *See* THEATER.

Philip II (ca. 382–336 B.C.E.) *Macedonian king who reigned 359–336 B.C.E. and fell to an assassin's knife at about age 46*
A brilliant soldier and diplomat, Philip took his backward Greek kingdom of MACEDON and turned it into the mightiest nation in the Greek world. His creation of a new-style army and his subjugation of mainland Greece both proved essential for the subsequent career of his son, ALEXANDER THE GREAT. Although he did not live to see Alexander's conquest of the Persian Empire (334–323 B.C.E.), Philip made it possible.

In the absence of better surviving sources, our knowledge of Philip comes mostly from book 16 of the *World History* of DIODORUS SICULUS, a later Greek writer (ca. 60–30 B.C.E.) prone to distortion. However, the following narrative seems plausible. Philip (Philippos, "horse lover") was the youngest son of the Macedonian king Amyntas. As a hostage for three years at the powerful city of THEBES, in central Greece, the teenage Philip probably had contact with the great Theban leader EPAMINONDAS. Another model that may have inspired the young Philip was the dynasty of rulers at Pherai, in the northern Greek region called THESSALY. In 359 B.C.E. Philip's brother Perdiccas, king of Macedon, was killed in battle. Philip, then about 23, became king.

Soon he began his military reforms, which were destined to change ancient warfare. Previously, the Macedonian army had consisted of a capable, aristocratic CAVALRY alongside a ragamuffin light infantry of peasant levies. With training and new equipment, Philip created an expert heavy infantry, armed with 13- to 14-foot-long pikes, fighting in the formation known as the PHALANX. Philip also pioneered new tactics of siege warfare, daring to storm fortified sites in direct attacks using siege-towers and arrow-shooting catapults. Among his other accomplishments, Philip was the most successful besieger of his day.

His early imperialism involved two strategies: the subjugation of Macedon's warlike, non-Greek neighbors, the Thracians and Illyrians; and the seizure of Greek cities of the north Aegean coast, to provide revenue and shipping outlets. Philip's rival for possession of this seacoast was the distant city of ATHENS, with its mighty navy.

In 357 B.C.E., the second year of his reign, Philip captured the north Aegean city of AMPHIPOLIS, a former Athenian colony located near the GOLD- and SILVER-mining region of Mt. Pangaeus. The Athenians declared war, but hostilities trailed off amid Athenian reluctance to commit land troops so far from home (a recurring factor that worked to Philip's advantage during the next two decades). Meanwhile the Pangaeus mines provided Philip with an enormous yearly sum of 1,000 TALENTS.

Another foreign policy success of 357 B.C.E. was Philip's MARRIAGE to Olympias, a young noblewoman from the northwestern Greek region called EPIRUS. For 20 years Olympias was the foremost of Philip's multiple wives. (Eventually he had seven.) Although the royal marriage proved unhappy, it produced a son and a daughter; the boy, born in 356 B.C.E., was Alexander.

By involving himself in the Third Sacred War against the central Greek state of PHOCIS (35–346 B.C.E.), Philip began to influence affairs in Greece. Soon he dominated the leadership of Thessaly and made an alliance with formidable Thebes. Amid these events, Philip lost an eye when he was hit by an arrow during his siege of the rebellious Macedonian city of Methone (354 B.C.E.)

In 349 B.C.E. Philip moved to devour the Greek cities of the north Aegean region known as CHALCIDICE. He besieged the Chalcidic capital, OLYNTHOS, whose inhabitants appealed for help to Athens. The Athenians again declared war on Philip but again declined to send troops, despite the fiery oratory of the Athenian statesman DEMOSTHENES (1). Captured by Philip, Olynthos was leveled to the ground.

The year 346 B.C.E. saw Philip preparing to conquer mainland Greece. As was typical of his style, he first made peace with Athens. When the Third Sacred War finally ended in Phocis's defeat, Philip marched his Macedonians unchallenged through THERMOPYLAE and into Phocis. At meetings of the influential AMPHICTYONIC LEAGUE, at DELPHI, Philip was admitted in place of the

Phocian delegates and was personally awarded the two votes previously controlled by the Phocian people. Through influence, he also controlled the votes of the Thessalian delegates and others. King of Macedon, overlord of Thessaly, master of Phocis, and boss of Delphi—he was by now the most powerful man in Greece.

It was in this year that the Athenian orator ISOKRATES published his pamphlet *Philip*, urging the Macedonian king to liberate the Greek cities of ASIA MINOR from Persian rule. No doubt Philip welcomed the propaganda value of this romantic plea, but he also took the idea to heart. In his way, Philip was a lover of Greek culture. He may have sincerely wished to lead a united Greece against its traditional enemy, PERSIA.

The idea of conquest also held a strong financial appeal for Philip, who was running out of money, despite his Mt. Pangaeus revenues. His ceaseless military campaigning and frequent resort to bribery had taken a heavy financial toll. Only the booty of a rich conquest could save him from bankruptcy and downfall.

Meanwhile his Greek enemies organized against him, with funding from the alarmed Persian king, Artaxerxes III. Supported by the Athenian navy, the northeastern Greek colonies of BYZANTIUM and Perinthus held out against Philip's siege (340 B.C.E.). Then his erstwhile Greek ally Thebes turned against him, ejecting his garrison from Thermopylae (338 B.C.E.).

Philip invaded central Greece in the spring of 338 B.C.E. Bypassing the Theban garrison at Thermopylae, he marched through Phocis toward Thebes. In response, Athens and Thebes, although traditional enemies, patched together a hasty alliance and faced Philip's advancing army at the Battle of CHAIRONEIA, northwest of Thebes.

The battle was a complete Macedonian victory, and Thebes and Athens surrendered. Philip treated Athens leniently but Thebes harshly, staging executions and selling war prisoners as SLAVES. After 20 years of scheming, he had conquered Greece in one campaign.

Almost immediately, Philip began preparations for an invasion of Persian-held Asia Minor, for which his trusted general Parmenion secured a crossing of the HELLESPONT (337 B.C.E.). But in 336 B.C.E. Philip was assassinated at the old Macedonian royal city of Aegai (modern Vergina), on the morning of his daughter's wedding. The killer, an aggrieved Macedonian noble, probably acted at the instigation of Olympias (whom Philip had recently divorced) and the 20-year-old Alexander. Philip's new number-one wife had recently borne Philip a son, and no doubt Olympias feared this threat to Alexander's succession to the throne. The young wife and child were later murdered on Olympias's orders. Alexander, acclaimed as king, took up Philip's invasion plan and crossed to Asia Minor in 334 B.C.E.

In 1977–1980 C.E. archaeological excavations at Vergina uncovered two tombs dating from the 300s B.C.E.

that were filled with treasure. The cremated remains in the tombs are thought to be those of Alexander's father and son (Alexander IV, who was murdered at age 13, in 310 B.C.E.). The skull believed to be Philip's apparently shows signs of an injured right eye socket—the wound from an arrow at the siege of Methone.

See also ARCHAEOLOGY; ILLYRIS; THRACE; WARFARE, LAND; WARFARE, SIEGE.

Further reading: W. Lindsay Adams and Eugene N. Borza, eds., *Philip II, Alexander the Great, and the Macedonian Heritage* (Washington, D.C.: University Press of America, 1982); John Bunkler, *Philip II and the Sacred War* (Leiden, Netherlands: E. J. Brill, 1989); N. Sawada, "Philip II's Policy toward Greece. A Reconsideration of the Peace of Philocrates," *Kodai. Journal of Ancient History* 4 (1993): 21–50; A. J. N. W. Prag, "Reconstructing King Philip II. The Nice Version," *American Journal of Archaeology* 94 (1990): 237–247; Elin C. Danien, ed., *The World of Philip and Alexander: A Symposium on Greek Life and Times* (Philadelphia: University Museum of Archaeology and Anthropology, University of Pennsylvania, 1990); James R. Ashley, *The Macedonian Empire: The Era of Warfare under Philip II and Alexander the Great, 359–323 B.C.* (Jefferson, N.C.: McFarland, 1998).

Philip V (238–179 B.C.E.) *Last great king of* MACEDON *(reigned 221–179 B.C.E.)*
Seeking to enlarge Macedon's traditional control over mainland Greece, Philip came to grief against a rival contender—the Italian city of ROME.

Philip ascended the Macedonian throne at age 17, on the death of his grandfather, Antigonus III. During the so-called Social War against the powerful Aetolian League in Greece, Philip led an army into the heart of enemy AETOLIA and sacked its capital, Thermon (218 B.C.E.). Faced with Roman domination of the nearby Illyrian coast, Philip in 215 B.C.E. made an anti-Roman alliance with the North African city of CARTHAGE (whose brilliant general Hannibal seemed on the verge of capturing Rome in the Second Punic War).

The Carthaginian alliance proved to be a disastrous decision. The Romans, despite their troubles with Hannibal, declared war on Philip and dispatched a fleet and land troops to Greece. This First Macedonian War (214–205 B.C.E.) saw Philip campaigning in Greece against an alliance of Romans and Aetolians. Hostilities ended in a treaty. A few years later, however, after defeating Carthage (201 B.C.E.), the Romans lent a ready ear to reports from their Greek allies PERGAMON and RHODES, complaining of Philip's naval aggression in the eastern Mediterranean.

Again the Roman senate declared war on Philip. The Second Macedonian War (200–197 B.C.E.) culminated in Philip's defeat by a Roman-Aetolian army at the Battle of Cynocephalae ("dog heads," a hill in THESSALY). At the battle, the Roman general Titus Quinctius Flamininus managed to send his troops around the flank of the

Macedonian PHALANX, to destroy it from behind. Cyno-cephalae marked the end of an independent Macedon; more significantly, it marked the end of the military era of the phalanx.

Philip was compelled to pay the Romans a huge cash penalty, hand over his son Demetrius as a hostage, and withdraw his troops forever from mainland Greece, which was declared by the Romans to be free of foreign taxation and interference. Philip became Rome's ally; his life's last decade was spent repairing Macedon's finances and warring against non-Greek peoples in the Balkans. Philip died on a military campaign and was succeeded by his son Perseus, Macedon's last king.

See also ILLYRIS; WARFARE, LAND.

Further reading: F. W. Walbank, *Philip V of Macedon* (Hamden, Conn.: Archon Books, 1967, 1940); E. S. Gruen, "The Last Years of Philip V," *Greek, Roman, and Byzantine Studies* 15 (1974): 221–246; D. Mendels, "Polybius, Philip V, and the Socio-Economic Question in Greece," *Ancient Society* 8 (1977): 155–174; E. S. Gruen, "Philip V and the Greek Demos," in *Ancient Macedonian Studies in Honor of Charles F. Edson* (Thessaloníki: Institute for Balkan Studies, 1981), 161–182; W. E. Thompson, "Philip V's Peloponnesian Campaigns in the Social War," *Rheinisches Museum für Philologie* 132 (1989): 141–148; A. Meadows, "Four Rhodian Decrees. Rhodes, Iasos, and Philip V," *Chiron* 26 (1996): 251–266.

Philoktetes This mythical hero of the TROJAN WAR was an expert archer from Central Greece. Philoktetes' name means "lover of possessions," and he led five ships in the allied Greek expedition against TROY. En route he went ashore on Lemnos or another Aegean island and was bitten on the foot by a serpent. The wound was agonizing, foul-smelling, and incurable, and so the Greeks—on ODYSSEUS's advice—abandoned Philoktetes on Lemnos. There he languished, neither dying nor recovering. He lived by hunting, using the unerring bow and arrows that had once belonged to the hero HERAKLES (and that had been bequeathed by Herakles to Philoktetes' father, Poeas).

Nearly 10 years went by. As the Greek siege of Troy became stalled, the Greeks learned of a prophecy that said the city could be captured only with the aid of Herakles' bow and arrows. Consequently two Greek leaders—in most versions, Odysseus and DIOMEDES—sailed to Lemnos and brought Philoktetes and the charmed weapons to the siege of Troy. There, at the Greek camp, Philoktetes was healed by the physician sons of ASKLEPIOS, Machaon and Podalirius. Taking to the field with Herakles' bow, Philoktetes killed the Trojan prince PARIS in an archery duel. After Troy's fall, Philoktetes survived the homeward voyage that claimed the lives of many other Greeks. He was said to have traveled to the West to establish Greek cities in eastern SICILY and southern ITALY.

The Athenian tragedian SOPHOKLES wrote a *Philoktetes* (performed in 409 B.C.E.), which survives today. In presenting the tale of the wounded hero on Lemnos, the play investigates the question of private wishes versus public duty. In Sophokles' version, the two arriving Greek captains are Odysseus and NEOPTOLEMOS (ACHILLES' son). Philoktetes loathes Odysseus as the one responsible for his being abandoned; but finally the honest, young Neoptolemos, with help from the gods, persuades Philoktetes to accompany them to the war to fulfill his destiny.

See also FATE.

Further reading: Joe Park Poe, *Heroism and Divine Justice in Sophokles' Philoctetes* (Leiden, Netherlands: E. J. Brill, 1974); Oscar Mandel, *Philoctetes and the Fall of Troy: Plays, Documents, Iconography, Interpretations* (Lincoln: University of Nebraska Press, 1981); S. J. Harrison, "Sophokles and the Cult of Philoctetes," *Journal of Hellenic Studies* 109 (1989): 173–175; R. G. Ussher, ed., *Philoloctetes/Sophokles* (Warminster, U.K.: Aris & Phillips, 1990); I. Malkin, "The Middle Ground. Philoktetes in Italy," *Kernos* 11 (1998): 131–141.

philosophy *Philosophia* is a Greek word, literally meaning "love of wisdom," but, in effect, translating to something like "love of arcane knowledge" or "a desire to find out the truth." The Greeks invented the concept of philosophy; for them, it meant a way of looking for reality and truth without strict reference to the traditional gods of RELIGION and mythology.

Philosophy began as a form of SCIENCE. The first philosophers, such as THALES of MILETUS (ca. 560 B.C.E.), sought to discover the essential element in the material world and to explain the causes of physical change. The Italian-Greek philosopher PARMENIDES (ca. 515–445 B.C.E.) revolutionized Western thought by theorizing that ultimate reality lies outside of the material world. Parmenides' younger contemporary SOCRATES of ATHENS (469–399 B.C.E.) redirected philosophy toward the pursuit of ethical truths and such moral questions as "What is virtue?" Both of these thinkers helped pave the way for PLATO (427–347 B.C.E.), who produced the first surviving philosophical system, in which questions about reality might shed light on ethical and epistomological questions. Plato's onetime pupil ARISTOTLE (384–322 B.C.E.) developed a system of logic and forever divorced science from philosophy by reorganizing them as separate disciplines. During the HELLENISTIC AGE (around 300–150 B.C.E.) new Greek philosophies such as STOICISM and EPICUREANISM sought to assure people about their place in the universal order.

See also ACADEMY; ANAXAGORAS; ANAXIMANDER; ANAXIMENES; CYNICS; DEMOCRITUS; EMPEDOCLES; HERACLITUS; LEUCIPPUS; LYCEUM; PYTHAGORAS; SKEPTICISM; SOCRATES; XENOPHANES.

Further reading: Robert Trundle, *Ancient Greek Philosophy: Its Development and Relevance to Our Time*

(Aldershot, U.K.: Avebury, 1994); R. W. Sharples, *Stoics, Epicureans, and Sceptics. An Introduction to Hellenistic Philosophy* (London: Routledge, 1996); A. A. Long, ed., *The Cambridge Companion to Early Greek Philosophy* (New York: Cambridge University Press, 1999); Julia Annas, *Ancient Philosophy: A Very Short Introduction* (New York: Oxford University Press, 2000); Richard Gotshalk, *The Beginnings of Philosophy in Greece* (Lanham, Md.: University Press of America, 2000); Jonathan Barnes, *Early Greek Philosophy*, 2d ed. (London: Penguin, 2001); Hans-Georg Gadamer, *The Beginning of Knowledge,* translated by Rod Coltman (New York: Continuum, 2002); David Sedley, ed., *The Cambridge Companion to Greek and Roman Philosophy* (New York: Cambridge University Press, 2003); Christopher Shields, *Classical Philosophy: A Contemporary Introduction* (London: Routledge, 2003).

Phocaea (Greek: Phokaia) This Greek city of IONIA is situated on the central west coast of ASIA MINOR. During the 600s and 500s B.C.E. Phocaea was at the forefront of long-range Greek TRADE and COLONIZATION, particularly in the western Mediterranean.

Located on the north shore of the entrance to the Bay of Smyrna, Phocaea was established around 1050 B.C.E. by IONIAN GREEKS who had emigrated from mainland Greece. The Phocaeans developed as brilliant seamen and began establishing anchorages and colonies to enlarge their shipping network. Probably one of their earliest colonies was Lampsacus, on the HELLESPONT (around 650 B.C.E.).

Around 600 B.C.E., in a westward drive for raw tin, SILVER, IRON, and other resources, the Phocaeans founded their famous colony, MASSALIA (modern-day Marseille), at the mouth of the Rhone on the southern coast of France. This depot facilitated trade with the local Ligurians and CELTS. Farther west, the Phocaeans traded with the Celtic kingdom of Tartessus, in southern Spain. Such ventures brought Phocaean sailors into battle with the Carthaginians, a non-Greek people who had previously held a monopoly on maritime trade in the West.

The Greek historian HERODOTUS describes Phocaea's abrupt decline. Around 545 B.C.E. the city was besieged by the invading Persians under King CYRUS (1). The Phocaeans, taking to their ships en masse, abandoned their home to the enemy. By way of an oath, they dropped an iron ingot into the sea and swore never to return until the metal should float up. (Nevertheless, half of them did decide to return.) The refugees sailed west. Rebuffed from Corsica by allied fleets of Carthaginians and ETRUSCANS, these Phocaeans eventually founded a new colony, Elea, on the southwestern coast of ITALY.

Phocaea, repopulated by the group that had returned, endured reduced fortunes under Persian rule. The city joined the doomed IONIAN REVOLT against the Persians (499–493 B.C.E.). After Ionia was liberated at the end of the PERSIAN WARS (479 B.C.E.), Phocaea became part of the Athenian-controlled DELIAN LEAGUE.

Like the rest of Ionia, Phocaea passed to Spartan control at the end of the PELOPONNESIAN WAR (404 B.C.E.) and was handed back to the Persians by the terms of the KING'S PEACE (386 B.C.E.). Liberated by ALEXANDER THE GREAT's conquest of the region in 334 B.C.E., Phocaea later passed to the Macedonian-Greek SELEUCID EMPIRE, then to the kingdom of PERGAMON, and finally, in 129 B.C.E., to the domain of ROME.

See also BRONZE; CARTHAGE; SHIPS AND SEAFARING.

Further reading: Donald F. McCabe and Allen Hilton, *Phokaia Inscriptions: Texts and List* (Princeton, N.J.: Institute for Advanced Study, 1989); W. Trillmich, "Early Iberian Sculpture and Phocaean Colonization," in *Greek Colonists and Native Populations. Proceedings of the First Australian Congress of Classical Archaeology, Sydney 9–14 July 1985,* edited by Jean-Paul Descoeudres (New York: Oxford University Press, 1990), 607–611; Ö. Özyigit, "The City Walls of Phokaia," *Revue des études anciennes* 96 (1994): 77–109.

Phocis This small region is located among the mountains of central Greece. The Phocians' significance was their intermittent control of the important sanctuary of the god APOLLO at DELPHI, located within Phocian territory. Their designs on Delphi brought them into periodic conflict with Apollo's priests and administrators there, who sometimes went so far as to declare holy war against Phocis.

Settlement in Phocis centered on two separate valleys: in the west, the Crisaean valley, adjoining the northern Corinthian Gulf; in the east, the valley of the middle Cephissus River, bordering BOEOTIA. Between the two Phocian valleys stood the traversible southern spur of Mt. Parnassus, where Delphi was located.

Coveted for its envelopment of Delphi and for its communication routes through mountainous central Greece, Phocis was surrounded by hostile Greek neighbors: Boeotia (to the east), West LOCRIS and Doris (to the west), and East Locris (to the north). Farther north lay another occasional enemy, THESSALY. In response to these pressures, the Phocians had by 600 B.C.E. become a unified, warlike people. They extended their power north of their home territory, even walling up the distant pass of THERMOPYLAE against southward attacks by the Thessalians. The Phocians' major conflicts with their neighbors were the three "Sacred Wars," so named because each involved Delphi's declaration of war. The Sacred Wars were consequential in allowing opportunities for intervention to such powerful states as ATHENS, SPARTA, THEBES, and MACEDON.

In the First Sacred War (around 590 B.C.E.), Phocis was overrun by an alliance of Sikyonians, Thessalians, Locrians, and Athenians. The Phocians were deprived of the fertile Crisaean plain (which was henceforth left as an uncultivated offering to Apollo), and control of Delphi was handed over to a league of neighboring states (including Phocis) known as the AMPHICTYONIC LEAGUE. At regular meetings of the League delegates, the Phocians had two of the 12 votes.

In 457 B.C.E. Delphi was recaptured by the Phocians, by now in alliance with the powerful city of Athens. There followed the bloodless Second Sacred War (448 B.C.E.), in which the Spartans marched into Phocis and restored Delphi to the Amphictyonic League. As soon as the Spartans had withdrawn, the Athenians—on PERIKLES' direction—marched to Delphi and returned it to the Phocians. But sometime in the next decades, the Phocians lost Delphi again and ceased to be Athenian allies. In the PELOPONNESIAN WAR (431–404 B.C.E.) and years following, Phocis was allied with SPARTA against Athens.

The Third Sacred War (355–346 B.C.E.) involved most of mainland Greece and gave the Macedonian king PHILIP II a chance for serious involvement in Greek affairs. The war began as a struggle between Phocis and the powerful Boeotian city of Thebes. At Thebes's prompting, Delphi declared war against certain Phocians who were impiously growing food on the Crisaean plain. But the Phocians seized Delphi and used funds stolen from the sanctuary to hire a mercenary army. With this force the Phocians fought back a coalition of Boeotians, Locrians, and Thessalians. A Phocian army even invaded Thessaly, where the Phocian commander was killed in battle against Macedonian Philip, who had entered the war as a Theban-Thessalian ally (352 B.C.E.). But in 346 B.C.E. an exhausted Phocis, its stolen funds depleted, surrendered to Philip. He garrisoned the region, occupied Delphi, and personally took over Phocis's two votes on the Amphictyonic council. The Phocians were made to pay an indemnity against their theft of Apollo's treasure, and the Crisaean plain was once more left fallow for the god.

In the 200s B.C.E. Phocis ceased to be important in Greek politics, as new Greek powers, such as AETOLIA, arose to dominate Delphi.

See also KLEISTHENES (2).

Further reading: B. V. Head, *Catalogue of Greek Coins. Central Greece (Locris, Phocis, Boeotia, and Euboea)* (Bologna, Italy: A. Forni, 1981); J. M. Fossey, *The Ancient Topography of Eastern Phokis* (Amsterdam: J. C. Gieben, 1986); J. McInerney, *The Folds of Parnassus. Land and Ethnicity in Ancient Phokis* (Austin: University of Texas Press, 1999).

Phoenicia This region corresponds roughly to modern-day Lebanon, located on the southern part of the east Mediterranean coast of ancient Syria. The Phoenicians were non-Greeks of Semitic race. They called themselves the Kinanu, and it is their ancestors who are known as

Canaanites in the Bible. In the late second millennium B.C.E. these Canaanites were battered by foreign invaders, including the Jewish tribes led by Joshua (around 1230 B.C.E.) and the Philistines (who may have been Mycenaean Greeks displaced by turmoil at home, around 1190 B.C.E.). But by 1000 B.C.E. the Canaanites had compensated for lost territory by becoming the greatest seafarers of the ancient world.

Our word *Phoenician* comes from the Greeks, who called these people Phoinikes, "red men"—probably a reference to skin color (not, apparently, to the purple murex dye, *porphyra*, which was among the Phoenicians' most precious commodities). By about 900 B.C.E. Phoenician sea traders were visiting Greece as part of their middleman's network that stretched throughout the ancient Near East to the Red Sea and Persian Gulf, touching on EGYPT, Assyria, Babylonia, and the kingdoms of ASIA MINOR. Also by 900 B.C.E. (as ARCHAEOLOGY reveals) the Phoenicians had begun exploring the western Mediterranean, seeking out suppliers of SILVER, tin, and other coveted metals. To facilitate western TRADE, the Phoenicians founded colonies, notably CARTHAGE (Kart Hadasht, "new city,") in what is now Tunisia, and Gaddir ("walled place," modern Cádiz) in southern Spain.

At home, the three Phoenician seaports of BYBLOS, Sidon, and Tyre became wealthy commercial and manufacturing centers. The primary industry at Sidon was the manufacture of beautiful glass vessels, while Tyre was the center of production for the purple murex dye. It was probably at Tyre prior to 1000 B.C.E. that the Phoenicians invented their 22-character Semitic ALPHABET, a vast improvement over their prior, cuneiform script. When the Greeks learned to adapt this Phoenician alphabet to represent the Greek language (before 750 B.C.E.), Greek literature was born.

In other ways as well, the brilliant Phoenicians deeply affected the formative Greek culture of 900–700 B.C.E. Near Eastern textiles and bronzework, brought to Greece by Phoenician traders, helped to spark the Greek artistic revolution of the "Orientalizing period" (around 730–630 B.C.E.). Certain oddities of Greek MYTH—such as the filial violence of both CRONUS and ZEUS, the flood of Deucalion, and the dying ADONIS—are best understood as being Near Eastern ideas that made their way to Greece via the Phoenicians (before 700 B.C.E.). Other Phoenician exports to Greece include the chicken (first domesticated in India) and the Semitic custom of reclining at meals, which the Greeks adapted to their drinking party known as the SYMPOSIUM.

The Greeks copied Phoenician shipbuilding techniques, around 900–700 B.C.E. It was surely also in emulation of the Phoenicians that the Greeks embarked on their own seaborne trade and COLONIZATION in the 800s–500s B.C.E. Inevitably the Greeks came into conflict with their former mentors, in competition for western trade privileges. Around 600 B.C.E., related to the founding of a Phocaean-Greek colony at MASSALIA (in southern France), a first sea battle was fought between Greeks and Carthaginian Phoenicians. Many such conflicts were to follow, particularly between Greeks and Carthaginians in SICILY.

Phoenicia surrendered to the conquering Persian king CYRUS (1) around 540 B.C.E., and henceforth the Phoenicians, like other subject peoples, supplied levies for the Persian armed forces. Phoenician ships and crews were the pride of the Persian navy. Phoenician squadrons fought fiercely against the Greeks in the PERSIAN WARS, in 499–480 B.C.E.

Phoenicia revolted unsuccessfully from Persian rule in the 300s B.C.E. When the Macedonian king ALEXANDER THE GREAT invaded the Persian Empire, the Phoenicians surrendered readily except for the Phoenician fortress of Tyre, which fell only after a monumental siege (332 B.C.E.).

In the HELLENISTIC AGE (300–150 B.C.E.), Phoenicia became a province of the SELEUCID EMPIRE, providing fleets and revenues. By the time of the Roman conquest (63 B.C.E.), Phoenicia had ceased to exist as a separate entity.

See also AL MINA; CADMUS; CYPRUS; SHIPS AND SEAFARING; THALES; WARFARE, NAVAL.

Further reading: Labib Boutros, *Phoenician Sport: Its Influence on the Origin of the Olympic Games* (Amsterdam: J. C. Gieben, 1981); E. Lipinski, ed., *Phoenicia and the East Mediterranean in the First Millennium B.C.* (Leuven, Belgium: Peeters, 1987): R. J. Harrison, *Spain at the Dawn of History. Iberians, Phoenicians, and Greeks* (London: Thames and Hudson, 1988); C. Grottanelli, "Of Gods and Metals. On the Economy of Phoenician Sanctuaries," *Scienze dell'antichità* 2 (1988): 243–255; D. W. J. Gill, "Silver Anchors and Cargoes of Oil. Some Observations on Phoenician Trade in the Western Mediterranean," *Papers of the British School at Rome* 56 (1988): 1–12; J. W. Shaw, "Phoenicians in Southern Crete," *American Journal of Archaeology* 93 (1989): 165–183; H. G. Niemeyer, "The Phoenicians in the Mediterranean. A Non-Greek Model for Expansion and Settlement in Antiquity," in *Greek Colonists and Native Populations. Proceedings of the First Australian Congress of Classical Archaeology, Sydney 9–14 July 1985*, edited by Jean-Paul Descoeudres (New York: Oxford University Press, 1990), 469–489; Glenn Markoe, "The Emergence of Phoenician Art," *Bulletin of the American Schools of Oriental Research* 279 (1990): 13–26; R. J. Clifford, "Phoenician Religion," *Bulletin of the American Schools of Oriental Research* 279 (1990): 55–64; John Grainger, *Hellenistic Phoenicia* (New York: Oxford University Press, 1991); Glenn Markoe, *Phoenicians* (Berkeley: University of California Press, 2000); Muriel Moity, Murielle Rudel, and Alain-Xavier Wurst, *Master Seafarers: The Phoenicians and the Greeks* (London: Periplus, 2003).

phratry   *See* KINSHIP.

Phrygia   *See* ASIA MINOR.

Phrynichus (late 500s–early 400s B.C.E.) *Athenian tragic playwright*
A pioneer of early Athenian tragedy, Phrynichus was reportedly the first to introduce female characters onstage. He exerted a strong influence on the younger tragedian AESCHYLUS, particularly with his innovative use of recent events from the PERSIAN WARS. Only a few fragments of Phrynichus's work survive.

Competing at the annual drama festival known as the City Dionysia, Phrynichus won his first victory in about 510 B.C.E. In around 492 B.C.E. he presented *The Capture of Miletus,* based on the recent ravaging of that Greek city by the Persians after the failed IONIAN REVOLT. The Athenian audience burst into tears at the rendition of their ally's fate, but Phrynichus was fined 1,000 drachmas for reminding the Athenians of their woes, and future performance of the play was banned.

In around 476 B.C.E. he presented another historical drama, *The Phoenician Women,* giving the tragic, Persian viewpoint of the recent Greek naval victory at SALAMIS (1). This play surely inspired Aeschylus's tragedy *The Persians* (472 B.C.E.).

See also MILETUS; THEATER.

Further reading: E. J. Bloedow, "Phrynichus, the Intelligent Athenian," *Ancient History Bulletin* 5 (1991): 89–100.

phyle   *See* KINSHIP.

Pindar (Greek: Pindaros) (ca. 518–438 B.C.E.) *Greatest choral poet of ancient Greece*
Born near the central Greek city of THEBES but often traveling, Pindar apparently claimed kinship with the noble Aegid clan, which had branches at SPARTA and other Greek cities. Much of his poetry beautifully conveys the old-fashioned values of the aristocratic class, whose power was waning throughout Greece during Pindar's own lifetime. Pindar wrote various types of LYRIC POETRY, most of it choral poetry—that is, intended for public performance by a chorus. He is best remembered for his victory odes (*epinikia*), composed in honor of various patrons' triumphs at such important Greek sports festivals as the OLYMPIC GAMES. In ornate language that often attains magnificence, Pindar combines a sense of joyous occasion with a sublime religious piety and a sadness over human transience or human injustice.

Forty-five of Pindar's victory odes survive whole, having come down to us numbered and arranged by a later ancient editor into four categories—Olympians, Pythians, Nemeans, and Isthmians. These categories reflect the four major sports festivals that occasioned nearly all the poems. The odes' honorees include winners in WRESTLING, PANKRATION, footraces, and the four-horse chariot race.

In Pindar's day, international athletes were always rich and male, and were usually members of the traditional noble class, for whom the games were part of a distinctive aristocratic identity. Pindar's patrons, from many Greek cities, included three rulers: King Arcesilas IV of CYRENE (1), the tyrant Theron of ACRAGAS, and the tyrant HIERON (1) of SYRACUSE, the most powerful individual in the Greek world. Pindar wrote four odes for Hieron; of these, two are usually considered the poet's masterpieces—Olympian 1 and Pythian 1.

Perhaps invented by the poet IBYCUS (ca. 530 B.C.E.), the Greek victory ode was composed for a fee paid by the victor or his family, and was performed by a chorus of men or boys at the athlete's home city sometime after the sports event. Like most choral verse, Pindar's odes are written in a Doric Greek dialect (although Pindar himself would have spoken a different dialect, Aeolic). The meters and lengths vary; most of Pindar's odes run between about 45 and 120 lines.

Employing an associative flow of ideas and images, the typical Pindaric ode salutes the athlete's home region, praises the inherited superiority of the upper class, and broods over the precariousness of human happiness. Many odes recount one or another Greek MYTH in such a way as to compare the mythical hero with the poem's patron. Beyond flattery, these comparisons convey the message that victory—for hero or athlete—is proof of divine favor. Pindar's frequent use of myth makes him one of our important sources for these stories; among many examples are Pythian 9's tale of APOLLO and the nymph CYRENE (2), and Nemean 10's tale of CASTOR AND POLYDEUCES. But the reverent Pindar always minimizes or bowdlerizes the god's cruelty and injustice, in comparison with other extant versions of such myths.

We know little of Pindar's life. His parents' names are variously reported. As a boy he studied poetry at ATHENS when that city had recently emerged as the world's first DEMOCRACY (508 B.C.E.). Significantly, Pindar's Athenian contacts came from right-wing, aristocratic circles; these friends included Megakles of the noble Alcmaeonid clan and Melesias, a champion wrestler who was the future father of the conservative Athenian politician THUCYDIDES (2). Both Megakles and Melesias represented Athenian upper-class forces that were soon destined to come to grief against the radical policies of the democracy. Megacles was ostracized by the Athenians in 486 B.C.E., and Pindar's ode Pythian 7—written to celebrate Megakles' chariot victory at the PYTHIAN GAMES at DELPHI that same year—is partly a consolation for his friend's political misfortune.

Pindar's fateful connection with Greek SICILY was forged in 490 B.C.E., when he wrote ode Pythian 6 for Xenocrates, a nobleman of the Sicilian Greek city of Acragas. (Xenocrates' brother was Theron, who was destined to become dictator of Acragas and one of Pindar's patrons.) Xenocrates had won the chariot race, which was the most prestigious event and one of the few in which contestants did not have to compete personally: The drivers were usually professionals, and the official contestants were considered to be the chariot's owners.

Xenocrates had a teenage son named Thrasybulus. Pythian 6 is remarkable for its frank expression of Pindar's infatuation with Thrasybulus. Homosexual attachments were a prominent part of Greek aristocratic life in that era, and Thrasybulus was probably the sort of glamorous youth who created a sensation amid the games' intense social atmosphere. We know that Pindar also wrote a drinking song for Thrasybulus and a later ode, Isthmian 2, for a chariot victory by him (around 470 B.C.E.). Pindar's tone in these verses—confident, personal, not at all subservient in addressing his eminent employers—is a sign of his high social status.

Pindar's comfortable world was soon shaken, however, when Persian armies invaded mainland Greece in 490 and 480 B.C.E. The allied Greeks' victory over the Persians brought on changes that eventually swept away the aristocrats' traditional way of life. Pindar's Thebes fell into deep disgrace for having collaborated with the occupying Persian forces, and the two cities that had led the Greek defense—Sparta and Athens—emerged as rival leaders of Greece.

Meanwhile, in Sicily, the Greek city of Syracuse had become the foremost power of the western Mediterranean, having led the Sicilian Greeks in defeating a Carthaginian invasion (480 B.C.E.). And it was at Syracuse that Pindar would deliver his greatest poetry.

He visited in 476 B.C.E., probably at the invitation of the dictator Hieron, who had won the horse-and-rider race at that summer's Olympic Games. (Like the chariot race, the horse race was officially won by the owner, not the rider.) Pindar's victory ode for Hieron that year is perhaps the most famous lyric poem of antiquity, placed by ancient editors at the beginning of the Pindaric corpus, as Olympian 1:

> Best of things is water. And gold,
> Like a fire at night, outshines all other wealth.
> And if you wish to sing of glory in the Games,
> Look no further in the daytime sky for any star
> More warming than the sun,
> Nor any contest grander than at Olympia. (lines 1–8)

The 116-line ode celebrates Hieron's victory by telling the legend of PELOPS, who supposedly established the first Olympic Games. Just as Pelops was beloved by the god POSEIDON, so is Hieron blessed by some god.

While in Sicily, Pindar may have indulged in a feud with the poet SIMONIDES of Keos and his poet-nephew BACCHYLIDES, who were likewise guests at Hieron's court. Pindar's Olympian 2 contains a mysterious reference to a pair of crows who "chatter vainly against the sacred eagle of ZEUS"—which is sometimes interpreted as the poet's rebuke to his rivals.

Pindar left Sicily in around 475 B.C.E. In 474 B.C.E. Hieron defeated an Etruscan invasion of Greek southern ITALY, at the sea battle of CUMAE. Soon thereafter Hieron founded a new Sicilian city, Aetna, near volcanic Mt. Etna. Then, in 470 B.C.E., Hieron won the chariot race at the Pythian Games and commissioned an ode from Pindar.

Pindar's resultant poem, Pythian 1, is probably his best. The 100-line ode successfully interweaves the above-mentioned events with a worldview of harmony versus discord, justice versus evil. The poem contains an unforgettable description of the mythical monster TYPHON, the god Zeus's defeated enemy, who now lies shackled beneath Mt. Etna and whose fire-breathing fury supposedly causes the volcano's eruptions. Cleverly linked to local geography, Pindar's Typhon serves as a cosmic symbol for the ETRUSCANS, Carthaginians, and other defeated enemies of Hieron and Greek civilization. Yet the poem ends with a bold warning to Hieron not to abuse his power, lest he too provoke the gods' anger.

In 468 B.C.E. Hieron, then dying, crowned his achievements with a chariot victory at the Olympic Games. But he hired Bacchylides, not Pindar, to commemorate this triumph. The ruler may have been offended by Pythian 1's presumptuous warning.

Pindar's last years saw the final erosion of his familiar world, with Greece divided by hostility between Sparta and the imperialist Athens of PERIKLES. One prominent victim of Athenian aggression was the Greek island of AEGINA. The anti-Athenian anger of Pindar's friends is suggested in the anxious tone of Pindar's last surviving victory ode, Pythian 8, written in 446 B.C.E. for a boy wrestler of Aegina. The poem also contains (lines 95–97) a poignant expression of Pindar's aristocratic religious outlook, which saw victory in SPORT as a god-given gift providing a brief triumph over the doom that awaits all mortals:

> We are creatures of a day. What is someone? What is
>   he not?
> A human being is a shadow in a dream.
> But when a god grants a brightness,
> Then humans have a radiant splendor and their life
>   is sweet.

Pindar lived until age 80. Supposedly he had a wife and three children, but we hear also of another young male friend, Theoxenus of Tenedos, in whose arms the poet is said to have died at the city of ARGOS. Pindar's memory was revered for centuries. Supposedly the priests of APOLLO at Delphi would close the temple daily with the words "May Pindar join the gods at dinner." And when the Macedonian king ALEXANDER THE GREAT captured and destroyed Thebes in 335 B.C.E., he is said to have spared the house that had been Pindar's.

See also ALCMAEONIDS; ARISTOCRACY; CATANA; CHARIOTS; CORINNA; FATE; GREEK LANGUAGE; HIMERA; HOMOSEXUALITY; ISTHMIAN GAMES; NEMEAN GAMES; PERSIAN WARS.

Further reading: G. Nagy, "Pindar's Olympian I and the Aetiology of the Olympic Games," *Transactions of the American Philological Association* 116 (1986): 75–81; H. M. Lee, "Pindar and Classical Art," in *Studies in Honor of T. B. L. Webster,* 2 (Bristol, U.K.: Bristol Classical Press, 1988): 75–81.

Piraeus (Greek: Peiraieus) The main port and naval base of ATHENS, Piraeus is located about four miles southwest of the city.

The westward-jutting peninsula known as the Piraeus was neglected in early Athenian times, when ships sheltered at the more southerly beachfront of Phalerum. In 510 B.C.E. the Athenian tyrant HIPPIAS (1) built a citadel on the Piraeus's hilltop, which was called Munychia. But it was the Athenian statesman THEMISTOKLES who, in 492 B.C.E., began developing the harbor for a growing Athenian war fleet.

By the mid-400s B.C.E. a walled town proper had arisen, laid out on a rectilinear grid by the city planner HIPPODAMUS. The naval base contained dockyards, arsenals, and ship sheds (covered drydocking for individual ships, the pride of Athenian naval technology). In addition, the port was a bustling commercial center, home to many of the METICS (resident aliens) who conducted Athens' import-export TRADE. It was also home to working-class Athenian citizens of left-wing loyalties, staunch supporters of such democratic politicians as PERIKLES.

Piraeus had three harbors, whose entrances—flanked by half-immersed stone walls—could be sealed completely by the raising of massive chains. By 448 B.C.E. the town and harborfront were enclosed on north and south by the LONG WALLS, running up to Athens. The Long Walls made Piraeus and Athens into a single, linked fortress; even the Spartan land invasions in the PELOPONNESIAN WAR could not breach these defenses or obstruct Athens' communications with its naval base. The Long Walls were torn down after Athens's defeat in the war (404 B.C.E.), but were rebuilt by the Athenian general KONON (393 B.C.E.).

From 322 until 196 B.C.E. the citadel at Munychia held a Macedonian garrison—one of the Macedonians' four "fetters" of Greece. Today Piraeus remains vital as the harbor of modern Athens.

See also GREECE, GEOGRAPHY OF; MACEDON; THIRTY TYRANTS, THE; WARFARE, NAVAL.

Further reading: M. Chambers, "Themistokles and the Piraeus," in *Studies Presented to Sterling Dow on His Eightieth Birthday,* edited by Alan L. Boegehold (Durham, N.C.: Duke University Press, 1984), 43–50; H. Conwell, "Topography and Toponyms between Athens and Piraeus," *Rivista di topografia antica* 3 (1993): 49–64; S. v. Reden, "The Piraeus. A World Apart," *Greece and Rome* 42 (1995): 24–37; Robert Garland, *The Piraeus: From the Fifth to the First Century B.C.,* 2d ed. (Bristol, U.K.: Bristol

Classical Press, 2001); A. Michalopoulos, *The Museums of Athens: Piraeus, Attica, and the Islands of the Argosaronic Gulf* (Athens: Erevnites Editions, 2001).

Pithecusae (Greek: **Pithekoussai**, "monkey island") This Greek trading colony is located on a volcanic island now called Ischia, off the western coast of southern ITALY, near modern-day Naples. First occupied by Greeks from CHALCIS and ERETRIA around 775 B.C.E., Pithecusae was apparently the earliest substantial Greek settlement in the West. It was the first landfall in a wave of westward Greek COLONIZATION that swept across southern Italy and SICILY over the following two centuries.

Most knowledge of Pithecusae comes from modern ARCHAEOLOGY on the site. The first Greeks found the island unoccupied. Their settlement site—atop a tall peninsula with two harbors, on the island's north shore—was chosen with an eye toward local seafaring. The island provided a safe base from which Greek merchant ships could sail the six miles to the Italian mainland, to conduct TRADE with the non-Greek peoples there. Foremost of these Italian trading partners were the ETRUSCANS, whose home region lay far to the north but who had an outpost at Capua, inland of the Bay of Naples.

What brought Greek traders from mainland Greece to western Italy was the lure of raw metals—IRON, SILVER, tin (for making BRONZE), and others—that would fetch high prices in the Greeks' home cities of Chalcis and Eretria. The Etruscans mined large amounts of iron ore on the island of Elba, off the western coast of northern Italy, and at least some of this valuable ore was then traded to the Greeks at Pithecusae. Archaeology at Pithecusae has yielded the remnants of ancient Greek foundries, probably indicating that the acquired iron was refined and forged into ingots by Greek smiths right there, before being shipped to Greece.

In exchange for Italian metals, the Pithecusae Greeks supplied WINE, painted POTTERY, worked metal, and other luxury goods. Modern discoveries at Pithecusae of ceramics and metalwork from ancient EGYPT and ASIA MINOR suggest that some of the Greeks' luxury items originated in the non-Greek Near East, traveling west via Greek trade networks.

By about 750 B.C.E. Pithecusae was crowded and prosperous. Affluence is suggested by the quantities of imported Near Eastern artifacts found in Greek tombs there. The most important archaeological item from Pithecusae is the so-called cup of Nestor, made between about 750 and 700 B.C.E. This is a Greek clay drinking cup, painted in Geometric style and inscribed with one of the earliest surviving examples of Greek alphabetic WRITING.

Pithecusae was largely abandoned in the late 700s B.C.E. One cause may have been the start of the LELANTINE WAR, which pitted Chalcidean Greeks against Eretrian Greeks as enemies. At least some of the Pithecusans—possibly the Chalcidean party—founded a new colony, CUMAE, on the Italian mainland opposite Pithecusae.

See also ALPHABET.

Further reading: David Ridgway, *The First Western Greeks* (New York: Cambridge University Press, 1992); Giorgio Buchner and David Ridgway, *Pithekoussai* (Rome: G. Bretschneider, 1993); David Ridgway, "The Trading Port of Pithekoussai," in *Old World Civilization: The Rise of Cities and States,* edited by Göran Burenhult (San Francisco: HarperSanFrancisco, 1994), 148–149; David Ridgway, "Seals, Scarabs, and People in Pithekoussai," in *Periplous: Papers on Classical Art and Archaeology Presented to Sir John Boardman,* edited by G. R. Tsetskhladze, A. J. N. Prag, and A. M. Snodgrass (London: Thames and Hudson, 2000), 235–243.

Pittacus Constitutional dictator of the city of MYTILENE, on the island of LESBOS around 580 B.C.E. Among his enemies was the poet ALCAEUS, whose loathing of Pittacus has been immortalized in verse. Nevertheless, Pittacus seems to have governed well, calming the civil strife at Mytilene between the nobles and the middle class. His rule supplied an alternative to the brutal TYRANTS who in those years were arising throughout the Greek world to wrest power from the ARISTOCRACY. Pittacus later was listed among the SEVEN SAGES.

Born of noble blood, he was an illustrious soldier, having once killed an enemy champion in single combat during Mytilene's war against Athenian settlers at Sigeum, in northwestern ASIA MINOR, around 600 B.C.E. Later Pittacus was elected as dictator for a term of 10 years. Like his contemporary, SOLON of ATHENS, he made new laws that loosened the aristocrats' monopoly on political power. By turning his back on the partisan interests of his own noble class, Pittacus earned the hatred of old-fashioned aristocrats such as Alcaeus.

Further reading: Nigel Spencer, "Exchange and Stasis in Archaic Mytilene," in *Alternatives to Athens: Varieties of Political Organization and Community in Ancient Greece,* edited by Roger Brock and Stephen Hodkinson (New York: Oxford University Press, 2000), 68–81.

Plataea This town of southern BOEOTIA, in central Greece, lies just north of Mt. Cithaeron, by the River Asopus. Due to fear of its powerful neighbor THEBES, Plataea formed an alliance with ATHENS in about 519 B.C.E. and remained a staunch ally during the PERSIAN WARS and PELOPONNESIAN WAR. Alone among the Greek states, Plataea sent soldiers to fight alongside the Athenians against the Persians at the Battle of MARATHON (490 B.C.E.). During the invasion of the Persian king XERXES, Plataea was occupied and sacked by the Persians (480 B.C.E.). Near the town in 479 B.C.E. the allied Greeks won the Battle of Plataea, which destroyed the Persian threat in Greece.

At the outbreak of the Peloponnesian War in 431 B.C.E., Plataea was unsuccessfully attacked by Thebes. Plataea's civilians were soon evacuated to Athens. A garrison, left to defend Plataea, surrendered and was massacred after a grueling, two-year siege by the Spartans and Thebans (427 B.C.E.). Later the empty town was razed to the ground.

Rebuilt, Plataea was again destroyed by Thebes in 373 B.C.E. After conquering Greece in 338 B.C.E., the Macedonian king PHILIP II rebuilt Plataea in order to humiliate Thebes, and the town survived down to Roman times.

See also: PLATAEA, BATTLE OF.

Further reading: G. S. Shrimpton, "When Did Plataea Join Athens?" *Classical Philology* 79 (1984): 295–304; E. Badian, "Plataea between Athens and Sparta. In Search of Lost History," in *Boiotika. Vorträge vom 5. Internationalen Böotien-Kolloquium, München 13–17 Juni 1986,* edited by Hartmut Beister and John Bucker (Munich: Editio Maris, 1989), 95–111; N. G. L. Hammond, "Plataea's Relations with Thebes, Sparta, and Athens," *Journal of Hellenic Studies* 112 (1992): 143–150; E. Badian, *From Plataea to Potidaea. Studies in the History and Historiography of the Pentecontaetia* (Baltimore: Johns Hopkins University Press, 1993).

Plataea, Battle of   This climatic land battle took place during the Greeks' defense of their homeland in the PERSIAN WARS. This hard-fought Greek victory occurred in the late summer of 479 B.C.E., on the plain near the Boeotian town of PLATAEA. Coming about a year after the Greek naval triumph at SALAMIS (1), the Battle of Plataea destroyed the last remaining Persian force in Greece and ended the Persian king XERXES' dream of conquering Greece.

After his unexpected defeat at Salamis, Xerxes led most of his troops home in 480 B.C.E. To pursue the subjugation of Greece, he left behind his able general (and brother-in-law) Mardonius, with an army numbering perhaps 60,000. Mardonius's army included Greek soldiers from the mainland regions of THESSALY and BOEOTIA, whose cities were actively collaborating with the Persians.

After wintering in Thessaly, Mardonius and his army marched south in the spring of 479 B.C.E. On receiving news of a Greek allied army's approach from the south, Mardonius withdrew toward friendly THEBES, the chief city of Boeotia. About five miles south of Thebes, just north of Plataea, where the level terrain favored his CAVALRY, Mardonius and his army awaited the Greeks.

The Greek army, commanded by the Spartan general Pausanias, contained about 38,700 HOPLITES—armored infantry—with perhaps as many light-armed troops. The largest hoplite contingents came from SPARTA, ATHENS, and CORINTH. The town of Plataea fought on the Greek side, as a staunch ally of Athens and longtime enemy of Thebes.

The allied Greeks had the advantage of heavier armor and the high morale of a patriotic army. The Persians' advantage was their mighty cavalry, drawn from the Iranian plateau, from Scythia, and from Thessaly and Boeotia. In action against foot soldiers, these horsemen would ride up, send out arrows and javelins, then spur quickly out of reach, only to wheel and attack elsewhere. On flat land, they proved highly effective against the allied Greeks, who had no horse soldiers.

The battle was preceded by 12 days of waiting and skirmishing. The two main armies faced each other, separated by the Asopus River; they stood in battle array in the hot summer sun all day and retired to camps at night. Trying to provoke an attack, Mardonius repeatedly sent his horsemen to harass the Greeks and raid their arriving supply wagons. Both sides suffered from lack of food and fresh water. Pausanias was unwilling to risk an attack, yet each passing day made his army's position more difficult.

At dawn on the 13th day the Persians saw that the entire Greek force had withdrawn toward Plataea. The Greeks were marching in some disarray, having split into three different groups in the dark. Seizing his chance, Mardonius led a full-scale attack across the plain.

The Persian army rushed upon the two nearer Greek contingents. One of these numbered about 11,500 hoplites and contained the best soldiers in Greece, the Spartans, commanded by Pausanias. The other embattled Greek contingent was from Athens and (fittingly enough) Plataea; it numbered about 8,600 and was commanded by the Athenian general ARISTIDES. The Battle of Plataea consisted of two simultaneous actions, separated by perhaps a mile. Meanwhile the third Greek division, farthest away, began marching back toward the fighting.

In attacking so eagerly, Mardonius evidently underestimated the Greeks' discipline and defensive strength. Near a rural temple of DEMETER, the Spartans and their allies formed into battle order, while Mardonius, atop a white charger, brought on his elite Persian infantry. Equipped as archers, the Persians halted a distance from the Greeks and shot volleys of arrows. Greek hoplites, although armored, tended to be vulnerable at the neck, legs, and groin, and many were felled by the arrows before the command finally came to charge.

The hoplites pushed forward into the Persian ranks. The melee wore on until Mardonius was killed, hit in the head with a stone thrown by a Spartan. Seeing their general fall, the Persians broke ranks and fled. At the other end of the battlefield, the Athenians were locked in combat with Boeotian Greeks serving on the Persian side. But at the sight of their Persian masters running away, the Boeotians retreated toward Thebes.

Many Persians ran to a large wooden palisade that Mardonius had built before the battle. This fort became a slaughterhouse, as the pursuing Greeks broke through and massacred the fugitives within. Although a sizable

Persian contingent may have escaped back to Asia, the battle was a stunning Greek victory.

But Plataea marked a fleeting glory. Before the battle, the Greeks had sworn an oath of camaraderie—the famous Oath of Plataea—pledging, among other things, never to harm Athens, Sparta, or the town of Plataea. Yet within a few years hostilities had erupted between Athens and Sparta, and in the PELOPONNESIAN WAR Plataea itself was destroyed by the Spartans.

See also WARFARE, LAND.

Further reading: P. Hunt, "Helots at the Battle of Plataea," *Historia* 46 (1997): 129–144; Philip De Souza, *The Greek and Persian Wars, 499–386 B.C.* (New York: Routledge, 2003).

Plato (Greek: Platon "wide", perhaps a nickname) (ca. 427–347 B.C.E.) *Athenian philosopher*

Plato was one of the most influential thinkers in world history. He founded the Western world's first important institution of higher learning, the ACADEMY, which helped shape the course of PHILOSOPHY for the next 1,000 years. Among Plato's teachings, his theory of Forms provided a revolutionary concept of reality—a concept that he tied into corresponding theories of ethics and human knowledge, in a way that seemed to explain the universe.

Most earlier Greek philosophers had searched for the universe's primal elements by examining the physical world. Plato, however, influenced by the earlier Greek philosopher PARMENIDES, theorized that true reality is not to be found in the visible, physical world but in an ideal world of eternal Forms. Our earthly phenomena are just imperfect copies of these Forms, Plato said. Such earthly copies include not only material items such as beds and tables, but human virtues such as justice and knowledge. Above all other Forms stands the Form of the Good, whose central and nutritive role in the universe in analogous to that of the Sun in the visible world.

To later generations, Plato's concept of a supreme Form of the Good seemed to anticipate Christian monotheism, and so Plato's teachings enjoyed great prestige in the Christian-influenced Roman Empire, around 100–400 C.E. when a movement called Neoplatonism arose. Probably because of his posthumous association with Christianity, Plato is almost unique among ancient Greek authors in that every major written work by him has been preserved.

For his philosophical writings, Plato chose a style that was unusual in his day—prose dialogue. We have about 30 of these. (A few, ascribed to Plato, are probably forgeries.) Each dialogue typically presents a philosophical discussion among several characters, many of whom are fictionalized versions of real-life personages of fifth-century-B.C.E. ATHENS. The characters debate a specific topic, such as the nature of courage. The beauty of Plato's technique is that it draws the reader directly into the inquiry. Of the dialogues, Plato's masterpiece is the *Republic* (Greek: Politeia, better translated as "form of government"), written circa 385–370 B.C.E. The *Republic* first addresses the question "What is justice?" and proceeds to sketch Plato's ideal government, run by a philosopher-king. Plato's theory of Forms receives its classic explanation in the lengthy *Republic*.

The scanty knowledge of Plato's life comes partly from information in the works of later ancient writers, such as the biographers Diogenes Laertius (200s C.E.) and PLUTARCH (ca. 100 C.E.). Also preserved are a number of epistles supposedly written by Plato. Although these letters seem to be forgeries, many scholars today accept as accurate the autobiographical information in the famous "Seventh Letter."

Plato was born into a rich and aristocratic Athenian clan with strong political links; his mother's family claimed descent from the lawgiver SOLON. Plato grew up entirely during the epic PELOPONNESIAN WAR (431–404 B.C.E.). Like other wealthy Athenian youths, Plato probably did military service in the CAVALRY, perhaps on patrol in the countryside around Athens, around 409–404 B.C.E.

Possibly through association with his slightly older kinsmen KRITIAS and Charmides, the young Plato joined the circle of the dynamic Athenian philosopher SOCRATES (ca. 469–399 B.C.E.). Socrates' ethical-political inquiries proved to be the single greatest influence on Plato's thought. In most of his dialogues, written after Socrates' death, Plato immortalized his old mentor by making him the central speaker. Plato's choice of the dialogue form was undoubtedly an attempt to convey the mental excitement of Socrates' discussions.

The convulsive end of the Peloponnesian War changed Plato's life. After Athens's defeat (404 B.C.E.), Kritias and Charmides became central figures in the dictatorship of the THIRTY TYRANTS. Invited to join them, Plato hesitated, and meanwhile the Thirty fell from power; Kritias and Charmides were killed (403 B.C.E.). In 399 B.C.E., under the restored Athenian DEMOCRACY, Socrates was tried and executed—partly because of his association with Kritias. As Socrates' disciple, Plato himself may have been in danger; in any case he seems to have been sickened by the bloody excesses of both right wing and left wing, and he rejected any plan of a political career, choosing instead a life of travel and reflection. But Socratic-type questions about politics and human nature remained foremost in Plato's mind, and he concluded (to use his later words) that there could be no end to human troubles until "either philosophers should become kings, or else those now ruling should become inspired to pursue philosophical wisdom" (*Republic* 473c).

Between about 399 and 387 B.C.E. Plato probably wrote many or all of the dialogues that modern scholars classify as "early." This group begins with the *Euthyphro*,

Apology, and *Krito*—concerning Socrates' arrest, trial, and imprisonment—and culminates in the *Protagoras* and *Gorgias.* The early dialogues mainly explore ethical issues, of which the most important is the *Protagoras'* question, "Is moral virtue teachable?"

During these years Plato traveled to Greek southern ITALY, where he met followers of the early philosopher PYTHAGORAS. Aspects of Plato's views on death and the soul's immortality seem influenced by Pythagorean belief. Also, historical memories of a Pythagorean ruling class—which in prior centuries had existed in certain Italian-Greek cities—may have helped to shape Plato's goal to create a government of philosophers.

In about 387 B.C.E., at about age 40, Plato made his fateful first voyage to SICILY, to the important Greek city of SYRACUSE, where the ruthless dictator DIONYSIUS (1) reigned. There Plato became both friend and teacher of a kinsman of the ruler—a handsome young nobleman named Dion. In keeping with prevalent Greek upper-class mores of the day, this male relationship was probably sexual: Plato's homosexual feelings are evident in surviving verses that he wrote for Dion. At the same time, the friendship may have suggested to Plato that he could win followers from among the Syracusan ruling circle and thus create his philosophers' government.

According to one story, the Sicilian visit became a fiasco when the cruel Dionysius, tiring of Plato's criticism, arranged for the philosopher to be sold into slavery; Plato's friends bought back his freedom. In any case, Plato soon returned to Athens and bought land and buildings in a park sacred to the mythical hero Academus, about a mile north of Athens's Dipylon Gate, in about 386 B.C.E. This holding became Plato's Academy, a university dedicated to philosophical inquiry and the preparation of future leaders of Athens and other Greek cities.

Plato devoted nearly the next 20 years to supervising the Academy and to writing the dialogues that modern scholars assign to his "middle" period. In addition to the *Republic,* these include the *Phaedo* (which combines an account of Socrates' last days in prison with Plato's introduction of his own theory of Forms) and the *Symposium* (on the nature of sexual love). The modern, popular notion of nonsexual, "Platonic" love is a distortion of Plato's views: Specifically addressing the aristocratic, male HOMOSEXUALITY of his own day, Plato believed that such feelings could ennoble and educate those partners who channeled their passion into a spiritual, not just a sexual, union. There is no evidence that Plato ever married, and from his writings he seems to have been of an abstemious homosexual nature.

Much of Plato's thought surely developed from life at the Academy—especially from his informal discussions and disputations with his colleagues (a procedure that derived from Socratic technique). This method of ques-

tion-and-answer disputation was called dialectic (Greek: *dialektikē,* "discussion" or "dialogue"). In Plato's dialogues, Socrates employs dialectic to refute his opponents' preconceptions, by showing that certain conclusions logically drawn from those preconceptions are false. Plato saw dialectic as the premier philosophical technique, "the coping-stone set atop the other types of learning" (*Republic* 534e).

Only through dialectic can people hope to gain some knowledge of reality—that is, of the Forms. Otherwise we are in the dark. In the most famous allegory in all philosophical literature, the *Republic* compares nonphilosophical inquiry with the plight of prisoners trying to learn about reality by observing shadows in firelight on the wall of a cave.

In 367 B.C.E. Dionysius of Syracuse died and was succeeded by his son, Dionysius II. The 60-year-old Plato—at the invitation of his old friend Dion—again voyaged to Syracuse, in the hope of making a philosophical convert of the new ruler. But the younger Dionysius proved to be a weak and decadent leader, and was eventually ejected in a coup led by Dion himself (357 B.C.E.). Plato meanwhile returned to Athens (361 B.C.E.), having despaired of ever creating an ideal state in Sicily.

The third and last stage of Plato's career covers the years from about 360 B.C.E. until his death, in 347 B.C.E. These years at the Academy saw the advancement of the brilliant "graduate student" ARISTOTLE, whom some considered to be Plato's likely successor as head of the school. Plato's dialogues of this period include the *Timaeus* (presenting Plato's picture of the physical cosmos) and the *Laws* (his longest and probably final work). Like the *Republic,* the *Laws* portray an ideal Platonic city-state, but in this later dialogue Plato's authoritarian bent is more pronounced—the laws of his utopian "Cretan city" include generous use of the death penalty—and the *Laws* can be read as evidence of an old man's embitterment. Plato died at age 80, pen in hand (according to legend). He was succeeded as head of the Academy by his nephew Speusippus.

See also AFTERLIFE; ATLANTIS; EDUCATION; GORGIAS; MATHEMATICS; PROTAGORAS; SOPHISTS; SYMPOSIUM.

Further reading: C. J. de Vogel, *Rethinking Plato and Platonism,* 2d ed. (Leiden, Netherlands: E. J. Brill, 1988); R. B. Rutherford, *The Art of Plato: Ten Essays in Platonic Interpretation* (Cambridge, Mass.: Harvard University Press, 1995); Thanassis Samaras, *Plato on Democracy* (New York: P. Lang, 2002); Ann N. Michelini, ed., *Plato as Author: the Rhetoric of Philosophy* (Leiden, Netherlands: E. J. Brill, 2003); Christopher Rowe, *Plato* (Bristol, U.K.: Bristol Classical Press, 2003); Julia Annas, *Plato: A Very Short Introduction* (Oxford: Oxford University Press, 2003); Rosemary Desjardins, *Plato and the Good: Illuminating the Darkling Vision* (Leiden, Netherlands: E. J. Brill, 2004).

Plutarch (Greek: Ploutarchos) (ca. 50–125 C.E.) *Greek biographer and moral essayist who lived during the early Roman Empire*

Born in the central Greek region of BOEOTIA, Plutarch lived in Greece but was also a Roman citizen, and may have held the local Roman post of procurator. He traveled, read, and wrote widely, and for the last 30 years of his life was a priest at the god APOLLO's shrine at DELPHI. Plutarch embodies the Greek-Roman assimilation under the Roman Empire.

Although he did not exactly write history, he happens to be a major source of information for events in the Greek world of around 600–200 B.C.E. This is due to one of his writings, known by the title *Parallel Lives of the Noble Greeks and Romans,* which in its surviving form consists of 22 paired short biographies ("Lives"), one of a Greek leader, one of a Roman. Most of these biographical subjects lived in the great centuries of classical Greece and the Roman Republic, prior to Plutarch's time. Among his more important Greek Lives are those of SOLON, PERIKLES, ALCIBIADES, and ALEXANDER THE GREAT. Although often sloppy about chronology, the Lives are full of historical and personal detail.

Further reading: A. Podlecki, "Plutarch and Athens," *Illinois Classical Studies* 13 (1988): 231–243; S. C. R. Swain, "Hellenic Culture and the Roman Heroes of Plutarch," *Journal of Hellenic Studies* 110 (1990): 126–145; Judith Mossman, "Plutarch's Use of Statues," in *Georgica. Greek Studies in Honor of George Cawkwell,* edited by Michael Flower and Mark Toher (London: University of London, Institute of Classical Studies, 1991), 98–119; L. van der Stockt, ed., *Plutarchea Lovaniensia. A Miscellany of Essays on Plutarch* (Leuven, Belgium: Universitas catholica lovaniensis, 1996); Judith Mossman, ed., *Plutarch and His Intellectual World: Essays on Plutarch* (London: Duckworth, 1997); F. E. Brenk, *Relighting the Souls. Studies in Plutarch, in Greek Literature, Religion, and Philosophy, and in the New Testament Background* (Stuttgart, Germany: Steiner, 1998); D. A. Russell, *Plutarch,* 2d ed. (Bristol, U.K.: Bristol Classical Press, 2001); Robert Lamberton, *Plutarch* (New Haven, Conn.: Yale University Press, 2001); C. B. R. Pelling, *Plutarch and History: Eighteen Studies* (Swansea: Classical Press of Wales, 2002).

polis *Polis* (from which word is derived the English word "politics") refers to the ancient Greek city-state and was the basic political unit of the classical Greeks. Between about 800 B.C.E. and 300 B.C.E., the map of Greece was a patchwork of autonomous city-states, some linked together by alliance or kinship, and some vying to dominate their neighbors, but each one capable of ruling itself as a self-contained political entity. Beginning as aristocracies, city-states developed as democracies or oligarchies in the 500s–400s B.C.E. The most important DEMOCRACY was ATHENS.

Two factors contributed to the emergence of the city-state. One was the geography of Greece; mountains, islands, and small farming valleys naturally created discrete, small population centers, many with their own dialects and religious cults. The second reason, more specific to the 900s–800s B.C.E., has to do with the rejection of kingship in Greece during that era. A king may strive to unite various peoples under his single rule, because he is the government. But members of an aristocratic clan—who may rely for their power on local lands and on local religious cults, for which they supply the priesthood—might be prone to concentrate their rule in a smaller, more homogeneous area.

In population, the polis consisted of the following social groups: full citizens (usually males over age 18, born of citizen parents); female and children citizens (protected by the law but without any voice in government); second-class citizens, such as PERIOIKOI; resident aliens or METICS; and SLAVES.

The age of the polis ended with the Macedonian conquest of Greece (338 B.C.E.), the campaigns of ALEXANDER THE GREAT (334–323 B.C.E.), and the subsequent rise of rich and powerful Greco-Macedonian kingdoms in the eastern Mediterranean and Near East. In the HELLENISTIC AGE (300–150 B.C.E.), individual Greek cities were not strong enough to survive independently.

See also APOLLO; ARISTOCRACY; GREECE, GEOGRAPHY OF; HELOTS; HOPLITE; LAWS AND LAW COURTS; OLIGARCHY; TYRANTS; WOMEN.

Further reading: Roger Brock and Stephen Hodkinson, eds., *Alternatives to Athens: Varieties of Political Organization and Community in Ancient Greece* (New York: Oxford University Press, 2000); Pernille Flensted-Jensen, Thomas Heine Nielsen, and Lene Rubinstein, eds., *Polis and Politics: Studies in Ancient Greek History* (Copenhagen: Museum Tusculanum Press, 2000); Pernille Flensted-Jensen, *Further Studies in the Ancient Greek Polis* (Stuttgart, Germany: F. Steiner, 2000); Rainer Kattel, *The Constitution of the Polis* (Tartu, Estonia: Tartu University Press, 2001); Thomas Heine Nielsen, ed., *Even More Studies in the Ancient Greek Polis* (Stuttgart, Germany: F. Steiner, 2002); Catherine Morgan, *Early Greek States Beyond the Polis* (New York: Routledge, 2003); Thomas Heine Hielsen, ed., *Once Again: Studies in the Ancient Greek Polis* (Stuttgart, Germany: F. Steiner, 2004).

Polycrates (ca. 600s B.C.E.) *Dynamic tyrant of the Greek island of SAMOS*

Reigning circa 540–522 B.C.E., Polycrates was the last great Greek ruler in the eastern Aegean, in the path of the advancing Persians. Usurping power at Samos with the help of his two brothers, Polycrates soon ruled alone, executing one brother and banishing the other. He made an alliance with the Egyptian pharaoh Amasis and built a navy of 100 longboats, arming them with bowmen.

Under him, Samos became the preeminent eastern Greek state—replacing Samos's nearby rival, MILETUS, now under Persian rule.

Polycrates was a visionary of naval power. The historian HERODOTUS (the main source for Polycrates' story) called him "the first Greek to plan an empire by sea," and the historian THUCYDIDES (1) saw his domain as a forerunner of the Athenian sea empire of the 400s B.C.E.

True to his name ("ruling much"), Polycrates led his fleet east and west across the Aegean, mainly against his fellow Greeks. Many of his ventures were probably aiming to drive the Persians from the ASIA MINOR coast and capture the Greek cities there for himself. Like other tyrants, Polycrates glorified his capital city (also named Samos), while providing employment and amenities for the common people. He completed Samos's grand temple of the goddess HERA, which was one of the largest existing Greek temples at that time. He developed Samos's harbor and built or completed a tunneled aqueduct, an engineering marvel of its day, bringing water to Samos city.

Polycrates maintained the most magnificent court of the Greek world. With generous retaining fees, he attracted the distinguished physician Democedes of CROTON and the famous lyric poets IBYCUS of RHEGIUM and ANACREON of Teos. In keeping with the upper-class tastes of the era, Polycrates (although married and a father) was an enthusiastic lover of boys and young men. It was probably for Polycrates that Anacreon wrote many of his extant poems of homosexual content.

Eventually the shadow of disaster fell across this glamorous despot, as he became caught between the unstoppable Persian advance and the antityrant elements of the Greek world. Around 525 B.C.E. the skippers of a Samian war fleet rebelled and attacked Polycrates on Samos. They were defeated, but the survivors sailed west to get help from SPARTA, the foremost antityrant state of mainland Greece. The Spartans sent out an overseas expedition, their first in recorded history. However, Polycrates held out against their six-week siege of Samos city, and they went home.

Polycrates did not survive for long. Around 522 B.C.E. the Persian governor of western Asia Minor lured Polycrates in person to the mainland, then had him seized and killed. A few years later the Persian king DARIUS (1) conquered Samos and installed, as his vassal, Polycrates' surviving brother, Syloson ("preserver of booty"). Samos's sea holdings were lost, and henceforth Samos's warships served in the Persian navy.

Among the folktales that sprang up around Polycrates, one has been retold in variations over the centuries. According to Herodotus, Polycrates, at the height of success, was warned that—because the gods are jealous of human happiness—he should offset the danger by throwing away whatever he valued most in the world. He

decided to discard his priceless signet ring, an engraved emerald set in GOLD. Aboard one of his ships, he threw the ring into the sea. But a few days later, as Polycrates sat down to dinner, his servants brought in that very ring; it had been found in the belly of a fine fish being prepared for the ruler's meal. The gods had rejected Polycrates' offering, and he was doomed to die a miserable death.

See also FATE; HOMOSEXUALITY; TYRANTS; WARFARE, NAVAL.

Further reading: H. T. Wallinga, "Polycrates and Egypt. The Testimony of the Samaina," in *Achaemenid History, 6. Asia Minor and Egypt. Old Cultures in a New Empire. Proceedings of the Groningen 1988 Achaemenid History Workshop*, edited by H. Sancisi-Weerdenburg and A. Kuhrt (Leiden, Netherlands: Nederlands Instituut voor het Nabije Oosten, 1991), 179–197.

Polygnotus *See* PAINTING.

Polykleitos (mid-late 400s B.C.E.) *Prominent sculptor known for his idealized view of the male body*
Polykleitos was born at ARGOS. Working mainly in BRONZE, he established his reputation with a number of commissioned statues of victorious Olympian athletes, displayed at OLYMPIA. Two famous nudes by Polykleitos have survived in the form of later marble copies—the Doryphoros (spear carrier, in the Naples Museum), representing a muscular athlete; and the more sensual Diadumenos (ribbon binder, in the Athens National Museum and elsewhere), showing a youth tying an athlete's ribbon around his head. The Doryphoros illustrated Polykleitos's Canon—his concept of the ideal human properties. It also brought to perfection the Contrappositio ("counterpoise") stance: weight on one leg, knee locked, the other leg drawn back. This stance became a standard pose for statuary down through Renaissance times.

Polykleitos's masterpiece was considered to be the giant GOLD and ivory cult statue of the goddess HERA, sculpted for Hera's temple at Polykleitos's native Argos (ca. 420 B.C.E.). The statue, now lost, showed the goddess seated, with a scepter in one hand and a pomegranate in the other. The statue was in ancient times compared with the colossal statue of Olympian ZEUS sculpted by Polykleitos's rival, PHEIDIAS. The Roman geographer Strabo considered the Hera to be the more lovely in technique, although smaller and less magnificent than the Zeus.

See also SCULPTURE.

Further reading: Cornelius Vermeule, *Polykleitos* (Boston: Museum of Fine Arts, 1969); Warren G. Moon, *Polykleitos, the Doryphoros, and Tradition* (Madison: University of Wisconsin Press, 1995); Adolf H. Borbein, "Polykleitos," in *Personal Styles in Greek Sculpture*, edited by Olga Palagia and J. J. Pollitt (New York: Cambridge University Press, 1996), 66–90.

Polynices   *See* SEVEN AGAINST THEBES.

Polyphemos   In HOMER's epic poem the *Odyssey* (written down around 750 B.C.E.) Polyphemos ("much fame") is a CYCLOPS—one of a race of gigantic, savage, one-eyed creatures who inhabit a legendary region in the West, vaguely associated with SICILY. Polyphemos is the son of the god POSEIDON and the nymph Thoösa. In what is probably the *Odyssey*'s best-known episode, Polyphemos captures the Greek hero ODYSSEUS (book 9).

Odysseus discovers the monster's cave after landing his ship in the Cyclopes's territory on his voyage home from the TROJAN WAR. With 12 of his men, Odysseus enters the deserted cave to steal supplies, then willfully remains inside the cave, hoping to have a look at the Cyclops. But when Polyphemos returns with his goats and sheep, he immediately traps the Greeks by sealing the cave mouth with a slab of rock, too large for humans to drag away. Then, catching two of the Greeks in his hands, Polyphemos beats out their brains and eats them raw for dinner. Stretching out amid his sheep, he falls asleep. The Greeks do not attack him, realizing that they can never escape without Polyphemos to move that massive boulder.

The next morning Polyphemos eats two more men for breakfast, leaves the Greeks penned inside as he pastures his flock and herd for another day, and then eats two more men for supper. By then Odysseus has a plan. He makes Polyphemos drunk by giving him a goatskin-full of WINE. When the Cyclops falls into a drunken sleep, Odysseus and his men ram a sharpened post into the monster's one eyeball, blinding him forever. The other Cyclopes, hearing Polyphemos's cries, gather outside the cave and ask what's wrong; Polyphemos shouts out that "Nobody" is hurting him—Nobody (Outis) being the false name by which Odysseus had identified himself to the giant. The other Cyclopes wander off, assuming that Polyphemos's affliction must come from the gods. Then the blind Polyphemos drags away the door boulder and, squatting at the cave mouth, waits furiously for the Greeks to try to run out.

Again Odysseus has a scheme. He ties each of his six remaining men to the underbellies of three sheep abreast, and himself takes hold of the fleecy underbelly of a big ram. As the Cyclops's sheeps and goats move out of the cave for grazing, the Greeks ride concealed among them. The giant strokes each animal's back as it passes, but he misses the Greeks hiding underneath.

The Greeks escape back to their beached ship and shipmates. Once safely aboard and headed out to sea, Odysseus cannot resist the impulse to shout out taunts to Polyphemos and tell him his own true name and lineage. Guided by the voice, Polyphemos hurls a boulder that nearly smashes the departing ship, then he prays to his divine father, Poseidon, to curse Odysseus. Thereafter, in the *Odyssey*, Poseidon is Odysseus's enemy, working to disrupt the hero's voyage home.

Centuries later, in the HELLENISTIC AGE, Polyphemos became the subject of poetic elaboration. The Sicilian Greek poet THEOKRITUS (ca. 275 B.C.E.) wrote two poems describing how, prior to the Odysseus episode, Polyphemos loved and wooed the sea nymph Galatea. The idea of turning a savage, ugly giant into a romantic hero is typical of the frivolous intellectual tastes of the Hellenistic era.

Unrelated to the Cyclops story, the name *Polyphemos* also belonged to one of the Argonauts who sailed with the Thessalian hero JASON (1) in search of the Golden Fleece.

Further reading: Gösta Säflund, *The Polyphemus and Scylla Groups at Sperlonga* (Stockholm: Almqvist & Wiksell, 1972); J. Glenn, "The Polyphemus Myth. Its Origins and Interpretation," *Greece and Rome* 25 (1978): 141–155; M. Knox, "Polyphemos and His Near Eastern Relations," *Journal of Hellenic Studies* 99 (1979): 164–165; Bernard Evslin, *The Cyclopes* (New York: Chelsea House, 1987).

Poseidon   The Greek god of the sea and all other bodies of water, Poseidon was also the god of earthquakes and horses. According to the Greek creation legend, Poseidon received the sea as his domain when he and his brothers, ZEUS and HADES, drew lots for their portions of the world, after deposing their royal father, CRONUS. Poseidon was variously described as younger or older than Zeus, but he was subordinate to Zeus in wisdom and moral significance.

A patron god of mariners and fishermen, Poseidon had important temples in certain Greek coastal regions in historical times. These sanctuaries included Cape MYCALĒ, on the central west coast of ASIA MINOR, and Cape Sunium, in the Athenian territory of ATTICA. The god was commemorated in the names of seaport cities such as POSEIDONIA and POTIDAEA. But his most famous shrine was at the Isthmus of CORINTH, in south-central Greece, where the biennial ISTHMIAN GAMES were held in his honor.

Poseidon was especially associated with storms at sea, which posed a deadly hazard to ancient shipping. In the god's sea-front temples, voyagers prayed for safe passage, and survivors of shipwrecks gave thanks for deliverance. When storms off the Thessalian coast in 480 B.C.E. destroyed part of the invading Persian fleet during the PERSIAN WARS, the Greeks paid thanks to Poseidon.

The name Poseidon clearly contains the Greek root *pos-*, "lord," but the rest of the meaning is lost to us. In Greek RELIGION, Poseidon (like Zeus) probably dates back to the earliest Greek-speaking tribesmen who arrived in Greece around 2100 B.C.E. Poseidon's earliest form was probably not that of a sea god. (According to modern scholarship, the Greeks originally came from a landlocked region, the Danube basin, and at first lacked a word for "sea.") The prehistoric Poseidon may have been a deity of lakes, rivers, and mountain torrents. He became associated with earthquakes because they were thought to be caused by underground watercourses. In historical times, Poseidon's most common titles were "shaker of the Earth" (Ennosigaios) and "holder of the Earth" (Gaieochos).

Probably before or during the years of MYCENAEAN CIVILIZATION (around 1600–1200 B.C.E.), Poseidon took on his familiar role as the sea god. This change surely occurred as the early Greeks learned shipbuilding and ventured out to sea for food supply, war, and TRADE. Poseidon is mentioned frequently in the surviving LINEAR B tablets from the late Mycenaean era, circa 1400–1200 B.C.E., but his precise roles in those years are unclear.

In taking over the sea, Poseidon's cult seems to have displaced the worship of certain pre-Greek sea deities. Apparently some of these survived in Greek MYTH in the guise of lesser sea gods, such as NEREUS and his mermaid daughters, the Nereids. Poseidon was said to have married a Nereid named Amphitritē, after subduing her by pursuit and abduction. She bore him a son, Triton. The sound *trit*, which the names of mother and son share, is considered by scholars to be non-Greek and may represent a prehellenic word for "sea."

Poseidon's function as the horse god may date back to his earliest roots among prehistoric Greek-speaking tribes, who evidently arrived in mainland Greece with domesticated horses. In historical times there was a widespread cult of Poseidon Hippios (of the horse); images in some shrines showed the god as a horseman. According to one myth, the first horse had been born out of a rock where Poseidon's semen had fallen. Poseidon oversaw the horse- and chariot-racing at all Greek sports festivals, not just at his own Isthmian Games. He was said to have been the mentor of the hero PELOPS, founder of the OLYMPIC GAMES.

Mythologically, Poseidon embodied the raw power found in his elements—the sea, earthquakes, and horses. Legends portrayed him as strong, yet brutish and not

An array of gods watching the progress of humans, from the Parthenon frieze. Poseidon, god of the sea, is at the left; his trident is missing from his hands. Apollo and Artemis are to his left. *(Alison Frantz Photographic Collection, American School of Classical Studies at Athens)*

clever, sometimes in contrast with the wise goddess ATHENA. Poseidon was an important god for the Athenians—he was associated with the hero THESEUS, and he had a shrine inside the patriotic-cult building known as the Erectheum, on the ACROPOLIS. But he was said to have lost a contest with Athena over who would become the chief Athenian deity. HOMER's *Odyssey* echoed this competition: Poseidon failed to destroy the wily hero ODYSSEUS, who was aided by Athena. Other legends described Athena as a civilizing influence over Poseidon's realm—she invented shipbuilding and the bridle, to bring humans to the sea and to tame the horse.

Poseidon's myths tended to associate him with monsters. He was the lover of the demon MEDUSA, and lover or father of the HARPIES. His beautiful mistress SCYLLA was transformed into a hideous sea monster by the jealous Amphitritē. His liaison with the earth goddess GAEA (who was technically his grandmother) produced the fierce giant Antaeus, later killed by HERAKLES. With the nymph Thoösa, Poseidon was father of the brutal POLYPHEMOS. Less grotesquely, the Elean princess Tyro bore Poseidon twin sons, Neleus (later king of PYLOS and father of NESTOR) and Pelias (later king of Iolcus, in THESSALY, and enemy of JASON [1]).

In Greek art, Poseidon supplied a study in pure strength. He was often shown holding his trident—a three-pronged fish spear used by Greek fishermen. He resembled Zeus in his beard, physique, and mature age. A superb classical Greek statue found in the sea off Cape ARTEMISION in the 1920s C.E., now identified as a likeness of Zeus, was for decades thought to represent Poseidon.

See also CHARIOTS; GREEK LANGUAGE; SHIPS AND SEAFARING.

Further reading: Elizabeth Gebhard, "Caves and Cults at the Isthmian Sanctuary of Poseidon," in *Peloponnesian Sanctuaries and Cults: Proceedings of the Ninth International Symposium at the Swedish Institute at Athens, 11–13 June 1994,* edited by Robin Hägg (Stockholm: Svenska Institutet i Athen, 2002), 63–74.

Poseidonia   This Greek city is situated on the southwestern coast of ITALY, on the Bay of Salerno. Located at the edge of a wide plain, Poseidonia was founded by colonists from the Italian Greek city of SYBARIS in the last quarter of the 600s B.C.E. and was named for the sea god POSEIDON. It was a sprawling city, encircled by a wall nearly three miles long but without natural defenses, and it thrived from FARMING and seaborne TRADE. Captured around 390 B.C.E. by neighboring Italian tribesmen, the Lucanii, the city passed in 273 B.C.E. into the hands of the Romans, who called it Paestum.

The site now boasts the standing remnants of three Doric-style temples, built between about 550 and 450 B.C.E., which are among the best-preserved examples of Greek monumental ARCHITECTURE. Of these, the famous "Temple of Neptune" (actually a temple of HERA) rivals the Athenian PARTHENON in magnificence. The site also contains tombs of the 400s and 300s B.C.E. that have provided some of the few surviving Greek wall paintings.

See also PAINTING.

Further reading: J. G. Pedley, *Paestum. Greeks and Romans in Southern Italy* (London: Thames and Hudson, 1990); Emanuele Greco, Ilaria D'Ambrosio, and Dinu Theodorescu, *Archaeological and Historical Guide to the Excavations, the Museum, and the Antiquities of Poseidonia Paestum,* translated by B. Marenco and V. Romano (Taranto, Italy: Scorpione editrice, 1996); J. G. Pedley, "Problems in Provenance and Patronage. A Group of Late Hellenistic Statuettes from Paestum," in *Regional Schools in Hellenistic Scupture. Proceedings of an International Conference Held at the American School of Classical Studies at Athens, March 15—17, 1996,* edited by Olga Palagia and William Coulson (Oxford: Oxbow Books, 1998), 199–209; Ernesto De Carolis, *Paestum; A Reasoned Archaeological Itinerary* (Naples: T & M, 2002).

Potidaea   (Greek: Poteidaia, a form of the name of the god Poseidon)   This important Corinthian colony was founded around 600 B.C.E. on the northern Aegean seacoast known as CHALCIDICĒ. Located on the narrow neck of the westernmost of Chalcidicē's three peninsulas, Potidaea had a fine harbor, facing west into the Thermaic Gulf and protected in later years by walls and by moles across the harbor mouth. Potidaea was the only major Chalcidic city founded by Greeks who were not IONIAN GREEKS; it was also the only Corinthian colony located in the Aegean rather than in the Adriatic or farther west. Potidaea's location made it a gateway from Greece to the north Aegean. Exporting to Corinth, it was a source for TIMBER, SILVER, and SLAVES, available from nearby THRACE.

Potidaea became a foremost Chalcidic city, later surpassed only by its neighbor OLYNTHOS. With Thracian silver, Potidaea was minting coins by about 550 B.C.E. It led the local Greek resistance to the invading Persians of 480–479 B.C.E., its formidable defenses withstanding a Persian siege. After the Persian retreat, Potidaea joined the Athenian-led DELIAN LEAGUE. However, the city maintained close ties with Corinth—for instance, it received its chief political executives from Corinth every year.

As Athenian-Corinthian relations worsened in the mid-400s B.C.E., Potidaea became the object of increasing Athenian mistrust. In 434 B.C.E. the Athenians raised Potidaea's Delian annual tribute from six to 15 TALENTS. In resistance to Athenian demands, Potidaea rebelled, appealing to Corinth for help. Soon ATHENS and Corinth were in collision over Potidaea. At the Battle of Potidaea, fought outside the city (432 B.C.E.), an Athenian expeditionary force of 2,000 HOPLITES defeated a slightly smaller Corinthian-led army. This episode—like similar

Athenian-Corinthian hostilities at the Adriatic city of CORCYRA—was a major cause in igniting the PELOPON-NESIAN WAR.

Potidaea finally was captured by the Athenians in early 429 B.C.E., after an immense siege in which the Athenian army suffered from plague and the starving defenders were reduced to cannibalism. The Athenians allowed the Potidaeans to evacuate, and the city was repopulated with Athenian colonists. But after Athens's defeat in the Peloponnesian War (404 B.C.E.), the local Chalcidic Greeks took over the city.

As the second city (after Olynthos) of the powerful Chalcidic League, Potidaea again became a target of Athenian imperialism, in the early 300s B.C.E. It was captured by Athenian troops in 363 B.C.E. The Athenians were expelled by the Macedonian king PHILIP II in 358 B.C.E., but Potidaea probably was destroyed by Philip in 348 B.C.E., in his war against Olynthos.

In around 316 B.C.E. the city was refounded as the capital of MACEDON under the ruler KASSANDER; the city's new name was Kassandreia. In the HELLENISTIC AGE (300–150 B.C.E.) it remained a major port of the north Aegean, and passed into the empire of ROME after the Romans dismantled the Macedonian kingdom in the mid-100s B.C.E.

Knowledge about Potidaea comes mostly from a few ancient literary sources: HERODOTUS, THUCYDIDES, XENOPHON, and DEMOSTHENES (1). The site has not been systematically excavated, but some of its archaeological remains have been discovered due to the cutting of a canal through the isthmus of the peninsula in 1935–1937 C.E. There are numerous silver and bronze coins from the site, as well as some bronze and terra-cotta sculptures. In addition, one of the treasuries at DELPHI was built by the Potidaeans.

See also PERIANDER; PERSIAN WARS.

Further reading: John A. Alexander, *Potidaea: Its History and Remains* (Athens, Ga.: University of Georgia Press, 1963); A. Alexander, "Cassandreia During the Macedonian Period: An Epigraphical Commentary," in *Ancient Macedonia*, edited by B. Laourdas and C. Makaronas (Thessaloníki: Institute for Balkan Studies, 1970); G. S. Shrimpton, "Strategy and Tactics in the Preliminaries to the Siege of Potidaea (Thuc. 1.61–65)," *Symbolae Osloenses* 59 (1984): 7–12; E. Badian, *From Plataea to Potidaea. Studies in the History and Historiography of the Pentecontaetia* (Baltimore: Johns Hopkins University Press, 1993).

pottery   The term *Greek pottery* refers mainly to ceramic vessels—storage jars, drinking cups, mixing bowls, plates, and the like—shaped from wet clay on a potter's wheel and fired to brittleness in a kiln heated to about 1,000 degrees Fahrenheit. In addition to hardening the pot, the baking permanently sets any glaze or paint, often with predictable changes of color.

Athenian amphora of the mid-700s B.C.E., 16 inches tall, painted in the style known as Geometric. Geometric vase painting provides the first surviving sign of an awakened Greek artistic genius after the Dark Age (1100–900 B.C.E.). This impressive example shows how painters began to break up their abstract designs with renderings of live figures—in this case, deer (above), goats (middle), and geese (below). The repeated key pattern, sometimes called a meander, remained a familiar design on Greek textiles and other goods throughout antiquity. *(Margaret Bunson)*

Items of ceramic (Greek: *keramos,* "potter's clay") obviously played a large role in the TRADE and daily life of all ancient cultures. However, for modern archaeologists, pottery takes on a paramount importance well beyond its importance in ancient times, due to the simple fact that pottery is nearly indestructible. A fired clay pot may shatter easily, but the sherds will last for 10,000 years once buried in the ground. Pottery is thus different from such perishable materials as textiles or wood, which also served major uses in ancient times but which have disappeared with barely a trace. Pottery provides the most available material link to the ancient world. Not every ancient site has a PARTHENON to offer, but almost every site has a buried wealth of potsherds, full of data for the archaeologist.

For example, Greek pottery is the best-surviving medium for ancient Greek PAINTING. The painted scenes that once adorned walls, wooden panels, and canvases in ancient Greece are lost, but the scenes on pottery, baked onto the clay, have survived. Such vase paintings suggest the developing techniques of all Greek painting, and the rendered scenes also provide priceless information about life in ancient Greece—for RELIGION, FARMING, warfare, and the like. Many of the illustrations in this book depict scenes that were originally painted on pottery.

More generally, the geographic distribution of pottery remnants can reveal ancient trade routes and waves of migrations. Mycenaean potsherds found in southern CYPRUS reveal that the early Greeks probably settled there around 1300 B.C.E. Similarly, the huge troves of Corinthian and Athenian pottery found at sites in former Etruria (in northern ITALY, a region where the Greeks never settled) are a dramatic sign of the insatiable market for Greek goods that existed among the ETRUSCANS, around 600–500 B.C.E.

The invention of pottery predates by thousands of years the dawn of Greek civilization, starting with pots shaped without a potter's wheel in Mesopotamia and eastern China, around 5000 B.C.E. By 2500 B.C.E. pottery was being produced in the pre-Greek CYCLADES and by the Minoan people of CRETE. Technique was improved by introduction of the potter's wheel around 2100 B.C.E.

Mainland Greece, with its soil rich in clay, was producing pottery before the Greeks arrived. The invading Greeks' conquest of Greece (around 2100 B.C.E. and after) is probably signified by the disappearance of prior styles of pottery and the abrupt emergence (around 1900 B.C.E.) of a new type, known to modern archaeologists as Minyan ware. Distinguished by its unadorned gray or gray-yellow glazing and its shape that resembles vessels of beaten metal, Minyan ware was discovered and named in 1880 C.E. by the great archaeologist Heinrich Schliemann. This pottery has been found throughout Greece and is the earliest surviving vestige of those people whose descendants would create the MYCENAEAN CIVILIZATION (around 1600–1200 B.C.E.)

A sampling of Greek pottery designs from the 500s and 400s B.C.E. Several of these types had their specialized use at the upper-class drinking party known as the symposium. (a) Amphora, meaning "two handled"—the classic Greek wine-storage vessel; sealed with a lid or plug, the amphora was used for domestic storage and (in a modified shape) for seaborne export. (b) Pelike, another type of storage vessel. (c) Krater ("mixer"), used for mixing wine and water at a meal or symposium; this particular design is known as a volute (curl-handled) krater. (d) Bell Krater. (e) Loutrophorous, a ceremonial water vase, used at Athens or the special bath on the wedding day and for the funerary washing corpse. (f) Stamnos, a jar for storing wine or oil. (g) Psykter ("cooler"), used to cool undiluted wine prior to mixing and serving; the psykter's shape allowed it to fit partly inside a bowl of cold water. (h) Hydra, a water jug. (i) Lebes, a basin used like a krater, for mixing wine and water. (j) Lekythos, an oil flask. (k) Oinochoë, a "wine pourer," for dispensing wine from the krater. (l) Kantharos, a type of wine cup. (m) Kylix, another type of wine cup; the shallow bowl was suited to a drinker reclining at a symposium. (n) Rhyton, a decorative form of wine cup, ending at bottom, in an animal's head or other shape. (o) Skyphos, another wine cup. (p) Alabastron, a jar for perfumes and unguents; the jar acquired its name, in ancient times, because many specimens were carved from alabaster. (*Margaret Bunson*)

More imaginative pottery shapes and painted designs emerge at the height of Mycenaean culture (around 1400—1200 B.C.E.). Clearly influenced by Minoan pottery, Mycenaean ware included many shapes—such as the drinking cup (kylix), pitcher (lekythos), and storage jar (amphora)—that would see use in later centuries in classical Greece. Mycenaean artists typically painted brown on pale yellow. Designs include concentric bands and floral patterns, but a few discovered Mycenaean pots show animal figures such as birds and an octopus. One spectacular vase shows a column of soldiers.

The downfall of Mycenaean society (by 1100 B.C.E.) was followed by the gradual emergence of new pottery shapes and painted designs, recognizably derived from Mycenaean types. This new style, emerging specifically at ATHENS around 1050 B.C.E., is today called Protogeometric—the forerunner to the Geometric style that developed around 900 B.C.E. Protogeometric vase painting is distinguished by certain brown or black designs: concentric circles or half circles (drawn with a compass on the vase's side), triangles, cross-hatching, and the earliest appearance of the typically Greek right-angle pattern known as the meander.

The Geometric period (around 900–700 B.C.E.) saw new methods of decoration, along with certain new pottery shapes. On a background of tan or light yellow, the best Geometric ware shows a density of design, including (after about 800 B.C.E.) silhouette stick figures representing animal life or human activity, at first confined to horizontal panels around the vase. One of the most characteristic Geometric human scenes (around 750 B.C.E.) is on the Dipylon amphora, named because it was discovered near Athens's ancient Dipylon Gate. Amid bands of meanders and diamond shapes, a panel shows triangular-torsoed stick figures in postures of mourning around a skirted figure on a bier. Appropriately, the five-foot-tall vase was deposited as an offering in an aristo-cratic tomb. This vase's artist, named the Dipylon painter by scholars, is considered to be the first recognizably individual Greek artist.

Geometric style spread to workshops throughout Greece, but by about 730 B.C.E. artists at the mighty commercial center of CORINTH had abandoned Geometric in favor of new designs, strongly influenced by artwork imported from the Near East. The first stage of this development—part of a larger Orientalizing movement in all Greek art—is known as the protocorinthian style (730–625 B.C.E.). Next came the ripe Corinthian style (ca. 625–550 B.C.E.). Widely popular, Corinthian-made potteries monopolized the market, both inside the Greek world and beyond, for nearly 150 years.

Protocorinthian and Corinthian vase painting shows mainly human or animal scenes, with some intervening decorations (typically floral, copied from Near Eastern motifs). Gone are the dark stick figures of Geometric art; there is wide use of color and detail, with attempts at foreshortening. One of the most admired such works is the Chigi Vase (around 650 B.C.E.), illustrated with a warfare scene. Under influence of the emerging Athenian black-figure technique, the full Corinthian style (around 560 B.C.E.) combined color with solemnity in a packed, friezelike scene. New pottery shapes also came into use in this era.

In imitation of Corinthian technique, the region of SPARTA produced a school of pottery painting in the early 500s B.C.E. A number of lively scenes survive on the inside bottoms of Spartan cups.

Meanwhile Athenian black-figure pottery, destined to oust Corinthian ware from the world market, was being produced by 600 B.C.E. Early black figure saw the vast reduction of decorative designs in favor of scenes from MYTH; later scenes from daily life—farming, seafaring—become more common. The name *black figure* refers to the fact that men's skin was painted dark and rendered into black by glazing and firing; in contrast, women's flesh was shown as white. Incisions helped create detail and fire lines. One early epitome of the style is the Athenian-made Francoise Vase (ca. 570 B.C.E.), discovered in what used to be Etruscan territory and now in the Florence archaeological museum. The small vase (a volute krater, or form of mixing bowl) uses a light background to present lively mythological scenes in miniature. The black-figure technique reached its zenith in about 550–525 B.C.E., with the work of such Athenian artists as the Amasis Painter.

But by 520 B.C.E. a new Athenian style had emerged, now called red figure. Red figure reversed the black-figure technique; the human and animal figures were left open to the clay's red color, and now the background was painted and fired black. This represented a breakthrough for creating realistic figures and precise detail. The style reached perfection in the work of the artist now known as the Berlin Painter (ca. 480 B.C.E.), who was able to show beautifully realistic musculature and detail.

A terra-cotta cart with amphorae from Euboea ca. 560 B.C.E. This was a decorative way to keep perfumed oils nearby. *(Alison Frantz Photographic Collection, American School of Classical Studies at Athens)*

Another popular Athenian style of the 400s B.C.E. was the white-ground technique, which rendered figures in delicate lines against a white background. This style was used particularly for *lekythoi* (pitchers) deposited as offerings in tombs.

The decline of Athenian red-figure style around 400 B.C.E. marks the end of the great phases of Greek vase painting. But red-figure continued—the painted scenes become more crowded, the figures more florid—into the 300s B.C.E., especially in Greek south Italy and SICILY (where Athenian-influenced vase-painting movements arose in the 440s B.C.E.). By 300 B.C.E. the new trade routes of the Hellenistic world were making metal pots and vessels more accessible, thereby removing any rich market for vase painting. But the 200s B.C.E. saw a renaissance of sorts, in the polychrome ware from Greek Sicily.

See also ARCHAEOLOGY; FUNERAL CUSTOMS; MINOAN CIVILIZATION.

Further reading: R. M. Cook, *Greek Painted Pottery,* 2d ed. (London: Methuen, 1972); Joseph V. Noble, *The Techniques of Painted Attic Pottery,* 2d ed. (London: Thames and Hudson, 1988); Brian A. Sparkes, *Greek Pottery: An Introduction* (New York: St. Martin's Press, 1991); Ioana E. Phoca and Panos D. Valavanis, *Greek Pottery: A Culture Captured in Clay,* translated by Timothy Cullen (Athens: B. Kagia, 1992); Michael Vickers and David Gill, *Artful Crafts: Ancient Greek Silverware and Pottery,* 2d ed. (Oxford: Clarendon Press, 1996); Toby Schreiber, *Athenian Vase Construction: A Potter's Analysis* (Malibu, Calif.: J. Paul Getty Museum, 1999); Dyfri Williams, *Greek Vases,* 2d ed. (London: British Museum Publications, 1999).

Statue of the god Hermes holding the infant Dionysus, sculpted by Praxiteles ca. 340 B.C.E., considered one of his existing masterpieces. *(Alison Frantz Photographic Collection, American School of Classical Studies at Athens)*

Praxiteles (ca. 400–325 B.C.E.) *Important Greek sculptor* An Athenian, Praxiteles worked in the mid-300s B.C.E. and was famous for his gorgeous, idealized nudes. He developed marble (as opposed to BRONZE) as a medium for free-standing statuary, and in keeping with the emerging tastes of the late classical period, he promoted the female nude as an object of artistic reverence, alongside the male.

Praxiteles' most celebrated work was his statue of APHRODITE for that goddess's temple at KNIDOS in ASIA MINOR (ca. 350–340 B.C.E.). Originally made for and rejected by the island of Kos, the statue was the first major cult statue showing a goddess in the nude. It eventually became one of the most famous statues in the world and was considered to be the most beautiful image of Aphrodite ever created. It showed the goddess having disrobed for her bath, with one hand vainly attempting to conceal her naked body. Many copies of this statue were created during the Roman period; one now stands in the Vatican Museum.

Another famous statue by Praxiteles, made around 340 B.C.E., showed the god HERMES holding the divine infant DIONYSUS. The Roman traveler PAUSANIAS mentions seeing this statue in the sanctuary of ZEUS at OLYMPIA. A statue of this type found there is the subject of debate among modern art historians; it is either Praxiteles' original or a slightly later copy, probably of the HELLENISTIC AGE (ca. 300–150 B.C.E.). It shows Hermes teasing the baby Dionysus with a bunch of grapes that he dangles above him (the grapes are not preserved but are known from a Roman wall painting of the group). This amusing, very human view of the gods is typical of Praxiteles' compositions and is one reason for his fame.

See also SCULPTURE.

Further reading: Christine M. Havelock, *The Aphrodite of Knidos and Her Successors: A Historical Review of the Female Nude in Greek Art* (Ann Arbor: University of Michigan Press, 1995); A. Ajootian, "Praxiteles," in *Personal Styles in Greek Sculpture,* edited by Olga Palagia and J. J. Pollitt (New York: Cambridge University Press, 1996), 91–129; A. Corso, "The Hermes of Praxiteles," *Numismatica e antichità classiche* 25 (1996): 131–153; A. Corso, "Love as Suffering. The Eros of Thespiae of Praxiteles,"

Bulletin of the Institute of Classical Studies 42 (1997–1998): 63–91.

prayer In the ancient Greek world, worshippers asked for favors from the gods through prayer and sacrifice. Images of people praying generally show them standing, with both arms raised and outstretched. Public prayers followed specific formulas and generally ended with the promise of a sacrifice or votive offering to the deity in thanks for the positive fulfillment of the request. Prayers did not necessarily take place in a sanctuary or near a temple, but sometimes people might choose to visit a cult space in the hopes that the god would respond more quickly and favorably.

Prayers to the gods were sometimes accompanied by votive offerings, and numerous such offerings (often works of SCULPTURE) survive. One is the so-called *Mantiklos Apollo*, a bronze statue from THEBES that dates to around 700 B.C.E. In this instance, the donor (Mantiklos) was not praying for anything specific, just for good fortune. The inscription on the male figure reads as follows: "Mantiklos offers me (the statue) as a tithe to APOLLO of the silver bow. Do you, Phoibos (Apollo), give some pleasing favor in return."

Further reading: J. Maringer, "Adorants in Prehistoric Art. Prehistoric Attitudes and Gestures of Prayer," *Numen* 26 (1979): 215–230; H. S. Versnel, ed., *Faith, Hope, and Worship. Aspects of Religious Mentality in the Ancient World* (Leiden, Netherlands: E. J. Brill, 1981); B. Rutkowski, "Prayer (Adoration) Gestures in Prehistoric Greece," *Archeologia. Rocznik Instytutu archeologii i etnologii Polskiej akademii nauk.* 41 (1990): 9–20; Christopher Faraone and Dirk Obbink, eds., *Magika Hiera: Ancient Greek Magic and Religion* (New York: Oxford University Press, 1991); P. W. van der Horst, "Silent Prayer in Antiquity," *Numen* 41 (1994): 1–25; D. Lateiner, "Homeric Prayer," *Arethusa* 30 (1997): 241–272; M. Kiley, ed., *Prayer from Alexander to Constantine. A Critical Anthology* (London: Routledge, 1997); M. Depew, "Reading Greek Prayers," *Classical Antiquity* 16 (1997): 229–258; Simon Pulleyn, *Prayer in Greek Religion* (New York: Oxford University Press, 1997).

Priam In MYTH, Priam was the last king of TROY, killed in the Greeks' capture of the city in the TROJAN WAR. He was the son and successor of King Laomedon and the husband of HECUBA, by whom he had 17 sons, including HECTOR and PARIS. Between wife and concubines, Priam had 50 sons and 12 daughters in all.

In HOMER's epic poem the *Iliad*, which describes events of the 10th year of the war, Priam appears as an important secondary character, elderly and wise. He disapproves of Paris's abduction of the Spartan princess HELEN, which has caused the war, but he shows nobility in his courtesy to her and his determination not to give her back to the Greeks against her will. Near the poem's end, after Hector has been slain by the Greek hero ACHILLES, Priam journeys, with the supernatural aid of the gods ZEUS and HERMES, to the Greek camp. There he successfully pleads with Achilles for the privilege of ransoming back Hector's corpse. The old king's grief and suppliant posture clearly foreshadow the destruction of his city.

The story of Priam's death was originally told in another Greek epic poem titled *The Capture of Troy (Iliou Persis)*, which has not survived but whose general plot is known. During the Greeks' sack of the city, Priam took refuge at an altar of Zeus but was impiously slain there by Achilles' son, NEOPTOLEMUS. For the classical Greeks, Priam represented the extremes of good and bad fortune that can visit a man in his lifetime.

Priam's name is apparently not Greek, and he may represent a memory of a real-life Trojan king of the historical Trojan War, around 1220 B.C.E.

See also EPIC POETRY; HELEN OF TROY.

Further reading: J. D. Madden, "The Palms Do Not Weep. A Reply to Professor Hurwit and a Note on the Death of Priam in Greek Art," *Classical Journal* 78 (1982–1983): 193–199; Margaret C. Miller, "Priam, King of Troy," in *The Ages of Homer: A Tribute to Emily Townsend Vermeule*, edited by Jane B. Carter and Sarah P. Morris (Austin: University of Texas Press, 1995), 449–466.

Priapus This east Greek fertility god and guardian of orchards and gardens is often pictured as a puny or misshapen man with an enormous, erect penis. Priapus originated in the non-Greek regions of ASIA MINOR, and in classical times (400s B.C.E.) his worship among the Greeks was confined mainly to Lampsacus, on the east shore of the HELLESPONT. During the HELLENISTIC AGE (ca. 300–150 B.C.E.), however, Priapus's cult spread and became popular at ALEXANDRIA (1) and later at ROME. His worship involved the non-Greek custom of sacrificing donkeys. He seems to have had no MYTH, being described merely as the son of APHRODITE and DIONYSUS. His name is commemorated in the modern English adjective *priapic*.

Priapus's monstrous organ signified his guardian powers as well as his fertilizing aspect, for the Greeks had a notion that trespassers and thieves (male or female) are liable to rape by the rightful owners of a territory.

See also HERMES.

Further reading: C. Johns and M. Henig, "A Statuette of a Herm of Priapus from Pakenham, Suffolk," *The Antiquaries Journal* 71 (1991): 236–239.

Procrustes In MYTH, this sadistic brigand was the son of the god POSEIDON; he preyed upon travelers in ATTICA until slain by the Athenian hero THESEUS.

Meeting a wayfarer on the road, Procrustes ("hammerer-out") would deceptively offer him lodging for the night and then force the victim to lie down on one of two beds. He would place tall men on the shorter bed and saw off their lower legs in order to make them fit; he placed short men on the longer bed and stretched them out (for the bed was a rack).

The modern English adjective *procrustean* describes an attempt to fit facts or individual examples into a preconceived, inappropriate theory or rule.

Further reading: Bernard Evslin, *Procrustes* (New York: Chelsea House, 1987).

Prometheus   In MYTH, this benevolent Titan (demigod) championed the cause of humankind against the gods. Although several characters in Greek myth defied or challenged the great god ZEUS, Prometheus is the only one who appears in a heroic light. Classical Greeks saw him as an example of the wily "trickster"—a type also represented by the god HERMES, the hero ODYSSEUS, and the real-life Athenian statesman THEMISTOKLES. Appropriately enough, *Promētheus* means "having forethought."

According to one version of the myth, it was Prometheus himself who created the first humans, shaping them out of clay while the goddess ATHENA breathed life into them. Zeus then called on Prometheus to decide the question of how humans should sacrifice to the gods—that is, which part of the sacrificed beast should be assigned as the gods' portion and which part should be eaten by mortals. In this arbitration, Prometheus chose to deceive and humiliate Zeus. As described in HESIOD's epic poem *Theogony* (ca. 700 B.C.E.), Prometheus butchered an ox and disguised the bones in a wrapping of fat, but hid the ox's flesh and edible organs inside the stomach. He showed both items to Zeus, inviting him to choose between a bundle glistening with fat or a tripe. The king of the gods chose the inviting-looking bundle, and that is why (according to the legend) humans customarily keep the best sacrificial portions for themselves to eat, while burning only the animal's bones and hide for the gods.

Zeus retaliated by withholding the use of fire from humankind, but Prometheus stole fire from heaven inside a fennel stalk and bestowed it on mortals.

Enraged at Prometheus's defiance, Zeus plotted revenge against him and his race of mortals (who up until then had included only one gender, the male). Zeus ordered the craftsman god HEPHAISTOS and other gods to create a new kind of human, lovely but treacherous: This was Pandora ("all gifts"), the first woman. She was sent to earth, where she married Prometheus's simple-minded brother, Epimetheus ("having afterthought"). Pandora brought with her, or otherwise acquired, a supernatural clay jar containing pain, toil, illness, and other evils not yet known in the world. When, out of curiosity, she opened the jar, the hateful contents flew out and propagated, leaving only hope inside the jar, to delude mortals.

For Prometheus himself, Zeus had a more terrible punishment. Hephaistos chained Prometheus to a lonely mountain crag; every day an eagle would fly up and tear out the prisoner's liver, devouring it. Prometheus never died, however and every night his liver was restored, so that the torture could be repeated daily. Eventually the hero HERAKLES released Prometheus, with Zeus's permission.

Prometheus's punishment is the subject of the stage tragedy *Prometheus Bound* (ca. 455 B.C.E.), which traditionally has been ascribed to the Athenian playwright AESCHYLUS, but which currently is thought not to be his work.

See also RELIGION; TITANS; WOMEN.

Further reading: Larry J. Kreitzer, *Prometheus and Adam: Enduring Symbols of the Human Situation* (Lanham, Md.: University Press of America, 1994); Karl Kerényi, *Prometheus: Archetypal Image of Human Existence,* translated by Ralph Manheim (Princeton, N.J.: Princeton University Press, 1997).

prophecy and divination   Because the ancient Greeks believed that the gods had a hand in human events, they also believed that humans could interpret the gods' wishes. While prayer and sacrifice sought to win the gods' favor, the interpretation of divine will was the goal of certain other activities, which the Greeks called *manteia*, denoting prophecy and other forms of divination. Prophets and soothsayers abounded in Greek MYTH, but they also remained important among living Greeks right down to the end of the ancient world.

In its strictest English-language use, the word *prophecy* refers to a form of soothsaying in which the god speaks directly through the mouth of the human prophet (Greek: *prophētēs*). "Divination," a more general word, includes less inspirational forms of future-telling. The most famous ancient Greek example of inspirational prophecy was the Delphic oracle. The oracle was a priestess of APOLLO, at the god's most holy sanctuary at DELPHI in central Greece. In response to an inquirer's question, she would go into a trance and deliver frenzied utterings, which a male priest would interpret and write down in verse. Similar oracles of Apollo were found at CUMAE and elsewhere.

Apollo's father, ZEUS, was the other main god of prophecy. At Zeus's very ancient sanctuary at DODONA, in northwestern Greece, the priests gave answers after listening for Zeus's prompting in the rustle of leaves in the god's sacred oak tree.

Other modes of divination were practiced by a seer (*mantis*), whose methods might involve observation of animal life, such as the flights and cries of passing birds—a practice now called augury. But the most common of the seer's duties was extispicy—that is, examining the removed organs (particularly the liver) of a newly sacrificed animal: A healthy-looking liver meant that the gods approved of the inquirer's intended course of action; an unhealthy one meant disapproval.

Still other forms of divination sought to find messages in dreams, in random consultations of texts of HOMER's poems, or in events of everyday life. A sneeze, for instance, was considered a good omen, applicable to whatever was being discussed or thought of at the moment. One peculiar rite, known as *kledon,* was practiced at various shrines of the god HERMES. After whispering a question into the ear of the god's cult statue, the worshipper would immediately stop up his or her own ears and leave the temple; outside, beyond the town marketplace, the worshipper would unplug his or her ears and listen for the god's answer delivered in the chance conversations of passersby.

Despite the scorn of intellectuals such as the philosopher XENOPHANES (ca. 520 B.C.E.) and the historian THUCYDIDES (1) (ca. 410 B.C.E.), a belief in divination ran

As his tenth labor, Herakles had to steal the cattle of Geryon, a fierce, three-bodied warrior. Herakles advances, and one of Geryon's bodies senses defeat and tries to run. The eagle is shown flying toward Herakles, an omen foretelling his victory. *(The J. Paul Getty Museum)*

deep and wide in Greek society. City governments employed official seers, and in times of crisis populations sought guidance in oracles and published prophecies. A Greek army on the march brought along a detail of seers, to determine divine will for military purposes; they usually did this by examining the entrails of sacrificial birds. The poet SIMONIDES wrote an epitaph for a Spartan seer, Megistias, killed at the Battle of THERMOPYLAE (480 B.C.E.). Supposedly Megistias foresaw the Spartans's annihilation, but chose to remain beside his fighting king.

See also CASSANDRA; RELIGION.

Further reading: S. Price, "Delphi and Divination," in *Greek Religion and Society,* edited by P. E. Easterling and J. V. Muir (New York: Cambridge University Press, 1985), 128–154; H. W. Parke, *Sibyls and Sibylline Prophecy in Classical Antiquity* (London: Routledge, 1988); Samson Eitrem, "Dreams and Divination in Magical Ritual," in *Magika Hiera. Ancient Greek Magic and Religion* (New York: Oxford University Press, 1991), 175–187; F. Graf, "Magic and Divination," in *The World of Ancient Magic. Papers from the First International Samson Eitrem Seminar at the Norwegian Institute at Athens, 4–8 May 1997,* edited by David Jordan, Hugo Montgomery, and Einan Thomassen (Bergen: Norwegian Institute at Athens, 1999), 283–298; Robert Temple, *Netherworld* (London: Century, 2002).

Propontis   *See* MARMARA, SEA OF.

Propylaea   *See* ACROPOLIS.

prostitutes   A society such as ancient Greece—with its slave population, discrimination against female employment, and lack of charitable relief for the poor—was bound to have many prostitutes of both genders, drawn from a needy underclass. There was also a strong demand for prostitutes because the unromantic nature of most ancient Greek marriages, combined with the enforced seclusion of citizen WOMEN, led many married men to seek sexual adventure outside the home. A market for teenage boys was fueled by the homosexual atmosphere of upper-class life in the 600s–300s B.C.E.

As with other aspects of ancient Greek society, most of our evidence for prostitution comes from ATHENS in the 400s–300s B.C.E. References to male or female prostitution occur in such Athenian writers as the comic playwright ARISTOPHANES (ca. 410 B.C.E.) and the orator AESCHINES (ca. 340 B.C.E.). The practice was legal at Athens, so long as the prostitute was not an Athenian citizen. If a male citizen was proved to have prostituted himself, he would basically lose his citizenship rights; a prostituted female citizen might suffer a similar penalty, while criminal charges could be brought against her male guardian. Prostitutes at Athens typically came from two social classes: METICS (resident aliens, meaning any

Greeks not born of Athenian parents) and SLAVES. The slaves would be women or boys sent out by their owners to earn money, which the owner then took.

No doubt many prostitutes lived the grim life of the streetwalker. But among females, the Greeks distinguished this lower-class type of prostitute, whom they called a *pornē,* from the high-class *hetaira* (literally "companion," often translated as "courtesan"). The *hetairai* were women skilled in flute-playing, singing, dancing, or acrobatics, skilled also in flirtation and sexual techniques, artful in conversation, and better educated than most citizen women. A number of extant Athenian vase paintings of the 400s B.C.E. give an idea of the *hetaira's* typical appearance and activities, while a later Greek writer, Athenaeus (ca. 200 C.E.), has preserved a collection of the sayings and exploits of famous Athenian *hetairai.*

Hetairai were often organized into "houses" run by managers, who would protect the women and supervise their schedules and fees. Such houses flourished at all commercial centers of the Greek world, including CORINTH and NAUKRATIS, in addition to Athens. Only SPARTA—austere, anticommercial, and with notoriously promiscuous citizen women—was said to have no prostitutes at all.

The natural setting for *hetairai* was the upper-class drinking party known as the SYMPOSIUM. Hired for the night, or perhaps owned as slaves of the host or guests, the *hetairai* might dance or provide flute music, but they were also obliged to give sexual favors to the guests, all of whom would be men. Certain verses of the poet ANACREON convey his infatuation with one or another *hetaira* at a symposium.

Such women were the only ones permitted to socialize with men informally outside of their homes. In one speech, the Athenian orator DEMOSTHENES (1) maintains that a certain woman cannot be an Athenian citizen, for she has been observed dining and drinking in male company, "just as a *hetaira* would do." Prostitutes, especially *hetairai,* were frequent subjects on Greek vase paintings. Since many of the vessels were used for serving or drinking wine at the symposium, scenes of these drinking parties were common. Because respectable citizen women were not permitted at the symposium, the women shown in these scenes are clearly *hetairai,* present for the purposes of entertainment, companionship, and sex. The women are thin, beautiful, and elegant, usually wearing fine garments (when clothed) and jewelry. They are often represented nude or bare-breasted, sometimes playing the flute or drinking and sometimes in the act of having sex.

The hazard of *hetairai*—from the established male viewpoint—was that they might captivate rich young men, who would squander entire fortunes on them. From the *hetaira's* viewpoint, the best she could hope for was to win a rich man's heart, so that he would purchase her freedom (if she were a slave) and set her up as his wife or mistress. At Athens, where a *hetaira* could not legally marry a citizen, she might at least become a common-law wife, or *pallakē.* Among the best-known *hetairai* were Thaïs, who was the mistress and mother of three children of PTOLEMY (1), and Phryne, who served as the sculptor PRAXITELES' model for his celebrated statue of APHRODITE.

Crude forms of birth control were no doubt an essential skill of the prostitute; unfortunately, little is known about this aspect. Ancient medical writers mention vaginal suppositories of woven fabric that were used for contraception, as well as herbal potions thought to suppress fertility. Probably more significant are the several ancient references to abortion. A clause of the ancient Hippocratic Oath, for example, forbade physicians from inducing abortion, while the Roman poet Ovid (ca. 20 B.C.E.) wrote a short poem lamenting his mistress's serious illness following a self-induced abortion.

See also ASPASIA; HIPPOCRATES; HOMOSEXUALITY; MARRIAGE; MUSIC; SAPPHO.

Further reading: Daniel Ogden, *Polygamy, Prostitutes, and Death: The Hellenistic Dynasties* (London: Duckworth, 1999); Jenifer Neils, "Others within the Other. An Intimate Look at Hetairai and Maenads," in *Not the Classical Ideal. Athens and the Construction of the Other in Greek Art,* edited by Beth Cohen (Leiden, Netherlands: E. J. Brill, 2000), 203–226; Julie Velissaropoulos-Karakostas, "Merchants, Prostitutes, and the 'New Poor': Forms of Contract and Social Status," in *Money, Labor, and Land: Approaches to the Economies of Ancient Greece,* edited by Paul Cartledge, Edward Cohen, and Lin Foxhall (London: Routledge, 2002), 130–139; Debra Hamel, *Trying Neaira: The True Story of a Courtesan's Scandalous Life in Ancient Greece* (New Haven, Conn.: Yale University Press, 2003).

Protagoras (ca. 485–415 B.C.E.) *The first and most famous of the* SOPHISTS

Born at the Greek city of ABDERA, Protagoras had a long and lucrative career. He traveled from city to city, instructing students in intellectual skills such as disputation and the arts of reasoning. Protagoras was the first thinker to acquire the title *sophistēs,* "professor" or "disputer." One of Protagoras's doctrines—that any question could admit two contradicting but equally true answers—became the hallmark of later sophists, who were notorious for their ability to debate a controversy from either side.

Visiting ATHENS, Protagoras may have influenced the thinking of the young SOCRATES. Protagoras was also a friend of the Athenian statesman PERIKLES, who once spent a whole day arguing with him over a famous criminal case, in which a boy at a GYMNASIUM had been accidentally killed by a thrown javelin: Was the javelin-thrower guilty in the death, or was the javelin itself guilty? In 443 B.C.E., when the Athenians organized a colonizing expedition to Thurii, in southern ITALY, Protagoras was chosen, no doubt on Perikles' influence, to draw up the law code for the departing colonists.

Protagoras taught an extreme form of moral relativism—that is, that there are no absolute truths, neither morally nor scientifically. Rather, he said, human convention and opinion determine completely what we can call "right" and "wrong" or "hot" and "cold." By Protagoras's teaching, perception *is* reality, for reality is determined by what we perceive. This was the background of Protagoras's best-known statement, which opened his treatise titled *Truth*: "Man is the measure of all things." Rather than extolling the beauty of the human spirit (as it is sometimes interpreted), the statement simply introduces the idea that there are no absolute truths outside of what humans agree upon.

Protagoras's writings survive only as quotations or references by later authors. He appears as a fictionalized character in PLATO's dialogue *Protagoras*, where he debates with Socrates the question, "Can moral virtue (*aretē*) be taught?"

See also ANTIPHON; LAWS AND LAW COURTS.

Further reading: Larry Goldberg, *A Commentary on Plato's Protagoras* (New York: P. Lang, 1983); J. K. Newman, "Protagoras, Gorgias, and the Dialogic Principle," *Illinois Classical Studies* 11 (1986): 43–61; J. Sihvola, *Decay, Progress, the Good Life? Hesiod and Protagoras on the Development of Culture* (Helsinki: Societas Scientiarum Fennica, 1989); Oded Balaban, *Plato and Protagoras: Truth and Relativism in Ancient Greek Philosophy* (Lanham, Md.: Lexington Books, 1999); Edward Schiappa, *Protagoras and Logos: A Study in Greek Philosophy and Rhetoric,* 2d ed. (Columbia: University of South Carolina Press, 2003).

Psyche   *See* EROS.

Ptolemy (1) (ca. 367–282 B.C.E.) *Macedonian general and, eventually, founder of a ruling dynasty in EGYPT*
Ptolemy (*Ptolemaios,* "warlike") was born the son of a Macedonian nobleman at the court of King PHILIP II; Ptolemy's mother, Arsinoë, was probably at some point the king's mistress. The young Ptolemy was a friend of Philip's son, later known as ALEXANDER THE GREAT; after Alexander became king (336 B.C.E.), Ptolemy was appointed to his bodyguard and general staff. He accompanied Alexander on the conquest of the Persian Empire (334–323 B.C.E.) and later published a campaign memoir that, although now lost, served as a major source for the surviving account written by Arrian.

When Alexander died in 323 B.C.E., Ptolemy was serving as his governor in Egypt. In the ensuing turmoil, Ptolemy emerged as one of the DIADOCHOI (Successors), who seized great chunks of Alexander's empire for themselves. Ptolemy's dangerous adversary in these years was the Macedonian general ANTIGONUS (1), who, from his base in ASIA MINOR, sought to reknit the old empire under his own rule. By 315 B.C.E. Ptolemy had joined the coalition of secessionist Diadochoi—SELEUCUS (1), KAS-

SANDER, and LYSIMACHOS—against Antigonus and his son, DEMETRIUS POLIORKETES.

At the sea battle of Cyprian Salamis (360 B.C.E.), Ptolemy suffered a major defeat at Demetrius's hands, and lost control of the AEGEAN SEA, but his Egyptian fleets remained strong in the southeastern Mediterranean. In 304 B.C.E. Ptolemy officially declared himself king of Egypt—modern scholars denote him henceforth as Ptolemy I. In 301 B.C.E. his army joined in the massive campaign that destroyed his enemy Antigonus. Ptolemy took the honorary title *Sotēr* (savior) to commemorate this victory. The next 15 years saw Ptolemy pushing to acquire or recapture territory in Antigonus's old empire, including CYPRUS, Asia Minor, and the Aegean.

Ruling from his capital at ALEXANDRIA (1), Ptolemy began organizing his Egyptian kingdom along lines that would last 700 years, down through the Roman Empire. He instituted such important "Ptolemaic" features as careful registration and taxation throughout the land, and established military colonies for the breeding of the vital Macedonian soldiering class.

In his private life, Ptolemy was devoted to his mistress, Thaïs, who bore him three children. More officially, his third wife, Berenice—who was also his half sister—bore him two children: a girl, Arsinoë, and a boy, PTOLEMY (2) II (born in 308 B.C.E.). In 285 B.C.E. the younger Ptolemy became joint ruler with his ailing father. Ptolemy's descendants would rule Egypt until 30 B.C.E.

See also CLEOPATRA; COLONIZATION; WARFARE, NAVAL.

Further reading: C. A. Kincaid, *Successors of Alexander the Great: Ptolemy I, Pyrrhus of Epirus, Hiero of Syracuse, Antiochus III* (Chicago: Ares, 1980); B. R. Brown, "Art History in Coins. Portrait Issues of Ptolemy I," in *Alessandria e il mondo ellenistico-romano. Studi in onore di Achille Adriani* (Rome: L'Erma di Bretschneider, 1983–1984), 405–417; W. M. Ellis, *Ptolemy of Egypt* (London: Routledge, 1994); N. L. Collins, "The Various Fathers of Ptolemy I," *Mnemosyne* 50 (1997): 436–476.

Ptolemy (2) II (309–246 B.C.E.) *Macedonian-descended king of EGYPT*
Ptolemy II reigned ca. 283–246 B.C.E., after succeeding his father, PTOLEMY (1). Under the younger Ptolemy's rule, the land of Egypt—already rich, powerful, and ancient—became home to a great Greek culture. Ptolemy turned his capital at ALEXANDRIA (1) into the cultural center of the Hellenistic world, a magnet for Greek thinkers, poets, and craftsmen, far surpassing contemporary ATHENS. It was Ptolemy II who built, at Alexandria, those famous institutions of learning and patronage, the Library and Museum, and who sponsored such "Alexandrian" poets as KALLIMACHUS and APOLLONIUS. It was also Ptolemy who built the lighthouse at Pharos, considered one of the SEVEN WONDERS OF THE WORLD.

Ptolemy developed his father's administrative system for the kingdom, creating an efficient bureaucracy to tax, govern, and police Egypt. Militarily, Ptolemy clashed with the SELEUCID EMPIRE, with which Egypt shared a shifting, uneasy border in the Levant. The resulting First Syrian War (ca. 274–271 B.C.E.) ended with important Ptolemaic gains in Syria and ASIA MINOR. The Second Syrian War (266–253 B.C.E.), less conclusive, ended with the MARRIAGE of Ptolemy's daughter Berenice to the Seleucid ruler Antiochus II.

Around 289 B.C.E. Ptolemy married Arsinoë, daughter of LYSIMACHUS, the Macedonian-born king of THRACE. She bore Ptolemy three children but was eventually banished for plotting to kill him. Then in about 276 B.C.E. he married his own full sister, also named Arsinoë. This Arsinoë II died within a few years, but her influence was great and her reign marked the most brilliant years of the Alexandrian court. It was this marriage to his sister that earned Ptolemy the title—which he bore with pride—of Philadelphos (lover of his sibling). Brother-sister marriage among members of the royal family was an Egyptian tradition dating back to the pharaohs, and many subsequent Ptolemies embraced this custom so as to minimize the range for court intrigues and problems of succession.

When Ptolemy died, he was succeeded by Ptolemy III, his son by the first Arsinoë.

See also HELLENISTIC AGE; JEWS; WOMEN.

Further reading: E. E. Rice, *The Grand Procession of Ptolemy Philadelphos* (New York: Oxford University Press, 1983); R. A. Hazzard, "The Regnal Years of Ptolemy II Philadelphos," *Phoenix* 41 (1987): 140–158; V. Foertmeyer, "The Dating of the Pompe of Ptolemy II Philadelphos," *Historia* 37 (1988): 90–104; W. S. Greenwalt, "Argaeus, Ptolemy II, and Alexander's Corpse," *Ancient History Bulletin* 2 (1988): 39–41.

Ptolemy (3)   *See* ASTRONOMY.

Pygmalion   This mythical king of CYPRUS sculpted an ivory statue of the goddess APHRODITE and then fell in love with it. The goddess herself, taking pity on him, breathed life into the statue, which became a living woman named Galatea. She and Pygmalion had a daughter, Paphos, after whom the Cypriot city was named.

Further reading: Geoffrey Miles, ed., *Classical Mythology in English Literature: A Critical Anthology* (London: Routledge, 1999); Esseka Joshua, *Pygmalion and Galatea: The History of a Narrative in English Literature* (Aldershot, U.K.: Ashgate, 2001).

Pylos   This coastal area of the southwest PELOPONNESE, encompasses the Bay of Navarino. In historical times, Pylos ("the gate") was part of the larger region known as MESSENIA.

Sheltered by the mile-and-a-half-long island of Sphacteria ("wasp place"), the bay provided an excellent harbor, one of the few of the entire Peloponnese. North and east of the harbor stretched the narrow but fertile coastal plain of western Messenia.

In Greek MYTH, Pylos was the home of King NESTOR, a Greek hero of the TROJAN WAR. Modern ARCHAEOLOGY confirms that the Pylos area was a western center of MYCENAEAN CIVILIZATION; excavations in the foothills eight miles northeast of the bay have uncovered the foundations of an elaborate palace complex. This palace, built 1400 B.C.E., was one of the largest Mycenaean citadels, after only MYCENAE and TIRYNS. Archaeologists have named this fortress the Palace of Nestor.

The palace consisted of three buildings, each two stories in height; their construction slightly resembled Tudor-style half-timbering. Their outer walls were made of limestone; interior elements included wooden columns and wainscoting. The complex was destroyed by fire around 1200 B.C.E., probably amid the internecine wars that ended Mycenaean society.

Among the items recovered from the ruins by archaeologists are more than 1,200 clay tablets inscribed in LINEAR B script. A few of these tablets (datable to a spring season just before the palace's destruction) record the inhabitants' keeping of a coastal watch, presumably against enemy naval attack. It was probably just such an attack that demolished the palace.

Despite Pylos's rich natural resources and geographical features, the region remained unoccupied for centuries after the Mycenaean era (although it retained its name). In 425 B.C.E., during the PELOPONNESIAN WAR, the Athenian general DEMOSTHENES (2) fortified and garrisoned Pylos's harbor, which lay only 50 miles west of the enemy city of SPARTA. The establishment of an Athenian naval base in Messenia was especially crucial to the war effort because the leaders hoped that the region's subjugated population might be incited to rebel against their Spartan overlords.

The threat of an Athenian-inspired Messenian revolt brought Spartan naval and land forces rushing against Pylos. In the ensuing sea battle, the victorious Athenians trapped 420 Spartan hoplites on the island of Sphacteria. The loss of these soldiers—then confined by Athenian naval patrols around the island—was disastrous for Sparta; all the young men belonged to the dwindling Spartan warrior class, and perhaps a third of them were "Spartiates" (*Spartiatai*), members of the military elite.

At the end of the summer of 425 B.C.E., Sphacteria was overrun by an Athenian force of 800 hoplites and several thousand light-armed troops, under the leadership of Demosthenes. Of the Spartans, 292 surrendered and survived. The political impetus for this Athenian assault had come from KLEON, who was present at Pylos as an elected Athenian general.

After the battle, the Athenian fort at Pylos remained garrisoned until 409 B.C.E. Thereafter, the harbor front was uninhabited for the rest of antiquity. The general region is now home to the modern Greek city of Pylos, also called Navarino, located at the south end of Navarino Bay.

Archaeological exploration at Pylos began in 1932 under the American archaeologist Carl Blegen. He discovered the above-mentioned Linear B tablets in the first trench he dug on the site. His work was interrupted by World War II, and he returned in 1952 to work for 12 years. Currently, a project known as PRAP (Pylos Regional Archaeological Project) is focusing on surveying the area around the Palace of Nestor and understanding the settlement patterns of the region during the BRONZE AGE.

See also KLEON.

Further reading: Thomas G. Palaima, *The Scribes of Pylos* (Rome: Edizioni dell'Ateneo, 1988); Piotr Dyczek, *Pylos in the Bronze Age: Problems of Culture and Social Life in Messenia* (Warsaw: Wydawnictwa Uniwersytetu Warszawskiego, 1994); P. A. Mountjoy, "The Destruction of the Palace at Pylos Reconsidered," *Annual of the British School at Athens* 92 (1997): 109–137; Yannos Lolos, *The Capital of Nestor and Its Environs: Sandy Pylos: Palace of Nestor, Museum of Chora, History, Monuments,* translated by John Davis (Athens: Oionos, 1998); Michael L. Galaty and William A. Parkinson, eds., *Rethinking Mycenaean Palaces: New Interpretations of an Old Idea* (Los Angeles: University of California, 1999); Carl William Blegen, *A Guide to the Palace of Nestor: Mycenaean Sites in Its Environs and the Cora Museum,* revised by Jack L. Davis and Cynthia W. Shelmerdine (Princeton, N.J.: American School of Classical Studies at Athens, 2001).

Pyrrhus (318–272 B.C.E.) *King of the Molossian tribes in the northwestern Greek region called* EPIRUS, *reigning 297–272 B.C.E.*

With his magnetic but erratic personality, Pyrrhus brought his kingdom to a brief preeminence in Greek affairs. However, his ambition of conquering a western empire was destined to fail against the Romans' growing power in ITALY. Pyrrhus was the first Greek commander ever to fight the Romans, and is best remembered for his "Pyrrhic victory" at Ausculum, in southeastern Italy, where he lost so many men that he supposedly declared, "Another such victory and we are ruined."

Pyrrhus ("fiery") was the son of the Molossian king Aiacides. The family was related by blood to the recently deceased Macedonian king ALEXANDER THE GREAT; they also claimed descent from the mythical hero NEOPTOLEMOS. When Aiacides was desposed and banished in 317 B.C.E., Pyrrhus began an exile that eventually involved him with some of the greatest personages of the day. As a teenager, Pyrrhus served as an officer for the Macedonian dynast DEMETRIUS POLIORKETES, who had married Pyrrhus's sister Deidameia. At about age 20, Pyrrhus married Antigone, the stepdaughter of King PTOLEMY (1) of EGYPT. With Ptolemy's support, Pyrrhus in 297 B.C.E. became a joint king of the Molossians. (He never officially called himself king of Epirus, although he is always referred to as such.) His partner-king was his kinsman Neoptolemos, whom he soon had murdered.

Discontented with the confines of humble Epirus, Pyrrhus spent much of his reign trying to conquer—or otherwise win the throne of—the nearby kingdom of MACEDON, the great realm to the northeast. In these years Macedon was ruled by Pyrrhus's former friend (now enemy) Demetrius, and later by Demetrius's son, Antigonus II.

At the same time, Pyrrhus sought to expand his domain westward toward the Adriatic and Italy. After his first wife died, Pyrrhus married Lanissa, the daughter of the Syracusan dictator AGATHOKLES (295 B.C.E.). Lanissa's dowry included the important Adriatic-Greek city of CORCYRA, to which Pyrrhus soon added other northwestern acquisitions, such as AMBRACIA, which he made into his capital. But when he polygamously took two more wives, Lanissa left him and married Demetrius (who soon claimed Corcyra).

In late 281 B.C.E. Pyrrhus received an appeal from the Greek city of TARAS, on the "heel" of Italy. The Tarentines had been contacting various Greek rulers, requesting military aid against the encroaching Romans. Lured by the hope of conquest, Pyrrhus sailed to Italy with 22,500 men and 20 Indian war ELEPHANTS. In the spring of 280 B.C.E. the fighting began at Heraklea, on the Italian south-coast "instep," not far from Taras. The Romans—terrified by Pyrrhus's elephants (beasts they had never seen before)—retreated before the massed pikes of the Greek PHALANX. The Romans lost 7,000 men, with another 1,800 captured but Pyrrhus lost 4,000.

Pyrrhus marched his army north to within 40 miles of ROME, but—discouraged by the lack of local Italian help—turned back south. The next year he experienced the costly victory at Ausculum that inspired his famous lament. After abruptly removing his forces to SICILY, to defend the Greek cities there against the Carthaginians, Pyrrhus returned to Italy to renew his Roman war. But he was defeated in battle near Capua, at Beneventum (where the Romans stampeded his elephants by shooting fire arrows), and he sailed back to Epirus, reportedly having lost two-thirds of his army (275 B.C.E.).

In a war against Antigonus II, Pyrrhus nearly conquered Macedon (274–272 B.C.E.). But he abruptly abandoned his advantage, marching far south to invade the territory of SPARTA. There the Spartans and Macedonians combined against him. Battling his way back northward, he encountered street-fighting in ARGOS and was killed—supposedly when an old woman threw a roof tile down onto his head.

A romantic figure and brilliant battlefield commander, Pyrrhus lacked the perseverance and long-range judgment to win an empire.

See also DODONA; WARFARE, LAND.

Further reading: Petros Garoufalias, *Pyrrhus King of Epirus* (London: Stacey International, 1979); C. A. Kincaid, *Successors of Alexander the Great: Ptolemy I, Pyrrhus of Epirus, Hiero of Syracuse, Antiochus III* (Chicago: Ares, 1980); Tony Hackens, ed., *The Age of Pyrrhus; Papers Delivered at the International Conference, Brown University, 8–10 April, 1988* (Providence: Center for Old World Archaeology and Art, Brown University, 1992); Blanche Brown, *Royal Portraits in Sculpture and Coins: Pyrrhos and the Successors of Alexander the Great* (New York: P. Lang, 1995).

Pythagoras (ca. 570–500 B.C.E.) *Greek philosopher, mathematician, and reputed miracle-worker*

No writings by Pythagoras survive, and his life and work are clouded in mystery; most information comes from statements by later writers.

Pythagoras apparently pioneered the study of MATHEMATICS in the Western world. Today he is best remembered for the discovery, made by him or one of his disciples, that the square of the hypotenuse of a right triangle is equal to the sum of the squares of the two other sides—the famous Pythagorean theorem.

Born on the island of SAMOS, Pythagoras emigrated west in about 531 B.C.E., reportedly to escape the power of the Samian tyrant POLYCRATES. Settling at CROTON, the foremost Greek colony of south ITALY, Pythagoras founded a religious-philosophical society. He is said to have risen to great local influence. He wrote new laws for Croton and in effect governed the town with his followers, who numbered 300 and came from the Crotonian elite. This OLIGARCHY eventually provoked a people's revolution, and Pythagoras and his followers withdrew to the nearby Greek colony of Metapontum, where Pythagoras died and where his tomb stood in later days.

Two reported tenets of his teachings stand out. One is that the universe's secrets can be learned through the study of numbers. Pythagoras apparently drew great significance from his discovery that musical notes comprise an arithmetic progression; if a lyre string is stopped at its halfway point, the note produced by plucking the half-string is exactly one octave above the whole string's note. Since the Greeks associated MUSIC with the civilizing power of the god APOLLO, this discovery was thought to reveal part of the gods' scheme for the world. Similarly, Pythagoras saw the number 10 as a key to knowledge, mainly because 10 is the sum of the first four integers: 1 + 2 + 3 + 4. The Pythagoreans were known to observe a mystic symbol of 10 dots arranged in rows forming an equilateral triangle:

The second major Pythagorean concept was the transmigration of souls, meaning that the individual soul does not descend to the Underworld at the body's death (as taught by Greek RELIGION) but passes into a new bodily form. In this, Pythagoras may have been influenced by the mystical cult of ORPHISM, which was popular in Greek southern Italy. Like the Orphics, the Pythagoreans viewed the human soul as a fallen divinity, imprisoned in the body and condemned to a series of reincarnations as human, animal, or even vegetable life, until the soul's impurities are cleansed away. As the soul becomes purified in successive lives, it is rewarded with higher forms of incarnation, such as statesmen or poets, until at last it wins some kind of release among the gods; more often, however, the soul might descend from human to beast. One tale records how Pythagoras saw a man beating a puppy and asked him to stop, because (said Pythagoras) he recognized in the puppy's howls the human voice of a deceased friend.

To purify the soul, Pythagoras developed elaborate rules of right conduct for his followers; several such rules are described by later writers. The eating of certain meats was prohibited, since an animal might house a human soul. (It is unclear, however, whether Pythagoras was a complete vegetarian.) The most famous Pythagorean taboo, forbidding the eating of beans probably involved a belief that beans contain little souls (whose attempts to escape are the cause of the bean-eater's flatulence).

The list of Pythagorean commandments strikes a modern reader as odd. The emphasis is not on ethical conduct but on what might be called superstition. Disciples were forbidden to wear rings, to stir a fire with IRON, or to speak of Pythagorean matters in the dark. On rising from bed, a Pythagorean was obliged to smooth away the body's impression in the bedclothes. These and other precepts apparently involved an attempt to avert the "evil eye" or similar bad luck.

Such superstitions reveal how primitive Pythagoras's society was, and how great were his achievements in mathematics and other areas. Pythagoras was said to admit WOMEN to his following on an equal footing with men—which, if true, represents a revolutionary notion in sixth-century-B.C.E. Greek society. The Pythagorean doctrine of transmigration influenced the Sicilian Greek philosopher EMPEDOKLES (mid-400s B.C.E.) and the Athenian philosopher PLATO (early 300s B.C.E.).

After Pythagoras's death, his followers split into two sects. Of these, the group known as the Mathematicians became a force in early Greek ASTRONOMY. It was these Pythagoreans who first concluded that the Earth is spherical, not flat. They also originated the famous theory of the music of the spheres, which imagined that the Earth,

Sun, Moon, and planets all revolve around a central fire and create a harmonious sound by virtue of their synchronized speeds; the music is inaudible to us humans.

The political history of the Pythagoreans was unhappy. In the late 400s B.C.E. they were nearly exterminated in a civil war at Metapontum. The next century saw the school reorganize itself at the Italian-Greek city of TARAS, before dying out by 300 B.C.E.

See also AFTERLIFE.

Further reading: Peter Gorman, *Pythagoras, A Life* (London: Routledge, 1979); R. R. R. Smith, "A New Portrait of Pythagoras," in *Aphrodisias Papers 2. The Theatre, a Sculptor's Workshop, Philosophers, and Coin Types,* edited by R. R. R. Smith and Kenan T. Erim (Ann Arbor: Department of Classical Studies, University of Michigan, 1991), 159–167; K. I. Boudouris, ed., *Pythagorean Philosophy* (Athens: International Center for Greek Philosophy and Culture, 1992); Christopher Bamford, ed., *Homage to Pythagoras: Rediscovering Sacred Science* (Hudson, N.Y.: Lindisfarne Press, 1994); John Strohmeier and Peter Westbrook, *Divine Harmony: The Life and Teachings of Pythagoras* (Berkeley, Calif.: Berkeley Hills Books, 1999); Charles Kahn, *Pythagoras and the Pythagoreans: A Brief History* (Indianapolis: Hackett, 2001).

Pythia   *See* DELPHI.

Pythian Games   This event was the second-most important of the great religious sports festivals of the ancient Greek world, after the OLYMPIC GAMES. The Pythian Games were held every four years in honor of the god APOLLO, at Apollo's holiest shrine, DELPHI. The name refers to Delphi's inner sanctum, known as Pytho.

An eight-yearly festival of Apollo at Delphi, featuring competitions of the lyre and choruses, was the ancient forerunner of these games. In 582 B.C.E., after an allied Greek coalition had broken the local power of PHOCIS during the First Sacred War, the Pythian Games were reorganized in their classic form and were placed under the administration of the AMPHICTYONIC LEAGUE. But the games never lost their original aspect—celebrating Apollo as the god of MUSIC.

Unlike other panhellenic fetes, these games included competitions in singing and drama. The footraces were held in a stadium on the slopes of Mt. Parnassus, near Delphi; the horse and chariot races took place far below, on the Crisaean plain.

The prize for victors in the Pythian Games was a garland of bay laurel leaves. The laurel tree was sacred to Apollo because when he was pursing his beloved Daphne, she fled from him and prayed to her father, the river god Peneus, for help. As a result, she was transformed into a laurel tree, which was subsequently considered to be sacred to Apollo. In modern times, the tradition of the laurel victory wreath is preserved in the title of the *poet laureate,* an honorary office that has existed in England since 1668 and in America since 1937.

The four-yearly Pythian Games fell halfway along the four-yearly Olympic cycle; that is, in the second spring after the last Olympics, and two years before the next one.

Further reading: Olga Tzachou-Alexandri, ed., *Mind and Body: Athletic Contests in Ancient Greece* (Athens: Ministry of Culture; National Hellenic Committee I.C.O.M., 1989).

R

religion The ancient Greeks believed that their gods had a guiding hand in human affairs. Events as diverse as the annual sprouting of crops, disease epidemics, victory or defeat in war, and individual victories in sports events—which modern observers might assign to scientific causes—were seen by the Greeks as proof of the gods' involvement in human events great and small. Greek MYTH told of gods in "the old days" who had actually descended to Earth to make love or war among mortals. Although the Greeks of 400 B.C.E. did not expect to meet a god in the street, they did expect their gods to be invisibly present—at least for major, public events.

This made the Greeks generally more pious than we are today, but also more legalistic and practical-minded in religious matters. Feeling close to their gods, the Greeks expected the gods to be influenced by prayers and sacrifices of animals or crops. The Greeks expected *results* from their faith. A farmer sowed his seeds in the field, then prayed to the gods to send the proper weather. To the ancient Greeks, both activities seemed equally practical.

Modern American society views religion as a purely private concern, legally separated from civic life. But the Greeks had the opposite view; religion was a public matter. The goodwill of the gods toward the community was something to be carefully maintained (like the water supply or military defense). Greek states therefore kept certain priesthoods and temples at public expense, to oversee festivals, offer sacrifices, and generally safeguard the gods' benefaction. Relatedly, the crime of impiety (*asebeia*) was a serious one. When an Athenian jury condemned the philosopher SOCRATES to death on charges including impiety (399 B.C.E.), it was because some Athenians believed that Socrates' philosophical questioning had genuinely offended the gods and had threatened their care of ATHENS.

As is well known, Greek religion was polytheistic. This means that—unlike the JEWS, but like most other ancient peoples—the Greeks generally worshipped more than one god. Their gods were anthropomorphic, that is, they were pictured in human shape, male or female. The major gods were 12 in number; each was imagined as having power over one or more important aspects of human life. ATHENA was the goddess of handicraft and wisdom, but in "wisdom" she might overlap somewhat with APOLLO, whose province included reason and intellect, while in "handicraft" she might overlap with HEPHAISTOS, god of metallurgy. The king of the gods was ZEUS, sky-father, lord of justice and of universal order. Below him were HERA, POSEIDON, Athena, Apollo, ARTEMIS, APHRODITE, DIONYSUS, DEMETER, HERMES, HEPHAISTOS, and ARES. Because they were imagined as dwelling in Zeus's palace in the sky atop Mt. OLYMPUS, these 12 were known as the Olympian gods.

The Greeks also recognized a second important group of gods, called the chthonians (from the Greek word *chthon,* earth). These were deities of the earth and the Underworld, chief of whom were HADES and PERSEPHONE, the Underworld's king and queen. In SICILY and other parts of the western Greek world, Persephone became an important object of worship, as a guardian and judge of souls after death. The Greeks worshipped chthonian deities with rites different from those used for Olympian gods.

In addition to the Olympians and chthonians, there were lesser gods, demigods, and heroes, who might have shrines and cults confined to specific locales (such as the cult of HYACINTHOS in the region of SPARTA). Heroes were usually worshipped as the spirits of extraordinary, deceased mortal men. A few major heroes, such as HERAKLES, were worshipped throughout the Greek world and were imagined as having turned into immortal gods after their death.

Worship of the gods involved the use of idols—manmade images, usually statues of wood, clay, stone, or BRONZE. With the advances in Greek marble carving in the 600s B.C.E. and the discovery of improved bronze-casting techniques in the 500s B.C.E., the representation of the gods became the highest calling of ancient Greek SCULPTURE. A god's idol might be miniature, life-size, or colossal (from the Greek *kolossos,* "a giant statue"). The god inhabited the idol, but not exclusively; a god could be everywhere at once, and many official statues of the same god might stand within a single city. All gods were portrayed as physically beautiful. They had been born but would never die; they lived forever in young adulthood or vigorous middle age. They were omniscient regarding human affairs and were able to assume any shape. Every city probably kept a shrine to each of the major gods, but certain deities had special care of specific places. Athena for instance, was the guardian of Athens, Poseidon of CORINTH, and Hera of ARGOS and SAMOS.

The gods were imagined as concentrations of energy; the faces of their statues might be painted red, signifying life and power. But the gods were also capable of human flaws and emotions, such as anger, cruelty, and brutal sexual desire. In the latter 500s B.C.E. the philosopher XENOPHANES complained that conventional religion had ascribed to the gods "everything that is shameful and disgraceful among human beings—thieving and adultery and deceiving one another." One reason why Greek mythology has cast a spell over readers through the centuries is its vivid, endearing character portrayal of the gods, particularly in the epic poems of HOMER.

Modern scholars believe that the religious system presented by Homer (around 750 B.C.E.) and HESIOD (around 700 B.C.E.) arose gradually, starting with a fusion of two or three different cultures after 2100 B.C.E. The facts are lost in prehistory, however, and scholars must rely on scant evidence from ARCHAEOLOGY in order to trace this process of religious fusion.

The Greeks were an Indo-European people, with a language and social patterns akin to other Indo-European peoples, such as the ancient Romans, Germans, and Persians. Almost certainly the Greek-speaking tribesmen who first invaded mainland Greece around 2100 B.C.E. brought a patriarchal, warrior religion whose chief god was the skyfather, Zeus (a figure that scholars recognize under other names in other Indo-European mythologies). Over time, the Greek conquerors absorbed certain religious elements from the subjugated, pre-Greek inhabitants of the land (an agrarian, non-Indo-European folk with possible origins in ASIA MINOR). This people, like the non-Greeks of Asia Minor in later centuries, may have worshipped a central mother goddess or family of goddesses. Similarly, the non-Greek MINOAN CIVILIZATION of the Aegean islands, which strongly influenced the emerging Greek culture around 2000–1400 B.C.E. evidently had important female deities. The prime result of these influences was the introduction into Greek religion of a few major goddesses not originally Greek; eventually they became known by the names Hera, Athena, Artemis, and Persephone.

By 1600 B.C.E. the mainland Greeks had organized themselves into the warlike and technologically advanced MYCENAEAN CIVILIZATION. It is this era that offers modern scholars the first clear glimpse at Greek religion, in the LINEAR B tablets excavated at Mycenaean KNOSSOS (ca. 1400 B.C.E.) and PYLOS (ca. 1200 B.C.E.). In their lists of religious ceremonies performed for various gods, the tablets reveal that the Mycenaean faith was surprisingly similar to the Greek religion of 700 or 1,000 years later. The tablets mention Zeus and Poseidon as important gods, as well as Hera, Athena, Dionysus, and other deities (some with names unfamiliar).

Of the 12 gods later to be known as the Olympians, only Apollo and Aphrodite definitely are not mentioned on the existing Linear B tablets. Scholars believe that these two latecomers entered Greek religion during the DARK AGE, after the collapse of Mycenaean society around 1200 B.C.E. Both deities probably reached Greece from the Near East, via the mercantile island of CYPRUS. In general, Greek religion remained open to foreign deities, particularly goddesses; later in ancient times various Greek locales had important cults of the Egyptian goddess Isis, the Anatolian goddess Cybele, and the Thracian goddess Bendis.

By the 600s B.C.E., the principal gods and forms of worship were well established. Statues of the gods were housed in temples of simple design but elaborate craftsmanship. In the 600s B.C.E. wooden temples began to be replaced by buildings largely of stone, either limestone or marble. The famous Greek "orders" of ARCHITECTURE—the Doric, Ionic, and Corinthian—originated as styles of temples.

A Greek temple was the sanctuary of a particular god; rarely would more than one god be worshipped in the same building. Unlike a modern church, a temple was not a place where congregations gathered. It had no rows of pews for multitudes of worshippers. Rather, the temple receive individuals or small groups for prayer or sacrifice. The temple's priests or priestesses might be minor functionaries under the direction of a high priest who typically came from an aristocratic family associated with that specific sanctuary. At Athens, for example, a noble family named the Eteoboutadai traditionally supplied the priest and priestess for the two major cults on the ACROP-OLIS. But Greek religion was noteworthy for the lack of power exercised by its priests (one important exception being Apollo's priesthood at DELPHI). Technically, prayer and sacrifice could be conducted by worshippers without any priest.

A society as intellectual as the Greeks' was bound to produce religious doubt. Independent thinkers such as the sophist PROTAGORAS (mid-400s B.C.E.) and the trage-dian EURIPIDES (later 400s B.C.E. were rumored to be atheists, disbelieving in the gods. Certain philosophers, such as Xenophanes, PLATO (early 300s B.C.E.), and ARISTOTLE (mid-300s B.C.E.), believed in a single, universal god. During the HELLENISTIC AGE (around 300–150 B.C.E.), the rise of giant Greco-Macedonian kingdoms created a new social order, and traditional religion—expressing as it did the public life of the old-fashioned Greek city-state—came in for questioning and modification. The philosophy STOICISM inclined toward a monotheism built around Zeus; the rival school of EPICUREANISM claimed that multiple gods existed but had no concern for humankind. Meanwhile there arose fringe "mystery" religions (Greek: *mystēria,* from *mystēs,* "an initiate"), offering to their followers a more personal faith and the promise of a happy life after death. These became increasingly popular during the course of the Hellenistic period, probably due in part to their all-inclusiveness. Divinities from the eastern Mediterranean, such as Isis and Mithras, also became more and more popular. Related trends, such as magic and astrology, also gained new followings in the Hellenistic age.

The great society of the Roman Empire saw further religious percolation, including the rise of Christianity among Greek communities of the eastern Mediterranean in the first century C.E. But many Greeks were still worshipping the old-fashioned gods in 391 C.E. when the Byzantine emperor Theodosius closed all pagan temples throughout his realm and decreed Christianity to be the only legal religion.

The religious beliefs and practices of the ancient Greeks had a tremendous influence on later cultures, including those of the Romans, the Jews, and the early Christians, as did their iconography, symbolism, and sacred architecture. The image of Christ as the good shepherd, for example, evolved from idyllic pastoral scenes of pagan shepherds with their flocks in classical art.

See also ADONIS; AFTERLIFE; ASKLEPIOS; CASTOR AND POLYDEUCES; ELEUSINIAN MYSTERIES; FATE; FUNERAL CUSTOMS; FURIES; HECATĒ; HESTIA; NYMPHS; OLYMPIA; ORPHISM; PAN; PARTHENON; PHILOSOPHY; PHOENICIA; PINDAR; POLIS; PROPHECY AND DIVINATION; ROME; SAMOTHRACE; THEATER.

Further reading: Irad Malkin, *Religion and Colonization in Ancient Greece* (Leiden, Netherlands: E. J. Brill, 1987); John Ferguson, *Among the Gods. An Archaeological Exploration of Ancient Greek Religion* (London: Routledge, 1989); Jon D. Mikalson, *Athenian Popular Religion* (Chapel Hill: University of North Carolina Press, 1989); Robert Parker, "Spartan Religion," in *Classical Sparta. Techniques behind Her Success,* edited by Anton Powell (London: Routledge, 1989), 142–172; Robert Parker, *Athenian Religion: A History* (New York: Oxford University Press, 1996); Richard Buxton, ed., *Oxford Readings in Greek Religion* (New York: Oxford University Press, 2000); Matthew Dillon, *Girls and Women in Classical Greek Religion* (London: Routledge, 2002); Erika Simon, *Festivals of Attica: An Archaeological Commentary* (Madison: University of Wisconsin Press, 2002); Jon Mikalson, *Ancient Greek Religion* (Oxford: Blackwell, 2004).

Rhadamanthys   *See* AFTERLIFE; MINOS.

rhapsodes   *See* EPIC POETRY.

Rhegium (Greek: *Rhēgion*)   This Greek seaport on the west coast of the "toe" of ITALY commanded the Straits of Messina. Rhegium was founded in the late 700s B.C.E. by Ionian Greek colonists from CHALCIS; a second group founded a sister-city, ZANCLĒ, across the straits in SICILY. With its strategic position, Rhegium became one of the most important Ionian Greek cities of the West. Accordingly, it was an enemy of such powerful Dorian Greek cities as SYRACUSE, in eastern Sicily, and LOCRI, on the eastern Italian "toe."

Rhegium's most famous citizen was the lyric poet IBYCUS (ca. 535 B.C.E.). The city reached a peak under its energetic tyrant Anaxilas (reigned 494–476 B.C.E.), who fortified the straits against Etruscan war fleets and enlarged the city population with refugees from the Spartan-dominated, Peloponnesian region of MESSENIA. In 433 B.C.E. Rhegium made an alliance with ATHENS for protection against Syracuse and Locri. In 415–413 B.C.E. during the PELOPONNESIAN WAR, Rhegium served as a naval base for the Athenians' campaign against Syracuse.

In about 387 B.C.E. the Syracusan tyrant DIONYSIUS (1) captured Rhegium and destroyed it. Rebuilt, it eventually passed into the hands of ROME. The site is now the Italian seaport of Reggio.

Recent archaeological excavation at Rhegium has discovered traces of the city wall, the AGORA, a concert hall, temples, bath buildings, houses, and nearby cemeteries. Numerous inscriptions, pieces of POTTERY, and evidence of the city's water supply system have also been found.

See also DORIAN GREEKS; ETRUSCANS; IONIAN GREEKS.

Further reading: E. Ruoff-Väänänen, "The Roads Leading to Rhegium," *Arctos* 9 (1975): 93–98; E. E. Clain-Stefanelli, "Late Silver Issues of Rhegium. A Janus Head Type in Rhegium," in *Florilegium numismaticum. Studia in honorem U. Westermark edita* (Stockholm: Svenska Numismatiska Föreningen, 1992), 119–126.

rhetoric Meaning the art of public speaking, the word rhetoric in modern English often implies empty or overblown verbiage. For the ancient Greeks, however the skill of *rhētorikē* meant nothing less than the ability to communicate in public. Rhetoric (also called oratory) was considered an essential skill for any active citizen in a DEMOCRACY because, in an age before telecommunications, newspapers, or advertising, the one way for an individual citizen to help shape public policy was to stand up before the citizen ASSEMBLY and make a speech. Although speeches might also play decision-making roles in an OLIGARCHY such as SPARTA or CORINTH, it was at the democratic cities—and particularly at the greatest of these, ATHENS—that the best speakers emerged. Among the more famous Athenian orators were DEMOSTHENES (1) (ca. 340 B.C.E.) and the statesman PERIKLES (ca. 440 B.C.E.). The philosopher ARISTOTLE (ca. 340 B.C.E.) wrote an extant treatise on rhetoric, one of many produced in antiquity.

The roots of Greek rhetoric go back to the war councils of the Mycenaean princes (around 1200 B.C.E.) and the civic councils of the early Greek aristocratic states (around 800 B.C.E.). The poems of HOMER (written down around 750 B.C.E.) show the assembled Greek heroes delivering speeches in turn at war council. There an artful speaker such as ODYSSEUS is admired for his ability to persuade his fellow captains toward a certain course of action.

It was in the 400s B.C.E. that rhetoric emerged as an organized study, under the impetus of the developing Greek democracies. The strong poetic traditions of SICILY also may have played a role, because it was a Sicilian Greek who first brought advanced rhetoric to Athens—GORGIAS of Leontini who amazed the sophisticated Athenians with his spoken "display pieces" (427 B.C.E.).

Aside from the assembly, the other great arena for public speaking was the law courts, where citizens spoke as defendants or prosecutors in front of juries usually numbering several hundred. Some of the best-known surviving speeches are Athenian courtroom speeches from the 300s B.C.E. delivered by such powerful arguers as LYSIAS. Other men became rich as speechwriters, who did not usually deliver speeches personally but who would, for a fee, compose a courtroom speech for a client. Among the best known of these was ISOKRATES, who opened a school of rhetoric (the first one known) in around 390 B.C.E.

See also AESCHINES; ANTIPHON; EDUCATION; ISAEUS; LAWS AND LAW COURTS; SOPHISTS.

Further reading: Ian Worthington, ed., *Persuasion: Greek Rhetoric in Action* (London: Routledge, 1994); Thomas Cole, *The Origins of Rhetoric in Ancient Greece*, 2d ed. (Baltimore: Johns Hopkins University Press, 1995); S. E. Porter, ed., *Handbook of Classical Rhetoric in the Hellenistic Period, 330 B.C.–A.D. 400* (Leiden, Netherlands: E. J. Brill, 1997); Robert Wardy, The Birth of Rhetoric: Gorgias, Plato, and their Successors (London: Routledge, 1998); Edward Schiappa, *The Beginnings of Rhetorical Theory in Classical Greece* (New Haven, Conn.: Yale University Press, 1999).

Rhetra *See* LYKOURGOS (1).

Rhodes This large Greek island is located off the southwest coast of ASIA MINOR. By 300 B.C.E. Rhodes had emerged as one of the foremost maritime powers of the Hellenistic world—wealthy from commerce and with a strong navy.

ARCHAEOLOGY has shown that the island engaged in Mycenaean-Greek TRADE and perhaps received settlers around 1300 B.C.E., following an era of Minoan domination. But the main inhabitants at this time were most likely of non-Greek, Carian stock. Rhodes's recorded history begins around 1000 B.C.E. with the arrival of DORIAN GREEKS, who sailed east from mainland Greece and founded three cities on the island—Ialysos, at the northern tip, Kameiros, on the northwest coast, and Lindos (the largest of the three), in the east. These three cities formed part of a local Dorian federation that included the nearby island of Kos and the city of KNIDOS, on the Asia Minor coast. The Greek name *Rhodos* probably did not refer to the roses (*rhodai*) that still grow throughout the island, but rather came from some Carian name.

The Rhodian Greeks acquired certain non-Greek traditions from the East, chief of which was their national cult of the sun god, worshipped under his Greek name, HELIOS. Rhodes was unique among early Greek states in having a sun cult. According to one myth, Helios had chosen Rhodes as his own kingdom and had populated it with the descendants of his seven sons.

Rhodes's location made it a natural middleman between East and West, although it was overshadowed initially by other east Greek sea powers, such as MILETUS and SAMOS. The Rhodians took part in the trading and colonizing expansion in the 700s–500s B.C.E. Rhodian Geometric POTTERY is among the main types found by archaeologists at the ancient Greek trade depot at AL MINA (on the Syrian coast), and it is known that Rhodians helped establish colonies in SICILY and south ITALY. By the 500s B.C.E. popular dictators known as TYRANTS had arisen in the Rhodian cities, as elsewhere in the Greek world. One such ruler, Kleobulos of Lindos, was later reckoned among the SEVEN SAGES of Greece.

After being conquered by the Persians in around 494 B.C.E. Rhodes was liberated in 478 B.C.E. by the mainland Greeks, at the end of the PERSIAN WARS. Over the next 65 years the three Rhodian cities were members of the Athenian-dominated DELIAN LEAGUE. By then the Rhodian cities were governed as Athenian-inspired democracies—as they would remain, with one interruption, until the Roman conquest. But in 411–407 B.C.E., during the PELOPONNESIAN WAR, the Rhodian cities joined the widespread Delian revolt and won independence from ATHENS.

Then the three Rhodian cities agreed to combine their individual governments and form a union, with a new capital city, Rhodos. This Rhodes city—a seaport at the island's northern tip, near Ialysos—eventually became one of the most spectacular Greek cities, thriving from the shipping of grain and other essentials across the eastern Mediterranean. The city of Rhodes received its urban plan from the architect HIPPODAMUS of MILETUS, and it displays the rectangular grid design typical of his work (as at, for instance, PIRAEUS). Since the modern city of Rhodes sits on top of the ancient remains, excavation has been sporadic but has revealed parts of this city grid plan.

Rhodes was recaptured by the Persians in 355 B.C.E. but regained independence and DEMOCRACY after the Macedonian king ALEXANDER THE GREAT invaded the Persian Empire (334 B.C.E.). Amid the turmoil following Alexander's death (323 B.C.E.), the island became a tempting target for the various DIADOCHOI (Successors) who battled over Alexander's vast empire, and in 305–304 B.C.E. Rhodes city withstood a huge siege by the Macedonian prince DEMETRIUS POLIORKETES.

In the burst of self-confidence following this defense, the Rhodians erected a giant BRONZE statue of Helios in about 290 B.C.E. that became known as the Colossus of Rhodes.

Designed by one Chares of Lindus, the 90-foot-tall Colossus (Greek: *Kolossos,* "giant statue") was counted as one of the SEVEN WONDERS OF THE WORLD. Although it collapsed in an earthquake after only about 65 years, its general appearance is known from ancient coins and an ancient writer's description. The Colossus may have stood alongside the city's harbor or in the city center; it did not bestride the harbor entrance, legs apart, with ships passing between, as is sometimes claimed. The statue consisted of bronze plating over a frame with an interior staircase. The god, with a halo of sun rays, was shown holding up a torch, which workmen inside operated as a beacon fire to aid ships at sea. The design of the Colossus helped to inspire New York City's Statue of Liberty, erected in 1886 C.E.

The Rhodians were among the first east Greek allies of the emerging power of ROME; it was complaints from Rhodes and PERGAMON that brought the Romans into the Second Macedonian War against the Macedonian king PHILIP V (200–197 B.C.E.). But Rhodes lost its prosperity when the Romans—seeking to punish Rhodes for its insufficient help in the Third Macedonian War (172–167 B.C.E.)—promoted the Aegean island of DELOS as the new center of east Mediterranean trade. Rhodes later became a Roman subject.

See also COLONIZATION; SHIPS AND SEAFARING; WARFARE, NAVAL.

Further reading: R. M. Berthold, *Rhodes in the Hellenistic Age* (Ithaca, N.Y.: Cornell University Press, 1984); S. Dietz and I. Papachristodoulou, eds., *Archaeology in the Dodecanese. Symposium Copenhagen, April 7th to 9th, 1986*

(Copenhagen: National Museum of Denmark, 1988); Vincent Gabrielsen, *The Naval Aristocracy of Hellenistic Rhodes* (Aarhus, Denmark: Aarhus University Press, 1997); Vincent Gabrielsen, ed., *Hellenistic Rhodes: Politics, Culture and Society* (Aarhus, Denmark: Aarhus University Press, 1999).

Rome This non-Greek city of west-central ITALY is located in Latium, about 16 miles from the Tyrrhenian coast. After being strongly influenced by the Greeks in such cultural rudiments as its ALPHABET and RELIGION, Rome emerged in the 300s B.C.E. as a dynamic military force, destined to conquer an empire that (by 117 C.E.) stretched from Britain to Mesopotamia. The Romans subdued many peoples, but their conquest of the Greek world, accomplished between about 338 and 30 B.C.E., deeply affected their own civilization by introducing them to the material and literary splendors of the Greeks. As the Roman poet Horace wrote (ca. 19 B.C.E.): "Captive Greece took mighty Rome captive, forcing culture onto rustic folk."

The Romans belonged to the Latin ethnic group, but early on they were dominated by another Italian people, the ETRUSCANS. The name *Roma* may be of Etruscan origin; its meaning is unclear. Supposedly founded in 753 B.C.E. Rome surely partook of the pro-Greek atmosphere of Etruscan society in the 600s B.C.E. Greek goods and customs made their way north from Greek colonies of Campania, such as CUMAE and Neapolis (Naples). The Roman alphabet, used today for English as well as for most other European languages, was first adapted by the Romans (perhaps around 600 B.C.E.) from an Etruscan model, itself based on the Greek alphabet. By the 400s B.C.E. the Romans were vigorously assimilating Greek gods, heroes, and MYTH into their own religion.

Rome supposedly expelled its last Etruscan king in 510 B.C.E. The next 150 years saw political strife between rich and poor; eventually Rome's government took shape as a republic, in which a wide citizen base was governed by a well-born elite, sitting on a legislative body called the senate.

These centuries also saw the spread of Roman control through Italy. First came the unification of Latium. By the mid-300s B.C.E. the Romans had reached Campania, where they entered into their first diplomatic relations with Italian-Greek cities. There followed an accelerated hellenization of Roman culture, including the first Roman copying of Greek ARCHITECTURE, COINAGE, and POTTERY.

After subduing the central-Italian people known as the Samnites, the Romans had by 290 B.C.E. won all of central Italy. In the extreme south, conflict with the Greek city of TARAS brought the Romans into their first war against a Greek army, led by the Epirote king PYRRHUS. The hard-won defeat of Pyrrhus (275 B.C.E.) left the Romans masters of all Italy south of the Po River. Rome had become a world power, comparable with the

Hellenistic kingdoms of the eastern Mediterranean or—closer to home—the African-Phoenician city of CARTHAGE. By this era the formidable Roman army could draw on a manpower pool of several million men, due to Rome's policy of requiring military service from its Italian-ethnic subject peoples.

Rome now became drawn into conflict with other great Mediterranean powers—particularly Carthage and MACEDON—which led eventually to the Romans' subjugation of the Mediterranean Greek world. First came two bitter wars with Carthage. The First Punic (Carthaginian) War was fought from 264 to 241 B.C.E. It turned Rome into a naval power and left the victorious Romans in possession of SICILY, with the important Sicilian-Greek city of SYRACUSE as a Roman ally.

The Second Punic War (218–201 B.C.E.) saw Rome fighting for its life on Italian soil against the brilliant Carthaginian general Hannibal. Syracuse, siding this time with Carthage, was captured, plundered, and annexed by the vengeful Romans (211 B.C.E.). Another ally of Carthage was the dynamic Macedonian king PHILIP V, whose domain included most of mainland Greece. In a Punic War sideshow, the Romans invaded Philip's Greek territories—their first advance into Greece (214 B.C.E.). This First Macedonian War ended in a truce (205 B.C.E.), but Philip was by then a hated enemy of an increasingly eastward-looking Rome.

After the Second Punic War ended with Carthage's defeat, the Romans turned a receptive ear to complaints from their eastern Greek allies PERGAMON and RHODES against Philip's adventuring. The Second Macedonian War (200–197 B.C.E.) saw the second Roman invasion of mainland Greece. With the help of Greek allies from AETOLIA, the Roman general Titus Quinctius Flaminius in 197 B.C.E. won a total victory against Philip's army at the Battle of Cynocephalae ("dog heads"), in THESSALY. The battle broke Macedon's imperial power forever and incidentally established the superiority of Roman battle tactics against the more cumbersome Macedonian PHALANX. But by the terms of a lenient treaty, Macedon was allowed to continue as an independent state.

It was at the ISTHMIAN GAMES of 196 B.C.E.—after Macedonian control of Greece had been removed—that Flamininus issued his famous proclamation declaring freedom for the mainland Greeks; neither Macedon nor Rome would be overlord there. In 194 B.C.E. Roman troops evacuated Greece.

Even unwillingly, however, the Romans found themselves embroiled in Greek events. The Aetolians, disgruntled over Rome's light treatment of their defeated enemy Philip, invited the Seleucid king ANTIOCHUS (2) III to invade Greece as a new liberator. Reentering Greece in response, Roman forces defeated Antiochus at THERMOPYLAE (191 B.C.E.) and pursued him to ASIA MINOR—the Romans' first campaign in Asia—where they defeated him again, at the Battle of Magnesia (190 B.C.E.). This victory foreshadowed the future Roman conquest of the entire Greek East. By the treaty of Apamea (188 B.C.E.), Antiochus lost most of Asia Minor, which the Romans parceled to their allies Pergamum and Rhodes. In Greece, meanwhile, the Aetolians were defeated and their power curtailed.

The accession of Philip's ambitious son Perseus brought new Macedonian adventurism, and another Roman invasion. The Third Macedonian War (172–167 B.C.E.) ended with Perseus's complete defeat at the Battle of Pydna, in southern Macedon. Deposed, Perseus died in a Roman prison. His kingdom was dismantled and was later annexed as a Roman province called Macedonia. In Greece, the League of ACHAEA was punished for its pro-Macedonianism with the removal of 1,000 well-born hostages to Rome. (One of these, named Polybius, was destined to become the last great Greek historian; so impressed was he by Roman power that he chose to write, in Greek, about the rise of Rome.)

When the Achaean League resumed anti-Roman agitation in 148 B.C.E. Roman patience with Greece was at an end. Marching south from the province of Macedonia, a Roman army defeated the Achaeans in battle. CORINTH, the league's major city, was besieged and captured. By order of the Roman senate the city was leveled to the ground as a warning to the Greeks (146 B.C.E.).

Greece's freedom was at an end, and the country was then incorporated into the Roman province of Macedonia. In the following centuries the Greek East fell. Much of Asia Minor was legally bequeathed to the Romans by the last Pergamene king, Attalus III, in 133 B.C.E. In 64 B.C.E. the Roman general Pompey annexed Syria, once the Seleucid heartland. And in 30 B.C.E. the Romans captured the last remaining Hellenistic Kingdom, EGYPT.

Despite being under Roman control, Greece (along with the rest of the eastern Mediterranean) continued to prosper and, in fact, retained much of its cultural heritage. The Romans, in fact, became strongly influenced by numerous aspects of Greek culture such as SCULPTURE, ARCHITECTURE, PHILOSOPHY, THEATER, and RELIGION.

See also AENEAS; CASTOR AND POLYDEUCES; CLEOPATRA; HELLENISTIC AGE; HERAKLES; SELEUCID EMPIRE.

Further reading: Sarah Macready and F. H. Thompson, eds., *Roman Architecture in the Greek World* (London: Thames and Hudson, 1987); Susan Walker and Averil Cameron, eds., *The Greek Renaissance in the Roman Empire: Papers from the Tenth British Museum Classical Colloquium* (London: University of London, Institute of Classical Studies, 1989); S. E. Alcock, *Graecia Capta: The Landscapes of Roman Greece* (New York: Cambridge University Press, 1993); Erik Nis Ostenfeld, ed., *Greek Romans and Roman Greeks: Studies in Cultural Interaction* (Aarhus, Denmark: Aarhus University Press, 2002); Fergus Millar, *Rome, the Greek World, and the East* (Chapel Hill: University of North Carolina Press, 2002).

Roxane *See* ALEXANDER THE GREAT.

S

Sacred Wars *See* DELPHI; PHOCIS.

sacrifice The rite of sacrifice—practiced in various forms by many ancient religions—probably dates back to Stone Age hunters' rituals. The Greeks saw it as the essential way to win divine favor. "Gifts persuade the gods," a proverb ran. Although "bloodless" sacrifices of grain, cakes, or fruit might be offered, a more significant act involved the slaughter of a domestic animal. The noblest victim was a bull; the most common was a sheep. Goats, pigs, and chickens were also used. To the best modern knowledge, human sacrifice was extremely rare among the Greeks; one of the few such cases was the sacrifice of Persian prisoners during the national emergency of the PERSIAN WARS.

Greek sacrifice involved the notion that the god somehow fed upon the victim's blood—an essential rite was the splashing of the blood onto the altar (typically located outside the temple). First, however, the live animal would be led to the altar in a procession featuring the priest and the person who was providing the animal. The worshippers would be dressed in clean finery, their heads decked with garlands of leaves appropriate to the god: oak for ZEUS, laurel for APOLLO, and so on. A flute player would provide stately background MUSIC.

Preliminary rituals included pelting the altar and the live animal with barley grains. Then the priest would cut the animal's throat. The carcass would be skinned and gutted. The inedible organs and bones would be burned at the altar for the god, the smoke ascending to the god's heavenly realm (for Olympian gods; for chthonian deities, the sacrifice emphasized the act of pouring blood into the ground). Then the edible flesh would be cooked as a meal for the celebrants. Large-scale animal sacrifices, sometimes at public expense, might provide community feasts for holidays.

See also PROMETHEUS.

Further reading: Nanno Marinatos, *Minoan Sacrificial Ritual: Cult Practice and Symbolism* (Stockholm: P. Aström, 1986); Marcel Detienne and Jean-Pierre Vernant, *The Cuisine of Sacrifice among the Greeks,* translated by Paula Wissing (Chicago: University of Chicago Press, 1989); Vincent Rosivach, *The System of Public Sacrifice in Fourth-century Athens* (Atlanta: Scholars Press, 1994); Fritz Graf, "What Is New about Greek Sacrifice?" in *Kykeon: Studies in Honour of H. S. Versnel,* edited by H. F. J. Horstmanshoff (Leiden, Netherlands: E. J. Brill, 2002), 113–126; Walter Burkert, "From Homo Necans: The Anthropology of Ancient Greek Sacrificial Ritual and Myth," in *Understanding Religious Sacrifice: A Reader,* edited by Jeffrey Carter (London: Continuum, 2003), 210–238.

Salamis (1) An inshore island in the northern Saronic Gulf, in central Greece, Salamis's eastern side is separated from the coast of ATTICA by a curved channel less than a mile wide in the narrows. It was there that the crucial sea battle of the PERSIAN WARS was fought in late summer of 480 B.C.E., after the invading army of the Persian king XERXES had overrun northern and central Greece. The allied Greek victory at Salamis broke the Persian navy and stopped the invasion, opening the way for the Greeks' final land victory, at PLATAEA, the following summer.

Well before the sea battle, Salamis was an important place, associated with the mythical hero AJAX (1). Salamis lay close offshore between the territories of ATHENS and MEGARA (1), and not far from the powerful island state of AEGINA. In the 600s B.C.E. the island was a bone of contention among those three warring states. By the mid-500s B.C.E. it was held by Athens.

In 480 B.C.E. the Persians and their allies overran a Spartan-led force at the Battle of THERMOPYLAE and swept southward into central Greece. The Persian navy sailed in escort. Reaching Athens, Xerxes' army found the city abandoned. The noncombatants had been evacuated, while most of Athens' fighting men were in the allied Greek navy, stationed inside Salamis' eastern channel.

Rounding the southern tip of Attica, the Persian navy sailed north into the Saronic Gulf. Not literally "Persian," this navy was manned largely by subject peoples—Phoenicians, Egyptians, and even IONIAN GREEKS—who were fighting for Xerxes. The Phoenician crews seem to have been superior seamen to any Greeks. Battered by prior fighting and storms, the Persians' warships by then probably numbered less than 400. Waiting at Salamis was a combined Greek fleet of perhaps 300 warships, with Athens supplying the largest contingent, almost 180 ships. The fleet's commander was Eurybiades, a Spartan.

The Greek plan to make a stand at Salamis probably originated with the brilliant Athenian soldier-statesman THEMISTOKLES, who foresaw that the way to offset the Persians' advantage in numbers and faster ships would be to lure them to battle inside the narrow straits. By vision and force of personality, he convinced Eurybiades and the other Greek sea commanders to stay together and risk a major fight, rather than dispersing to defend their homes.

According to two fifth-century-B.C. writers—the Athenian playwright AESCHYLUS (who may have fought at Salamis) and the historian HERODOTUS—Themistokles tricked the Persian king by sending him an untruthful message, couched as a plea for personal favor, saying that the Greeks were ready to disband and flee. Supposedly Xerxes actually believed this report from an enemy commander. Whether this is true or not, we do know that Xerxes, overconfident and impatient, ordered his fleet to enter the Salamis channel at night and attack the Greeks at dawn. What followed was one of the most dramatic events in world history—the saving of Greece from foreign domination.

At dawn the Greeks sang their battle paean and launched their fleet in a concave crescent formation in the narrow waterways around Salamis. By filling the entire width of the channel, the Greeks minimized the advantage provided by the greater numbers of ships in the Persian fleet. If the battle were to take place in more open waters, the Greeks realized that the overwhelming size of the enemy force might result in a defeat. With the Persian ships rowing into this Greek "net," the two fleets collided.

As Themistokles had expected, the Persians' advantage in numbers and skill was lost in the crowded narrows. Whereas boarding tactics had been the rule at the recent sea battle at ARTEMISION, Salamis saw more use of Greek ramming techniques. The Persian ships—jammed together by the Greek enveloping tactic, and not as able to withstand ramming as the heavier ships of the Greeks—soon began to get the worst of it. Aeschylus gives a vivid description, presented from the Persian viewpoint, in his tragedy *The Persians* (472 B.C.E.). "The Greek ships, arrayed in a circle around us, bore in and rammed: our ships capsized, the sea was hidden in wrecks and corpses, and all the shores and reefs were heaped with dead . . ."

After most of the elite Phoenician squadron had been destroyed, the other Persian allies broke off and rowed away, pursued by the Greeks. At this point an amphibious landing of Athenian HOPLITES, under the general ARISTIDES, overran a contingent of Persian infantry on the nearby islet of Psytalleia.

The battle was over. The Greek side had lost 40 ships, the Persians (probably) several times that number. Among the Persian dead was the admiral Ariabignes, a brother of Xerxes.

Xerxes himself had watched the battle from a throne set up on the shore, and was so alarmed by his fleet's ruin that he soon started overland for home. Then vulnerable by sea, he was anxious to reach the HELLESPONT before the Greek navy could destroy his bridges there, to trap him inside Europe. Along with most of his huge invasion force, Xerxes crossed back into Asia, leaving behind a small army under his general Mardonius to continue the campaign on land. This army, in turn, was later destroyed by the Greeks at Plataea.

For the Athenians, who had abandoned their city yet still supplied the bulk of the Greek navy, the Battle of Salamis was a patriotic triumph and a springboard to Athens's naval empire in the following decades. For the Persians, Salamis marked the turning point on their western frontier; no longer would they be purely the aggressors, as they had been for 70 years. With their naval power crippled for a decade, the Persians would subsequently go on the defensive—first against Athenian naval action in the eastern Mediterranean, and later, in the 300s B.C.E., against Spartan and Macedonian invasions of Asia. The process that would end with ALEXANDER THE GREAT's conquest of PERSIA (334–323 B.C.E.) began in the narrows at Salamis.

See also WARFARE, NAVAL.

Further reading: Peter Green, *Xerxes at Salamis* (New York: Praeger, 1970); B. Jordan, "The Honors for Themistokles after Salamis," *American Journal of Philology* 109 (1988): 547–571; J. Barron, "All for Salamis," in *Owls to Athens. Essays on Classical Subjects Presented to Sir Kenneth Dover,* edited by E. M. Craik (New York: Oxford University Press, 1990), 133–141; J. S. Morrison, "The Greek

Ships at Salamis and the 'diekplous'," *Journal of Hellenic Studies* 111 (1991): 196–200; Martha Taylor, *Salamis and the Salaminioi: The History of an Unofficial Athenian Demos* (Amsterdam: J. C. Gieben, 1997); C. Higbie, "The Bones of a Hero, the Ashes of a Politician. Athens, Salamis, and the Usable Past," *Classical Antiquity* 16 (1997): 278–307; Hans Rupprecht Goette, *Athens, Attica, and the Megarid: An Archaeological Guide* (London: Routledge, 2001).

Salamis (2)   This Greek city is situated on the east coast of the island of CYPRUS and was apparently founded sometime in the 1000s B.C.E. as a successor to the Mycenaean city of Enkomi when that harbor was silted up. Salamis became the most important city of Cyprus in the 500s B.C.E. In its early history, the entire island was under the control of various imperial powers: the Assyrians (673–669 B.C.E.), the Egyptians (560–545 B.C.E.), and the Persians (545–332 B.C.E.). The Cypriots rebelled against Persian domination under King Onesilos around 500 B.C.E., but this freedom was short-lived. A later king, Euagoras I (reigned 411–373 B.C.E.), also attempted to escape the control of the Persians but eventually failed and was forced to resubmit to the Persian king.

After the death of the Macedonian king ALEXANDER THE GREAT in 323 B.C.E., two of his successors (DIADOCHOI) fought for control of Salamis, DEMETRIUS POLIORKETES and PTOLEMY (1). Ptolemy finally defeated Demetrios and took over Salamis and all Cyprus. Another city, Paphos, grew in importance and supplanted Salamis as the primary city of the island. Later, in the 300s C.E., Salamis regained its dominance and became the metropolis of Christian Cyprus.

Salamis was first excavated in the late 1800s C.E., and additional archaeological work has been done there in recent years. Its major monuments include the gymnasium, public bath buildings, theater, reservoir, AGORA, a temple dedicated to the god ZEUS, part of the city wall, two early Christian churches, and the Royal Tombs. Much of the city, however, has not yet been excavated.

Further reading: Vassos Karageorghis, *Sculptures from Salamis* (Nicosia: Department of Antiquities, Cyprus, 1964); ———, *Salamis in Cyprus: Homeric, Hellenistic, and Roman* (London: Thames and Hudson, 1969); ———, *Salamis: Recent Discoveries in Cyprus* (New York: McGraw-Hill, 1969); ———, *Excavating at Salamis in Cyprus, 1952–1974* (Athens: A. G. Leventis Foundation, 1999).

Samos   This fertile and mountainous Aegean island, 190 square miles in area, is located two miles off the central west coast of ASIA MINOR. Samos was among the most prosperous and powerful Greek states of the 600s–400s B.C.E. The Samians were known for their seafaring, their domestic WINE, and their national cult of HERA, patron goddess of the island.

Occupied before 1200 B.C.E. by Greek colonists of the MYCENAEAN CIVILIZATION, Samos was resettled around 1100–1000 B.C.E. by a new wave of immigrants—IONIAN GREEKS, fleeing from the Dorian invasion of mainland Greece. A capital city, also named Samos, arose in the southeast part of the island, opposite the Asia Minor coast; today it is the site of the modern village of Tigani. Outside the ancient city was the important sanctuary of Hera.

Samos island became a foremost state of the eastern Greek region called IONIA, and played a major role in the Greek world's expansion through seaborne TRADE and COLONIZATION in the 800s–500s B.C.E. The principal Samian colony was at the north Aegean island of SAMOTHRACE (which, as the name suggests, served as an anchorage between Samos and THRACE). To buy luxury goods and raw metals, the Samians exported domestic products such as wine and woolens, along with Thracian SLAVES and SILVER acquired via Samothrace. Markets included both mainland Greece and Near Eastern kingdoms such as EGYPT. One Samian sea captain made a famously lucrative trading stop at the Celtic kingdom of Tartessus, in southern Spain, around 650 B.C.E.

In this era Samos was governed as an ARISTOCRACY, with a ruling class known as *geomoroi*, "landholders." The island was home to famous craftsmen such as the architect Rhoikos, whose temple of Hera, begun around 560 B.C.E., was the largest Greek building of its day (320 × 160 feet). All that survives of that proud structure today is a single Ionic column, standing at the site of ancient Samos city.

The island reached its zenith under POLYCRATES, who held supreme power around 540–522 B.C.E. Polycrates carved out an Aegean sea empire and glorified Samos with engineering marvels such as an underground aqueduct and sea walls to defend the harbor entrance. His palace, of which no trace remains, was situated on the ACROPOLIS of the city, and his lavish court attracted many intellectuals and artisans. But Samos's most important citizen, the philosopher and mathematician PYTHAGORAS, fled Polycrates' rule and emigrated to south ITALY.

After Polycrates was captured and murdered by the encroaching Persians under King DARIUS (1), Samos became a Persian holding, ruled by Greek puppet rulers. Joining the IONIAN REVOLT against the Persians, Samos contributed its entire navy, 60 ships. But at the revolt's climactic sea battle of Lade, fought near Samos, the Samian ships deserted for Persian offers of preferential treatment (494 B.C.E.). In 480 B.C.E., under Persian command, Samian crews fought against their fellow Greeks in King XERXES' invasion of Greece. The following year, Samos was liberated by the victorious Greek counteroffensive.

Then under the heavy influence of ATHENS, Samos became a DEMOCRACY and foremost member of the Athenian-run DELIAN LEAGUE. Samos was one of the few

Delian states to supply warships and crews in lieu of silver tribute. In 440 B.C.E. however the island rebelled against Athens. The nine-month-long revolt amounted to an Athenian crisis: An attacking Athenian fleet was defeated by 70 ships under the Samian leader Melissus, but eventually Samos fell to an Athenian siege and blockade commanded by PERIKLES himself. The island was purged of anti-Athenian elements and reduced to subject status, paying a yearly tribute as well as a huge war penalty of 1,400 TALENTS.

Samos remained a staunch Athenian ally—although no longer contributing warships—throughout the PELOPONNESIAN WAR (431–404 B.C.E.). After 413 B.C.E. the island was a major Athenian naval base. During the right-wing coup of the FOUR HUNDRED at Athens, the Samians supported the Athenian democratic government-in-exile, formed by the Athenian fleet and troops at Samos (411 B.C.E.). For their loyalty, the Samians received the unique honor of being made Athenian citizens (405 B.C.E.). But in the following year, at the war's end, Samos was captured by SPARTA.

In the next decades an independent Samos again fell into conflict with the Athenians, who captured the island and repopulated it with Athenian colonists (365 B.C.E.). Later the native population was allowed to return, by edict of the Macedonian conqueror ALEXANDER THE GREAT (effected posthumously, in 321 B.C.E.).

A bone of contention among the warring DIADOCHOI (Successors) who divided up Alexander's empire after his death, Samos eventually passed to King PTOLEMY (2) II of Egypt (ca. 281 B.C.E.). By then Samos was waning as an east Greek sea power, surpassed by the growing commercial might of RHODES. In 127 B.C.E. Samos was annexed by the Romans.

Samos, especially the Sanctuary of Hera, has been visited and explore by European travelers since the early 1700s C.E. Some small-scale archaeological excavation took place on the site in the early 20th century, first in 1902–1903 by the Archaeological Society of Athens and then in 1910–1914 (until interrupted by World War I) by the Koenigliche Museen of Berlin. Systematic excavation began in 1925 under the auspices of the German Archaeological Institute at Athens and has continued to the present day, with the exception of the period from 1939 to 1951, when World War II and the Greek civil war intervened. The major monuments of the Hera sanctuary include the temple itself, a few subsidiary buildings, the Great Altar, and the "Sacred Road" leading back to the city of Samos.

See also BRONZE; PERSIAN WARS; SHIPS AND SEAFARING; TYRANTS.

Further reading: T. J. Quinn, *Athens and Samos, Lesbos, and Chios, 478–404 B.C.* (Manchester, U.K.: Manchester University Press, 1981); Graham Shipley, *A History of Samos, 800–188 B.C.* (Oxford: Clarendon Press, 1987); H. Kienast, "The Tunnel of Eupalinos at the Island of Samos,"

in *Ancient Technology. Symposium Athens 30.3–4.4.1987* (Helsinki: Museum of Technology, 1990), 38–45; Helmut Kyrieleis, "The Heraion at Samos," in *Greek Sanctuaries. New Approaches,* edited by Nanno Marinatos and Robin Hägg (London: Routledge, 1993), 125–153.

Samothrace A small Greek island of the northeast AEGEAN SEA. Samothrace sits 25 miles south of the northern coast, which in antiquity belonged to the non-Greek land of THRACE. The oval island, only 68 square miles, consists of a single mountain, rising to 5,250 feet and heavily forested in ancient times. The pre-Greek inhabitants were probably of Thracian stock. Sometime between 700 and 550 B.C.E., Samothrace was conquered by seafaring Greeks, who sought it as a safe anchorage from which to make the trading run to the Thracian coast. (The mainland Thracians were a potentially hostile folk who nevertheless could offer such precious goods as SILVER and SLAVES.) As suggested by the name Samothrakē (Samos's Thrace), the island was probably occupied by Greeks from the island state of SAMOS; possibly the Samians were preceded by Greeks from another (and nearer) Greek island state, LESBOS. Samothrace seems to have been a mixed settlement, where Greek and Thracian inhabitants lived in harmony; modern archaeological excavations have uncovered a cemetery that (as inscriptions reveal) was used by both peoples in the latter 500s B.C.E.

In classical times, Samothrace was known for its unique Greek religious cult, colored by the place's pre-Greek origins. This cult worshipped the Kabeiroi—male deities, originally non-Greek, possibly from Thrace or Phrygia (in ASIA MINOR). The Kabeiroi varied between two and four in number and were patron gods of smiths and sailors as well as of fertility. Also called the Great Gods, they were sometimes identified with the Greek deities CASTOR AND POLYDEUCES. If the name Kabeiroi is Greek (which is uncertain), it probably means "the burners," in reference to the forge fire of an ancient smithy.

The Kabeiroi had cults at several shrines in the Greek world, but their main sanctuary was at Samothrace city, high in the island's hills. There were held the Mysteries of Samothrace—a secret cult, open only to initiates. These Mysteries (Greek: *mystēriai,* from *mystēs,* "an initiate") are often mentioned but rarely discussed by ancient writers, who feared to divulge secret details lest they provoke the Kabeiroi's wrath. Unlike the mysteries at ELEUSIS, the Samothracian cult could be joined by anyone—male or female, free or slave—and initiations could take place at any time of the year, not only during the annual festival. The initiation consisted of two stages, *myesis* and *apopteia.* At least some of the rituals took place at night, but their details remain unknown. Although access to certain buildings was limited to those who had undergone the initiation, the sanctuary itself was open to visitors. Since the Great Gods were special patrons of sea travel in an era when this mode of transportation was quite dangerous, many travelers did visit the sanctuary to make offerings. The cult became popular in the HELLENISTIC AGE (300–150 B.C.E.); men and WOMEN flocked to Samothrace for initiation and worship. King PTOLEMY (2) II of EGYPT (ca. 270 B.C.E.) was an important patron of the sanctuary; remnants of the buildings that he financed can be seen today. Among the costly offerings that adorned the site was the wonderful second-century-B.C.E. marble statue known as the Winged Victory of Samothrace, excavated by French archaeologists in 1863 C.E. and now displayed at the Louvre.

Politically Samothrace became an ally of ATHENS, serving as a member of the Athenian-controlled DELIAN LEAGUE (478–404 B.C.E.) and the subsequent SECOND ATHENIAN LEAGUE (378–338 B.C.E.). Attractive as a naval base and propagandistic pawn, in Hellenistic times the island changed hands frequently, among the Macedonians, Ptolemaic Egyptians, and Seleucids.

The first archaeological exploration in the sanctuary at Samothrace was conducted around the Nike monument by the French consul M. Champoiseau in 1861. Other French teams excavated the area of the theater in 1866 and 1891. More systematic excavations were done under Austrian archaeologists in 1873 and 1875. The current archaeological project was begun in 1938 by New York University, directed by Karl Lehmann until his death in 1960 and from then (until the present) by James McCredie.

See also AFTERLIFE; SCULPTURE.

Further reading: S. G. Cole, *Theoi Megaloi. The Cult of the Great Gods at Samothrace* (Leiden, Netherlands: E. J. Brill, 1984); Yiannis Kizis, *Samothrace,* translated by Philip Ramp (Athens: Melissa Publishing House, 1991); Walter Burkert, "Concordia discors. The Literary and the Archaeological Evidence on the Sanctuary of Samothrace," in *Greek Sanctuaries. New Approaches,* edited by Nanno Marinatos and Robin Hägg (London: Routledge, 1993), 178–191; J. Bouzek, "Notes on the Topography of the City of Samothrace," *Eirene* 30 (1994): 169–173; Ira S. Mark, "The Victory of Samothrace," in *Regional Schools in Hellenistic Sculpture. Proceedings of an International Conference Held at Athens, March 15–17, 1996,* edited by Olga Palagia and William Coulson (Oxford: Oxbow Books, 1998), 157–165.

Sappho (ca. 630–570 B.C.E.) *Lyric poet of* MYTILENE *on the island of* LESBOS

Sappho's verses, of which perhaps two short poems and some 150 fragments survive today, have been much admired since ancient times for their directness of expression and personal honesty. Most of her poems were composed for solo recitation to the accompaniment of the lyre. She wrote in the Aeolic dialect and vernacular of Lesbos, a place whose strong lyric tradition had already produced such poets as TERPANDER, ARION, and Sappho's

contemporary ALCAEUS. Sappho is one of the few female poets whom we know of from ancient Greece.

The typical subject of Sappho's verse is her physical love for several of the young WOMEN who were her comembers in a local cult of the goddess APHRODITE. The clearly homosexual nature of Sappho's poetry (and the presumably homosexual atmosphere of her female circle on Lesbos) gave rise in the 19th century C.E. to the word *lesbian,* meaning "a woman who has sexual feelings for other women."

The only reliable facts about Sappho's life are those that can be gleaned from her verses. She was born into an aristocratic family of Mytilene. Although her poetry does not deal with politics, she apparently shared in the privileges and hazards of upper-class life. She went into brief exile in SICILY during a period of civil unrest on Lesbos circa 600 B.C.E., and she writes of happier days when her brother Larichus served as cupbearer at aristocratic drinking parties in Mytilene. Sappho had another brother, Charaxus, who sailed as a trader to NAUKRATIS, in EGYPT, where he squandered a fortune on a courtesan named Doricha; in certain verses Sappho rails against Doricha and wishes Charaxus a return to sanity. Later writers say that Sappho was married—as most women of her social class were bound to be—and we know that she had a daughter, Cleïs; in one poem Sappho expresses joy at the beauty of her daughter's face. In later centuries there arose a ridiculous tale that Sappho had died by jumping off a cliff for hopeless love of a sturdy ferryman.

Modern writers often assume that Sappho was a music teacher or similar, but her poems show only that she led a group of younger women, probably teenagers, in an official worship of Aphrodite—specifically, in observing the goddess' religious calendar and in maintaining various shrines in and around Mytilene. Some of Sappho's loveliest verses show the women venturing into the countryside or plaiting wildflower garlands to adorn a cult statue or altar. Sappho's sexual involvements with her young colleagues would seem to grow out of this sincere devotion to the goddess of sex and nature. The one poem by Sappho that definitely survives in its complete form is a hymn to Aphrodite in which the goddess, appearing before Sappho, promises to help the poet woo her beloved.

Not that love always means happiness in Sappho's poetry. "O Atthis," she writes to a girlfriend, "you have come to hate me in your mind, and flee to Andromeda!" (Andromeda was a rival of Sappho's, possibly the leader of a rival cult.) There was also the melancholy fact that, no matter what liaisons might arise between the girls in Sappho's group, all of these aristocratic maidens were detained to be married off by their families. (In ancient Greece girls were usually married by age 18; often by 14 or even 12.) Several of Sappho's poems are wedding songs, while other verses show distress within the group as members depart for MARRIAGE. Sappho's most famous poem, which survives nearly complete, records her own unabated desire as she watches a girlfriend talk with a handsome young man—probably the girl's husband and evidently at their wedding feast. He looks calm and god-like, the poet writes, "but whenever I even glance at you, my voice is lost, my tongue is stopped, and a delicate fire has spread under my skin . . ."

In another poem, which survives only as a mutilated fragment, Sappho recalls how she consoled a girlfriend who was departing from the group. "'Honestly I want to die,'" the fragment begins, with the other woman talking. "'Sappho, I swear it's against my will that I'm leaving you.' And I answered her thus: 'Go gladly and remember me, for you know how we cherished you. Or let me remind you, if you forget, what blissful days we enjoyed—how at my side you often put on garlands of violets and roses and crocuses . . . and on soft mattresses gently you satisfied desire. And there was . . . nothing sacred from which we kept away . . .'"

In the modern age of commercialized sex and sexual politics, it takes some effort to imagine the innocence of Sappho's world. Although Sappho has been appropriated as a feminist forerunner since the 1970s, the poems suggest a woman with an open and honest heart living in a land of private emotion, completely removed—as almost all women of those days were—from politics or grand social concerns. Certain verses by the male Spartan poet ALCMAN (ca. 630 B.C.E.) seem to commemorate similar emotional tides within a Spartan girls' chorus.

The private world of Sappho and her lovers represents the female response to an outside world created by men—a world of politics, war, and male HOMOSEXUALITY, which excluded even upper-class women except as wives and mothers. One of Sappho's best-known poems involves a gentle rejection of male militarism: "Some say that a host of cavalry is the loveliest sight on earth, some say foot soldiers, some say warships. But I say it is the person you love."

What makes such verses great, despite their self-absorption, is their apparent honesty and unselfconsciousness. Sappho's eroticism is miles apart from the amused, detached male homosexuality in the poetry of IBYCUS or ANACREON (mid- and late 500s B.C.E.). Sappho's genius lies in her ability to convey her sincere feelings, in simple lyric meters and vocabulary. Her metaphors and similes are beautifully apt and often come from the natural world, as when she writes of a maiden who outshines other women as the Moon outshines the stars. Among Sappho's admirers in later generations was the philosopher PLATO, who called her the tenth Muse. The Roman poet Catullus (ca. 55 B.C.E.) imitated her verses in at least two of his poems.

See also ARISTOCRACY; LYRIC POETRY; MUSES.

Further reading: H. N. Parker, "Sappho Schoolmistress," *Transactions of the American Philological Association* 123 (1993): 309–351; J. M. Snyder, "Sappho in Attic Vase Painting," in *Naked Truths. Women, Sexuality, and Gender in Classical Art and Archaeology*, edited by Ann Olga Koloski-Ostrow and Claire L. Lyons (London: Routledge, 1997), 108–119; Margaret Reynolds, ed., *The Sappho Companion* (New York: Palgrave for St. Martin's Press, 2001); André Lardinois, "Keening Sappho: Female Speech Genres in Sappho's Poetry," in *Making Silence Speak: Women's Voices in Greek Literature and Society*, edited by André Lardinois and Laura McClure (Princeton, N.J.: Princeton University Press, 2001), 75–92; Marilyn B. Skinner, "Aphrodite Garlanded: Eros and Poetic Creativity in Sappho and Nossis," in *Among Women: From the Homosocial to the Homoerotic in the Ancient World*, edited by Nancy Sorkin Rabinowitz and Lisa Auanger (Austin: University of Texas Press, 2002), 60–81; Ellen Greene, "Subjects, Objects, and Erotic Symmetry in Sappho's Fragments," in *Among Women: From the Homosocial to the Homoerotic in the Ancient World*, edited by Nancy Sorkin Rabinowitz and Lisa Auanger (Austin: University of Texas Press, 2002), 82–105; Anne Carson, trans., *If Not, Winter: Fragments of Sappho* (New York: Alfred A. Knopf, 2002).

satyrs The *satyrai* were mythical spirits of the countryside and wilderness, personifying fertility and sexual desire. Satyrs were semihuman in form, with the ears, tail, legs, and hooves of a goat (or, in some earlier versions, of a horse). They were favorite subjects in vase painting and other art, and were always shown naked, with beards and pug noses, often with bald heads, and usually with erect penises. Satyrs were typically shown getting drunk or pursuing sexual gratification with their female counterparts, the NYMPHS.

The satyrs were associated with DIONYSUS, the god of WINE and fertility. Processions honoring Dionysus and the satyrs were held in the Athenian countryside (among other places), and these bawdy ceremonies apparently supplied the origin for Athenian stage comedy. Classical Athens retained a form of stage farce, less elaborate than formal comedy, known as the satyr play (*satyrikon*).

See also THEATER.

Further reading: Guy Hedreen, *Silens in Attic Black-figure Vase-painting* (Ann Arbor: University of Michigan Press, 1992); Francois Lissarrague, "On the Wildness of Satyrs," in *Masks of Dionysus*, edited by Thomas H. Carpenter and Christopher A. Faraone (Ithaca, N.Y.: Cornell University Press, 1993), 207–220; N. Vogeikoff, "A Smiling Satyr in Context," in *Stephanos: Studies in Honor of Brunilde Sismondo Ridgway*, edited by Kim J. Hartswick and Mary C. Sturgeon (Philadelphia: University Museum, University of Pennsylvania, 1998), 235–239; J. M. Padgett, "The Stable Hands of Dionysus. Satyrs and Donkeys as Symbols of Social Marginalization in Attic Vase Painting," in *Not the Classical Ideal. Athens and the Construction of the Other in Greek Art*, edited by Beth Cohen (Leiden, Netherlands: E. J. Brill, 2000), 43–70; J. M. Padgett, "Horse Men: Centaurs and Satyrs in Early Greek Art," in *The Centaur's Smile: The Human Animal in Early Greek Art,* edited by J. M. Padgett (New Haven, Conn.: Yale University Press, 2003), 3–48.

science   The ancient Greeks were the first Europeans to make inquiries into ASTRONOMY, physics, and biology, yet they were slow to recognize a separate discipline that might be called science. Greek scientific studies in the 500s and 400s B.C.E. were bound up in the concept of *philosophia* (love of arcane knowledge) and the search for philosophical truth. Such studies were conducted in imitation of MATHEMATICS, with emphasis on theory rather than on experiment and observation. It took the categorizing genius of ARISTOTLE (384–322 B.C.E.) to identify a separate discipline that he called *physikē* (natural studies), in contrast to mathematics or PHILOSOPHY.

The origin of Western science is associated with the philosopher THALES of MILETUS (ca. 585 B.C.E.). Thales was the first Greek to try to explain the universe without appeal to MYTH or RELIGION, but rather with reference to a primary physical substance (which he identified as water). Further crude theorizing in physics came from Thales' disciples ANAXIMANDER (ca. 560 B.C.E.) and ANAXIMENES (ca. 550 B.C.E.), and from such later philosophers as HERAKLEITOS (ca. 500 B.C.E.), PARMENIDES (ca. 490 B.C.E.), EMPEDOKLES (who originated the concept of four primal elements—earth, fire, water, and air, ca. 450 B.C.E.), and the atomists LEUKIPPOS (ca. 440 B.C.E.) and DEMOCRITUS (ca. 430 B.C.E.). These thinkers all addressed, in highly original ways, the basic problem of physical change: How is it that matter apparently comes into being and grows out of nothing? (For instance, how is it that trees sprout leaves?)

But the single most important figure in ancient science was Aristotle, whose voluminous inquiries into all existing branches of knowledge served to create certain scientific categories still recognized today, such as physics and biology. Aristotle introduced the practice of studying by empirical observation, purely for the sake of scientific knowledge—a practice that became traditional at his Athenian school of higher learning, the LYCEUM (founded in about 335 B.C.E.).

In zoology specifically, Aristotle's inquiries were simply epoch-making. His zoological writings make reference to over 500 animal species, including about 120 kinds of fish and 60 kinds of insects, observed either in their natural habitat or in dissection. Although not the first Greek to practice animal dissection, he was the first to do so with a wide variety of species and to document his researches.

Aristotle tackled the problem of change with typical restraint and common sense, suggesting that a thing can come to be both what it already is and what it is not—in the sense that it fulfills an inborn potential, or *telos*. For example, the acorn "is" an oak tree, in terms of its *telos*. In physics, Aristotle pioneered the study of motion, which is now called dynamics.

Aristotle's work dominated Western science, for better or worse, for over 2,000 years, down to the 1600s A.D. His acceptance of Empedocles' notion of four elements guaranteed that that theory would remain for centuries the authoritative theory of chemistry. Even Aristotle's grosser errors became canonical; his treatise *On the Heavens* contains the notoriously inaccurate statement that a heavier object will fall at a proportionately faster speed than a lighter one. Although questioned in late antiquity, this false law of physics was taught in European schools until it was finally disproved by Galileo in around 1590 C.E.

Aristotle's successor at the Lyceum, THEOPHRASTUS (president ca. 323–287 B.C.E.), carried on the master's studies in biology and physics, as did Theophrastus's successor, Straton (president ca. 287–269 B.C.E.). Theophrastus's achievements in botany were particularly important contributions to later scientific thought. Meanwhile, the Athenian philosophical movement of STOICISM popularized the Empedoclean-Aristotelian theory of four elements, while the rival school of EPICUREANISM adapted Leucippus's and Democritus's concept of atoms (*atomoi*, "indivisible particles"). But by the early 200s B.C.E. the center of scientific research was shifting from Athens to the wealthy court of the Ptolemies at ALEXANDRIA (1), where the Library and Museum attracted scholars from around the Greek world. Whereas the scientific studies in Greece during the HELLENISTIC AGE tended to be very theoretical, Egyptian science focused on more practical issues and solutions.

The main scientific advances at Alexandria were in the previously neglected field of mechanical engineering. From at least the 500s B.C.E. onward, the Greeks had possessed such simple mechanical devices as the lever, pulley, and winch, but in the 200s B.C.E. Alexandrian scientists explored new constructions and mechanical theories. Fueling this advance was the Ptolemies' eager financing of military technology, specifically the creation of bigger and better siege artillery, powered by torsion. The Alexandrian inventor Ktesibios (ca. 270 B.C.E.) is credited with improvements in catapult design as well as with such peaceful inventions as the water pump and the water clock (which measured the passing hours through the controlled dripping of water). Ktesibios also pioneered the study of pneumatics (the action of air under pressure).

The century's greatest Greek scientist—and one of its greatest mathematicians—was ARCHIMEDES (active 260–212 B.C.E.), a lifelong citizen of the Sicilian-Greek city of SYRACUSE. Among his many accomplishments, Archimedes invented the branch of physics known today as hydrostatics (the study of properties of standing water). Archimedes added one important invention to Mediterranean technology—the Archimedes screw, still used today to draw water uphill continually, without suction. Another significant Hellenistic scientist was Euclid, whose basic mathematical "Elements" remains a fundamental part of modern geometry.

One technological breakthrough of the late Greek world (around 100 B.C.E.) was the simple expedient of powering a millstone by means of a donkey tethered to a pole, treading a circle. Further advances appeared under the Roman Empire, although these tended to be mainly in the fields of medicine and engineering. One significant event was the Alexandrian inventor Hero's famous experiment with steam power around 60 C.E. The relatively slow advance of Greek technology can be explained partly by the availability of slave labor and by a lack of government funding for nonmilitary research.

See also SLAVES; WARFARE, SIEGE.

Further reading: G. E. R. Lloyd, *The Revolution of Wisdom. Studies in the Claims and Practice of Ancient Greek Science* (Berkeley: University of California Press, 1987); Robin Waterfield, *Before "Eureka": The Presocratics and Their Science* (New York: St. Martin's Press, 1989); George Sarton, *Ancient Science through the Golden Age of Greece* (New York: Dover, 1993); Patrick H. Byrne, *Analysis and Science in Aristotle* (Albany: State University of New York Press, 1997); Malcolm Wilson, *Aristotle's Theory of the Unity of Science* (Toronto: University of Toronto Press, 2000).

sculpture Arguably the greatest artistic achievement of the ancient Greeks was their development of high-quality marble and metal sculpture, particularly their representation of the human body. By the mid-400s B.C.E., Greek sculptors (working mainly at the preeminent city of Athens) had attained a level of realism in portraying human forms that went unequaled for the next 2000 years, until the Italian Renaissance. Modern art historians refer to the years 480–323 B.C.E. (from the PERSIAN WARS to the death of ALEXANDER THE GREAT) as the Greek Classical era. (This terminology indicates many scholars' belief that that was when the Greeks established standards of excellence—in sculpture as well as in ARCHITECTURE— that helped to define those art forms for all time.) Prior to the Classical period, from about 600 to 480 B.C.E., is the time period called "archaic," and the following time period, from 323 to 31 B.C.E. (the battle of Actium and the conquest of ROME), is called "Hellenistic."

Relatively few original Greek sculptures have survived from ancient times. During late antiquity and the Middle Ages, numerous pieces were lost to neglect or plundered for their raw material. Today, many ancient sculptures exist only as Roman copies of vanished Greek works. Most of these Roman copies are made of marble, even in those instances where the Greek original was BRONZE.

There were several media for ancient Greek sculpture. Statues are by definition freestanding and carved in the round. Greek statues frequently represented a human

Clay female figurine from Boeotia, in central Greece, late 700s B.C.E. The bell-shaped body was molded on a potter's wheel, then painted and baked in a kiln; the legs were made separately and fastened inside. *(Alison Frantz Photographic Collection, American School of Classical Studies at Athens)*

figure, male or female, mortal or divine. Among the most important statues were cult images of gods or goddesses set up in those deities' temples. Another important category of sculpture is architectural sculpture meant to be fastened to panels on the outside of temples and other public buildings. These figures were carved of limestone or marble and were either carved in the round (like a statue) or left unfinished in back, where they would be fixed to the building. Another type of architectural sculpture was relief, in which case a panel of stone would be carved so that the figure or group of figures would rise three-dimensionally from the surface of the panel. In addition to appearing on buildings, relief sculpture was also used for gravestones and public plaques.

The earliest Greek sculptors probably worked in wood, but none of these pieces survives in the archaeological record since wood is a perishable material. Even as late as the 400s B.C.E., wooden idols were still being worshipped in some Greek sanctuaries. Other early small-scale figures were made of ivory, clay, or metals such as bronze or GOLD. The earliest extant large-scale Greek sculpture is in stone—specifically, the soft limestone plentiful in the mountains of mainland Greece. The best-known early work of carved limestone is the relief slab over the gateway of MYCENAE, called the Lion Gate (around 1250 B.C.E.).

After the collapse of the MYCENAEAN CIVILIZATION, the grim DARK AGE (around 1100–900 B.C.E.) saw artistic impoverishment throughout the Greek world. Sculpture may have been reduced largely to wood carving and the shaping of clay. Sculpture in stone reemerged around 600 B.C.E., at the beginning of the archaic era. Influenced by the monumental statuary carved in granite and porphyry that could be seen in EGYPT, Greek sculptors chose the most suitable hard stone found in Greece—marble (a compacted form of limestone). The Greeks also copied from the Egyptians the typical pose of their human figures: frontal, arms stiffly at sides, left leg advanced. The Greek statues, however, were more freestanding than the Egyptian ones and soon developed new postures and movements. A number of these Greek archaic statues survive, with the earliest dating from around 600 B.C.E. They are the figures known today as *kouroi* ("male youths," singular: *kouros*); typically they show a naked young man, slightly larger than life-size. The *kouroi* and their somewhat later female counterparts, the clothed figures known as *korai* ("maidens," singular: *kore*), were works commissioned by wealthy families to stand at a young person's grave or as a dedicatory offering in a temple. Most extant *kouroi* and *korai* come from Athens and ATTICA.

A comparison of individual *kouroi* made between 600 and 500 B.C.E. reveals the advances made by Greek sculptors during this time. Figures made in the later part of the century show more realistic musculature, facial expressions, and posture. Greek statues begin to show the famous "archaic smile"—intended to represent, not happiness necessarily, but the vividness of a living human face.

The defeat of the invading Persians in 480–479 B.C.E. opened a new phase in Greek art—the Classical period—in which artistic confidence, religious piety, and prosperity all combined to produce one of the greatest cultural eras in world history. From about 450 to 404 B.C.E., the rich, imperial city of Athens—with its lavish public-building program begun by the statesman PERIKLES—dominated the field. Greek sculptors broke away from the styles of previous generations and developed a new realism in showing the posture and proportions of the human form, particularly the male form. This breakthrough is embodied in the Athenian marble statue that modern scholars call the "Kritios Boy," carved around

480 B.C.E. By the mid-400s B.C.E., the Argive sculptor POLYKLEITOS had perfected the proportions of the standing male figure, with his statue known as the Doryphoros ("Spear bearer").

The fifth century B.C.E. also saw an improved ability to show bodies in motion or in emotional poses. The beginning of this development is evident when comparing different figures from one building, the temple of Aphaia at AEGINA, which was carved at the very beginning of the Classical period. The best-known surviving examples of such figures are the marble sculptures that adorned the temple of ZEUS at OLYMPIA (ca. 470–456 B.C.E.) and the Athenian PARTHENON (ca. 447–432 B.C.E.).

Greek sculpture was also revolutionized in the early 400s B.C.E. by improvements in metal casting technology. Around this time, artists invented a method of casting molten bronze around a wooden core, thus creating a hollow metal figure rather than (as in previous bronze

During the 300s B.C.E. sculpture began capturing the female form. This statuette attempts to show the woman's body draped yet visible through thin and thick clothing. (*Alison Frantz Photographic Collection, American School of Classical Studies at Athens*)

sculptures) a solid one. The new method allowed for greater realism in the rendering of musculature, clothing, and such fine details as beards and hair. Relatively few original Greek bronze statues survive today (many were melted down in late antiquity for reuse); among the most famous extant examples are the Charioteer of DELPHI (478 or 474 B.C.E.) and the Artemision Zeus (460–450 B.C.E.). The new metal-casting method also helped to create the century's two most famous statues—the colossal gold and ivory images of ATHENA and Zeus, both sculpted by the Athenian PHEIDIAS in the 430s B.C.E. but now lost.

Athens's defeat in the PELOPONNESIAN WAR (404 B.C.E.) saw the start of a less confident, less public-minded, but still innovative artistic era. In place of the former patriotism and piety, tastes in sculpture during the 300s B.C.E. turned to more personal subjects. Portraiture of living people became a growing field. In mythological subjects, the prior era's fascination with the male form was finally counterbalanced by an interest in the female form (usually show clothed, sometimes partially or completely nude). At the same time, sculptors worked to achieve better realism in the rendering of flowing clothing fabric and facial expression. The spirit and values of the mid-300s B.C.E. were embodied in the work of the Athenian sculptor PRAXITELES.

The conquests of the Macedonian king Alexander the Great (334–323 B.C.E.) re-created the map of the Greek world, with new centers of Greek culture and patronage arising in the eastern Mediterranean. The classical era was followed by the HELLENISTIC AGE (323–31 B.C.E.), which saw further advances in conveying emotion or movement through pose, facial gesture, and clothing. Among the masterpieces of Hellenistic sculpture are the reliefs carved on the Great Altar of Zeus from the Greek city of PERGAMON in ASIA MINOR, carved around 180 B.C.E. Now displayed in the Staatliche Museum in Berlin, the Pergamene sculptures show a favorite mythological subject—the primeval battle between the gods and the GIANTS, representing the triumph of civilization over savagery.

Most ancient Greek sculpture, both marble and metal, was painted. The flesh, clothing, jewelry, and other attributes of sculpted figures were vividly colored so as to be clearly seen from a distance. On buildings, architectural sculptures stood out against dark painted backgrounds of red or blue. Today the paint on most of the surviving Greek sculpture has faded away through time, but traces of it remain visible in some instances.

See also FUNERAL CUSTOMS; LAOCOON; MELOS; RELIGION; RHODES; SAMOTHRACE; SEVEN WONDERS OF THE WORLD; WOMEN.

Further reading: J. J. Pollitt, *Art and Experience in Classical Greece* (Cambridge: Cambridge University Press, 1972); Andrew Stewart, *Greek Sculpture: An Exploration* (New Haven, Conn.: Yale University Press, 1990); R. R. R. Smith, *Hellenistic Sculpture: A Handbook* (New York: Thames and Hudson, 1991); Olga Palagia and J. J. Pollitt, eds., *Personal Styles in Greek Sculpture* (New York: Cambridge University Press, 1996); Diana Buitron-Oliver, ed., *The Interpretation of Architectural Sculpture in Greece and Rome* (Washington, D.C.: National Gallery of Art, 1997); Brunilde S. Ridgway, *Prayers in Stone: Greek Architectural Sculpture ca. 600–100 B.C.E.* (Berkeley: University of California Press, 1999); Nikolaos Kaltsas, *Sculpture in the National Archaeological Museum, Athens,* translated by David Hardy (Athens: Kapon Editions, 2002); Katerina Karakasi, *Archaic Korai* (Los Angeles: J. Paul Getty Museum, 2003).

Scythia *See* BLACK SEA.

Second Athenian League This name is given by modern historians to the alliance formed by ATHENS and various other Greek states in 378 B.C.E. and modeled after the DELIAN LEAGUE, which had been founded exactly 100 years before. The league arose in response to Spartan repression in the generation following SPARTA's victory in the PELOPONNESIAN WAR (404 B.C.E.) and particularly as a result of the unpopular Spartan-Persian treaty known as the KING'S PEACE (386 B.C.E.).

To entice Greek allies into the league, Athens had to promise to avoid its previous imperialistic excesses of the Delian League, including the levying of tribute and the imposition of Athenian garrison colonies; the latter promise was not kept scrupulously. The most important ally in the league was THEBES. But, after defeating the Spartans at the Battle of LEUKTRA in 371 B.C.E., Thebes led other central Greek states in seceding from the league. Indeed, the rapid decline of Sparta after 371 B.C.E. removed much of the league's original reason for being.

The league received another blow in 357 B.C.E., when three major east Greek member states—CHIOS, RHODES, and BYZANTIUM—revolted. The league was dissolved by the Macedonian king PHILIP II, after he had seized mainland Greece in 338 B.C.E.

Further reading: Jack Cargill, *The Second Athenian League: Empire or Free Alliance?* (Berkeley: University of California Press, 1981); Jack Cargill, "Hegemony, not Empire. The Second Athenian League," *Ancient World* 5 (1982): 91–102; R. M. Kallet-Marx, "Athens, Thebes, and the Foundation of the Second Athenian League," *Classical Antiquity* 4 (1985): 127–151; C. M. Fauber, "Was Kerkyra a Member of the Second Athenian League?" *Classical Quarterly* 48 (1998): 110–116.

Seleuceia *See* ANTIOCH; SELEUCID EMPIRE.

Seleucid Empire This was the largest of several Hellenistic kingdoms that emerged from the eastern conquests of the Macedonian king ALEXANDER THE GREAT (died 323 B.C.E.). At its greatest secure extent, around 280 B.C.E., the Seleucid Empire occupied much of what had been Alexander's domain, from ASIA MINOR and the Levant to Afghanistan, but excluding EGYPT. The Seleucids' governing and soldiering classes came from a Greek and Macedonian minority based in the western cities and in military colonies throughout; these people ruled a population of Syrians, Persians, Phoenicians, Babylonians, JEWS, and others. Unfortunately, this unwieldy domain lacked a unifying identity and had trouble replenishing its Greco-Macedonian soldiery. For most of its 250-year history, the empire was losing territory.

The term *Seleucid Empire* is a translation of the kingdom's Greek name, Seleukis, which was derived from the name of the founding dynast, SELEUCUS (1), who lived ca. 358–281 B.C.E. Seleucus began his career as a Macedonian nobleman and soldier under Alexander. After Alexander's death, he was one of several Macedonian generals, known collectively as the DIADOCHOI (Successors), who seized portions of the conqueror's domain; Seleucus's share was by far the largest.

In 300 B.C.E. Seleucus built the Syrian coastal city of ANTIOCH, which later became the Seleucid capital, superseding the prior capital of Seleuceia-on-the-Tigris, in Mesopotamia. Brilliantly located to be a gateway between the Mediterranean and the East, Antioch became the seat of a lively Syro-Greek culture, personified for us by the poet and anthologist Meleager of Gadara (ca. 100 B.C.E.) Antioch was named for Seleucus's son and eventual successor, Antiochus, who reigned 281–261 B.C.E. The names Antiochus and Seleucus (also Demetrius) became traditional for the Seleucid royal house.

Despite their Eastern holdings, the Seleucid rulers tended to look westward, being preoccupied with territorial conflicts against Ptolemaic Egypt. The six Syrian Wars (274–168 B.C.E.), fought over the two empires' shared frontier in the Levant, involved use of war elephants and huge phalanxes of heavy infantry. Meanwhile the city of PERGAMON, revolting from Seleucid rule, established a rival domain in Asia Minor (around 262 B.C.E.). Farther east, the hellenized kingdom of BACTRIA rebelled (around 250 B.C.E.), and the non-Greek kingdom of Parthia emerged to deprive the Seleucids of territories on PERSIA and Mesopotamia (mid-200s–mid-100s B.C.E.).

ANTIOCHUS (2) III (reigned 223–187 B.C.E.), the greatest Seleucid king, re-created much of the old empire; but he came to grief against the overseas armies of the Italian city of ROME. The Romans defeated Antiochus in battle in Greece (191 B.C.E.) and Asia Minor (190 B.C.E.), and forced him to relinquish his holdings in Asia Minor (188 B.C.E.). Weakened by palace factions and by the Maccabean Revolt of the Palestinian Jews (167 B.C.E.), the Seleucid realm gradually shrank into the region that was called Syria (including modern Syria and Lebanon). The Seleucid kingship was dismantled in 64 B.C.E., when Syria became a Roman province.

The Seleucid Empire's significance for history is its role in hellenizing the Levant. This effect can be seen today in Greek-style ruins at such sites as Palmyra, in the Syrian desert. Long after the end of the Seleucid Empire, Greek was still the language of commerce, government, and higher learning in the Near East. Under Roman rule, in the first century C.E., the Bible's New Testament was written in Greek—rather than in Hebrew, Aramaic, or Latin—as a result of the Seleucid legacy.

See also CELTS; HELLENISTIC AGE; WARFARE, LAND.

Further reading: P. Bilde, T. Engberg-Pedersen, and L. Hannestad, eds., *Religion and Religious Practice in the Seleucid Kingdom* (Aarhus, Denmark: Aarhus University Press, 1990); A. Kuhrt and S. Sherwin-White, "Aspects of Seleucid Royal Iconography. The Cylinder of Antiochus I from Borsippa," *Journal of Hellenic Studies* 111 (1991): 71–86; S. Sherwin-White and A. Kuhrt, *From Samarkhand to Sardis. A New Approach to the Seleucid Empire* (London: Duckworth, 1993); L. MacKenzie, "Problems in Seleucid Administration. Macedonian or Near Eastern?" *Mediterranean Archaeology* 7 (1994): 61–68.

Seleucus (1) (ca. 358–281 B.C.E.) *Founder and first king of the Seleucid Empire, which was named after him*
Seleucus was one of the most capable of the DIADOCHOI (Successors), who fought over the dismembered empire of ALEXANDER THE GREAT. He assumed the surname "Nikator" (Victor), and the kingdom that he received was the largest of any Successor's, extending from the Levant to the Indus River valley.

This Oriental despot was born—neither Oriental nor royal—in MACEDON, as the son of a Macedonian nobleman in the service of the Macedonian king PHILIP II. At about age 24, Seleucus (Shining one) accompanied Philip's son and successor, Alexander, on his invasion of the Persian Empire (334 B.C.E.). Although not mentioned as a prominent commander, Seleucus may have been a close friend of the young king, who was his near contemporary.

Following Alexander's spectacular conquests and his death, Seleucus became the Macedonian governor at Babylon (321 B.C.E.). Coming into conflict with ANTIGONUS (1), who was based in ASIA MINOR, in 316 B.C.E. Seleucus fled to the protection of PTOLEMY (1), in EGYPT, but in 312 B.C.E. he returned to Babylon with an army and recaptured the city. Later Seleucus conquered eastward to seize an empire that nearly compared with Alexander's. Soon Seleucus, like the other Diadochoi, was calling himself "king" (*basileus*). In 301 B.C.E. he and the Macedonian dynast LYSIMACHUS destroyed Antigonus at the Battle of Ipsus, in central Asia Minor. An essential element in the victory was Seleucus's 480 trained Indian war ELEPHANTS, acquired from an Indian king in exchange for Seleucid territorial concessions in the Indus region.

The Ipsus victory left Seleucus with secure gains in Syria and southeastern Asia Minor. He then sought westward outlets; no doubt he saw that his domain could survive only by remaining a part of the Greek world and by attracting Greek immigration. Having established an eastern capital, Seleuceia, on the River Tigris (in about 312 B.C.E.), he then founded a western capital, the great city of ANTIOCH, near the Syrian seacoast (300 B.C.E.).

Antioch was named for Seleucus's son and eventual successor, Antiochus. Prince Antiochus's mother was Apama, a noblewoman of BACTRIA whom Seleucus had married under Alexander's supervision, in 324 B.C.E. In 298 B.C.E., without divorcing, the 60-year-old Seleucus took a second wife—Stratonicē, the 20-year-old daughter of his prior enemy, DEMETRIUS POLIORKETES (Antigonus's son). Later, when the dynamic but unstable Demetrius invaded Asia Minor, Seleucus captured him (285 B.C.E.) and chivalrously provided a comfortable captivity in which Demetrius ate and drank himself to death.

In 281 B.C.E. Seleucus took aim at what would be his last great acquisition—Asia Minor, most of which was held by his former ally, Lysimachus, now king of Macedon. For Seleucus, Asia Minor represented the crucial westward link to the central Greek world. Seleucus defeated Lysimachus at the Battle of Corupedium, near Sardis. Lysimachus's death in the fighting inspired the 77-year-old Seleucus with dreams of seizing the vacant Macedonian throne. Seleucus invaded Macedon and was on the point of capturing the kingdom when he was murdered by one of his followers, a son of Ptolemy who wanted the throne for himself. Seleucus was succeeded by Antiochus, who had been reigning as his father's partner since 292 B.C.E.

The Seleucid Empire continued under Seleucus's descendants for nearly another 220 years, but the vast conquests of Seleucus I gradually were eroded.

See also WARFARE, LAND.

Further reading: A. Houghton, "A Colossal Head in Antakya and the Portraits of Seleucus I," *Antike Kunst* 27 (1986): 52–62; J. D. Grainger, *Seleukos Nikator. Constructing a Hellenistic Kingdom* (London: Routledge, 1990).

Seleucus (2) *See* SELEUCID EMPIRE.

Selinus The westernmost Greek city in SICILY, ancient Selinus is now uninhabited and boasts one of the grandest collections of Greek temple ruins from the 400s B.C.E.

Founded in about 628 B.C.E. by Dorian-Greek colonists from the city of Megara Hyblaea (on Sicily's east coast), Selinus occupied a terrace of land overlooking the southwestern Sicilian coastline, just south of modern Castelvetrano. According to one tale, Selinus was named for local growths of wild celery (Greek: *selinon*). Selinus enjoyed access to rich coastal farmland and sea trade, but it also lay within the territory of the Greeks' traditional enemies, the Carthaginians, who occupied western Sicily. This menace was decreased by the immense Greek victory over the Carthaginians at the Battle of HIMERA (480 B.C.E.), after which the Selinuntines became allies of the preeminent Sicilian-Greek city, SYRACUSE.

It was during these years—late 500s–early 400s B.C.E.—that the prosperous Selinuntines constructed the eight Doric-style temples whose remnants grace the site today. They were constructed on the ACROPOLIS, to the south of the city itself, and on a second hill west of the city. Scholars have speculated about the deities to whom the temples were dedicated, and it appears as though Temple C was dedicated to APOLLO, Temple A to Leto, Temple O to ARTEMIS, Temple D to APHRODITE, Temple E to HERA, Temple F to ATHENA, and Temple G to ZEUS. Of these buildings, the one now known as Temple G must have been planned as one of the largest buildings in the Greek world; it was left incomplete around 480 B.C.E. The temples all seem to have been toppled by earthquake in ancient times.

A traditional enmity existed between Selinus and the northwestern city of Segesta (inhabited by a non-Greek native people, the Elymi). This conflict took on international proportions in 415 B.C.E., when the Segestans appealed for help to the powerful city of ATHENS, in mainland Greece. During the subsequent, ill-fated Athenian invasion of Sicily, Selinuntine troops fought alongside their Syracusan allies, against the Athenians (415–413 B.C.E.). But soon Segesta had found a new ally, CARTHAGE, and in 409 B.C.E. Selinus was destroyed by the Carthaginians in their drive to reconquer Sicily.

Reinhabited by refugees, Selinus probably remained a Carthaginian vassal until 250 B.C.E., when it was again destroyed in the course of the First Punic War, between Romans and Carthaginians.

Archaeological exploration at Selinus began in the early 1800s C.E., at which time three sculpted relief panels (*metopes*) were discovered from one of the Doric temples (Temple C). Sporadic surveys of the site have continued since then, but there has been no systematic excavation of the city, and the ACROPOLIS remains almost entirely unexcavated.

See also ARCHITECTURE; DORIAN GREEKS; PELOPONNESIAN WAR; ROME.

Further reading: C. Arnold-Biucchi, "The Beginnings of Coinage in the West. Archaic Selinus," in *Florilegium numismaticum. Studia in honorem U. Westermark edita* (Stockholm: Svenska Numismatiska Föreningen, 1992), 13–19; P. Danner, "Megara, Megara Hyblaea, and Selinus. The Relationship between the Town Planning of a Mother City, a Colony, and a Sub-colony in the Archaic Period," *Acta Hyperborea. Danish Studies in Classical Archaeology* 7 (1997): 143–165.

Semele *See* DIONYSUS.

Semonides (late 600s B.C.E.) *Early Greek lyric poet*
Semonides came from the island of SAMOS but emigrated—possibly because of social unrest—to Amorgos, an island of the CYCLADES.

Semonides' work survives in one apparently complete poem and one fragment, both written in iambic meter, a form associated with satire. The poem—a social satire on the nature of WOMEN—is typical of the misogyny of Greek male culture of the 600s–400s B.C.E. The gods (the poem explains) made women from different materials or animals: from mud, the changeable sea, the weasel, the donkey, and so forth. According to the poem, only one type is good to marry: the one made from the quiet, industrious bee.

Semonides should not be confused with the more famous SIMONIDES of Keos, who lived a century later.

See also LYRIC POETRY.

Further reading: Hugh Lloyd-Jones, *Females of the Species: Semonides on Women* (Park Ridge, N.J.: Noyes Press, 1975); David Mulroy, trans., *Early Greek Lyric Poetry* (Ann Arbor: University of Michigan Press, 1992); M. L. West, trans., *Greek Lyric Poetry: The Poems and Fragments of the Greek Iambic, Elegiac, and Melic Poets (excluding Pindar and Bacchylides) down to 450 B.C.* (New York: Oxford University Press, 1994); Douglas E. Gerber, ed., *A Companion to the Greek Lyric Poets* (Leiden, Netherlands: E. J. Brill, 1997); Douglas E. Gerber, ed., *Greek Iambic Poetry: From the Seventh to the Fifth Centuries B.C.* (Cambridge, Mass.: Harvard University Press, 1999).

Sestos This small Greek city on the European shore of the HELLESPONT is situated midway along the strait, at the narrowest section. Sestos was the fortress of the Hellespont, with a hilltop citadel whose walls ran down to flank the best harbor in the region. Ideally situated to control shipping in the channel, Sestos served as a naval base for ATHENS in the 400s–300s B.C.E., protecting Athenian imports of precious grain from the BLACK SEA.

Sestos was founded by colonists from LESBOS in the 600s B.C.E. Around 512 B.C.E. The city was annexed by the Persian king DARIUS (1). The Persian king XERXES, in his campaign to conquer Greece, marched his vast army across the Hellespont on two pontoon bridges that reached the European shore near Sestos (480 B.C.E.). After the Persian defeat in Greece, Sestos was immediately captured and occupied by Athenian forces (479 B.C.E.). For nearly the next 75 years, Sestos was a member of the Athenian-led DELIAN LEAGUE.

Athenian-held Sestos played a prominent role in naval campaigns for the Hellespont in the later PELOPONNESIAN WAR. After Athens's defeat (404 B.C.E.), Sestos was taken over by SPARTA. Sestos became Athens's subject again in 365 B.C.E. but soon rebelled. The Athenians crushed and rebellion, captured the city, sold the inhabitants as SLAVES, and repopulated the place with Athenian colonists (357 B.C.E.). In 334 B.C.E. the Macedonian king ALEXANDER THE GREAT brought his army to Sestos for his shipborne invasion of Persian territory across the Hellespont.

On the Asian shore opposite Sestos, one mile away, stood the Greek city of Abydos. In later Greek times there arose the legend of Hero and Leander, about a man of Abydos (Leander) who swam the Hellespont every night to visit his sweetheart in Sestos.

See also EUROPE AND ASIA; PERSIAN WARS.

Further reading: John Boardman, *The Greeks Overseas: Their Early Colonies and Trade,* 4th ed. (London: Thames and Hudson, 1999).

Seven against Thebes, the This well-known MYTH is part of the so-called Theban Cycle, about the legendary woes of the royal house of THEBES (a city in central Greece). By the 600s B.C.E. the myths of Thebes had been collected in an epic poem, now lost, called the *Thebaïd.* Like other episodes in the Theban Cycle, the tale of the Seven was presented onstage by the great Athenian playwright AESCHYLUS, in his tragedy *Seven against Thebes* (467 B.C.E.). In the early Roman period (ca. 80–92 C.E.), the poet Statius composed another epic poem about the expedition of the Seven against Thebes; this poem was also called the *Thebaïd.*

According to the legend, the Theban king OEDIPUS had two sons, Eteokles ("True Glory") and Polynices (Greek: Polyneikes, "Much Strife"). The brothers' destiny was not happy. After Oedipus's death, they argued as to who should be king—Eteokles was the elder, but the law of primogeniture did not apply among the Greeks—and they finally agreed to reign in alternate years. Eteokles drew the lot allowing him to rule first, and Polynices withdrew to the city of ARGOS, awaiting his turn.

With the year's passing it became obvious that Eteokles would not relinquish his throne. So Polynices enlisted the aid of Adrastus, king of Argos, whose daughter (Argeia) he had married. Polynices and Adrastus collected a mighty army, to be led by Polynices and six other champions, usually identified as Tydeus of Calydon; Amphiaraus of Argos; Capaneus of Argos; Hippomedon of Argos; Parthenopaeus of ARCADIA (son of the huntress ATALANTA); and, in most versions, King Adrastus.

Foremost among the Seven was Tydeus, a small but valiant man who had gone to Argos after being banished from Calydon for homicide. Like Polynices, Tydeus had married one of Adrastus's daughters, Deipyle. Their baby son, DIOMEDES, was destined to outshine even his father, as a hero in the TROJAN WAR.

Also notable among the Seven was Amphiaraus, a seer who foresaw that the expedition would be a disaster and that he himself would never return if he accompanied it. Amphiaraus knew that his wife, Eriphyle, would be approached to convince him to join the campaign, and he forbade her to accept any gift from Polynices. She disobeyed, and was bribed by the fabulous necklace that had once belonged to Polynices's great-grandmother Harmonia (wife of the hero CADMUS). As a result, Eriphyle successfully convinced Amphiaraus to join the doomed expedition—an odd concession by him, given his foreknowledge, but so runs the myth. In departing, Amphiaraus compelled his son ALCMAEON (1) to pledge to avenge his death by killing Eriphyle (i.e., Alcmaeon's own mother); he also made the boy vow to launch his own attack on Thebes someday.

The tale of Amphiaraus was a favorite among the Greeks, who liked stories, mythical or otherwise, about people choosing a course of certain death. Amphiaraus's fateful departure from Argos is the subject of one of the most beautiful surviving Corinthian-style vase paintings, made around 560 B.C.E.

The Seven's attack on Thebes was, as Amphiaraus had predicted, a failure. At each of the seven gates of Thebes, one of the Seven fought a Theban champion in single combat. Polynices and Eteokles killed each other, and the rest of the Seven died, with the exception of King Adrastus, who escaped on his superlative horse. Amphiaraus, attempting to flee in his chariot, was swallowed up in the earth.

In the next generation, Amphiaraus's son Alcmaeon, true to his vow, marched to Thebes with six other heroes, including Tydeus's son, Diomedes; this time the city fell to the attackers. Alcmaeon's exploit was known as the Expedition of the Epigoni (Descendants) and was described in a now-lost epic poem titled *Epigonoi* (ca. 600 B.C.E.).

Because Greek myths often provide distorted reflections of events in the distant Mycenaean age (around 1600–1200 B.C.E.), this tale may contain a kernel of historical truth. Thebes and Argos represent the two heartlands of Mycenaean Greek civilization, with Argos equivalent to the royal city of MYCENAE. The legends of the Seven and the Epigoni surely commemorate repeated attempts by the king of Mycenae to capture Thebes and its fertile plain, perhaps around 1350 B.C.E.

See also ANTIGONE; MYCENAEAN CIVILIZATION.

Further reading: William G. Thalmann, *Dramatic Art in Aeschylus's Seven against Thebes* (New Haven, Conn.: Yale University Press, 1978); Froma Zeitlin, *Under the Sign of the Shield: Semiotics and Aeschylus' Seven Against Thebes* (Rome: Edizioni dell'Ateneo, 1982); D. R. Shackleton Bailey, ed. and trans., *Thebaid, Books I-VII/Statius* (Cambridge, Mass.: Harvard University Press, 2003); ———, *Thebaid, Books VIII–XII; Achilleid/Statius* (Cambridge, Mass.: Harvard University Press, 2003).

Seven Sages, the   This list consisted of seven men said to be the wisest in ancient Greece. Each of the sages (Greek: *sophoi*) was a real person, typically a statesman, active in the 500s or late 600s B.C.E. One or two were benign TYRANTS. The list first appears in PLATO's dialogue *Protagoras,* written circa 390 B.C.E.; but the tradition probably dates back another 200 years. The seven were: (1) THALES, a philosopher and scientist of MILETUS; (2) PITTACUS, an elected ruler of MYTILENE, on the island of

LESBOS (3) Bias, a judge and diplomat of Priēnē (in IONIA); (4) SOLON, an elected ruler and lawgiver at ATHENS; (5) Kleobulus, tyrant of Lindos, on the island of RHODES; (6) CHILON, an EPHOR (chief official) at SPARTA; and (7) Myson of Chenae (in Trachis in central Greece), a rustic sage.

In other versions, the obscure Myson is replaced by PERIANDER, tyrant of CORINTH.

Further reading: R. P. Martin, "The Seven Sages as Performers of Wisdom," in *Cultural Poetics in Archaic Greece. Cult, Performance, Politics,* edited by Carol Dougherty and Leslie Kurke (New York: Cambridge University Press, 1993), 108–128; Constantine Cavarnos, *The Seven Sages of Ancient Greece: The Lives and Teachings of the Earliest Greek Philosophers* (Belmont, Mass.: Institute for Byzantine and Modern Greek Studies, 1996).

Seven Wonders of the World, the   By a popular tradition in the HELLENISTIC AGE (among 300–150 B.C.E.), the Greeks counted seven monuments as preeminent in size or grandeur among all man-made works. In the most usual list, five of the seven wonders belonged to the Greek world; the other two—the oldest—were built by non-Greek civilizations. The seven included the following monuments:

1. the pyramids of EGYPT, built between about 2700 and 1800 B.C.E.
2. the hanging gardens of Babylon, dating from the early 500s B.C.E.
3. the temple of the goddess ARTEMIS at EPHESOS, constructed over the period 550–430 B.C.E.
4. the giant cult statue of ZEUS fashioned around 430 B.C.E. by the Athenian sculptor PHEIDIAS for the god's temple at OLYMPIA.
5. the Mausoleum, or tomb of the ruler Mausolus, at HALICARNASSUS, built around 350 B.C.E.
6. the Colossus of RHODES—a statue of the sun god, HELIOS, erected beside the harbor at Rhodes city around 285 B.C.E.
7. the lighthouse at ALEXANDRIA (1), built on the isle of Pharos, outside Alexandria harbor, around 270 B.C.E.

Of all these works, only the pyramids of Egypt survive today.

Further reading: Peter A. Clayton and Martin Price, eds., *The Seven Wonders of the Ancient World,* 2d ed. (New York: Barnes and Noble, 1993); John and Elizabeth Romer, *The Seven Wonders of the World: A History of the Modern Imagination* (New York; Henry Holt, 1995); Paul Jordan, *The Seven Wonders of the Ancient World* (Harlow, U.K.: Longman, 2002); Diana Bentley, *The Seven Wonders of the Ancient World* (New York: Oxford University Press, 2002).

ships and seafaring   "We live around a sea like frogs around a pond," the Athenian philosopher SOCRATES is reported to have said (ca. 410 B.C.E.), summarizing the ancient Greeks' reliance on seaborne TRADE and transport. Like the Phoenicians, but unlike many other Mediterranean peoples, the Greeks had a genius for seamanship. Seafaring was proverbially dangerous in ancient times, but it was also far faster, more efficient, and more lucrative than overland freighting; mule teams or ox-drawn carts could never compare with the speed and efficiency of ships carrying cargo (or troops) under sail or oar. New cities were established regularly to take advantage of nearby natural harbors or waterways. The great expansion of the Greek world in 800–500 B.C.E. was largely the story of seaborne trade, COLONIZATION, and conquest, along ever-enlarging shipping routes. On the military side, sea power came to mean (by the mid-500s B.C.E.) something like what air power means to modern generals—the fastest way to bring harm to enemies at various points, including the ability to stop their imports and starve them. Sea power became the necessary condition for imperial strength among classical Greek states. It was by sea that ATHENS became great in the 400s B.C.E.

Seafaring was encouraged by the geography of mainland Greece—with its mountains, scarce farmland, and immensely long overall coastline, nearly 2,000 miles total. Many Greeks, such as the people of the island AEGINA, took to the sea to compensate for their home region's lack of space or fertility.

Aside from Athens and Aegina, major Greek seagoing states in various eras of history included CHALCIS, CORINTH, MILETUS, PHOCAEA, SAMOS, CHIOS, LESBOS, and RHODES.

The Mediterranean Sea—including its northeastern corner, the Greeks' AEGEAN SEA—offered inducements to seafaring. Unlike the Atlantic Ocean, the Mediterranean has no tides and is broken by many islands and peninsulas, with a reliable "window" of calm weather in summer. Against these natural advantages, the ancient Greeks were burdened by primitive means of navigation. Lacking the compass and sextant, they depended on visible reckonings, such as coastal landmarks and position of the stars. This need for landmarks—along with a fear of straying too far from shelter—explains the ancient seafarers' persistent reliance on coastal routing. A Greek colony such as CORCYRA, on the Adriatic coast, long remained an important anchorage between Greece and ITALY, even though on a map it looks to be a northern detour.

Ancient vessels were made from TIMBER and relied on two forms of power—wind and oars. Most ships carried a single mast, capable of hoisting one square sail typically made of patchwork linen (from the flax plant) or canvas (from Egyptian cotton). Unlike modern sailboats, ancient square-riggers could make direct progress only if the wind was fully or nearly astern; a wind from the side (abeam) required the ship to sail close-hauled, on a zigzag course of tacking, and a wind forward of the beam tended to be unusable. Still, heavier ships, such as the larger merchant vessels, had to rely mostly on wind power. Smaller craft, such as warships, could make progress under oars alone if that was preferable to using the sail. War squadrons always rowed when moving into battle, for better control and uniformity.

Despite changes in ship design during the Greek epoch of 1600–100 B.C.E., these two basic categories persisted: merchant vessel and war vessel. The merchantmen were by far the larger type, designed to carry freight; such ships had deep drafts, wide beams, and heavy masts; their hulls were usually closed at top by a deck. They carried only a small crew. A war craft, by contrast, was designed for speed and was slender, shallow-drafted, and low-riding. Like a canoe or modern racing shell, the warship's hull was typically undecked (or only partly decked), and almost every foot of space was taken by oarsmen or shipboard soldiers.

The major difference in handling between warships and merchantmen was that war crews, sitting at their crowded benches, could not spend the night aboard ship easily. To rest or cook, they needed to pitch camp ashore. Merchant freighters, on the other hand, could sail day and night. Sheltered under the top decking, the off-duty crew could rest on mattresses and could feed from supplies aboard. Under proper conditions, a freighter might leave the shore behind and course out over the open sea; with a favoring wind, such a ship might reach between four and six knots, traveling 100 or more miles in 24 hours.

Because a merchant ship was capable of long-range travel, ancient Greek merchant voyages tended to be ambitious and dangerous. Shipwrecks were common—as suggested by vase paintings, written references, and modern underwater ARCHAEOLOGY. Many harbors had temples where mariners went to pray and sacrifice for a safe voyage. The main patron gods of seafaring were POSEIDON, ATHENA, APHRODITE, and CASTOR AND POLYDEUCES.

For safety, shipping and naval operations normally were confined to the season from May to mid-September, when Mediterranean weather tends to be sunny and calm. But even this period seemed too long to HESIOD (ca. 700 B.C.E.), whose epic poem *Works and Days* mentions that seafaring is safe for only the 50 days following the summer solstice—roughly June 21 to mid-August. Only the extremes of war or greed could induce ships to put to sea during autumn or winter. The hazard of winter seafaring lay partly in violent storms, but also in reduced visibility due to rain, fog, and short daylight. The apostle Paul's shipwreck of 57 C.E. (described in the New Testament book *Acts of the Apostles*, Chapter 27) occurred because the skipper had risked sailing from CRETE after the season's end.

See also CYPRUS; GREECE, GEOGRAPHY OF; MASSALIA; MINOAN CIVILIZATION; MYCENAEAN CIVILIZATION; PHOENICIA; WARFARE, NAVAL.

Further reading: A. F. Tilley and V. H. Fenwick, "Ours Is to Reason Why. The Iconography of Ancient

Ships," *International Journal of Nautical Archaeology* 9 (1980): 151–154; J. Morrison, *Long Ships and Round Ships. Warfare and Trade in the Mediterranean, 3000 B.C.–500 A.D.* (London: H.M.S.O., 1980); P. F. Johnston, "Bronze Age Cycladic Ships. An Overview," in *Trade and Travel in the Cyclades during the Bronze Age. Temple University Aegean Symposium, 7. Philadelphia, March 5, 1982* (Philadelphia: Temple University Press, 1982), 1–8; Harry E. Tzalas, ed., *First International Symposium on Ship Construction in Antiquity, Piraeus, 30 August–1 September 1985* (Athens: Institute for the Preservation of Nautical Traditions, 1989); ———, ed., *Second International Symposium on Ship Construction in Antiquity, Delphi, 27–29 August 1987* (Athens: Institute for the Preservation of Nautical Traditions, 1990); D. M. Goodburn, "Some Further Thoughts on Reconstructions, Replicas, and Simulations of Ancient Boats and Ships," *International Journal of Nautical Archaeology* 22 (1993): 199–203; H. T. Wallinga, *Ships and Sea Power before the Great Persian War. The Ancestry of the Ancient Trireme* (Leiden, Netherlands: E. J. Brill, 1993); J. Coates, "Power and Speed of Oared Ships," in *Crossroads in Ancient Shipbuilding. Proceedings of the Sixth International Symposium on Boat and Ship Archaeology, Roskilde 1991,* edited by Christer Westerdahl (Oxford: Oxbow Books, 1994), 249–255; J. P. Stronk, "Greek Sailing Merchant-ships, c. 500–330 B.C. A Preliminary Research," *Talanta* 24–25 (1992–1993): 117–140; Lionel Casson, *Ships and Seafaring in Ancient Times* (Austin: University of Texas Press, 1994); Lionel Casson, *Ships and Seamanship in the Ancient World,* 2d ed. (Baltimore: Johns Hopkins University Press, 1995); Harry Tzalas, ed., *Third International Symposium on Ship Construction in Antiquity, Athens, 24–27 August 1989* (Athens: Hellenic Institute for the Preservation of Nautical Tradition, 1995); J. S. Morrison and J. F. Coates, *Greek and Roman Oared Warships* (Oxford: Oxbow Books, 1996); R. Gardiner, ed., *The Earliest Ships. The Evolution of Boats into Ships* (London: Conway Maritime Press, 1996; Harry Tzalas, ed., *Fourth International Symposium on Ship Construction in Antiquity, Center for the Acropolis Studies, Athens, 28–31 August 1991* (Athens: Hellenic Institute for the Preservation of Nautical Tradition, 1996); O. Dickinson, "The Catalogue of Ships and All That," *Aegaeum* 20 (1999): 207–210; Harry Tzalas, ed., *Fifth International Symposium on Ship Construction in Antiquity, Nauplia, 26–28 August 1993* (Athens: Hellenic Institute for the Preservation of Nautical Tradition, 1999); J. S. Morrison, J. F. Coates, and N. B. Rankov, *The Athenian Trireme: The History and Reconstruction of an Ancient Greek Warship,* 2d ed. (New York: Cambridge University Press, 2000); Harry Tzalas, ed., *Sixth International Symposium on Ship Construction in Antiquity, Lamia, 28–30 August 1996* (Athens: Hellenic Institute for the Preservation of Nautical Tradition, 2001); ———, ed., *Seventh International Symposium on Ship Construction in Antiquity, Pylos, 26–29 August 1999* (Athens: Hellenic Institute for the Preservation of Nautical Tradition, 2002).

Sicily The largest (9,860 square miles) island of the Mediterranean, Sicily is situated just west of the "toe" of ITALY. It is shaped roughly like an isosceles triangle, with the base facing east.

Renowned in ancient times for its fertile coastlands, Sicily attracted waves of Greek settlers at the outset of the great colonizing epoch (beginning after 750 B.C.E.). The island became a major part of the Greek world, producing a dozen or so noteworthy Greek cities, particularly the Corinthian colony of SYRACUSE, which grew to be the greatest Greek city of the West (400s–200s B.C.E.). Syracuse and other Sicilian-Greek cities supplied precious grain for CORINTH and other populous mainland Greek cities.

Despite prosperity, Greek Sicily had a tragic history, full of social unrest within cities and conflicts between cities inhabited by DORIAN GREEKS and those inhabited by IONIAN GREEKS. But worst of all were the repeated wars with the non-Greek, Carthaginian settlers of western Sicily.

The name Sicily (Greek: Sikelia) commemorates the Sicels—a native, non-Greek people of the island's east coast, whose prime land at Syracuse and on the plain of Catania was seized by the early Greek colonists. Other native peoples included the Sicani, in the island's west-central region; and the Elymi, in the west. The relatively unsophisticated level of these peoples no doubt helped to attract early Greek settlers. (The Greeks tended to plant colonies where they knew they could subdue local inhabitants.)

Sicily's earliest Greek colonies—NAXOS (2), Syracuse, CATANA, and Leontini—arose around 734–728 B.C.E. along the island's 200-mile-long eastern coast. Among the coast's distinctive geographic features are volcanic Mt. Etna (over 11,000 feet tall) and the plain of Catania (whose fertility is due in part to volcanic lime, washed down from Etna's slopes). Toward the coast's southern end is the promontory of Syracuse, with its superb natural harbor and nearby farmland.

Most of the eastern coast was Ionian Greek, with the exception of Dorian Syracuse. But a Dorian bloc soon arose on Sicily's southern coast, with the founding of GELA (around 688 B.C.E.) and ACRAGAS (around 580 B.C.E.). After Syracuse, Acragas became the second most important city of Greek Sicily (400s B.C.E.).

Sicily's western side, meanwhile, had been occupied by settlers from the African-Phoenician city of CARTHAGE (which lay only about 135 miles southwest of Sicily). By about 500 B.C.E. Greeks and Carthaginians had settled into a bitter conflict that lasted over 250 years and monopolized the energies of Greek Sicily. The constant Carthaginian threat largely shaped the authoritarian nature of Sicilian Greek politics. Long after the age of TYRANTS had passed away in mainland Greece, Sicilian

Greek cities were still relying on military tyrants who could promise protection against the hated Carthaginians. Foremost among such powerful rulers were the Syracusan tyrants: GELON (reigned ca. 490–478 B.C.E.), his brother HIERON (1) (478–467 B.C.E.), DIONYSIUS (1) (ca. 400–367 B.C.E.), and AGATHOKLES (317–289 B.C.E.). Under these men, Syracuse dominated the other Greek cities and several times came close to driving the Carthaginians from the island. At other times leaders from mainland Greece were called in to help the beleaguered Sicilian Greeks. For example, the Corinthian commander TIMOLEON (345–340 B.C.E.) defeated the Carthaginians in battle and gave the Greek cities new governments. King PYRRHUS OF EPIRUS arrived and beat the Carthaginians (279 B.C.E.), then hurried away before exploring his advantage.

The conquest of Sicily remained an elusive and dangerous dream for Syracuse, for Carthage, and for the mainland Greek city of ATHENS, whose attempt to capture Syracuse during the PELOPONNESIAN WAR proved a disaster (415–413) B.C.E.). It took the emerging might of Italian ROME to conquer Greeks and Carthaginians alike. Sicily became a battlefield between Rome and Carthage in the First Punic War (264–241 B.C.E.), before it passed to Roman control. A defiant Syracuse was besieged and captured by the Romans in 213–211 B.C.E., during the Second Punic War. Sicily was then made a province of the Roman Empire.

See also COLONIZATION; CYCLOPS; HIMERA; PERSEPHONE; SELINUS; ZANCLĒ.

Further reading: R. S. Bianchi, "The Greek Temples of Sicily," *Archaeology* 37 (1984): 26–32; S. C. Bakhuizen, "Italy and Sicily in the Perception of the Early Greeks," *Mededelingen van het Nederlands Instituut te Rome* 48 (1988): 9–25; A. Di Vita, "Town Planning in the Greek Colonies of Sicily from the Time of Their Foundations to the Punic Wars," in *Greek Colonists and Native Population. Proceedings of the First Australian Congress of Classical Archaeology, Sydney, 9–14 July, 1985,* edited by Jean-Paul Descoeudres (New York: Oxford University Press, 1990), 343–363; R. R. Holloway, *The Archaeology of Ancient Sicily* (London: Routledge, 1991); S. Berger, *Revolution and Society in Greek Sicily and Southern Italy* (Stuttgart, Germany: F. Steiner, 1992); N. K. Rutter, *The Greek Coinages of Southern Italy and Sicily* (London: Spink, 1997); R. Leighton, *Sicily before History. An Archaeological Survey from the Palaeolithic to the Iron Age* (London: Duckworth, 1999); C. Smith and J. Serrati, eds., *Sicily from Aeneas to Augustus. New Approaches in Archaeology and History* (Edinburgh: Edinburgh University Press, 2000).

siege warfare   *See* WARFARE, SIEGE.

Sigeum   *See* HELLESPONT.

Sikyon   An important city of the northeast PELOPONNESE, Sikyon is situated about 15 miles west of CORINTH. It is located two miles inland, on a fertile coastal plain beside the Corinthian Gulf, at the foot of a lofty hill that served as the city's ACROPOLIS. The city had a mixed Dorian and Achaean population, having been founded (probably) from Dorian ARGOS around 1000 B.C.E. Supposedly Sikyon was named for its local growths of cucumbers (*sikyai*).

Sikyon was one of the first Greek cities to be seized by TYRANTS. The dynasty created around 660 B.C.E. by the tyrant Orthagoras lasted for over a century and made Sikyon into a great power. Orthagoras's descendant KLEISTHENES (2) ruled ca. 600–570 B.C.E., leading the First Sacred War against PHOCIS and later celebrating his daughter's wedding with Homeric magnificence. This era saw construction of the Sikyonians' treasury house at DELPHI, prominently occupying the start of the Sacred Way up to APOLLO's temple.

Under Kleisthenes wealthy Sikyon was a center for manufacturing and art, particularly SCULPTURE and PAINTING. A Sikyonian poet, Egigenes, is said to have been a pioneer in the writing of "tragic choruses" in the early 500s B.C.E. The city's schools of art remained important for centuries; Sikyon's most famous artist was the sculptor Lysippos (ca. 330 B.C.E.).

The Sikyonian tyranny was extinguished around 550 B.C.E. by the Spartans. Sikyon became an OLIGARCHY and a Spartan ally. Sikyonians fought alongside the Spartans in the PERSIAN WARS (480–479 B.C.E.) and PELOPONNESIAN WAR (431–404 B.C.E.). In the mid-200s B.C.E. Sikyon's most famous son was the statesman and commander Aratus.

See also ACHAEA; DORIAN GREEKS; THEATER.

Further reading: Audrey Griffin, *Sikyon* (Oxford: Clarendon Press, 1982); Nicos Papahatzis, *Ancient Corinth: The Museums of Corinth, Isthmia, and Sicyon,* translated by Kay Cicellis (Athens: Edotike Athenon, 1989).

Silenus   A mythical semihuman creature, Silenus is distinguished by his horse ears, horse tail, pot belly, shaggy hair, bald head, and pug nose. Like the SATYRS, whom he resembled, Silenus was associated with the wine god DIONYSUS. On vase paintings of the 500s–400s B.C.E., Silenus was portrayed cavorting in the god's retinue or lustily pursuing the NYMPHS. Sometimes he was shown as several creatures (called by the plural, Silenoi or Sileni). A widespread Athenian joke of the late 400s B.C.E. claimed that Silenus resembled the living philosopher SOCRATES.

Further reading: A. Ajootian, "Silenus at Sparta," in *Sculpture from Arcadia and Laconia. Proceedings of an International Conference Held at the American School of Classical Studies at Athens, April 10–14, 1992,* edited by

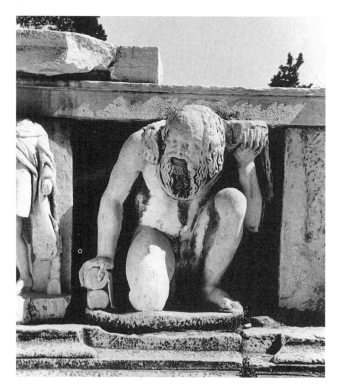

Statue of Silenus, a mythical semihuman creature, at the theater of Dionysos, identified by his bald head, shaggy hair, and pug nose. *(Alison Frantz Photographic Collection, American School of Classical Studies at Athens)*

Olga Palagia and William Coulson (Oxford: Oxbow Books, 1993), 251–256.

silver   A precious metal in both ancient and modern times, silver traditionally has been less prized than GOLD, partly because silver ore is more common and less malleable for shaping.

Throughout antiquity, silver was used for luxury items such as plates, goblets, statuary, and jewelry; it was particularly favored for cups and plates with repoussé work. More important, silver was the prime substance for Greek COINAGE (first appearing just after 600 B.C.E.). Even before the invention of coinage, silver was being used in ingot form for high-level exchange, in the monetary unit known as the TALENT.

Unlike gold, silver existed as a natural mineral deposit in mainland Greece. The publicly owned silver mines at Laurion, 15 miles south of ATHENS, played a large role in Athenian greatness in the 500s–400s B.C.E. The Laurion mines helped finance naval fleets and the social programs of the DEMOCRACY.

But the main supplier of raw silver for the Greek world was the north Aegean coast (in the non-Greek land of THRACE) and particularly Mt. Pangaeus, near the lower Strymon River. From there—where silver seems to have been available by panning in local rivers—the precious ore reached Greek hands by TRADE and eventually by conquest. In the 600s–500s B.C.E., Greek traders began operating out of THASOS, SAMOTHRACE, ABDERA, and AENUS, acquiring raw silver from local Thracian kings. From the Thracian shore, this silver—typically in the form of large, bowtieshape ingots—would be shipped to markets in the Greek world or to foreign markets such as EGYPT and PHOENICIA. In this early era (650–480 B.C.E.), raw silver was one of the few goods that Greek traders could offer to the sophisticated Near Eastern markets.

During the mid-400s B.C.E., Mt. Pangaeus seems to have come under control of imperial Athens, through the Athenian colony at AMPHIPOLIS. In the mid-300s B.C.E. the region fell to the cash-hungry Macedonian king PHILIP II. Other sources of raw silver included non-Greek Asian kingdoms such as LYDIA and Phrygia, fabled for their wealth. Another source, around 600–500 B.C.E., was the Celtic kingdom in southern Spain known as Tartessus (the Tarshish of the Bible). To this distant domain sailed Greek traders from SAMOS and PHOCAEA.

In the HELLENISTIC AGE (300–150 B.C.E.), silver became more plentiful among the Greeks, due to the formerly Persian-owned mines and treasure hordes acquired by ALEXANDER THE GREAT. The silver mines of Thrace, Asia Minor, and Mesopotamia made possible the beautiful, large-denomination coins of the Hellenistic Greek kings.

Further reading: Dionysios Kounas, ed., *Studies on the Ancient Silver Mines at Laurion* (Lawrence, Kans.: Coronado Press, 1972); H. Mussche, P. Spitaels, and F. Goemaere-De Poerck, eds., *Thorikos and the Laurion in Archaic and Classical Times: Papers and Contributions of the Colloquium held in March, 1973, at the State University of Ghent* (Ghent, Belgium: Belgian Archaeological Mission in Greece, 1975); N. H. Gale, "Some Aspects of Lead and Silver Mining in the Aegean," *Thera and the Aegean World. Papers and Proceedings of the Second International Scientific Congress, Santorini, Greece, August 1978*, edited by Christos Doumas (London: Thera and the Ancient World, 1980), 161–195; B. S. Strauss, "Philip II of Macedon, Athens, and Silver Mining," *Hermes* 112 (1984): 418–427; J. E. Jones, "Laurion, Agrileza, 1977–1983. Excavations at a Silver-mine Site," *Archaeological Reports* 31 (1984–1985): 106–123; D. Harris, "Gold and Silver on the Athenian Acropolis. Thucydides 2, 13, 4 and the Inventory Lists," *Horos* 8–9 (1990–1991): 75–82; Robert Shepherd, *Ancient Mining* (London: Elsevier Applied Science, 1993); M. Vickers and D. Gill, *Artful Crafts: Ancient Greek Silverware and Pottery* (Oxford: Clarendon Press, 1994); Michail Yu Treister, *The Role of Metals in Ancient Greek History* (Leiden, Netherlands: E. J. Brill, 1996); K. M. V. Shipton, "The Prices of the Athenian Silver Mines," *Zeitschrift für Papyrologie und Epigraphik* 120 (1998): 57–63.

Simonides (ca. 556–468 B.C.E.) *Lyric poet from the island of Keos, in the* CYCLADES

Over his long lifetime, Simonides enjoyed success with many genres of poetry. He was famous for the epitaphs he wrote to commemorate the Greek dead in the PERSIAN WARS (490–479 B.C.E.). He developed the choral song known as the victory ode (*epinikion*), thereby in effect clearing the way for his younger and greater contemporary, the Theban poet PINDAR. The only poems by Simonides that survive complete are epigrams—short poems in elegiac verse, written to be carved in stone. Fragments of his victory odes and his dirges exist, but other categories are largely lost, including Simonides' dithyrambs—narrative poems on mythological topics, performed by choruses.

Simonides' work was admired in the ancient world for its clarity, word choice, and sympathy for human transcience and suffering. His simple language went right to the heart—particularly in its expressions of sorrow—and was considered more effective than the grandiose phrasings of other great poets such as AESCHYLUS.

Simonides was also the first poet to work for hire—that is, to compose poetry for a one-time fee from successive patrons rather than in a permanent position in the retinue of some wealthy man. Simonides was said to be fond of money and shrewd in business dealings. He seems to have had an affable, worldly personality.

Keos—where Simonides, son of Leoprepes, was born into an upper-class family—was an Ionian-ethnic island, 15 miles off the Athenian coast. After gaining repute for his victory odes, Simonides was summoned to ATHENS (in about 525 B.C.E.) by Hipparchus, the brother and cultural minister of the Athenian tyrant HIPPIAS (1). There Simonides enjoyed high payments from Hipparchus, whose majestic court hosted another famous poet, ANACREON.

At Athens in these years, Simonides surely wrote some of his many dithyrambs, now lost. Late in life Simonides set up an inscription commemorating his 56 victories in dithyramb contests at Athens; the inscription mentions that he himself taught the choruses, which were composed of men.

Simonides left Athens around 514–510 B.C.E., as the tyranny crumbled. He traveled to THESSALY, and there found employ with the wealthy Aleaud and Scopad clans. But his stay ended after the Scopads were decimated by the collapsing roof of a banquet hall. The disaster later inspired Simonides to write a poem containing one of his much-admired reflections on the brevity of human happiness: "Since you are mortal, never say what tomorrow will bring nor how long a man may be happy. For the darting of the dragonfly is not so swift as change of fortune."

By the early 490s B.C.E., Simonides, then approaching 60, was back in Athens, his former intimacy with the tyrants apparently pardoned. Amid the great events of the Persian Wars he found a new calling as the poet laureate of Greece. After the Athenian victory at MARATHON (490 B.C.E.), the Athenians honored their dead with an epitaph by Simonides, chosen over one submitted by the young poet Aeschylus (himself an Athenian who had fought at the battle). According to the story, the Athenians decided that Simondes' poem conveyed a keener sympathy.

In 479 B.C.E., after the invasion by the Persian king XERXES had been repelled, Simonides was again commissioned to write patriotic verse. He produced choral odes about the sea battles at ARTEMISION and SALAMIS (1) and several much-admired epitaphs for the Greek dead.

In 476 B.C.E., at age 80, Simonides left Athens again, this time for the grand court of the tyrant HIERON (1) of SYRACUSE, in SICILY. Simonides' departure might have been related to the political downfall at Athens of his friend THEMISTOKLES. At Syracuse, Simonides—with his nephew and protégé, the poet BACCHYLIDES—is said to have indulged in a feud with Pindar, who was also in Sicily at that time. Another tale claims that Hieron's wife once asked Simonides which is better, to acquire wisdom or wealth. "Wealth," the poet replied. "For I see the wise sitting at the doorsteps of the rich."

Simonides died in Sicily and was buried at ACRAGAS.

See also IONIAN GREEKS; LYRIC POETRY; THEATER; THERMOPYLAE.

Further reading: John H. Molyneux, *Simonides: A Historical Study* (Wauconda, Ill.: Bolchazy-Carducci Publishers, 1992); M. A. Flower, "From Simonides to Isocrates. The Fifth-century Origins of Fourth-century Panhellenism," *Classical Antiquity* 19 (2000): 65–101; Deborah Boedeker and David Sider, eds., *The New Simonides: Contexts of Praise and Desire* (New York: Oxford University Press, 2001); Anne Carson, *Economy of the Unlost: Reading Simonides of Keos with Paul Celan* (Princeton: Princeton University Press, 2002).

Sinope   This prosperous Greek city on the BLACK SEA was founded in about 625 B.C.E. by colonists from MILETUS. Sinope (modern Sinop, in Turkey) is located halfway along the north coast of ASIA MINOR, where the coast bulges advantageously northward. The city was built at the neck of a lofty promontory with a fine double harbor—the only first-rate harbor on the Black Sea's southern shore.

Isolated by mountains inland, Sinope depended for its prosperity on seaborne TRADE. The city was probably an export center for goods shipped in from other Greek ports of the Black Sea. Such goods would include the metals of Asia Minor—GOLD, SILVER, IRON, and copper and tin for BRONZE making—as well as "Sinopic earth" (cinnabar, or red mercuric sulfide, used for making a prized red dye). Sinope is located 220 miles due south of the eastern Crimean peninsula, which was home to PANTICAPAEUM and other Greek seaports in antiquity; the shipping run between Sinope and the Crimea was a vital link in the Greek navigation of the Black Sea.

Sinope founded its own colonies, farther east on the Black Sea coast. Chief among these daughter cities was Trapezus ("the table," named for a mountain landmark), which is now the Turkish city of Trabzon. Unlike mountain-girt Sinope, Trapezus had access to the Asia Minor interior and the land route to the Near East.

Sinope probably offered nominal submission to the Persian kings who had conquered Asia Minor by 545 B.C.E. The city was being ruled by a Greek dictator in the mid-400s B.C.E., when an Athenian fleet under the commander PERIKLES arrived on a Black Sea expedition. The Athenians established DEMOCRACY at Sinope and settled Athenian colonists there. The city may have henceforth had some trading agreement with ATHENS, but it never became a member of the DELIAN LEAGUE.

Occupied briefly by Persian troops in around 375 B.C.E., Sinope was liberated by ALEXANDER THE GREAT's conquest of the Persian Empire (334–323 B.C.E.). The city seems to have remained independent of the several Hellenistic kingdoms that subsequently dominated Asia Minor, but was captured by the Iranian-ethnic kingdom of Pontus in 183 B.C.E. and became the Pontic capital. After the Romans' conquest of Pontus (63 B.C.E.), Sinope became a city of the Roman Empire.

Sinope was a center of Greek culture in the East, with grand temples, markets, and a tradition of learning. Its most famous citizen was the Cynic philosopher DIOGENES (mid-300s B.C.E.).

Sinope was first excavated in the 1950s C.E. by a Turkish archaeologist, Ekrem Akurgal, who concentrated on the city center and the surrounding cemeteries. He discovered several monumental tombs as well as a Hellenistic temple dedicated to the Egyptian god Sarapis. Currently, an American team of archaeologists is conducting the Black Sea Trade Project, intended to investigate thoroughly the area around Sinope and its trade relations, using traditional land archaeology as well as underwater archaeological techniques in the Black Sea.

Further reading: Owen Doonan, *Sinop Landscapes: Exploring Connection in a Black Sea Hinterland* (Philadelphia: University of Pennsylvania Museum of Archaeology and Anthropology, 2004).

Sirens   In Greek MYTH the Seirēnes were sea witches who lured sailors to their deaths. The sailors, hearing the Sirens' enchanting song, would land their ship and go ashore, where the Sirens would kill them.

The Sirens are first mentioned in book 12 of HOMER's epic poem the *Odyssey* (written down around 750 B.C.E.). There they are two in number; their appearance is never described. The seafaring hero ODYSSEUS defies the Sirens by plugging his crewmen's ears with beeswax beforehand. However, wishing to hear the song himself, he has his men bind him to the ship's mast. As they row past the Sirens' island, Odysseus is bewitched by the song and pleads to be untied. His crew pays him no heed, however,

and eventually the ship passes out of earshot. The Sirens, whose name may mean "Scorchers" or "Binders," are among several female threats that Odysseus encounters on his voyage home.

Later generations of Greeks named 11 Sirens and pictured them as half woman, half bird. These Sirens resemble other winged, malevolent, female creatures of Greek myth—the HARPIES and the FURIES.

Further reading: Jenifer Neils, "Les Femmes Fatales. Skylla and the Sirens in Greek Art," in *The Distaff Side. Representing the Female in Homer's 'Odyssey',* edited by Beth Cohen (New York: Oxford University Press, 1995), 175–184; Méri Franco-Lao, *Sirens: Symbols of Seduction* (Rochester, Vt.: Park Street Press, 1998); W. R. Biers, "Plastic Sirens from Corinth. An Addendum to Amyx," *Hesperia* 68 (1999): 135–146.

Sisyphus   Mentioned in book II of HOMER's epic poem the *Odyssey*, Sisyphus is one of three infamous sinners—betrayers of the gods' friendship and thus eternally damned—encountered by the hero ODYSSEUS. In his visit to the Underworld, Odysseus observes Sisyphus's punishment, which is to roll a great boulder up a hill but, on nearing the top, to have it slip backward past him, back down the slope. Sisyphus must pursue this frustrating and exhausting labor forever. In theory, his punishment would end if he could ever reach the summit and push the boulder down the *far* slope, but the vindictive gods would never allow this to happen.

The *Odyssey* does not mention Sisyphus's original offense, but later writers describe him as the conniving founder of the city of CORINTH. In exchange for receiving a perpetual water source for his city's citadel, Sisyphus informed the god Asopus that the great god ZEUS had abducted Asopus's daughter. When angry Zeus sent the god HADES to fetch Sisyphus to the Underworld, the hero outwitted Hades and tied him up, thus unnaturally stopping all death in the world. Eventually the gods captured Sisyphus.

Sisyphus was a hero of the "trickster" type—a category that included the god HERMES, the Titan PROMETHEUS, and Odysseus himself (sometimes said to be Sisyphus's illegitimate son).

See also AFTERLIFE; TANTALUS.

Further reading: C. Sourvinou-Inwood, "Crime and Punishment. Tityos, Tantalos, and Sisyphos in 'Odyssey' 11," *Bulletin of the Institute of Classical Studies* 33 (1986): 37–58.

Skepticism   This Greek school of thought believed than no positive knowledge is possible because everything is in a constant state of flux. This notion appears early in ancient Greek philosophy, related to statements made by HERACLITUS (ca. 500 B.C.E.) and the belief of the SOPHISTS (late 400s B.C.E.) that any argument could be met by an equally true counterargument. The Skeptics

(Greek: Skeptikoi) withheld judgment on all matters, stating no positive doctrines but accepting tentatively the outward appearances of things for the sake of daily life. This outlook was supposed to bring the Skeptic to the desired state of imperturbability (*ataraxia*).

The term "skepticism" derives from the Greek word *skepsis*: "examination," "inquiry," "consideration." The founding of a formal school of Skepticism was the work of Pyrrhon (363–273 B.C.E.), a native of ELIS (in the western PELOPONNESE) who had accompanied ALEXANDER THE GREAT on his conquest of the Persian Empire (334–323 B.C.E.).

Alongside STOICISM and EPICUREANISM, Skepticism became one of the major philosophies of the HELLENISTIC AGE (ca. 300–150 B.C.E.). It had its greatest influence at the ACADEMY, the prestigious philosophical school founded at ATHENS by PLATO in about 385 B.C.E. Skepticism was introduced as a course of study at the Academy around 270 B.C.E., and for nearly the next two centuries it provided the basis of much Academic thought. Rejecting many of their founder Plato's doctrines, the Academics of these years saw Skepticism as connecting back to Socrates' statement, "All I know is that I know nothing." They sought to prove the impossibility of positive knowledge and also used Skepticism to attack the rival Stoics, whose beliefs relied on sensory perception.

Further reading: Leo Groarke, *Greek Scepticism: Anti-realist Trends in Ancient Thought* (Montreal: McGill-Queen's University Press, 1990); P. de Lacy, "Galen's Response to Skepticism," *Illinois Classical Studies* 16 (1991): 283–306; Frederick F. Schmitt, *Knowledge and Belief* (London: Routledge, 1992); R. J. Hankinson, *The Sceptics* (London: Routledge, 1995); R. W. Sharples, *Stoics, Epicureans, and Sceptics: An Introduction to Hellenistic Philosophy* (London: Routledge, 1996); Juha Sihvola, *Ancient Scepticism and the Sceptical Tradition* (Helsinki: Philosophical Society of Finland, 2000).

Skopas *See* SCULPTURE.

Skylla A mythical, female sea monster, semihuman in shape, Skylla is described in HOMER's epic poem the *Odyssey* (book 12). She lived in a narrow sea channel sometimes identified as the Straits of Messina, between SICILY and the "toe" of ITALY. Opposite her cave, the whirlpool Charybdis operated; ships moving through the channel had to risk encountering either Skylla at one side or Charybdis at the other. Skylla ("Mangler") had six heads and 12 legs, and normally fed herself on fish; but she would attack any passing ship, grabbing men from shipboard and devouring them.

In the *Odyssey* the hero ODYSSEUS, having been forewarned by the witch CIRCE, steers his ship close by Skylla to avoid the worse danger, Charybdis. Skylla, snatches six of Odysseus's men overboard, but the ship passes by, rowed by the surviving crew. Odysseus's adventure has given rise to the expression "Steering on Skylla to avoid Charybdis," meaning to choose the lesser of two evils.

Later writers described Skylla as having genitalia consisting of ferocious, snarling dogs' heads. This deformity was said to be the result of a magic spell. Skylla had once been a beautiful woman who became the lover of the sea god POSEIDON and was then hideously bewitched in a magical bath prepared by Poseidon's jealous wife, Amphitritē.

Further reading: G. Säflund, *The Polyphemus and Scylla Groups at Sperlonga* (Stockholm: Almqvist & Wiksell, 1972); G. B. Waywell, "The Scylla Monument from Bargylia," *Antike Plastik* 25 (1996): 75–119; D. Buitron-Oliver and B. Cohen, "Between Skylla and Penelope. Female Characters of the 'Odyssey' in Archaic and Classical Greek Art," in *The Distaff Side. Representing the Female in Homer's 'Odyssey,'* edited by Beth Cohen (New York: Oxford University Press, 1995), 29–58; Jenifer Neils, "Les Femmes Fatales. Skylla and the Sirens in Greek Art," in *The Distaff Side. Representing the Female in Homer's 'Odyssey,'* edited by Beth Cohen (New York: Oxford University Press, 1995), 175–184; E. Walter-Karydi, "Dangerous Is Beautiful. The Elemental Quality of a Hellenistic Scylla," in *Regional Schools in Hellenistic Sculpture. Proceedings of an International Conference Held at Athens, March 15–17, 1996,* edited by Olga Palagia and William Coulson (Oxford: Oxbow Books, 1998), 271–279.

slaves Slave labor was a fundamental part of the ancient Greek economy. No less a thinker than ARISTOTLE (ca. 330 B.C.E.) believed that the use of slaves, although lamentable, was unavoidable; to him, a slave was "a living tool." Only the mystical PLATO (ca. 360 B.C.E.) imagined a society where slavery would be abolished (and where WOMEN would be equal citizens). Unfortunately, we know little about ancient Greek slavery; no extant ancient Greek writer discusses it at length, and modern scholars must rely on a patchwork of references in ancient Greek poetry, written history, stage comedy, and courtroom and political speeches. Archaeological evidence, such as tombstone inscriptions, add valuable details. Inevitably—as in all studies of ancient Greek society—the available information focuses on the rich and literate city of ATHENS, specially from the 300s B.C.E. onward.

Generally, a slave is a person without civil rights, owned as a possession, usually by another individual. The owner might have the power of life and death over the slave; at Athens however, an owner could not legally kill a slave at will, but needed state permission. To his or her master, the slave owes all labor and service—including, if required, sexual favors. In exchange, the master shelters, clothes, and feeds his slaves, just as he would be expected to care for his dogs or cattle. The origins of this brutal institution are lost in prehistory; certainly slavery was not confined to the Greeks. In HOMER's epic poem the *Iliad* (written down around 750 B.C.E.), slaves are shown to be war captives; the proud Trojans preordained fate is death or slavery at the Greeks' hands.

War was a major source of slaves. A defeated people would face slavery at the victors' discretion. These enslaved captives could be either Greeks or non-Greeks. To take one of many examples: After subduing the defiant Greek island of MELOS in 416 B.C.E., during the PELOPONNESIAN WAR, the Athenians put to death the entire adult male population and sold the women and children into slavery. Rather than being transported back to the conquerors' home city, such captives probably were sold on the spot to slave traders, who followed every Greek army. These traders were businessmen, with access to cash and transport, who would bring their newly purchased slaves to some major market for resale. The east Greek states of CHIOS and EPHESOS were important slave markets in the 400s B.C.E.; other commercial centers, such as Athens and CORINTH, played their roles.

The fate of war captives was surely ghastly. Families must have been broken up. The demand for adult male slaves (purchased for heavy labor) was far less than the demand for women, teenagers, and children (purchased for domestic duties). Children were especially prized as being pliant, physically pleasing, and long-term investments, but the mothers surely were often left behind on the auction block.

In times of peace, slaves might originate outside the Greek world. References in Homer, along with other documents, show Greek pirates of the 700s B.C.E. swooping down on the coast of ASIA MINOR or THRACE to carry away captives. Thracian slaves are mentioned regularly in Greek literature, and the Greek colonies founded on Thrace's Aegean coast—such as ABDERA and AMPHIPOLIS probably were active in acquiring slaves. This was done with the help of the feuding Thracian chieftains of the interior, who would bring their war captives to the Greek town, to sell.

In Greek cities the "exposure" of unwanted infants, particularly girls, was a legal, common practice. Exposed infants—that is, babies abandoned outdoors by their parents—automatically assumed slave status and would become the property of whoever rescued them. However, Greek cities typically had laws forbidding, within the city, the enslavement of any recognized citizen, whether child or adult. The Athenian lawgiver SOLON (ca. 594 B.C.E.) wrote famous legislation prohibiting the enslavement of any Athenian for debt.

Except for SPARTA—with its large numbers of HELOTS, or serfs—Greek cities tended to depend heavily on slave labor. The Athenian state-run SILVER mines at Laurion may have employed as many as 30,000 slaves in the 400s–300s B.C.E. Modern ARCHAEOLOGY has revealed the hellish work conditions at Laurion, where slaves, including children, worked 10-hour shifts in black crawl-tunnels with poor ventilation; it seems to have been cheaper

to let the workers sicken and die than to improve conditions. Smaller and less gruesome were privately owned factories, where skilled slaves produced beds, knives, and other household goods. The largest such operation now known of was an Athenian shield factory, owned by the family of the orator LYSIAS, which employed 120 slaves.

Some Athenian slaves probably worked semiindependently of their owners. A slave might practice a trade or keep a shop, delivering the profits to his master; a slave might be bailiff of a country estate, overseeing the slave farmhands and selling produce for the absentee owner. Slaves might be educated men, serving as clerks or tutors. Such slaves could earn wages and, by saving enough money, might eventually buy their freedom. In other instances, a trusted worker might be freed by his or her master (perhaps in a legal last will). At Athens, a freed slave took on the status of a metic, or resident alien.

Slave-population numbers are difficult to guess. Modern estimates suggest that, at the outbreak of the PELOPONNESIAN WAR (431 B.C.E.), Athenian territory was home to slightly over 100,000 slaves; this figure is probably equivalent to the number of nonslaves living there at that time. The ratio of 1:1 implies that slave ownership went fairly far down the social ladder. At the bottom of the scale might be (for example) a cobbler owning one slave to assist him in the shop and to do domestic work in the evening. Purely domestic slaves, bringing in little or no income, were a sign of wealth; the richest Athenian families might have 50 household slaves. No doubt many Athenians were too poor to afford even one slave, but this was viewed as a hardship.

With a 1:1 ratio, the Athenian slave population seems ominously large; yet there never was a slave revolt comparable to that led by Spartacus against the Romans in 73 B.C.E. The closest we come to this is the Athenian historian THUCYDIDES' (1) statement that 30,000 skilled slaves ran away from Athens during the latter part of the Peloponnesian War (413–404 B.C.E.). Reasons for this relative lack of unrest include the diverse origins and languages of the slaves, and their piecemeal segregation by owners and duties. In fact, when a Greek army marched to war, each HOPLITE had a servant (probably a slave) to carry armor and supplies. This would seem to provide a golden opportunity for revolt or escape, but the slaves lacked the motive and organization.

Slavery continued to be a fundamental social institution through the HELLENISTIC AGE and into the Roman period. Modern theories estimate that 15 to 20 percent of the entire population of the Roman Empire in the first century C.E. were slaves (i.e., one out of every five or six people). Slavery continued throughout antiquity, gradually becoming replaced by other sources of cheap labor such as low-wage workers and serfs.

See also METICS; NICIAS; PROSTITUTES.

Further reading: Michael Grant, *A Social History of Greece and Rome* (New York: Scribner, 1992); Sarah

Pomeroy, *Goddesses, Whores, Wives, and Slaves: Women in Classical Antiquity* (New York: Schocken Books, 1995); Peter Hunt, *Slaves, Warfare, and Ideology in the Greek Historians* (New York: Cambridge University Press, 1998); Gary Reger, "Enslavement and Manumission in Ancient Greece," in *Race and Racism in Theory and Practice*, edited by Berel Lang (Lanham, Md.: Rowman and Littlefield, 2000), 99–110; Robin Osborne, "The Economics and Politics of Slavery at Athens," in *Ancient Greek Democracy: Readings and Sources*, edited by Eric Robinson (Malden, Mass.: Blackwell, 2004), 265–280.

Smyrna *See* ARCHAEOLOGY; IONIA.

Socrates (469–399 B.C.E.) *Athenian philosopher*
Although Socrates left no writings, he is of landmark importance in Western thought. By his example, PHILOSOPHY was turned away from its prior emphasis on natural SCIENCE and became directed more toward questions of ethics—that is, the right conduct of life. In the words of the Roman thinker Cicero (ca. 50 B.C.E.), "Socrates was the first to call philosophy down from the sky."

Socrates profoundly influenced his pupil PLATO. Socrates' central conclusions—that happiness depends solely on living a moral life, and that moral virtue is equivalent to knowledge and is therefore teachable—became the springboard for Plato's elaborate theory of reality and system of ethics. Socrates' equation of virtue with knowledge led to the daring corollary that evil is ignorance and hence unintentional. According to Socrates, the evildoer acts mistakenly in harming his or her own soul.

Socrates himself taught no doctrine, claiming simply, "I know nothing." This professed ignorance was denoted by the Greek word *eironeia*: that is, the famous Socratic irony. Unlike other philosophers, he never founded a school or charged fees for lessons. At ATHENS he attracted a following of young, aristocratic men, with whom he would dispute ethical or political issues. Since he took no money, his goal was evidently to prepare these students for public office by teaching them to think for themselves. His "Socratic method" consisted of asking questions, particularly in pursuit of definitions. For example: "You say that this man is a better citizen than his opponent? Let us consider therefore what we mean by 'good citizen.'" This question-and-answer process forced the respondent to examine his own preconceptions, in a search for general truths.

Socrates' disputations and skeptical outlook led him to be associated—unfairly, from his viewpoint—with those well-paid teachers of intellectual skills, the SOPHISTS. One famous sophist, PROTAGORAS OF ABDERA, who taught at Athens around 455–415 B.C.E., is recorded as believing that expertise (Greek: *aretē*) in most fields is teachable. Protagoras surely inspired Socrates' similar but more profound view that moral virtue (likewise denoted by the Greek word *aretē*) is teachable.

Among Socrates' well-heeled students were two destined for great importance in Athenian politics: the brilliant but erratic ALCIBIADES and the extreme right-winger KRITIAS (who was killed in 403 B.C.E. while trying to abolish Athenian DEMOCRACY). The link with Kritias was probably responsible for Socrates' death. In 399 B.C.E. the 70-year-old philosopher was prosecuted for corrupting the youth (a charge implicitly referring to Kritias and Alcibiades) and for impiety. After making a flamboyantly nonconciliatory defense speech, Socrates was found guilty by the jury of 501 Athenians and was sentenced to die by being given poison. The famous prison scene, in which Socrates discusses the soul's immortality with his visitors before drinking the fatal hemlock, is recounted in Plato's dialogue *Phaedo*.

Information about Socrates comes mainly from two sources. Plato's fictional dialogues contain much biographical information about Socrates while also foisting onto him Plato's own more complex philosophical theories. Here the insoluble question arises: What aspects of Plato's Socrates show us the real Socrates, and how much is just a mask for Plato's own thought? Probably a more biographical Socrates is portrayed in Plato's early work (such as the *Krito* or *Euthyphro*), while the Socrates in the *Republic* and later dialogues is a more fictionalized character, who discusses concepts that the real Socrates never explored. The other source is XENOPHON, a stolid Athenian soldier and historian who was one of Socrates' disciples and who wrote about him in three nonfiction memoirs, *Memorabilia*, *Symposium*, and *Apology*. (The latter two titles also belong to works by Plato.) That Socrates could be the beloved mentor of two such different people as Plato and Xenophon is itself revealing. Other information comes from ARISTOPHANES' stage comedy *Clouds* (performed in 423 B.C.E.), in which a crackpot scientist named Socrates operates a "Thinking Shop." Clearly the real Socrates was a dynamic personality who fascinated friend and foe alike. When one contemporary Athenian asked the oracle at DELPHI who was the wisest of all men, the answer came back "Socrates."

He was born into the Athenian middle class, the son of a stonecutter or sculptor named Sophroniskos. Socrates came of age during the political primacy of PERIKLES, when Athens reached its zenith as a radical democracy and imperial naval power—twin developments that alienated many conservative Athenians. As a youth, Socrates supposedly studied under a disciple of the philosopher ANAXAGORAS, but became discouraged by the emphasis on physics and cosmology rather than ethics.

During the PELOPONNESIAN WAR between Athens and SPARTA (431–404 B.C.E.), Socrates served as foot soldier in the POTIDAEA campaign (432–430 B.C.E.), at the disastrous Battle of Delium (424 B.C.E.), and at AMPHIPOLIS

(422 B.C.E.), by which time he would have been about 47 years old. On campaign, he distinguished himself by his physical endurance and courage. One anecdote describes Socrates striding calmly amid the Athenian retreat from Delium, defying the pursuing enemy CAVALRY.

In later life he repeatedly resisted the political hysteria of Athens in crisis. In 406 B.C.E., while serving a citizen's normal duty on the council panel to prepare the agenda for the Athenian ASSEMBLY, Socrates refused to go along with an illegal motion ordering a group trial for six commanders charged with negligence after the sea battle of Arginusae. In 403 B.C.E. Socrates defied his old pupil Kritias, who had seized power in the coup of the THIRTY TYRANTS: Brought before the Thirty, Socrates refused to help them arrest a certain intended victim. No doubt Socrates himself would have become a victim of the Thirty, had not their reign of terror soon ended. Instead, Socrates was denounced by prominent accusers after the restoration of democracy.

That Socrates should have been prosecuted under the democracy is significant. An original thinker who defied convention, Socrates was known for his antidemocratic sentiments. As Xenophon's memoirs make clear, he criticized the democracy's inability to entrust its government to the most apt and expert people. Without advocating revolution or dictatorship, Socrates seems to have favored a meritocracy, with power entrusted to a worthy ruling class. Such beliefs—although purely theoretical—must have seemed damning after Critias' right-wing coup. Following the Thirty's downfall, the Athenians' wrath turned against Socrates.

Across the centuries, Socrates' eccentric personality communicates itself. Although magnetic in character, he was physically unattractive in middle age—balding, pug-nosed, and paunchy. His contemporaries humorously compared him to the mythical figure SILENUS. Socrates was famous for his austerity: Impervious to cold and fatigue, he almost always went barefoot, even over frozen winter ground at the siege of Potidaea.

He had three sons by his wife, Xanthippe (whom several sources describe as a bad-tempered shrew). Socrates may have practiced a stonecutter's trade, like his father, but he evidently spent most of his time at the Athenian sports grounds where educated men of leisure congregated. There he would conduct semipublic debates with his followers or rivals.

Socrates' disciples (all male) included several of the most glamorous youths of the day in the homosexual society of aristocratic Athens. A homosexual ambiance pervades many of Plato's dialogues, such as the *Symposium*, where the topic is love and where the mutual attraction between Socrates and Alcibiades is discussed. But as so much is said about his indifference to physical needs, it remains unclear whether Socrates actually was intimate with these young men.

See also GYMNASIUM; HOMOSEXUALITY; LAWS AND LAW COURTS; SKEPTICISM.

Further reading: Eugene Kelly, ed., *New Essays on Socrates* (Lanham, Md.: University Press of America, 1984); M. Montuori, *Socrates, an Approach* (Amsterdam: J. C. Gieben, 1988); K. J. Boudouris, ed., *The Philosophy of Socrates* (Athens: International Center for Greek Philosophy and Culture, 1991); G. Vlastos, *Studies in Greek Philosophy, 2. Socrates, Plato, and Their Traditions* (Princeton, N.J.: Princeton University Press, 1995); Mark McPherran, *Wisdom, Ignorance, and Virtue: New Essays in Socratic Studies* (Edmonton: Academic Printing and Publishing, 1997); Mark Lutz, *Socrates' Education to Virtue: Learning the Love of the Noble* (Albany: State University of New York Press, 1998); Mark Munn, *The School of History. Athens in the Age of Socrates* (Berkeley: University of California Press, 2000); Debra Nails, *The People of Plato: A Prosopography of Plato and Other Socratics* (Indianapolis, Ind.: Hackett, 2002).

Solon (ca. 638–559 B.C.E.) *Athenian statesman who in the early 500s B.C.E. drafted a new code of law*
Solon's reforms averted a revolution at ATHENS and laid the foundations for Athenian DEMOCRACY. They came at a time of major class tensions, both between the nobles and the increasingly confident middle class, and also between the country landowners and the tenant farmers who paid rent under onerous conditions. Solon alleviated the burdens of the poor farmers and, at the upper end of the social scale, broke the nobles' traditional monopoly on political power.

Later generations revered Solon as one of the SEVEN SAGES of Greece. The texts of his laws, carved into wooden tablets, were kept on display in the Athenian AGORA. These laws supplied the code at Athens for nearly 200 years, until the legal revisions of 410–400 B.C.E., even afterward, the Athenians still called their code "the laws of Solon."

Solon was also a poet. A number of his verses are preserved in two later written works—ARISTOTLE's *Constitution of Athens* (ca. 340 B.C.E.) and PLUTARCH's biography of Solon (ca. 100 C.E.). But because Solon is the earliest important figure in Athenian history, much of his life and work remain unclear to us.

Born into an aristocratic Athenian family, Solon first distinguished himself in a war against MEGARA (1). His patriotism won the respect of his fellow citizens, and they asked him to serve as arbitrator and lawgiver, to avert civil war. It was probably in 594 B.C.E., the year in which he served as chef ARCHON, that Solon instituted his famous reforms.

The most grievous social problem facing Athens at that time was the plight of the rural poor in ATTICA, the 1,000-square-mile district surrounding Athens. It seems that the rich landowners were crushing the tenant farmers who paid part of their produce as rent. The law allowed loans to be secured on the person of the borrower; that is, defaulting debtors were liable to be sold as SLAVES. Tenant farmers who forfeited on their rent (in bad harvest years, for example) were faced with catastrophe, for both themselves and their families.

In the city, meanwhile, the better-off commoners had their own grievances, directed against the government. Citizens of the middle class—who supplied the backbone of Athens's army, serving as HOPLITE infantry—were chafing at being excluded from government. At this time, Athens was still an ARISTOCRACY. All political power was held by a few ancient, upper-class families (of which Solon was a member). Only aristocrats could hold executive posts or be admitted to the powerful decision-making council and supreme court known as the AREOPAGOS. All of the law courts, overseen by aristocrats, showed a strong upper-class bias; the existing law code, devised around 620 B.C.E. by the nobleman DRACO, was mainly repressive.

By the early 500s B.C.E. there was fear at Athens that these two aggrieved classes—the peasantry and the hoplite class—would join forces and place a dictator, or *tyrannos,* on the throne. TYRANTS had seized power at CORINTH and Megara, and Athens itself had seen a failed coup by a would-be tyrant named KYLON in around 620 B.C.E. In this volatile atmosphere Athens turned to Solon, whom all parties trusted. He could have exploited the situation to make himself tyrant, but he was a greater man than that.

Solon rescued the tenant farmers and other poor Athenians by forbidding that loans be secured on the borrower's person—henceforth no Athenian could be enslaved for debt—Solon also cancelled all such existing debts. "I plucked up the marker-stones," he declares in one poem, referring to the hated signs standing at repossessed farms. He also freed Athenians who had been enslaved, bringing home many who had been sold abroad. Solon's poverty-relief measures were known as the seisachtheia, "the shaking off of burdens."

Solon overhauled the crude Draconian law code and created political changes that broke the aristocrats' monopoly on power. He devised a new system of social ranking, with four citizen classes based entirely on income level. This new emphasis on income worked against the traditional emphasis on noble birth. The upper classes might still be full of rich aristocrats, but now other men—commoners—could be admitted to these classes. Since a man's social rank determined his eligibility for various political offices, this was a significant democratic change.

Solon enfranchised the lowest income class, the Athenian peasants, admitting them as citizens and allowing them to vote in the ASSEMBLY. He created a new deliberative COUNCIL, of 400 members, open to the upper three income classes; the council members served for one year, after being chosen by lot. This new council, very influential in that it helped prepare the agenda for the assembly, served to counterbalance the old aristocratic Areopagos. It was probably also Solon who set up the Athenian "people's court," to which any citizen had the right of appeal; this assured that a defendant could be heard by a jury of his peers rather than by a court consisting of nobles.

The principal beneficiaries of Solon's reforms were the rich commoners—nonaristocratic landowners, traders, and manufacturers who could now take their place in Athens's upper classes and enjoy greater political voice. Solon was not a complete democrat; he was more of a timocrat. As his poetry makes clear, he believed that the populace should be governed by a worthy, fair-minded ruling class.

Certain embittered verses by Solon indicate that his reforms came as a disappointment to both extremes. The nobles resented their losses, and the poorer classes were angry that Solon had stopped short of redistributing the land. Having made the Athenians promise to obey his laws unchanged for 10 years, Solon left Athens to travel (some say) to EGYPT and LYDIA. Returning home, he lived long enough to see his kinsman PEISISTRATUS make himself tyrant in Athens (in about 561 B.C.E.)—the very outcome that Solon had tried to prevent. But Solon's laws and political apparatus survived in Athens (the tyrants did not) and set the stage for KLEISTHENES' (1) reforms (508 B.C.E.) and the radical democracy of the 400s B.C.E.

See also LAWS AND LAW COURTS.

Further reading: T. W. Gallant, "Agricultural Systems, Land Tenure, and the Reforms of Solon," *Annual of the British School of Athens* 77 (1982): 111–124; M. H. Hansen, "Solonian Democracy in Fourth-century Athens," in *Aspects of Athenian Democracy [Conference, Boston, June 18–21 1987],* edited by W. R. Connor (Copenhagen: Museum Tusculanum Press, 1990), 71–99; L. Foxhall, "A View from the Top. Evaluating the Solonian Property Classes," in *The Development of the Polis in Archaic Greece,* edited by Lynette Mitchell and P. J. Rhodes (London: Routledge, 1997), 113–136; Bernard Randall, *Solon: The Lawmaker of Athens* (New York: Rosen, 2004).

sophists *Sophistai* (experts or professors) were itinerant teachers who, in the latter 400s B.C.E., went from city to city in the Greek world, tutoring young men in disputation and other intellectual skills. These lessons, for which the sophists charged hefty fees, were designed to help students achieve practical success as lawyers, politicians, speechwriters and so on. The visiting sophists caused a cultural sensation at the wealthy, intellectual city of ATHENS, but they also earned a reputation for amoral cleverness; the hallmark of a sophist was the ability to argue any question from two opposing sides. The modern English word *sophistry* (meaning "clever but false reasoning") retains the negative associations of this rationalistic movement.

Yet not all sophists were amoral. The best were genuine thinkers, breaking new intellectual ground and answering a need for "college-level" EDUCATION in their day—the sophist Hippias of ELIS, for instance, taught a method of memory training, among many offered courses (ca. 430 B.C.E.).

The earliest and most famous sophist was PROTAGORAS of ABDERA (ca. 445 B.C.E.); another prominent one was Prodicus of Keos (ca. 430 B.C.E.). The orator GORGIAS of Leontini (ca. 427 B.C.E.) was associated with the sophists, due to the ingenuity of the arguments he used in public speaking. And in the eyes of many Athenians, the philosopher SOCRATES (469–399 B.C.E.) was a sophist, on account of his question-and-answer method of inquiry.

Further reading: J. V. Muir, "Religion and the New Education. The Challenge of the Sophists," in *Greek Religion and Society*, edited by P. E. Easterling and J. V. Muir (New York: Cambridge University Press, 1985), 191–218; M. W. Gleason, *Making Men. Sophists and Self-presentation in Ancient Rome* (Princeton, N.J.: Princeton University Press, 1995); R. W. Wallace, "The Sophists in Athens," in *Democracy, Empire, and the Arts in Fifth-century Athens,* edited by Deborah Boedeker and Kurt Raaflaub (Cambridge, Mass.: Harvard University Press, 1998); Jacqueline de Romilly, *The Great Sophists in Periclean Athens,* translated by Janet Lloyd (New York: Oxford University Press, 1998); John Dillon and Tania Gergel, trans., *The Greek Sophists* (London: Penguin, 2003).

Sophokles (ca. 496–406 B.C.E.) *Athenian tragic playwright*

Sophokles is reckoned among the three great classical tragedians (the other two being AESCHYLUS and EURIPIDES). His work has been seen as Greek tragedy's high point, wherein the separate requirements of plot and character are fused most successfully. He is said to have written 123 plays, of which only seven survive today; among these is the play that the philosopher and critic ARISTOTLE admired more than any other Greek tragedy, *Oedipus the King.*

Sophokles ("famed for wisdom") was born the son of a rich manufacturer at the Athenian DEME of Colonus—the beauty of which he would commemorate in a famous choral ode in his tragedy *Oedipus at Colonus.* His life spanned the near century of Athenian greatness. Growing up during the PERSIAN WARS, he partook of the spirit of Athenian confidence following the miraculous victory over the Persians. After the Greek sea victory at SALAMIS (1) (480 B.C.E.), the teenage Sophokles was honored with the assignment of dancing and singing, naked and anointed, at the trophy monument. To win this commission he must have been a performer of considerable tal-

ent and beauty. Supposedly, in his earlier plays he occasionally appeared in roles onstage, but gave that up due to a weak voice.

At about age 28 Sophokles won his first tragedy-competition, at the major annual drama festival known as the City Dionysia (468 B.C.E.). We know that one of the playwrights whom he defeated this year was the well-established Aeschylus, but the centuries have not preserved the three Sophoklean tragedies (and one satyr-play) that comprised this winning entry. Sophokles went on to win a total of 24 victories in over 65 more years of writing. Of the seven times (only) when he failed to win first prize, he always took second prize, never third. This remarkable record makes Sophokles the most successful tragedian of his day; Euripides, by contrast, won first place only five times. Relatedly, Sophokles was highly popular as a social figure. Several ancient writings testify to his charming personality and many friends—who included the historian HERODOTUS and the Athenian statesman KIMON.

In the development of Greek THEATER, Sophokles is credited by ancient writers with making several changes in the way tragedy was performed. Most important, he raised the number of speaking actors from two to three—which greatly increased the possible number of speaking parts, since an actor could play multiple roles. Sophokles supposedly ended the custom of presenting tragedies as linked trilogies, in favor of presenting three tragedies on unrelated topics. And he is said to have increased the size of the chorus from 12 to 15 men and to have developed the use of painted backdrops as scenery.

Outside the theater, Sophokles played a substantial role in Athenian public life prior to and during the PELOPONNESIAN WAR (431–404 B.C.E.). He was devoted to ATHENS, and—unlike Aeschylus, Euripides, and other artists—he refused all lucrative invitations to visit other cities of the Greek world. In 443 B.C.E. Sophokles was elected to the office of treasurer of the DELIAN LEAGUE. In 441 B.C.E., reportedly in recognition of his play *Antigone,* he was elected for the following year as a general of the Athenian armed forces. Under PERIKLES' senior command, General Sophokles served in the campaign against the rebellious island of SAMOS. Possibly (we do not know for sure) Sophokles was later elected as general a second time.

In 420 B.C.E. Sophokles was active in developing the god ASCLEPIUS's cult at Athens, which may mean that he helped establish a public hospital. In 413 B.C.E., amid the state emergency following the Athenian military disaster at SYRACUSE, the Athenians appointed Sophokles, age 83, to a special executive post.

Sophokles married twice and we hear of two sons. One of them became a successful writer of tragedies, as did one of Sophokles' grandsons. Like other Greek men of his era, Sophokles may have pursued a private life that we would call bisexual. An anecdote in the memoirs of the writer ION (2) describes Sophokles relaxing at a SYM-POSIUM during the Samian military campaign; Sophokles coaxed a kiss from a handsome slave boy, then commented to the other guests, "So you see, I am not so bad a strategist as Perikles believes." Another famous quotation is preserved in the philosopher PLATO's treatise *The Republic;* when Sophokles in old age was asked if he was still able to have sex with a woman, he replied that he had happily escaped from his sex urge, "as from a cruel and insane master."

In about 406 B.C.E., after Euripides died, the 90-year-old Sophokles presented his chorus dressed in mourning, to commemorate his dead rival. Soon afterward Sophokles himself died, and he was remembered in ARISTO-PHANES' comedy *Frogs* (405 B.C.E.), which is set in the Underworld: "He was a good fellow up there and now he's a good fellow down here."

The first performance dates for most of Sophokles' seven existing tragedies are unknown. But the following sequence is plausible: *Ajax* (performed perhaps in about 450–445 B.C.E.), *Antigone* (perhaps around 442 B.C.E.), *The Women of Trachis* (perhaps around 429–420 B.C.E.), *Oedipus the King* (perhaps around 429–420 B.C.E.), *Electra* (perhaps around 418–410 B.C.E.), *Philoctetes* (409 B.C.E.), and *Oedipus at Colonus* (performed in 401 B.C.E., after Sophokles' death). These tragedies survived because they were chosen in later antiquity to be taught in schools. Of the lost plays, the titles of many are known and there exist some fragments of text; apparently about a third of them were drawn from legends of the TROJAN WAR. All of Sophokles' plays, in keeping with the custom of the day, retold tales already familiar from EPIC POETRY and other sources.

A brief description of a few of the plays must suffice here. *The Women of Trachis* presents the horrible death of the hero HERAKLES, poisoned by a venom-smeared robe given to him by his innocent wife, Deineira (who wrongly believes the robe to be a magic charm to reclaim her husband's love). The play is named for the characters portrayed by the chorus, local women in the region of central Greece where Herakles legendarily met his end. The action emphasizes Herakles' agony in death and the tragic irony that the world's mightiest hero, vanquisher of monsters, should die at the unintending hands of his gentle, loving, naive wife.

Oedipus the King and *Antigone* are today among the most accessible and widely read of all existing Greek tragedies. *Oedipus* is often misunderstood as the tragedy of a man undone by arrogance, or *hubris.* But like much of Sophokles' work, the play is really about the limits of human knowledge and power. The Theban king OEDIPUS, at the play's outset, seems as blessed as a human can be: young, wise, powerful, just, beloved by his people. By the play's end he is blind, accursed, and homeless; his prior happiness has been revealed as an illusion. Unlike certain other Greek tragic heroes, Oedipus onstage does not do

anything evil or foolhardy to bring on the gods' wrath. Although he does show pride and anger early in the play, these do not lead to bad action—rather, Oedipus's destructive actions lie buried, unbeknownst to him, in the past. *Oedipus the King* presents his gradual discovery of his own calamity; ironically, it is Oedipus's intelligence and perseverance that bring about this discovery.

The tightly plotted play opens with King Oedipus's city of THEBES ravaged by plague and famine; the oracle at DELPHI has revealed that the land lies under a curse because the murderer of the prior king, Laius, has not been punished. Since the killer's identity is unknown, Oedipus vows to discover it. The blind seer TEIRESIAS is summoned for questioning. The ensuing scene is perhaps the finest in all extant Greek tragedy. As Oedipus grows puzzled and enraged, Teiresias at first refuses to speak, then angrily replies that Oedipus himself is the defiler of the land; Oedipus himself is the murderer. Oedipus ignores the stated message and shrewdly assumes that Teiresias is trying to discredit him as king, perhaps in league with the ambitious nobleman Kreon.

Teiresias, alone of all the characters, understands that Oedipus slew King Laius years ago, in a quarrel at a crossroads far from Thebes. Oedipus, traveling from CORINTH (where he had grown up as the son of the king and queen there), did not know the identity of the arrogant older man whom he killed. Worse, he did not know that Laius was his own father. Worst of all, Oedipus has since married Laius's widow, Jocasta, and had children by her—who is really Oedipus's mother. He had been taken from her at his birth, and she did not recognize him as a young man.

The tragedy moves toward its climax as Oedipus, like an ideal courtroom judge, gradually uncovers the truth by interrogating witnesses, including Jocasta and a Theban shepherd who is the sole survivor of Laius's fatal fight. At one point Oedipus realizes that it was he who killed Laius, but he holds onto the hope that at least Laius was not his father (and Jocasta his mother). When finally the whole truth is publicly revealed, Oedipus in horror gouges out his own eyes and Jocasta hangs herself (both offstage). The final scenes show the blind Oedipus departing into self-imposed exile, cursed by his revealed parricide and incest. The tragedy ends with the statement—appearing in the writings of Sophokles' friend Herodotus—that no human being should be called happy until he is safely dead. Sophokles' *Oedipus at Colonus* presents the hero's final days, when he finds sanctuary and divine forgiveness under protection of the mythical Athenian king THESEUS.

Antigone presents the classic conflict of public duty versus private conscience. In the aftermath of the destructive war of the SEVEN AGAINST THEBES, Oedipus's daughter ANTIGONE chooses to disobey an edict of Kreon (who is now ruler of Thebes) in favor of her religious and familial obligations. Kreon has forbidden anyone on pain of death to grant funeral rites to the slain attacker Polynices, Antigone's brother. In breaking this law, Antigone discards all happiness, including her betrothal to Kreon's son, Haemon. But death comes as a triumph for her and a curse for Kreon and his family. It is Antigone who has upheld the higher, unwritten law of social obligation.

The Sophoklean hero or heroine tends to be a splendid individualist, set apart from other people by a refusal to compromise. These protagonists are larger than life—stronger, wiser, or more pious than others—yet they inevitably succumb to circumstance or FATE. This two-sided view is essential to Sophokles' work; the hero may be called "godlike," but usually he fails due to his human flaws, such as anger or ignorance. Ignorance in particular interests Sophokles. He portrays both Oedipus and Herakles as violently undone by an imperfect, human understanding of the facts.

Above human beings stand the gods. Where Aeschylus's surviving tragedies convey a faith in divine wisdom and Euripides' show gods who are malicious and capricious, Sophokles' work falls somewhere in between. In Sophokles, the great god ZEUS controls mortal destiny, but Zeus's purpose may be mysterious to the onstage characters and to the audience. "All of these events are Zeus," the chorus announces at the end of *The Women of Trachis,* amid Herakles' gruesome death. Zeus's purpose seems needlessly cruel, except that Herakles will win blessed immortality after his suffering. Sophokles refuses to clarify or justify the workings of the gods. Rather, his plays mirror the religious questions of real life.

See also AJAX [1]; DEMOCRACY; ELECTRA; HOMOSEXUALITY; HUBRIS; MYTH; ORESTES; PHILOKTETES; RELIGION.

Further reading: Harold Bloom, ed., *Sophokles* (New York: Chelsea House, 2003); Marianne McDonald, *The Living Art of Greek Tragedy* (Bloomington: Indiana University Press, 2003); Josh Beer, *Sophokles and the Tragedy of Athenian Democracy* (Westport, Conn.: Praeger, 2004).

Sounion (Sunium)   The site of Sounion is situated on the coast of ATTICA, about 40 miles from ATHENS. It is famous for its sanctuary dedicated to the god POSEIDON; much of the marble temple constructed on the promontory in the mid-400s B.C.E. remains standing today. It is clearly visible to ships at sea and was a popular attraction for European travelers in the 18th and 19th centuries C.E. Among the many names carved as graffiti on one of the temple's columns is that of the British romantic poet Lord Byron.

The classical temple of Poseidon replaced an earlier cult building that was destroyed, unfinished, by the invading Persians in 480 B.C.E. It was decorated with architectural SCULPTURE: a relief frieze depicting the battle of the CENTAURS and the Lapiths, the battle of the gods and the GIANTS, and the deeds of THESEUS. There were also sculptures in the pediments, but these do not survive. The sanctuary also contained two colonnaded stoas and a monumental gateway.

Down the hill from the Poseidon sanctuary was another cult site, dedicated to the goddess ATHENA. Two small temples were built here in the mid-late 400s B.C.E.

A number of domestic buildings have been located at Sounion, some of which have been excavated. They were occupied continuously from the 400s B.C.E. into the Roman era. The residents were protected by a fortification wall, 300 feet long and punctuated with square watchtowers.

The site of Sounion was first excavated by the German archaeologist Dörpfeld in 1884, then by the Greek Archaeological Society in 1899–1915. Some restoration work has been done since 1958, including the re-erection of two of the temple's columns.

Further reading: William B. Dinsmoor, *Sounion,* 2d ed. (Athens: Lycabettus, 1974); Costis Dararas, *Sounion: Archaeological Guide* (Athens: General Direction of Antiquities and Restoration, 1979); A. B. Tataki, *Sounion: The Temple of Poseidon* (Athens: Ekdotike Athenon, 1984); G. Behor, *Ancient Greece: The Famous Monuments Past and Present* (Athens: Muses, 1997); Hans Goette, *Athens, Attica, and the Megarid: An Archaeological Guide* (London: Routledge, 2001); John Camp, *The Archaeology of Athens* (New Haven, Conn.: Yale University Press, 2001).

Sparta   One of the greatest city-states of mainland Greece, Sparta was often in rivalry with ATHENS. Located in the southern Greek region known as the PELOPONNESE, the city dominated southern Greece after 600 B.C.E. in 404 B.C.E. Sparta became the supreme Greek city, having defeated Athens in the PELOPONNESIAN WAR. But a declining birthrate among Sparta's citizens, poor relations with its subject cities, a constant fear of serf revolt, and a resistance to change all made the failure of the Spartan Empire inevitable. In 371–369 B.C.E. Sparta was unexpectedly defeated and crippled (although not captured) by its erstwhile ally THEBES. Thereafter Sparta confined itself mainly to intrigues in the Peloponnese, often in defense against armies of the kingdom of MACEDON. In 222 B.C.E., amid internal political convulsions, Sparta was defeated and captured by the Macedonian king Antigonus III. Within the next 80 years, however, both Macedon and Sparta surrendered to the armies of ROME.

Sparta was unique among Greek cities, because of its program of patriotic indoctrination and full-time military service for males. This program arose in the mid-600s B.C.E., probably at the hands of a Spartan statesman named LYKOURGOS (1), who was revered as a hero by later generations of Spartans. Today nothing is known for sure about Lykourgos's life, but he evidently shaped Sparta into an authoritarian state, devoted to maintaining the bravest and most disciplined of all HOPLITE armies. Between about 600 B.C.E. and 371 B.C.E. the Spartans could justifiably claim to be the best infantry in the Greek world (also superior to the one foreign infantry they encountered, the Persians). Eventually, however, the Spartans' reliance on traditional battle tactics left them vulnerable to new tactics, developed by the Thebans and Macedonians.

The grim world of Sparta was the "other" Greece, in contrast to the exuberant life and literature of classical Athens. The Spartans were secretive and anti-intellectual. They rarely let in visitors and left behind few writings. Most modern knowledge of Sparta comes from information preserved by ancient Greek writers who were not themselves Spartan—the historians HERODOTUS, THUCYDIDES (1), and XENOPHON, the philosopher ARISTOTLE, and the biographer PLUTARCH. Still, much remains mysterious about the Spartans today.

Although militaristic and austere, Sparta was not necessarily repulsive to all other Greeks. In a Greek world where ideals of DEMOCRACY (rule by the many) vied against those of OLIGARCHY (rule by the few), Sparta was the model oligarchy. It maintained its dominance over other Greek cities by supporting the ruling classes of those cities. In so doing, Sparta counterbalanced the appeal of Athens, which was trying to export democracy to the lower-income classes everywhere. In southern Greece, aristocrats and other wealthy people welcomed Spartan protection and leadership. And many other Greeks admired Sparta's army and stable government.

Even Athens itself contained pro-Spartan individuals. Typically these Athenians were aristocrats. The best remembered of them is the gentleman-soldier-historian Xenophon (ca. 428–354 B.C.E.). Similarly, Xenophon's contemporary, the Athenian philosopher PLATO, used Spartan government as inspiration for the authoritarian utopias imagined in his writings the *Republic* and the *Laws*.

Sparta ("sown land," or possibly "broom shrub") was located in the region called LACONIA, or Lacedaemon, in the southeastern Peloponnese. Nestled between lofty mountain ranges on the west and the east, the city sat at the northern tip of the Laconian plain, which fans out triangularly 25 miles southward to the sea. Just west of the city, the River Eurotas flowed southward through the widening plain. Nowadays a Greek provincial capital, Sparti, stands near the ancient site.

Long before the city of Sparta arose, the fertile and rain-nourished Laconian plain was home to pre-Greek inhabitants in the third millennium B.C.E. and to Mycenaean Greeks in the second millennium B.C.E. According to legend, this was the kingdom ruled by MENELAUS at the time of the TROJAN WAR (around 1220 B.C.E.). Archaeological excavations reveal that the town of Amyclae, just south of the future site of Sparta, was a civic center containing a sanctuary of a pre-Greek god named HYAKINTHOS. Later Amyclae became an important shrine

of the Greek god APOLLO, one of the patron gods of the Spartan region.

Sparta itself was founded by descendants of the DORIAN GREEKS who overran most of the Peloponnese around 1100–1000 B.C.E., after the collapse of MYCENAEAN CIVILIZATION. Around 950 B.C.E. four local Dorian villages became amalgamated around a shared civic center. This multipart beginning probably explains the odd Spartan institution of dual monarchy, whereby Sparta always had two joint kings, drawn from two royal families, the Agiads and Eurypontids. One reason the double kingship survived for the next 700 years was that Spartan kings were primarily military leaders, commanding armies in the field. Certainly by the 600s B.C.E.—and probably long before—the king's power at home was being curtailed by other governmental branches, specifically the EPHORS (Greek: *ephorai,* "overseers") and the COUNCIL.

In appearance Sparta remained a sprawling village, interspersed with trees. Disdaining wealth and pomp, the Spartans of later centuries continued to make their houses out of wood and to build very few public stone monuments. Sparta at its height of power had no perimeter wall; the Spartans preferred to trust in their army and their protective mountains. Not until 318 B.C.E. did an enclosing wall finally go up, against the threat of a Macedonian invasion. Similarly, the Spartan ACROPOLIS was a puny, unwalled mound (very unlike the lofty citadels of other Greek cities), whose main job was to hold the temple of the city's patron deity, ATHENA. The building itself was known as the temple of Athena Chalkioikos ("Athena in Bronze"), so named because its walls were covered in BRONZE plates showing mythical scenes.

This temple and that of ARTEMIS Orthia, which stood to the west, by the Eurotas bank, were Sparta's two main monuments. Thucydides, writing during the Spartan heyday (around 400 B.C.E.), contrasted such physical simplicity with the elaborate grandeur of Athens. In a famous passage, Thucydides commented that if Sparta were to become deserted and only its empty structures viewed by future generations, people would never believe that the city had been so great a power.

The earliest events of Spartan history saw Sparta still governed as an old-style ARISTOCRACY, prior to Lykourgos's reforms. By about 700 B.C.E. this aristocratic Sparta had conquered Laconia (including the seaport of Gytheum, about 25 miles south of Sparta, to serve as the Spartans' maritime link).

The capture of Laconia and its inhabitants created three distinct social levels. At the top were the original Spartans, called Spartiatai (or "Spartiates"). Below them were the PERIOIKOI ("dwellers around"), second-class citizens who were descendants of the earliest-subdued Laconian villagers. As their name suggests, the perioikoi lived in towns that roughly formed a circle around the Spartiates' prime land on the central plain. The perioikoi were obligated to pay taxes and serve alongside the Spartiates in the army; they enjoyed legal protections, rights of ownership, and so on but were excluded from the political process. Spartiates and perioikoi together comprised the people known as the Lacedaemonians.

Below these was another group, far inferior in status. They were the serfs, or HELOTS (Greek: *helotai*), supposedly named for the Laconian coastal village of Helos ("marsh"). It seems that the Spartans, at some point in their expansion, changed their policy toward the villagers they subdued: instead of admitting them as lesser citizens, they began to subjugate them as serfs. This brutal serf system existed elsewhere in the Greek world, but the Spartans used it the most.

The helot population increased enormously after the Spartan capture of the fertile Greek region called MESSENIA, in the southwestern Peloponnese. Invading across the high Tagytus mountain range that borders Sparta to the west, Spartan armies descended into the Messenian plain and fought a long war (735–715 B.C.E.) to seize the farmlands and helotize the people. Sparta's victory in this First Messenian War is associated with a Eurypontid king, Theopompus, the earliest reliably real figure in Spartan history.

The annexation of Messenia made Sparta rich, with control of two-fifths of the Peloponnese. In a land where famine was a constant threat, Sparta alone had solved the food problem, with supplies from Messenia abundant to its needs: no other Greek state ever managed to subdue an entire Greek region and population. Yet the helots in Messenia and Laconia were also a source of fear. They outnumbered their Spartan masters—by the mid-400s B.C.E. the ratio would be seven to one. Fear of helot uprisings, which occurred periodically, kept Spartan armies close to home and created a mass neurosis in the Spartan mentality. Every year the ephors would formally declare war on the helots, thus allowing them to be killed with impunity; Spartan youths were enrolled in the Krypteia, or Secret Society, whose job it was to murder subversive helots. Conversely, the helots became a magnet for intrigues by Sparta's external enemies, such as Athens in the 400s B.C.E. But helot freedom had to wait until 369 B.C.E., when the triumphant Theban leader EPAMINONDAS liberated the helots of Messenia (although not those of Laconia), setting up an independent Messenian state.

Meanwhile, Sparta came into conflict with the one southern Greek power that could challenge Spartan ambition—the city of ARGOS, in the northeastern Peloponnese. In 669 B.C.E. a Spartan army was defeated by an Argive army at Hysiai, on the road to Argos. Modern scholars believe that the battle involved the victory of organized hoplite tactics, as perfected by the Argive king PHEIDON, over the old-fashioned, individualistic fighting of the aristocratic Spartan army. Scholars further believe

that the defeat fully discredited the aristocratic leadership at Sparta and brought on drastic changes in government, society, and military organization, through the reforms of Lykourgos.

Lykourgos changed Sparta from a narrow aristocracy to a broad-based oligarchy. That is, he brought middle-class Spartan men into the government as voters and soldiers, creating an enlarged citizen body of about 9,000 adult males. Henceforth, perhaps once a month, all citizens over age 30 gathered at the *apella,* or ASSEMBLY, to vote on proposals framed by a 30-man council called the *gerousia* ("the elders"), which included the two kings. The assembly could vote only "yes" or "no" and not initiate any business. But its voting included such duties as declaring war or peace, ratifying the appointment of military leaders, and electing ephors and council members aside from the kings. Council members had to be 60 or more years old; they held office for the rest of their lives. Although elected annually, ephors had immense power as chief legal officials and as monitors controlling the kings' conduct.

In theory any citizen could be elected to the council or ephorate, but in practice these offices probably tended to be filled by members of a few rich and prestigious families. Both the council and the ephorate were probably survivals of the old aristocratic government, now adapted to the Lykourgan government.

Most significant, Lykourgos's system created a large, full-time hoplite army, supported by Sparta's captured territories. The 9,000 full-rank citizens—the Spartiates—henceforth were barred from practicing any profession aside from soldiering; crafts and TRADE became solely the province of the perioikoi. Instead, every male Spartiate (excepting perhaps the rich) received an allotment of public land in Messenia or Laconia. Farmed by helots overseen by state officers, the allotment produced food that supported the citizen and his family; the citizen was thus free to devote himself to lifelong military drill and campaigning.

Of all Greek city-states, only Sparta had a permanent soldiering class, free of the need to earn a livelihood as farmers or craftsmen. Spartan armies, for example, could campaign through late summer and autumn, when other states' farmer-soldiers might feel obliged to return home for their various sowings and harvests.

The Spartiates—the full-rank male Spartan citizens—sometimes called themselves *homoioi,* "equals." They were equal in that each man had a land allotment (although rich families undoubtedly kept their traditional estates in Laconia) and each had one vote in the assembly. But *homoioi* also means "those who are all the same," and this nuance reveals the essence of Lykourgos's reforms. Sparta became a city where concepts of the individual and the family were erased, in favor of a grim system of conformity and state service.

An individual Spartiate reached full citizenship by meeting three requirements: legitimate birth to Spartiate-rank parents, completion of a 13-year-long boyhood training program called the *agogē,* and election at age 20 to one of the communal dining messes that were the center of Spartan adult male life. The *agogē* process is described in the writings of Plutarch and Xenophon. At birth, boys (and girls) were examined for health and were accepted or rejected by state officials—not by the family father, as elsewhere in the Greek world. Those rejected were killed. At age seven, boys were taken from their mothers, to be brought up in "packs" under supervision of older boys who reported to a state officer. By age 12, boys lived in barracks, sleeping on mattresses of river rushes that they gathered themselves. Year round they went shoeless and were allowed only one outer garment, a kind of cloak. Their staple diet was a kind of pork-boiled porridge—the famous "Spartan broth"—which they were encouraged to supplement by stealing food from local storages and farms. If caught stealing, they were beaten for their clumsiness.

Boys received schooling in traditional Spartan musical art forms, such as competitive choral singing and dancing, but book-learning was minor. Their EDUCATION was mainly physical—combat-type sports and games. They exercised naked outdoors in all weather. They were subjected to routine hazing and abuse by the older boys, intended to toughen them. Homosexual pairings between older and younger boys were officially encouraged, as being helpful to patriotic esprit.

Foremost, boys were taught to obey orders and endure hardship without complaint. Scrutinized and judged by their elders, they grew up fearing disgrace more than death. Plutarch recounts how a Spartan boy somehow stole a fox cub and hid it under his cloak, only to have the animal start biting out his insides. Rather than cry out or otherwise reveal his theft, the child collapsed and died without a whimper.

The training program was designed to prepare boys for a soldiering life and to weed out anyone unsuitable for full citizenship. For each young male the reckoning came at age 20, when he sought admittance to one of the Spartan dining messes (Greek: *sussitia*). Each *sussition* probably consisted of about 15 men, who voted among themselves whether to admit or reject a candidate. Once selected, a new member remained part of the mess for life, barring expulsion, and he contributed a portion of his land's produce to help feed the group. (Their diet seems to have been far more ample and varied than the boyhood fare.) A man's mess-mates—not his family—were the center of his life and identity.

Thus, at Sparta, a man's most intense feelings were normally directed at other males. Men were still expected to marry citizen-rank WOMEN and breed children, but MARRIAGE was not a deeply emotional affair. Probably until age 30 a male Spartan continued to live with his mess-mates, visiting his wife only in secret. And Spartan law even allowed a husband to arrange for his wife to sleep with another suitable man, possibly at her request—a custom that other Greeks found outrageous.

The Spartan screening system inevitably created classes of citizens in between the Spartiates and perioikoi. Spartiates who failed to win admittance to a sussition—or who were expelled because of cowardice or inability to provide a share of food—ceased to be Spartiates and descended to a rank known as Inferiors. Conversely, individual perioikoi boys might be selected for the rugged Spartiate training program, but it is unclear whether such boys could ever attain full citizenship. A tendency to exclude groups on grounds of inferior birth was a deeply ingrained aspect of Spartan mentality: as early as 700 B.C.E. (probably before Lykourgos's reforms) a rejected group called "the sons of virgins" sailed off to found Sparta's only major colony, TARAS, in southern ITALY.

Sparta's extreme social conditions created an unusual life for women, as well. Sparta was unique among ancient Greek cities in the freedom it granted to its female citizens—this was partly due to reliance on women to manage estates while men were away at war. Somewhat similarly to boys, Spartan girls received training in choral singing, dancing, and gymnastics. Scandalously (as it seemed to other Greeks), Spartan girls exercised in public, naked or scantily clad. Like boys, Spartan girls apparently might experience homosexual love affairs in the course of their upbringing—as suggested in extant verses by the poet ALCMAN (ca. 620 B.C.E.). Spartan women had a unique reputation for heterosexual initiative and promiscuity. At least some of these conditions were intended to mold Spartan females into healthy and capable child-bearers, to supply future soldiers for the state.

Yet for reasons that are not clear, Sparta eventually faced a dwindling of its Spartiate population (as opposed to the perioikoi or helots). Perhaps Spartan marriages were unproductive, with the problem worsened by the brutal screening system. The shrinkage reached crisis proportions after 464 B.C.E., when a catastrophic earthquake wiped out large numbers of Spartiates in the city center. By 425 B.C.E. the Spartiates numbered no more than 3,000—whereas Lykourgos in the mid-600s B.C.E. had made arrangements based on a population of 9,000.

In theory, Sparta's population problem could have been eased by promoting large numbers of perioikoi up to Spartiate status. Although this drastic measure was proposed amid Sparta's political turmoil of the 200s B.C.E. it was never carried out. Spartiates viewed themselves as an ethnically distinct elite, raised from birth to dominate "lesser" peoples. Their mentality did not allow for mass enrollments of new citizens.

Another long-term result of Lykourgos's reforms was loss of trade and arts. Although the late 600s B.C.E. saw Sparta's cultural heyday—with verses being written by choral poets such as Alcman and TYRTAEUS, and Laconian perioikoi bronzesmiths producing a valued metalwork for export—in the 500s B.C.E. Sparta's crafts declined, even as the city thrived. A major reason for this was Sparta's decision not to adopt COINAGE, an invention that revolutionized Greek trade soon after 600 B.C.E. Instead of using coins, Sparta retained a primitive, awkward currency of IRON rods, thereby assuring itself, intentionally, of economic and cultural isolation.

The 500s B.C.E. saw Sparta dominate the Peloponnese, to become the foremost mainland Greek city. After an attempt to conquer ARCADIA met with defeat (around 570 B.C.E.), Sparta changed its policy toward its Peloponnesian neighbors: instead of seeking to crush and helotize them (which was certain to inspire fierce resistance), Sparta began offering them a place in a Spartan-led alliance that modern scholars call the Peloponnesian League. This "league policy" is sometimes associated with the Spartan ephor CHILON, ca. 556 B.C.E. Eventually the league embraced most Peloponnesian states except Argos, which remained Sparta's enemy but was badly defeated in wars in 546 and 494 B.C.E. Sparta's staunchest allies in the league included TEGEA, CORINTH, and ELIS.

Sparta reached its peak under its most capable king, the first KLEOMENES (1), who reigned ca. 520–490 B.C.E and tried to organize all of Greece against the coming Persian invasion. During the PERSIAN WARS (490–479 B.C.E.), Sparta led the land-army defense of mainland Greece, alongside the Athenian-led defense at sea. The final victory brought Sparta immense prestige—which it soon lost to Athens.

The years 478–431 B.C.E. saw a steady worsening of Sparta's relations with Athens. Thucydides relates that the Spartans feared the growth of Athenian power—specifically Athens's naval empire organized through the DELIAN LEAGUE. Sparta also feared the appeal and aggressive export of Athenian democracy, so dangerous to Sparta's oligarchic friends in its allied cities. Spartan-Athenian hostility culminated in the huge Peloponnesian War (431–404 B.C.E.). A hard-fought victory left Sparta dominant over an exhausted Greece.

Sparta had by now acquired a navy and an important foreign ally, the empire of PERSIA, but Sparta's turn as an imperial power was destined to last barely a generation. By harsh rule in Greece and adventuring in ASIA MINOR, Sparta managed to unite several of its former allies and enemies, including Persia, Corinth, Thebes, Athens, and Argos, in a war against itself. This CORINTHIAN WAR ended with Spartan hypocrisy exposed by the shameful terms of the KING'S PEACE (386 B.C.E.); far from seeking to liberate the Greek cities of Asia Minor from Persian rule as they claimed, the Spartans just wanted to retain power in Greece.

Growing anti-Spartan anger fueled the emergence of a challenger state, Thebes. The Spartan king AGESILAUS, despite personal virtues, proved blind to the danger posed by the Theban leader Epaminondas. At the Battle of LEUKTRA (371 B.C.E.) the age-old myth of Spartan invincibility was shattered: A Spartan army was destroyed

and Sparta thrown forever on the defensive. Invading Laconia for the first time in its history, Epaminondas decided not to attack Sparta itself. But he proceeded to dismantle the Spartan empire, by freeing Messenia and Arcadia from Spartan domination (369–368 B.C.E.). Messenia's liberation in particular was devastating to Sparta, since it removed the city's source of surplus food. With these events, the Peloponnesian League more or less dissolved.

Sparta remained resistant to Thebes and then to the Macedonians, who conquered Greece in 338 B.C.E. While the Macedonian king ALEXANDER THE GREAT campaigned through distant Persia, the Spartan king Agis III led a few Peloponnesian states in revolt. But he was defeated and killed at the Battle of Megalopolis, at the hands of the Macedonian regent ANTIPATER (331 B.C.E.).

By the mid-200s B.C.E. Sparta was a relatively poor state, its citizen body shrunken to a mere 700 Spartiates, vastly outnumbered by perioikoi and helots. In foreign policy, Sparta lay on the defensive against the Achaean League, which was now the dominant Peloponnesian power. This era saw the final significant moments of Spartan history. Hoping to revive the city's prior greatness, the young king Agis IV tried to abolish debts, redistribute land, and enroll perioikoi as new citizens. Opposed by conservative Spartiates, Agis died violently (241 B.C.E.), but his revolutionary plan inspired a new king, Kleomenes III.

After a few years on the throne, Kleomenes discarded constitutional kingship and seized absolute power (226 B.C.E.). He abolished the ephorate, redistributed the land into 4,000 lots, and enrolled perioikoi as full citizens. Next, seeking to recover Sparta's military supremacy in the Peloponnese, he waged war with the armies of the Achaean League. But when the Achaean League leader Aratus invited the powerful Macedonian king Antigonus III to intervene, Sparta's revival was doomed. At the Battle of Sellasia, just north of Sparta, Antigonus destroyed a Spartan army (222 B.C.E.). Kleomenes fled into exile, soon to die, while Antigonus seized Sparta and canceled Kleomenes' reforms.

Of the Spartan kings who came later, Nabis was a noteworthy adventurer during and after the Second Macedonian War (220–197 B.C.E.) By 146 B.C.E., however, Sparta and all of Greece had passed into Roman hands. During the first century C.E., under the Roman Empire, Sparta enjoyed a revival as a tourist attraction. Spectators were regaled by the sight of such age-old endurance contests as Spartan boys running the gauntlet of whips at the altar of Artemis Orthia.

Excavation on the ACROPOLIS of Sparta was begun by Greek and American archaeologists in the late 1800s C.E. Since 1905, work at the site has been under the auspices of the British Archaeological School at Athens. This team investigated the sanctuary of Artemis Orthia in 1906–1910. A new program of excavation (still by the

British Archaeological School) was undertaken in the 1990s, concentrating on the area around the THEATER and the shops.

See also ACHAEA; AGIAD CLAN; EURYPONTID CLAN; HOMOSEXUALITY; KIMON; LYSANDER; MUSIC; TYRANTS; WARFARE, LAND.

Further reading: L. F. Fitzhardinge, *The Spartans* (London: Thames and Hudson, 1980); Richard J. A. Talbert, trans., *Plutarch on Sparta* (New York: Penguin Books, 1988); Anton Powell, ed., *Classical Sparta: Techniques Behind Her Success* (Norman: University of Oklahoma Press, 1989); Paul Cartledge, *Hellenistic and Roman Sparta: A Tale of Two Cities* (London: Routledge, 1992); Michael Whitby, ed., *Sparta* (Edinburgh: Edinburgh University Press, 2002).

Speusippus *See* ACADEMY; PLATO.

sport As early as the 700s B.C.E., the ancient Greeks revered competitive sports, especially for men and boys. Sport was seen as a character-building facet of a youth's EDUCATION and as a means of demonstrating the gods' favor for certain contestants. Individual events were overwhelmingly preferred to team sports. The most popular events at public competitions included foot races (200 yards, 400 yards, long distance, and the race in armor), field events (long jump, discus throw, and javelin throw), combative events (WRESTLING, BOXING, and PANKRATION), and the horse races and chariot races.

The Greeks' love of sport was also closely related to the glorification of male strength and beauty. In most public competitions, males competed naked or nearly so, their bodies anointed with oil. Most of the prestigious athletic festivals were restricted to men, since this type of public physical display was considered inappropriate for Greek WOMEN. Women and girls, however, were not completely barred from sports in ancient Greece. SPARTA, for instance, maintained a vigorous program of girls' gymnastics, and the Olympic Games included a foot race for girls (dedicated to the goddess HERA and held outside the main sanctuary where the other events took place). When they did compete, the female athletes wore tunics.

The Greeks constantly associated sport with RELIGION. Their major competitions took place at festivals held in the honor of the gods; the most famous of these were the OLYMPIC GAMES, sacred to the great god ZEUS. Every Greek city-state had its own schedule of local festivals, where athletes might compete in honor of the city's patron gods. In every city, the GYMNASIUM was an important public institution, where the wealthier men might pass the day in socializing and political discussions, as well as sports practice. The Greeks' serious approach to sports was an aspect of Greek culture that attracted many non-Greek peoples—including ETRUSCANS, Romans, and certain JEWS—who came into contact with the Greeks in the Classical and Hellenistic eras.

See also CHARIOTS; HOMOSEXUALITY; ISTHMIAN GAMES; NEMEAN GAMES; PENTATHLON; PINDAR; PYTHIAN GAMES.

Further reading: Wendy J. Raschke, ed., *The Archaeology of the Olympics: The Olympics and Other Festivals in Antiquity* (Madison: University of Wisconsin Press, 1988); David Sansone, *Greek Athletics and the Genesis of Sport* (Berkeley: University of California Press, 1988); Stephen G. Miller, ed., *Arete: Greek Sports from Ancient Sources,* 2d ed. (Berkeley: University of California Press, 1991); Thomas F. Scanlon, *Eros and Greek Athletics* (New York: Oxford University Press, 2002); Stephen G. Miller, *Ancient Greek Athletics* (New Haven, Conn.: Yale University Press, 2004); William Blake Tyrrell, *The Smell of Sweat: Greek Athletics, Olympics, and Culture* (Wauconda, Ill.: Bolchazy-Carducci Publishers, 2004).

statues *See* SCULPTURE.

Stesichorus (632–552 B.C.E.) *Important Greek lyric poet, usually associated with the Sicilian-Greek city of* HIMERA

Stesichoros, meaning "chorus master," may have been a title; according to one story, the man's real name was Tisias. Prolific and inventive, Stesichoras was the first west Greek literary celebrity, and he strongly influenced later generations of Greek poets. He was known for his long narrative poems on mythological subjects, perhaps 26 in number. Of these, much has been lost; the remnants survive mainly in quotations by later writers and in some recovered ancient papyrus fragments, published in 1973 C.E., containing portions of Stesichorus's poem *Geryoneis* (about the mythical creature Geryon, who was slain by HERAKLES).

Writing in the Doric Greek dialect, Stesichorus told tales inspired by HOMER's verses and by other poems of the epic cycle. In the *Wooden Horse,* the *Capture of Troy,* and *Homecomings,* he described the TROJAN WAR and its aftermath. His *Oresteia*—about the murder of AGAMEMNON and the vengeance taken by his son, ORESTES—almost certainly later influenced the *Oresteia* stage trilogy by the Athenian playwright AESCHYLUS.

Stesichorus was both clever and verbose. The *Geryoneis* ran at least 1,300 lines (probably much longer) and featured a sympathetic portrait of the three-bodied Geryon, who traditionally had been presented as a fierce monster.

It is not known how Stesichorus's poems were performed. He usually is called a choral poet, meaning that his work typically would have been sung or chanted by a trained chorus at a public event. However, his more recently discovered verses seem to lack certain hallmarks of choral song, leading certain scholars to believe that at least some of Stesichorus's poems were written for a solo singer accompanying himself on the lyre. Perhaps this performer was the poet himself.

Stesichorus is traditionally credited with inventing the "triad"—a three-stanza metrical grouping that became an essential element in lyric verse and Athenian stage drama. The triad consisted of the *strophē*, or "turn," the *antistrophē*, "counterturn," and the *epodos*, "after-song." This sequence was repeated throughout the poem. The strophe and antistrophe had to be metrically identical; the epode was different. Supposedly the names denote the chorus' motions in singing the parts—dancing rightward on the strophe, leftward on the antistrophe, and standing still for the epode.

One well-known story claims that Stesichorus wrote two different poems dealing with the mythical HELEN OF TROY. The first was a conventional treatment of Helen's adulterous elopement with the Trojan prince PARIS. The second poem, entitled the *Palinodia* (retraction), claimed that the first version was untrue and that Helen had never left her Spartan husband, MENELAUS. This version instead said that the gods had sent a phantom-Helen to TROY, so that the city's doom might be fulfilled.

The daring contrivance of this palinode was much admired in the ancient world and gave rise to a legend: Supposedly, after writing the first Helen poem, Stesichorus was struck blind. Only after publishing the retraction did the poet regain his sight.

A recently rediscovered fragment of poetry by Stesichorus has become the focus of a scholarly debate about the foundation of the city of ROME. The poet describes a woman named Roma fleeing Troy after the TROJAN WAR with a fleet of ships and landed in Italy, where they founded the new city. Most ancient authors claimed instead that the city was named after the hero Romulus, with its foundation traditionally dated to 753 B.C.E. Stesichorus, having lived just about a century after this date, is an older source and thus perhaps a more accurate one. It is an interesting question about which more research is needed, perhaps through the discovery of additional fragments by Stesichorus and other ancient Greek and Roman poets.

See also LYRIC POETRY; MUSIC.

Further reading: M. Davies, "Stesichorus' 'Geryoneis' and Its Folk-tale Origins," *Classical Quarterly* 38 (1988): 277–290; G. O. Hutchinson, *Greek Lyric Poetry: A Commentary on Selected Larger Pieces: Alcman, Stesichorus, Sappho, Alcaeus, Ibycus, Anacreon, Simonides, Bacchylides, Pindar, Sophokles, Euripides* (New York: Oxford University Press, 2001).

Stoicism   This school of Greek PHILOSOPHY was founded at ATHENS around 300 B.C.E. by Zeno, a Cypriot of Phoenician-Greek descent. With its ideal of a virtuous life impervious to misfortune, and its assurance of an ordered universe in which the individual person played a role, Sto-

icism addressed certain feelings of change and doubt that accompanied the start of the HELLENISTIC AGE.

During Hellenistic times (around 300–150 B.C.E.), Stoicism remained a modest influence, about equal to its major rival philosophy, EPICUREANISM. But once introduced at the non-Greek city of ROME in about 144 B.C.E., Stoicism captured the Roman mentality (more so than the Greek) and grew into the major intellectual movement of the early Roman Empire. Unlike Epicureanism, Stoicism encouraged its followers to engage in the public life of government, and many ruling-class Romans were Stoics, such as the statesman Seneca the Younger (ca. 60 C.E.) and the emperor Marcus Aurelius (ca. 170 C.E.).

Stoicism's long history is divided by scholars into three phases, called the Early, Middle, and Late Stoa. The Middle Stoa, around 144–30 B.C.E., saw Stoicism transplanted to Rome, where it flourished as the Late Stoa, around 30 B.C.E.–mid-200s C.E. Although finally submerged by the spread of Christianity, Stoicism helped to shape the ethical outlook of early Christian thinkers. Most modern knowledge of Stoicism comes from extant Greek and Latin writings of the late period. The early Stoic writings survive only in brief quotations or summaries by later authors.

Zeno, the Stoic founder, immigrated to Athens as a young man and probably studied the teachings of the Athenian CYNICS. By about age 33 he had created his own philosophy, borrowing Cynic ethical theories of self-sufficiency along with select teachings of PLATO and others. Zeno presented his new ideas in public lectures and disputations in a part of the Athenian AGORA known as the Stoa Poikilē, or Painted Colonnade. This locale gave the new movement its name.

Zeno died around 261 B.C.E., bequeathing his school to a disciple named Cleanthes. Cleanthes' successor was Chrysippus (president 232–207 B.C.E.), a highly important thinker. His writings (not extant today) clarified Zeno's teachings and fused Stoic ethics, scientific theories, and theories of knowledge into a coherent, interconnected system.

Although most ancient Greeks worshipped many gods, the Stoics inclined toward belief in a single divinity. They pictured a universe imbued with a divine purpose or intelligence, variously referred to as reason (Greek: *logos*), fire, breath, or FATE. Every human being, they believed, contained a small version of the divine purpose, which is demonstrated in the human ability to reason, plan and give speech (*logos*).

This idea of a shared divine spark is background to one of Stoicism's most appealing teachings: the essential brotherhood of all people. The Stoic was taught to ignore distinctions of wealth and birth and to see all humans, including WOMEN and SLAVES, as being spiritually the same material.

Stoicism recognized only two classes of people: the virtuous and the wicked. Like SOCRATES and Plato, the

Stoics described virtue (Greek: *aretē*) as a form of knowledge or wisdom. Courage, moderation, and other virtues were evidence of this wisdom; greed, fear, sensuality were symptoms of ignorance. Wisdom produced virtue and virtue produced happiness; the greedy or dishonest person could not, by definition, be happy. In life, virtue was to be exercised, not in the cloistered setting that Epicureanism favored, but in areas of social responsibility: earning a living, raising a family, holding public office.

Contrary to some popular belief, the Stoics did not seek out pain. But they believed that pain, poverty, and death were not to be feared, since those ills could not harm a person's virtue. The Stoic therefore, could find consolation in adversity: Happiness dwelt within, unaffected by external misfortune or external success. "Only the wise man is rich," a Stoic proverb ran. The Stoic tried to emulate the calm and grandeur of the universe, by accepting all events in life with a serene mind. This state of mind the Stoics called *apatheia*, "absence of passion."

Stoicism involved many other beliefs in fields such as logic and SCIENCE, but it was its noble, reassuring ethical system that made Stoicism so popular in later antiquity. Today we still use the adjectives "stoic" and "stoical" to denote an indifference to pain or misfortune.

Further reading: Brad Inwood, *Ethics and Human Action in Early Stoicism* (Oxford: Clarendon Press, 1987); Andrew Erskine, *The Hellenistic Stoa: Political Thought and Action* (Ithaca, N.Y.: Cornell University Press, 1990); Julia Annas, *Hellenistic Philosophy of Mind* (Berkeley: University of California Press, 1992); Brad Inwood, ed., *The Cambridge Companion to the Stoics* (New York: Cambridge University Press, 2003); John Sellars, *The Art of Living: The Stoics on the Nature and Function of Philosophy* (Burlington, Vt.: Ashgate, 2003).

Styx *See* AFTERLIFE.

Sybaris This affluent Greek city on the Gulf of Taranto is located on the "instep" of the southern coast of ITALY. Founded by colonists from ACHAEA in around 720 B.C.E., Sybaris grew rich from its fertile farmland and its TRADE with the ETRUSCANS of the north. The city's reputation for luxury has produced the English word *sybarite*, meaning "someone excessively devoted to pleasure."

Sybaris enlarged its territory at the expense of local non-Greeks and founded Italian colonies of its own, including POSEIDONIA (Paestum). But rivalry with the nearly Greek city of CROTON led to a war, in which Sybaris was defeated and obliterated (510 B.C.E.). Nearly 70 years later, the Athenians established the colony Thurii near the site of Sybaris.

Further reading: F. G. Rainey and C. M. Lerici, *The Search for Sybaris, 1960–1965* (Rome: Lerici Editori, 1967); F. G. Rainey, "The Location of Archaic Greek Sybaris," *American Journal of Archaeology* 73 (1969): 261–173; O. H. Bullitt, *Search for Sybaris* (Philadelphia: Lippincott, 1969); N. K. Rutter, "Sybaris, Legend and Reality," *Greece and Rome* 17 (1970): 168–176; O. C. Colburn, "A Return to Sybaris," *Expedition* 18 (1975–1976): 2–13.

symposium A type of all-male, after-dinner drinking party, the symposium (Greek: *symposion*, "drinking together", plural: *symposia*) played a vital role in ancient Greek aristocratic life. Only the rich could afford to host symposia; and the symposium's expense, its male homosexual or bisexual aspect, and its intellectual games were all part of a separate aristocratic identity.

Symposia were frequent subjects on Greek vase paintings, often decorating the very vessels that would be used at the party, particularly the cups used for drinking wine (*kylikes*, singular: *kylix*). These scenes show groups of older men (usually bearded) reclining on couches and attended by young male SLAVES. The parties seem to have taken place in specially designated rooms of the host's house, with wine pitchers and cups often visible hanging on hooks in the background. The occasional WOMEN who appear are HETAIRAI, PROSTITUTES or courtesans. Such women might be dancers or flute girls, but they would also be obliged to give sexual favors.

The feasting of kings and their retainers goes back to prehistoric times. The poems of HOMER, written down around 750 B.C.E. describe aristocratic warriors sitting at banquets. By the 600s B.C.E. the symposium had arisen, probably through Phoenician influence, as a new form of social gathering. Snacks such as sesame cakes might be served, but the symposium's central activity was the semiritualistic drinking of WINE. All the drinkers were men, of equal noble status. The servers and entertainers were typically young female and male SLAVES chosen for their beauty.

The symposium was the natural setting for hetairai and extramarital heterosexual encounters. Similarly, according to ancient Greek aristocratic taste, the symposium would be the scene of various homosexual attractions, whether between guests or involving a guest and slave. One anecdote tells how the great Athenian playwright SOPHOKLES coaxed a kiss from a slave boy at a symposium (around 440 B.C.E.). A surviving tomb painting from POSEIDONIA (around 480 B.C.E.) shows a youthful guest warding off a caress from his couchmate, a slightly older man.

The symposium was governed by rules. The typical "symposiast" (reveler) did not sit but rather reclined on a couch, propped up on his left elbow, Phoenician style. There were usually between seven and 15 couches, with two men to each. One of the drinkers was appointed "king," or master of ceremonies, to decide on the sequence of activities.

Symposia had their own equipment, including many of the forms of Greek POTTERY that are known from

ARCHAEOLOGY. The men drank from cups such as the *kylix*—wide and shallow, for sipping on the recline. According to Greek custom, the wine was diluted with water, usually one part wine to two or three water. The mixture was prepared in a large bowl, the *kratēr*, and from there distributed by slaves to the drinkers' cups. During the festivities the wine-to-water ratio might be altered according to the wishes of the "king," but drinking undiluted wine was considered very unhealthy. Games included *kottabos* (in which wine dregs were flicked from the cup at a target) and competitive singing by individual symposiasts to flute accompaniment—the origin of the Greek verse form known as the elegy.

Undoubtedly events could grow wild as men got drunk—for example, more than one vase painting shows *hetairai* climbing onto couches to embrace guests. The party might end in a *komos*, a drunken torchlight procession in honor of DIONYSUS, the wine god.

But symposia were also the setting for philosophical and, especially, political discussion. The symposiasts were usually men of right-wing views, and the symposium was designed to foster a sense of exclusivity in an atmosphere of male bonding. At ATHENS and other democracies, such a strong minority could be subversive. The right-wing conspiracies that threatened democratic Athens in 457, 411, and 404 B.C.E. were surely hatched in gatherings such as symposia.

The symposium's dual intellectual-sexual nature is conveyed in idealized terms by the philosopher PLATO, in his dialogue titled the *Symposium*. In this fictional account, SOCRATES, ARISTOPHANES, ALCIBIADES, and other notable fifth-century-B.C.E. Athenians meet to drink and discuss the nature of sexual love.

See also ALCAEUS; ANACREON; ARISTOCRACY; HOMO-SEXUALITY; LYRIC POETRY; MUSIC; OLIGARCHY; PHOENICIA; POTTERY; PROSTITUTES.

Further reading: Michael Vickers, *Greek Symposia* (London: Joint Association of Classical Teachers, 1978); O. Murray, ed., *Sympotica. A Symposium on the Symposion* (Oxford: Oxford University Press, 1990); William J. Slater, *Dining in a Classical Context* (Ann Arbor: University of Michigan Press, 1991); Susan Rotroff and John Oakley, *Debris from a Public Dining Place in the Athenian Agora* (Princeton, N.J.: American School of Classical Studies at Athens, 1992).

Syracuse The preeminent Greek city of SICILY, Syracuse was also one of the grandest and most violent cities of Greek history. Under a series of military dictators in the 400s–200s B.C.E., the city led the Sicilian Greeks in their constant struggle against the Carthaginians, who occupied Sicily's western corner. Syracuse played a major role in the downfall of ATHENS during the PELOPON-NESIAN WAR, when the Syracusans totally destroyed an Athenian invasion force (413 B.C.E.). By the first half of the 300s B.C.E., Syracuse vied with North African CARTHAGE for control of the western Mediterranean, before falling to the expansionism of ROME (211 B.C.E.).

Syracuse (now the Sicilian city of Siracusa) was one of the earliest Greek colonies. Located on the south part of Sicily's east coast, it was founded in about 733 B.C.E. by shipborne Corinthian settlers who subdued the local native Sicels. The site combined fertile coastal farmland with the best harbor of eastern Sicily—a double harbor, formed by the inshore island Ortygia ("quail island"). The Greeks fortified Ortygia and the mainland opposite, eventually linking them with a causeway and bridge.

The Syracuse colony was undoubtedly intended as a breadbasket for its mother city, CORINTH. Syracuse's surplus harvest of barley and wheat was probably offered first for sale to the Corinthians.

Like Corinth, Syracuse in the 700s–500s B.C.E. was governed as an ARISTOCRACY. The descendants of the first settlers became a ruling class known as the Gamoroi, "landholders," who lived in the city and whose farms occupied the best land of the plain. Lower on the social ladder were the descendants of later Greek arrivals, who might be craftsmen in the city or have smallholdings in the hills. Lowest of all were the Sicel-ethnic serfs, who tilled the land for their Greek masters (and whose condition resembled that the Spartan HELOTS). These distinctive social layers created class hatreds, which—when added to the external menace of the Carthaginians and native Sicilian tribes—were destined to have important political consequences. By the 400s B.C.E. Syracuse saw TYRANTS (*tyrannoi,* "dictators") arising, as champions of the common people and as promisers of military security.

The first tyrant was GELON; ruler of the nearby Greek city of GELA, who seized Syracuse under pretext of aiding the beleaguered Gamoroi (485 B.C.E.). Gelon transferred his capital to Syracuse and from there ruled as the most powerful individual in the Greek world. He led Greek Sicily to victory against the Carthaginians at the Battle of HIMERA (480 B.C.E.), and he extended the Syracusan empire westward, subjugating Carthaginians, Greeks, and natives across two-thirds of Sicily.

Gelon was succeeded by his brother HIERON (1), who ruled 478–467 B.C.E. and extended Syracusan power to Greek ITALY with his defeat of the Etruscans at the sea battle of CUMAE (474 B.C.E.). Under Hieron, Syracuse became a cultural capital, attracting literary artists of old Greece, such as AESCHYLUS, PINDAR, SIMONIDES, and BACCHYLIDES. The Greek amphitheater, ancient Syracuse's best-known surviving remnant, was first built under Hieron, quite possibly for the performance of Aeschylus's play *Women of Etna* (476 B.C.E.). A Sicilian Greek playwright Epicharmus, probably a Syracusan, is said to have pioneered the writing of stage comedy in the early 400s B.C.E.

After Hieron's death, the tyranny was overthrown (466 B.C.E.). A Syracusan DEMOCRACY, based on the Athenian model, lasted for about 60 years. During this time

Syracuse remained the foremost Dorian-Greek city of Sicily, and was hostile to such local Ionian-Greek cities as Leontini. Eventually Syracuse's enemies appealed to the great city of Athens for help. The ambitious Athenians dreamed of capturing Syracuse's wheatfields and other riches, and in 415 B.C.E. they dispatched an ill-fated armada that eventually totaled perhaps 50,000 troops and 173 warships. The attackers besieged Syracuse but, after two years' fighting, were annihilated. The architects of this Syracusan triumph were the Spartan general Gylippus and the Syracusan statesman-general Hermocrates.

In 410 B.C.E. a new threat emerged, as the Carthaginians began a series of eastward campaigns in Sicily. Following so close after the Athenian attack, this crisis threw the Syracusan democracy into turmoil, and in about 405 B.C.E. there emerged a new dictator, DIONYSIUS (1), a military officer and former follower of Hermocrates (since killed in civil war). Seizing power, Dionysius married Hermocrates' daughter and embarked on a war that rolled the Carthaginians back from the very walls of Syracuse to Sicily's western corner. The ensuing peace (397 B.C.E.) left Greek Sicily securely under Syracusan protection and rule.

The prosperous years until Dionysius's death (367 B.C.E.) saw Syracuse as the magnificent capital of the western Greeks. Dionysius made Ortygia island his private citadel and fortified Syracuse's inland heights, called the Epipolae ("above the city"); still standing are the remains of one of his forts, now called the Castle of Euryalus. Like Hieron, Dionysius sought to attract poets and thinkers to his court. In 387 B.C.E. the Athenian philosopher PLATO made the first of his ill-fated visits to Syracuse. (The philosopher was unimpressed, complaining that in Sicily everyone overate twice a day and never slept alone.)

Dionysius's son and successor, Dionysius II, lacked his father's ability to rule successfully, and was ousted after 10 years. Greek Sicily relapsed into civil strife, and Syracuse's power declined.

The reorganization of Greek Sicily by the Corinthian commander TIMOLEON (345–ca. 340 B.C.E.) left Syracuse with a moderate OLIGARCHY on the Corinthian pattern. Yet, once again, a dictator emerged: AGATHOKLES, who ruled 317–287 B.C.E. The hectic events of his reign saw Syracuse again besieged by the Carthaginians and again leading the defense of Greek Sicily.

After Agathocles' death, a new autocrat emerged from the ranks of military officers: Hieron II, who in 269 B.C.E. declared himself king and whose 54-year reign brought Syracuse to its final peak of glory. Hieron wisely made an alliance with the emerging power of Rome.

Under him, Syracuse was one of the three great Greek cities of the HELLENISTIC AGE, along with ALEXANDRIA (1) and ANTIOCH. Syracuse's most famous citizen of this era was the mathematician-scientist ARCHIMEDES.

Syracuse's downfall came amid the conflict between Rome and Carthage. After Hieron's death (215 B.C.E.), his successor made a foolhardy alliance with Carthage that soon brought Syracuse under attack by Roman forces. From 213 to 211 B.C.E. the city's huge fortifications withstood the Roman siege: According to legend, the aged Archimedes invented a giant glass lens, designed to focus sun rays on Roman warships in the harbor and set them afire. But eventually the city's outer wall fell to night assault and its inner wall to treason. The Romans captured Syracuse amid slaughter and looting. Among the booty shipped back to Rome were statues and other art objects that spurred the Romans' fascination with Greek culture. Later, Syracuse became the chief city of Roman Sicily and eventually lost its Greek identity.

The main part of ancient Syracuse lies completely underneath the modern city, making it difficult to conduct extensive archaeological excavation. A few monuments have been located and investigated, including the theater, an altar of Gelon II, and a Roman amphitheater. The island of Ortygia, by contrast, is sparsely occupied today and preserves several buildings erected by the Greek colonists. The most important of these is the temple dedicated to the god APOLLO, built in the early 700s B.C.E. with numerous later architectural phases. The temple was discovered in 1862 C.E. and excavated in 1943. A second temple, dedicated to the great god ZEUS, was probably also built in the 700s B.C.E. Two other elaborate but unindentified temples sit on the highest point of the island. One, begun around 550 B.C.E., was never finished and represents the only Ionic-style temple known in Sicily (all the rest are constructed using the Doric order). The other temple was erected in the early 400s B.C.E., probably after Gelon's victory at the Battle of Himera in 480 B.C.E.

See also THEATER.

Further reading: Rita Salerno Carusi, *Syracuse and Its Province* (Syracuse, Italy: Istituto editoriale siciliano, 1985); *Syracuse: Art, History, Landscape* (Milan: Co. Graf. Editrice, 1986); Bonna Daix Wescoat, ed., *Syracuse, The Fairest Greek City: Ancient Art from the Museo Archeologico Regionale 'Paolo Orsi'* (Rome: De Luca edizioni d'arte, 1989); Brian Caven, *Dionysius I, War-lord of Sicily* (New Haven, Conn.: Yale University Press, 1990).

T

talent This large monetary unit was equivalent to a certain weight (Greek: *talanton*) of SILVER, usually about 58 pounds. The talent measure was in use well before the beginnings of Greek COINAGE (around 595 B.C.E.), and no talent coin existed. In ATHENS in the 400s to 300s B.C.E., a talent was considered equivalent to 6,000 of the silver coins known as drachmae.

Further reading: A. S. Henry, "Polis, Acropolis, and the Ten Talent Fund," *Chiron* 12 (1982): 91–118; M. L. Cook, "Timokrates' 50 Talents and the Cost of Ancient Warfare," *Eranos* 88 (1990): 69–97; John Melville-Jones, *Testimonia numaria: Greek and Latin Texts Concerning Ancient Greek Coinage* (London: Spink, 1993); David Schaps, *The Invention of Coinage and the Monetization of Ancient Greece* (Ann Arbor: University of Michigan Press, 2004).

Tantalus In HOMER's epic poem the *Odyssey,* the hero ODYSSEUS visits the Underworld (book 11), where he sees three great sinners who are suffering eternal punishment for having betrayed the friendship of the gods. The sinners are the giant Tityus and the mortals SISYPHUS and Tantalus. Described as an old man, Tantalus is tortured by unrelieved thirst and hunger. He stands in a cool pond up to his neck, with the boughs of fruit trees hanging above his head; but when he lowers his head to drink, the water drains away instantly, and when he reaches up for fruit, the boughs are lifted away by the wind. Tantalus's fate has given rise to our English word *tantalize,* meaning "to cause torment by showing but withholding something desirable." In Greek, the name Tantalus may have meant "sufferer."

Tantalus was described as a wealthy king in ASIA MINOR and a son of the great god ZEUS, but his good fortune brought on insane arrogance (HUBRIS). To test the omniscience of the gods, he invited them to a banquet, then he killed his own young son, PELOPS, and cooked him as the dish. Zeus and the other gods detected the trick; only the goddess DEMETER—distracted by grief for her lost daughter, PERSEPHONE—ate a few bites, from the shoulder. The divinities brought Pelops back to life, replacing the missing part of his shoulder with ivory. Tantalus was sent off to an eternal pain that mirrors his crime somewhat. Through Pelops, Tantalus was the ancestor of the mythical kings who eventually ruled MYCENAE, in Greece. This family of the Pelopidae included ATREUS, AGAMEMNON, and ORESTES; the misfortunes of this royal house can be understood partly as originating with Tantalus's crime.

See also AFTERLIFE; MYTH.

Further reading: C. Sourvinou-Inwood, "Crime and Punishment. Tityos, Tantalos, and Sisyphos in 'Odyssey' 11," *Bulletin of the Institute of Classical Studies* 33 (1986): 37–58.

Taras This Greek city was founded by Spartan colonists in the late 700s B.C.E. on the "instep" of the southern coast of ITALY. Often known by its Latin name, Tarentum, this city is now the Italian seaport of Taranto, located beside the Gulf of Taranto.

As the only colony established by SPARTA, Taras maintained a Spartan form of government until switching to DEMOCRACY, around 475 B.C.E. Taras thrived from FARMING, manufacturing (including POTTERY and jewelry), and Adriatic TRADE, despite the hostility of local Italian tribes. By the mid-400s B.C.E. it was the foremost Greek city of south Italy. The city's peak came in the 300s

B.C.E., when it was producing such luminaries as the philosopher-engineer Archytas and the philosopher-musical theorist Aristoxenus. But by midcentury Taras was being threatened by its Italian enemies—the nearby Lucanii and the more distant, expansionist city of ROME.

For help, Taras appealed to other Greek states. The last and best known of these episodes came in 280 B.C.E., when the dynamic King PYRRHUS of EPIRUS arrived with his army to fight the Romans. After early victories gave way to defeat, Pyrrhus withdrew.

Taras was captured by the Romans and became a Roman subject state (272 B.C.E.). Later it was an important port city of Roman Italy. Ancient Taras lies underneath the modern town of Taranto, so the visible archaeological remains are few and far between. There is a Doric temple on the ACROPOLIS, built around 575 B.C.E., and remains of domestic buildings have been located throughout the lower city, but these have not been systematically excavated or recorded. Another public building was discovered in 1880 C.E. on the grounds of the Villa Peripato. Numerous tombs have also been excavated, ranging in date from 800 to 100 B.C.E., many of which contained fine grave goods such as decorated Greek POTTERY. Neither of the two theaters known to have been in the ancient city has been found.

Further reading: Joseph C. Carter, *The Sculpture of Taras* (Philadelphia: American Philosophical Society, 1975); M. Philippides, "The Partheniai and the Foundation of Taras," *Ancient World* 2 (1979): 79–82; George C. Brauer Jr., *Taras: Its History and Coinage* (New Rochelle, N.Y.: A. D. Caratzos, 1986); M. Nafissi, "From Sparta to Taras. Nomina, Ktiseis, and Relationships between Colony and Mother City," in *Sparta. New Perspectives,* edited by Stephen Hodkinson and Anton Powell (London: Duckworth, 1999), 245–272.

Tarentum *See* TARAS.

Tartarus *See* AFTERLIFE.

Tegea This city in the southeastern part of the plain of ARCADIA was located along the main route between SPARTA, to the south, and ARGOS, to the northeast. Tegea was one of the two original Arcadian cities, the other being MANTINEIA, Tegea's rival.

Tegea arose around 600 B.C.E. from an amalgamation of local villages, formed to resist Spartan aggression. Renowned as fighters, the Tegeans defeated a Spartan invasion around 585 B.C.E., but in the mid-500s B.C.E. they made peace and became staunch Spartan allies. Tegean troops had the traditional privilege of occupying the left wing of the battle line in a Spartan-led army.

Tegean troops played a prominent role alongside the Spartans in the PELOPONNESIAN WAR (431–404 B.C.E.). But after Sparta's defeat by THEBES in 371 B.C.E., Tegea turned against the crippled Sparta and fought on the Theban side at the Battle of Mantinea (362 B.C.E.). Later, however, enmity with Mantinea brought Tegea back to a treaty with Sparta.

The glory of ancient Tegea was its temple of the goddess ATHENA. Destroyed by fire in 390 B.C.E., this shrine was rebuilt as the largest and grandest temple in southern Greece. The site lies three miles outside Tegea; the later temple's foundations and column fragments are visible today.

Excavations at Tegea were begun by the French Archaeological School in 1888–1889 C.E., under the direction of archaeologists G. Fougères and V. Bérard. The Temple of Athena Alea itself was first investigated by A. Milchhofer in 1879 and by W. Dörpfeld in 1882, and it was fully excavated by the French School between 1900 and 1910. Further excavations took place at Tegea in the 1960s, and the current program of work, begun in 1990, is being conducted by the Norwegian Institute at Athens under the leadership of E. Ostby.

Further reading: Andrew F. Stewart, *Skopas of Paros* (Park Ridge, N.J.: Noyes Press, 1977); Naomi J. Norman, "The Temple of Athena Alea at Tegea," *American Journal of Archaeology* 88 (1984): 169–194; E. Ostby, "The Archaic Temple of Athena Alea at Tegea," *Opuscula Atheniensia* 16 (1986): 75–102; Naomi J. Norman, "Asklepios and Hygeia and the Cult Statue at Tegea," *American Journal of Archaeology* 90 (1986): 425–430; Mary E. Voyatzis, *The Early Sanctuary of Athena Alea at Tegea and Other Archaic Sanctuaries in Arcadia* (Göteborg, Sweden: P. Aströms, 1990); ———, "Current Fieldwork at the Sanctuary of Athena Alea at Tegea," *Archaeological News* 17 (1992): 19–25; G. C. Nordquist, J. M. Luce, and E. Ostby, "The Sanctuary of Athena Alea at Tegea. First Preliminary Report (1990–1992)," *Opuscula Atheniensia* 20 (1994): 89–141; E. Ostby, "Recent Excavations in the Sanctuary of Athena Alea at Tegea, 1990–1993," in *Archaeology in the Peloponnese. New Excavations and Research,* edited by Kenneth Sheedy (Oxford: Oxbow Books, 1994), 39–63; G. C. Nordquist, "Evidence for Metalworking in Late Geometric Tegea," in *Trade and Production in Premonetary Greece. Production and the Craftsman. Proceedings of the 4th and 5th International Workshops, Athens 1994 and 1995,* edited by Carole Gillis, Christina Risberg, and Birgitta Sjöberg (Jonsered, Sweden: P. Aströms, 1997), 197–207; Jari Pakkanen, *The Temple of Athena Alea at Tegea. A Reconstruction of the Peristyle Column* (Helsinki, Finland: Department of Art History at the University of Helsinki, 1998); G. C. Nordquist, "Early Cult in the Sanctuary of Athena Alea at Tegea, Arcadia," in *Classical Archaeology towards the Third Millennium. Reflexions and Perspectives. Proceedings of the XVth International Congress of Classical Archaeology, Amsterdam, July 12–17, 1998* (Amsterdam: 1999), 282–284; Robin Hägg, ed., *Peloponnesian Sanctuaries and Cults: Proceedings of the Ninth International Symposium at the Swedish Institute at Athens,*

11–13 June 1994 (Stockholm: Svenska Institutet i Athen, 2002).

Teiresias In MYTH, this blind Theban seer was renowned for his wisdom and longevity; he was said to have lived for seven generations. In HOMER's epic poem the *Odyssey* (book 11), the hero ODYSSEUS visits the Underworld to consult the ghost of Teiresias, who prophesies as to what FATE awaits the hero at home and mentions certain precautions to observe on the return voyage.

Teiresias was not born blind; the best-known story about him tells how he lost his sight. Out walking one day, he encountered two snakes mating and hit them with his walking stick, killing the female. Immediately he was transformed into a woman, and remained so until, some time later, he again encountered two snakes mating. This time he killed the male and so regained his prior gender. Because Teiresias had had this unique experience, the god ZEUS and his wife, HERA, asked Teiresias to settle their argument as to who gets more pleasure from sexual intercourse, men or WOMEN. Zeus claimed it was women, but Hera insisted it was men. When Teiresias declared that women get nine times more pleasure than men, Hera angrily blinded him. But Zeus, to compensate, gave him long life and the inner sight of prophecy.

See also PROPHECY AND DIVINATION; SOPHOKLES.

Further reading: M. J. Alden, "Tiresias. A Boiotian Prophet in the 'Odyssey'," *EpetBoiotMel* 1 (1988): 183–193.

Telemachos In MYTH, this character was the son of King ODYSSEUS and PENELOPE. Telemachos's name, "distant battle," refers to his father's part in the TROJAN WAR, which began just when the boy was born. A subplot in HOMER's epic poem the *Odyssey* traces Telemachos's passage to maturity. At the *Odyssey's* opening, Telemachos, about 20 years old, is a dutiful but timid prince, overawed by the confident nobles who crowd his absent father's palace at ITHACA and compete for Penelope's hand in MARRIAGE. Unable to make them leave, Telemachos voyages by ship to the Peloponnesian courts of NESTOR and MENELAUS, to ask about the whereabouts of the father he has not seen since he was a baby. With the goddess ATHENA's help, Telemachos sails back to Ithaca (evading an ambush by the suitors en route and encounters his father, who has returned in disguise. By now the boy is showing considerable confidence and initiative. In the climactic scene, where Odysseus slaughters the suitors (book 22), Telemachos fights bravely alongside his father, sustaining a wrist wound.

Other legends add a few details about his life. Supposedly Telemachos later married his father's former paramour, CIRCE.

Further reading: Eva Brann, *Homeric Moments: Clues to Delight in Reading the Odyssey and the Iliad* (Philadelphia: Paul Dry Books, 2002).

Teos *See* IONIA.

Terpander (mid-600s B.C.E.) *Lyric poet*
Terpander came from the island of LESBOS but composed and performed at SPARTA. His name means "delight of man," and legend claims that his poetry soothed the Spartans at a time of civil crisis. Only a few lines ascribed to Terpander survive, and even these were probably not really written by him. He was apparently an important early figure in creating choral poetry as an art form and in making Sparta a center for that art. Almost certainly, he influenced the younger Spartan choral poet ALCMAN.

Terpander may have pioneered certain techniques in playing the lyre. However, the story crediting him with inventing the seven-stringed lyre (in place of four strings) is not true, as the seven-stringed type dates back to the second millenium B.C.E.

See also LYRIC POETRY; MUSIC.

Further reading: M. L. West, trans., *Greek Lyric Poetry: The Poems and Fragments of the Greek Iambic, Elegiac, and Melic Poets (excluding Pindar and Bacchylides) down to 450 B.C.* (New York: Oxford University Press, 1994).

Thales (ca. 634–546 B.C.E.) *Greek scientist and philosopher*
The first Greek thinker to try to explain the universe in nonreligious, rationalistic terms. Thales can be considered both the first scientist and the first philosopher in the West. He lived in MILETUS, in the flourishing Greek region called IONIA, in ASIA MINOR. Although he left no writings, he is best remembered for his theory that water is the fundamental constituent of all matter.

Thales and two of his followers, ANAXIMANDER and ANAXIMENES, comprise the first known philosophical movement: the Milesian School of natural philosophers. These men used physical observations to inquire about a primary substance in the universe. The significance of such thinkers is that they were the first to look for answers without reference to the traditional myths of the gods. Later generations considered Thales to be one of the SEVEN SAGES of Greece. He was famous in his lifetime, and took part in great events. In around 545 B.C.E., when Ionia was under attack by the Persian king CYRUS (1), Thales proposed the creation of a federated union of Ionian cities.

He established—probably on the basis of Babylonian or Egyptian learning—the studies of ASTRONOMY and geometry among the Greeks; he was believed to be the first Greek to accurately predict the year of a solar eclipse (probably in 585 B.C.E.). Like other Greek wise men, he is said to have traveled to EGYPT, where he supposedly calculated a pyramid's height by measuring its shadow simultaneously with that of his walking stick and calculating the ratios.

Thales was of partial Phoenician descent, and Near Eastern influences may lurk behind his emphasis on water and his theory that the earth floats like a log in a cosmic watery expanse. (This resembles the Semitic myth of watery creation in the biblical book of Genesis.) In Thales' mind however such ideas became scientific.

See also MATHEMATICS; PHILOSOPHY; PHOENICIA; SCIENCE.

Further reading: A. A. Mosshammer, "Thales' Eclipse," *Transactions of the American Philological Association* 111 (1981): 145–155; Patricia O'Grady, *Thales of Miletus: The Beginnings of Western Science and Philosophy* (Aldershot, U.K.: Ashgate, 2002).

Thasos This wealthy island of the northern AEGEAN SEA, lies six miles offshore of the non-Greek mainland of THRACE. Thasos is a round island, about 13 miles in diameter and rises to a central peak. The Greek poet ARCHILOCHUS sourly described it as sticking up like a donkey's back, topped with forests (ca. 670 B.C.E.). The main city was a seaport, also named Thasos (site of the modern Greek town of Limen); it lay at the north of the island, opposite the mainland.

As one of the very few Aegean sites to offer mineral deposits of GOLD, Thasos attracted Greek colonists at an early date, around 700 B.C.E. These colonists—of whom Archilochus eventually was one—came from the island of Paros in the CYCLADES. Although Thasos's mines were soon exhausted, the island served as a base from which to pursue mining and panning on the nearby Thracian mainland. The most important mainland prospecting area lay on the eastern slopes of Mt. Pangaeus, at a site called Skaptē Hulē ("dug-out wood"), about 25 miles due northwest of Thasos.

But the Pangaeus fields existed amid a hostile native people—the warlike Thracians. Much of Archilochus's surviving poetry describes fierce fighting against the "mop-haired men of Thrace," and what these verses seem to portray is Greek military protection for miners and for convoys of raw gold and SILVER, moving from the slopes of Pangaeus to the safe anchorage at Thasos.

The island grew rich from its exports of precious ore, TIMBER, local marble, and, probably, SLAVES acquired as Thracian war captives.

Thasos had a renowned school of SCULPTURE in the 600s and 500s B.C.E. and was the birthplace of the painter Polygnotus (ca. 475 B.C.E.).

The island surrendered to the advancing Persians under King DARIUS (1) in 491 B.C.E. After the Persian defeat in 479 B.C.E., Thasos joined the Athenian-controlled DELIAN LEAGUE, and, like most other Delian allies, reorganized its government as a DEMOCRACY.

In 465 B.C.E. however, Thasos revolted from the Delian League, over Athenian interference in its crucial mining operations on the mainland. An Athenian war fleet defeated the Thasians in a sea battle, and besieged and captured the capital city (465–463 B.C.E.). Relatedly,

the Athenians began colonizing the west foot of Mt. Pangaeus, at the site later known as AMPHIPOLIS.

The Athenians apparently now took over Thasos's mainland mines, at least temporarily. We know that in 454 B.C.E. Thasos was paying only three TALENTS of Delian tribute a year—a tiny assessment for that rich state, unless it was no longer rich. But by 446 B.C.E. the Thasian tribute had jumped to 30 talents a year, which may signify the Thasians' recovery of their mainland possessions.

In 411 B.C.E., amid the widespread Delian revolt against a beleaguered ATHENS in the PELOPONNESIAN WAR, Thasos rebelled again and went over to the Spartan side. But the common people resisted this defection, and the next years saw civil war on Thasos, followed by recapture by the Athenians (407 B.C.E.). In 404 B.C.E., at the war's end, the exhausted island's Athenian loyalists were massacred by the Spartan general LYSANDER.

In 389 B.C.E. the island joined the SECOND ATHENIAN LEAGUE, of which it remained a faithful member. Thasos was seized by the Macedonian king PHILIP II in 340 B.C.E., by about 300 B.C.E. he and his successors had depleted the Pangaeus mines. Thasos remained a part of the Macedonian kingdom until 196 B.C.E., when it was freed by the Romans in their liberation of Greece.

As befits a rich capital, Thasos city boasted a number of grand buildings. Among the remnants visible today are parts of the AGORA and of a temple of HERAKLES (400s B.C.E.). Most impressive is the partly surviving ancient city wall, dating back to the Thasians' preparation for revolt in 411 B.C.E.

See also PAINTING; PERSIAN WARS; ROME.

Further reading: R. J. L. Wynne-Thomas, *Legacy of Thasos* (London: Springwood Books, 1978); Robin Osborne, "Island Towers. The Case of Thasos," *Annual of the British School at Athens* 81 (1986): 167–178; J. Des Courtils and A. Pariente, "Excavations in the Herakles Sanctuary at Thasos," in *Early Greek Cult Practice. Proceedings of the Fifth International Symposium at the Swedish Institute at Athens, 26–29 June 1986*, edited by Robin Hägg, Nanno Marinatos, and G. C. Nordquist (Stockholm: Svenska Institutet i Athen, 1988), 121; N. Herz, "Classical Marble Quarries of Thasos," in *Antike Edel- und Buntmetallgewinnung auf Thasos* (Bochum, Germany: Selbstverlag des Bergbau-Museens, 1988), 232–240; Stergios Stephanou, *Thasos,* translated by Philip Ramp (Athens: Melissa Publishing House, 1991); A. J. Graham, "Thasos: The Topography of the Ancient City," *Annual of the British School at Athens* 95 (2000): 301–327; S. Owen, "New Light on Thracian Thasos. A Reinterpretation of the Cave of Pan," *Journal of Hellenic Studies* 120 (2000): 139–143.

theater Many cultures have produced some original form of public performance that might be called drama or theater. It was the ancient Greeks, specifically the

Athenians of the 400s B.C.E., who perfected the two genres known as tragedy and comedy, which defined European theater for centuries following. Shakespeare (ca. 1600 C.E.) wrote tragedies and comedies because those were playwriting's two principal forms, inherited from the Greeks.

Greek tragedy drew on tales from MYTH. This meant that in most cases the entire audience would be familiar with the story's plot beforehand (similar to an audience at a modern Easter pageant). The playwright's skill would lie in shaping the material so as to communicate a particular world view or character portrait.

Most Greek tragedy presents the downfall of a hero or other lofty protagonist. In the more sophisticated tragedies, this downfall is shown to be due to HUBRIS (arrogance): Having attracted the anger of the gods, the hero is destroyed by a disastrously arrogant decision of his own. The clearest example of this pattern is in AESCHYLUS's *Agamemnon*, where the hero displays his hubris by walking atop a priceless tapestry.

The philosopher ARISTOTLE, in a famous passage in his literary-critical *Poetics*, explains that tragedy's artistic goal is to arouse the audience's emotions of pity and fear in a way that purges these feelings and provides relief; this purging is called *katharsis*. Greek tragedy also strives to examine the nature—or absence—of divine justice, and the role of humankind in the universe.

Comedy, on the other hand, was always meant to be funny and riotous, with characters less noble and complicated than those in tragedy or even real life. ARISTOPHANES' 11 surviving comedies, dating between 425 and 388 B.C.E., are farcical, fantastical works that celebrate the city's political life, while mocking specific individuals and institutions.

Ancient Greek theater was a form of poetry, with all dialogue being spoken or sung in verse. Theater was also

The theater at Epidaurus dates from the mid-300s B.C.E. and has excellent acoustics. Its 55 rows of limestone benches could seat 12,000. Actors performed on the 66-foot-wide beaten circle of earth. *(Alison Frantz Photographic Collection, American School of Classical Studies at Athens)*

mass culture, intended for an audience that included several social classes, and it thrived in democracies such as ATHENS (although it is unclear whether WOMEN, even female citizens, were allowed to attend). Because the theater audiences comprised much the same constituency as the democratic ASSEMBLY, Greek drama often conveyed strong political messages.

Tragedy apparently was invented at Athens in the 500s B.C.E. (although the city of SIKYON claimed this honor, too). Comedy was developed at various Greek states, including SYRACUSE and other cities of SICILY, before being instituted most grandly at Athens. Both genres probably emerged from the public performances of choral singers at religious festivals in honor of DIONYSUS, the god of WINE and fertility, who was a favorite deity of the masses. Greek comedy, with its farce and obscenity, seems clearly derived from the riotous Dionysian procession known as the *komos*, held at many Greek states; *komoidia* means "song of the *komos*." Vase paintings show the *komos* as a parade of masked men costumed as SATYRS and carrying a log carved as a huge penis. The *komos* was probably an occasion for rude jokes exchanged with onlookers; out of this interplay there may have developed the *parabasis* (a direct choral address to the audience that was a hallmark of Athenian stage comedy). The belief that Dionysus could spiritually possess his worshippers probably led to individual speaking or singing roles in the god's character.

The origins of tragedy are less clear than those of comedy. According to Aristotle's *Poetics*, tragedy emerged from the narrative choral song known as the dithyramb. Like the *komos*, the dithyramb was performed at certain festivals of Dionysus, but was more solemn and rehearsed than the *komos*. The meaning of the word *dithyramb* is unclear now, but it is known, from extant dithyrambs written by the poet BACCHYLIDES (mid-400s B.C.E.), that these songs told tales from Greek myth, not necessarily relating to Dionysus. The chorus would sing or chant the story and probably dance interpretively.

Assuming that what Aristotle said was accurate, there must have come a time at Athens when certain types of performance broke away from the rules governing the dithyramb's poetic meter, size of chorus, and so on. Most significantly, individual performers began stepping out of the chorus, to sing or speak roles in the character of a mythical figure in the story. This step is traditionally credited to a shadowy genius named Thespis (ca. 535 B.C.E.), who also may have introduced the single actor's wearing of a mask to signify character. Thespis's actor apparently delivered set speeches in between the chorus' presentations; the actor may have changed masks to assume multiple roles.

This new Athenian art form was called *tragoidia*, "goat song," perhaps referring to its presentation of festivals of Dionysus. (The sacrifice of goats was part of the god's cult.) By about 534 B.C.E., under the enlightened tyrant PEISISTRATUS, tragedy performance was installed officially at the important Athenian early springtime festival called the City Dionysia. By 500 B.C.E. this festival had developed into the annual, publicly funded, three-way competition that was the famous occasion for all performances of new tragedy. Performances were held in a theater—first of wood or earth, later of marble—at the south base of the Athenian ACROPOLIS.

The Dionysia contest typically presented three authors' new work—in each case, a tragic trilogy and a satyr play (*satyrikon*), for comic relief. The satyr play, an offshoot of comedy, featured a clownish chorus always represented as satyrs. In a typical plot, this gang would "wander into" one of the great myths, such as that of PERSEUS (1). Today only one complete satyr play survives: the *Cyclops* of EURIPIDES (ca. 410 B.C.E.).

The three groups of plays performed at the Dionysia would have been selected previously, in written form, by an official who judged the applicants. Qualifying entrants were assigned a paying sponsor (*chorēgos*), who paid part of the cost out of pocket as a form of state service; the balance came directly out of state funds. At the festival a panel of judges, consisting of ordinary citizens chosen by lottery, awarded first, second, and third prize to the three playwrights. SOPHOKLES is said to have won first prize 24 times, second prize seven times, and never third.

Comedy, less esteemed than tragedy, was installed as a competition at the City Dionysia only around 488 B.C.E. The entries were single plays, one by each playwright. By 440 B.C.E. a second contest had been introduced, at the Lenaea (a Dionysian festival in midwinter). Normally five comedies competed. The two earliest comedy-writers about whom any information exists are KRATINUS and KRATES (mid-400s B.C.E.).

Comedy employed a chorus of 24 members; tragedy used 12 at first, later 15. Comic choruses tended to be more important to the play's action and message than were their tragic counterparts—at least by the time of Aeschylus (525–456 B.C.E.), who was remembered for having reduced the tragic chorus' speaking role. All Athenian actors and stage choruses were male, although the roles might be female.

The first Athenian tragedian about whom any information exists is PHRYNICHUS (ca. 540–475 B.C.E.). His tragedies may have been a form of costumed oratorio, with a simple narrative. The story would unfold around a single speaking actor (the *protagonistēs*), who might assume multiple roles by changing masks and who would deliver his speeches in alternation with the chorus.

Stagecraft, plotting, and characterization were improved by Aeschylus, whose *Persians* (472 B.C.E.) is the earliest extant tragedy. Emphasizing individual roles over the chorus, Aeschylus introduced a second speaking actor, which allowed for better-developed conflicts onstage and which greatly increased the number of available roles. Sophockles (ca. 496–406 B.C.E.) introduced a third speaking actor, and he emphasized characterizations of his protagonists that tended to remove the chorus from the plot. His younger rival Euripides (ca. 485–406 B.C.E.) produced innovations in plotting and in characterization of mythical characters that often seem intended to disturb the audience. These three tragedians—along with a fourth, AGATHON (late 400s B.C.E.)—were recognized in their own day as being the greatest practitioners of the art.

With the deaths of Euripides and Sophokles (both in 406 B.C.E.) and Athens's defeat in the PELOPONNESIAN WAR (404 B.C.E.), the great age of Athenian theater had passed. New tragedies were still performed—the Syracusan tyrant DIONYSIUS (1) wrote one that won a single-play prize at Athens in 367 B.C.E.—but in the absence of steady new talent, a tradition arose of restaging the plays of the three classic tragedians.

Comedy at Athens enjoyed a resurgence with MENANDER, Philemon, and other writers of "New Comedy," in the late 300s B.C.E. This socially satirical comedy of manners—so different from the directly political invective of Aristophanes of EUPOLIS—went on to influence the work of the Roman comedy-writers Plautus and Terence (100s B.C.E.).

Outside Athens, monumental theater buildings had arisen before about 470 B.C.E., when the Syracusan tyrant HIERON (1) constructed a theater for the production of a tragedy by the visiting Aeschylus. By the HELLENISTIC AGE (300–150 B.C.E.), every major Greek city had a marble theater, seating as many as 24,000, where performances might consist largely of restaged plays of the three great Athenian tragedians. Today admirable ancient theaters have been reconstructed at EPIDAURUS, DODONA, PERGAMON, and EPHESOS, among other sites.

Further reading: J. Herington, *Poetry into Drama. Early Tragedy and the Greek Poetic Tradition* (Berkeley: University of California Press, 1985); L. Rodley, ed., *Papers Given at a Colloquium on Greek Drama in Honour of R. P. Winnington-Ingram* (London: Society for the Promotion of Hellenic Studies, 1987); Arthur Pickard-Cambridge, *The Dramatic Festivals of Athens* (New York: Oxford University Press, 1988); D. J. Mastronarde, "Actors on High. The Skene Roof, the Crane, and the Gods in Attic Drama," *Classical Antiquity* 9 (1990); 247–294; J. J. Winkler and F. I. Zeitlin, eds., *Nothing to Do with Dionysus? Athenian Drama in Its Social Context* (Princeton, N.J.: Princeton University Press, 1990); J. Henderson, "Women and the Athenian Dramatic Festivals," *Transactions of the American Philological Association* 121 (1991): 331–147; J. Aronen, "Notes on Athenian Drama as Ritual Myth-telling within the Cult of Dionysus," *Arctos* 26 (1992): 19–37; A. H. Somerstein, S. Halliwell, and J. Henderson, eds., *Tragedy, Comedy, and the Polis. Papers for the Greek Drama Conference, Nottingham, 18–20 July 1990* (Bari, Italy: Levante Editori, 1993); A. Griffiths, ed., *Stage Directions. Essays in Ancient Drama in Honour of E. W. Handley* (London: Institute of Classical Studies, 1995); David Wiles, *Tragedy in*

Athens: Performance Space and Theatrical Meaning (New York: Cambridge University Press, 1997); Jennifer Wise, *Dionysus Writes: The Invention of Theatre in Ancient Greece* (Ithaca, N.Y.: Cornell University Press, 1998); David Taylor, *The Greek and Roman Stage* (Bristol, U.K.: Bristol Classical Press, 1999); Clifford Ashby, *Classical Greek Theatre: New Views of an Old Subject* (Iowa City: University of Iowa Press, 1999).

Thebes (Greek: Thēbai) This major city of central Greece is situated in the eastern plain of BOEOTIA. Seven-gated Thebes enjoyed wide farmlands and control of overland routes both north and south. Today the ancient city's central fortress, the Cadmea (named for Thebes's legendary founder, King CADMUS) lies buried directly under the modern Greek town of Thivai.

Thebes was known for its first-rate army, which included a strong CAVALRY arm, and throughout its history the city usually dominated all of Boeotia. In the 300s B.C.E. Thebes became the foremost Greek power for a brief time, after defeating and displacing its former ally SPARTA.

Along with its neighbor and rival ORCHOMENOS, Thebes seems to have been preeminent in the earlier centuries of MYCENAEAN CIVILIZATION, around 1600–1350 B.C.E. Archaeological excavations at Thebes, hampered by the site's modern town, have yielded portions of a Mycenaean palace as well as LINEAR B tablets and Near Eastern seal stones (which may add credence to the legend that King Cadmus originally came from the Levant). Thebes's importance in this era is reflected in the city's large role in Greek MYTH. The ruling caste's fortunes and misfortunes are recounted in the tales of HERACLES, OEDIPUS, and the SEVEN AGAINST THEBES. The legend of the Seven—with its sequel, the tale of the Epigoni—possibly commemorates Thebes's downfall at the hands of the rival Greek kingdom of MYCENAE, around 1350 B.C.E.

By the 500s B.C.E. the tales of Thebes had been organized into three epic poems, the *Oedipodia,* the *Thebaïd,* and the *Epigoni,* collectively known as the Theban Cycle. These stories later became favorite material for the Athenian tragic playwrights.

In historical times Thebes's hegemony over the other Boeotian cities took the form of a federation—the Boeotian League, wherein Thebes supplied two or more of the 11 delegates, and every other represented state supplied one. Thebes shared an ill-defined, mountainous frontier with ATHENS, which lay about 40 miles southeast. The two cities were enemies in the late 500s–early 300s B.C.E., due largely to Athens's alliance with Thebes's neighbor PLATAEA. The creation of the Athenian DEMOCRACY (508 B.C.E.) further alarmed the Thebans, whose government was an OLIGARCHY.

During the Persian king XERXES invasion of Greece (480–479 B.C.E.), Thebes was the major Greek city to submit to the Persians, and it contributed soldiers and a base of operations for the Persian war effort. After the Persian defeat, Thebes fell into deep discredit. Stripped of its Boeotian hegemony by the vindictive Spartans, the city remained a minor power until the mid-400s B.C.E., when the Spartans revived it as an ally against their common enemy, Athens. As a staunch Spartan ally, Thebes again became the chief city of Boeotia. The Thebans' attack on Plataea precipitated the PELOPONNESIAN WAR (431–404 B.C.E.). In 424 B.C.E. the Thebans defeated an Athenian invasion at the Battle of Delium.

Victory in the war added to Thebes's prestige and territory, gained at the expense of its small Boeotian neighbors. But alienated by Spartan arrogance, Thebes soon made alliance with Athens, ARGOS, and CORINTH against Sparta, in the CORINTHIAN WAR (394–386 B.C.E.).

The following decades saw the acme of Theban power, under the city's greatest statesman and general, EPAMINONDAS. He led his countrymen against the Spartans—supposing the greatest soldiers in Greece—and defeated them at the Battle of LEUKTRA (371 B.C.E.). The Thebans then dismantled Sparta's empire, marching into the PELOPONNESE and freeing MESSENIA and ARCADIA from Spartan control. The Theban army of these years was distinguished by the Sacred Band (Hieros Lochos), an elite corps of 300 HOPLITES consisting of paired male lovers. Classical Thebes in general was known for its military male homosexual society.

In the mid-300s B.C.E. Thebes was confronted with the emerging power of MACEDON. Initially siding with the Macedonian king PHILIP II, Thebes switched sides to join the Athenian-led alliance that opposed Philip. After taking part in the disastrous Greek defeat at CHAIRONEIA (338 B.C.E.), Thebes was stripped of power and garrisoned by Philip's vengeful troops. A Theban revolt after Philip's death brought the city to complete destruction at the hands of Philip's successor, ALEXANDER THE GREAT; 6,000 Thebans were supposedly killed and 30,000 sold as SLAVES (335 B.C.E.). Thebes was rebuilt in 316 B.C.E. by the Macedonian ruler KASSANDER but was never again a great power. By the first century B.C.E. it was little more than a village.

Greek Thebes had nothing to do with the magnificent ancient Egyptian city called Thebes (modern Luxor and Karnak). Thēbai was a hellenized name, given to the Egyptian site by Greek visitors. One ancient Egyptian name for the city was Apet; to the Greek ear, this apparently sounded enough like Thēbai for the two names to become assimilated.

See also ANTIGONE; DIONYSUS; EPIC POETRY; HOMOSEXUALITY; PERSIAN WARS; WARFARE, LAND.

Further reading: S. Symeonoglou, "Thebes, Greece. An Archaeological and Sociological Problem," *Architectura* 2 (1972): 81–91; N. H. Demand, *Thebes in the Fifth Century. Herakles Resurgent* (London: Routledge, 1982); S. Symeonoglou, *The Topography of Thebes from the* *Bronze Age to Modern Times* (Princeton, N.J.: Princeton University Press, 1985); R. M. Kallet-Marx, "Athens, Thebes, and the Foundation of the Second Athenian League," *Classical Antiquity* 4 (1985): 127–151; N. G. L. Hammond, "Plataea's Relations with Thebes, Sparta, and Athens," *Journal of Hellenic Studies* 112 (1992): 143–150; S. C. Bakhuizen, "Thebes and Boeotia in the Fourth Century B.C.," *Phoenix* 48, (1994): 307–330; J. C. Trevett, "Demosthenes and Thebes," *Historia* 48 (1999): 184–202; P. J. Rhodes, "Thebes, Sparta, and Autonomia," *Eirene* 35 (1999): 33–40.

Themistokles (524–459 B.C.E.) *Athenian statesman and general*

In the history of ATHENS, Themistokles is second in importance only to PERIKLES (who was his political successor). By urging the Athenians to create a powerful navy in the early 480s B.C.E., Themistokles provided his city and all of Greece with an effective defense against invasion in the PERSIAN WARS (480 B.C.E.). This Athenian navy then became the means by which Athens acquired and held its sea empire of 479–404 B.C.E. In domestic politics, Themistokles was a radical left-winger who helped broaden the base of the Athenian DEMOCRACY, in opposition to the rich and noble-born. He was also an inveterate enemy of SPARTA, foreseeing, as few Athenians did in the 470s B.C.E., that Sparta would be Athens's next great foe.

Themistokles remained a controversial figure long after his death. His deeds are described by the historical HERODOTUS (ca. 435 B.C.E.), by the biographer PLUTARCH (ca. 100 C.E.), and briefly by the historian THUCYDIDES (1) (ca. 410 B.C.E.). Herodotus and Plutarch show signs of having used anti-Themistoklean source material, which condemns the man for his greed and flawed patriotism. But Thucydides praises Themistokles' foresight and decisiveness, summarizing him with these words: "With his inborn genius and speed of action, he was the best for doing at a moment's notice exactly what the emergency called for" (book 1, 103).

Themistokles' father Neocles was of an aristocratic Athenian family. Themistokles' mother is sometimes described as a non-Athenian—which, if true, would have placed the future statesman in a relatively humble social category. Themistokles rose quickly as a left-wing politician in the newly created democracy, being elected chief ARCHON at about age 35 and organizing the development of PIRAEUS as Athens's harbor and naval base (493 B.C.E.).

The years after the Battle of MARATHON (490 B.C.E.) saw political turmoil at Athens, with at least five prominent politicians banished by OSTRACISM—but not Themistokles, who emerged as the city's leading statesman. It was then he made his great contribution to Athens's future. In 483 B.C.E. the publicly owned SILVER mines at Laurion, outside Athens, produced a bonanza yield. Although it was customary for such surpluses to be distributed as cash to each citizen, Themistokles convinced the Athenian ASSEMBLY to use the revenue to build new warships. His ostensible reason was Athens's current war against the nearby Greek state of AEGINA, but his real reason seems to have been his expectation of the Persian invasion. Within three years Athens had acquired the biggest navy in the Greek world—going from 70 warships to 200—and all its new vessels were the superior type of warship known as the trireme.

When the Greek states allied against the attack of the Persian king XERXES (480 B.C.E.), Themistokles served as a fleet commander and as one of the strategy-planning chiefs of staff. (He was not, however, the top-ranking Greek admiral; that honor went to a Spartan.) To Themistokles can be ascribed the strategy of confronting the southward-sailing Persian fleet inside certain narrow channels, where the invaders' superior numbers and seamanship would be canceled out. After moderate success at the sea battle of ARTEMISION, this strategy resulted in a total Greek victory at SALAMIS (1), inside a mile-wide channel not far from Athens, specially chosen by Themistokles long before the event.

Even before the war was over, Themistokles foresaw that Sparta would be Athens's next enemy. Although the Spartans respected him, Themistokles began to steer his city against them. The walls of Athens, destroyed by the Persians, were rebuilt despite Spartan disapproval (479 B.C.E.), and alliances were formed with ARGOS and THESSALY, two enemies of Sparta.

But Themistokles' downfall soon followed. The creation of the DELIAN LEAGUE and the naval counteroffensive against the Persians brought new Athenian soldier-politicians to the fore, particularly the young, conservative, pro-Spartan KIMON. In about 471 B.C.E. the Athenians voted to ostracize Themistokles, who was by then nearly 60. He spent the next years traveling around the PELOPONNESE, where his activities seem connected with the establishment of anti-Spartan democracies at Argos, at MANTINEIA, and elsewhere. The alarmed Spartans appealed to Athens, claiming to have proof that Themistokles was conducting treasonous intrigues with the Persian king. Indicted by the Athenians for treason, Themistokles fled Greece for ASIA MINOR (467 B.C.E.). Eventually making his way to the Persian court at Susa, he became a valued adviser to King Artaxerxes I (464 B.C.E.). For about the last year of his life, the hero of Salamis served as a local Persian governor at the city of Magnesia-on-the-Maeander, in Asia Minor. He died, probably of natural causes, at age 65.

Themistokles was married twice, to Athenian women; his second wife, Archippe, accompanied or followed him to Asia with the youngest of their children. Two of Themistokles' daughters had the unusual names Italia and Sybaris, which may indicate yet another of his foreign-policy visions—namely, the extension of Athenian influence westward to the Greek cities of southern ITALY.

See also AESCHYLUS; ARISTIDES; ATTICA; SYBARIS; WARFARE, NAVAL; XANTHIPPUS.

Further reading: A. J. Podecki, *The Life of Themistocles. A Critical Survey of Literary and Archaeological Evidence* (Montreal: McGill-Queens University Press, 1975); Frank J. Frost, *Plutarch's Themistocles: A Historical Commentary* (Princeton, N.J.: Princeton University Press, 1980); A. J. Holladay, "The Forethought of Themistocles," *Journal of Hellenic Studies* 107 (1987): 182–187; B. Jordan, "The Honours for Themistocles after Salamis," *American Journal of Philology* 109 (1988): 547–571; E. M. Carawan, "Thucydides and Stesimbrotus on the Exile of Themistocles," *Historia* 38 (1989): 144–161; J. Marr, "The Death of Themistocles," *Greece and Rome* (1995): 159–167; Arthur Keaveney, *The Life and Journey of Athenian Statesman Themistocles (524–460 B.C.?) as a Refugee in Persia* (Lewiston: E. Mellen Press, 2003).

Theocritus (ca. 300–260 B.C.E.) *One of the best-known poets of the HELLENISTIC AGE*
Theocritus was born in the Sicilian Greek city of SYRACUSE but spent most of his career at Egyptian ALEXANDRIA (1), in the wealthy and literary court of King PTOLEMY (2) II Philadelphus. Theocritus seems to have had a close friendship with another famous Alexandrian poet, CALLIMACHUS, but otherwise little is known of his life.

Theocritus composed poems in several different genres, but his most significant works were his innovative pastoral poems. These influenced generations of later poets, from the Roman period through the European Renaissance. Of his poems, 31 survive today, including several of the bucolic poems, set in the countryside. Other extant pieces of Theocritus's work include mimes (Greek: *mimoi,* realistic or satirical scenes rendered into hexameters) and epyllia ("little epics," hexameter poems of several hundred lines presenting a heroic MYTH or romance).

Further reading: Heather White, *Studies in Theocritus and Other Hellenistic Poets* (Amsterdam: Gieben, 1979); Steven Walker, *Theocritus* (Boston: Twayne, 1980); M. A. Rossi, "Theocritus. A Select Bibliography," *L'Antiquité classique* 56 (1987): 290–295; P. Bing, "Theocritus' Epigrams on the Statues of Ancient Poets," *Antike und Abendland* 34 (1988): 117–123; G. O. Hutchinson, *Hellenistic Poetry* (New York: Clarendon Press, 1990); Judith Haber, *Pastoral and the Poetics of Self-contradiction* (New York: Cambridge University Press, 1994); M. A. Harder, R. F. Regtuit, and G. C. Wakker, eds., *Theocritus* (Groningen, Netherlands: Egbert Forsten, 1996); R. L. Hunter, *Theocritus and the Archaeology of Greek Poetry* (New York: Cambridge University Press, 1996).

Theognis (ca. 570–485 B.C.E.) *Lyric poet of the Greek city of* MEGARA (1)

Little is known of Theognis's life other than that he was born in Megara to a noble family; much of his poetry is strongly political and reflects his aristocratic sympathies. He was exiled for a time, along with the leaders of his city's oligarchical party, and most of his poems were written during this period.

Theognis's work survives as a collection of nearly 700 elegiac couplets, many of which apparently were actually written by later anonymous poets in imitation of Theognis's poems. Within this collection (known as the Theognidia), modern scholars have tentatively identified a core of about 300 poems that seem to reflect a consistent poetic personality (supposedly that of Theognis himself) and a composition date in the mid-500s B.C.E.

Further reading: S. I. Dost, "The Megara of Theagenes and Theognis," *Classical Philology* 68 (1973): 186–196; T. J. Figueira, ed., *Theognis of Megara. Poetry and the Polis* (Baltimore: Johns Hopkins University Press, 1985).

Theophrastus (ca. 372–287 B.C.E.) *Greek philosopher and essayist from the islands of* LESBOS

Theophrastus was first introduced to philosophy at Lesbos and then went to ATHENS, where he studied first under PLATO and, later, ARISTOTLE. When Aristotle died, his will made Theophrastus the guardian of his children and bequeathed his library to him. He also designated Theophrastus as his successor as the head of Aristotle's philosophical school, known as the LYCEUM. As the leader of the Lyceum, Theophrastus maintained the school's broad range of study and caused it to flourish. He eventually moved the location to a larger building complex, called the Peripatos; by the time he died, Theophrastus had presided over the Lyceum for about 35 years. He had thousands of students, including the comic poet MENANDER, and was highly regarded by the Athenian people, as well as by several Hellenistic kings.

Theophrastus wrote on a variety of scientific and philosophical subjects, but he is best known today for his extant work entitled *Characters*, a collection of 30 sketches of eccentric or abnormal personality types. His surviving texts also include works on botany and geology.

Further reading: J. Scarborough, *Pharmacy's Ancient Heritage. Theophrastus, Nicander, and Dioscorides* (Lexington, Ky.: College of Pharmacy, 1985); William Fortenbaugh and Dimitri Gutas, eds., *Theophrastus: His Psychological Doxographical, and Scientific Writings* (New Brunswick, N.J.: Transaction, 1992); R. W. Sharples, *Theophrastus of Eresus. Sources for His Life, Writings, Thought, and Influence* (Leiden, Netherlands: E. J. Brill, 1995); P. G. Maxwell-Stuart, "Theophrastus the Traveller," *La Parola del Passato* 51 (1996): 241–267; P. G. Maxwell-Stuart, "Theophrastus and the Peloponnese," *La*

Parola del Passato 53 (1998): 81–114; Johannes M. van Ophuijsen and Marlein van Raalte, eds., *Theophrastus: Reappraising the Sources* (New Brunswick, N.J.: Transaction, 1998).

Thera This Greek island of the mid AEGEAN SEA, is situated at the southern edge of the island group known as the CYCLADES. The island's alternative, Italian-derived name, Santorini, commemorates St. Irene of Salonika. Covering only 29 square miles, Thera consists of an irregular, westward-opening crescent that rises dramatically from the sea. This odd shape marks the remnant of an ancient volcanic cone, which—as geology and ARCHAEOLOGY show—erupted in about 1628 B.C.E., blasting itself in half.

Before the eruption, Thera was home to a branch of the pre-Greek MINOAN CIVILIZATION. Modern excavations at Akrotiri, in southern Thera, have uncovered the most important Minoan site known to us outside of CRETE, with remnants of streets and villas, and some fine frescoes. This settlement was preserved for millennia by being buried in lava after its inhabitants had fled.

Thera's cataclysmic eruption probably resembled that of the Indonesian island Krakatoa in 1883 C.E. The resultant tidal waves must have battered other Aegean islands, including Crete, 70 miles to the south. It used to be thought that the Theran eruption occurred in about 1480 B.C.E. and that it was perhaps the direct cause of a sharp social decline observable in Crete at that time, including the depopulation of Crete's coastlines. Now, however, due to modern scientific dating techniques such as dendrochronology (tree-ring dating), archaeologists have realized that the volcano erupted about 150 years earlier and are studying the evidence to reconcile the dates and relationships of the Theran and Cretan destructions. It is thought by some that Thera's destruction might lie behind the later Greek legend of ATLANTIS.

Around 1000 B.C.E., Thera was occupied by DORIAN GREEKS from the mainland, who founded Thera city, in the south mid-island. An impressive temple of Carnean APOLLO, datable to the 500s B.C.E., is among the city's early monuments revealed by excavation. Scratched onto rocks nearby are ancient Greek graffiti, many with jocular homosexual messages, which represent some of the earliest surviving examples of Greek alphabetic WRITING (600s B.C.E.).

Despite prosperity, early Dorian Thera was badly enough afflicted by drought to send out large numbers of its young men to found a colony in North Africa, around 630 B.C.E. This colony was CYRENE (1), which became one of the foremost cities of the Greek world within just a few decades.

Although Dorian-Greek and not Ionian, Thera was a subject ally of ATHENS in the DELIAN LEAGUE (400s B.C.E.). In the 200s B.C.E. the island became a naval base for Ptolemaic EGYPT, before being annexed by the Romans in the first century B.C.E. Most of Thera city's physical remains, including the AGORA, colonnades, and temple of the god DIONYSUS, date from the Ptolemaic and Roman occupations.

Exploration of the island of Thera began in 1845, and the first systematic archaeological excavation took place in 1895–1903. After World War II, work was resumed under Greek archaeologist S. Marinatos, and the current program of excavations on the site are being conducted by a Greek team under the direction of C. Doumas.

See also COLONIZATION; HOMOSEXUALITY.

Further reading: Lyvia Morgan, *The Miniature Wall Paintings of Thera: A Study of Aegean Culture and Iconography* (New York: Cambridge University Press, 1988); Christos Doumas, *The Wall-Paintings of Thera,* translated by Alex Doumas (Athens: Thera Foundation, 1992); ———, *Santorini: A Guide to the Island and Its Archaeological Treasures* (Athens: Ekdotike Athenon, 1996); Phyllis Young Forsyth, *Thera in the Bronze Age* (New York: P. Lang, 1999); Spyridon Marinatos, *Excavations at Thera,* 2d ed. (Athens: Archaeological Society at Athens, 1999); C. Palyvou, "Theran Architecture through the Minoan Looking Glass," *Aegaeum* 20 (1999): 609–615; S. W. Manning, *A Test of Time: The Volcano of Thera and the Chronology and History of the Aegean and East Mediterranean in the Mid Second Millennium B.C.* (Oxford: Oxbow Books, 1999); S. W. Manning, C. B. Ramsey, and C. Doumas, "New Evidence for an Early Date for the Aegean Late Bronze Age and Thera Eruption," *Antiquity* 76 (2002): 733–744.

Theramenes (d. 404 B.C.E.) *Athenian commander and right-wing politician of the late* PELOPONNESIAN WAR *and its aftermath*
Theramenes was instrumental in arranging the Athenian surrender to SPARTA at the war's end (404 B.C.E.). More important, he was involved in both of the oligarchic coups at ATHENS in these years—that of the FOUR HUNDRED (411 B.C.E.) and that of the THIRTY TYRANTS (404–403 B.C.E.). As leader of the moderate faction within the Thirty, Theramenes lost his life for opposing the extremist leader, KRITIAS.

The contemporary Athenian historian XENOPHON, who knew Theramenes, portrays him as a cynical opportunist. But later writers (including ARISTOTLE in his *Constitution of Athens*) have seen Theramenes as a true moderate and patriot, trying to steer his city through disaster.

See also OLIGARCHY.

Further reading: M. L. Lang, "Theramenes and Arginousai," *Hermes* 120 (1992): 267–279; R. J. Buck, "The Character of Theramenes," *Ancient History Bulletin* 9 (1995): 14–24; C. Ehrhardt, "Lysias on Theramenes," *Ancient History Bulletin* 9 (1995): 125–126; E. David,

"Thermenes' Speech at Colonus," *L'Antiquité classique* 64 (1995): 15–25; W. J. McCoy, "The Political Debut of Theramenes," in *Polis and Polemos: Essays on Politics, War, and History in Ancient Greece in Honor of Donald Kagen,* edited by Charles D. Hamilton and Peter Krentz (Claremont, Calif.: Regina Books, 1997), 171–192.

Thermopylae This seaside mountain pass connects the frontiers of THESSALY and East LOCRIS, at the eastern edge of the Mt. Oeta range, in northeast-central Greece. In 480 B.C.E., during the PERSIAN WARS, Thermopylae was the site of a famous three-day battle in which 5,000 Greek HOPLITES, led by the Spartan king Leonidas, blocked a Persian army of perhaps 200,000, marching south under the command of King XERXES.

Long before the battle, Thermopylae was recognized as the strategic weak point on the main route into central Greece. Just under four miles long and less than 50 feet wide at its narrowest point, the pass was hemmed (to the west) by a wall of cliffs and (to the east) by the waters of the Gulf of Malis. Around 600 B.C.E. the pass was further closed by a wall, built by inhabitants of the central Greek region of PHOCIS to block the southward incursions of their enemies, the Thessalians.

North of the pass, the river Spercheios flows into the gulf. The river's alluvial deposits have changed the coastline since ancient times, resulting in a seaward widening of the pass. No longer is Thermopylae the grim "catwalk" it once was. The name *Thermopulai,* "hot gates," refers to local sulfur springs. Ancient Thermopylae also served as a sanctified meeting place for the local peoples of the AMPHICTYONIC LEAGUE.

The Battle of Thermopylae was fought in the late summer of 480 B.C.E., simultaneous with the sea battle of ARTEMISION, 40 miles away. On the Greek side, the object of both battles was to stop the enemy at narrow points on land and sea, north of the Greek heartland. Unfortunately, the Thermopylae effort was undermined by the indecision of leaders at SPARTA, who sent an advance guard under Leonidas, but then declined to send the main army—in part because their religious festival of the Carneia officially forbade the dispatching of troops during that time. So Leonidas was left to hold Thermopylae with his small force.

The Persian infantry entered the northern mouth of the pass and charged against the Greek hoplites, who had formed up alongside and behind the stone wall. The Greek historian HERODOTUS, the main source for information on the Persian Wars, describes how the Persians and their countrymen, the Medes—unable to use their superior numbers in the narrow space—fell back repeatedly with heavy losses. Even Xerxes' elite legion of Immortals failed to push through. The invaders were disadvantaged by having shorter thrusting spears and lighter armor than the Greeks, and perhaps by having inferior morale and discipline. But, after two days, with the help

Bust of the warrior Leonidas, hero of the Battle of Thermopylae. The Greeks died holding off an invading Persian force. *(Alison Frantz Photographic Collection, American School of Classical Studies at Athens)*

otic terms. Like other suicidal exploits, the Spartan defense at Thermopylae inspired strong reverence in the Greek mind. Monuments to the slain were erected at Sparta and in the pass itself, where the defenders were buried. The poet SIMONIDES wrote one of the epitaphs:

Here is the tomb of that famous Megistias
Whom the Mede slew crossing the River Spercheios.
A seer, he clearly saw the goddesses of death approach,
Yet could not desert his Spartan king.

But the most enduring Thermopylae epitaph is an anonymous elegiac couplet, from a commemorative column in the pass:

Go tell the Spartans, O passerby,
That here we lie, complying with their orders.

The Thermopylae pass remained a strategic bone of contention throughout Greek history. In 352 B.C.E. it was occupied by the Macedonian king PHILIP II, in a military-diplomatic maneuver against ATHENS. In 279 B.C.E. a united Greek army defended the pass—again unsuccessfully—against the southward invasion of the CELTS.

See also LYRIC POETRY; PROPHECY AND DIVINATION.

Further reading: Konstantinos Kontorlis, *The Battle of Thermopylae* (Athens: K. Kontorlis, 1972); Ernle Bradford, *The Year of Thermopylae* (London: Macmillan, 1980); Ernle Bradford, *The Battle for the West: Thermopylae* (New York: Da Capo, 1993); Philip Steele, *Thermopylae* (New York: New Discovery Books, 1993); L. A. Curchin, "The Unburied Dead at Thermopylae (279 B.C.)," *Ancient History Bulletin* 9 (1995): 68–71; G. J. Szemler, *Thermopylai: Myth and Reality in 480 B.C.* (Chicago: Ares, 1996); N. G. L. Hammond, "Sparta at Thermopylae," *Historia* 45 (1996): 1–20.

Theron *See* ACRAGAS.

Theseus Theseus was a mythical Athenian hero and king. Whereas many Greek legendary heroes were connected with the cities of THEBES or MYCENAE, relatively few figures were attached to ATHENS. Theseus therefore came to be viewed as an Athenian national hero—not only a great warrior and lover, but a civilizer, who rid the countryside of brigands and who unified the villages of ATTICA into a single federation, centered at Athens. In historical times, he was honored at an annual festival, the Theseia, held in the fall.

Being an Athenian cultural treasure, the Theseus MYTH was reworked by generations of poets and storytellers. Several of Theseus's adventures seems specifically modeled on those of HERAKLES, in an attempt to make Theseus as important as that greatest Greek hero. Some of this nationalistic myth-making perhaps occurred in the 500s B.C.E., under the Athenian tyrants PEISISTRATUS and HIPPIAS (1).

The mythical Theseus probably commemorates some actual Athenian king of the Mycenaean era, perhaps circa

of a traitorous local Greek named Ephialtes, the Persians found a mountain footpath that brought their troops down behind the Greek lines.

Leonidas, learning that he was being outflanked, sent most of the army south to safety. The battle's climax, on the third day, was the heroic last stand of Leonidas with his royal guard of 300 Spartans and 1,100 other Greek troops, from BOEOTIA. The Persian troops, lashed on by the whips of their commanders, attacked from both ends of the pass; in the crush, some fell into the sea or were trampled underfoot. The Greeks fought until their spears were broken, then fought on with their swords. Leonidas was killed, as were all his 300 Spartans—except for one man, who had been sent home ill. The Boeotians died, too, or surrendered. On the Persian side, the dead included two of Xerxes' brothers. But the invading hordes marched through, into central Greece.

Although in military terms Thermopylae was a Greek failure—with more men and better organization they might have seriously stalled the Persian land invasion—the battle became very significant in emotional and patri-

1300 B.C.E., whose lasting achievement was to consolidate the 1,000-square-mile region of Attica under his rule. Possibly this king's name really was Theseus ("Settler"). Alternatively, the king's accomplishments were eventually ascribed to an existing legendary hero. The historical essence of the Theseus legend appealed to PLUTARCH (ca. 100 C.E.), who wrote a biography of Theseus among his biographies of more strictly historical Greeks and Romans.

According to the myth, the Athenian king Aegeus, being childless, consulted the god APOLLO's oracle at DELPHI. He received the advice to return home but that, until arriving, he should not "loosen the wineskin's jutting foot." In fact this was a warning, not against alcohol, but against sexual intercourse; however, Aegeus, failing to understand, dallied with King Pittheus's daughter, Aethra, at the city of Troizen (in the northeastern PELOPONNESE). Departing from Troizen, Aegeus left behind a sword and a pair of sandals underneath a huge boulder; he secretly instructed Aethra that when their future son—whom Aethra was confident she had conceived—was strong enough to shift the boulder and recover the items of proof, he should go to Athens.

The son was born at Troizen and named Theseus. King Pittheus, to protect his daughter's reputation, claimed that Theseus's father was the god POSEIDON, who supposedly had seduced Aethra. On reaching manhood, Theseus easily pushed the boulder away from the sandals and sword. Taking these tokens of identity, he went to find his father at Athens. Rather than use the quick sea route across the Saronic Gulf, Theseus chose to travel by land, around the top of the gulf, for adventure's sake.

On the journey, he encountered a series of sadistic brigands and slew them all. Reaching Athens, Theseus was acknowledged by his father, King Aegeus. Soon, however, Theseus came into danger from Aegaeus's paramour, the Colchian princess MEDEA, who feared Theseus's influence and right of succession. At Medea's prompting, Aegeus sent Theseus against the Bull of MARATHON, which was ravaging the countryside. (This adventure is clearly based on Herakles' Seventh Labor, against the Cretan Bull.) Theseus captured the animal and sacrificed it to Apollo.

Next came the hero's most famous adventure. Athens (according to the myth) was at this time a subject city of Crete, having been subdued by the Cretan king MINOS. The Athenians were compelled to pay a yearly tribute of seven youths and seven maidens, who were sent by Athenian ship to Crete to be locked up inside the maze of the LABYRINTH. There the young people would be devoured by the ferocious Minotaur (bull of Minos), who was the monstrous half-man, half-bull offspring of Minos's wife, Queen Pasiphaë. Theseus, deciding to put a stop to this oppression, volunteered to sail to Crete amid the next batch of young people.

Reaching Crete, he met the princess Ariadne, daughter of Minos and Pasiphaë. She fell in love with him and, to guide him through the dark Labyrinth, gave him a thread, one end of which he fastened near the entrance. Then he slew the Minotaur, escaped from the Labyrinth, and fled from Crete with Ariadne aboard the waiting Athenian tribute ship. But Theseus callously abandoned Ariadne on the island of Naxos, where she was later found and wed by the god DIONYSUS.

Theseus's ship sailed on toward Athens. The hero had arranged with his father that, if he were successful on Crete, he would substitute the tribute ship's black sail for another one, colored white. In the excitement of the return Theseus forgot this agreement, and Aegeus, seeing the ship approach under a black sail, assumed that his son had been killed. The remorseful Aegeus immediately threw himself into the sea and drowned. Supposedly, from this, the AEGEAN SEA was named.

Succeeding his father as king, Theseus brought about the unification of Attica. He then departed on a campaign against the distant-dwelling AMAZONS, the tribe of fierce female warriors. One version says that Theseus accompa-

The Greek hero Theseus battles the Minotaur. The hero has just stabbed the beast and blood streams from the wound. A youth and a girl—representative of those saved from sacrifice by Theseus's victory—stand at each side watching. (The J. Paul Getty Museum)

nied Herakles' Amazon expedition, another that Theseus went on his own, but in either case he brought back to Athens, as his captive, the Amazon queen, Hippolyta. In pursuit, the mass of Amazons marched to Athens and besieged the city, but were repulsed. (In classical times, the Amazonomachy, or Battle with the Amazons, was a favorite subject of monumental Athenian SCULPTURE and PAINTING.) Hippolyta died after bearing Theseus a son, HIPPOLYTUS. Later Theseus married Phaedra, the younger sister of Ariadne, and this young wife conceived an illicit passion for her stepson, resulting in the tragic deaths of both.

One of Theseus's last adventures was his visit to the Underworld with his friend Peirithoos, king of the Lapiths. Their ambitious goal was to carry off the goddess PERSEPHONE, to be Peirithoos's wife. However, Persephone's husband, HADES, captured the two heroes by tricking them into sitting on an enchanted bench, which held them fast. Theseus eventually was rescued by Herakles, who managed to rip him out of his chair, but Peirithoos remained in the nether world.

The end of Theseus's life was unhappy. Ousted from Athens by a rebellion, he voyaged to the island of Skyros, where he was murdered by the king, Lykomedes, who disputed Theseus's claim to a local estate.

The myth has a historical aftermath. In about 476 B.C.E. the Athenian commander KIMON brought back from Skyros a skeleton and relics said to be those of Theseus. The hero was reburied in a monumental tomb in the middle of Athens. The writer Plutarch mentions that the tomb became a sanctuary for runaway SLAVES and the needy, because, in his lifetime, Theseus was the champion of the oppressed.

See also MYCENAEAN CIVILIZATION; PROCRUSTES.

Further reading: J. N. Davie, "Theseus the King in Fifth-century Athens," *Greece and Rome* 29 (1982): 25–34; Jenifer Neils, *The Youthful Deeds of Theseus* (Rome: Bretschneider, 1987); H. Alan Shapiro, "The Marriage of Theseus and Helen," in *Kotinos. Festschrift für Erika Simon*, edited by Heide Froning, Tonio Hölscher, and Harald Mielsch (Mainz am Rhein, Germany: P. von Zabern, 1992), 232–236; Henry J. Walker, *Theseus and Athens* (New York: Oxford University Press, 1995); L. Press, "The Victory of Theseus over Minotaur. Durability and Significance of That Myth," in *Studia in Honorem Georgii Mihailov* (Sofia, Bulgaria: 1995), 385–393; E. Simon, "Theseus and Athenian Festivals," in *Worshipping Athena. Panathenaia and Parthenon*, edited by Jenifer Neils (Madison: University of Wisconsin Press, 1996), 9–26; Sophie Mills, *Theseus, Tragedy, and the Athenian Empire* (New York: Oxford University Press, 1997).

Thespis *See* THEATER.

Thessaly A large, northeasternly region of Greece, Thessaly's best-known landmark is Mt. OLYMPUS. The region consists of two wide and fertile plains, enclosed on four sides by mountains. To the south rises the range of Mt. Oeta, which—in ancient Greek geographical terms—separated Thessaly from PHOCIS and the rest of central Greece; the principal route through this barrier was the pass of THERMOPYLAE. On Thessaly's western and southwestern frontiers stood the Pindus mountain range, beyond which lay the Greek states of EPIRUS and AETOLIA. On the north, more mountains divided Thessaly from the kingdom of MACEDON. And, in the east, the north-to-south line of Mt. Olympus, Mt. Ossa, and Mt. Pelion occupied the Aegean coast and rendered the shoreline harborless and unusable for shipping.

The only suitable harbor in all Thessaly was located at the top of the Gulf of Pagasae (the modern Gulf of Volos), nestled behind the southward-jutting peninsula called Magnesia. There two seaports emerged in different phases of history: First was Iolcus (modern Volos), a major city of the MYCENAEAN CIVILIZATION (around 1600–1200 B.C.E.), fabled as the home of the hero JASON (1). Later came nearby Pagasae, which flourished in the 400s and 300s B.C.E.

The name Thessaly commemorates the Thessaloi, a Greek people of the Aeolian ethnic group who subjugated the area around 1100 B.C.E., soon after the Mycenaean collapse. The inhabitants retained an Aeolic dialect in ancient times. Thessaly's wealth lay in its wide plains, which provided grain, cattle, and—the region's hallmark—horses. The Thessalians were famous horsemen; their armies, unlike most Greek forces, consisted mainly of CAVALRY.

Isolated by its mountain perimeter, Thessaly developed as a self-contained, horse-ranching ARISTOCRACY. During the great centuries of Greek history (800–300 B.C.E.) it remained politically and culturally backward, with power and ownership concentrated in the hands of a few immensely rich families. One such family was the Aleudae, based at the city of Larissa, in the northern plain. These aristocrats resisted both kingship and DEMOCRACY, and it was not until about 374 B.C.E. that Thessaly became united under one leader, the tyrant JASON (2) of the city of Pherae.

In the 350s B.C.E. Thessaly fell under the sway of the Macedonian king PHILIP II, and Thessalian cavalry did important service in the army of Philip and of his son ALEXANDER THE GREAT. Valuable as a doorway into central Greece, Thessaly received a Macedonian garrison, which was housed (293 B.C.E.) in a newly built fortress called Demetrias, adjoining Pagasae. The region remained under Macedonian control until the Romans broke Macedon's power, in 168 B.C.E.

Several archaeological sites in Thessaly have been excavated. At Larissa, the remains of two theaters have been discovered and are visible today. Pelinna, the main city of western Thessaly, is another place that has been partially investigated; archaeologists have located the remains of two city walls and numerous traces of roads and buildings. Just outside Pelinna are several tombs, a monumental tumulus excavated in 1906 and two Hellenistic cist graves found in 1969.

See also AEOLIAN GREEKS; GREECE, GEOGRAPHY OF; GREEK LANGUAGE; ROME; TYRANTS.

Further reading: Bryan Feuer, *The Northern Mycenaean Border in Thessaly* (Oxford: B.A.R., 1983); Marija Gimbutas, Shan Winn, and Daniel Shimabuku, *Achilleion: A Neolithic Settlement in Thessaly, Greece, 6400–5600 B.C.* (Los Angeles: Institute of Archaeology, UCLA, 1989); Kostas Gallis and Laia Orphanidis, *Figurines of Neolithic Thessaly* (Athens: Academy of Athens, 1996); I. Georganas, "Early Iron Age Tholos Tombs in Thessaly, c. 1100–700 B.C.," *Mediterranean Archaeology* 13 (2000): 47–54; Nicholas Konsolas, *Regional Development in Greece* (New York: Springer, 2001).

Thetis   *See* ACHILLES; PELEUS.

Thirty Tyrants, the   This name is commonly given to the 30-man committee that ruled in ATHENS as a dictatorial puppet government for the Spartans immediately after Athens's surrender in the PELOPONNESIAN WAR (404 B.C.E.). The Thirty ruled for over a year, from spring of 404 until early autumn of 403 B.C.E., in a reign of terror.

The 30 men were right-wing Athenians, elected by the Athenians at a rigged meeting of the ASSEMBLY under the watchful eye of the occupying Spartan general, LYSANDER. Elected ostensibly to draft a new law code, they seized the government, with Lysander's approval, and dismantled the Athenian DEMOCRACY. They disbanded the democratic COUNCIL, abolished the people's law courts, and convinced Lysander to install a Spartan garrison on the ACROPOLIS. With their private police force of 300 "whip-bearers," the Thirty conducted arrests and executions to eradicate opposition and raise funds by confiscation. As many as 1,500 citizens and METICS (resident aliens) are said to have lost their lives; many others fled.

Eventually division arose within the Thirty, between the extremist KRITIAS and the more moderate THERAMENES. At length, KRITIAS had Theramenes put to death.

When a resistance band under the exiled Athenian soldier Thrasybulus seized a fortress in the Attic countryside, the Thirty began preparing a refuge for themselves at the town of Eleusis, outside Athens. This led to their worst atrocity—the execution of 300 men of Eleusis—perhaps the town's entire adult male population.

But the despots' days were numbered. When Thrasybulus's rebels seized Athens's harbor town of PIRAEUS, the Thirty brought out an army against them and were defeated (winter of 404–403 B.C.E.). Kritias was killed in the fighting, as was his nephew and lieutenant Charmides. The remnants of the Thirty were deposed, and full democracy was restored by the autumn of 403

B.C.E. Individual members of the Thirty were executed thereafter.

Remarkably, the Spartans made little effort to save their puppet government. This inactivity owed much to a political rift at Sparta, where King Pausanias was repudiating Lysander's policies. Pausanias soon came to terms with the new Athenian government.

The Thirty represent the worst of three different oligarchic attempts to subvert the Athenian democracy during the 400s B.C.E. The first of these was the plot to hand over the LONG WALLS to the Spartans in 457 B.C.E.; the second was the coup d'état of the FOUR HUNDRED in 411 B.C.E. All three attempts were inspired by an upper-class desire to rid the government of its lowest-income class of citizens, the *thētes*. Such plots failed because they inevitably did harm to the middle class—the HOPLITE class—as well as causing patriotic outrage.

See also OLIGARCHY; PLATO; SOCRATES; SYMPOSIUM.

Further reading: D. Whitehead, "The Tribes of the Thirty Tyrants," *Journal of Hellenic Studies* 100 (1980): 208–213; Peter Krentz, *The Thirty at Athens* (Ithaca, N.Y.: Cornell University Press, 1982); D. Whitehead, "Sparta and the Thirty Tyrants," *Ancient Society* 13–14 (1982–1983): 105–130; Andrew Wolpert, *Remembering Defeat: Civil War and Civic Memory in Ancient Athens* (Baltimore: Johns Hopkins University Press, 2002); Nicole Loraux, *The Divided City: On Memory and Forgetting in Ancient Athens* (New York: Zone Books, 2002).

Thrace   This non-Greek land extends for about 300 miles across the top of the AEGEAN SEA and the Sea of MARMARA, with a further coastline on the southwestern BLACK SEA, south of the Danube River. The region is now divided among the modern nations of Greece, Turkey, and Bulgaria. Relevant geographical features include three large rivers that empty southward into the Aegean; these are (from west to east) the Strymon, Nestus, and Hebrus. The largely mountainous interior rises to the Rhodope chain, which runs east-west along southern Bulgaria and the modern Greek border.

The ancient Greek name Thraikē probably renders the sound of some native name for the homeland. The Thracians spoke a non-Greek language and possessed northern European physical features, such as red hair. They brewed beer but for WINE they depended on Greek imports; they craved many Greek goods. The Thracians were renowned for their ferocity in battle (they used heavy slashing swords) and for their drunken devotions to the god DIONYSUS (a deity who may have originally been a Thracian beer god).

Throughout most of their history the Thracians remained grouped into various warlike tribes, chief of which were the Odrysae, in the east. Only in the mid-400s B.C.E. did a united Thracian kingdom emerge, briefly, under the Odrysian king Sitalces and his successors. The Thracians lived in villages, with no cities until Roman times (after the mid-100s B.C.E.).

Although Greece and Thrace had no common border—being buffered by the kingdom of MACEDON, northeast of Greece—Greek traders and settlers gravitated to Thrace's Aegean coast early on, to acquire the land's precious resources. GOLD and SILVER deposits at Mt. Pangaeus brought the Greek colonists to nearby THASOS (around 700 B.C.E.) and Maroneia (mid-600s B.C.E.), in defiance of hostile local tribes. Other Greek colonies in Thrace included BYZANTIUM (mid-600s B.C.E.), AENUS (around 600 B.C.E.), Perinthus (around 600 B.C.E.), the CHERSONESE region (mid-500s B.C.E.), ABDERA (545 B.C.E.), and AMPHIPOLIS (437 B.C.E.).

Besides resources for mining, Thrace offered wheat, TIMBER, and SLAVES to the Greeks. The slaves were often freeborn Thracian war captives, acquired in internal Thracian feuds and then sold to local Greek traders. Thracians might even sell their own children (according to the Greek historian HERODOTUS). Thracian slaves, particularly females, are mentioned periodically in writings from ancient Greece.

The internal history of Thrace consists mainly of the rise of the Odrysian state in the 400s B.C.E., followed by its collapse in the 300s B.C.E. The Macedonian kings PHILIP II and ALEXANDER THE GREAT invaded Thrace repeatedly (340s–330s B.C.E.), annexing the Strymon valley and other locales and subjugating the entire land. After Alexander's death, Thrace briefly became a sovereign power under the Macedonian dynast LYSIMACHUS (reigned 323–281 B.C.E.), before returning to Macedonian control. After the Roman conquest of Macedon in 167 B.C.E., Thrace became an uneasy section of the Roman province of Macedonia.

The primary city of ancient Thrace was Abdera, and it has been excavated by Greek archaeologists since the 1950s C.E. Remains have been discovered of the city walls, the roads (revealing an orthogonal urban plan), and several buildings of the HELLENISTIC AGE. The region's smaller towns have been the subject of very little archaeological exploration.

See also COLONIZATION; ORPHEUS.

Further reading: Gerda von Bülow, *Treasures of Thrace* (New York: St. Martin's Press, 1987); Manolis Andronikos, *Thessalonike Museum* (Athens: Ekdotike Athenon, 1993); General Secretariat of the Region of East Macedonia-Thrace, *Thrace* (Athens: Idea Advertising-Marketing SA, 1994); Zofia Archibald, *The Odrysian Kingdom of Thrace: Orpheus Unmasked* (New York: Oxford University Press, 1998); J. P. Stronk, "Crossing the Straits. The Persians in Thrace," *Talanta* 30–31 (1998–1999): 55–72; Nikola Theodossiev, *North-western Thrace from the Fifth to First Centuries B.C.* (Oxford: Archaeopress, 2000); M. Tonkova, "Classical Jewellery in Thrace. Origins and Development, Archaeological Context," *Talanta* 32–33 (2000–2001): 277–288; N. Theodossiev, "Mountain Goddesses in Ancient Thrace. The Broader Context," *Kernos* 15 (2002): 325–329.

Thucydides (1) (ca. 460–400 B.C.E.) *Athenian historian* Thucydides is best known for his detailed but unfinished account of the PELOPONNESIAN WAR (431–404 B.C.E.), which he had lived through. This work is one of the most valuable and impressive writings surviving from ancient Greece.

Although he was not the first Greek to write history—his main predecessor was HERODOTUS—Thucydides was in many ways the first real historian, the first author to apply rationalistic standards in inquiring about the past. Unlike Herodotus, Thucydides keeps strict chronology and avoids fables, biographical anecdotes, and (usually) digressions, instead focusing austerely on the most important events. In Herodotus's work, war and politics can result from the gods, FATE, or sexual passion. In Thucydides there are no such fairy-tale causes of action; Thucydides, like a modern political scientist, explains events in terms of a fundamental human drive for power and self-advantage.

In modern terms, Thucydides was as much a journalist as a historian, because much of what he reported was current or very recent as he was writing. He was no mere library scholar; already an adult when the Peloponnesian War began, he served (briefly and unsuccessfully) as an Athenian general. He states in his opening sentence that he began writing as soon as fighting broke out, since he believed that the war would be bigger and more worth recording than any prior conflict. He says that, for all events described, he either witnessed them firsthand or carefully interviewed participants afterward. Also (implicitly contrasting himself with the crowd-pleasing Herodotus), Thucydides announces that his opus will be the last word on the subject, and that it contains only strictly relevant information: "My work is written not as a display piece for an immediate audience, but as a prize to last forever" (book 1).

Thucydides belonged to a very distinguished Athenian family with wealth from GOLD- and SILVER-mining privileges in the Mt. Pangaeus region of THRACE. His father, although Athenian, bore the Thracian royal name Olorus. According to a plausible reconstruction of Thucydides' family tree, the eminent Athenian soldier and statesman KIMON was Thucydides' granduncle, while Thucydides's maternal grandfather was the right-wing politician THUCYDIDES (2), in whose honor the future historian was named. Yet the younger Thucydides at some point deserted his family's politics and followed the radical democrat PERIKLES, the bitter enemy of both Kimon and the elder Thucydides. In his writing, Thucydides the historian (normally sparing of praise) extolls Perikles' intelligence and leadership.

The young Thucydides probably heard the historian Herodotus give public readings in ATHENS, around

445–425 B.C.E. The earliest episode in Thucydides' life that is known today comes from a rare autobiographical mention in his history. Early in the Peloponnesian War, probably in 430 B.C.E., Thucydides caught the deadly plague that was sweeping through Athens. Unlike many Athenians, he survived, and in one passage he describes with scientific detachment the bodily symptoms of the disease and its devastation of the city (book 2).

By 424 B.C.E. he had been elected as one of Athens's 10 annual generals. He was assigned to the strategically vital coast of Thrace, where he already wielded influence as a mining mogul, but there (as he coolly relates in his history) he failed to prevent the Spartan commander BRASIDAS from capturing the Athenian colony of AMPHIPOLIS. For this failure, Thucydides was banished by the Athenians and lived away for 20 years, returning only when the exiles were recalled in 404 B.C.E., after Athens's final defeat.

Ironically, it was exile that allowed him to produce so fine a history. As an independently wealthy member of the international ARISTOCRACY in the days before general suspicion of espionage, Thucydides was able to travel through the theaters of war. "Because of my exile, I saw what was happening on both sides, particularly on the Peloponnesian side," he relates (book 5). He may have made the Thracian mining region his base, but he journeyed to SPARTA, whose paltry physical monuments he comments on (book 1), and to SYRACUSE, which looms large in his written work. He must have been a relentless seeker of truth—observing battles, interviewing soldiers and politicians, consulting archives, collating notes, and rejecting items in a drive for accuracy. Much of his information is amazing in its detail, but he rarely allows the details to submerge his story.

According to a later writer, Thucydides was married and had children. Apparently he died only a few years after his return to Athens. He never completed his history, which breaks off in midsentence describing events of 411 B.C.E. (The last seven years of the war are recounted by the historian XENOPHON, in his *Hellenica*.)

Thucydides' history was organized by later scholars into eight "books," but in content it can be broken down into four unequal sections: (1) books 1–5 (partial), on the Archidamian War and Peace of NIKIAS, 431–421 B.C.E., (2) book 5 (remainder), on the troubled years of temporary peace, 421–415 B.C.E., (3) books 6 and 7, a beautifully polished section describing the calamitous Athenian invasion of Syracuse, 415–413 B.C.E., and (4) book 8, describing naval events in the eastern Aegean and the right-wing coup of the FOUR HUNDRED in Athens, 412–411 B.C.E. Both book 5 and the unfinished book 8 are clearly unrevised drafts. The work's well-known set pieces include Perikles' funeral oration over the Athenian dead (book 2), the description of civil war and moral breakdown at the city of CORCYRA (book 3), and the Melian Dialogue, in which notions of Might versus Right are debated prior to

the Athenians' devastation of the helpless island of MELOS (book 5). Writing in his native Attic prose, Thucydides uses a uniquely clipped and condensed style that is sometimes difficult to understand. He seems to want to fit as much meaning into as few words as possible.

The writer's intelligence and mastery of his material tend to disguise certain flaws or quirks. It may be that Thucydides overrates Perikles as a soldier and glosses over a major Periklean military setback, the failed siege of the Peloponnesian city of EPIDAURUS in 430 B.C.E. Conversely, Thucydides surely underrates the motives and abilities of the Athenian politician KLEON; Thucydides seems to have disliked him personally—perhaps Kleon proposed the edict banishing General Thucydides in 424 B.C.E. Also, Thucydides shows himself totally uninterested in finance, despite its importance for the Athenian empire and war effort. His treatment of Greek-Persian affairs is skimpy, insofar as it was PERSIA's funding of the Spartan navy, 413–404 B.C.E., that enabled Sparta to defeat Athens. But some of these shortcomings might have been corrected had the historian lived to complete his work.

Another idiosyncrasy is Thucydides' way of ignoring questions of emotional motive, such as patriotism or religious piety, as not being true causes of events. Modern historians believe that emotional issues were important in such gatherings as the Athenian democratic ASSEMBLY, where demagogues might whip up the citizens to get them to vote a certain way. But in Thucydides' world it is only the victims, such as the doomed Melians in the Melian Dialogue, who make emotional appeals to the gods or to justice; the winners always speak in rational terms of selfadvantage and expediency.

Nevertheless, Thucydides stands as a monumental early figure in history writing. The personal impression he creates is that of an Olympian intellectual, patterned after his hero, Perikles. An atheist and a loner, enamored of intelligence and power, Thucydides could combine icy objectivity with a fascination for human affairs. He was a cynical genius, well suited to recording the suicidal event that toppled the classical Greek world.

Further reading: Michael Palmer, *Love of Glory and the Common Good: Aspects of the Political Thought of Thucydides* (Lanham, Md.: Rowman & Littlefield, 1992); Karl Maurer, *Interpolation in Thucydides* (Leiden, Netherlands: E. J. Brill, 1995); June W. Allison, *Word and Concept in Thucydides* (Atlanta: Scholars Press, 1997); Mary Frances Williams, *Ethics in Thucydides: The Ancient Simplicity* (Lanham, Md.: University Press of America, 1998); Gregory Crane, *Thucydides and the Ancient Simplicity: The Limits of Political Realism* (Berkeley: University of California Press, 1998); Tim Rood, *Thucydides: Narrative and Explanation* (New York: Oxford University Press, 1998); Robert Luginbill, *Thucydides on War and National Character* (Boulder, Colo.: Westview Press, 1999); Lowell S. Gustafson, ed., *Thucydides' Theory of International Relations: A Lasting Possession* (Baton Rouge: Louisiana State University Press,

2000); Jonathan Price, *Thucydides and Internal War* (New York: Cambridge University Press, 2001).

Thucydides (2) (b. ca. 500 B.C.E.) *Athenian politician in the 440s B.C.E.*

Thucydides led the rightwing opposition to the radical democrat PERIKLES and was ostracized by Perikles' efforts. Thucydides' defeat brought on a 14-year period of Periklean supremacy in the Athenian DEMOCRACY. This Thucydides probably was the maternal grandfather and namesake of the historian THUCYDIDES (1).

The future politician's father, Melesias, an Athenian nobleman and celebrated wrestler, was a friend of the poet PINDAR. Thucydides grew up in the cosmopolitan world of Greek aristocrats and married a sister of the great Athenian soldier KIMON. After Kimon's death (ca. 450 B.C.E.), Thucydides succeeded him as leader of the conservative opposition. He organized a system whereby all his followers sat together in the ASSEMBLY, in order to create more noise and effect during public debate.

An able orator, in around 448 B.C.E. Thucydides attacked Perikles' public-building policy, whereby allied DELIAN LEAGUE funds, contributed for defense against PERSIA, were to be used instead to erect grand monuments in ATHENS (such as the PARTHENON). Thucydides may have been sincerely offended by Athens's domination of other Greek states, as well as by Periklean domestic policies that opened up political opportunities to the Athenian lower-income classes.

But Perikles' support was overwhelming, and the Athenians voted to ostracize Thucydides (in about 443 B.C.E.). He seems to have returned to Athens after his term of exile ended, around 433 B.C.E., but we hear of no more political activity.

See also OSTRACISM; WRESTLING.

Thurii *See* SYBARIS.

timber In ancient mainland Greece, thick forests flourished in the foothills and mountains, which were cooler and far less heavily farmed than the arable plains. Trees carpeted mountainous regions such as ARCADIA and the Ossa-Pelion massif of southern THESSALY. The wood of these trees was a crucial construction material for public buildings, private homes, furnishings, machinery, and ships.

Foothills and lower mountain slopes supported a natural growth of deciduous trees; the most common was the oak, in several varieties. The oak's strong, heavy wood was an important source of timber for building beams and furniture. A tall, majestic tree, the "king" of the Greek forests, the oak was from an early period associated with ZEUS, king of the gods.

Other timber-producing trees of the middle-altitude region might include cypress, elm, and ash. Ash provides a tough, flexible wood that early on was used for military purposes. In HOMER's poems, the warriors' spears are described as being of ash.

Above 4,000 feet over sea level, the mountain regions produced the tallest conifers—fir, juniper, and cedar—which as a group supplied much of the best building timber in the ancient Mediterranean. Cedars produce large, durable beams, prized for big constructions such as a temple's roof supports. The fir tree, which grew in several varieties, was the seagoing tree; its lengthy, flexible, lightweight wood was well suited to the building of warships. Alternatively, the shipwright could use pine or cypress, which grew at lower altitudes than fir and were more accessible throughout the Greek world, but which gave the disadvantage of somewhat heavier planking. Merchant ships usually were made of pine.

Like grain, timber was a crucial import for the populous, powerful cities of central and southern Greece in the classical period. For the imperial ATHENS of the 400s B.C.E., with its need to maintain a large war fleet, foreign policy was partly a matter of ensuring friendship with—or else conquering—those states that had access to valuable forests of fir trees (such as MACEDON or the CHALCIDICE region).

In RELIGION, the Greeks associated certain trees with the Olympian gods. As mentioned above, the oak was linked to Zeus; similarly, the olive "belonged" to ATHENA, the laurel to APOLLO, the cedar and nut trees to ARTEMIS, and the myrtle to APHRODITE. DIONYSUS, the god of WINE and vegetation in general, was associated with the pine, the plane tree, and most fruit-bearing trees as well as with the grape and ivy vines. Despite these divine associations, such trees generally were not immune from being cut down. In most Greek communities, however, there existed sacred groves dedicated to a god or local hero, where the trees were sacrosanct.

See also DODONA; FARMING; SHIPS AND SEAFARING.

Further reading: Russell Meiggs, *Trees and Timber in the Ancient Mediterranean World* (Oxford: Clarendon Press, 1982); E. Raptou, "Contribution to the Study of the Economy of Ancient Cyprus. Copper, Timber," in *The Development of the Cypriot Economy. From the Prehistoric Period to the Present Day*, edited by V. Karageorghis and D. Michaelides (Nicosia, Cyprus: Lithographica, 1996), 249–259; Oliver Rackham, *Trees, Wood, and Timber in Greek History* (Oxford: Leopard's Head Press, 2001); K. Bringmann, "Grain, Timber, and Money. Hellenistic Kings, Finance, Buildings, and Foundations in Greek Cities," in *Hellenistic Economies*, edited by Zofia H. Archibald (London: Routledge, 2001), 205–214.

Timoleon (ca. 411–337 B.C.E.) *Corinthian-born commander and statesman who in the 340s B.C.E. became the political savior of Greek Sicily*

Liberating the various cities from their dictatorial TYRANTS, Timoleon led the Greeks in resistance to Carthaginian invaders.

Timoleon was a soldier and aristocrat of middle age, living in CORINTH in 345 B.C.E., when the Corinthians sent him with a small mercenary force to Sicily, in response to a request for help from the aristocrats of SYRACUSE. (Syracuse was the foremost Sicilian Greek city, and a Corinthian colony and ally.) The Syracusans were seeking aid against the tyrant Dionysius II, who, after a period of exile, had reinstated himself as master of the city. By combining military strategy with diplomacy, Timoleon ousted Dionysius. Then he reorganized the Syracusan government, creating a liberal OLIGARCHY on the Corinthian model. Thereafter he began a campaign to oust the tyrants of the other Sicilian-Greek cities and reorganize those governments.

Amid these events, in 341 B.C.E., a seaborne Carthaginian invasion force landed in Sicily. Timoleon won an initial victory over the invaders at the Crimisus River, in northwestern Sicily, but he was forced to sue for peace with the Carthaginians, after the Greek tyrants joined the war against him. Having made this peace, he was then free to defeat the tyrants separately (around 340–337 B.C.E.) and to complete his reorganization of the cities' governments. He spent his final few years as a revered private citizen at Syracuse and died there.

Timoleon's political significance and success are attested by the fact that Sicily continued to flourish for several years after his death. Unfortunately, however, within a generation chaos returned to the island, and a new Syracusan tyrant, AGATHOKLES, arose.

See also CARTHAGE.

Further reading: Richard Talbert, *Timoleon and the Revival of Greek Sicily, 344–317 B.C.* (New York: Cambridge University Press, 1974); R. R. Holloway, "Syracusan Coinage between Dion and Timoleon," *Numismatica e antichità classiche* 20 (1991): 57–62; Lars Karlsson, "The Symbols of Freedom and Democracy on the Bronze Coinage of Timoleon," in *Ancient Sicily*, edited by Tobias Fischer-Hansen (Copenhagen: Museum Tusculanum Press, 1995), 149–170.

tin   See BRONZE.

Tiryns   This ancient Greek city is located in the Argolid region of the northeastern PELOPONNESE, near modern Nauplion. With its spectacular fortifications, first excavated by archaeologist Heinrich Schliemann in 1884 C.E., Tiryns provides the best surviving example of a fortress city of the MYCENAEAN CIVILIZATION (around 1300 B.C.E.).

Tiryns was ideally located, atop a rocky hill in the southeast Argive plain, beside the sea (which now lies a mile away, due to coastal changes since ancient times). The site was inhabited long before the Greek era; the name Tiryns was not originally Greek for its ending resembles the distinctive *nth* sound found in such other pre-Greek names as CORINTH and OLYNTHOS. Archaeological evidence suggests that Tiryns was among the first sites in Greece to be taken over by Greek-speaking invaders. The Greeks' arrival probably is indicated in the destruction of the pre-Greek palace known as the House of the Tiles, at nearby Lerna (around 2100 B.C.E.).

In the Mycenaean age (1600–1200 B.C.E.) Tiryns served as the port for the overlord city of MYCENAE, nine miles to the north. Tiryns received its famous encircling walls, at two separate levels of its terraced hill, after 1400 B.C.E. These fortifications, made of huge limestone blocks weighing as much as 14 tons each, rose about 65 feet, with a typical thickness of 20–30 feet. In the east there stood a tall gateway, protected by an enfilading wall, similar to the Lion Gate at Mycenae. Greeks of later centuries ascribed these works to the mythical giant creatures known as Cyclopes, and they coined the adjective *Cyclopean*, which still is used today to denote Mycenaean grand masonry.

Within the walls stood a city complex, ascending to the summit's two royal halls (east and west), built in different eras. These two palaces were made of limestone and wood; a bathhouse and remnants of frescoes throughout suggest a primitive luxury. Tiryns's prominence in this epoch is reflected in Greek MYTH, which claimed that the hero HERAKLES was born there or that his family came from there.

Like Mycenae and other cities, Tiryns shows clear signs of having been destroyed by fire around 1200 B.C.E., amid the collapse of Mycenaean society. Reinhabited on a reduced scale, the town survived into historical times. But by then the nearby city of ARGOS was the dominant power of the plain, and in around 470 B.C.E. the Argives destroyed Tiryns.

See also ARCHAEOLOGY; CYCLOPS; GREEK LANGUAGE.

Further reading: Heinrich Schliemann, *Tiryns: The Prehistoric Palace of the Kings of Tiryns* (New York: Arno Press, 1976, reprint of the 1885 edition); E. Zangger, "Landscape Changes around Tiryns during the Bronze Age," *American Journal of Archaeology* 98 (1994): 189–212; N. Claire Loader, *Building in Cyclopean Masonry: With Special Reference to the Mycenaean Fortifications on Mainland Greece* (Jonsered: P. Aström, 1998); Alkestis Papademetriou, *Tiryns: A Guide to the History and Archaeology*, translated by Alexandra Doumas (Athens: Hesperos Editions, 2001).

Titans   In MYTH, the Titans were a race of primeval gods who preceded the Olympian gods. They were the offspring of the goddess GAEA (Mother Earth) and the god Uranus (Greek: Ouranos, Sky); the most important of their number was CRONUS, who ruled the universe prior to his son ZEUS.

The Titans represent the brutal era before Zeus's civilizing reign. As recounted in HESIOD's epic poem the *Theogony* (around 700 B.C.E.), Zeus became king after leading his fellow gods in a 10-year war against Cronus and the other Titans. (But two Titans, PROMETHEUS and Themis, fought beside the gods, as did other supernatural beings—the Cyclopes and the Hekatoncheires, or "hundred-handed ones.") Defeated, the enemy Titans now lie shackled forever in the lowest level of the Underworld—all except ATLAS, whose immense strength is employed in holding up the sky.

If the name Titan (plural: Titanes) is actually a Greek word, it may mean "honored one." More probably it is not Greek, but derives from the lost language of the pre-Greek inhabitants of Greece. The legend of the defeated Titans may distortedly commemorate the Greeks' conquest of a native people, around 2100 B.C.E.

See also AFTERLIFE; CYCLOPS; GIANTS; OLYMPUS, MT.; ORPHISM; RELIGION.

Further reading: N. Leipen, "Atlas, the Titan Who Supported the Sky," in *Tranquillitas. Mélanges en l'honneur de Tran tam Tinh,* edited by Marie-Odile Jentel and Gisèle Deschênes-Wagner (Quebec: Université Laval, 1994), 333–342; A. Annus, "Are There Greek Rephaim? On the Etymology of Greek Meropes and Titanes," *Ugarit-Forschungen* 31 (1999): 13–30.

trade   The Greeks (along with their neighbors, the Phoenicians) were the greatest traders and seafarers of the ancient Mediterranean world. They sailed far and wide, constantly searching for new commercial markets and trade opportunities; through these excursions Greek civilization made its tremendous impact on other ancient cultures, including the ETRUSCANS, the CELTS, the Romans, and the Scythians.

Greek trade routes can be reconstructed using archaeological evidence such as Greek POTTERY and metalwork found in non-Greek lands. Written references by such authors as the Greek historian HERODOTUS or the Roman geographer Strabo also help complete the picture. It is known that as early as about 1300 B.C.E., long before the invention of COINAGE, Mycenaean-Greek merchants were spanning the Mediterranean and trading by barter. Archaeologists have discovered that these early Greeks had trade depots in the Lipari Islands (near SICILY) as well as on CYPRUS, in western ASIA MINOR, and in the northern Levant. During the Greek trading and colonizing expansion around 800–500 B.C.E., Greek merchants visited southern France and Spain and the farthest corners of the BLACK SEA. In about 308 B.C.E., a Greek skipper named Pytheas of MASSALIA explored the Atlantic seaboard, sailing around Britain and perhaps reaching Norway in his search for new trade routes.

In many cases, Greek traders were inspired to travel these amazing distances by the need to acquire certain valuable resources unavailable in Greece. Southern Spain, for example, offered raw tin, a necessary component of the alloy BRONZE, a metal essential to many aspects of ancient Greek society for centuries. In the elaborate trade network of the ancient Mediterranean, tin was quarried by Celtic peoples in British Cornwall and (possibly) in northwest Spain, and it was brought to the Greek market, overland to the Mediterranean, by Celtic middlemen. Other prized resources of the western Mediterranean included SILVER ore and lead. In exchange, the Greeks offered metalwork, textiles, and WINE, brought from mainland Greece or from the Greek cities of Asia Minor.

In other instances, Greek exchange networks were forged because of the desire for exotic luxury goods. To acquire the carved ivories, metalwork, and textiles of EGYPT, for example, the ancient Greeks would have to offer SLAVES, silver ore, or other basic resources that the wealthy Egyptians lacked. Perhaps most desirable of all Egyptian goods was the grain surplus of the Nile valley, which Greek merchants could ship to hungry Greece for lucrative resale. Grain, along with TIMBER, was also a major attraction of Sicily, ITALY, THRACE, and the northern Black Sea coast. Among valuable Greek exports were the painted pottery of CORINTH (600s B.C.E.) and ATHENS (500s B.C.E.), and the woolen textiles of MILETUS and other cities of IONIA.

The conquests of the Macedonian king ALEXANDER THE GREAT (334–323 B.C.E.) flooded the Greek market with luxury goods and changed the trading map of the ancient world. For instance, the greater availability of metalwork greatly reduced the demand for ceramic vessels. During the HELLENISTIC ERA, travel increased even further, as did international commerce (particularly eastward, to central Asia). Improved harbors, as well as roads, bridges, and canals, all contributed to the growth of trade in the 200s and 100s B.C.E., and this trend continued after the Roman conquest of the eastern Mediterranean.

See also AEGINA; AL MINA; CARTHAGE; CHALCIDICĒ; CHALCIS; CHIOS; COLONIZATION; CRETE; GOLD; ILLYRIS; PITHECUSAE; PHOENICIA; RHODES; SAMOS; SHIPS AND SEAFARING; TROY.

Further reading: Fik Meijer, *Trade, Transport, and Society in the Ancient World. A Sourcebook* (London: Routledge, 1992); Helen Parkins and Christopher Smith, eds., *Trade, Traders, and the Ancient City* (London: Routledge, 1998); Jane Shuter, *Builders, Craftsmen, and Traders* (Des Plaines, Ill.: Heinemann Library, 1999); C. M. Reed, *Maritime Traders in the Ancient Greek World* (New York: Cambridge University Press, 2003); Sitta von Reden, *Exchange in Ancient Greece* (London: Duckworth, 2003).

Early Mediterranean Trade Routes

tragedy   *See* THEATER.

trees   *See* TIMBER.

tribes   *See* KINSHIP.

trireme   *See* WARFARE, NAVAL.

Troilus   The son of the mythical Trojan king PRIAM and his wife, HECUBA, Troilus was slain by the Greek champion ACHILLES in the early days of the TROJAN WAR.

Although Troilus had only a small role in Greek MYTH, he became important later, in the medieval European legend of Troilus and Cressida.

Further reading: A. Cambitoglou and J. Wade, "Achilles and Troilos," *Antike Kunst* 15 (1972): 90–94; Martin Robertson, "Troilos and Polyxene. Notes on a Changing Legend," in *Eumousia: Ceramic and Iconographic Studies in Honour of Alexander Cambitoglou*, edited by Jean-Paul Descoeudres (Sydney: Meditarch, 1990), 63–70.

Trojan War   The legend of the Trojan War is today the best-known story from Greek MYTH. Amazingly rich in its many characters and events, the Trojan War legend describes how the allied Greeks—under the command of King AGAMEMNON of MYCENAE—sailed from Greece and laid siege to the non-Greek city of TROY (also called Ilion or Ilium), located outside the mouth of the HELLESPONT sea channel, in northwest ASIA MINOR. The Greeks had come at Agamemnon's behest to avenge the abduction of the beautiful Helen—wife of Agamemnon's brother MENELAUS—by the Trojan prince PARIS. The Trojans, then sheltering Paris and the compliant Helen within their walls, had refused the Greeks' demand for Helen's return. This was the official reason for the war, although the Greeks also craved Troy's wealth.

The siege, consisting mainly of battlefield fighting on the plains outside the city, lasted for 10 years and saw the death of many heroes on both sides, including the Trojan prince HECTOR and the Greek champion ACHILLES. Finally Troy fell to a stratagem devised by the wily Greek hero ODYSSEUS. Pretending to abandon the siege, the Greeks sailed away, leaving behind a huge wooden horse they had constructed—the so-called Trojan Horse. Hidden within this hollow monument was a picked force of Greek soldiers, but the unsuspecting Trojans believed the horse to be a Greek offering to the gods and brought it into the city. After nightfall, the Greeks emerged from the horse and opened Troy's gates to the waiting Greek army (which had hurried back under cover of darkness).

Destruction of the rich and proud city followed, with the inhabitants all massacred or captured as SLAVES. The Greeks' arrogant and impious behavior at the sack of Troy

however, angered the gods, who decreed that many of the surviving Greek heroes would be killed on the voyage home.

The immense saga—of which HOMER's *Iliad* and *Odyssey* present only a portion—was the product of Greek oral poetic tradition over several centuries, approximately 1200–550 B.C.E. The legend produced a body of EPIC POETRY, describing major episodes of the war. The earliest and greatest of the heroic epics were the two poems written down around 750 B.C.E. and ascribed to the poet Homer—namely, the *Iliad*, or *Tale of Ilium*, recounting the "passion" of the Greek hero Achilles during the war's 10th year; and the *Odyssey*, describing the homecoming of the Greek hero Odysseus, with several back references to the last days of the war.

These two Homeric poems, however, were not the only epic poems dealing with the Trojan War. The classical Greeks (400s B.C.E.) knew at least six other Trojan-related epics, not ascribed to Homer. These poems did not survive antiquity, but their story plots are summarized by later writers. The lost Trojan War epics were: (1) the *Cypria* ("Tales from CYPRUS"), describing the war's causes and outset; (2) the *Aethiopis*, recounting Achilles' slaying of the Ethiopian king MEMNON (a Trojan ally) and Achilles' own death in battle; (3) *The Little Iliad*, describing the madness of the Greek hero AJAX (1) and the episode of the Wooden Horse; (4) the *Capture of Troy (Iliou Persis)*, recording the Greeks' bloody capture of the city; (5) the *Homecomings*, recording the calamitous homeward voyages of the surviving Greek heroes other than Odysseus; and (6) the *Telegonia*, describing Odysseus's last days and the related adventures of Telegonus, who was his son by the witch CIRCE.

In 1870–1890 C.E. the pioneering German archaeologist Heinrich Schliemann discovered and excavated the ancient site of Troy, which—amid its various ancient strata—showed clear signs of having been destroyed by a great fire around 1220 B.C.E. Since this epoch-making discovery, scholars have universally come to agree that the Trojan War of legend was based on some genuine event of the late Mycenaean age. Certainly the Mycenaean Greeks possessed the wealth, manpower, and organization to launch such an expedition, and they probably had sufficient cause; even if we dismiss the abduction of Spartan Helen as a fiction, there remains that fact that ancient Troy must have controlled the Hellespont waterway and was probably preying on the Mycenaeans' vital imports of raw metals.

See also AJAX (2); ARCHAEOLOGY; ANDROMACHE; BRONZE; CASSANDRA; DIOMEDES; HECUBA; HELEN OF TROY; LAOCOÖN; NEOPTOLEMUS; NESTOR; PHILOKTETES; PRIAM; TRADE; WARFARE, LAND; WARFARE, SIEGE.

Further reading: S. Woodford, *The Trojan War in Ancient Art* (London: Duckworth, 1993); Jonathan Burgess, *The Tradition of the Trojan War in Homer and the Epic Cycle* (Baltimore: Johns Hopkins University Press,

2001); Donna Wilson, *Ransom, Revenge, and Heroic Identity in the Iliad* (New York: Cambridge University Press, 2002); Diane Thompson, *The Trojan War: Literature and Legends from the Bronze Age to the Present* (Jefferson, N.C.: McFarland, 2004); M. S. Silk, *Homer: The Iliad,* 2d ed. (New York: Cambridge University Press, 2004); Barry Powell, *Homer* (Malden, Mass.: Blackwell, 2004).

Troy This ancient city of ASIA MINOR is usually described as being inhabited by a non-Greek people. In the late BRONZE AGE (around 1300 B.C.E.), Troy was evidently one of the most powerful cities of the eastern Mediterranean. The site of ancient Troy—at the village of Hissarlik, in modern-day Turkey—was discovered by the German archaeologist Heinrich Schliemann in 1870 C.E. But Troy had been famous for 3,000 years prior, immortalized in the ancient Greek epic cycle of the TROJAN WAR, of which the two greatest poems are HOMER's *Iliad* and *Odyssey.* Schliemann's epoch-making discovery revealed that the historical Troy had achieved affluence in the early second millennium B.C.E., before being destroyed in an immense fire, at the archaeological level known as Troy VIIa (around 1220 B.C.E.). Modern scholars tend to believe that this destruction marks the real event commemorated in the mythical Trojan War.

The name *Troy* comes to us from the poet Homer and other Greek writers who called the city Troia and Ilion. These names seem to have no meaning in the Greek language, and may simply preserve the ancient Trojans' names for their city. Greek MYTH mentions two Trojan founding fathers—Tros and his son Ilus—who gave the city its two names; but this sounds like a later rationalization. The first founder of Troy, according to Greek myth, was Tros's grandfather Dardanus.

Troy is situated at the very northwestern corner of Asia Minor, about four miles south of the western mouth of the HELLESPONT waterway and about four miles inland of the AEGEAN SEA. Set on a height commanding the seaside plain, ancient Troy could raid or toll the merchant shipping in the Hellespont without itself being blockaded inside the strait; its inland site left it safe from surprise raids by sea. Troy's control of the Hellespont must have been a crucial factor in the city's prosperity and was probably the reason why the real Trojan War was fought; the Mycenaean Greeks of the mid-1200s B.C.E. may have decided to destroy Troy because it was blocking their badly needed imports of metals from Asia Minor.

Schliemann's excavations uncovered no fewer than nine levels of habitation at Troy, dating from around 2500 B.C.E. to the early first century C.E. The significant levels for our purpose begin with Troy VI (about 1900–1300 B.C.E.), which marks the arrival of certain invaders—an accomplished people, with horses and superior building techniques, who enlarged and refortified the city. These Trojans may have been Luwians, displaced from interior Asia Minor by the Hittites. Or these Trojans may have been kinfolk of the first Greeks, who in the same centuries were descending through the Greek peninsula, overrunning or assimilating the prior inhabitants there.

This impressive Troy VI was devastated by an earthquake around 1300 B.C.E. Troy VIIa represents the survivors' rebuilding in the wreckage, along the plan of the preceding city. This Troy was destroyed by fire around 1220 B.C.E., in what may have been the Trojan War.

Scholars have always noted that the small size of Schliemann's Troy VIIa seems at odds with Homer's picture of a mighty and defiant fortress city. Until archaeologists can find convincing evidence of wider ancient city limits, it must be assumed that the Trojan War legends greatly exaggerate the grandeur of the real Troy of the 1200s B.C.E.

Schliemann excavated at the site of Troy from 1871 to 1891, followed by Carl Blegen (University of Cincinnati, Ohio) from 1932 to 1938. The current program of work began in 1988, under the direction of the German archaeologist Manfred Korfmann, with the cooperation of the American archaeologist Brian Rose from the University of Cincinnati. This project is using modern techniques to review the findings of the early excavations, as well as exploring new areas of the site and the greater Troad region. Documentation, conservation, and restoration of the archaeological remains are also essential components of the fieldwork program.

See also ARCHAEOLOGY.

Further reading: Robert Payne, *The Gold of Troy: The Story of Heinrich Schliemann and the Buried Cities of Ancient Greece* (New York: Dorset Press, 1990); Caroline Moorhead, *The Lost Treasures of Troy* (London: Weidenfeld and Nicolson, 1994); Michael Wood, *In Search of the Trojan War* (London: Penguin Books, 1996); Susan Heuck Allen, *Finding the Walls of Troy: Frank Calvert and Heinrich Schliemann at Hisarlik* (Berkeley: University of California Press, 1999); Andrew Erskine, *Troy between Greece and Rome: Local Tradition and Imperial Power* (New York: Oxford University Press, 2001); Manfred Korfmann and Dietrich Mannsperger, *A Guide to Troia* (Istanbul: Ege Yayinlari, 2001); D. F. Easton, *Schliemann's Excavations at Troia, 1870–1873* (Mainz am Rhein, Germany: von Zabern, 2002).

Tydeus *See* SEVEN AGAINST THEBES.

Typhon One of several mythical monsters that arose to challenge the might of ZEUS soon after the beginning of the world. Typhon (or Typhoeus) was a son of the earth goddess, GAEA. The epic poet HESIOD, in his *Theogony* (around 700 B.C.E.), vividly describes Typhon as having a vaguely human form with 100 serpents' heads that sparked fire and made the deafening noise of many different beasts. This grotesque creature tried to take over the world but was incinerated by Zeus's thunderbolts. Being immortal, Typhon could not die and was imprisoned for eternity in Tartarus (the lowest abyss of the Underworld).

Like other hybrid creatures described in Hesiod, Typhon probably represents a mythological borrowing from the Near East. Greek legend often associated Typhon with the southeastern ASIA MINOR region called Cilicia, and perhaps Typhon was originally a spirit of Cilician volcanoes.

As Greek exploration opened up SICILY and southern ITALY in about 800–600 B.C.E., Typhon became "reassigned" to that new frontier (as did other Greek mythical figures). At that time he was said to be imprisoned under Mt. Etna, in Sicily, where his fire and rage were the cause of that volcano's eruptions.

In surviving artwork, Typhon is sometimes shown as a snake-footed man in combat with Zeus. For the Greeks, the battle provided a picturesque emblem of savagery versus civilization.

See also GIANTS; PINDAR.

Further reading: J. G. Griffiths, "The Flight of the Gods before Typhon. An Unrecognized Myth," *Hermes* 88 (1960): 374–376; Anne Rockwell, *The One-eyed Giant and Other Monsters from the Greek Myths* (New York: Greenwillow Books, 1996).

tyrants The Greek tyrants were dictators who first arose at various Greek cities on a wave of middle-class anger in the mid 600s B.C.E. and seized the government from the aristocrats who had hitherto ruled. The Greek title tyrant (*tyrannos*) did not at first denote the cruel abuse of power, as it does now; rather, it had a neutral meaning—"usurper with supreme power." The word *tyrannos* apparently was imported to Greece from the Near East, where it had been used to describe the usurping Lydian king Gyges (ca. 670 B.C.E.). The point of this newly minted Greek word was that, for the first time in Greek memory, these despots were coming from outside the narrow ruling circles.

What brought the first tyrants to power was a growing Greek middle class that was ready for political and social privileges that the aristocrats had denied them. By the mid-600s B.C.E. CORINTH and other cities had been active in seaborne TRADE for probably 200 years. This trade had created a class of merchants and manufacturers with wealth but no prestige or political voice. When a revolution in military tactics brought these middle-class men into the army to serve as HOPLITES, their potential power increased greatly. There followed, throughout the greater Greek cities, a wave of tyrants' revolutions.

The first Greek *tyrannos* now known is PHEIDON OF ARGOS (ca. 670 B.C.E.). Other famous tyrants include KYPSELOS of Corinth (and his son PERIANDER), KLEISTHENES (2) of SIKYON, PEISISTRATUS OF ATHENS (and his son HIPPIAS (1)), and POLYCRATES of SAMOS. Tyrants also held power at MEGARA (1), MILETUS, and many other Greek cities. These rulers spanned the period from about 670–510 B.C.E. Their dynasties rarely lasted for more than two generations, since it was impossible to maintain or repeat constructively the popular discontent that had raised the tyrant to power in the first place.

Like other popular dictators throughout history, the tyrants sought to bring amenities to the poor and to relieve unemployment with public works. Tyrants such as Polycrates were known for improving local water supplies as well as for their monumental building programs, which glorified themselves and their cities. Tyrants might also be known for their unbridled passions and sexuality.

The enemy of the tyrants was the Panhellenic class of the ARISTOCRACY, who had most to fear from revolution. But the tyrants also had an enemy in the Greek city of SPARTA, which by the 500s B.C.E. had developed into a kind of Greek police force, sending out troops in response to appeals from displaced aristocrats of Samos, Athens, and elsewhere. In 510 B.C.E. the Spartans ejected the last important tyrant of mainland Greece, Hippias of Athens; in his place, the Athenians soon established the first Greek DEMOCRACY.

The great supporter of the tyrants was the Eastern kingdom of PERSIA, which used Greek tyrants as puppet rulers in its conquest of Greek ASIA MINOR. The Persians also negotiated in secret with independent tyrants in mainland Greece, in hopes of winning collaborators.

Tyrants played a major role in the history of Greek SICILY, particularly at the preeminent city of SYRACUSE. This was due in part to bitter class divisions within Sicilian-Greek society. But another factor was the abiding external menace of the Carthaginians, who inhabited the western corner of Sicily and who periodically launched massive campaigns to subjugate the island's Greek cities. There thus arose a demand for capable Greek military dictators who could organize defense. The early 400s B.C.E. saw a series of grand Sicilian tyrants, culminating in GELON of Syracuse (ca. 480 B.C.E.), his brother HIERON (1) (ca. 470 B.C.E.), and Theron of ACRAGAS (ca. 480 B.C.E.), all of whom were known for their wealth and magnificent court.

Although Syracuse saw periods of democracy, conditions there remained ripe for tyrants down through the 200s B.C.E., long after tyranny had faded away elsewhere in the Greek world. The most famous or notorious of the later Syracusan tyrants were DIONYSIUS (1) (ca. 390 B.C.E.) and AGATHOKLES (ca. 300 B.C.E.); Agathokles was the first tyrant to assume the title king.

See also PERSIAN WARS.

Further reading: Brian Lavelle, *The Sorrow and the Pity: A Prolegomenon to a History of Athens under the Peisistratids, c. 560–510 B.C.* (Stuttgart, Germany: F. Steiner, 1993); J. A. Smith, *Athens under the Tyrants* (Bristol, U.K.: Bristol Classical Press, 1989); H. Alan Shapiro, *Art and*

Cult under the Tyrants in Athens (Mainz am Rhein, Germany: von Zabern, 1989); M. M. Austin, "Greek Tyrants and the Persians, 546–479 B.C.," *Classical Quarterly* 40 (1990): 289–306; J. Salmon, "Lopping Off the Heads? Tyrants, Politics, and the Polis," in *The Development of the Polis in Archaic Greece*, edited by L. G. Mitchell and P. J. Rhodes (London: Routledge, 1997), 60–73; Heleen Sancisi-Weerdenburg, ed., *Peisistratos and the Tyranny: A Reappraisal of the Evidence* (Amsterdam: J. C. Gieben, 2000); H. van Wees, "Tyrants, Oligarchs, and Citizen Militia," in *Army and Power in the Ancient World*, edited by A. Chaniotis and P. Ducrey (Stuttgart, Germany: Steiner, 2002), 61–82; S. E. Harrell, "King or Private Citizen. Fifth-century Sicilian Tyrants at Olympia and Delphi," *Mnemosyne* 55 (2002): 439–464.

Tyre *See* PHOENICIA.

Tyrtaeus (mid-600s B.C.E.) *Spartan lyric poet*
Tyrtaeus was born in the region of Attica but spent most of his life and career in Sparta. According to legend, he was sent to Sparta at the instruction of the oracle at DELPHI to assist the Spartans in the Second Messenian War. A later tale also claims that Tyrtaeus was originally a lame Athenian schoolmaster. The Athenians supposedly chose to send him to Sparta as someone they thought would never assist the Spartans in their conquest of the PELOPONNESE, but his poetry turned out to be the most inspiring aid possible, and his poems encouraged the Spartans in their difficult fight during the Second Messenian War.

Tyrtaeus wrote elegiac verse, a form of poetry intended for recital to flute accompaniment, but only fragments of his work survive today. His poems were patriotic and instructional—reminding his listeners, for example, how beautiful it is to die for one's country and urging them to adhere to the specific tactics of HOPLITE warfare. His propagandistic poetry belonged to a larger program by which SPARTA transformed itself in those years into a militaristic society, with the best army in Greece.

Tyrtaeus is said to have composed military marching songs (now lost) in the Spartan Doric dialect, but he wrote his elegies in Ionic Greek, following the literary convention of his day. His verses contain epic-style language with many echoes of HOMER. He lived at least through the end of the Second Messenian War (668 B.C.E.), but the exact date and circumstances of his death are uncertain. Depending on how late in the century Tyrtaeus lived, he may have been influenced by the Ionian poet KALLINUS of EPHESOS, who also developed the elegy for patriotic themes.

See also GREEK LANGUAGE; LYRIC POETRY; MESSENIA.

Further reading: Douglas Gerber, *A Companion to the Greek Lyric Poets* (Leiden, Netherlands: E. J. Brill, 1997); Hans van Wees, "Tyrtaeus' Eunomia: Nothing to Do with the Great Rhetra," in *Sparta: New Perspectives*, edited by Stephen Hodkinson and Anton Powell (London: Duckworth, 1999), 1–42; Douglas Gerber, ed., *Greek Elegiac Poetry: From the Seventh to the Fifth Centuries B.C.* (Cambridge, Mass.: Harvard University Press, 1999); Peter J. Steinberger, ed., *Readings in Classical Political Thought* (Indianapolis, Ind.: Hackett, 2000).

U–W

Ulysses   *See* ODYSSEUS.

Underworld   *See* AFTERLIFE; HADES.

Uranus   *See* CRONUS; GAEA.

vase-painting   *See* POTTERY.

vines and viticulture   *See* FARMING; WINE.

voting   *See* DEMOCRACY.

warfare, land   The famous land battles of ancient Greece were primarily collisions of heavy infantry, who met on open ground by mutual consent. CAVALRY remained secondary, partly due to the mountainous Greek terrain and partly due to technical matters, such as the small size of Greek horses and the absence of stirrups. It took the tactical genius of the Macedonian king PHILIP II and his son ALEXANDER THE GREAT (mid-300s B.C.E.) to make cavalry at least partly effective against infantry.

It is less obvious why light-armed foot soldiers were underemployed until the 400s B.C.E. Commanders in mountainous Greece might have been expected to develop guerrilla tactics using projectile troops—javelin men, archers, and slingers. However, for social and psychological reasons, such tactics did not arise among the major Greek states until the PELOPONNESIAN WAR (431–404 B.C.E.). Instead, the Greeks (a sporting people) tended to think of war as a manly and consensual contest of strength. "Whenever the Greeks declare war on one

another, they go find the most smooth and level piece of ground and fight their battle there," states an observer cited by the historian HERODOTUS (ca. 435 B.C.E.). In classical Greece, as in Europe of the 18th century C.E., brutal warfare was conducted along certain gentlemanly guidelines.

Greek military history falls into three major phases: (1) Mycenaean and post-Mycenaean warfare, around 1600–750 B.C.E., (2) the age of the HOPLITE, or heavily armed infantryman, around 650–320 B.C.E.; and (3) the era of the Macedonian-developed PHALANX, perfected by Alexander the Great and employed by his successors. The HELLENISTIC AGE (around 300–150 B.C.E.) saw larger armies, commanded by absolute monarchs, battling for vast tracts of land in the eastern Mediterranean and using such innovative war "machines" as elephants. In the end, phalanx and elephant fell to the superior maneuverability of the legions of Republican ROME (100s B.C.E.).

To understand Mycenaean warfare, modern scholars rely on such archaeological evidence as arms and armor from burial sites and artistic depictions of soldiering on surviving artwork. Also helpful if approached cautiously are the battle descriptions in HOMER's *Iliad* (written down around 750 B.C.E. but purporting to describe the TROJAN WAR, fought around 1220 B.C.E.).

Mycenaean warfare (somewhat like medieval European warfare) revolved around armored noblemen who would take the field at the head of their kinsmen and retainers. These warlords are commemorated in such Homeric heroes as ACHILLES and DIOMEDES. In battle, such champions would seek out their social equals on the enemy side, to duel it out with javelins, jabbing spears, and stabbing swords. As IRON was yet unknown, the

This warrior vase from Mycenae shows soldiers carrying the jabbing spears and body-covering oxhide shields that were obsolete by 1450 B.C.E. *(Alison Frantz Photographic Collection, American School of Classical Studies at Athens)*

choice metal for war was BRONZE. The most dramatic Mycenaean armament—the body-covering shield of oxhide, stretched on a wooden frame, such as AJAX (1) carries in the *Iliad*—was obsolete by about 1450 B.C.E., replaced by wooden shields faced with bronze. CHARIOTS were used for war—perhaps to convey champions across the plain to the fighting, or perhaps for chariot battles, on the model of contemporary Egyptian and Hittite warfare. The rough terrain of Greece does not generally lend itself to chariots, but the plains of ARGOS and BOEOTIA would have sufficed.

The depressed years of the DARK AGE (1100–900 B.C.E.) continued the Mycenaean pattern on an impoverished scale. War was still a job for aristocrats and their followers. Bronze armor became scarcer then, but iron—more plentiful than bronze—made its first appearance, in swords and spear points.

The emergence of the hoplite (after 700 B.C.E.) eliminated the old, individualistic approach to war. Henceforth battles were decided not by dueling champions but by large concentrations of armored hoplites, arrayed in tight rows, who fought by pushing with their spears and shields in an organized effort to break the enemy formation. The hoplite era includes the most famous conflicts of mainland Greece: the PERSIAN WARS and Peloponnesian Wars (400s B.C.E.), and the wars of SPARTA and THEBES (300s B.C.E.).

The precise origins of hoplite warfare are unclear. It is known that in 669 B.C.E. the army of ARGOS decisively defeated a Spartan force at Hysiae in the eastern PELOPONESE; evidence suggests that the Argives at this battle were the first Greeks to use large-scale hoplite tactics,

against Spartans who were still fighting in the disorganized old manner.

The hoplite's name came from his new-style shield, the *hoplon,* made of bronze-faced wood. The *hoplon* was round, wide (about three feet in diameter), heavy (about 16 pounds), and deeply concave; in battle it enclosed the soldier's torso while extending toward his neighbor on the left. Other hoplite armament included a bronze helmet and breastplate, a six- to eight-foot-long jabbing spear, and a stabbing or slashing sword of forged iron, for use after the spear had broken. A hoplite's armor, weighing about 60 pounds, would not be worn on the march, but would be carried in wagons or by personal SLAVES or servants.

One difference between the hoplite and previous Greek warriors was that the hoplite was nearly helpless on his own. He remained an effective fighter so long as he stayed grouped with his fellows. Should soldiers leave the battle formation—whether by turning and fleeing from the rear ranks or by breaking ranks in front to chase an enemy—the whole structure was endangered. This obligation to stand fast in battle shaped the classical Greek values of steadfastness, calmness in danger, and the ability to endure fatigue and pain.

Another difference between the hoplite and the armored warrior of prior centuries was that the hoplite was probably not an aristocrat. (Aristocrats comprised the cavalry at this time.) The hoplite was a middle-class citizen, levied in defense of his city-state and fighting against analogous citizens in the enemy army. Cities henceforth relied for their defense on large numbers of uniformly equipped citizens, not on a few noble heroes; the coming of the hoplite thus saw the democratization of warfare.

Ancient writers use the word *othismos,* the "push," to describe hoplite battle. Down to the 300s B.C.E., the battle line typically was formed six to eight rows deep, with a front of several hundred men. The men in the first three rows advanced with spears leveled; behind them, the soldiers held their spears pointing upward. As the two armies collided, sometimes at a full run, the front ranks of both sides met the enemy spear points while thrusting overhand with their own spears. But at the same time, the rear ranks kept pushing forward—each man actually leaning his shield into the back of his countryman ahead and shoving him toward the enemy. The armies tried to push each other apart.

For the front hoplites, battle must have been hellish and exhausting. There are tales of soldiers dying of suffocation, pinned upright by the press of men. More usually, of course, soldiers died of wounds—possibly to the neck or genitals (areas not always protected by shield or breast plate), or possibly to the head or chest (the armor splitting under the spear point). When a hoplite fell, the man behind him took his place with leveled spear, and most men who went down alive would be very lucky not to be trampled to death.

The heart of the battle, the excruciating *othismos*, lasted probably less than an hour. As one army started to get the worst of it, soldiers on that side would begin fleeing (rear rows first), and suddenly the entire losing army might be reduced to a chaotic rout as every man dropped his shield and spear, running in panic. Then the cavalry might come into play, either in slaughtering a fleeing enemy or in covering its own side's retreat.

Unlike modern armies, the Greeks did not usually make war all year long. The campaign season lasted from March until October, when weather conditions were right for encamping and moving large numbers of men. Furthermore, since most Greek soldiers were farmers by trade, the end of summer usually saw a consensus to stop campaigning and go home for the autumn sowings and vintage. One reason for the military superiority of SPARTA in the 500s to 400s B.C.E. was that its citizens were professional soldiers; they had no job but war. (Their fields at home were worked by a society of serfs, the HELOTS.)

In strategy, hoplite warfare was very simple, and relied on an element of cooperation between antagonists. The aggressor army would march into enemy territory, and the defending army would march out to meet it. Defenders did not like to stay confined behind their city walls—the Athenian statesman PERIKLES' strategy for the Peloponnesian War was unique in its passive defense. Rather, defending armies would come out to protect the farms of the countryside, upon which the city's food supply might depend.

The size of hoplite armies could vary greatly. At the Battle of PLATAEA, against the Persians (479 B.C.E.), the allied Greek force was said to number over 38,000 hoplites. At the Battle of MANTINEIA (418 B.C.E.), the opposing armies had about 3,600 hoplites each, plus light-armed troops. Other armies, fielded in local disputes, might be much smaller.

By the late 400s B.C.E. military minds had begun adjusting hoplite tactics. It had long been observed that an army's right wing tended to outperform its left wing—partly because the better troops were stationed on the right, but partly because the battle line itself would drift rightward on the approach to battle, as each man leaned right to gain the protection of his neighbor's shield; this rightward drift meant that each army advantageously outflanked the other on the right. To increase this advantage, the Boeotians at the Battle of Delium used a fortified right wing, 25 rows deep, and defeated an Athenian army (424 B.C.E.).

In the Classical period, the city of SPARTA developed a military force that was superior in many ways to the armies of other Greek city-states. Every Spartan boy received extensive military training, and boys' upraising included the teaching that dying in battle, protecting one's city, was the most honorable fate possible. The Spartan army also had excellent equipment and supplies. The Spartans' superior tactics involved speedily gaining the upper hand on their right wing and then wheeling the right wing leftward, rolling up the enemy from the side. However, at the Battle of LEUKTRA (371 B.C.E.), the Theban general EPAMINONDAS beat the "invincible" Spartans by stacking his *left* wing 50 men deep and crushing the 12-man-deep Spartan right wing before it could destroy him.

Theban triumphs partly inspired the innovations of King Philip II of MACEDON (reigned 359–336 B.C.E.) who brought land warfare into its third stage with his development of the formation that modern scholars call the phalanx. To make his Macedonian peasantry effective against Greek hoplites, Philip forged a new-style heavy infantry—lighter-armored than hoplites and equipped with an innovative, 13- to 14-foot-long pike, the *sarissa*. The phalanx formation consisted of about 9,000 such infantry, arrayed 16 rows deep, with the first five rows presenting their pikes forward. On the model of Spartan organization, Philip's phalanx was articulated into 1,500-man battalions, for maneuverability. A well-trained phalanx enjoyed advantages over a hoplite army in terms of its weapons' reach and probably its level of fatigue. (The phalanx men were not crowded together as closely as the hoplites, nor were they so heavily armored.)

In battle Philip employed the phalanx mainly for defense—to halt and punish an enemy attack—while using his cavalry to charge against any gap that opened in the enemy formation. The phalanx was the anvil; the cavalry was the hammer. The superiority of Philip's tactics was proven at the Battle of CHAIRONEIA (338 B.C.E.), where his troops totally defeated a hoplite army of allied Greeks. The hoplite age was passing, 330 years after the Battle of Hysiae.

Philip's innovations helped produce the spectacular victories won by his royal son, Alexander the Great (reigned 336–323 B.C.E.). In military history, Alexander opened the door to further development of cavalry, under Persian influence and using larger Persian horse breeds. More important, Alexander's conquests changed the social-political basis of ancient warfare, by creating several large and wealthy Greco-Macedonian kingdoms around the eastern Mediterranean. The incessant warfare of these Hellenistic kingdoms—particularly Ptolemaic EGYPT against the Levantine SELEUCID EMPIRE (274–168 B.C.E.)—saw the use of huge, unwieldy phalanxes, upward of 20,000 men. These kingdoms were constantly trying to perpetuate a Greco-Macedonian soldiering class, so as to reduce reliance on mercenaries.

When the armies of ROME began to invade the Greek world, various features of the Roman military made it immediately superior to the Greek forces. The Romans fought the Greek phalanxes with their more flexible legions, with their built-in reserves. Such advances in land warfare organization and tactics led to Rome's eventual conquest of the Mediterranean and other lands.

See also CRETE; DEMOSTHENES (2); LELANTINE WAR; PHEIDON; PHILIP V; PYRRHUS.

Further reading: Victor Davis Hanson, *Hoplites: The Classical Greek Battle Experience* (London: Routledge, 1993); M. M. Sage, *Warfare in Ancient Greece. A Sourcebook* (London: Routledge, 1996); H. van Wees, "Homeric Warfare," in *A New Companion to Homer,* edited by Ian Morris and Barry Powell (Leiden, Netherlands, E. J. Brill, 1997), 668–693; R. Osgood, S. Monks, and J. Toms, *Bronze Age Warfare* (Stroud, U.K.: Sutton, 2000); H. van Wees, ed., *War and Violence in Ancient Greece* (London: Duckworth, 2000); J. A. Thorne, "Warfare and Agriculture. The Economic Impact of Devastation in Classical Greece," *Greek, Roman, and Byzantine Studies* 42 (2001): 225–253; T. Bekker-Nielsen and L. Hannestad, eds., *War as a Cultural and Social Force. Essays on Warfare in Antiquity* (Copenhagen: Reitzels, 2001); A. B. Bosworth, *The Legacy of Alexander: Politics, Warfare, and Propaganda under the Successors* (New York: Oxford University Press, 2002); I. G. Spence, *Historical Dictionary of Ancient Greek Warfare* (Lanham, Md.: Scarecrow Press, 2002); H. van Wees, *Greek Warfare: Myths and Realities* (London: Duckworth, 2004).

warfare, naval In the earliest centuries of Greek history (ca. 1600–700 B.C.E.), warships served primarily as troop transports—the troops in question were the oarsmen, who would leave their benches to go ashore as infantry. Eventually the sea itself became the scene of fighting, as defending states learned to send out ships to oppose an oncoming enemy fleet on the water. The historian THUCYDIDES (1) writes that the earliest remembered sea battle was fought in about 664 B.C.E. between the navies of two Greek states, CORINTH and CORCYRA. Thucydides mentions another early naval battle, around 600 B.C.E., between Phocaean Greeks and Carthaginians in the western Mediterranean.

Such early sea fights, tactically crude, were probably conducted as infantry battles on water—that is, the opposing fleets would crowd together, allowing boarding parties of spearmen to fight it out hand to hand. But naval warfare was changed by two developments around 700–430 B.C.E.: the invention and gradual spread of the superior Greek warship type known as the trireme; and the acceptance of ramming tactics over boarding tactics, as a more effective way to destroy the enemy without sustaining harm oneself. The famous Greek sea battles of the 400s B.C.E.—such as the Battle of SALAMIS (1) (480 B.C.E.)—featured trireme warships maneuvering to ram and sink the enemy.

The trireme was invented in response to a specific challenge: how to fit as many oarsmen as possible into a vessel that would still be seaworthy. Throughout Greek history, the oar was the main power source for any warship. Most war vessels carried one midship mast, capable of hoisting a single square sail; but the mast was not always used and typically could be removed. The oarsmen powered the ship through battle and in passage through contrary winds or calms.

The more oarsmen, the greater the power—up to a point. The practical limit in length for an undecked wooden ship is about 100 feet; beyond that, the hull is liable to break apart. In a simple ship design, this 100-foot limit confined the total number of rowers to about 50—whence the Greek term *pentekontoros*, or penteconter, meaning a 50-oared, single-leveled vessel. Images in vase paintings and other surviving art show penteconters as resembling Viking longboats, with the oarsmen seated along one level in the open air. There was no deck—that is, no layer of planking across the hull's top. The rowers sat in double file—two men side by side on each bench, each man handling his own oar, which projected out (left or right) through thole-pins above the gunwale.

Around 900–700 B.C.E., Greek shipwrights—probably copying Phoenician designs—learned to fit more oarsmen into a 100-foot hull. They did so by laying the benches at two different levels (still without any deck) and providing oarports below the gunwales for the lower row of oars.

This two-leveled type of Greek warship is known by modern scholars as the bireme. But the real breakthrough came around 700 B.C.E., with the Greeks' development of a three-leveled warship (again, probably based on a Phoenician model). This was the ship that the Greeks called the *triērēs* (three-rowing or three-fitted) and that is now called the trireme—the ancient Greek warship par excellence.

However, the trireme caught on slowly. Penteconters, cheaper and easier to build, were still being used by some Greek states as late as the PERSIAN WARS (490–479 B.C.E.). The universal change to trireme navies came after 479 B.C.E.

A trireme typically carried 160 to 170 oarsmen, far more than prior designs could hold. The oars emerged in three rows on each side—one above the gunwale and two below. The added power meant greater speed, hence greater maneuverability in battle. The ample power also meant that triremes could take on more weight; therefore, they carried such array as partial decking fore and aft, vertical defensive screens, and an overhead central catwalk running the length of the vessel. These structures created room for a contingent of archers and HOPLITES, who did not row but served purely as ship's soldiers, to aim projectiles in battle and fend off enemy boarding attempts. By the time of the Peloponnesian War, the number of shipboard hoplites had settled at 10. Including crew, officers, and soldiers, the trireme might carry 215 men in all.

With its partial decking, the trireme hull could be built to about 120 feet long. The design was narrow, with a width at the gunwales of only 12 to 16 feet. There was scant room for passengers or any cargo aside from drinking water—most food supplies had to come from shore or from supply ships. A trireme had no accommodations for eating or resting. Confined to their crowded benches, the crew could not easily spend a night at sea; to cook and sleep, they had to camp ashore every night.

This basic restriction applied to all ancient warships and influenced all Greek naval strategy. A navy could conduct operations only within range of a friendly harbor or beaching place. To fight an offensive naval war, a state would have to create and maintain forward naval bases (as SPARTA did against Athenian interests in western ASIA MINOR in the later PELOPONNESIAN WAR, 413–404 B.C.E.). Relatedly, naval blockades of enemy harbors tended to be faulty, since fleets could not ride off the coast day and night.

Ramming tactics favored the faster and more skillful ship or fleet. The Greek ship's ram was a wooden post—sheathed in BRONZE, often styled as a boar's head—jutting forward of the prow at water level. The challenge in ramming was to avoid a head-on collision (which could sink both ships) and instead strike the enemy vessel abeam or astern. The classic ramming maneuver was called *diekplous*, "going through and out." When two opposing fleets moved to battle, each side would typically deploy in rows abreast. In *diekplous*, a fleet would suddenly shift from row-abreast to single-file formation, with ships prow to stern, and then veer inward, perhaps by squadrons, to penetrate the enemy's row-abreast formation. Proceeding through the enemy line, the attackers would come around to ram from behind.

Because the *diekplous* required sea room, a commander wishing to defend against this tactic could seek to offer battle inside a confined area—as the Greeks did at Salamis, against a superior Persian fleet. A way to equalize terms further was to try to compel a battle of boarding tactics—as the Syracusans did in their three victories over the Athenians inside SYRACUSE's harbor (414–413 B.C.E.). A commander intent on boarding tactics might outfit his ships beforehand with raised platforms to hold more soldiers. Generally, the superior-skilled fleets in Greek naval history sought to force battle on the open sea, where there was room for ramming by *diekplous*.

A fleet's skill and speed depended on crews' training and ships' maintenance (since wooden hulls need periodic drying out, caulking, etc.). The top Greek naval power of the 400s–early 300s B.C.E. was the city of ATHENS, with its standing fleet of 200 triremes (ca. 431 B.C.E.) and its elaborate shipbuilding and drydocking facilities at PIRAEUS. The creator of this navy was the Athenian statesman THEMISTOKLES, ca. 488 B.C.E. The heir to Themistokles' program was the statesman PERIKLES (active around 462–429 B.C.E.). Unlike many Greek states that employed foreign mercenary oarsmen, Athens employed its lower-income citizens as rowers. This military reliance on large number of poorer citizens effectively increased their political power in the DEMOCRACY.

Athens aside, the important navies in Greek history down to the late 300s B.C.E. belonged to Corinth, Corcyra, SAMOS, PHOCAEA, AEGINA, CHIOS, LESBOS, and Syracuse. Sparta, not originally a sea power, developed a navy with Persian funding in order to defeat Athens in the Peloponnesian War. Among non-Greek peoples, the Phoenicians (ruled by PERSIA by the mid-500s B.C.E.) were the Greeks' most dangerous enemies at sea. Farther west, the Greeks' naval opponents included the ETRUSCANS and those Phoenician colonists, the Carthaginians.

New navies and naval tactics arose in the later 300s B.C.E. Partly as a result of ALEXANDER THE GREAT's studious contact with powerful Phoenician fleets (332 B.C.E.), Greek shipwrights began building warships larger than the trireme. There are types called "four-rowing" (*tetrērēs*), "five-rowing" (*pentērēs*), and others, eventually up to "16," and even "30" and "40." Modern scholars believe that these names describe three-leveled ships containing multiple oarsmen per oar at one or more levels. The "five" type, usually called the quinquereme, may have employed two men per oar on the upper two rows, with one man per oar on the lowest row. The quinquereme was favored by Greek and Roman navies of the HELLENISTIC AGE (300–150 B.C.E.).

The late 300s–200s B.C.E. saw two Hellenistic empires battling for control of the eastern Mediterranean—Ptolemaic EGYPT and the dynasty of ANTIGONUS (1) (based first in Asia Minor, then in MACEDON). The best-known sea battle of this era is also called the Battle of Salamis, fought near a different Salamis, on the island of CYPRUS, in 306 B.C.E. There a fleet of 108 warships under Antigonus's son DEMETRIUS POLIORKETES destroyed 140 ships of PTOLEMY (1). This era also saw the rise of RHODES as a naval and mercantile power.

Ramming remained the primary battle tactic, but a more remote means of attack emerged in the form of shipborne catapults, shooting arrows. Too bulky for a trireme or quinquereme, a catapult might be fitted onto a merchant ship or onto two warships lashed together. Historians report the first use of such naval artillery at Alexander the Great's siege of Tyre. Demetrius Poliorketes used naval arrow-catapults in his Battle of Cyprian Salamis and at his siege of Rhodes (305–304 B.C.E.). Later navies of the Hellenistic era probably also employed rock-throwing catapults.

The deadly use of fire against wooden ships is at least as old as the Peloponnesian War, when the Syracusans sent out a fire-ship against Athenian vessels in Syracuse harbor (413 B.C.E.). Later, around 190 B.C.E., Rhodian warships carried fire-pots—containers of pitch, set ablaze and then slung by long poles onto nearby enemy ships. But the more fiendish tactic of shooting burning naphtha ("Greek fire") across the water at enemy vessels was not invented until the late 600s C.E., by the medieval Byzantines.

In the second half of the 200s B.C.E., naval control of the Mediterranean was won by the Romans, who had copied and adapted the designs and tactics of Hellenistic and Carthaginian navies.

See also AEGEAN SEA; AEGOSPOTAMI; ARTEMISIUM; BOSPORUS; CARTHAGE; CORINTHIAN WAR; CYZICUS; DELIAN LEAGUE; HELLESPONT; HIERON (1); IONIAN REVOLT; KIMON; KONON; LYSANDER; PHOENICIA; POLYCRATES; ROME; SHIPS AND SEAFARING; TIMBER; WARFARE, SIEGE.

Further reading: William L. Rodgers, *Greek and Roman Naval Warfare; A Study of Strategy, Tactics, and Ship Design from Salamis (480 B.C.) to Actium (31 B.C.)* (Annapolis, Md.: United States Naval Institute, 1964); B. S. Strauss, "Democracy, Kimon, and the Evolution of Athenian Naval Tactics in the Fifth Century B.C.," in *Polis and Politics. Studies in Ancient Greek History Presented to Mogens Herman Hansen on his Sixtieth Birthday, August 20, 2000*, edited by P. Flensted-Jensen, T. H. Nielsen, and L. Rubinstein (Copenhagen: Museum Tusculanum Press, 2000), 315–326; V. Gabrielsen, "Naval Warfare. Its Economic and Social Impact on Ancient Greek Cities," in *War as a Cultural and Social Force. Essays on Warfare in Antiquity*, edited by Tønnes Bekker-Nielsen and Lise Hannestad (Copenhagen: Det Kongelige Danske Videnskabernes Selskab, 2001), 72–89.

warfare, siege Siege warfare entails the capture of forts and fortified cities. For much of Greek history, this process remained crude. An attacking army might try to take a site by storm—that is, by massed assault using scaling ladders. Alternatively, there was siege—the attackers would encircle the enemy walls with earthworks (a procedure known as circumvallation) and wait to starve out the defenders or to win treasonous help from within. The legend of a 10-year-long siege of TROY surely reflects the frustrations of primitive siege warfare.

By the late 700s B.C.E. the armies of Near Eastern empires (well in advance of the Greeks) were using machines and scientific methods to reduce enemy fortifications. The Greeks, impressed by Persian siegecraft in the era 546–479 B.C.E., began copying these tactics. These included use of battering rams to tear open an enemy wall, siege mounds to bring attackers to the top of a wall, and miners tunneling under walls. Yet the PELOPONNESIAN WAR (431–404 B.C.E.) saw only a few successful sieges, such as at PLATAEA or BYZANTIUM. Siege was still largely a waiting game, and a fortress city with a harbor (such as ATHENS) could almost never be captured without being completely blockaded, by both warships at sea and troops on land.

A breakthrough came in about 399 B.C.E. with the Greeks' development of the catapult. Credit goes to the engineers of the Syracusan dictator DIONYSIUS (1), who probably were copying the machines used by their enemies, the Carthaginians. The earliest type of Greek catapult resembled a giant medieval crossbow, set atop a stand. This wooden device shot a single, six-foot-long arrow and was typically aimed at troops visible at the parapet of the enemy wall. Although unable to knock down walls, the arrow could easily pierce a man's armor, hence the Greek name *katapeltēs*, "shield-piercer."

Volleys from multiple catapults provided valuable "covering fire" for troops conducting siege operations. Typically the besiegers' catapults would be perched inside of siege towers. The siege tower was a wooden structure, built as tall as the enemy wall and used as a kind of multistory armored car, with catapults set on internal parapets and sighted through portholes. Pushed forward on wheels, the tower approached the enemy wall gradually, while engineers prepared a roadbed ahead. Some towers were apparently designed to be pushed right up to the city wall, in order to bring up attacking troops on internal ladders or to employ a ground-level battering ram.

The first recorded use of Greek catapults and siege towers was at Dionysius's capture of the Carthaginian stronghold of Moyta, in western SICILY (397 B.C.E.). Dionysius's dramatic successes brought swift imitation and improvement by other Greek commanders. A more powerful type of arrow-shooting catapult arose, perhaps under the Thessalian dictator Jason of Pherae (reigned ca. 385–370 B.C.E.). This new design used the principle of torsion. Instead of a horizontal, bending wooden bow, the torsion catapult featured two vertical cylinders of taut skeining (composed of human hair or animal sinew), set on either side of the front of a long wooden stock. Into each skein was slotted one wooden arm, extending outward; the arms' outer ends were attached to a bowstring. Winched back, the bowstring brought great tension from the twisting skeins to the arrow waiting in the groove of the stock.

Siegecraft in the Greek world reached its mature stage under the Macedonian king PHILIP II (reigned 359–336 B.C.E.), who successfully coordinated the use of tower, catapult, and battering ram. Philip's catapults were torsion-powered arrow-shooters. It was Philip's son ALEXANDER THE GREAT who (among other achievements) pioneered the use of rock-firing catapults. Alexander's "stone-throwers" (*lithoboloi* or *petroboloi*) could hurl 170-pound boulders more than 190 yards, to batter apart enemy walls. Mounted aboard ships, these deadly machines helped Alexander to capture the island fortress of Tyre, in one of history's monumental sieges, conducted simultaneously by land and sea (332 B.C.E.).

Stone-throwing catapults were made of wood and were torsion-powered, looking much like the foregoing arrow-shooting type. This design remained the basic form for Greek catapults. (A different design, with one vertical arm, has been popularized by medieval European artwork and now represents what most people think of as a catapult. Although probably invented by the Greeks, this type was used later, by Roman armies.)

Alexander and his successors of the HELLENISTIC AGE (around 300–150 B.C.E.) were the most ambitious besiegers the world had yet seen. The Macedonian prince DEMETRIUS POLIORKETES won his surname (Poliorkētēs means "city besieger") from his huge—but unsuccessful—siege of RHODEA in 305–304 B.C.E. Demetrius's armament included two massive battering rams (iron-clad treetrunks, perhaps 130 feet long, hung inside mobile sheds and worked by hundreds of men) and an armor-plated siege tower called the Hēlēpolis, or "taker of cities," containing nine levels of stone-throwers and arrow-catapults.

Tactics of defense also improved in this era—with catapults on city walls shooting flaming projectiles against wooden siege machines—but generally the advantage had now swung to the besiegers. The Romans of the late 200s B.C.E. adopted Hellenistic siege tactics and brought them to new technical heights in conquering the Mediterranean. In 213–211 B.C.E. the Romans besieged and captured the Greek fortress city of SYRACUSE, which 200 years before had defied and destroyed a besieging Athenian army.

See also ROME; SCIENCE; THESSALY; WARFARE, LAND; WARFARE, NAVAL.

Further reading: J. P. Romane, "Alexander's Sieges of Miletus and Halicarnassus," *Ancient World* 25 (1994): 61–76; P. B. Kern, *Ancient Siege Warfare* (Bloomington: Indiana University Press, 1999); Duncan B. Campbell, *Greek and Roman Siege Machinery, 399 B.C.–A.D. 363* (Oxford: Osprey, 2003).

wine An alcoholic beverage produced by controlled fermentation of grapes, wine remains an important agricultural commodity in the Mediterranean today. The Greeks' development of wine-making skills may be reflected in legends describing the arrival of a newcomer god, DIONYSUS, lord of viticulture and wine.

The earliest surviving archaeological evidence for winemaking in ancient Greece is a stone press from a Minoan villa on the island of CRETE, dating to about 1600 B.C.E., but it appears that the Minoans had been producing wine for some time already by this date. During the time of the Minoan and Mycenaean civilizations, wine played an important role in the economy and recreation of the Greeks. Archaeologists are uncertain about the initial introduction of winemaking to ancient Greece; it may have been brought to CRETE by traders from PHOENICIA, or it may have arrived over land from the north.

By the 500s B.C.E., the Greeks had perfected their wine production to the point where Greek wines were an important trade item, prized throughout the Mediter-

ranean. The Greeks exported wine to such advanced Eastern kingdoms as EGYPT, while Greek traders in THRACE, southern Gaul, and elsewhere used wine to exploit the local populations and to acquire goods cheaply (much as European fur traders used brandy to affect the northeast American Indians in the 1600s C.E.).

The hilly terrain of Greece was (and is) well suited to vine growing, and renowned wines were produced in particular by some of the islands, including THASOS, CHIOS, LESBOS, RHODES, Lemnos, and Kos. Certain Greek colonies, such as MASSALIA (modern Marseilles, in southern France), also proved to have ideal conditions for growing grapes. Wine was made throughout the Greek world, however, and was cherished by both the peasantry (as a mode of riotous release, on festival days sacred to Dionysus) and by the upper classes (as an object of ritualized consumption, at the type of male drinking party known as the SYMPOSIUM).

In Greece, grapes were harvested in September. Juice was produced by workers first treading the grapes in vats and then crushing the remaining pulp in wine presses. The juice was stored indoors in tubs and allowed to ferment for six months; then it was filtered through cloth and sealed inside storage jars (*amphorai*). Unlike modern winemakers, the Greeks could not halt the natural fermentation process. Greek wines therefore had to be consumed within three or four years. These wines had more natural sugar than modern wines, and thus more alcohol, perhaps 18 percent (versus 12.5 percent for most modern consumer wines).

Not surprisingly, the ancient Greeks customarily mixed water into their sweet, potent wine just before drinking—the typical ratio was two or three parts water to one part wine. Several distinctive Greek POTTERY forms, including the psychter (cooler) and krater (mixing bowl), were developed expressly for the chilling and diluting of wine. Once cooled in a psychter, the straight wine would be poured into a krater, mixed with water, and ladled out into drinking cups (*kylikes*; singular: *kylix*). Undiluted wine was considered unhealthy, but water wine, if imbibed moderately, was viewed as medicinal—as wine is still viewed today in some Mediterranean countries.

See also CELTS; FARMING.

Further reading: Virginia Grace, *Amphoras and the Ancient Wine Trade*, rev. ed. (Princeton, N.J.: American School of Classical Studies at Athens, 1979); Ruth Palmer, *Wine in the Mycenaean Palace Economy* (Austin: University of Texas at Austin, Program in Aegean Scripts and Prehistory, 1994); Patrick McGovern, Stuart Fleming, and Solomon Katz, eds., *The Origins and Ancient History of Wine* (Philadelphia: Gordon and Breach, 1995); Peter Franke and Irini Marathaki, *Wine and Coins in Ancient Greece* (Athens: Hatzimichalis Estate, 1999); Clementina Panella and Andre Tchernia, "Agricultural Products

Transported in Amphorae: Oil and Wine," in *The Ancient Economy*, edited by Walter Scheidel and Sitta von Reden (New York: Routledge, 2002), 173–189; Patrick E. McGovern, *Ancient Wine: The Search for the Origins of Viniculture* (Princeton, N.J.: Princeton University Press, 2003).

women The inferior role of women in ancient Greek society reminds us that the Greeks remained in some ways a primitive people. Even in classical ATHENS, at its height of democratic enlightenment (mid-400 B.C.E.), women were considered second-class citizens at best. A female Athenian citizen, protected by law, was far better off than a slave or a metic (resident alien); but the citizen woman also was forbidden to own much property, to inherit in her own name, to vote, or to attend political debate in the ASSEMBLY. Women might practice humble trades such as street-cleaning, but this was a sign of hardship, and very few skilled or lucrative trades were open to women. Instead, a woman was considered to be the ward of a man—her husband, her father, or her guardian (such as a brother).

Female SLAVES might run errands in public, but a respectable woman's place was in the home—specifically, in the house's interior and secluded "women's chambers." There the wife or mature daughter was expected to perform—or, if the household was wealthy, to oversee—such domestic duties as child care, cleaning, and spinning and weaving. The only crucial public role of citizen women was to give birth to young citizens for the state.

Of all the major Greek city-states, only warlike SPARTA granted its citizen women any degree of freedom, allowing them to own quantities of property and encouraging such male-imitative pastimes as girls' gymnastics. The unusual freedom of Spartan women probably arose from their roles as estate managers during the absences of their soldiering husbands and kinsmen. Spartan women also had a unique reputation for promiscuity. The philosopher ARISTOTLE (mid-300s B.C.E.) criticized Spartan society for allowing its women too much freedom and influence. Of all Greek thinkers, only PLATO, in his dialogue *The Republic* (ca. 360 B.C.E.), could imagine a utopian society where women and men would be equally eligible for roles in government.

As with all other social topics from ancient Greece, the existing evidence for women's lives comes overwhelmingly from Athens in the 400s–300s B.C.E. This evidence includes extant stage drama, courtroom speeches, and archaeological remains such as tombstone inscriptions.

Nothing is known for certain about the role of women during the era of MYCENAEAN CIVILIZATION (around 1600–1200 B.C.E.). But a cautious reading of Greek MYTH and particularly HOMER's poems suggests that Mycenaean baronial society did allow considerable power to a few highborn ladies. For example, the queens PENELOPE and KLYTEMNESTRA in the *Odyssey* are each shown as managing a kingdom in her husband's absence.

The segregation and devaluation of women in Greece began sometime in the era 1100–700 B.C.E. and may be connected to two related changes: the emergence of the Greek city-state, with its wide, citizen-based military organization, and the idealization of male strength and beauty, as expressed most fully in institutionalized male HOMOSEXUALITY. The misogyny expressed by the poets HESIOD (ca. 700 B.C.E.) and SEMONIDES (late 600s B.C.E.)—in contrast with Homer's often charming portrayal of women—surely indicates this social shift.

In archaic and classical Greece, around 800–300 B.C.E., women were seen as the opposites or subjugated

Woman as ideal beauty. This statue of an aristocratic maiden (kore) was carved in marble ca. 515 B.C.E. and set up as an offering on the Athenian acropolis. (*Alison Frantz Photographic Collection, American School of Classical Studies at Athens*)

opponents of men. Male Greek society valued rational discourse, military courage, and physical endurance and self-restraint. Women were believed to be irrational, fearful, and ruled by physical desires. One reason why women were kept secluded at home is that they were thought liable to sexual seduction (or other mischief) if they ventured out unescorted. "The highest honor for a woman is to be least talked about by men, whether in praise or criticism," declared the Athenian statesman PERIKLES in his famous funeral oration of 431 B.C.E.

Only in RELIGION were Greek women allowed to participate in public life to any degree. Holy days, such as the autumn sowing festival of the Thesmophoria, provided occasions when women were expected to leave the house and congregate for religious ceremonies. Also, certain priesthoods were reserved for women, such as the office of Pythia or priestess of APOLLO at DELPHI. These religious duties probably date back to a prehistoric belief in the magical properties of female fertility. Similarly, the large role played in Greek mythology by such goddesses as ATHENA or HERA may represent vestiges of a non-Greek religion, adopted by the first arriving Greek tribes around 2100 B.C.E.

There is some evidence that female infanticide was regularly practiced at classical Athens and elsewhere. A father could choose whether to officially accept a child or not, and many men might prefer to raise sons, who could help with the farmwork, inherit the estate, and so on.

Girls had a narrow upbringing. A girl of the middle and upper classes grew up in the women's chambers of the house, perhaps rarely seen by her father. At age seven, she might start attending a girls' school, but only long enough to acquire literacy and numeracy. In various Greek cities, she might be considered ready for MARRIAGE by age 14 or even 12. The poet SAPPHO (ca. 580 B.C.E.) has some poignant verses on the plight of an aristocratic girl who must go from the beautiful security of childhood to the strangeness and anxiety of marriage.

Marrying young, women bore children young and died young. Medical examination of extant skeletons from ancient Greece suggest that women typically died around age 36, having borne an average of four children. The estimated life expectancy for men was 45, but (since husbands might be 20 years older than their wives) many wives must have survived their husbands and remarried. At Classical Athens and elsewhere, a woman's inheritance would legally pass to her new husband's hands at her remarriage, and so heiresses and widows were in great demand.

The oppression of women seems to have lightened somewhat in the changed world of the HELLENISTIC AGE (around 300–150 B.C.E.). The royal court of ALEXANDRIA (1), ANTIOCH, and PELLA created a breed of rich, ruling-class women who were able to influence public and cultural life. These royal examples probably created new opportunities for other women—at least for wealthy citi-

zen women. A surviving public inscription from CYMĒ honors a certain Archippe for her public donations (100 B.C.E.), while papyrus documents from Ptolemaic EGYPT show women to have been active as lessors, creditors, and debtors much more so than at Athens in prior centuries.

Relatedly, Hellenistic culture placed a new, greater value on female intelligence and sexuality. The Athenian philosopher Epicurus (ca. 300 B.C.E.) is said to have admitted women to his school on equal terms with men. Female beauty reemerged as an ideal for painters and sculptors—most famously in the Athenian sculptor PRAXITELES' celebrated nude statue of the goddess APHRODITE (mid-300s B.C.E.). In literature, poets such as APOLLONIUS (ca. 270 B.C.E.) showed a new interest in female psychology and male-female romance.

See also ALCMAN; AMAZONS; EPICUREANISM; ERINNA; EURIPIDES; FUNERAL CUSTOMS; MAENADS; METICS; POLIS; PROSTITUTES; SCULPTURE.

Further reading: Mary Lefkowitz and Maureen Fant, eds., *Women's Life in Greece and Rome: A Source Book in Translation,* 2d ed. (Baltimore: Johns Hopkins University Press, 1992); Elaine Fantham et al., *Women in the Classical World: Image and Text* (New York: Oxford University Press, 1994); Riet van Bremen, *The Limits of Participation: Women and Civic Life in the Greek East in the Hellenistic and Roman Periods* (Amsterdam: J. C. Gieben, 1996); M. Lightman and B. Lightman, *Biographical Dictionary of Ancient Greek and Roman Women. Notable Women from Sappho to Helena* (New York: Facts On File, 2000); D. Miron, "Transmitters and Representatives of Power. Royal Women in Ancient Macedonia," *Ancient Society* 30 (2000): 35–52; A. Kosmopoulou, "Working Women. Female Professionals on Classical Attic Gravestones," *Annual of the British School at Athens* 96 (2001): 281–319; Lloyd Llewellyn-Jones, ed., *Women's Dress in the Ancient Greek World* (London: Duckworth, 2002); Sian Lewis, *The Athenian Woman: An Iconographic Handbook* (London: Routledge, 2002); S. B. Pomeroy, *Spartan Women* (Oxford: Oxford University Press, 2002); M. Dillon, *Girls and Women in Classical Greek Religion* (London: Routledge, 2002); Diane Bolger and Nancy Serwint, eds., *Engendering Aphrodite: Women and Society in Ancient Cyprus* (Boston: American Schools of Oriental Research, 2002).

wrestling Among the sports-loving Greeks, wrestling was a highly popular and well-organized event. Less brutal than BOXING and PANKRATION, the other two major Greek combat sports, wrestling was considered a valuable element in a boy's EDUCATION and military training as well as an appropriate exercise for well-bred adult men. Most sizable Greek towns of the classical age contained at least one *palaistra* (enclosed wrestling court).

Wrestling was among the most prestigious events at great athletic festivals such as the OLYMPIC or PYTHIAN GAMES. In addition to separate competitions for men and

Two wrestlers from a statue base, ca. 510 B.C.E. Note the two men's difference in size; the Greeks observed no weight classes, and size could be a distinct advantage. *(Alison Frantz Photographic Collection, American School of Classical Studies at Athens)*

boys, there were wrestling contests that served as the final round in the five-event PENTATHLON.

The patron deity of wrestlers was the god HERMES, who was said to have invented the sport. In fact, wrestling predates the Greek world, having been practiced in the ancient Near East. The Greeks adopted the sport early in their history, maybe in the Mycenaean era (1600–1200 B.C.E.). Wrestling is described in HOMER's poems—in the *Iliad*, for example, the heroes ODYSSEUS and AJAX (1) engage in a friendly match (book 23). Other mythical wrestlers included the hero HERAKLES, who in the course of his 12th Labor had to grapple the giant Antaeus to death.

In its rules, the classical Greek sport was much like modern collegiate free-style wrestling, only tougher. There were no weight classes for the ancient Greeks—advantage favored size and weight. Punching was forbidden, but other harmful moves, such as strangleholds, shoulder-throws, or breaking an opponent's finger, were allowed.

Like other Greek athletes, wrestlers competed naked and were typically slicked down with olive oil (which prevented abrasions but also had a ritualistic significance). They competed atop soft ground; practice sessions were generally held in a mud pit, and formal matches took place on the *skamma*, a special bed of fine sand. At grand events, the matches might be held in a stadium full of spectators.

The bout began with the two competitors standing, facing each other, and ended with a "fall," when one man was forced down in such a way that his back, his shoulders, or his chest and stomach touched the ground.

(Alternatively, a man could lose by being thrown off the wrestling ground.) To win in an official contest, a man had to gain three falls against his adversary; therefore, a single match could run to as many as five bouts.

See also SPORT.

Further reading: R. Katzoff, "Where Did the Greeks of the Roman Period Practice Wrestling?" *American Journal of Archaeology* 90 (1986): 437–440; Michael Poliakoff, *Combat Sports in the Ancient World: Competition, Violence, and Culture* (New Haven, Conn.: Yale University Press, 1987).

writing   The use of written symbols to convey words or ideas predates the Greeks by many centuries. In the third millennium B.C.E., well before the start of Greek civilization, the Sumerians and other Mesopotamian peoples had developed a script called cuneiform. The Egyptians of this era had several forms of writing, including the famous hieroglyphic pictograms that can still be seen on inner pyramid walls and other Egyptian artifacts.

The earliest form of writing known from ancient Greece is one developed in the second millennium B.C.E. by the MINOAN CIVILIZATION on CRETE; this was a pictogram script that modern scholars call Linear A, and it has not yet been deciphered. By 1400 B.C.E., the Mycenaean Greeks on the mainland had adapted the Minoan script and developed their own form of writing, which scholars refer to as LINEAR B. This was deciphered in 1952 C.E. and recognized as an early form of the Greek language.

The use of Linear B ended with the collapse of the MYCENAEAN CIVILIZATION around 1200 B.C.E. The invention of the versatile Greek ALPHABET around 775 B.C.E. brought new, widespread literacy to the Greek world and allowed the Greeks to produce a great literary culture. The emergence of the first Greek literature in the eighth century B.C.E. is clearly a result of the invention of this alphabet, allowing scribes to write down stories that had been composed through a long oral tradition. The earliest and best-known examples of such stories are HOMER's epic poems *Iliad* and *Odyssey,* written down around 750 B.C.E.

The earliest surviving example of Greek alphabetic script is a verse inscription scratched onto a ceramic cup, found in a grave at the Greek colony of PITHECUSAE, in western ITALY, and dated to about 725 B.C.E.: *I am the cup of Nestor and this I say: whoever drinks from me will instantly be smitten by lovely Aphrodite.* This inscription, coming from what was then the western frontier of the Greek world, is striking evidence of the spread of the alphabet among the Greeks within only one or two generations. General literacy is also indicated by extant graffiti and public inscriptions of the latter 600s B.C.E. from THERA, CHIOS, and elsewhere. One of the most dramatic specimens of early Greek writing is the graffito scratched onto the left leg of a colossal statue of the Egyptian pharaoh Ramses II at Abu Simbel, 700 miles up the Nile. Written in about 591 B.C.E. by Greek mercenary soldiers in the service of Pharaoh Psamtik II, the message (still visible today) records the names of the expedition's leaders. It is the earliest known announcement that "Kilroy was here."

More typical early Greek writing materials included clay tablets, wax-coated wooden tablets, or animal skins that could be pumiced smooth and stitched together to form a roll. For scratching in clay or wax, a stylus was used, but animal skins took pen and ink. The pen was usually a feather quill, and the ink often was a vegetable mixture. By the 600s B.C.E., papyrus—cheaper and plentiful—had replaced animal skins for Greek writing. The papyrus plant, which grew only in the Egyptian Nile delta, had a pith that, when cut into strips, could be arranged and pressed so as to create a page of paperlike material. These pages would then be glued together to form a continuous sheet, normally 30–35 feet in length. When two wooden pins were fastened to the ends of the sheet, the result was a scroll, which could be rolled back and forth around the pins. The papyrus scroll was the ancient Greeks' "book" (*biblion*), the primary tool for reading and writing. Long works were produced in multiple scrolls, or "books." Most lengthy writings from the Greco-Roman world—such as those of Homer or Virgil—are still divided by modern editors into different books, even if the whole work is now contained in a single volume.

The drawback of papyrus as a Greek writing material was that it came exclusively from Egypt. Around 200 B.C.E., the Greek-Egyptian king Ptolemy V discontinued papyrus exports, supposedly to hamper the rival book-collecting of King Eumenes II of PERGAMON. In response, the Pergamenes invented parchment (Greek: *pergamene*). Parchment (or vellum, as it is now known) was made from cattle, goat, or sheep skin processed in an improved way so as to smooth it down to papyruslike quality. Today, important documents such as college diplomas are still printed on vellum, hence the nickname "sheepskin."

See also BYBLOS; EPIC POETRY.

Further reading: Deborah Steiner, *The Tyrant's Wit: Myths and Images of Writing in Ancient Greece* (Princeton, N.J.: Princeton University Press, 1994); Roger Woodard, *Greek Writing from Knossos to Homer: A Linguistic Interpretation of the Origin of the Greek Alphabet and the Continuity of Ancient Greek Literacy* (New York: Oxford University Press, 1997); Barry Powell, *Writing and the Origins of Greek Literature* (New York: Cambridge University Press, 2002); Harvey Yunis, ed., *Written Texts and the Rise of Literate Culture in Ancient Greece* (New York: Cambridge University Press, 2003).

Xanthippus

Xanthippus (ca. 525–475 B.C.E.) *Athenian soldier and politician who was active in the* PERSIAN WARS

Xanthippus ("Yellow Horse") was born to an aristocratic family at ATHENS. In the days after KLEISTHENES' (1) democratic reforms (508 B.C.E.), Xanthippus began his political career by marrying Kleisthenes' niece Agariste. Uncle and niece both belonged to the noble and ambitious Alcmaeonid clan. Agariste and Xanthippus had three children, the youngest of whom was the future left-wing leader PERIKLES, born in 494 B.C.E.

With family wealth and connections, Xanthippus rose to political prominence in 489 B.C.E., when he prosecuted the soldier-statesman MILTIADES on a charge of deceiving the people. With Miltiades' downfall, Xanthippus briefly became the foremost politician in Athens, but was himself soon on the defensive, probably at the hands of the left-wing leader THEMISTOKLES. In 484 B.C.E. Xanthippus was ostracized by the Athenians—one of five important OSTRACISMS in the 480s B.C.E.

Although the normal term of banishment in an ostracism was 10 years, Xanthippus was recalled early, in the state emergency created by the Persian king XERXES' invasion of Greece (480 B.C.E.). Elected as a general for the year 479 B.C.E., Xanthippus commanded the Athenian contingent at the land battle of MYCALE, where the Greeks liberated IONIA. Elected general again, for 478 B.C.E., he led a Greek fleet against the Persian-held fortress of SESTOS, on the HELLESPONT; after a grueling siege, Xanthippus captured the city and crucified the hated Persian governor. Xanthippus returned to great acclaim at Athens but died within a few years, perhaps from injuries received at Sestos. By 472 B.C.E. the young Perikles had inherited his father's estate (the other son had died) and was embarked on his own political career.

See also ALCMAEONIDS.

Further reading: T. J. Figueira, "Xanthippos, Father of Perikles, and the Prutaneis of the Naukraroi," *Historia* 35 (1986): 257–279; B. S. Ridgway, "An Issue of Methodology. Anakreon, Perikles, Xanthippos," *American Journal of Archaeology* 102 (1998): 717–738; Anthony Podlecki, *Perikles and His Circle* (London: Routledge, 1998).

Xenophanes (570–478 B.C.E.) *Greek poet and philosopher*
Xenophanes was born at Colophon, in ASIA MINOR but was active in Greek SICILY and southern ITALY. There he traveled from city to city, presenting his PHILOSOPHY in verses (some of which have survived as quotations in later writers' work). Xenophanes apparently lived into his 90s. He is said to have founded the philosophical school at the Italian-Greek city of Elea and to have tutored there the student destined to be the most famous Eleatic philosopher, PARMENIDES.

It is known that Xenophanes left Colophon at age 25—probably to escape the invading Persians under King CYRUS (1). Like his contemporary PYTHAGORAS, Xenophanes brought to the western Greeks the rationalism and sophistication of his native IONIA, and he seems to have caused an intellectual sensation with his attack on traditional Homeric theology. "HOMER and HESIOD," Xenophanes wrote, "have attributed to the gods everything that is shameful and disgraceful among human beings—theft and adultery and deceiving each other." Xenophanes also expressed the enlightened theory that humans have created gods in their own image: The Ethiopians say that their gods are black and snub-nosed; the Thracians make their gods blue-eyed and red-haired. "But if cattle or horses or lions had hands," Xenophanes wrote, "then horses would portray their gods as horses, and cattle as cattle." Rather, said Xenophanes, there is one god, who is in no way like humans, either in form or thought. Xenophanes' concept of God—as a single, unmoved mover—may have inspired Parmenides' more elaborate concept of a unified, motionless Reality.

Remarkably, Xenophanes' also intuited the nature of fossils. Observing the impressions of fish and seaweed in rock quarries near SYRACUSE, Xenophanes supposedly guessed that that area had once been under water and that the earth's land in general is created from, and returns to, the sea.

A brilliant, dilettantish observer rather than a deep thinker, Xenophanes stands as an embodiment of Ionian rationalism and as an intellectual "pollenizer" for Greek Sicily and Italy. His lifetime saw the violent end of the Ionian Enlightenment and the emergence of new intellectual centers, among the mainland and western Greeks. One poignant fragment by Xenophanes gives a brief self-portrait of a wanderer, dispossessed by the Persians' conquest of his native land: "In winter, as you lie by your fire after dinner, drinking wine and cracking nuts, speak thus to the wayfarer at your door: 'What is your name, my friend? Where do you live? What is your age? How old were you when the Persians came?'"

See also PERSIAN WARS; RELIGION.

Further reading: P. J. Bicknell, "Xenophanes' Account of Solar Eclipses," *Eranos* 65 (1967): 73–77; J. H. Lesher, trans., *Xenophanes of Colophon: Fragments* (Toronto: University of Toronto Press, 1992); Jonathan Barnes, ed., *Early Greek Philosophy,* 2d ed. (London: Penguin, 2001).

Xenophon (431–354 B.C.E.) *Athenian historian, soldier, and gentleman*

Xenophon wrote several histories and treatises, but he is best remembered for producing the most exciting memoir from the ancient world—the *Anabasis* ("expedition to the interior"), describing his adventures in leading 10,000 beleaguered Greek mercenary soldiers out of the heart of the Persian Empire (401–400 B.C.E.). Among Xenophon's other surviving work is his valuable but biased history titled *Hellenica* ("Greek history"). Beginning at the point where THUCYDIDES' (1) history of the PELOPONNESIAN WAR abruptly breaks off, with the events of 411 B.C.E., *Hellenica* recounts the turbulent events of his own lifetime, from the later years of the war to the rise of THEBES and the destruction of Spartan hegemony in Greece (411–362 B.C.E.). In terms of breadth, objectivity, and analysis, Xenophon as a historian is far inferior to his predecessor Thucydides.

Like other Athenian aristocrats, he showed strong pro-Spartan sympathies during his life, and these are reflected constantly in his writings. Nevertheless, his work remains invaluable because it provides modern scholars with their primary source of evidence for the period from the final years of the Peloponnesian War to the rise of MACEDON in the late fourth century B.C.E.

Born into a rich, aristocratic family at ATHENS, Xenophon was a contemporary of the philosopher PLATO. Like Plato, the young Xenophon, although not a deep thinker, became a disciple of the Athenian philosopher SOCRATES. Today our most important source of information about the real-life Socrates (as opposed to the Socrates of Plato's scheme) is Xenophon's memoir titled *Memorabilia.*

The Peloponnesian War was being waged throughout Xenophon's childhood and youth, and—like other Athenian aristocrats—Xenophon was to show strong pro-Spartan sympathies during his life. He probably participated in the war's last years—perhaps in the naval battle at Arginusae (406 B.C.E.), which looms large in his *Hellenica,* and perhaps in CAVALRY patrols outside the city. Also in these years, he married an Athenian woman, Philesia, and had two sons, Gryllus (named for Xenophon's father) and Diodorus.

In 401 B.C.E., after Athens's defeat in the war and the disastrous reign of the THIRTY TYRANTS, Xenophon left his native city for what was fated to be an absence of 35 years. As a member of the discredited Socratic circle, he probably felt uncomfortable in the restored DEMOCRACY. (And, in fact, within two years the Athenians would condemn and execute Socrates.) Xenophon went to ASIA MINOR as one of about 10,000 Greek mercenary HOPLITE soldiers in the service of the Persian prince Cyrus but, as it turned out, Cyrus used this force in his attempt to seize the Persian throne from his brother, Artaxerxes II. After Cyrus was killed and his army defeated at the Battle of Cunaxa, near Babylon (401 B.C.E.), the frightened and demoralized surviving Greek troops elected Xenophon to lead them the 1,500 miles out of hostile territory. Four months later, the Greeks finally emerged from the Persian interior, at the Greek colony of Trapezus, on the southeast coast of the BLACK SEA. These exploits are recounted in the *Anabasis.*

In about 399 B.C.E., during Xenophon's absence, the Athenians declared him exiled forever; the probable causes were Xenophon's pro-Spartanism and prior friendship with Socrates. The following years saw Xenophon doing military service under the Spartan king AGESILAUS. During the CORINTHIAN WAR (in which Sparta and Athens were enemies, 395–386 B.C.E.), Xenophon probably served against his fellow Athenians. Xenophon remained a close associate of Agesilaus, whose deeds are recounted in the *Hellenica* and in Xenophon's laudatory biography *Agesilaus.*

In around 388 B.C.E. Xenophon and his family were settled by their Spartan friends at an estate near OLYMPIA. There Xenophon devoted himself to writing and to the pursuits addressed in his treatise *On Household Management.* In a spirit of gratitude toward Sparta, he wrote a laudatory account of the Spartan governmental system, the *Lakedaimonion politeia.* Other works of the 380s and 370s B.C.E. include the treatise *On Horsemanship* (our only surviving full account from ancient Greece on this subject) and the *Cyropaedia* ("Education of Cyrus"), a historical novel that imagines the ideal tutoring received by the old-time Persian ruler CYRUS (1) (not the Cyrus of the *Anabasis*). Some of these works seem to have developed out of Xenophon's notes toward the EDUCATION of his two sons. Another treatise, *On Hunting,* was previously attributed to Xenophon but is now considered to have been written by someone else.

In 371 B.C.E., after Sparta's defeat at Theban hands at the Battle of LEUKTRA, the people of ELIS (near Olympia) rose in defiance of Sparta and reclaimed local lands, including Xenophon's estate. Xenophon, then nearly 60, was eventually allowed by the Athenians to return.

At Athens he lived his last decade or so, finishing the *Hellenica* (which ends with a description of the Theban victory over the Spartans at the second Battle of MANTINEIA in 362 B.C.E.). Xenophon's own son Gryllus was killed at this battle, fighting on the Spartan side. On receiving the tragic news, Xenophon is said to have replied, "I knew my son was mortal."

Xenophon rewards modern study because he is the complete Athenian gentleman. He embodied many of the values and interests of his social class—soldiering, horsemanship, estate management, pro-Spartanism (exaggerated, in Xenophon's case), respect for education, and so on. He had verbal skill (his prose is plain and workmanlike) and a strong interest in right and wrong. However, his youthful dabbling in PHILOSOPHY clearly had more to do with Socrates' dynamic personality and the intellectual milieu of late-fifth-century B.C.E. Athens than with any genius of Xenophon's.

His flaws as a historian are apparent in his failure to present a full, unbiased account in his magnum opus, the *Hellenica.*

Further reading: J. K. Anderson, *Xenophon* (New York: Charles Scribner's Sons, 1974); Vivienne Gray, *The Character of Xenophon's Hellenica* (Baltimore: Johns Hopkins University Press, 1989); P. Georges, *Barbarian Asia and the Greek Experience. From the Archaic Period to the Age of Xenophon* (Baltimore: Johns Hopkins University Press, 1994); J. P. Stronk, *The Ten Thousand in Thrace. An Archaeological and Historical Commentary on Xenophon's 'Anabasis,' books 6, 3–6 and 7* (Amsterdam: Gieben, 1995); J. Dillery, *Xenophon and the History of His Times* (London: Routledge, 1995); G. Hutchinson, *Xenophon and the Art of Command* (London: Greenhill Books, 2000); R. Seager, "Xenophon and Athenian Democratic Ideology," *Classical Quarterly* 51 (2001): 385–397; V. Parker, "Ephorus and Xenophon on Greece in the Years 375–372 B.C.," *Klio* 83 (2001): 353–368; Christopher Nadon, *Xenophon's Prince: Republic and Empire in the 'Cyropaedia'* (Berkeley: University of California Press, 2001).

Xerxes (ca. 518–465 B.C.E.) *Persian king who led the failed invasion of Greece in 480 B.C.E.*
Our knowledge of Xerxes comes mainly from the ancient Greek historian HERODOTUS, whose viewpoint is hostile; he portrays the king as sometimes reflective and aesthetic-minded, but also intoxicated by power and capable of great lust, cruelty, anger, and cowardice. "Xerxes" is the Greek form of the name, which in Persian sounded like Khshah-yar-shan and meant "king of kings." In the biblical book of Esther, Xerxes is called King Ahasuerus and is pictured favorably.

As son and heir of the brilliant king DARIUS (1), Xerxes was about 32 years old when he came to the throne in late 486 B.C.E. Soon he turned his attention westward, to resume his father's conflict with the mainland Greeks. Various Persian inscriptions of Xerxes' reign make it clear that he was a pious worshipper of Ahura Mazda, the Zoroastrian supreme god, and he may have thought he was on a divine mission to conquer Greece.

After four years' preparation, including the spanning of the HELLESPONT with elaborate twin bridges of boats, Xerxes led a mighty host—perhaps 200,000 troops and 600 warships—to Europe. Descending through THRACE and MACEDON, he subdued northern and central Greece, but his navy was first eroded due to storms and a sea battle, and then destroyed when Xerxes overconfidently decided to attack the Greek fleet inside SALAMIS (1) channel. After the Salamis defeat in late summer of 480 B.C.E., Xerxes hurried back to Asia with most of his force, leaving behind a Persian army, which the Greeks smashed at PLATAEA the following summer.

Little is known of Xerxes' life afterward. He apparently devoted himself to construction of royal buildings at Persepolis, the empire's summer capital, and was assassinated in a palace intrigue. He was succeeded by his son Artaxerxes I.

To the Greeks, Xerxes supplied the prime living example of the sin of HUBRIS—insane pride that leads to divinely prompted self-destruction. The abiding picture of him in Western tradition (whether true or false) is a vainglorious emperor who, after a Hellespont storm had wrecked his boat bridges, ordered his men to punish the channel by lashing its waters with whips.

See also PERSIA; PERSIAN WARS.

Further reading: H. Sancisi-Weerdenburg, "The Personality of Xerxes, King of Kings," in *Archaeologia iranica et orientalis. Miscellanea in honorem Louis Vanden Berghe,* edited by L. de Meyer and E. Haerinck (Ghent, Belgium: Peeters Presse, 1989), 549–561; B. S. J. Isserlin, "The Canal of Xerxes. Facts and Problems," *Annual of the British School at Athens* 86 (1991): 83–91; P. R. Barkworth, "The Organization of Xerxes' Army," *Iranica Antiqua* 27 (1992): 149–167; N. G. L. Hammond and L. J. Roseman, "The Construction of Xerxes' Bridge over the Hellespont," *Journal of Hellenic Studies* 116 (1996): 88–107; Pierre Briant, *From Cyrus to Alexander: A History of the Persian Empire* (Winona Lake, Ind.: Eisenbrauns, 2002); Philip De Souza, *The Greek and Persian Wars, 499–386 B.C.* (New York: Routledge, 2003).

Z

Zanclē This Greek city of northeast SICILY is located beside the three-mile-wide Strait of Messina, which separates Sicily from the "toe" of ITALY. Located on a crescent-shaped peninsula enclosing a fine harbor, Zanclē (now the modern Sicilian city of Messina), was founded around 725 B.C.E. by Greek settlers from CUMAE and CHALCIS. Its sister city was RHEGIUM, across the strait.

Zanclē's original settlers were of the Ionian-Greek ethnic group, but around 490 B.C.E., Zanclē was repopulated by settlers of Dorian-Greek identity, commanded by the powerful tyrant Anaxilas of Rhegium. Chief among these newcomers were refugees from the Peloponnesian region of Messenia, which was suffering under Spartan domination. Anaxilas, whose ancestral home was Messenia, then renamed Zanclē as Messana (in the Doric dialect) or Messene (in Ionic form).

Zanclē-Messana eventually became an ally of Syracuse against ATHENS and the Carthaginians in the latter 400s and early 300s B.C.E. In 264 B.C.E. the city was captured by the Carthaginians—an episode that eventually brought on the titanic First Punic War between CARTHAGE and ROME (264–241 B.C.E.). After the Roman victory, Messana thrived as a Roman ally.

The ancient town of Zanclē lies underneath modern Messina; its location makes archaeological excavation of the site somewhat difficult. Two Roman cemeteries, one to the north and one to the southwest, seem to mark the settlement's boundaries. A monumental tomb dated to the late 300s and 200s B.C.E. has been excavated and restored and is now open to visitors. Remains of the Greek city plan have also been located, with the streets arranged in an orthological grid pattern.

See also DORIAN GREEKS, IONIAN GREEKS.

Further reading: D. Ridgway, *The First Western Greeks* (New York: Cambridge University Press, 1992); Gocha Tsetskhladze and Franco De Angelis, eds., *The Archaeology of Greek Colonisation: Essays Dedicated to Sir John Boardman* (Oxford: Oxford University Committee for Archaeology, distributed by Oxbow Books, 1994); G. Pugliese Carratelli, ed., *The Western Greeks: Classical Civilization in the Western Mediterranean* (London: Thames and Hudson, 1996); ———, ed., *The Greek World: Art and Civilization in Magna Graecia and Sicily* (New York: Rizzoli, 1996).

Zeno (1) *See* STOICISM.

Zeno (2) *See* PARMENIDES.

Zeus The king of all the Olympian gods, Zeus was the dispenser of divine justice in the universe, according to Greek RELIGION and MYTH. Zeus was worshipped at least as early as the Mycenaean era, since the name appears on LINEAR B tablets dated to 1400 B.C.E., but his cult is probably even older than that. Unlike many of the Classical Greek gods, Zeus was truly Greek in origin. He was probably a Sky Father originally—a weather god and chief deity—worshipped by the Greek tribes who came southward from the Balkans into the Greek mainland around 2100 B.C.E. In name and function, this primitive Zeus seems related to celestial father gods of other ancient Indo-European peoples, such as the Roman Jupiter (*Zeupater*) and the Germanic Tiu. The name *Zeus* is also related to the Greek word *dios,* "bright."

373

Throughout antiquity, Zeus never lost his identity as a weather god. He is portrayed as sending thunderstorms against his enemies in HOMER's epic poem the *Iliad* (written down around 750 B.C.E.), and in art he is often shown hurling a thunderbolt.

Zeus's most important function in Greek civilization was his role as the orderer of the universe. During the Mycenaean period (1600–1200 B.C.E.), Zeus was the supreme king over a human society organized around kings. From his cloud-shrouded palace on top of Mt. OLYMPUS in THESSALY, Zeus ruled the subordinate gods and oversaw human events in the mortal world below.

As the age of Greek kings dissolved during the 1100s–900s B.C.E., Zeus retained his preeminence, developing into a kind of chief judge, peacemaker, and civic god. The poet HESIOD (ca. 700 B.C.E.) involves Zeus as the lord of justice, and the god's epithets include *Kosmetas* (orderer), *Polieos* (overseer of the *polis*—the city), *Soter* (savior), and *Eleutherios* (guarantor of political freedom). He maintained the laws, protected suppliants, instituted festivals, gave prophecies (such as at his important oracle at DODONA), and generally oversaw most aspects of civilized life. This high moral conception of Zeus reaches its epitome in the tragedies of the great Athenian playwright AESCHYLUS—for instance, in *The Suppliants* (performed 472 B.C.E.) and in *The Eumenides* (458 B.C.E.). By the 200s B.C.E., the Stoic philosophers tended to consider Zeus the single, universal deity.

Zeus's central myths—as recorded primarily by Hesiod in his epic poem *Theogony*—tell how the young Zeus usurped the heavenly kingdom from his father, CRONUS, then reorganized this kingdom and defended it against attacks by monstrous demigods. In the myth, Cronus, king of the race of TITANS, always ate each of his newborn children, but baby Zeus was spirited away by his mother, Rhea, and brought up on the island of CRETE. Returning, Zeus led a revolt against his father, banished him, and installed himself as king of a new race of immortals, many of whom were his own children. As king of the gods, Zeus ruled the sky; his brothers, POSEIDON and HADES, ruled the sea and the Underworld, respectively.

Zeus and the other gods defended their kingdom from three separate assaults by the violent offspring of GAEA (Mother Earth), including the GIANTS, the serpent-headed TYPHON, and the twin brothers called the Aloadae, who stacked two other mountains on top of Mt. Olympus in their attempt to storm the heavens. Such mythical battles originally may have commemorated the first Greeks' conquest of mainland Greece and the subjugation of the prior inhabitants' religion by the invaders' cult of Zeus.

During the TROJAN WAR (as described in Homer's *Iliad*), Zeus sided with the aggrieved Greek hero ACHILLES and brought misfortune to the Greeks until Achilles' quarrel with King AGAMEMNON was resolved. Even Zeus had to yield to FATE, however, and so was unable to save his mortal son Sarpedon from his preordained death in the fighting at TROY (*Iliad*, book 16).

Zeus also had another, more grotesque mythological dimension, which certain Greek thinkers found puzzling or repugnant. For "the father of gods and men" (as the poet Homer calls him) was quite literally that, insofar as his numerous love affairs produced many offspring, both human and immortal. With his wife and sister, the goddess HERA, Zeus fathered the gods ARES, HEPHAISTOS, and Hebe. His other children included the deities ATHENA, APOLLO, ARTEMIS, HERMES, and DIONYSUS, the hero HERAKLES, produced through extramarital liaisons with other goddesses and mortal women (often involving rape or deception). Zeus raped or seduced several humans, including the Spartan queen Leda (whom he approached in the form of a swan and who gave birth to two pairs of twins—CASTOR AND POLYDEUCES and HELEN OF TROY and KLYTEMNESTRA), the Argive princess Danae (whom he visited as a shower of gold and who bore him the hero PERSEUS [1]), the Phoenician princess EUROPA (whom he abducted in the form of a bull and who bore him MINOS and Rhadamanthys), and the Trojan prince GANYMEDE (who was abducted by an eagle, perhaps Zeus in disguise, to become Zeus's lover and cupbearer on Mt. Olympus).

The legends of Zeus's sexual exploits with human women probably arose during the Mycenaean age, in an attempt to connect the great god with some noble family's genealogy. These myths, however, contained an unsavory discrepancy, with the god of justice descending to earth to commit rape and adultery. This incongruity was commented on by intellectuals such as the Ionian philosopher XENOPHANES (latter 500s B.C.E.) and was exploited in the tragedies of the innovative Athenian playwright EURIPIDES (latter 400s B.C.E.).

In Greek art, Zeus was often represented as a bearded, kingly figure in vigorous middle age, frequently holding a scepter. His weapons were the thunderbolt and the aegis (a magic cloak or shield, originally imagined as a storm cloud), and his sacred bird was the eagle. Of the innumerable shrines throughout the Greek world dedicated to Zeus, probably the most magnificent was the Doric-style temple built in the mid-400s B.C.E. at OLYMPIA. Inside the temple was an immense GOLD-and-ivory statue of the enthroned god, sculpted by PHEIDIAS and considered one of the SEVEN WONDERS OF THE World for its size and grandeur. Olympia was the site of the greatest athletic festival in antiquity: the OLYMPIC GAMES, held in honor of Olympian Zeus.

See also PROMETHEUS; STOICISM.

Further reading: Arthur B. Cook, *Zeus: A Study in Ancient Religion* (New York: Biblio and Tannen, 1964–1965);

H. W. Parke, *The Oracles of Zeus: Dodona, Olympia, Ammon* (Cambridge, Mass.: Harvard University Press, 1967); Karl Kerényi, *Zeus and Hera: Archetypal Image of Father, Husband, and Wife,* translated by Christopher Holme (London: Routledge and Kegan Paul, 1976); Hugh Lloyd-Jones, *The Justice of Zeus,* 2d ed. (Berkeley: University of California Press, 1983); K. W. Arafat, *Classical Zeus: A Study in Art and Literature* (New York: Oxford University Press, 1990).

Zeuxis *See* PAINTING.

BIBLIOGRAPHY

Aird, Hamish. *Pericles: The Rise and Fall of Athenian Democracy.* New York: Rosen Publishing Group, 2004.

Atchity, Kenneth, ed. *The Classical Greek Reader.* New York: Henry Holt and Co., 1996.

Austin, M. M., ed. *The Hellenistic World from Alexander to the Roman Conquest: A Selection of Ancient Sources in Translation.* New York: Cambridge University Press, 1981.

Avery, Catherine B., ed. *The New Century Classical Handbook.* New York: Appleton-Century-Crofts, 1962.

Barber, Robin. *Blue Guide: Greece.* 6th ed. New York: W. W. Norton, 1996.

Barnes, Jonathan. *Aristotle: A Very Short Introduction.* Rev. ed. Oxford: Oxford University Press, 2000.

———. *Early Greek Philosophy.* 2d rev. ed. London: Penguin Books, 2001.

Beer, Josh. *Sophocles and the Tragedy of Athenian Democracy.* Westport, Conn.: Praeger, 2004.

Belozerskaya, Marina, and Kenneth Lapatin. *Ancient Greece: Art, Architecture, and History.* Los Angeles: J. Paul Getty Museum, 2004.

Bérard, Claude, et al. *A City of Images.* Princeton, N.J.: Princeton University Press, 1989.

Biers, William R. *The Archaeology of Ancient Greece: An Introduction.* 2d ed. Ithaca, N.Y.: Cornell University Press, 1996.

Blanchard, Paul. *Blue Guide: Southern Italy: From Rome to Calabria.* 10th ed. New York: W. W. Norton, 2004.

Bloom, Harold, ed. *Euripides: Comprehensive Research and Study Guide.* Philadelphia: Chelsea House, 2003.

———. *Greek Drama.* Philadelphia: Chelsea House, 2004.

Blundell, S. *Women in Ancient Greece.* Cambridge, Mass.: Harvard University Press, 1995.

———. *Women in Classical Athens.* London: Bristol Classical Press, 1998.

Boardman, John. *Athenian Black Figure Vases. A Handbook.* New York: Thames and Hudson, 1974.

———. *Athenian Red Figure Vases: The Archaic Period. A Handbook.* New York: Thames and Hudson, 1975.

———. *Greek Sculpture: The Archaic Period. A Handbook.* New York: Thames and Hudson, 1978.

———. *Greek Sculpture: The Classical Period. A Handbook.* New York: Thames and Hudson, 1985.

———. *Greek Art.* New York: Thames and Hudson, 1987.

———. *Athenian Red Figure Vases: The Classical Period. A Handbook.* New York: Thames and Hudson, 1989.

———. *Greek Sculpture: The Late Classical Period and Sculpture in Colonies and Overseas.* New York: Thames and Hudson, 1995.

———. *The Greeks Overseas: The Early Colonies and Trade.* 4th ed. London: Thames and Hudson, 1999.

———. *The Archaeology of Nostalgia: How the Greeks Recreated Their Mythical Past.* London: Thames and Hudson, 2002.

Boardman, John, and N. G. L. Hammond, eds. *The Cambridge Ancient History: The Expansion of the Greek World, Eighth to Sixth Centuries B.C.,* vol. 3, part 3. 2d ed. New York: Cambridge University Press, 1982.

Boardman, John, et al., eds. *The Cambridge Ancient History: Persia, Greece, and the Western Mediterranean c. 525–479 B.C.,* vol. 4. 2d ed. New York: Cambridge University Press, 1988.

Boardman, John, Jasper Griffin, and Oswyn Murray, eds. *The Oxford Illustrated History of Greece and the Hellenistic World.* Oxford: Oxford University Press, 2001.

Bowra, C. M. *Greek Lyric Poetry from Alcman to Simonides.* 2d rev. ed. New York: Oxford University Press, 2000.

Bremmer, Jan. *Greek Religion.* New York: Oxford University Press, 1994.

Brulé, Pierre. *Women of Ancient Greece.* Translated by Antonia Nevill. Edinburgh: Edinburgh University Press, 2003.

Buckley, Terry. *Aspects of Greek History, 750–323 BC: A Source-Based Approach.* London: Routledge, 1996.

Burkert, Walter. *Ancient Mystery Cults.* Cambridge, Mass.: Harvard University Press, 1987.

———. *Greek Religion.* Translated by John Raffan. Cambridge, Mass.: Harvard University Press, 1985.

Burn, Andrew Robert. *The Lyric Age of Greece.* New York: St. Martin's Press, 1960.

———. *The Penguin History of Greece.* 2d ed. New York: Penguin Books, 1990.

Bury, J. B., S. A. Cook, and F. E. Adcock, eds. *The Cambridge Ancient History: Athens 478–401 B.C.*, vol. 5. New York: Cambridge University Press, 1964.

———. *The Cambridge Ancient History: Macedon: 401–301 B.C.*, vol. 6. New York: Cambridge University Press, 1964.

Bury, J. B., and Russell Meiggs. *A History of Greece to the Death of Alexander the Great.* 4th ed. London: Macmillan, 1975.

Cameron, Pat. *Blue Guide: Crete.* 5th ed. New York: W. W. Norton, 1988.

Camp, John M. *The Archaeology of Athens.* New Haven, Conn.: Yale University Press, 2001.

Carpenter, Thomas. *Art and Myth in Ancient Greece.* London: Thames and Hudson, 1991.

Cartledge, Paul, ed. *The Cambridge Illustrated History of Ancient Greece.* Rev. ed. Cambridge: Cambridge University Press, 2002.

Casson, Lionel. *Ships and Seamanship in the Ancient World.* Princeton, N.J.: Princeton University Press, 1971.

Cawkwell, George. *Philip of Macedon.* Boston: Faber & Faber, 1978.

Ceram, C. W. *Gods, Graves, and Scholars: The Story of Archaeology.* Translated by E. B. Garside. New York: Alfred A. Knopf, 1952.

Childe, Gordon. *What Happened in History.* 2d ed. Foreword and footnotes by Grahame Clarke. Baltimore: Penguin Books, 1964.

Cook, R. M. *Greek Painted Pottery.* London: Methuen, 1960.

Cotterell, Arthur, ed. *The Encyclopedia of Ancient Civilizations.* New York: Mayflower Books, 1980.

Csapo, Eric, and William J. Slater. *The Context of Ancient Drama.* Ann Arbor: University of Michigan Press, 1995.

Dalby, Andrew. *Siren Feasts: A History of Food and Gastronomy in Greece.* London: Routledge, 1996.

Davies, J. K. *Democracy and Classical Greece.* Atlantic Highlands, N.J.: Humanities Press, 1978.

Demand, Nancy. *Birth, Death, and Motherhood in Classical Greece.* Baltimore: Johns Hopkins University Press, 1994.

Detienne, M. *Masters of Truth in Archaic Greece.* Cambridge, Mass.: MIT Press, 1996.

Dover, K. J. *Aristophanic Comedy.* Berkeley: University of California Press, 1972.

———. *Greek Homosexuality.* Cambridge, Mass.: Harvard University Press, 1978.

———, ed. *Ancient Greek Literature.* 2d ed. New York: Oxford University Press, 1997.

Easterling, P. E. *Greek and Roman Actors.* Cambridge: Cambridge University Press, 2002.

Easterling, P. E., et al., eds. *The Cambridge History of Classical Literature.* New York: Cambridge University Press, 1989.

Edwards, I. E. S., et al., eds. *The Cambridge Ancient History: The Middle East and the Aegean Region, circa 1380–1000 B.C.*, vol. 2, part 2. 3d ed. New York: Cambridge University Press, 1975.

Edwards, Paul, ed. *The Encyclopedia of Philosophy,* vols. 1–8. New York: Macmillan, 1967.

Eisner, Robert. *Travelers to an Antique Land: The History and Literature of Travel to Greece.* Ann Arbor: University of Michigan Press, 1991.

Ellis, Walter M. *Alcibiades.* New York: Routledge, 1989.

Errington, R. M. *A History of Macedonia.* Berkeley: University of California Press, 1990.

Evans, J. A. S. *Herodotus.* Boston: Twayne, 1982.

Fantham, Elaine, et al. *Women in the Classical World: Image and Text.* New York: Oxford University Press, 1994.

Ferrari, Gloria. *Figures of Speech: Men and Maidens in Ancient Greece.* Chicago: University of Chicago Press, 2002.

Finley, M. I. *Early Greece: The Bronze and Archaic Ages.* 2d ed. London: Chatto and Windus, 1981.

———. *The Ancient Economy.* Rev. ed. Berkeley: University of California Press, 1999.

Fomara, Charles W., ed. and trans. *Archaic Times to the End of the Peloponnesian War.* Baltimore: Johns Hopkins University Press, 1977.

Fomara, Charles W., and Loren J. Samons. *Athens from Cleisthenes to Pericles.* Berkeley: University of California Press, 1991.

Fox, Robin Lane. *The Search for Alexander.* Boston: Little, Brown, 1980.

Fullerton, Mark D. *Greek Art.* New York: Cambridge University Press, 2000.

Gagarin, Michael. *Early Greek Law.* Berkeley: University of California Press, 1986.

Gantz, Timothy. *Early Greek Myth: A Guide to Literary and Artistic Sources.* Baltimore: Johns Hopkins University Press, 1993.

Grady, Ellen. *Blue Guide: Sicily.* 6th ed. New York: W. W. Norton, 2003.

Graf, Fritz. *Greek Mythology: An Introduction.* Translated by Thomas Marier. Baltimore: Johns Hopkins University Press, 1993.

Graves, Robert. *The Greek Myths,* vols. 1 and 2. Baltimore: Penguin, 1955.

Green, J. R. *Theatre in Ancient Greek Society.* London: Routledge, 1994.

Green, Peter. *Alexander of Macedon, 356–323 B.C.* Berkeley: University of California Press, 1991.

———. *A Concise History of Ancient Greece.* London: Thames and Hudson, 1979.

Griffin, Jasper. *Homer on Life and Death.* New York: Oxford University Press, 1980.

Guthrie, W. K. C. *Socrates.* New York: Cambridge University Press, 1971.

Habicht, Christian. *Athens from Alexander to Antony.* Cambridge, Mass.: Harvard University Press, 1999.

Hale, William H. *Ancient Greece.* New York: American Heritage, 2001.

Halperin, David. *One Hundred Years of Homosexuality.* New York: Routledge, 1990.

Hammond, N. G. L. *Alexander the Great: King, Commander, and Statesman.* 2d ed. Bristol, U.K.: Bristol Press, 1989.

———. *Philip of Macedon.* Baltimore: Johns Hopkins University Press, 1994.

————. *The Genius of Alexander the Great.* Chapel Hill: University of North Carolina Press, 1997.

Hammond, N. G. L., and H. H. Scullard, eds. *The Oxford Classical Dictionary.* New York: Oxford University Press, 1970.

Hansen, M. H., ed. *The Ancient Greek City-State.* Copenhagen: Royal Danish Academy, 1993.

————. *Studies in the Ancient Greek Polis.* Stuttgart, Germany: Franz Steiner Verlag, 1995.

Hanson, Victor Davis. *The Western Way of War: Infantry Battle in Classical Greece.* 2d ed. Berkeley: University of California Press, 2000.

Hare, R. M. *Plato.* New York: Oxford University Press, 1982.

Harris, Edward, and Lene Rubinstein. *The Law and the Courts in Ancient Greece.* London: Duckworth, 2004.

Hignett, C. *A History of the Athenian Constitution.* New York: Oxford University Press, 1952.

Holliday, Peter, ed. *Narrative and Event in Ancient Art.* New York: Cambridge University Press, 1993.

Hornblower, Simon. *Thucydides.* Baltimore: Johns Hopkins University Press, 1987.

How, W. W., and J. Wells. *A Commentary on Herodotus,* vols. 1 and 2. New York: Oxford University Press, 1975.

Hurwit, Jeffrey. *The Art and Culture of Early Greece.* Ithaca, N.Y.: Cornell University Press, 1985.

Hussey, Edward. *The Presocratics.* London: Duckworth, 1972.

James, Vanessa. *The Genealogy of Greek Mythology: An Illustrated Family Tree of Greek Myth from the First Gods to the Founders of Rome.* New York: Gotham Books, 2003.

Janson, H. W. *History of Art.* 6th ed. New York: Harry N. Abrams, 2001.

Jones, A. H. M. *Athenian Democracy.* 2d ed. Baltimore: Johns Hopkins University Press, 1986.

————. *Sparta.* 2d ed. Cambridge, Mass.: Harvard University Press, 1993.

Kagan, Donald. *Pericles of Athens and the Birth of Democracy.* New York: Simon & Schuster, 1991.

————. *The Peloponnesian War.* New York: Viking, 2003.

Kirk, G. S. *Homer and the Oral Tradition.* New York: Cambridge University Press, 1976.

————. *The Songs of Homer.* New York: Cambridge University Press, 1962.

Knox, Bernard. *The Oldest Dead White European Males and Other Reflections on the Classics.* New York: W. W. Norton, 1993.

Konstam, Angus. *Historical Atlas of Ancient Greece.* New York: Checkmark Books, 2003.

Konstan, David, and Keith Rutter. *Envy, Spite, and Jealousy: The Rivalrous Emotions in Ancient Greece.* Edinburgh: Edinburgh University Press, 2003.

Lawrence, A. W. *Greek Architecture.* 5th ed. Revised by R. A. Tomlinson. New Haven, Conn.: Yale University Press, 1996.

Lefkowitz, Mary R. *The Lives of the Greek Poets.* Baltimore: Johns Hopkins University Press, 1981.

Levi, Peter. *Atlas of the Greek World.* New York: Facts On File, 1984.

Lewis, David, et al., eds. *The Cambridge Ancient History: The Fifth Century,* vol. 5. 2d ed. New York: Cambridge University Press, 1992.

Liddell, H. G., ed. *An Intermediate Greek-English Lexicon* (abridgement of the 7th edition of Liddell and Scott's Greek-English Lexicon). New York: Oxford University Press, 1889.

Llewellyn-Jones, Lloyd. *Aphrodite's Tortoise. The Veiled Women of Ancient Greece.* Swansea, U.K.: Classical Press of Wales, 2003.

Lloyd, G. E. R. *Aristotle: The Growth and Structure of His Thought.* New York: Cambridge University Press, 1968.

————. *Early Greek Science: Thales to Aristotle.* London: Chatto and Windus, 1970.

————. *Greek Science after Aristotle.* London: Chatto and Windus, 1973.

Long, A. A. *Hellenistic Philosophy: Stoics, Epicureans, Sceptics.* London: Duckworth, 1974.

Longrigg, James. *Greek Medicine: From the Heroic to the Hellenistic Age: A Source Book.* New York: Routledge, 1998.

Luce, J. V. *An Introduction to Greek Philosophy.* New York: Thames and Hudson, 1992.

MacDowell, Douglas M. *The Law in Classical Athens.* Ithaca, N.Y.: Cornell University Press, 1978.

MacKendrick, Paul. *The Greek Stones Speak: The Story of Archaeology in Greek Lands.* New York: W. W. Norton, 1962.

Mackie, Hilary. *Graceful Errors: Pindar and the Performance of Praise.* Ann Arbor: University of Michigan Press, 2003.

Martin, Roland. *Greek Architecture.* Milan, Italy: Electa-architecture, 2003.

Mattusch, Carol. *Classical Bronzes.* Ithaca, N.Y.: Cornell University Press, 1996.

McCarthy, George E. *Classical Horizons: The Origins of Sociology in Ancient Greece.* Albany: State University of New York Press, 2003.

McDonagh, Bernard. *Blue Guide: Turkey: The Aegean and Mediterranean Coasts.* 3d ed. New York: W. W. Norton, 2001.

McGlew, James. *Tyranny and Political Culture in Ancient Greece.* Ithaca, N.Y.: Cornell University Press, 1993.

McLeish, Kenneth. *The Theatre of Aristophanes.* New York: Taplinger, 1980.

Meiggs, Russell. *The Athenian Empire.* New York: Oxford University Press, 1972.

Meiggs, Russell, and David Lewis, eds. *A Selection of Greek Historical Inscriptions.* New York: Oxford University Press, 1969.

Michelakis, Pantelis. *Achilles in Greek Tragedy.* Cambridge: Cambridge University Press, 2002.

Miller, Stephen G. *Ancient Greek Athletics.* New Haven, Conn.: Yale University Press, 2004.

Morgan, Kathryn, ed. *Popular Tyranny: Sovereignty and Its Discontents in Ancient Greece.* Austin: University of Texas Press, 2003.

Morris, Ian Macgregor. *Themistocles: Defender of Greece.* New York: Rosen Publishing Group, 2004.

————. *Leonidas: Hero of Thermopylae.* New York: Rosen Publishing Group, 2004.

Murray, Oswyn. *Early Greece.* 2d ed. Cambridge, Mass.: Harvard University Press, 1993.

Murray, Oswyn, and Simon Price, eds. *The Greek City from Homer to Alexander.* New York: Oxford University Press, 1990.

Nardo, Don. *Ancient Greece.* San Diego: Kidhaven Press, 2002.

Neils, Jenifer. *The Parthenon Frieze.* New York: Cambridge University Press, 2001.

Neils, Jenifer, and John H. Oakley. *Coming of Age in Ancient Greece: Images of Childhood from the Classical Past.* New Haven, Conn.: Yale University Press, 2003.

The New York Times *Atlas of the World.* New York: Time-Life Books, 1993.

Ogden, Daniel, ed. *The Hellenistic World: New Perspectives.* London: Classical Press of Wales and Duckworth, 2002.

Oldfield, Adrian. *Ordered Cities, Ordered Souls. An Introduction to Greek Political Thought.* London: Routledge, 2003.

Ostwald, Martin. *From Popular Sovereignty to the Sovereignty of Law: Law, Society, and Politics in Fifth-Century Athens.* Berkeley: University of California Press, 1986.

Paine, Mike. *The Pocket Essential Ancient Greece.* Harpenden, U.K.: Pocket Essentials, 2002.

Parton, Sarah. *Cleisthenes: Founder of Athenian Democracy.* New York: Rosen Publishing Group, 2004.

Pedley, John. *Greek Art and Archaeology.* 3d ed. Englewood Cliffs, N.J.: Prentice Hall, 2002.

Picard-Cambridge, A. W. *Dithyramb, Tragedy, and Comedy.* New York: Oxford University Press, 1962.

Podlecki, A. J. *The Life of Themistocles.* Montreal: McGill-Queen's University Press, 1975.

Poliakoff, Michael B. *Combat Sports in the Ancient World.* New Haven, Conn.: Yale University Press, 1987.

Pollitt, J. J. *Art and Experience in Classical Greece.* Cambridge: Cambridge University Press, 1972.

————. *Art in the Hellenistic Age.* New York: Cambridge University Press, 1986.

————. *Art and Ancient Greece: Sources and Documents.* New York: Cambridge University Press, 1990.

Pomeroy, Sarah B. *Goddesses, Whores, Wives, and Slaves: Women in Classical Antiquity.* New York: Schocken Books, 1975.

————. *A Brief History of Ancient Greece: Politics, Society, and Culture.* New York: Oxford University Press, 2004.

Powell, Barry. *Homer.* Malden, Mass.: Blackwell, 2004.

Race, William H. *Pindar.* Boston: Twayne, 1986.

Randall, Bernard. *Solon: The Lawmaker of Athens.* New York: Rosen Publishing Group, 2004.

————. *Alexander the Great: Macedonian King and Conqueror.* New York: Rosen Publishing Group, 2004.

Reden, Sitta von. *Exchange in Ancient Greece.* London: Duckworth, 2003.

Reeder, Ellen. *Pandora: Women in Classical Greece.* Baltimore: Trustees of the Walters Art Gallery, in association with Princeton University Press, 1995.

Renault, Mary. *The Nature of Alexander.* New York: Pantheon Books, 1975.

Rhodes, P. J. *A Commentary on the Aristotelian Athenaion Politeia.* New York: Oxford University Press, 1981.

Richter, Gisela M. A. *A Handbook of Greek Art.* London: Phaidon Press, 1959.

Ridgway, Brunilde Sismondo. *Prayers in Stone: Greek Architectural Sculpture ca. 600–100 B.C.E.* Berkeley: University of California Press, 1999.

Roberts, Jennifer, and Tracy Barrett. *The Ancient Greek World.* New York: Oxford University Press, 2004.

Robertson, Alec, and Denis Stevens, eds. *The Pelican History of Music,* vol. 1. Baltimore: Penguin Books, 1960.

Robertson, Martin. *A History of Greek Art.* London: Cambridge University Press, 1975.

————. *The Art of Vase-Painting in Classical Athens.* Cambridge: Cambridge University Press, 1992.

Robinson, Eric, ed. *Ancient Greek Democracy: Readings and Sources.* Malden, Mass.: Blackwell, 2004.

Roebuck, Derek. *Ancient Greek Arbitration.* Oxford: Arbitration Press, 2001.

Rose, H. J. *A Handbook of Greek Literature.* New York: E. P. Dutton, 1934, 1961.

————. *A Handbook of Greek Mythology.* New York: E. P. Dutton, 1959.

————. *Religion in Greece and Rome.* New York: Harper and Row, 1959.

Rose, Martha. *The Staff of Oedipus: Transforming Disability in Ancient Greece.* Ann Arbor: University of Michigan Press, 2003.

de Ste. Croix, G. E. M. *The Origins of the Peloponnesian War.* London: Duckworth, 1972.

Salmon, J. B. *Wealthy Corinth: A History of the City to 338 B.C.* New York: Oxford University Press, 1984.

Samuel, Alan. *Greek and Roman Chronology: Calendars and Years in Classical Antiquity.* Munich, Germany: C. H. Beck, 1972.

Scanlon, Thomas. *Eros and Greek Athletics.* Oxford: Oxford University Press, 2002.

Scodel, Ruth. *Sophocles.* Boston: Twayne, 1984.

Sealey, R. A. *A History of the Greek City States, ca. 700–338 B.C.* Berkeley: University of California Press, 1976.

Senker, Cath. *Everyday Life in Ancient Greece.* North Mankato, Minn.: Smart Apple Media, 2004.

Sherratt, Andrew, ed. *The Cambridge Encyclopedia of Archaeology.* New York: Crown Cambridge University Press, 1980.

Simon, Erika. *Festivals of Attica: An Archaeological Commentary.* Madison: University of Wisconsin Press, 2002.

Smith, R. R. R. *Hellenistic Sculpture.* London: Thames and Hudson, 1991.

Snodgrass, A. M. *Arms and Armour of the Greeks.* Ithaca, N.Y.: Cornell University Press, 1967.

Snowden, Frank M., Jr. *Blacks in Antiquity: Ethiopians in the Greco-Roman Experience.* Cambridge: Belknap Press/ Harvard University Press, 1970.

Sommerstein, Alan H. *Greek Drama and Dramatists.* New York: Routledge, 2002.

Sourvinou-Inwood, Christianne. *Tragedy and Athenian Religion.* Lanham, Md.: Lexington Books, 2003.

Sparkes, Brian A. *Greek Pottery: An Introduction.* New York: Manchester University Press, 1991.

Spence, Iain. *Historical Dictionary of Ancient Greek Warfare.* Lanham, Md.: Scarecrow Press, 2002.

Stewart, Andrew. *Greek Sculpture: An Exploration,* vols. 1 and 2. New Haven, Conn.: Yale University Press, 1990.

———. *Faces of Power: Alexander's Image and Hellenistic Politics.* Berkeley: University of California Press, 1993.

Stillwell, Richard, ed. *The Princeton Encyclopedia of Classical Sites.* Princeton, N.J.: Princeton University Press, 1976.

Stockton, David. *The Classical Athenian Democracy.* New York: Oxford University Press, 1990.

Stone, I. F. *The Trial of Socrates.* Boston: Little, Brown, 1988.

Taylour, Lord William. *The Mycenaeans.* 2d ed. New York: Thames and Hudson, 1983.

Thomas, Carol G. *Citadel to City-state: The Transformation of Greece, 1200–700 B.C.* Bloomington: Indiana University Press, 1999.

Tsigakou, Fani-Maria. *The Rediscovery of Greece: Travellers and Painters of the Romantic Era.* London: Thames and Hudson, 1981.

Tyrrell, William Blake. *The Smell of Sweat: Greek Athletics, Olympics, and Culture.* Wauconda, Ill.: Bolchazy-Carducci, 2004.

Vivante, Bella. *Events That Changed Ancient Greece.* Westport, Conn.: Greenwood Press, 2002.

Walbank, F. W., et al., eds. *The Cambridge Ancient History: The Hellenistic World,* vol. 7, part 1. 2d ed. New York: Cambridge University Press, 1984.

———. *The Cambridge Ancient History: The Rise of Rome to 220 B.C.,* vol. 7, part 2. 2d ed. New York: Cambridge University Press, 1989.

———. *The Cambridge Ancient History: Rome and the Mediterranean to 133 B.C.,* vol. 8. 2d ed. New York: Cambridge University Press, 1989.

Walker, Steven F. *Theocritus.* Boston: Twayne, 1980.

Weidman, Thomas. *Greek and Roman Slavery.* Baltimore: Johns Hopkins University Press, 1981.

West, M. L. *Ancient Greek Music.* New York: Oxford University Press, 1994.

Whitby, Michael, ed. *Sparta.* Edinburgh: Edinburgh University Press, 2002.

Whitley, James. *The Archaeology of Ancient Greece.* New York: Cambridge University Press, 2001.

Wiles, David. *Greek Theatre Performance: An Introduction.* New York: Cambridge University Press, 2000.

Winnington-Ingram, R. P. *Sophocles: An Interpretation.* New York: Cambridge University Press, 1980.

Wood, Michael. *In Search of the Trojan War.* New York: Facts On File, 1985.

Zaidman, L. B., and P. S. Pantel. *Religion in the Ancient Greek City.* Cambridge: Cambridge University Press, 1992.

Zimmerman, Bernhard. *Greek Tragedy: An Introduction.* Translated by Thomas Marier. Baltimore: Johns Hopkins University Press, 1991.

ANCIENT AUTHORS IN GREEK AND IN TRANSLATION

Aeschylus. *Septem quae supersunt tragoediae.* Greek text. 2d ed. Edited by Denys Page. New York: Oxford University Press, 1972.

———. *The Complete Plays.* Translated by Carl R. Mueller. Hanover, N.H.: Smith and Kraus, 2002.

———. *Prometheus Bound.* Edited and translated by A. J. Podlecki. Warminster, U.K.: Aris & Phillips, 2003.

———. *Agamemnon.* Translated by Philip de May. Cambridge: Cambridge University Press, 2003.

———. *The Oresteia.* 2d ed. Translated by Simon Goldhill. New York: Cambridge University Press, 2004.

Archilochus et al. *Greek Lyric Poetry.* Edited and translated by Willis Barnstone. New York: Schocken Books, 1967.

———. *The Penguin Book of Greek Verse.* Greek text. Translated and edited by Constantine A. Trypanis. New York: Penguin Books, 1971.

———. *Greek Lyrics.* Edited and translated by Richmond Lattimore. Chicago: University of Chicago Press, 1981.

———. *Greek Iambic Poetry: From the Seventh to the Fifth Centuries BC.* Edited and translated by Douglas E. Gerber. Cambridge, Mass.: Harvard University Press, 1999.

Aristophanes. *Frogs, Assemblywomen, Wealth.* Edited and translated by Jeffrey Henderson. Cambridge, Mass.: Harvard University Press, 2002.

———. *Lysistrata.* Translated by Sarah Ruden. Indianapolis: Hackett Publishers, 2003.

———. *Peace.* Greek Text. Edited by S. Douglas Olson. New York: Oxford University Press, 2003.

———. *Acharnians.* Edited by Charles Platter. Bryn Mawr, Pa.: Bryn Mawr College, 2003.

Aristotle. *Politics.* Edited and translated by Ernest Baker. New York: Oxford University Press, 1946.

———. *On the Art of Poetry.* Edited and translated by Lane Cooper. Ithaca, N.Y.: Cornell University Press, 1947.

———. *The Athenian Constitution, The Eudemian Ethics, On Virtues and Vices.* 1952. Greek text. Reprint, translated by H. Rackham. Cambridge, Mass.: Harvard University Press (Loeb Classical Library), 1992.

———. *The Nicomachean Ethics.* Rev. ed. Translated by J. A. K. Thomson. Introduction and further reading by Jonathan Barnes. London: Penguin, 2004.

Arrian. *The Campaigns of Alexander.* Translated by Aubrey de Sélincourt. Introduced and notes written by J. R. Hamilton. New York: Penguin Book, 1971.

Demosthenes. *On the Crown.* Edited and translated by S. Usher. Classical Texts Series: Greek Orators, vol. 5. Warminster, U.K.: Aris & Phillips, 1993.

Euripides. *Hippolytus.* Bryn Mawr, Pa.: Department of Greek, Bryn Mawr College, 1980.

———. *Hecuba.* Translated by Timberlake Wertenbaker. Woodstock, Ill.: Dramatic, 1996.

———. *Euripides' Medea.* Greek text. Commentary in English by Michelle Kwinter. Bryn Mawr Greek Commentaries. Bryn Mawr, Pa.: Thomas Library, Bryn Mawr College, 1999.

———. *Bacchae.* Translated by David Franklin. Cambridge: Cambridge University Press, 2000.

———. *Alcestis, Heracles, Children of Heracles, Cyclops.* Translated by Robin Waterfield. New York: Oxford University Press, 2003.

———. *Medea and Other Plays.* Translated by John Davie. London: Penguin Books, 2003.

———. *Euripides' Alcestis.* Greek text. Notes and commentary by C. A. E. Luschnig and H. M. Roisman. Norman: University of Oklahoma Press, 2003.

Herodotus. *Herodotus.* Greek text. Translated by A. D. Godley. Cambridge, Mass.: Harvard University Press (Loeb Classical Library), 1981–1982.

———. *Histories, Book 1.* Greek text. Edited with introduction and notes by J. H. Sleeman. Bristol, U.K.: Bristol Classical Press, 2002.

———. *Histories. Book IX.* Edited by Michael Flower and John Marincola. New York: Cambridge University Press, 2002.

Hesiod. *Theogony and Works and Days.* Translated with introduction and notes by M. L. West. New York: Oxford University Press, 1999.

Homer. *The Iliad,* vols. 1 and 2. Greek text. Edited and translated by A. T. Murray. Cambridge, Mass.: Harvard University Press (Loeb Classical Library), 1939, 1942.

———. *The Iliad.* Translated by Robert Fagles. New York: Penguin Books 1991.

———. *The Odyssey,* vols. 1 and 2. Greek text. Edited by W. B. Stanford. New York: St. Martin's Press, 1965.

———. *The Odyssey.* Translated by Robert Fitzgerald. New York: Farrar, Straus and Giroux, 1998.

Menander. *The Dyskolos.* Edited with translation, introduction, and commentary by Stanley Ireland. Warminster, U.K.: Aris & Philips, 1995.

Pausanias. *Guide to Greece,* vols. 1 and 2. Translated with introduction by Peter Levi. New York: Penguin Books, 1979.

Pindar. *The Odes of Pindar.* Translated by Geoffrey S. Conway. London: Dent, 1972.

———. *New Selected Odes of Pindar.* Greek text. Commentary by Eleanor Dickey and Richard Hamilton. Bryn Mawr, Pa.: Bryn Mawr College, 1991.

Plato. *Gorgias.* Translated with introduction by Walter Hamilton. Harmondsworth, U.K.: Penguin, 1971.

———. *Plato's Crito.* Greek text. Commentary and notes by Gilbert P. Rose. Bryn Mawr, Pa.: Bryn Mawr College, 1981.

———. *Plato's Republic.* Translated by B. Jowett. New York: Modern Library, 1982.

———. *Plato's Symposium.* Greek text. Commentary and notes by Gilbert P. Rose. 2d ed. Bryn Mawr, Pa.: Bryn Mawr College, 1985.

———. *Plato's Republic.* Greek text. Edited by Lewis Campbell and Benjamin Jowett. New York: Garland Press, 1987.

———. *Plato's Apology.* Greek text. Commentary and notes by Gilbert P. Rose. Bryn Mawr, Pa.: Bryn Mawr College, 1989.

———. *Gorgias: A Revised Text.* 2d ed. Greek text. Introduction and commentary by E. R. Dodds. New York: Oxford University Press, 1990.

———. *Euthyphro.* Greek text. Introduction and commentary by Chrys Emlyn-Jones. London: Bristol Classical Press, 1991.

———. *Ion; Hippias Minor, Laches; Protagoras.* Translated with commentary by R. E. Allen. New Haven, Conn.: Yale University Press, 1996.

———. *Plato's Symposium.* Translated with introduction and notes by Avi Sharon. Newburyport, Mass.: Focus/R. Pullins, 1998.

Plutarch. *The Rise and Fall of Athens.* Translated and introduced by Ian Scott-Kilvert. New York: Penguin Books, 1960.

———. *Plutarch's Lives,* vols. 1–7, 9. Greek text. Translated by Bernadotte Perrin. Cambridge: Harvard University Press (Loeb Classical Library), 1968.

———. *The Age of Alexander.* Translated by Ian Scott-Kilvert. Introduced by G. T. Griffith. New York: Penguin Books, 1973.

———. *Plutarch on Sparta.* Translated, introduced, and notes written by Richard J. A. Talbert. New York: Penguin Books, 1988.

Sappho et al. *Greek Lyric,* vol. 1. Greek text. Edited and translated by David Campbell. Cambridge, Mass.: Harvard University Press (Loeb Classical Library), 1982.

Sophocles. *The Complete Plays of Sophocles.* Translated by Richard Claverhouse Jebb. Introduced by Moses Hadas. New York: Bantam Books, 1971.

———. *Oedipus Rex.* Greek text. Edited by R. D. Dawe. New York: Cambridge University Press, 1982.

———. *Ajax.* Translated by H. Golder. New York: 1999.

Stesichorus et al. *Greek Lyric,* vol. 3. Greek text. Edited and translated by David Campbell. Cambridge, Mass.: Harvard University Press (Loeb Classical Library), 1991.

Thucydides. *Historiae,* vols. 1 and 2. Greek text. Edited by Henry Stuart Jones and Enoch Powell. New York: Oxford University Press, 1960, 1963.

———. *The Peloponnesian War.* Translated and introduced by Rex Warner. Baltimore: Penguin Books, 1954.

Xenophon. *Conversations of Socrates: Socrates' Defense, Memoirs of Socrates, The Dinner Party, The Estate-manager.* Translated by Hugh Tredennick and Robin Waterfield. Edited by Robin Waterfield. New York: Penguin Books, 1990.

———. *A History of My Times (Hellenica).* Translated by Rex Warner. Introduced and notes written by George Cawkwell. New York: Penguin Books, 1979.

———. *The Persian Expedition.* Translated by Rex Warner. Introduced and notes written by George Cawkwell. New York: Penguin Books, 1972.

INDEX